Where the classroom comes to life!

From watching actual classroom video footage of teachers and students interacting to building standards-based lessons and web-based portfolios . . . from a robust resource library of the "What Every Teacher Should Know About" series to complete instruction on writing an effective research paper . . . **MyLabSchool** brings together an amazing collection of resources for future teachers. This website gives you a wealth of videos, print and simulated cases, career advice, and much more.

Use **MyLabSchool** with this Allyn and Bacon Education text, and you will have everything you need to succeed in your course. Assignment IDs have also been incorporated into many Allyn and Bacon Education texts to link to the online material in **MyLabSchool** . . . connecting the teachers of tomorrow to the information they need today.

PEARSON AB

VISIT www.mylabschool.com **to learn more about** **this invaluable resource and Take a Tour!**

Here's what you'll find in **mylabschool**

Where the classroom comes to life!

VideoLab ▶

Access hundreds of video clips of actual classroom situations from a variety of grade levels and school settings. These 3- to 5-minute closed-captioned video clips illustrate real teacher–student interaction, and are organized both topically *and* by discipline. Students can test their knowledge of classroom concepts with integrated observation questions.

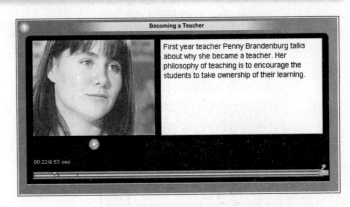

Becoming a Teacher

First year teacher Penny Brandenburg talks about why she became a teacher. Her philosophy of teaching is to encourage the students to take ownership of their learning.

00:22/4:53 sec

◀ Lesson & Portfolio Builder

This feature enables students to create, maintain, update, and share online portfolios and standards-based lesson plans. The Lesson Planner walks students, step-by-step, through the process of creating a complete lesson plan, including verifiable objectives, assessments, and related state standards. Upon completion, the lesson plan can be printed, saved, e-mailed, or uploaded to a website.

Here's what you'll find in mylabschool™

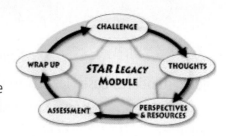

Where the classroom comes to life!

Simulations ▶

This area of MyLabSchool contains interactive tools designed to better prepare future teachers to provide an appropriate education to students with special needs. To achieve this goal, the IRIS (IDEA and Research for Inclusive Settings) Center at Vanderbilt University has created course enhancement materials. These resources include online interactive modules, case study units, information briefs, student activities, an online dictionary, and a searchable directory of disability-related web sites.

◀ Resource Library

MyLabSchool includes a collection of PDF files on crucial and timely topics within education. Each topic is applicable to any education class, and these documents are ideal resources to prepare students for the challenges they will face in the classroom. This resource can be used to reinforce a central topic of the course, or to enhance coverage of a topic you need to explore in more depth.

Research Navigator ▶

This comprehensive research tool gives users access to four exclusive databases of authoritative and reliable source material. It offers a comprehensive, step-by-step walk-through of the research process. In addition, students can view sample research papers and consult guidelines on how to prepare endnotes and bibliographies. The latest release also features a new bibliography-maker program—AutoCite.

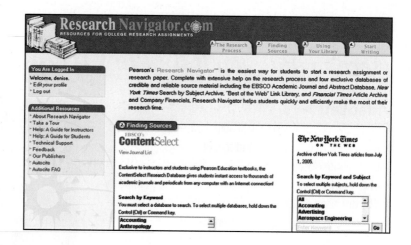

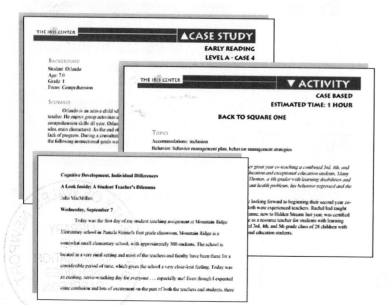

◀ Case Archive

This collection of print and simulated cases can be easily accessed by topic and subject area, and can be integrated into your course. The cases are drawn from Allyn & Bacon's best-selling books, and represent the complete range of disciplines and student ages. It's an ideal way to consider and react to real classroom scenarios. The possibilities for using these high-quality cases within the course are endless.

Fifth Edition

Teaching Students with Special Needs in Inclusive Settings

Tom E. C. Smith
University of Arkansas

Edward A. Polloway
Lynchburg College

James R. Patton
University of Texas, Austin

Carol A. Dowdy
University of Alabama at Birmingham

PEARSON

Boston   New York   San Francisco
Mexico City   Montreal   Toronto   London   Madrid   Munich   Paris
Hong Kong   Singapore   Tokyo   Cape Town   Sydney

Executive Editor: Virginia Lanigan
Senior Development Editor: Virginia L. Blanford
Series Editorial Assistant: Matthew Buchholz
Marketing Manager: Kris Ellis-Levy
Production Editor: Paula Carroll
Editorial Production Service: NK Graphics and Black Dot Group
Composition Buyer: Linda Cox
Manufacturing Buyer: Megan Cochran
Electronic Composition: NK Graphics and Black Dot Group
Interior Design: Glenna Collett
Photo Researcher: Kate Cook Cebick
Cover Administrator: Linda Knowles

For related titles and support materials, visit our online catalog at www.ablongman.com.

Between the time website information is gathered and then published, it is not unusual for some sites to have closed. Also, the transcription of URLs can result in typographical errors. The publisher would appreciate notification where these errors occur so that they may be corrected in subsequent editions.

Cataloging-in-Publication Data not available at press time:
ISBN 0-205-53057-5
ISBN 978-0-205-53057-1

Photo Credits

Pages ix, 2, © Kat Wade/San Francisco Chronicle/Corbis; **page 9,** © Janine Wiedel Photolibrary/Alamy; **page 11,** courtesy of John Colbert; **page 21,** © Ellen B. Senisi/The Image Works; **page 25,** Will Hart/PhotoEdit, Inc.; **pages ix, 34,** © Ellen Senisi/The Image Works; **page 41,** © Bob Daemmrich/The Image Works; **page 49,** Elizabeth Crews Photography; **page 57,** Brian Smith; **pages x, 66,** AP Images/Bob Child; **page 73,** courtesy of Tracy Corriveau; **page 78,** Will & Deni McIntyre/Photo Researchers; **page 82,** Robert E/ Daemmrich/Getty Images; **page 90,** © Laura Dwight/CORBIS; **pages x, 94,** Will Hart; **page 102,** Frank Siteman Photography; **page 111,** Laura Dwight Photography; **page 124,** Will Faller; **pages xi, 132,** Will Hart/PhotoEdit, Inc.; **page 139,** Elizabeth Crews Photography; **page 149,** © Marla Sweeney/Getty Images; **page 152,** Will Hart/PhotoEdit, Inc.; **page 162,** Elizabeth Crews Photography; **page 166,** courtesy of Larry Silver; **page 174,** Will Hart/ PhotoEdit, Inc.; **pages xii, 178,** Dennis MacDonald/PhotoEdit, Inc.; **page 188,** Nancy Richmond/The Image Works; **page 198,** courtesy of Mike Kelly; **page 200,** Elizabeth Crews Photography; **page 201,** Dennis MacDonald/PhotoEdit, Inc.; **page 202,** Dennis MacDonald/ PhotoEdit, Inc.; **pages xii, 210,** © Michael Greenlar/The Image Works; **page 231 top,** © Michael Greenlar/The Image Works; **page 231 bottom,** © Ellen Senisi/The Image Works; **page 235,** Tom Lindfors Photography; **pages xiii, 238,** Vickie D. King/The Clarion-Ledger; **page 242,** Will Hart; **page 253,** Will Hart/PhotoEdit, Inc.; **page 264,** courtesy of David Birt; **page 268,** Vickie D. King/The Clarion-Ledger; **page 269,** © Ellen B. Senisi/The Image Works; **pages xiii, 276,** © Grace/zefa/Corbis; **page 299 top,** courtesy of Kim Carper; **page 299 bottom,** Paul Conklin/PhotoEdit, Inc.; **page 301,** © Grace/zefa/Corbis; **page 302,** © Grace/zefa/Corbis; **pages xiv, 304, 313, 318,** © Ellen Senisi/The Image Works; **page 327,** Will Faller; **page 336,** Richard Hutchings/PhotoEdit, Inc; **page 343,** Brian Smith; **pages xv, 350,** Robin Sachs/PhotoEdit, Inc.; **page 358,** Robert Harbison; **page 359,** Brian Smith; **page 361,** Robin Sachs/PhotoEdit, Inc.; **page 364,** Robin Sachs/PhotoEdit, Inc.; **page 375,** courtesy of Martha Drennan; **page 376,** Will Hart; **pages xvi, 384,** Photodisc Royalty Free/Getty Images; **page 397,** Will Hart/PhotoEdit, Inc.; **page 414,** courtesy of Joy Katoka; **page 416,** © Jim Cummins/CORBIS; **pages xvii, 422,** Brian Smith; **page 430,** courtesy of Sara Gillison; **page 433,** © Sandra Seckinger/zefa/Corbis; **page 446,** AP Images/Michael Dwyer; **page 451,** Richard Hutchings/PhotoEdit Inc.; **pages xvii, 454,** Catherine Ledner/Stone/Getty Images; **page 459,** Will Hart/PhotoEdit, Inc.; **page 477,** Elizabeth Crews Photography; **page 485,** courtesy of Karen Weeks Canfield; **pages xvii, 490,** Ariel Skelley/Blend Images Royalty Free/Getty Images; **page 500,** Jeff Greenberg/ PhotoEdit, Inc.; **page 506,** courtesy of Val Sharpe; **page 507,** © Ellen Senisi/The Image Works; **page 513,** Ariel Skelley/Blend Images Royalty Free/Getty Images; **pages xviii, 522,** Will Hart; **page 534,** Jose I. Pelaez/Stock Market/Corbis; **page 542,** courtesy of the Flowers Family.

About the Authors

Tom E. C. Smith is currently Professor and Head, Department of Curriculum and Instruction, University of Arkansas. He has been on the faculties of the University of Arkansas at Little Rock, University of Alabama at Birmingham, and the University of Arkansas for Medical Sciences. Prior to receiving his Ed.D. from Texas Tech University, he taught children with mental retardation, learning disabilities, and autism at the elementary and secondary levels. President Clinton appointed him to three terms on the President's Committee on Mental Retardation. He has served as the Executive Director of the Division on Developmental Disabilities of the Council for Exceptional Children since 1996. His current professional interests focus on legal issues and special education.

Edward A. Polloway is the Rosel H. Schewel Professor of Education and Human Development at Lynchburg College in Virginia, where he has taught since 1976. He also serves as Vice President for Community Advancement and Dean of Graduate Studies. He received his doctoral degree from the University of Virginia and his undergraduate degree from Dickinson College in Pennsylvania. He has served twice as president of the Division on Developmental Disabilities of the Council for Exceptional Children and on the board of directors of the Council for Learning Disabilities. He also served on the committee that developed the 1992 definition of mental retardation for the American Association on Intellectual Disabilities. He is the author of 20 books and over 100 articles in the field of special education with primary interests in the areas of learning disabilities and mental retardation.

James R. Patton is an Educational Consultant and Adjunct Associate Professor at the University of Texas at Austin. He received his Ed.D. from the University of Virginia. He is a former high school biology teacher and elementary-level special education resource teacher. He has also taught students who were gifted and those who were gifted/learning disabled. His professional interests include transition, life skills instruction, adult issues related to individuals with special needs, behavioral intervention planning, and classroom accommodations. He has served on national boards of the Division on Developmental Disabilities, the Council for Learning Disabilities, and the National Joint Committee on Learning Disabilities.

Carol A. Dowdy is Professor of Special Education at the University of Alabama at Birmingham, where she has taught since receiving her Ed.D. degree from the University of Alabama, Tuscaloosa. She has written eight books on special education and published 34 articles on learning disabilities. She has served on the national board of the Council for Learning Disabilities and the Professional Advisory Board for the Learning Disabilities Association of America, and she has worked closely with the federal department of Vocational Rehabilitation to assist in their efforts to better serve adults with learning disabilities.

Brief Contents

Contents

Chapter 3 Home–School Collaboration: Working with Families   66

Chapter 4 Identifying and Programming for Student Needs   94

Chapter 8 Teaching Students with Attention Deficit/Hyperactivity Disorder   238

Chapter 9 Teaching Students with Autism Spectrum Disorders   276

Chapter 10 Teaching Students with Low-Incidence Disabilities: Sensory Impairments, Traumatic Brain Injury, and Other Severe Disabilities   304

Chapter **11**   Teaching Students with Communication Disorders   350

Chapter **12**   Teaching Students with Special Gifts and Talents   384

Special Features

RIGHTS AND RESPONSIBILITIES

TECHNOLOGY TODAY

PERSONAL SPOTLIGHT

Preface

The fifth edition of *Teaching Students with Special Needs in Inclusive Settings* comes more than ten years after we wrote the first edition. In that time, the field of special education has evolved significantly. Undoubtedly, the movement to include students with disabilities in general classrooms has taken hold; the debate is far less about whether inclusion should be used and more about how we can use it better and more effectively.

In these last ten years, the discussion about how we educate all students who differ in their learning and behavior has come to the national forefront. Faced with increasingly diverse classroom populations, educators must address meeting the needs of all students. The education of students with disabilities is part of national legislation, in particular IDEA, which was reauthorized with significant changes in 2004.

While professionals, advocates, parents, and individuals with disabilities themselves may disagree over some issues, one thing remains constant: the commitment to provide *all* students, regardless of their abilities or disabilities, with an equal opportunity to receive an appropriate education. This is not an easy challenge, but one that must be addressed. Meeting the needs of some students while not meeting the needs of others is simply not an option in our public school system.

Making the Connections

A key priority for us in creating this fifth edition was to help our readers make the necessary, practical, and satisfying connections involved in successful inclusive teaching: connections between a conceptual understanding of the nature and characteristics of the various disabilities with which many students struggle, and the practical (and often required) procedures, collaborative practices, and instructional strategies that good educators employ to help those students learn well, be accepted within their school communities, and ultimately achieve their fullest academic and social potential.

Inclusive education is an evolving, problem-solving, and recursive process, and as educators, we need constantly to ask ourselves, "How is my plan working for this child? What changes do I need to make going forward? How are these changes working?" To that end, each chapter begins with the story of a particular student or teacher in the context of that chapter's topic, and the student or teacher is then revisited throughout most chapters in several features. Complete IEPs for three students (one each in elementary school, middle school, and secondary school) are also included in the Appendices to help you connect the needs of your students with specific interventions intended to help them become more successful in school and afterwards.

As in earlier editions, you will find emphases throughout this book on three areas: collaboration; planning, assessment, and evaluation; and diversity.

- **Collaboration.** Not only do we devote a complete chapter to professional collaboration (Chapter 2), but we continue to include a unique complete chapter on home-school collaboration and working with families (Chapter 3).

- **Planning, assessment, and evaluation.**   The IEP continues to be the basis for providing appropriate instruction and meeting all the needs of students with disabilities and special needs. We provide a wealth of information and resources for working with IEPs, including sample goals for the students whose stories appear in the opening vignettes in most chapters and model IEPs in the three appendices, as well as a complete chapter on identifying and programming for students with special needs (Chapter 4).
- **Diversity.**   As cultural and linguistic diversity increases in U.S. society, it becomes critical that school personnel possess a thorough understanding of this diversity, and how to use it to enhance the education of all students. New Diversity Forums in every chapter underline the strategies needed for teaching in diverse classrooms.

How This Book Is Organized

Teaching Students with Special Needs in Inclusive Classrooms is organized around in-depth explorations of the characteristics of specific disabilities, including detailed descriptions of the disabilities, information on how to assess students with these disabilities, and specific strategies for providing appropriate instruction. The chapters fall into three major groups:

- **Chapters 1–4** present an **overview of the inclusion process**. In addition to the introduction to inclusion in Chapter 1, Chapters 2 and 3 explore the particular collaborative possibilities offered by inclusion programs, both between professionals and between educators and families, and Chapter 4 offers clear explanations of the challenges of identifying and programming for students with special needs.
- **Chapters 5–13** focus on **specific categories of disabilities and other special needs**. Chapters 5–11 provide detailed explorations of specific disabilities, while Chapters 12 and 13 explore the needs of students identified as gifted and at risk.
- **Chapters 14–16** provide specific information about **management and instruction in inclusive settings**. Chapter 14 looks at the classroom management and organization needs specific to inclusion classrooms. Chapters 15 and 16 focus on the curriculum and instruction particular to elementary and secondary inclusion programs, with a look in Chapter 14 at preschool programs and in Chapter 15 at transition from high school.

Features in the Fifth Edition

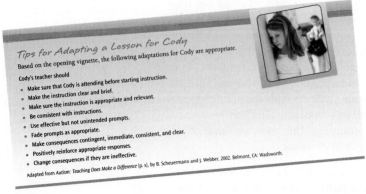

Tips for Adapting a Lesson for Cody
Based on the opening vignette, the following adaptations for Cody are appropriate.

Cody's teacher should
- Make sure that Cody is attending before starting instruction.
- Make the instruction clear and brief.
- Make sure the instruction is appropriate and relevant.
- Be consistent with instructions.
- Use effective but not unintended prompts.
- Fade prompts as appropriate.
- Make consequences contingent, immediate, consistent, and clear.
- Positively reinforce appropriate responses.
- Change consequences if they are ineffective.

Adapted from *Autism: Teaching Does Make a Difference* (p. x), by B. Scheuermann and J. Webber, 2002. Belmont, CA: Wadsworth.

- **Chapter opening scenarios** provide mini case studies of students and teachers who exemplify the chapter topics and offer Questions to Consider to focus the reader's attention on key issues to be covered in the chapter.
- **IEP Goals and Objectives** and **Tips for Adapting a Lesson** in Chapters 6–11 present sample IEP goals for the students profiled in the chapter opening scenarios, as well as practical strategies for modifying instruction to meet the particular needs of these students.
- **NEW! Evidence-Based Practice** boxes offer practical, specific, research-supported strategies for working with students with special needs in inclusive classrooms.

- **NEW and REVISED! Diversity Forums**, contributed by Shernaz Garcia and her colleagues at the University of Texas/Austin, now appear in every chapter. These boxes provide both vignettes of authentic situations and practical, research-driven information to help teachers in inclusive classrooms understand and meet the needs of culturally and linguistically diverse students.

EVIDENCE-BASED PRACTICE

Teaching Strategies to Help Problem Listeners in the Classroom

- Allow for clarification and repetition of questions during oral tests.
- Avoid use of figurative language and complex or passive sentences.
- Be an interesting speaker—use gestures, facial expressions, movement, and variety in your voice.
- Encourage students to ask questions.
- Identify problem and at-risk listeners and pair them with "study buddies."
- Keep sentence structures simple and direct.

- Limit concentrated listening time to short intervals.
- Make simple adaptations in your classroom to improve the acoustics.
- Reduce noise levels in the classroom during listening tasks.
- Refer problem listeners for hearing screenings.
- Repeat and rephrase.
- Seat problem listeners strategically.
- Speak slowly and pause between thoughts.

- Use advanced organizers and preview questions to help focus listening.
- Use the blackboard and other visual aids.

Adapted from *It's Time to Listen: Metacognitive Activities for Improving Auditory Processing in the Classroom* (2nd ed., pp. 9–15), by P. A. Hamaguchi, 2002, Austin, TX: Pro-Ed.

DIVERSITY FORUM

Cultural Contexts of Developmentally Appropriate Curriculum

Susan, a 13-year old Navajo student, is receiving services under the category of mild mental retardation. Her teacher, Mr. Villarreal, has developed a buddy system to help Susan learn new material and practice new skills. He is concerned that Susan prefers to work on her own instead of collaborating with her buddies. During a conference with Susan's family to discuss his goals, Mr. Villarreal is surprised to learn that the family wants Susan to be more independent. Her grandmother is reluctant to pressure Susan to work with a buddy because in their Navajo community, pre-adolescent children are expected to become more self-reliant and to make their own decisions.

When working with exceptional learners from diverse cultural backgrounds, teachers should keep in mind that the primary caregiver's goals for a student may reflect cultural values than those held by educators; i.e., the age at which children are expected to master self-help and academic skills can vary widely, depending on the family's cultural background and level of acculturation (Roe & Malach, 2004). For example, youth in traditional Navajo families may be expected to master the skills necessary to travel about town independently two to three years earlier than peers from the mainstream. Further, children as young as nine years of age are encouraged to make their own decisions and accept the consequences of those choices. This could include attending school, as traditional families believe that children should not be forced to do something against their will (Dehyle & LeCompte, 1999).

Culturally responsive special education services begin by integrating the student's and family's cultural values and beliefs with goals and objectives in the IEP. Factors to be considered may include:

- Parameters of acceptable behavior
- The view of child independence in the student's community
- The amount and extent of interaction desired with the community
- Gender-specific roles
- Expectations for economic self-sufficiency, and

- Independent living for people with disabilities.

Questions

1. What sources could provide you with reliable information about a family's cultural beliefs regarding child development in light of disability?
2. Who could help you develop the skills necessary to integrate home and school expectations into a coherent set of goals?

REFERENCES

Roe, J. R., & Malach, R. S. (2004). Families with American Indian roots. In, E. W. Lynch, & M. J. Hanson, (Eds.), *Developing cross-cultural competence: A guide for working with children and their families* (3rd ed.) (pp. 109-134). Baltimore, MD: Brookes.

Dehyle, D. & LeCompte, M. (1999). Cultural differences in child development: Navajo adolescents in middle schools. In R. H. Sheets & E. R. Hollins (Eds.), *Racial and ethnicity in school practices: Aspects of human development* (pp. 123-139). Mahwah, NJ: Erlbaum.

Personal Spotlight

Pam Underwood graduated from the University of Alabama at Birmingham a decade later than she originally planned. She had big dreams and excellent scholarships when she left high school to pursue a degree in social work, but the diagnosis of a disease she was told was incurable and her poor health led her to drop out of college. Thirteen years later, Pam had beaten the disease, and she returned to college full time. She raised her daughter as a single parent and still kept an A average. In fact Pam was recognized as the Outstanding Undergraduate in the Collaborative Teacher Program and was also honored as the Most Outstanding Undergraduate Campus-wide.

Although she received several offers of teaching positions, Pam chose to work with the local inner city school system that has challenging students and working conditions that are not always optimal. She decided that those students needed her, and she was up to the job. By chance I interviewed Pam at the end of her first day with students in the middle school setting in which she had been assigned. She admitted that she was overwhelmed and had a big headache! She had wanted to begin teaching right away, but found that she had several students needing to be tested first and at least one student that had been tested by last year's teacher but needed an IEP meeting right

away. She wanted to start some collaborative teaching, but paperwork seemed to be most pressing.

Alabama recently revised the IEP process to include a standards-based format that had been added since she had her college class on writing IEPs. Pam liked the new practice of using goals from the general education curriculum, because she thought it helped special and general education teachers get on the "same page" faster. However, Pam did admit that with the added step, her first IEP took her a day and a half to write. She credited her internship experience as preparing her the most for her job because in addition to teaching, she was able to follow a student from the initial referral throughout the special education process. Although college was difficult, she was grateful for all those challenges. She said, "This is the real deal! I am not in school anymore, but I still have a lot to learn!" Now with a 13 year old, a one year old, and a challenging new job, Pam has also begun graduate school. She says she plans to make it one day at a time.

Pam Underwood
First Year Special Education Teacher

- **Personal Spotlights** profile real teachers, parents of children with special needs, and students with special needs themselves, letting readers connect chapter content with real-life situations and providing insight into the multifaceted experiences of people most affected by the challenges of inclusion.
- **Technology Today** boxes provide practical updates on the emerging technologies and online resources available to help *all* students learn in today's classrooms.
- **Rights and Responsibilities** boxes examine legal cases and issues that impact the instructional process for students with special needs.
- **Sample IEPs**, found in the appendices at the back of this book, provide models for developing programs appropriate for three students: a girl in fourth grade and boys in eighth and twelfth grades.
- **Marginal notes.** Throughout, three kinds of marginal notes provide a variety of useful information for readers. *Teaching Tips* offer brief, specific instructional suggestions related to chapter content. *Cross References* point out related information to be found in other parts of the text. *Consider This* notes present issues that require problem-solving or creative thinking related to a challenging topic.

New to This Edition

- **A new chapter on autism spectrum disorders.** Because of the emerging importance of autism spectrum disorders in the student population, we chose in this edition to increase our emphasis on autism and its related disorders. As a result, we have reorganized some existing material and added a significant amount of new material to create a new chapter, Chapter 9, *Teaching Students with Autism Spectrum Disorders*. As with the other chapters covering specific disorders, this one provides basic concepts about autism (including its history and definition, information about identifying it in children and about its causes); information about the characteristics of autistic behavior, strategies for curriculum and instruction with students who are autistic, and guidance for promoting inclusion with this challenging population. A concluding section explores the particular issues of working with students with Asperger's Syndrome.

- **A new chapter on low-incidence disabilities.** To provide a more practical reflection of the range of disabilities teachers will probably face in inclusion classrooms, we have consolidated two chapters from earlier editions on sensory impairments and physical disabilities into a new chapter, Chapter 10, *Teaching Students with Low-Incidence Disabilities: Sensory Impairments, Traumatic Brain Injury, and Other Severe Disabilities*.

- **Questions to Reconsider.** We now repeat the questions that accompany each chapter opening scenario at the end of that chapter and ask readers to reconsider their responses in light of what they have learned from the chapter.

- **Marginal standards correlations.** More and more, instruction is aligned with Standards developed by various professional groups. We have added marginal notes throughout this book that connect the contents of each chapter to the Standards of both the Council on Exceptional Children and INTASC. These notes lead readers to the summaries provided [in the front matter] of the CEC and INTASC Standards. You will also find marginal correlations to the PRAXIS II Special Education: Knowledge-Based Core Principles (0351).

- **MyLabSchool activities** at the end of every chapter offer students the opportunity to explore the wealth of resources in Allyn & Bacon's unique umbrella website for education and engage in activities and assignments related to chapter content.

- **New IEP for middle school.** In addition to two new elementary and secondary student IEPs, we have added an IEP for an eighth grade boy who has been diagnosed with Attention Deficit/Hyperactivity Disorder.

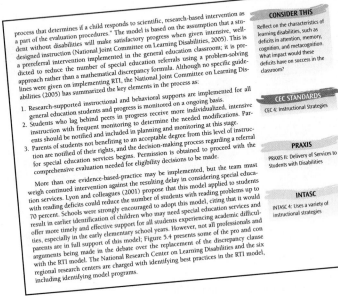

Supplements for Instructors and Students

Resources for Instructors

Instructor's Resource Manual and Test Bank. The Instructor's Resource Manual includes a wealth of interesting ideas and activities designed to help instructors teach the course. Each chapter includes a chapter-at-a-glance grid, chapter objectives, key terms, key legislation/litigation, discussion questions, activities, additional resources, and handouts. There is also a test bank for each chapter. (Please request this item from your local Allyn & Bacon sales representative; also available for download from the Instructor's Resource Center at www.ablongman.com/irc.)

Computerized Test Bank. The printed Test Bank is also available electronically through the Allyn & Bacon computerized testing system, TestGen EQ. Instructors can use TestGen EQ to create exams in just minutes by selecting from the existing database of questions, editing questions, and/or writing original questions. (Please request this item from your local Allyn & Bacon sales representative; also available for download from the Instructor's Resource Center at www.ablongman.com/irc.)

PowerPoint™ Presentation.   Ideal for lecture presentations or student handouts, the PowerPoint™ Presentation created for this text provides dozens of ready-to-use graphic and text images. (Available for download from the Instructor's Resource Center at www.ablongman.com/irc.)

Allyn & Bacon Transparencies for Special Education.   A set of 100 acetate transparencies related to topics in the text.

Videotapes for Lecture Presentation.   These videos provide a way to bring video into your course for maximized learning.

- **Snapshots: Inclusion Video** (22 minutes in length). This videotape profiles three students of differing ages and with various levels of disability in inclusive class settings. In each case, parents, classroom teachers, special education teachers, and school administrators talk about the steps they have taken to help the student succeed in inclusive settings.
- **Snapshots: Learning Disabilities, Mental Retardation, Emotional or Behavioral Disorders; Snapshots: Hearing Impairment, Visual Impairment, Traumatic Brain Injury** (each tape 20–25 minutes in length). These tapes are designed specifically for use in college classrooms. The segment for each category of disability profiles three individuals and their families, teachers, and experiences. These programs are of great interest to students; instructors who have used the tapes in their courses have found that they help disabuse students of stereotypical viewpoints and "put a human face" on the course material.
- **Professionals in Action Videotape: Teaching Students with Special Needs** (120 minutes in length). This Professionals in Action video consists of five 15- to 30-minute modules presenting viewpoints and approaches to teaching students with various disabilities in general education classrooms, in separate education settings, and in various combinations of the two. Each module explores its topic via actual classroom footage and includes interviews with general and special education teachers, parents, and students themselves.

VideoWorkshop for Introductory Special Education: Inclusion, Version 2.0.   An easy way to bring video into your course for maximized learning! This total teaching and learning system includes quality video footage on an easy-to-use CD-ROM plus a Student Learning Guide and an Instructor's Teaching Guide—both with questions and activity suggestions. The result? A program that brings textbook concepts to life with ease and that helps students understand, analyze, and apply the objectives of the course. VideoWorkshop is available for students as a value-pack option with this textbook.

Course Management.   Powered by Blackboard and hosted nationally, Allyn & Bacon's own course management system, CourseCompass, helps you manage all aspects of teaching your course. For colleges and universities with WebCT™ and Blackboard™ licenses, special course management packages can be requested in these formats as well, and the Test Item file for this text can be prepared in the appropriate format for porting into your system. Allyn & Bacon is proud to offer premium content for Special Education in these platforms. (Your sales representative can give you additional information.)

- Allyn & Bacon CourseCompass for Special Education (Access code required)
- Allyn & Bacon Blackboard for Special Education (Access code required)
- Allyn & Bacon WebCT for Introduction to Special Education (Access code required)

Resources for Students

mylabschool   Available as a value-package item with student copies of *Teaching Students with Special Needs in Inclusive Settings,* MyLabSchool is a collection of online tools for student success in the course, in licensure exams, and the teaching career. Visit www.mylabschool.com to access the following: **video clips** from real classrooms, with opportunities for students to reflect on the videos and offer their own thoughts and suggestions for applying theory to practice; an extensive archive of **text and multimedia cases** that provide valuable perspectives on real classrooms and real teaching challenges; Allyn & Bacon's **Lesson and Portfolio Builder** application, which includes an integrated state standards correlation tool; help with research papers using **Research Navigator™**, which provides access to three exclusive databases of credible and reliable source material including EBSCO's ContentSelect Academic Journal Database, *New York Times* Search by Subject Archive, and "Best of the Web" Link Library. MyLabSchool also includes a **Careers** center with resources for PRAXIS exams and licensure preparation, professional portfolio development, job search, and interview techniques.

Companion Website.   Created to accompany *Teaching Students with Special Needs in Inclusive Settings, Fifth Edition,* this online site offers **tools and activities** to help students understand and extend the text discussion and study more effectively. It includes for each text chapter learning objectives, essays, practice tests, web links, flash cards, and Questions to Consider with Expert Responses. The website also features standards correlation grids, an interactive timeline, and selected *New York Times* articles. Visit www.ablongman.com/sppd5e.

Acknowledgments

The fifth edition of *Teaching Students with Special Needs in Inclusive Settings* is the result of a great deal of effort on the part of many people. We would like to acknowledge the tremendous contribution made by numerous professionals in the field of special and general education whose daily work inspires and helps provide us with the information to share in this textbook, and we also acknowledge those authors whose works we cite regularly, who make a significant contribution to the education of children with special needs. We would also like to thank every member of our families who put up with our time away from them, whether it is physically or just mentally away while we ponder permissions, references, or the changes we need to make in that one last chapter. Especially we thank our spouses, Debi, Carolyn, Joy, and Jim. And, we could never have the energy to write about children without having the wonderful opportunities presented by the children in our own lives, namely Jake, Alex, Suni, Lyndsay, Kimi, Cameron, and Meredith.

We are especially grateful to Dr. Shernaz B. García at the University of Texas at Austin, who coordinated and edited the contribution of the new Diversity Forum features. The writing team included Mary Ellen Alsobrook, doctoral candidate at the University of Texas (Chapters 3, 7), Dr. Rocio Delgado, Trinity University (Chapter 2), Drs. Barbara Dray and Satasha Green, Buffalo State College (Chapters 10, 11, 14, 15), Dr. Peggy Hickman, Arcadia University (Chapters 1, 13), Dr. Ying Hui, Rhode Island College (Chapter 4), Won Gyoung Kim, doctoral candidate at the University of Texas (Chapters 1, 6), Dr. Audrey Trainor, University of Wisconsin/Madison (Chapters 8, 16), and Dr. Brenda-Jean Tyler, Austin Independent School District (Chapter 5).

As always, our extended family at Allyn & Bacon deserve thanks. We acknowledge in particular Virginia Lanigan, our Editor, Ginny Blanford, our Developmental Editor, Paula Carroll, our Production Editor, and Kris Ellis-Levy, our Marketing Manager. We also owe a great deal of thanks to individuals who were involved in the production and marketing of the text. These include editorial and production personnel at NK Graphics and Black Dot Group.

Finally, we want to thank those persons who have reviewed our text through various editions and whose ideas have informed our work in this fifth edition. These include:

Lynn A. Cadle, Augusta State University

Mitra Fallahi, Saint Xavier University

Jennifer Buie Hune, University of Arkansas at Little Rock

Karen L. Kelly, University of Montana, Missoula

Kevin A. Koury, California University of Pennsylvania

Loretta Salas, New Mexico State University

Qaisar Sultana, Eastern Kentucky University

Georgia Ronna Vanderslice, Southwestern Oklahoma State University

Inclusive Education: An Introduction

After reading this chapter, you should be able to:

1. Describe the evolution of services for students with special needs.
2. Describe different disabilities served in public schools.
3. Describe the key components of IDEA, Section 504, and the ADA.
4. Describe the advantages and disadvantages of different service delivery models for students with special needs.
5. Discuss methods that enhance the inclusion of students with disabilities.
6. Discuss the role of school personnel in inclusion.
7. Describe issues facing special education.
8. Describe the role of philosophy and ethics in serving children with disabilities.

Questions to Consider

1. How would Kevin's life have been different had he been born in 1950 rather than in the 1980s?

2. Would more inclusion in secondary schools have had a positive or negative impact on Kevin's future success?

3. Has IDEA been a success or failure for Kevin and many other individuals with disabilities?

Kevin is twenty-five years old. He is intelligent; however, he has very limited oral language skills and displays many characteristics expected of an adult with severe autism. When Kevin was three years old he was diagnosed with autism. He was immediately enrolled in a preschool program for children with disabilities under Part H (now Part C) of the Individuals with Disabilities Education Act (IDEA). At the age of six, Kevin transitioned to kindergarten. He was in a self-contained special education classroom for children with severe disabilities for the first three years. Beginning in the third grade, Kevin was included in a regular classroom for a small portion of each day. Surprisingly, to his parents and many teachers, he did better in his new placement than the special education placement. His behavior improved; his oral language improved; and his general academic performance improved. As a result of his success, Kevin's time in the inclusive setting was increased over the next several years until he was included for approximately 80 percent of the school day by the sixth grade. Kevin continued to progress. When he went to junior high school, Kevin's time in a special education setting was again increased; he was placed in some regular classes, mostly those with lower academic expectations. In high school Kevin's placement in special education settings increased again, primarily because of his difficulty with higher academic tasks. His individualized education program (IEP) focused more on functional classes and prevocational activities.

Since Kevin completed his high school program at the age of twenty-two, he has been attending an adult day-service program. He recently moved to a group home for individuals with moderate to severe disabilities. Kevin's educational program provided him with many benefits. Had he been born twenty years earlier, he would have been school age before the passage of Public Law 94–142. This likely would have meant that Kevin would not have had access to public education; his parents could have easily placed him in an institutional setting because there would have been no other programming options. While Kevin would have likely benefited from more inclusion in middle and secondary schools, his earlier inclusion improved his social skills and enabled him to learn some basic academic skills that he still uses and enables him to live semi-independently.

The public education system in the United States continues to be unequaled in the world. Rather than serving the needs of certain groups of students, such as those who are wealthy, those with certain academic potential, or those of certain genders, the U.S. education system is for all children. It attempts to offer thirteen or more years of free, equal educational opportunities to all children, including those with parents who are not educated and those from families without financial means. Children with disabilities and those who have learning or behavior problems are included in this educational system. Students do not have to pass certain tests to attend various schools, nor do their families need to pay for a comprehensive educational program. Students do not have to choose, early in their school years, the school track that they will follow.

PRAXIS

PRAXIS II: Legal and Societal Issues

The U.S. Constitution, which guarantees equal opportunities for all citizens, is the basis for the free public educational system. Since beginning in the mid-1800s, public schools have evolved into a system that provides educational opportunities for all students. Initially that was not the case. Girls did not secure their right to equal educational opportunities until the early 1900s; racial minorities not until the 1950s and 1960s; and students with disabilities not until the 1970s and 1980s. Litigation and legislation played important roles as each group secured the right to participate in public educational programs (Murdick, Gartin, & Crabtree, 2007).

History of Education for Students with Disabilities

Prior to federal legislation passed in the mid-1970s, many schools did not provide any programs for students with disabilities, or the programs they provided were very minimal. In fact, in 1970, only 20 percent of all children with disabilities were served in public school programs (U.S. Department of Education, 2006). Until the 1970s, it was estimated that 3 million children with disabilities received inappropriate or inadequate services, while up to 1 million were totally excluded from the educational system (U.S. Department of Education, 2000). The only recourses available for most parents were private educational programs or programs specifically designed for "handicapped" students. In many cases, parents paid for these educational programs out of their own resources. And in many situations, students with disabilities stayed home and received no formal education (Katsiyannis, Yell, & Bradley 2001).

CEC STANDARDS

CEC 1: Foundations

In a few schools, students with physical disabilities or mental retardation were provided with services; however, these services were nearly always in self-contained, isolated classrooms, and the students rarely interacted with nondisabled students. Services for this group of children were simply slow to develop because of limited financial resources and public apathy (Alexander & Alexander, 2001).

Some children with disabilities received services in **residential programs**. Typically, children with mental retardation and with sensory deficits were placed in these settings (Crane, 2002). In 1965 approximately 100,000 children, from birth to twenty-one years old, lived in institutions for people with mental retardation in the United States (White, Lakin, Bruininks, & Li, 1991). The first school for children with deafness in the United States was established in 1817 as the American Asylum for the Education of the Deaf and Dumb (now the American School for the Deaf) (Stewart & Kluwin, 2000). The first school for children with visual problems, the New England Asylum for the Blind, was founded in 1832. In 1963 nearly 50 percent of children classified as legally blind in the United States lived in residential schools for the blind. These residential programs offered daily living support as well as some education and training.

Since the mid-1970s services to students with disabilities have changed dramatically. Not only are more appropriate services provided by schools, but they are also frequently provided in both **resource rooms** and general education classrooms with collaboration between special education and general classroom teachers (U.S. Department of Education, 2003). Many different developments brought about this change, including parental advocacy, legislation, and litigation. The federal government played a major part in the evolution of special education services, primarily through legislation, litigation, and funding.

Services for students with disabilities evolved in four distinct phases: relative isolation, integration (mainstreaming), inclusion, and empowerment (Polloway, Smith, Patton, & Smith, 1996). In the **relative isolation** phase, which included the first sixty to seventy years in the twentieth century, students were either denied access to public schools or permitted to attend only in isolated settings. In the **integration** phase, which began in the 1970s, students with disabilities were mainstreamed, or integrated, into general education programs when appropriate. During the **inclusion** phase, starting in the mid-1980s, emphasis was placed on students with disabilities being included in all school programs and activities. This phase differed from the integration phase in a minor but very significant way.

Although students with disabilities were in general classrooms under both integration and inclusion, in the inclusion phase it was assumed that these students belonged in general classrooms, whereas in the integration phase they were considered to be special education students who were simply placed in the general classroom part of the time, primarily for socialization. Most recently, the fourth phase of services, empowerment and self-determination, has been the focus of inclusion efforts, to better prepare students for the highest degree of independence possible (Lee, Palmer, Turnbull, & Wehmeyer, 2006; Wehmeyer, Garner, Yeager, Lawrence, & Davis, 2006). The idea of student-led conferences is a prime example of the focus on self-determination (Test et al., 2004). Figure 1.1 depicts the historical changes in the education of students with disabilities in public education. While the changes in special education during the past twenty-five years have been dramatic, probably the most significant change has been acceptance of the idea that special education is a service, not a place. In other words, special education is not a classroom in a building; rather, it is the specialized instruction and services provided for students with disabilities. It is not a place; it is a service.

Because all children are entitled to a public education in the United States, teachers in today's public schools must provide instruction and other educational services that meet the needs of a growingly diverse student population. In fact, the diversity of students in today's schools is far greater than in the past. Compare students in today's schools with students in U.S. schools in the 1950s. Table 1.1 shows the primary differences between these two groups of students. Traditionally, teacher education programs have focused on teaching students who learn in similar ways and at similar levels. However, today's teachers do not have the luxury of teaching only students who learn easily and behave in a manner the teachers deem appropriate based on their own standards. They must be prepared to deal effectively with all kinds of students. The following summarizes some of the major types of student groups found in today's schools.

> **CONSIDER THIS**
>
> Should all children, even those with very different learning needs, have access to free educational services in public schools? Why or why not? What about the high costs that may be incurred?

Figure 1.1

Historical Changes in Education for Students with Disabilities

From "Historic Changes in Mental Retardation and Developmental Disabilities," by E. A. Polloway, J. D. Smith, J. R. Patton, and T. E. C. Smith, 1996, *Education and Training in Mental Retardation and Developmental Disabilities, 31*, p. 9. Used by permission.

Table 1.1	Differences between Students in 1950 and 2005
Students in 1950	**Students in 2005**
Two-parent homes	One-parent homes, most often single mothers
Stay-at-home mothers	Mothers working outside of home
All students speak English	Many students do not speak English as their primary language
Most students from lower to middle class economically	Many students living below the poverty line; many students in upper economic status
Parents mostly support school over child	Many parents support the child over the the school
Most students and their families from the area	Many students and their families from other regions of the country
Extended families in the area	Extended families not present

Defining Students with Special Needs

CONSIDER THIS

What is a typical child? Is there such a thing as an average child or person? Can schools afford to look at each child as a unique learner?

PRAXIS

1: Understanding exception-alities

INTASC

2: Teacher understands how students differ

CEC STANDARDS

1: Foundations

Many students do not fit the mold of the "typical" student. They include those with identi-fied disabilities, those who are classified as gifted and talented, and those who are "at risk" for developing problems. It has been estimated that 11.5 percent of school-age children, or approximately 5.9 million students, are classified as disabled and are served in special edu-cation programs (U.S. Department of Education, 2006). Another group of students experi-ence a degree of disability that is not significant enough to result in special education eligibility. Many of these students, approximately 1–3 percent of the student population, are eligible for certain services and protections under Section 504 and the Americans with Disabilities Act (Smith, 2001; Smith, 2002; Zirkell, 1999). Still other students need special attention because of poverty, difficulties with language, or other at-risk factors (Gollnick & Chinn, 2006). These students exhibit various characteristics that often result in school problems (Morgan, 1994a). Adding all these students together, plus gifted students, who are considered to be an additional 3–5 percent of the school population, shows that 20–30 percent of all students in public schools have some special needs. Although many of these students do not meet the specific criteria to be classified as "disabled" and are therefore not eligible for special education or 504 services, school personnel cannot afford to ignore the special problems presented by these students (Barr & Parrett, 2001).

Diversity among students in public schools represents the norm rather than the exception (Gollnick & Chinn, 2006). If public schools are to be effective, school per-sonnel must address the needs of all children, including children with special needs. They must be able to identify these students and help develop and implement effective programs. A first step for classroom teachers is to understand the types of students they need to serve.

Students with Disabilities Served under IDEA

One of the largest and most visible groups of students with special needs in the public school system includes those formally classified as having disabilities as defined by the **Individuals with Disabilities Education Act (IDEA)**. Students with disabilities are defined as those who exhibit one of several specific conditions that result in their need for special education and related services. The number of children with disabilities has grown significantly since the mid-1970s (U.S. Department of Education, 2006). Table 1.2

Table 1.2	**Number of Students Ages Three to Twenty-One Served under IDEA in the 1989–1990 and 2002–2003 School Years**	
	1989–1990	**2002–2003**
Specific learning disabilities	2,062,076	2,839,311
Speech and language impairments	974,256	1,103,091
Mental retardation	563,902	580,375
Emotional disturbance	381,639	480,187
Multiple disabilities	87,957	130,443
Hearing impairments	57,906	71,112
Orthopedic impairments	48,050	73,617
Other health impairments	52,733	390,295
Visual impairments	22,866	25,520
Autism	NA	118,092
Deaf-blindness	1,633	1,536
Traumatic brain injury	NA	21,384
Developmental delay	NA	58,075
All disabilities	4,253,018	5,893,038

From U.S. Department of Education, 2006.

shows the number of children, by disability, served during the 1989–1990 and 2002–2003 school years.

Many different types of students are found in these thirteen categories. For example, the broad area of **other health impairments** includes hemophilia, diabetes, epilepsy, and sickle-cell anemia. Even the category of learning disabilities comprises an extremely heterogeneous group of students. The fact that disability categories are composed of different types of students makes it impossible to draw simple conclusions about them. The following paragraphs provide a general description of the categories of disabilities recognized in IDEA.

Mental retardation The disability category that has been recognized for the longest time in most school districts is mental retardation (Crane, 2002). Students with mental retardation are usually identified through intelligence tests and measures of adaptive behavior, which indicate a person's ability to perform functional activities expected of age and cultural norms. By definition, individuals with mental retardation score less than 70–75 on individual intelligence tests and have concurrent deficits in adaptive behavior (American Association on Mental Retardation, 2002). Their general characteristics include problems in learning, memory, problem solving, and social skills (Taylor, Richards, & Brady, 2005).

Learning disabilities The learning disabilities category accounts for more than 50 percent of students served in special education (U.S. Department of Education, 2006). This category is beset with problems of definition and programming, but it continues to include more children than all other special education categories combined (Lyon et al., 2001; Smith, Dowdy, Polloway, & Blalock, 1997). In general, the achievements of students with learning disabilities are not proportionate with their abilities. Although the cause of learning disabilities is unclear, the controversial assumption is that a neurological dysfunction causes the learning disability (Hallahan, Lloyd, Kauffman, Weiss, & Martinez, 2005).

Emotional disturbance Students with emotional disturbance exhibit inappropriate behaviors or emotions that result in disruptions for themselves or others in their environment. Whereas the federal government uses the term "emotional disturbance,"

CEC STANDARDS
1: Foundations   **CEC**

PRAXIS
1: Understanding exceptionalities

INTASC
2: Teacher understands how students differ   *INTASC*

specifically eliminating from the category children and youth who are socially maladjusted, other groups prefer the terms emotional and behavior disorders or behavior disorders. Mental health professionals use still other terms, such as conduct disorder and depression. In addition to differing on terminology, professionals serving children with these problems also differ on definitions of the problems and the types of services they provide (Coleman & Webber, 2002).

Deafness/Hearing Impairments   Students with hearing impairment include those whose permanent or fluctuating impairments in hearing adversely affect their educational performance. Those considered deaf have impairments that result in difficulties in processing linguistic information through hearing, with or without amplification (IDEA, 2004). Students classified as hard of hearing can process linguistic information through hearing with assistance (Stewart & Kluwin, 2001).

Visual Impairments   Students' educational performance may be adversely affected because of impairments in vision, even with correction. This category includes students who are partially sighted and those who are blind (IDEA, 2004). Students who are partially sighted can generally read print, whereas those classified as blind cannot (Freiberg, 2005).

Orthopedic Impairments   Many students experience problems related to their physical abilities. Students with cerebral palsy, spina bifida, amputations, or muscular dystrophy are a few examples. For these students, physical access to educational facilities and problems with writing and manipulation are important concerns.

Other Health Impairments   Students are classified as having other health impairments when they have limited strength, vitality, or alertness due to chronic or acute health problems. Examples of such problems include asthma, diabetes, epilepsy, hemophilia, and leukemia. Attention deficit disorder (ADD) or attention deficit hyperactivity disorder (ADHD) may be included in this category (IDEA, 2004). As with orthopedic impairment, this category includes a wide variety of disabling conditions.

Autism   In the 1990 reauthorization of Public Law (PL) 94–142, Congress added autism as a separate disability category. Autism is a lifelong disability that primarily affects communication and social interactions. Children with autism typically relate to people, objects, and events in abnormal ways; they insist on structured environments and display many self-stimulating behaviors (Tryon, Mayes, Rhodes, & Waldo, 2006).

Traumatic Brain Injury   In 1990, Congress also added traumatic brain injury (TBI) as a separate disability category. TBI "means an acquired injury to the brain caused by an external physical force, resulting in total or partial functional disability or psychosocial impairment, or both, that adversely affects a child's educational performance" (IDEA, 2004). TBI applies to both open or closed head injuries that affect a variety of areas, including cognition, memory, attention, judgment, and problem solving (Best, 2005).

Speech or Language Impairments   For some children, speech difficulties are a serious problem. When the impairment results in a need for special education and related services, children are considered eligible for services under IDEA. Most of these children need speech therapy (Polloway, Miller, & Smith, 2003). Teachers need to work closely with speech and language specialists when dealing with this group of students.

PRAXIS

PRAXIS II: Legal and Societal Issues

Students Eligible for Section 504 and the ADA

Students who need special assistance do not all fit neatly into disability categories defined by IDEA. Other federal statutes, namely Section 504 of the Rehabilitation Act and the Americans with Disabilities Act (ADA), use a very different definition of disability, employing a functional, not a categorical, model. Under Section 504 and the

ADA, a person is considered to have a disability if that individual (1) has a physical or mental impairment that substantially limits one or more major life activities; (2) has a record of such an impairment; or (3) is regarded as having such an impairment. The acts do not provide an exhaustive list of such impairments but require the functional criterion of "substantial limitation" to be the qualifying element (Smith, 2001; Smith & Patton, 2007).

As previously noted, many students not eligible for IDEA services may have disabilities that are covered under Section 504, because the definition of disability in Section 504 and the ADA is broader than the definition used in IDEA. Eligibility for Section 504 and the ADA is based on impairments that result in substantial limitations of such major life activities as breathing, walking, seeing, hearing, and learning. Schools are required to refer students who are thought to be eligible for services and protections under Section 504 and the ADA for evaluation. If students are determined eligible, schools must provide accommodations for them in academic and nonacademic areas that enable them to receive a free appropriate public education (Smith, 2002; Smith & Patton, 2007).

Students Classified as Gifted and Talented

Some students differ from their peers by having above-average intelligence and learning abilities. These students, classified as gifted and talented, were traditionally defined and identified using intelligence quotient (IQ) test scores. IQ scores of 120 or higher were the primary criterion, but current criteria are much broader. Although no single definition is accepted by all groups, most focus on students who are capable of making significant contributions to society in a variety of areas, including academic endeavors and creative, mechanical, motor, or fine arts skills.

Students At Risk for School Problems

Some students who do not have a specific disability category and do not have an above-average capacity to achieve also present problems for the educational system. These students, considered to be **at risk** for developing problems, manifest characteristics that could easily lead to learning and behavior problems (Morrison, 2006). Some of these students considered at risk include the following:

CONSIDER THIS

Should students who are considered at risk for developing learning and behavior problems be provided special services?

- Drug and alcohol abusers
- Students from minority cultures
- Students from low-income homes
- Teenagers who become pregnant
- Students who speak English as a second language
- Students who are in trouble with the legal system

These students may present unique problems for teachers who attempt to meet their educational needs in general education classrooms. Since students in the at-risk group are not eligible for special education services, classroom teachers bear the primary responsibility for their educational programs, which may need to be modified to meet these students' needs.

Teenage girls who have babies are at risk for dropping out of school.

Current Services for Students with Special Needs

Most students with special needs receive a portion of their education from classroom teachers in general education classrooms. In 2003 the U.S. Department of Education stated that "most students with disabilities (around 96 percent) are being educated in regular school buildings, and almost half are in regular classrooms for most of the day" (U.S. Department of Education, 2006). For students who are gifted or at-risk, this has always been the norm. Students in these two groups have always remained in general education classes for most, if not all, of their instruction. Similarly, students who are eligible for services under Section 504 and the ADA are served in general classrooms because they are not eligible for IDEA services (Smith, 2002).

Since the mid-1980s, the movement to serve students with disabilities in general education classrooms with their nondisabled peers has become the trend (U.S. Department of Education, 2003). As early as 1998, McLeskey, Henry, and Hodges noted that educating students with disabilities in general education settings was one of the most significant changes in public education during the previous fifteen years. Since the beginning of the twenty-first century, the inclusion movement has only expanded. Since the 1991 school year, the number of students with disabilities who are educated outside the regular classroom not more than 20 percent of the day has increased by more than 60 percent (U.S. Department of Education, 2006).

Inclusion entails more than merely physically locating students with special needs in classrooms with their chronological-age peers; it requires that they be included in all aspects of the classroom and that their educational needs be met through services provided within the general education classroom.

Actions Leading to Inclusion of Students with Disabilities

CEC STANDARDS

CEC 1: Foundations

From 1950 to 1970 the self-contained classroom was the primary setting for serving students with disabilities. This service model greatly limited the interaction among students with disabilities and general education teachers and students, thus isolating these students. In the late 1970s this segregated service approach gave way to mainstreaming students with disabilities into general education classrooms, either full time or for part of each school day. The process of mainstreaming came about as a result of several factors. These included the civil rights movement, federal and state legislation, litigation, actions by advocacy groups, and actions by professionals.

PRAXIS

PRAXIS II: Legal and Societal Issues

The Civil Rights Movement   Prior to the 1950s many students from minority racial groups were educated in "separate but equal" schools. Most communities had separate schools for African American children and separate schools for white children. Often, Mexican American and Asian children were educated in the "white" schools. The civil rights movement to eliminate discrimination based on racial differences emerged as a significant social force in the 1950s. It culminated in the 1960s with the dismantling of the system of school segregation on the basis of race. State and federal court cases and legislation mandated equal access to all schools by children from all backgrounds, including all races.

CONSIDER THIS

How available do you think services for students with disabilities would be today were it not for the civil rights movement of the 1960s? Would services be better or worse for these students?

The critical event in the civil rights movement that supported the education of students with disabilities was the *Brown v. Board of Education* court case in 1954. In this case, the U.S. Supreme Court unanimously struck down laws allowing for racial segregation (Smith & Kozleski, 2005). Parents of students with disabilities soon realized that they could emulate the successful actions of civil rights groups and gain better services for their children. This court decision "laid the foundation for litigation to challenge the constitutionality of 'separate but equal' as it related to public school

Personal Spotlight

A Principal's Perspective on Education

John Colbert has been an elementary principal for more than twenty years. During that time he has witnessed major changes in the way students with disabilities are taught. For the most part, John thinks these changes have been very positive. For example, he says that "having students with disabilities in our school building, and indeed our regular classrooms, has done more than anything else in getting these students accepted by their classmates." John notes that while the movement to include students with disabilities has been mostly positive, there have been some bumps in the road. Dealing with teachers who have not wanted these students in their rooms has been one of the most difficult barriers to successful inclusion. He says that the best way to deal with teachers who have reservations about inclusion is to have them talk with teachers who have been successful. "I can talk to them all day long, but they really don't think I know the problems created by some of these students. On the other hand, when they talk to other teachers who have had success, they tend to believe them."

John thinks that full inclusion is not an appropriate solution for many students who need to be pulled out periodically for special instruction. He is a strong supporter of the resource room model where students spend most of their days in regular classes but are pulled out into the resource room for specialized instruction. John believes that this model provides the best of all worlds—opportunities to be with peers for socialization purposes and opportunities for specialized instruction by special education teachers. John believes that one of the easiest groups to deal with regarding inclusion is students. He says that students, in general, think that including students with disabilities is not a problem at all. His view is that barriers to this movement, while very fixable, are primarily adult based, not child based.

John Colbert
Principal
Holcomb Elementary School, Fayetteville, AR

opportunities for students with disabilities" (Blanchett, Mumford, & Beachum, 2005, p. 73).

Using legislation, litigation, and advocacy, parents sought to gain equal opportunities for their children, who had been denied access to public education solely on the basis of having a disability. "Whereas the movement to desegregate schools racially and the movement to integrate students with disabilities have operated in parallel universes, activists for the desegregation of schools for students with disabilities have capitalized on the arguments and strategies used for racial desegregation." (Smith & Kozelski, 2005, p. 274).

CONSIDER THIS

How are students with disabilities similar to students from racial minorities? Are similar educational services being offered to both groups of students?

Legislation Probably the factor most responsible for the inclusion of students with disabilities was legislation, which was often enacted in response to litigation. Parents of students with disabilities noted that the civil rights legislation passed in the 1960s helped break down racial segregation barriers in schools. Therefore, they advocated for legislation that would have the same result for their children. In advocating for appropriate legislation, parents also noted that funds needed to be provided and teachers appropriately trained to meet the needs of students with disabilities. The most important legislation to help students with disabilities access general education programs was PL 94–142, which was passed in 1975 and implemented in 1978, and reauthorized numerous times (Smith, 2005). However, prior to its passage, several other legislative acts helped pave the way. These included the following:

- PL 83–531 (1954), which provided funding for research into mental retardation.
- PL 89–313 (1965), which provided funds for children in hospitals and institutions.
- PL 93–112 (1973), Section 504 of the Rehabilitation Act of 1973.
- PL 93–380 (1973), the precursor to PL 94–142.
- PL 94–103 (1974), Developmentally Disabled Assistance and Bill of Rights Act of 1974.

An in-depth discussion of PL 94–142/IDEA, Section 504, and the ADA will be presented in a later section.

CEC STANDARDS

CEC 1: Foundations

Litigation   In addition to legislation, litigation has played a major role in the development of current services to students with disabilities. The *Brown v. Board of Education* case set the stage by supporting the notion that equal opportunities in education were just as applicable to students with disabilities as to students from racial minorities (Blanchett, Brantlinger, & Shealey, 2005). Important litigation has focused on numerous issues, including (1) the right to education for students with disabilities; (2) nonbiased assessment for students; (3) procedural safeguards for students with disabilities; (4) the right to an extended school year at public expense for some students; (5) related services for students; (6) the right to be educated in general education classrooms; and (7) the interpretation by the U.S. Supreme Court of the intent of Congress in PL 94–142 (Turnbull & Turnbull, 2000). Several landmark court cases from the 1970s, 1980s, and

---

DIVERSITY FORUM

Inclusive Education in an Era of Accountability: Counting Each and All

Ms. Goodman, principal of a Title I school, held a faculty meeting to discuss the results of the recent state accountability assessment. During the last two years, the school has focused on improving instruction for all students. Ellen, a special educator, mentioned that her two-year collaboration with a bilingual education teacher has given her new insights into addressing the cultural and linguistic needs of her students. Doug, a general educator, shared his successes with differentiating instruction in response to students' learning styles, skill levels, and interests. Ms. Goodman said, "Our analysis of academic needs of our students on the benchmark assessments, and attention to instruction that targets those needs, has paid off in better student understanding and scores. I applaud you for accepting responsibility for ensuring that all children at our school can succeed."

The accountability provisions in No Child Left Behind (2001) and IDEA (2004) provide schools with structured ways to examine student achievement data to ensure that *all* students are experiencing academic success. This includes students with disabilities, students from low-income backgrounds, English language learners, and students who are African American, Latino, Native American, and Asian/Pacific Islander. By analyzing scores, school personnel are able to identify struggling learners whose instruction can then focus on these skills areas, using evidence-based practices.

In Mrs. Goodman's school, the expectation that teachers will collaborate to ensure student success creates a climate in which teachers seek to create responsive learning environments through various means. In today's era of inclusion and accountability, each and every teacher must take responsibility for understanding how to meet the needs of students who may have special education needs, who are culturally and linguistically diverse, or come from nonmainstream economic or social backgrounds (Hickman, 2004; Scheurich & Skrla, 2003). In a school climate of shared responsibility, *all* professionals collaborate to address the learning needs of *each* and *all* students.

Questions

1. What types of information might special education teachers share with general education teachers (including bilingual education and English-as-a-second language teachers), and vice-versa, to support effective instruction and learning for students with disabilities?

2. How might personnel in a school work to directly meet the academic needs of all students? For example, how might physical education teachers, music teachers, or counselors contribute to a school climate of shared responsibility for student learning?

3. What types of school-level and administrative supports might be necessary to develop and maintain shared responsibility for all learners?

REFERENCES

Hickman, P. (2004). *Sociocultural dimensions of White principal leadership in multicultural elementary schools.* Unpublished doctoral dissertation, The University of Texas at Austin.

Scheurich, J. J., & Skrla, L. (2003). *Leadership for equity and excellence: Creating high-achievement classrooms, schools, and districts.* Thousand Oaks, CA: Corwin Press.

1990s helped shape current special education services by setting legal precedents and encouraging Congress to act to pass critical federal legislation (Katsiyannis et al., 2001). These cases are summarized in Table 1.3.

PRAXIS

PRAXIS II: Legal and Societal Issues

Parental Advocacy   The third primary force that facilitated the inclusion of students with disabilities in general classrooms was parental advocacy. Parents not only encouraged schools to integrate students with disabilities, but they were also directly involved with the legislation and litigation that broke down barriers for these students. Without them, Congress would not have passed PL 94–142. Also, parental advocacy was directly

Table 1.3   **Legal Cases**

Supreme Court Cases		
Case	**Key issue**	**Ruling**
Board of Education of the Hendrick Hudson Central School District v. Rowley (1982)	FAPE	• Schools would be considered to have met the FAPE provision of IDEA if the IEP, developed through the act's procedures, is reasonably calculated to enable the child to receive educational benefits.
Irving Independent School District v. Tatro (1984)	Related services	• Health services must be necessary to assist the student to benefit from special education, and the service must be performed by a nonphysician, to be considered a related service.
Burlington School Committee of the Town of Burlington v. Department of Education of Massachusetts (1985)	Tuition reimbursement	• Parents who unilaterally place their children with disabilities in a private school are entitled to reimbursement for tuition and living expenses if a court finds that the public school's proposed IEP was inappropriate.
Honig v. Doe (1988)	Discipline	• Schools must abide by the stay-put provision (during administrative or court proceedings, the student must remain in his or her present placement). • Students cannot be excluded unilaterally for misbehavior that is related to their disability. • Exclusions over ten days constitute a change of placement.
Florence County School District Four v. Carter (1993)	Tuition reimbursement	• Parents can be reimbursed for private school tuition if the public school failed to offer an appropriate education and if the private school offered an appropriate education. • Private schools do not have to be on a state-approved list for a court to order reimbursement.
Zobrest v. Catalina Foothills School District (1993)	Establishment clause and services in parochial schools	• The establishment clause of the U.S. Constitution does not bar interpreter services to a student with a disability unilaterally placed by his or her parents in a parochial school. • The services must be provided in a religiously neutral manner, and IDEA funds must not find their way into a parochial school's coffers.
Cedar Rapids Community School District v. Garrett F. (1999)	Related services	• Health services deemed necessary for a qualified child with a disability by the IEP team must be provided as long as a nonphysician can perform the services.

Note. FAPE = free appropriate public education; IDEA = Individuals with Disabilities Education Act; IEP = individualized education program.

Table 1.3   **Legal Cases (Continued)**

Lower Court Cases		
Key issue	**Court case**	**Ruling**
Zero reject	• _Timothy W. v. Rochester, New Hampshire School District_ (1989)	• FAPE must be available to all qualified students with disabilities, without exception. • Schools cannot use a student's ability to benefit educationally as a condition of eligibility for special education services.
Least restrictive environment	• _Daniel R. R. v. State Board of Education_ (1989)	• To determine whether a school has adhered to the LRE mandate of the IDEA, a court must ask (a) if education in the regular classroom with supplementary aids and services can be achieved satisfactorily, and (b) if a student is placed in a more restrictive setting, whether the student is integrated to the maximum extent appropriate.
	• _Hartmann v. Loudoun County Board of Education_ (1997)	• The IDEA's mainstreaming provision is a presumption, not an inflexible mandate. • Mainstreaming is not required when (a) a student with a disability would not receive benefit from such placement; (b) any marginal benefits would be significantly outweighed by benefits that could feasibly be obtained in a separate setting; and (c) the student's presence is a disruptive force.
Extended school year	• _Armstrong v. Kline_ (1979)	• Students with disabilities are entitled to extended school year services if necessary to receive a FAPE.
Private schools	• _K. R. v. Anderson Community School Corporation_ (1996)	• If a public school has offered a FAPE to a student with disabilities unilaterally placed in a private school by his or her parents, the school has no further obligation.
Discipline	• _S-I v. Turlington_ (1981)	• A manifest determination is necessary before expulsion for students with disabilities; disciplinary exclusions are subject to IDEA procedural safeguards; and cessation of services is prohibited.
Placement	• _Spielberg v. Henrico Public Schools_ (1988)	• The school's determination to change a student's placement prior to developing an IEP violates a parent's right to participate in its development and therefore violates the IDEA.

Note. FAPE = free, appropriate public education; LRE = least restrictive environment; IDEA = Individuals with Disabilities Education Act; IEP = individualized education program.

From "Reflections on the 25th Anniversary of the Individuals with Disabilities Education Act," by A. Katsiyannis, M. L. Yell, and R. Bradley, 2001, _Remedial and Special Education 22_, pp. 328–329. Used with permission.

INTASC

INTASC 10: The teacher fosters relationships with school colleagues, families, . . .

responsible for litigation that forced many schools to include students with disabilities in general education classrooms. The result was a powerful coalition that targeted discriminatory practices that excluded students with disabilities from public education (Smith, Gartin, Murdick, & Hilton, 2006).

Parents have unified their efforts and maximized their influence by forming advocacy groups. The power of such organizations frequently results in changes in educational systems. The ARC (formerly the Association for Retarded Citizens), formed in 1950 as the National Association of Retarded Children, played a major role in getting local school districts, state education agencies, and the federal government to require the inclusion of students with disabilities in general education classrooms (Yell, Rogers, & Rogers, 1998). Following the lead of the Arc, other groups, such as the Association for Children with Learning Disabilities (ACLD) (now the Learning Disabilities Association), continued to pressure schools to provide appropriate educational services in the least restrictive setting.

PL 94–142/IDEA

CEC STANDARDS

CEC 1: Foundations

Public Law 94–142, the Education for All Handicapped Children Act (EHA), literally opened the doors of public schools and general education classrooms to students with disabilities (Katsiyannis et al., 2001). It was the result of much debate that followed the PARC and Mills cases (Yell et al., 1998). Under PL 94–142, now called the Individuals with Disabilities Education Improvement Act (IDEA), schools are required to seek out and implement appropriate educational services for all students with disabilities, regardless of the severity; to provide appropriate, individualized services to students with disabilities; and to actively involve parents in the educational process. For general education teachers, the most important part of the legislation is the requirement that students with disabilities be educated with their nondisabled peers as much as possible (Smith, 2005).

PRAXIS

PRAXIS II: Legal and Societal Issues

Since its original passage in 1975 as PL 94–142, IDEA has been reauthorized by Congress several times. Though each reauthorization has made changes in the original law, the basic requirements have remained relatively intact. The 1983 reauthorization provided incentives for serving preschool children. In 1986, the IDEA reauthorization mandated services for children with disabilities ages three to five. The 1990 reauthorization renamed the law to the Individuals with Disabilities Education Act (IDEA), and replaced the word handicap with the word disability. In addition, two new separate categories of disabilities were added—autism and TBI—and schools were required to develop transition planning for students when they turned sixteen years old (Smith, 2005). The most recent reauthorization of the act was in 2004. The following paragraphs describe some of the most important elements found in IDEA. Table 1.4 summarizes each of the act's reauthorizations. Table 1.5 summarizes the key components of IDEA 2004.

Child Find IDEA requires schools to seek out students with disabilities. This provision was a "hallmark of the 1975 statute and subsequent amendments" because so many children had been excluded from services before the legislation was passed (U.S. Department of Education, 2000, p. vii). To meet this mandate, schools have conducted

---

Table 1.4	Key Components of Reauthorizations of PL 94–142/IDEA

Reauthorization	Key components
1983 (PL 98–199)	1. Provided incentives for states to serve preschool children with disabilities. 2. Required states to collect information and address issues related to students transitioning from school to postschool.
(PL 101–457)	1. Mandated services for children ages three to five, lowering all of the requirements of PL 94–142 to include three- to five-year-old children. 2. Provided for attorney's fees in due process or court cases where parents prevailed.
(PL 101–476)	1. Added autism and traumatic brain injury to the list of disabilities covered under IDEA. 2. Changed the name of the act from the Education for All Handicapped Children Act to the Individuals with Disabilities Education Act. 3. Required schools to initiate transition services no later than age sixteen.
1997 (PL 105–17)	1. Required schools to initiate transition planning no later than age fourteen. 2. Required schools to include behavior intervention plans for students with behavior problems.

From IDEA 2004: Another round of re-authorization. Smith, 2005. *Remedial and Special Education 26,* p. 316.

Table 1.5	Key Components of the Individuals with Disabilities Education Act (IDEA) (2004)
Provisions	**Description**
Least restrictive environment	Children with disabilities are educated with nondisabled children as much as possible.
Individualized education program	All children served in special education must have an individualized education program.
Due-process rights	Children and their parents must be involved in decisions about special education.
Due-process hearing	Parents and schools can request an impartial hearing if there is a conflict over special education services.
Nondiscriminatory assessment	Students must be given a comprehensive assessment that is nondiscriminatory in nature.
Related services	Schools must provide related services, such as physical therapy, counseling, and transportation, if needed.
Free appropriate public education	The primary requirement of IDEA is the provision of a free appropriate public education to all school-age children with disabilities.
Mediation/Resolution	Parents have a right, if they choose, to mediation or a resolution session to resolve differences with the school. Using mediation should not deny or delay a parent's request for a due-process hearing.
Transfer of rights	When the student reaches the age of majority, as defined by the state, the school shall notify both the parents and the student and transfer all rights of the parents to the child.
Discipline	A child with a disability cannot be expelled or suspended for ten or more cumulative days in a school year without a manifest determination as to whether the child's disability is related to the inappropriate behavior.
State assessments	Children with disabilities must be included in districtwide and statewide assessment programs with appropriate accommodations. Alternative assessment programs must be developed for children who cannot participate in districtwide or statewide assessment programs.
Transition	Transition planning and programming must begin when students with disabilities reach age sixteen.

a number of activities, including the dissemination of "child find" posters, commercial and public television announcements, newspaper articles, and other widespread public relations campaigns. IDEA requires schools to identify highly mobile children, such as homeless children and migrant children, who may qualify for special education.

Nondiscriminatory Assessment Before students can be classified as disabled and determined to be eligible for special education services, they must receive a comprehensive evaluation. While results of assessments are also used for labeling purposes, the focus should be on determining the educational needs of students (Prasse, 2006). The evaluation must not discriminate against students from minority cultural groups. The requirement for **nondiscriminatory assessment** resulted from evidence that certain norm-referenced standardized tests are inherently discriminatory toward students from minority racial and disadvantaged socioeconomic groups. Teachers and other school personnel must be extremely cautious when interpreting standardized test scores for their students. The scores may not reflect an accurate estimate of the student's abilities.

CONSIDER THIS

Should students without disabilities have an IEP? What would be the advantages, disadvantages, and impact of such a requirement?

Individualized Education Program (IEP) A key requirement of IDEA is that all students with disabilities have an IEP. Gartin and Murdick (2005) go as far as to say that the IEP is "the cornerstone of the Individuals with Disabilities Education Act of 2004" (p. 327). IEPs have served as guides for academic planning for students with disabilities since the original passage of Public Law 94–142 (Martin et al., 2006). The IEP, based on information collected during the comprehensive assessment, is developed by a group of individuals knowledgeable about the student (Gartin & Murdick, 2005). For students who are sixteen years old who have transition plans, additional individuals should attend the IEP/transition planning meeting. The participation of parents is critical (Lytle & Bordin, 2001), although schools may proceed to develop and implement an

IEP if a parent simply does not wish to meet with the team. However, parents are uniquely qualified to provide important information during the development of an appropriate program for their child (Drasgow et al., 2001).

Another key requirement related to the IEP is access to the general curriculum. The 2004 reauthorization of IDEA requires that students with disabilities have access to the general education curriculum. This requirement means that "educators must ensure that all students have the opportunity to participate and progress in the general curriculum, including students with significant cognitive disabilities" (Clayton, Burdge, Denham, Kleinert, & Kearns, 2006, p. 20)

Progress monitoring is a key component of the IEP. The specific requirement in IDEA is for monitoring the child's progress toward annual goals and for informing parents of the child's progress. Often schools develop an IEP but fail to monitor adequately the student's progress (Etscheidt, 2006).

Least Restrictive Environment   IDEA also requires that a student's education take place in the **least restrictive environment (LRE)**. The law further states that special classes, separate schooling, or other issues concerning the removal of students with disabilities from general educational settings should be used only when students cannot succeed in general education classrooms, even with supplementary aids and services. "In the 1997 Amendments to the IDEA, for the first time supplementary aids and services were expressly defined as 'aids, services, and other supports that are provided in regular education classes or other education-related settings to enable children with disabilities to be educated with nondisabled children to the maximum extent appropriate' " (Etscheidt & Bartlett, 1999, p. 164). This definition adds emphasis and clarification to the purpose of supplementary aids and services; it was continued in the 2004 reauthorization.

The LRE requirement obviously results in the inclusion of many students with disabilities in general education classrooms. Exactly how much each student is included depends on the student's IEP. Some students are able to benefit from full-time inclusion, whereas others may be able to benefit from minimal placement in general education classrooms. IDEA requires that schools provide a continuum of placement options for students, with the IEP determining the most appropriate placement. Therefore, if the IEP committee determines that the least restrictive environment for a particular child is a special classroom, then that is the LRE for that child. The decision about how much to include students with disabilities in general education settings is complex; it is based on a wide variety of factors. Wolfe and Hall (2003) note that the optimal placement is primarily determined based on the student's IEP objectives and the activities occurring in the general education setting.

> **CONSIDER THIS**
>
> Why should students with severe disabilities not be served in institutional or other segregated services? Are there some children who you think should be placed in these types of settings? Why or why not?

For the majority of students with disabilities and other special needs, placement in general education classrooms for at least a portion of each school day is the appropriate option. Students with more severe disabilities may be less likely to benefit from inclusion and will generally spend less time with their peers. The implementation of the LRE concept means that all classroom teachers will become more involved with students with special needs. General education teachers and special education teachers must share in the responsibility for educating students with disabilities (Wolfe & Hall, 2003). Close communication among all teachers involved with specific students is required (Cramer, 1998; Walther-Thomas, Korinek, McLaughlin, & Williams, 2000).

Due-Process Safeguards   Providing **due-process safeguards** to students with disabilities and their parents is another requirement of IDEA. Prior to this legislation, school personnel often made unilateral decisions about a student's education, including placement and specific components of the educational program; parents had little input and little recourse if they disagreed with the school. Due-process safeguards make parents and schools equal partners in the educational process. Parents must be notified and give their consent before schools can take certain actions that affect their child.

When the school and parents do not agree on the educational program, either party can request a due-process hearing. In this administrative appeals process, parents and schools present evidence and testimony to an impartial hearing officer who decides on the appropriateness of an educational program. The process ensures that children with disabilities and their families have equal opportunities in the school (Getty & Summy, 2004). The decision of the hearing officer is final and must be implemented unless it is appealed to state or federal court. Table 1.6 provides a brief description of the due-process safeguards provided by IDEA.

Functional Behavior Assessment and Behavior Intervention Planning   Discipline is a controversial area of PL 94–142 and the IDEA. Advocates for children with disabilities are adamant that a child's disability should not be the cause of punitive actions. In other words, if a student's inappropriate behaviors are related to his or her disabilities, then any punitive actions must take into consideration the role played by the disability.

The 2004 reauthorization of IDEA requires that schools conduct a functional behavior analysis and develop behavior intervention plans for students with disabilities who have behavior problems. A complete description of the requirements and best practices for behavior intervention planning is in Chapter 14.

Transition   "By 1990, researchers and practitioners had recognized the importance of careful planning to help students with disabilities move from school to adult life" (U.S. Department of Education, 2000, p. xi). The result was that IDEA was amended to require transition planning and programming. The 2004 reauthorization of IDEA requires that a student's IEP include a statement, beginning not later than the first IEP in effect when the student is sixteen, and updated annually, of appropriate measurable postsecondary goals based on age appropriate transition assessments related to needs.

Table 1.6	Due-Process Requirements of IDEA	
Requirement	**Explanation**	**Reference**
Opportunity to examine records	Parents have a right to inspect and review all educational records.	300.501
Independent evaluation	Parents have a right to obtain an independent evaluation of their child at their expense or the school's expense. The school pays only if it agrees to the evaluation or if it is required by a hearing officer.	300.502
Prior notice; parental consent	Schools must provide written notice to parents before the school initiates or changes the identification, evaluation, or placement of a child.	300.503
	Consent must be obtained before conducting the evaluation and before initial placement.	300.505
Contents of notice	Parental notice must provide a description of the proposed actions in the written native language of the home. If the communication is not written, oral notification must be given. The notice must be understandable to the parents.	300.504
Impartial due-process hearing, mediation, resolution	A parent or school may initiate a due-process hearing, engage in mediation, or a resolution session to resolve a dispute.	300.507

From *IDEA 2004,* Washington, DC: U.S. Government Printing Office.

Key Changes in the 2004 Reauthorization of IDEA   The most recent reauthorization of IDEA leaves much of the original IDEA intact, but does make some changes. In general, the reauthorization "aligned IDEA with the Elementary and Secondary Education Act, as amended by the No Child Left Behind Act" (Turnbull, 2005, p. 320). In so doing, the trend to further blur the lines between special education and general education continues. "We are moving away from rather rigid, categorical approaches for serving children and toward approaches that are intended to make additional resources dependent on educational needs rather than on categorical criteria resulting in years of frustration and failure" (Prasse, 2006, p. 14). However, "the basic requirement of IDEA—to provide a free, appropriate public education to children with disabilities—has not changed" (Smith 2005, p. 318). Most notable changes include the requirement that special education teachers meet the highly qualified mandate of the No Child Left Behind Act; some flexibility in the identification of children with learning disabilities; changes in the IEP; and modifications in the area of discipline. Table 1.7 summarizes the most significant changes made by this reauthorization.

Section 504 and the Americans with Disabilities Act

In addition to IDEA, Section 504 of the Rehabilitation Act of 1973 and the Americans with Disabilities Act (ADA), passed in 1990, provide a strong legal base of appropriate educational services for students with disabilities. Unlike the IDEA, which is an entitlement funding program, 504 and the ADA are both civil rights statutes. These laws ensure that individuals with disabilities are not discriminated against on the basis of disability (Smith, 2001; Smith, 2002).

CEC STANDARDS

CEC 1: Foundations

Section 504 and the ADA extend coverage to individuals who meet the definition of disability, in the laws, who are "otherwise qualified." Section 504 states: "No otherwise qualified individual with a disability, shall solely by reason of her or his disability, be excluded from participation in, be denied the benefits of, or be subjected to discrimination under any program or activity receiving federal financial assistance" (29 U.S.C.A. § 794). "In other words, if a person with a disability wants to participate in some activity in which he or she is not otherwise qualified to participate, not allowing the person to participate would not be considered discrimination" (Smith, 2001, p. 336). Discrimination is a factor only if the person with the disability is qualified to engage in the activity.

PRAXIS

PRAXIS II: Legal and Societal Issues

Section 504 applies to programs and institutions that receive federal funds. The ADA, however, applies to just about everything except churches and private clubs. As a result, virtually every public accommodation and governmental agency must comply with the ADA, regardless of whether it receives federal funds. Private schools that do not receive federal funds do not have to comply with Section 504, but unless they are associated with a church, they do have to comply with the ADA.

Section 504 and the ADA use a very different approach to defining disability than the IDEA uses. Under the IDEA, individuals are considered eligible for services if they have one of the recognized disabilities and need special education. Under 504 and the ADA, a person must have a mental or physical impairment that substantially limits a major life activity. Because the definition is broadly stated, some individuals who are classified as disabled under 504 and the ADA do not meet the eligibility criteria of the IDEA.

Section 504 and the ADA, like IDEA, require schools to provide students with disabilities with a free appropriate public education (FAPE). FAPE, under 504 and the ADA, is defined as "the provision of regular or special education, related aids and services, designed to meet the individual needs of students with disabilities as well as the needs of individuals without disabilities are met." Remember, 504 and the ADA are both civil rights statutes. Equal opportunity is a key factor in these two laws (Smith, 2002).

Comparison of IDEA, Section 504, and ADA

Rights & Responsibilities

Area	IDEA	504	ADA
Who is covered?	All children ages three to twenty-one who have one of the designated disability areas who need special education.	All individuals who have a disability as defined; no age restrictions.	Same as 504
Who must comply?	All public schools in states that participate in IDEA.	An entity that receives federal funds of any kind or amount.	Any business, governmental agency, or public accommodation other than churches or private clubs.
What is the basic requirement?	Provide eligible children with a free appropriate public education.	Do not discriminate against any individual because of a disability.	Same as 504
Due-process requirements	Provide notice and gain consent before taking specific actions with a child.	Provide notice.	Same as 504
Specific requirements	IEP Nondiscriminatory assessment Least restrictive environment	Accommodation plan Same as IDEA Same as IDEA	Same as 504 Same as IDEA Same as IDEA
Definition of free appropriate public education (FAPE)	A student's individual program determined by an IEP.	An individual program designed to meet the disabled student's educational needs as well as the needs of nondisabled students are met.	Same as 504
Transition requirements	Begin transition planning at age sixteen.	No requirement	No requirement
Assessment	Nondiscriminatory comprehensive assessment before determining eligibility and developing an IEP; required every three years unless determined not needed.	Nondiscriminatory preplacement assessment before determining eligibility for 504 services and protections; required before any significant change of placement.	Same as 504
Complaints	Due-process hearing, mediation, and resolution session must be offered. Attorney's fees may be granted to parents or school.	Administrative appeals must be offered; parents may go straight to federal court or file complaint with the Office for Civil Rights.	Same as 504; may file complaint with Department of Justice.
Designated coordinator	No requirement	At least one person in each district must be designated in writing as the district 504 coordinator.	Same as 504 (ADA coordinator)
Self-study	No requirement	Each district must form a committee and do a self-study to determine any areas where physical or program discrimination occurs. A plan to correct deficiencies must be developed.	Same as 504. Only areas added since 504 self-study must be reviewed.
Monitoring agency	U.S. Department of Education—Office of Special Education	Office for Civil Rights	Department of Justice

There are many similarities and differences between IDEA and 504/ADA. The nearby Rights & Responsibilities feature compares the elements of the IDEA, Section 504, and the ADA. Although school personnel must adhere to the requirements and criteria established by the U.S. Department of Education, they must also remember that many students who are ineligible for classification as disabled still need assistance if they are to succeed in educational programs.

Where Should Students with Disabilities Be Educated?

The setting in which students with disabilities should receive educational and related services is a much-discussed, much-debated topic. In fact, as early as 1989, Jenkins and Heinen wrote that the issue has "received more attention, undergone more modifications, and generated even more controversy than have decisions about how or what these students are taught" (p. 516). The topic has continued to be much discussed and remains one of the key issues in the field of education for children with disabilities. Simply saying the word inclusion "is likely to engender fervent debate" (Kavale & Forness, 2000, p. 279).

CEC STANDARDS

CEC 7: Instructional Planning

Most students with disabilities experience mild disabilities and are included in general education classrooms for at least a portion of each school day (Prater, 2003). A smaller number of students, with more severe disabilities, are more typically educated in segregated special education environments (McLeskey, Henry, & Hodges, 1999). However, even some students with more severe disabilities are included in general education classrooms part of the time (Wolfe & Hall, 2003).

INTASC

INTASC 5: Creating an appropriate learning environment

Approximately 75 percent of all students with disabilities are included for at least 40 percent of each day in general education classrooms and taught by general education classroom teachers, and almost half of all children with disabilities are educated in general education classrooms most of the day (U.S. Department of Education, 2006). In addition to these students, some students with disabilities continue to spend a significant portion of their school days outside general education settings. Table 1.7 provides the percentage of students, by disability category, and their school placement.

PRAXIS

PRAXIS II: Delivery of Services to Students with Disabilities

While still raging, the debate about where students should be educated has shifted in favor of more inclusion, which can be implemented in many different ways. Students can be placed in general education classrooms for a majority of the school day and

For most students with disabilities and other special needs, general education classroom placements are appropriate for at least part of the day.

Table 1.7   **Percentage of Students with Disabilities, Ages Six to Twenty-One, Served in Different Educational Environments during the 2001–2002 School Year**

	Served Outside the Regular Classroom					
	0–21% of the Day	21–60% of the Day	>60% of the Day	Separate Facilities	Residential Facilities	Home/ Hospital
All disabilities	48.21	28.50	19.23	2.90	0.73	0.44
Specific learning disabilities	46.83	38.33	13.83	0.65	0.21	0.17
Speech or language impairments	87.05	7.43	4.66	0.75	0.04	0.06
Mental retardation	12.04	29.97	52.26	4.78	0.56	0.40
Emotional disturbance	28.72	22.52	30.94	12.54	4.00	1.30
Multiple disabilities	12.26	16.63	45.80	20.76	3.61	1.94
Hearing impairments	43.07	18.86	24.28	6.28	7.32	0.19
Orthopedic impairments	46.31	21.75	27.31	2.62	0.27	1.73
Other health impairments	49.39	30.87	15.77	1.80	0.37	1.90
Visual impairments	52.43	16.97	16.87	5.30	8.07	0.62
Autism	24.28	16.83	46.15	11.24	1.12	0.39
Deaf-blindness	17.27	19.04	28.53	20.37	12.72	2.09
Traumatic brain injury	35.20	27.40	26.25	8.72	1.15	1.18

From U.S. Department of Education 2006.

"pulled out" periodically and provided instruction in resource settings by special education teachers. Or they can be placed full time in general education classrooms. In this latter model, special education teachers may go into general education classrooms and work with students who are experiencing difficulties or collaborate directly with classroom teachers to develop and implement methods and materials that will meet the needs of many students. Schools use the model that best meets the individual's needs, developed through the IEP process.

The specific placement of students with disabilities falls along a continuum of options. This **continuum-of-services model** provides a range of placements, from institutions to full-time general education classrooms. It was first described by Deno in 1970. Wolfe and Hall (2003) refer to it as "the cascade of integration options." The 2004 reauthorization of IDEA continues to require schools to have a continuum of alternative placements available "to meet the needs of children with disabilities for special education and related services" (IDEA, 2004). The regulations specifically include instruction in regular classes, special classes, special schools, home instruction, and instruction in hospitals and institutions. Therefore, while IDEA mandates that services be provided in the least restrictive environment, it also acknowledges that schools should have options available along a continuum of placement options. As previously noted, the placement decision is based on numerous factors, but should primarily hinge on the student's IEP.

The Special Education Classroom Approach

Traditionally, students with disabilities received their educational programs in specialized classrooms, typically called self-contained classrooms. Serving students with disabilities in special programs was based on the presumption that general educators did not have the skills necessary to meet the needs of all students representing different learning needs (Shanker, 1994–1995). This placement option has been considered a "stage" in the movement from isolation for students with disabilities to inclusion (Safford & Safford, 1998). The result was the removal of students from the general education environment and an education provided by specialists. In the special-education-classroom approach, students receive the majority of their educational program from a special education teacher specifically trained to serve the population of students with mental retardation, learning disabilities, or some other specific disability.

Self-contained special education classes were the preferred and dominant service model between 1950 and 1970 (Podemski et al., 1995; Smith, 1990; Smith et al., 1986). Special education teachers were trained to teach students with disabilities, but usually only students with one kind of disability, in all subject areas. However, the primary focus was on a functional curriculum. Students placed in self-contained special education classrooms rarely interacted with their nondisabled peers, often even eating lunch separately. Likewise, the special education teacher interacted very little with nondisabled students or general classroom teachers.

Many general education teachers liked the self-contained special class model because they did not have to deal with students who differed from their view of "typical" children. The role of classroom teachers in the self-contained model was extremely limited. They might have indirect contact with students with disabilities but rarely had to instruct them. The primary role of general education teachers in the self-contained model was to refer students to the special education program. This assignment primarily occurred in lower elementary grades, where the majority of students with disabilities are identified.

During the late 1960s and early 1970s, parents and professionals began questioning the efficacy of the self-contained model (Smith et al., 1986). Indeed, Dunn's classic 1968 article concluded that segregated classes did not result in improved academic performance for students with mental retardation. With the passage of PL 94–142 and the requirement to serve students with disabilities in the least restrictive environment, the special class model was doomed as the preferred service model (Blackman, 1989). In the 1997–1998 school year, only 20.4 percent of all students with disabilities were served outside the general education classroom, in separate classes, compared to nearly 100 percent of students with disabilities prior to passage of PL 94–142 (U.S. Department of Education, 2000).

The movement away from special class programs has not been without dissent. Advocates for special classes have noted several problems with inclusion. Arguing against including all students with disabilities in general education classes, Fuchs and Fuchs (1994–1995) note that separate settings have several advantages:

CONSIDER THIS

Think about services for students with disabilities when you were in school. Did you have much contact and interaction with students with disabilities? Why or why not?

- Education is provided by well-trained special educators.
- Education is selected from a variety of instructional methods, curriculums, and motivational strategies.
- The system monitors student growth and progress.

Regardless of these advantages, the self-contained model has had many critics. The movement away from self-contained classrooms was sparked by several factors, including the following:

- Students served in special classes are isolated from their nondisabled peers.
- Students do not have "typical" role models.
- Students may be isolated from many of the activities that are engaged in by nondisabled students.
- Special education teachers in special class models have limited interaction with general education teachers.
- Special education students are considered to "belong" to the special education teacher and program.
- Nondisabled students do not have the opportunity to interact with students with disabilities.
- Teachers are required to teach all areas rather than relying on colleagues with specialized expertise in selected areas.

One final reason for the demise of the self-contained special class model was a growing awareness of the diversity of students with disabilities. Although the special class was the predominant model, the majority of students with disabilities served in special education were those with mild mental retardation. As exceptional populations, such as students with learning disabilities and emotional problems, were recognized, the number of students needing special education grew significantly. Serving all these students in isolated special classes became less attractive and less feasible.

The Resource Room Model

CONSIDER THIS

Public Law 94–142 (IDEA) greatly changed services for students with disabilities. Was such change good or bad? Why or why not?

As a result of PL 94–142 and its LRE requirement, as well as the growing criticism of the self-contained model, the primary service delivery option used for most students with disabilities (except for those with speech impairments) became, and continues to be, the resource room (U.S. Department of Education, 2006). Unlike the self-contained special class, where students spend their entire day, students go to the resource room only for special instruction. Students who use resource rooms spend part of each school day with their nondisabled, chronological-age peers and attend resource rooms for special assistance in deficit areas.

CONSIDER THIS

What problems are created by students coming and going from general education classrooms? How can teachers deal with some of these problems?

Advantages of the Resource Room Model   Several obvious advantages make the resource room model preferable to the self-contained special class. Most important, students with disabilities have an opportunity to interact with their chronological age peers. Other advantages include these:

- Students are more visible throughout the school and are more likely considered to be a part of the school.
- Students have the opportunity to receive instruction from more than one person.
- Students have the opportunity to receive instruction from "specialists" in specific academic areas.
- Special education teachers have the opportunity to interact with general education teachers and be an active part of the school staff.

CROSS-REFERENCE

Chapter 2 focuses extensively on creating environments for successfully including students in general education classrooms.

Disadvantages of the Resource Room Model   Despite the numerous advantages of the resource room model, this approach does not offer the ultimate answer to the complex question of where students with disabilities should be educated. Identifying students as needing special education and requiring them to leave the general education classroom, even for only part of the day, can be detrimental.

Dunn's article in 1968 questioned the efficacy of serving students with disabilities in separate classes. His article, along with others, helped move the field from segregated to integrated services. Research currently being reported is similarly questioning the efficacy of resource room services. While there are many advantages to serving students with disabilities in resource rooms, there are some obvious disadvantages, including these:

- Pull-out programs are disruptive to the routine of the general classroom.
- Students who exit the classroom to receive specialized services are ostracized.
- Communication between the resource room teacher and general classroom teachers, which must be mandatory for programs to be successful, is often difficult.
- Students may become confused if teachers use different strategies to teach similar content.
- Students may miss some favorite activities when they are pulled out for resource room time.

Role of Special Education Personnel   In the resource room model, a key role of special education personnel is to collaborate with classroom teachers to deliver appropriate programs to students with disabilities. Resource room teachers cannot simply focus on their students only when they are in the special education classroom. Close collaboration between the resource room teacher and the classroom teacher must occur to ensure that students receiving instruction in the special education room and general education classroom are not becoming confused by contradictory methods, assignments, curricula, and so on. The special education teacher should take the lead in opening up lines of communication and facilitating collaborative efforts.

Role of Classroom Teachers   Unlike the special class model, the resource room model requires that classroom teachers play numerous roles related to students with disabilities. One primary role is referral. The majority of students with mild disabilities and other special needs are referred for services by classroom teachers. Students with mild mental retardation, learning disabilities, and mild behavior problems are usually in elementary classrooms before their problems become apparent enough to warrant a referral for special education. General education teachers are often the first to recognize that a student is experiencing problems that could require special education services.

Classroom teachers also play the important role of implementing interventions that can bring improvement in problem areas and thereby prevent unnecessary referrals, with the result that fewer students will be labeled with a disability and served in special education programs. Many states and local school districts actually require classroom teachers to implement and document intervention strategies prior to a formal referral (Smith et al., 1997). These strategies, called prereferral interventions, will be discussed in Chapter 4.

Inclusive Education Programs

Just as full-time special class placement of students with disabilities received criticism in the early 1970s, resource room programs began to be criticized in the 1980s. Madeline Will, formerly assistant secretary of the U.S. Department of Education, helped formulate the criticism of the resource room model and spur the movement toward inclusion. In 1986 she stated, "Although well-intentioned, this so-called 'pull-out' approach to the

Children with disabilities were often educated in isolated, self-contained classes between 1950 and 1970.

CROSS-REFERENCE

Read Chapter 7 on serious emotional disturbance to see how modeling appropriate behaviors can impact students with this type of disability.

PRAXIS

PRAXIS II: Delivery of Services to Students with Disabilities

educational difficulties of students with learning problems has failed in many instances to meet the educational needs of these students and has created, however unwittingly, barriers to their successful education" (Will, 1984, p. 412).

CONSIDER THIS

Why are some people opposed to merging special education and general education into one system?

Since the mid-1980s there has been a call for dismantling the dual education system (general and special) in favor of a unified system that attempts to meet the needs of all students. Rather than spend a great deal of time and effort identifying students with special problems and determining whether they are eligible for special education services, proponents of a single educational system suggest that efforts be expended on providing appropriate services to all students. In the early 1980s this model was advocated for students classified as gifted and talented by Renzulli and Reis (1985). Their model, called **schoolwide enrichment**, offered gifted programming services to all students without their having to meet restrictive eligibility criteria.

The model for more fully including students with special needs in general education programs was originally called the **Regular Education Initiative (REI)**. More recently, the term "inclusion" has been used to identify this program model. Inclusion has been defined in many different ways. Unfortunately, the term "full inclusion" was originally used, suggesting that all students with disabilities, regardless of the severity of the disability, be included full time in general education classes (Kavale & Forness, 2000). This approach was advocated by several professional and advocacy groups, most notably **The Association for the Severely Handicapped (TASH)** and the Arc. Their encouragement of full-time general education classroom placement for all students was met with a great deal of criticism and skepticism. In advocating such an approach, proponents basically asserted that there was no need for a continuum of placement options for students, since the least restrictive environment was always the general education classroom for all students (Kavale & Forness, 2000).

CONSIDER THIS

How can terms such as "mainstreaming," "inclusion," and "full inclusion" complicate services for students with disabilities? What could be done to clarify terminology?

Currently, the terms "inclusion" and "responsible inclusion" are used to identify the movement to provide services to students with disabilities in general education settings (Smith & Dowdy, 1998). It is acknowledged that within the context of inclusion, some services to students may be necessary outside the general education classroom. While acknowledging that some students with disabilities may need some services outside the general classroom, proponents suggest that all students with disabilities belong with their nondisabled peers. Lamar-Dukes and Dukes (2005) state that "the move toward including students with disabilities in general education is fundamentally about the delivery of services in environments where students with disabilities have sufficient and systematic opportunities to engage with students without disabilities" (p. 55). When successful, inclusive schools result in a unified educational system for all students (Burstein, Sears, Wilcoxen, Cabello, & Spagna, 2004).

As early as 1984, Stainback and Stainback suggested the following reasons to support inclusion:

1. *"Special" and "regular" students:* The current dual system of general and special education assumes that there are two distinct types of children, special and regular. In reality, all students display a variety of characteristics along a continuum; there simply is no way to divide all students into two groups. All students exhibit strengths and weaknesses that make them unique.

2. *Individualized services:* There is no single group of children who can benefit from individualized educational programming. The dual system of special and general education adopts the notion that students with disabilities require individual education, whereas other students do not. In fact, some research suggests that students with diverse characteristics do not benefit from different instructional techniques. If future research concludes that individualized instruction does indeed result in improved education, then all students should be afforded the opportunity.

3. *Instructional methods:* Contrary to many beliefs, there are no special teaching meth-

ods that are effective only with students who have disabilities. Good, basic instructional programs can be effective for all students.

4. *Classification:* A dual system of education, general and special, requires extensive, time-consuming, and costly efforts to determine which system students fit into and, in the case of those students determined to be eligible for special education, into which disability category they fit. Unfortunately, classification often is unreliable, results in stigma, and does not lead to better educational programming.

5. *Competition and duplication:* Perpetuating the general and special systems has resulted in competition between professionals as well as duplication of effort. If the educational system is to improve, all educators must work together, sharing expertise, effective methods, and educational goals.

6. *Eligibility by category:* The dual system results in extensive effort being spent on determining who is eligible for special services. The programs for students are often based on which category they are placed in, not on their specific needs. Placements and even curricular options are often restricted on the basis of clinical classification. For example, students classified as having mental retardation may be placed in work-study programs without having the opportunity to participate in regular vocational education.

7. *"Deviant" label:* A major negative result of the dual system is the requirement to place "deviant" labels on students. To determine that a student is eligible for the special system, a clinical label must be attached to him or her. Few, if any, would argue that clinical labels result in positive reactions. The routine reaction to the labels "mental retardation," "emotionally disturbed," and even "learning disabled" is an assumption that the student is not capable of functioning as well as other students.

> **CONSIDER THIS**
>
> How can serving students based on their individual needs benefit all students, not just those fitting into certain disability categories? Do the benefits outweigh the disadvantages?

Although proponents of inclusion have articulated numerous reasons to support the model, many oppose its implementation (Fuchs & Fuchs, 1994–1995). Al Shanker (1994–1995), past president of the American Federation of Teachers, noted that "we need to discard the ideology that inclusion in a regular classroom is the only appropriate placement for a disabled child and get back to the idea of a 'continuum of placements,' based on the nature and severity of the handicap" (p. 20).

Several professional and advocacy groups also support the continued use of a continuum of placement options. These include the Council for Exceptional Children (CEC), American Council on the Blind, Commission on the Education of the Deaf, the Division on Mental Retardation and Developmental Disabilities of CEC, and the Council for Children with Behavior Disorders of CEC. It also should be noted that the U.S. Department of Education does not mandate inclusion. Rather, the most recent reauthorization of IDEA in 2004 continues to require that schools provide a continuum of alternative placement options for students (IDEA, 2004). If an IEP committee determines that a child needs a self-contained placement to receive an appropriate education, then failing to provide such an opportunity would be a violation of IDEA.

Advantages of Inclusion   There are many different advantages to inclusion, including opportunities for social interaction (Peck & Scarpati, 2004); ease in accessing the general curriculum (Abell, Bauder, & Simmons, 2005); academic improvement (Hunt et al., 2001); and positive outcomes for students with and without disabilities (Idol, 2006). Inclusion also creates learning opportunities for students with severe disabilities (Downing & Eichinger, 2003).

Although not mandatory, parental and teacher support for inclusion is very important. Hobbs and Westling (1998) note that many parents have mixed views. While they believe that inclusion has some obvious benefits for their children, they also worry about their children being in integrated placements. The concept has simply "not been embraced by all parents" (Palmer, Fuller, Arora, & Nelson, 2001, p. 481).

> **CONSIDER THIS**
>
> How can some of the problems caused by inclusion be addressed in order to facilitate success in school for all students?

Teachers, for the most part, have expressed support for inclusion. After reviewing several studies, Scruggs and Mastropieri (1996) noted that most teachers support inclusion, are willing to teach students in their classrooms (although those who respond in this way are fewer than those who support the concept), and believe that inclusion results in positive benefits for students with disabilities and does not harm other students or the instructional process. Idol (2006) conducted a recent program evaluation of eight schools to determine the extent of inclusion of students with disabilities. Perceptions of staff related to inclusion were also studied. Idol's findings included: (1) teachers had a positive attitude toward inclusion; (2) administrators supported inclusion; (3) few teachers preferred that students with disabilities should be educated in special classes; and (4) educators thought that inclusion had a positive impact on other students. "Overall, there was a trend among the participating educators of moving more and more toward the inclusion of students with disabilities in the general education classes" (Idol, 2006, p. 91).

Disadvantages of Inclusion   Just as there are many supporters of inclusion and reasons for its implementation, there are also professionals and parents who decry the movement. Among the reasons they oppose inclusion:

- General educators have not been involved sufficiently and are therefore not likely to support the model.
- General educators as well as special educators do not have the collaboration skills necessary to make inclusion successful.
- There are limited empirical data to support the model. Therefore, full implementation should be put on hold until sound research supports the effort.
- Full inclusion of students with disabilities into general education classrooms may take away from students without disabilities and lessen their quality of education.
- Current funding, teacher training, and teacher certification are based on separate educational systems.
- Some students with disabilities do better when served in special education classes by special education teachers.

Although some of these criticisms may have merit, others have been discounted. For example, research indicates that the education of nondisabled students is not negatively affected by inclusion (National Study on Inclusion, 1995). Therefore, though the movement has its critics, research on inclusion provides support for its continuation.

PRAXIS

PRAXIS II: Delivery of Services to Students with Disabilities

CONSIDER THIS

How would you feel if you were a classroom teacher who was suddenly asked to teach a student with a disability and you did not have any skills in special education?

Role of Special Education Personnel   The inclusion of students in general classrooms results in changes in the roles of all school personnel (Burstein et al., 2004). In the inclusion model, special education personnel become much more integral to the broad educational efforts of the school; they take on a very challenging role (Lamar-Dukes & Dukes, 2005). Some special education personnel are unsure of their exact role in an inclusive classroom (Dover, 2005). In the dual system, special education teachers provide instructional programming only to students identified as disabled and determined eligible for special education programs under state and federal guidelines. In inclusive schools, these teachers work with a variety of students, including those having difficulties but not identified specifically as having a disability. The special education teacher works much more closely with classroom teachers in the inclusion model, with the result being increased opportunities for all students. Collaboration among school personnel is "the foundation of successful inclusive environments" (Volts, Sims, Nelson, & Bivens, 2005, p. 18).

Role of Classroom Teachers   Teachers must develop strategies to facilitate the successful inclusion of students with disabilities in general education classrooms (Prater, 2003). Neither classroom teachers nor special education teachers want students with disabilities simply "dumped" into general education classes (Banks, 1992), and the successful inclusion of students does not normally happen without assistance. School personnel must work on effective, cooperative methods to provide appropriate programs to all students.

Two methods are generally used to implement inclusion: facilitating the acceptance of the students with disabilities and providing services to support their academic success. Chapter 2 provides extensive information on creating classroom environments to enhance acceptance and provide academic support; later chapters provide specific, practical suggestions for providing academic support.

King-Sears and Cummings (1996) note seven practices that teachers can use to help students succeed in inclusive settings: (1) curriculum-based assessment; (2) cooperative learning; (3) self-management; (4) peer tutoring; (5) strategy instruction; (6) direct instruction; and (7) goal setting. Figure 1.2 depicts the comfort of teachers in using these seven different methods. Clearly, some practices are only moderately or slightly comfortable, suggesting that in order for inclusion to be successful, teacher training and preparation need to be modified.

Classroom teachers play a vital role in the education of students with disabilities. As noted by Hobbs and Westling (1998), teachers possibly play the most important role in the success of inclusion. Classroom teachers must be able to perform many different functions, such as:

- Acting as a team member on assessment and IEP committees
- Advocating for children with disabilities when they are in general education classrooms and in special programs
- Counseling and interacting with parents of students with disabilities
- Individualizing instruction for students with disabilities
- Understanding and abiding by due-process procedures required by federal and state regulations
- Being innovative in providing equal educational opportunities for all students, including those with disabilities

Sharing responsibility among classroom teachers, special education teachers, and other specialists, such as reading teachers, is the key to providing effective educational programs for all students (Voltz, Brazil, & Ford, 2001).

Figure 1.2   **Comfort Level of Implementing Various Strategies**

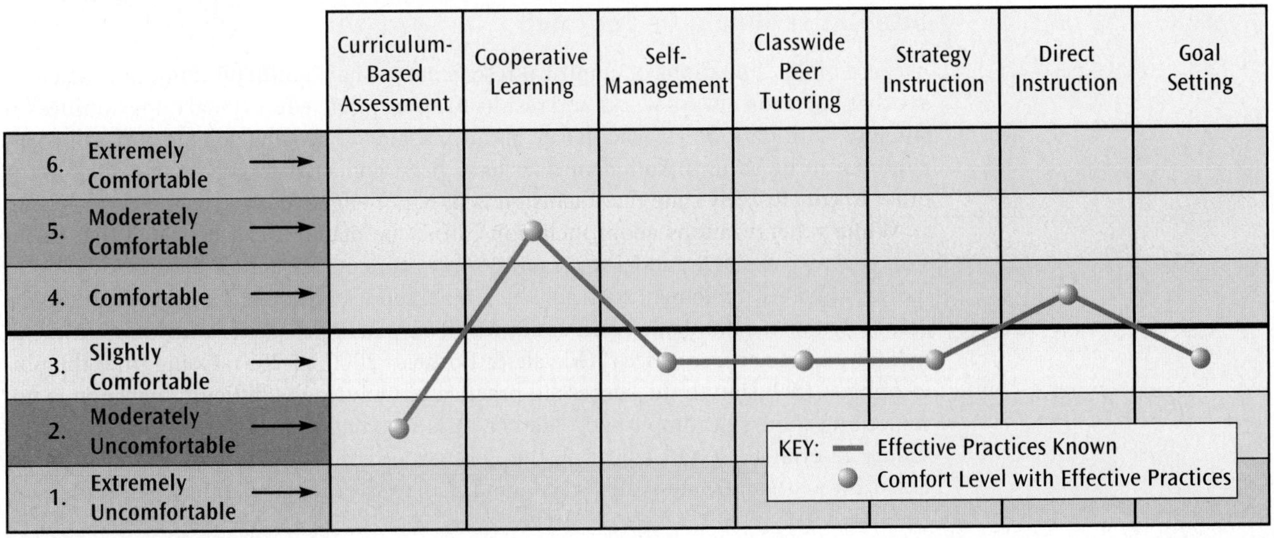

From "Inclusive Practices of Classroom Teachers," by M. E. King-Sears and C. S. Cummings, 1996 *Remedial and Special Education, 17*, p. 218. Used by permission.

TECHNOLOGY Today

Libraries and media centers can be excellent places to support students with disabilities. The following list provides suggestions for software and physical accommodations that might be installed to aid students with disabilities. Of course, the most helpful "installation" is a skilled, knowledgeable librarian or media specialist who understands the needs of all students and is willing to take time to listen to them.

- Universal design in the library or media center
- Low-tech items for students

- Microsoft Windows XP
- JAWS for Windows
- ZoomText
- Kurzweil 3,000 Version 9
- Texthelp Read and Write 7.1EGold
- Inspiration
- Boardecisionmaker
- Activation switches
- DAISY Ebooks
- Intellikeys
- Reading Pen II
- PocketTalker Pro

- Keyguards for computers
- Adjustable workstations
- Listening station
- SMART Board

Adapted from J.D. Neal and D. Ehlert (2006). Add Technology for Students with Disabilities to the Library or Media Center. *Intervention in School and Clinic, 42*, 119–123.

CONSIDER THIS

What tips would you give teachers to enhance the inclusion of students with special needs in general education classrooms?

In general, the classroom teacher controls the educational programs for all students in the classroom, including students with disabilities, students at risk for developing problems, and those classified as gifted and talented. The attitude of the teacher toward students and the general climate the teacher establishes in the classroom have a major impact on the success of all students, particularly those with disabilities.

Classroom teachers need to be able to use a variety of techniques when meeting the needs of students included in their classes. Technology can be a great asset. The primary function of teachers, both general education and special education, is to teach. Good teaching has been described in many different ways. Researchers have attempted to define good teaching based on student outcomes, parental opinions, peers, supervisor ratings, and self-evaluations.

Conclusions Concerning Where Students with Disabilities Should Be Educated

Because of the limitations of empirical research, it remains difficult if not impossible to say that inclusion always works and results in appropriate educational opportunities for students with disabilities. The debate about placement remains volatile and will likely continue to be so until sufficient data have been collected to enable one side or the other to conclusively state that inclusion is or is not effective.

While generalizations about inclusion cannot be made, it can be stated that inclusion is a very effective model for serving some students with disabilities. However, to indiscriminately implement such an educational model without adequate preparation is definitely not recommended and could result in placing students with disabilities "at risk for adverse consequences" (Kavale & Forness, 2000, p. 287). Going from the philosophy of inclusion to the successful practice of inclusion is difficult; inclusion is not something that is accomplished. "Rather, it is a dynamic process that involves constantly re-evaluating and adjusting the delivery of educational services and supports based on a student's individual needs and achieved outcomes" (Dymond & Russell, 2004, p. 138).

In light of the limited empirical information and the emotional nature of the debate, it is currently recommended that the inclusion movement continue to proceed slowly. Because "requisite attitudes, accommodations, and adaptations for students with disabilities" are not yet in place, "a more tempered approach that formulates and implements policy on the basis of research and evaluation findings as well as ideological and political considerations is necessary" (Kavale & Forness, 2000, p. 290). In the meantime, using the LRE approach appears to be the prudent means of providing services to students with disabilities.

Philosophical and Ethical Issues in Special Education

School personnel involved in the education of students with disabilities must have a positive attitude about serving this group of students. If teachers feel that they are being asked to do things that are unnecessary, the entire classroom climate may be affected. Teachers set the example for students in their classrooms by either accepting and supporting students with disabilities or rejecting them. Therefore, the philosophy of educators regarding special education is critical to the success of these students.

CEC STANDARDS

CEC 9: Professional and Ethical Practice

School personnel must view students with disabilities as their students. Having a disability in no way should result in some students not being a part of the school body. This philosophy is a large part in the underpinning of the inclusion movement. All students belong. As part of this sense of belonging, the language used to refer to individuals with disabilities becomes important. Person-first language, or language that always acknowledges the individual with a disability as an individual first, should be used by all professionals. Person-first language is described in Figure 1.3.

INTASC

INTASC 9: Reflective practitioner

In addition to having a personal philosophy of education that forms the basis for meeting the needs of all children, including those with special needs, educators must be aware of the code of ethics that is used to govern meeting the needs of students with special needs. The CEC, the primary professional group of special education personnel, has a code of ethics that could be adopted by all educators serving this group of students. Figure 1.4 presents their code of ethics. All educators should adhere to professional ethics in meeting the needs of the diverse group of students in our schools, including those with special needs.

Figure 1.3 **Using "People-First" Language**

One of the results of the inclusion movement has been a change in the way individuals with disabilities are labeled. "People-first" language has become the appropriate nomenclature for individuals with disabilities. The following list provides examples of using "people-first" language:

Say	Do Not Say
Person with a disability	The disabled person
Billy with mental retardation	Mentally retarded Billy
Children with autism	The autistic children
Classroom for students with mental retardation	The mentally retarded classroom
Students with visual impairments	The blind students
Bus for students with disabilities	The special education bus
Individuals with disabilities	Disabled individuals
Disability or disabled	Handicap or handicapped
The boy with cerebral palsy	The cerebral palsied boy
The girl with a hearing impairment	The deaf girl
Mary with a learning disability	The learning-disabled girl

Figure 1.4   **Code of Ethics for Educators of Persons with Exceptionalities**

We declare the following principles to be the Code of Ethics for educators of persons with exceptionalities. Members of the special education profession are responsible for upholding and advancing these principles. Members of the Council for Exceptional Children agree to judge and be judged by them in accordance with the spirit and provisions of this code.

A. Special education professionals are committed to developing the highest educational and quality of life potential of individuals with exceptionalities.
B. Special education professionals promote and maintain a high level of competence and integrity in practicing their profession.
C. Special education professionals engage in professional activities which benefit individuals with exceptionalities, their families, other colleagues, students, or research subjects.
D. Special education professionals exercise objective professional judgment in the practice of their profession.
E. Special education professionals strive to advance their knowledge and skills regarding the education of individuals with exceptionalities.
F. Special education professionals work within the standards and policies of their profession.
G. Special education professionals seek to uphold and improve where necessary the laws, regulations, and policies governing the delivery of special education and related services and the practice of their profession.
H. Special education professionals do not condone or participate in unethical or illegal acts, nor violate professional standards adopted by the Delegate Assembly of CEC.

http://cec.sped.org/ps/code.html

Summary

Students with Special Needs
- The U.S. public school system attempts to provide thirteen years of equal educational opportunity to all its citizens.
- Today's student population is very diverse and includes students with a variety of disabilities.
- During the 1950s and 1960s, students from minority cultures won the right to equal educational opportunities.
- Many students in today's schools have specific special needs.
- A sizable percentage of students are at risk for developing problems, present learning or behavior problems, or may be classified as having a disability.
- The largest group of students with special needs in the public school system consists of those formally classified as having disabilities.
- Although there are thirteen recognized categories of disabilities in schools, many students do not fit neatly into a specific category.
- Mental retardation, learning disabilities, and emotional and behavior disorders make up the majority of student disabilities.
- Students who are at risk for developing problems, as well as those considered gifted and talented, also require special attention from school personnel.

Current Services for Students with Special Needs
- Services for students with disabilities have evolved significantly during the past twenty years.
- Services for students with disabilities focus on inclusion—including students in general education classroom situations as much as possible.
- The civil rights movement, legislation, litigation, and parental advocacy all helped shape the service system for students with disabilities.
- Public Law 94–142, now the IDEA, provides the framework for services to students with disabilities in school settings.
- IDEA requires that students with disabilities be educated in the least restrictive environment, using an IEP.

Where Should Students with Special Needs Be Educated?
- About 70 percent of all students with disabilities spend a substantial portion of each school day in general education classrooms.
- The preferred service model for students with disabilities between 1950 and 1970 was segregated classroom settings.
- In the self-contained model, special education teachers were trained to teach specific types of students, primarily based on clinical labels.

- Classroom teachers had a very limited role in special education in the self-contained classroom model.
- Many parents advocated more inclusion of their students than was possible in the self-contained classroom. The LRE mandate of PL 94–142 was the impetus for the development of the resource room model.

Classroom Teachers and Students with Disabilities

- General education teachers play a very critical role in providing services to students with disabilities.
- The attitudes of classroom teachers are extremely important in the quality of services rendered to students with disabilities.

Questions to Reconsider

Think back to the scenario about Kevin that you read at the beginning of this chapter. Would you answer the questions raised there any differently after reading the chapter itself?

1. How would Kevin's life be different had he been born in 1950 rather than in the 1980s?

2. Would more inclusion in secondary schools have had a positive or negative impact on Kevin's future success?
3. Has IDEA been a success or failure for Kevin and many other individuals with disabilities?

Further Readings

Alexander, K., & Alexander, M. D. (2001). *American public school law* (5th ed.). Belmont, CA: Wadsworth/Thomson Learning.

Coleman, M. C., & Webber, J. (2002). *Emotional and behavioral disorders: Theory and practice* (4th ed.). Boston: Allyn & Bacon.

Elksnin, L. K., Bryant, D. P., Gartland, D., King-Sears, M., Rosenberg, M. S., Scanlon, D., Strosnider, R., & Wilson, R. (2001). LD summit: Important issues for the field of learning disabilities. *Learning Disability Quarterly, 24,* 297–305.

Halvorsen, A. T., & Neary, T. (2001). *Building inclusive schools: Tools and strategies for success.* Boston: Allyn & Bacon.

Katsiyannis, A., Yell, M. L., & Bradley, R. (2001). Reflections on the 25th anniversary of the Individuals with Disabilities Education Act. *Remedial and Special Education, 22,* 324–334.

Kavale, K. A., & Forness, S. R. (2000). History, rhetoric, and reality: Analysis of the inclusion debate. *Remedial and Special Education, 21,* 279–296.

King-Sears, M. E. (2001). Three steps for gaining access to the general education curriculum for learners with disabilities. *Intervention in School and Clinic, 37,* 67–76.

Lyon, G. R., Fletcher, J. M., Shaywitz, S. E., Shaywitz, B. A., Torgesen, J. K., Wood, F. B., Schulte, A., & Olson, R. (2001). Rethinking learning disabilities. In C. E. Finn, A. J. Rotherham, & C. R. Hokanson Jr. (Eds.), *Rethinking special education for a new century.* (47–61). Washington, DC: Thomas B. Fordham Foundation.

Scheuermann, B., & Webber, J. (2002). *Autism: Teaching does make a difference.* Belmont, CA: Wadsworth/Thomson.

Smith, T. E. C. (2001). Section 504, the ADA, and public schools: What educators need to know. *Remedial and Special Education, 22,* 335–343.

Voltz, D. L., Brazil, N., & Ford, A. (2001). What matters most in inclusive education: A practical guide for moving forward. *Intervention in School and Clinic, 37,* 3–8.

Yell, M. L., Rogers, D., & Rogers, E. L. (1998). The legal history of special education: What a long, strange trip it's been! *Remedial and Special Education, 19,* 219–228.

(mylabschool
Where the classroom comes to life

Go to Allyn & Bacon's MyLabSchool (www.mylabschool.com) and enter Assignment ID SPV2 into the Assignment Finder. View the video clip called *The Inclusive Classroom.* Then consider what you have seen along with what you've read in Chapter 1 to answer the following questions.

1. This chapter notes that research data about inclusion suggests that student outcomes are positive. Does what you see in the video support that? In what ways?
2. How does Penny Brandenburg insure that the general education students in her classroom receive the atten-

tion they need, while providing additional help to the students with special needs? Cite specific examples from the video clip.

You may also answer the questions at the end of the clip and e-mail your responses to your instructor.

Now go back and enter Assignment ID CS09 into the Assignment Finder. Read the case study, *A Look Inside: A Student Teacher's Dilemma,* and answer the questions raised at the end of it.

Effective Inclusion Practices and Professional Collaboration

After reading this chapter, you should be able to:

1. Discuss the concept of diversity.
2. Explain different perceptions among teachers, students, and parents regarding inclusion.
3. Delineate critical dimensions of inclusive classrooms.
4. Describe the role of classroom management, curricular options, and accommodative practices in inclusive classrooms.
5. Discuss the range of personnel supports in inclusive classrooms.
6. Create and maintain successful inclusive classrooms.
7. Describe different methods of maintaining inclusive programs after they are initiated.
8. Describe the consultation-collaboration and co-teaching strategies used in inclusive classrooms.

Libby is one of the favorites in Ms. Jordan's third-grade class. She is popular among her peers and an excellent student, and she never gets into trouble. At the beginning of this school year, a new student was placed in her classroom. This student, Rhonda, has cerebral palsy and mild mental retardation. At first Libby was sort of afraid of Rhonda. Rhonda rarely talked, did not follow Ms. Jordan's directions very well, and could read hardly anything. The students thought Rhonda was really dumb. Libby, and all the other students in the class, did not want anything to do with Rhonda in the classroom, on the playground, or in the lunchroom.

After Rhonda had been in the class for about a week, a new teacher came into the room. Ms. Baker, the special education teacher, started working with Rhonda on some specific activities, such as reading at a much lower level than third-graders were reading. Libby and all her friends thought this proved that Rhonda was dumb and really did not belong in the class. About two weeks later, Ms. Baker asked if any of the students in Ms. Jordan's class wanted to be a peer tutor. None of the students knew what a peer tutor was, but it sounded pretty important. Libby, of course, volunteered and was chosen, partly because she was doing so well in all her subjects. When Ms. Baker and Ms. Jordan met with Libby and talked to her about being a peer tutor, they explained that Rhonda had some learning problems and needed some extra help in the classroom. Libby didn't know she would have to work with Rhonda when she volunteered, but she hated to back out, so she decided to go ahead for a little while. Ms. Baker and Ms. Jordan talked to Libby a long time about what it means to be a peer tutor.

Finally, the day to begin tutoring came, and Libby discovered that she loved helping others. She also learned a very important fact that she quickly spread to all her classmates—Rhonda was okay. In fact, Rhonda was pretty cool. Getting to know Rhonda made Libby stop to think about people's differences. From then on, Rhonda was considered by all the students in Ms. Jordan's class as an equal. The big step in getting her to be accepted was to get one of the most popular students in the room to accept her as a fellow classmate.

*I*ncluding students with special needs in general education classrooms continues to receive significant attention on a philosophical level. It is implemented for a variety of reasons; chief reasons are to improve educational opportunities and social development (Wolfe & Hall, 2003) and to give all students equal opportunities. However, too little discussion has focused on specific ways to implement inclusion successfully. Addressing the needs of a growing, diverse student population is a daunting challenge for today's schools. Adding students with disabilities to the mix only increases the challenges faced by general educators. This chapter discusses some of the key features of sound inclusive settings. It also addresses how to create and maintain these settings and the collaborative relationships that are critical to help them function well.

Accepting Diversity

The most important issue underlying successful inclusion of students with disabilities is the acceptance of diversity in general. Today's students bring a much more diverse set of backgrounds than ever before (Rapp, 2005). This includes differences in language, race, ethnic, socioeconomic, gender, sexual orientation, and academic (Morrison, 2006). Morrison (2006) goes on to say that "we can count on the fact that an increase in diversity will be the demographic norm rather than the exception"(p. 114). Our increasingly diverse society is reflected in our student population. Teachers today have to deal with a wide variety of language and learning abilities (Rueda, Monzo, Shapiro, Gomez, & Blacher, 2005). Unfortunately, acceptance of diverse students is not likely to happen easily or without major changes in the way many schools operate (Smith et al., 2006). While some teachers and administrators readily accept diverse students, others may not (Nieto, 2004). Teachers need to "recognize and celebrate unique individual characteristics and group affiliations" (van Garderen & Whittaker, 2006, p. 14).

While diversity is generally viewed as a good thing, it can create difficulties for teachers and schools. For example, students who do not speak English as their primary language can cause difficulties for classroom teachers, not to mention their own educational opportunities. Likewise, students with disabilities can also create challenges for classroom teachers. It is important to remember that one teacher can have a dramatic effect on the lives of all students, including those who are different and who have learning challenges. It should also be remembered that steps toward the successful inclusion of diverse students can be taken on a classroom-by-classroom and school-by-school basis. While a great idea, the "successful inclusion of students with disabilities requires fundamental change in the organizational structures of schools and in the roles and responsibilities of teachers" (Burstein, Sears, Wilcoxen, Cabello, & Spagna, 2006, p. 105).

While the merits of inclusion continue to be debated, the reality is that the movement has taken hold. A comparison of national placement figures from the early 1980s to the present reveals a significant increase in the number of students with disabilities educated in general classrooms at least part of the day. The U.S. Department of Education (2006) noted that approximately 96 percent of all school-age students are in their home school buildings and almost half are educated in general education classrooms for most of the day. More than 46 percent of all students were served outside their general classrooms less than 21 percent of the school day.

The discussion of inclusion and how to make it work has focused mostly on students with disabilities. However, gifted students, at-risk students, and students from diverse backgrounds often face the same obstacles to acceptance and the same problems gaining access to appropriate educational programming. Consequently, the ideas in this chapter apply to students with all sorts of special needs, not only those classified as having disabilities.

CEC STANDARDS

CEC 1: Foundations

CONSIDER THIS

What does the term "diversity" include? Is our society becoming more or less diverse?

CONSIDER THIS

What factors would make teachers who support inclusion more willing to accept students with disabilities into their classrooms?

Developing effective inclusive classrooms has relevance for students' immediate needs as well as their long-term needs. In the short term, students need to learn in settings along with their peers (that is, inclusive schools). Extensive research findings show that students with disabilities in inclusive settings learn as well as or better than they do in segregated settings, while enjoying opportunities for social interactions that they do not have in segregated settings (Rea, McLaughlin, & Walther-Thomas, 2002). In the long term, we want these students, as adults, to live, work, and play along with their peers in their home communities (i.e., inclusive living). Without the opportunity to grow and learn with nondisabled peers throughout their lives, individuals with disabilities will not be able to accomplish these goals as adults. Inclusion must begin in the early years. Expecting students with disabilities who have been isolated in segregated settings the first eighteen to twenty years of their life to assimilate into society is unrealistic.

Perceptions of Inclusion

A significant amount of discussion has surrounded the movement toward inclusion. On the philosophical level, only a few arguments have been levied against this movement. Who, for example, would argue against the idea of educating students together and giving all students equal opportunities? It is, however, primarily on the implementation level that concerns have arisen. "Ideology may be useful in discussions attempting to establish goals and objectives, but actual practice is best derived from scientific inquiry" (Kavale & Forness, 2000, p. 289). Although most teachers and administrators agree that inclusion is a good thing, making decisions about how to achieve it is often problematic. Studies focusing on attitudes toward inclusion have involved two primary groups: general education teachers and parents.

Weiner (2003) found that teachers believe that the most important factor related to successful inclusion was teacher attitudes toward their students. Teachers who focused on these kinds of factors, rather than on factors such as the availability of alternate placement options, were much more successful in inclusion. In 2004, Burstein and colleagues determined that the satisfaction of general classroom teachers and special education teachers concerning inclusion increased over time. They viewed inclusion as benefiting both students with disabilities and their nondisabled peers. In a program evaluation of eight schools, Idol (2006) found that elementary and secondary teachers were supportive of inclusion and believed that it was beneficial to both students with disabilities and without disabilities. In the same study, it was also determined that school administrators supported inclusion. These more recent studies appear to confirm earlier findings from Scruggs and Mastropieri (1996), who through analyzing studies between 1958 and 1995 found that nearly two-thirds of general education classroom teachers support, for the most part, the concept of inclusion.

Results of these studies have a direct impact on teacher preparation. Teacher education programs must do a better job of preparing teachers, both general and special education, to work together to effectively implement inclusion in their schools, and schools must provide professional development for their staff to better prepare them for inclusive schools and classrooms (Weiner, 2003). The inclusion movement continues to dim the line between general education and special education. The nearby Rights & Responsibilities feature addresses this issue.

The support of parents in the inclusion of their children with disabilities in general education settings has a great deal to do with the ultimate success the child experiences (Duhaney & Salend, 2000). Some parents support inclusion, while others are opposed (Palmer, Borthwick-Duffy, & Widaman, 1998). For parents of students with disabilities, the reaction to the inclusion movement is mixed, ranging from complete support of the idea (i.e., as propounded by the Arc) to skepticism, especially concerning the concept

CEC STANDARDS

5: Learning environments and social interactions

PRAXIS

3: Delivery of services to students with disabilities

INTASC

3: Understands how students differ

INTASC

2: Understands how children learn and develop

CONSIDER THIS

Often parents of students with mental retardation are more supportive of inclusion than parents of students with less severe disabilities. Why do you think this is the case?

CEC STANDARDS

7: Collaboration

Where Does General Education Stop and Special Education Begin?

The distinction between regular education and special education has become increasingly less clear over time. In the mid-1970s, when special education laws were first enacted, the special education and "regular" education domains were very distinct. Increased inclusion means that many special education students now spend most or all of their day in the regular education setting. This means that both regular and special education teachers must be fully involved in programming for these students.

Identification, Referral, and Evaluation

Through the "child find" process, as defined in the Individuals with Disabilities Education Act, 20 U.S.C. § 1400 *et seq.,* students are referred for special education assessment to determine if services are needed. In Minnesota, before being referred, a district must conduct and document at least two instructional strategies, alternatives, or interventions that were implemented while the student was in the regular classroom. The student's teacher must provide this documentation, unless the assessment team determines that there is an urgent need for assessment. After a referral is submitted to the assessment team, but before conducting the assessment, the team must review the student's performance, including prereferral interventions. Districts must use alternative intervention services to serve at-risk students who demonstrate a need for alternative instruction strategies.

When it is determined that a child initially qualifies for special education services, at least one regular education teacher must be a member of the IEP team. A representative of the district who is knowledgeable about the school's general curriculum must also participate in the IEP team. In developing an IEP for a child with a disability, districts are required to take steps to ensure that the disabled child has access to the same services that are available to nondisabled peers. These services may include various programs such as music, industrial arts, consumer and homemaking education, and vocational education.

Planning and Implementation

The child's IEP should be accessible to each regular education teacher, special education teacher, related service provider, and any other service provider who is responsible for implementation of the goals, objectives, or adaptations contained in the IEP. Each teacher and service provider must be informed of his or her specific responsibilities related to the implementation of the IEP. Further, all specific accommodations, modifications and support services should be communicated to the appropriate parties and monitored to ensure compliance with the IEP.

Coordination of Responsibilities

The coordination of regular and special education requires that teachers and service providers understand how the child's services will be delivered. To accomplish this goal, administrators, teachers, service providers, and counselors should be well trained. Service coordinators should carefully monitor the delivery of services. This can be done through regular contact with teachers and other providers to confirm that the child is receiving the services delineated in the IEP.

Documentation of Progress or Lack of Progress

The IEP team should track student progress to ensure that the current program is providing meaningful benefit to the child. Teachers and service providers should maintain accurate, logically compiled data regarding progress in regular classes and on IEP goals. The student's progress, or lack thereof, should be communicated to all team members, including the parents. Similarly, specific information about progress is important where the team wants to support a proposed action or discontinue service based on a student's success or lack of progress.

Discipline

Applying disciplinary standards to students with disabilities can be a challenge for districts. According to 34 C.F.R. § 300.527, "a child who has not been deemed eligible for special education may assert any of the protections provided for under the IDEA, if the district had knowledge that the child was a child with a disability *before* the behavior that precipitated the disciplinary action occurred" (emphasis added).

A district is deemed to have knowledge that a child is a child with a disability if:

• The parent of the child has expressed concern in writing, or orally to personnel of the district that the child is in need of special education and related services;
• The behavior or performance of a child demonstrates the need for special education services;
• The parent of the child has requested an evaluation of the child; or
• The child's teacher or other district personnel has expressed concern about the behavior or performance of the child to the director of special education or to other personnel in accordance with the district's established child-find or special education referral system.

When a child with a disability engages in conduct that violates district policies, a manifestation determination must be made by a team knowledgeable about the student. If the

team determines that the behavior is a manifestation of the child's disabling condition, the student is not subject to standard disciplinary procedures regarding expulsion. If the team determines that the behavior is not a manifestation of the child's behavior, and the district initiates disciplinary procedures applicable to all children, including exclusion or expulsion, the district must ensure that the special education and disciplinary records of the child with a disability are transmitted for consideration by the person making the final determination regarding disciplinary action.

Records

Critical stages of educational planning should include a review of records and information. The records review should include the child's cumulative file, attendance data, grades, discipline records, counselor information, child

study, nurse's files, health records, parent notes and communications, e-mails, teacher files, and information regarding any past services and referrals. A careful review of current information can help in avoiding overlooking factors that may be critical to legal compliance.

From "Where Does General Education Stop and Special Education Begin?" by S. E. Torgerson & K. H. Boyd, 2001, *Special Education Law Update, 10*(4), pp. 7-8. Used with permission. Susan E. Torgerson and Kimberly H. Boyd are education-law attorneys with the Minneapolis law firm Rider, Bennett, Egan and Arundel LLP. They can be reached via e-mail at setorgerson@riderlaw.com and khboyd@riderlaw.com, respectively. The firm's website is www.riderlaw.com. The foregoing article was based on their presentation "Where Does General Education Stop and Special Education Begin?" as part of Rider, Bennett, Egan and Arundel's first annual "Back to School Legal Seminar," held in Bloomington, Minnesota, on August 17, 2001.

of full-time inclusion. This latter orientation is reflected in the position statements of various parent organizations, most notably the Learning Disabilities Association of America.

Duhaney and Salend (2000) did a literature review of parental perceptions of inclusive educational settings. After reviewing seventeen studies published since 1985, they concluded that "parents of children with disabilities have mixed but generally positive perceptions toward inclusive educational placements" (p. 125). In the study by Burstein and colleagues (2004), parents of children with and without disabilities reflected positive reactions to inclusion, stating that the process was beneficial for all students in the school.

Many parents who oppose inclusion are concerned that their children will simply not receive the amount of attention they would in a special education setting and that their child will be ostracized, or they are worried that many general education teachers need additional training (Strong & Sandoval, 1999). These results were confirmed in the literature review by Duhaney and Salend (2000). As a result of these concerns, school personnel should assess the impact on individual children with disabilities to insure that inclusion does not have a negative impact.

Attitudinal research provides a glimpse of the task faced by professionals who support teaching students with special needs in inclusive settings. First, accurate information about inclusion in general and about individuals who need to be included must be distributed to teachers, parents, and the general public. Yet the greatest challenge will be changing an educational system that presents great barriers to inclusion, since teachers' perceptions, attitudes, and opportunities for collaboration are directly related to the success of inclusion (Weiner, 2003).

CONSIDER THIS

How are the attitudes of administrators linked to the attitudes of teachers regarding inclusion? Is this link important?

Critical Dimensions of Inclusive Classrooms

The concept of inclusion purports that students with special needs can be active, valued, fully participating members of a school community in which diversity is viewed as the norm and high-quality education is provided through a combination of meaningful curriculum, effective teaching, and necessary supports (Halvorsen & Neary, 2001). Anything less is unacceptable. Inclusion is distinctly different from the notion of integration or mainstreaming, in which students with special needs are educated in physical proximity to their age peers, yet without significant attention paid to the qualitative features of this arrangement. Both integration and mainstreaming begin with the notion that students with disabilities belong in special classes and should be integrated as much as possible in general classrooms. Inclusion, however, assumes that all students belong in the general education classroom and should be pulled out only when appropriate services cannot be provided in the inclusive setting. While seemingly a simple difference, these two approaches vary significantly (Halvorsen & Neary, 2001). Several key structural and philosophical differences distinguish the inclusive model and more traditional special education models. Figure 2.1 depicts some of these differences.

Many different factors are critical to the success of inclusion. Webber (1997) identified five essential features that characterize successful inclusion of students with special needs: (1) a sense of community and social acceptance; (2) an appreciation of student diversity; (3) attention to curricular needs; (4) effective management and instruction; and (5) personnel support and collaboration. Voltz, Brazil, and Ford (2001) list three

TEACHING TIP

Teachers can create opportunities for students with disabilities to be full members of their classrooms with such methods as peer support systems.

Figure 2.1   **Structure and Philosophy: Differences between Traditional and Inclusive Models**

Traditional Models	Inclusive Educational Models
1. Some students do not "fit" in general education classes.	1. All students "fit" in general education classrooms.
2. The teacher is the instructional leader.	2. Collaborative teams share leadership responsibilities.
3. Students learn from teachers and teachers solve the problems.	3. Students and teachers learn from one another and solve problems together.
4. Students are purposely grouped by similar ability.	4. Students are purposely grouped by differing abilities.
5. Instruction is geared toward middle-achieving students.	5. Instruction is geared to match students at all levels of achievement.
6. Grade-level placement is considered synonymous with curricular content.	6. Grade-level placement and individual curricular content are independent of each other.
7. Instruction is often passive, competitive, didactic, and/or teacher-directed.	7. Instruction is active, creative, and collaborative among members of the classroom.
8. Most instructional supports are provided outside the classroom.	8. Most instructional supports are provided within the classroom.
9. Students who do not "fit in" are excluded from general classes and/or activities.	9. Activities are designed to include students though participation levels may vary.
10. The classroom teacher assumes ownership for the education of general education students, and special education staff assume ownership for the education of students with special needs.	10. The classroom teacher, special educators, related service staff, and families assume shared ownership for educating all students.
11. Students are evaluated by common standards.	11. Students are evaluated by individually appropriate standards.
12. Students' success is achieved by meeting common standards.	12. The system of education is considered successful when it strives to meet each student's needs. Students' success is achieved when both individual and group goals are met.

Adapted from "Problem-Solving Methods to Facilitate Inclusive Education," by M. F. Giangreco, C. J. Cloniger, R. E. Dennis, and S. W. Edelman, 1994, in *Creativity and Collaborative Learning: A Practical Guide to Empowering Students and Teachers*, edited by J. S. Thousand, R. A. Villa, and A. J. Nevin. Baltimore: Paul H. Brookes Publishing. Used by permission.

critical elements—(1) active, meaningful participation in the mainstream; (2) sense of belonging; and (3) shared ownership among faculty. Finally, Mastropieri and Scruggs (2001) add administrative support to the list. The five dimensions for successful inclusion identified by Webber (1997) are discussed in the following sections.

Sense of Community and Social Acceptance

In desirable inclusive settings, every student is valued and nurtured. Such settings promote an environment in which all members are seen as equal, all have the opportunity to contribute, and all contributions are respected. Students with special needs are truly included in their classroom communities only when they are appreciated by their teachers and socially accepted by their classmates. An understanding teacher more effectively meets students' instructional and curricular needs, and social acceptance among classmates contributes to students' self-perception of value. Both these goals are equally critical to creating effective inclusive settings and responsible learning environments. It is imperative that we address the need for acceptance, belonging, and friendship (Murray & Greenberg, 2006).

Teachers play a very critical role in creating a positive classroom environment (Favazza, Phillipsen, & Kumar, 2000). Several factors controlled by teachers are essential to establishing a successful inclusive setting. These include teacher attitude, teacher expectations, teacher competence, teacher collaborative skills, and teacher support (Mastropieri & Scruggs, 2001; Salend, 1999). Some of these factors are directly related to a positive classroom environment.

Teachers must have a positive attitude about students with special needs being in their classrooms and also have high expectations of these students. Students often achieve at a level that is expected of them; if teachers expect less, they get less. A great deal of research has shown that teachers actually treat students whom they consider underachievers differently than they treat other students (Jones & Jones, 2004). Also, students are aware of the support given by their teachers to students with disabilities, and they have a tendency to model these attitudes and behaviors. As a result, teachers "need to examine their own attitudes and behaviors as they relate to interactions with students and the acceptance of individual differences" (Salend, 1999, p. 10). If they are not supportive of the inclusion of these students, other students will detect this attitude and be less likely to accept them as equal class members (Salend, 1999).

Teachers also must prepare students to interact with others whose physical characteristics, behaviors, or learning-related needs require special consideration. Sometimes students need to be educated about diversity and disabilities to reduce the fear of differences. While teachers can serve as excellent role models for acceptance of diversity, they can also facilitate interactions and acceptance by orchestrating situations where students with and without disabilities interact. In studying the importance of social relationships in the lives of students, Murray and Greenberg (2006) concluded that school personnel must develop intervention strategies to help students with disabilities develop better relations with their peers and with adults. Remember the chapter-opening vignette, where the teacher's actions resulted in a student without a disability interacting positively with a student with a disability.

If students with special needs are to enjoy a sense of acceptance in general classrooms, teachers must play a critical role.

CEC STANDARDS

CEC 5: Learning Environment and Social Interactions

INTASC

INTASC 3: Understands how students differ

CONSIDER THIS

How likely is it that students with special needs will be successfully included if teachers leave peer acceptance of these students to chance? Why?

CEC STANDARDS

CEC 5: Learning Environment and Social Interactions

INTASC

INTASC 5: Understanding of individual and group motivation

When determining if the school does promote a sense of community and social acceptance, school personnel can ask the following questions:

- Are students with disabilities disproportionately teased by other students?
- Do students with disabilities seem to enjoy being in the general education classroom?
- Do students without disabilities voluntarily include students with disabilities in various activities?
- Do students without disabilities seem to value the ideas and opinions of students with disabilities? Do students with disabilities seem to value the ideas and opinions of nondisabled students?
- Do students with disabilities consider the general education classroom to be their "real class"? Do they consider the general education teacher to be one of their "real teachers"? (Voltz et al., 2001, p. 25)

While students may develop friendships and a classroom community naturally, teachers can do some things to facilitate the process. Friendship facilitation should be an integral part of both special education and general education teachers' roles in inclusive settings (Turnbull, Pereira, & Blue-Banning, 2000). Facilitation can occur through organized group activities, pairing students for various tasks, seating arrangements, buddy systems, and other methods.

Appreciation of Student Diversity

To maximize learning, a teacher needs to understand each individual in the classroom as well as possible. The increasing diversity of today's classrooms makes teaching a very complex activity that will likely only get more complex in the future as our culture becomes more diverse (Maheady, Harper, & Mallette, 2001). In addition to recognizing and responding to each student's educational needs, teachers must be sensitive to the cultural, community, and family values that can have an impact on a student's educational experience. For instance, the nature of teacher-student interactions may be directly affected by certain cultural factors, or the type of home-school contact will be dictated by how the family wants to interact with the school.

Attention to Curricular Needs

Many discussions of inclusion lose track of an important consideration: what the student needs to learn. Teachers must seriously look at the curriculum and ask what students are learning and how students with disabilities can access the curriculum (Pugach & Warger, 2001). If the individual curricular needs of a student are not being met, the curriculum must be modified or the educational placement must be reexamined. Not meeting the curricular needs of students will definitely make it difficult for the student to learn, but it will also likely lead to behavior problems (Jones & Jones, 2004). Good teachers vary their curricula to meet the needs of the students (Walther-Thomas, et al., 2000). While some students with disabilities included in general classrooms may be able to deal effectively with the curricula, many need substantial modifications (Van Laarhoven, Coutinho, Van Laarhoven-Myers, & Repp, 1999).

Effective Management and Instruction

Another essential component of successful inclusive settings is the effective management of the classroom and effective instruction provided by the teacher to meet the wide range of needs of students (Cangelosi, 2004). These practices include four elements: successful classroom management, effective instructional techniques, appropriate accommodative practices, and instructional flexibility. Without effective practices in these areas, successful inclusion is improbable.

CONSIDER THIS

Describe the ways in which today's school population can be diverse. What kinds of actions can school personnel take to show sensitivity to this diversity?

CONSIDER THIS

Can you imagine a situation in which a student with special needs cannot be taught in a general education classroom? What would be an appropriate action if this were the case?

CEC STANDARDS

CEC 2: Development and Characteristics of Learners

CONSIDER THIS

How can appropriate accommodative practices benefit all students, including those without special needs?

PRAXIS

PRAXIS II: Delivery of Services to Students with Disabilities

INTASC

INTASC 7: Plans instruction on knowledge of students

Planning as a Team, Learning Together

Dinora is a seven-year-old in Mrs. Gomez's bilingual (English/Spanish) second grade classroom. She was recently identified as having a learning disability and has begun receiving reading instruction in Mrs. Emerson's special education resource classroom. Her IEP goals include letter recognition, recognizing letter-sound relationships, blending letter sounds, sight word vocabulary development, and reading comprehension. Because Mrs. Emerson does not speak Spanish, all instruction is provided in English. Given Ms. Emerson's limited experience with teaching English language learners (ELLs), Mrs. Gomez is concerned that Dinora will not benefit from her special education reading instruction.

This scenario documents the challenges of providing appropriate special education services for English language learners with disabilities when special educators are monolingual and inadequately prepared to modify instruction to address the cultural and linguistic needs of their students. When used with ELLs with disabilities, special education interventions must provide appropriate language supports so that instruction is comprehensible (García & Dray, 2007; Santamaria, Fletcher, & Bos,

2002). Because Dinora's teachers understood the importance of collaboration, they met regularly to plan together (Delgado, 2006). As a result, they were able to learn from each other's expertise in working with students like Dinora, who are ELLs with disabilities. Mrs. Emerson spent time in Mrs. Gomez' class to model instructional adaptations that could support Dinora's reading during social studies, math, and science. In turn, Mrs. Gomez shared her knowledge of English as a second language (ESL) instruction and suggested ways that Mrs. Emerson could respond to Dinora's English proficiency level and simultaneously support her reading achievement in English. Both teachers also combined efforts in communicating Dinora's progress to her mother. Mrs. Gomez assisted with translations during the Individualized Education Plan (IEP) meeting; through these facilitated conversations Dinora's mother was able to actively participate in the decision-making process about the services her child should receive in school.

Questions

1. What factors contributed to successful collaboration between these two teachers?

2. In what other ways could general and special education teachers collaborate to increase Dinora's participation in the general education classroom during reading instruction?

3. What are other possibilities for collaboration between Dinora's teachers and the student's home/parents?

REFERENCES

García, S. B., & Dray, B. (2007). Bilingualism and special education. In F. E. Obiakor (Ed.), *Multicultural special education* (pp. 18–33). Columbus, OH: Merrill.

Delgado, R. (2006). *Teachers' instructional practices when working with Latino English language learners with reading-related disabilities.* Unpublished doctoral dissertation, The University of Texas at Austin.

Santamaría, L. J., Fletcher, T. V., & Bos, C. S. (2002). Effective pedagogy for English language learners in inclusive classrooms. In A. J. Artiles & A. A. Ortiz (Eds.), *English language learners with special education needs: Identification, assessment, and instruction* (pp. 133–157). Washington, DC: Center for Applied Linguistics and Delta Systems.

Successful Classroom Management   Classrooms that encourage learning are characterized by sound organizational and management systems. Classroom management—including physical, procedural, instructional, and behavior management—sets the stage for the smooth delivery of instruction. Effective classroom management is required if students are to benefit from any form of instruction, especially in inclusive classrooms where students display a wide range of diversity (Jones & Jones, 2004). Without effective classroom organization and management, learning will not be optimal for any student.

CEC STANDARDS

CEC 4: Instructional Strategies

PRAXIS

PRAXIS II: Delivery of Services to Students with Disabilities

Effective Instructional Techniques   Teachers must feel comfortable using a wide variety of instructional techniques to meet the needs of diverse classrooms (Voltz et al., 2001). Students with disabilities, especially those eligible for special education services, by definition, have learning problems. As a result, effective instructional techniques must be used if these students are to be successful.

EVIDENCE-BASED PRACTICE

Music and Art Activities to Promote Friendships

- Teach students songs that deal with the theme of friendship, including recorded songs such as "Friends" (Linhart & Klingman, 1976), "You've Got a Friend" (Taylor, 1971), "That's What Friends Are For" (Bayer Sager & Bacharach, 1985), and "A Little Help from My Friends" (Lennon & McCartney, 1967), and nonrecorded songs that appear in music books, such as "All I Need Is a Friend" (Worsley, 1995), "Best of Friends" (Fidel

& Hohnston, 1986), and "Best Friends" (Ravosa & Jones, 1981).
- Teach students group sing-along songs.
- Teach students songs that require two or more students to perform accompanying physical gestures and movements.
- Teach students humorous songs.
- Ask students to draw pictures of scenes depicting friendships.
- Have students work on group art projects such as a friendship mural, a

friendship book with illustrations, and a friendship bulletin board.
- Have students make silhouettes and collages of their friends.
- Have students make friendship posters that include the qualities that contribute to making someone a good friend.

From "Facilitating Friendships among Diverse Students," by S. J. Salend, 1999, *Intervention in School and Clinic*, 35, p. 11. Used with permission.

CROSS-REFERENCE

Refer to Chapters 12 and 13 on gifted students and students at risk to determine how inclusion applies to these groups of students.

Appropriate Accommodative Practices   Some students require special adaptations to the physical environment, the curriculum, the way instruction is provided, or the assignments given to them. Scruggs and Mastropieri (1994) note that instructional supports are a key variable in classrooms where inclusion is successful. Chapters 5–11 provide examples of disability-specific accommodations that might be needed.

Instructional Flexibility   The ability to respond to unexpected and changing situations to support students with special needs is a key characteristic of responsible inclusive settings. As Schaffner and Buswell (1996) note, classroom teachers need to develop the capabilities that families have acquired to react successfully and spontaneously to challenges that arise on a day-to-day basis. Teachers must be flexible; they must be able to handle behavior problems, provide extra support during instruction, modify assessment techniques, and orchestrate social interactions (Jones & Jones, 2004).

Differentiated instruction has become an important focus for facilitating the success of students with disabilities in general education classrooms. Originally used as a tool for meeting the needs of gifted students, differentiated instruction is now considered an appropriate tool for meeting the needs of students with disabilities (van Garderen &

EVIDENCE-BASED PRACTICE

Practices to Improve Reading Skills: *PALS* and *Modified PALS*

PALS—Peer-mediated program; high-performing student acts as tutor first and the low-performing student is the reader first; then roles are reversed. The coach or tutor provides prompts, feedback, praise, and corrective feedback for each reading activity. Activities can include letter-sound recognition, sight word recognition, decoding, and comprehension.

Modified PALS—Similar to PALS. Teacher selects a high-performing reader as the coach or tutor. This student models appropriate reading skills. The reader reads materials at his/her reading level. Fewer sounds and words are introduced in the Modified PALS, and there is more emphasis on phonological awareness and decoding.

From "Nonresponders: How to Find Them? How to Help Them? What Do They Mean for Special Education?" by D. Fuchs, L. S. Fuchs, K. L. McMaster, L. Yen, & E. Svenson, 2004, *Teaching Exceptional Children, 37,* pp. 72–77.

Web Resources on Inclusion and Disability

Inclusion	**Disability Resources**
www.ici.coled.umn.edu/ici	www.iser.com
www.asri.edu/cfsp/brochure/abtcons.htm	www.ed.gov/offices/OSERS/OSEP/index.html
www.tash.org	www.schwableaming.org
interwork.sdsu.edu	www.mankato.msus.edu/dept/comdis/kuster2/welcome.html
www.nyise.org/college.htm	www.ldonline.org
www.ldonline.org	www.downsyndrome.com
	www.iltech.org
	www.hsdc.org
	www.ncldd.org

From *Quick Guide to the Internet for Special Education 2000 Edition* (p. 13), by M. Male and D. Gotthoffer, 2000. Boston: Allyn & Bacon.

Whittaker, 2006). Differentiated instruction can be described as planning and implementing curricula and instruction to address the diverse learning needs of students. Table 2.1 provides an overview and examples of differentiated instruction.

Prater (2003) summarizes strategies that will facilitate the success of students with special needs in inclusive settings. This set of strategies, titled SHE WILL SUCCEED, provides a set of guidelines for teachers in inclusive classrooms. Figure 2.2 summarizes the SHE WILL SUCCEED process.

Personnel Support and Collaboration

Students with special needs require personnel support to allow them to benefit from placement in inclusive settings, in addition to the instructional support noted earlier (accommodative practices and assistive technology). Special education teachers, **para-educators**, and other related service professionals—such as speech and language pathologists, occupational and physical therapists, and audiologists—are typically involved in providing supports to students with disabilities. They also assist general education teachers in inclusive settings through a variety of collaborative models, including collaboration-consultation, peer support systems, teacher assistance teams, and co-teaching. Table 2.2 summarizes these approaches. A more in-depth discussion of these approaches will be presented in the following section. Equally important is administrative support for inclusion, as reflected by attitudes, policies, and practices at the district and individual school level (Mastropieri & Scruggs, 2001). The next section focuses on collaboration as a critical element in successful inclusive practices.

The use of teams to provide services to students with disabilities, especially students included in general education classrooms, has grown significantly over the past several years. A primary reason for this growth is the realization that it takes a creative use of manpower to effectively implement an inclusion teaching model. Special education teachers and general education teachers must share knowledge of teaching strategies and curricula in order to implement effective instruction. "Through collaborative teaming, teachers set the stage for student achievement of goals" (Wolfe & Hall, 2003, p. 57).

CROSS-REFERENCE

For more information on appropriate classroom management techniques for inclusive settings, see Chapter 14.

INTASC

INTASC 10: Fosters relationships with school colleagues

CEC STANDARDS

CEC 10: Collaboration

CONSIDER THIS

How can administrators make time available for teams of teachers to plan? Why is it important for administrators to support this planning effort?

INTASC

INTASC 10: Fosters relationships with school colleagues

Table **2.1**   **Overview and Examples of Key Concepts for Differentiated Instruction**

Elements	Examples
Content: What is taught and how access to the information and ideas that matter is given.	• Texts at varied reading levels • Provision of organizers to guide note-taking • Use of examples and illustrations based on student interest • Present in visual, auditory, and kinesthetic modes • Provide materials in the primary language of second-language learners
Process: How students come to understand and "own" the knowledge, skills, and understanding.	• Vary the pacing of student work • Use cooperative grouping strategies (e.g., Think-Pair-Share, Jigsaw) • Develop activities that seek multiple perspectives on topics and issues • Highlight critical passages in a text • Tiered assignments
Product: Student demonstration of what he or she has come to know, understand, and be able to do.	• Provide bookmarked Internet sites at different levels of complexity for research sources • Develop rubrics for success based on both grade-level expectations and individual student learning needs • Teach students how to use a wide range of product formats (e.g., presentation software)
Affect: Student linking of thought and feeling in the classroom.	• Modeling respect • Help students examine multiple perspectives on important issues • Ensure consistently equitable participation of every student
Learning Environment: Classroom function and feeling.	• Rearrange furniture to allow for individual, small-group, and whole-group work • Availability of supplies and materials (e.g., paint, paper, pencil) • Procedures for working at various places in the room and for various tasks

From "Planning Differentiated Multicultural Instruction for Secondary Classrooms," by D. van Garderen and C. Whittaker, 2006, *Teaching Exceptional Children*, p. 14. Used with permission.

CEC STANDARDS

CEC 10: Collaboration

INTASC

INTASC 10: Fosters relationships with school colleagues

Several critical variables must be in place for these teams to be successful, ranging from knowing the purpose of the team to making sure that the team appreciates disagreement. Figure 2.3 lists variables for success determined by Fleming and Monda-Amaya in a 2001 study. Cooperative teams should be evaluated periodically to ensure their effectiveness. Salend, Gordon, and Lopez-Vona (2002) recommend that, to review their effectiveness, teams should be evaluated using information on team-member experiences and their reactions to working together.

Professional Collaboration

Collaboration among professionals has been discussed in the social services research since the early 1900s; it is not a new concept. Collaboration in schools for serving children with special needs occurs both formally, when teams are formed around a particular child, and informally, when two teachers get together and discuss how to meet a child's specific need (Friend, 2000). Collaboration can be defined as "a system of planned cooperative activities where general educators and special educators share roles and responsibilities for student learning" (Wiggins & Damore, 2006, p. 49).

Figure 2.2 **The SHE WILL SUCCEED Process**

S	Show concern for the targeted student.
H	Have faith in yourself and your targeted student.
E	Examine your classroom.
W	Write down the targeted student's strengths and limitations.
I	Include skills, learning preferences, and behaviors specific to your classroom.
L	Line up student and classroom characteristics as those that facilitate, provide barriers, or are neutral for the individual student's learning success.
L	List 1–3 classroom characteristics you could modify and skills you could teach.
S	Select and implement adaptation(s) and goal(s).
U	Use effective teaching principles to teach goals.
C	Collaborate with others as needed.
C	Change adaptations and instruction as necessary.
E	Evaluate results.
E	Exit here OR
D	Do again.

From "She Will Succeed!" by Mary Anne Prater, 2003, *Teaching Exceptional Children, 35*, p. 58. Used with permission.

CEC STANDARDS

CEC 10: Collaboration

INTASC

INTASC 10: Fosters relationships with school colleagues

PRAXIS

PRAXIS II: Delivery of Services to Students with Disabilities

Professional collaboration has become a key component of effective schools and a necessity for successful inclusion. Collaboration can occur in a variety of settings and activities, including prereferral efforts and IEP meetings (see Chapter 4), consulting and cooperative teaching arrangements, and teacher assistance teams. Still another form of collaboration is peer tutoring or some other peer support framework.

Collaboration is not successful without a great deal of planning and effort (Clark, 2000). It "requires commitment on the part of each individual to a shared goal, demands careful attention to communication skills, and obliges participants to maintain parity throughout their interactions" (Friend, 2000, p. 131). In general, collaboration should be accomplished to ensure (1) natural inclusion of students in all activities of the general education classroom; (2) appropriate specialized instruction of students; and (3) adaptations of curriculum and materials necessary for each student (Halvorsen & Neary, 2001).

Table 2.2 **Types of Collaborative Efforts**

Approach	Nature of Contact with Student	Description
Collaboration-Consultation	Indirect	General education teacher requests the services of the special education teacher (i.e., consultant) to help generate ideas for addressing an ongoing situation. The approach is interactive.
Peer Support Systems	Indirect	Two general education teachers work together to identify effective solutions to classroom situations. The approach emphasizes the balance of the relationship.
Teacher Assistance Teams	Indirect	Teams provide support to general education teachers. The team is made up of core members plus the teacher seeking assistance; it emphasizes analyzing the problem situation and developing potential solutions.
Co-teaching	Direct	General and special education teachers work together to provide direct service to students. The approach employs joint planning and teaching, and emphasizes the joint responsibilities of instruction.

From *Cooperative Teaching: Rebuilding the Schoolhouse for All Students* (p. 74), by J. Bauwens and J. J. Hourcade, 1995, Austin, TX: Pro-Ed. Used by permission.

Figure 2.3 **Critical Variables for Team Efforts and Effectiveness, Ranked by Categories**

Team Goals
Purpose of the team is clear.
Team goals are understood by all members.
Team goals are regularly reviewed.
Team goals are established by team members.
Team goals are clearly stated.
Team goals are modified by team members.
Team goals are supported by the family.
Team goals are attainable.
Team goals are prioritized.
Members anticipate both positive and negative outcomes.
Members are satisfied with goals that have been selected.

Team Roles and Team Membership
Team members are committed to the team process.
The team has a leader.
Members are accountable to the team.
Team roles are clearly understood.
Team roles are perceived by members as being important.
New team members are added when practical.
The team leader is unbiased.

Team Communication
Decisions are made for the good of the student.
Team members have adequate listening time.
Decisions are alterable.
Team members have equal opportunities to speak.
Decisions are reached by consensus.

Team Cohesion
Members feel safe sharing ideas.
The team has trust among members.

Members (especially parents) feel equally empowered.
The team has a unified goal.
The team has time to celebrate.
The team has support from superiors.
Members have respect for one another.
The team has recognition for efforts.
The team has autonomy for decision making.
The team has a healthy regard for disagreement.

Team Logistics
Progress is evaluated internally, by members.
Team procedures are clearly understood.

Team Outcomes
The team makes modifications to the plan as needed.
Members are clear about their responsibilities for the plan.
Members are committed to implementing the plan.
Solutions are practical.
A plan was implemented.
The team reviews the impact of the plan.
A plan was developed.
Parent satisfaction is part of the evaluation.
Outcomes are evaluated internally, by members.
The family is generally feeling better.
A plan was agreed on.
A decision was made.
Outcomes are evaluated at regularly scheduled times.
Members are satisfied with the plan.

From "Process Variables Critical for Team Effectiveness," by J. L. Fleming and L. E. Monda-Amaya, 2001, *Remedial and Special Education, 22*, p. 168. Used with permission.

Unfortunately, many schools implement collaborative models because "everyone else is doing it." To make it work effectively, collaboration should be introduced through professional development for general and special education personnel (Wiggins & Damore, 2006). Schools can use several different models that rely on collaboration among school staff. One particular model is no better than another. Schools need to understand the variations that are possible and implement the approach that best meets their needs and the needs of their students.

Collaboration-Consultation

Collaboration-consultation is a model that emphasizes a close working relationship between general and special educators. "Effective collaboration consists of designing and using a sequence of goal-oriented activities that result in improved working relationships between professional colleagues. The responsibility for collaborating can either be the sole responsibility of one individual who seeks to improve a professional relationship, or a joint commitment of two or more people who wish to improve their working relationship" (Cramer, 1998, p. 3).

There are several benefits of collaboration:

1. Collaboration facilitates the ongoing planning, evaluation, and modification necessary to ensure the success of included placements.

2. Collaboration enables general education classrooms to meet the needs of students with and without disabilities in new and exciting ways.
3. Collaboration can provide the personal and professional support of highly skilled colleagues.
4. Collaboration can result in personal and professional growth for all participants.
5. Collaboration helps teachers identify ways to access the skills, knowledge, and expertise of other teachers (Mundschenk & Foley, 1997, p. 58).

Through collaborating with one another, general education and special education teachers can bring more ideas and experiences to help students achieve success. Through consultation, teachers can assist one another in utilizing skills that also result in positive outcomes for students.

A critical skill in collaboration is effective communication. Without the ability to communicate with one another, school personnel will not be able to collaborate effectively (Hollingsworth, 2001). The more individuals involved in a child's educational program, the more effective communication must be. Communication allows the sharing of information about a student, expertise, perceptions, concerns, ideas, and questions (Halvorsen & Neary, 2001).

To facilitate communication, school staff must have time for planning. Regardless of the collaboration approach used, planning time is critical. Unfortunately, the logistics of arranging planning time is often complicated. Teachers may not share planning periods, and in elementary schools teachers may not even have planning periods. Also, students with disabilities included in secondary schools may have six or seven general classroom teachers. Trying to sit down to plan with so many players is extremely difficult (Halvorsen & Neary, 2001).

Making planning time available for school staff requires the support of school administrators. If school administrators support inclusion, they generally find a way to arrange for planning opportunities for professionals and paraprofessionals. However, if they are not supportive of inclusion or do not see the need for planning time, then they are less likely to make the time available.

Making time for teachers and other staff members to plan for specific students can be accomplished in several ways. Arranging for team members to have the same planning periods, having split schedules for teachers, using roving aides to cover classes, and providing financial incentives are only a few methods for finding planning time. Regardless of how it is accomplished, the fact remains that without time to plan, many attempts to provide supports for students with disabilities in general education classes will be unsuccessful. The Personal Spotlight provides a glimpse of a general education teacher and her thoughts on collaboration.

Teachers often need to work together to solve some of the challenges created by inclusion.

CONSIDER THIS

How could the use of paraprofessionals be a detriment to the successful inclusion of students with special needs in a general education classroom?

Co-teaching

Another model to provide support for students in general education classrooms is **co-teaching**. Cooperative teaching, or co-teaching, "helps provide students with disabilities access to the general education teacher and the general education curriculum, providing the required accommodations from the students' IEPs" (Magiera, Smith, Zigmond, & Gebauer, 2005, p. 20). Co-teaching is an arrangement of two or more teachers or other school staff who collectively assume the responsibilities for the same group of students on a regular basis (Magiera et al., 2005). This model is becoming very popular as the movement to include students with disabilities expands (Wilson, 2005).

TEACHING TIP

Teachers who use the co-teaching model should determine which team members have expertise in specific areas and take advantage of those skills.

Personal Spotlight

Inclusion from a First Grade Teacher's Perspective

Debi Smith is a first grade teacher at Washington Elementary School in Fayetteville, Arkansas. She has taught kindergarten and first grade for more than fifteen years. She has also taught in special education classrooms for three years. During the years she has taught regular classes, she has frequently had students with special needs included in her classroom. Most recently she had three students with significant disabilities included in her classroom. These included Rebecca, with Down Syndrome, Johnathan with autism, and Andrea with severe mental retardation. Rebecca spent approximately half of each day in Debi's classroom, while Johnathan and Andrea were included between one and two hours daily. A special education paraprofessional, Jessica, always accompanied the students when they were in the first grade classroom. Debi says that the first two weeks were very difficult, primarily getting the students to understand the differences in routines and expectations between the special education classroom and her classroom. Once the students understood these expectations and routines, things went much better. Debi strongly supports inclusion as a way of helping non-disabled students understand and accept differences. Her non-disabled students enjoyed the included students and provided a great deal of spontaneous peer support. The non-disabled students learned to be more tolerant, while the included students with disabilities learned appropriate behaviors from modeling. The biggest challenge created by the included students was simply time. Debi noted that she spent a great deal of time in special education meetings, and she also had to develop some parallel programs for the students, since they were not able to do the same academic tasks as the non-disabled students. Too often, Debi noted, general classroom teachers are simply not prepared to deal effectively with included students. Her experiences as a special education teacher helped prepare her to develop and implement programs for her students with special needs. Debi's big focus with students with disabilities is to ensure that they are truly included in her classroom activities, not simply physically included in the classroom.

Debi Smith
Fayetteville, AR

Cooperative teaching is a logical outgrowth of collaborative efforts between teachers that include consultative arrangements, additional help given by special education teachers to children not identified as eligible for special services, and the sharing of teaching assistants, especially to accompany students who are disabled in the general education classroom. Cooperative teaching involves a team approach to supporting students within the general classroom, combining the content expertise of the classroom teacher with the pedagogical skills of the special education teacher. Co-teaching is perhaps the best vehicle for attaining successful inclusive classrooms; it truly provides supported education, the school-based equivalent of supported work in which students are placed in the LRE and provided the necessary support (e.g., by the special educator) to be successful.

Co-teaching usually occurs at set times, such as during second period every day or certain days of each week. When students with disabilities are included in general education classrooms, the special education teacher, who becomes a co-teacher, is usually present (Friend & Bursuck, 2005). Co-teachers perform many tasks jointly, including planning and teaching, developing instructional accommodations, monitoring and evaluating students, and communicating student progress (Walther-Thomas et al., 2000). Co-teaching can take the form of one teaching, one supporting; station teaching; parallel teaching; team teaching; complementary teaching; supportive learning activities; and alternative teaching (Halvorsen & Neary, 2001). Table 2.3 summarizes the advantages and disadvantages of several variations.

Austin (2001) studied 139 co-teachers from nine school districts, kindergarten through twelfth grade. He found that although the majority of co-teachers had not volunteered for the role, "a major percentage indicated that they considered co-teaching

Table 2.3	**Variations of Coteaching: Advantages and Disadvantages**	
Variation	**Advantages**	**Disadvantages**
Interactive Teaching (Whole group) Partners alternate roles presenting new concepts, reviewing, demonstrating, role playing, and monitoring.	• Provides systematic observation/data collection • Promotes role/content sharing • Facilitates individual assistance • Models appropriate for academic, social, and help-seeking behaviors • Teaches question-asking • Provides clarification (e.g., concepts, rules, vocabulary)	• May be job sharing, not learning enriching • Requires considerable planning • Requires modeling and role-playing skills • Becomes easy to "typecast" specialist with this role
Station Teaching (Small group) Students in groups of three or more rotate to various teacher-led and independent work stations where new instruction, review, and/or practice is provided. Students may work at all stations during the rotation.	• Provides active learning format • Increases small-group attention • Encourages cooperation and independence • Allows strategic grouping • Increases response rate	• Requires considerable planning and preparation • Increases noise level • Requires group and independent work skills • Is difficult to monitor
Parallel Teaching (Small group) Students are divided into mixed-ability groups, then each partner teaches a group. The same material is presented in each group.	• Provides effective review format • Encourages student responses • Reduces pupil–teacher ratio for group instruction/review	• Not easy to achieve equal depth of content coverage • May be difficult to coordinate • Requires monitoring of partner pacing • Increases noise level • Encourages some teacher–student competition
Alternative Teaching (Big group; small group) One partner teaches an enrichment lesson or reteaches a concept for the benefit of a small group, while the other partner teaches and/or monitors the remaining members of the class.	• Facilitates enrichment opportunities • Offers absent students "catch up" time • Keeps individuals and class on pace • Offers time to develop missing skills	• May be easy to select the same low-achieving students for help • Creates segregated learning environments • Is difficult to coordinate • May single out students

From *Collaboration for Inclusive Education* (p. 190), by C. Walther-Thomas, L. Korinek, V. L. McLaughlin, and B. T. Williams, 2000. Boston: Allyn & Bacon. Used by permission.

worthwhile" (p. 252). Also, the majority felt that co-teaching actually contributed to academic gains made by all students in their classrooms. Austin's study found that the important co-teaching activities included providing feedback to one another, sharing classroom management, having daily planning time, and using cooperative learning techniques. In another study, Willson and Pace (2002) found that 84 percent of their special education administrators rated their co-teaching efforts as very good or higher.

Cooperative teaching is not a simple solution for the many challenges of accommodating a broad range of students with disabilities. Certain difficulties may create barriers for effective co-teaching, such as limitations of time, cooperation with others, and workload (Langerock, 2000; Bauwens et al., 1989; Harris, 1998). Time problems can be alleviated through careful planning, regularly scheduled discussions on teaching, and support for planning periods from administrators. The issue of cooperation is best addressed through training in the use of cooperative teaching, experience with the process, development of guidelines specific to the program, and attention to effective communication accompanied, as needed, by conflict resolution. The concern for work-load should be addressed as the team relationship develops, delegating tasks in a way that allows each individual to focus on areas of expertise and interests. Evaluation should be a component of the workload as well.

Another critical issue regarding cooperative teaching is voluntary involvement. Set-ting up cooperative teaching arrangements without regard to input from the teachers themselves will not set the stage for success for teachers or ultimately for the students. Teachers should be given some choice and flexibility—for example, allowing general and special education teachers to select partners with whom to collaborate has worked well.

Teachers, both general and special education, involved in coteaching activities have rated having scheduled planning time and administrative support as either very impor-tant or important (Austin, 2001). Figure 2.4 reflects the ratings of other areas by coteachers.

One of the obvious difficulties in implementing the co-teaching model is insuring the compatibility of the individuals working together. Mastropieri and colleagues (2005) found that "when co-teachers are getting along and working well together, students with disabilities are more likely to be successful and have successful experiences in the inclusive environment" (p. 268). Common characteristics of successful co-teachers include the following (Walther-Thomas et al., 2000):

- Professional competence
- Personal confidence
- Respect of colleagues
- Professional enthusiasm
- Respect for colleagues' skills and contributions
- Good communication and problem-solving skills
- Personal interest in professional growth
- Flexibility and openness to new ideas
- Effective organizational skills
- Previous experience teaming with others
- Willingness to invest extra time in the process as needed
- Commitment to planning weekly with partner
- Voluntary participation in co-teaching

Still another characteristic of effective co-teaching teams is a shared work ethic (McCormick, Noonan, Ogata, & Heck, 2001). Co-teaching works extremely well when the coteachers are committed to the success of students and find a common ground for working together. Since it requires the development of a unique relationship, it will not work in all situations. In a study by McCormick and colleagues (2001), it was con-cluded that "the extent to which co-teachers perceive themselves to be similar to one another in personal characteristics and traits, professional style, and philosophical beliefs and biases may affect their ability to provide a quality environment" (p. 128).

Cooperative Teaching Arrangements Although cooperative teaching can be imple-mented in many ways, it essentially involves collaboration between special and general education teachers in the environment of the general education classroom, typically for several periods per day. Bauwens, Hourcade, and Friend (1989) discuss three distinct yet related forms of cooperative teaching: complementary instruction, team teaching, and supportive learning activities. Complementary teaching involves teaching the skills related to success in learning, commonly referred to as study skills or learning strategies.

In **team teaching**, the general and special education teachers plan one lesson jointly and teach it to all students, both with and without disabilities. Each teacher may take responsibility for one aspect of the teaching. Peterson and Hittie (2003) note that this is the most common model for classes being taught by two teachers. In this model, two teachers teach the same content to two smaller groups. The intent of this arrangement is

Figure 2.4   **Comparison of Percentages of Very Important and Important Responses of Co-teachers in Value versus Access Categories**

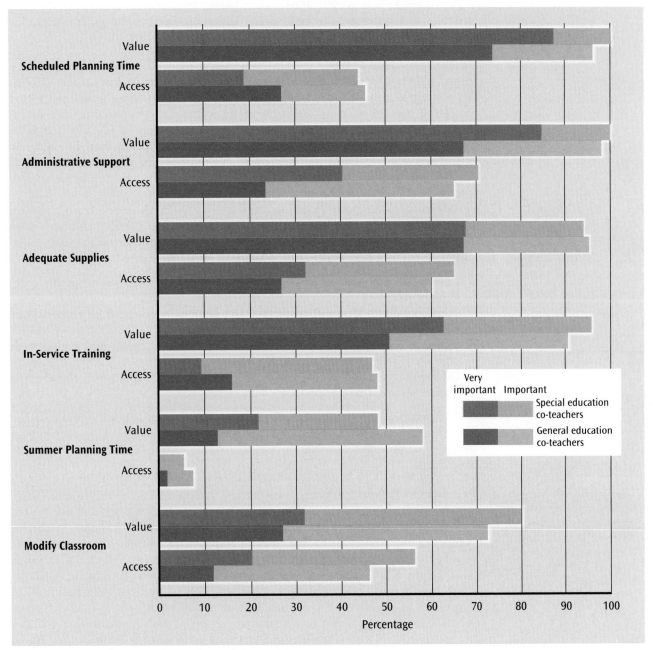

From Austin, *Remedial and Special Education* 4(22). July/August 2001.

to provide further opportunities for students to be actively involved in the instruction, to respond to the teacher and peers, and to have their responses monitored by the teacher. It can serve as a wrap-up session for the larger group instruction (Vaughn et al., 1997).

In **supportive learning activities**, the general and special educators plan and teach the lesson to the whole class. The general educator typically delivers the main content; the special educator then plans and implements activities that reinforce the learning of the content material (e.g., cooperative learning groups, tutoring, reciprocal teaching, or simulations).

Unfortunately, although the use of co-teaching and other collaborative staffing patterns is increasing along with inclusive programs, preservice programs have not kept up with preparing teachers for their new roles. These programs must develop curricula and activities that better prepare both special education teachers and general education teachers for their roles in collaborative teaching models (Austin, 2001).

Teacher Assistance Teams   Another collaborative model to provide support to students in general education classrooms is the use of **teacher assistance teams.** Teacher assistance teams can be defined as "school-based, problem-solving teams designed to enable all teachers to meet the needs of their students demonstrating difficulties" (Walther-Thomas et al., 2000, p. 140). These teams comprise teachers and other instructional support personnel, either elected or voluntary; they provide a forum where problems are raised and discussed, and solutions are developed. The use of teacher assistance teams enables educators to bring a diverse set of skills and experience to bear on specific problems.

Westling, Cooper-Duffy, Prohn, Ray, and Herzog (2005) describe a teacher support program that incorporates different types of support. While a teacher assistance team provides useful collaborative opportunities around particular students, the teacher support program includes a wider array of supports for teachers. These include:

1. Collaborative-problem solving and mutual support sessions, where specific problems are discussed.
2. Electronic networking and communication sessions, where teachers communicate via online chat rooms to discuss various issues.
3. Information and materials search, where teachers request specific information about different problems they are encountering.
4. On-site/in-class consultation, where a consultant actually comes to a classroom to observe and provide specific suggestions and supports.

This broader range of supports is intended to help teachers deal with stress and burnout. In a study to validate the system, it was determined that the teacher support program did provide substantial supports (Westling, Herzog, Cooper-Duffy, Prohn, & Ray, 2006).

Peer Support Systems   Educators must realize that the staffing needed to successfully support students with disabilities in inclusive settings is increasing, and one way to help meet that growing need is through **peer support systems** (Kroeger & Kouche, 2006). In this model, students with disabilities in general education classrooms receive social or instructional help from their nondisabled peers (Dobbs & Block, 2004). While not the same as professional collaboration, peer support systems do result in collaborative efforts on behalf of students with disabilities. Peer support systems are some of the best means to provide support to students with disabilities in general education classrooms because students rely on the natural support of other students; they facilitate access by students with disabilities to the general curriculum (Copeland et al., 2004). "Students learn a lot from one another—particularly about things that matter to them in their world" (Collins, Hendricks, Fetko, & Land, 2002, p. 56). Peer support for instruction can be provided in several different ways, such as peer tutoring, peer assessment, peer modeling, and cooperative learning (Ryan, Reid, & Epstein, 2004). These peer supports assist not only students with disabilities, but also students with language and other needs (Burks, 2004; Fuchs & Fuchs, 2005). Table 2.4 summarizes various peer support models.

Peers can also provide support to one another through cooperative learning activities. Cooperative learning, which takes advantage of small groups of students working together in a cooperative rather than competitive manner, helps teach social skills as well as academic skills (Goodwin, 1999). When using cooperative learning, teachers should do the following:

Table 2.4	**Types of Peer-Mediated Interventions**
Intervention	**Description**
Classwide Peer Tutoring (CWPT)	Entire class simultaneously participates in tutoring dyads. During each tutoring session, students can participate as both tutor and tutee, or they can participate as only the tutor or tutee.
Cooperative Learning	Small teams composed of students with different levels of ability use a variety of learning activities to improve their understanding of a subject. Each member of a team is responsible not only for learning what is taught but also for helping teammates learn.
Cross-Age Tutoring	Older students are matched with younger students to deliver instruction. Tutors are typically at least two years older than the tutees. Large differences in skill levels between the tutor and tutee are not needed.
Peer Tutoring	Students who need remedial support are paired with select tutors (perhaps highly skilled peers, peers also in need of remedial work, or cross-age tutors). Each member of the dyad may receive and provide tutoring in the same content area, or tutors can provide instruction in a content area in which they are highly skilled.
Peer-Assisted Learning Strategies (PALS)	A version of CWPT where teachers identify children who require help on specific skills and the most appropriate children to help them learn those skills. Pairs are changed regularly, and over time as students work on a variety of skills, all students have the opportunity to be "coaches" and "players."
Peer Assessment	Peers are used to assess the products or outcomes of learning of other students of similar status.
Peer Modeling	Students acting as peer models receive instruction in desired behaviors, then engage in these behaviors in front of students deficient in these areas. The teacher draws the student's attention to the peer model and identifies the desired behaviors the student should emulate.
Peer Reinforcement	Peers provide reinforcement for appropriate responses within the natural environment. The purpose is to reinforce appropriate behaviors of students with disabilities by their peers.

From "Peer Medicated Intervention Studies on Academic Achievement for students with EBD," by J. B. Ryan, R. Reid, and M. H. Epstein, 2004, *Remedial and Special Education, 25,* p. 332.

- Start slowly.
- Teach beginning social skills with nonacademic activities.
- Use pairs and threes, which work better than large cooperative groups.
- Gradually extend applications to new subject matter.
- Make changes incrementally.
- Have a parent meeting to dispel fear of group grades.
- Keep things simple.
- Use old tennis balls to fit on desk legs to cut down on noise when students are moving into groups.
- Fine-tune procedures to improve functioning.
- Pick and choose from a variety of cooperative structures.
- Share concerns with a "veteran" teacher.
- Have a written ongoing evaluation of social skills progress for both the group and individuals (Goodwin, 1999, p. 32).

When implementing any peer support system, school personnel must always remember that while these approaches may work extremely well in some situations, the peers providing the support are also students. They may provide a great deal of help, but providing the necessary support to enable students to be successful remains a professional responsibility. Nine guidelines should be considered before implementing a peer tutoring system (Figure 2.5). These guidelines emphasize the importance of planning before implementing any peer support system.

There are benefits to both the peers receiving supports and the peers providing the supports (Hughes et al., 2001). Peer support networks enhance a sense of classroom community, student motivation, and student learning (Korinek et al., 1999). One way to implement a peer support system is through service learning activities. "Service learning experiences allow students to extend their learning by applying their knowledge and skills to actual problems outside their classroom environments" (Hughes et al., 2001, p. 343). When implementing a peer buddy system using service learning, the general education students would receive academic credit for their work. Activities that could easily be included in a service learning, peer support program could include (Hughes et al., 2001):

- Accompanying their special education peers to general education classes and activities.
- Helping their peers become included in the mainstream of everyday high school life.
- Assisting their peers in performing activities in the community or at employment training sites.
- Providing friendship.

In a study of peer buddy systems implemented through service learning, nearly 50 percent of all peer buddies felt that the program resulted in their providing assistance to their buddies, while enabling them to perform service activities (Hughes et al., 2001).

Using Paraprofessionals

The use of paraprofessionals to provide direct support to students with significant learning problems is occurring more commonly (Giangreco et al., 2001). The most recent IDEA amendments specifically note that "paraprofessionals who are adequately trained and supervised may assist in the delivery of special education and related services" ([Part B, Sec. 612 (a) (15)]). Therefore, IDEA provides regulatory support for using

---

Figure 2.5   **Implementation Guidelines for Peer Tutoring Programs**

1. Explain the purpose and rationale for the technique. Stress the idea of increased opportunities for practice and "on-task" behavior.
2. Stress collaboration and cooperation rather than competition.
3. Select the content and instructional materials for tutoring sessions.
4. Train students in the roles of tutor and tutee. Include specific procedures for (a) feedback for correct responses, (b) error correction procedures, and (c) score-keeping.
5. Model appropriate behaviors for tutor and tutee. Demonstrate acceptable ways to give and accept corrective feedback.
6. Provide sample scripts for student practice of roles. Divide the class into practice pairs and teams.
7. Let pairs practice roles of tutor as teacher circulates and provides feedback and reinforcement.
8. Conduct further discussion regarding constructive and nonconstructive pair behavior. Answer questions and problem-solve as needed.
9. Let pairs switch roles and practice new roles as teacher circulates and provides feedback, and reinforcement. Repeat Step 8.

From "Classwide Peer Tutoring at Work," by B. M. Fulk and K. King, 2001, *Teaching Exceptional Children, 34*, p. 49. Used with permission.

Paraeducators can provide direct services to some students with special needs in general classrooms.

paraprofessionals in a direct support role for students with disabilities (Carroll, 2001) and indicates that paraprofessionals should have adequate training. Carroll (2001) suggests that this training should be in professional interaction, communication, and conflict-management skills. The U.S. Department of Education (2003) noted that in the 2000–2001 school year, 321,657 paraprofessionals were involved in providing education services to children with disabilities.

However, the mere presence of paraprofessionals in inclusive classrooms is not positive. Depending on individual paraprofessionals to be tied all day to a particular student can actually be detrimental. Having an individual paraprofessional for one child could result in his separation from classmates, unnecessary dependence, and even interference with the teacher's efforts at instruction (Giangreco, Yuan, McKenzie, Cameron, & Fialka, 2005). Paraprofessionals can have great potential at facilitating inclusion as long as proper safeguards ensure that paraprofessionals implement support services effectively.

The role of paraprofessionals is often unclear. Whereas sometimes they take a major responsibility for the education of some students with disabilities, in other settings they

CONSIDER THIS

Why is preparing school staff for inclusion important? How could a prepared staff make a difference in the success of inclusion?

EVIDENCE-BASED PRACTICE

Increasing Peer Interactions for Students with Severe Disabilities through Training for Paraprofessionals

Peer interactions between individuals with disabilities and their nondisabled peers can be increased by training paraprofessionals to facilitate such interactions. Four topics included in the training activities might be:

1. *Enhancing paraprofessionals' perspective of their social interactions:* Ask paraprofessionals to complete a worksheet to reflect on their own social relationships and then on the students with whom they work.

2. *Establishing the importance of peer interactions:* Discuss the importance of peer interactions involving paraprofessionals in discussing why such relationships are important.

3. *Clarifying the paraprofessional's role in facilitating interactions:* Use discussions about how paraprofessionals could facilitate interactions to help them understand their important role in facilitating such interactions.

4. *Increasing paraprofessionals' knowledge base:* Present and discuss specific strategies for enhancing interactions. Present examples of such strategies.

From "Increasing Peer Interactions for Students with Severe Disabilities via Training for Paraprofessionals," by J. N. Causton-Theoharis and K. W. Malmgren, 2005, *Exceptional Children, 71,* pp. 431–444.

function primarily as clerical aides. Still, their role in providing instruction appears to be increasing. There are several roles that paraprofessionals can be invaluable, including:

- Doing clerical tasks that free teachers to spend more time instructing students.
- Engaging in follow-up instruction, tutoring, or homework help.
- Providing supervision in group settings (e.g., cafeteria, playground, bus boarding).
- Assisting students with personal care needs (e.g., bathroom use, eating, dressing).
- Facilitating social skills, peer interactions, and positive behavior support plans (Giangreco et al., 2005, p. 29).

Once roles are determined, regardless of what those roles are, then appropriate training must be afforded paraprofessionals to enable them to be prepared to successfully implement those roles (Giangreco et al., 2005).

Creating and Maintaining Inclusive Classrooms

PRAXIS

PRAXIS II: Delivery of Services to Students with Disabilities

This section presents practical ways to establish responsible inclusive classrooms and to ensure that they continue to provide appropriate educational programs to students. Specific ideas for preparing staff and students who do not have special needs as well as mechanisms for developing collaborative relationships are discussed.

Preparing Staff for Inclusion

CEC STANDARDS

CEC 4: Instructional Strategies

A comprehensive program for preparing a school setting for inclusion must consider the involvement of all staff members. As Roach (1995) points out, "Successful planning models ensure that all teachers, paraprofessionals, and related service personnel are included in the process" (p. 298). Although many preservice training programs acquaint teachers-in-training with working with students with diverse needs, the nature of this preparation varies greatly. Moreover, many teachers who are already in the field have not been exposed to information important for implementing good inclusive practices. This conclusion is supported by the data discussed earlier in this chapter.

INTASC

INTASC 3: Understands how students differ

The primary goals of all preservice and in-service training of general education teachers include creating positive attitudes about working with students with diverse needs and allaying apprehensions and concerns teachers might have about their competence to address the needs of these students. These goals are achieved by three major training-related activities: (1) opportunities to see good examples of inclusion; (2) provision of information about inclusion, student diversity, and inclusion-related practices, together with the development of skills that a teacher needs to feel comfortable and competent when working with students with special needs; and (3) time to plan with team members.

CONSIDER THIS

If examples of good inclusion classrooms are unavailable in a school district, how can teachers in that district be exposed to such examples?

Exposure to Good Inclusive Classrooms   Nothing is more encouraging and motivating than to see wonderful examples of what one wants to achieve. It is essential that teachers have opportunities to visit schools or classrooms that demonstrate the five critical dimensions of inclusion discussed earlier in this chapter. It is one thing to talk about these practices, and yet another thing to see them being implemented. A number of projects in the United States have developed model inclusion classrooms. These settings can serve as demonstration sites that teachers can observe and imitate.

CONSIDER THIS

How could having a guest speaker with a disability backfire on a teacher's effort to prepare the class for the inclusion of students with special needs?

Information and Skills Needed   Teachers regularly express a desire to know more about the inclusion process, the needs of students with learning-related challenges, and ways to address these needs. Teachers must find practical ways of matching individual needs with sound instructional practices. For teachers to become comfortable in making and implementing such decisions, they must have sufficient training in management techniques, instructional strategies, and curriculum adaptation tactics.

Teachers can also benefit from instruction in topics such as social skills, self-determination, learning strategies, and study skills. From time to time, updates and new ideas in these important areas can be offered to teaching staff to spark strategies and deepen knowledge. In turn, teachers can enhance the social acceptance of students with special needs by instructing their classes in social skills, such as how to make and keep friends.

Other skills are also needed in most inclusive arrangements. First and foremost are skills in collaboration. General education teachers will need to work collaboratively with other professionals within the school setting, especially special education staff, and with parents or other individuals who are responsible for students at home.

Preparing Students for Inclusion

Like those for staff, the goals for preparing students for inclusion focus on developing positive attitudes and allaying concerns. Ultimately, we want students to understand the needs of others who are different and to welcome them into the classroom community as valued members. Many nondisabled students have not been involved with students with special needs. As a result, the movement to inclusive schools often results in students being unprepared for dealing with such diverse classrooms. While nondisabled students are generally supportive of inclusion, they need to be prepared for the changes that accompany this educational model. Awareness programs, class discussions, simulations, guest speakers, and social interactions can pave the way for inclusion.

Awareness Programs   Over the years, an assortment of formal programs has emerged to help change the attitudes of nondisabled students toward their classmates who have special needs. Tovey (1995) describes three programs that promote this type of awareness: Friends Who Care, New Friends, and Kids on the Block. These programs are highlighted in Table 2.5.

Discussions   In-class discussion is a good way to address topics related to students with special needs. Topics for discussion can be found in a variety of sources, including books and films about disabilities or famous people with special needs who have been successful in a variety of fields. Guest speakers can also be effective. Schulz and Carpenter

> **TEACHING TIP**
>
> When attempting to prepare students for the inclusion of students with special needs, teachers should use a variety of techniques and not rely on only one method.

Table 2.5	Disability Awareness Programs
Program	**Description**
Friends Who Care (National Easter Seals Society)	• Elementary level curriculum. • Information about major types of disabilities. • Hands-on activities. • Recommends inviting guest speakers. • Package contains teacher's guide, videotape, worksheet activities, guest speaker guidelines, posters, etiquette bookmarks, and attitude survey.
New Friends (Chapel Hill Training Outreach Project)	• Goal—to promote awareness and understanding of disabilities. • Parents and children make dolls out of cloth patterns—the dolls are used for instructional purposes.
Kids on the Block	• Lifesize puppets include disabled and nondisabled. • Skits are scripted—puppeteers follow the scripts. • Presents various situations in which certain information is discussed. • Audience is given an opportunity to ask the puppets questions after the skit is over. • Uses volunteers as puppeteers.

From "Awareness Programs Help Change Students' Attitudes toward Their Disabled Peers," by R. Tovey, 1995, *Harvard Educational Letter, 11*(6), pp. 7–8. Used by permission.

(1995) warn, however, that "caution must be taken to ensure that the discussions are based on accurate information, avoiding the possibility that uninformed biases would form the core of the exchanges" (p. 400).

Imaginative literature offers many examples of characters with special needs. A great source of information for elementary students is children's literature. A number of books have been written about disabilities or conditions that might directly relate to students who are about to be included in a general education class.

For secondary-level students, films can stimulate discussion about people with special needs. A listing of such films can be found in Table 2.6. However, a note of caution is warranted, as this table includes some films containing characterizations that are "disablist" (an updated term for "handicapist"). This means that they may make generalizations about individuals with disabilities that relate to their inability to do things that nondisabled persons can do.

Salend (1994) recommends the development of lessons about successful individuals with disabilities, focusing on their achievements and the ways they were able to deal with the challenges their disabilities have presented. Teachers can generally find suc-

Table 2.6   Motion Pictures with Characters Who Are Disabled or Gifted

Title	Identifier	Title	Identifier
Key		King of Hearts	BD
Behavior Disorder	BD	La Strada	MR
Gifted	G	Last Picture Show, The	MR
Hearing Impairment	HI	Little Man Tate	G
Learning Disability	LD	Lorenzo's Oil	PHI
Mental Retardation	MR	Man without a Face, The	PHI
Physical or Health Impairment	PHI	MASH	VI, PHI (H)
Traumatic Brain Injury	TBI	Miracle Worker, The	VI, PHI (H)
Visual Impairment	VI	Moby Dick	PHI
		My Left Foot	PHI
Awakenings	BD	Of Mice and Men	MR
Bedlam	MR	One Flew Over the Cuckoo's Nest	BD
Being There	MR	Ordinary People	BD
Benny and Joon	BD	Other Side of the Mountain, The	PHI
Best Boy	MR	Patch of Blue, A	VI
Bill	MR	Philadelphia	PHI
Blackboard Jungle	At Risk	Places in the Heart	VI
Born on the Fourth of July	PHI	Rain Man	Autism
Butterflies Are Free	VI	Regarding Henry	TBI
Camille Claudel	BD	Rudy	LD
Charley	MR	Scent of a Woman	VI
Children of a Lesser God	PHI (H)	See No Evil, Hear No Evil	VI
Coming Home	PHI	Sneakers	VI
Deliverance	MR	Stand and Deliver	At Risk
Dr. Strangelove	PHI	Sting, The	PHI
Dream Team	BD	Sybil	BD
Edward Scissorhands	PHI	Tim	MR
Elephant Man, The	PHI	Tin Man	PHI (H)
Fisher King, The	BD	To Kill a Mockingbird	MR
Forrest Gump	MR	To Sir, with Love	At Risk
Gaby: A True Story	PHI (P)	Wait until Dark	VI
Hand That Rocks the Cradle, The	MR	Whatever Happened to Baby Jane?	PHI
Heart Is a Lonely Hunter, The	PHI (H)	What's Eating Gilbert Grape?	PHI
I Never Promised You a Rose Garden	BD	Young Frankenstein	PHI
If You Could See What I Hear	VI	Zelly and Me	BD

cessful individuals with disabilities in their own communities. These persons, plus famous people with disabilities, such as Tom Cruise (learning disabilities) and the late Christopher Reeve (physical disabilities), can be the focus of lessons that can help nondisabled students understand the capabilities of individuals with disabilities.

Guest speakers with disabilities provide positive role models for students with disabilities, give all students exposure to individuals who are different in some way, and generate meaningful class discussion. However, the choice of guest speakers must match the intended purposes of the teacher. For example, securing a guest speaker who is in a wheelchair and who has a negative attitude about his or her condition may not serve a positive purpose for the class. Advance planning and communication ensure that maximum benefit is achieved from this type of experience and also avoid inappropriate presentations. Guest speakers who are comfortable and effective when talking with students usually can be identified through local agencies and organizations.

Simulations   Simulating a specific condition, to give students the opportunity to feel what it might be like to have the condition, is a common practice. For example, visual impairment is often simulated by blindfolding sighted students and having them perform activities that they typically use their vision to perform. In another simulation, students can use a wheelchair for a period of time to experience this type of mobility.

Although simulations can be effective in engendering positive attitudes toward individuals with special needs, this technique should be used with caution. Bittner (cited in Tovey, 1995) warns that "it is impossible to pretend to have a disability. An able-bodied kid sitting in a wheelchair knows he can get up and walk away" (p. 8). Also, some simulation activities seem to be amusing, rather than meaningful, to students. Therefore, teachers must use caution when simulations are conducted to ensure that they serve their intended purpose.

Maintaining Effective Inclusive Classrooms

Setting up a responsible inclusive classroom does not guarantee that it will remain effective over time. Constant vigilance concerning the critical dimensions of inclusive settings and ongoing reevaluation of standard operating procedures can ensure continued success. Too often teachers, both special education and general education, become disenchanted with the process and often burn out (Westling et al., 2006). A system needs to be in place to monitor and evaluate inclusion programs as well as provide appropriate support for teachers involved in delivering the programs.

Westling and colleagues (2006) describe a teacher support program designed to provide the necessary supports for teachers involved in delivering services in inclusive settings. The program was founded on five principles:

1. Teachers can help each other through collaborative problem solving as well as other types of mutual support, but can also benefit from additional expertise.
2. A support program for teachers should be available to all teachers but not required of any, should offer multiple types of support, and should allow for flexible participation.
3. A support program should provide valid information and assistance to deal with practical problems, and teachers should have the opportunity to specify the type of information or assistance they need and how it should be delivered.
4. Support must be disassociated from evaluation or judgment.
5. A support program should not create additional problems or increase stress (Westling et al., 2006, p. 137).

The teacher support program provides for problem-solving meetings, electronic networking, information materials search, peer mentoring, on-site class consultation, teacher release, and staff development workshops. After an initial review of the program it was found to have a positive impact on dealing with issues (Westling et al., 2006).

CONSIDER THIS

Why is ongoing monitoring of the effectiveness of an inclusion program necessary? Why not evaluate effectiveness only every five years?

CONSIDER THIS

Some schools think all they have to do in order to implement inclusion is place students with disabilities in general classrooms. Why does this action alone not guarantee good inclusive practices?

PRAXIS

PRAXIS II: Delivery of Services to Students with Disabilities

Maintaining flexibility contributes to long-term success; rigid procedures cannot adequately address the unpredictable situations that arise as challenges to management and instruction. Unforeseen problems will inevitably surface as a result of including students with special needs in general education classrooms. The more flexible a school can be in dealing with new challenges, the more likely it is that responsible inclusion will continue.

Figure 2.6   **Steps in the Development of a Plan to Support Successful Inclusion of Students with Disabilities**

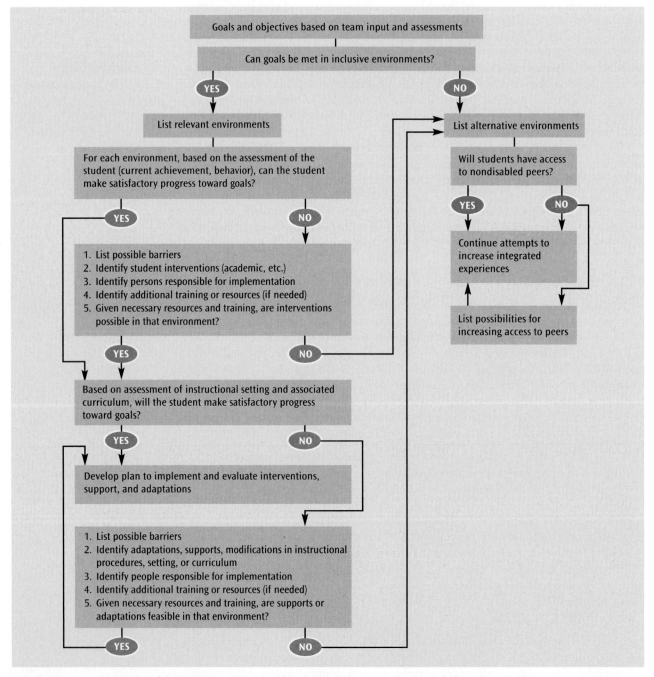

From "Assessment and Adaptation of the Student, Instructional Setting, and Curriculum to Support Successful Integration," by T. Van Laarhoven, M. Coutinho, T. Van Laarhoven-Myers, and A. C. Repp (p. 163), in *Inclusion: The Integration of Students with Disabilities,* edited by M. J. Coutinho and A. C. Repp, 1999. Belmont, CA: Wadsworth. Used by permission.

Planning for Successful Inclusion, One Student at a Time

CEC STANDARDS

CEC 4: Instructional Strategies

Regardless of how much time and effort have been expended to create an environment that is conducive for students with disabilities to achieve success in general education classrooms, the fact remains that planning must be accomplished for students on an individual basis. Students with disabilities cannot simply be placed in a school regardless of the supports provided or teaching methods used and be expected to succeed. School personnel must develop a planning model that provides opportunities for school staff to develop supportive, individualized inclusive environments for each student.

INTASC

INTASC 7: Plans instruction based on knowledge of students

Van Laarhoven and colleagues (1999) provide a planning model for determining the support needed for each student prior to implementing inclusion. The model, depicted in Figure 2.6, includes both a list of possible environments for a student and steps to ensure an inclusive environment that is geared to each student. When determining the least restrictive environment for an individual student during the IEP process, school personnel should be sure that each student's unique characteristics have been considered in the planning process.

CEC STANDARDS

CEC 5: Learning Environment and Social Interactions

School personnel must routinely review their programs to ensure that their buildings, programs, and instructional techniques support the inclusion of students with disabilities and other special needs. Figure 2.7 includes ten questions that can facilitate a discussion among school personnel around reviewing school programs and inclusion.

Figure 2.7   **Ten Discussion Questions Related to Inclusion**

Using the scale below, rate the extent to which you agree or disagree with each statement. After rating the items independently, discuss your responses with your partner(s). Identify the area(s) that you and your partner(s) feel could be strengthened. Jointly identify strategies that could be used to strengthen these areas.

1—strongly disagree   2—disagree   3—unsure   4—agree   5—strongly agree

	1	2	3	4	5
1. Students with disabilities are engaged in classroom learning activities along with their nondisabled peers.	1	2	3	4	5
2. Students with disabilities participate productively in classroom learning activities.	1	2	3	4	5
3. Effective instruction strategies are used to meet the educational needs of students with disabilities.	1	2	3	4	5
4. Students with and without disabilities interact frequently.	1	2	3	4	5
5. Students with disabilities seem to enjoy being in the general education classroom.	1	2	3	4	5
6. Nondisabled students voluntarily include students with disabilities in various activities.	1	2	3	4	5
7. Students with disabilities consider the general education classroom to be their "real" class.	1	2	3	4	5
8. When general and special educators are discussing students with and without disabilities, words like "our" and "we" are used more often than words like "your" or "you."	1	2	3	4	5
9. Students with disabilities are included in any school accountability system that may be used.	1	2	3	4	5
10. The problems and successes involving students with and without disabilities are shared by general and special educators.	1	2	3	4	5

Comments: _____
_____
_____
_____
_____
_____
_____
_____
_____

From "What Matters Most in Inclusive Education: A Practical Guide for Moving Forward," by D.L. Voltz, N. Brazil, and A. Ford, 2001, *Intervention in School and Clinic, 37,* p. 28. Used with permission.

Summary

Perceptions of Inclusion

- Inclusion of students with special needs in general education classes has received more attention on a philosophical level than on a practical level.
- The critical issue of successful inclusion is the acceptance of diversity.
- Effective inclusive settings have an impact on the student's immediate as well as long-range needs.
- On a philosophical level, there are few arguments against inclusion.
- Although many teachers support the concept of inclusion, a large percentage are uncomfortable about teaching students with special needs in their own classrooms.
- The opinions of parents regarding inclusion vary greatly.

Critical Dimensions of Inclusive Classrooms

- Five essential features must be in place to ensure maximum success of inclusion, including creating a sense of community and social acceptance, appreciating student diversity, attending to curricular needs, effectively managing and instructing students, and offering access to adequate personnel supports.
- The concept of inclusion affirms that students with special needs can be active, valued, and full participating members of the school community.

- Students with special needs will be truly included in their classrooms only when they are appreciated by their teachers and socially accepted by their classmates.
- Teachers play a critical role in the success of inclusion.
- The curricular needs of students cannot be lost in the philosophical and political debate on inclusion.
- Effective classroom management is an important component in a successful inclusive classroom.
- Accommodative practices that are good for students with special needs are usually good for all students.

Creating and Maintaining Inclusive Classrooms

- Appropriately trained personnel, in adequate numbers, are a major factor in successful inclusion programs.
- Both staff and students must be prepared for inclusion.
- Once inclusion is initiated, its effectiveness must be monitored to ensure its ongoing success.

Planning for Successful Inclusion, One Student at a Time

- To be effective, planning an appropriate environment for students with disabilities must be carried out one student at a time.
- School personnel must develop supports that provide each student with the least restrictive environments possible that still meet the individual needs of each student.

Questions to Reconsider

Think back to the scenario about Libby you read at the beginning of this chapter. Would you answer the questions raised there any differently after reading the chapter itself?

1. Do you think that Ms. Jordan and Ms. Baker planned for this result?

2. Can events be planned to orchestrate social interactions among students with and without disabilities in the classroom?
3. Who is responsible for facilitating the acceptance of students with disabilities into general education classrooms?
4. What are some other ways that Ms. Jordan could have encouraged the students in the class to accept Rhonda?

Further Readings

Cramer, S. (1998). *Collaboration: A successful strategy for special education.* Boston: Allyn & Bacon.

Deno, S. L., Foegen, A., Robinson, S., & Espin, C. (1996). Commentary: Facing the realities of inclusion for students with mild disabilities. *Journal of Special Education, 30,* 345–357.

Fox, T., & Williams, W. (1991). *Implementing best practices for all students in their local school.* Burlington: University of Vermont.

National Association of State Boards of Education. (1992). *Winners all: A call for inclusive schools* (chapter 5). Alexandria, VA: Author.

Schwartz, S. E., & Karge, B. D. (1996). *Human diversity: A guide for understanding* (2nd ed.). New York: McGraw-Hill.

mylabschool
Where the classroom comes to life

Go to Allyn & Bacon's MyLabSchool (www.mylabschool.com) and enter Assignment ID SPV3 into the Assignment Finder. View the video clip called *The Collaborative Process*. Then consider what you have seen along with what you've read in Chapter 2 to answer the following questions.

1. What characteristics of successful coteaching do these two teachers exhibit? Provide specific examples from the video clip.
2. What form of coteaching do the teachers in the video appear to be implementing? What other forms of coteaching might be appropriate in this classroom? What should determine the form that coteaching should take?

You may also answer the questions at the end of the clip and e-mail your responses to your instructor.

Now enter Assignment ID CS09 into the Assignment Finder. Read the case called *Back to Square One,* and answer the questions raised at the end of it.

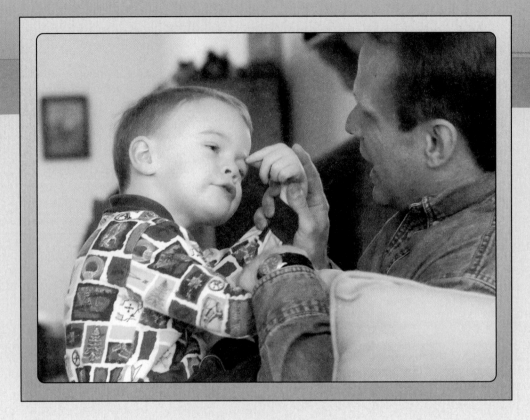

Home–School Collaboration: Working with Families

After reading this chapter, you should be able to:

1. Discuss the particular challenges experienced by parents of individuals with disabilities.
2. Discuss effective ways to involve the family in educational programs.
3. Understand the perspectives of parents of children with special needs.
4. List principles of effective communication with parents.
5. Delineate support roles that parents and family members can play.

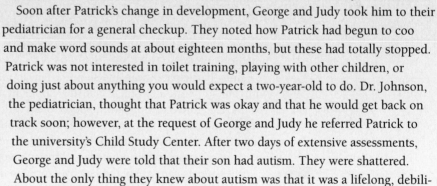

Questions to Consider

1. Analyze George's and Judy's potential feelings and possible reactions upon learning that Patrick has a disability.

2. What advice, recommendations, and help would you provide for these parents?

3. What would you tell them about the advantages and challenges of inclusive preschool programs?

4. What influence could Patrick's condition have on George and Judy's marriage?

5. How could other parents, with children like Patrick, help George and Judy deal with their crisis?

People always said what wonderful parents George and Judy were to their son, Patrick. They shared in child-rearing activities and seemed to love every moment when they were with their son. Patrick was healthy and seemed to be developing exactly on time, if not a little ahead of those infamous developmental milestones associated with rolling over, sitting, standing up, walking, smiling, and cooing. When Patrick was about twenty-four months old he began doing some odd things. He stopped smiling, would withdraw from adults and other children, and seemed to be perfectly content "doing his own thing." He began waking up multiple times during the night, wanting to get up to play. He began to focus on particular objects, one being a toy car that he had played with for several months. Rather than playing with the car in an appropriate way, he would only spin the wheels, over and over and over. He would pick up objects, such as crumpled paper, and not want to have them taken away from him.

Soon after Patrick's change in development, George and Judy took him to their pediatrician for a general checkup. They noted how Patrick had begun to coo and make word sounds at about eighteen months, but these had totally stopped. Patrick was not interested in toilet training, playing with other children, or doing just about anything you would expect a two-year-old to do. Dr. Johnson, the pediatrician, thought that Patrick was okay and that he would get back on track soon; however, at the request of George and Judy he referred Patrick to the university's Child Study Center. After two days of extensive assessments, George and Judy were told that their son had autism. They were shattered.

About the only thing they knew about autism was that it was a lifelong, debilitating disorder. Their hopes and dreams for Patrick went out the window. The next two years were very difficult on the family. George and Judy took Patrick to several doctors and clinics, hoping for a different diagnosis, which never came. George and Judy's relationship suffered. It seemed as if they were always getting up in the middle of the night or constantly on vigil when Patrick was awake to ensure that he did not do something that could be dangerous. George's and Judy's lives had been changed forever.

Prior to the enactment of Public Law 94–142 (IDEA), schools frequently did not encourage parents of children with special needs to actively participate in the education of their children. However, given the numerous concerns that parents may have (such as those mentioned in the chapter-opening vignette), and given the value of family input into educational programs, increasing parental involvement is a welcome trend. This chapter highlights the challenges facing parents, examples of perspectives provided by parents, and strategies for collaboration between educators and parents. The chapter also discusses the potential influences on marriage and siblings when raising a child with disabilities.

Federal law formally established the role of parents relative to students with special needs through IDEA (Werts, Harris, Tillery, & Roark, 2004). IDEA requires schools to:

- Inform parents in understandable language of impending actions regarding their child's education.
- Involve parents in decisions regarding the education of their child.
- Honor parents' decision for no special education services.
- Make available due-process rights for parents and their child.
- Enable parents to request a due-process hearing, or engage in mediation or resolution efforts in cases of disagreements with schools.

Decisions about children with disabilities are so important that parents must be involved. For example, a child cannot be placed in a special education program without parental approval. Two IDEA principles underlie collaboration between schools and parents—parent participation and procedural due process (Lake & Billingsley, 2000). "In recognition of the important role of parents in the decision-making process, IDEA mandated that parents receive a document explaining their educational rights and responsibilities any time their child is referred for an evaluation, and at other times throughout the special education process" (Fitzgerald & Watkins, 2006, p. 497). This document should outline all of the legal rights of parents and help them understand these rights.

Legislation and parental advocacy have established an increasingly higher degree of family involvement in the education of students with disabilities. School personnel acknowledge the merit of having parents actively participate in the educational process, including identification, referral, assessment, program planning, and implementation. Comprehensive programs of family involvement begin when children with disabilities are young and continue through the transition process out of school and into adulthood.

The challenge for educators is to consider effective ways to involve families in the education of children with disabilities. Table 3.1 describes six categories of **family support** principles.

Family participation can and should occur in many areas. These include involvement with the student's assessment and development of the IEP, involvement with parent groups (e.g., for education and support), observation of the student in the school setting, and communication with educators. Participation in developing the IEP process typically occurs the most frequently. Some families are very involved in their child's special education program, while others have limited involvement (Dabkowski, 2004).

Professionals can satisfy the law by simply inviting parental participation; however, school personnel should develop strategies to facilitate parental involvement or, more appropriately, family involvement. Although some parents create challenges for the school because of their intense level of involvement, for the most part educational programs are greatly strengthened by parental support.

The Family

The viewpoint of what constitutes a family has changed dramatically in recent decades. Traditionally, a family was thought of as a group of individuals who live together, including a mother, a father, and one or more children. However, this stereotypical

CONSIDER THIS

The enactment of federal laws mandating special education ended a laissez-faire period of home-school relationships. What do you think the situation would be like today without these federal laws mandating parental involvement?

CROSS-REFERENCE

See Chapter 8 to review how supports have been provided to families of students with mental retardation.

CONSIDER THIS

Not unexpectedly, the degree of parental participation in the IEP process is correlated with socioeconomic level. Why do you think this is the case?

INTASC

INTASC 10: Fosters relationships with families

CEC STANDARDS

CEC 10: Collaboration

Table 3.1	Major Categories and Examples of Family Support Principles
Category/Characteristic	**Examples of Principles**
1. **Enhancing a Sense of Community** Promoting the coming together of people around shared values and common needs in ways that create mutually beneficial interdependencies.	• Interventions should focus on the building of interdependencies between members of the community and the family unit. • Interventions should emphasize the common needs and supports of all people and base intervention actions on those commonalities.
2. **Mobilizing Resources and Supports** Building support systems that enhance the flow of resources in ways that assist families with parenting responsibilities.	• Interventions should focus on building and strengthening informal support networks for families rather than depending solely on professionals' support systems. • Resources and supports should be made available to families in ways that are flexible, individualized, and responsive to the needs of the entire family unit.
3. **Shared Responsibility and Collaboration** Sharing of ideas and skills by parents and professionals in ways that build and strengthen collaborative arrangements.	• Interventions should employ partnerships between parents and professionals as a primary mechanism for supporting and strengthening family functioning. • Resources and support mobilization interactions between families and service providers should be based on mutual respect and sharing of unbiased information.
4. **Protecting Family Integrity** Respecting the family's beliefs and values and protecting the family from intrusion upon its beliefs by outsiders.	• Resources and supports should be provided to families in ways that encourage, develop, and maintain healthy, stable relationships among all family members. • Interventions should be conducted in ways that accept, value, and protect a family's personal and cultural values and beliefs.
5. **Strengthening Family Functioning** Promoting the capabilities and competencies of families necessary to mobilize resources and perform parenting responsibilities in ways that have empowering consequences.	• Interventions should build on family strengths rather than correct weaknesses or deficits as a primary way of supporting and strengthening family functioning. • Resources and supports should be made available to families in ways that maximize the family's control over and decision-making power regarding services they receive.
6. **Proactive Human Service Practices** Adoption of consumer-driven human service delivery models and practices that support and strengthen family functioning.	• Service-delivery programs should employ promotion rather than treatment approaches as the framework for strengthening family functioning. • Resource and support mobilization should be consumer-driven rather than service provider–driven or professionally prescribed.

From "Family-Oriented Early Intervention Policies and Practices: Family-Centered or Not?" by C. J. Dunst, C. Johanson, C. M. Trivette, and D. Hamby, 1991, *Exceptional Children, 58,* p. 117. Copyright 1991 by the Council for Exceptional Children. Used by permission.

picture has been challenged by the reality that many, perhaps most, families do not resemble this model. As early as 1992, Allen noted, "The idealized nuclear family of yesteryear with the stay-at-home, take-care-of-the-children mother and the outside-the-home breadwinner father no longer represents the typical American family" (p. 319). Since the early 1990s, the family structure in the United States has continued to evolve. Families depicted in *The Cosby Show, Roseanne, Still Standing,* and *Everybody Loves Raymond* are no longer the norm (Smith et al., 2006). The family of today, unlike the family of the early twentieth century, more simply can be described as a group of individuals who live together and care for one anothers' needs. Table 3.2 describes the typical family in the 1950s and the typical family today.

Unlike the typical family of the mid-twentieth century, today there are numerous family arrangements. For example, many families are single-parent families, most frequently with the father absent. A growing number of families are now headed by grandparents, with the children's parents unable or unwilling to accept parental responsibility. And, although not as common as they once were, some families constitute

Table 3.2	Typical Families in the 1950s and Today
Family in the 1950s	**Family in the Twenty-first Century**
Mother and father in the home Two or three siblings Father works; mother stays home Grandparents nearby Children attend school in a culturally homogeneous environment	One-parent family Both parents work Grandparents not nearby Children attend school in a culturally heterogeneous environment

extended family units, with grandparents living with parents and children. Some children also live in foster homes, wherein foster parents fill all legal parental roles. Finally, school personnel must also be able to interact with families headed by parents living in gay or lesbian relationships.

An additional twenty-first-century challenge to the family is the increase in diversity in the United States. Families today represent numerous races, cultures, socioeconomic levels, and religions. They reflect the social changes that have occurred in our society during the past fifty years. Some of these societal changes include (Smith et al., 2006):

- Increased diversity
- Increased litigation in education
- Increased involvement of the federal government in education
- Mandatory services for children with disabilities
- Civil rights laws for minorities, women, and individuals with disabilities
- Increased divorce rates
- Increased levels of poverty
- Increased number of single parent homes

Despite undergoing major changes in its structure, the family remains the basic unit of U.S. society. It is a dynamic, evolving social force that remains the key ingredient in a child's life. Teachers must be sensitive to the background of the family to ensure that cultural differences do not interfere with school–family relationships. In addition, school personnel must remember that students' parents or guardians should be involved in educational programs regardless of the specific composition of the family. School personnel must put aside any preconceived notions they may have about various lifestyles and work with students' families to develop and implement the most effective programs for the students. Finally, professionals should adopt a family systems perspective to involve the whole family—rather than just the child—in efforts to enhance programs (Turnbull & Turnbull, 2005).

Cultural Considerations

The success of parent–professional partnerships often hinges on the ability of professionals to develop a level of cultural competence. "The cultural context through which both parents and professionals form their personal value systems contributes to their ability to make joint decisions" (Dabkowski, 2004, p. 36). Several issues that can create barriers for parent–professional partnerships related to culture include (Dabkowski, 2004):

- Disparate beliefs about disability
- Value placed on parent–professional partnerships
- Language barriers, including non-English speakers as well as professional jargon
- Seemingly indifferent attitude of professionals

Rueda and colleagues (2005) also note that different cultural beliefs related to transition goals can also create problems. Regardless of the issues, professionals must be aware of their own cultural biases and attitudes to ensure that they do not negatively impact home–school partnerships (Montgomery, 2005).

Montgomery (2001) notes that culturally responsive classrooms acknowledge diversity represented in students and helps find connections for these students and other students in the classroom. Because many teachers do not fully understand different cultures, a self-assessment of culture should be completed. This self-assessment is intended to help teachers understand diversity that is present in their classroom and how to respond to such diversity. One of the primary actions that teachers can take is to establish a classroom atmosphere that is respectful of all cultures. In establishing such an atmosphere, Montgomery (2001) notes that teachers should (1) pay attention to their bulletin boards; (2) maintain reading books that deal with cultural diversity; (3) engage in cross-cultural literature discussions with students; and (4) use language arts and social studies programs to promote opportunities for students to learn about other cultures.

Families and Children with Disabilities

The arrival of any child results in changes in family structure and dynamics. Obviously, children change the lives of the mother and father and siblings, and each child alters the dynamics of the family unit, including finances, the amount and quality of time parents can devote to individual children, the relationship between the husband and wife, and the family's future goals. The arrival of a child with a disability exacerbates the challenges that such changes bring. When a child with a disability becomes a member of the family, whether through birth, adoption, or later onset of the disability, the entire family must make adjustments. Families with children with disabilities have unique experiences and challenges (Hutton & Caron, 2005). The almost immediate financial and emotional impact can create major problems for family members, including siblings.

In addition to these problems, a primary difficulty may be accepting and understanding the child and the disability. Parents with a limited understanding of a diagnosis will probably have difficulty in developing realistic expectations of the child, possibly creating major problems within the family. On one hand, parents might not understand the nature of a learning disability and therefore accuse the child of being lazy and not trying. On the other hand, parents may overlook the potential of students with mental retardation and develop low expectations that will limit the child's success. For example, parents of adolescents might not support a school-work program for their son or daughter because they believe that adults with retardation are not capable of holding a job.

Families who discover that their child has a disability obviously undergo a wide variety of feelings and reactions. Some of these may include the following (Smith et al., 2006):

- Grief
- Loss
- Denial
- Guilt
- Bargaining
- Anger
- Depression
- Acceptance
- Stress

CONSIDER THIS

What are some problems faced by families following the birth of a child with a disability or the identification of a child's disability?

CROSS-REFERENCE

Review Chapters 5–11, which discuss specific disabilities that can affect children. Then reflect on how different types of problems can cause different reactions in parents.

CONSIDER THIS

As a teacher, how could you deal with families experiencing various reactions to a child with a disability? What role, if any, should a teacher play in helping parents work through their reactions?

TEACHING TIP

Teachers need to be aware of the different reactions that parents may have and know some specific strategies for dealing with these reactions.

Although it cannot be assumed that all or even most parents have these particular reactions, many must deal with complicated emotions, often experienced as a "bombardment of feelings" that may recur over many years (Hilton, 1990). Some parents and other family members experience all these different reactions; others may experience only some of them. Regardless of specific reactions, family members almost always experience some negative reactions upon learning that a child has a disability. Sileo, Sileo, and Prater (1996) refer to the "shattering of dreams" that underlies many of these feelings. School personnel—including teachers, school social workers, counselors, and administrators—need to be aware of these dynamics and be prepared to deal with family members who are experiencing various feelings. For example, when parents say that they feel guilt after learning that their child has a disability, school personnel should listen with acceptance to the parents and help them understand the nature of the disability and the fact that they are not responsible for it. The Personal Spotlight provides a vivid portrait of the reactions of one family to these emotions.

Some models of potential parental reactions reflect a **stage theory** approach to understanding these responses (i.e., a series of presumed phases in response to learning that a child has a disability). However, parental responses rarely follow any formal stage process (e.g., shock-denial-anger-rejection-acceptance). Rather, the preceding reactions more often reflect responses that individual parents may experience when accepting that they have a child with a disability and that they need to meet that child's needs. For example, Elisabeth Kübler-Ross, who originated the stage theory in her book *On Death and Dying* (1969), discovered that stages can be skipped or a person can become "stuck" in a single stage.

School personnel need to support family members' acceptance of children with disabilities. This effort begins with assisting parents in understanding the needs of their child; at the same time, the educator should listen to the parents, to better understand the child from their perspective. Further, teachers must be sensitive to the fact that many parents do not see the school as a welcoming place for various reasons (e.g., problems the parents experienced as students themselves, negative responses communicated to them as advocates for their child). Professionals must understand that all of their actions can have a profound impact on families. For example, "the way in which diagnostic information is conveyed to the family can have a long-term influence on parents' attitudes, families' level of stress and acceptance, and coping strategies" (Hutton & Caron, 2005, p. 180).

Families of children with disabilities cope in many ways, some good and some bad. Hutton and Caron (2005) interviewed twenty-one families of children who had been diagnosed with autism to determine their reaction and coping. Their findings indicated that 43 percent felt grief and loss; 29 percent shock and surprise; and 10 percent self-blaming. Of the families in the study, 52 percent did say that the diagnosis resulted in some relief in knowing what was wrong with their child. Figure 3.1 lists some of the statements made by respondents during the interviews.

Parents' Views on Inclusion

Parents, like professionals, struggle with the issue of inclusion. On the one hand, some parents of students with learning disabilities (such as those represented by the Learning Disabilities Association) have remained cautious about inclusion; on the other hand, the Arc has actively favored it. Fisher, Pumpian, and Sax (1998) noted, "The success and enhancement of any educational program depends on the attitude and involvement of many stakeholders, including parents, in its design and renewal" (p. 179).

Parents of children with disabilities generally have positive perceptions toward inclusion; however, often these feelings are mixed (Duhaney and Salend, 2000). As noted in Chapter 2, Burstein and colleagues (2004) found that parents of children with

Personal Spotlight

A Mother's Perspective

We have a beautiful, vibrant, intelligent, and mischievous six-year-old little girl, Kayla, who is a big sister to our nineteen-month-old son, Joey, a boy who lights up the room with his blond hair, blue eyes, and brilliant smile. When I was pregnant with Joey, the doctors grew concerned about his prenatal growth and delivered him three weeks early. The delivery was uneventful, and I held my four-pound fifteen-ounce baby boy in my arms as my husband and I decided on a name. When it came time to visit my son in the nursery, however, he was not there and had been transferred to the neonatal intensive care unit (NICU). And so begins our "story." He stayed in the NICU for one week. Leaving the hospital without my son was the beginning of the emotional roller coaster on which I have found myself a passenger.

Joey was released with a clean bill of health and a huge sigh of relief; however, I noticed a difference in my son as compared to my daughter. His arm had a tendency to arbitrarily jerk, and he didn't move quite as fluently as other babies. Because of time spent in the NICU, coupled with his prematurity, Joey was scheduled for a three-month checkup at the neonatal clinic. It was there that my suspicions were confirmed—Joey showed signs of developmental delay, and as he grew older, the gap between his chronological and developmental age widened.

Sixteen months and what seems like a million tests after his first checkup, the doctors remain unable to determine what caused his delays, so they have labeled him with a mild form of cerebral palsy. To me this means that Joey will have to work harder to do what comes naturally to many others. It took my son ten months to learn to sit, fourteen months to stand, and sixteen months to crawl. Now, at nineteen months, he is able to walk behind an object while pushing it across the floor. Joey cannot speak, but he babbles incessantly and loudly! Kayla has sisterly intuition; she dotes on her baby brother and always seems to understand what he is communicating. She realizes that her brother is different, although she does not fully comprehend why he cannot do the things that the other children his age can do. When Joey reaches a milestone, Kayla is equally as excited as we are, as each milestone reached brings him one step closer to playing with her as a toddler who is not disabled might.

Accepting that my son is different has been both easy and difficult. There are moments when I look at him and forget that he has a disability, yet there are times when his imperfections glare at me from behind his sweet smile. My heart aches when I think of the teasing he will encounter from the mouths of unmerciful children who know no better. I worry about how my daughter has been affected by her brother's disability; have I been remiss in showing an equal amount of attention to both children?

I have learned a great deal from my son. I detect a sense of determination that is not often found in people. It is at these moments that I mentally pledge to do everything in my power to foster this determination and optimism, as these are the qualities that will assist him in overcoming any obstacles, whether physical, mental, or emotional. It is because of my son that I have converted from a "glass half empty" point of view to a "glass half full" approach.

I also have learned how to be a better friend, knowing when to keep quiet and when to offer advice. I have become more patient and tolerant of others, although I continue to find myself becoming frustrated with the endless questions and constant probing into my personal life—it is not easy to open your heart and your home to strangers (e.g., doctors, therapists, early intervention personnel).

Raising a child with a disability has also strengthened my marriage. My husband and I have leaned on each other for emotional support on numerous occasions. He has validated my feelings, assuring me that he, too, feels the same myriad emotions. One of the hardest aspects of dealing with Joey's disability is believing that I am a bad parent for feeling certain emotions (e.g., anger, disappointment). Understanding that these emotions are normal, and even acceptable, and felt by others brings a great sense of relief.

I thank God every day for the life and the family he has given me. I love my husband more than I can express, yet somehow, some way, I love my children even deeper. Where others may feel sorry for my family or my son, I feel proud that I have two children who will understand firsthand that being different is not something of which to be ashamed but rather to embrace. Thank you for allowing me to share my story with you.

Tracey Corriveau and Family
Lynchburg, VA

Figure 3.1   **Reactions to the Diagnosis of Autism**

I went to the doctor when my son was two because he did not talk—I knew something was wrong but I was told to wait—that he will be fine. I took him to Child Development Services when he was two and a half, and I had to wait five months before seeing a psychologist, who eventually diagnosed him with autism.

When I went to my doctor and told him something was wrong, he said not to worry—that sometimes boys are just slower than girls.

I didn't challenge the diagnosis because everything fit into place. After reading about autism, I said, "This is so much like her."

Yes, I accepted the diagnosis. I knew it was autism by that time, since I had been doing a lot of my own research.

I accepted the psychologist's diagnosis. We had figured it out.

When the doctor told me, I had the same feeling as when my grandmother died.

This wasn't supposed to happen to us. I thought this was something he would grow out of.

I cried when I left the office. I felt that it was my fault, since I had been exposed to shingles early in the pregnancy.

One doctor told me, "Your son has autism and there is nothing you can do about it so just live with it." Yet I knew that wasn't the case.

The psychologist treated me like it was my fault. He said my child's behavior was because of his home environment.

I was treated with respect—in fact, one doctor said I knew more than he did!

It has been an honor to be given a child like this—to parent a child like this.

It was heartbreaking, stressful, and devastating—especially for my husband. We were quite overwhelmed with the demands and needs of our child.

Some days it is a living hell; 30 percent of the time you feel like you are in a normal family, and 70 percent of the time you feel like you are juggling so many things you don't know where you are going.

We have not taken a vacation as a family since the diagnosis.

He (my son) never gets invited anywhere and doesn't have friends over to the house.

I had a career before my child's diagnosis. Now all that doesn't seem important anymore. I work a part-time job so I can be home with my son.

Our daily life is a routine—if you throw anything different and unpredictable in, our son melts down, which affects the whole family.

When our child with autism was born, his sister was just turning two. We had the PEC System done at home, with the sister learning also; they are inseparable.

From "Experiences of Families with Children with Autism in Rural New England," by A. M. Hutton and S. L. Caron, 2005, *Focus on Autism and Other Developmental Disabilities, 20,* p. 184–187. Used with permission.

disabilities, as well as parents with nondisabled children, reflected positive reactions to inclusion, noting that the process was beneficial for all students in the school. Often, parents who do not support inclusion are mainly concerned that their children will not receive an appropriate education or be harassed by nondisabled children (Strong & Sandoval, 1999; Duhaney & Salend, 2000).

In an enlightening study of parental views of inclusion, Palmer and colleagues (2001) surveyed 460 parents of children with severe disabilities. The comments of the parents are quite informative. (Selected comments are included in Table 3.3.) Overall, they show that teachers should be sensitive to the fact that individual parents and groups of parents may have quite different views of the benefits of inclusionary educational practices, and teachers should involve these parents in discussions related to the development of the most effective programs for their children. When inclusion is perceived as successful by parents, a strong working relationship can be created.

Table 3.3	**Written Statements by Parents Explaining Why They Are or Are Not Supportive of Inclusive Placement**
Statements Reflecting Parental Support for Inclusion:	**Statements Reflecting Parental Rejection of Inclusion:**
• The "special education" program is very limiting and acts to confine people to "expected limitations," closing the door to the ability or opportunity to learn because they are not expected to or thought able. • My son has recently in the past six months improved his language, and he's using more words, and I know he will do better mainstreamed in a "regular" classroom. • I also feel the program she is in through the county isn't enough, she isn't challenged . . . she is in a class with others who have such low skills that she is bored or ignored. • Lots of kids I see are working down to someone's level when they would blossom in a more demanding environment. • Teaches nondisabled children to be sensitive to other children who do not have the same capabilities. • I see mainstreaming as a plus, and both sides benefit— besides getting a great education in the triumphs and difficulties of life. • I am adamantly opposed to any segregation by disability or ability because the situation created . . . is not representative of the society their children will live to grow up and eventually work in.	• Jennifer has many medical conditions that I feel need a special classroom and teacher. She will never learn to take care of herself. I feel she needs to be in a protective class. • My child would be stuck in her wheelchair most of the day, unless the classroom were completely modified with carpet, and room to move. A lot of special equipment would be needed. • Until she can communicate expressively, she does not need inclusion. She has cerebral palsy and can't verbalize or sign so others can understand. • It would be extremely difficult for a teacher to take care of regular students, let alone students with severe disabilities, even with help. • Regular classrooms are so overbooked with students already who are struggling to learn, that neither the student nor the teacher needs the additional . . . diversion of a severely disabled child. • Our thirteen-year-old is attention deficit. His teachers have been at their wit's end with him year after year. How will they help my autistic son? • This has got to be an expense that most parents of regular schoolchildren would resent. • Most severely disabled children . . . need to learn living skills so as to survive in the outside world. Vocational training and independent living training are more necessary than what is taught in the regular classroom. • My child is fourteen years old, and I don't think he is capable of learning academic subjects at a nineth-grade level, nor would that be particularly helpful. He needs to learn to behave appropriately, speak as much as possible, get along with others, and be as independent as possible. • I also think that she needs to see other children who are having the same level of instruction so that she won't feel that she is the only one who needs special attention, and she needs to be around children who can relate to what she is dealing with.

Adapted from "Taking Sides: Parent Views on Inclusion for Their Children with Severe Disabilities," by D. S. Palmer, K. Fuller, T. Arora, & M. Nelson, 2001, *Exceptional Children, 67,* pp. 474–479.

Involvement of Fathers

Frequently when people say that families should be involved in a child's education, the "family" is defined as the child's mother. The involvement of the entire family should be the primary goal, but the father is often left out of the planning process. Governmental research indicates that fathers are only half as likely to be highly involved in their child's special education program (U.S. Department of Education, 1997). This report also concluded:

• Children are more likely to get [good grades] and are less likely to repeat a grade if their fathers are involved in their schools.
• Children do better in school when their fathers are involved, regardless of whether their fathers live with them and whether their mothers are also involved.

Websites for Families of Children with Disabilities

The Alliance	www.taalliance.org
Federation of Families for Children's Mental Health	www.ffcmh.org
The Center for Law and Education	www.cleweb.org
Family Voices	www.familyvoices.org
National Down Syndrome Congress	www.ndsccenter.org
National Council on Independent Living	www.ncil.org
National Indian Child Welfare Association	www.nicwa.org
National Coalition for Parent Involvement in Education	www.ncpie.org
Fiesta Educativa	www.fiestaeducativa.org
National Association for Parents of Children with Visual Impairments	www.spedex.com/napvi/
The Arc of the United States	www.thearc.org
Autism Society of America, Inc.	www.autism-society.org
Brain Injury Association of America	www.biausa.org
Epilepsy Foundation of America	www.efa.org
Learning Disabilities Association of America	www.ldanatl.org
Spina Bifida Association of America	www.sbaa.org
UCP National (aka United Cerebral Palsy)	www.ucpa.org

- Many fathers in two-parent families, as well as fathers not living with their children, have low involvement.
- The relationship between fathers' involvement and children's success in school is important, regardless of income, race/ethnicity, or the parents' education (U.S. Department of Education, 1997, p. 3).

Hietsch (1986) described a program to encourage fathers to get involved in the educational program of their child. The program focuses on Father's Day, when the fathers of children in the class are invited to participate in a specific activity. However, teachers need to be sensitive to single-parent (i.e., mother only) homes in arranging such events. The inclusion of a grandfather or an uncle may be a good alternative.

Involvement of Siblings

Like adults, siblings are important in developing and implementing appropriate educational programs. Because over 10 percent of the school population is identified as disabled, the number of children with siblings who are disabled is significant: a working estimate of 15–20 percent or more seems realistic. Although not all siblings experience adjustment problems, some doubtlessly have significant difficulties responding to the disability. Hutton and Caron (2005) found that 38 percent of siblings in their survey reacted with resentment or jealousy; 12 percent with fear; 12 percent with sadness. The survey found an additional 12 percent were accepting of their sibling, while 6 percent felt awkward by having a sibling with a disability. Regardless of the reactions of siblings, the presence of a child with a disability does present a unique opportunity to learn about the diversity of individual needs.

CONSIDER THIS

The recent emphasis on family (rather than parental) involvement reflects the importance of siblings and others in supporting the child. Is it a good idea to include siblings in the education of a brother or sister with a disability? Why or why not?

EVIDENCE-BASED PRACTICE

Parent-Delivered Interventions

The involvement of parents and other family members in intervention strategies has been described a great deal in the literature. In fact, as the role of families in the lives of individuals with disabilities increases, parent-delivered interventions will likely increase. DiPipi-Hoy and Jitendra (2004) identify six general rules for parent-delivered interventions related to teaching purchasing skills to young adults with disabilities outside the home setting. These include:

1. Review the target skill prior to leaving the house.
2. Refrain from jumping in to help too quickly
3. Do not complete the entire step when providing assistance.
4. Allow for self-correction of errors prior to intervening.
5. Direct a store clerk's attention to the student when the clerk attempts to communicate with the parent.
6. Discuss the routine, provide praise for appropriate behaviors, and address areas that need improvement with the student on the way home.

From DiPipi-Hoy & Jitendra, 2004, p. 145.

Meyer (2001) summarized the literature and noted these areas of concern expressed by siblings:

- A lifelong and ever-changing need for information about the disability or illness.
- Feelings of isolation when siblings are excluded from information available to other family members, ignored by service providers, or denied access to peers who share their often ambivalent feelings about their siblings.
- Feelings of guilt about having caused the illness or disability, or being spared having the condition.
- Feelings of resentment when the child with special needs becomes the focus of the family's attention or when the child with special needs is indulged, overprotected, or permitted to engage in behaviors that are unacceptable if done by other family members.
- A perceived pressure to achieve in academics, sports, or behavior.
- Increased care-giving demands, especially for older sisters.
- Concerns about their role in their sibling's future (Meyer, 2001, p. 30).

Siblings of children with disabilities need support from family members as well as other adults. Teachers and other adults should be aware of the stress and other impact a sibling with a disability can have (Smith et al., 2006). Some considerations adults should make when dealing with children who have siblings with disabilities include:

- Express love for the sibling.
- Provide siblings with information concerning the disability.
- Keep the sibling informed concerning changes and stress on the family.
- Include the sibling in family and school meetings.
- Work for equity within the family duties and responsibilities.
- Prevent siblings from becoming second parents in the areas of care and discipline.
- Be aware that the needs of all the children will change through the family life cycle (Smith et al., 2006, p. 61).

Parent Education

Many educators believe parents of children with disabilities benefit tremendously by attending parent education classes. One reason is that parents too frequently attribute normal and predictable misbehavior to a child's disability rather than to the age and stage of a child. Seeing that all parents face similar challenges with their children can be

A father's direct involvement with his child with disabilities increases the child's chance for success in school and in the community.

both comforting and empowering to parents (West, 2002). Some helpful hints parents learn through parent education include the following (West, 2002):

1. Never compare children.
2. Notice the improvements and accomplishments of each child in the family, and always reinforce the positive.
3. Hold family meetings that allow children a weekly opportunity to voice their concerns, accept chores, and plan enjoyable family nights and outings.
4. Learn to help children become responsible by the use of logical and natural consequences rather than using punishment or becoming permissive.
5. Spend special time alone with each child in the family. Be sure that no child feels lost or left out because others require more attention.
6. Plan family events that allow children to enjoy being together.
7. Reduce criticism and increase encouragement.
8. Be sensitive to the possibility that children functioning at a higher academic level in the family may be finding their place through perfectionism and a need to excel at all costs.
9. Invest time in your marriage. A strong marriage is important to your children's sense of well-being.
10. All families experience stress. The more stress is encountered, the more time they need together to share their feelings, plan ahead, solve problems mutually, and plan time to enrich relationships.

TEACHING TIP

Teachers and other school personnel must keep in mind that parents are the senior partners in the education of their children and should be involved in all major decisions.

Home–School Collaboration

Educators and parents of children with disabilities must be partners in ensuring that appropriate education is available to children. In reality, parents should be seen as the "senior partners" because they are responsible for their child every day. To meet the child's needs best, classroom teachers, special education teachers, administrators, and support personnel need to be actively involved with families. "Parents who are supported in their initial attempts to participate in decision making will likely continue these efforts later in their child's school career" (Dabkowski, 2004, p. 38).

Unfortunately, too often partnerships between families and school personnel fall short. These shortcomings can be the result of several reasons, including (Summer et al., 2005):

- Professionals feeling unprepared to work with families.
- Professionals feeling like they do not have administrative support.
- Communication difficulties.
- Failure to recognize and adapt to cultural differences.
- Disagreement on appropriate services for the child.

In working with parents of students with special needs, educators find that parents vary tremendously in knowledge and expertise about disabilities. Some parents may be well-versed in special education laws and practices and may have informed opinions that must be considered in effective instructional planning. Other parents may be limited in their knowledge and their understanding of special education law. In this case, educators are responsible to inform parents so that they can become effective advocates for their child and partners in educational programming. (See the Rights & Responsibilities feature.)

Although effective collaboration cannot be based on professionals' presumptions that they understand the way a parent feels, it is useful to consider the advice that parents give other parents in learning how to respond effectively to the needs of their child and also of themselves. Figure 3.2 provides a summary of some parent-to-parent suggestions.

Rights & Responsibilities

Recommendations for Parental Involvement

In 2002 the President's Commission on Excellence in Special Education released a report titled "A New Era" that included two recommendations related directly to parents and family:

1. **Increase parental empowerment and school choice:** Parents should be provided with meaningful information about their children's progress, based on objective assessment results, and with educational options. The majority of special education students will continue to be in the regular public school system. In that context, IDEA should allow state use of federal special education funds to enable students with disabilities to attend schools or to access services of their family's choosing, provided states measure and report outcomes for all students benefiting from IDEA funds. IDEA should increase informed opportunities for parents to make choices about their children's education. Consistent with the No Child Left Behind Act, IDEA funds should be available for parents to choose

services or schools, particularly for parents whose children are in schools that have not made adequate yearly progress under IDEA for three consecutive years.

2. **Prevent disputes and improve dispute resolution:** IDEA should empower parents as key players and decision-makers in their children's education. IDEA should require states to develop early processes that avoid conflict and promote individualized education program (IEP) agreements, such as IEP facilitators; require states to make mediation available anytime it is requested and not only when a request for a hearing has been made; permit parents and schools to enter binding arbitration and ensure that mediators, arbitrators, and hearing officers are trained in conflict resolution and negotiation.

From "A New Era: Revitalizing Special Education for Children and Their Families," by the President's Commission on Excellence in Special Education, 2002, retrieved from www.ed.gov/inits /commissionboards/ whspecialeducation/reports/intro.html.

Figure 3.2   **Parent-to-Parent Suggestions**

- Seek the assistance of another parent of a child with a disability.
- Communicate feelings with spouse, family members, and significant others.
- Rely on positive sources in your life (e.g., minister, priest, rabbi, counselor).
- Take one day at a time.
- Learn the key terminology.
- Seek accurate information.
- Do not be intimidated by medical or educational professionals.
- Do not be afraid to show emotion.
- Learn how to deal with natural feelings of bitterness and anger.
- Maintain a positive outlook.
- Keep in touch with reality (e.g., there are some things that can be changed and others that cannot be changed).
- Find effective programs for your child.
- Take care of yourself.
- Avoid pity.
- Keep daily routines as normal as possible.
- Remember that this is your child.
- Recognize that you are not alone.

Adapted from "You Are Not Alone: For Parents When They Learn That Their Child Has a Disability," by P. M. Smith, 1997, *NICHY News Digest, 2,* pp. 3–5.

Parents like to feel that professionals really care about their child. In a study by Nelson, Summers, and Turnbull (2004), it was determined that parents like professionals to go above and beyond their job descriptions; this shows to parents a commitment that leads them to believe that the professional is doing everything possible for the child. Parents also like professionals to be flexible in their availability (Nelson et al., 2004). Things that parents indicated as positive in establishing close partnerships with professionals included being available when parents want them, going beyond the narrow limitations of their job descriptions, and sometimes being a friend.

Communicating with Parents

Many parents feel that too little communication takes place between them and the school. Perhaps this response is to be expected—approximately 50 percent of both general and special education teachers indicate that they have received no training in this area and consequently rate themselves as only moderately skilled (e.g., Buck et al., 1996; Epstein et al., 1996). This deficiency is particularly unfortunate because problems between parents and school personnel often can be avoided with proper communication by school professionals. They should make a conscious effort to begin the year with a discussion of roles and responsibilities in terms of communication (Munk et al., 2001). Parents need to know information for parent–professional communication to be effective. For example, sharing assessment information with parents will foster collaboration (Pemberton, 2003). One thing that parents of children with disabilities want is access to their child's teachers (Nelson et al., 2004).

Communication is not only required by IDEA; it also represents best practice (Ulrich & Bauer, 2003). True family involvement in the education of their child cannot occur without good communication. Brandes (2005) makes the following recommendations to enhance communication between school and parents.

- Give parents your undivided attention, and be an active listener.
- Stand or sit alongside parents when communicating.

DIVERSITY FORUM

Working Toward Cultural Reciprocity

Ms. Santos, a kindergarten teacher, has made repeated attempts to modify the disruptive behavior of two students with attention deficit disorder. Cami interrupts story time with numerous questions and comments while Elise tends to echo lines of text or engage in word play. When the teacher calls the families to discuss this problem, she discovers that the girls are engaging in behaviors that reflect the storytelling traditions in their respective cultures.

How should Ms. Santos deal with the girls' behavior without offending their families or disregarding their cultural traditions? Kalyanpur and Harry (1999) offer a four-step process that can help us, as educators, to build relationships with families through cultural reciprocity.

1. *We must identify our own beliefs, values and expectations that lead us to view the behavior as problematic.* Ms. Santos would realize that, like many teachers, she expects students to remain quiet during teacher-directed activities and that

she views interruptions as inappropriate, off-task behavior.

2. *We need to establish whether each family shares these values and expectations, and how their views may be different from our own.* Ms. Santos would realize that the parents do not share her concern. In her conversation with them she would also be sure to find out how they feel about her classroom expectations for their child.

3. *We should make sure that parents understand the underlying cultural basis for our perspective, while honoring and respecting the cultural differences that have been identified.* Ms. Santos would recognize that the girls' interruptions demonstrate, in fact, that they are paying attention. She would explain that, in school, students are expected to demonstrate that they are paying attention by listening quietly, and to wait to be called on to participate.

4. *Through dialogue and collaboration with the family, we should identify ways to adapt our interpretations to*

accommodate the value system of the home. Ms. Santos might decide that she will accept a few interjections during storytelling. Similarly, the parents may be willing to set aside time to practice the storytelling routine of school with their daughters while maintaining their traditions at other times.

Questions

1. What values, assumptions, and beliefs do you hold about teacher-student interaction that reflect the cultural values and beliefs with which you were raised?
2. What can you do to learn more about the cultural values and beliefs of the families you serve, so you can resolve these types of culture clashes in your classroom?

REFERENCE

Kalyanpur, M. & Harry, B. (1999). *Cultural reciprocity: Building reciprocal family-professional relationships.* Baltimore, MD: Brookes.

- Take notes openly while conversing with parents.
- When first meeting parents, engage them in conversation and pay close attention to what they choose to discuss.
- View parents who are challenging as an opportunity for you to grow.
- When working with angry parents, maintain a respectful demeanor and take notes rather than defend your actions at the time of the accusations.
- Allow parents to regard you as one of the experts in their child's education.
- Share the relevance of the curriculum to the student's goals.
- Share specific behavioral expectations early and regularly.
- Explain that you will try to resolve any conflict their child may have at school before you engage the parents.
- Model respect for the student by frequently acknowledging his or her efforts and achievements.
- Share some of the student's positive events that happen at school, such as successfully serving on a committee.
- Set up regular and frequent positive communication avenues such as a weekly newsletter that is sent home each Thursday.
- Be specific about when you will return phone calls, e-mails, and notes.

PRAXIS

PRAXIS II: Delivery of Services to Students with Disabilities

- Communicate often.
- Let parents know you appreciate their support and follow-through at home.
- Encourage parents to make provisions for their children who do not need to be at a meeting.
- Try to have both parents present when "major" topics are discussed.
- Start every meeting with a welcome, introductions, and review; clarification of the purpose of the current meeting and the ending time; and a recap of the meeting before everyone leaves.
- Never assume parents know how to help with homework (Brandes, 2005, pp. 52–54).

Effective communication must be regular and useful. Communicating with parents only once or twice per year, such as with IEP conferences, or communicating with parents regularly but with information that is not useful, will not facilitate meeting educational goals.

One good way to communicate with parents is the home-to-school notebook. The home-to-school notebook is simply a notebook that the child takes daily from school to home back to school containing notes from the teacher and parent about the child's activities. This particular communication device serves three functions. First, the notebook can encourage problem-solving; second, the notebook helps parents and school personnel analyze information; and finally, the notebook provides documentation of program implementation (Hall, Wolfe, & Bollig, 2003). Table 3.5 provides procedural recommendations for parents and school personnel in using a home-to-school notebook. Without both parties engaged in the day-to-day activities of the notebook, it will unlikely be a successful communication tool.

Communication between school personnel and parents does not have to be formal written communication. Effective communication can be informal, including telephone calls, written notes, e-mail, or newsletters. When communicating with parents, school personnel should be aware of how they convey messages. For example, they should never "talk down" to parents. They should also choose their words thoughtfully. Some words convey very negative meanings, while other words are just as useful in transmitting the message and are more positive. Table 3.6 lists words that should be avoided along with preferred alternatives.

Teachers must communicate regularly with parents to keep them informed about their child's progress and needs.

Table 3.5	Procedural Recommendations for Using Home-to-School Notebook
Procedural Recommendations for School	**Procedural Recommendations for Parents**
• Entry to classroom, collect journals. • Morning routine to discuss with student what parent wrote. • Keep journals in one place during day. • Respect confidentiality. • Structure journal writing during daytime routine, versus at the end of a busy day. • Get input from specialists/teachers and others working with student (personal care aide). • If student is included in a general education setting for a substantial part of day, the journal should travel to that setting and that teacher should make an entry. • Analyze the journal; look for patterns of behavior. • Establish a routine to return journal home. • Avoid educational jargon.	• Establish routine to review journal with student. • Keep journal available. • Include information from specialists (e.g., medical personnel, occupational and physical therapists). • Obtain input from family members to include in journal entry (e.g., siblings). • Establish a consistent, quiet time to write in journal. • Review journal entries, analyze data, look for patterns of behavior. • Review journal: Are your questions being addressed?

From "The Home-to-School Notebook," by T. E. Hall, P. S. Wolfe, and A. A. Bollig, 2003, *Teaching Exceptional Children, 36,* p. 72. Used with permission.

When communicating with parents, school personnel should also be aware of cultural and language differences. Taking these factors into consideration enhances the quality of communication with family members. School personnel must remember that the use of professional jargon can be just as much a barrier as communicating with parents whose primary language is not English (Dabkowski, 2004).

Informal Exchanges   Informal exchanges can take place without preparation. Teachers may see a parent in the community and stop to talk momentarily about the student. Teachers should always be prepared to talk briefly to parents about their children but should avoid talking about confidential information, particularly in the presence of

Table 3.6	Making Positive Word Choices
Avoid	**Use Instead**
Must	Needs to
Lazy	Is motivated toward less helpful interests
Culturally deprived	Culturally different, diverse
Troublemaker	Disturbs class
Uncooperative	Needs to work more with others
Below average	Works at his (her) own level
Truant	Absent without permission
Impertinent	Disrespectful
Steals	Takes things without permission
Dirty	Has poor grooming habits
Disinterested	Complacent, not challenged
Stubborn	Has a mind of his or her own
Wastes time	Could make better use of time
Sloppy	Could be neater
Mean	Has difficulty getting along with others
Time and time again	Usually, repeatedly
Poor grade or work	Works below his (her) usual standard

Adapted from *Parents and Teachers of Children with Exceptionalities: A Handbook for Collaboration* (2nd ed., p. 82), by T. M. Shea and A. M. Bauer, 1991. Boston: Allyn & Bacon. Used by permission.

individuals who do not need to know about it. If the conversation becomes too involved, the teacher should request that it be continued later, in a more appropriate setting.

Parent Observations   Parents should be encouraged to visit the school to observe their children in the classroom. Although the parents' presence could cause some disruption in the daily routine, school personnel need to keep in mind that parents have a critical stake in the success of the educational efforts. Therefore, they should always feel welcome. If the teacher feels that one time would be better than another, this information should be conveyed to the parent. Also, both teacher and parents should realize that children tend to behave differently when being observed by parents.

Telephone Calls   Many teachers use telephone calls effectively to communicate with parents. Parents feel that teachers are interested in their child if the teacher takes the time to call and discuss the child's progress with the parent. Teachers should remember to call when there is good news about the child as well as to report problems the child is experiencing. For example, teachers can make notes of positive behaviors and follow through with a call. Again, understanding the language and culture of the home is important when making telephone calls. Giving parents your home telephone number is an option that may reassure parents. Used appropriately, voice mail may enhance ongoing communication, especially when contact times are not mutually convenient.

Written Notes   Written communication to parents is also an effective method of communication. Teachers should consider the literacy level of the parents and use words and phrases that will be readily understandable. They should also be aware of the primary language of the home. Written communications that are not understood can be intimidating for parents. When using written communication, teachers should provide an opportunity for parents to respond, either in writing or through a telephone call.

Electronic Communication   Increasingly, e-mail offers opportunities for ongoing communication (Smith et al., 2006). However, as Patton, Jayanthi, and Polloway (2001) noted, "Although the use of new technologies [is] attractive in terms of their immediacy and efficiency, such use poses a dilemma, as a significant number of families may not have access to technology" (p. 228). As more and more families do have access to e-mail communication, teachers should take advantage of this form of communication. Not only is it expedient, but it also provides a record of the communication.

Home Visits   A home visit is the best way to get an understanding of the family. When possible, school personnel should consider making the extra effort required to arrange and make home visits. Home visits are a way that parents view school personnel of really caring about their child (Nelson et al., 2004). When visiting homes, school personnel need to follow certain procedures. Figure 3.3 includes a home-visit checklist that could be useful for school personnel to follow.

Although home visits are an important option, there is a low "teacher acceptability" of this practice. General education teachers report that they consider home visits the least effective (and perhaps least desirable) alternative available to them in terms of home–school collaborations (Polloway et al., 1996). Among other possible concerns, home visits for a potentially large number of children simply may be unrealistic. They tend to be more common, and perhaps more effective, at the preschool level. However, this form of communication can be essential in some instances and can take on greater significance when parents decline invitations to visit the school.

Formal Meetings   Parent-teacher meetings and conferences provide an important opportunity for collaboration. As Patton and colleagues (2001) indicated, "Conferences are called for one of three primary reasons: administrative purposes (e.g., assessment or

Figure 3.3   **Home-Visit Checklist**

Before the visit:
M   Have you scheduled the home visit around the family's needs?
M   Did you send any materials home for family members to review before the home visit?
M   Did you explain to family members the purpose of the home visit?
M   Do you have good directions on how to get to the house?
M   Do you have other school staff making the home visit with you?
M   Are you familiar with the family situations (e.g., number of children, employment status, composition of family)?
M   Are you appropriately dressed for the home visit (professional but not in a way to make family members feel uncomfortable)?

During the meeting:
M   Did you arrive on time?
M   Did you make family members feel comfortable?
M   Did you provide structure to the meeting (e.g., time, topics, etc.)?
M   Did you provide a summary of the meeting at the end?
M   Did you appropriately respond to offers of food/drink?

After the meeting:
M   Did you provide some follow-up information to the family after the meeting?
M   Did you schedule another meeting, if necessary?

From *Families and Children with Special Needs* (p. 96), by T. E. C. Smith, B. A. Gartin, N. Murdick, & A. Hilton, 2006. Columbus, OH: Merril. Used with permission.

eligibility issues); crisis situations (e.g., disciplinary actions); and routine progress reporting, which is typically held at the end of grading periods" (p. 228).

Under federal special education law, formal meetings include conferences to develop the IEP, the individualized family service plan (IFSP), the individualized transitional plan (ITP) (see Chapter 16), and, as applicable, behavioral intervention plans (BIPs) (see Chapter 14). Regardless of the purpose of the meeting, school personnel should focus attention on the topics at hand. They should send advance information home (e.g., a week before the meeting) to parents and make them feel at ease about their participation. Directing their attention to academic, social, and transitional goals before such meetings enhances their participation.

When preparing to meet with parents to discuss children who are experiencing problems, school personnel need to anticipate the components of the discussion. Figure 3.4 provides typical questions raised at such conferences. To increase parental participation in formal conferences, school personnel may wish to consider whether parents should have an advocate present at formal conferences. The advocate could be a member of the school staff or, in some cases, will be privately contracted by the parents. An advocate can facilitate parental participation by enhancing communication, encouraging parental participation, and providing them a summary of the discussions and decisions at the end of the conference. State regulations govern this practice; teachers should consult with administrative colleagues concerning this practice.

IEP and IFSP Meetings   Parents should be involved in the development of students' individualized programs, IEPs or IFSPs, for two reasons. First, IDEA requires that parents be invited to participate in the development of the child's individualized program, and must "sign off" on the completed plan. The more important reason for involvement, however, is to gain the input of parents. Parents know more about their children than school personnel do. They have been involved with the child longer, and beyond the hours of a school day. Schools need to take advantage of this knowledge about the child in the development of the IEP and IFSP.

CEC STANDARDS

CEC 1: Foundations

PRAXIS

PRAXIS II: Legal and Social Issues

CROSS-REFERENCE

For more information on the IDEA requirements for family involvement, see Chapter 2.

Figure 3.4   **Common Questions Asked by Parents and Teachers**

QUESTIONS PARENTS MAY ASK TEACHERS

- What is normal for a child this age?
- What is the most important subject or area for my child to learn?
- What can I work on at home?
- How can I manage her behavior?
- Should I spank?
- When will my child be ready for community living?
- Should I plan on her learning to drive?
- Will you just listen to what my child did the other day and tell me what you think?
- What is a learning disability?
- My child has emotional problems; is it my fault?
- The doctor said my child will grow out of this. What do you think?
- Will physical therapy make a big difference in my child's control of his hands and arms?
- Have you become harder on our child? Her behavior has changed at home.
- Can I call you at home if I have a question?
- What is the difference between delayed, retarded, and learning disabled?
- What kind of after-school activities can I get my child involved in?
- Can my child live on his own?
- What should I do about sexual activity?
- What's he going to be like in five years?
- Will she have a job?
- Who takes care of him when I can no longer care for him?
- What happens if she doesn't make her IEP goals?

QUESTIONS TEACHERS SHOULD ASK PARENTS

- What activities at home could you provide as a reward?
- What particular skill areas concern you most for inclusion on the IEP?
- What behavior at home do you feel needs to improve?
- Would you be interested in coming to a parent group with other parents of my students?
- When is a good time to call you at home?
- May I call you at work? What is the best time?
- Is there someone at home who can pick up the child during the day if necessary?
- Would you be interested in volunteering in our school?
- What is the most difficult problem you face in rearing your child?
- What are your expectations for your child?
- How can I help you the most?
- What is your home routine in the evenings? Is there a quiet place for your child to study?
- Can you or your spouse do some special activity with your child if he or she earns it at school?
- Can you spend some time tutoring your child in the evening?
- Would you like to have a conference with your child participating?
- When is the best time to meet?

Adapted from *The Special Educator's Handbook* (pp. 208–209), by D. L. Westling and M. A. Koorland, 1988. Boston: Allyn & Bacon. Used by permission.

Too often, for a variety of reasons, parents do not fully participate in IEP/IFSP meetings. They are present, but often feel intimidated or unworthy of contributing to the discussion. School personnel can facilitate the active involvement of parents at these meetings. In reflecting on how professionals encourage parental participation, Dabkowski (2004) suggests asking the following questions:

1. Are parents equal partners with you in the education of students with disabilities?
2. Do you actively invite parents, accommodate their schedules, and welcome their differing cultural contributions?
3. Are you aware of cultural and linguistic team processes or environments that might make parents uncomfortable?
4. Are you wondering how to improve parent participation in your decision-making processes? (Dabkowski, 2004, p. 34)

By asking these questions, it is hoped that professionals will have a better understanding of not only how involved parents are in the process but also how to increase the level of involvement.

Mediation   The legal requirements concerning the involvement of parents in their child's education provide a foundation for appropriate practices in home–school collaboration. Nevertheless, even when careful efforts at compliance are made by school personnel and when educators attempt to fulfill both the letter and spirit of the law, some conflicts are inevitable in such an emotionally charged area as the determination of an appropriate education for a student with a disability. Local education agencies are mandated by law to offer **mediation** to resolve disagreements between parents and school personnel. In mediation, the parties share their concerns and then work to develop a solution that is mutually acceptable, typically through the facilitation of a third party (Smith et al., 2006).

CEC STANDARDS
CEC 1: Foundations

IDEA 2004 also provides an opportunity for parents to engage in a resolution session with school personnel in situations where there is disagreement. The resolution session is required when a due-process hearing has been requested, unless the school and parents agree not to have one. If effective, a mediation or the resolution process can result in the avoidance of a hearing, the subsequent cost of attorney fees, and the potential for an adversarial relationship developing as a result of due-process hearings.

Cross-Cultural Considerations   A particularly sensitive area for teachers is working with families from another cultural background. Parents, for example, may have a different view than the teacher about issues such as the nature of a presenting problem or the preferred solution. One suggestion for dealing with these challenges is a four-step, two-way communicative process to share information and establish reciprocity across cultures.

CEC STANDARDS
CEC 10: Collaboration

Step 1: Identify the cultural values that are embedded in your interpretation of a student's difficulties or in the recommendation for service. Ask yourself which values underlie your recommendation. For many of us, the values of equity, independence, and individuality are central to our recommendation. Next, analyze your experiences that contributed to these values. Consider the roles of nationality, culture, socioeconomic status, and professional education in shaping your values. (Note that within some cultures, families may perceive relationships as more important than school achievement.)

Step 2: Find out whether the family being served recognizes and values your assumptions, and if not, how their view differs from yours.

| *Table* 3.7 | **What Do Parents Want?** |

What Do Parents Want for Their Children?	What Do Parents Expect of Teachers?	What Do Parents Expect of Schools?
Personal and Social Adjustment "To belong to more groups." "More socialization." "To open up a little bit so he can learn to mix and mingle more." **Accommodation and Adaptation** "One-to-one learning environment for academics." "More hands-on learning." "Sometimes the test should be given verbally." **Responsibility and Independence** "To buckle down and study [to get better grades]." "To learn to finish his tasks." "To be able to set limits with people she goes out with [when she is on her own]." **Academic and Functional Literacy** "To read better." "To get every opportunity to learn what he should know . . . and continue to progress every year." **Supportive Environment** "A sense of accomplishment, success." "A positive environment." "Constant encouragement to stick to the tasks he is [working] on."	**Personal Characteristics** "Enjoy what they are teaching." "Love what they are doing." "Be enthusiastic." "Be open-minded, friendly, and down-to-earth." "Be caring and patient." **Accountability and Instructional Skills** "Evaluate themselves instead of turning to outside sources to evaluate what they are doing." "Direct the students toward resources and information that can further their studies." **Management Skills** "Make [students] follow through with assignments." "Be very well-organized." "Be fair in remediating disputes between students." **Communication** "Consider parents as part of a team for learning." "Keep in touch with parents at times other than IEP meetings."	**Responsibility and Independence** "Help them make decisions." "Train them to be self-sufficient." "[Help] them handle a checking and savings account." **Academic and Functional Literacy** "[Help them] meet certain proficiency requirements to get their high school degree or whatever." "Prepare him to go on to [further education]." **Supportive Environment** "Keep kids interested [in learning]." "Provide an atmosphere for learning." "[Provide an environment] where they feel safe and respected. . . . Warmth is important."

Adapted from "Parents' Perspectives on School Choice," by C. M. Lange, J. E. Ysseldyke, and C. A. Lehr, 1997, *Teaching Exceptional Children, 30*(1), pp. 17–19.

Step 3: Acknowledge and give explicit respect to any cultural differences identified, and fully explain the cultural basis of your assumptions.

Step 4: Through discussion and collaboration, set about determining the most effective way to adapt your professional interpretations or recommendations to the value system of this family (Harry, cited in *Research Connections*, 2001, p. 4).

Common Concerns   The preceding discussion highlighted vehicles for effective communication among teachers, other school personnel, parents, and other family members. Note the value for teachers in anticipating possible concerns that parents may express about their child's education. Table 3.7 identifies three domains of possible concerns of parents: expectations for their child, expectations of schools, and expectations of teachers. These examples provide a picture of ways in which teachers can anticipate and respond to parents effectively.

Home-Based Intervention

Families can become involved with the education of a family member with a disability through home-based intervention. For preschool children, home-based services are fairly common; however, parents less frequently provide instruction at home for older students. Nevertheless, such support can be very beneficial to all students with disabilities.

Parents and other family members at home can get involved in the student's educational program by providing reinforcement and instructional support, as well as by facilitating homework efforts. At the same time, teachers should be sensitive to the numerous roles parents must play in addition to supporting their child with special needs. The purpose of this section is to briefly outline some considerations in each of these three areas; elements of each are discussed further in Chapters 14, 15, and 16.

Providing Reinforcement and Encouragement

Most students with disabilities experience some failure and related frustration. This failure cycle becomes difficult to break, especially after it becomes established over several years. Reinforcing success is an important strategy to interrupt the failure cycle. Parents can work with school personnel to provide positive reinforcement and encourage students to strive for school success.

Parents are in an excellent position to provide reinforcement. They are with the child more than school personnel and are involved in all aspects of the child's life. As a result, parents can provide reinforcement in areas where a child most desires rewards, such as time with friends, money, toys, or trips. For many students, simply allowing them to have a friend over or stay up late at night on a weekend may prove reinforcing. School personnel do not have this range of reinforcers available to them; therefore, parents should take advantage of their repertoire of rewards to reinforce the positive efforts of students.

A special example of reinforcement is home–school contingencies, which typically involve providing reinforcement in the home that is based on the documentation of learning or behavioral reports from school. The basic mechanism for home–school contingencies is written reports that highlight a student's behavior with regard to particular targets or objectives. Two popular forms are daily report cards and passports.

Daily report cards give feedback on schoolwork, homework, and behavior. They range in complexity from forms calling for responses to simple rating scales to more precisely designed behavioral instruments with direct, daily behavioral measures of target behaviors. Passports typically take the form of notebooks that students bring to each class and then take home daily. Individual teachers (or all of a student's teachers) and parents can make regular notations. Reinforcement is based both on carrying the passport and on meeting the specific target behaviors that are indicated on it (Walker & Shea, 1995). A comprehensive discussion of other specific reinforcement strategies is presented in Chapter 14.

Some overarching considerations will enhance reinforcement programs in the home. Discipline in the home involves two types of parental action: (1) imposing consequences for misbehavior, and (2) reinforcement of positive behavior. Rushed and stressed parents frequently are better in one area than another. School personnel need to let parents understand that reinforcement of positive behaviors is crucial to a child's self-esteem and growth. To see a new positive behavior or achievement and fail to reinforce it is a form of neglect that is unintentional but damaging. Parents need to train themselves to see and to reinforce positive behaviors, attitudes, and achievements.

Providing Instructional Support

Parents and other family members may become directly involved with instructional programs at home, which can be critical to student success. Unfortunately, many family members provide less direct instruction as the child gets older, assuming that the student is capable of doing the work alone. Too often, the reverse is true; students may need more assistance at home as they progress through the grades. While older children sometimes resist their parents' attempts to help, parents nevertheless should endeavor to remain involved at an appropriate level.

CEC STANDARDS

CEC 10: Collaboration

CROSS-REFERENCE

A description of the principles of reinforcement is presented in Chapter 14.

TEACHING TIP

Regardless of the format, the key element in home–school contingencies is ongoing, effective communication between school personnel and parents.

CONSIDER THIS

Parents generally know more about their children than school personnel. In what ways can this knowledge be used to develop programs that meet the needs of children?

Lack of clear communications from teachers about homework expectations can lead parents to be either underinvolved or overinvolved.

CROSS-REFERENCE

School-based aspects of homework are discussed in Chapters 15 and 16.

Since parents are generally with the child more than are school personnel, it is logical to involve them in selected instructional activities. Advocates for expanding the role of parents in educating their children adhere to the following assumptions:

- Parents are the first and most important teachers of their children.
- The home is the child's first schoolhouse.
- Children will learn more during the early years than at any other time in life.
- All parents want to be good parents and care about their child's development (Ehlers & Ruffin, 1990, p. 1).

Although the final assumption may not always be reflected in practice, it provides a positive foundation for building home programs.

Devlin and Harber (2004) describe a program where parents and professionals collaborated with discrete trial training in the treatment of a child with autism. The program used the collaboration among family members, special education teachers, resource room teacher, and speech/language therapist to achieve various goals and objectives for the child. The end result was that after twenty-eight weeks of intervention, significant progress was made toward the goals and objectives. The study concluded that such an intervention program, using family members as part of the intervention team, could result in significant gains by the child. In another study, Skoto and colleagues (2004) concluded that parental involvement with reading stories could result in positive gains by young girls with Rett syndrome.

Interventions that promote self-determination are another area that parents can be involved. Lee and colleagues (2006) describe a model for parent–teacher collaboration that focuses on improving self-determination. Using the program, Self-Determined Learning Model of Support (SDLMS), parents are able to influence the self-determination of children with and without disabilities. Using such a program at home facilitates partnerships between schools and families (Lee et al., 2006).

Providing Homework Support

We conclude this chapter with the topic of homework, an area that may be in many ways the most problematic for successful home–school collaboration. As Polloway, Bursuck, and Epstein (2001) noted, "The challenge of homework for students with special needs who are served in inclusive settings remains a significant concern for American education, one that tends to escalate as more students are educated in these settings" (p. 196).

Jayanthi, Nelson, Sawyer, Bursuck, and Epstein's (1994) report on communication problems within the homework process reveals significant misunderstandings among general and special education teachers and parents regarding the development, implementation, and coordination of homework practices for students with disabilities in inclusive settings. Teachers and parents indicated concerns about failures to initiate communication (in terms of informing the other of a student's learning and behavior characteristics as well as the delineation of roles and responsibilities) and to provide follow-up communications, especially early on, when problems first become evident. In addition, respondents identified several variables that they believed influence the severity of these problems (e.g., lack of time, student-to-teacher ratio, student interference, not knowing whom to contact). Munk and colleagues' survey research (2001) on 348 parents confirmed this pattern of findings.

As Epstein and colleagues (1996) reviewed these problem areas, they found that general education teachers reported the following key communication problems: lack of follow-through by parents, lateness of communication, the relative lack of importance placed on homework, parental defensiveness, and denial of problems. These concerns were generally consistent with the reports of special education teachers in a parallel study (Buck et al., 1996). However, these data are open to interpretation because they are survey responses by teachers about parents.

The concerns raised in these two studies focus primarily on underinvolved parents. Teachers should also be sensitive to over-involved parents and, when appropriate, encourage them not to teach their children to be helpless but to teach them to do as much for themselves as possible.

Despite the numerous problems associated with homework, solutions can be found. Based on their study, Bursuck and colleagues (1999) found that special education teachers indicated the following recommendations:

- General educators and parents need to take an active and daily role in monitoring and communicating with students about homework.
- Schools should find ways to provide teachers with the time to engage in regular communication with parents and should provide students with increased opportunities to complete homework after school.
- Teachers need assistance in taking advantage of technological innovations (e.g., homework hotlines, computerized student progress records).
- Students need to be held responsible for keeping up with their homework.
- Special educators need to share with general educators more information about the needs of students with disabilities and appropriate instructional accommodations.

Examples of strategies that general education teachers ranked most effective in resolving homework dilemmas are provided in Figure 3.5. Note that many of these strategies have validity for all students, not only those with special needs.

Figure 3.5   **Effective Strategies Relative to Homework**

Parents' Efforts to Communicate

Parents should

- check with their child about homework daily.
- regularly attend parent–teacher conferences.
- sign their child's assignment book daily.

Adopting Policies to Facilitate Communication

Schools should

- provide release time for teachers to communicate with parents on a regular basis.
- require frequent written communication from teachers to parents about homework (e.g., monthly progress reports).
- schedule conferences in the evenings for working parents.

General Education Teachers' Roles

Teachers should

- require that students keep a daily assignment book.
- provide parents at the start of school with a list of suggestions on how parents can assist with homework.
- remind students of due dates on a regular basis.

Technologies to Enhance Communication

Schools should

- establish telephone hotlines so that parents can call when questions or problems arise.
- regularly provide computerized student progress reports for parents.
- establish systems that enable teachers to place homework assignments on audiotapes so that parents can gain access by telephone or voice mail.

From "Strategies for Improving Home–School Communication Problems about Homework for Students with Disabilities," by M. H. Epstein, D. D. Munk, W. D. Bursuck, E. A. Polloway, and M. M. Jayanthi, 1999, *Journal of Special Education, 33*, pp. 166–176.

Callahan, Redemacher, and Hildreth (1998) developed an intensive program that included parent training, student training, systematic homework procedures, and self-management strategies followed by home- and school-based positive reinforcement programs. They reported that homework completion as well as the quality of homework significantly increased for children of those parents who were able to follow the homework program and that significant increases in achievement in mathematics also were the result. See Inclusion Strategies for a further strategy of how parents and educators can work together to solve the homework dilemma.

As Patton and colleagues (2001) noted, "Even conscientious parents who understand the significance of homework in their children's lives and the importance of their own role in supporting, nurturing, and helping their children have successful homework experiences sometimes simply fail at their daily responsibilities of checking the assignment book or asking 'What homework did you get today?' and 'Have you completed it?'" (p. 240). Thus, teachers should reflect an understanding in communication with parents that homework may be a lower priority for families when compared with other issues (e.g., school attendance, family illness) and respond accordingly by helping to address these other issues first.

Strategies for use by elementary and secondary teachers in the area of homework are explored in further detail in Chapters 15 and 16. Although calls for an end to, or a reform of, homework are increasing (e.g., Kralovec & Buell, 2000), the coincidental trend toward testing of students for accountability purposes is likely to have the effect of increasing homework. Therefore, until such time occurs (if ever) that homework's role in education is diminished, concerns in this area will greatly influence home–school partnerships.

Final Thoughts

Establishing good working relationships with parents and families enhances the school experience of their children. Thus an important objective for the schools should be to achieve and maintain such relationships. Most professionals acknowledge the importance of the involvement of families in the schooling of their children, and this importance can be especially critical for students with disabilities. However, programs that promote home–school collaboration must aim for more than students' classroom success. Often, parental involvement has been focused on children's goals (i.e., student progress), with less attention given to parental outcomes (i.e., their particular needs). Teachers and family members all should gain from cooperative relationships that flow in both directions and are concerned with success in both home and school settings. Both general and special education teachers need to help family members understand the importance of their involvement, give them suggestions for how to get involved, and empower them with the skills and confidence they will need. Students with disabilities, and those at risk for developing problems, require assistance from all parties in order to maximize success. Family members are critical components of the educational team.

Summary

The Family
- A major change in the past several decades in provision of educational services to students with special needs is the active involvement of families.
- Encouraging parents to participate in school decisions is essential.

- Schools need to take proactive steps to ensure the involvement of families of students with disabilities. Regardless of their own values, school personnel must involve all family members of a student with special needs, regardless of the type of family.

- All family members must make adjustments when a child with a disability becomes a family member.
- Siblings of students with disabilities may experience special problems and challenges.
- Overriding attention needs to be given to cultural differences in families as a basis for collaborative programs.

Home–School Collaboration

- Families and schools must collaborate to ensure appropriate educational programs for students with disabilities. IDEA requires that schools involve families in educational decisions for students with disabilities.

- A critical component in any collaboration between school personnel and family members is effective communication. All types of communication, formal and informal, between school and families are important.

Home-Based Intervention

- Family members should be encouraged and taught how to become involved in the educational programs implemented in the school. A variety of strategies are available to facilitate successful home intervention programs (i.e., reinforcement, instruction, homework support).

Questions to Reconsider

Think back to the scenario about Patrick and his parents that you read at the beginning of this chapter. Would you answer the questions raised there any differently after reading the chapter?

1. Analyze George and Judy's potential feelings and possible reactions upon learning that Patrick has a disability.
2. What advice, recommendations, and help would you provide for these parents?

3. What would you tell them about the advantages and challenges of inclusive preschool programs?
4. What influence could Patrick's condition have on George and Judy's marriage?
5. How could other parents, with children like Patrick, help George and Judy deal with their crisis?

Further Readings

Darling, R. B., & Baxter, C. (1996). *Families in focus: Sociological methods in early intervention*. Austin, TX: Pro-Ed.

Hanson, M. J., & Carter, J. J. (1996). Addressing the challenges of families with multiple risks. *Exceptional Children, 62*, 201–211.

Klein, S. D., & Schive, K. (Eds.). (2001). *You will dream new dreams: Inspiring personal stories by parents of children with disabilities*. New York: Kensington Books.

Palmer, D. S., Fuller, K., Arora, T., & Nelson, M. (2001). Taking sides: Parent views on inclusion for their children with severe disabilities. *Exceptional Children, 67*, 467–484.

Rosenkoetter, S. E., Hains, A. H., & Fowler, S. A. (1994). *Bridging early services for children with special needs and their families*. Baltimore: Brookes.

Turnbull, A. P., & Turnbull, H. R. (1997). *Families, professionals, and exceptionality: A special partnership*. Columbus, OH: Merrill.

Welch, M., & Sheridan, S. M. (1995). *Educational partnerships: Serving students at risk*. Fort Worth, TX: Harcourt Brace.

West, K. (2000). *The Shelbys need help: A choose-your-own solutions guidebook for parents*. Atascadero, CA: Impact.

(mylabschool
Where the classroom comes to life

Go to Allyn & Bacon's MyLabSchool (www.mylabschool.com) and enter Assignment ID SPV4 into the Assignment Finder. View the video clip called *Working with Parents and Families*. Then consider what you have seen along with what you've read in Chapter 3 to answer the following questions.

1. When a child has a disability, family members must often wear many hats including medical caregiver, therapist, and comforter in addition to the more traditional roles of parent or sibling and friend. How might these additional roles place a burden on the family of a child with a disability? How might they enrich the life of that family? Use specific examples from the video to support your comments.

2. What kinds of support would you say the parents or caregiver of a child with a disability might find most valuable from a teacher?

3. Some teachers might feel apprehensive about having parents in the classroom. How do you think you might feel? What might be the positive benefits of having a parent of a child with a disability spend time in the classroom? Might there be any negative effects?

You may also answer the questions at the end of the clip and e-mail your responses to your instructor.

Identifying and Programming for Student Needs

1. Describe the steps in the special education process.

2. Identify the rights and responsibilities of students with disabilities and their parents in the special education process.

3. Explain the prereferral intervention process and identify successful strategies in the general education classroom.

4. Discuss the uses of assessment throughout the special education process.

5. List the major components of an IEP.

6. Highlight the major elements of behavioral intervention planning.

7. Discuss the intent and recommended practices associated with transition services.

8. Identify the key components of Section 504.

9. Describe the role of the general education teacher in the various services and programs provided to students with special needs.

Questions to Consider

1. What suggestions can you make to help Jessica succeed in the general education classroom?

2. How would you feel about making accommodations to keep Jessica if you were Jessica's teacher?

3. Do you think treating Jessica differently was fair to the other students?

Last year was my first year to teach! I was so happy to be assigned a fourth-grade class of twenty-five students. My class had children from several cultures; I met with parents and planned activities to expose the class to these rich cultural differences. The special education teachers contacted me about the needs of several children who were in my class for some or all of a day.

My lack of experience was balanced by my eagerness and enthusiasm. Each day I spent several hours planning exciting learning experiences. I was so caught up in the process of teaching that it took me a couple of months to realize that one of my students was floundering, despite my efforts. Jessica was new to our school, so I could not consult with other teachers to gain insight. She was a puzzle. Some days were better than others. She had difficulty following directions, seldom finished her work or handed in homework; her desk and papers were a mess, and she spent too much time looking for pencils and supplies needed to complete an activity. She read slowly and laboriously and had problems decoding and predicting unknown words. I tried to talk to her, but she had little to say. She was a loner with only one or two friends with whom she seemed comfortable. I wasn't ready to refer her for a special education evaluation, but I knew she and I both needed help!

Fortunately, the school had a prereferral intervention team (PIT) that met weekly to discuss children like Jessica who were experiencing problems in general education classrooms. I didn't like admitting that I needed help, but I was glad that the resource was available. I let Jessica's parents know I was concerned about her progress and was seeking help within the school. I filled out the required form requesting a brief summary of the problems and attached examples of Jessica's work.

The PIT meeting, held at 7:00 A.M., gave us uninterrupted time. The team was composed of an experienced teacher from each grade, the assistant principal, the counselor, and a special education teacher. Other teachers were there to discuss children having difficulties in their classrooms. When Jessica's case was discussed, I came up with some strategies, and the team agreed they would be appropriate. I guess I just needed the peer support to give me ideas and confidence to help Jessica. Thanks to the assistance from this team, Jessica's achievement improved, and she finished fourth grade. I never had to refer her for additional testing. Both she and her parents were pleased. I think she will be successful in fifth grade. I'm glad the PIT is in place so that Jessica and others like her will have help if problems arise.

In the preceding vignette, a concerned teacher identified Jessica's needs and reached out for resources that would help keep her successfully learning in the general education classroom. This chapter focuses on identifying the unique needs of students like Jessica and programming for those needs in an inclusive classroom whenever possible.

A comprehensive process should be in place in every school system for a student who needs to be evaluated to determine if he or she is eligible for special educational services. This process is governed by the Education for All Handicapped Children Act (EHA; PL 94–142) and its successor, the Individuals with Disabilities Education Act (IDEA; PL 101–476) (1990, 1997, 2004), as well as by regulations developed in each state. This chapter reviews key steps in the process: prereferral intervention, referral, assessment, and the development, implementation, and review of IEPs. In addition, the chapter examines other services that are mandated under IDEA and Section 504 of the Rehabilitation Act.

All educational procedures must be consistent with the due-process clause under the U.S. Constitution, which ensures that no person will be deprived of legal rights or privileges without appropriate established procedures being followed. The implications of the due-process clause have resulted in regulations in IDEA (2004) that give parents and students with disabilities significant rights throughout the special education process. These are listed in the Rights & Responsibilities feature. While these basic rights are guaranteed nationwide, specific procedures guiding the special education process will vary from state to state.

The process for addressing the classroom challenges presented by students with special needs is discussed throughout this chapter. The flowchart provided in Figure 4.1 shows that procedures begin with efforts to address students' challenges that are focused on improving academic and behavioral performance and keeping the student in the general education classroom. If these are ineffective, a formal referral to evaluate eligibility for special education services results. Based on the eligibility determination, either special education–related services, along with the various services specified by IDEA, are provided, or other considerations such as Section 504 eligibility are pursued.

The key players in the process include the student, if appropriate, the parents, at least one special and one general education teacher, a qualified administrative staff member, and other professional staff who have knowledge or special expertise regarding the student (e.g., school psychologists; various therapists, including speech/language, occupational, and physical; school social workers; and school nurse). Even though teamwork is required by IDEA (2004), involving several individuals should not be simply an issue of compliance or happenstance. Many people should have a vested interest in the educational program for a student, and consideration of a student's needs is best accomplished by a team approach. Thus, a team, representing various disciplines and relationships with the student, makes key decisions in regard to the student. Important decisions that have to be made include whether the student should be referred for an evaluation, eligibility for special services, design of the IEP, development of the BIP (if needed), evaluation of annual progress made on implementation of the IEP, and reevaluation of eligibility and placement.

All teams, when dealing with the important issue of a student's educational program, must keep in mind certain guidelines during this process. Doing so will increase the chances that positive outcomes will be realized. Some of the most crucial guidelines are the following:

1. The best interests of the student and their unique needs and strengths should dictate all aspects of the decision-making process.
2. Sensitivity to family values and cultural differences must pervade all activities.
3. Ongoing and effective home-school collaboration efforts should be established.
4. Parents and students have a right to and should be given information about the educational performance of the student, the special education programs and services to which the student is entitled and from which the student may receive benefit, and what will happen after formal schooling ends.

CEC STANDARDS

CEC 1: Foundations

CROSS-REFERENCE

Refer to Chapter 1 for a comprehensive summary of the provisions of IDEA.

PRAXIS

PRAXIS II: Legal & Societal Issues

CEC STANDARDS

CEC 1: Foundations

INTASC

INTASC 7: The teacher plans instruction based on students

CONSIDER THIS

The three-year reevaluation is a good time to update the levels of knowledge about students and make adjustments to their program of studies if the decision is to continue providing special education services.

IDEA 2004

According to IDEA 2004 school personnel must

- make reasonable efforts to ensure parental participation in group discussions relating to the educational placement of their child.
- notify parents of meetings early enough to ensure they will have an opportunity to attend and use conference or individual calls if they cannot attend.
- inform parents of the purpose, time, and location of a meeting and who will attend it.
- notify parents that they, or school personnel, may invite individuals with special knowledge or expertise to IEP meetings.
- notify parents of their right to refuse special education services.
- schedule the meetings at a mutually agreed upon time and place.
- provide written notification (in the parent or guardian's native language) before any changes are initiated or refused in the identification, evaluation, educational placement, or provision of a free, appropriate public education.
- obtain written consent from parents before the initial evaluation, preceding initial provisions of special education

and related services, or before conducting a new test as part of a reevaluation. Parents have a right to question any educational decision through due-process procedures.
- inform parents that they have the right to an independent educational evaluation that may be provided at public expense if the evaluation provided by the education agency is determined to be inappropriate.
- inform parents of requirements for membership on the IEP committee, including an invitation to the student to attend beginning at age sixteen or younger if appropriate.
- use interpreters or take other action to ensure that the parents understand the proceedings of the IEP meetings.
- inform parents of requirement to consider transition services needed for students by age sixteen.
- consider the student's strengths and the parental concerns in all decisions.
- provide the parents with a copy of the IEP at no cost.
- inform parents of their right to ask for revisions to the IEP or invoke due-process procedures if they are not satisfied.
- notify parents of their right to mediation, resolution session, or due-process hearing.
- allow parents to review all records and request amendments if deemed appropriate.

5. Each student should be taught and encouraged to participate as an active, contributing member of the team.
6. Programs and services, including the rules and regulations that apply, should be reviewed regularly, and improvements should be made whenever possible and allowable under the law.

The most recent reauthorization of IDEA (2004) maintains the basic requirements for home–school collaboration. IDEA continues to require schools to involve parents in every phase of the special education process. While future reauthorizations of IDEA will likely result in some changes, the basic intent of the law—providing a free appropriate public education to children with disabilities with parental involvement—will remain.

Prereferral Intervention

Most schools have developed and implemented a process to study and intervene in the general education classroom before referring a student for formal evaluation. The **prereferral intervention** process is designed to address the needs of students who exhibit learning and behavioral problems and who have not yet been referred for special education. (Remember, it was the PIT that helped Jessica and her new teacher in the opening vignette.) The essence of the process is that intervention within the general education classroom is facilitated by providing assistance to classroom teachers and, ultimately, the students so the students' learning and/or behavior will be improved to the extent that a formal referral for special education services will not be needed. As Buck, Fad, Patton, and Polloway (2003) point out, while the prereferral intervention practice is widely supported, this particular process has not yet been mandated by federal law.

Figure 4.1

**Flowchart of Services for
Students with Special Needs**

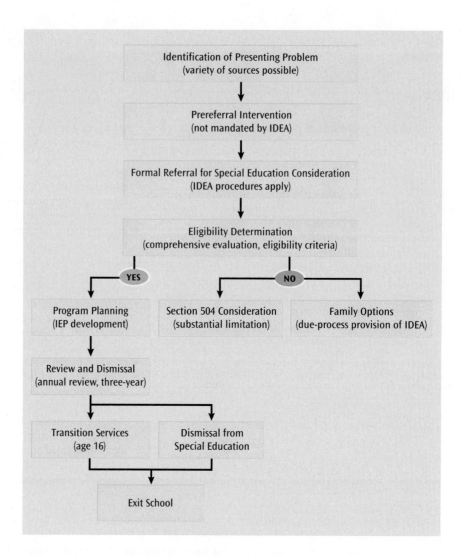

CEC STANDARDS

CEC 3: Individual Learning
Differences

However, the 2004 reauthorization of IDEA allows schools to use up to 15 percent of federal funds to provide these interventions. A survey reported recently found that 86 percent of the states either required or recommended the use of PITs (Truscott, Cohen, Sams, Sanborn, & Frank, 2005). Because this prereferral process is not regulated by government standards, much variation exists between schools. More research and leadership is needed to standardize these procedures and develop a model for best practice.

Although this process might seem like a way for some school systems to avoid providing costly special education services, the process has merit, as it can be a powerful way to address student needs within inclusive settings. However, the prereferral intervention process should be considered a first level of intervention and definitely will not be an answer for all students. The prereferral process itself involves four major phases:

1. Initial indication that a classroom-based problem exists.
2. Systematic examination of the presenting problem(s) that have been indicated by the referral source.
3. Development of an intervention plan that contains strategies and other suggestions for addressing the presenting problem.
4. Evaluation and monitoring of the effectiveness of the interventions and decision on what to do next if the interventions have not yielded the outcomes originally desired.

The prereferral intervention process ordinarily begins with concerns voiced by a classroom teacher about the performance, progress, or behavior(s) of a student. Other sources

CONSIDER THIS

Estimate the elapsed time from a teacher's initial concern about a student to implementation of special education services. Is this time frame reasonable from the perspective of the student? The parent? The teacher?

for a referral to the PIT could be parents, end-of-year reviews of student progress, or an external service provider. Hopefully, schools will establish procedures to inform parents of these initial concerns if the parents are not part of the referral process. Most schools provide a simple form for teachers and others to use when making this referral. Information requested might include a brief description of the presenting problem, documentation of any support services the child currently receives and any interventions attempted, and the child's strengths (Buck, Polloway, Patton, & McConnell, in press).

When the form is completed, a group of school-based personnel meet to review the information provided. This team is referred to as the **prereferral intervention** team, or PIT, throughout this text; however, these teams may also be called the *child assistance team, teacher intervention team, teacher assistance team,* or *building-based support team* depending on the geographical location (Buck, Wilcox-Cook, Polloway, & Smith-Thomas, 2002). Frequently, the PIT will need more in-depth information on the student and will seek information in the following areas:

- student's school history
- previous evaluations performed: psychological, educational, speech/language, functional behavioral assessments, outside agency evaluations
- observations (previous and new)
- interviews (previous and new): teachers, family, student

Once the team has sufficient information to understand the nature of the presenting problem(s), members will attempt to generate suggestions to address the student's difficulties. At the outset, the team attempts to assist the teacher in targeting the most significant problems in the classroom by identifying intervention goals and the criteria by which a successful change will be measured. Then, the task is to identify effective strategies such as accommodations or modifications to the environment or instructional strategies; less often, the curriculum might be modified or an alternative teaching method implemented (IDEA mandates that these be research- or evidence-based). When a student's behavior is interfering with learning, strategies will be designed and implemented to help in this area. Emphasis should be placed on choosing the most positive interventions that rely on the natural support systems within a classroom and result in the least change to the general education setting and curriculum. Sometimes well-meaning educators and parents err by recommending too many accommodations or modifications, when it is actually in the child's best interest to implement the least number of changes that still result in the desired outcome.

Although some professionals and texts use the terms accommodations and modifications interchangeably, the following distinctions made by Cohen and Spenciner (2007) are helpful in seeing the range of adaptations available and the implications of each. *Accommodations* are changes made during assessment or to a child's education that do not substantially change the curriculum content, the level of instruction, or the assessment criteria. In other words, the changes do not lower the standards expected on a subject or test. Examples would be giving extra time to complete an assignment made for all students or changing a child's proximity to the teacher to increase attention or improve behavior. *Modifications* are more significant departures from the general education assessment and/or instructional program and might include substituting a text written on the same subject but using simpler wording, or requiring only half of the math problems assigned to the rest of the class. Modifications do alter the assessment criteria, curriculum content, or level of work; these changes are less likely to be made at the prereferral level of intervention and are usually documented on an IEP if the team agrees to the need. Table 4.1 provides examples of accommodations and modifications frequently used in assessment.

Typically adaptations made for instructional programming are also available during assessment. However, some states do not allow accommodations or modifications during statewide assessment if the changes interfere with the test validity. For example, the

CEC STANDARDS

CEC 4: Instructional Strategies

Table 4.1   **Frequently Used Accommodations and Modifications**

Type of Accommodation or Modification	Example of Accommodations	Example of Modifications
Presentation mode	• Test is administered individually rather than administered in a group. • Examiner reads items out loud (except when student is tested in reading). • Student takes a computer-administered form of the test. • Large print forms are used. • Braille form of the test is used. • Test directions and items are signed. • A specific examiner may be chosen who is able to develop (or who already has) rapport with the student.	• Examiner uses prompts or cues.
Location of the test administration	• Test is administered in an area with reduced distractions. • Test is administered while student is using special furniture. • Test is administered in space that has special lighting.	
Response mode	• Teacher or helper marks the responses as indicated by the student. • Student indicates responses on paper that has lines or a grid. • Student uses a communication device. • Time limits for responding are extended or modified.	• Student is allowed to use a calculator for mathematics calculation. • Examiner accepts key word responses instead of complete sentences required by the test. • Student is allowed to use a spell checker, specialized software, or dictionary for writing test.
Test content	• Number of items per page is reduced but student completes all test items. • Use of bilingual glossaries and dictionaries (for English language learners).	• Fewer test items are presented.
Test format	• Test items are magnified.	• Key words in the test directions are highlighted or color-coded. • Test items are reworded. • Pictures or graphics are substituted for words.

From *Assessment of Children and Youth with Special Needs* (p. 5), by L. G. Cohen and L. J. Spenciner, 2007. Boston: Allyn & Bacon.

reading comprehension portion of a test could not be read to the student because it would no longer be a valid measure of reading ability; however, the math portion of the test might be read to the student. The IEP team can also identify alternative assessments as needed for students with more severe disabilities. Figure 4.2 provides a form that might be used to document the decisions and recommendations of the PIT. Note that the form also documents the person responsible for implementing the plan, support given, and timelines.

Prereferral intervention techniques are generally implemented for at least one grading period, typically six to nine weeks; however, the teacher and the team may be flexible and specify a different time period, according to the needs of the individual student. When a teacher implements a new method for teaching a student, the teacher and team must carefully monitor the student's response to that intervention. The team may also recommend that more than one research-based intervention be implemented if the first attempt fails to show improvement (Cohen & Spenciner, 2007); however, care should be taken that unnecessary delays are not made to the referral process. Contact with the classroom teachers should be an ongoing part of the PIT activities to determine whether the recommended interventions are being implemented properly

Student: _____ Grade: _____ Teacher: _____

G O A L

Intervention Goal # _____

What observable, measurable changes do we want to see in the student?

_____

_____

What criteria for success will be used? _____

_____

I N T E R V E N T I O N – F O L L O W U P

Curricular Changes	Environmental Adjustments
Instructional Adaptations	Behavioral Strategies

Who is responsible for implementing the plan? _____

What supports will be available? _____

_____

How will effectiveness be evaluated? _____

When will the team reconvene to review intervention? _____

Figure 4.2

Child Study Intervention Plan

From *The Prereferral Resource Guide,* by G. Buck, E. A. Polloway, J. R. Patton, and K. McConnell, in press, Austin, TX: Pro-Ed.

and whether they are successful. However, at the end of the agreed-upon period, the team more formally evaluates the success of the prereferral intervention to determine whether the intervention goals have been met and whether a formal referral for a comprehensive special education evaluation is warranted. Note that the purpose of the prereferral team is to review concerns and design interventions, rather than to pass cases on for special education consideration. Far too often in the past, the easy action to take for a student who exhibited learning or behavioral problems was to refer him or her immediately to special education. The learning and behavioral needs of many students can, and should, be handled in the general education classroom. To do so, however, requires a system (i.e., prereferral) that offers a timely response to teachers' dilemmas and fulfills a collaborative role of providing consultation and ongoing support to benefit the student.

The prereferral process appears to be both effective in helping teachers and students and efficient in forwarding referrals of only those students who need specialized services. In research settings, the PITs have also been shown to reduce unnecessary testing

Members of a child study team may help develop prereferral interventions for students having problems.

and placements in special education, improve student performance and improve the attitude of teachers and their skill in handling more challenging students (Truscott et al., 2005).

The Special Education Process

Unfortunately, prereferral intervention sometimes is not able to achieve the goals that were set by the PIT after reasonable and robust interventions have been tried. Moreover, in some instances in which students display significant learning and behavioral problems, prereferral intervention is never attempted. Regardless of how a student gets to this particular stage, a referral for special education consideration marks the official beginning of the special education process.

Figure 4.3 provides a flowchart of how the special education process works. Inherent in this process are specific timelines and actions that must be followed to be compliant with federal and state law. This figure relates closely to the major elements presented in Figure 4.1 (see page 98) and provides more detail of the formal special education process. Again, this formal referral to evaluate the student to determine eligibility for special education services follows the lack of success of the prereferral intervention as determined by the PIT or suggests that the difficulties are too severe to delay the special education process.

Formal Referral

The format of the written referral varies across school systems; however, the form generally contains basic descriptive information (e.g., birth date, grade) and evidence of the severity and duration of the problem(s) in the classroom. Individual school systems may require that documentation be written as a summary or ask that evidence be attached; the information needed usually includes:

- work samples showing areas of weakness
- samples of classroom tests
- behavioral assessment/behavioral log
- report cards
- test information from cumulative folder
- description and results of prereferral intervention
- parent information, including summaries of contact documenting their concerns

At the point of referral, a new team is formulated to work together throughout the special education process. This team is referred to as the **Individualized Education Program** (IEP) team. The federal regulations of IDEA stress that every school district ensure that the IEP team assembled for each student with a disability includes the following:

1. the parents of a child with a disability
2. at least one regular education teacher of the child (if the child is, or may be, participating in the regular education environment)
3. at least one special education teacher or, where appropriate, at least one special education provider of the child
4. a representative of the local educational agency who
   a. is qualified to provide, or supervises the provision of, specially designed instruction to meet the unique needs of children with disabilities
   b. is knowledgeable about the general education curriculum
   c. is knowledgeable about the availability of resources of the local education agency

| *Figure* 4.3 | **Special Education Process** |

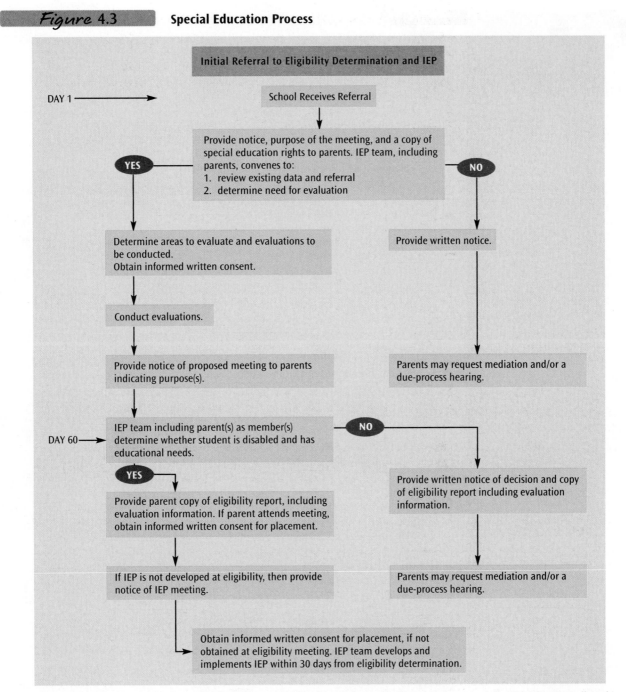

Note: The 2004 reauthorization of IDEA allows schools to pursue evaluation through due process if parents deny permission. Schools are not allowed to pursue due process if the parents deny consent for services.

5. an individual who can interpret the instructional implications of evaluation results
6. other individuals who have knowledge or special expertise regarding the child, including related services personnel as appropriate
7. whenever appropriate, the child with a disability

Submitting a referral to a designated school official initiates a set of formal activities. First and foremost, a letter is sent to the parents to notify them of the referral, to inform them of their rights throughout the special education process, and to invite them and their child, if appropriate, to participate along with "other qualified professionals" in the first meeting of their child's IEP team. Figure 4.4 provides a sample of a letter that

CEC STANDARDS

CEC 1: Foundations

PRAXIS

PRAXIS II: Legal & Societal Issues

CROSS-REFERENCE

Methods for modifying the curriculum and instruction in elementary and secondary general education settings are described in Chapters 15 and 16. Many of these techniques are appropriate at the prereferral stage.

Figure 4.4   **A Sample IEP Invitation**

Dear Parents,

As you know, we recently determined that your daughter Abigail was eligible for an Individualized Education Program (IEP) to meet her special academic, social, behavioral, physical, or other needs. She is now legally entitled to: (1) special education, which is specially designed instruction to meet those unique needs; (2) related services such as transportation or physical therapy, which may be necessary to enable her to benefit from her special education; and (3) any necessary services, aids, modifications or accommodations if and when she is in regular education classes, including support for the personnel working with her.

We need to have a meeting to plan Abigail's IEP. At this meeting, we will discuss her strengths, her unique characteristics and needs, the services appropriate to address these, and the ways we should judge how well the services are helping Abigail to make progress at school. You are a full and equal partner with the school personnel in deciding what will be in Abigail's IEP. The enclosed sample IEP for a fictional child will give you an idea of what kinds of things an IEP might include. Please give some thought to these matters ahead of time, so we can exchange ideas at the meeting.

You are welcome to bring anyone you wish to the meeting. Some parent groups (e.g., Learning Disabilities Association, Association for Retarded Citizens) have advocates available to attend IEP meetings with parents. You may choose to have Abigail present for all or part of the meeting. It is often useful for the student to participate, and she may feel more involved with and committed to her IEP objectives. If you decide Abigail won't be at the meeting, please consider bringing a picture of her to remind us all that the only purpose of the meeting is to plan an educational program just for her. Pam Brown, who helped evaluate Abigail, and Nancy Janes, her regular classroom teacher, will be at this first IEP meeting. The principal, Denise Smith, will attend the IEP meeting as the district representative, and I will be there as Abigail's Special Education teacher.

We have tentatively scheduled this meeting for Feb. 2 at 3:00 P.M. here at McAuliffe Elementary. If this is not convenient, please call and we will arrange another time. In addition to the sample IEP, I have enclosed a brochure explaining your legal rights. Please look it over. If you have any questions, we can discuss them at the meeting.

Sincerely,

Anita Hall

Anita Hall
Abigail's Teacher

From: *Better IEPs: How to Develop Legally Correct and Educationally Useful Programs* (p. 119), B. D. Bateman and M. A. Linden, 2006. Verona, WI: Attainment.

meets all the legal requirements and provides a warm invitation to the parents. This meeting is usually held at the child's school and is scheduled at a mutually agreed upon time. Some schools hold meetings in the evenings or on the weekend to accommodate working parents. Although face-to-face meetings are always desirable, computer conferencing or conference calls have been used to facilitate parental participation.

At this meeting a decision is made by the IEP team as to whether a comprehensive evaluation should be undertaken (i.e., whether the referral has merit). If the decision is yes, then the parents are asked for written consent for the evaluation. The school is allowed up to sixty days to collect the needed information and to complete the required and requested assessment. At the next meeting of the IEP team, this data is used to determine whether the child meets the eligibility criteria for a particular disability as developed within that state and whether the child needs special education and/or related services.

Determination of Eligibility

If the decision to proceed with a **comprehensive evaluation** is affirmed, and parents consent, then the eligibility phase begins. The evaluation must be comprehensive enough to gather functional, developmental, and academic data sufficient to determine if the student has one of the disabilities covered by IDEA, to identify his or her educational needs and present levels of performance, and to determine if the student needs special education and/or related services (Bateman & Linden, 2006). The assessment instruments and techniques used, along with the personnel who will administer them, will vary greatly within and across states. Nevertheless, the evaluation process and any assessment battery chosen must be sensitive to age, grade level, and culture, and must be comprehensive and flexible enough to address the learning and behavioral difficulties of any student referred. Because the vast majority of students who are disabled are referred during the elementary years, the process is often less visible at the secondary level. However, since the demands of the middle school and high school settings are more complex, prereferral intervention and referral must be available and operative at these levels as well.

During the eligibility determination phase, the general education teacher will likely be called on to provide background information on the student. The teacher might be interviewed or asked to complete rating scales or checklists or participate in functional assessments. On occasion, the teacher will be asked to conduct some observations of a student. The teacher will likely be asked to provide samples of the student's academic work. Additional aspects of the evaluation process are discussed more fully at the end of the chapter.

Ultimately, the IEP team, "a team of qualified professionals and the parent," is responsible for making the eligibility decision. After the pertinent assessment information is compiled on the student, the team meets again, this time to examine the data to determine whether a disability exists, whether the student meets the state eligibility guidelines for a particular disability, and whether, even if the student has a disability, the student needs special education services. At this point, a determination of whether a student qualifies for special education is made (see Figure 4.3). If the answer is yes, and the parents agree (providing written consent for placement), the team can proceed with the development of the IEP and placement decisions. If the team wishes to wait, the IEP and placement decision must be completed within thirty days of the eligibility meeting. Placement should immediately follow determination of eligibility unless issues such as transportation must be addressed.

The IEP team can pursue an evaluation of a child through due process without the parents written consent; however, the 2004 reauthorization of IDEA notes that children will not be determined eligible for services if their parents do not consent to placement. Placement can also be denied if the child's problems are determined to result from a lack of appropriate instruction in reading or math, or from limited English proficiency. One of the most challenging tasks often faced by an IEP team is making the determination of whether the academic difficulties are the direct result of language or learning differences (Salend & Salinas, 2003).

Individualized Education Program

An IEP is a requirement for every child determined eligible to receive special education services. It is a well-described legal document under IDEA and contains a summary of a child's strengths, limitations, and needs, and the corresponding special education and related services planned to address those needs. This written document is reviewed at

CEC STANDARDS

CEC 1: Foundations

least once annually thereafter. The overriding concept behind the IEP is that all educational programming should be driven by the unique needs of the student and may involve changing methodology or delivery of instruction or adapting content to ensure the child's access to and participation in the general curriculum (Bateman & Linden, 2006). Further, the plan should be written to allow the child "reasonable educational benefit." If academic, behavioral, or social needs are identified, then goals need to be written to address these needs. In other words, services are determined by individual need, not by availability. Every individual on the IEP team, including the parents, should ideally come to the meeting with personal notes on the child's unique needs and related goals and services they would like to see included on the IEP. Any differences are resolved through the team process; any issues that cannot be resolved are continued under the due process procedures described in Chapter 1.

Federal Regulations for IEPs   The 2004 IDEA Reauthorization specifies the content for IEPs in general, the content for transition services for students beginning no later than age sixteen, and the special requirements for plans for young children from birth to age three. The law also requires that a student be notified of the transfer of his or her rights at least one year prior to reaching the age of majority specified by law in his or her state. For example, in many states, the **age of majority** is eighteen; so, by this age, the student must sign the IEP verifying that this right has been explained. After this birthday, students can make decisions regarding school, independent living, and work. In extreme cases, when students are judged incapable of making their own decisions and protecting their own rights, the courts will award guardianship to parents or another advocate. One method of developing independence is to encourage and train

Personal Spotlight

Pam Underwood
First Year Special Education Teacher

Pam Underwood graduated from the University of Alabama at Birmingham a decade later than she originally planned She had big dreams and excellent scholarships when she left high school to pursue a degree in social work, but the diagnosis of a disease she was told was incurable and her poor health led her to drop out of college. Thirteen years later, Pam had beaten the disease, and she returned to college full time. She raised her daughter as a single parent and still kept an A average. In fact Pam was recognized as the Outstanding Undergraduate in the Collaborative Teacher Program and was also honored as the Most Outstanding Undergraduate Campus-wide.

Although she received several offers of teaching positions, Pam chose to work with the local inner city school system that has challenging students and working conditions that are not always optimal. She decided that those students needed her, and she was up to the job. By chance I interviewed Pam at the end of her first day with students in the middle school setting in which she had been assigned. She admitted that she was overwhelmed and had a big headache! She had wanted to begin teaching right away, but found that she had several students needing to be tested first and at least one student that had been tested by last year's teacher but needed an IEP meeting right

away. She wanted to start some collaborative teaching, but paperwork seemed to be most pressing.

Alabama recently revised the IEP process to include a standards-based format that had been added since she had her college class on writing IEPs. Pam liked the new practice of using goals from the general education curriculum, because she thought it helped special and general education teachers get on the "same page" faster. However, Pam did admit that with the added step, her first IEP took her a day and a half to write. She credited her internship experience as preparing her the most for her job because in addition to teaching, she was able to follow a student from the initial referral throughout the special education process. Although college was difficult, she was grateful for all those challenges. She said, "This is the real deal! I am not in school anymore, but I still have a lot to learn!" Now with a 13 year old, a one year old, and a challenging new job, Pam has also begun graduate school. She says she plans to make it one day at a time.

students with disabilities to assume leadership at the IEP meeting and participate in the decision making process (Torgesen, Miner, & Shen, 2004). This approach will be discussed in greater detail in Chapter 16.

The general requirements of an IEP for students between ages three and twenty-one are as follows:

1. a statement of the child's present levels of academic achievement and functional performance, including
    a. how the child's disability affects the child's involvement and progress in the general education curriculum
    b. for preschool children, as appropriate, how the disability affects the child's participation in appropriate activities
    c. for children with disabilities who take alternative assessments aligned to alternative achievement standards, a description of benchmarks or short-term objectives
2. a statement of measurable annual goals, including academic and functional goals, designed to meet the child's needs and to enable the child to be involved in and make progress in the general education curriculum
3. a description of how the child's progress toward meeting the annual goals will be measured and when periodic reports on the progress the child is making toward meeting the annual goals will be provided
4. a statement of the special education and related services and supplementary aids and services, based on peer reviewed research to the extent practicable, to be provided to the child and a statement of the program modifications or supports that will be provided for the child
5. an explanation of the extent, if any, to which the child will not participate with nondisabled children in the regular class and other activities
6. a statement of any individual appropriate accommodations that are necessary to measure the academic achievement and functional performance of the child on state and districtwide assessments; and if the IEP team determines that the child should take an alternate assessment on a particular state and districtwide assessment of student achievement, a statement of why the child cannot participate and the particular alternative assessment selected
7. the projected date for the beginning of the services and modifications, and the anticipated frequency, location, and duration of those services and modifications
8. beginning not later than the first IEP to be in effect when the child is sixteen and updated annually thereafter, components related to the transition of the child

Other special considerations include these:

- For students whose behavior impedes their learning or that of others, positive behavioral strategies, supports, and interventions, when appropriate (described in more detail later in this chapter).
- For students who are blind or visually impaired, Braille instruction, unless the IEP team determines that use of Braille is not appropriate.
- For students with hearing impairments or language and communication needs, opportunities for communication with peers and teachers in each student's language and communication mode, including direct instruction in the mode.

Key Components of an IEP   Following is a brief description of major components in an IEP. Figure 4.5 provides a format for an IEP that addresses each IEP requirement discussed. (A sample IEP using this format is included in Appendix A.)

Present level of performance (PLOP)   The first major component in an IEP is the present level of educational performance section (PLOP). This provides the written summary of assessment data on a student's current levels of functioning that subsequently serves as the basis for establishing annual goals. The information should include data for each

CROSS-REFERENCE

Transition for adolescents from school to life after school is discussed again in Chapter 16.

CONSIDER THIS

See if you can locate each of the required IEP components in Figure 4.5.

Figure 4.5   **Individualized Education Program (IEP)**

Student's name _____   IEP meeting date _____

Date of birth _____   Grade _____   Case manager _____

*Copies of this IEP will circulate among staff members who are working with this student. Please observe the federal and state laws that protect the student's right to confidentiality of education records. Do **not** share with unauthorized persons, and do **not** include such sensitive information as disability category or IQ.*

Special factors to consider	**Participation in statewide or other large-scale assessments**
For all students, consider: ☐ The student's strengths ☐ Concerns of the parent(s) for enhancing the student's education ☐ Need for assistive technology devices and services ☐ Communication needs	The following individual appropriate accommodations are necessary to measure the student's academic achievement and functional performance on state and districtwide assessments:
If behavior impedes learning of student or others, consider: ☐ Positive behavioral interventions and support strategies, including positive behavioral interventions ☐ Other strategies to address behavior	The IEP team has determined that the student should take an alternative assessment because:
If student has limited English proficiency, consider: ☐ Language needs as they relate to student's IEP	
If student is blind or visually impaired, consider: ☐ Instruction in use of Braille (unless IEP team decides that instruction in Braille is not appropriate)	The IEP team has determined that the student should take the following alternative assessment:
If a student is deaf or hard of hearing, consider: ☐ Opportunities for direct communication with peers and professionals in student's language and communication mode ☐ Opportunities or direct instruction in student's language and communication mode	

Additional comments about this student relevant to developing an appropriate IEP:

CEC STANDARDS

CEC 8: Assessment

CEC STANDARDS

CEC 8: Assessment

priority area in which instructional support is needed. Depending on the individual student, consideration might be given to reading, math, and other academic skills, written and oral communication skills, vocational strengths and needs, social skills, behavioral patterns, study skills, self-help skills and other life skills, and motor skills. While the special education teacher may have more of a role in reporting the evaluation results, the input from parents, general education teachers, and other team members into this student profile is critical.

Performance levels can be provided in various forms, such as formal and informal assessment data, behavioral descriptions, and specific abilities delineated by checklists or skill sequences. Functional summary statements of an individual's strengths and weaknesses draw on information from a variety of sources rather than relying on a sin-

Figure 4.5   **Continued**

Transition services

The IEP team has developed a transition plan because
☐ although the student will not yet be 16 during the effective period of this IEP, the team has determined that the transition planning is appropriate at this time,
☐ the student will be 16 during the effective period of this IEP, or
☐ the student has reached the age of 16.

Transition services must address the student's individual needs, taking into account his/her strengths, preferences, and interests as described here:

Based on these factors, this IEP includes services and appropriate measurable postsecondary goals on page _____, that draw upon age-appropriate transition assessments related to training, education, employment, and, where appropriate, independent living skills.

The transition services, including the course of study needed to assist the student in reaching those goals, include:
☐ instruction
☐ related services
☐ community experiences
☐ the development of employment and other post-school adult living objectives
☐ If appropriate, acquisition of daily living skills and functional vocational evaluation

The student has been informed of the IDEA rights that will transfer to him/her upon reaching the age of majority.

Student's signature

Progress report

Parents will receive reports on the student's progress toward annual goals through:
☐ IEP progress report completed per the report card schedule on these dates:

_____   _____   _____   _____

☐ Other progress reporting systems as follows:

Progress toward each annual goal must be measured through the criteria and evaluation measures established for each goal.

Participation with nondisabled students

Explanation of extent to which the student will **not** participate with nondisabled children:
(a) In regular classes:

(b) In special education services:

IEP team members

Signature	Position

---

gle source. Test scores in math, for example, might be combined with a description of how the child performed on a curriculum-based measure such as a computational checklist or an observation from the parents.

In general, the phrasing used to define levels of performance should be positive and describe things the child can do. For example, the same information is conveyed by the two following statements, but the former demonstrates the more positive approach: "The student can identify 50 percent of the most frequently used occupational vocabulary words," versus "The student does not know half of the most frequently used occupational vocabulary words." Appropriately written performance levels provide a broad range of data to help generate relevant and appropriate annual goals. Federal requirements also mandate that the IEP include some sense of how the disability affects the student's

 **Continued**		
Unique educational needs, characteristics, and measured present levels of academic achievement and functional performance (PLOPs) (Including how the disability affects student's ability to participate and progress in the general curriculum)	Special education, related services, and supplemental aids and services (based on peer-reviewed research to the extent practicable); assistive technology and modifications or personnel support (Including anticipated starting date, frequency, duration and location for each)	Measurable annual goals and short-term objectives (progress markers),[1] including academic and functional goals to enable students to be involved in and make progress in the general curriculum and to meet other needs resulting from the disability (Including progress measurement method for each goal)

From: *Better IEPs: How to Develop Legally Correct and Educationally Useful Programs* (pp. 124–126), by B. D. Bateman and M. A. Linden 2006. Verona, WI: Attainment.

[1]For students who take an alternative assessment and are assessed against other than grade level standards, the IEP **must** include short-term objectives (progress markers). For other students, the IEP **may** include short-term objectives. The IEP **must** for all students clearly articulate how the student's progress will be measured, and that progress must be reported to parents at designated intervals.

involvement and progress in the general curriculum. An example of a PLOP statement that conforms to these criteria is presented in Figure 4.6. (See Appendixes A and B for more examples of PLOPs and other components of an IEP.)

CEC STANDARDS

CEC 1: Foundations

PRAXIS

PRAXIS II: Delivery of Services to Students with Disabilities

Measurable annual goals   The second, and central, IEP instructional component is annual goals. Each student's goals should be individually determined to address unique needs and abilities. Since it is obviously impossible to predict the precise amount of progress a student will make in a year, goals should be reasonable projections of what the student will accomplish. To develop realistic expectations, teachers can consider a number of variables, including the chronological age of the child, the expected rate of learning, and past and current learning profiles.

Annual goals should be measurable, positive, student-oriented, and relevant (Polloway, Patton, & Serna, 2001). Measurable goals provide a basis for evaluation. Statements should use terms that denote action and can therefore be operationally defined (e.g., pronounce, write), rather than vague, general language that confounds evaluation and observer agreement (e.g., know, understand). Positive goals provide an appropriate direction for instruction. Avoiding negative goals creates an atmosphere conducive to good home–school relationships and makes it easier to chart student progress. Goals should also be oriented to the student. Developing a student's skills is the intent, and the only measure of effectiveness should be what is learned, rather than what is taught. Finally, goals must be relevant to the individual's actual needs in terms of remediation and other desirable skills.

Prior to the 2004 reauthorization of IDEA, all IEPs had to include **short-term objectives**. The 2004 reauthorization requires short-term objectives in IEPs only for students with disabilities who complete alternative assessments aligned with alternative achievement standards. While the reauthorization does not require short-term objectives in IEPs, developing them is a good way to operationalize the annual goals for students. Since the requirement to monitor progress and report to parents is still required by IDEA 2004, the development of short-term objectives would facilitate this effort. **As a result, short-term objectives will be provided throughout this text as examples of how goals should be broken down for instructional purposes.** The four criteria applied to annual goals are also appropriate to short-term objectives. Since objectives are more narrow in focus, an objective's measurability should be enhanced with a criterion for mastery. For example, a math short-term objective might read, "Given twenty multiplication facts using numbers 1–5, John will give correct answers for 90 percent."

These benchmarks or objectives should be obtained from the general education curriculum being used by the student's nondisabled peers. The IEP included in Appendix A is from a state that connects each goal and objective to a specific, numbered goal from the general education curriculum. Figure 4.7 contains a portion of four IEPs using the IEP format included earlier in this chapter (see Figure 4.5); this figure provides examples of academic and nonacademic challenges. Throughout Chapters 6–11, the IEP goals and objectives feature will illustrate the goals and objectives portion of the IEP for the students featured in the chapter-opening vignettes. Remember that no IEP is perfect—it reflects the thinking of a group and reflects a team effort!

Special Education and Related Services IDEA provides a general paragraph describing commonly used related services, such as transportation and speech, occupational, and physical therapy; the more recent regulations also provide an expanded list with definitions. However, many of our most effective education strategies and related services have been spelled out in litigation judgments. Many of the examples cited by Bateman and Linden (2006) came from federal judges; these include:

- small classes
- computer access
- texts on tape
- highly structured environment
- a need for reteaching and repetition
- frequent teacher feedback
- distraction reduced environment
- schoolwide positive behavior support program
- extended school year
- intensive, effective remedial reading
- a peer tutor

No list should be considered exhaustive, because the key is to identify any service or special education technique required for the child with a disability to benefit from special education. Parents as well as other members of the IEP team should come to the IEP meeting with notes on how they would like the child's educational program

Sammy is a seventh-grade student whose disability inhibits his ability to understand vocabulary associated with occupations and employment. Sammy can define orally thirty-seven out of fifty-two words correctly from a list of the most frequently used occupational vocabulary words.

Figure 4.6 **Example of a present-level-of-educational-performance statement**

From *Understanding Occupational Vocabulary*, by S. Fisher, G. M. Clark, and J. R. Patton, 2003. Austin, TX: Pro-Ed.

CEC STANDARDS
CEC 1: Foundations

CEC STANDARDS
CEC 1: Foundations

PRAXIS
PRAXIS II: Delivery of Services to Students with Disabilities

Parental involvement in the development of the individualized education program is both a legal requirement as well as an important aspect in the design of appropriate school programs.

Figure 4.7 Partial IEP Academic Examples

Unique educational needs, characteristics, and measured present levels of academic achievement and functional performance (PLOPs)	Special education, related services, and supplemental aids and services (based on peer-reviewed research to the extent practicable); assistive technology and modifications or personnel support	Measurable annual goals and short-term objectives (progress markers),[1] including academic and functional goals to enable students to be involved in and make progress in the general curriculum and to meet other needs resulting from the disability
(Including how the disability affects student's ability to participate and progress in the general curriculum)	(Including anticipated starting date, frequency, duration, and location for each)	(Including progress measurement method for each goal)
James James is a very bright sixteen-year-old who is functionally illiterate, i.e., cannot distinguish "ladies" from "gentlemen" on doors. By shrewd guessing and a few sight words he can score from 1st to high 2nd grade on comprehension tests. His word attack skills are few, random, and ineffective.	Intensive, systematic, synthetic phonics reading instruction, 1:1 or small group (no more than four with a teacher or aide trained in the methodology used. Minimum one hour daily, plus same methodology to be used in all language arts areas consistently. Resource room and classroom.	End 1st 9 weeks: James will be able to decode all regular CVC words at 50 WPM w/ 0 errors. End 2nd 9 weeks: James will write and read the Dolch 220. End 3rd 9 weeks: James will read from 3rd-grade material at 60 WPM w/ 0-2 errors. End 4th 9 weeks: James will score above 3.5 grade equivalent on 2 standardized reading tests.
Todd Todd's reading level is between the 4th- and 5th-grade level. His oral reading fluency rate is 70 words per minute with 5–6 errors, in 4th-grade material.	Small group instruction from a reading specialist 30 minutes per day in a resource room beginning 11/24.	**Goal:** In 3 one-minute timed passages, Todd will increase his oral reading fluency to 150 WPM with 0-1 error by 11/24. **STO 1:** In 3 one-minute timed passages, Todd will increase his oral reading fluency to 90 WPM with 2–3 errors by 4/24. **STO 2:** In 3 one-minute timed passages, Todd will increase his oral reading fluency to 110 WPM with 1–2 errors by 9/24.
Tarah Tarah's expressive language skills are underdeveloped, although she scores in the average range on nonlanguage measures of intelligence. She doesn't initiate conversation and answers questions with 1- or 2-word sentences. She has a spoken vocabulary of approximately 50–100 words. Her articulation is only slightly delayed (r, l not yet perfect) at the age of 7.	One-on-one direct instruction in vocabulary provided by a speech and language pathologist (SLP) three times a week/20 min. a session. Small group, SLP-led discussions with same-age peers twice a week/20 min. a session.	**Goal:** Tarah will initiate conversation with peers at least twice a day. 1. By November, Tarah will initiate a conversation with peers or with an adult on at least one occasion per week as monitored by teacher, instructional assistants, parent volunteers, recess teachers, special ed. teacher, or SLP. 2. By March, Tarah will initiate conversation with same-age peers during speech class, or during work or play activities at least once a day.
Jeremy Jeremy lacks understanding of the processes of multiplication and division and does not know the multiplication facts beyond x2. **PLOP:** Jeremy scored 10 correct problems out of 100 on the district comprehensive test of multiplication and division.	1. 20 minutes per school day, small group (< 5) instruction with remedial math specialist in the resource room. 2. Computerized drill and practice in multiplication and division for 15 minutes each school day.	**Goal:** By the end of the school year, Jeremy will be able to complete 85 percent of multiplication and division problems correctly, on the district math test. **Obj. 1:** By Nov. 15 Jeremy will be able to complete a test of two-digit multiplication with at least 22 out of 25 score. **Obj. 2:** By Feb. 15 Jeremy will be able to complete a test of simple division with at least a 22 out of 25 score.

[1]For students who take an alternative assessment and are assessed against other than grade level standards, the IEP **must** include short-term objectives (progress markers). For other students, the IEP **may** include short-term objectives. The IEP **must** for all students clearly articulate how the student's progress will be measured, and that progress must be reported to parents at designated intervals.

From *Better IEPs: How to Develop Legally Correct and Educationally Useful Programs* (4th ed., pp. 160–162), by B. D. Bateman and M. L. Linden, 2006. Verona, WI: Attainment. Adapted with permission.

individualized to meet his or her unique needs. Bateman and Linden (2006) share their concern that computer software is being used in some locations that in effect controls the development and the format of an IEP. Any predetermination of services, goals, or placements based on the disability, not on the individual, is totally outside of the intent of the law. For example, a few years ago, if you were a student with mental retardation, you were usually placed in a self-contained class where the focus was on self-care skills, and your only experience in the regular classroom was usually for music or art instruction. A student with learning disabilities was seldom given instruction in self-help or social skills, even it they were mentioned in the PLOP as a need.

The law also requires that special education methods and other services be based on peer-reviewed research to the extent that it is practical. It is important for the members of the IEP team to be familiar with these legal requirements and the multitude of services available with the potential to secure an effective individualized education plan (Downing, 2004). Old methods that are simply within a teacher's comfort level must now be reevaluated; this process should result in more effective education, especially in reading and behavioral support strategies where research has validated many new techniques. The IEP must also provide documentation of the amount of service to be provided (e.g., speech therapy, three thirty-minute sessions weekly), and the date the service is to begin, the duration, and the location.

Role of the general education teacher in the IEP   Although IEPs are supposed to be jointly developed by the whole IEP team, in practice the task has often largely fallen to special education teachers. Some abuses of the system have occurred in which general education teachers were asked to "sign off" on an IEP or had to ask to see an IEP for one of their students! This is clearly not the intent of the law; in fact, the 1999 changes in IDEA require that teachers not in attendance at the IEP meeting be given a copy of the document. This is an important practice because a student with a disability will almost always require some accommodation or modification to benefit from regular classroom activities, and these should be known to all teachers (Bateman & Linden, 2006).

The role of general education teachers in the development of IEPs will vary with each child, often depending on how much time the child is in the general classroom. The 2004 reauthorization of IDEA states that a regular education teacher of the child, as a member of the IEP team, shall, to the extent appropriate, participate in the development of the IEP of the child, including the determination of appropriate positive behavioral interventions and supports, the determination of supplementary aids and services needed, the need for program modifications or content adaptations, and support for school personnel.

Ideally, the classroom teacher is very involved in the IEP meeting; this is especially true with the current emphasis on access to the general education curriculum. When the general education teacher is not in attendance, a different means of teacher input should be developed (e.g., a pre-IEP informal meeting or note); otherwise, the document may not reflect the student's needs in the inclusive classroom. In particular, teachers should keep the goals and benchmarks at hand so that the IEP can influence instructional programs.

An IEP's annual goals and short-term objectives, when included, ultimately should be reflected in instructional plans in the classroom; however, they are not intended to be used as weekly plans, let alone daily plans. Teachers should refer to the document periodically to ensure that instruction is consistent with the long-term needs of the student. When significant variance is noted, it may become the basis for the IEP team to reconvene to make a change in instructional strategy or even the goals of the IEP. Bateman and Linden (2006) indicate that teachers must not lose sight of the spirit of individualization that should guide the IEP process. Teachers need to view the documents not just as a process of legal compliance but also as a tool for focusing on the unique needs of a child and meeting those needs through specially designed instruction.

The IEP should be written to ensure access to the general education curriculum and to allow the student to benefit educationally. Unless guided by the rationale and spirit that infused the original development of the IEP concept, the process can degenerate into a mere bookkeeping activity. Instead, well-thought-out IEPs should form the foundation for individually designed educational programs for students with disabilities. The teacher should continue to include parents in the implementation and evaluation of the IEP. Extra effort is required, especially if the parents have limited English skills, but the effect on outcomes is significant.

Behavioral Intervention Planning

The requirement for **behavioral intervention planning** (BIP) was introduced in the 1997 amendments to IDEA and remains in the 2004 reauthorization. Although the fundamental concept is not new and has been used in various settings previously, the fact that BIPs were required stunned many school-based professionals.

In general, behavioral intervention plans are required for (1) students whose behaviors impede their learning or that of others; (2) students who put peers at risk because of their behaviors; and (3) students with disabilities for whom serious disciplinary action is being taken. A BIP is required on any student who is dismissed from school for more than ten days for misbehavior. The major assumptions underlying the development of BIPs include the following points:

- Behavior problems are best addressed when the causes (i.e., function) of the behaviors are known.
- Interventions that are based on positive intervention strategies are more effective than punitive ones.
- Dealing with difficult behaviors demands a team approach.

Many teachers reacted negatively to the notion of having to develop behavioral plans, citing the lack of time as the leading reason for their lack of enthusiasm. However, students with behavior problems require some time and effort. Dedicating time and effort to understanding the true function of a behavior and then intervening appropriately seems like a better way to expend effort than reacting to inappropriate behavior on an ongoing basis.

The BIP Process   The behavioral intervention planning process typically includes the following specific steps (Fad et al., 2000):

- Collect background information to provide context for the presenting problems.
- Conduct a functional behavioral assessment (FBA), where you analyze the relationship of the target behavior to environmental antecedents and consequences and you explore the purpose of the behavior.
- Determine whether the behavior in question is directly related to the student's disability (i.e., whether the behavior is a manifestation of the disability).
- Determine specific goals that teach and support positive alternative behavior and decrease or eliminate negative behavior.
- Develop intervention strategies, preferably of a positive nature, that will be used and identify the person(s) who will be responsible for implementation.
- Implement the plan and evaluate its effectiveness.
- Use information from the implementation of the intervention to revisit the assessment information as a basis for further intervention efforts.

The topic of behavioral intervention planning is revisited in Chapters 6 and 14. A sample of a completed BIP is shown in Figure 4.8.

Role of the General Education Teacher in the BIP Process   General education teachers can be involved in all aspects of the BIP process. During the first stage of collecting background information, the general education teacher plays a crucial role in supplying

| *Figure 4.8* | **Behavioral Intervention Plan (BIP)** |

Specific Goal(s)	Proposed Intervention(s)	Person(s) Responsible	Methods	Criterion	Schedule	
					Date	Code
1. Casey will increase respectful language in class, including saying "yes, sir" or "yes, ma'am" when requested to do something.	1. Contract for • positive comments • saying "yes, ma'am" or "yes, sir" • refrain from verbal threats	1. Student Teachers Counselor	–Contract forms –Discipline referrals	1. Respectful language 90% of time	9/1/99 10/15/99 12/1/99 1/15/00 3/1/00 4/15/00 6/1/00	
2. Casey will decrease verbal threats and teasing.	2. Delay release from classroom to hallway by 5 minutes	2. Teachers		2. Contract • positive comments: 5 per day • "yes" responses: 80% of time • verbal threats: fewer than 8 per 6 weeks		
3. Casey will decrease aggressive incidents toward peers (fighting, hitting, tripping).	3. Continuum of responses to aggression: • Parent–Asst. Principal conference and suspension to AEP for 3 days • Go to antiaggression classes • Notify probation officer	3. Parents Assistant Principal Counselor		3. Aggression: No incidents in next 6 weeks		

Evaluation

Progress Codes:
/ = ongoing
X = mastered
D = discontinued

These goals were developed with consideration of the following information:

☐ Parent concerns regarding special circumstances: _____ _____ _____

☐ Teacher/administrator concerns regarding special circumstances: _____ _____ _____

☑ Outside agency/professional concerns regarding special circumstances: _____ Probation officer requires notification. _____

From *Behavioral Intervention Planning: Completing a Functional Behavioral Assessment and Developing a Behavioral Intervention Plan* (p. 21), by K. Fad, J. R. Patton, and E. A. Polloway, 2000. Austin, TX: Pro-Ed.

classroom-related information about the behaviors under review. Although the FBA is likely to be conducted by someone other than the classroom teacher, on occasion the general education teacher might be asked to be involved in generating it. Classroom teachers are quite likely to be involved in the identification of the positive interventions, strategies, and services to be used because many students requiring a BIP will receive their education in a general education classroom. Last, classroom teachers will be intricately involved in monitoring the effectiveness of the interventions when students with BIPs are in their classes.

PRAXIS

PRAXIS II: Delivery of Instruction to Students with Disabilities

Transition Services

The 1990 amendments to the Education for All Handicapped Children Act (EHA) of 1975, which changed the name of the law to the Individuals with Disabilities Education Act (IDEA), had a significant effect on transition services. Up to this point, no federal mandate had existed for implementing transition planning. Under the amendments of 1990, 1999, and 2004, one of the purposes of the annual IEP meeting for students with disabilities, upon reaching sixteen years of age, is to plan for necessary transition services.

Definition of Transition Services   The 2004 reauthorization of IDEA defines transition services as a coordinated set of activities for a child with a disability that

1. Is designed to be within a results-oriented process that is focused on improving the academic and functional achievement of the child with a disability to facilitate the child's movement from school to postschool activities, including postsecondary education, vocational education, integrated employment (including supported employment), continuing and adult education, adult services, independent living, or community participation.
2. Is based on the individual child's needs, taking into account the child's strengths, preferences, and interests.
3. Includes instruction, related services, community experiences, the development of employment, and other postschool adult living objectives, and, when appropriate, acquisition of daily living skills and functional-vocational evaluation.

Essential Elements   Individual planning for transition services, as prescribed in the legislation and accompanying regulations, stresses a number of critical concepts. First, the student and his or her family need to be actively involved in the process, and the student's strengths as well as interests and preferences must be taken into account. Second, activities and services should be results-oriented—leading to improved academic and functional achievement to facilitate the movement from school to postschool life. Third, the complexity of adult life needs to be recognized and planned for. Any agency personnel who might be involved in or pay for a transition service should be invited to the transition IEP meetings; however, if cooperation is not forthcoming, schools are ultimately responsible for meeting the transitional needs of the student (Bateman & Linden, 2006). Unfortunately, the nature and quality of transition services vary widely from one school district to another across the country, ranging from minimal compliance activities to what could be considered best practices in transition (Patton, 2001).

IDEA 2004 requires that postsecondary goals that are appropriate and measurable and based on age-appropriate transition assessments, and the services needed to achieve those goals, be included in the IEP by the time the child turns sixteen. Also, one year before reaching majority age, the IEP must state that the child has been informed of his or her rights that will transfer to the child at the age of majority (in most states, age eighteen). Finally, schools are required to provide a summary of performance (SOP) to students and parents as the students exit high school. This report should include relevant information about current functional and academic skill levels, progress toward meeting the IEP transition goals, and recommendations to help the student meet the postsecondary goals (O'Leary, 2006).

Role of the General Education Teacher in the Transition Process   The general education teacher can contribute to the transition process in two primary ways. First, the classroom teacher, mindful of adult outcomes (i.e., the demands of everyday living) can integrate real-life topics of current or future importance into the existing curriculum, as a way to cover topics that will be relevant and meaningful to students in their classes (see Patton, Cronin, & Wood, 1999). Second, classroom teachers can participate by contributing information to the transition assessment phase. Here, teachers who know the academic, social, and behavioral competence of their students can provide valuable information to the transition planning process.

Assistive Technology

Assistive technology is broadly defined by IDEA as "any item, piece of equipment, or product system, whether acquired commercially off the shelf, modified, or customized, that is used to increase, maintain or improve the functional capabilities of a child with a disability" (excluding a medical device that is surgically implanted, or the replacement of such a device). Assistive technology must be a part of a child's IEP and must be provided if it is necessary to provide a free, appropriate public education. Assistive technology can be considered "low tech" and be as simple as using graph paper to help hold proper spacing during math problems, or "high tech" and consist of use of a computer to read text to a student. The following chapters will offer examples of assistive technology used effectively for students with disabilities.

Extended School Year Services

Another service to which some students with disabilities are entitled is summer school, or, more appropriately, "the extended school year." The provision of special education and related services beyond the normal school year and at no cost to the parents emerged as a way to ensure that a natural disruption of services (i.e., summer) did not interfere with a student's continued educational progress and that there was no "regression" or loss of skills. The IEP team determines whether summer programming is necessary for the provision of a "free, appropriate public education." Parents must be informed of their child's right to this service.

Annual Assessment of IEP and Reevaluation

Two additional critical features of the special education process are (1) the ongoing monitoring of a student's progress in special education, and (2) reevaluation to determine the continued need for special education and related services. By law, a student's IEP must be reviewed and revised on an annual basis. This annual review is essential for updating the student's goals and evaluating the overall results of the modifications and instructional plans implemented during the year. The IEP meeting when this topic is discussed should not only look closely at existing goals but also be open to the development of new goals in areas of need. For example, new goals may need to be written into the IEP during the transition assessment process. Further, the IEP team can identify areas needing instructional attention after examining a student's competence across a range of areas.

> **CEC STANDARDS**
>
> CEC 7: Instructional Planning

Reevaluation refers to testing to determine if a child is still eligible to receive special educational services. This must occur not more than once a year and at least once every three years, unless the parents and school agree it is not necessary.

Although being admitted to special education is too frequently a one-way street, many students can and should reach levels of academic competence whereby they will no longer need special education or related services. The process to dismiss students from special education can be politically charged. Some parents may not want the cessation of services for their son or daughter; some school-based professionals do not like to see services cease when they feel support may be needed to continue success in the general education curriculum. The benefits and ramifications of dismissal from special educational services should be considered carefully by the IEP team. However, it is ultimately the parents who can discontinue placement at any time.

Individualized Family Service Plan

The written plan for children from birth to age three and their families, the IFSP, serves as a guide for available early intervention services. The basic philosophy underlying the IFSP is that infants and toddlers with known or suspected disabilities, medical conditions, or other development issues are uniquely dependent on their families and can best be understood within the context of their families. Thus, the intent of the IFSP is to focus on the family unit and to support the natural care-giving role of families. Many of the components of the IFSP are the same as those of the IEP; however, they have several important differences. For example, the goals in the IFSP are called outcome statements, which reflect changes that families want to see for their child and for themselves. The outcome statements on the IFSP are family-centered rather than child-centered, as they are on the IEP. In addition, a service coordinator must be identified for each family. The coordinator is responsible for the implementation of the IFSP and coordination with other agencies and people. Finally, a transition plan must be included to support the child and family when moving to the next stage of services at age three.

Section 504 Eligibility and Planning

As noted in Chapter 1, Section 504 is an antidiscrimination statute. It prohibits discrimination against any individual because of a disability. It applies to any organization that receives federal funds and includes public and private schools.

Eligibility

Eligibility for Section 504 is based on a student having a physical or mental impairment that results in a substantial limitation in one or more major life activities (e.g., seeing, hearing, learning). A "substantial limitation" is related to two primary factors: severity of the impairment and duration (i.e., permanence of the condition).

As previously suggested, Section 504 rights should be a considered for any student who is referred for special education services but does not qualify under IDEA. For example, a student with a disability of a medical nature, such as epilepsy, might not require special education services and, therefore, would not be eligible for services under IDEA. However, this student does have a documented disability and might be eligible for protection under Section 504. Every public school should have a committee and process for handling 504 eligibility and planning activities. Schools should document that a logical and reasonable process for determining eligibility is used. A good plan is to have someone on staff who is knowledgeable about 504 and to develop a coherent system for addressing 504 queries Although not required by law, a written 504 eligibility determination form is a good practice for documentation.

Reasonable Accommodations

If a student is determined to be eligible for services under 504, schools are required to provide reasonable accommodations for the student in academic and nonacademic areas. Accommodations may range from providing extended time on tests for a student with ADHD to providing dry marker boards for a student with severe allergies to chalk dust. A student with epilepsy should not be held to the same standards for attendance if frequent seizures are responsible for the absences. A reasonable accommodation provided under Section 504 might include a more liberal attendance requirement. Most accommodations are easy to implement and do not cost much money. Some accommodations that require the use of technology may be more costly. See the Technology Today feature for some forms of technology that are inexpensive and some that would be expensive.

Typically, a written accommodation plan is developed that specifies the nature and scope of the accommodations to be implemented. This document differs greatly from an IEP because it has no specifically mandated components. As a result, many accommodation plan formats have emerged, ranging from very basic to semi-elaborate. Figure 4.9 is an example of a basic accommodation plan.

CONSIDER THIS

A relatively small number of people even know that Section 504 applies to students, and even fewer know what it means. What do you consider its most important points?

CEC STANDARDS

CEC 1: Foundations

PRAXIS

PRAXIS II: Understanding Exceptionalities

CONSIDER THIS

Why is a written accommodation plan important? What is its main function?

Technological Applications in the Special Education Process

Without question, technology pervades the full spectrum of the education in schools today. Significant changes can be seen in the curriculum (e.g., teaching keyboarding in grade 6 versus teaching it at the beginning of high school, as in previous times) and instruction (e.g., the large number of multimedia materials that are available commercially). Technology has had an impact on the various elements of the special education process, as discussed in this chapter and highlighted in Figure 4.1. Some selected examples of what is available today to improve the efficiency of requisite activities in the special education process are the following:

Identification of the presenting problem:

1. Videotaping capabilities to provide observational data.

2. Computerized assessment systems for collecting and graphing student performance.

Prereferral intervention:

1. Sophisticated school record management systems.

2. Software programs that assist in the compilation of data.

Formal referral and eligibility determination:

1. Systems for submitting referrals electronically.

2. Assessment instruments that can now be given using a computer.

3. Many assessment instruments that have computer scoring software.

Program planning and delivery:

1. Computer-based IEP systems.

2. Vast array of teacher utilities (grade books, activity-generating software—e.g., crossword puzzles, calendars).

3. Lesson plans and ideas available online.

4. Computer-based instruction systems (e.g., reading programs, brainstorming).

5. Innovative curricular programs that incorporate extensive use of the Internet.

6. Availability of easy-to-use multimedia devices and delivery systems (e.g., digital photography and video).

7. Use of personal digital assistants in instruction.

8. Various assistive technology devices for use with students with specific needs.

9. Curriculum-based assessment systems for monitoring student progress.

Review and dismissal:

1. See ideas under "formal referral and eligibility determination."

Transition services:

1. Computer-based systems for determining occupational interests and transition needs.

2. Curricular materials on CD for addressing real-world topics.

3. Individual transition portfolios.

Role of the General Education Teacher in Section 504 Activities

General education teachers play a crucial role in identifying students who might qualify for services under Section 504. Being knowledgeable about what Section 504 provides and how one qualifies for services contributes to a classroom teacher's resourcefulness. Classroom teachers may be contacted during the eligibility determination phase to provide information to the committee to assist with the decision-making task. Teachers may also be required to monitor the effectiveness of the accommodations that are suggested.

Assessment Practices throughout the Special Education Process

Assessment applied to the educational setting is the process of observing, gathering, recording, and interpreting information to answer questions and make instructional and legal decisions about students (Cohen & Spenciner, 2007). It is a dynamic, continuous process that guides and directs decisions about students with suspected or known disabilities to the extent that much of what educators do is addressed in regulations. However, the states still vary in the types of procedures used, the specific approaches to assessment, and the criteria used to determine student eligibility.

CEC 8: Assessment

Figure 4.9

A Section 504 Accommodation Plan

Name: _Ricky Rives_

School/Class: _Mablevale Junior High—7th grade_

Teacher: _Mr. Barnes; Ms. Johns_   Date: _10/8/06_

General Strengths: _Ricky wants very much to be successful in his classes. He tries very hard and wants to please his parents. His motivation is strong._

General Weaknesses: _Ricky has a learning disability. Although his discrepancy was not significant enough to make him eligible for special education, he still has major problems in reading. Recently his behavior has become problematic due to his being frustrated in classes._

Specific Accommodations:

Accommodation #1

Class: _Science_   Accommodation(s): _Mr. Barnes will give Ricky a note-taking guide before he lectures. He will also allow Ricky to use a tape recorder in class._

Person Responsible for Accommodation #1: _Mr. Barnes—teacher_

Accommodation #2

Class: _Science_   Accommodation(s): _Mr. Barnes will have Ricky's test read orally to him and give him extra time to complete the examination._

Person Responsible for Accommodation #2: _Mr. Barnes—teacher_

Accommodation #3

Class: _Social Studies_   Accommodation(s): _Ms. Johns will allow Ricky to use a tape recorder during class. She will also highlight Ricky's textbook, pointing out the important facts for each chapter._

Person Responsible for Accommodation #3: _Ms. Johns—teacher_

Accommodation #4

Class: _Social Studies_   Accommodation(s): _Ms. Johns will give Ricky extra time on written assignments and provide feedback and allow Ricky to redo work that needs improvement._

Person Responsible for Accommodation #4: _Ms. Johns—teacher_

Accommodation #5

Class: _All classes_   Accommodation(s): _A behavior management plan will be developed and used in all of Ricky's classes. The plan will focus on positive reinforcement of appropriate behaviors._

Person Responsible for Accommodation #5: _Mr. Frank—asst. prin._

General Comments:

Ricky's plan will be reviewed at the end of the fall term to determine if additional modifications are required.

Individuals Participating in Development of Accommodation Plan:

John Barnes—teacher   _Ralph Frank—asst. prin. and 504 coor._

Linda Johns—teacher

Darlene Rives—mother

Teachers play four major roles in regard to school-based assessment and, as a result, need to have skills in all four areas.

1. Teachers are consumers of assessment information—in this role, they must be able to understand assessment information.
2. Teachers are producers of assessment information—they must be able to generate assessment information by administering tests, conducting observations, and so on.
3. Teachers are communicators of assessment information—because much of what we do in schools today is team-based, teachers must be able to share assessment information with others (professionals, parents, students).
4. Teachers are developers of assessment instruments—most teachers will find that they have to create assessment techniques to accomplish some education-related tasks.

PRAXIS

PRAXIS II: Delivery of Services to Students with Disabilities

Although assessment has always played a critical role in the special education process, the importance of assessment for all students and school personnel has increased dramatically since the passing of the No Child Left Behind Act of 2001 (NCLB). The central theme of this act is accountability for all students to have positive academic outcomes (Simpson, LaCava, & Graner, 2004). Specifically, every student, including those with special needs, is to make adequate yearly progress and ultimately meet state identified standards measured by performance markers identifying what students should know in each academic area at each grade level. The NCLB mandates combined with the standards set forth in IDEA—that every child eligible for special education services have "access to the general education curriculum" and "make progress in that curriculum"—bring a new increased focus on the assessment process.

Purpose of Assessment

Assessment is critical in each of the major phases of the special education process. During the **screening** phase, including the steps of prereferral and referral discussed previously, the concerns expressed by teachers and parents are the result of their informal "assessment" of the student's lack of progress. Their concern comes from their observations and interactions with the student in the natural environment. When parents and teachers get concerned, they may consult others who have worked with the child or review previous records or current work. At this point, these students are acknowledged to be at risk for failure, and the first level of assessment for special education services has begun.

If a referral is made and the IEP team accepts the referral, the **identification and eligibility** phase of assessment begins. During this phase the child is formally evaluated in all areas related to the suspected disability to determine if he or she has a disability and is eligible for special education services. This might include evaluating a student's intellectual ability, health, vision, hearing, academic achievement, social and emotional needs, level of communication, or motor skills (Bateman & Linden, 2006); the evaluations are performed individually by trained professionals. These results are studied by the IEP team along with the information gathered during the screening, prereferral, and referral phases.

If the student is determined to be eligible, assessment data are needed to identify the unique needs of the child for **program planning**. Existing data are studied further, and new data may be collected to help the IEP team select goals and objectives or benchmarks, as well as identify the most effective research-validated methods of instruction to include in the IEP. After the IEP has been implemented, ongoing assessment is conducted to **monitor** and **evaluate** the student's progress. The IEP team predetermines the methods used for reporting and how often progress will be reported to parents throughout the year. The student is assessed annually to evaluate the outcome of the IEP and provide a measure of accountability. In addition, the student's eligibility or need for services is reconsidered by the IEP team every three years. The IEP team may agree that no changes are

DIVERSITY FORUM

Looking Beyond Model Minority Stereotypes: Asian American Struggling Learners

Amy is a quiet, reserved Vietnamese American student in Mrs. Richards' 5th grade classroom. Although she follows instructions well and always stays on task, she almost never speaks up in class. She earns mostly Cs in academic subjects, struggling the most in math and science. Mrs. Richards, who has great respect for Asian cultures, often praises her as a hard worker. She also comments that Amy is sweet and sincere. Mrs. Richards does not seem to recognize Amy's academic struggles and predicts that she will do fine in upcoming state achievement tests.

Teachers like Mrs. Richards who have positive stereotypes about Asian culture and assume that all Asian American students are academically successful are more likely to overlook those who struggle academically but display acceptable classroom behavior. As a result, Asian American students who may have learning disabilities are often overlooked for special education evaluation (Hui, 2005). It is important for Mrs. Richards to become aware that she is relying on the 'model minority' stereotype about Asian American students, so that she can develop strategies to ensure

accurate interpretations of student performance. Factors that should be considered in this process include (García & Ortiz, 2004):

- *Academic history.* Amy failed the state's reading and math tests in 3rd grade. She barely passed the reading and writing portions in 4th grade, failing again in math. Information about prior efforts to address these areas can contribute to understanding the nature of her difficulties.

- *Prior instruction as an English language learner (ELL).* Amy received English-as-a-second language (ESL) services until the 3rd grade when she was classified as "English proficient". It would be helpful for Mrs. Richards to know if Amy's 3rd and 4th grade instruction was responsive to her ELL status. If so, her ELL status may not be the *primary* explanation for her current difficulties.

- *Input from the family and other professionals.* Information from Amy's parents and ESL teachers can assist in determining if cultural and/or linguistic factors are contributing to Amy's academic difficulties.

Questions

1. How might Amy's cultural and linguistic backgrounds influence her academic performance?

2. How could Mrs. Richards overcome her positive stereotypes and develop realistic perceptions of Asian American students?

3. What are your perceptions and expectations for students whose cultural, linguistic or socioeconomic backgrounds are different from your own? How are these views likely to influence your instruction and interactions with these groups?

REFERENCES

Hui, Y. (2005). *Teachers' perceptions of Asian American students: Implications for special education.* Unpublished Doctoral Dissertation, The University of Texas at Austin.

García S. B., & Ortiz, A. A. (2004) *Preventing disproportionate representation: Culturally and linguistically responsive prereferral intervention.* Denver, CO: National Center for Culturally Responsive Educational Systems (NCCREST).

needed in placement and services and agree not to reevaluate, or they may decide that additional assessments are required to make that decision. The results of each phase of this assessment determine which of several approaches to assessment are used.

Approaches to Assessment

Salvia and Ysseldyke (2001) identified four approaches used to gather information on students: (1) observation; (2) recollection (by means of interview or rating scale); (3) record or portfolio review; and (4) testing. Data collected through naturalistic observation can be highly accurate and provide detailed, relevant information on how the student performs in the natural environment. The observer may be systematically looking for one or more specific behaviors, such as inattention or inappropriate comments. In this approach, the frequency, duration, and intensity of the behavior(s) are usually recorded for study. The student's behavior can then be compared to normal standards of his or her peers or to the individual's previous behavior. Another method of collecting observational data is more anecdotal, in which case the observer records any behavior that seems significant. This type of data may be more subjective than the systematic recordings and harder to validate. Observational data may also be collected using audiotape or videotape.

In data collection involving **recollection**, individuals familiar with the student are asked to recall events and interpret the behaviors. The most commonly used are interviews or ratings scales that can be obtained from the students through a self-report or from peers, family members, teachers, counselors, or others. Through interviews, parents' concerns and preferences can be determined. Since interviews are generally held in person, reactions to questions can be observed and, when appropriate, questions can be explored more thoroughly. **Ratings scales** offer a structured method of data collection involving asking the rater to respond to a statement by indicating the degree to which an item describes an individual. When using rating-scale data, care should be taken to confirm the rater's ability to understand the scale and determine the possibility of bias in reporting. For example, comparisons should be made between responses from parents, teachers, and self-reports from students.

Another important component of assessment is record or **portfolio review**. Existing information such as school cumulative records, databases, anecdotal records, nonschool records, or student products (often found in a student's portfolio) should be reviewed carefully for insight into the student's needs and strengths. To maintain consistency a school will usually consider the same kinds of records for each child being considered.

The most common method of gathering information on students is through formal or informal testing. **Formal assessment** instruments are generally available commercially. They typically contain detailed guidelines for administration, scoring, and interpretation, as well as statistical data regarding **validity**, reliability, and **standardization procedures**. They are most often **norm-referenced**; that is, the tests provide quantitative information comparing the performance of an individual student to others in his or her norm group (determined, for example, by age, grade, or gender). Test results are usually reported in the form of test quotients, percentiles, and age or grade equivalents. These tools are most useful early in an assessment procedure, when relatively little is known of a student's strengths and weaknesses, and thus they may help identify areas in which informal assessment can begin. The ability to compare the student to his or her age and grade peers is also an advantage in making eligibility and placement decisions and fulfilling related administrative requirements. Table 4.2 is a useful assessment resource that shows the relationship across various types of scores obtained through standardized testing.

Professionals can make more informed decisions about the use of formal instruments if they study the instrument and become familiar with its features, benefits, and possible liabilities. One way to do so is to consult one or more of the excellent resources on tests. For recommendations, see the "Further Readings" section at the end of the chapter.

Although formal testing provides quantitative and sometimes qualitative data based on student performance, tests can obtain a measure of a student's best performance only in a contrived situation; they cannot broadly represent a student's typical performance under natural conditions. When considered in isolation, the results of formal tests can also result in lost data that can lead to poor decisions in placement and instructional planning. Rigid administration and interpretation of test results can obscure, rather than reveal, a student's strengths and weaknesses. It has become increasingly apparent that traditional, formal approaches must be augmented with assessment techniques that more accurately represent a student's typical skills.

Informal tests and measurements are usually more loosely structured than formal instruments and are more closely tied to teaching. Such tools are typically devised by teachers to determine what skills or knowledge a child possesses. Their key advantage is the direct application of assessment data to instructional programs. By incorporating informal tests and measurements and by monitoring students' responses each day, teachers can achieve a more accurate assessment of growth in learning or behavioral change. Following is a brief discussion of general types of informal assessment procedures.

CONSIDER THIS

Why do you think parents often find test scores confusing? The information in Table 4.2 will help you convey students' scores more accurately to parents. Notice that the 50th percentile rank is in the nondeficit range. A score indicating a mild disability begins with a score of 16th percentile, and a moderate deficit begins with a score of 5th percentile.

Table 4.2   Relation of Various Standard Scores to Percentile Rank and to One Another

| Percentile Rank | Standard Scores | | | | | Deficit |
	Quotients	NCE Scores	T-scores	Z-scores	Stanines	
99	150	99	83	+3.33	9	
99	145	99	80	+3.00	9	
99	140	99	77	+2.67	9	
99	135	99	73	+2.33	9	
98	130	92	70	+2.00	9	
95	125	85	67	+1.67	8	
91	120	78	63	+1.34	8	None
84	115	71	60	+1.00	7	
75	110	64	57	+0.67	6	
63	105	57	53	+0.33	6	
50	100	50	50	+0.00	5	
37	95	43	47	−0.33	4	
25	90	36	43	−0.67	4	
16	85	29	40	−1.00	3	
9	80	22	37	−1.34	2	Mild
5	75	15	33	−1.67	2	
2	70	8	30	−2.00	1	Moderate
1	65	1	27	−2.33	1	
1	60	1	23	−2.67	1	Severe
1	55	1	20	−3.00	1	

From "The Role of Standardized Tests in Planning Academic Instruction," by D. D. Hammill and B. R. Bryant, 1991, *Handbook on the Assessment of Learning Disabilities,* edited by H. L. Swanson, p. 377. Austin, TX: Pro-Ed Copyright 1991 by Pro-Ed, Inc. Used by permission.

Curriculum-based assessment can focus attention on changes in a student's academic behavior.

Criterion-referenced testing (CRT) compares a student's performance with a criterion of mastery for a specific task, disregarding his or her relative standing in a group. This form of informal assessment can be especially useful when documentation of progress is needed for accountability because the acquisition of skills can be clearly demonstrated. As Taylor (2000) stresses, CRTs are quite popular because they focus attention on specific skills in the curriculum, provide measures of progress toward mastery, and assist teachers in designing instructional strategies. Traditionally, teachers have developed most criterion-referenced instruments, but publishers have begun to produce assessment tools of this type.

One important and popular form of criterion-referenced assessment is **curriculum-based assessment**, which, unlike norm-referenced tools, uses the actual curriculum as the standard and thus provides a direct link between assessment and instruction (Cohen & Spenciner, 2007). This type of assessment can have a role in many important tasks: identification, eligibility, instructional grouping, program planning, progress monitoring, and program evaluation.

Alternative assessment procedures have emerged as dissatisfaction with group-administered standardized tests has increased. Two terms commonly used to describe these procedures are **authentic assessment** and **portfolio assessment**. These assessment methods use similar techniques such as requiring students to construct, produce, perform, or demonstrate a task. These types of student responses are considered alternatives to typical testing responses, such as selecting from multiple-choice items, a technique commonly used on standardized, formal tests. An example of an authentic assessment would be setting up a ministore in a classroom and asking the students to make purchases involving counting money and making change. Portfolio assessment was described in the previous section on assessment approaches. Approximately half of the fifty states use portfolio assessment to measure progress on state goals and standards for students with such severe disabilities that they cannot take the state and districtwide assessments even with accommodations (Johnson & Arnold, 2004).

Ecological assessment is another approach used with many types of informal assessment. As educational assessment has increasingly begun to reflect a trend toward appreciating the ecology of the student, data obtained are now more frequently analyzed in relation to the child's functioning in his or her various environments. Although a full discussion of ecological assessment is beyond the scope of this chapter, the following information highlights some basic considerations, and Figure 4.10 provides a format for assessing the physical environment, the behavioral structure, instructional strategies, and student-to-student and student-to-teacher interactions.

The focus of ecological assessment is to place the evaluation process within the context of the student's environment. Its central element is functionality—how well the student operates in the current environment or the one into which he or she will be moving. This focus shifts a program's emphasis from correcting deficits toward determining how to build on strengths and interests. This type of assessment is particularly useful in early childhood.

Legal Requirements for Assessment

PL 94–142, the first major law dealing with special education policy, introduced many of the assessment mandates that exist today. The most recent reauthorization of IDEA in 2004 continues to address and refine the assessment process. The law specifically addresses the concept of nondiscriminatory evaluations. Only tests that are not racially or culturally biased can be used to determine a disability and the extent of special education and related services that a student needs. Tests are to be administered in the child's' native language or other form of communication most likely to yield accurate information. Those professionals using assessment procedures for a student with limited English proficiency have to ensure that they are measuring the disability and the need for special education, not the student's English language skills. Eligibility also cannot be determined if the deficits are found to be a reflection of a lack of instruction in reading or math.

Any assessment measures must be validated for the specific purpose for which they are used and administered by an individual trained to give the test. No single procedure or test can be the sole criterion for determining eligibility for special education. The student must be assessed in all areas of suspected disability. These areas might include health, vision, hearing, social and emotional status, intelligence, academic performance, communication status, and motor abilities. The variety of assessment tools and strategies used must provide relevant, functional information to directly assist in determining eligibility and the educational, functional, and developmental needs of the student. Information provided by parents must also be considered. Finally, the information must address how to enable the student to participate and progress in the general education curriculum (or for a preschool student, to participate in appropriate activities).

Significant trends in the area of assessment include a focus on the informal assessment procedures that produce more relevant, functional information, as described in the previous section. This type of assessment offers information helpful in eligibility determination as well as IEP development. The increase of the importance of parental

CEC STANDARDS

CEC 8: Assessment

PRAXIS

PRAXIS II: Legal Societal Issues

Figure 4.10   **Assessment of Academic Environment**

Name of Student _____ Date: _____

Class: _____

Duration of observation: _____ minutes.

Check all that are observed during this observational period.

Physical Environmental Factors
_____ Seating: Individual student desks
_____ Seating: Group tables
_____ Seating: Student desks grouped in pairs or groups of four
_____ Material organized for quick student access and use
_____ Target student's materials organized

Classroom Behavioral Structure
_____ Classroom expectations (rules) posted
_____ Verbal praise for effort of students
_____ Verbal praise for target student
_____ Quiet redirection for target student when needed
_____ Inconsequential minor behaviors are ignored
_____ Transitions were smooth
_____ Time lapse to begin task less than 3 minutes (for class)
_____ Time lapse to begin task less than 3 minutes (for target student)
_____ Time lapse to begin task 5 minutes or more (for class)
_____ Time lapse to begin task 5 minutes or more (for target student)
_____ Noise level consistent with task demands
_____ Classwide behavior plan used

Classroom Teacher's Instructional Behaviors
_____ Task expectations explained verbally
_____ Task expectations explained visually (on board, etc.)
_____ Task modeled by teacher
_____ Cognitive strategies modeled by teacher first (thinking aloud)

Teacher-Students Interactions
_____ Academic behavior/responses shaped by teacher for all students
_____ Teacher used proximity as a monitoring technique for all students
_____ Teacher used proximity for reinforcement technique for all students
_____ Teacher used one-on-one instruction to clarify task for all students

Teacher-Target Student Interactions
_____ Academic behavior/responses shaped by teacher for target student
_____ Teacher used proximity as a monitoring technique for target student
_____ Teacher used proximity for reinforcement technique for target student
_____ Teacher used one-on-one instruction to clarify for target student

input is apparent in the IDEA amendments of 2004, as is the focus on increasing the student's chances for successful participation in the general education classroom. This includes participation in statewide or districtwide assessments given to all students. The increased emphasis on participation in the general education curriculum is not useful without a measure of the student's progress in the curriculum.

The IEP team may decide that the student with a disability should not participate in the traditional testing program without accommodations. Table 4.3 provides a checklist

Figure 4.10   **Continued**

Classroom Academic Structure
_____ Anticipatory set for lesson/activity
_____ Task completed by group first before individuals are expected to complete task
_____ Academic behavior/responses modeled/assisted by peers
_____ Expected response or task made by pairs, groups, or teams
_____ Expected response made by individual students
_____ Tasks, instructions were structured and clear to students
_____ Tasks, instructions were unclear to target student
_____ A variety of teaching methods (direct instruction, media, manipulatives) used
_____ Advanced organizers used; cues, prompts, presented to class

Extended Learning Experiences
_____ Homework assignment appropriate (at independent level, not emerging skill level)
_____ Homework instructions are clear
_____ Homework assignment is displayed in consistent place in room (board, etc.)
_____ Students use daily planner or other technique for homework/classwork
_____ Homework assignment is planned for reinforcement of skill rather than extension of
        work not completed during class

Other concerns of academic environment:

From: "Promoting Academic Success through Environmental Assessment," by T. Overton, 2006, *Intervention in School and Clinic, 39*(3), pp. 147–153.

of recommended accommodations and modifications for test taking that may be considered by the IEP team for a student. The team also may decide that participation in standardized testing is not appropriate even with accommodations. In this case, the team must identify an alternate assessment procedure that allows the student to demonstrate what he or she has learned. The decision to use an alternative means of assessment is made only for the students with the most severe disabilities; the assessments developed to measure their progress should also be aligned with the same curriculum standards used by all students. A rare number of students (no more than 2 percent of the entire grade level population) may be reported "proficient" under alternate standards. It is clearly the focus of NCLB and IDEA to move away from a "special education curriculum" and toward the use of regular assessment techniques measuring progress toward meeting grade level standards in the general education curriculum (Bateman & Linden, 2006).

Issues of Bias in Assessment

By 2010 in the United States, the number of K–12 students from diverse cultures is expected to increase by 37 percent, rising to approximately 24 million students. This trend will present one of the greatest challenges for special educators—accurately assessing culturally and linguistically diverse students for disabilities (CEC, 1997). The importance of addressing these challenges through the use of fair and equitable assessment procedures clearly was emphasized in IDEA. This basic assumption of the law

TEACHING TIP

When the results of standardized tests differ significantly from your observations and experiences with a student, consult the examiner. Additional assessment may be necessary.

CEC STANDARDS

CEC 8: Assessment

Table 4.3 **Suggested Adaptations for Test Taking: Checklist**

Behavioral and Environmental Adaptations

Distracted/off task

- ❒ Provide both written and verbal instructions
- ❒ Provide additional space between work areas
- ❒ Place student near teacher and/or in the front of the class
- ❒ Develop a secret signal for on-task behavior
- ❒ Keep work area free from unnecessary materials (e.g., books, pencils)
- ❒ Provide positive feedback
- ❒ Enforce behavior management system
- ❒ Seat apart from others

Completion of Task-Related Adaptations

Getting started and completing tasks

- ❒ Reduce length of test (e.g., select questions to be answered)
- ❒ Allow additional time
- ❒ Break test into shorter tasks (e.g., break every 10 minutes)
- ❒ Establish a reward system
- ❒ Set timer for designated amount of work time and allow student to take a one-minute break after the timer is complete
- ❒ Provide checklist of appropriate behaviors

Processing difficulties

- ❒ Allow use of manipulatives (e.g., counting blocks)
- ❒ Provide both written and verbal instructions

- ❒ Take frequent breaks
- ❒ Break test into shorter tasks
- ❒ Provide list of things to do

Difficulty keeping place when reading

- ❒ Provide large-print version
- ❒ Allow use of place keeper (e.g., bookmark, paper)
- ❒ Create version of test with fewer questions per page

Academic Adaptations

Difficulty with reading comprehension

- ❒ Identify key vocabulary (e.g., highlight or underline)
- ❒ Review key vocabulary
- ❒ Read questions or passages to student

Difficulty with writing

- ❒ Allow oral response
- ❒ Have proctor or teacher write student response
- ❒ Allow the use of computer or word processor

Difficulty with mathematics

- ❒ Have calculation read to student
- ❒ Allow the use of a calculator
- ❒ Break task into smaller parts
- ❒ Reduce the number of questions to be answered (e.g., answer only even-numbered questions)

From *Step-by-Step Guide: For Including Students with Disabilities in State and District-wide Assessments* (p. 29) by D. P. Bryant, J. R. Patton, & S. Vaughn, 2000, Austin, TX: Pro-Ed.

stated that assessment procedures must be established to make sure that assessments and other evaluation materials are

1. selected and administered so as not to be discriminatory on a racial or cultural basis
2. provided and administered in the language and form most likely to yield accurate information, unless not feasible to do so
3. used for purposes for which the assessments are valid and reliable
4. administered by trained and knowledgeable personnel
5. administered in accordance with instructions provided by the producer of such assessments (IDEA, 2004).

It is important for teachers to understand the historical and legal foundations for many policies regarding test bias so that injustices will less likely be repeated. For example, tracking of students based on scores from an IQ test was made unconstitutional in *Hobsen v. Hansen* (1967). The use of culturally biased tests or tests not given in a child's native language was ruled illegal to be used for special education placement decisions in *Diana v. Board of Education* (1970). In *Larry P. v. Riles* (1979) the courts mandated that IQ tests could not be used as the sole basis for a special education placement. Despite this type of critical litigation, research continues to confirm inequities such as the disproportionate representation of students of color in special education classes (Salend & Garrick Duhaney, 2005). Educators and school districts must continue to collect information regarding bias and search for better methods to elicit change.

In addition to racial or cultural bias in assessment, a separate concern is the accurate assessment of individuals who experience sensory or motor disabilities. For example, individuals who have hearing impairments may require a nonverbal test, whereas people who have visual impairments require measures that do not rely on object manipulation and do not include cards or pictures (Hoy & Gregg, 1994). An individual with a severe motor impairment may have limited voluntary responses and may need to respond using an eye scan or blink. Other students may have limited receptive or expressive language capabilities.

Students who have multiple disabilities compound the difficulties of administering the assessment task. Browder and Snell (1988) note that some individuals simply lack "test behaviors." For example, they may refuse to stay seated for an assessment session or may exhibit interfering self-stimulatory behavior (e.g., hand flapping, rocking). Such disabilities or behaviors may cause the test to measure problems rather than assess functioning. Considered collectively, these problems can make traditional testing procedures ineffective, resulting in discriminatory practices despite the best intentions of the tester (Luckasson et al., 1992). Implementation of accommodations or modifications appropriate for the needs of each student with a disability greatly reduces this type of test bias. Refer to Table 4.1 for the list of commonly used adaptations.

Role of the General Education Teacher in Assessment

The list that follows suggests ways in which the general education professional can take an active role in the assessment process.

- Ask questions about the assessment process. Special education teachers and school psychologists should be committed to clarifying the nature of the assessments used and the interpretation of the results.
- Encourage family participation in school activities to better understand values and differences, and let parents know that their input is valued. If communication is a problem, special education teachers may offer the support you need during a conference.
- Provide input. Formal test data should not be allowed to contradict observations in the classroom about a student's ability, achievement, and learning patterns. A valid diagnostic picture should bring together multiple sources of data, including learning journals, curriculum-based measures, and portfolio assessment from the general education classroom.
- Observe assessment procedures. If time and facilities are available (e.g., a one-way mirror), observing the testing process can be educational and can enhance your ability to take part in decision making.
- Consider issues of possible bias. Since formal assessments are often administered by an individual relatively unknown to the child (e.g., a psychologist), inadvertent bias factors between examiner and examinee may be more likely to creep into the results. Work with other staff to ensure an unbiased process.
- Avoid viewing assessment as a means of confirming a set of observations or conclusions about a student's difficulties. Assessment is exploratory and may not lead to expected results. Too often, after a student is not judged eligible for special services, various parties feel resentment toward the assessment process. However, the key commitment should be to elicit useful information to help the student, not to arrive at a foregone eligibility decision that may please the student, parent, or teacher.

Final Thoughts

The intent of this chapter is to provide an overview of the special education programs and services that are available in schools today. Despite the availability of services, certain conditions must exist for teachers to address the needs of students with challenging characteristics who are placed in inclusive classrooms.

CONSIDER THIS

Access to the general education curriculum is a major theme of IDEA.

TEACHING TIP

When entering a new school system, ask the principal or lead teachers to describe the assessment instruments typically used. If curriculum-based assessment has not been developed, organize a grade level team to begin this important process.

CEC STANDARDS

CEC 8: Assessment

PRAXIS

PRAXIS II: Delivery of Services to Students with Disabilities

CONSIDER THIS

Do you feel that the role of the classroom teacher in the assessment process is realistic? In what areas do you feel comfortable participating? In what areas are you uncomfortable?

The special education process discussed in this chapter provides essential services to students who need them. This process does require that efficient and effective procedures are in place in schools. More important, for this process to work the dedication of administration and staff to fulfilling the goals of providing an appropriate education to students with special needs is essential.

Summary

Prereferral Intervention

- All procedures associated with special education programs must be consistent with due-process requirements.
- Each state provides timelines that govern the referral, assessment, and IEP processes.
- Prereferral intervention is a process of assisting students in the general education classroom prior to referral for full assessment.
- Child study or teacher assistance committees are responsible for helping teachers modify instruction for a student experiencing learning difficulties.
- Well-trained child study teams can assist teachers and limit referrals.

The Special Education Process

- The formal referral process initiates a series of activities.
- Not all referrals have merit and therefore require evaluation.
- A comprehensive evaluation precedes eligibility determination.
- The IEP includes many required components.
- The essential elements of the IEP document are present levels of educational performance and measurable annual goals.
- BIPs are required for certain students.
- Transition services are mandated for all students with IEPs who are age sixteen.
- Some students can qualify for extended school year services.
- Goals within the IEP are reviewed annually, and a comprehensive reevaluation is conducted no less than every three years.
- The 2004 reauthorization of IDEA contain very specific mandates for assessment, developing the IEP or IFSP, and ensuring parental involvement throughout the special education process.

Section 504 Eligibility and Planning

- Some students who do not qualify under IDEA may qualify for services under Section 504.
- Eligibility is determined by whether a person has a physical or mental impairment that results in a substantial limitation in one or more major life activities.
- If a student qualifies under 504, an accommodation plan is typically developed.

Assessment Practices throughout the Special Education Process

- Assessment includes testing and a broader range of methods that help define a student's strengths and problems leading to the development of educational interventions.
- Formal assessment is based on the administration of commercial instruments, typically for survey or diagnostic purposes.
- Informal assessment includes a variety of tools that can enhance a teacher's knowledge of students' learning needs.
- Curriculum-based measures are tied to the class curriculum and assess a student within this context.
- Ecological assessment places the evaluative data within the context of a student's environment.
- Authentic and portfolio assessment documents a student's ability to construct, perform, produce, or demonstrate a task.
- The control of bias in assessment is not only essential to accurate and fair evaluation, but is also a legal requirement.
- Classroom teachers may not administer the formal assessments but nevertheless are important members of any assessment process and should be informed about the assessment process and the IEP.

Questions to Reconsider

Think back to the scenario about Jessica that you read at the beginning of this chapter. Would you answer the questions raised there any differently, after reading the chapter?

1. What suggestions can you make to help Jessica succeed in the general education classroom?

2. How would you feel about making accommodations to keep Jessica if you were Jessica's teacher?
3. Do you think treating Jessica differently was fair to the other students?

Further Readings

Bateman, B., & Golly, A. (2003). *Why Johnny doesn't behave: Twenty tips and measurable BIPs* (2nd ed.) Verona, WI: Attainment.

Bateman, B., & Herr, C. M. (2006). *Writing measurable IEP goals and objectives* (2nd ed). Verona, WI: Attainment.

Buck, L. H., Polloway, E. A., Smith-Thomas, A., & Cook, K. W. (2003). Prereferral intervention processes: A survey of state practices. *Exceptional Children, 69,* 349–360.

Cohen, L. G., & Spenciner, L. J. (2007). *Assessment of children and youth with special needs.* Boston: Allyn & Bacon.

Crone, D. A., Horner, R. H., & Hawken, L. S. (2004). *Responding to problem behavior in schools: The behavior education program.* New York: Guilford Press.

Dabkowski, D. (2004). Encouraging active participation in IEP team meeting. *Teaching Exceptional Children, 36*(3), 34–39.

Gartin, B., & Murdick, N. (2005). IDEA 2004: The IEP. *Remedial & Special Education, 26*(6), 327–331.

Goh, D. S. (2004) *Assessment accommodations for diverse learners.* Boston: Allyn & Bacon.

Herr, C. M., & Bateman, B. (2006). *Better IEP meetings.* Verona, WI: Attainment.

Kamens, M. W. (2004). Learning to write IEPs: A personalized, reflective approach for preservice teachers. *Intervention in School and Clinic, 40*(2), 76–80.

Keyes, M. W., & Owens-Johnson, L. (2003). Developing person-centered IEPs. *Intervention in School and Clinic, 38*(3), 145–152.

Miller, L., & Hoffman, L. (2002). *Linking IEPs to State learning standards: A step by step guide.* Austin, TX: Pro-Ed.

Reed, P., & Lahm, E. (2005). *A resource guide for teachers and administrators about assistive technology.* Oshkosh: Wisconsin Assistive Technology Initiative.

Reick, W. A., & Wadsworth, D. E. (2005). Assessment accommodations: Helping students with exceptional learning needs. *Intervention in School and Clinic, 41*(2), 105–109.

Sherer, M., & Craddock, G. (2002). Matching person & technology (MPT) assessment process. *Technology and Disability, 14,* 125–131.

Tam, K. Y., & Heng, M. A. (2005). A case involving culturally and linguistically diverse parents in prereferral intervention. *Intervention in School and Clinic, 40*(4), 222–230.

Wright, P. W. D. (2004). The Individuals with Disabilities Education Improvement Act of 2004: Overview, explanation, and comparison IDEA 2004 vs IDEA 97. Available at www.wrightslaw.com/idea/idea.2004.all.pdf

Zhang, C., & Bennett, T. (2003). Facilitating the meaningful participation of culturally and linguistically diverse families in the IFSP and IEP process. *Focus on Autism and Other Developmental Disabilities, 18*(1), 51–59.

mylabschool

Go to Allyn & Bacon's MyLabSchool (www.mylabschool.com) and enter Assignment ID CS13 into the Assignment Finder. Read the case study called *Is This Child Mislabelled?* and, using both the case and the information in this chapter, answer the questions raised at the end of it and e-mail your answers to your instructor.

Now enter Assignment ID SPV9 into the Assignment Finder. View the video clip called *Inclusion of Students with Hearing Impairments.*

1. What instructional accommodations are made for the student with the hearing impairment in the video clip? Does the placement of this student in a general education classroom meet the provision of *least restrictive environment?* Do you feel this is the most supportive placement for this student?

Enter Assignment ID SPV2 into the Assignment Finder. Now view the video clip called *Assessment of Special Needs Students.*

2. Many students with special needs are unable to be assessed by standardized testing, but schools are still accountable for the progress made by these students. What alternate kinds of assessments might be used? How might you as a teacher ensure that the right skills are being measured?

You may also answer the questions at the end of these clips and e-mail your responses to your instructor.

Teaching Students with Learning Disabilities

After reading this chapter, you should be able to:

1. Identify the characteristics of learning disabilities (LD).

2. Discuss the impact of cultural diversity on identification of and intervention for LD.

3. Describe the criteria for eligibility for LD services.

4. Discuss the pros and cons of using "response to treatment" as a criteria for identification of LD.

5. Compare the traditional approaches to intervention for individuals with LD at the preschool, elementary, and secondary levels.

6. Describe the impact of learning disabilities during the adult years.

7. Make modifications in teaching methods and classroom management to address academic, social, emotional, and cognitive differences.

Questions to Consider

1. What alerted Emmanuel's teacher to a possible learning disability?
2. How might his move have been a factor in his school performance?
3. Would "response to intervention" have been a viable option for Emmanuel?
4. How might that have changed Emmanuel's life?

Emmanuel was six years old when he eagerly started first grade. Problems began to emerge as the reading program expanded from picture books with lots of repetition to books containing unknown words. Emmanuel had difficulty using context clues, and he had limited phonemic awareness in decoding a new word. His first report card showed "needs improvement" in reading, listening, and following directions. The bright spot in Emmanuel's first-grade achievement was his above-average functioning in math, his ability to pay attention, and good social skills. Emmanuel was promoted to second grade.

Over the summer, his family moved to another state. Emmanuel adjusted to the new school and everything was fine for the first nine weeks of review, and then he began to have trouble finishing his work. He became frustrated with written assignments and often complained of stomachaches, asking to stay home from school. His teachers felt that he was still adjusting to a new school.

By the middle of the year, his parents, teacher, and child-study team agreed that accommodations were needed. The special education teacher put together material to develop phonemic awareness skills Emmanuel had not mastered. His parents agreed to work on this material at home. He also worked with a fifth-grade peer helper who read with him one-on-one three days a week. The classroom teacher agreed to restate oral instructions, to continue working on phonics, and to encourage Emmanuel to predict unknown words based on meaning and evaluate whether the word he guessed fit with the rest of the words in the sentence.

After six weeks the child-study team still felt that Emmanuel was struggling too much, so they recommended a special education referral. His tests showed average intelligence and significant deficits in reading skills, writing, and listening despite the interventions that had been made. The IEP team determined that Emmanuel had a learning disability and needed special education services to make adequate progress in the general education curriculum; Emmanuel's IEP was developed to allow him to benefit from his educational experience. Although signs of learning disabilities were present, the school proceeded cautiously in identifying Emmanuel as a child with a learning disability. (As discussed in Chapter 1, school personnel and parents often want to avoid labeling because it can be detrimental to children.) Emmanuel attended a resource class in third grade. Through these services, his reading of multisyllable words greatly improved as did his writing and listening skills. By fourth grade, he remained in the general education classroom full time, needing only periodic support from the learning disabilities teacher.

*J*ust as it is difficult to distinguish children with LD from their peers by looks, you cannot distinguish adults with learning disabilities from other adults. You may be surprised to find that many important and famous people have made significant achievements in spite of experiencing a severe learning disability. Adults with learning disabilities can be found in all professions. They may be teachers, lawyers, doctors, blue-collar workers, or politicians. Read the examples that follow, and see whether you can identify the names of the individuals with learning disabilities.

1. During his childhood, this young man was an outstanding athlete, achieving great success and satisfaction from sports. Unfortunately, he struggled in the classroom. He tried very hard, but he always seemed to fail academically. His biggest fear was being asked to stand up and read in front of his classmates. He was frequently teased about his class performance, and he described his school days as sheer torture. His only feelings of success were experienced on the playing field.

   When he graduated from high school, he didn't consider going to college because he "wasn't a terrific student, and never got into books all that much." Even though he was an outstanding high school pole vaulter, he did not get a single scholarship during his senior year. He had already gone to work with his father when he was offered a $500 football scholarship from Graceland College. He didn't accept that offer; instead he trained in track and field. Several years later, he won a gold medal in the Olympics in the grueling decathlon. This story is about Bruce Jenner.

2. This individual was still illiterate at age twelve, but he could memorize anything. Spelling was always impossible for him, and as he said, he "had trouble with the A, B, and that other letter." He also was a failure at math. He finally made it through high school, but he failed his first year at West Point. He did graduate, with the help of tutors, one year late. His special talent was in military strategy, and during World War II he became one of the United States' most famous generals, George Patton.

Other famous people with LD include Charles Schwab, Tom Cruise, Cher, Nelson Rockefeller, Winston Churchill, Woodrow Wilson, F. W. Woolworth, Walt Disney, Ernest Hemingway, Albert Einstein, George Bernard Shaw, and Thomas Edison (see discussions at www.dyslexiaonline.org). These and other individuals with learning disabilities were often misunderstood and teased early in life for their inadequacies in the classroom. To be successful, they had to be creative and persistent. Adults with learning disabilities succeed by sheer determination in overcoming their limitations and focusing on their talents.

Perhaps the most difficult aspect of understanding and teaching students with learning disabilities is that the disability is hidden. When students with obviously normal intelligence fail to finish their work, interrupt inappropriately, never seem to follow directions, and turn in sloppy, poorly organized assignments, it is natural to blame poor motivation, lack of effort, and even an undesirable family life.

However, the lack of accomplishment and success in the classroom does have a cause; the students are not demonstrating these behaviors to upset or irritate their teachers. A **learning disability** is a cognitive disability; it is a disorder of thinking and reasoning. Because the dysfunction is presumed to be in the central nervous system, the presence of the disability is not visible.

The individuals with learning disabilities described earlier have experienced the frustration of living with a disability that is not easily identified. Children with learning disabilities look like other students in their grade. They can perform like other students in some areas, but not in others. Like Emmanuel in the chapter-opening vignette, a child may have good social skills and make good grades in math, but fail in reading. Another child may be able to read and write at grade level but fail in math and get in trouble for misconduct. Students with learning disabilities also may perform inconsistently. They may know spelling words on Thursday and fail the test on Friday.

In this chapter you will study the patterns of strengths and weaknesses of children, youth, and adults who experience "unexpected underachievement." Professionals from

CONSIDER THIS

Reflect on the students who were your classmates during elementary and secondary school. Do you remember someone who had good academic abilities in some areas and low achievement in others? Was he or she ever accused of not trying or being lazy? This may have been a misunderstood child with a learning disability.

many fields have joined the search for a definition and causes of these disabilities, as well as methods to identify affected children and to accommodate or remediate areas of the disability. Yet many questions remain.

In August 2001 a Learning Disability Summit was held in Washington, D.C., to advance the "science" of LD and to provide leadership in this area for future reauthorizations of IDEA. Research presented at the summit is discussed throughout this chapter and papers from the conference are listed in "Further Readings" at the end of the chapter. You will see that the answers are still evolving, but much progress has been made in this exciting field (Polloway, 2002).

Basic Concepts about Learning Disabilities

Learning Disabilities Defined

Hallahan and Mercer (2001) discuss the history of LD, noting that the concept has longstanding recognition, dating back to a period they call the European Foundation Period (1800–1920). The early research focused on brain function. This era was followed by the Foundation Period (1920–1960), focusing on research on brain-injured adults with deficits in perception, attention, and the perceptual-motor area, and children with reading and language deficits. Since that time, more than ninety terms have been introduced into the literature to describe these individuals. The most common terms include minimal brain dysfunction (MBD), brain damage, central processing dysfunction, and language delay. To add to the confusion, several definitions were also offered to explain each term. The term "specific learning disabilities" was first adopted publicly in 1963 at a meeting of parents and professionals. Kirk (1962) developed the generic term "learning disabilities" in an effort to unite the field, which was torn between individuals promoting different theories regarding underachievement. The term was received favorably because it did not have the negative connotations of the other terms and did describe the primary characteristic of the children.

The Emergent Period (1960–1975) describes the development of professional and parent organizations to promote awareness of LD. During the Solidification Period (1975–1987), IDEA (then called PL 94–142) was passed, and it included LD as a disability category, citing a definition developed originally by a committee chaired by Kirk in 1968.

This definition, modified only slightly over the years, was reformatted into the following three sections in IDEA (2004):

- IN GENERAL: The term "specific learning disability" means a disorder in one or more of the basic psychological processes involved in understanding or in using language, spoken or written, which disorder may manifest itself in an imperfect ability to listen, think, speak, read, write, spell, or to do mathematical calculations.
- DISORDERS INCLUDED: Such term includes such conditions as perceptual disabilities, brain injury, minimal brain dysfunction, dyslexia, and developmental aphasia.
- DISORDERS NOT INCLUDED: Such term does not include a learning problem that is primarily the result of visual, hearing, or motor disabilities, of mental retardation, of emotional disturbance, or of environmental, cultural, or economic disadvantage (IDEA 2004).

Hallahan and Mercer (2001) describe the period since 1988 as the Turbulent Era. Dissension still exists over the most effective methods to teach children with LD, as well as to identify and define them. A majority of states use the IDEA definition, but it has been criticized over the years for including concepts that are unclear or difficult to use to identify children with a learning disability (Swanson, 2000). For example, the concept of deficits in "psychological processes" is the most nebulous and has been

PRAXIS

PRAXIS II: Understanding Exceptionalities

CEC STANDARDS

CEC 2: Development and Characteristics of Learners

INTASC

INTASC 3: Understanding how students differ

interpreted in several ways, including perceptual-motor deficits, deficits in the process of taking in information, difficulty in making sense of information and expressing knowledge effectively, and deficits in cognitive processes such as attention, memory, and metacognition (the way one thinks about and controls his or her cognitive processing, e.g., self-monitoring, predicting, and planning). As a result, the U.S. Office of Education (USOE) did not include a measure of psychological processes when publishing the original criteria for identifying students with learning disabilities (USOE, 1977). The agency focused instead on identifying a discrepancy between a child's ability and his or her achievement in reading, math, written language, speaking, or listening.

Most recently the practice of documenting a discrepancy between IQ and achievement for LD identification has been made optional for states (IDEA, 2004), so more changes will be forthcoming. This exciting field requires a professional commitment to continue reading the literature to stay current with the latest research and policy. To this end, the National Research Center on Learning Disabilities was federally funded in 2002. To follow the activities of this center, log on to www.NRCLD.org.

Prevalence and Causes of Learning Disabilities

There are by far more students in today's schools with LD than with any other disability. Critics propose that the debate over the definition and eligibility criteria is to blame for the huge rise in the prevalence of LD. The number of students labeled as learning disabled has tripled since it first was recognized as a disability, causing Swanson (2000) to refer to the increase as epidemic. A 2002 report from the U.S. Department of Education (www.ideadata.org) shows that over half the students between the ages of six and twenty-one with disabilities were learning disabled; the state average for school-aged children with learning disabilities is 5.74 percent.

It should be noted that this prevalence figure can vary widely among states and within a state, depending on the stringency of the method used to determine eligibility. For example, Kentucky reports the lowest prevalence figure (2.85 percent) and Rhode Island the highest (9.43 percent). A study completed in Michigan compared the learning disabilities eligibility criteria and procedures for identification across the fifty-seven regional education service agencies (RESA) in that state (Haight, Patriarca, & Burns, 2001). The results showed that 21 percent of the RESAs had no written eligibility criteria or policies, the length of the written policies varied from one sentence to 112 pages, and the severe discrepancy formula score varied from 15 to 30 standard score points! It is possible for a student to move a few miles to the next school district and no longer be considered to have a learning disability. These results are also supported by a study in Georgia that looked at the variability of minority representation across systems, with some systems identifying three to four times as many African Americans in learning disabilities classes as European Americans, and other systems showing the opposite. National data suggest an equal distribution of European American and African American students in learning disability classes (5.7 percent) (Colarusso, Keel, & Dangel, 2001). Disproportionality in gender is decreasing, with recent data suggesting that males are about twice as likely as females to be identified with LD (Coutinho & Oswald, 2005).

What causes learning disabilities? The advances in methods such as computerized imaging techniques that are reasonably reliable in detecting brain abnormalities have led to the generally accepted view that LD are the result of differences in brain function or structure (Hallahan et al., 2005). The literature suggests several causes for neurological differences or dysfunction, primarily hereditary factors and trauma experienced before birth, during birth, and after birth. Following is a summary provided by Hallahan and colleagues (2005).

PRAXIS

PRAXIS II: Understanding Exceptionalities

1. *Genetic factors:* Many studies have cited the large number of relatives with learning problems in children identified with learning disabilities. Chromosomal abnormalities and structural brain differences have been linked to learning disabilities. Raskind

(2001) describes the progress that has been made identifying the gene location for a learning disability in reading. Research in this area continues to show promise.

2. *Causes occurring before birth:* Learning problems have been linked to injuries to the embryo or fetus caused by the mother's use of alcohol, cigarettes, or other drugs, such as cocaine and prescription and nonprescription drugs. Through the mother, the fetus is exposed to the toxins, causing malformations of the developing brain and central nervous system. Although significant amounts of overexposure to these drugs may cause serious problems, such as mental retardation, no safe levels have been identified.

3. *Causes occurring during the birth process:* Traumas during birth may include prolonged labor, anoxia, prematurity, and injury from medical instruments such as forceps. Although not all children with a traumatic birth are found to have learning problems later, a significant number of children with learning problems do have a history of complications during this period.

4. *Medical and environmental causes occurring after birth:* High fever, encephalitis, meningitis, stroke, diabetes, and pediatric AIDS have been linked to LD. Malnutrition, poor postnatal health care, and lead ingestion can also lead to neurological dysfunction.

Advances in neurological research and use of computerized neurological techniques such as computerized axial tomography (CAT) scans and positron emission tomography (PET) scans have made professionals more inclined to believe in a neurological explanation of learning disabilities. Widespread use of these tests to identify a learning disability has not been forthcoming for several reasons: such procedures are expensive and invasive, and the documented presence of a neurological dysfunction does not affect how the child is taught (Hallahan et al., 2005). However, this research is important to advance knowledge of this type of disability and in the future may help determine the effectiveness of various treatment techniques. Studies are under way to monitor the impact of various reading interventions on the results of neuroimaging (Pugh et al., 2001). A neurophysicist has recommended using neuroimaging to identify young children with reading problems for treatment purposes, noting that learning to read can cause the brain to change and become like the brain of good readers (Richards, 2001). It is interesting to think about the possibility that one day brain imaging could be used to determine the best methods for teaching.

Characteristics of Students with Learning Disabilities

Learning disabilities are primarily described as deficits in academic achievement (reading, writing, and mathematics) and/or language (listening or speaking). However, children with learning disabilities may have significant problems in other areas, such as social interactions and emotional maturity, attention and hyperactivity, memory, cognition, metacognition, motor skills, and perceptual abilities. It is also important to understand that students with LD tend to be overly optimistic regarding some of their abilities, masking strategy and skill deficits. They may need more support in these areas than they report that they need (Klasson, 2002). Since LD are presumed to be a central nervous system dysfunction, characteristics may be manifested throughout the life span, preschool through adult (Bender, 2001).

The most common characteristics of students with LD are described briefly in the following sections, concentrating on the challenges they may create in a classroom. Students with LD are a heterogeneous group. A single student will typically not have deficits in all areas. Also, any area could be a strength for a student with LD, and the student might exceed the abilities of his or her peers in that area. An understanding of the characteristics of children with learning problems is important in developing prereferral interventions, in making appropriate referrals, and in identifying effective accommodations, modifications, and intervention strategies. Figure 5.1 displays the possible strengths and weaknesses of children with learning disabilities.

TEACHING TIP

Often parents will ask teachers what causes a learning disability. To respond, you might discuss some of the possible causes and suggest that the specific cause is seldom identifiable for individual children. Reassure parents that pinpointing the cause is not important in planning and implementing effective intervention strategies.

PRAXIS

PRAXIS II: Understanding Exceptionalities

CEC STANDARDS

CEC 3: Individual Learning Differences

Figure 5.1

Areas of Possible Strengths and Deficits of Students with Learning Disabilities

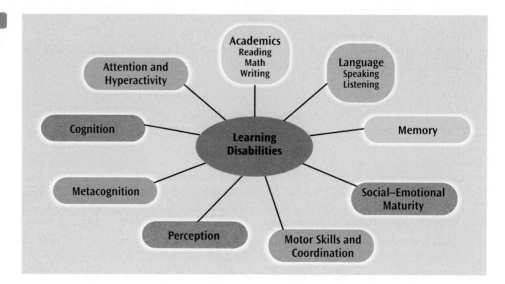

CEC STANDARDS

CEC 3: Individual Learning Differences

Academic Deficits   During the elementary school years a child's ability and his or her achievement across academic areas begin to vary significantly in students with LD. Often puzzling to teachers and parents, these students seem to have strengths similar to their peers in several areas, but their rate of learning in other areas is unexpectedly slower. The term "unexpected underachievement" is frequently used to describe LD; Smith (2004) described an unexpected failure "despite adequate intelligence, schooling, and their parents' best attempts at nurturing" (p. 2). The vignette that began this chapter profiles a typical child with LD: above-average ability in math; average ability in language, attention, and social skills; and severe deficits in reading, written expression, and listening. (See the IEP goals and objectives for Emmanuel later in the chapter.)

The academic problems that identify a learning disability fall into the areas of reading, math, and written expression. The most prevalent type of academic difficulty for students with LD is reading. Lyon and colleagues (2001) report that approximately 80 percent of children identified as learning disabled have primary deficits in the area of reading and related language functions. Problems may be noted in basic reading skills and reading comprehension. Children with LD may struggle with oral reading tasks. They may read in a strained voice with poor phrasing, ignore punctuation, and grope for words, as would a much younger child. Oral reading problems cause tremendous embarrassment to these children. Polloway, Patton, and Serna (2001) confirm that a student's self-image and feelings of confidence are greatly affected by reading experience. Deficits in reading skills can also lead to acting-out behavior and poor motivation.

Some children with learning disabilities may be able to say the words correctly but not remember what they have read. Comprehension problems may include one or more of the following: (1) identifying the main idea; (2) recalling basic facts and events in a sequence; and (3) making inferences or evaluating what has been read. A child with a specific deficit in reading may be described as having **dyslexia**.

Another major academic problem area is mathematics. Students with LD may have problems in math calculations or math reasoning (USOE, 1977). These conceptual and skill areas include deficits in the four operations, the concept of zero, regrouping, place value, basic math concepts (e.g., one-to-one correspondence, sets), and solving math problems. Children may have abilities in calculation but have disabilities in math reasoning; they may make many errors in calculations but be able to perform calculations to solve a math word problem. Often the rate of response interferes with success in math; for example, a child may be able to perform the skill, but unable to complete the number of problems required during the time allowed. Robinson, Manchetti, and Torgeson (2002) proposed that for some children this math difficulty may be due to either deficits in the phonological processing of the features of spoken numbers or failure to grasp meaningful aspects of numbers. They note that 43 percent of students with a math disability also have reading problems. It is hoped that math disabilities will soon be studied as intensely as reading disabilities. A disability in math may be called **dyscalculia**.

Learning disabilities in the area of written expression are beginning to receive more recognition as a potentially serious problem. The three main areas of concern are handwriting, spelling, and written expression, including mechanics and creativity. The impact of written-language problems increases with a student's age because so many school assignments require a written product. A learning disability in writing may be referred to as **dysgraphia**.

Language Deficits   Language deficits are found in the areas of oral expression (expressive language) and listening comprehension (receptive language). Since these two areas control our ability to communicate with others, a deficit can have a major impact on quality of life—including life in a general education classroom. Common oral language problems include difficulty in retrieving correct words; children often use a less-appropriate word because the word they are searching for will not come to them. The response rate of children with LD may be slower than that of their nondisabled peers, and they may speak more slowly. If ample time is not allowed for a response, the student's behavior may be misinterpreted as failure to understand or refusal to participate. Children with LD tend to use simpler, less mature language and confuse sequences in retelling a story. Listening problems also can be easily misinterpreted. A child with a disability in listening demonstrates that disability in a negative way—for example, by failing to follow directions or by appearing oppositional or unmotivated. A teacher's careful observation and assessment of a student's language ability is important for ensuring the student's success. Figure 5.2 provides examples of how speech can become "twisted" for students with receptive language (e.g., listening) deficits; these deficits may be referred to as auditory processing deficits.

A new area of concern and research for children with language-learning disabilities is the area of **pragmatics**, or use of language in social situations. Children with these disabilities are often unsuccessful in fully participating in conversation. They may change the subject of a conversation or ask inappropriate questions. They may miss nonverbal language cues such as frowns. They may not understand jokes; they may laugh inappropriately or at the wrong times. Group work is often difficult, as is giving or following directions. Language disabilities can contribute significantly to difficulties in other social situations as well.

Social-Emotional Problems   Some children with LD have a real strength in the area of social skills; they are well-liked by peers and teachers. However, several characteristics of learning disabilities, like those noted in the area of language, can create difficulties in social and emotional life. Social skills deficits of children with LD include resolving conflict, managing frustrations, initiating or joining a conversation or play activities,

During grades 2 through 6, academic problems begin to become very obvious.

These are actual "mis-heard" sayings from an individual who has a receptive language/listening learning disability.

1. ROCKER BUY BAY BEE INNER TREE HOPS
2. TURNIP OUT FIR PLAY
3. ROLAND'S TONE GADDERS NOME HOSS
4. SINKER'S HONKERS SICK SPENTZ
5. LAW TENT BRITCHES FULL IN TOWN

Figure 5.2

Family Air Sangs (Familiar Sayings)

Source: "Recognizing and Responding to Cultural Differences in the Education of Culturally and Linguistically Diverse Learners," by S. P. Chamberlain, 2005, *Intervention in School and Clinic, 40*(4), p. 207.

CEC STANDARDS

CEC 3: Individual Learning Differences

CROSS-REFERENCE

Often students with learning disabilities who have social-emotional difficulties will present challenges in behavior management in the classroom. Refer to Chapter 14 for more information in this area.

CROSS-REFERENCE

Many students with LD have ADHD. This topic is covered more extensively in Chapter 8.

CONSIDER THIS

Think of the impact long-term memory deficits would have on your daily life. If you were not able to efficiently recall experiences or facts and information you previously learned, would others doubt your intelligence or motivation?

listening, demonstrating empathy, maintaining a friendship, and working in groups. About a third of the students with LD have nonverbal, or social, disabilities (Morris, 2002). These students and those with ADHD have also been shown to have lower self-concept in academics and social relations (Tabassam & Grainger, 2002).

Often positive interactions and exchange of information do not occur between children with LD and their peers or teachers. Because of behavior and language differences, children with LD need more guidance and structure. Over time, this need can create feelings of overdependency, and eventually "learned helplessness" can occur. Social deficits have even been known to lead to school failure (Bryan, Burstein, & Ergul, 2004), and years of failure can create other concerns. Researchers have reported psychological problems, including feelings of anxiety, depression, inadequacy, frustration, and anger (Bender, 2002). Confusion and frustration can also result in aggressive behavior (Allsopp, Santos, & Linn, 2000). By adolescence, a student's combined cognitive and language deficits can interfere significantly with deciding how to act in the new social situations brought about by increased independence. When interacting with normal adolescents who have advanced language skills, students with disabilities may experience greater failure in communication and may suffer more rejection (Morris, 2002).

In summary, Weiner and Schneider (2002) found that LD are often found along with an increase in emotional distress. Emotional issues may mask or exacerbate a child's LD; however, positive emotional health can enhance the performance of students with LD. By being sensitive to emotional issues, teachers can take care to include students with LD in supportive situations and provide reinforcement for specific successes. General praise statements such as "Good work!" or "You are really smart!" will not have much impact because they are not believable to the students. Commenting on or rewarding specific accomplishments will be more effective. Additional examples of appropriate interventions are discussed later in this chapter and in future chapters.

Attention Deficits and Hyperactivity   Attention is a critical skill in learning. Conte (1991) suggests that to be effective learners, children must be able to initiate attention, direct their attention appropriately, sustain their attention according to the task demands, and shift attention when appropriate. Deficits in these areas can have an impact on all aspects of success in school. When children are "not paying attention," they cannot respond appropriately to questions, follow directions, or take notes during a lecture. The excess movement of a hyperactive student can draw sharp criticism when it negatively affects the learning environment. Social problems occur when the student interrupts others and does not listen to his or her peers. Students with attention problems often have trouble finishing assignments or rush through their work with little regard for detail. Approximately 51 percent of students with LD are also reported to have attention problems, and it is estimated that 3.7 percent of school-aged children have both LD and ADHD (Smith & Adams, 2006). The comorbid occurrence of these two disabilities have also been found to create an increase in the need for special education services. In a recent survey, 64.7 percent of children with both LD and ADHD were receiving special education services compared to 45.9 percent of children with LD only and 11.7 percent of students with ADHD alone (US DHHS-CDCP, 2002). Attention deficits will be explored further in Chapter 8.

Memory Deficits   Students with LD have deficits in short-term memory, working memory, and long-term memory (Hallahan et al., 2005). Short-term memory problems show up when a child has difficulty repeating information heard less than one or two minutes earlier. Working memory problems occur when students are trying to take recent information and organize it for storage or link it to information previously stored in long-term memory to broaden their knowledge about a subject. Work by McNamara and Wong (2003) confirms that memory problems of students have a negative impact on everyday tasks and situations as well as academic demands. Teachers and parents add that the memory skills are inconsistent in children with LD—for example, a student may know the multiplication facts on Thursday and fail the test on Friday. The good news is that when children with learning disabilities are taught memory strategies, they make substantial gains at all grade levels (Scruggs & Mastropieri, 2000).

Cognition Deficits   **Cognition** refers to the ability to reason or think (Hallahan et al., 2005). Students with problems in this area may make poor decisions or frequent errors. They may have trouble getting started on a task, have delayed verbal responses, require more supervision, or have trouble adjusting to change. Understanding social expectations may be difficult. They may require concrete demonstrations. They often have trouble using previously learned information in a new situation.

Metacognition Deficits   Hallahan and colleagues (2005) refer to **metacognition** as "thinking about thinking." Students with problems in this area might have difficulty focusing on listening, purposefully remembering important information, connecting that information to prior knowledge, making sense out of the new information, and using what they know to solve a problem. They often lack strategies for planning and organizing, setting priorities, and predicting and solving problems. An important component of metacognition is the ability to evaluate one's own behavior and behave differently when identifying inappropriate behavior or mistakes.

Perceptual Differences   Perceptual disorders affect the ability to recognize stimuli being received through sight, hearing, or touch, and to discriminate between and interpret the sensations appropriately. A child with a learning disability might not have any problems in these areas, or he or she might have deficits in any or all of them. Identification of deficits and training in the perceptual processes or reference to a child's "learning style" was emphasized in the early 1970s; however, it is no longer a prominent consideration in the education of children with LD.

Motor Skill and Coordination Problems   This area has also been de-emphasized in the identification of an intervention for children with learning disabilities because it is not directly related to academics. However, it is common for children with LD to display problems in gross motor areas; they often cannot throw and catch a ball or may have a clumsy gait. Common fine motor deficits include difficulties with using scissors, buttoning clothing, and handwriting. Individuals with LD may also have a slow reaction time. Consideration of exceptionalities or disabilities in motor skills and coordination is especially important in the selection of postsecondary educational programs and, ultimately, in the identification of a career.

Identification, Assessment, and Eligibility

Because of the difficulty in measuring some of the nebulous constructs included in the definition of LD (e.g., psychological processes), the federal government has specified stronger criteria to assess and identify LD and to determine eligibility for special education services. Following a national debate that lasted for two years after PL 94–142 was passed in 1975, the federal regulations for definition and identification criteria for LD were published in the *Federal Register* (USOE, 1977). These are considered minimal standards, and states may require additional criteria. The criteria include the following:

INTASC

INTASC 8: Formal and informal assessment

PRAXIS

PRAXIS II: Delivery of Instruction

- *Multidisciplinary team:* A group of individuals, including a classroom teacher, at least one individual qualified to perform diagnostic examinations of children, and a learning disabilities specialist, is required to determine eligibility.
- *Observation:* A student must be observed by at least one member of the team in the general education classroom. The purpose of the observation is to document the manifestation of the disability in the classroom.

- *Criteria for determining a learning disability:*
  1. The team must determine the existence of a severe discrepancy between achieve-ment and intellectual ability in one or more of the following areas: (a) reading skills; (b) reading comprehension; (c) mathematical calculations; (d) mathemati-cal reasoning; (e) written expression; (f) oral expression; and (g) listening com-prehension. (An example is presented in Figure 5.3.)
  2. The team may not identify a student as having a specific learning disability if the severe discrepancy between ability and achievement is primarily the result of (a) a visual, hearing, or motor handicap; (b) mental retardation; (c) emotional dis-turbance; or (d) economic disadvantage.
  3. The team must document that appropriate learning opportunities have been pro-vided.
- *Written report:* A written report is required to provide information to document that each of the above criteria was met. It must be noted on the report whether all team members agree with the findings (USOE, 1977, p. 65083).

Despite widespread criticism, the definition and criteria above have been left unchanged since 1977. Recently, however, government leaders in Washington, D.C., have begun to emphasize the importance of developing a "genuine science" for dealing with LD (Elksnin et al., 2001). The recent reauthorization of IDEA (2004) reflected the thinking that significant changes were needed in the policies used to identify and serve students with LD; specifically, section one above requiring documentation of a discrep-ancy between achievement and IQ, was determined to be unnecessary and not suffi-cient for identifying individuals with specific learning disabilities (SLD):

> Schools shall not be required to take into consideration whether a child has a severe discrepancy between achievement and intellectual ability in oral expression, listening comprehension, written expression, basic reading skill, reading comprehension, mathematical calculation, or mathematical reasoning.

The use of a discrepancy model was replaced by the model referred to as the responsiveness-to-intervention (RTI) model. IDEA describes this approach "as a

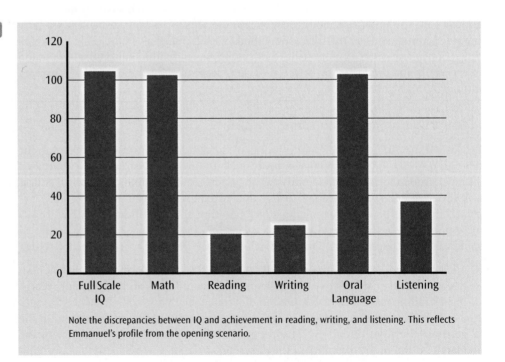

Figure **5.3**

**Profile of a Student with
Learning Disabilities**

Note the discrepancies between IQ and achievement in reading, writing, and listening. This reflects Emmanuel's profile from the opening scenario.

process that determines if a child responds to scientific, research-based intervention as a part of the evaluation procedures." The model is based on the assumption that a student without disabilities will make satisfactory progress when given intensive, well-designed instruction (National Joint Committee on Learning Disabilities, 2005). This is a prereferral intervention implemented in the general education classroom; it is predicted to reduce the number of special education referrals using a problem-solving approach rather than a mathematical discrepancy formula. Although no specific guidelines were given on implementing RTI, the National Joint Committee on Learning Disabilities (2005) has summarized the key elements in the process as:

1. Research-supported instructional and behavioral supports are implemented for all general education students and progress is monitored on a ongoing basis.
2. Students who lag behind peers in progress receive more individualized, intensive instruction with frequent monitoring to determine the needed modifications. Parents should be notified and included in planning and monitoring at this stage.
3. Parents of students not benefiting to an acceptable degree from this level of instruction are notified of their rights, and the decision-making process regarding a referral for special education services begins. Permission is obtained to proceed with the comprehensive evaluation needed for eligibility decisions to be made.

More than one evidence-based-practice may be implemented, but the team must weigh continued intervention against the resulting delay in considering special education services. Lyon and colleagues (2001) propose that this model applied to students with reading deficits could reduce the number of students with reading problems up to 70 percent. Schools were strongly encouraged to adopt this model, citing that it would result in earlier identification of children who may need special education services and offer more timely and effective support for all students experiencing academic difficulties, especially in the early elementary school years. However, not all professionals and parents are in full support of this model; Figure 5.4 presents some of the pro and con arguments being made in the debate over the replacement of the discrepancy clause with the RTI model. The National Research Center on Learning Disabilities and the six regional research centers are charged with identifying best practices in the RTI model, including identifying model programs.

Steps in the Assessment Process   When a student with continued deficits in areas of academic achievement is referred, the IEP team reviews the concerns stated on the referral and develops a comprehensive evaluation plan. RTI data will be an important consideration in determining eligibility but it cannot be the sole measure in the evaluation for special education services; data should come from parents, classroom assessments and observations, and standardized and statewide assessments (Bateman & Linden, 2006). One member of the evaluation team is assigned to observe the student in the general education classroom. This individual looks for any behaviors that might pose a limitation to success, such as inattention, impulsivity, or difficulties following directions. The student's academic deficits are noted, as well as the teacher's instructional style, to determine whether accommodations or modifications could be made to reduce deficits in learning. For example comprehension of reading passages might be given in timed and untimed formats to see if extended time would increase comprehension and be an effective accommodation.

The student is also evaluated for possible vision and hearing problems to determine whether these areas could be the cause of the learning problems. A professional with specialized training is assigned to administer an individualized intelligence test and evaluate the student in any academic areas in which there is a suspected deficit. Kavale (2001) recommends a combination of standardized, norm-referenced, and informal tests to measure achievement. In addition to measuring achievement, one or more teachers familiar with the student and often the student's parents complete a behavior-

CONSIDER THIS

Reflect on the characteristics of learning disabilities, such as deficits in attention, memory, cognition, and metacognition. What impact would these deficits have on success in the classroom?

CEC STANDARDS

CEC 4: Instructional Strategies

PRAXIS

PRAXIS II: Delivery of Services to Students with Disabilities

INTASC

INTASC 4: Uses a variety of instructional strategies

CEC STANDARDS

CEC 8: Assessment

| *Figure* 5.4 | **Issues Raised at the LD Summit and in the Literature** |

With the negative impact of the LD label (Higgins, Raskind, Goldberg, & Herman, 2002), some feel it is critical that we apply the label only to those who are truly learning disabled. Others have asked why students with specific LD are any more entitled to resources than those students who struggle for other reasons or are just slow (Finn, Rotherham, & Hokanson, 2002). MacMillian and Siperstein (2001) suggest that public schools are using low achievement alone without considering the discrepancy from aptitude, essentially making LD a "category of failure" or low achievement. Kavale and colleagues (2006) suggest that without the discrepancy factor, the existence of LD as a category is endangered. However, he suggests that determining discrepancy should be only one component of the assessment process. Wise and Snyder (2001), primarily focusing on reading, recommend the use of clinical judgment to determine disability and to identify the most effective instructional interventions. Other researchers also studying reading found that the students with low achievement had scores that were higher than the students with LD, especially on timed measures requiring skills in comprehension. Their research suggests that students with learning disabilities may be the lowest of the low achievers. Still others suggest that it is the lack of response to intervention that separates LD from other low achieving groups, and they recommend that this be considered in identification (Fuchs, Fuchs, Mathes, Lipsey, & Roberts, 2001). Kavale, and colleagues (2006) warn that using the RTI model to identify those with LD creates the potential for "diagnostic chaos." They propose that at best the RTI model will identify students at such risk for reading failure that they will require intensive intervention to have any chance for success. Conversely, Francis and colleagues (2005) purport that the weakness of using a discrepancy score is that the measurement is one point in time, using norm-referenced testing that has low reliability, whereas the RTI uses behaviors related to classroom performance and has more reliability than the norm-referenced testing.

rating scale. This behavioral assessment is completed to rule out the possibility that the primary cause of the deficit(s) in academic achievement is emotional or behavioral factors, suggesting that the child might be more appropriately served under the category of seriously emotionally disturbed.

At this point the IEP teams in states that choose to continue to use the discrepancy model will determine whether there is a severe discrepancy between the student's ability and achievement in one or more of the areas in which he or she was evaluated. This determination is typically made by obtaining a discrepancy score using a formula to quantify the severe discrepancy between achievement and potential (Kavale 2001). As noted earlier, IDEA 2004 does not require a discrepancy; in this case the IEP team would look at the RTI data to determine if the student should be further evaluated for possible special education placement due to lack of responsiveness to the evidence-based-teaching method implemented to allow the child to benefit from the general education curriculum. In either case, the IEP team must also consider whether the discrepancy or lack of progress could primarily be the result of a vision or hearing problem, mental retardation, emotional disturbance, or a disadvantaged economic status.

The team must also consider the student's history and document that appropriate learning opportunities have been provided. A child might not be determined eligible, for example, if a student's school attendance is reviewed and the team notes that the child has moved frequently during the school years, thus causing him or her to miss out on content as a result of the differences in each school's curriculum. If, after the review, the IEP team, including the parents, determines that the student is eligible for services, the team may decide to write the individualized educational plan immediately or return to develop the plan at a separate meeting. More information on educational plans is found in Chapter 4.

The criteria published in the Federal Register for identification of a learning disability (USOE, 1977) focus on the language, academic, and exclusion concepts and do not address the identification of deficits in areas such as attention and memory. However, it is often these characteristics and others noted in the characteristics section that create the biggest barriers to success in the general education classroom and later in the workforce. Teachers should be very familiar with the characteristics of LD and the impact they might have on functioning in a general education classroom. They should also understand that these characteristics are not manifested intentionally but occur as a result of a presumed central nervous system dysfunction.

Difficulty of Identifying Preschool Students with Learning Disabilities   Because the federal criteria for determining a learning disability mainly involve academic and language deficits that emerge in the elementary school years, the identification of LD and the delivery of special education services for preschoolers have been difficult and often controversial. One approach described by Hallahan and colleagues (2005) has been to identify students with a generic label such as "developmental delay." In this model students are determined to be at risk for school failure and receive assistance with language, academic, or motor skills in which they are generally found to be lagging behind as compared to their peers. The advantage of this approach is that it helps a large number of students if the criterion is a small developmental delay. However, if a significant delay is required to be eligible for services, the students with potential LD may be excluded, as it is much easier to identify mental retardation using more stringent criteria and less easy to identify the more subtle indicators of a learning disability.

The alternative to the generic approach is the identification of the specific disability. Mercer and Pullen (2005) describe several issues that make this approach difficult. The greatest complication is the tremendous differences in growth and maturation that children manifest, that are normal and may not represent a learning disability. They as well as Hallahan and colleagues (2005) offer caution against early identification of LD. Other concerns include the difficulty in diagnosis that results from the inadequacy of assessment tools and procedures for this age group. Young children may have language and other skills that are lower than expected based on IQ, but it is difficult to determine whether these are the result of a learning disability, a maturational lag, or the effect of diverse educational experiences, language, and/or culture. An additional concern is the risk of diagnosing a learning disability where none exists, thus labeling and burdening the child unnecessarily. However, this argument does not address the fact that an equal risk is taken when a student who needs special educational services is not diagnosed and appropriately assisted; this student may be burdened by difficulties and failure that could have been avoided. Many authors of the summit papers referenced at the end of the chapter in "Further Readings" stress the need for early intervention and use this argument to support the concept of RTI.

Critics call current practice for learning disabilities identification the "wait and fail" effect as the gap or discrepancy between ability and achievement becomes large enough to be labeled as a severe discrepancy that warrants services (MacMillian & Siperstein, 2001). Lyon and colleagues (2001) concluded that a child must be nine years old before discrepancy from IQ can be measured reliably. Thus, under the discrepancy model, potentially life-changing failure occurs for several years. They suggest that early intervention can be so critical for disabilities in the area of reading that children with a strong family history of attention difficulties or reading failure should be labeled at-risk and placed in a preventive intervention program to strengthen their deficit areas. Currently each state determines the proper age for identifying a child with a learning disability or one who is at risk for early school failure. Hammill (2004) identifies the following skills as effective screening items for identifying young

CEC STANDARDS

CEC 8: Assessment

INTASC

INTASC 8: Formal and informal assessment

PRAXIS

PRAXIS II: Delivery of Services to Students with Disabilities

children at risk for future reading failure: "Handling books; copying letters and numbers, writing their names; distinguishing print from nonprint markings; naming and writing letters and numbers; knowing the meaning of a few abbreviations and acronyms; discriminating among letters, numbers, and words; identifying and spelling some preprimer words."

CONSIDER THIS

A child's having a language and vocabulary other than English has a significant impact on the assessment process. Inappropriate referrals, identification of a disability, and/or inappropriate programming might result.

Cultural and Linguistic Diversity

The number of Americans who are a race other than European American has increased from one out of every eight in 1900 to one out of four in 2000 (Hallahan et al., 2005). Since learning disabilities are found in over 5 percent of the school-age population and the number of school-age children with cultural and language diversity is growing steadily, inevitably many children will fall into both groups. Much of the literature on special education supports the idea that there is overrepresentation of culturally and linguistically diverse (CLD) learners. Chamberlain (2005) suggests that this is due to multiple variables, some of which, like poverty, are beyond the realm of education; oth-

DIVERSITY FORUM

What Is Evidence-Based Practice for Teaching Reading to Middle School English Language Learners with LD?

Many of the English language learners (ELLs) with disabilities in my 6th and 7th grade reading groups have recently made the transition from bilingual (often, bilingual special education) to all-English instruction (like my class). These students lag behind the others in English vocabulary, spelling, grammar and syntax; their ability to express themselves and understand classroom English also trails that of their native English-speaking peers. My district has adopted a commercially-available reading program for all students (including ELLs) who are reading significantly below grade level that I'm expected to use with my students to build decoding skills. We were assured that the program has produced outstanding results, but I've been using the program for about six weeks now, and I'm worried that it does not teach some of the key skills I think my ELLs need.

This teacher is wise to examine his reading program with an eye to evaluating how well the program addresses some of the critical areas ELLs need to develop (Tyler, 2006). Many programs are designed primarily with the needs of elementary native English-speakers

in mind, and have been evaluated with primarily younger, mainstream, native English-speaking populations. To ensure that a commercially available, 'scientifically-based' reading program is appropriate for their students, teachers should verify that it has been validated for populations similar to those with whom it will be used (Hibbert & Iannacci, 2005). Specifically, the program's evaluation data should demonstrate effectiveness with:

- students at similar grades, and
- English language learners and speakers of non-standard English dialects.

In addition to teaching decoding, fluency, and comprehension, a solid reading curriculum for ELLs with LD must also build English language proficiency by emphasizing vocabulary and language use through the inclusion of language-rich discussions and regular opportunities to write (Echevarria & Graves, 1998).

Questions

1. In what ways and domains might a student's culture, language, and life experiences influence his or

her reading? How might a teacher adjust the reading curriculum and intervention strategies to be responsive to these characteristics?

2. How can reading instruction accomplish the goals of increasing decoding skills and fluency, while concurrently developing students' abilities to think about their reading in more complex ways and thus develop higher order comprehension?

REFERENCES

Hibbert, K. N., & Iannacci, L. (2005). From dissemination to discernment: The commodification of literacy instruction and the fostering of "good teacher consumerism." *Reading Teacher, 58*(8), 716–727.

Echevarria, J., & Graves, A. (1998). *Sheltered content instruction: Teaching English-language learners with diverse abilities.* Boston: Allyn & Bacon.

Tyler, B.-J. (2006). *Teaching reading to middle school English-language learners with learning disabilities in reading.* Unpublished doctoral dissertation, The University of Texas at Austin.

ers, like inadequate instruction and assessment practices, should be addressed. Accurately identifying a learning disability in the presence of cultural diversity is no small challenge. School personnel must carefully determine that the differences related to diversity in language or culture are not the primary cause of a student's learning difficulties. In other words, the student's learning difficulties must be significantly different when compared to peers in age, grade, and culture.

Gregory (2004) reports that too often a diagnosis of learning disability is based on intelligence and achievement tests administered in English without considering cultural and language differences. The discrepancy model is considered especially problematic when applied to CLD students because of the problems in using standardized tests with this population. The referral itself may be made because a teacher has been ineffective in teaching a student who comes from another culture or who understands little of the language of the classroom. In this case, the child's failure to make progress may not be the result of a learning disability but the failure of the educational system to respect and adequately respond to cultural and language differences (Garcia & Guerra, 2004). Chamberlain (2005) refers to these as "cultural clashes" and suggests that teachers sometimes expect less from students from diverse cultural backgrounds and may view special education as the most viable placement option for them. As a result, a disproportionate number are referred for assessment and ultimately funneled into special education settings. However, it is certainly possible that a child with a low socioeconomic level or one who speaks English as a second language could have a central nervous system dysfunction that results in a learning disability.

The IEP committee often has a big challenge in considering the diversity variable. Fuchs, Mock, Morgan, and Young (2003) propose that the RTI prereferral model is a promising approach to reduce the overrepresentation of CLD students in special education. In this model underachievement is addressed by more intense instruction with ongoing monitoring of progress by a team of individuals and a variety of nonstandardized measurement techniques. Recommendations for anyone involved in the assessment of CLD students are found in Figure 5.5.

Figure 5.5   Addressing Cultural and Linguistic Diversity in the Assessment Process

Following are recommendations for anyone involved in assessment of students. These were compiled by Chamberlain (2005) from a variety of sources.

1. Understand nondiscriminatory assessment practices. Bias may occur when English tests are used for students more fluent in another language, when tests have items that are biased, and when eligibility is determined using tests covering material the student has not had an opportunity to learn.
2. Know the law. IDEA requires nondiscriminatory and valid testing instruments, tests given in the child's native language, use of more than one source of data for eligibility determination, and use of an interdisciplinary team.
3. Rely less on norm-referenced data and more on comprehensive sets of data such as curriculum-based assessment techniques that measure directly what is being taught in the classroom
4. Support well-designed prereferral intervention to lessen referrals and lead to properly identified students receiving special education services.
5. Advocate for students by using a comprehensive set of assessment procedures, being alert for the possibility of bias, and validating the results of norm-referenced tests.

From: "Recognizing and Responding to Cultural Differences in the Education of Culturally and Linguistically Diverse Learners," by S. P. Chamberlain, 2005, *Intervention in School and Clinic, 40*(4), p. 207.

CEC STANDARDS
CEC 8: Assessment

PRAXIS
PRAXIS II: Delivery of Services to Students with Disabilities

INTASC
INTASC 8: Formal and informal assessment

Strategies for Curriculum and Instruction for Students with Learning Disabilities

Treatment procedures for individuals with learning disabilities have been controversial over the years. In the 1970s, advocates for perceptual training of auditory and visual processes debated those who advocated direct instruction in the deficit academic area(s) (Engelmann & Carnine, 1982). A convincing article by Hammill and Larsen (1974) analyzed research showing that perceptual training did little to improve basic academic skills. This triggered a move toward a skills approach, in which direct instruction was implemented in the areas of academic deficit. More recently, language, social-emotional, and cognitive-metacognitive areas have received positive attention. Many approaches have gained acceptance as research-based methods for improving the skills and developing the abilities of children and adults with learning disabilities; the methods used are typically determined by school policy or teacher preference. However, the 1999 regulations of IDEA expanded the definition of specially designed instruction to include the term "methodology," thus opening the door for the IEP team to specify the particular teaching method(s) that defines individualized instruction for a student.

Ideally the IEP team decisions will be developed by parents and professionals with knowledge of and support for methods that are backed by research and demonstrate evidence of benefit to children with disabilities. Unfortunately all teaching methods are not supported by research; some are considered nontraditional approaches by most professionals in the field but may have a large following in literature that is not research-based (Silver, 2003). Teachers need to be well informed on all approaches so they can provide objective information to parents who seek to understand and address their child's difficulties. Both parents and educators need to closely monitor the child's "ability to benefit" from the method of instruction being used to teach new skills; this data will help the team determine when a new intervention is needed if the child fails to make adequate progress. The following section discusses the evidence-based, traditional approaches for each age level and a brief overview of some of the nontraditional approaches.

Evidence-Based Approaches

In a review of various treatment approaches, Elksnin and colleagues (2001) conclude that no single approach to learning disabilities can be cited as the best. They suggest that each model has a "partial view of the truth" and "each individually is too narrow to be useful for all students" (p. 189). The following approaches are time-tested and research-based. They can be implemented in a general education classroom and may benefit many nondisabled students as well. The strategies are discussed according to age levels—preschool, elementary, secondary, and adult. The largest section concerns the elementary school student; however, many elementary-level techniques are equally effective at the secondary level. An understanding of these approaches is critical, as recent federal data indicate that the majority of students with LD received at least 60 percent of their instruction in the general education classroom (U.S.Department of Education, 2002).

Preschool Services   In addition to the controversy surrounding assessment and identification of learning disabilities in preschool children, much has been written for and against the educational effectiveness and cost-effectiveness of early intervention programs for these children. Bender (2001) summarizes research in this area by stating that early intervention for some preschool children with learning disabilities—particularly those from low socioeconomic minority groups—is effective. One of the expected benefits from RTI is the reduction of the overidentification of minority students. The National

Joint Committee on Learning Disabilities, (NJCLD) (2005) reports a study in Minneapolis in which the number of referrals and special education placements was reduced for African American students during a four-year period when the RTI approach was implemented (Marston et al., 2003). Congress emphasized the need for early intervening services for students in kindergarten through third grade, although they may be implemented in any grade level. The focus is on behavioral interventions and research-based literacy programs; however, services may include evaluation of educational or behavioral needs and any service or support needed (Bateman & Linden, 2006).

Mercer (2005) provides an overview of the curriculum models primarily used in preschool programs for children with LD. These include developmental, cognitive, and behavioral models. The **developmental model** stresses provision of an enriched environment. The child is provided numerous experiences and opportunities for learning. Development is stimulated through language and storytelling, field trips, and creative opportunities. These activities are particularly effective with diverse learners (Craig et al., 2001).

The **cognitive model** (or constructionist model) is based on Piaget's work. Stimulating the child's cognitive or thinking abilities is the primary focus. Activities are designed to improve memory, discrimination, language, concept formation, self-evaluation, problem solving, and comprehension. This new area of research is experiencing great success.

Concepts learned by direct instruction and the theory of reinforcement form the basis for the **behavioral model**. Measurable goals are set for each student, behaviors are observed, and desirable behavior is reinforced. Direct instruction is provided to accomplish goals, and progress is charted to provide data that determine the next instructional task. Coyne, Zipoli, and Ruby (2006) use the term "conspicuous instruction" and stress the importance of this type of intentional teaching in the five "big ideas" in literacy and beginning reading identified by the National Reading Panel (2000). These are described in detail in Table 5.1. The nearby Evidence-Based Practice box provides an example of a first grade lesson for teaching phonemic awareness.

Most children with learning disabilities are identified during early elementary grades.

Table 5.1   Big Ideas in Beginning Reading Instruction

Big Idea	Example
Phonemic Awareness: The ability to hear, identify, and manipulate the individual sounds in spoken words.	• Blending: Combining individual spoken sounds to form a word. Example: The sounds mmm . . . ooo . . . p make the word *mop*. • Segmentation: Separating a spoken word into individual sounds. Example: The word *mop* is made up of the sounds mmm . . . ooo . . . p.
Phonics: Understanding the relationship between the letters of written language and the individual sounds of spoken language, and using these relationships to read and spell words.	• Letter–sound correspondences: Knowing the sounds that correspond to letters and the letters that correspond to sounds. Example: The letter *b* represents the sound /b/; the sound /aaa/ is represented by the letter *a*. • Regular word decoding/spelling: Reading/spelling words in which each letter represents its most common sound. Example: mat, sled, fast • Advanced phonics skills: Reading/spelling words that include more advanced spelling patterns and multiple syllables. Example: make, train, mu-sic, re-port
Fluency: The effortless, automatic ability to read quickly and accurately in connected text.	• Accuracy: Reading grade-level text accurately. • Speed: Reading grade-level text quickly and automatically. • Prosody: Reading grade-level text with expression.
Vocabulary: The ability to understand and use words to acquire and convey meaning.	• Vocabulary knowledge: Possessing a well-developed vocabulary acquired directly through instruction or indirectly through exposure to vocabulary in oral and/or written language. • Strategy knowledge: Applying strategies for determining the meanings of unknown words by using context or meaningful word parts (e.g., roots, affixes).
Comprehension: The complex cognitive process involving the intentional interaction between reader and text to construct meaning.	• Priming prior knowledge/previewing/predicting. • Identifying the main idea/summarizing. • Organizing information/using text structure/using graphic organizers. • Answering and asking questions. • Self-monitoring understanding.

From: "Beginning Reading Instruction for Students at Risk for Reading Disabilities: What, How, and When" (p. 163), by M. D. Coyne, R. P. Zipoli, and M. F. Ruby, 2006, *Intervention in School and Clinic, 41* (3), pp. 161–168.

CEC STANDARDS

CEC 4: Instructional Strategies

Mercer (2005) recommends a program that combines features from each approach. He suggests some structure, availability of free-choice activities, direct instruction in targeted areas, daily charting and feedback, developmental activities, and spontaneous learning experiences. McCordle and colleagues (2001) speak to the importance of the birth-to-five period as the foundation for learning as children acquire knowledge and develop abilities—particularly in the area of reading. They, like others, speak against the "wait to fail" approach where children are not identified as struggling readers until the third or fourth grade. These researchers recommend a focus on book reading, writing, and fine-motor activities like coloring and drawing, as well as on developmental experiences that enhance vocabulary and increase language and communication skills.

These methods allow individual needs to be met in an inclusive setting without stigmatizing the children. Since children at this age are more likely to be falsely identified

EVIDENCE-BASED PRACTICE

Evidence-Based Instruction: Sound Blending

Phonemic awareness activities that you may see in the first grade classrooms

Phoneme deletion: Children recognize the word that remains when you take away a phoneme.

Example
Teacher: What is *space* without the /s/?
Children: *Space* without the /s/ is *pace*.

Phoneme addition: Children make a new word by adding a phoneme to a word.

Example
Teacher: What word do you have if you add /p/ to the beginning of *lace*?
Children: *Place*.

Phoneme substitution: Children substitute one phoneme for another to make a new word.

Example
Teacher: The word is *rag*. Change /g/ to /n/. What's the new word?
Children: *Ran*.

Teaching phonics and word recognition
The teacher…
explicitly teaches the children letter-sound relationships in a clear and useful sequence. The teacher also teaches children "irregular" words they will see and read often, but that do not follow the letter-sound relationships they are learning. These are often called **sight words**—words such as *said, is, was, are*.

The children…
learn to blend sounds to read words—first one-syllable words and, later, words with more than one syllable. They read easy books that include the letter-sound relationships they are learning as well as sight words that they have been taught. They recognize and figure out the meaning of compound words (words made of two words put together, such as *background*). They practice writing the letter-sound relationships in words, sentences, messages, and their own stories.

From: *A Child Becomes a Reader* (p. 33) by National Institute for Literacy.

---

as learning disabled because of a maturational lag or lack of educational opportunities, it is particularly important to teach them in inclusive settings if at all possible. Lyon and colleagues (2001) agreed that the most efficient way to intervene early in reading is through general education. They were instrumental in designating that schools could use up to 15 percent of federal funds for RTI efforts. They summarized several studies stating that when intervention is used with the bottom 18 percent of the student population and works on 70 percent, the number of at-risk children requiring services drops from 18 to 5.4 percent.

Elementary Services The importance of intervention during the early elementary years is validated by Lyon and colleagues (2001), suggesting that over 70 percent of the children with a reading disability in the third grade remained disabled in the twelfth grade. As discussed in the section on characteristics, many of these deficits remain a problem throughout an individual's life. The intervention begun during elementary school years may be equally important at the secondary level and for some adults. Intervention is important in academic and language deficits, social-emotional problems, and cognitive and metacognitive deficits.

Children with learning disabilities may have academic and language deficits in any or all of the following areas:

- basic reading skills
- reading comprehension
- math calculation
- math reasoning
- written expression
- oral expression
- listening

Since these areas are usually the focus of an elementary school curriculum, they can very often be addressed in the general education classroom. Both general and special education

CONSIDER THIS

According to Lyon's study, intervention in reading skills in grades 1–3 is critical. Should all students who are behind their peers in reading ability be helped during these years? What are possible positive and negative outcomes of providing a special education program for all these children who are at risk for later failure?

IEP Goals and Objectives for Emmanuel*

The chapter-opening vignette explains that Emmanuel is struggling primarily in the areas of reading, listening, and writing. The following sample from his IEP shows his top three goals and the objectives necessary to meet them.

Goal 1: Reading   Emmanuel will read orally and demonstrate comprehension of text on the third-grade level.

Objective 1:   Given a list of Dolch sight words, Emmanuel will read words through third-grade level with 80% accuracy three times in a row.

Objective 2:   Given a paragraph on his reading level, Emmanuel will use context clues to predict unknown words with 70% accuracy.

Objective 3:   Given a list of 10 multisyllable words in isolation and a list of 10 multisyllable words in text, Emmanuel will correctly apply phonetic patterns in decoding the words with an 80% accuracy rate.

Objective 4:   Given a paragraph at his reading level, Emmanuel will read the text and respond to comprehension questions orally or in writing with an 80% accuracy rate.

Goal 2: Listening   Emmanuel will increase his listening skills.

Objective 1:   Given a list of words orally, Emmanuel will display his increased phonemic awareness skills by repeating them in order with 80% accuracy.

Objective 2:   After listening to a story read by the teacher, Emmanuel will retell it with age-appropriate detail, with 80% accuracy.

Objective 3:   Given a multistep set of oral directions, Emmanuel will follow each step with 100% accuracy.

Goal 3: Writing   Emmanuel will develop age-appropriate writing skills.

Objective 1:   Given a list of Dolch words through third-grade level, Emmanuel will spell the words correctly with 80% accuracy.

Objective 2:   Given a list of Dolch words through third-grade level, Emmanuel will apply phonetic patterns to spell multisyllable words with 80% accuracy.

Objective 3:   Given the assignment to write in his daily journal, Emmanuel will write daily journal entries using age-appropriate vocabulary.

Objective 4:   Given the assignment to write in his daily journal, Emmanuel will construct complete sentences, including correct capitalizations, punctuation, and grammar, with 80% accuracy.

Objective 5:   Given a topic sentence, Emmanuel will generate a paragraph with at least five sentences, including a topic sentence, supporting details, and a concluding sentence, with 80% accuracy.

*IDEA 2004 does not require short-term objectives except for students taking alternative assessments.

CEC STANDARDS

CEC 8: Assessment

INTASC

INTASC 7: Instruction based on knowledge of subject matter

teachers have been trained to provide instruction in these areas, so collaborative teaching is possible. Because of the uneven skill development in children with LD, individualized assessment is generally required to identify areas that specifically need to be addressed. Informal methods, such as the curriculum-based assessment discussed in Chapter 4, are usually effective for planning instruction. This assessment should include an evaluation of the student's strengths that may indicate the most effective method for instruction.

Because student strengths and weaknesses are so diverse, a single method of teaching may not meet the needs of all students with LD. For example, in the area of reading instruction, many general education teachers use a reading approach based on reading literature for meaning; development in areas such as phonics is assumed to occur naturally as the reader becomes more efficient. In this method, often referred to as the **whole language method**, the teacher might note difficulty with a phonetic principle during oral reading and subsequently develop a minilesson using text to teach the skill. Unfortunately, many children with LD do not readily acquire the alphabet code because of limitations in processing the sounds of letters.

Research has shown a dramatic reduction in reading failure when comprehensive, explicit instructions are provided in **phonemic awareness**, a structured sequential phonics program for decoding and fluent word recognition, processing text to construct meaning, vocabulary, spelling, and writing. A small number of children will need an intense small-group or one-on-one format (Foorman & Torgesen, 2001). A survey of teaching practices used by special education teachers nominated as effective literacy teachers showed that they used direct instruction and the best of whole language. See Table 5.2 to learn the practices and philosophies of these outstanding teachers. Evidence supporting teaching strategies is found in the literature. Hammill (2004) reviewed over 450 studies of reading and concluded that educators concerned with teaching reading should focus on direct teaching of reading skills, especially programs linking reading to writing and including the following:

PRAXIS

PRAXIS II: Delivery of Services to Students with Disabilities

- print awareness and alphabet knowledge
- phonics (e.g., letter-sound correspondence), word attack, and word identification
- comprehension
- oral and silent reading fluency
- written composition, spelling and sentence punctuation, and textual composition

The activity in the near-by evidence-based instruction includes incorporating writing to strengthen comprehension skills and using text to reinforce the phonic skill being taught through direct instruction.

Another way to facilitate success for students with learning disabilities in inclusive settings is teaching a **strategy** to apply during the process of learning new information or skills. A strategy is defined by Lenz, Deshler, and Kissam (2004) as an individual's approach to a task. Teaching a strategy provides a specific set of steps for thinking strategically, including how to approach difficult and new tasks, guide actions and thoughts, and finish tasks successfully and in a timely manner. Students with learning disabilities may not automatically develop strategies for learning, or the ones they develop may be inefficient. With the increased emphasis on state competency tests, it is more important than ever to remember academic content.

Using mnemonic strategies can help students with learning disabilities having problems with memory. For example, to remember $4 \times 8 = 32$, the student might associate "door" for "4" and "gate" for "8" and a "dirty shoe" for "32," so the association to visualize would be a door on a gate by a dirty shoe (Wood & Frank, 2000). One very simple but effective strategy for increasing reading comprehension is a questioning strategy where students are taught how to ask and then answer these summarization strategy questions

- Who or what is the paragraph about?
- What is happening to whom or what?
- Create a summary sentence in your own words using less than ten words.

Mastropieri, Scruggs, and Graetz (2003) provide this strategy and the research to support it; however, they note that the set of instructional features found in Figure 5.6 are critical to successful strategy instruction. (Additional examples of strategy instruction are discussed in Chapter 16.)

Students with learning disabilities in the area of mathematics have been described by Gersten, Jordan, and Flojo (2005) as lacking in "number sense." They propose that the traditional method of math instruction for students in special education that focuses on teaching algorithms and being drilled on number facts has led to a lack of general understanding. Their work supports the use of "responseness to intervention" for

CEC STANDARDS

CEC 4: Instructional Strategies

Table 5.2	**Philosophies, Learning Environments, and Instructional Processes and Practices Frequently Reported by Effective Special Education Teachers of Reading and Writing**

General Philosophies and Learning Environments

Identify with a Whole Language Philosophy

Use of the language experience approach

Create a literate environment in the classroom, including in-class library, chart stories, signs and labels, and word lists

Use of themes to organize reading and writing instruction, with these themes extending into other curricular areas

Attempt to motivate literacy encouraging positive attitudes, providing positive feedback, reducing risks for attempting literacy activities, accepting where students are and working from that point, creating an exciting mood, encouraging personal interpretations, and conveying the importance of reading and writing in daily life

Encourage ownership and personal decision making

General Teaching Processes

Ability grouping for half of instruction, however, not in the form of traditional reading groups

Small-group and individualized instruction is predominant

Direct instruction of attending behaviors

Direct instruction of listening skills

Assess learning styles and adjustment of instruction accordingly

Parent communication and involvement—specific reading and writing activities occurring with parents at home

Monitor progress several times a week by both formal and informal methods

Teaching of Reading

Types of Reading and Materials

Total class and individual silent reading

Individual oral reading, including round-robin reading

Different types of materials used—materials with controlled reading level, outstanding children's literature, materials that provide practice in specific phonetic elements and patterns (about half as often as the others)

What Is Taught

Concepts of print, including punctuation, sounds associated with print, concept of words and letters, parts of a book, directionality of print; taught both in context and isolation

Alphabetic principle and alphabet recognition; taught in context, isolation, with games and puzzles

Letter–sound associations, auditory discrimination, and visual discrimination; taught in context, isolation, with games and puzzles

Decoding skills taught several times a day in both context and isolation, most frequently teaching sounding out words and use of context cues

Explicit teaching of phonics based on individual student needs

Explicit teaching of sight words

Develop new vocabulary, using words from stories, other reading and writing, and student-selected words

Direct teaching of comprehension strategies, most frequently teaching prediction of upcoming events, finding the main idea, and activation of prior knowledge

Explicit attempts to develop background knowledge

Teach text elements, including character analysis, sequence of events, theme, details, and plot

Teach about various illustrators

Instructional Practice—Both Traditional and Whole Language

Use of worksheets and workbooks for specific instructional purposes

Use of frequent drill and repetition (for learning such things as sight words, phonic elements, spelling words, letter recognition), occurring both in the context of reading and writing and in more traditional practice methods

Tracing and copying of letters and words

Daily reading, both independent and in groups

Read stories to students with students "reading along"

Overt modeling of reading and writing

Comprehension questions asked for nearly all stories read

Weekly use of literature discussions

Use of story mapping or webbing to teach text elements

Publish students' work

Teaching Writing

Frequent writing (several times a week to several times a day)

Model the writing process

Students write stories, journals, and books

Guided writing

Write in response to reading

Teach planning, drafting, and revising as part of writing

Teach punctuation, both in context of real writing and in isolation

Teach spelling, including high-frequency words, words from spelling and reading curriculum, and words from students' writing

Acceptance and encouragement of invented spelling

From "Literacy in Special Education" (p. 221), by J. L. Rankin-Erickson and M. Pressley, 2000, *Learning Disabilities Research and Practice, 15*(4), pp. 206–225.

young children showing math difficulties; this intervention should focus on teaching math combinations, counting strategies, and number sense (Gersten et al., 2005). Additional strategies proposed by Furner, Yahya, and Duffy (2005) include: teaching vocabulary; demonstrating with real objects; relating vocabulary and math problems to prior knowledge and daily life experiences; using manipulatives and drawing pictures to solve math problems; using the computer and cooperative learning activities with heterogeneous student groupings; connecting math to other disciplines such as history

INTASC

INTASC 4: Variety of Instructional Strategies

EVIDENCE-BASED PRACTICE

Main Idea Activity

Book Title	Chapter 1 Illustration Main Idea	Chapter 2	Chapter 3	Chapter 4
Chapter 5	Chapter 6	Chapter 7	Chapter 8	Student Name

Directions:

1. Fold a piece of paper into the appropriate number of squares.

2. After reading chapter one, write the main idea on your main idea poster.

3. Illustrate the main idea (see chart for a visual direction).

4. Go on to the next chapter.

Phonics Activity

Directions:

1. Fold a piece of paper to resemble a bookmark.

2. Draw a picture at the top of your bookmark. (Make sure it relates to your book.)

3. Locate words in your book that address the skill you are working on.

4. As you find words in your book, write them on the inside of the bookmark.

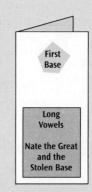

First Base

Long Vowels

Nate the Great and the Stolen Base

From: "Engaging Students in Meaningful Reading" (p. 17), by A. Rossow and C. Hess, 2001. *Teaching Exceptional Children, 33*(6), pp. 15–20.

and literature; and making cultural connections when teaching math, for example, taking "Internet field trips." Figure 5.7 contains excellent websites for math activities and help with math anxiety.

Written language is often difficult to master for children and adults with LD. Unfortunately, making too many adaptations in this area may result in underdeveloped skills. For example, if a student is always allowed to use another student's notes or allowed to take tests orally in place of written exams, the short-term benefits may be helpful, but instruction and experience in taking notes and writing essay answers must be continued if growth is to occur in these areas. This is another area that strategy instruction can be used to develop important skills. Figure 5.8 shows a motivating strategy to prompt a five-paragraph theme using a graphic organizer. An impressive method for team-teaching a report writing strategy in a general education classroom is described by Graham, Harris, and MacArthur (2006), in which the special education teacher takes the lead in introducing the strategy and working with the struggling writers, and the general education

PRAXIS

PRAXIS II: Delivery of Instruction to Students with Disabilities

Figure 5.6 **Effective Intervention Components**

- Use clear objectives
- Follow specific sequence for teaching
  - state the purpose
  - provide instruction
  - model
  - guided practice
  - corrective feedback
  - independent practice
  - generalization practice
- Inform the students of importance of the strategy
- Monitor performance
- Encourage questions that require students to think about strategies and text
- Encourage appropriate attributions
- Teach for generalized use of the strategy

From: "Reading Comprehension Instruction for Secondary Students: Challenges for Struggling Students and Teachers," (p. 106), by M. A. Mastropieri, T. E. Scruggs, and J. E. Graetz, 2003, *Learning Disability Quarterly, 26,* pp. 103–116.

TEACHING TIP

Many students with learning disabilities resist the challenge to write because of prior negative feedback. Try giving them multiple opportunities without grading, and then grade only one or two skills at a time. For example, one week you might grade punctuation, and the next, spelling. You can also give one grade for content and another for mechanics, and then average the two scores for the final grade.

teacher participates in all phases of instruction. The authors point out that by explicitly teaching these strategies for planning, drafting, and revising text, the struggling writers, as well as their classmates, are helped with better writing skills.

Improvement in oral language can be stimulated by promoting a better self-concept, teaching the skills of language production directly, and enriching the language environment. When students speak, listen closely to the message and respond appropriately; save corrections for a later teaching moment. The respect you show for attempts at communication will increase conversation and confidence. Providing opportunities for students to share their experiences and expertise is also a nonthreatening way to promote use of oral language. Listening and praise help reinforce talking. Bos and Vaughn

Figure 5.7 **Websites that Address Math Anxiety and Teach Mathematics**

www.mathpower.com
This website by Professor Freedman offers great resources for both teachers and students. Students can take a math anxiety test to evaluate their level of math anxiety, and they can learn math study skills and get help with basic math and algebra. The Student's Math Anxiety Bill of Rights is great for hanging in the classroom. For teachers, the website provides a plethora of information on math anxiety and ways to help students who are math anxious.

www.funbrain.com
This website, designed for teachers, parents, and students, provides great math activities and games that offer practice in a gamelike setting. It also offers teachers tools for making tests and activity sheets and provides a grade book. Parents will find the site wonderful for teaching and motivating their children to learn math, as well as language arts, science, history, music, geography, art, technology, and physical education.

funschool.kaboose.com
This great site for teachers, parents, and children is like educational software presented through the Internet. It offers a wide variety of math and literacy games and activities to keep any child engaged and motivated mathematically for a long time.

coolmath.com
One of the most exciting websites for children, it is full of color and offers exciting activities in math and science, including many interesting math facts and statistics. Kids can practice running a business selling lemonade while dealing with the weather and other factors, using both math and science skills in a real-life application.

From: "Equity for All students in the New Millenium: Disabling Math Anxiety" (p. 73), by J. M. Furner and M. L. Dubby, 2002. *Intervention in School and Clinic, 38*(2), pp. 67–74.

| Figure 5.8 | **Graphic Organizer for Five-Paragraph Essay** |

Graphic Organizer A
(one of the five organizers students can choose in this plan sheet)

Introduction

First Idea

Second Idea

Third Idea

Conclusion

From: "Effects of a Motivational Intervention for Improving the Writing of Children with Learning Disabilities" (p. 146), by J. N. García and A. M. deCaso, 2004. *Learning Disability Quarterly, 27*, pp. 141–159.

(2002) reviewed the research in the area of spoken language and made the following additional recommendations:

- Increase wait time to allow sufficient time for comprehension and a response.
- Model good language.
- Take the student's words and briefly elaborate or expand on ideas.

CEC STANDARDS

CEC 4: Instructional Strategies

- Use parallel talk and self-talk to describe what you and others are doing and thinking.
- Use a structured language program and build in activities in a variety of settings to develop generalization.

Poor listening skills also limit individuals with LD, influencing success both in the classroom and in social interactions. It is important for teachers to analyze the amount of listening required in their classrooms, study the barriers to good listening such as distracting noises, and teach and reinforce specific listening strategies (Swain, Friehe, & Harrington, 2004). Following is a simple strategy to cue listening behaviors that can be modified for older students (Heaton & O'Shea, 1995).

L	Look at the teacher.
I	Ignore the student next to you.
S	Stay in your place.
T	Try to visualize and understand the story.
E	Enjoy the story.
N	Nice job! You're a good listener.

Computers and other technology can assist in teaching individuals with learning disabilities in inclusive classrooms. Olsen and Platt (1996) describe the following advantages of technology that still hold true today:

- It is self-pacing and individualized.
- It provides immediate feedback.
- It has consistent correction procedures.
- It provides repetition without pressure.
- It confirms correct responses immediately.
- It maintains a high frequency of student response.
- It builds in repeated validation of academic success.
- It is an activity respected by peers.
- It is motivating.
- It encourages increased time on task.
- It minimizes the effects of the disability.

The computer can be used effectively for curriculum support in math, writing, language arts, social studies, science, and other areas. Various types of software provide instructional alternatives such as tutoring, drill and practice, simulation, and games. With so many choices available, teachers should carefully evaluate each program for ease of use and appropriateness for exceptional students.

Intervention related to social interactions and emotional maturity is critical for many students with LD. The inclusion movement provides opportunities for interactions; the question is how to best prepare both the children with disabilities and nondisabled children for positive interactions. Changing a student's self-image, social ability, and social standing is difficult. Until recently, the research and literature on LD focused primarily on the efficacy of treatments for the most obvious characteristic—academic deficits. The importance of social skills is just now being recognized and given the attention it deserves.

Intervention in the area of social standing and interaction can take two courses: changing the child or changing the environment. Optimally, both receive attention. Good teaching techniques can lead to academic achievement and eventually to higher self-esteem. Teachers can create a positive learning environment, incorporate praise and encouragement for specific accomplishments, such as making positive comments about themselves and others. Teachers should also set goals and be very explicit about expectations for academic work and behavior in the class; they should monitor progress closely and provide frequent feedback (Polloway et al., 2001).

Improvement in low academic self-concept has also been made by correcting maladaptive **attributional styles**, or teaching students to take credit for their successes.

Students with higher academic self-concepts have been found to work harder to achieve (Tabassam & Grainger, 2002).

Modeling prosocial skills and positive self-talk is important, as well as is providing natural opportunities for conversation and conflict resolution. A forum during group time can be used to pose potential problems and generate discussions to brainstorm possible solutions before the situations occur (Morris, 2002). Role-playing successful cooperation followed by experience in collaborative group projects can also provide positive social experiences if the teacher monitors closely. Figure 5.9 provides a lesson plan in which the goal is to provide direct instruction to teach students to interact with other individuals.

The overall goal of social programs is to teach socially appropriate behavior and social skills that are self-generated and self-monitored. The cognitive problems of students with LD often make this type of decision making very difficult and often these skills that seem to develop naturally in most children have to be taught. Areas potentially in need of instruction are included in Figure 5.10. Although the effectiveness of social skills training has had little empirical support, it seems that this is too important a life skill to ignore, and research efforts should continue (Kavale & Mostert, 2004).

Intervention in cognitive and metacognitive skills has only recently received support from LD professionals. Powerful techniques are being studied to improve learning. Some of the ideas are relatively simple and require only common sense. First, and most important, is being sure a child is paying attention to the stimulus being presented. This purpose might be achieved by dimming the lights, calling for attention, or establishing eye contact. Without attention, learning will not take place. A fun and effective strategy for gaining students' attention is presented in Figure 5.11. The strategy is introduced,

| *Figure* 5.9 | **Teaching Interaction** |

Nonverbal Behavior
1. Face the student.
2. Maintain eye contact.
3. Maintain a neutral or pleasant facial expression.

Paraverbal Behavior
4. Maintain a neutral tone of voice.
5. Speak at a moderate volume.

Verbal Teaching Behavior
6. Begin with a compliment related to the student's efforts and achievements.
7. Introduce the social skill and define what the social skill means.
8. Give a rationale for learning the skill and for using the skill with others.
9. Share an experience when you used the social skill or could have used the social skill.
10. Specify each behavior (e.g., nonverbal and verbal behavior) to be considered when exhibiting the skill.
11. Demonstrate or model the use of the skill.
12. Have the student rehearse the social skill. (Observe the student's behavior.)
13. Provide positive corrective feedback.
    State what the student did correctly.
14. Practice the social skill with the student. (Make sure you do not prompt.)
15. Continue to provide corrective feedback to practice until the student masters (100 percent) the social skill in a novel situation.
16. Plan, with the student, when and where to use the social skill.

Remember: Make sure the student participates throughout the lesson. To do so, ask questions and let the student share ideas and thoughts. Always praise the student for participating and rehearsing the social skill.

From: *Strategies for Teaching Learners with Special Needs* (p. 212), by E. A. Polloway, J. R. Patton, and L. Serna, 2001. Upper Saddle River, NJ: Merrill.

Figure 5.10   **Examples of Social Skills**

Starting a conversation	Expressing your feelings	Using self-control
Asking a question	Negotiation	Keeping out of fights
Introducing yourself	Setting goals	Feeling sad
Asking for help	Working cooperatively	Responding to aggression
Learning how to listen	Dealing with frustration	Responding to failure
Apologizing	Controlling anger	Decision-making

From: "Social skills Interventions for Individuals with Learning Disabilities" (p. 33), by K. A. Kavale and M. P. Mostert, 2004, *Learning Disability Quarterly, 27,* pp. 31–43.

modeled, and practiced with and then without teacher guidance. The chart can be posted in the room or on individual desks. New lessons can begin with the exciting prompt, "Give me five!"

CEC STANDARDS

CEC 4: Instructional Strategies

Secondary Services   Academic and language deficits, social and emotional problems, and differences in cognitive and metacognitive functioning continue to plague many adolescents with LD. With the focus on content classes in middle and high school,

Figure 5.11   **Give Me Five Strategy Used to Increase Listening Skills**

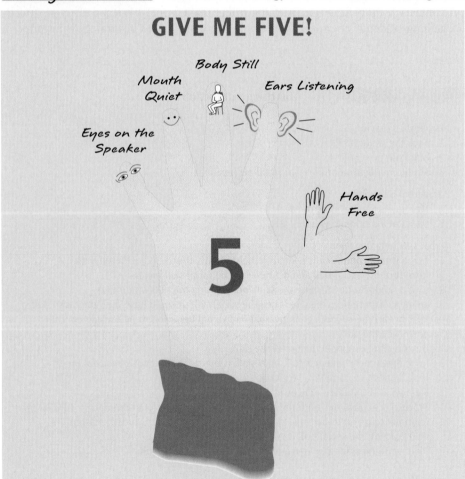

From: *Language Strategies for Children,* by Vicki Prouty and Michele Fagan, 1997. Eau Claire, WI: Thinking Publications (1-800-225-4769; www.ThinkingPublications.com). Copyright 1997 by Thinking Publications. Reprinted with permission.

remediation of basic skills often is minimal. This situation can be problematic for students having difficulty passing the high school graduation exam required in many states for a regular diploma, and for those unable to read the content material at the secondary level. Students who continue to benefit from remediation should be provided these opportunities. Research-based strategies are available to teach secondary students who are struggling readers to read the all important multisyllabic words. Several of these are described by Archer, Gleason, and Vachon (2003); the Evidence-Based Practice box demonstrates one strategy in which students are taught to decode these words by breaking them into smaller, more readable parts, while the teacher also introduces the new content vocabulary. Chapter 16 will include more on this evidence-based practice.

The adaptations described in the next section and the learning strategies described in the previous section can also be used with secondary students to facilitate basic skill acquisition and to make learning and performance more effective and efficient (Chamberlain, 2006). For example, instead of trying to bring basic skills to a level high enough to read a chapter in a content area textbook written on grade level, a teacher might assist students in comprehension by reading the heading and one or two sentences in each paragraph in a chapter. Students can be taught self-questioning strategies such as "What or who is the paragraph about?" and "What is happening to whom or what?" to increase their comprehension (Mastropieri et al., 2003). Strategies can enable a student to handle the increased amount of content information, but it is equally important to be sure that the cognitive level of the student is sufficient to handle the strategy. Don Deshler, credited with validating the learning strategies model, warns that other elements also important to content learning include teaching critical vocabulary skills, building prior knowledge to connect to new information, and teaching an understanding of the structure of text (Chamberlain, 2006).

The teacher can also make an impact on student learning and performance by accounting for individual differences when developing and implementing lesson plans. Many students fail, not because of an inability to perform but because they do not understand directions, cannot remember all the information, or cannot process verbal information fast enough. Most adults and older children automatically lower the language they use when speaking to younger children or individuals with obvious disabilities. Unfortunately they do not typically do so when speaking to school-age children and adults with LD—even though the latter may have language-based learning disabilities. Johnson (1999) suggests the following strategies to meet the needs of students with language difficulties in an inclusive classroom setting:

- Be conscious of the level of language used, including rate of presentation, complexity of vocabulary, and sentence structure.
- Prepare a list of relevant terms prior to instruction; pretest students to determine their level of understanding.
- Adjust the level of language until students have basic concepts.
- Use demonstrations as needed.
- Repeat instructions individually to students if necessary.
- Select a method of testing knowledge to match the student's best method of communication. For example, a student may be able to select the correct answer from options given but not be able to answer open-ended questions (p. 6).

As noted earlier in the chapter, a major problem for secondary students with LD is low self-concept and social and emotional problems that often stem from years of school failure. To help ameliorate unhappiness, school environments must be structured to create successful experiences. One method involves **self-determination**, or making students more active participants in designing their educational experiences and monitoring their own success; this can be done by teaching self-awareness and self-advocacy skills. Students should use these skills as active participants in their IEP meetings. Such participation is particularly important when a student is deciding whether to continue postsecondary education or to obtain employment after high school (Pocock et al., 2002).

CONSIDER THIS

Many parents are drawn to nontraditional approaches to treating LD because the approaches promise a quick cure. How will you respond when a parent asks your opinion of the value of one of these approaches for his or her child?

PRAXIS

PRAXIS II: Delivery of Services to Students with Disabilities

EVIDENCE-BASED PRACTICE

Part-by-Part Decoding Instruction when Preteaching Content Area Words

Overt Strategy

1. Circle the word parts (prefixes at the beginning of the word.
2. Circle the word parts (suffixes) at the end of the word.
3. Underline the letters representing vowel sounds in the rest of the word.
4. Say the parts of the word.
5. Say the parts fast.
6. Make it a real word.

EXAMPLE

Covert Strategy

1. Look for word parts at the beginning and end of the word, and vowel sounds in the rest of the word.
2. Say the parts of the word.
3. Say the parts fast.
4. Make it a real word.

From: "Decoding and Fluency: Foundation Skills for Struggling Readers" by A. L. Archer, M. C. Gleason, and V. L. Vachon, 2003, *Learning Disability Quarterly 26*, 89-103.

While giving students more power and responsibility for determining their life outcome is very important at the secondary level, it is also important to maintain communication with parents and involve them in this process (Jayanthi et al., 1999). Parents can promote responsibility in their children by setting clear expectations and consequences in regard to school achievement. Teachers can help by:

- Giving parents and students information on course assignments for the semester, available adaptations, and policies.
- Providing progress reports, including descriptive comments on the quality of homework.
- Putting assignment calendars on brightly colored paper to prevent misplacement.
- Collaborating with other teachers to prevent homework overloads.
- Communicating with parents regarding the amount of time students spend completing homework and adjusting workload correspondingly.
- Understanding that homework may be a low priority in some families where other stressors, such as family illness or school attendance, may be a priority.

High school students with LD especially need to acquire transition skills (e.g., abilities that will help students be successful after high school in employment and independent living). For students in inclusive settings, teachers can find ways to integrate transition topics into the regular curriculum. For example, when an English teacher assigns letter writing or term papers, students might focus their work on exploring different career opportunities. Math teachers can bring in income tax and budget forms to connect

Adolescents should be active participants in meetings concerning them.

them to a variety of math skills. When planning any lesson, ask yourself, "Is there any way I can make this meaningful to their lives after high school?" See Table 5.3 for more examples.

Adult Services   The instruction provided in high school classes can have a powerful impact on the outcome for adults with LD. The life skills applications of various school activities and lessons are described in Chapter 16. Relevant lessons in the general education curriculum can help adults be more successful in many aspects of independent living. Individuals with LD are often deficient in choosing and carrying out strategies, and they do not automatically generalize previously learned information to new challenges.

An important study by Raskind and colleagues (2002) identified characteristics of highly successful adults with learning disabilities. Development of many of these factors can be encouraged by teachers and other individuals; however, some factors seem to be innate personality traits of the individuals themselves, like emotional stability. One of the strongest predictors for success was the desire and willingness to persist and work

CONSIDER THIS

What are your personal strengths and challenges? How are you alike and different from your family members and your peers? We are all different. Can we learn to celebrate our differences?

CONSIDER THIS

Should instruction in high schools always be relevant to post-secondary needs? Why or why not?

Table 5.3	**Examples of Study Skill Functions in and out of the Classroom**	
Study Skill	**School Examples**	**Life Skills Applications**
Reading Rate	Reviewing an assigned reading for a test Looking for an explanation of a concept discussed in class	Reviewing an automobile insurance policy Reading the newspaper
Listening	Understanding instructions about a field trip Attending to morning announcements	Understanding how a newly purchased appliance works Comprehending a radio traffic report
Note Taking/Outlining	Capturing information given by a teacher on how to dissect a frog Framing the structure of a paper	Writing directions to a party Planning a summer vacation
Report Writing	Developing a book report Completing a science project on a specific marine organism	Completing the personal goals section on a job application Writing a complaint letter
Oral Presentations	Delivering a personal opinion on a current issue for a social studies class Describing the results of a lab experiment	Describing car problems to a mechanic Asking a supervisor/boss for time off from work
Graphic Aids	Setting up the equipment of a chemistry experiment based on a diagram Locating the most densely populated regions of the world on a map	Utilizing the weather map in the newspaper Deciphering the store map in a mall
Test Taking	Developing tactics for retrieving information for a closed-book test Comparing notes with textbook content	Preparing for a driver's license renewal test Participating in television self-tests
Library Usage	Using picture files Searching a computerized catalog	Obtaining travel resources (books, videos) Viewing current periodicals
Reference Materials	Accessing CD-ROM encyclopedias Using a thesaurus to write a paper	Using the yellow pages to locate a repair service Ordering from a mail-order catalog
Time Management	Allocating a set time for homework Organizing a file system for writing a paper	Maintaining a daily "to do" list Keeping organized records for tax purposes
Self-Management	Ensuring that homework is signed by parents Rewarding oneself for controlling temper	Regulating a daily exercise program Evaluating the quality of a home repair

From: *Teaching Students with Learning Problems to Use Study Skills: A Teacher's Guide* (p. 7), by J. J. Hoover and J. R. Patton, 1995. Austin, TX: Pro-Ed. Reprinted by permission.

extremely hard. Understanding one's strengths and limitations, identifying appropriate goals, and working proactively to meet them were also important. The successful adults developed a plan and then worked hard to accomplish their goals. They also developed and used support groups. These characteristics were more powerful predictors of success than academic achievement, IQ, life stressors, social-economic status, or race.

The adults also were able to reframe their feelings about having a learning disability, gradually identifying and accepting their own strengths and weaknesses. Once the weaknesses were identified, they took creative action to build strategies, techniques, and adaptations to offset the impact of the disability. The study also showed that it was important to find a "goodness of fit": choosing goals that would be possible to attain. Finally, successful adults were willing to seek help from supportive people, such as a spouse or an individual at an agency. As one highly successful adult with learning disabilities said, "You must learn where your strengths are and how you can use them and where your weaknesses are and how to avoid them or compensate. I have learned to accept who I am, what I can do, what I cannot do, who I should not try to be, and who I should try to be" (Ginsberg, Gerber, & Reiff, 1994, p. 210).

The level of commitment and persistence shown by these successful adults is remarkable. A study by Madaus (2006) identified the most frequently used strategies for success as:

- setting goals and priorities
- time management
- arrive to work early
- stay at work late

One highly successful individual was told by his new boss that he was promoted to a higher level because he had a work ethic that had never been seen before. He never left until the job was done perfectly, and he was willing to do whatever was asked of him without complaining (Guyer, 2002).

Unfortunately, many adults leave high school without the skills and confidence necessary to find employment to help them realize their maximum potential and to live independently. According to Madaus (2006), 72 percent of workers with LD reported that their learning disabilities did impact work at least occasionally. The biggest problems noted were writing skills, rate of processing information, reading comprehension, organizational skills, math computation, and time management.

These skills can be taught and should be addressed in a secondary curriculum. For adults with learning disabilities who still need support, a variety of agencies are available to address needs such as improving literacy skills, obtaining a high school equivalency certificate (called a GED or general equivalency diploma), and meeting goals in areas such as financial aid for further education, employment, and independent living. Figure 5.12 lists examples of these important resources. The primary adult agency that offers treatment and intervention to promote employment for adults with learning disabilities is the Rehabilitation Services Administration. An office of this vocational rehabilitation agency is located in every state. Vocational evaluators are trained to identify each individual's strengths and the characteristics that will limit employment. Counselors provide a variety of employment-related services to those who are eligible, often including financial support for postsecondary training. Other helpful agencies are explored in a text on adult agencies by Cozzins, Dowdy, and Smith (1999).

TEACHING TIP

Ask students with disabilities to call the agencies listed in Figure 5.12 to identify services available in your local area. Have them research others and then create a resource directory. They might organize each entry by referral process, range of services, or cost.

Controversial Approaches

Some interventions, often presented to the public through television or newsstand magazines, are controversial and have not been validated as effective for students with LD. Educators may be asked for an opinion on these therapies by parents who are attempting to find solutions to their children's frustrating problems. The traditional, evidence-

Figure 5.12	**Adult Agencies**

GED Hotline (1-800-626-9433) General Education Development (GED) provides information on local GED classes and testing services, including an accommodations guide for people taking the GED test who have a learning disability.

National Literacy Hotline (1-800-228-8813) The hotline has a twenty-four-hour bilingual (Spanish/English) operator service that provides information on literacy/education classes, GED testing services, volunteer opportunities, and a learning disabilities brochure.

HEATH Resource Center (1-800-544-3284) National clearinghouse on postsecondary education for individuals with disabilities has information specialists available 9:00 A.M.–5 P.M. ET (Monday–Friday) who provide resource papers, directories, information on national organizations, and a resource directory for people with LD.

Learning Resources Network (LERN) (1-800-678-5376) Has an operator service 8:00 A.M.–5:00 P.M. ET (Monday–Friday) that provides information to practitioners of adult continuing education. It also gives consulting information, takes orders for publications, and provides phone numbers of organizations that deal with learning disabilities.

ABLE DATA (1-800-227-0216) Provides information on more than 27,000 assistive technology products; www.abledata.com.

Association on Higher Education and Disability (AHEAD) Provides information on full participation in postsecondary education for people with disabilities; www.ahead.org.

Job Accommodation Network (JAN) (1-800-526-7234) Provides information on job accommodations and employment.

From "Useful Resources on Learning Disability Issues," 2005, *LDA Newsbriefs*, January/February, pp. 12–16. Used by permission. Adapted with permission.

based interventions often take time, and although they are shown to be successful, results may take years, and still progress may not be at the desired level. Parents are understandably drawn to the promise of a "quick cure," even if the treatment carries a big price tag. Educators and parents must be armed with techniques to study these controversial therapies as they appear, claiming to be the new panacea.

Dr. Larry Silver (see Personal Spotlight) (2003) has been a national leader in helping identify those treatments backed by research and those that have no scientific basis. He suggests that caution be used when therapies are presented with a claim that is broad and offer a cure and when research is implied but not presented. One controversial therapy he describes involves the prescription of **tinted glasses** as a cure for dyslexia. In this approach, light sensitivity, said to interfere with learning, is treated by identifying a colored lens to reduce sensitivity. Another treatment provides **orthomolecular therapy**, involving vitamins, minerals, and diet claiming to straighten out the biochemistry of the brain to reduce hyperactivity and to increase learning. Hair analysis and blood studies are used to determine the doses needed. The research on the efficacy of these diet-related interventions usually consists of clinical studies without control groups. When control groups are used, the diets do not substantiate the claims made for them. Only a small percentage of children benefit from them.

Vision therapy or training is another controversial treatment for individuals with a learning disability. It is based on the theory that LD are the result of visual defects that occur when the eyes do not work together and that these deficits can be cured by visual training. This widespread practice has been supported primarily by groups of optometrists. The American Academy of Ophthalmology (1984) issued a statement clearly stating that "no credible evidence exists to show that visual training, muscle exercises, perceptual, or hand/eye coordination exercises significantly affect a child's Specific Learning Disabilities" (p. 3); however, clinics are still offering this expensive therapy.

Silver (2003) and the International Dyslexia Association (2001) have issued a warning against one of the latest proposals that purports LD are due to **cerebella developmental delay** in which the brain cannot process information quickly enough. Centers offer children exercises to stimulate the underdeveloped cerebellum, claiming the brain will then function faster with improved cognitive and motor skills. In studying the information on this approach at their website, the Dore Achievement Centers, Silver found reference to "a major research program to measure the possible effectiveness of the novel

CONSIDER THIS

Why are parents of children with disabilities so eager to find a "cure" for their child?

A Family History of Learning Disabilities

It was a Tuesday morning last December. I was getting ready to attend a staffing meeting at a nearby school to discuss a ten-year-old girl, who was in the fifth grade gifted-and-talented program. She breezed through grades one through four then was selected for the gifted program. She was a happy child with lots of friends who always loved school. In November of her fifth grade year, she began to cry each morning and not want to go to school. We discussed what was happening. She was very verbal and explained that her hand did not work right and that she could not keep up with the need to copy or to take notes or to do all the math or so many papers. Her teacher was angry with her for not completing her class work. With tears she said, *I never had a teacher mad at me before. I can't help it if writing is so hard for me.* She told me that she did her homework at different places around the house. The problem was that she often left it where she did it. She showed me her notebook and binders. It was a mess, with everything shoved everyplace. She admitted that she lost and forgot things. *Sometimes when we clean out my backpack on the weekend, my mom finds work I should have turned in earlier in the week. Then, the teacher tells me I am just lazy and not trying hard enough.* She cried again. We discussed her other problems.

With her parents' agreement, I requested that the school professionals do a psycho-educational evaluation, because I suspected learning disabilities. Their response, *She is so bright. Anyone in a gifted program and succeeding does not qualify for testing.* Fortunately, these parents could afford a private evaluation. The results were clear. Very bright, yes; nonverbal learning disabilities, yes. (I think of the many parents who cannot afford private testing and have to wait until their child fails to get help.)

I arrived at the staffing. Most of the school professionals knew me and had worked with me over the years, so the meeting was friendly. Her parents sat down. At my request, this young student was at the meeting. She sat between her mother and me. I presented the test results and we discussed my recommendation for services and accommodations. The meeting chairperson ended the discussion by saying, *She is not far enough behind to qualify for services.* How many times have I heard this? Some of the professionals sitting around the table looked down to avoid looking at me. I had planned a fall-back proposal with her parents in advance. I said that this family could not wait for their

daughter to fail and to lose her self-confidence as a student. Thus, I mentioned that she also had ADHD and was on medication. Would the school do a 504 Plan to cover accommodations? Her parents would pay privately for the needed special education services. They could not say no. I could document the ADHD. I thought to myself, accommodations don't cost the school system money. I also thought of the many families who could not afford private services. The proposal was accepted. I did not tell them that the private special education services had already started.

Larry Silver and granddaughter
Rockville, MD

I said good-bye to the team, kissed the mother, who is my daughter, hugged the father, who is my son-in-law, and kissed my granddaughter. Then I quickly left the room. I quickly left because I did not want anyone to see the tears welling in my eyes.

I had been there as a student. Public school was a struggle. I did not really learn how to learn until mid-college. Life can be a struggle if I have a lot of reading to do or I have to write something by hand rather than by computer or I have to spell. How many times have people commented that I said the wrong word or name in a conversation? Another daughter, not this one, had been there. Fortunately, we gave her help through college. She is now a successful social worker. But she will tell you how she feels when she makes mistakes in writing or misreads something. Now, my granddaughter. A third generation. Yes, she will get all the help possible. Yes, she will have to face teachers who blame the victim by saying the student is lazy or unmotivated. I knew that each time this happens, her parents or I will be on the phone to that teacher. Yes, she will be successful. But I cannot take away her frustration and pain. Like her grandfather and aunt, she will have to deal with it. I walked out of the school with mixed feelings. Guilt for causing this. Relief that she will get all the help possible. Sadness that her path through education will not be as easy as others. And, more tears.

From: "What Does It Mean to Have Learning Disabilities," by L. Silver, 2002, *LDA Newsbriefs,* January/February, p. 3.

treatment," but no published data. In responding to the claims of the centers using this treatment approach, the International Dyslexia Association (IDA, 2001) shares the concern for the cost of this treatment in terms of the exceptional expense to the families and, more important, the human cost incurred by postponing research-based intervention, and reading instruction that is sequential, systematic, and phonetically based. Parents

Figure 5.13	Websites with Information about Evidence-Based Practice

Many websites maintain information on research-based practices. In addition to searching your university library databases such as ERIC or Academic Search Premier, you may want to begin with one or more of the following:

- What Works Clearinghouse (www.w-w-c.org) identifies current research studies on effective practices and intervention.
- ERIC/OSEP Special Project (www.ericec.org/osep-sp.html#recon) disseminates federally funded special education research.
- The Center for Innovations in Education (www.cise.missouri.edu/links/research-ep-links.html) at the University of Missouri at Columbia maintains links to research-based practices leading to effective instruction.
- www.abledata.com provides information on assistive technology and products used to assist in daily living activities.
- www.ncddr.org provides research outcomes for over 350 projects funded by the National Institute on Disability and Rehabilitation Research.
- www.nichhd.nih.gov/crmc/cdb/reading.html links to the National Institute of Child Health and Human Development, Reading Research Resources.
- education.umn.edu/NCEO is the website for the National Center on Education Outcomes.
- ncal.literacy.upenn.edu provides information about research in literacy.

and professionals are encouraged to refer to research funded by the National Institute of Child Health and Human Development and the National Institute on Disability and Rehabilitation Research. Figure 5.13 contains a list of websites from projects funded through a national peer review process to serve as centers of excellence and to disseminate information of evidence-based knowledge and practice.

Classroom Modifications for Students with Learning Disabilities

One of the most important roles of inclusive educators is to identify and implement modifications (accommodations and adaptations) that address the unique learning needs of a student and at the same time maintain the integrity of the lesson (Fisher, Frey, & Thousand, 2003) or assessment process. In fact, IDEA requires a statement of program modifications and supports be included in every child's IEP. Although there are differences in the way modifications, accommodations, and adaptations are defined, for our purposes accommodations are "changes to the delivery of instruction, method of student performance, or method of assessment that do not significantly change the content or conceptual difficulty level of the curriculum" (Miller, 2002, p. 292). For example, a teacher might allow extra time for an assignment or a test to be completed. An adaptation, frequently referred to as a modification, is a greater change or modification that does alter expectations and the level of content to be learned (Miller, 2002). Table 5.4 includes examples of modifications ranging from simple accommodations to adaptations that are more complex and difficult to implement.

One important consideration for individuals of all ages with disabilities, including learning disabilities, is the appropriate use of accommodations or modifications during testing. Use of these helps ensure that common characteristics of LD such as poor reading, distractibility, or slow work rate do not lower the results of an assessment of the child's learning. Care must be taken when implementing these accommodations or modifications because, while disallowing fair changes prevent a student from demonstrating his or her knowledge, overly permissive changes will inflate scores. Inflated

CONSIDER THIS

What happens when teachers don't want to implement modifications?

INTASC

INTASC 3: Understands how students differ in their approaches to learning

PRAXIS

PRAXIS II: Delivery of Services to Students with Disabilities

Table 5.4   **Nine Types of Modifications**

Type of Modification	Description	Examples
Size	Change the amount or number of items the student is expected to learn or complete.	Have student complete the even-numbered problems in their math text. Have student learn 10 rather than 20 vocabulary terms.
Time	Change the amount of time allowed for learning; change amount of time for completing assignments or tests.	Give student extra week to complete science project. Give student 1½ hours instead of 1 hour to complete unit exam.
Input	Change the way instruction is presented.	Use cooperative learning. Use visual displays. Use computer-assisted instruction.
Output	Change the way students respond.	Allow student to say answers into a tape recorder rather than writing responses. Allow students to complete projects rather than take tests.
Difficulty	Change the skill level required for task completion.	Allow open-book test. Allow students to use spell-checker.
Participation	Allow for various levels of student involvement.	One student counts and distributes 20 manipulative devices to each student; other students use the devices to solve subtraction problems. One student writes report; another student draws accompanying illustrations.
Level of support	Change the amount of individual assistance.	Have paraeducator work one-to-one with student needing additional help with assignment. Arrange peer tutoring.
Alternative goals	Use same materials, but change the expected outcomes.	Given a diagram of the parts of the eye; one student labels the parts; others label the parts and their function. One student identifies the ingredients in a recipe; other students identify, measure, and mix the ingredients.
Substitute curriculum	Change the materials and instruction.	Some students read and discuss novel; some students participate in reading mastery lessons.

From *Validated Practices for Teaching Students with Diverse Needs and Abilities* (p. 290), by S. P. Miller, 2002. Boston: Allyn & Bacon. Copyright © 2002 by Pearson Education. Reprinted by permission of the publisher.

scores may give students an overestimate of their abilities and may lead to unrealistic postsecondary goals. They also may reduce pressure on schools to maintain high expectations and offer students a challenging program with intense instruction (Fuchs & Fuchs, 2001). These researchers note, however, that when students can be penalized for low test scores, as is the case for "high stakes" assessment—the gateway to promotion or graduation—a more liberal allowance of accommodations or modifications should be made. Examples of reasonable modifications and accommodations are presented in Rights & Responsibilities.

When you are developing classroom accommodations/modifications, remember the wide range of behaviors identified earlier that might characterize individuals with learning disabilities. The heterogeneity in this population is sometimes baffling. No child with a learning disability is going to be exactly like any other, so teachers must provide a wide range of accommodations/modifications to meet individual needs. In the following sections, these are discussed for each of the areas described earlier: academic and language deficits, social-emotional problems, and other differences such as attention, memory, cognition, metacognition, perception, and motor skills.

Rights & Responsibilities

Examples of Accommodations and Modifications for Assessment

Timing/Scheduling
- Time of day
- Breaks during test
- Multiple test sessions
- Order of test administration
- Extend the time to complete the test
- Administer the test over several days

Setting
- Preferential seating (e.g., at the front of the room or in a study carrel)
- Small-group testing
- Individual testing (one-on-one)
- Special lighting
- Adaptive or special furniture
- Test administration in locations with minimal distractions
- Noise buffers
- Auditory trainers
- Hospital/home

Presentation
- Braille
- Large print
- Enlarging the answer sheet
- Reading directions to students
- Simplifying directions
- Interpreting/transliteration directions (e.g., sign language, cued speech)
- Written directions to accompany oral directions
- Clarifying directions
- Computer

- Increased spacing between items or (fewer?) items per page
- Reading test questions
- Interpreting/transliteration test items (e.g., sign language, cued speech)
- Audiotape version of test items
- Amplifying equipment
- Magnifying glass
- Templates
- Mask or markers to maintain place
- Highlight key word or phrases in directions
- Provide cues (e.g., arrows and stop signs) on answer form
- Secure papers to work areas with tape/magnets
- Short-segment testing booklets

Response Mode
- Student marks booklet
- Student responds verbally to scribe
- Student points to response
- Abacus
- Brailler
- Calculators
- Pencil grip
- Large diameter/special grip pencil
- Word processor/computer/typewriter
- Answer recorded on audiotape
- Augmentative or alternative communication devices
- Spell check
- Dictation to a scribe
- Use sign language
- Use template for recording

From: "State and Districtwide Assessments and Students With Learning Disabilities: A Guide for States and School Districts" (p. 75), by the National Joint Committee on Learning Disabilities, 2004, *Learning Disability Quarterly, 27*, pp. 67–76.

Academic and Language Deficits

Recall that students with LD may manifest deficits in the academic areas of reading skill, reading comprehension, math calculation, math applications, listening, speaking, and written language. Chapters 15 and 16 provide extensive accommodations and modifications for students with LDs at the elementary and secondary school levels. Following are some general guidelines written by a high school student with learning problems and ADHD with the help of his teachers (Biddulph, Hess, & Humes, 2006):

- Provide copies of notes and overheads for students so they won't have to worry about getting all the information down, and they can pay attention and concentrate better.
- Read tests to students so they can process the information better by hearing it as they read it.

TEACHING TIP

Go to www.cresst96.cse.ucla. edu/resources/justforteachers/ ACCCOMMODATIONS.pdf to download a helpful document: "Students with Disabilities Performance Assignments Accommodations Reference Guide."

CONSIDER THIS

Should general classroom teachers provide these accomodations for all children?

PRAXIS

PRAXIS II: Delivery of Services to Students with Disabilities

INTASC

INTASC 6: Communication technologies

TEACHING TIP

Each word-processing program has unique features. Try to have several programs available so students can experiment and find the one that works best for them. Dyslexic is a medical term to describe an individual with severe reading difficulties.

INTASC

INTASC 6: Communication technologies

- Let a student sit close to the front of the class and not by a window. This helps the student focus on the important information and not be distracted by other students or things happening outside.
- Let a student sit with another student he or she is are comfortable with and can ask for help.
- Provide a decreased amount of homework, for example, fewer math problems, or let the student have extra time to complete homework.
- Have math formulas posted for quick reference.
- Have books on tape available to help with focus and comprehension.
- Provide examples for how to complete homework.
- Make sure the student has everything needed to complete homework and understands the assignment.
- Have students use an organized binder with dividers and color-coding; have a different folder for each class.
- Let students take tests in a quiet place.
- Create study guides for tests.

For students with learning difficulties in writing, a word processor can be invaluable. It allows students to see their work in a more legible format and simplifies proofreading and revising, allowing students to focus more on developing content. The spell-checker and grammar-checker of many word-processing programs can encourage success in writing, and a talking word processor may provide valuable assistance for students who also have difficulty in reading. The following list describes recommended programs (Bryant & Bryant, 2003):

- *Write:OutLoud* has a speech-feedback component that highlights each word as it is "read" out loud to students as they write (Don Johnson Inc.).
- *IntelliTalk II* is a talking word processor that adds a built in scanner and has picture menus that make it easy to use (IntelliTools Inc.).
- *Inspiration* is a tool that helps students develop visual aids such as concept maps as they brainstorm (Inspiration Software Inc.).
- *Writing with Symbols 2000* is a symbol-supported writing and reading program that has over 8,000 pictures (Mayer-Johnson Inc.).
- *Stanley's Sticker Stories* has a word-processing program with animated characters (Edmark Inc.).

These and other types of technology can be critically important in facilitating success in inclusive settings for students with LD. Technology Today demonstrates the improvement made by a seventh-grade student, J.T., using the software *Write:OutLoud* and *Co:Writer*. When he began the program, J.T., who received all his instruction in an inclusive classroom, read on preprimer level and had many difficulties in the writing process. The assistive technology plan for J.T. was successful; however, some students are given assistive technology that is not a good match for their abilities or interests. The use of technology should be monitored closely to determine whether devices are being used successfully (Beigel, 2000). Guidelines are available in Figure 5.14; specific examples of technology used for students with LD are included in Table 5.5.

Students and adults with LD in the area of reading are also eligible to apply for services from Reading for the Blind and Dyslexic. A catalog of services and application forms are available by calling 800-221-4792. The forms require verification of the disability by a professional in disability services. This agency will provide a cassette tape of any book requested. The tapes are available at no cost; however, there may be a one-time charge for the special equipment needed to play the tapes. Taped trade books and textbooks would be an excellent adaptation for Emmanuel as his reading skills improve to allow him to be successful with printed material on his grade level. Other adaptations appropriate for Emmanuel are identified in Tips for Adapting a Lesson.

TECHNOLOGY Today

J.T.'s Writing Samples— Before and After

Each day during the study, J.T.'s class received a descriptive writing prompt, and then had twenty minutes to address this prompt in a journal entry. The entries shown here depict a prompt and J.T.'s corresponding journal response. On November 21, J.T. had not been introduced to the features of Co:Writer and was using word-processing capabilities Write:OutLoud with the speech component disabled. By February, J.T. was using the intervention software when he composed his journal entries. This

entry is a typical example of the longer entries he generated using Co:Writer and Write:OutLoud.

November 21

Prompt: Describe your idea of the "ideal" Thanksgiving dinner

MY FAVORITE FOOD IS A GRILL HOG IN A PUMPKIN IN A ROAST HAM IN A MAYBE A TURKEY my favorite DESSERT food strawberry pie THE END

February 27

Prompt: Describe your favorite clock

The clock that I have it is very old it was the first clock that my grandpa had it run off of current and it might go to the time it will go off in a little bird will comes at of the box. The box look like a house in it has a to pendulums on the bottom of the house inside of the house it has people in it. On the outside it has to door on it in it has to windows the color is color is brown on the top of the clock it is black.

From "How Speech-Feedback and Work-Prediction Software Can Help Students Write" by S. Williams, 2002, *Teaching Exceptional Children, 34*(3), pp. 72–78. Adapted with permission.

Social-Emotional Problems

As discussed earlier, the social and emotional problems of individuals with LD may be closely tied to academic failure. Many of the academic modifications already described will encourage success in the classroom, which ultimately leads to a better self-concept, increased emotional stability, and greater confidence in approaching new academic tasks. A student who has deficits in social skills may need previously described training. However, some accommodations may still be needed even as the training begins to show results. Students may need to work in an isolated setting in the classroom during particularly challenging times. Distractions caused by peers may interfere with meeting academic challenges successfully. However, if teachers encourage the student with LD to sit in a segregated portion of the room all the time, it sends a bad message to others. Including students with disabilities in group activities, such as cooperative learning, provides them with models of appropriate interactions and authentic opportunities to practice social skills. Identify the students in the classroom who seem to work best with individuals with a learning disability, and give them more opportunities to interact. When conflicts arise, provide good modeling for the student by verbalizing the bad choices that were made and the good choices that could have been made.

Because many of these individuals have difficulty responding appropriately to verbal and nonverbal cues, teachers should avoid sarcasm and use simple concrete language when giving directions and when teaching. If the student has difficulty accepting new tasks without complaint, consider providing a written assignment that the student can refer to for directions. When a student frequently upsets or irritates others in the classroom, you might agree on a contract to reduce the inappropriate behavior and reinforce positive peer interaction. Periodically review the rules for the classroom, and keep them posted as a quick reference. To assist students who have difficulty making and keeping friends, you can subtly point out the strengths of the individual with the learning disability to encourage the other students to want to be his or her friend. Allowing the student to demonstrate his or her expertise in an area or to share a hobby may stimulate conversations that can eventually lead to friendships.

CONSIDER THIS

Why do you think students with disabilities often have social-emotional problems?

PRAXIS

PRAXIS II: Understanding Exceptionalities

INTASC

INTASC 2: How children learn and develop

Figure 5.14   **Assistive Technology Evaluation Guide: The ABCDs of Students with Learning Disabilities**

Assistive technology garners much attention these days in the discussion of students with learning disabilities. LDOnline (www.ldonline.org) provides a wealth of information about this topic, including a thorough evaluation guide for teachers and parents. The site provides a no-nonsense approach to determining what types of assistive technology (no-tech, low-tech, or high-tech) may be right for students in writing, reading, math, studying/organizing, and listening. The evaluation begins with the ABCDs:

A. What difficulties is the student experiencing in the school environment for which assistive technology intervention is needed?

1. What are the student's strengths and weaknesses?
2. What educational task(s) is the student unable to perform because of the student's disability, and will the use of assistive technology help the student accomplish task(s) more independently and within the least restrictive environment?
3. Will the use of assistive technology enable the student to compensate for difficulties in various settings?

B. What strategies, materials, equipment, and technology tools has the student already used to address the concerns?

C. What new or additional assistive technology or accommodations should be tried?

1. What is the student's prior experience with technology, and does the student want to use the assistive technology device and/or service recommended?
2. Will the student be involved in the decision-making process to determine the most appropriate assistive technology device and/or service?
3. Is the teacher comfortable with the assistive technology? If not, will training and support be available?

D. What will the criteria be for determining whether the student's needs are being met while using assistive technology?

1. What plan will be in place to integrate the technology effectively?
2. What will the time frame be for evaluating the potential success of using assistive technology?
3. Who will be responsible for determining if the criteria are being met?
4. Are the assistive technology devices and/or services being utilized? If not, explain why.
5. Does the use of assistive technology enable the student to meet IEP goals?

The evaluation guide also provides a sampling of strategies, materials, equipment, and technology tools to consider when answering these questions. (The entire evaluation guide can be retrieved from www.ldonlineorg/ld_indepth/technology/evaluation.pdf.)

From _Learning Disabilities: Foundations, Characteristics, and Effective Teaching_ (p. 252), by D. P. Hallahan et al., 2005. Boston: Allyn & Bacon.

Because many of these students cannot predict the consequences of negative behavior, teachers need to explicitly explain the consequences of rule breaking and other inappropriate behavior. Though you can implement many behavior management techniques to reinforce positive behavior, it is important to train the student in methods of self-monitoring and self-regulation. The ultimate goal is for the student to be able to identify socially inappropriate behavior and get back on track.

Cognitive Differences

Cognitive problems described earlier include deficits in attention, perception, motor abilities, problem solving, and metacognition. Modifications and accommodations for individuals exhibiting problems in attention are described more fully in Chapter 8. To

- Use advance organizers to help orient students before reading or listening to new information.
- Activate the students' prior knowledge or help them build a bridge from long-term memory to new information.
- Give continuous feedback and offer practice by repeating important information at intervals to promote frequent review.
- Think out loud for students, showing them your strategies for learning new information.
- Help students develop self-efficacy by explicitly communicating expectations.
- Use active learning techniques so students can use executive functioning and memory techniques to store and retrieve new information.

Promoting Inclusive Practices for Students with Learning Disabilities

After identifying an appropriate educational plan for individuals with learning disabilities and determining the accommodations or modifications that should lead to a successful educational program, the next challenge is to be sure the students in the general education classroom and the student with the learning disability understand the disability and the need for special education. Primarily, children should be made aware that all people are different. The Personal Spotlight shares the thoughts of a nationally recognized pediatrician who experiences the pain of LD personally and professionally. His story provides insight into the importance of promoting a sense of security and acceptance in inclusive classrooms.

According to Bryan and colleagues (2004), research suggests that merely placing a student in an inclusive classroom does not insure social acceptance or inclusion. Direct instruction in areas of academic and social skill deficits as well as creating a positive, accepting atmosphere in the general education classroom is needed to facilitate educational benefit. Following are simple methods to empower students and build a sense of classroom community:

- Believe in a positive classroom community and the importance of empowered students; students will follow your lead.
- Facilitate a sense of inclusion by helping students get to know and trust one another.
- Have students create a map of the people and places in the school/classroom to help them understand their place in the community.
- Have students interview one another and adults in the school.
- Highlight commonalities like characteristics and favorite activities among students.
- Play bingo, matching names with personal items (e.g., owns a pet).
- Guide students in conducting classroom meetings to facilitate a sense of power in knowing what they say is important.
- Give students choices of activities or assignments.
- Reduce rewards for individuals and reward the group, especially for inclusive behaviors.
- Assign classroom jobs and encourage community service.
- Use a "sharing chair" technique, where students lead a group discussion of personal importance.
- Teach active listening skills, where students validate others' thoughts even if they disagree.
- Display a celebration board highlighting group accomplishments and good citizenship.

An important part of promoting acceptance is having the student with the disability, family members, other teachers, and professionals understand the disability, as well as how it can be manifested and successfully addressed in home and school environments.

CEC STANDARDS

CEC 5: Learning Environments and Social Interactions

PRAXIS

PRAXIS II: Delivery of Services to Students with Disabilities

INTASC

INTASC 5: Creating learning environments

CONSIDER THIS

How can simply placing a student with a disability in a general classroom actually restrict inclusiveness?

Summary

Basic Concepts about Learning Disabilities

- LD is frequently misunderstood because it is hidden. It may be mistaken for purposely uncooperative behavior.
- The study of LD is a relatively young field, and basic definitions, etiology, and criteria for special education eligibility remain controversial.
- The most widely used criterion for identifying LD has been a severe discrepancy between ability and achievement that cannot be explained by another disabling condition or lack of learning opportunity; IDEA 2004 does not require this.
- IDEA 2004 allows states to implement a responsiveness-to-intervention program that provides struggling students with more intense, evidence-based teaching methods.
- Students not responding to the new teaching efforts may be identified as potentially needing special education and support services; the evaluation process may begin at that time, as decided by the IEP team.
- School personnel must determine that the primary cause of a student's learning difficulties is not cultural or linguistic diversity, lack of educational opportunity, vision, hearing, mental retardation, or motor deficits.
- Cultural and linguistic differences need to be taken into account when any assessment of a student's skills occurs so that the student is not mistakenly referred to a special education setting.
- Characteristics of LD are manifested across the life span.
- LD is manifested in seven areas of academics and language: reading skills, reading comprehension, mathematical calculations, mathematical reasoning, written expression, oral expression, and listening comprehension.
- Other common characteristics of LD include social-emotional problems and difficulties with attention and hyperactivity, memory, cognition, metacognition, motor skills, and perceptual abilities.

Strategies for Curriculum and Instruction for Students with Learning Disabilities

- Teaching strategies for preschool children with LD include developmental, cognitive, and behavioral models.
- Interventions for elementary school children with LD address academic and language deficits, social-emotional problems, and cognitive and metacognitive problems.
- Secondary school students with LD continue to need remediation of basic skills, but they also benefit from strategies that will make them more efficient learners.
- A secondary curriculum that includes application of life skills can produce successful outcomes for adults with LD.
- Successful adults with LD are goal-directed, work hard to accomplish their goals, understand and accept their strengths and limitations, are advocates for themselves, and accept appropriate support.

Classroom Modifications for Students with Learning Disabilities

- Modifications and/or accommodations in the general education classroom can address the academic, social-emotional, and cognitive, metacognition, and attentional differences of students with LD.
- The role of the classroom teacher includes using effective teaching strategies and adaptations to address the challenges of students with LD.

Promoting Inclusive Practices for Students with Learning Disabilities

- Classroom teachers need to help children with learning disabilities and other children in the general classroom understand and accept a learning disability.
- Students need to be aware that all people are different; this awareness will promote a positive, accepting atmosphere in the general education classroom.

Questions to Reconsider

Think back to the scenario you read at the beginning of this chapter. Would you respond any differently to the questions asked there, now that you have read the chapter?

1. What alerted Emmanuel's teacher to a possible learning disability?

2. How might his move have been a factor in his school performance?

3. Would "response to intervention" have been a viable option for Emmanuel? How might that have changed Emmanuel's life?

Further Readings

Baker, S., Gersten, R., & Lee, D. (2002). A synthesis of empirical research on teaching mathematics to low-achieving students. *The Elementary School Journal, 103,* 51–73.

Denton, C. A., Vaughn, S., & Fletcher, J. M. (2003). Bringing research-based practice in reading intervention to scale. *Learning Disabilities Research & Practice, 18,* 201–211.

Finn, C. E., Rotherham, A. J., & Hokanson, C. R., Jr. (2001). *Rethinking special education for a new century.* Washington, DC: Thomas B. Fordham Foundation. Available at www.edexcellence.net/library/special ed/index.html.

Fuchs, D., Fuchs, L. S., Mathes, P. G., Lipsey, M. W., & Roberts, P. H. (2001). Is "learning disabilities" just a fancy term for low achievement: A meta-analysis of reading differences between low achievers with and without the label. LD Summit: Building a Foundation for the Future. Available at www.air.org/ldsummit.

Fuchs, D., Mock, D., Morgan, P. L., & Young, C. L. (2003). Responsiveness-to-intervention: Definitions, evidence, and implications for the learning disabilities construct. *Learning Disabilities Research & Practice, 18,* 157–171.

Geary, D. C. (2004). Mathematics and learning disabilities. *Journal of Learning Disabilities, 37,* 4–15.

Graham, S., & Harris, K. R. (2006). Cognitive strategy instruction. In C. MacArthur, S. Graham, & J. Ditzgerald (Eds.), *Handbook of writing research* (pp. 187–207). New York: Guildford.

Justice, L. M., & Kaderavek, J. (2002). Using shared storybook reading to promote emergent literacy. *Teaching Exceptional Children, 34*(4), 8–13.

Kavale, K. A. (2001). Discrepancy models in the identification of learning disability. LD Summit: Building a Foundation for the Future. Available at www.air.org/ldsummit.

Latham, P. S., & Latham, P. H. (1993). Learning disabilities and the law. Washington, DC: JKL Communication.

Lenz, B. K., Deshler, D. D., & Kissam, B. R. (2004). *Teaching content to all: Evidence-based inclusive practices in middle and secondary schools.* Boston: Allyn & Bacon.

Making the "No Child Left Behind Act" Work for Children Who Struggle to Learn: A Parent's Guide. Available at www.LD.org/NCLB and www.SchwabLearning.org/NCLB.

McCordle, P., Mele-McCarthy, J., & Leos, K. (2005). English language learners and LD. Research agenda and implications for practice. *Learning Disabilities Research and Practice, 20*(1), 68–78.

National Reading Panel Report. (2000). *Report of the National Reading Panel: Teaching children to read.* Washington, DC: National Institutes of Health.

Swanson, H. L. (2000). Issues facing the field of learning disabilities. *Learning Disabilities Quarterly, 23*(1), 37–50.

Swanson, H. L., Harris, K. R., & Graham, S. (2003). *Handbook on learning disabilities.* New York: Guildford.

Times Tables the Fun Way! Times/Division and Addition/Subtraction Kits, available from www.citycreek.com.

Wise, B. W., & Snyder, L. (2001). Judgments in identifying and teaching children with language-based reading difficulties. LD Summit: Building a Foundation for the Future. Available at www.air.org/ldsummit.

mylabschool

Go to Allyn & Bacon's MyLabSchool (www.mylabschool.com) and enter Assignment ID SPV7 into the Assignment Finder. View the video clip called *Learning Disabilities.* Then consider what you have seen along with what you've read in Chapter 5 to answer the following questions.

1. One issue that Bridget discusses at length in the video clip is social acceptance of students with dyslexia by other students. Based on suggestions in this chapter, what strategies do you believe could help promote social acceptance in Bridget's high school? Be specific.

2. In Chapter 1, you read about the advantages and disadvantages of the resource room model. Do you support Bridget's rejection of that model? Why or why not?

3. Choose a common learning disability and write a brief summary of its characteristics. Include information on strategies for working with students with that disability. Expand on the information in this chapter by using Research Navigator on *MyLabSchool* and doing a key word search on the name of the disability.

You may also answer the questions at the end of the clip and e-mail your responses to your instructor.

Teaching Students with Emotional and Behavioral Disorders

After reading this chapter, you should be able to:

1. Define emotional and behavioral disorders (E/BD).

2. Describe the characteristics of children and youth with emotional and behavioral disorders.

3. Discuss ways to identify and evaluate students with E/BD.

4. Identify effective interventions for students with E/BD.

5. Discuss the role of teachers in meeting the needs of students with E/BD in general education classrooms.

Travis is a seven-year-old first-grader often in trouble. On the first day of school, he stole some crayons from one of his classmates. When confronted with the fact that they belonged to another student, Travis adamantly denied stealing them. His behavior became more difficult during the first six months of the school year. Ms. Holke, Travis's teacher, uses a classroom management system that rewards students with check marks for appropriate behaviors. Students can redeem their check marks at the end of the week for various toys. Travis has never earned enough check marks to get a toy. Now he openly states that he doesn't care if he ever receives any check marks.

Travis's primary difficulty is his inability to leave his classmates alone. He is constantly pinching, pulling hair, or taking things from other students. Ms. Holke has separated his desk from the other students in an attempt to prevent him from bothering them. Still, he gets out of his chair and manages to create disturbances regularly. Ms. Holke has sent him to the principal's office on numerous occasions. Each time he returns, his behavior improves, but only for several hours. Then he returns to his previous behavioral patterns. Travis's schoolwork suffers as a result of his behavior problems. While many of his classmates are reading and writing their names, he still has difficulties associating sounds with letters and can print his name only in a rudimentary fashion.

The teacher has had four parent conferences regarding Travis. His mother indicates that she does not know what to do with him. Ms. Holke and Travis's mother are both concerned that his behavior will get worse unless some solution is found. They are currently discussing whether to retain him in first grade.

Although many children and youth are occasionally disruptive, few display negative behaviors sufficient to create serious problems in school. Most comply with classroom and school rules without needing extensive interventions. However, some students' behaviors result in significant problems for themselves, their peers, and/or their teachers. These problems may be exacerbated as a consequence of the way school personnel deal with these student behaviors. Students with significant school problems may require specialized intervention. (Wagner et al., 2005)

Wagner and colleagues provided a summative statement on the challenges of students with E/BD and, thus, also the teachers who work with them. They noted from their research (2005): "Children and youth with ED are a group that has serious, multiple, and complex problems. Parents report that a wide range of disabilities affect their children, including anxiety, bi-polar disorder, depression, oppositional behavior, and psychosis. Almost two-thirds of the students were reported to have ADHD, and one-fourth were reported to have a learning disability in addition to ED" (p. 91). This chapter addresses these challenges and provides recommendations for successfully educating students with E/BD.

Basic Concepts about Emotional and Behavioral Disorders

CONSIDER THIS

What kinds of children do you think of when you hear the term "emotionally disturbed"? How does this term have an impact on teachers' expectations of children?

CEC STANDARDS

CEC 2: Development and Characteristics of Learners

PRAXIS

PRAXIS II: Understanding Exceptionalities

INTASC

INTASC 2: How children learn and develop

CONSIDER THIS

What impact can a definition that is vague, like the federal definition of emotionally disturbed, have on identification of, and services to, children?

Students who experience emotional and behavioral disorders receive a variety of labels. The federal government historically has identified this group as **seriously emotionally disturbed (SED)**, and later as emotionally disturbed, under IDEA. Whereas SED is the category used in most states, others classify this group of children as having behavioral disorders. The most widely accepted term by professionals in the field is **emotional and behavioral disorders (E/BD)** because this term better describes the students who receive special education services. As a result, E/BD is the term that will be used throughout this chapter.

This section provides basic information about emotional and behavioral disorders. Understanding children with these problems will aid teachers and other educators in developing appropriate intervention programs. To provide a broader initial view, Figure 6.1 illustrates a parent's perspective on intervention programs for students with E/BD.

Emotional and Behavioral Disorders Defined

For students with E/BD to be identified accurately, and appropriately served in educational programs, a critical prerequisite is an acceptable definition. The challenges of developing an acceptable definition for emotional/behavioral disorders have been frequently stated. Kauffman (1995, 2005) indicated that the definitional problem has been made more difficult by the different conceptual models that have been used in the field (e.g., psychodynamic, biological, sociological, behavioral, ecological, educational); the different purposes for definition (e.g., educational, legal, mental health); the difficulties in measuring both emotions and behavior; the range and variability of normal and deviant behavior; the complex relationships of E/BD to other disabilities; and the transient nature of many emotional/behavioral problems.

The definition used by the federal government for its category of emotionally disturbed derives from the classic work of Bower (1969) and is as follows:

(i) The term means a condition exhibiting one or more of the following characteristics over a long period of time and to a marked extent, which adversely affects educational performance:

(A) An inability to learn which cannot be explained by intellectual, sensory, or health factors;

(B) An inability to build or maintain satisfactory relationships with peers and teachers;

(C) Inappropriate types of behavior or feelings under normal circumstances;

(D) A general pervasive mood of unhappiness or depression; or

Figure 6.1   **A Parent's Perspective on E/BD: Patti Childress (Lynchburg, VA)**

From: pchildress [mailto: patti@inmind.com]

Sent: Tuesday, June 6, 2000 11:42 PM

TO: Polloway, Edward 'Ed'

Subject: Re: Concerns

Dr. Polloway:

    Thanks for trying to help and please keep thinking about resources that can
assist me as both a teacher and a parent.

    It bothers me tremendously when I see children with E/BD often getting a
"raw deal." People seem to think that it is fine for these children to have a
disorder and maybe/maybe not receive special services, but heaven forbid if they
can't control themselves or if they do something that appears to be a bit
irrational. At times I feel like I am jumping in front of a firing squad to protect
that [child whom some seem to see as that] "bad kid that shouldn't be in school
anyway." I would like to work with a group that supports parents, provides
understanding and advocacy regarding disorders, and seeks support and additional
resources for help, etc. What is available in this field? Much is needed.

    I have always had a huge heart for "the kid who is a little bit or a long
way out there" even before I became a parent of a child with a mood disorder.

    From an educational perspective, I know that these children can be very
difficult in a group; however, they seem to function much better when they feel in
control, are able to make choices, and are spoken to in a calm tone.

    From a parent's perspective, I am an educated individual with a traditional
home makeup: dad, mom, daughter, and son. . .and I know the difficulties of
saying, "Yeah, we've got a very bright child with mood problems." We've been
through every medication from ritalin to cylert and clonodone. The next stop would
be lithium, weekly counseling, and psychiatric treatment to regulate the
medications. I want teachers to understand that getting "meds" is not an easy task
or a quick fix. It has taken us over a year of trying various medications until we
have, hopefully, found the right combination for now. It requires the constant
efforts of counselor, doctor, parents, and teachers working together and exchanging
information.

    Children without support have got to have advocates to help them get help.
These children are very fragile and need to be treated as such. My heart goes out
to such a child and the family that simply does not understand why their child is
not like everybody else's. In the school environment, even when I listen to special
education teachers, I do not find the same level of empathy and understanding for
children with E/BD as for those with LD.

(E) A tendency to develop physical symptoms or fears associated with personal or school problems.
(i) The term includes children who are schizophrenic. The term does not include children who are socially maladjusted unless it is determined that they are seriously emotionally disturbed. (*Federal Register,* 1999, p. 12422; Algozzine, Serna, & Patton, 2001)

The applicability of this definition as a framework for viewing the characteristics has been studied by Cullinan and Sabornie (2004). Their research is discussed later in the chapter on page 187.

Although the Bower federal definition has been used by most states and local educational agencies (e.g., Skiba, Grizzle, & Minke, 1994; Cullinan & Sabornie, 2004), it leaves much to be desired. It is vague and may leave the reader wondering just what a child with emotional disturbance is like. When this definition is interpreted broadly, many more children are served than when it is interpreted narrowly. As evidenced by the underserved nature of this disability category, most states and local school districts seem to interpret the definition narrowly and serve far fewer children in the category than prevalence data would project as needing services.

Most agencies other than schools that provide services to children and adolescents with emotional problems use the definition and classification system found in the *Diagnostic and Statistical Manual of Mental Disorders* (DSM-IV-TR) (American Psychiatric Association, 2000). With multiple definitions in use, some children may be considered disabled according to one system but not according to the other.

Algozzine (2001) presented an alternative definition to guide educational practices. While not adapted by any governmental agencies, it illustrates an educationally relevant approach to defining this population:

> Students with behavior problems are ones who, after receiving supportive educational services and counseling assistance available to all students, still exhibit persistent and consistent severe behavioral disabilities that consequently interfere with their productive learning processes as well as those of others. The inability of these students to achieve adequate academic progress and satisfactory interpersonal relationships cannot be attributed primarily to physical, sensory, or intellectual deficits. (Algozzine, 2001, p. 37)

Classification of Emotional and Behavioral Disorders

Children who experience E/BD constitute a heterogeneous population. Professionals typically have subcategorized the group into smaller, more homogeneous subgroups so that these students can be better understood and served. Several different classification systems are used to group individuals with E/BD.

One classification system focuses on clinical elements. This system is detailed in DSM-IV-TR (American Psychiatric Association, 2000), which is widely used by medical and psychological professionals, though far less frequently by educators. The manual categorizes emotional and behavioral problems according to several subtypes, such as developmental disorders, organic mental disorders, and schizophrenia. Educators need to be aware of this classification system because of the periodic need to interact with professionals from the mental health field. Figure 6.2 lists the major types of disorders according to this system.

A second commonly used classification system was developed by Quay and Peterson (1987). They described six major subgroups of children with E/BD as follows:

1. Individuals are classified as having a **conduct disorder** if they seek attention, are disruptive, and act out. This category includes behaving aggressively toward others.
2. Students who exhibit **socialized aggression** are likely to join a group of peers who are openly disrespectful to their peers, teachers, and parents. Delinquency and truancy are common among this group.

Figure 6.2	**Major Components of the DSM-IV-TR Classification System**

Organic mental syndromes and disorders	Sexual disorders
Psychoactive substance-use disorders	Sleep disorders
Schizophrenia	Factitious disorders
Delusional disorders	Impulse control disorders not elsewhere classified
Psychotic disorders not elsewhere classified	
Mood disorders	Adjustment disorders
Anxiety disorders	Psychological factors affecting physical condition
Somatoform disorders	
Dissociative disorders	Personality disorders

Adapted from American Psychiatric Association (2000). *Diagnostic and Statistical Manual of Mental Disorders* (4th ed.). Washington, DC: American Psychiatric Publishing.

3. Individuals with **attention problems-immaturity** can be characterized as having attention deficits, being easily distractible, and having poor concentration. Many students in this group are impulsive and may act without thinking about the consequences.
4. Students classified in the **anxiety/withdrawal** group are self-conscious, reticent, and unsure of themselves. Their self-concepts are generally very low, causing them to retreat from immediate activities. They are also anxious and frequently depressed.
5. The subgroup of students who display **psychotic behavior** may hallucinate, deal in a fantasy world, and exhibit bizarre behavior.
6. Students with motor excess are **hyperactive.** They have difficulties sitting still, listening to other individuals, and keeping their attention focused.

At one time, children with autism spectrum disorders (ASD) were included in the federal definition of SED. Since these children frequently displayed behaviors that were considered extremely atypical, it initially was thought that they were experiencing emotional problems. However, professionals and advocates no longer classify autism as an emotional problem as defined within the concepts of SED or E/BD. The consequence has been the removal of autism from the SED (or E/BD) category. ASD will be discussed in full in Chapter 10.

Classification becomes less important when school personnel use a functional behavioral assessment and intervention model. This approach primarily emphasizes determining which environmental stimuli influence inappropriate behaviors. Once these stimuli are identified and altered, the inappropriate behaviors may decrease or disappear (Foster-Johnson & Dunlap, 1993; McConnell, Patton, & Polloway, 2006). In such instances, the process of clinically classifying a student's problem becomes less relevant to the design of educational programs.

Prevalence of Emotional and Behavioral Disorders

Traditionally the category of E/BD along with learning disabilities (LD) and mental retardation have been referred to as high-incidence disabilities (Polloway, 2005). However, as compared to children classified as having LD, in particular, the category of E/BD represents a much smaller number of children. In terms of prevalence, the 25th Report to Congress on the Implementation of the Individuals with Disabilities Education Act noted that .91 percent of the school population (ages six to seventeen) was served as EB/D during the 2001–2002 school year (U.S. Department of Education, 2005).

Because of the difficulty in defining and identifying emotional and behavioral disorders, the range of estimates of the prevalence of the disorder has historically, and routinely, been significant (Knitzer, Steinberg, & Fleisch, 1990). The overall federal figure of .91 percent cited above reflects the number of students ages six to seventeen being

TEACHING TIP

Whenever possible, teach appropriate social skills in the context in which they will be used. If they must be taught in a different context, plan for their transfer to more typical settings.

CONSIDER THIS

What factors would likely lead to larger or smaller numbers of children being identified as having E/BD?

served under this category. This national average masks significant state variance, ranging from 2.32 percent in the District of Columbia to 0.12 percent in Arkansas. In all cases, these data for children receiving special services contrast sharply with foundational estimates for moderate and severe disorders, such as 22 percent (Cotler, 1986) or 14 to 20 percent (Brandenburg, Friedman, & Silver, 1990). The specific number depends on the definition used and the interpretation of the definition by individuals who classify students. However, the clear consensus is that E/BD is a dramatically underserved category of disability with far more students in need of supports than the approximately 1 percent currently identified on average in U.S. schools across the fifty states.

It is therefore a safe assumption that students with E/BD are typically the most underidentified in the school setting. Lambros and colleagues (1998) indicated that the reasons for this situation include the following: the ambiguity of definitions used by states; the limited training of school psychologists in conducting assessments for these students; the financial limitations of districts; and the general professional hesitation to apply labels such as behavioral disorder or seriously emotionally disturbed.

Demographic Data   Among students classified as having E/BD, the clear majority are males (Reid et al., 2004). While gender variance is common in disability categories, it is most pronounced in the E/BD area. Some studies have revealed that as many as ten times more boys than girls are found in programs for students with behavioral disorders (e.g., Rosenberg et al., 1992). Wagner and colleagues (2005) reported that estimates from research range as high as 80 percent male for this population; their own study confirmed this trend. Federal data indicate that 80 percent of students in E/BD programs, ages six to twelve, and 77.1 percent of students in E/BD programs, ages thirteen to seventeen, are male (U.S. Department of Education, 2005).

A second demographic focus is the ethnicity of students who have E/BD. An important way to view these data is through risk ratios (i.e., determining the likelihood that a student will be identified with a given disability as compared to that of all students, ages six to twenty-one). Given that a risk ratio of 1.0 indicates no differences between ethnic groups, and that data above 1.0 indicate increased risk of identification, the data are as follows: Native American/Native Alaskan, 1.26; Asian/Pacific Islander, 0.29; African American, 2.21; Hispanic, 0.52; and European American, 0.87 (U.S. Department of Education, 2005).

Causation and Risk Factors

Many factors can cause students to display E/BD or can create risks for problems. These factors can be viewed through five theoretical frameworks: biological, psychoanalytical, behavioral, phenomenological, and sociological/ecological. Within each framework are specific causal factors. Table 6.1 summarizes these variables by theoretical framework. (See Kauffman and Landrum [2006] for a historical analysis of the development of these models.)

When considering causation, it is typically difficult to analyze whether school failure is the source of emotional and behavioral problems, or if the reverse is true. (See Figure 6.5, which is discussed later in the chapter.) It is critical to note that many students experience E/BD because of the environmental factors that affect their lives. In American society, potential causative elements may include variables related to family, school, and community factors. In Figure 6.3, a model designed in reference to antisocial youth outlines this interaction of factors. The model underscores the importance of taking a broad view in understanding the problems experienced by students.

There is substantial support for the fact that students identified with E/BD are far more likely to come from backgrounds that are characterized as being economically disadvantaged. While this finding is not direct evidence of causation, the correlational data in this area suggest that people from lower socioeconomic backgrounds are at increased risk for having mental disorders. Wagner and colleagues (2005) elaborated on this point as follows:

Table 6.1	**Causes of Emotional and Behavioral Disorders**
Theoretical Framework	**Etiologies/Causal Factors**
Biological	Genetic inheritance Biochemical abnormalities Neurological abnormalities Injury to central nervous system
Psychoanalytical	Psychological processes Functioning of the id, ego, and superego Inherited predispositions (instinctual process) Traumatic early-childhood experiences
Behavioral	Environmental events 1. Failure to learn adaptive behaviors 2. Learning of maladaptive behaviors 3. Developing maladaptive behaviors as a result of stressful environmental circumstances
Phenomenological	Faulty learning about oneself Misuse of defense mechanisms Feelings, thoughts, and events emanating from the self
Sociological/Ecological	Role assignment (labeling) Cultural transmission Social disorganization Distorted communication Differential association Negative interactions and transactions with others

Adapted from *Human Exceptionality* (8th ed., pp. 243–246), by M. L. Hardman, C. J. Drew, and M. W. Egan, 2005. Boston: Allyn & Bacon. Used with permission.

Youth identified as [emotionally disturbed] tend to live in households in which there are multiple risk factors for poor life outcomes. Approximately one-third live below the poverty level and in households headed by a single parent, and one-fifth live in households in which the head of the house is unemployed and not a high school graduate. Further indication of potential stress . . . is the finding that almost half (45%) of these students are reported to live in a household with another person who has a disability. All of these differences between children and youth with [emotional disturbances] and both those with other disabilities and those in the general population are statistically significant and large, indicating that the children and youth with [emotional disturbances] are more likely to have each of these risk factors that are strongly associated with the poor life outcomes. (p. 90–91)

An area that is often overlooked but is related to both economic disadvantage and school achievement is school instability (Rothstein, 2006). This phenomenon of changing schools is particularly a concern with students with E/BD because they experience more school environmental instability than other students. Wagner and colleagues (2005) summarized this issue as follows:

They change schools more often than students in other disability groups and nondisabled peers, with one-third of the elementary/middle school students and two-thirds of the secondary students attending at least four different schools. Furthermore, an examination of the most recent move indicates that the students with [emotional disturbances] are reassigned to new schools by their school district at a rate much higher than that of both their nondisabled peers and those in other disability groups. In addition, almost half of the elementary/middle school students and three fourths of the secondary students have been suspended or expelled. These rates are more than four times that of peers in other disability categories and of students in the general population. (p. 92)

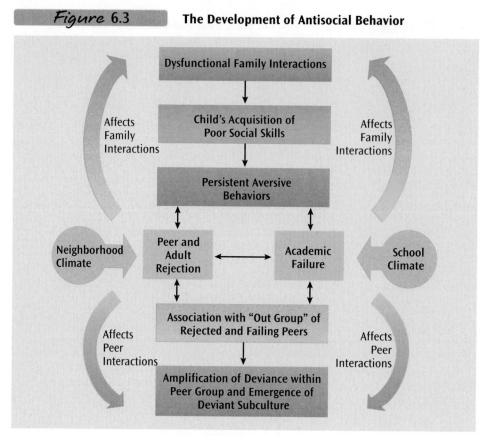

Figure 6.3   **The Development of Antisocial Behavior**

From "Antisocial Behavior, Academic Failure, and School Climate: A Critical Review," by A. McEvoy and R. Welker, 2000, *Journal of Emotional and Behavioral Disorders, 8,* p. 133.

Although risk factors cannot be adjudged to be causes in the typical way that causation is conceptualized, nevertheless, a consideration of risks provides a broad view of the issues that may exacerbate the functioning of students who are identified with E/BD. Table 6.2 lists common risk factors across the domains of child, family, school, and culture.

Characteristics of Students with Emotional and Behavioral Disorders

Students with emotional and behavioral problems exhibit a wide range of characteristics that differ in type as well as intensity. According to Reid and colleagues (2004), for example, students with E/BD are frequently behaviorally disruptive, often noncompliant, aggressive, and verbally abusive. This wide range of behaviors and emotions reflects the broad variety of characteristics associated with individuals with emotional and behavioral problems.

According to the current federal definition of emotional disturbance, there are five key eligibility characteristics: inability to learn, relationship problems, inappropriate behavior, unhappiness or depression, and physical symptoms or fears. Cullinan and Sabornie (2004) investigated these five characteristics to confirm whether students with E/BD in middle and high school settings could be differentiated from their peers across these characteristics. Overall, their data confirmed that these adolescents who are identified as having E/BD did, in fact, exceed their peers who were not disabled on measures for each of the five characteristics. At the same time, these researchers posed several key questions that relate to both the definition and to the research on these characteristics:

Table 6.2	Examples of Risk Factors Common to Students with Emotional Disorders		
Child	**Family**	**School**	**Cultural**
Biological factors (e.g., autism)	Maternal stress/depression	Insufficient training	Low socioeconomic status
Difficult temperament	Large families	High student–teacher ratios	High-crime neighborhoods
Substance use	Divorce	Poor instruction	Negative peer relationships
Neuropsychological deficits (e.g., language deficits)	Antisocial parent/sibling	Maladaptive working conditions	Peer rejection
Antisocial	Ineffective behavior management	Poor behavior management	Cultural expectations
Academic deficits	Abuse	Inconsistent expectations	
Low intelligence	Harsh or coercive parenting	Little academic emphasis	

From "Achievement and Emotional Disturbance: Academic Status and Intervention Research," by M. H. Epstein, J. R. Nelson, A. L. Trout, and P. Mooney, 2005, in *Outcomes for Children and Youth with Emotional and Behavioral Disorders and Their Families,* p. 454, edited by M. H. Epstein, K. Kurash, and A. Duchnowski, 2005. Austin, TX: Pro-Ed.

To what extent is each characteristic related to the likelihood that a student will be referred to a multidisciplinary team for consideration or ultimately identified as [emotionally disturbed]? How do these characteristics change over the course of middle school and high school, and how are such changes affected by different interventions in education environments? What school-based interventions should be available to students who differently manifest the characteristics? (Cullinan & Sabornie, 2004, pp. 165–166)

A common and helpful way to conceptualize E/BD is to categorize them as externalizing or internalizing behaviors. The lists in Table 6.3 provide such an illustration. The discussion in the remainder of this section addresses key domains related to the characteristics of students with E/BD.

Social and Behavioral Problems

Students with E/BD present unique challenges that require professional attention. They typically engage in behaviors that are rated by teachers, and by parents, as more challenging than those of students with learning disabilities and mental retardation (Sabornie et al., 2005).

CEC STANDARDS

CEC 2: Development and Characteristics of Learners

Table 6.3	Categorizing Emotional and Behavioral Disorders
Externalizing Behaviors and Emotions	**Internalizing Behaviors and Emotions**
• Aggressive toward people and objects • Temper tantrums • Defiant • Jealous • Disobedient • Distrustful, blames others • Noncompliant • Pattern of lying and stealing • Argumentative • Lack of self-control • Destructive	• Withdrawn • Apathetic, restricted activity levels • Fixated on certain thoughts • Avoids social situations • Fearful, anxious • Inferiority • Sad, moody, depressed • Self-conscious, overly sensitive • Irritable • Inappropriate crying

From *Childhood Behavioral Disorders: Applied Research and Educational Practices* (2nd ed.), p. 69, by R. Algozzine, L. Serna, and J. R. Patton, 2001. Austin, TX: Pro-Ed.

Depression is a characteristic of students with emotional and behavioral disorders.

Behavioral problems typically associated with children who experience E/BD vary significantly, with common examples including the following:

- aggressive/acting-out behaviors (Grosenick et al., 1991; Kauffman et al., 1995)
- social deficits (Smith & Luckasson, 1995)
- inadequate peer relationships (Searcy & Meadows, 1994)
- hyperactivity/distractibility
- lying, cheating, and stealing (Rosenberg et al., 1992)
- academic deficits (Bullock, 1992)
- anxiety (Kauffman et al., 1995; Wicks-Nelson & Israel, 1991)

These students have been presumed to frequently display deficits in social skills (Knitzer, 1990; Rosenberg et al., 1992) (see Figure 6.4). Wagner and colleagues (2005), however, reported the surprising finding that only one-quarter of elementary and middle school children, and one-third of older peers, had deficiencies in social skills. Nevertheless, deficits in this domain present challenges in the classroom. Elksnin and Elksnin (1998) stress the complexity of social skills, indicating that they include both overt, observable behaviors and covert actions that may relate more to problem solving.

Depression

A problem often overlooked is depression. According to national estimates, approximately 2–4 percent of elementary school children and 4–8 percent of adolescents suffer from depression (CEC, 1999). Further, Forness (cited by CEC, 1999) has estimated that between 30 and 40 percent of students in E/BD classes suffer from depression. Depression may be a particularly significant issue for girls, which unfortunately may be underdiagnosed, because depression is a "silent" disorder, unlike acting-out problems. While depression may be more prevalent in young boys, Marcotte and colleagues (2002) reported that this trend reverses during the teenage years. Negative body image and self-esteem as well as stressful life events were found to be related to this trend. Issues such as the stigma of being labeled, biological factors related to the causation of the disability, and failure experiences can all promote feelings of depression.

Teachers should be alert to signs of depression in order to assist students in the classroom, where depression may be associated with an inability to concentrate or achieve. More dramatically, depression can be associated with suicide, estimated to be the third leading cause of death for adolescents and young adults.

CEC STANDARDS

CEC 6: Language

Language Development

An area that has received limited attention in terms of the characteristics of students with E/BD is language development. However, this is an area of importance and problems have been noted (Wagner et al., 2005). Based on a recent review of research on the language skills of students with E/BD, Nelson, Benner, and Cheney (2005) noted the common co-occurrence of language deficits and problem behaviors. These researchers noted that children who experience language deficits were ten times more likely than those in the general school population to also exhibit antisocial behaviors. The relatively limited research in this area suggests that receptive, expressive, and pragmatic language problems are more likely to place students at risk for inappropriate behavior than are speech disorders, for instance.

| *Figure* 6.4 | **Types of Social Skills** |

Interpersonal Behaviors: "Friendship-making skills," such as introducing oneself, asking a favor, offering to help, giving and accepting compliments, and apologizing.
Peer-Related Social Skills: Skills valued by classmates and associated with peer acceptance. Examples include working cooperatively and asking for and receiving information.
Teacher-Pleasing Social Skills: School success behaviors, including following directions, doing one's best work, and listening to the teacher.
Self-Related Behaviors: Skills that allow a child to assess a social situation, select an appropriate skill, and determine the skill's effectiveness. Other self-related behaviors include following through, dealing with stress, and understanding feelings.
Assertiveness Skills: Behaviors that allow children to express their needs without resorting to aggression.
Communication Skills: Listener responsiveness, turn taking, maintaining conversational attention, and giving the speaker feedback.

From "Teaching Social Skills to Students with Learning and Behavioral Problems," by L. K. Elksnin and N. Elksnin, 1998, *Intervention in School and Clinic, 33,* p. 132.

Based on their research concerning E/BD and language development, Nelson and colleagues (2005) further highlighted three findings. First, they indicated that 68 percent of the students in their sample of children with E/BD met established criteria for a language deficit. Second, these deficits appear to be stable over time and that consequently students continue to have difficulty with expressive and receptive language problems. Third, the magnitude of problems was reported to be greater in expressive rather than receptive skills. They also looked at distinctions between those individuals who expressed externalizing versus internalizing problem behaviors. They concluded that students with E/BD who exhibited externalizing behaviors were more likely to experience key language problems than those who had internalizing behavior problems.

The area of language development and related interventions is discussed in more significant detail in Chapter 11. That discussion will provide further information to complement these summative findings about the language development of students with E/BD.

Academic Achievement

While the focus of research on the characteristics of students with E/BD is often on social and behavioral concerns, it should not be overlooked that academic problems are often documented as a key concern as well (Sabornie et al., 2005; Wagner et al., 2005).

Students with E/BD have routinely been described as having difficulties in academic achievement. As Reid and colleagues (2004) noted, the behaviors in which these students too often engage can "inhibit a child's ability to build and maintain social relationships with peers, teachers, and adults. . . . These children often arouse negative feelings in others, alienating schoolmates and adults and ultimately robbing these children of the benefits of learning opportunities. Inevitably, these behaviors significantly impair a child's ability to succeed in school and in society" (p. 130).

Most of the research on academic achievement and behavioral disorders shows the interrelationship of these two considerations. It can be hypothesized that behavioral problems impede academic achievement but also that academic achievement deficits are predictive of subsequent behavioral problems in the classroom (see Table 6.4). Regardless of which hypothesis is more valid, it appears clear that the vast majority of students with E/BD experience difficulties in academic achievement (Reid et al., 2004).

Reid and colleagues (2004) reviewed existing research on students with E/BD and summarized their findings by indicating that these students typically perform one to two years below their assigned grade level; their problems are identified at an early age and persist throughout elementary and secondary school; they achieve at lower levels in reading and math; and they consequently experience higher rates of failure and ultimately grade retention, which then biases their future in terms of lower graduation rates and a reduced likelihood of enrollment in postsecondary education programs.

CEC STANDARDS

CEC 2: Development and Characteristics of Learners

PRAXIS

PRAXIS II: Understanding Exceptionalities

Table 6.4		The Co-occurrence of Emotional Disorders and Academic Underachievement: A Theoretical Model		
Model	**Hypothesis**	**Directionality of Influence**
1	Poor grades—aggression	Poor grades ——→ Aggression
2	Aggression—poor grades	Aggression ——→ Poor grades
3	Reciprocal causation	Academic failure ←——→ Emotional disorders
4	Spurious relationship	Underlying factors ——→ Emotional disorders and academic failure

From "Achievement and Emotional Disturbance: Academic Status and Intervention Research," by M. H. Epstein et al., 2005, in *Outcomes for Children and Youth with Emotional and Behavioral Disorders and Their Families,* p. 452, edited by M. H. Epstein, K. Kutash, and A. Duchnowski, 2005. Austin, TX: Pro-Ed.

Anderson, Kutash, and Duchnowski (2001) noted that students with E/BD, as well as those with LD, often are frequently observed to exhibit "below-average achievement in content area courses, deficits in basic academics, a general lack of motivation toward school, and deficiencies in school-related skills such as note-taking and test-taking" (p. 6). Further, Anderson and colleagues, in their five-year study of elementary school students, noted that students with E/BD made limited progress in academic achievement when compared to their peers identified as LD.

The difficulty that students with E/BD experience in reading has been noted in several studies and reviews of the literature (e.g., Nelson, Benner, & Gonzalez, 2005). This difficulty is compounded because, as Nelson and colleagues (2005) noted, research indicates a likely poor response by the students to otherwise generally effective interventions for prereading and reading. Given the common findings of significant problems in reading and lack of responsiveness to some effective practices, they stressed the vital importance of the use of appropriate interventions for young children as a way to prevent significant, subsequent problems.

While the academic performance deficits of students with E/BD are often generalized across subject areas, the most common focus has been in reading and literacy. However, Reid and colleagues (2004) reported in their review of research that math and spelling problems were even more significant than those of reading, albeit the difference was not statistically significant. For all academic areas, however, the deficits are substantial enough, and wearisome enough, that teachers should use research-validated interventions to enhance academic achievement.

The relationship between academic achievement and behavioral disorders may be most pronounced in instances of more significant antisocial behavior. McEvoy and Welker (2000) summarized these issues as follows:

> Antisocial behavior and academic failure reinforce one another within the context of ineffective school practices and ineffective parenting strategies. . . . A pattern of academic failure provides few opportunities for the student to receive positive reinforcement. From the failing student's perspective, school then takes on aversive properties that increase the likelihood of escape, rebellion, uncooperativeness, and other negative behaviors. This cycle often results in school failure, dropping out, and involvement in delinquent groups. Conversely, ineffective school responses to antisocial conduct have negative implications and influence the academic performance of students in general. (p. 131)

Postsecondary and Adult Outcomes

A critical concern for all students, including those with emotional and behavioral disorders, is postschool outcomes. In a longitudinal study, Greenbaum and colleagues (1999) reported on students who were identified as SED and were served in either a publicly funded residential mental health facility or a community-based special education program. While the severity of the disorders that these students experienced is likely to be greater, in general, than those of students in general education classrooms, this information should alert educators to the potential challenges that these students face. Educational outcomes were generally poor. For those who were young adults (ages eighteen and older) at the time of the follow-up, 75.4 percent were assessed to be below age-appropriate reading levels, and 96.9 percent were below age-appropriate levels in math achievement. Only one in four had obtained a regular high school diploma; an additional 17.4 percent had completed a GED. Approximately 43 percent had dropped out of school programs.

These data are consistent with the challenging picture that emerges from the annual federal reports on IDEA, which indicate that students with E/BD are the most likely, of all students with disabilities, to drop out of school (65.1 percent of students with E/BD exit school in this manner [U.S. Department of Education, 2005]). In addition, these students, along with students with mental retardation, are the least likely to receive a high school diploma or certificate (28.9 percent) (U.S. Department of Education, 2005).

Students with emotional and behavioral disorders often have significant challenges in adjustment within the community. Maag and Katisyannis (1998) noted that successful adjustment is affected by the high dropout rate, which makes it difficult to establish and address transition goals within the student's IEP and individual transition plan. In addition, successful transition is affected by the high rates of unemployment, the increased likelihood of incarceration, and the persistence of mental health problems in adulthood.

Following up (after three years) on a group of adolescents who participated in a statewide system of care, Pandiani, Schacht, and Banks (2001) reported that these individuals, when compared to other young people, were eight times more likely to be hospitalized for behavioral health care. The young men in the sample were five times as likely to be incarcerated.

Greenbaum and colleagues (1999) reported that approximately two-thirds (66.5 percent) of the individuals had at least one contact with police in which the person was believed to be the perpetrator of a crime, and 43.3 percent had been arrested at least once. The most commonly reported crimes were property-related.

In the area of employment, critical to successful transition, Rylance (1998) reported that the key variables that increase an individual's chances of employment include basic academic skills, high functional competence levels in school-related areas, and high school graduation. Successful school programs for these students tended to be ones that included effective vocational education and counseling programs, and that motivated students to persist in school and obtain a diploma. Chapter 16 provides more information about preparing students with disabilities for successful transitions to adult life.

One somewhat encouraging finding is that students with E/BD had greater success in adult education programs. Scanlon and Melland (2002) hypothesized that the context of adult programs may contribute to this success because such programs may be "less antagonizing and more accepting of any emotional or behavioral problems" (p. 253).

A study reported by McConaughy and Wadsworth (2000) provided some guidance in predicting which individuals would fare better as adults. Based on life histories of these individuals, they concluded that young adults with good outcomes:

> tended to have more stable and quality living situations, better family relationships, more positive relationships with friends, were more goal-oriented, and experienced more successes and fewer stresses than did young adults with poor outcomes. In addition, more young adults with good outcomes held full-time jobs in the community, and fewer associated with friends who used drugs or who were in trouble with the law or violent. (pp. 213–214)

In conclusion, (Burns, Hoagwood, and Maultsby, 1999) "There is little disagreement among families and school personnel concerning the outcomes for children with emotional and behavioral disorders. The difficulty is in achieving such outcomes."

CEC STANDARDS

CEC 8: Assessment

INTASC

INTASC 8: Formal and informal assessment

PRAXIS

PRAXIS II: Delivery of Services to Students with Disabilities

Identification, Assessment, and Eligibility

Students with E/BD are evaluated for several purposes, including identification, assessment to determine appropriate intervention strategies, and determination of eligibility for special services. The first step is for students to be identified as potentially having emotional and behavioral problems. Teachers' awareness of the characteristics of students with these problems is critical in the identification process. Behavioral checklists can be used to identify students for possible referral for assessment.

Once students are identified as possibly having problems, they are referred for formal assessment to determine their eligibility for special education programs and to ascertain appropriate intervention strategies. Kaplan (1996) lists clinical interviews, observations, rating scales, personality tests, and neurological examinations as methods for obtaining relevant information. Figure 6.5 summarizes these procedures.

One encouraging approach to the assessment of students with emotional and behavioral disorders is through the use of **strength-based assessment**. Unlike widely used deficit-oriented assessment models, strength-based assessment focuses on the student and his or her family "as individuals with unique talents, skills, and life events as well as with specific unmet needs. Strength-based assessment recognizes that even the most challenged children in stressed families have strengths, competencies, and resources that can be built on in developing a treatment approach" (Epstein, 1999, p. 258).

Strength-based assessment is based on the following principles:

1. All children have strengths.
2. Assessing a child's strengths in addition to his or her deficits may result in enhanced motivation and improved performance from the child.
3. Deficits should be viewed as opportunities to learn rather than as fixed or stable.
4. Families and children are more likely to positively engage in treatment when service plans include a focus on strengths (Harniss & Epstein, 2005, p. 126).

| *Figure* **6.5** | **Assessment Procedures for Students with Emotional and Behavioral Disorders** |

Clinical Interview
- The interview is the most common tool for assessment.
- Questions are directed to the child and others regarding behaviors and any relevant relationships.
- Some questions are planned; some are developed as the interview progresses.
- The interview can be highly structured, using questions generated from the DSM-IV-TR criteria.

Observation
- The observation can be structured with time limitations, or unstructured.
- Observations should occur in a variety of settings and at different times.

Rating Scales
- A rating scale contains a listing of behaviors to note.
- It provides for much more structure than observation.
- It ensures that certain behaviors are observed or asked about.

Personality Tests
- The two kinds of tests include self-completed inventories and projective tests.
- Both kinds can provide insightful information.
- Interpretation is subjective and needs to be done by a trained professional.

Adapted from *Pathways for Exceptional Children: School, Home, and Culture,* by P. Kaplan, 1996. St. Paul, MN: West Publishing.

Epstein and Charma (1998) developed a scale that complements assessment instruments focusing on difficulties experienced by the student in the school or home setting. As they noted: "Strength-based assessment is defined as the measurement of those emotional/behavioral skills and characteristics that create a sense of personal accomplishment; contribute to satisfying relationships with family members, peers, and adults; enhance one's ability to deal with adversity and stress; and promote one's personal, social, and academic development" (p. 3).

Given the difficulties of assessing students with emotional and behavioral problems, the use of strength-based assessments is promising in terms of their contributions to understanding the nature and needs of students with E/BD. Uhing, Mooney, and Ryser (2005) reported on their studies using the Behavioral and Emotional Rating Scale, second edition (BERS-2) (Epstein, 2004). They confirmed that this scale was effective for distinguishing between students with and without emotional and behavioral disorders. They also indicated support for the use of this instrument in providing further information about students with E/BD to assist in the development of educational programs.

Functional Behavioral Assessment

One important approach to assessment warrants separate consideration because of its clear implications for intervention efforts. Functional behavioral assessment (FBA) provides a consideration of specific behaviors and behavioral patterns set within an environmental context. It has been defined as "an analysis of the contingencies responsible for behavioral problems" (Malott, Whaley, & Malott, 1997, p. 433).

An FBA is a "systematic procedure . . . [to explain] why a behavior occurs by analyzing the behavior and generating hypotheses about its purpose or intended function. Ultimately, these hypotheses should assist school personnel in identifying interventions that change the student's undesirable behavior" (McConnell et al., 2006, p. viii). For analyzing behavior, a sample form is presented in Figure 6.6.

When determining appropriate intervention strategies, FBA provides extensive information for teachers. A functional assessment helps teachers better understand disruptive behaviors; improved understanding can lead to an insightful intervention approach. Foster-Johnson and Dunlap (1993) identified the following variables that may influence behavior:

1. **Physiological factors**
   - Sickness or allergies
   - Side effects of medication
   - Fatigue
   - Frustration due to a fight, missing the bus, or a disrupted routine
2. **Classroom environment**
   - High noise level
   - Uncomfortable temperature
   - Over- or understimulation
   - Poor seating arrangement
   - Frequent disruptions
3. **Curriculum and instruction**
   - Few opportunities for making choices
   - Lack of predictability in the schedule
   - Inadequate level of assistance provided to the student
   - Unclear directions provided for activity completion
   - Few opportunities for the student to communicate
   - Activities that are too difficult
   - Activities that take a long time to complete
   - Activities for which the completion criterion is unclear
   - Activities that might not be perceived as relevant or useful

CEC STANDARDS

CEC 8: Assessment

PRAXIS

PRAXIS II: Delivery of Services to Students with Disabilities

INTASC

INTASC 8: Formal and informal assessment

CONSIDER THIS

How can using FBA help teachers focus on specific issues related to inappropriate behaviors?

Figure 6.6 **Functional Behavioral Assessment: Analysis of Behavior**

Student: _____

Analysis of Behavior
Prioritized Behavior #

Antecedents (Events or conditions occurring before or triggering the behavior)	Behavior (Exactly what the student does or does not do)	Consequences (Actions or events occurring after the behavior)	Function of Behavior (Hypothesized purpose of the behavior)
Setting, subject, or class:	Behavior in observable, measurable terms:	Behavior in ignored Planned Unplanned	Avoidance or escape Avoid a directive or request Avoid an assignment Escape a situation or a person
Time of day:		Peer attention	
Person(s):	Baseline measures of behavior Frequency of behavior:	Adult attention Reminder(s) Repeated directive or request	Attention Gain peer attention Gain adult attention
Interruption in routine:	per	Private meeting or conference Reprimand or warning	Self-control issue Express frustration Express anger
	Duration of behavior:		Vengeance Power or control
Directive or request to:		Change in directive or request	Intimidation
	per incident		Sensory or emotional reaction
Consequences imposed:		Loss of privilege:	Fear or anxiety
	intensity of behavior:		Sensory relief or stimulation
Lack of social attention:		Time out in classroom	Other(s):
Difficulty or frustration:		Administrative consequences:	
Other(s):		Parent contact	
		Other(s):	

From *Behavioral Intervention Planning (BIP-III)* (3rd ed.) by K. McConnell, J. R. Patton, and E. A. Polloway, 2006. Austin, TX: Pro-Ed.

CEC STANDARDS

CEC 8: Assessment

Manifestation of the Disability

A key issue in the field of E/BD is the relationship between the disability itself and the behaviors that are exhibited in school. Under IDEA guidelines, educators must determine whether the behavior in question functions as a **manifestation of the student's disability**. The key questions, as outlined in IDEA 2004, are whether the behavior was caused by, or had a direct and substantial relationship to the child's disability, or if the behavior was the direct result of the school's failure to implement the IEP. The function of the guidelines is not to prevent educators from taking action to redirect troublesome behavior. Rather, the purpose is to prevent the misapplication of disciplinary actions that, owing to the student's particular disability, may fail to achieve the desired objective and create needless frustration for everyone involved (Buck et al., 1999; McConnell et al., 2006).

To complete a manifestation determination for students with E/BD (as well as for other disabilities), school personnel should carefully consider the disability and the nature of the behavior to determine a possible relationship.

After reviewing research on manifestation determination, Katsiyannas and Maag (2001) developed a model for conceptualizing key questions to consider. The four issues they identified are summarized in Rights & Responsibilities. In Figure 6.7, a flowchart for manifestation determination, developed by McConnell and colleagues (2006) in response to the changes in federal law under IDEA 2004, is presented.

Classroom teachers should be aware of the concept of manifestation of disability within the continuing debate about disciplinary procedures for students with disabilities, including those with E/BD. The debate revolves around the issues of equity, discipline, school safety, and the legal rights of students with disabilities for a free and appropriate public education with accommodations designed to be consistent with students' individual needs.

PRAXIS

PRAXIS II: Delivery of Services to Students with Disabilities

CEC STANDARDS

CEC 4: Instructional Strategies

INTASC

INTASC 4: Uses a Variety of Strategies

Strategies and Adaptations in Curriculum and Instruction

Students with emotional and behavioral disorders often present significant problems for teachers in general education settings. Their behavior may affect not only their own learning but the learning of other students as well.

The intransigence of these problems underscores the importance of preventative programs as does the common delay between identification and services initiation (Wagner

---

Rights & Responsibilities

Manifestation Determination Model

1. Does the student possess the requisite skills to engage in an appropriate alternative behavior? The team would break the behavior down into its subcomponents using task analysis, list the subcomponents on a checklist to note their presence or absence, and select a powerful reinforcer. The reinforcer is designed to motivate the student to use the targeted skills if they exist in his repertoire. If necessary, a relevant scenario would then be generated, and the student would be asked to role-play the skills for dealing with teasing appropriately in order to earn the reinforcer. . . .

2. Is the student able to analyze the problem, generate solutions, evaluate their effectiveness, and select one? . . . The evaluator would generate a scenario in which the aggressive behavior occurred. She would then determine how well the student could answer the following questions:
   - Can the student define the problem to be solved?
   - Can the student set realistic and concrete goals to solve the problem?
   - Can the student generate a wide range of possible alternative courses of action?

   - Can the student imagine and consider how others might respond if asked to deal with a similar problem?
   - Can the student evaluate the pros and cons of each proposed solution and rank order the solutions from least to most practical and desirable?

3. Does the student interpret the situation factually or distort it to fit some existing bias? . . . A cognitive distortion exists when a student does not factually interpret aspects of the situation. . . . In addition, an evaluator can interview a student to identify any discrepancies between the event and activated thoughts.

4. Can the student monitor the behavior? This deficit area is perhaps the most difficult to evaluate because the assessment and intervention techniques for this deficit area are identical. Namely, if we want to assess a student's skill at self-monitoring, we have him self-monitor. However, the process of self-monitoring results in reactivity—obtaining a positive change in the target behavior by virtue of the student observing and recording it.

Adapted from "Manifestation Determination as a Golden Fleece," by A. Katsiyannis and J. W. Maag, 2001, *Exceptional Children, 68,* pp. 93–94.

| Figure 6.7 | **Manifestation Determination Flowchart** |

If the student has violated the student code of conduct, school personnel may consider unique circumstances for this specific student when deciding whether to order a change in placement.

Is a placement change to an IAES, another setting, or suspension for **NOT MORE than 10 school days** being considered?

If this alternative is applied to other students without disabilities for the same violation, then the student may be removed and **no Manifestation Determination is needed.**

Is a placement change to an IAES, another setting, or suspension for **MORE than 10 school days** being considered?

Is a placement change to an IEAS, another setting, or suspension that is part of a **series of removals totaling more than 10 school days and constituting a pattern** being considered?

Conduct a Manifestation Determination

If the decision is made to remove the student for more than 10 school days, within 10 school days of that decision the school district, parents, and relevant IEP team members shall review all relevant information, including the following:
- The IEP
- Teacher observations
- Relevant information provided by parents

The purpose of the review is to determine if either of the following instances applies. If *either* of these two applies, the behavior is a manifestation of the disability.
1. The conduct was *caused by, or had a direct and substantial relationship to* the student's disability.
2. The conduct was a *direct result of the Local Education Agency's (school district's) failure to implement the IEP.*

Is the behavior a manifestation of the disability?

If the behavior is a manifestation of the disability, the student must
1. continue to receive educational services enabling progress toward IEP goals and participation in the general education curriculum; and
2. if appropriate, receive
   - a functional behavioral assessment (FBA), and
   - behavioral intervention services and modifications (BIP and modifications).

In addition, the IEP team shall
1. conduct a functional behavioral assessment, if there is not one in place;
2. implement a BIP or review a previous plan for modification; and
3. return the student to his or her previous placement, unless parents and school district agree to a change in placement as part of a modified BIP or if the violation involved weapons, drugs, or infliction of serious bodily injury.*

If the behavior is not a manifestation of the disability, you may apply the same disciplinary action applicable to students without disabilities, in the same manner, and for the same duration. This *does* include placement to an IEAS.

The student must
1. continue to receive educational services enabling progress toward IEP goals and participation in the general education curriculum; and,
2. if appropriate, receive
   - a functional behavioral assessment (FBA), and
   - behavioral intervention services and modifications (BIP and modifications).

* Either the parents or the school district may request an appeal. During appeal, the student remains in the IAES pending a decision or until expiration of the time period allowed for students without disabilities, whichever occurs first, unless parents and the school district agree otherwise.

From *Behavioral Intervention Planning (BIP-III)* (3rd ed.), by K. McConnell, J. R. Patton, and E. A. Polloway, 2006. Austin, TX: Pro-Ed.

et al., 2005). Walker and colleagues (2005) have developed a comprehensive program to serve this purpose, shown in the Evidence-Based Practice box.

The challenges of appropriately serving students with E/BD are emphasized by the realities of how schools respond to these students. See the Personal Spotlight for one educator's experience with these challenges.

Educational Placements

Students with E/BD are commonly included in general education classrooms, albeit to a lesser extent than students with other types of disabilities (e.g., learning disabilities). According to the 25th Annual Report to Congress on the Implementation of IDEA (U.S. Department of Education, 2005), 26.8 percent of all students identified as emotionally disturbed were taught in the regular class setting (i.e., general education) at least 79 percent of the time, while an additional 23.4 percent were served in these settings between 40 percent and 79 percent of the time. Combining these figures, we can conclude that approximately 50 percent of students identified as E/BD will spend much of their time in general education–based programs. At the same time, according to these data for the 2001–2002 year, 31.8 percent of students with E/BD were out of the general education classroom at least 60 percent of the time, and an additional 18.1 percent were educated in separate environments. The latter settings included 13.12 percent of students with E/BD (ages 6–21) in separate public (7.72 percent) or private (5.40 percent) day facilities, 1.63 percent in public or private residential facilities, and 1.30 percent in home or hospital environments.

The challenge of inclusion for students with E/BD has given rise to a number of perspectives on the relative advantages of inclusive versus restrictive settings, which can

PRAXIS

PRAXIS II: Delivery of Services to Students with Disabilities

CEC STANDARDS

CEC 4: Instructional Strategies

INTASC

INTASC 4: Uses a variety of strategies

PRAXIS

PRAXIS II: Delivery of Services to Students with Disabilities

EVIDENCE-BASED PRACTICE

First Step to Success: A Preventive Program for Behaviorally At-Risk Children (K–2)

First Step to Success was designed as an early intervention program to address emerging patterns of antisocial behavior. The program includes three components:

1. A screening and early detection procedure that provides four different options for use by adopters.
2. A school intervention component that teaches an adaptive behavior pattern to facilitate successful adjustment to the normal demands of schooling.
3. A parent training component, called HomeBase, that teaches parents how to develop their child's school success skills (e.g., cooperation, accepting limits, sharing, doing one's work). The program is set up and operated initially in the classroom by a behavioral coach (school psychologist, counselor, early interventionist, behavioral specialist) who invests approximately fifty to sixty hours of time during the approximately three-month implementation period.

Coaches must be school professionals who can coordinate the roles of these participants and contribute approximately sixty hours during the implementation period. Typically, coaches are trained in the First Step screening, implementation, and parental training procedures during one- and two-day training sessions for staff members.

The coach conducts screening activities, identifies candidates who meet eligibility criteria, and secures parental consent for the child's participation as well as teacher cooperation. The coach explains to the child and classmates how the First Step program works and then he operates it during two brief daily sessions for the first five program days. On day six, the coach turns the program over to the general education classroom teacher, who operates it as part of his or her ongoing teaching routine, with supervision, assistance, and support provided by the coach.

After day ten, First Step is operated independently by the regular classroom teacher. The behavioral coach then contacts the target child's parents to enlist their cooperation in learning how to teach the child school success skills at home. Parents meet for approximately an hour and a half weekly with the First Step coach for a six-week period. During each weekly session, parents and caregivers learn to teach one of the following school success skills: communication and sharing, cooperating, setting limits, solving problems, making friends, and developing self-confidence. The general education classroom teacher looks for, recognizes, and praises the child's display of these skills.

From "The Oregon First Step to Success Replication Initiative: Statewide Results of an Evaluation of the Program's Impact," by H. Walker et al., 2005, *Journal of Emotional and Behavioral Disorders, 13,* p. 165.

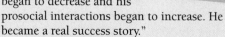

Middle School Principal

Mike Kelly took a circuitous route to becoming a school administrator. After completing his undergraduate degree in special education, Mike taught students with learning disabilities and those with emotional and behavioral problems for eleven years. He then completed two master's degrees, one in school administration and the other in special education. He was an elementary school principal for twelve years and has been a middle school principal for the past five years.

Mike finds inclusion powerful because it provides excellent learning opportunities for all students. At the same time, his experiences as a teacher and administrator reinforce the fact that successful inclusion stands or falls on access to necessary supports and resources. Reflecting back on his own teaching experience, Mike notes there had been more limited opportunities for his own students to experience inclusion when he was teaching children with disabilities.

As a principal, Mike has seen a number of successes that relate to inclusion. In particular, for students with E/BD, the benefits of inclusion are most clearly seen when a student's behavior begins to change as a result of interaction with peers and his or her social skills develop to a corresponding degree. In many instances, though certainly not all, dramatic changes in terms of appropriate behavior were seen after inclusion. As he notes, "One student identified as E/BD was placed in a general education classroom and initially continued the kinds of behaviors that had previously characterized his school performance. After a while, however, he seemed to realize that he was not getting the 'audience' that he had anticipated, and consequently, his inappropriate behaviors began to decrease and his prosocial interactions began to increase. He became a real success story."

Mike continues, "While some indicate that inclusion may be difficult in schools with academically talented students, I believe that there are some special advantages in such a school. Because the students are quite committed to the learning process, they often consequently serve as very effective models for students who are experiencing both learning and behavioral difficulties."

While some students have made remarkable progress in social adjustment, Mike finds that there is a significant need for supports in the classroom to make it work from an academic perspective. Paraprofessionals and the substantive involvement of special educators in support of classroom teachers can make the difference between successful and less successful inclusion experiences for individual learners as well as for their peers.

Mike Kelly
Bedford County, VA

prove helpful to teachers as they plan inclusive programs. McConnell's (2001) perspectives are presented in Table 6.5.

Because many students with E/BD are included in general education classrooms, teachers and special education teachers need to collaborate in developing and implementing intervention programs. Without this collaboration, appropriate interventions will be difficult to provide. Consistency in behavior management and other strategies among teachers and family members is critical. If students receive feedback from the special education teacher that significantly differs from the feedback received from the classroom teacher, then confusion often results.

As more students with disabilities are included in general education classrooms, many students with serious emotional disturbances and behavioral disorders are being reintegrated into general classrooms from more restrictive settings. The ability of students and teachers to deal with behavior problems effectively is critical for successful reintegration (Carpenter & McKee-Higgins, 1996). Rock, Rosenberg, and Carran (1995) studied the variables that affected this reintegration and reported that programs that were more likely to have success at reintegration included those with a more positive reintegration orientation; those with certain demographic characteristics, such as being located in a wing of the general classroom building; and those whose teachers had particular training experiences, such as having reintegration training at several sites.

Table 6.5	Advantages and Disadvantages of More and Less Restrictive Placements	
Placements	**Advantages**	**Disadvantages**
Less Restrictive Regular classrooms (with and without support) Resource rooms	Prevents the regular educator from giving up on the student and turning to "experts" Permits students to model appropriate behavior of their peers; increased interaction Possibly less expensive May be able to serve more students Students do not experience problems with reintegration Students follow general curriculum more easily	Expense and time required to train general educators to work with students and special educators to work collaboratively with general educators Problems with classroom management and discipline Lack of consistent expectations for the students Time and materials required for individualization Fear and frustration of general education
More Restrictive Separate classes Separate campuses Residential facilities Hospitals	Flexibility to provide different curricula and different goals Progress can be more closely monitored Accountability of program is more clearly defined Intervention can be more consistent Student follows only one set of guidelines and expectations One team for consistent discipline	Student's opportunities for peer interactions are limited, especially when student is not at neighborhood school with peers from neighborhood Travel time for students can be excessive No possible modeling of appropriate peers; no opportunities for socialization with nondisabled peers Difficulties with reintegration back into regular school or class

From "Placements," by K. McConnell, 2001, in *Childhood Behavior Disorders: Applied Research and Educational Practices* (2nd ed.), p. 324, edited by R. Algozzine, L. Serna, and J. R. Patton, 2001. Austin, TX: Pro-Ed.

Special Curricular Needs

In addition to the importance of implementing validated academic curricular strategies for all students, a particular area of concern for students with E/BD is social skills instruction. Social skills are best learned from observing others who display appropriate skills, but there are times when a more formal instructional effort must be made. When using a formal instructional process to teach social skills, the first step is to determine the student's level of social competence.

Assessing social skills requires eliciting informed judgments from people who interact regularly with the student (Smith et al., 1993). Many checklists are available to assist in assessing social competence. In addition, self-monitoring charts and sociometric measures may be used.

Following the assessment process, an instructional approach for eliminating deficiencies in social skills must be developed. Numerous methods may be used to teach social skills and promote good social relations, including modeling, direct instruction, prompting, and positive practice (Searcy & Meadows, 1994). Teachers must determine the method that will work best with a particular student.

Quinn and colleagues (1999) reported a comprehensive research analysis of the use of social skills training with students with E/BD. In general, they caution that it has been demonstrated that only about half of students with E/BD have benefitted from social skills training, particularly when the focus was on the broader dimensions of the social domain. Greater success was obtained when the focus was on specific social skills (e.g., social problem-solving, social interaction, cooperation). Forness (1999) and Kavale (2001b) hypothesized that the reason more substantive positive effects have not been obtained from training may be that the programs within the research studies were too limited in duration and intensity.

CROSS-REFERENCE

For information on autism spectrum disorders, see Chapter 10.

CEC STANDARDS

CEC 4: Instructional Strategies

Another reason why social skills instruction may be problematic is that its effectiveness is challenged by the difficulty of achieving generalization across settings. Scott and Nelson (1998) cautioned teachers to realize that educational practices for achieving generalization in academic instruction are often insufficient for achieving similar outcomes in social skills instruction. They stress that any such instruction in artificial contexts will create difficulty in generalization, and therefore schoolwide instruction, modeling, and the reinforcement of appropriate social behaviors taught within the context of the classroom are likely to be most effective. This instruction may be more effective when students who are not disabled are involved in the training. While they stress the complexity of teaching social skills, Scott and Nelson (1998) also similarly stress the critical nature of learning within this area. Teachers are advised to consider social skills programs cautiously, implement them experimentally, and confirm that positive outcomes are obtained.

Effective Instruction

A key to effective instruction is the use of empirically validated strategies. Research offers promising directions for effective instructional practices. As adapted from Wehby and colleagues (1998), these practices should include the following:

- Providing appropriate structure and predictable routines.
- Establishing a structured and consistent classroom environment.
- Establishing a consistent schedule with set rules and consequences and clear expectations.
- Fostering positive teacher-student interaction with adequate praise and systematic responses to problem behaviors.
- Frequently implementing instructional sequences that promote high rates of academic engagement.
- Creating a classroom environment in which independent seat work is limited and sufficient time is allotted for establishing positive social interaction. (p. 52)

The behavior of teachers can have great impact on effective behavior management.

An important emphasis in effective instruction for students with E/BD is to use FBA procedures (discussed earlier in the chapter) as a basis for making effective classroom adaptations. For example, Kerr and colleagues (2001) demonstrated that adaptations based on assessment data—which identified activities associated with problem behavior and also activities not associated with such behavior—resulted in increased task employment, decreases in challenging behavior, and increased academic productivity—all without significant difficulties in implementation by the teacher. Further, Reid and Nelson (2002) reported that FBA provides a promising approach with research validation for planning positive behavioral interventions, which can have a significant effect on improving student behavior. FBA-based approaches offer exciting opportunities to enhance instruction and influence successful inclusion practices. McConnell and colleagues (2006) provide a detailed approach for developing behavioral intervention plans based on the use of FBA.

Physical Adaptations

The physical arrangement of the classroom has an impact on the behaviors of students with E/BD. Attention to the classroom arrangement can both facilitate learning and minimize disruptions (Zabel & Zabel, 1996). The following considerations can help maintain an orderly classroom:

- Arranging traffic patterns to lessen contact and disruptions.
- Arranging student desks to facilitate monitoring of all students at all times.

IEP Goals and Objectives for Travis*

The following IEP goals and objectives are consistent with the chapter-opening vignette of Travis if he were subsequently identified as having E/BD and found eligible for special education.

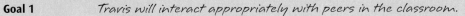

Goal 1   *Travis will interact appropriately with peers in the classroom.*

Objective 1:   *In classroom settings, Travis will ask permission to borrow or use items from classmates 90 percent of the time.*

Objective 2:   *In classroom settings, Travis will engage in disruptions of peers no more than three times per day.*

Objective 3:   *In classroom settings, Travis will participate in group projects with peers without disruptions, independent of teacher monitoring of his behavior, 70 percent of the time.*

Goal 2   *Travis will complete the in-class and homework assignments successfully.*

Objective 1:   *Given an in-class assignment, Travis will work independently for a minimum of fifteen minutes with one or no disruptions 80 percent of the time.*

Objective 2:   *Given homework assignments for one week, Travis will complete 75 percent of assignments on time.*

Objective 3:   *Given in-class assignments, Travis will complete 80 percent of them within the appropriate time frame.*

Goal 3   *Travis will demonstrate the ability to make sound-symbol correspondences for vowels and consonant sounds.*

Objective 1:   *Given a series of common consonants (i.e., b, d, f, l, m, n, p, r, s, t), Travis will correctly identify the associated sounds with 80 percent accuracy.*

Objective 2:   *Given a list of vowels, Travis will correctly identify all short vowel sounds with 90 percent accuracy.*

Objective 3:   *Given a set of vowels, Travis will correctly identify all long vowel sounds with 90 percent accuracy.*

*IDEA 2004 does not require short-term objectives (STOs) except for students taking alternative assessments. However, they are included here both to illustrate learning benchmarks for teachers, and because many school discussions continue to use STOs.

- Physically locating students with tendencies toward disruptive behaviors near the teacher's primary location.
- Locating students away from stored materials that they may find tempting.
- Creating spaces where students can do quiet work, such as a quiet reading area.

Strategies for Behavioral Change

Effective Classroom Procedures   Classroom rules and procedures are a critical management tool for students with E/BD. A complete discussion of classroom management procedures is included in Chapter 14. In relation to classroom management, rules should be developed with the input of students and should be posted in the room. Remember that "the process of determining rules is as important as the rules themselves" (Zabel & Zabel, 1996, p. 169). The following are examples of classroom rules:

- Be polite and helpful.
- Keep your space and materials in order.
- Take care of classroom and school property.
- Raise your hand before speaking.
- Leave your seat only with permission.
- Only one person in the rest room at a time (Walker & Shea, 1995, p. 252).

CEC STANDARDS

CEC 5: Learning Environments and Social Interactions

INTASC

INTASC 5: Create learning environments

PRAXIS

PRAXIS II: Delivery of Services to Students with Disabilities

Tips for Adapting a Lesson for Travis

Based on the chapter-opening vignette, the following sample classroom adaptations might be considered to enhance Travis's learning and respond to his IEP goals and objectives.

His teacher could:

- Establish a reinforcement system based on check marks earned for appropriate behavior with redemption for rewards or special activities twice daily on an initial basis.

- Use peer-mediated interventions such as the "hero" technique, in which Travis's appropriate social interactions with peers result in whole class reinforcement (e.g., special activity).

- Use a peer tutor from an upper elementary grade to drill Travis on vowel and consonant sounds.

- Set up a system of pictures to symbolize work assignments so Travis can monitor his own work completion as a basis for reinforcement.

- Establish a home-school contract in which appropriate classroom behavior is linked with special opportunities provided by his mother.

- Assign homework that can be completed in ten to fifteen minutes to reinforce effective work habits and task completion.

CROSS-REFERENCE

For more information on classroom management considerations, see Chapter 14.

CONSIDER THIS

How can classroom rules and procedures result in improved behavior for children with E/BD?

TEACHING TIP

When students cannot reach a target behavior immediately, reinforce their efforts and their progress toward reaching the behavior.

Teachers should establish classroom procedures to ensure an orderly environment. These include procedures for the beginning of a period or the school day, use of classroom equipment, social interaction, the completion of work, group and individual activities, and the conclusion of instructional periods and the school day (Walker & Shea, 1995). Effective procedures undergird the concept of preventive discipline discussed below.

Positive Behavior Supports The development of **positive behavior supports (PBS)** has been a significant achievement in the education of students with special needs and has particular relevance for students with E/BD. Carr and colleagues (2002) describe PBS as follows:

> Positive behavior includes all those skills that increase the likelihood of success and personal satisfaction in . . . academic, work, social, recreational, community, and family settings. Support encompasses all those educational methods that can be used to teach, strengthen, and expand positive behavior and . . . increase opportunities for the display of positive behavior. The primary goal of PBS is to help an individual change his or her lifestyle in a direction that gives . . . teachers, employers, parents, friends, and the target person him- or herself the opportunity to perceive and to enjoy an improved quality of life. An important but secondary goal of PBS is to render problem behavior irrelevant, inefficient, and ineffective by helping an individual achieve his or her goals in a socially acceptable manner. (pp. 4–5)

PBS interventions provide an alternative to an emphasis on punitive disciplinary strategies and provide guidance to students with behavioral problems to make appropriate changes in their behavioral patterns. PBS emphasizes proactive, preventive strategies and early intervention with students deemed to be at risk. Further, those programs that are organized on a schoolwide basis have an increased likelihood of success (Nelson et al., 2005). A key component of such programs is administrative support (see the Personal Spotlight on Mike Kelly, p. 198).

An effective positive behavioral support program for a school should include the following components:

- specialized individual behavior support for students with chronic behavior problems
- specialized group behavioral support for students with at-risk problem behavior
- universal group behavior support for most students (Lewis & Sugai, 1999, p. 4).

DIVERSITY FORUM

Teaching Students with Emotional/ Behavioral Disorders—Disproportionate Representation: Is There a Problem?

Ms. Luce is preparing for conferences with parents of two of her students at their request. Kay is well-behaved but almost never participates verbally even when called on, and rarely interacts with other children. Although Ms. Luce feels helpless she has assumed that Kay will participate more as she learns English as a second language. The second student, Jordan, presents quite a different challenge. During literature circle, Jordan complains loudly about reading assignments and refuses to follow directions. Ms. Luce is planning to discuss the possibility of a special education referral with his parents.

As discussed earlier in this chapter, disproportionate representation by race, ethnicity, and gender raises questions about appropriate identification of emotional or behavioral disorders (E/BD). Because socio-cultural and linguistic characteristics can greatly influence students' learning and social behavior, care is needed when interpreting responses that are inconsistent with expectations for classroom

behavior. Classroom teachers like Ms. Luce must be able to accurately identify behaviors that may be symptoms of a potential E/BD because they usually make the initial referral of students for special education evaluation.

In both instances above, information from multiple sources can validate students' learning or behavioral difficulties, and ensure that interventions developed to address them will be appropriate. Ms. Luce would carefully observe and monitor Kay's behavior to determine if her silence primarily reflects limited English proficiency. Kay's parents have noticed changes in her behavior at home, and she received lower-than-usual grades on her last report card. Ms. Luce may find that there is sufficient data to supports Kay's referral for a special education evaluation. On the other hand, Jordan's parents perceive that Jordan is becoming less motivated to learn in Ms. Luce's class. From talking with Jordan's parents, she may learn that Jordan responds well to a flexible and interactive learning envi-

ronment. His behavior may improve if he can participate in selecting reading assignments or work in a small group with opportunities for social interaction and movement (Bondy & Ross, 1998).

Questions

1. What other types of socio-cultural and linguistic information should be gathered when conducting a functional behavioral assessment of Kay's and Jordan's classroom behavior to assist Ms. Luce in accurately identifying the sources of each student's difficulties?

2. If Kay qualifies for services under the category of E/BD, what cultural and linguistic factors would have to be considered to ensure that positive behavioral supports are responsive to her needs?

REFERENCES
Bondy, E., & Ross, D. (1998). Confronting myths about teaching black children: A challenge for teacher educators. *Teacher education and special education, 21*(4), 241-254.

The system that Lewis and Sugai (1999) have developed emphasizes schoolwide programs that put in place a preventive, proactive system and provide a foundation for the appropriate design of programs for individuals experiencing significant behavior problems.

Representative behavioral strategies that have merit for use with students with E/BD include the good behavior game, contingency contracting, and individual behavior management plans (see Chapter 14 for a comprehensive discussion of strategies for students in general education as well as those identified as having E/BD). Cognitive approaches are of particular importance to students with E/BD. These interventions were discussed in Chapters 4 and 5. For students with E/BD, a particular focus should be on the development of behavioral self-control in which students are taught to use self-management strategies throughout the day. A sample self-control plan is presented in Figure 6.8.

Another technique, the use of peer mediation, has also been used effectively with students with emotional and behavioral disorders. As Gable, Arllen, and Hendrickson (1994) noted, while most behavioral programs rely on adults to monitor and provide reinforcement for desirable behaviors, this technique instead relies on peers. After reviewing peer interaction studies, they concluded that peer behavior modifiers could be effective among students with emotional and behavioral problems. "The generally positive results surfacing from the modest number of investigations in which E/BD students have served as behavior modifiers underscore the relevance of this procedure for those facing the

TEACHING TIP

When using peers to assist with the implementation of a behavior-change program, make sure that the students involved in the process are appropriately trained.

INTASC

INTASC 4: Variety of instructional strategies

Figure 6.8   **Sample Behavioral Self-Control Plan to Improve Math Scores**

1. Rules needed to meet goal:
   a. Every day, after school, I will go to the library.
   b. I will study math for two hours at the library.
   c. I will monitor my time so only the time spent working on math will be attributed to the two-hour period.
   d. If I have trouble with my math assignment, I will ask the proctoring teacher for help.
   e. After the two-hour period, I can spend time with my friends, talk on the phone, or have leisure time alone.
2. Goal: I will improve my math grade by at least one letter grade in a six-week period.
   a. I will complete all my daily homework assignments.
   b. I will review each lecture on a daily basis.
   c. I will develop strategies that will help me remember problem-solving procedures for math problems.
   d. I will practice and review math problems.
3. Feedback: Prior to turning in my homework, I will ask my parent or teacher to check my work. I will correct any wrong answers.
4. Measurement-monitoring of rules and subgoals:
   a. Rules: Develop a monitoring system that indicates the time spent studying at the library and asking for help when needed.
   b. Subgoals: Develop a monitoring system that indicates whether the homework, review of lecture, strategies, or practice was completed during the two-hour period.
   c. Products: Improvement on math scores should indicate progress toward goal; if progress is not seen after a two-week period, reevaluate the plan.

From *Childhood Behavior Disorders: Applied Research and Practices* (2nd ed.) p. 212, edited by R. Algozzine, L. Serna, and J. R. Patton, 2001. Austin, TX: Pro-Ed.

PRAXIS

PRAXIS II: Delivery of Services to Students with Disabilities

CEC STANDARDS

CEC 4: Instructional Strategies

daunting task of better serving students with emotional/behavioral disorders" (Gable et al., 1994, p. 275). Peer mediation strategies are discussed further in Chapter 15.

Table 6.6 provides some sample hypothesis statements and possible interventions related to functional behavioral assessment-based interventions. Such an approach does not lock teachers into specific strategies, thus allowing them to tailor interventions to specific behaviors and causes (Kauffman et al., 1995).

Behavioral Intervention Planning   According to federal guidelines under the 1997 and 2004 amendments to IDEA, school district personnel are required to address the strategies to be employed for students with disabilities who exhibit significant behavioral problems. The required component is the development of a **behavioral intervention plan (BIP)**. This plan is required in certain instances of serious misbehavior (e.g., using weapons or drugs) but also may be an effective response to other significant behavioral problems. The development of the BIP parallels the development of the IEP and includes input from professionals and parents. Detailed discussion on the development of BIPs is provided by McConnell and colleagues (2006) and is elaborated on in Chapter 14.

Wraparound Services

The focus of this text is on the inclusion of students with disabilities in general education classrooms and the implications of this process for educators. However, for students with E/BD, the school setting is only one environment that must be responsive to their needs. In addition, other services include mental health organizations, social services, and the juvenile and criminal justice systems. Kamradt, Gilbertson, and Lynn (2005) emphasized the importance of this broad-based approach to meeting students' needs. The core elements of their wraparound program are listed in Figure 6.9. For a portrait of a wraparound program, see the Personal Spotlight on "Jake."

Windle and Mason (2004), focusing on emotional and behavioral problems in adolescents, validated a model for predicting such problems in these students that clearly illustrates the complexity of problems and hence programmatic needs. Based on their research, the key predictors formed a four-factor model of behavioral and emotional problems. These variables included polydrug use (alcohol, marijuana, cigarettes,

Table 6.6	Sample Hypothesis Statements and Possible Interventions	
	Intervention	
Hypothesis Statements	**Modify Antecedents**	**Teach Alternative Behavior**
Suzy pinches herself and others around 11:00 A.M. every day because she gets hungry.	Make sure Suzy gets breakfast. Provide a snack at about 9:30 A.M.	Teach Suzy to ask for something to eat.
Jack gets into arguments with the teacher every day during reading class when she asks him to correct his mistakes on the daily reading worksheet.	Get Jack to correct his own paper. Give Jack an easier assignment.	Teach Jack strategies to manage his frustration in a more appropriate manner. Teach Jack to ask for teacher assistance with the incorrect problems.
Tara starts pouting and refuses to work when she has to sort a box of washers because she doesn't want to do the activity.	Give Tara half of the box of washers to sort. Give Tara clear directions about how much she has to do or how long she must work.	
Frank kicks other children in morning circle time and usually gets to sit right by the teacher.	Give each child a clearly designated section of the floor that is his or hers.	Teach Frank how to ask the children to move over. Teach Frank how to ask the teacher to intervene with his classmates.
Harry is off task for most of math class when he is supposed to be adding two-digit numbers.	Ask Harry to add the prices of actual food items. Intersperse an easy activity with the more difficult math addition so Harry can experience some success.	Teach Harry how to ask for help. Teach Harry how to monitor his rate of problem completion, and provide reinforcement for a certain number of problems.

From "Using Functional Assessment to Develop Effective, Individualized Interventions for Challenging Behaviors," by L. Foster-Johnson and G. Dunlap, 1993, *Teaching Exceptional Children, 25,* p. 49. Used by permission.

drugs); delinquency (vandalism, theft, personal offenses); negative affect (depressed affect, sense of well-being, somatic complaints, interpersonal relationships); and academic orientation (school grades, educational aspirations). Based on this research, it appears reasonable to conclude that these areas represent focal areas of concern both within and outside the school setting. While schools may be able to address some of these variables to a greater extent (i.e., academic orientation), successful programs for adolescents with behavioral and emotional problems often require a wraparound approach to services that reflects general community commitment.

Figure 6.9	Core Elements of Wraparound Approaches

- Community-based care
- Individualized services based on the needs of the client
- Adherence to culturally competent services and supports
- Family involvement in the design and delivery of services
- Team-driven planning process
- Flexible funding
- Balance of formal and informal services to support families
- Collaboration among child-serving systems
- Unconditional care (never giving up on a child)
- Presence of an ongoing evaluation process

From "Wraparound Milwaukee," by B. Kamradt, S. A. Gilbertson, and N. Lynn (p. 307), in *Outcomes for Children and Youth with Emotional and Behavioral Disorders and Their Families,* edited by M. H. Epstein, K. Kurash, and A. Duchnowski, 2005. Austin, TX: Pro-Ed.

School-Based Wraparound: Jake's Story

Jake is a thirteen-year-old student being raised by his maternal grandmother. By the beginning of his fifth-grade year, he had enrolled in five schools across three states. Jake's family changed schools frequently as a result of the inability to address his behavior within the school system.

Jake currently attends a school that is participating in [a special project]. Jake is beginning his second year at the school. Since enrolling there, he has had a total of three office referrals. In the past, he averaged three office referrals a week!

In other schools, Jake worked from the time he got home until bedtime, trying to finish his homework, but he was still failing almost all classes. . . . He now completes his homework quickly in the evening, and he consistently receives A's and B's.

In other programs, professionals encouraged Jake's family to put him on medication, but they did not discuss the importance of other supportive services. His grandmother describes past school and mental health services as disjointed and prescriptive. Due to the coordinated supports provided to Jake and his family by school and mental health personnel . . ., Jake's grandmother receives fewer calls from the school and can focus on supporting her family rather than leaving work to meet with school personnel. She reports feeling that she is now working in partnership with the school rather than fighting against them. . . .

Jake's grandmother has learned about how to survive his disability. She is always getting ideas about new things to try and how to modify them if they don't work. . . . She has called it a "life-changing experience." . . . The improvements in the family's quality of life testify to the importance of providing coordinated services, focusing on strengths rather than deficits, and including the family as an equal partner at all levels of decision making. . . .

In addition to himself and his grandmother, Jake's wraparound team includes a service coordinator, intervention specialist, two teachers, and the school principal. Extended team members include his aunt, a family friend, and his coach. Initial conversations revealed that Jake is bright, is motivated, wants to succeed, and enjoys positive adult attention.

Given Jake's history and identified strengths, the team developed the following mission statement: "Jake will interact successfully with peers and succeed in the classroom." The majority of needs identified by Jake's team fell into the educational/vocational and social/recreational life domains. Due to the severity of school-related problems, the team chose to prioritize needs in the educational/vocational domain. These needs centered on classroom behavior problems and difficulty with completion of schoolwork. All core team members accepted responsibility for ensuring that the plan was implemented as written and modified as needed to meet Jake's behavioral and academic needs.

As Jake met with success at school as evidenced through a reduction in office referrals and improved grades, the team reconvened and determined that the next priority was to improve his peer-interaction skills. To meet this need, Jake began participating in a highly structured after-school program with an emphasis upon prosocial development. Currently, Jake is working with his intervention specialist to appropriately apply the skills he learned in the after-school program to school and classroom settings.

Adapted from "Wraparound Milwaukee," B. Kamradt, S.A. Gilbertson, and N. Lynn (pp. 362–363), in *Outcomes for Children and Youth with Emotional and Behavioral Disorders and Their Families*, edited by M. H. Epstein, K. Kurash, and A. Duchnowski, 2005. Austin, TX: Pro-Ed.

Medication

CONSIDER THIS

What role should mental health professionals play in serving students with E/BD? How can schools involve mental health professionals more?

Many students with emotional and behavioral problems experience difficulties in maintaining attention and controlling behavior. For students experiencing these problems, "medication is the most frequently used (and perhaps overused) intervention" (Ellenwood & Felt, 1989, p. 16). Many different kinds of medication have been found to be effective with students' behavior problems (Forness & Kavale, 1988), including stimulants, tranquilizers, anticonvulsants, antidepressants, and mood-altering drugs. The U.S. Department of Education (2005) cites the following data on the use of medication with students with E/BD (ages six to twelve and thirteen to seventeen respectively): antidepressant/antianxiety (40 percent, 29 percent), antipsychotic (24 percent, 29 percent), and other drugs (16 percent, 34 percent).

The use of medication to help manage students with emotional and behavior problems is controversial but nevertheless can be an important component of comprehensive intervention programs. Some key considerations are as follows:

1. Medication can result in increased attention of students.
2. Medication can result in reduced aggressive behaviors.
3. Various side effects can result from medical interventions.
4. The use of medication for children experiencing emotional and behavioral problems should be carefully monitored. (Smith et al., 1993, p. 214)

Numerous side effects may accompany medications taken by children for emotional and behavioral problems. For example, Ritalin is commonly prescribed to help students with attention and hyperactivity problems. Several potential side effects of Ritalin include nervousness, insomnia, anorexia, dizziness, blood pressure and pulse changes, abdominal pain, and weight loss. Teachers can monitor side effects by keeping a daily log of student behaviors that could be attributed to the medication. Chapter 10 provides a comprehensive analysis of the use of medications for students with ASD that has validity for students with E/BD as well.

Promoting Inclusive Practices

CEC STANDARDS

CEC 5: Learning Environments and Social Interactions

Classroom teachers usually make the initial recommendation for prereferral review for child study or teacher accommodations for students with E/BD. Unless the problem exhibited by the student is severe, it may have gone unrecognized until the school years. In addition to referring students for initial review, classroom teachers must be directly involved in implementing the student's IEP because the majority of students in this category receive a portion of their educational program in general education classrooms. General education classroom teachers must deal with behavior problems much of the time because there are large numbers of students who occasionally display inappropriate behaviors, although they have not been identified as having E/BD.

INTASC

INTASC 5: Create a learning environment

Community and Social Acceptance

Because students with emotional and behavioral disorders are generally placed in general education classrooms rather than in isolated special education settings, teachers must ensure their successful inclusion. Several tactics that teachers can adopt include:

PRAXIS

PRAXIS II: Delivery of Services to Students with Disabilities

- Using programs in which peers act as buddies or tutors.
- Focusing on positive behaviors and providing appropriate reinforcements.
- Using good-behavior games in which all students work together to earn rewards.

Teachers must make a special effort to keep themselves, as well as other students, from developing a negative attitude toward students with E/BD.

CONSIDER THIS

Can general education teachers effectively deal with students with E/BD? What factors will enhance the likelihood of success?

Supports for General Education Teachers

Since students with emotional and behavioral disorders are most frequently educated in general classrooms, classroom teachers are the key to the success of these students. Too often, if these students do not achieve success the entire classroom may be disrupted. Therefore, appropriate supports must be available to teachers. These supports may include special education personnel, psychologists and counselors, and mental health service providers.

INTASC

INTASC 10: Relationships with school colleagues

Special educators should be available to collaborate with teachers regarding the development of behavioral as well as instructional supports. A particularly helpful way to assist classroom teachers involves modeling methods of dealing with behavior problems. At times, it is best for students with emotional and behavioral problems to leave the general education setting and receive instruction from special educators.

School psychologists and counselors are other critical team members in providing a comprehensive program for students with E/BD. They can provide intensive counseling to students with E/BD; they may also consult with teachers on how to implement

What Kinds of Assistive Technology Are Available?

Writing difficulties: word processors, spell-checkers/talking spell-checkers, proofreading programs (grammar-checkers), speech synthesizers/screen readers (convert electronic text to synthetic speech), outlining programs, graphic organizers (create diagrams of ideas before writing), word prediction programs (predict and offer suggestions), alternative keyboards (customize key appearance and placement), and speech recognition systems (convert the spoken word to electronic text).

Reading difficulties: tape recorders (e.g., books on tape), speech synthesis/screen reading systems, and optical character recognition/speech synthesis systems (scan hard copy text, convert to electronic text and synthetic speech).

Math difficulties: talking calculators (use speech synthesis to speak numbers) and electronic computer-based worksheets (provide automatic alignment of numbers).

Listening difficulties: personal FM listening devices (small transmitter and receiver that "brings" speaker's voice directly to the listener's ear) and variable speech-control tape recorders (slow down or speed up the recording).

Organization and memory difficulties: personal data managers (store and retrieve phone numbers, addresses, notes, etc.), free-form databases (note storage and retrieval software), and tape recorders.

Selecting the appropriate device . . . requires careful analysis of the interplay among (a) the individual's specific strengths, limitations, special abilities, prior experience/knowledge, and interests; (b) the specific tasks/functions to be performed (e.g., compensating for a reading, writing, or memory problem); (c) the specific contexts of interaction (across settings—school, home, work, and over time—over a semester or a lifetime); and (d) the specific device (e.g., reliability, operational ease, technical support, cost).

From *Assistive technology,* by M. Raskind. Information sheet, Council for Learning Disabilities, September 2002.

---

specific programs, such as a student's individual behavior management plan. Finally, mental health personnel can provide helpful support for teachers. Too often, mental health services are not available in schools; however, some schools are beginning to develop school-based mental health programs that are jointly staffed by school personnel and mental health staff and provide support for teachers as well as direct interventions for students. If mental health services are not available, teachers should work with school administrators to involve mental health specialists with students who display emotional and behavioral problems.

Technology

INTASC

INTASC 6: Communication Technologies

Assistive technology offers a number of ways for teachers to promote successful learning in inclusive settings by responding to the needs of students with E/BD. According to IDEA 1997, an assistive technology (AT) device refers to "any item, piece of equipment, or product system . . . that is used to increase, maintain or improve the functional capabilities of a child with a disability." This definition is "broad and encompasses devices that are electronic (e.g., computer, scanner, tape recorder) and nonelectronic (e.g., pencil grip, manual typewriter). . . . In addition, the federal definition includes items such as computer-aided instructional software programs for reading and mathematics that can be used to remediate skill deficits" (Raskind, 2002, p. 1). Technology Today above provides information on assistive technology products.

Summary

Basic Concepts
- Most children and youth are disruptive from time to time, but most do not require interventions. Some students' emotional or behavioral problems are severe enough to warrant interventions.

- Many problems complicate serving students with E/BD, including inconsistent definitions of the disorder, the large number of agencies involved in defining and treating it, and limited ways to measure objectively the extent and precise parameters of the problem.

- Determining the eligibility of students with E/BD is difficult because of problems with identification and assessment.
- The estimated prevalence of students with emotional and behavioral problems ranges from a low of less than 1 percent (actually served in special education nationwide) to a high of 30 percent.
- Students with emotional and behavioral problems are significantly underserved in schools.

Strategies for Curriculum and Instruction

- Students with E/BD are commonly included in general education classes. General education teachers and special education teachers must collaborate so that there is consistency in the development and implementation of intervention methods.

- A variety of curricular, classroom, and management strategies is available to enhance the educational programs for students with E/BD.
- Social skills development is important for students with E/BD.
- Interventions based on FBA and PBS are important methods for reducing the impact of problems or for keeping problems from occurring.

Promoting Inclusive Practices

- The skills, attitudes, and beliefs needed to work effectively with students with E/BD may vary from those that are effective for students who are nondisabled.
- Special education teachers and mental health personnel need to be available to provide guidance for general education teachers who are implementing a student's behavior management plan.

Questions to Reconsider

Think back to the scenario you read about Travis at the beginning of this chapter. Would you answer the questions raised there any differently now that you have read the chapter itself?

1. Why did the behavior management system used by Ms. Holke not work with Travis?

2. What positive behavior support strategies can Ms. Holke use that might result in an improvement in Travis's behavior?
3. What other preventative strategies should be considered?
4. How would it potentially help or hurt Travis if he were labeled as E/BD?

Further Readings

Algozzine, R., Serna, L., & Patton, J. R. (2001). *Childhood behavior disorders: Applied research and educational practices* (2nd ed.). Austin, TX: Pro-Ed.

American Psychiatric Association. (2000). *Diagnostic and statistical manual of mental disorders* (DSM-IV-TR). Washington, DC: American Psychiatric Publishing.

Epstein, M. H., Kutash, K., & Duchnowski, A. J. (2005). *Outcomes for children and youth with emotional and behavioral disorders* (2nd ed.). Austin, TX: Pro-Ed.

Katsiyannas, A., & Maag, J. W. (2001). Manifestation determination as a golden fleece. *Exceptional Children, 68,* 85–96.

Kauffman, J. M. (2005). *Characteristics of emotional and behavioral disorders of children and youth* (9th ed.). Columbus, OH: Merrill.

Kauffman, J. M., & Landrum, T. J. (2006). *Children and youth with emotional and behavioral disorders: A history of their education.* Austin, TX: Pro-Ed.

McConnell, K., Patton, J. R., & Polloway, E. A. (2006). *Behavioral intervention planning (BIP-III)* (3rd ed.). Austin, TX: Pro-Ed.

⟨mylabschool™
Where the classroom comes to life

Go to Allyn & Bacon's MyLabSchool (www.mylabschool.com) and enter Assignment ID SPV10 into the Assignment Finder. View the video clip called *Behavior Disorder.* Then consider what you have seen along with what you've read in Chapter 6 to answer the following questions.

1. What kinds of inappropriate behavior does Nick demonstrate? How have the special educators at Nick's school addressed these behaviors?
2. Nick's teacher notes that he has academic strengths and, while he has behavior problems, he is manageable and responds to feedback and redirection. How might these

management strategies be used to reintegrate Nick into a general education classroom? Use specific information from this chapter to support your answer.
3. Nick has experienced success in controlling his behavior in self-contained programs for several years. His academic achievement indicates an ability to learn in a general education setting. What *social skills* strategies would you use to help Nick reintegrate into the general education classroom? Use specific information from this chapter to support your choices.

You may also answer the questions at the end of the clip and e-mail your responses to your instructor.

Teaching Students with Intellectual Disabilities/Mental Retardation

After reading this chapter, you should be able to:

1. Discuss the concepts of intellectual disabilities and mental retardation.
2. Summarize key definitions and classifications.
3. Identify the instructional implications of common characteristics of students with intellectual disabilities.
4. Describe the transitional needs of students with mild disabilities.
5. Apply considerations of the needs of students to curriculum design.
6. Identify strategies to enhance successful inclusion.

Questions to Consider

1. How can Jason's curriculum include peers who are not disabled and use the functional curriculum designed by special educators?

2. How can the curriculum balance short-term objectives and preparation for competitive employment and independent living?

3. What strategies can enhance a positive influence from peers?

4. What available community resources will aid his transition to independent living?

Jason is currently a junior at Afton High School. He has been receiving special education supports throughout his school career. Prior to kindergarten, he had been identified as "at-risk" because of language delays and also in part because of the difficult home situation in which he was raised (his grandmother has been his guardian since his mother was incarcerated when Jason was four; his father has not been part of his life since he was an infant).

When Jason began elementary school, he was identified as developmentally delayed, a term that allows the school division to provide special education services in primary school without a formal categorical label. However, when assessments were completed at age eight, his language, academic, and social skills were deemed consistent with the label of mild retardation.

Jason has progressed well in part because of his continued involvement in general education classrooms through both middle and high school. With in-class support and periodic remedial instruction, he has developed his reading skills to the fourth-grade level with comparable achievement in mathematics and other academic areas. Currently, the focus of his program is on building his academic skills in the inclusive classroom and complementing these with a functional curriculum to prepare him for success in the community.

Jason has become an active participant in the development of his IEP and his individual transition plan. A key current objective is to obtain his driver's license. He is currently enrolled in both an instructional program to complete the written portion of the test and the behind-the-wheel component. A longer-term focus is to prepare him for competitive employment in the community.

Through a series of community-based instructional programs, he has become aware of the options available to him; and an apprenticeship program in maintenance at the local IGA grocery store will be available next year. Jason's success is a combination of his motivation to succeed, detailed planning by key individuals in his life, and ongoing support provided by teachers, his grandmother, and several significant peers who are more academically able.

Basic Concepts about Mental Retardation

CEC STANDARDS

CEC 2: Development and Characteristics of Learners

Mental retardation (MR) is a powerful term used to describe a level of functioning significantly below what is considered to be "average." It may conjure up a variety of images, including a stereotypical photo of an adolescent with Down syndrome, a young child living in poverty and provided with limited experience and stimulation, and an adult striving to adjust to the demands of a complex society. Since it is a generic term representing a very diverse group of individuals, ironically all the images of MR and, at the same time, none of these images may be accurate ones. Smith (in press) aptly notes this point:

> The term mental retardation has been used to describe people who are more different than they are alike. . . . It has been used as an amalgam for very diverse human conditions. The core of mental retardation as a field is the assumption that somehow there is an "essence" that eclipses all of the differences that characterize people described by the term. It is truly a box of chocolates, however. "You don't know what you're gonna get" when you reach into the category. Maybe it will be someone who needs constant care, or maybe it will be someone much like yourself but who needs help with academic skills. Maybe it will be someone with severe physical disabilities, or maybe it will be someone who you would pass on the street without notice. What is certain about the category is that it is a stigmatizing label with universally negative connotations. That may be the only "glue" that holds it together.

PRAXIS

PRAXIS II: Understanding Exceptionalities

CONSIDER THIS

Why do you think the prevalence of mental retardation varies so much from state to state?

The U.S. Department of Education (2006) reported that the percentage of children between the ages of six and seventeen served under the category of MR was 1.04 percent. Across individual states, the range was substantial, from 3.1 percent (West Virginia) to 0.37 percent (New Jersey). Because of the common use of the term developmental delay (DD) (see p. 213) for children under the age of nine, it is illustrative to note that an additional 0.12 percent of six–seventeen-year-olds were so identified; given that these children were all ages six–eight, we can extrapolate that approximately 0.44 percent of children in that age range are likely to be identified as developmentally delayed; many, though not all, of these students may later receive the label of mental retardation.

Even a naive observer would at once conclude that the concept is not defined, or the condition is not conceptualized, in the same way across the states. Further, the prevalence of MR in individuals of school age tends to be higher than in adults because of the challenges of formal education for school-age individuals as well as the relative lack of identification in adulthood; thus, Larson et al. (2001) estimated prevalence to be 0.78 percent for the general population.

Terminology

Adding complexity to the discussion of concepts, the term "mental retardation" is so powerful that it is increasingly avoided. The common, negative response to the term by professionals, parents, as well as the people so labeled, has given rise to alternative terminology, just as retardation was an option to earlier terms such as feebleminded and moron. Receiving the greatest contemporary attention is the term **intellectual disabilities (ID)**. This term endeavors to convey a broad-based concept that places under it deficits in varied cognitive and adaptive ability areas. The term has received broad acceptance internationally, though less so in the United States (Greenspan, in press). The American Association on Mental Retardation has changed its name to reflect this new term. The organization's emerging focus in its definitional work will emphasize ID.

A broader term is **developmental disabilities**. Defined by federal guidelines, the term has become popular particularly for reference to programs for adults and professional organizations (Stodden, 2002), although it is used far less frequently in the schools. One difficulty with the term is that a precise rendering of the definition would suggest that developmental disabilities would exclude perhaps 40 percent of those people who might otherwise have been identified as mildly mentally retarded (AAMR, 2002).

For a number of years, professionals have been reluctant to use the term "mental retardation" to refer to young children, and certainly this reluctance has been championed by parents as well. As a consequence, the term is rarely used for children during the preschool years and, in many states, is deferred until children reach approximately the age of nine. The preferred term for younger children is "developmental delay," a term recognized by the federal government that brings with it an assumption that it is most appropriately used for children through age eight. It is likely that many young children who previously might have been identified as mentally retarded are now instead identified as developmentally delayed. This decision is a positive one in that it may delay the use of a stigmatizing term such as retardation, although for some children, and their families, the label of retardation nevertheless may be applied once the child reaches the age of nine or so.

Finally, the term "mild retardation" requires some careful consideration, even if the term retardation is accepted, such as by a given state department of education. Mild retardation presents as an oxymoron and may convey the fact that mild is relatively insignificant (e.g., a mild cold). For this reason, many people advocate an avoidance of the term because it serves as a judgment and thus they rather encourage a term such as "high-incidence disability," which is more of a fact in terms of the numbers of children who are identified in the schools (Polloway, 2005). However, no term is without criticism and, certainly, the term "high incidence disabilities" creates confusion because it also embraces learning disabilities and E/BD.

It is noteworthy that although the term "mental retardation" has been widely criticized and proposals for alternative terms have been made periodically (e.g., Terrill, 2001; Schalock, 2001; Smith, in press), a survey still found that educational departments in twenty-six states (51 percent) continued to use the term, while an additional fourteen states (27.4 percent) used similar terms (e.g., mental disability, mental impairment) (Denning, Chamberlain, & Polloway, 2000).

Thus, while we continue to use the term "mental retardation" in this text, we caution the reader that it is value-laden. Indeed, the underlying message is clear: without question, being labeled mentally retarded can be stigmatizing and the label is often seen as offensive by people to whom it refers. Avoiding labels or using more positive labels, such as "intellectually disabled," as well as providing opportunities to be with peers who are not disabled, must be pursued to ensure the prospect of a positive quality of life for those people who traditionally have been identified as mentally retarded. Smith (in press) provides an important perspective on the term: "Yes, the term is dead and deserves a decent burial. But no, we cannot allow a recognition of the needs of numbers of children and adults to 'pass away.' It is incumbent upon the many of us who began our careers in the field of mild retardation that we strive to rekindle interest in and commitment to the students who have escaped a negative identity, but who are now adrift with little help for their significant learning needs" (p. 23). Further, as Polloway (2004) noted:

> In our appropriate efforts to downplay the deficits associated with mental retardation and emphasize the importance of a supports-based model, we may lose sight of the educational and life needs of persons traditionally identified as having mild retardation. The movement to inclusion is admirable, but a parallel commitment to ensuring the success of these individuals is also essential . . . the question is unanswered as to whether the passing of this category is best classified as lack of interest, lack of awareness, or deliberate attempts to bring about its demise. Regardless of cause, it is important that we continue to focus on making sure that these students will not be disadvantaged by our ignorance of their educational needs. (p. 8)

In this field, the late twentieth century witnessed momentous changes that have washed away the realities of restricted, and often abusive, settings that characterized many of the so-called services through the 1970s. Shifts in public attitudes and the resulting development and provision of services and supports have been truly phenomenal. Consequently, this is an exciting time to be participating in the changing perspectives on intellectual disabilities. Thus, while the discussion of definitional aspects unfortunately creates a focus on deficits, the more powerful and relevant message of the twenty-first century is that people with MR or intellectual disabilities are capable of substantial achievements as we develop their strengths and assets.

Within this chapter, we rely primarily on the term "mental retardation," even though "intellectual disabilities" is used as appropriate to reflect contemporary perspectives on this impairment. Both are broad concepts that have been used to refer to a wide range of functioning levels, from mild disabilities to more severe limitations. The primary focus of this chapter is on the former. While the overall discussion focuses on MR in general, the analysis of characteristics and the discussion of educational implications has its emphasis on this high incidence disability. Nevertheless, much of the discussion herein has broader applicability and is complemented by the subsequent attention to more significant disabilities in Chapter 10.

Definitions

While it is challenging to formulate a definition of mental retardation that can be used to govern practices such as assessment and placement, nevertheless a number of definitional concepts have been consistently followed during the years. Mental retardation has been most often characterized by two dimensions or prongs: limited intellectual ability and difficulty in coping with the social demands of the environment. In an illustrative way, Greenspan (1996) described mental retardation primarily as a problem in "everyday intelligence"; thus, people with retardation can be viewed as those who are challenged by adapting to the demands of daily life in the community. It is noteworthy that the less pejorative term of "intellectual disabilities" has as yet not been formally identified in a universally acceptable way; therefore, the focus here is on MR.

All individuals with MR must, by most definitions, demonstrate some degree of impaired mental abilities, traditionally said to be reflected in an IQ significantly below average. In addition, these individuals would necessarily demonstrate less mature adaptive skills, such as social behavior or functional academic skills, when compared to their same-age peers. For some individuals, this discrepancy can be somewhat subtle and not be readily apparent in a casual interaction in a non-school setting. These individuals may be challenged most dramatically by the school setting, and thus between the ages of six and twenty-one their inability to cope may be most evident, for example, in problems with peer relationships, with difficulty in compliance with adult-initiated directions, or in meeting academic challenges.

The American Association on Mental Retardation (AAMR), which became The American Association on Intellectual and Developmental Disabilities (AAIDD) in January 2001, has concerned itself for decades with developing and revising the definition of mental retardation. This organization's efforts are broadly recognized, and its definitions have often been incorporated, with modifications, into state and federal statutes. Although use of the definition in the states in terms of educational regulations and practice has been uneven (Denning et al., 2000; Frankenberger & Harper, 1988), the AAIDD's definitions are generally considered as the basis for diagnosis in the field and have been the most common basis for federal and state definitions.

Three concepts are central to the AAIDD's recent definitions: intellectual functioning, adaptive behavior or skills, and the developmental period (Grossman, 1983; Luckasson et al., 1992; Luckasson et al., 2002).

Intellectual Functioning   The concept of intellectual functioning was intended as a broad summation of cognitive abilities, such as the capacity to learn, solve problems, accumulate knowledge, adapt to new situations, and think abstractly. Operationally, however, it has often been reduced to performance on a test of intelligence, typically with a flexible upper IQ range of 70 to 75. This approximate IQ range is a relatively common component of state identification practices if an IQ cut-off score is required at all (Denning et al., 2000).

It is worth considering how an IQ score relates to this first criterion for diagnosis. Since an IQ of 100 is the mean score on such tests, a person receiving a score of 100 is considered to have an average level of cognitive functioning. Based on statistical analysis, approximately 2.3 percent of IQs would be expected to lie below 70 and a like percentage above 130. Thus, to limit the diagnosis of mental retardation to people with IQs of approximately 70 or below is to suggest that, hypothetically, about 2–3 percent of the tested population may have significantly subaverage general intellectual functioning. However, low IQ scores alone are not sufficient for diagnosis. Hence, we must next consider the adaptive dimension.

Adaptive Behavior An individual's **adaptive behavior** represents the degree to which the individual meets "the standards of maturation, learning, personal independence, and/or social responsibility that are expected for his or her age level and cultural group" (Grossman, 1983, p. 11). Particularly important to the concept of adaptive behavior are the skills necessary to function independently in a range of situations and to maintain responsible social relationships. The importance of adaptive behavior is reflected in the fact that 98 percent of all states required consideration of this dimension for eligibility (Denning et al., 2000). Table 7.1 lists key adaptive skill areas. These skills are each age-relevant and represent core areas of concern for both elementary and secondary educators.

Developmental Period The third definitional component is the **developmental period**. It has most often been defined as the period of time between conception and eighteen years of age. Below-average intellectual functioning and disabilities in adaptive behavior must appear during this period for an individual to be considered to have MR.

Based on the three dimensions noted in the table below, the contemporary MR definition is as follows (Luckasson et al., 2002):

> Mental retardation is a disability characterized by significant limitations both in intellectual functioning and in adaptive behavior as expressed in conceptual, social, and practical adaptive skills. This disability originates before age 18. The following

Table 7.1   Conceptual, Social, and Practical Adaptive Skills

Conceptual	Social	Practical

• Language (receptive and expressive)
• Reading and writing
• Money concepts
• Self-direction
	• Interpersonal
	• Responsibility
	• Self-esteem
	• Gullibility (likelihood of being tricked or manipulated)
	• Naïveté
	• Follows rules
	• Obeys laws
	• Avoids victimization
		• Activities of daily living
		  • Eating
		  • Transfer/mobility
		  • Toileting
		  • Dressing
		• Instrumental activities of daily living
		  • Meal preparation
		  • Housekeeping
		  • Transportation
		  • Taking medication
		  • Money management
		  • Telephone use
		• Occupational skills
		• Maintains safe environments

From *Mental retardation: Definition, classification, and systems of supports* (p. 42), by R. Luckasson et al., 2002. Washington, DC: American Association on Mental Retardation.

five assumptions are essential to the application of the stated definition of mental retardation.

1. Limitations in present functioning must be considered within the context of community environments typical of the individual's age peers and culture.
2. Valid assessment considers cultural and linguistic diversity as well as differences in communication, sensory, motor, and behavioral factors.
3. Within an individual, limitations often coexist with strengths.
4. An important purpose of describing limitations is to develop a profile of needed supports.
5. With appropriate personalized supports over a sustained period, the life functioning of the person with mental retardation generally will improve. (p. 1)

The foremost critic of definitional efforts in the field has been Greenspan (1979, 1997, in press). Greenspan's model of personal competence, inclusive of his focus on a design for considering adaptive functioning, was the basis for the AAMR (2002) definition and its identification of conceptual, practical, and social adaptive skills. In fact, Greenspan's model actually called these three, respectively, conceptual intelligence, practical intelligence, and social intelligence.

Although the focus here is on educational programming, it is important to note that a significant area of interest in recent years related to mild retardation has come ironically in the criminal justice system. For example, for many years the courts, both state and federal, have debated the wisdom of applying the death penalty to individuals with retardation. While many states historically have excluded people with retardation from this penalty (if they had the death penalty at all), nevertheless nationally the U.S. Supreme Court had simply required that MR be considered as a mitigating circumstance when sentencing occurred (*Penry v. Lynaugh* [1989, 1991]). This changed with the *Atkins v. Virginia* (2002) decision in which the U.S. Supreme Court declared that no individual identified as mentally retarded could be executed.

As a result of this case, renewed attention has now been given to the definition of mental retardation and the diagnostic process for making a determination of whether an individual is retarded. These issues now have become major legal concerns and people whose functioning level puts them on the borderline have now received increased scrutiny from attorneys, judges, and juries as our society seeks to determine how to implement the Atkins decision. Patton and Keyes (in press) provide a full discussion of the implications of this case for professionals in the field (see Rights and Responsibilities).

Classification

The classification system cited most often in the professional literature continues to be the deficit system recommended by Grossman (1983). This system uses the terms mild, moderate, severe, and profound retardation, which are summative judgments reflecting more significant degrees of disability as based on both intelligence and adaptive behavior assessment. Among the problems with this system was that the emphasis has primarily been on the former only, so IQ scores have frequently and unfortunately been equated with level of functioning.

Terms such as "educable" and "trainable" reflect an alternative system that has been used in school environments. These archaic terms remain in use today in many places; it is not uncommon to hear students referred to as **EMR (educable mentally retarded)** and **TMR (trainable mentally retarded)**. The terms roughly correspond to **mild** and **moderate/severe retardation**, respectively. However, by nature, these terms are inherently stereotypical and prejudicial, and consequently (and appropriately) have been criticized, thus leading to decreased use.

One alternative is to classify MR according to only two more general levels of functioning (i.e., mild and severe) and to avoid reliance on IQ scores in considerations of

Rights & Responsibilities

Mental Retardation and the Criminal Justice System: *Atkins v. Virginia* (2002)

Those of us who work in special education maintain an orientation and mindset of empowerment, capacity-building, and self-determination. The reality of the legal world, especially when it is about capital cases, is that the total focus is on deficits. . . . The special education community attempts to downplay labels and their pejorative connotations. The legal world, however, is all about labels and their less-than-positive implications. Those of us with special education/human service backgrounds must recognize and become comfortable in this legal venue if we are going to be effective in writing reports, declarations, and affidavits, participating in depositions, or offering expert testimony in open court.

The Court's majority opinion, delivered by Justice Stevens, cited the Eighth Amendment to the Constitution, which prohibits "cruel and unusual punishment," and that there was serious concern whether either justification underpinning capital punishment, retribution and deterrence, applies to such offenders because of their perceived reduced level of culpability. "Construing and applying the Eighth Amendment in the light of our 'evolving standards of decency,' we therefore conclude that such punishment is excessive and that the Constitution places a substantive restriction on the State's power to take the life of a mentally retarded offender," wrote Justice Stevens . . . (cited in Patton & Keyes, in press).

What is interesting is that the concept of mild mental retardation . . . has resurfaced as a primary area of professional focus. The salient issues and controversies associated with eligibility are now being raised on a level that has far more serious consequences than whether someone gets services or not. The issue is now about life or death. For those who have gotten involved in death penalty cases, the seriousness of these issues is professionally and personally challenging. . . .

We must find better ways to convey to judges, juries, and attorneys on *both sides* of the bar, just what mild retardation is and how it looks to the nonprofessional. As a result, experts in mental retardation are going to be badly needed in professional areas that they never could have even imagined. People whose backgrounds include extensive experience working with individuals who have mental retardation can play a variety of critical roles in this most important work. Not everyone needs to become a mental retardation expert in these cases; however, a great need exists to educate the key professionals who are more and more a vital part of the criminal justice system and the public in general about mental retardation. As long as the United States continues to impose a death penalty for capital offenses, a need will remain for determining whether certain individuals meet the criteria of mental retardation in judicial proceedings.

From "Death penalty issues following *Atkins*," by J. R. Patton and D. W. Keys (in press). *Exceptionality.*

---

level of severity. With such a less-formal approach, the consideration of levels of adaptive skills serves as the yardstick for determining level of retardation, resulting in a more meaningful and broad-based, though less precise, system of classification. This approach is commonly used in the field and is consistent in the distinctions made between mild and severe retardation in this text.

An alternative to this deficit approach is the revised AAIDD classification system of Luckasson and colleagues (1992, 2002). According to this system, classification is not derived from levels of deficit, but rather from needed **levels of support**. As defined by Luckasson and colleagues (2002), "supports are resources and strategies that aim to promote the development, education, interests, and personal well-being of a person and that enhance individual functioning" (p. 151). Thus, this system (Luckasson et al., 1992) classifies the needs rather than the deficits of the individual. The four general levels of support are intermittent, limited, extensive, and pervasive, and these are related to specific adaptive skill areas. Of course, in a given area, an individual may also not need any support to function successfully. These levels of support are defined as follows (see also Table 7.2):

> **Intermittent:** Support on an "as-needed basis," characterized by their episodic (person not always needing the support) or short-term nature (support needed during life-span transitions, e.g., job loss or acute medical crisis). Intermittent support may be high- or low intensity when provided.

CONSIDER THIS

What are some advantages to focusing classification on supports rather than on levels of deficit?

DIVERSITY FORUM

Cultural Contexts of Developmentally Appropriate Curriculum

Susan, a 13-year old Navajo student, is receiving services under the category of mild mental retardation. Her teacher, Mr. Villarreal, has developed a buddy system to help Susan learn new material and practice new skills. He is concerned that Susan prefers to work on her own instead of collaborating with her buddies. During a conference with Susan's family to discuss his goals, Mr. Villarreal is surprised to learn that the family wants Susan to be more independent. Her grandmother is reluctant to pressure Susan to work with a buddy because in their Navajo community, pre-adolescent children are expected to become more self-reliant and to make their own decisions.

When working with exceptional learners from diverse cultural backgrounds, teachers should keep in mind that the primary caregiver's goals for a student may reflect very different cultural values than those held by educators; i.e., the age at which children are expected to master self-help and academic skills can vary widely, depending on the family's cultural background and level of accul-

turation (Roe & Malach, 2004). For example, youth in traditional Navajo families may be expected to master the skills necessary to travel about town independently two to three years earlier than peers from the mainstream. Further, children as young as nine years of age are encouraged to make their own decisions and accept the consequences of those choices. This could include attending school, as traditional families believe that children should not be forced to do something against their will (Dehyle & LeCompte, 1999).

Culturally responsive special education services begin by integrating the student's and family's cultural values and beliefs with goals and objectives in the IEP. Factors to be considered may include:

- Parameters of acceptable behavior
- The view of child independence in the student's community
- The amount and extent of interaction desired with the community
- Gender-specific roles
- Expectations for economic self-sufficiency, and

- Independent living for people with disabilities.

Questions

1. What sources could provide you with reliable information about a family's cultural beliefs regarding child development in light of disability?
2. Who could help you develop the skills necessary to integrate home and school expectations into a coherent set of goals?

REFERENCES

Roe, J. R., & Malach, R. S. (2004). Families with American Indian roots. In, E. W. Lynch, & M. J. Hanson, (Eds.), *Developing cross-cultural competence: A guide for working with children and their families* (3rd ed.) (pp. 109-134). Baltimore, MD: Brookes.

Deyhle, D. & LeCompte, M. (1999). Cultural differences in child development: Navajo adolescents in middle schools. In R. H. Sheets & E. R. Hollins (Eds.), *Racial and ethnic identity in school practices: Aspects of human development* (pp. 123-139). Mahwah, NJ: Erlbaum.

Limited: An intensity of support characterized by consistency over time, time-limited but not of an intermittent nature, may require fewer staff members and less cost than more intense levels of support (e.g., time-limited employment training or transitional support during the school-to-adult period).

Extensive: Support characterized by regular involvement (e.g., daily) in at least some environments (e.g., school, work, or home) and not time-limited nature (e.g., long-term support and long-term home living support).

Pervasive: Support characterized by constancy, high intensity, provision across environments, potentially life-sustaining nature. Pervasive support typically involves more staff members and intrusiveness than does extensive or time-limited support (adapted from Luckasson et al., 2002, p. 152).

The support classification system received general endorsement in the field, particularly in the area of programs for adults with MR, although it did not have a significant impact on research and school practices after its initial development (Conyers, Martin, Martin, & Yu, 2002; Denning et al., 2000; Polloway, Smith, Chamberlain, Denning, & Smith, 1999). In Table 7.3, a portrait of the concept of support is provided by describing support functions and selected representative activities.

Table 7.2   **Levels of Supports X Intensity Grid**

	Intermittent	Limited	Extensive	Pervasive
Time Duration	As needed	Time limited, occasionally ongoing	Usually ongoing	Possibly lifelong
Time Frequency	Infrequent, low occurrence	Regular, anticipated, could be high frequency		High rate, continuous, constant
Settings Living, Work, Recreation, Leisure, Health, Community, etc.	Few settings, typically one or two settings	Across several settings, typically not all settings		All or nearly all settings
Resources Professional/ Technological Assistance	Occasional consultation or discussion, ordinary appointment schedule, occasional monitoring	Occasional contact or time limited but frequent regular contact	Regular, ongoing contact or monitoring by professionals typically at least weekly	Constant contact and monitoring by professionals
Intrusiveness	Predominantly all natural supports, high degree of choice and autonomy	Mixture of natural and service-based supports, lesser degree of choice and autonomy		Predominantly service-based supports, controlled by others

From "The 1992 AAMR Definition and Preschool Children: Response from the Committee on Terminology and Classification," by R. Luckasson, R. Schalock, M. Snell, and D. Spitalnik, 1996, *Mental Retardation, 34,* p. 250.

Prevalence

As discussed previously, prevalence data based on the twenty-sixth annual report from the U.S. Department of Education for IDEA indicated that 1.04 percent of the estimated enrollment (ages six to seventeen) was identified as having MR (U.S. Department of Education, 2006). This statistic represents a significant change from the time when the national school prevalence for MR was approximately 3 percent; MR was one of the two largest categories of disabilities, and mild retardation was the most significant high-incidence disability related to learning problems in the schools. Currently, it is likely that, of the approximately 1 percent of the school population that is identified with MR, approximately 50 percent might be viewed as mildly retarded, with the remainder having more severe disabilities.

A key reason for the decrease in the reported incidence of mild retardation relates to the concern about the overrepresentation of minority children under this label. However, while efforts have been made to prevent potential bias in the system (see MacMillan & Forness, 1998), African American students have been estimated to be 2.4 times more likely to be identified as having mild retardation than their non–African American peers (Oswald, Coutinho, Best, & Singh, 1999).

The data on racial and ethnic composition reported by the U.S. Department of Education (2006) indicates the following percentage breakdown within the category of mental retardation (the comparative data for all students with disabilities across all categories are provided in parentheses): 1.1 percent for Native Americans/Alaskans (1.5 percent), 1.8 percent for Asian/Pacific Islanders (2.0 percent), 34.5 percent for African Americans (20.4 percent), 12.5 percent for Hispanic (16.0 percent), and 50.6 percent for European Americans (60.2 percent).

According to the U.S. Department of Education (2005), 56 percent of all children identified were male. The gender odds ratio for males over females for the United States was reported at 1.33/1 by Coutinho and Oswald (2005).

CEC STANDARDS

CEC 3: Individual Learning Differences

CONSIDER THIS

Why do you think the prevalence of students has declined during the past thirty years?

Table 7.3	Support Functions and Representative Activities		
Support Function*	**Representative Activities**		
Teaching	Supervising Giving feedback Organizing the learning environment	Training Evaluating Supporting inclusive classrooms	Instructing Collecting data Individualizing instruction
Befriending	Advocating Car pooling Supervising Instructing	Evaluating Communicating Training Giving feedback	Reciprocating Associating and disassociating Socializing
Financial Planning	Working with SSI–Medicaid Advocating for benefits	Assisting with money management Protection and legal assistance	Budgeting Income assistance and planning/considerations
Employee Assistance	Counseling Procuring/using assistive technology devices	Supervisory training Job performance enhancement	Crisis intervention/assistance Job/task accommodation and redesigning job/work duties
Behavioral Support	Functional analysis Multicomponent instruction Emphasis on antecedent manipulation	Manipulation of ecological and setting events Teaching adaptive behavior	Building environment with effective consequences
In-home Living Assistance	Personal maintenance/care Transfer and mobility Dressing and clothing care Architectural modifications	Communication devices Behavioral support Eating and food management Housekeeping	Respite care Attendant care Home-health aides Homemaker services
Community Access and Use	Carpooling/rides program Transportation training Personal protection skills	Recreation/leisure involvement Community awareness opportunities Vehicle modification	Community use opportunities and interacting with generic agencies Personal protection skills
Health Assistance	Medical appointments Medical interventions Supervision Med Alert devices	Emergency procedures Mobility (assistive devices) Counseling appointments Medication taking	Hazard awareness Safety training Physical therapy and related activities Counseling interventions

*The support functions and activities may need to be modified slightly to accommodate individuals of different ages.

Adapted from *Mental Retardation: Definition, Classification, and Systems of Supports* (pp. 153–154), by R. Luckasson et al., 2002. Washington, DC: American Association on Mental Retardation.

Causes

There are hundreds of known causes of retardation, and at the same time, numerous cases for which the cause is unknown. Table 7.4 outlines some representative causes to show the complexity of this area of concern. This information is limited to selected causes and brief, related information; see Polloway and Smith (2006) for a fuller discussion of biological causes and prevention and Beirne-Smith, Patton, and Kim (2006) for an analysis of psychosocial aspects.

Characteristics

Given the diversity of people who may be identified as intellectually disabled, the drawing of a portrait of characteristics must be done with caution. Nevertheless, some generalizations related to mild retardation are reasonable.

Table 7.4	Selected Causes of Mental Retardation	
Cause	**Nature of Problem**	**Considerations**
Down syndrome	Trisomy 21 (3 chromosomes on this pair) IQ range from severe retardation to nonretarded	Wide variance in learning characteristics Classic physical signs Most common chromosomal anomaly
Environmental or Psychosocial Disadvantage	Elements of poverty environment (e.g., family constellation, resources, educational role models)	Can be related to mild disabilities Commonly associated with school failure
Fetal alcohol syndrome (FAS)	Caused by drinking during pregnancy Related to toxic effects of alcohol Fetal alcohol effects: less significant disorder	Associated with varying degrees of disability May be accompanied by facial and other malformations and behavioral disturbances Among the three most common biologically based causes of retardation
Fragile X syndrome	Genetic disorder related to gene or X chromosome	Most often transmitted from mother to son Frequently associated with retardation in males and learning disabilities in females (in some instances) May be accompanied by variant patterns of behavior (e.g., self-stimulation), social skills difficulties, language impairment
Hydrocephalus	Multiple causes (e.g., genetic, environmental) Disruption in appropriate flow of cerebrospinal fluid on the brain	Previously associated with enlarged head and brain damage Controlled by the implantation of a shunt
Phenylketonuria	Autosomal recessive genetic disorder	Associated with metabolic problems in processing high-protein foods Can be controlled via restrictive diets implemented at birth
Prader-Willi syndrome	Chromosomal error of the autosomal type	Associated with biological compulsion to excessive eating Obesity as a common secondary trait to retardation
Tay-Sachs	Autosomal recessive genetic disorder	Highest risk for Ashkenazic Jewish people Associated with severe disabilities and early mortality No known cure Prevention through genetic screening

CEC STANDARDS

CEC 2: Development and Characteristics of Learners

INTASC

INTASC 2: How children learn and develop

PRAXIS

PRAXIS II: Understanding Exceptionalities

Mental retardation, or ID, is associated with a number of characteristics that are in turn related to specific challenges to learning. For example, problems in attention are common; it is noteworthy, for instance, that federal data underscore that 10 percent of all students with ADHD have a primary diagnosis of MR. Table 7.5 identifies the most significant learning domains, lists representative problem areas, and notes certain instructional implications. In addition, the table summarizes information on motivation as well as cognitive, language, academic, and sociobehavioral development.

The U.S. Department of Education (2006) provides summative academic data on a variety of academic tasks. Within these data sets, the report notes the following: "For the standardized assessments, each student's performance is associated with a percentile score which reflects the proportion of the individuals of that student's age in the general population who received a lower score on that assessment. The [data] indicate the proportion of students whose percentile rank on the assessment fell within a given

Table 7.5   **Learning Characteristics and Educational Implications**

Domain	Representative Problem Areas	Instructional Implications
Attention	Attention span (length of time on task) Focus (inhibition of distracting stimuli) Selective attention (discrimination of important stimulus characteristics)	Train students to be aware of the importance of attention. Teach students how to actively self-monitor their attention. Highlight salient cues in instruction
Metacognition and Mediational Strategies	Production of strategies to assist learning Organizing new information Metacognition: thinking about thinking	Teach specific strategies (rehearsal, labeling, chunking). Involve student in active learning process (practice, apply, review). Stress meaningful content.
Memory	Short-term memory (i.e., over seconds, minutes)—common deficit area Long-term memory—usually more similar to that of people who are nondisabled (once information has been learned)	Because strategy production is difficult, students need to be shown how to use strategies to proceed in an organized, well-planned manner. Stress meaningful content.
Generalization Learning	Applying knowledge or skills to new tasks, problems, or situations Using previous experience to formulate rules that will help solve problems of a similar nature	Teach in multiple contexts. Reinforce generalization. Teach skills in relevant contexts. Remind students to apply what they have learned.
Motivational Considerations	External locus of control (attributing events to others' influence) Outerdirectedness (in learning style) Lack of encouragement to achieve and low expectations by others Failure set (personal expectancy of failure)	Create environment focused on success opportunities. Emphasize self-reliance. Promote self-management strategies. Teach learning strategies for academic tasks. Focus on learning to learn. Encourage problem-solving strategies.
Cognitive Development	Ability to engage in abstract thinking Symbolic thought, as exemplified by introspection and developing hypotheses	Provide concrete examples in instruction. Provide contextual learning experiences. Encourage interaction between students and the environment, being responsive to needs so they learn about themselves as they relate to people and objects around them.
Language Development	Delayed acquisition of vocabulary and language rules Possible interaction with cultural variance and language dialects Speech disorders (more common than in general population)	Create environment that facilitates development and encourages verbal communication. Provide appropriate language models. Provide opportunities for students to use language for varied purposes and with different audiences. Differentiate cultural variance and language delay or difficulties. Encourage student speech and active participation.
Academic Development	Delayed acquisition of reading, writing, and mathematical skills, decoding, and comprehension of text Problem-solving difficulties in mathematics	Use learning strategies to promote effective studying. Teach sight words with emphases on functional applications (see Polloway, Smith, & Miller, 2003). Teach strategies for decoding unknown words (Joseph & Seery, 2004) and place skills in context of literacy development (Katims, 2001). Provide strategies to promote reading comprehension and math problem solving. Adapt curriculum to promote success.
Sociobehavioral Considerations	Social adjustment Social perception and awareness Self-esteem Peer acceptance Suggestability, gullibility Classroom behavioral difficulties	Promote social competence through direct instruction of skills. Reinforce appropriate behaviors. Seek understanding of reasons for inappropriate behavior. Involve peers as classroom role models. Program for social acceptance. Use peers in reinforcing interventions. Teach resistance to social manipulation.

percentile range (e.g., 0–20, 21–60, 61–100). Thus the data provide comparative samples for students with specific disabilities as compared to the general population" (p. 57). These data are as follows for students with MR:

a. *Letter-word identification* (reading skills in identifying isolated letters and words; not necessary that the student knows the meaning of any words correctly identified): 91 percent of children fall into the bottom 20 percent of students in the general population.

b. *Passage comprehension* (measures skill in reading a short passage and identifying a missing key word based on a variety of comprehension and vocabulary skills): 88 percent of students fall into the lower 20 percent.

c. *Calculation* (measures ability to perform mathematical calculations; student is not required to make any decisions about what operations to use or what data to include): 82 percent of students with mental retardation fall into the lower 20 percent.

d. *Applied problems* (ability to analyze and solve problems; student must decide not only the appropriate operations to use but also which of the data to include in the calculations): 88 percent of students fall into the lowest 20 percent of the general population.

While a discussion of learning characteristics inevitably concerns deficiencies related to students with MR (Kavale & Forness, 1999), as noted with the academic descriptions above, nevertheless teachers must keep in mind the importance of retaining high expectations for their students. As Wehmeyer, Lattin, and Agran (2001) noted, the fact that these students are often held to low expectations can have a deleterious effect on outcomes and that may, in part, provide an explanation for limited achievement. A commitment to challenging these learners to succeed and build on their assets is clearly called for.

The key area of educational expectations is a foundation for understanding the characteristics and educational experiences of individuals with MR. The concept owes much of its early attention to the classic research (often maligned) of Rosenthal and Jacobson (1968). This so-called Pygmalion-in-the-Classroom research led to widespread popular acceptance of the concept of a self-fulfilling prophecy, even though it was not validated at the time by research.

While Rosenthal and Jacobson's research has been criticized numerous times, nevertheless the importance of expectation in determining an individual's achievement is intuitively strong and is supported by more modest research studies than the claims attached to the Pygmalion study. In a comprehensive study of this area, several researchers concluded that the impact of teacher behavior on student achievement was differentiated by whether students were high achievers or low achievers (McGrew & Evans, 2004).

In the context of MR, clearly students are likely to be low achievers and are potentially thus subject to the negative impact of teachers' expectations. The result may be a diminished level of achievement even beyond that which might be expected based on the intellectual level of the child. This hypothesis helps to explain the common finding that students with retardation experience even more significant difficulties in academic learning than might have been anticipated. Key expectancy effects related to level of achievement reported by McGrew and Evans (2004) are as follows:

- Students who are high achievers are nearly invulnerable to teacher perceptions that underestimate ability. When teachers overestimate ability, these students also exhibit increased achievement.
- Students who are low achievers are differentially responsive to teachers' over- and underestimation of predicted achievement growth. When growth is underestimated, students tend to achieve less. However, when achievement growth is overestimated, students achieve more.

Therefore, low achievers experience academic growth that matches teachers' predictions for achievement. Obviously, low achievers are more susceptible to self-fulfilling prophecies than most high-achieving students (McGrew & Evans, 2004).

Recent research on learning in students with MR has been relatively limited, and this group has been referred to as the "forgotten generation" (Fujiura, 2003). For example, Kavale and Forness (1999) reported that the majority of studies in this area useful for ascertaining learning characteristics were more than twenty-five years old. Quite simply, in considering the characteristics of individuals with mild mental retardation as well as the implications for curriculum and instruction, it is important to note that the rich research literature that developed in this field has been somewhat neglected for many years. This neglect led Polloway (2004) to suggest a eulogy for the field, in recognition of the relatively limited attention given, especially when compared to the areas of learning disabilities, E/BD, and severe disabilities.

As an example of this trend, the data reflect the relative emphases of papers published in the journal *Education and Training in Developmental Disabilities*. As noted, even though mild retardation is considered a high-incidence disability, the degree of attention in the literature is inconsistent with this fact (Barnett, 2006). Thus, while the population has changed over time, there has been rather limited attention to the study of these changes.

While the obvious focus in the field of MR has been on the cognitive, learning, and academic characteristics of students, practitioners should not overlook how socioemotional factors are also critical to successful functioning. For example, Masi, Mucci, and Favilla (1999) studied a group of adolescents with mild mental retardation and found depressed moods, psychomotor agitation, and loss of energy and interest as the more common problems experienced by these students.

Greenspan (in press) argues that an essential element of MR, and one that nevertheless draws attention to deficiency, is gullibility, or vulnerability to social manipulation, often by a negative benefactor. The attention that Greenspan's work has given to the social domain is particularly significant in the context of considering behavioral disorders in students with MR as well as criminal justice concerns in adolescents and adulthood. If accepted as a fundamental concept in MR, it provides some explanation for the disproportionate level of behavioral problems experienced by individuals with retardation as well as the related disproportionately in the criminal justice system. Further, it relates directly to questions of the death penalty in the aftermath of the *Atkins v. Virginia* decision (Rights and Responsibilities) by the U.S. Supreme Court (2002).

Finally, let's return to the question about weaknesses and strengths as well as deficits and supports. While the potentials and opportunities for students with intellectual disabilities are excellent, their success is most definitely determined in many instances by the support provided by others. Therefore, it is sobering to consider that these supports can result not only in successful school and community inclusion but also in difficulties because of vulnerability to a negative benefactor.

CEC STANDARDS

CEC 8: Assessment

INTASC

INTASC 8: Formal and informal assessment

PRAXIS

PRAXIS II: Delivery of Services to Students with Disabilities

Identification, Assessment, and Placement

Procedures for the identification of mental retardation proceed directly from the specific scheme as outlined in the 2002 AAMR manual (Luckasson et al., 2002), which provides a framework for the consideration of diagnosis, classification, and the planning of supports.

The key focus of the eligibility process is the application of professional judgment to data from the two key prongs or dimensions of the definitions of MR, which include intellectual functioning and adaptive behavior. For the former, data came primarily from a standardized test of intelligence (e.g., Wechsler, 1980) while the latter includes the results from instruments such as the Adaptive Behavior Assessment Scale (Harrison & Oakland, 2003).

The challenges of accurate identification, assessment, and eligibility criterion procedures have been faced by the field for many years. The Personal Spotlight feature provides a perspective on this process by offering a biographical sketch of the life effects of an individual who was diagnosed as having MR.

The history of educational placement for students with MR was characterized by research attention in the 1950s, 1960s, and 1970s followed by a long period of philosophical, rather than empirical, focus. Throughout this period, the most common service delivery system was the self-contained class, a special class-based program in which students spent the majority of their time in a pull-out program and were integrated for certain periods throughout the school day.

Gradually, this process has changed. There has been an increased commitment to inclusion in the field of MR as there has been in education in general. Nevertheless, the data indicate that this group of individuals are among the least likely to be educated in general education classrooms for most or all of the school day. For example, data from the U.S. Department of Education (2005) indicated that only 11 percent of children with MR between the ages of six and seventeen spend more than 79 percent of their time in the general education classroom.

> ### CROSS-REFERENCE
>
> See Chapters 1 and 2 to review the purposes of including students with disabilities in general education settings.

J. David Smith: Understanding Montgomery

Montgomery was well aware of the stigma associated with the term mental retardation. . . . He seemed to be laboring constantly to convince everyone that he was not retarded. From the beginning he made it evident that he did not need help or supervision during the [respite] camping weekend. Within a few hours of arriving, in fact, he asked that he be given a job as a counselor. He explained that he would help the college students assist and supervise the "handicapped people." His request was granted and he served as a counselor with distinction.

Later in that semester, I asked Montgomery to visit one of my classes. He agreed to talk about his experiences as a child, adolescent, and young adult. He spoke candidly about the impact of the stereotypes of mental retardation and Down syndrome on his life. He also spoke openly about living with a mother who would not, from his perspective, let him live an adult life. He felt she was treating him like a child even though he was twenty-seven. His younger brother was living on his own and doing the things Montgomery wanted desperately to do as a young adult (e.g., riding a motorcycle).

That evening I drove Montgomery home in my car. On the way he asked if we could stop at a 7-11. In the parking lot he insisted that I wait in the car while he went in for a soft drink. After a few minutes he returned with a Coke for each of us. Soon I delivered him to his front door. His mother . . . had apparently been listening for the car, and she made it obvious that she thought we were a bit late.

The next day Montgomery's mother called me. . . . She had just discovered a pack of cigarettes and a Playboy magazine in his room. . . . I told her that I could only assume that Montgomery had bought both at the 7-11 while I waited in the car. She was furious that I had allowed this to happen.

After several months, numerous apologies, and assurances that there would be no further 7-11 stops, Montgomery's mother agreed to allow him to speak with another of my classes. . . . Montgomery talked with my students about his recollection of being in special education classes. He also talked about his experiences at the workshop. He answered each of their questions with care. His observations and reflections were, as always, provocative. One of my students asked him what his wishes would be if he had three. Montgomery paused briefly and then replied that he wanted four wishes. "My four wishes," he said, "are to ride a motorcycle, smoke cigarettes, look at Playboy if I want to, and not be called retarded."

Along with my students, I was stunned by Montgomery's remarks. Regardless of the wisdom or political correctness of his choices, all of us were moved by his message of a yearning for freedom and a wish to escape the stigma of a term and concept that were dominating forces in his life. . . .

Montgomery's wish to free himself from the label of mental retardation has been found to be shared widely by those to whom it has been assigned . . . that escape from being labeled in this manner is a common quest for those who are asked for their own opinions of the diagnosis of mental retardation that has been assigned to them by others (Smith, in press, pp. 16–18).

For students between the ages of six and twenty-one, the U.S. Department of Education (2006) reported that children identified as mentally retarded were served as follows: 11.0 percent were in the regular classroom for 79 percent or more of the day; 30.6 percent were served outside of the regular classroom from 21–60 percent of the time; 52.6 percent were served outside of the regular classroom over 60 percent of the time; and 5.8 percent were in other separate environments (i.e., 4.0 percent served in public separate facilities and 0.9 percent in private separate facilities, 0.5 percent were served in public or private residential facilities, and 0.5 percent within the home or in a hospital environment).

When these numbers are compared with other areas of exceptionality (e.g., the average across disabilities is 48.2 percent of students served in regular classes more than 79 percent of the school day) (U.S. Department of Education, 2006), it is apparent that students with other disabilities are more commonly served in general education. However, the trend has been toward an increase in general education and resource placement and a decrease in separate (i.e., self-contained) placement (Katsiyannas, Zhang, & Archwamety, 2002).

When evaluating placement considerations, educators should realize that setting alone does not represent an effective intervention for the students. Too often the debate in education has concerned placement to the exclusion of a careful analysis of what constitutes effective instructional practices. In fact, it is quite likely that "features of instruction are probably the major influence on outcomes, but these are not unique to setting. Setting is thus a macro-variable; the real question becomes one of examining what happens in that setting" (Kavale & Forness, 1999, p. 70).

Transition Considerations

Occupational success and community living skills are among the critical life adjustment variables that ensure successful transition into adulthood. Numerous studies and case histories confirm the successes that individuals achieve, often thanks to the supports of teachers, family, and friends. Two general and equally critical considerations are these: (1) Through which means do students exit special education? and (2) What opportunities and supports are available to them during adulthood?

The U.S. Department of Education (2005) provides data on students aged fourteen and older exiting from special education. Students with MR exited as follows: 25 percent graduated with a diploma, 17.6 percent received a certificate, 3.7 percent reached the maximum age for public education, 4.1 percent no longer were receiving special education, 0.5 percent died during the school year, 24.7 percent moved and were known to continue their education, 8.6 percent moved and were not known to continue, and 15.8 percent dropped out. If one considers the data on dropouts in combination with those who moved, nearly 50 percent of the students experienced a disruption in their school experience. For students with disabilities, a deleterious effect on achievement and adult outcomes may be the likely result.

The key conclusion that can be drawn is that fewer than half of students with MR complete the designated academic curriculum with either a diploma or a certificate, while a large number of students instead either leave because of age or formally or less formally (i.e., moved, not known to continue) drop out of school. In terms of students with MR earning a diploma or a certificate, Katsiyannas and colleagues (2002, p. 143) note a "disturbing trend" of a decreased annual percentage having completed secondary school with this recognition. However, they urged caution in an interpretation of these findings because of the complexity of variables influencing these data. This complexity is underscored because the same federal report (U.S. Department of Education, 2005) indicates paradoxically that the number of children with MR who graduated with a standard diploma increased from 35 percent in 1994 to 37.8 percent in 2002. Conversely, the number of students dropping out of school was reported to have decreased from 35.4 percent in 1994 to 31.2 percent in 2002.

In terms of postschool adjustment, the transition period after leaving high school traditionally has been described as a time of "floundering" (Edgar, 1988), particularly for students with mild retardation who were not afforded effective transition programming. However, outcomes are far more optimistic when effective transition programs are in place. Examples of the challenges of adulthood in terms of life demands are summarized in Table 7.6.

In general, the clear majority of adults with intellectual disabilities can make successful transitions and obtain and maintain gainful employment. A number of critical factors influence their success. First, postschool adjustment hinges on their ability to demonstrate personal and social behaviors appropriate to the workplace. Second, the quality of the transition programming provided will predict subsequent success. Such programs recognize that programming must reflect a top-down perspective (i.e., from community considerations to school curriculum) that bases curriculum on the demands of the next environment in which the individual will live, work, socialize, and recreate.

Third, the workplace of the future poses special challenges. The more complex demands of the workplace will become increasingly problematic for this group. Many of the jobs that traditionally have been available to individuals with MR (e.g., in the service industry) may be in shorter supply. Finally, individuals with MR are likely to have increased leisure time. Thus an important component of transition planning should be preparing students to use their leisure time in rewarding and useful ways (Patton, Polloway, & Smith, 2000).

Table 7.6   Major Life Demands

Domain	Subdomain	Sample Life Demands
Employment/Education	General job skills	Seeking and securing a job Learning job skills Maintaining one's job
	General education/ training considerations	Gaining entry to postsecondary education/training settings (higher education, adult education, community education, trade/technical schools, military service) Finding financial support Utilizing academic and system survival skills (e.g., study skills, organizational skills, and time management)
	Employment setting	Recognizing job duties and responsibilities Exhibiting appropriate work habits/behavior Getting along with employer and coworkers
Home and Family	Home management	Setting up household operations (e.g., initiating utilities) Cleaning dwelling Laundering and maintaining clothes and household items
	Financial management	Creating a general financial plan (e.g., savings, investments, retirement) Paying bills Obtaining government assistance when needed (e.g., Medicare, food stamps, student loans)
	Family life	Preparing for marriage, family Maintaining physical/emotional health of family members Planning and preparing meals (menu, buying food, ordering take-out food, dining out)
Leisure Pursuits	Indoor activities	Performing individual physical activities (e.g., weight training, aerobics, dance, swimming, martial arts) Participating in group physical activities (e.g., racquetball, basketball)
	Outdoor activities	Engaging in general recreating activities (e.g., camping, sightseeing, picnicking)

CEC STANDARDS

CEC 7: Instructional Planning

INTASC

INTASC 7: Plans instruction

General education teachers would be quite unlikely to have full responsibility for meeting the transitional needs of all of their students; nevertheless, this focus is one of the most critical curricular and instructional aspects of their needs. Patton and Dunn (1998) summarized the essential features of transition, highlighting the following:

- Transition efforts must start early and planning must be comprehensive.
- Decisions must balance what is ideal with what is possible.
- Active and meaningful student participation and family involvement are essential.
- Supports are beneficial and used by everyone.
- Community-based instructional experiences have a major impact on learning.
- The transition planning process should be viewed as a capacity-building activity.
- Transition planning is needed by all students.

Transition planning is critical to success for students with MR, and therefore school districts can profit significantly from analyzing the life outcomes of their graduates.

Strategies for Curriculum and Instruction

Education in inclusive settings presents a unique opportunity for students with intellectual disabilities, their peers, and their teachers. Without question educators must deliver quality programs, or else the prognosis for young adults with MR, as noted earlier, will not reflect the positive quality of life to which they, like all people, aspire.

Challenges for General Education

CEC STANDARDS

CEC 7: Instructional Planning

INTASC

INTASC 7: Plans instruction

PRAXIS

PRAXIS II: Delivery of Services to Students with Disabilities

The data on postschool outcomes point to areas that teachers in inclusive settings must address. These concerns should be kept in mind as curricula and instructional plans are developed and implemented in conjunction with special education teachers. Patton and colleagues (1996) identified four primary goals: productive employment, independence and self-sufficiency, life skills competence, and opportunity to participate successfully within the schools and the community. These four overarching goals challenge teachers to structure educational programs so that these important emphases can complement the primary focus of curriculum and instruction on state learning standards.

In relation to *employment,* teachers should build students' career awareness and help them see how academic content relates to applied situations; at the secondary level, this effort should include training in specific job skills. This concern should be the primary focus of vocational educators who work with these students.

In terms of *independence and economic self-sufficiency,* young adults need to become responsible for themselves. As Miller (1995) states, the educational goal "is to develop self-directed learners who can address their own wants and concerns and can advocate for their goals and aspirations" (p. 12).

The successful inclusion of students with intellectual disabilities depends on the ability of teachers, peers, and the curriculum to create a climate of empowerment. Empowerment involves self-efficacy, a sense of personal control, self-esteem, and a sense of belonging to a group. Empowerment is not an automatic by-product of inclusive classrooms. However, when students are members of the group and retain the right to make decisions for themselves, they are being prepared for the challenges and rewards of life.

One essential element of empowerment is self-determination. As Wehmeyer (1993) noted:

Self-determination refers to the attitudes and abilities necessary to act as the primary causal agent in one's life, and to make choices and decisions regarding one's quality of life free from undue external influence or interference. (p. 16)

A series of specific behaviors constitute self-determination. Zhang (2001b) included the following: "making choices, making decisions, solving problems, setting and attaining goals, being independent, evaluating our performance, self-studying, speaking up for self, having internal motivations, believing in one's own abilities, being aware of personal strengths and weaknesses, and applying strengths to overcome weaknesses" (p. 339).

A third key consideration is the *inclusion of life skills in the curriculum,* focusing on the importance of competence in everyday activities. This area includes, but is not limited to, use of community resources, home and family activities, social and interpersonal skills, health and safety skills, use of leisure time, and participation in the community as a citizen (e.g., compliance with legal and cultural standards). With the increased commitment to inclusion, a particularly challenging consideration for both general and special educators will be ways to include a life skills and transitional focus within the general education curriculum beginning at the elementary school level and reflected throughout formal schooling. A critical concern is the successful blending of a standards-based curriculum with a focus on life skills and community preparation (Hoover & Patton, 2004).

A fourth consideration, *successful school and community involvement,* requires that students experience inclusive environments. Students with MR can learn to participate in school and the community by being included in general education classrooms. Although school inclusion may be viewed by some as an end in itself, it is better viewed as a condition that can provide instruction and training for success in subsequent inclusive community activities. Further information on the role of education in providing for successful adult adjustment is reflected in the IEP Goals and Objectives for Jason along with the Tips for Adapting a Lesson.

Finally, consideration must be given to the perspectives of the individuals themselves about educational programs and their outcomes. To provide a picture of the outcomes of interventions, Fox and Emerson (2001) solicited input from people with MR, parents, clinical psychologists, nurses, program managers, and direct-support workers. The focus was on two groups of individuals with MR who also had challenging behaviors: children and young adults living at home and young adults in group homes. The most salient outcomes for these two groups identified by stakeholders present an interesting contrast. While program managers, nurses, and psychiatrists, for example, stressed reductions in the severity of challenging behaviors for both groups of individuals, people with MR from both groups identified increased friendships and relationships as their priority outcome goals.

Considerations for Inclusion

The key to including students with intellectual disabilities in the general education classroom is providing necessary and appropriate support. These include personal supports (e.g., self-regulation, academic skills), natural supports (e.g., parents, friends), support services (e.g., specialized instruction), and technical supports (e.g., assistive technology). A focus on the concept of **supported education**, as a necessary complement to inclusion, assumes that individuals should be maintained in inclusive classroom settings to the maximum degree possible and supported in those settings to ensure successful learning.

There has been a too frequent tendency simply to physically place students in the general education classroom. Inclusion, as supported education, must focus on welcoming and involving people with disabilities in the general education classroom. Merely placing students in general education without active classroom participation is not the intent of inclusion and will be far less likely to result in positive gains for students. Likewise, adults with intellectual disabilities who live in the community but do not participate in community activities do not fulfill the true spirit of inclusion.

CEC STANDARDS

CEC 5: Learning Environments and Social Interaction

INTASC

INTASC 5: Learning environment

TEACHING TIP

Instructional activities should focus on the development of self-determination skills.

IEP Goals and Objectives for Jason

The importance of a focus on educational programs is reflected in this set of IEP goals and objectives for Jason (from the chapter-opening vignette). These are as follows:

Goal 1:   *To obtain a valid driver's license.*

    Objective 1:   *Given a teacher-developed test orally, which parallels the requirements for a driver's license, Jason will score at 80 percent accuracy.*

    Objective 2:   *Given a written form of a teacher-made driver's test, Jason will score at 80 percent accuracy (with graduated, less intrusive prompts).*

    Objective 3:   *Given the state-required written test, Jason will successfully pass the test.*

    Objective 4:   *Given the opportunity to enroll in the behind-the-wheel educational program, Jason will complete the program.*

    Objective 5:   *Given the opportunity to take behind-the-wheel driver's test, Jason will complete the program at an acceptable competency level.*

Goal 2:   *To successfully complete apprenticeship program at IGA.*

    Objective 1:   *Given a job application for IGA, Jason will accurately complete application for an apprentice position with 100 percent accuracy.*

    Objective 2:   *Given the opportunity to use public transportation, Jason will effectively use transportation to arrive on time for work on a daily basis with 100 percent accuracy.*

    Objective 3:   *Given a workplace setting, Jason will demonstrate correct application of safety rules with 100 percent accuracy.*

    Objective 4:   *Given necessary tools and equipment to clean the floor at work, Jason will demonstrate specific skills required for cleaning floor and emptying trash receptacles with 100 percent accuracy.*

Goal 3:   *To demonstrate the ability to handle personal finances in the areas of housing, food, leisure, and transportation.*

    Objective 1:   *Given a set income level, Jason will establish a realistic weekly budget to cover daily living expenses.*

    Objective 2:   *Given the opportunity to eat whatever he wants, Jason will identify elements of a nutritious diet with 80 percent accuracy.*

    Objective 3:   *Given the opportunity to live alone, Jason will be able to identify appropriate supports and be able to access assistance as needed for budget management 100 percent of the time.*

With the movement toward increased inclusion has come the parallel emphasis on the importance of access to the general education curriculum and a commitment to holding all students, including those with MR, to school standards. Wehmeyer and colleagues (Palmer, Wehmeyer, Gipson, & Agran, 2004; Wehmeyer, Lance, & Bashinski, 2002; Wehmeyer, in press) have been among the foremost advocates for the development of strategies, including the principles of universal design, to promote successful inclusion of students with MR. While they indicated that their research (e.g., Wehmeyer, Lattin, Lapp-Rincker, & Agran, 2003) has not been altogether encouraging of the response to teachers to this movement, nevertheless the work that has been done in this area has identified a number of strategies that can be used effectively to enhance successful inclusion and resultant school achievement.

Wehmeyer and colleagues (2001) developed a model related to access to the general curriculum. Presented in Figure 7.1, the model reflects the fact that a series of key decisions need to be made in curriculum development for students to succeed in the

Tips for Adapting a Lesson for Jason

The following selected adaptations reflect the learning and life needs as well as the classroom challenges for Jason (as described in the Chapter-opening vignette). They provide an illustration of adaptations that may be effective with students with special needs.

Jason's teacher can:

- use video-based training to learn the key elements in the driving manual;
- use a computer-simulated behind-the-wheel driving program;
- use community-based instruction to illustrate application of academic concepts (e.g., consumer math) in shopping;
- read test questions to Jason in social studies;
- use weighted grades to emphasize laboratory assessment (versus test grades) in assigning report card grades in science;
- develop cooperative learning groups and use group grades for literature projects in English.

general education classroom. Particular emphases include the use of assistive technology, the development of curricular adaptations (see the next section), the augmentation of the curriculum (to include emphases on strategy training, self-determination), and the availability of curricular alternatives (which stress a more functional emphasis often not present in the general curriculum). As noted earlier, one key consideration in the successful inclusion of students with intellectual disabilities is the application of universal design for learning. Wehmeyer (in press), drawing from the work of Rose, Meyer, and Hitchcock (2005), outlined the three essential qualities associated with curricular materials based on universal design. These include the following:

- *Multiple means of representation:* To promote learning opportunities for all students, content must be presented in alternative ways to printed text, particularly to facilitate learning by those students with reading difficulties. The advent of increased use of graphics, such as through the Internet, provide particularly apt opportunities.

A key to successful inclusion for students with mental retardation is provision of appropriate supports.

Figure 7.1   **Model for Gaining Access to the General Curriculum**

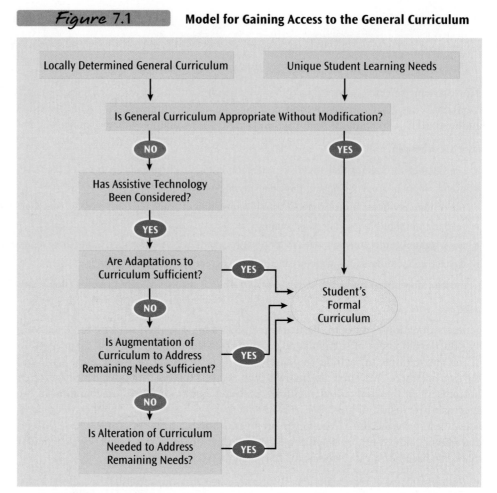

From "Achieving Access to the General Curriculum for Students with Mental Retardation: A Curriculum Decision-Making Model," by M. L. Wehmeyer, D. Lattin, and M. Agran, 2001, *Education and Training in Mental Retardation and Developmental Disabilities, 36.* pp. 327–342.

- *Multiple means of expression:* This principle indicates that materials based on universal design will offer students multiple ways in which to demonstrate the information that they have learned. As Wehmeyer (in press) noted, this could include "artwork, photography, drama, music, animation, and video that enable students to express their ideas and their knowledge" (p. 7).
- *Multiple means of engagement:* The third principle refers to ways in which curriculum based on the principles of universal design take into account the interests and preferences of individual students to find effective means of engaging those students in active class participation. Again, the basic premise is that successful inclusion is not defined by physical placement but rather by opportunities for active learning and social interaction.

The section at the end of the chapter on technology includes further information on innovations that reflect a commitment to universal design.

As described previously in the chapter, a significant concern for teaching students with intellectual disabilities is ensuring that the students are held to high expectations. To respond to the challenges related to teacher expectations, a number of principles are available to guide educational practice. Teacher behaviors that are associated with communicating low expectancies, and thus should be avoided, include (McGrew & Evans, 2004):

- Offering more limited opportunities to learn new material.
- Providing less "wait" time to answer questions.
- Providing answers for a student or calling on someone else.
- Using criticism for failure or offering insincere praise.
- Providing limited reinforcement and having it not be contingent on completed tasks.
- Engaging in differential treatment among students (e.g., less friendly or responsive, limited eye contact, fewer smiles).
- Providing briefer and less useful feedback to responses.
- Asking lower-level cognitive questions to the exclusion of those that challenge the students' thinking.

Classroom Adaptations

As inclusion has become the placement alternative of choice for students with disabilities in general, and individuals with intellectual disabilities in particular, the standard curriculum likewise has become the "program of choice" for more students with MR. Review of data on the preferences of general education teachers concerning modifications and adaptations for such students indicates that preferred adaptations typically revolve more around changes in instructional delivery systems and response modes (e.g., testing adaptations such as extended time) than in changes in the actual curriculum or the standards associated with the curricular content (e.g., Polloway, Epstein, & Bursuck, 2002; Polloway, Bursuck, Jayanthi, Epstein, & Nelson, 1996; see also Chapter 15). Therefore, to the extent that these observations are verified, it is likely that a specialized curriculum may less commonly be available for students with mild retardation (Patton et al., 2000). Nevertheless, given the preceding discussion, teachers need to be aware of the importance of a functional focus within the curriculum in order to enhance learning and adult outcomes for students with mental retardation.

Table 7.5 presented an outline of the common characteristics associated with retardation, along with their implications for instruction. When these characteristics are considered collectively, certain core instructional themes emerge. Teachers should focus on teaching and learning adaptations that:

- ensure attention to relevant task demands;
- teach ways to learn content while teaching content itself;
- focus on content that is meaningful to the students, to promote learning as well as to facilitate application;
- provide training that crosses multiple learning and environmental contexts;
- offer opportunities for active involvement in the learning process.

One promising approach that has merit for all students is the use of cognitively oriented instructional methods (e.g., strategy training). Based on the premise that learning problems experienced by low-achieving students are due more to a lack of knowledge regarding the processes involved in independent learning than to underlying deficits, these approaches incorporate learning strategies, metacognition, and cognitive behavior modification (e.g., self-monitoring) as alternatives to traditional instructional practices.

Clearly it remains critical for teachers to focus not only on the content to be learned but also on the learning process itself so that students can lessen their learning deficits through systematic strategy training. Kavale and Forness (1999) underscore the importance of focusing on strategy training so that students learn effective ways to acquire, retain, and master relevant skills within the curriculum. The potential of strategy usage for students with mild retardation is clear (e.g., Polloway, Patton, Smith, & Buck, 1997).

Curricular adaptations are likewise important to consider. One key focus should be on relevant and meaningful curricular content that students can master and apply to their current and future lives. Teachers should focus on the subsequent environments for which students will prepare (in terms of learning, working, residing) as a basis for

CEC STANDARDS

CEC 4: Instructional Strategies

INTASC

INTASC 4: Instructional Strategies

PRAXIS

PRAXIS II: Delivery of Services to Students with Disabilities

TECHNOLOGY Today

Assistive Technology: Enhancing Quality of Life

The potential for technology to contribute to "the good life" was a primary motivation behind the passage of Public Law 100–407, the Technology-Related Assistance for Individuals with Disabilities Act of 1988. . . . This legislation noted (p. 1044) that providing assistive technology devices and services to individuals with disabilities enables them to:

- have greater control over their own lives;
- participate in and contribute more fully to activities in their home, school, and work environments, and their communities;
- interact to a greater extent with nondisabled individuals;
- otherwise benefit from opportunities that are taken for granted by individuals who do not have disabilities.

People with and without disabilities universally value these goals of self-determination, inclusion, participation in school and community, and enhanced social relationships. This desire for greater control and inclusion and the potential of technology to lead to these outcomes are, presumably, no less true for people with disabilities than anyone else. . . .

What have we learned [at the Beach Center] in our research? First, we have described modifications that can improve access to technology for people with intellectual disabilities. These device modifications follow the principles of universal design. Universal design was first applied in architecture to create barrier-free buildings that were accessible to all people. Rather than adding special features to a building so people with disabilities could gain access, a building could be designed to be "universally" accessible for everyone. . . .

Universal design benefits everyone. For example, most scissors are designed for people who are right-handed; people who are left-handed must purchase specially designed scissors. Scissors that have been designed for people with limited hand strength or fine motor difficulties, however, are also easily used by people who are left-handed or right-handed. They're universally designed. . . .

A number of universal design features are important if people with intellectual and developmental disabilities are to be able to use technology. These features include the simplicity of the technology, the capacity of the technology to support repetition, and the consistency of presented information. In addition, the technology must be able to provide information on how to use a device in multiple modalities, including, in particular, audio and graphic representations.

From "Assistive Technology: Fulfilling the Promise for Individuals with Disabilities," 2006. *Beach Center Newsletter, 2.* pp. 2–4.

INTASC

INTASC 7: Plans instruction

curriculum design. The subsequent-environments rationale has applicability across the school levels as individuals prepare for successful transitions and life challenges. Most important is the assurance that the secondary school curriculum prepares students with MR (as well as all students) for adulthood, whether that means further education, job placement, or independent living.

To make the curriculum more appropriate, specific adaptations can enhance learning and increase relevance. Assistive technology can further enhance classroom adaptations. Although students with MR can benefit from a variety of technological applications, the key concern is that technology be used in a way that effectively enhances learning through conscious attention to the use of technology for each of the four respective stages of learning: the *acquisition* of new skills; the development of fluency and *proficiency*; the *maintenance* of skills over time; and the *generalization* of skills learned to other settings, including beyond the school and into the community. The Technology Today feature describes how assistive technology devices can affect the learning environment.

Promoting Inclusive Practices

Beyond the curricular and instructional considerations summarized previously, several other considerations are central to successful inclusion. The first is the creation of a sense of community in the school in general and the classroom in particular. As noted earlier, successful inclusion is best achieved as a by-product of supported education—an environment where students succeed because they are welcomed, encouraged, and involved (i.e., supported) in their learning.

CEC STANDARDS

CEC 5: Learning Environments and Social Interactions

Teachers need to promote an environment where social relationships can be developed.

The challenge for teachers seeking to successfully include students with intellectual disabilities reaches beyond the students' acquisition of, for example, specific academic skills. Rather, it requires finding ways to provide a "belonging place" for them in the general education classroom. Such a place can be created through friendships, a key priority outcome for the students themselves (Fox & Emerson, 2001).

Despite the broad support for inclusion, it does bring with it the potential loss of friendships present in traditional, self-contained classes. For example, Stainback, Stainback, East, and Sapon-Shevin (1994) noted the concern of adolescents (and their parents) over finding dating partners in general education classes. Teachers should be sensitive to this consideration and promote an environment in which the benefits of friendships can be realized.

A beneficial strategy for promoting social acceptance for students (and young adults) involves "circles of support," or "circles of friends." The Evidence-Based Practice feature discusses an example of such a program. As teachers consider developing such systems, they should not overlook the benefits to students who are not disabled of being part of these circles of friends, which may include enhanced attitudes, personal growth, and a sense of civic responsibility in addition to the benefits of friendship (Hughes et al., 2001).

Final Thoughts

As special and general education teachers jointly develop and implement educational programs, they should keep in mind that students with intellectual disabilities require a comprehensive, broad-based curriculum to meet their needs. The most effective programs will provide appropriate academic instruction consistent with state learning standards but adapted to facilitate learning. However, while the curriculum must reflect a commitment to high academic standards, it also should be complemented by emphases on developing social, life, and transition skills. In this way, it can facilitate not only the students' success in general education classrooms but also their subsequent inclusion into the community.

INTASC

INTASC 5: Learning environment

PRAXIS

PRAXIS II: Delivery of Services to Students with Disabilities

TEACHING TIP

The supports model emphasizes providing whatever supports are necessary to enable a student to be successful in a general education setting.

TEACHING TIP

Curricular decisions for students with intellectual disabilities should always be made with the students' future needs in mind.

EVIDENCE-BASED PRACTICE

Circles of Friends in Schools

Marsha Forest came away from her Joshua Committee experiences as if she had put on a better pair of glasses. Her position as a professor of special education suddenly seemed less important to her. She spent long hours on the road helping school boards, principals, and teachers to see how everybody can experience richness when someone with a disability is placed in a regular classroom, and the students are encouraged to form a circle of friends around that person.

Forest always believed in getting teaching down to meticulous detail when it came to educating people with disabilities. Now, however, she saw that some of the most valuable educational steps can come naturally from classmates, if the right conditions exist in the classroom.

She also knew that parents and teachers fear peer group pressure. After all, when kids get together these days, they can give one another quite an education—one that often shapes lives more powerfully than adults can shape them. But peer group education doesn't always lead to belligerence and destruction and drugs. It can lead to caring and nurturing

and helping others do healthy things they had never done before.

This twist, however, generated fears in some teachers when it dawned on them that a circle of friends might foster better growth and development in a student than they were capable of teaching.

And so Marsha worked hard at:

1. helping boards and principals understand the circles-of-friends process;
2. finding a teacher and class willing to include a person with a disability;
3. helping the teacher handle any initial fears about the venture;
4. letting the teacher and class call the shots as much as possible;
5. providing strong support people who would assist only when really needed;
6. finding a handful of kids willing to work at being friends with their classmate with the disability.

Forest sees building a circle of friends as a person-by-person process, not an all-encompassing program. So she focuses on students with disabilities one at a time, and sets up a framework that enables a circle to surround that person.

Because no two settings are alike, she watches as the circle, the regular teacher, and the rest of the students develop and coordinate their own routines for helping. Then, never predicting an outcome, she waits. And when new learning takes place in the person with the disability, Forest moves in and makes all the students, the teacher, the principal—even the board members—feel simply great.

According to her, the average school can handle up to twelve of these arrangements. After that, the efficiency of the process may diminish.

She doubts that circles of friends will work in every school. "If a school . . . has lost its zest and commitment for really helping kids learn—forget it. On the other hand, I'm sure that circles of friends can help make a good school—and especially the kids—better. Then coming to school takes on fresh values and meaning. Some enjoy coming to school as they never did before."

Adapted from *Circles of Friends: People with Disabilities and Their Friends Enrich the Lives of One Another* (pp. 39–40), by R. Perske, 1988. Nashville, TN: Abingdon Press.

The ultimate goal is not simply school inclusion but rather community or "life" inclusion; the curriculum that achieves that purpose most effectively is the most appropriate one. As Cassidy and Stanton (1959) suggested almost five decades ago, the key question in evaluating the efficacy of programs for students is *effective for what?* What are the knowledge and the skills that the schools are to impart to the students? The challenge of inclusion is to ensure that the curriculum students pursue prepares them for their future.

Summary

- The concept of MR has varying meanings to professionals and the public.
- The term intellectual disabilities has become a preferred term to refer to students experiencing cognitive and adaptive challenges.
- The three central dimensions of the definition are lower intellectual functioning, deficits or limitations in adaptive skills, and an onset prior to age eighteen.
- The 2002 AAMR definition also stresses the importance of assumptions related to cultural and linguistic diversity, an environmental context for adaptive skills, the strengths of individuals as well as their limitations, and the promise of improvement over time.
- Common practice in the field has been to speak of two general levels of MR, mild and severe, but emerging efforts in classification stress levels of needed supports rather than levels of deficits.
- The prevalence of mental retardation in schools decreased dramatically throughout the 1980s and early 1990s and has stabilized at approximately 1 percent.

- Social competence is a critical component of instructional programs for students with MR. Teaching social skills can have a positive effect on successful inclusion both in school and in the community.
- Educational programs must be outcomes-oriented and attend to transitional concerns so that students receive the appropriate training to prepare them for subsequent environments. The curriculum should thus have a top-down orientation.
- Teachers should teach not only content but also strategies that facilitate learning. Examples include rehearsal, classification, and visual imagery.
- Attention difficulties can be addressed by modifying instruction to highlight relevant stimuli and by training students to monitor their own attention.

- Cognitive development for students with MR can be enhanced by emphasizing active interaction with the environment and the provision of concrete learning experiences.
- Many students with a history of failure have an external locus of control, which can be enhanced by an emphasis on success experiences and by reinforcement for independent work.
- To enhance language development, teachers should provide a facilitative environment, structure opportunities for communication, and encourage verbal language.
- Opportunities for inclusion are essential and should focus on social benefits such as friendship.
- Curriculum must reflect high academic expectations but not neglect critical, functional curricular needs.

Questions to Reconsider

Think back to the scenario about Jason that you read at the beginning of this chapter. Would you answer the questions raised there any differently now that you have read the chapter itself?

1. How can Jason's curriculum include peers who are not disabled and use the functional curriculum designed by special educators?

2. How can the curriculum balance short-term objectives and preparation for competitive employment and independent living?
3. What strategies can enhance a positive influence from peers?
4. What available community resources will aid his transition to independent living?

Further Readings

Beirne-Smith, M., Patton, J., & Kim, S. (2006). *Mental retardation: An introduction to intellectual disabilities* (7th ed.). Columbus, OH: Merrill/Prentice-Hall.

Greenspan, S. (in press). Functional concepts in mental retardation: Finding the natural essence of an artificial category. *Exceptionality.*

Luckasson, R., Borthwick-Dubby, S., Butinx, W. H. E., Coulter, D. L., Craig, E. M., Reeve, A., Schalock, R. L., Snell, M. E., Spitalnik, D. M., Spreat, S., & Tassé, M. J. (2002). *Mental retardation: Definition, classification, and systems of supports.* Washington, DC: American Association on Mental Retardation.

Polloway, E. A. (Ed.). (in press). Mild mental retardation: The forgotten disability. *Exceptionality* (special issue).

Wehman, P., McLaughlin, P. J., & Wehman, T. (2005). *Intellectual and developmental disabilities* (3rd ed.). Austin, TX: Pro-Ed.

Wehmeyer, M. L. (in press). Universal design for learning, access to the general education curriculum, and students with mild mental retardation. *Exceptionality.*

Wehmeyer, M. L., & Patton, J. R. (2000). *Mental retardation in the 21st century.* Austin, TX: Pro-Ed.

mylabschool

Go to Allyn & Bacon's MyLabSchool (www.mylabschool.com) and enter Assignment ID SPV8 into the Assignment Finder. View the video clip called *Mental Retardation*. Then consider what you have seen along with what you've read in Chapter 7 to answer the following questions.

1. Teacher comments made in the video clip indicate that Carlyn has had a successful first year in preschool. Describe the teacher behaviors that contributed to Carlyn's success. Are there additional teacher behaviors described in this chapter that you might recommend for Carlyn's teachers?
2. To prepare Carlyn for transition to an integrated kindergarten, what skills would you target to help ensure that Carlyn's inclusion will continue to be successful?
3. How do we define *moderate, severe,* and *profound* mental retardation? From what you could see of Carlyn's learner characteristics and physical needs, at what level do you believe Carlyn is functioning? Provide examples to support your choice.

You may also answer the questions at the end of the clip and e-mail your responses to your instructor.

Teaching Students with Attention Deficit/Hyperactivity Disorder

After reading this chapter, you should be able to:

1. Discuss the legal basis for services to students with attention deficit/hyperactivity disorder (ADHD).

2. Describe the characteristics and identification process for students with ADHD, including the impact of cultural diversity.

3. Discuss educational, technological, and medical intervention.

4. Design strategies to enhance instruction and classroom adaptations.

5. Develop methods for promoting a sense of community and social acceptance.

Questions to Consider

1. How could Jake's early school years have been made more successful?

2. What rights did Jake have to get special accommodations from his teachers?

3. What might be Jake's most likely challenges in college? What reasonable accommodations could be made to help him be successful?

Jake was always described as a "handful." He was the second son, so his mom was used to lots of noise and activity, but nothing prepared her for Jake. He was always into something, he climbed everything, he pulled out all the toys at once, and he was fussy and seldom slept. As he entered school, his mom hoped that the scheduled day would help, but his teachers complained and called her often to discuss how difficult Jake was to manage. He was held back in kindergarten to allow him an extra year to mature, but he didn't make the progress that was hoped for. He was still disruptive and frequently in trouble with teachers.

At the same time, everyone else seemed to love Jake. He talked all the time and could really entertain a group. From the beginning, he was an excellent athlete. Baseball, swimming, football, wrestling, and basketball kept him busy but didn't really leave enough time for homework to be completed properly. He was described as "all boy!" Because he was so intelligent, he was able to make passing grades without much

effort, but he never excelled in school. Teachers always called him an underachiever and told his parents frequently that he just wasn't trying. He tried medication for one year for his hyperactivity, but that was dropped over the summer and never started again.

During high school Jake was state heavyweight champion and placed fourth in the nation in wrestling. He made the regional all-star football team, but his teachers still complained about his attitude and commitment to his studies; he had a short attention span and was easily distracted. Jake became frustrated as more effort was needed to pass all his subjects. He wanted to go to a good college and expected a scholarship, but he had to graduate with a grade point average that met the college standards. With this goal in mind, he agreed to begin taking medication, and he and his mom met with his teachers to develop a plan to improve his grades and behavior. Jake also met with a psychologist several times to discuss strategies that would make him more independent. The plan worked, and Jake got his scholarship. Without the adaptations, strategy training, and medication, Jake and his parents wonder how different his life would be.

Attention Deficit/Hyperactivity Disorder (ADHD) is a complex condition that has been a major concern in public education for several years. It is a complicated but intriguing condition and a real challenge for classroom teachers. This condition remains controversial because professional perspectives and personal opinions vary regarding the nature of ADHD and effective intervention techniques. In the past few years, awareness of this disability has significantly increased, along with successful intervention plans for students who struggle with it. The National Institutes of Health (NIH) released a consensus statement that, despite the controversy, there is enough scientific evidence to conclude that ADHD is a valid disorder (National Institutes of Health, 2000). It is a lifelong condition, and it has negative impact on an individual's social, educational, and occupational life (Weyandt, 2001).

CEC STANDARDS

CEC 1: Foundations

The legal basis for services and protection against discrimination for ADHD comes from IDEA and Section 504 of the Rehabilitation Act of 1973 (PL 93–112). When IDEA was reauthorized in 1990, a major debate took place as to whether to add ADHD as a separate handicapping condition. Some people were very disappointed when that change was not made. However, in 1991 the U.S. Department of Education did issue a policy memorandum indicating that students with attention deficit disorder (ADD, the department's term) who need special education or related services can qualify for those services under existing categories.

PRAXIS

PRAXIS II: Legal and Societal Issues

The category of "other health impaired" (OHI) was recommended as the appropriate classification for students whose primary disability is ADHD. This category includes "any chronic and acute condition that results in limited alertness and adversely affects educational performance" (U.S. Department of Education, 1991).

TEACHING TIP

The primary advocacy organization for people with ADHD is CHADD (Children and Adults with Attention Deficit Disorder); it was started in 1987 and now has 22,000 members.

The final regulations for implementation of the 1999 amendments to IDEA actually amended the definition of OHI to add ADD and ADHD to the list of conditions that could render a child eligible under OHI. The definition provides the explanation that a child with ADD or ADHD has a heightened awareness or sensitivity to environmental stimuli, and this results in a limited alertness to the educational environment (U.S. Department of Education, 1999). In other words, the child is so busy paying attention to everything going on around him or her that attention is directed away from the important educational stimuli, and school performance is negatively affected. The OHI category continues to include ADHD (IDEA, 2004).

CEC STANDARDS

CEC 1: Foundations

The number of students with ADHD requesting services under IDEA has grown dramatically, but a sizable number of students with ADHD are floundering in school and not qualifying for special education and support services that would promote academic success. In an effort to find a basis for services for this population, the U.S. Department of Education determined that Section 504 applies to these individuals and serves as a legal mandate to provide assessment and services. Section 504 has been and may continue to be the primary legal basis for services to this population.

PRAXIS

PRAXIS II: Legal and Societal Issues

Section 504 is not a special education law but a civil rights law. It mandates special education opportunities and related aids and services to meet individual educational needs for people with disabilities as adequately as the needs of those who are not disabled. Section 504 provides protection for a larger group of individuals with disabilities and differs in some respects from IDEA. It protects any individual with a disability, defined as "any physical or mental impairment that substantially limits one or more major life activities." Since learning is one of the stated life activities, it was determined that this law does apply to schools, specifically those receiving federal funding. If a school has reason to believe that any student has a disability as defined under Section 504, the school must evaluate the student. If the student is determined to be disabled under the law, the school must develop and implement a plan for the delivery of services that are needed (Smith & Patton, 2007).

CROSS-REFERENCE

Section 504 of the Rehabilitation Act of 1973 and IDEA are introduced in Chapter 1. Compare the provisions of these important legislative acts.

If a student with ADHD does not qualify for services under IDEA, services might be made available under Section 504. Although its required services and procedures are not as specific as those found in IDEA, Section 504 does provide an avenue for accom-

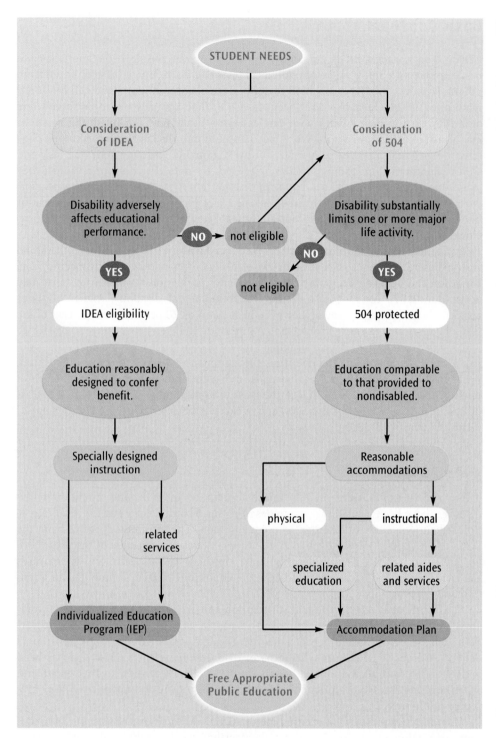

Figure 8.1

IDEA/504 Flowchart

From *Student Access: A Resource Guide for Educators: Section 504 of the Rehabilitation Act of 1973* (p. 25), by the Council for Administrators of Special Education, 1992. Reston, VA: Author. Used by permission.

modating the needs of students with ADHD in the schools. The intent of this law is to level the playing field for individuals with disabilities, creating an equal opportunity for success (Smith, 2002). Figure 8.1 is a flowchart demonstrating how both IDEA and Section 504 work together to provide appropriate services to students with ADHD.

Teachers must understand ADHD to recognize the characteristics and, most important, to implement effective intervention strategies and accommodations to facilitate success for affected children in their classrooms.

Basic Concepts about ADHD

ADHD encompasses four types of disabilities: inattention, hyperactivity-impulsivity, hyperactivity, and impulsivity.

ADHD is an invisible, hidden disability in that no unique physical characteristics and no definitive psychological or physiological tests can differentiate these children from others. However, ADHD is not hard to spot in the classroom. For some children their inattention is the clue; they don't seem to listen, their minds seem to be somewhere else, they turn in messy work with careless errors, they may not finish the work, or may finish but never turn it in. Work may be found months later crammed into a cluttered desk. These children may have trouble organizing and may start one task and shift to another before completing the first. They are not defiant or oppositional; they simply do not perform as expected based on their ability. Other children can be spotted more quickly; they are squirming, talking excessively, jumping out of their seat or interrupting the teacher at inappropriate times. They may be referred to as the "class clown."

Unfortunately, the disabling behaviors associated with ADHD may be misunderstood and misinterpreted as a sign of being lazy, unmotivated, and even disrespectful. The condition can be recognized only through specific behavioral manifestations that may occur during the learning process. As a developmental disability, ADHD becomes apparent before the age of seven; however, in as many as 70 percent to 80 percent of the cases, it continues to cause problems in adulthood (Heiligenstein, Conyers, Beirns, & Smith, 1998). ADHD may have an impact on success in both academic and nonacademic areas. It occurs in various countries throughout the world and across all cultural, racial, and socioeconomic groups. It can also affect children and adults with all levels of intelligence (Weyandt, 2001). In fact, the greatest limitation for someone with ADHD is difficulty in areas of self-sufficiency and what can be referred to as "street smarts" (Schuck & Crinella, 2005).

ADHD Defined

Although a variety of terms such as "minimal brain dysfunction" and "attention deficit disorder" have been used in the past to describe this disorder, currently the term "attention deficit/hyperactivity disorder" is most common. The terminology stems from the DSM-IV-TR (2000). On a global level, the *International Classification of Diseases* (10th ed.; ICD–10, 1992) is used to describe these children. This classification system uses the term "hyperkinetic disorders" to describe conditions related to problems in attention and hyperactivity.

ADHD primarily refers to deficits in attention and behaviors characterized by impulsivity and hyperactivity. A distinction must be made between ADHD and other disorders such as sleep disorders, conduct disorder (e.g., physical fighting), and oppositional defiant disorder (e.g., recurrent patterns of disobedience). The DSM-IV-TR has been widely adopted as a guide to the diagnosis of ADHD. According to this document, ADHD encompasses four types of disabilities. The diagnostic criteria for ADHD are presented in Figure 8.2.

The identification of the specific type of ADHD depends on the number of symptoms in sections 1 and/or 2 that can be ascribed to the individual. For example, ADHD, combined type, is designated if six or more symptoms are identified from each section. A diagnosis of ADHD, predominantly inattentive type, is indicated if six or more symptoms are identified from section 1 only. A third type of ADHD, predominantly hyperactive-impulsive type, has six or more of the hyperactivity-impulsivity behaviors. Last, a category called ADHD, not otherwise specified, is typically used for individuals who do not meet the full criteria for ADHD; for example, their age of onset may be after age seven, or they may have inattention behaviors described as sluggishness, daydreaming, and *hypoactivity* (defined as *underactive*).

Figure 8.2   **Diagnostic Criteria for ADHD**

A. Either (1) or (2):

1. six (or more) of the following symptoms of inattention have persisted for at least six months to a degree that is maladaptive and inconsistent with developmental level:
   Inattention:
   a. often fails to give close attention to details or makes careless mistakes in schoolwork, work, or other activities
   b. often has difficulty sustaining attention in tasks or play activities
   c. often does not seem to listen when spoken to directly
   d. often does not follow through on instructions and fails to finish schoolwork, chores, or duties in the workplace (not due to oppositional behavior or failure to understand instructions)
   e. often has difficulty organizing tasks and activities
   f. often avoids, dislikes, or is reluctant to engage in tasks that require sustained mental effort (such as schoolwork or homework)
   g. often loses things necessary for tasks and activities (e.g., toys, school assignments, pencils, books, or tools)
   h. is often easily distracted by extraneous stimuli
   i. is often is forgetful in daily activities

2. six (or more) of the following symptoms of hyperactivity-impulsivity have persisted for at least 6 months to a degree that is maladaptive and inconsistent with developmental level:
   Hyperactivity:
   a. often fidgets with hands or feet or squirms in seat
   b. often leaves seat in classroom or in other situations in which remaining seated is expected
   c. often runs about or climbs excessively in situations in which it is inappropriate (in adolescents and adults, may be limited to subjective feelings of restlessness)
   d. often has difficulty playing or engaging in leisure activities quietly
   e. is often "on the go" or acts as if "driven by a motor"
   f. often talks excessively
   Impulsivity:
   g. often blurts out answers to questions before the questions have been completed
   h. often has difficulty awaiting turn
   i. often interrupts or intrudes on others (e.g., butts into conversations or games)

B. Some hyperactive-impulsive or inattentive symptoms that caused impairment were present before age seven years.

C. Some impairment from the symptoms is present in two or more settings (e.g., at school [or work] and at home).

D. There must be clear evidence of clinically significant impairment in social, academic, or occupational functioning.

E. The symptoms do not occur exclusively during the course of a Pervasive Developmental Disorder, Schizophrenia or other Psychotic Disorder, and are not better accounted for by another mental disorder (e.g., Mood Disorder, Anxiety Disorder, Dissociative Disorder, or a Personality Disorder).

From *Diagnostic and Statistical Manual of Mental Disorders* (4th ed., text rev., pp. 92–93), by the American Psychiatric Association, 2000. Washington, DC: Author. Used by permission.

Identification of the characteristics associated with ADHD is critical in the diagnosis. The teacher often brings the ADHD-like behaviors to the attention of the parents. When parents initiate contact with the school to find help, as Jake's parents did, they will be served best by teachers who are already well informed about this condition and the special education assessment process.

CEC STANDARDS

CEC 8: Assessment

Prevalence and Causes of ADHD

ADHD is more common than any other child behavioral disorder (Scahill & Schab-Stone, 2000). Estimates of the prevalence of ADHD in school-age children range from a conservative figure of less than 2 percent to a more liberal figure of 30 percent; however, 3–7 percent is most probable (American Psychiatric Association, 2000). The extreme differences found in prevalence figures reflect the lack of agreement on a definition and the difficulty and variance in identification procedures. Regardless of the exact prevalence figure, a substantial number of students with this condition attend general education classrooms. The most common subtype is the combined type, accounting for about 50–75 percent of all individuals with ADHD; second most prevalent is the inattentive type (20–30 percent); and third is hyperactive-impulsive (less than 15 percent) (Wilens et al., 2002). Boys are more often diagnosed than girls; however, this gap is closing (Robinson, Skaer, Sclar, & Galin, 2002). Several individuals have noted that the prevalence of ADHD is increasing; however, it is generally felt that this perception is due to the increased media attention that alerts parents and teachers and to better training of clinicians and physicians (Weyandt, 2001).

Although the exact cause of ADHD is unknown, several theories have been proposed, and rigorous research is ongoing. Most professionals agree that ADHD is a neurobiologically based condition. Following is a summary of the research on possible causes as described by Weyandt (2001):

- *Neuroanatomical:* Related to brain structure. Unexplained differences such as smaller right frontal regions, smaller brain size in boys with ADHD, and a smaller cerebellum have been found. It is not known whether these differences are due to genetics or the environment, or if they are even related to or responsible for the symptoms of ADHD.
- *Neurochemical:* Related to a chemical imbalance in the brain or a deficiency in chemicals that regulate behavior. This research usually focuses on neurotransmitters, chemicals in the brain responsible for communication among brain cells and necessary for behavior and thought to occur. Stimulant medication is proposed to stimulate or regulate production of the neurotransmitters and increase brain activity. As a result of conflicting findings, this research is currently inconclusive.
- *Neurophysiological:* Related to brain function. Various medical tests such as the EEG and brain scans have suggested that individuals with ADHD have reduced brain activity (were found to be in a low state of arousal) and reduced blood flow in the right frontal region, an area that produces important neurotransmitters and helps regulate impulse control, attention, and planning. To be considered conclusive, these tests need to be validated on many more individuals at various ages and on both females and males.
- *Neuropsychological:* Dysfunction of the frontal lobes resulting in deficits in attention, self-regulation, impulsivity, and planning, collectively called executive function. Renowned researcher Dr. Russell Barkley (1997) proposed a unifying theory that individuals with ADHD have deficits in behavioral inhibition that is caused by physiological differences in the brain. These differences result in the executive function deficits listed previously in addition to impairments in working memory, problem solving, motor control, and using internal speech (i.e., self-talk) to guide behavior. Other studies support this model, but again, more research is needed.

Some data suggest that genetics plays a significant role in ADHD, evidenced by a higher prevalence rate in some families. Studies have shown that biological parents, siblings, and other family members of individuals with this disorder have higher rates of ADHD than expected in the general population. For example, Faraone and Doyle (2001) found that parents of children with ADHD are two to eight times more likely to have ADHD than parents of children without ADHD.

Barkley (2000) noted that pre- and postnatal events may cause ADHD. Premature birth is associated with ADHD; other events include complications during pregnancy, fetal exposure to tobacco or alcohol, head trauma, lead poisoning in preschool years, and strep infection. While many factors are still being seriously considered as a potential cause of ADHD, others have little or no evidence to support them. These include aspects of the physical environment such as fluorescent lighting, soaps, disinfectants, yeast, preservatives, food coloring, aspartame, certain fruits and vegetables, sugar, social factors, and poor parental management (Weyandt, 2001). For most students, the precise cause of the problem may never be understood. Although many parents want to understand why their children have a developmental disability such as ADHD, its cause is really not relevant to educational strategies or medical treatment. These can succeed without pinpointing the root of the problem.

Characteristics of Students with ADHD

The characteristics of ADHD manifest themselves in many different ways in the classroom. Recognizing them and identifying adaptations or strategies to lessen the impact in the classroom constitute a significant challenge for teachers. The characteristics listed in the DSM-IV-TR (2000) criteria highlight the observable behaviors. Barkley (2000) groups these characteristics into the following three most common areas of difficulty:

1. *Limited sustained attention or persistence of attention to tasks.* During tedious, long-term tasks, the students become rapidly bored and frequently shift from one uncompleted activity to another. They may lose concentration during long work periods and fail to complete routine work unless closely supervised. The problem is not due to inability to comprehend the instructions, memory impairment, or defiance. The instructions simply do not regulate behavior or stimulate the desired response. One study found limitations in sustained attention characterized most of the children, while deficits in selective attention, executive attention, and orienting attention were characteristic of over half (Tsal, Shalev, & Mevorah, 2005).
2. *Reduced impulse control or limited delay of gratification.* Individuals often find it hard to wait their turn while talking to others or playing. Students may not stop to think before acting or speaking. They may have difficulty resisting distractions while concentrating and working toward long-term goals and long-term rewards, preferring to work on shorter tasks that promise immediate reinforcement.
3. *Excessive task-irrelevant activity or activity poorly regulated to match situational demands.* Individuals with ADHD are often extremely fidgety and restless. Their movement seems excessive and often not directly related to the task—for example, tapping pencils, rocking, or shifting positions frequently. They also have trouble sitting still and inhibiting their movements when the situation demands it.

Other areas of difficulty in psychological functioning include: working memory or remembering to do things; sensing time or using time as efficiently as their peers; and using their internal language to talk to themselves in order to think about events and purposefully direct their own behavior. They have problems inhibiting their reaction to events, often appearing more emotional or hotheaded and less emotionally mature. They are easily frustrated and seem to lack willpower or self-discipline. They may have difficulty following instructions or rules, even following their own "to-do" lists. They demonstrate considerable variation in the quantity, quality, and speed with which they perform their assigned tasks. Their relatively high performance on some occasions, coupled with low levels of accuracy on other occasions, can be baffling. Low levels of performance often occur with repetitive or tedious tasks.

CONSIDER THIS

Refer to the opening vignette in this chapter. Identify Jake's characteristics that would lead a teacher or parent to suspect ADHD.

CEC STANDARDS

CEC 2: Development and Characteristics of Learners

INTASC

INTASC 2: How children learn and develop

PRAXIS

PRAXIS II: Understanding Exceptionalities

CONSIDER THIS

Sustained attention is attention paid to a specific task over time. *Selective attention* is the ability to focus on the relevant information and to ignore the irrelevant. *Orienting attention* is appropriately responding to a cue that should direct attention and then redirecting attention when presented another cue. *Executive attention* is the ability to inhibit responses to irrelevant stimuli, resulting in planned, organized activity (Tsal, Shalev, and Mevorah, 2005).

The symptoms are likely to change from one situation to another. More ADHD symptoms may be shown in group settings, during boring work, when students are without supervision, and when work has to be done later in the day. Individuals with ADHD behave better when: there is immediate payoff for doing the right thing; they enjoy what they are doing or find it interesting; they are in one-on-one situations; and they can work earlier in the day (Barkley, 2000). One researcher reported the following as the ADHD motto; it seems to summarize the challenge of ADHD in the classroom: "It's got to be fun! If it is not fun, it's got to be moving! If its not moving and I'm not moving, maybe I can make it mad!" (Zentall, 2006).

The characteristics of ADHD may also be present in adulthood; only an estimated 20 percent to 35 percent of children with the disorder will not be impaired as adults. For some individuals the condition continues to cause problems and limitations in the world of work, as well as in other life activities. Figure 8.3 provides a summary of common characteristics for varying age groups, including adults. Barkley (2000) reports that adults with ADHD are more likely to be fired, typically change jobs three times more often in a ten-year period than do adults without the disorder, are more likely to divorce, and typically have more traffic citations and accidents. On the positive side, the outcome is much brighter for individuals with ADHD who receive treatment such as medication, behavior management, and social-skills training. Many

---

Figure **8.3**

Common Characteristics of Individuals with ADHD

From *An ADHD Primer* (p. 17), by L. L. Weyandt, 2001. Boston: Allyn & Bacon.

Early Childhood
Excessive activity level
Talking incessantly
Difficulty paying attention
Difficulty playing quietly
Impulsive and easily distracted
Academic underachievement

Middle Childhood
Excessive fidgeting
Difficulty remaining seated
Messy and careless work
Failing to follow instructions
Failing to follow through on tasks
Academic underachievement

Adolescence
Feelings of restlessness
Difficulty engaging in quiet sedentary activities
Forgetful and inattentive
Impatience
Engaging in potentially dangerous activities
Academic underachievement

Adulthood
Feelings of restlessness
Difficulty engaging in quiet sedentary activities
Frequent shifts from one uncompleted activity to another
Frequent interrupting or intruding on others
Avoidance of tasks that allow for little spontaneous movement
Relationship difficulties
Anger management difficulties
Frequent changes in employment

adults with ADHD are very successful; Zentall (2006) proposes three possible reasons for this:

- Some professions have built-in support personnel such as computer operators, administrative assistants, and accountants.
- Some jobs have built in accommodations such as frequent travel or a stimulating work setting, such as a hospital or a high-volume sales floor.
- Some jobs require the personal qualities frequently found in individuals with ADHD, such as extroversion, spontaneity, humor, energy, risk-taking, multitasking, and entrepreneurship.

Crawford (2002) offers this insight into the challenge of becoming successful for an individual with ADHD and LD:

> It hurts so much to try hard every day, sometimes relearning what you learned the day before because you forgot it all, and comparing yourself to others and realizing you are different! If you fail, then you don't have to push on. Others can feel sorry for you—take care of you; it's easier, at least it seems so. But what happens when we give up is that we try to find other avenues to make up for what we lost. Often, those avenues are devastatingly more painful than struggling to get what we need to be independent. Giving up our independence, giving up our dream, is like dying. The key is not to give up but to be realistic, to be optimistic, and to find the support one needs. Then, apply the hard work. Though it may take a lifetime, it is time well spent. (pp. 139–140)

A large part of a successful outcome for any person with a disability is self-determination and persistence, but so much depends on the support of others. Teachers who can identify and plan meaningful interventions for students with ADHD can have a powerful impact on their success during the school years as well as their quality of life as adults.

Identification, Assessment, and Eligibility

For years the assessment and diagnosis of ADHD were considered the responsibility of psychologists, psychiatrists, and physicians, and typically these individuals are still involved in the identification process. However, the mandates of Section 504 of PL 93–112 as interpreted by the assistant secretary for civil rights (Cantu, 1993) charged public education personnel with responsibility for this assessment as needed. If a school district suspects that a child has a disability that substantially limits a major life activity such as learning, the district is required to provide an assessment. If the disability is confirmed, the school district must then develop a plan and provide services. Because teachers are often the first to suspect the presence of ADHD, they should be familiar with the specific behaviors associated with the disorder and the commonly used assessment techniques. Although specially trained school personnel must perform the formal assessment for ADHD, teachers should participate on the interdisciplinary team that reviews the assessment data to determine whether the attention problems limit learning and to plan the individualized program, if appropriate. Teachers may also be called on to complete informal assessment instruments that, with other data, will help in determining the presence of ADHD. Weyandt (2001) supports the participation of teachers as an important source of information in ADHD assessment. She notes that teachers spend a significant amount of time with students in a variety of academic and social situations and have a better sense of normal behaviors for the comparison group.

It is important to respect the rights that parents are guaranteed throughout this process; these are highlighted in Rights & Responsibilities. As soon as the school suspects that a child is experiencing attention problems, the parents should be notified and invited to meet with school personnel. Often the parents, the teacher, the principal, and

CONSIDER THIS

If your school has a policy stipulating that teachers should not recommend services that the school system might have to pay for (e.g., a medical exam), how will you proceed when you feel a child is in need of such services? What are your options?

TEACHING TIP

Begin a parent conference by talking about the strengths of the student. Give parents time to respond to the limitations observed in the school setting by having them report examples of behavior from home and other environments.

Rights & Responsibilities

Parent Rights Under Section 504

Section 504 of the Rehabilitation Act provides services for students identified as having a disability that substantially limits a major life activity. As parents, you have the following rights:

1. The right to be informed of your rights under Section 504 of the Rehabilitation Act.
2. The right for your child to have equal opportunities to participate in academic, nonacademic, and extracurricular activities in your school.
3. The right to be notified about referral, evaluation, and programs for your child.
4. The right for your child to be evaluated fairly.
5. The right, if eligible for services under 504, for your child to receive accommodations, modifications, and related services that will meet his/her needs as well as the needs of nondisabled students are met.

6. The right for your child to be educated with nondisabled peers as much as possible.
7. The right to an impartial hearing if you disagree with the school regarding your child's educational program.
8. The right to review and obtain copies of your child's school records.
9. The right to request attorney fees related to securing your rights under Section 504.
10. The right to request changes in the educational program of your child.

Signed: Parent(s): _____   Date: _____
            School Representative: _____   Date: _____

From *Section 504 and Public Schools: A Practical Guide* (p. 73), by T. E. C. Smith and J. R. Patton, 2007. Austin, TX: Pro-Ed. Adapted by permission.

the school counselor will attend the initial meeting. During this meeting parents should be asked to respond to the observations of the school personnel and describe their own experiences with problems in attention, impulsivity, and overactivity outside the school setting. If the team agrees that additional testing is needed, a trained individual should step in to direct the assessment process. This person must understand the impact of ADHD on the family; the bias that might occur during the assessment process because of cultural, socioeconomic, language, and ethnic factors; and other conditions that may mimic ADHD and prevent an accurate diagnosis.

Initially, a teacher who has been trained in identifying the symptoms of ADHD according to the school's criteria may begin to observe that a particular student manifests these behaviors in the classroom to a greater degree than his or her peers. At this point, the teacher should begin to keep an anecdotal record, or log, to document the child's ADHD-like behaviors, noting the times when behaviors appear to be more intense, more frequent, or of a longer duration. Figure 8.4 provides a simple format for this observational log. For example, a teacher might document behavior typical of ADHD, such as constantly interrupting, excessive talking, not following directions, leaving a designated area, not finishing assignments, or not turning in homework. When the teacher observes that the behaviors are severe enough to have a significant impact on academic or social functioning, the counselor or individual designated to lead the formal assessment process should be contacted.

Although schools are not required to use a specific set of criteria to identify ADHD, the DSM-IV-TR criteria described earlier are the most widely accepted and are highly recommended (Weyandt, 2001; Zentall, 2006). A variety of methods and assessment procedures will be needed to provide a thorough evaluation for ADHD. The school system will most likely interview the child, parents, and teachers; obtain a developmental

CEC STANDARDS

CEC 2: Development and Characteritics of Learners

Teacher: _____ School: _____

Child: _____ Grade: _____ Age: _____

Class Activity	Child's Behavior	Date/Time

***Figure* 8.4**

Sample Form for Documenting Classroom Manifestations of ADHD-like Behaviors

and medical history; review school records; review and/or evaluate intellectual and academic performance; administer rating scales to parents, teachers, and possibly peers; and document the impact of the behavior through direct observation. Figure 8.5 contains a rating form that can be used at home or at school to document activity. This form is especially helpful as it is configured to allow comparison of data for a child not suspected of having ADHD.

According to Weyandt (2001), an interview with parents might include the following topics:

- The student's medical, social-emotional, and developmental history
- Family history
- Parental concerns and perception of the problem
- The student's behavior at home
- Academic history and previous testing

An interview with the child is appropriate in many cases, to determine the child's perception of teacher reports, attitudes toward school and family, and perception of relationships with peers. Although the child's responses will be slanted by personal feelings, the interview still is an important source of information.

The assessment of achievement and intelligence is not required in the identification of ADHD. However, the results of achievement and intelligence tests might suggest that the child can qualify for services under IDEA (2004) in categories of learning disabilities or mental retardation. Also, knowing the levels of intelligence and achievement will help eventually in developing an intervention plan.

Rating scales that measure the presence of ADHD symptoms are widely used to quantify the severity of behaviors. They offer a way to measure the extent of the problem objectively. Several informants who know the child in a variety of settings should complete rating scales. The results should be compared to responses from interviews and the results of observations. Some rating scales are limited to an assessment of the primary symptoms contained in the DSM-IV-TR criteria; other assessment instruments are multidimensional and might address emotional-social status, communication, memory, reasoning and problem solving, and cognitive skills such as planning and self-evaluation.

A medical examination is not required to diagnose ADHD; however, because symptoms of certain medical conditions may mimic those of ADHD, a medical exam should be considered. No specific laboratory tests have been developed to diagnose ADHD

INTASC

INTASC 2: How children learn and develop

PRAXIS

PRAXIS II: Understanding Exceptionalities

Figure 8.5   **Home and Classroom Activity Indicators**

1. Activity—off chair/up and down, talk/noisemaking
2. Inattention—changes in the focus of play or free-time activities, visual off task, verbal off task (e.g., off the subject)
3. Social impulsivity—disrupt, interrupt
4. Social negativity
   - *Verbal*—disagree/argue/command/verbal statement
   - *Physical*—negative physical contact with another or noncompliance or nonperformance of a request or an assigned task (Zentall, 1985a)

This behavior has been converted to a data collection procedure (see below)

Coding Time Intervals

Child A:	1	2	3	4	5	6	7	8	9	10	11	12	13	14	15
Up/down, noise															
Change focus															
Disrupt/interrupt															
Social negative															
Child B:	1	2	3	4	5	6	7	8	9	10	11	12	13	14	15
Up/down, noise															
Change focus															
Disrupt/interrupt															
Social negative															

	Totals	
	Child A	Child B
Up/down, noise/activity	Activity /15	/15
Change focus/inattention	Inattention /15	/15
Disrupt/interrupt/impulsivity	Social impulsivity /15	/15
Social negative	Social negative /15	/15
	Child A	Child B
	/60	/60

The intervals are defined as 1 to 15. The observer needs to select time units of 1 to 4 minutes per interval. (If 4 minutes, then total time observed = 1 hour; if 2 minutes, then total time = 30 minutes; and if 1 minute, then total time = 15 minutes.)

From *ADHD and Education Foundations, Characteristics, Methods, and Collaboration* (p. 25), by S. S. Zentall, 2006. Upper Saddle River, NJ: Pearson.

(American Psychiatric Association, 2000). However, a physician might identify sleep apnea, anemia, allergies, lead poisoning, side effects from medication, or other medical conditions as the primary cause of problem behaviors.

When the interdisciplinary team reconvenes to review all of the data, the following DSM-IV-TR criteria should be considered:

- Six or more of the nine characteristics of inattention and/or six or more of the nine symptoms of hyperactivity-impulsivity should be demonstrated as present for longer than six months.
- The behaviors observed should be considered maladaptive and developmentally inconsistent.
- The symptoms should have been observed prior to or by age seven.
- The limitations that stem from the characteristics should be observed in two or more settings (e.g., home, school, work).
- The characteristics are not considered solely the result of schizophrenia, pervasive developmental disorder, or other psychiatric disorder, and they are not better attributed to the presence of another mental disorder, such as an anxiety disorder or mood disorder.
- The symptoms must cause clinically significant impairment or distress in social, academic, or occupational functioning.

The team reviewing the data should look for consistency across reports from the assessment instruments and the informants to validate the existence of ADHD. If it is confirmed, the team must determine whether it has caused an adverse effect on school performance and whether a special educational plan is needed.

After an educational plan has been developed under IDEA or 504 protection, the parents and school personnel should monitor the child's progress closely to ensure success. Adjustments may be needed occasionally to maintain progress. For example, reinforcement for good behavior may eventually lose its novelty and need to be changed. The ultimate goal is to remove accommodations and support as the child becomes capable of self-regulating his or her behavior. As the setting and school personnel change each year, reevaluating the need for special services will yield benefits. As the student becomes more efficient in learning and demonstrates better social skills under one plan, a new, less restrictive plan must be designed to complement this growth.

Cultural and Linguistic Diversity

DSM-IV-TR confirms that ADHD is known to occur in various cultures with varying prevalence figures, probably due to differences in diagnostic procedures. Since the racial, cultural, and linguistic diversity of our country is continuing to enlarge, teachers will find a significant number of languages and cultures represented in their classrooms across the years. When ADHD does coexist with cultural and linguistic diversity, it presents a special set of challenges to the educator. Failure to address the special needs of these children can be detrimental to their academic and social success. Issues related to assessment and cultural diversity have been discussed previously; the same concerns exist in the identification and treatment of students with ADHD. To address the needs of multicultural students with ADHD, teachers must become familiar with their own unique values, views, customs, interests, and behaviors as well as those of their students.

Gay (2003) proposes that the frequent mismatch between the cultures of teachers and their students in regard to language, culture, and socioeconomic background cause many students to display behaviors that may be misinterpreted as ADHD. For example, students learning English will likely have difficulty concentrating and attending to large amounts of information presented in their new language (Salend & Rohena, 2003).

CEC STANDARDS

CEC 2: Development and Characteristics of Learners

They may be observed as fidgety, distracted, or seeming not to listen, much like students with ADHD. Barkley (2000) raises the issue that the chaotic home environment of many minority populations existing below the poverty level exacerbates the problems of children with ADHD. DSM-IV-TR (American Psychiatric Association, 2000) requires that ADHD be distinguished from "difficulty in goal-directed behavior in children from inadequate, disorganized, or chaotic environments" (p. 91), although no guidance is given in making this differentiation. Certainly people being interviewed during the assessment process should be asked to describe how the student's behavior might be affected by their culture, language, or experiential background (Garrick Duhaney, 2000).

Accommodations can be important in both assessing and teaching children with racial, cultural, and linguistic diversity. Gestures, demonstrations, visuals, and simulations may help provide a context that promotes learning (Salend & Rohena, 2003). Teachers can also integrate personal and community experiences into teaching an academic concept to help make it relevant. The literature tells us that when teachers carefully organize and structure instruction, these students benefit. These and other strategies and accommodations appropriate for all students with ADHD, including the culturally diverse, are described more fully in the following sections.

CONSIDER THIS

Complete an in-depth study of the characteristics or educational needs of a particular culture. Share your findings with other groups in the class.

Strategies for Curriculum and Instruction for Students with ADHD

Treatment for students with ADHD is unique because professionals outside education are often involved in the process of identification and intervention. Although no magic cure has been discovered for this disorder, many treatments are effective in its management. Barkley (2000) suggests that the education of the school staff, the family, and the individuals with ADHD is one of the most important treatments. He also reports that parent training in child management is helpful, particularly when children are preadolescent, and that family therapy is often needed to improve communication, especially with teens. General and special education teachers need to work closely with parents, physicians, and support personnel to develop, monitor, and maintain successful interventions. For many students, accommodations implemented in general education classrooms are enough to improve learning; however, other students may need special education support services and placement or at least behavioral intervention. Although controversial, research has also concluded that evidence-based medical intervention is one of the most successful treatments to enhance learning for students with ADHD (Barkley, 2000; Weyandt, 2001), especially in combination with evidence-based behavioral therapy (Zentall, 2006). These and other issues will be discussed in the following sections.

Continuum-of-Placement Options

Under Section 504 and IDEA, a local education agency must provide a free appropriate public education to each qualified child with a disability. The U.S. Department of Education suggests that the placement of choice for children with ADHD should be the general education classroom, with appropriate adaptations and interventions.

Although students with ADHD may be found in a variety of special education settings, the majority of students classified as special education students spend more than 80 percent of the school day in general education classes (U.S. Department of Education, 2001). Since the general education teacher is responsible for the learning experience of students with ADHD most of the time, it is imperative that these teachers understand the condition and have strategies for dealing with it in their classrooms.

The U.S. Department of Education notes that most children with ADHD are in general education classrooms.

Special educators must be knowledgeable in order to collaborate effectively with general educators to develop educational plans that might adapt curriculum, instruction, and environment. Both special and general education teachers also need to be effective in providing behavioral support and skillful in teaching students to regulate their own behavior.

Developing Educational Plans

If a local education agency decides that a child has a disability under Section 504, the school must determine the child's educational needs for regular and special education or related aids and services. Although this law does not mandate a written individualized education program, implementation of a written IEP is recommended. Most school systems have opted to develop written plans; they are generally referred to as student accommodation plans, individual accommodation plans, or 504 plans.

It is recommended that this plan be developed by a committee that includes parents, professionals, and, as often as possible, the student. The areas identified as causing significant limitations in learning should be the targets of the intervention plan. The committee should determine the least amount of adaptations needed to stimulate success in learning and social development. If medication therapy is being used, the plan should also indicate the school's role in administering the medication and special precautions or considerations regarding side effects (Austin, 2003). When a conservative intervention plan has been developed and implemented, additional goals and interventions can be added as needed.

Each local education agency must have an identified 504 coordinator or officer responsible for maintaining a fair and responsive evaluation process and plan for developing 504 plans. They monitor students' needs and communicate with parents and teachers as necessary. Although it is much simpler than an IEP, a 504 plan serves to document legally the services agreed upon by the team members. Jake's 504 plan is included later in the chapter on page 260. If a student is served under IDEA under the area of "other health impaired," an IEP will be written by the team.

CEC STANDARDS

CEC 4: Instructional Strategies

INTASC

INTASC 4: Instructional strategies

PRAXIS

PRAXIS II: Delivery of Services to Students with Disabilities

TEACHING TIP

When you are employed in a new school district, meet the special education and 504 coordinators to obtain an overview of policies and procedures for assessment and delivery.

The Role of Medication

CONSIDER THIS

Adolescents often refuse to take medication prescribed for ADHD. What do you think happens during this developmental period that might account for this behavior?

Since many students with ADHD will be prescribed medication by their physicians, teachers need to understand the types of medications used, commonly prescribed dosages, intended effects, and potential side effects. Pharmacological therapy can be defined as treatment by chemical substances that prevent or reduce inappropriate behaviors, promoting academic and social gains for children with learning and behavior problems. Studies have shown that different outcomes occur for different children. In 70 percent to 80 percent of cases, children with ADHD (ages six and older) respond in a positive manner to psychostimulant medication (Baren, 2000; Barkley, 2000). One extensive study sponsored by the National Institute of Mental Health (MTA, 1999) found that medication was more effective than medication plus behavioral and educational treatments; however, other studies recommend the effectiveness of including behavioral intervention along with pharmacological interventions (Kollins, Barkley, & DuPaul, 2001). The desired outcomes from the intervention include increased concentration, completion of assigned tasks, increased work productivity, better handwriting and motor skills, improved social relations with peers and teachers, increased appropriate behaviors and emotional control, and reduction of inappropriate, disruptive behaviors such as talking out loud, getting out of the seat, and breaking rules. These changes frequently lead to improved academic and social achievement as well as increased self-esteem.

DIVERSITY FORUM

Alternatives to Medication as Intervention

Will, a European American 11-year old, is in middle school. His parents are concerned because his first progress report reflects inattention and low grades. While they associate high activity level with gender and maturity, teachers worry that he may have ADHD. They think medication might help him be more successful. In accordance with their religion, Will's parents believe in addressing physical and mental health problems through prayer; they oppose medical intervention. Will's parents and teachers meet to discuss a possible referral for special education evaluation.

Will's family and teachers have different beliefs about how to respond to Will's behavior; in this case, religious differences, rather than race/ethnicity or social class, will require cultural sensitivity and intercultural collaboration. Building upon student strengths, and developing a caring learning environment are important when collaborating with families whose beliefs vary from the dominant group (Delpit, 2006).

Documenting problematic behavior is just the first step in the referral process; placement in special education should not be viewed as inevitable. With ADHD, resources for interventions beyond medical treatment are widely available. Home- and school-based strategies can be implemented collaboratively so that teachers and parents consistently address Will's strengths and needs. Through discussion, they have identified several strengths including Will's capacity to build positive adult and peer relationships. One skill he needs to improve is working independently. Will's teachers and parents will verbally reinforce target behaviors and practice selectively ignoring attention-seeking behaviors (U.S. Department of Education, 2005). Similarly, they identify common sources of Will's inattention so teachers can modify the classroom environment. Will's parents share their success with checklists and direction sequences. Teachers, concerned about Will's ability to use strategies independ-

ently, will implement a self-management system with him so that he monitors his progress. More time is necessary to determine Will's progress; the discussion of medical treatment and special education referral is tabled.

Questions

1. How might the involvement of parents increase the effectiveness of prereferral interventions for students from diverse cultural/linguistic backgrounds?
2. If Will is diagnosed as having AD/HD, how could teachers meet his academic needs while honoring the religious beliefs of his family?

REFERENCES

Delpit, L. (2006). Lessons from teachers. *Journal of Teacher Education, 57,* 220–231.

U.S. Department of Education. (2005). *Teaching Children with Attention and Hyperactivity Disorder: Instructional Strategies and Practices.* Washington, DC: IDEAs that Work.

Side Effects Checklist: Stimulants

Child _____ Date Checked _____

Person Completing Form _____ Relationship to Child _____

I. SIDE EFFECTS

Directions: Please check any of the behaviors which this child exhibits while receiving his or her stimulant medication. If a child exhibits one or more of the behaviors below, please rate the extent to which you perceive the behavior to be a problem using the scale below (1 = Mild to 7 = Severe).

		Mild						Severe
1.	Loss of appetite	1	2	3	4	5	6	7
2.	Stomachaches	1	2	3	4	5	6	7
3.	Headaches	1	2	3	4	5	6	7
4.	Tics (vocal or motor)	1	2	3	4	5	6	7
5.	Extreme mood changes	1	2	3	4	5	6	7
6.	Cognitively sluggish/disoriented	1	2	3	4	5	6	7
7.	Excessive irritability	1	2	3	4	5	6	7
8.	Excessive nervousness	1	2	3	4	5	6	7
9.	Decreased social interactions	1	2	3	4	5	6	7
10.	Unusual or bizarre behavior	1	2	3	4	5	6	7
11.	Excessive activity level	1	2	3	4	5	6	7
12.	Light picking of fingertips	1	2	3	4	5	6	7
13.	Lip licking	1	2	3	4	5	6	7

II. PSYCHOSOCIAL CONCERNS

Please address any concerns you have about this child's adjustment to medication (e.g., physical, social, emotional changes; attitudes toward the medication, etc.).

III. OTHER CONCERNS

If you have any other concerns about this child's medication (e.g., administration problems, dosage concerns), please comment below.

IV. PARENT CONCERNS (FOR PARENTS ONLY)

Using the same scale above, please check any behaviors that this child exhibits while at home.

		Mild						Severe
1.	Insomnia; sleeplessness	1	2	3	4	5	6	7
2.	Possible rebound effects (excessive hyperactivity, impulsivity, inattention)	1	2	3	4	5	6	7

Figure 8.6

Stimulant Side Effects Checklist

From *ADHD Project Facilitate: An In-Service Education Program for Educators and Parents* (p. 10), by R. Elliott, L. A. Worthington, and D. Patterson, 1993. Tuscaloosa: University of Alabama. Used by permission.

For some children, the desired effects do not occur. In these situations the medication has no negative effect, but simply does not lead to the hoped-for results. However, parents and teachers often give up too soon, prematurely concluding that the medication did not help. It is important to contact the physician when no effect is noticed, because the dosage may need to be adjusted or a different type of medication may be needed. Barkley (2000) reports that when individuals continue to try different stimulants when one fails, the success rate rises to 90 percent.

Another possible response to medication is side effects. Side effects are changes that are not desired, such as insomnia. The most common side effect, loss of appetite, occurs more than 50 percent of the time; however, it has not been found to affect adult stature (Barkley, 2000). Figure 8.6 shows the most common side effects of the medications used for ADHD. Parents and teachers may use this rating scale when communicating with one another and physicians. Teachers should be on the lookout for signs of side effects and report any concerns to parents or the child's physician. Parents should also be informed that there are no studies on the long-term effects of using psychostimulants (Valente, 2001).

The most commonly prescribed medications for ADHD are psychostimulants, such as Ritalin and Concerta (methylphenidate); Adderall (amphetamine salts); and Cylert (dextroamphetamine); (Austin, 2003) . Studies have shown that Ritalin accounts for 90 percent of the market in stimulants prescribed (Weyandt, 2001). This medication is considered a mild central nervous system stimulant; it is effective for approximately four hours and is at its peak after one and a half to two and a half hours. A typical dosage of Ritalin for an initial trial is 5 mg, two to three times daily. The dosage will be increased until the optimal response is obtained with the fewest side effects. The medication is thought to stimulate the underaroused central nervous system of individuals with ADHD, increasing the amount or efficiency of the neurotransmitters needed for attention, concentration, and planning (Weyandt, 2001). Students who are described as anxious or tense, have tics, or have a family history or diagnosis of Tourette's syndrome are generally not given Ritalin. Adderall is gaining in use partly because it is effective for up to fifteen hours and a second dose does not have to be taken at school. The specific dose of medicine must be determined individually for each child. Generally, greater side effects come from higher dosages, but some students may need a high dosage to experience the positive effects of the medication. No clear guidelines exist as to how long an individual should take medication. Both adolescents and adults have been found to respond positively to these stimulants.

Antidepressants are also used to manage ADHD. They are prescribed less frequently than psychostimulants and might include Tofranil (imipramine), Norpramin (desipramine), and Elavil (amytriptyline). These medications are generally used when negative side effects have occurred with stimulants, when the stimulants have not been effective, or when an individual is also depressed. The long-term use of antidepressants has not been well studied. Again, frequent monitoring is necessary for responsible management. Other medications that are used much less frequently include antipsychotics such as Mellaril (thioridazine), Thorazine (chlorpromazine), Catapres (clonidine), Eskalith (lithium), and Tegretol (carbamazepine) (Austin, 2003). Whatever medication is prescribed by the child's physician, teachers should refer to the current *Physicians' Desk Reference* or ask the physician or pharmacist for a thorough description of the possible positive and negative outcomes for that medication. Table 8.1 contains a list of common myths associated with medication treatment for ADHD.

Remember, not all children diagnosed with ADHD need medication. The decision to intervene medically should come only after a great deal of thought about the possibility of a variety of interventions. Children whose impairments are minimal are certainly less likely to need medication than those whose severe impairments result in major disruptions. The following questions are recommended to be answered by the team before making the final decision to use medication (Austin, 2003):

- Is the child younger than six years? (Methylphenidate has not been approved for preschool children [Leo, 2002].)
- Have other interventions been tried and, if so, why were they ineffective?
- How severe are the child's current symptoms?
- Can the family afford the costs associated with pharmacological intervention?
- Can family members adequately supervise the use of medication and prevent abuse?
- What are the attitudes and cultural perspectives of family members toward medication?
- Is there a substance-abusing family member in the home?
- Does the child have concomitant disorders such as tics or mental illness?
- Is the child overly concerned about the effects of the medication?
- Does the physician seem committed to appropriate follow-up monitoring?

Table 8.1	**Common Myths Associated with ADHD Medications**
Myth	**Fact**
Medication should be stopped when a child reaches teen years.	Research clearly shows there is continued benefit to medication for those teens who meet criteria for diagnosis of ADHD.
Children tend to build up tolerance for medication.	Although the dose of medication may need adjusting from time to time due to weight gain or increased attention demands, there is no evidence that children build up a tolerance to medication.
Taking medicine for ADHD leads to greater likelihood of later drug dependency or addiction.	A study by the National Institutes of Health (2000) suggested that children and adolescents with ADHD who had used medication were less likely to engage in deviant behavior or substance abuse.
Positive response to medication is confirmation of a diagnosis of ADHD.	The fact that a child shows improvement of attention span or a reduction of activity while taking ADHD medication does not substantiate the diagnosis of ADHD. Even some normal children will show a marked improvement in attentiveness when they take ADHD medication.
Medication stunts growth.	ADHD medications may cause an initial and mild slowing of growth, but over time the growth suppression effect is minimal if not nonexistent in most cases.
Ritalin dulls a child's personality and can cause depression.	If a child's personality seems depressed or less spontaneous, the dosage should probably be lowered.
ADHD children who take medication attribute their success only to medication.	When self-esteem is encouraged, children taking medication attribute their success not only to the medication but to themselves as well.

Adapted from "What Teachers and Parents Should Know About Ritalin," by C. Pancheri and M. A. Prater, 1999, *Teaching Exceptional Children* (March/April), pp. 20–26.

- Is the child or adolescent involved in competitive sports or planning to enter the military? (The medication will be detected as a "controlled substance" in the course of urinalysis [Kollins et al., 2001].)

Although teachers and other school personnel are important members of a therapeutic team involved in exploring, implementing, and evaluating diverse treatment methods, the decision to try medication is primarily the responsibility of the parents and the physician. Figure 8.7 summarizes research providing guidance in the decisions leading to an optimal intervention plan that includes medication. Teachers are generally cautioned by their school systems not to specifically recommend medication because the school may be held responsible for the charges incurred. Educators, therefore, find themselves in a dilemma when they feel strongly that medication is needed to address the symptoms of ADHD. Since the studies are not conclusive, and individual parents may prefer not to use medication, it is best to prepare for a multimodal approach, including the cognitive and behavioral strategies addressed in the following section.

Occasionally teachers and parents will hear of alternative treatment therapies that seem to offer a "quick fix." These are often advertised in newspapers and popular magazines or seen on television, but they seldom appear in professional literature. Alternative approaches described by Silver (2000), and Weyandt (2001) include the use of megavitamins, diet restrictions (e.g., sugar or additives), caffeine, massage therapy, chiropractic skull manipulations, biofeedback, play therapy, and herbs. These authors caution that if an approach were that amazing, everyone would use it. They encourage asking to see the evidence supporting the treatment before submitting children to the treatment and investing resources.

| *Figure 8.7* | **Evidence-Based, Educationally Relevant Guidelines for Use of Medication** |

Guideline #1: When initiating medication treatment, be sure that your child is tested on a full range of doses. The optimum stimulant dosage for a child is not weight dependent, and it is not possible to predict in advance what the best dose—or most effective stimulant—will be for an individual child.

Guideline #2: Before medication treatment is implemented, parents should insist that a systematic procedure is in place to monitor the effectiveness of the different doses being tested. In a recent multisite study (the MTA Cooperative Group study, 1999), only 17 percent of the children with ADHD continued on the same medication and dosage throughout the entire thirteen-month maintenance period. The remaining children all experienced at least one change in drug or dosage during this period.

Determining the benefits of medication treatment needs to be far more systematic than anecdotal reports from a teacher that the child seems to be "doing better." In addition to ratings of core inattention and hyperactivity-impulsivity, it is important to obtain information on the child's academic functioning, social relations, and ability/willingness to follow rules at home and school. Effective treatment for ADHD should improve children's functioning in these key areas in addition to reducing core symptoms.

Guideline #3: Alternate types of stimulants should be tried before giving up on stimulant medication. As noted in the American Academy of Pediatrics (AAP) treatment guidelines, children may respond favorably to one stimulant but not another. For this reason, the guidelines recommend that two or three stimulant medications be tested across a full range of doses before nonstimulant medications are considered.

The only medications other than stimulants for which efficacy in treating ADHD in children has been demonstrated are tricyclic antidepressants, bupropion, and clonidine. These should be considered only after a child has not responded to a careful trial of two or three different stimulants. That is, there is not sufficient research supporting the safety and efficacy of combined pharmacotherapy for children with ADHD. Note: The use of Pemoline/Cylert is not recommended because of potential complications with liver functioning.

Guideline #4: The AAP guidelines compared behavioral techniques with stimulant medication. The guidelines indicated that the stimulants were more effective than behavioral techniques on the core symptoms of ADHD.

However, on some measures, children receiving combined behavioral and medication treatments:

1. showed greater improvement than children treated with medication alone.
2. required a significantly lower dose of medication over the fourteen-month study.
3. resulted in higher ratings of parent and teacher satisfaction with the treatment plan. As with stimulant medication, behavior therapy typically did not bring a child's behavior into the normal range and did not yield positive changes that persisted beyond the time it was being implemented (American Academy of Pediatrics, 2001).

From *ADHD and Education: Foundations Characteristics, Methods, and Collaboration* (p. 210), by S. S. Zentall, 2006. Upper Saddle River, NJ: Pearson.

Classroom Adaptations for Students with ADHD

Because no two children with ADHD are exactly alike, a wide variety of interventions and service options must be available to allow them to benefit from their education in the general education classroom. Any approach addressing the needs of students with ADHD must be comprehensive. Figure 8.8 depicts a model of educational intervention built on four areas: environmental management, instructional accommodations, student-regulated strategies, and medical management. The program planned for each student is developed by a team during a collaboration process and is based on the student's individual strengths and limitations identified during the assessment process. The medical management component of the model was described previously. Following is a discussion of the other strategies that might be used to make school a more positive experience for students with ADHD. Reread the story of Jake, the boy described in the opening vignette, and refer to his 504 plan that is shown on page 260.

Managing the Classroom Environment

A classroom with even one or two students with ADHD can be difficult to control if the teacher is not skilled in classroom management. Rather than reacting spontaneously—and often inconsistently—to disruptive situations, teachers should have a proactive

CONSIDER THIS

Do you think the team that developed Jake's 504 plan has addressed all the areas that will challenge Jake at school?

CEC STANDARDS

CEC 5: Learning Environments and Social Interactions

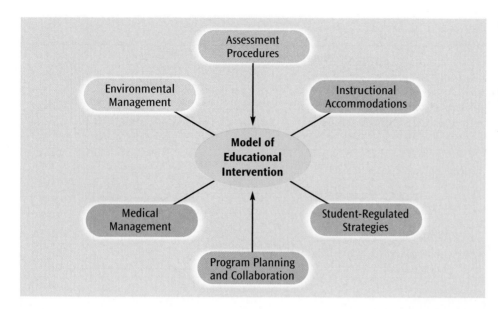

Figure 8.8

Model for ADHD Intervention

From *Attention-Deficit/Hyperactivity Disorder in the Classroom: A Practical Guide for Teachers* (p. 26), by by C. A. Dowdy, J. R. Patton, T. E. C. Smith, and E. A. Polloway, 1998. Austin, TX: Pro-Ed.

management system to help avoid crises. Good classroom management is beneficial for all students, including those with ADHD. Techniques that will be discussed include group management, management of the environment, and behavior management.

Group Management Group management techniques benefit all members of a class, but they are critical in managing the behavior of individual students with ADHD. One of the most basic and effective techniques is to establish classroom rules and consequences for breaking those rules. Children with ADHD need to understand the classroom rules and school procedures in order to be successful. Polloway, Patton, and Serna (2005) suggest that students feel more committed to following rules when they have contributed to developing them. The rules should be displayed prominently in the room and reviewed periodically if students with ADHD are to retain and follow them. It is important for teachers to apply the rules consistently, even though students can sometimes frustrate teachers and make them want to "give in." Teachers may start the process of rule development by offering one or two rules of their own and then letting the children pick up with their own ideas. The following is a list of recommendations for developing rules:

- State rules positively and clearly. A rule should tell students what to do instead of what not to do!
- Rules should be stated in simple terms so students can easily understand them. For young students, rules can be depicted with drawings and figures.
- The number of rules should be no more than five or six.
- Rules should be displayed conspicuously in the room.
- Rules should be practiced and discussed at the beginning of the year and periodically throughout the year.
- For students with ADHD, role-playing how to carry out the rules is an effective technique.
- Adopt rules and consequences that you are willing to enforce; then be consistent!
- Positively reinforce students who abide by the rules. It is more effective to reinforce the students who abide by the rules than to punish those who break them.
- To avoid misunderstandings, communicate rules and consequences to parents. It is helpful to have parents and students sign a contract documenting their understanding of the rules.

INTASC

INTASC 5: Learning environments

PRAXIS

PRAXIS II: Delivery of Services to Students with Disabilities

CROSS-REFERENCE

Teachers should develop a list of procedures to make the classroom run smoothly. For example, how should students request help? How should they respond during a fire drill? For more tips in this area, refer to Chapter 14.

CONSIDER THIS

What are some appropriate activities to begin and end the day or class period for elementary and secondary students?

Section 504 Plan for Jake

From *Section 504 and Public Schools* (p. 51) by T. E. C. Smith & J. R. Patton, 1998, Austin, TX: Pro-Ed. Used with permission.

Name: *Jake Smith*

School/Class: *11th grade — Central High School*

Teacher: *Pratt — History, Jordan — Literature*   Date: *9/29/97*

General Strengths: *Jake is a bright student, he wants to learn and make good grades. He is very ambitious and wants to go to college and become an engineer.*

General Weaknesses: *Jake has been diagnosed with ADHD. His attention span is very short and he is easily distracted. He frequently gets out of his seat and walks around the room.*

Specific Accommodations:

Accommodation #1

Class: *History*   Accommodation(s): *Jake will be given extra time to complete his assignments. He will be given assignments divided into shorter objectives so that his progress can be checked sooner.*

Person Responsible for Accommodation #1: *Mr. Pratt — teacher*

Accommodation #2

Class: *History*   Accommodation(s): *Jake will sit at the front of the class.*

Person Responsible for Accommodation #2: *Mr. Pratt — teacher*

Accommodation #3

Class: *Literature*   Accommodation(s): *Jake will work with selected other students in cooperative learning arrangements.*

Person Responsible for Accommodation #3: *Ms. Jordan — teacher*

Accommodation #4

Class: *Literature*   Accommodation(s): *An assignment notebook will be sent home each day with specific assignments noted. Parents will sign the assignment notebook daily and return it to school.*

Person Responsible for Accommodation #4: *Ms. Jordan — teacher*

Accommodation #5

Class: *All classes*   Accommodation(s): *A behavior management plan will be developed and implemented for Jake for the entire day. The plan will include time for Jake to take Ritalin and will focus on positive reinforcement.*

Person Responsible for Accommodation #5: *Ms. Baker — asst. prin.*

General Comments:
Jake's plan will be reviewed at the end of the fall term to ensure that it is meeting his needs.

Individuals Participating in Development of Accommodation Plan:

William Pratt — teacher   *Fred Haynes — 504 Coor.*

Bonita Jordan — teacher   *Hank Smith — father*

Mary Baker — asst. prin.

Time Management Time management is also important in effective classroom management. Students with ADHD thrive in an organized, structured classroom. Acting out and inappropriate behavior often occur during unscheduled, unstructured free time, when the number of choices of activities may become overwhelming. If free time is scheduled, limit the choices and provide positive reinforcement for appropriate behavior during free time. Encourage students to investigate topics that interest them and to complete projects that bring their strengths into play. Figure 8.9 provides information regarding the types of classroom events that might trigger negative behavior for children with ADHD and other types of disabilities. Understanding these antecedent events can help teachers make adjustments that allow more children to benefit from their education in a general education classroom.

Polloway and Patton (2005) suggest that teachers begin each day with a similar routine. The particular activity is not as important as the consistency. For example, some teachers like to start the day with quiet reading or music, whereas others might begin with singing, recognizing birthdays, or talking about special events that are coming up. This routine sets the stage for a calm orderly day, and students will know what to expect from the teacher. Secondary teachers need to advise students of scheduling changes (e.g., assembly, pep rally) and provide a brief overview of the topics and activities to be expected during the class period.

Like the beginning of the day, closure on the day's or the class period's activities is important for secondary students. Reviewing the important events of the day and describing the next day's activities help students with ADHD. This is also an excellent time for teachers to provide rewards for students who have maintained appropriate behavior during the day. If parents are involved in a contract, this is the time to discuss the transmitted notes and to review homework that might have been assigned during the day.

Teachers may want to offer incentives to individual students and groups to reward outstanding work. A teacher might place a marble in a jar each time students are "caught being good." When the jar is filled the class receives an award such as a picnic or a skating party. Another technique involves adding a piece to a puzzle whenever the teacher recognizes that the class is working especially hard. When the puzzle is complete, the class is rewarded. These group incentives can be very effective; however, some students will need an individual contract or behavior management plan to help direct their behavior. Babkie (2006) offers the following additional tips for proactive classroom management:

- Make boundaries clear for appropriate interactions with you and peers. Remember you are not your students' friend—you are their teacher. Be sympathetic and supportive but reinforce the boundaries.
- Cue students when activities are about to change and teach transitioning skills.
- Teach cognitive strategies to facilitate success in academic and social environments.
- Pace lessons and alter the workload based on student needs and responses instead of punishing students for not "keeping up."
- Give learning a purpose by providing real-world uses for new skills.
- Use activity-based activities that are not always a paper-and-pencil task or test.
- At all times, be respectful toward students. Consider how you would want to be treated. Ensure that students are comfortable in the classroom and feel like successful, contributing members.

Physical Management The physical environment of a classroom can also have an impact on the behavior of students with ADHD. The arrangement of the room is most important. The classroom needs to be large enough for students to have space between themselves and others, so they will be less likely to impose themselves on one another. Each student needs some personal space. The student with ADHD may need to be near the teacher in order to focus attention on the information being presented in the classroom; however, students should never be placed near the teacher as a punitive measure.

> **CONSIDER THIS**
>
> Become familiar with these triggers so you can apply your knowledge later in the chapter.

| *Figure 8.9* | **Antecedents That often Trigger Negative Behaviors for Children with Different Exceptionalies** |

Students with ADHD
Behavior difficulties will increase when:

- the task is effortful in its length, repetitiveness, and nonmeaningfulness;
- little opportunity exists for movement or choice;
- few opportunities exist for active involvement in learning;
- many students and only one teacher are present, and learning is large-group teacher directed;
- little supervision, feedback, or positive reinforcement takes place;
- periods of transition exist with little structure (for a review, see Zentall, 1993, 1995).

Students with ADHD Plus Aggression
Aggression occurs primarily:

- when entering new groups;
- when resources are scarce or information is needed;
- during low structure;
- during difficult tasks;
- when little flexibility exists;
- when few adults and much activity are present;
- when no apparent way to escape tasks or social demands is available;
- when a peer group values "toughness."

Students with ADHD Plus Learning Disabilities
Task avoidance behavior, such as off-task behavior, occurs primarily when:

- presented with a task that is within the student's area of specific learning disability (e.g., with reading requirements, mathematical calculations);
- presented with any kind of auditory input, such as listening tasks, group discussion, social interactions (in these contexts the child may be more likely to actively refuse, avoid, or act disruptively);
- presented with complex visual input, such as copying from the board or from dictionary to paper, art tasks using collage (with such tasks, the child may take a long time to produce work);
- asked to respond in certain ways (e.g., fine motor handwriting or talking) (with such response requirements, the child may avoid or become negative and noncompliant).

Students with ADHD and Giftedness
Off-task or disruptive behavior is observed primarily when:

- tasks are too easy;
- teachers believe that if the child can't do the easy work, he or she can't do the challenging work;
- tasks involve a lot of rote lower-level skills.

Students with ADHD and Developmental Disabilities
Disruptive behavior and poor performance occur primarily:

- during difficult, complex, higher-level tasks that require problem solving, analysis, synthesis, or reasoning abilities.

Students with ADHD and Anxiety
Avoidance, inflexible, or repetitive behavior occurs:

- when entering new groups;
- in the presence of a lot of activity and confusion;
- during difficult or unstructured (ambiguous) tasks;
- when it is noisy;
- when unpredictable activities that have not been scheduled are provided or changes in a schedule have been made.

From *ADHD and Education: Foundations, Characteristics, methods, and Collaboration* (pp. 73–74), by S.S. Zentall, 2006. Upper Saddle River, NJ: Pearson.

A seat near the front may help the student who is distracted by someone's new hairstyle or flashy jewelry.

There should also be various places in the room where: quiet activities can take place; small groups can work together; sustained attention for difficult tasks can be maintained; and a relaxed and comfortable environment can be enjoyed for a change of pace. At one time, classrooms with lots of visual stimulation were considered inappropriate for students with ADHD, leading to the creation of sterile environments with colorless walls and no bulletin boards. This is no longer considered necessary; however, order is needed in the classroom. Assignments should be posted in the same location daily, materials and completed assignments should be placed consistently in the same place so students will be able to return them, and bulletin boards should be uncluttered. Set aside places where students who seem to be overstimulated can work in a carrel or other private space with minimal visual and auditory stimuli, and have a place for a child who seems underaroused to be able to move around and get rejuvenated (Carbone, 2001). Make sure to consider transition skills for these students. Figure 8.10 provides a strategy to help with transition.

Behavioral Support   Behavioral support techniques can enhance the education of students with ADHD, especially those that reward desired behavior. For example, when students with ADHD are attending to their tasks, following classroom rules, or participating appropriately in a cooperative learning activity, their behaviors should be positively reinforced. Unfortunately, teachers often ignore appropriate behavior and call attention only to what is inappropriate. When students receive attention for actions that are disruptive or inconsiderate, the negative behaviors can be reinforced and may thus increase in frequency. The Personal Spotlight presents a unique example of a student with ADHD who experienced behavior problems in school.

Positive reinforcement tends to increase appropriate behavior. Teachers should consider which rewards appeal most to the individuals who will receive them. Common ones include small toys, candy and other edibles, free time, time to listen to music, time in the gym, opportunities to do things for the teacher, having lunch with the teacher, praise, or hugs. Because a reward that acts as a reinforcer for one student may not work for another, teachers might generate a menu of rewards and allow students to select their own. Rewards do not have to be expensive; in fact, simply allowing students to take a break, time to get a drink of water, or time to sharpen a pencil, or giving a homework pass may be just as effective as expensive toys and games.

Another behavior-management technique is cuing or signaling students with ADHD when they are on the verge of inappropriate behavior. First, student and teacher sit down privately and discuss the inappropriate behavior that has been creating problems in the classroom. The teacher offers to provide a cue when the behavior begins to be noticed. Teachers and students can have fun working together on the signal, which might involve flipping the light switch, tapping the desk lightly, or simple eye contact. These cuing techniques help establish a collegial relationship between the teacher and

CEC STANDARDS

CEC 5: Learning Environment and Social Interactions

INTASC

INTASC 5: Learning environment

PRAXIS

PRAXIS II: Delivery of Services to Students with Disabilities

CONSIDER THIS

These ideas are effective with elementary-age students. Generate some reinforcers that would be more effective in secondary settings.

Figure **8.10**   **The Change Strategy to Teach Transitioning Skills**

Collect my materials and put them away.
Have ready what I need for the next activity
Always watch my teacher for cues to move
Now take my seat quietly
Get my materials out and ready for the next activity
Encourage my peers to get started

From "Be Proactive in Managing Classrooms" (p. 185) by A. M. Babkie, 2006, *Intervention in School and Clinic,* 41(3).

Personal Spotlight

Growing Up with ADHD

Dave Birt has had ADHD as long as he can remember. Now age twenty-nine, he feels that he is still working to counteract the negative experiences of his school days. Upon entering kindergarten, he could already read, and throughout elementary school he felt impatient when waiting for his peers to catch up. He qualified for the gifted program with an IQ well into the genius range, but even that program couldn't give him enough to do. He says, "The teachers would repeat things over and over. They only had to tell me once, and I learned it." As a result, Dave filled his time entertaining himself, and he soon became a behavior problem in the classroom. He was shuffled around suburban Pennsylvania school districts, but no one knew what to do for him. Soon, he simply became labeled a "troublemaker."

In the eighth grade, Dave was officially diagnosed with ADHD, but teachers still didn't know how to instruct him in the traditional classroom. The primary problem with the adaptations was the social stigma attached to them. For example, teachers had him keep assignment journals, but this special treatment made him feel like an outcast, so he didn't do it. The same applied to Ritalin—he didn't think it would help, and he wanted to avoid the stigma, so he didn't take it. Finally, a rural school district placed him in the program for students with behavior problems. Dave remembers, "They put me in the 'sped shed,' a program where the teacher had fewer students and could keep a closer eye on them. It worked to a point, but it was based on the idea that bad kids are dumb. My misbehavior was rebellion against being treated like an idiot or an attempt

Dave Birt
Boston, MA

to keep myself entertained." Furthermore, the program was set up only for homeroom, study halls, and lunch, so it deprived students of important socializing opportunities with the rest of the school. Dave was reluctant to socialize with the other students in the program, some of whom are now in prison. He feels that the development of his social skills suffered as a result.

Eventually, Dave tired of this routine. He signed himself out of school in eleventh grade and took the GED, scoring in the 97th percentile. He later joined the army, but the ADHD didn't allow him the patience necessary to wait for his peers to catch on to whatever they were doing.

Finally, Dave discovered something that held his interest—computers. He started his own small business building custom computers for clients, and he also took night classes and earned IT certifications. Currently he works for the wireless communications company Nextel, and he is considering attending college, perhaps to become a computer teacher. Because of his school experiences, though, he is hesitant about going back into the classroom as a full-time student. "What if I have professors who don't understand ADHD?" he worries. "I'm not going through that again." Still, he says, "I think I could be a good teacher because I understand how kids think. You have to keep them interested in order for them to learn."

the student that says, "We are working on this together; we have a problem, but we also have a plan" (Wood, 2006).

A functional behavioral assessment may be needed to develop the most effective behavioral plan. Table 8.2 provides a guide for conducting a functional behavioral assessment. Often students need an individual contract that focuses on their particular needs. The student and teacher develop the goals to improve behavior together and then put these goals in writing. The contract provides structure and becomes an explicit way to communicate with children with ADHD and their parents. Downing (2002) offers the following guidelines for making and using such contracts:

- Determine the most critical area(s) of concern.
- Consider when the behavior usually occurs, the events that trigger it, and why you think the behavior is occurring.
- Specify the desired behavior in measurable terms, using clear, simple words.
- Specify the reinforcers that will be used and the consequences that will follow if the contract is not fulfilled.
- See that both teacher and student sign the contract (and the parents, when appropriate).
- Keep a record of the student's behavior.

> **TEACHING TIP**
>
> One of the reasons children with ADHD don't take their medication or follow through with classroom adaptations is their embarrassment in front of peers. As a teacher, how can you provide accommodations for students with ADHD in a way that minimizes the stigma of special treatment?

Table 8.2	Guidelines for Conducting a Functional Behavioral Assessment
Guidelines	**Questions**
1. Identify the problematic behavior.	What does the student do that causes a problem? How does the behavior affect the student's learning? Is there a relationship between the behavior and the student's cultural and language background?
2. Define the behavior.	Have I defined the behavior in observable and measurable terms?
3. Record the behavior using an observational recording system.	What observational recording system will use to record the behavior? (See Salend, 2001, for examples of recording systems—event recording, duration and latency recording, interval recording or time sampling, and anecdotal records.)
4. Obtain additional information about the student and the behavior.	Have I determined the student's skills, strengths, weaknesses, interests, hobbies, self-concept, attitudes, culture, language, and experiences?
5. Perform an antecedents-behavior-consequences (A-B-C) analysis.	Have I considered the events, stimuli, objects, actions, and activities that precede and trigger the behavior? Have I considered the behaviors that follow and maintain the behavior?
6. Analyze the data and develop hypotheses.	Have I examined the data to determine when, where, with whom, and under what conditions the behavior is most likely and least likely to occur? What is the purpose of the behavior? Is the behavior related to the student's disability?
7. Consider sociocultural factors.	Is the student's behavior related to her or his cultural perspectives and language background?
8. Develop a behavioral intervention plan.	Have I identified specific measurable goals that focus on the student's behavior, characteristics, and needs? Do these goals relate to the antecedents and consequences of the student's behavior?
9. Evaluate the plan.	Have I continued to collect data to determine the effectiveness of the behavior management plan? Does the plan need to be revised? Should the intervention (or interventions) be changed?

Adapted from *Creating Inclusive Classrooms: Effective and Reflective Practices* (4th ed.), by S. J. Salend, 2001: Upper Saddle River, NJ: Prentice Hall.

- Provide the agreed-upon consequences or reinforcements in a timely fashion.
- When the goal is reached, celebrate, and write a new contract! (A sample contract is provided in Figure 8.11)

Making Instructional Adaptations

Children with ADHD do not have a problem with skills, they have problems with performance. However, these students are often misunderstood and labeled lazy or unmotivated, as if they are choosing not to perform at their maximum potential. Teacher comments such as "I know you can do this work, because you did it yesterday," or "You can do better; you just aren't trying" probably suggest a lack of understanding of the inconsistent performance characteristic of this disability (Flick, 1998). Instead, teachers need to find ways to cope with the frustration and stress sometimes involved in working with these students, while modifying their teaching style, their curriculum, and possibly their expectations in order to engineer academic success for these students.

Modifying Teacher Behavior Since students with ADHD are not easily stimulated, they need novelty and excitement in their learning environment. Although complete and thorough directions, structure, and consistency are extremely important, students

Figure 8.11

An Example of a Contingency Contract

From "Individualized Behavior Contracts," by J. A. Downing, 2002, *Intervention in School and Clinic, 37*(3), p. 170.

I, Bobby, agree to:

▶ Follow the classroom rules and teacher's directions.

▶ Handle conflict situations appropriately, using the strategies I have learned rather than running away.

▶ Express my negative feelings in a calm, quiet voice without making threats and/or refusing to do what I am told.

For this effort, I will earn:

▶ Fifteen minutes of free time at the end of each successful day to play *The Magic School Bus Explores the Rainforest* computer game.

▶ A visit from Billy the Boa Constrictor at the end of every week if I am successful for at least 4 out of 5 days.

Date:

Student Signature:

Teacher Signature:

need challenging, exciting activities to keep them focused and learning. The Internet offers endless ideas for "jazzing up" lesson plans or developing new ones. See the nearby Technology Today feature to explore some options.

Weyandt (2001) reports that the incidence of inappropriate behavior increases during nonstimulating, repetitive activities. She suggests that teachers vary activities, allow and encourage movement that is purposeful and not disruptive, and even let students stand as they listen, take notes, or perform other academic tasks. "Legal movement," such as pencil sharpening or a hall pass for walking to the restroom or getting water, might be preapproved for a student's restless times (Guyer, 2000). Here are some recommendations from Zentall (2006) for best practice in teaching strategies:

- Don't try to accomplish so much in one time period.
- Give frequent beaks or shorter assignments.
- Increase novelty—use treasure hunts, games, group projects. For example, play the game "What's My Verb?" where one team acts out a verb for the other team to guess and use the word in a sentence.
- Use technology.
- Incorporate student interests.
- Use "real-world" projects. For example, "If we have $100 for a party, what could we afford for refreshments and entertainment?"
- Alternate high-interest and low-interest tasks.
- Increase opportunities for motor responses during or after a task. For example, use flash cards, games, and timed drills.
- Do not take away recess or other special classes. One young man said that he learned to dawdle more because he never got recess anyway.

- Assign unique topics and assignments.
- Allow students to "play" with objects during lectures or longer tasks.

During a long lecture period, teachers might also list main ideas or important questions on the chalkboard or by using the overhead projector, to help students focus on the most important information. When a student's attention does wander, a small, unobtrusive signal such as a gentle pat on the student's shoulder can cue the student to return to the task. To perk up tiring students, teachers can try a quick game of Simon Says or assign purposeful physical activities such as taking a note to the office, feeding the animals in the classroom, or returning books to the library.

Motivating these students can be difficult but should be a high priority. Smith, Salend, and Ryan (2001) suggest using a competency-oriented approach where students are referred to in terms of their strengths and where all students are given opportunities to assume leadership roles. They encourage teachers to offer the students choices and ask for their preferences. Establish rapport by talking to them about topics that interest them; attend after school events and cultural activities. Also important is creating a positive learning atmosphere by demonstrating your love of teaching and learning (Salend, 2001)!

Modifying the Curriculum   Although students with ADHD are typically taught in the general education classroom using the regular curriculum, they need a curriculum that focuses on "doing" and avoids long periods of sitting and listening. Such adaptations can benefit all students. For example, experience-based learning, in which students might develop their own projects, perform experiments, or take field trips, can help all students grow as active learners. Resources can be found in story problems included in traditional textbooks, curriculum-based experiments and projects, or extended activities such as writing letters to environmental groups to obtain more information than is offered in a textbook.

Teachers are also encouraged to vary their assessment techniques. Oral examinations, multiple-choice instead of essay or short answer, take-home tests, open-book or open-note exams, portfolio assessment, and informal measures are alternative assessment methods that provide a different perspective on what students know. Students with ADHD will generally be able to take the same tests as their peers; however, testing adaptations may be needed to specifically address the ADHD characteristics. These might include extra time to take the test (usually no more than time and a half), frequent breaks, taking the exam in a distraction-reduced environment, or using a computer to record responses. See the nearby feature "Tips for Adapting a Lesson for Jake" for examples of how to meet the needs of an individual student.

CONSIDER THIS

If you are currently teaching, complete the Time-on-Task Self-Assessment; if not, rewrite the questions and use them as an observation tool to evaluate a teacher who is willing to be observed. Analyze the results and identify changes that are indicated to improve learning in the classroom.

CEC STANDARDS

CEC 4: Instructional Strategies

TECHNOLOGY Today

Web Tools for Lesson Plans

Use tools available on the Internet like the following to enhance lesson plans and shorten preparation time:

- www.teach-nology.com/web_tools/rubrics/ Helps create assessment rubrics for any content area.

- www.classbuilder.com/
- www.edhelper.com/ Generates work sheets and puzzles for any content area.
- teachers.teach-nology.com/web_tools/ Generates planners, bingo cards, learning contracts, and more.
- www.educationalpress.org/educationalpress/ Focuses on flashcards and game boards for beginning reading skills.

- www.theeducatorsnetwork.com Provides comprehensive links to lessons.
- www.schoolexpress.com/ E-mails a free thematic unit each week.
- www.kimskorner4teachertalk.com Provides bulletin board ideas, icebreakers, and more.

Developing Student-Regulated Strategies

The previous sections on classroom environment and instructional accommodations focused on activities that the teacher directs and implements to increase the success of children with ADHD. This section describes student-regulated strategies. The following discussion provides an overview of four types of student-regulated strategies: study and organizational tactics, self-management, learning strategies, and social skills. These will be addressed in more detail in Chapters 15 and 16.

Study and Organizational Tactics   Students with ADHD have difficulty organizing their work and developing effective, independent study skills in general education classrooms. To help them with organization, teachers may designate space for students to keep materials that is periodically cleaned out and organized, establish the routine of students writing down their assignments daily in an assignment notebook, and provide notebooks or folders in different colors for each subject. Pierangelo and Giuliani (2006) suggest the following techniques to assist students with ADHD to develop study skills necessary for academic success:

- Teach children how to use Venn diagrams to organize new information in academic subjects.
- Teach children how to use a note-taking strategy such as Anita Archer's Skills for School Success (Archer & Gleason, 2002).
- Provide children with checklists that identify categories of items needed at home and school for various assignments. They can remember to check lists for themselves before departing.
- Teach children how to "unclutter" and organize their workspace for more efficient work.
- Involve children and parents in ongoing monitoring of homework.

Students should practice planning as an organizational strategy. Before being given an assignment such as a term paper, students should practice deciding how to break the task into small parts and how to complete each part. Students should also practice estimating

Tips for Adapting a Lesson for Jake

Since Jake's primary limitations include a short attention span, impulsive movement, and being easily distracted (as described in the chapter-opening vignette), the teacher's adaptations listed in his 504 plan and those recommended here should limit the impact of these challenges and help Jake make the good grades he needs to go to college.

Jake's teacher should:

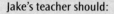

- allow Jake to sit by students who generally remain on task;
- provide a copy of notes and overheads;
- color-code or underline important concepts;
- give Jake permission to leave the room occasionally or to walk in back of the room to provide authorized movement and not create a disturbance;
- take tests in a distraction-reduced environment and give extra time as needed;
- check often for understanding and review;
- vary activities.

how much time is needed for various activities so they can establish appropriate and realistic goals. Outlining skills can also help with organization and planning. Students may want to use a word processor to order their ideas and to help organize their work.

Self-Management   The primary goal of programs that teach self-management or self-control is to "make children more consciously aware of their own thinking processes and task approach strategies, and to give them responsibility for their own reinforcement" (Reeve, 1990, p. 76). Here are some advantages of teaching self-control:

- It saves the teacher's time by decreasing the demand for direct instruction.
- It increases the effectiveness of an intervention.
- It increases the maintenance of skills over time.

Cuing or signaling students is one method that teachers can use to help get their attention.

Polloway and Patton (2005) cite four types of self-regulation. In self-assessment, the individual determines the need for change and also monitors personal behavior. In self-monitoring, the student attends to specific aspects of his or her own behavior. While learning to self-monitor, a student can be given a periodic beep or other cue to signal that it is time for him or her to evaluate "on" or "off" task behavior. In self-instruction, the student cues himself or herself to inhibit inappropriate behaviors or to express appropriate ones. In self-reinforcement, the student administers self-selected reinforcement for an appropriate behavior that has been previously specified. Figure 8.12 contains a self-management strategy used to help students deal with anger. Figure 8.13 provides a self-monitoring sheet for the student to use to reflect on his or her use of the strategy. Eventually the student will begin to automatically self-monitor and will begin to use the appropriate response to situations that previously triggered an inappropriate display of anger. Other behaviors commonly targeted for self-regulation include completing assignments, appropriate classroom behavior (such as staying in one's seat), accuracy of work (such as percent correct), and staying on task.

1. **W**ATCH for the "trigger."
    - Count to 10.
    - Use relaxation techniques.

2. **A**NSWER, "Why am I angry?"

3. **I**DENTIFY my options.
    - Ignore the other person.
    - Move away.
    - Resolve the problem.
    - "I feel this way when you . . ."
    - Listen to the other person.
    - Talk to the teacher.

4. **T**RY an appropriate option for dealing with my anger.

Figure **8.12**

A Self-Management Strategy for Dealing with Anger

From "Collaborating to Teach Prosocial Skills," by D. H. Allsopp, K. E. Santos, and R. Linn, 2000, *Intervention in School and Clinic,* 35(3), p. 145.

Figure 8.13 **A Self-Monitoring Sheet for Dealing with Anger**

What was the trigger?	Why was I angry?	Did I identify my options?	What option did I choose and was it successful?
1.			
2.			
3.			
4.			
5.			

From "Collaborating to Teach Prosocial Skills," by D. H. Allsopp, K. E. Santos, and R. Linn, 2000, *Intervention in School and Clinic, 35*(3), p. 146.

CEC STANDARDS

CEC 4: Instructional Strategies

INTASC

INTASC 4: Instructional strategies

PRAXIS

PRAXIS II: Delivery of Services to Students with Disabilities

Learning Strategies Deshler and Lenz (1989) define a learning strategy as an individual's approach to a task. It includes how an individual thinks and acts when planning, executing, or evaluating performance. The learning strategies approach combines what is going on in an individual's head (cognition) with what a person actually does (behavior) to guide the performance and evaluation of a specific task. All individuals use strategies; however, not all strategies are effective. Strichart and Mangrum (2002) recommend this approach to assist students who are inefficient learners.

Babkie and Provost (2002) encourage teachers and students to create their own strategies or cues to teach a difficult concept or behavior. A key word is identified that specifies the targeted area. A short phrase or sentence that tells the student what to do is written for each letter in the key word. Figure 8.14 shows a strategy developed to cue students to organize homework.

Social Skills Because students with ADHD often do not exhibit good problem-solving skills and are not able to predict the consequences of their inappropriate behavior, specific and direct instruction in social skills may be necessary. Although it is better for students to be able to assess their own inappropriate behavior and adjust it to acceptable standards, many students may need social-skills training first. For example, students who misread or totally miss social cues can benefit from role-playing situations where problems have previously occurred. A fight on the playground, inappropriately interrupting a teacher, or a

Figure 8.14

A Learning Strategy for Homework

Organization: **HOMEWORK**
Have a place to work
Organize assignments according to difficulty
Make sure to follow directions
Examine the examples
Weave my way through the assignments
Observe work for errors and omissions
Return work to school
Keep up the effort!

From "Select, Write, and Use Metacognitive Strategies in the Classroom" (p. 174) by A. M. Babkie and M. C. Provost, 2002, *Intervention in School and Clinic,* 37(3).

shoving incident in the lunchroom may be examples where reenacting the event under controlled circumstances allows students to proactively rehearse correct responses for future social encounters. Repeated opportunities to practice appropriate social skills may be needed for the correct responses to be internalized (Garrick Duhaney, 2003).

Promoting Inclusive Practices for ADHD

The Professional Group for Attention and Related Disorders (PGARD) proposes that most children with ADHD can be served in the general education program by trained teachers providing appropriate instruction and modifications. In addition to activities that teachers can use to promote a supportive classroom environment, Korinek, Walther-Thomas, McLaughlin, and Williams (1999) suggest that schoolwide support be promoted through disability-awareness activities, the use of positive discipline, and the use of adult volunteers. They add that the entire community can become involved through the establishment of business partnerships and the provision of organized activities like scouting and other forms of sports and recreation. Of course, school administrators have to make a commitment to dedicate resources for training and to facilitate change.

The two critical features for successful inclusion of students with ADHD are the skills and behaviors of the teachers and the understanding and acceptance of the general education peers.

Community-Building Skills for Teachers

One of the most important aspects of promoting success for children with ADHD is the teacher. Fowler (1992) suggests that success for children with ADHD might vary from year to year, class to class, teacher to teacher. She reports that the most commonly cited reason for a positive or negative school experience is the teacher. She cites the following seventeen characteristics of teachers as likely indicators of positive learning outcomes for students with ADHD; the effectiveness of these traits is timeless:

1. positive academic expectations
2. frequent review of student work
3. clarity of teaching (e.g., explicit directions, rules)
4. flexibility
5. fairness
6. active interaction with the students
7. responsiveness
8. warmth
9. patience
10. humor
11. structured and predictable approach
12. consistency
13. firmness
14. positive attitude toward inclusion
15. knowledge of and willingness to work with students with exceptional needs
16. knowledge of different types of effective interventions
17. willingness to work collaboratively with other teachers (e.g., sharing information, requesting assistance as needed, participating in conferences involving students) (p. 17)

Resources for Developing Awareness in Peers

Teachers with the traits listed in the preceding section will provide a positive role model for general education students in how to understand and accept children with ADHD. Teachers should confer with parents and the child with ADHD to obtain advice on explaining ADHD to other students in the classroom. The child with ADHD may wish to be present during the explanation or even to participate in informing his or her classmates. The following books and publications may help introduce this topic to students with ADHD and their peers.

Jumping Johnny Get Back to Work—A Child's Guide to ADHD/Hyperactivity
By Michael Gordon, Ph.D.,
Connecticut Association for Children with LD
18 Marshall Street
South Norwalk, CT 06854
203-838-5010

Shelley, the Hyperactive Turtle
By Deborah Moss
Woodbine House
5616 Fishers Lane
Rockville, MD 20852
800-843-7323

Sometimes I Drive My Mom Crazy, but I Know She's Crazy about Me!
Childworks
Center for Applied Psychology Inc.
P.O. Box 61586
King of Prussia, PA 19406
800-962-1141

You Mean I'm Not Lazy, Stupid, or Crazy?
By Peggy Ramundo and Kate Kelly
Tyrell & Jerem Press
P.O. Box 20089
Cincinnati, OH 45220
800-622-6611

Otto Learns about His Medicine
By Michael Gaivin, M.D.
Childworks
Center for Applied Psychology Inc.
P.O. Box 61586
King of Prussia, PA 19406
800-962-1141

Eagle Eyes: A Child's View of Attention Deficit Disorder
By Jeanne Gehret, M.A.
Childworks
Center for Applied Psychology Inc.
P.O. Box 61586
King of Prussia, PA 19406
800-962-1141

Collaborating with Parents of Students with ADHD

Evelyn Green, president of the CHADD National Board of Directors and a parent of a child with ADHD, stresses the importance of teachers and other professionals in supporting and helping parents. In an interview (Chamberlain, 2003), she offers the following insight:

I think professionals are not always sympathetic to the fact that for most parents, it is initially devastating when they discover that their child is not the "perfect" little person that they have dreamed about. But it isn't hopeless and doesn't have to remain devastating if you use a strength-based approach, if you help the child discover her or his talents and strengths and build from there. Professionals can be extremely helpful to parents in getting over the initial feelings of helplessness and in finding the child's strengths. . . . Parents absolutely have to have somebody who knows and understands, who does not blame them . . . who will let you know that there is a next step to get to and whatever challenges you are facing now will pass. Having that kind of support system has certainly been one of our [family's] keys to success.

Brandes (2005) stresses the importance of keeping parents involved in their child's education through meaningful communications. She offers these recommendations to promote healthy relationships based on respect:

- Be an active listener, sit or stand beside parents, and give them your undivided attention.
- Take notes while talking with parents and review them for accuracy as they leave; recap the meeting.
- View a challenging parent as an opportunity to grow. Be respectful when working with an angry parent, write down their concerns rather, and do not be defensive.
- Share specific behavioral and curricular goals early and provide their relevance.
- Communicate regularly and often; always share some of the positive events from school; let parents know how much you appreciate their support and follow-through at home; specify future communications.

Summary

Basic Concepts about ADHD
- ADHD is a complex condition that offers a real challenge to classroom teachers.
- The legal basis for service delivery and protection for students with ADHD comes from IDEA and Section 504 of the Rehabilitation Act of 1973.
- Under IDEA, students with ADHD may be served through the category of "other health impaired"; children with ADHD as a secondary disability may be primarily diagnosed as behaviorally disordered, learning disabled, or mentally retarded.
- ADHD is a hidden disability with no unique physical characteristics to differentiate children who have it from others in the classroom.
- The diagnosis of ADHD is primarily based on the criteria in the DSM-IV-TR.
- Many theories exist to explain the cause of ADHD; however, ADHD is considered primarily neurobiologically based.
- ADHD manifests itself across the life span; characteristics include limited sustained attention, reduced impulse control, excessive task, irrelevant activity, poor working memory, time-management problems, limited self-talk and behavior control, and greater-than-normal variability during task performance.
- The process for determining eligibility for services based on ADHD includes a preliminary meeting with parents and others to determine the need for further assessment, a formal assessment process, follow-up meeting of the team

to review the assessment results, a collaborative meeting to develop an intervention plan, and follow-up and progress reviews.
- Cultural and linguistic diversity complicates issues related to assessment and treatment for children with ADHD.

Strategies for Curriculum and Instruction for Students with ADHD
- A continuum of placement options is available to students with ADHD, and the selected placement is based on their individual needs and abilities.
- The majority of students with ADHD spend all or most of the school day in general education classes.
- An individual accommodation plan or IEP is written collaboratively with parents, professionals, and, when possible, the student to identify interventions that will create success in the general education classroom.
- Medication is frequently used to enhance the educational experience of students with ADHD.
- The most commonly prescribed medication is a psychostimulant such as Dexedrine, Ritalin, or Adderall.
- Both positive outcomes and negative side effects should be monitored for children taking medication for ADHD.

Classroom Adaptations for Students with ADHD
- Classroom adaptations include environmental management techniques, instructional adaptations, and student-regulated strategies.

- Techniques used to manage the classroom environment include strategies for group management, physical arrangement of the room, and individual behavior-management techniques.
- Through instructional adaptations, teachers modify their behavior to include novel and stimulating activity, to provide structure and consistency, to allow physical movement as frequently as possible, to include cooperative learning activities, and to give both spoken and written direction.
- The curriculum for students with ADHD should be stimulating and include experience-based learning as well as problem-solving activities.

- Student-regulated strategies include study and organizational tactics, self-management techniques, learning strategies, and social skills training.
- Effective teachers for students with ADHD provide positive classroom environments, frequently review student work, and are flexible, fair, responsive, warm, patient, consistent, firm, and humorous. They develop a knowledge of the strengths and needs of their students with ADHD and are knowledgeable about different intervention strategies. They are also willing to work collaboratively with other teachers, parents, and professionals.

Questions to Reconsider

Think back to the scenario about Jake that you read at the beginning of this chapter. Would you answer the questions raised there any differently now that you have read the chapter?

1. How could Jake's early school years have been made more successful?

2. What rights did Jake have to get special accommodations from his teachers?
3. What might be Jake's most likely challenges in college? What reasonable accommodations might be made to help him be successful?

Further Readings

Angold, A., Erkali, A., Egger, H. L., & Costell, J. E. (2000). Stimulant treatment for children: A community perspective. *Journal of the American Academy of Child and Adolescent Psychiatry, 39*(8), 975–987.

Bishop, B., & Olsen, L. (2000). *Clayton's path.* M. Eagle (illustrator). New York, NY Apogee Publishing.

Carpenter, P., & Ford, M. M. (2000). *Sparky's excellent misadventures: My ADD journal.* P. Horjus (illustrator). Magination.

Child, L. (2001). *I am not sleepy and I will not go to bed.* Cambridge, MA: Candlewick Press.

Dendy, C. A. Z. (2000). *Teaching teens with ADD/ADHD: A quick reference guide for teachers and parents.* Bethesda, MD: Woodbine House.

Fowler, M. C. (2001). *Maybe you know my teen? A parent's guide to helping your adolescent with attention deficit hyperactivity disorder.* New York: Broadway Books.

Hardmann, T. (2000). *Thom Hartmann's complete guide to ADHD: Help for your family at home, school, and work.* Grass Valley, CA: Underwood Books.

Hoagwood, K., Kelleher, K. J., Feil, M., & Comer, D. M. (2000). Treatment services for children with ADHD: A national perspective. *Journal of the American Academy of Child and Adolescent Psychiatry, 39*(2), 198–206.

Jensen, P. S. (2000). Commentary: The NIH ADHD consensus statement: Win, lose, or draw? *Journal of the American Academy of Child and Adolescent Psychiatry, 39*(2), 194–197.

Latham, P. S., & Latham, P. H. (1999). ADHD views from the courthouse. *The ADHD Report, 7*(4), 9–11, 14.

McKenzie, J. (1998). The WIRED classroom: Creating technology enhanced student-centered learning environments. *From Now On, 7*(6), 1–14. [Online]. Available at www.fromnowon.org/mar98/flotilla.html.

Mooney, J., & Cole, D. (2000). *Learning outside the lines: Two Ivy League students with learning disabilities and ADHD give you the tools for academic success and educational revolution.* New York: Fireside.

Munden, A. C., & Archelus, J. (2001). *The ADHD handbook: A guide for parents and professionals.* New York: Jessica Kingsley.

National Institutes of Health. (2000). Consensus and development conference statement: Diagnosis and treatment of attention-deficit/hyperactivity disorder. *Journal of the American Academy of Child and Adolescent Psychiatry, 39*(2), 182–193.

Semrul-Clikerman, M., Steingard, R. J., Filipek, P., Biederman, J., Bekken, K., & Renshaw, P. F. (2000). Using MRI to examine brain-behavior relationships in males with attention-deficit hyperactivity disorder. *Journal of the American Academy of Child and Adolescent Psychiatry, 39*(4), 477–484.

Silver, L. B. (1999). *Attention deficit hyperactivity disorder: A clinical guide to diagnosis and treatment for health and mental health.* Washington, DC: American Psychiatric Press.

Smith, T. E. C., & Patton, J. R. (2007). *Section 504 and public schools*. Austin, TX: Pro-Ed.

Web Sites:

American Academy of Pediatrics. Provides diagnostic and evaluation guidelines for children with ADHD. www.aap.org/policy/AC0002.html

ADDA: Attention Deficit Disorder Association www.add.org/

CHADD: Children and Adults with Attention Deficit Disorders www.chadd.org/index.cfm

AD-IN. Attention Deficit Information Network Inc. www.addinfonetwork.com

NIMH (National Institute on Mental Health) ADHD page www.nimh.nih.gov/publicat/adhd.cfm

Advice on behavior management and social skills development can be found at www.BehaviorAdvisor.com and www.ldonline.org/ld_indepth/teaching_techniques/class_manage.html

mylabschool

Go to Allyn & Bacon's MyLabSchool (www.mylabschool.com). And enter Assignment ID SPV7 into the Assignment Finder. View the video clip called *Attention Deficit / Hyperactivity Disorder*. Then consider what you have seen along with what you've read in Chapter 8 to answer the following questions.

1. In this video clip, a doctor and two teachers discuss the problems that Eric has with hyperactivity and aggression. They have determined that Eric needs to learn to work independently, express his needs verbally, and increase his compliance in the classroom. Using the information in this chapter about behavior contracts, write a contract for one of these goals.

2. Neither the doctor nor the teachers mention using medication for Eric. Based on both the video and information you've read in this chapter, would you raise that possibility? Why?

3. Do you believe Eric should be included in a general education classroom? Provide specific support for your decision.

You may also answer the questions at the end of the clip and e-mail your responses to your instructor.

Teaching Students with Autism Spectrum Disorders

After reading this chapter, you should be able to:

1. Define and describe students with autism spectrum disorder (ASD)
2. Discuss the causes and prevalence of ASD
3. Describe various intervention strategies for students with autism
4. Identify strategies for successful inclusion.

Questions to Consider

1. Is there a preferred placement for children with autism?

2. What kinds of supports should be available for Cody to facilitate her success in the general education classroom?

3. Is a child ever ready for inclusion, or does the school have to make the placement decision and provide the necessary supports to make it work?

Cody's parents noted something different about their child when she was about two years old. Up until that time she had developed perfectly. She walked at thirteen months, started babbling at about fifteen months, and loved to play with adults and other children. Then things began to change. Her babbling stopped. She developed sort of a blank stare. Her early success at toilet training seemed to be reversed, and she stopped paying any attention to other children and adults. When she was about three years old, her parents took her to the state children's hospital, and the diagnosis was autism. Cody was placed in a preschool program and has been in special education services ever since. In kindergarten and first grade, she was placed in a self-contained special education classroom. During these two years, Cody seemed to regress and started picking up some of the other children's stereotypical, self-stimulating behaviors. Her parents convinced the school to give Cody a try in the regular second grade, with supports. Now, in December, Cody is doing very well. While she has limited oral language, she enjoys being with her peers and is able to do much of the academic work with the assistance of a paraprofessional.

This chapter provides an introduction and discussion of ASD. Given the clear trend toward increased prevalence of ASD (U.S. Department of Education, 2006a) and the unique learning challenges faced by students so identified, teachers must have a clear understanding of the condition and its implications for education. Because schools and state education agencies provide support personnel for teachers and students with autism, teachers should not have to go it alone. A multidisciplinary approach to meeting the needs of students with ASD will be the key to successful education.

Basic Concepts about Autism

Autism spectrum disorders are pervasive developmental disorders (PDD) that primarily affect social interactions, language, and behavior. Although autism has been glamorized by several movies, such as *Rain Man* (1988), many students with this condition do not have the incredible abilities reflected in the movie. The characteristics displayed by individuals with autism vary significantly; some individuals are able to assimilate into community settings and activities, whereas others have major difficulties achieving such normality (Scheuermann & Webber, 2002). Needless to say, "children and youth with autism spectrum disorders are a particularly unique group, even when compared with other children with disabilities" (Simpson, 2001, p. 68).

In general, PDD and ASD are both considered to be "umbrella" concepts. The term "pervasive developmental disorder" was first used in the DSM in 1980, while the term "autism spectrum disorder" was initially coined in 1988. Thus, they are inclusive of the conditions of autism, Asperger syndrome, Rett syndrome, and childhood disintegrative disorder and PDD not otherwise specified.

Those who prefer the term PDD make reference to the broad scope of problems that "pervade" the individual's life as opposed to a global cognitive problem such as mental retardation. Those who prefer ASD may note that PDD is misleading because the condition may not be truly pervasive and uneven development and strengths are often noted. In education, there is a strong consensus for the use of ASD, and thus it will be the term used in this chapter.

Brief History

The study of autism has had a controversial history since the condition was first described by Leo Kanner (Scheuermann & Webber, 2002). Some of the early controversy centered on attempts to relate the cause of autism to poor mother-child bonding. Eventually this hypothesis was disproved, but it caused a great deal of guilt, confusion, and misunderstanding. Some professionals once believed that children with autism made a conscious decision to withdraw from their environment because of its hostile nature. However, during the 1980s, autism was found to be an organic disorder, thus eliminating much of this speculation (Eaves, 1992).

Autism was not a separate category under IDEA until 1990 (Kaplan, 1996). Prior to this change, children with autism were eligible for special education services only under the category of "other health impaired." Parents and other advocates for children with autism subsequently and successfully advocated that children with this disability deserved their own category. Asperger syndrome (AS), one of the conditions under the umbrella of ASD that has received a great deal of attention since the 1990s, was first described in 1944 by Hans Asperger (Griswold et al., 2002) but was somewhat ignored until it was initially included in DSM-IV-TR (Safran, 2002).

As discussed below (see Prevalence, p. 283), the epidemic-like recent increases in the number of people identified as having autism has given rise to new societal challenges that require a response on a greater scale than would have been anticipated even

---

CONSIDER THIS

What are some problems that may be encountered by general education teachers with which specialists could provide assistance?

CONSIDER THIS

How can movies that depict persons with disabilities help, as well as hurt, the cause of providing appropriate educational opportunities to students with disabilities?

CEC STANDARDS

CEC 1: Foundations

INTASC

INTASC 2: How children learn and develop

PRAXIS

PRAXIS I: Understanding Exceptionalities

CONSIDER THIS

How did making autism a separate category under IDEA promote appropriate services to this group of children?

in the mid-1990s. Steuernagel (2005) highlighted the policy implications as related to the need for:

- Enhanced teacher training
- Support for general education teachers to promote successful inclusion
- Increased vocational rehabilitation services for adults
- Increased commitment to research on etiology
- Advanced understanding of effective interventions for use by parents and teachers

Defining Autism

It is important to be familiar with two key definitions: the one in IDEA, primarily used by educators, and the one found in the DSM-IV-TR (APA, 2000), used more often by psychologists and medical professionals. IDEA defines autism as "a developmental disability that primarily results in significant deficits in verbal and non-verbal communication and social interactions, generally evidenced before the age of 3 years and adversely affects the child's educational performance" [34 CFR § 300.7(b)(1)]. Figure 9.1 provides the DSM-IV-TR definition and diagnostic criteria.

The IDEA and DSM-IV-TR definitions are the most widely used; however, there are other definitions popular among some groups. The Autism Society of America (ASA), the primary parent advocacy group associated with autism, defines autism as follows (ASA, 2000):

> Autism is a complex developmental disability that typically appears during the first three years of life. The result of a neurological disorder that affects the functioning of the brain, autism . . . is four times more prevalent in boys than girls and knows no racial, ethnic, or social boundaries. Family income, life-style, and educational levels do not affect the chance of autism's occurrence. Autism interferes with the normal development of the brain in the areas of social interaction and communication skills. Children and adults with autism typically have difficulties in verbal and non-verbal communication, social interactions, and leisure or play activities. The disorder makes it hard for them to communicate with others and relate to the outside world. They may exhibit repeated body movements (hand flapping, rocking), unusual responses to people or attachments to objects, and they may resist changes in routines. (p. 3)

Of the specific disorders under the ASD umbrella that have received significant attention, the most studied has been AS (APA, 2000). As outlined by Safran (2005), the DSM diagnostic criteria that define AS are as follows:

A. Qualitative impairment in social interaction, as manifested by at least two of the following:
1. Marked impairment in the use of multiple nonverbal behaviors such as eye-to-eye gaze, facial expression, body postures, and gestures to regulate social interaction.
2. Failure to develop peer relationships appropriate to developmental level.
3. A lack of spontaneous seeking to share enjoyment, interests, or achievements with other people. . . .
4. Lack of social or emotional reciprocity.
B. Restricted repetitive and stereotyped patterns of behavior, interests, and activities as manifested by at least one of the following:
1. Encompassing preoccupation with one or more stereotyped and restricted patterns of interest that is abnormal either in intensity or focus.
2. Apparently inflexible adherence to specific, nonfunctional routines or rituals.
3. Stereotyped and repetitive motor mannerisms (e.g., hand or finger flapping or twisting, or complex whole-body movements).
4. Persistent preoccupation with parts of objects.

CEC STANDARDS

CEC 2: Development and Characteristics of Learners

INTASC

INTASC 3: How children differ

PRAXIS

PRAXIS I: Understanding Exceptionalities

C. The disturbance causes clinically significant impairment in social, occupational, or other important areas of functioning.

D. There is no clinically significant general delay in language (e.g., single words used by age 2 years, communicative phrases used by age 3 years).

E. There is no clinically signficant delay in cognitive development or in the development of age-appropriate self-help skills, adaptive behavior (other than social interaction), and curiosity about the environment in childhood. (p. 45)

Within this chapter, the following referents are used: **ASD** to reflect broad considerations across the spectrum of the disorders; **autism** to be broad-based unless specified as being in specific reference to the autistic subtype under ASD; and **Asperger syndrome** to reflect only this specific subtype.

Identification of Children with ASD

A number of problems are related to the identification of children with ASD. As noted by Eaves (1992), these include:

- Children with autism display many characteristics exhibited by individuals with other disabilities, such as speech and language disorders.
- Many children with autism, because they exhibit disorders across multiple domains, are mistakenly classified as having multiple disabilities.
- No stable classification system is used among educators and other professionals who encounter children with autism.

| *Figure* 9.1 | **Definition of Autism: DSM-IV-TR** |

A. A total of six (or more) items from (1), (2), and (3), with at least two from (1), and one each from (2) and (3):

  (1) qualitative impairment in social interaction, as manifested by at least two of the following:
    (a) marked impairment in the use of multiple nonverbal behaviors such as eye-to-eye gaze, facial expression, body postures, and gestures to regulate social interaction
    (b) failure to develop peer relationships appropriate to developmental level
    (c) a lack of spontaneous seeking to share enjoyment, interests, or achievements with other people (e.g., by a lack of showing, bringing, or pointing out objects of interest)
    (d) lack of social or emotional reciprocity

  (2) qualitative impairments in communication as manifested by at least one of the following:
    (a) delay in, or total lack of the development of spoken language (not accompanied by an attempt to compensate through alternative modes of communication such as gesture or mime)
    (b) in individuals with adequate speech, marked impairment in the ability to initiate or sustain a conversation with others
    (c) stereotyped and repetitive use of language or idiosyncratic language
    (d) lack of varied, spontaneous make-believe play or social imitative play appropriate to developmental level

  (3) restricted repetitive and stereotyped patterns of behavior, interests, and activities, as manifested by at least one of the following:
    (a) encompassing preoccupation with one or more stereotyped and restricted patterns of interest that is abnormal either in intensity or focus
    (b) apparently inflexible adherence to specific, nonfunctional routines or rituals
    (c) stereotyped and repetitive motor mannerisms (e.g., hand or finger flapping or twisting, or complex whole-body movements)
    (d) persistent preoccupation with parts of objects

B. Delays or abnormal functioning in at least one of the following areas, with onset prior to age 3 years: (1) social interaction, (2) language as used in social communication, or (3) symbolic or imaginative play.

C. The disturbance is not better accounted for by Rett's Disorder or Childhood Disintegrative Disorder (two pervasive developmental disorders characterized by impairment in the development of reciprocal social interaction).

From *Diagnostic and Statistical Manual of Mental Disorders-TR* (4th ed., p. 75), 2000. Washington, DC: American Psychiatric Association. Used by permission.

Another problem in identifying children with autism is the large, diverse group of professionals involved in evaluation and diagnosis. In diagnosing some disabilities, educators function as the lead professionals; in the area of autism pediatricians, speech-language pathologists, psychologists, audiologists, and social workers are typically involved as well (Powers, 1989). Working with such a large group of individuals can cause logistical problems. Diverse definitions and eligibility criteria, different funding agencies, and varying services complicate the process of identifying and serving these children and adults. The "Rights & Responsibilities" feature summarizes some of the legal decisions concerning the rights of students with autism; a number of the cases relate to diagnostic as well as service issues.

Finally, the process of identification is further complicated by professional and parental disagreement as to whether ASD reflects a continuum of disorders or several discrete categories. Volkmar (2004) refers to "clumpers" (i.e., those who will include Asperger syndrome under ASD because all have social deficits) and "splitters" (e.g., those who keep Asperger on its own because of advanced language and higher cognitive functioning).

Addressing the question of an autism continuum versus discrete categories, Tryon et al. (2006) presented data on twenty-two children who had been identified as having AS. They found that twenty met the DSM-IV-TR criteria for autism and that none met the criteria for AS. They cited their data as consistent with:

> the mounting empirical evidence that Asperger's disorder is high-functioning autism [and thus encouraged that] Asperger's disorder be deleted from the next version of the *DSM*. High- and low-functioning autism would continue to be indicated, as before, by an Axis I diagnosis of autism with an Axis II diagnosis of mental retardation for low-functioning autism, and no Axis II diagnosis of mental retardation for high-functioning autism. According to the DSM-IV-TR, a child can still have autism even without language or cognitive delays, and a diagnosis of autism takes precedence over Asperger's disorder. If a child meets DSM-IV-TR autism criteria, the child cannot have Asperger's disorder. (p. 4)

Early Identification   A critical concern in the field of ASD is early identification. The common challenge has been to determine how early autism can be detected. Goin and Myers (FADD, 2004) indicated that, although there were better detection rates during the second year, nevertheless, some developmental anomalies may be noticed in year one. They stressed the value of multiple sources, including home videos, early screening devices, and parental reports.

The key characteristics identified in the literature (e.g., Goin & Myers, 2004; Gomez & Baird, 2005; Zwaigenbaum et al., 2005) for earliest detection included lack of eye contact and limited social skills; differences in postural and motoric characteristics; a lack of responsiveness to others and to one's own name; a pattern of solitary or unusual play; marked passivity; fixation on objects in the environment; delayed expressive and receptive language, including gestural communication; and difficulties in self-regulation that may be reflected in, for example, impulsivity, irritability, and interference with the formation of attachments.

Causes of ASD

There is no single specific cause of autism, but a variety of factors can result in this disability. Organic factors such as brain damage, genetic links, and complications during pregnancy may be contributors to this condition, though in most cases no single cause can be confirmed (Kaplan, 1996). In general, autism occurs across all segments of society.

The study of causation reflects a continued focus on efforts to unravel complexity. While the "cold mother" theory initially espoused by Bettelheim and others has long been discredited, the precise causative mechanism remains elusive. Most accepted models suggest a combination of a genetic base influenced by environmental events.

CEC STANDARDS

CEC 8: Assessment

INTASC

INTASC 8: Formal and informal assessment

PRAXIS

PRAXIS I: Understanding Exceptionalities

CEC STANDARDS

CEC 2: Development and Characteristics of Learners

INTASC

INTASC 2: How students differ

PRAXIS

PRAXIS I: Understanding Exceptionalities

Rights & Responsibilities

Selected Court Decisions Related to Interventions and Treatment Programs for Students with ASD

- **Delaware County IU#25 v. Martin K. (1993)** When programs are new or considered pilot programs, programs with documented benefits (e.g., the program developed by Lovaas) will be considered more effective.
- **Hartmann v. Loudoun County Board of Education (1997)** A student's IEP should reflect individual needs; an IEP that strictly focuses on a singular emphasis, such as social skills training, will likely be considered inappropriate.
- **Johnson v. Independent School District No. 4 of Bixby (1990)** In addition to regression/recoupment, other factors that must be included when determining the need for an extended school year for students with autism are the degree of impairment, the ability of the child to interact with others, the child's rate of progress, and professional opinion predicting the student's progress toward goals.
- **Byron Union School District 35, IDELR 49 (SEA CA 2001)** A district hearing officer ruled that an eleven-year-old student with autism did not require placement in a special day class to receive a free appropriate public education. Evidence and testimony supported the fact that the student was able to benefit from academic instruction in the general education classroom and therefore did not need to be placed in the special school.
- **West Des Moines Community School District, 36 IDELR222 (SEA-IA, 2002) (Gorn, 2005)** A fourteen-year-old boy with Asperger's syndrome who was also intellectually gifted had difficulty with social skills, friendship

relationships, eye-contact maintenance, conversation interactions, and eccentric behavior. The hearing officer and review panel held that the schools needed to focus not just on his academic strengths but also on the need for gifted education and related social skills training.
- **Sanford School Committee v. Mr. and Mrs. L., No. CIV.00–CV113 PH (D. Me.2001)** A student with autism was found to be denied his free appropriate public education when an IEP was developed that did not take into consideration his needs. In developing the IEP, it was determined that the district never considered whether the proposed placement would meet the needs of the student (Special Education Law Update, 2001).
- **West Des Moines Community School Dist., 36 IDELR 222 SEA(IA, 2002)** In this case, a federal judge ruled that a child with Asperger's syndrome has a disability and is thus entitled to special education services even though he or she is performing well in the classroom (e.g., appropriate behaviors, homework completion, test performance).

Adapted from: 1. "Interventions for Children and Youth with Autism: Prudent Choices in a World of Exaggerated Claims and Empty Promises," by L.J. Heflin and R. Simpson, 1998, *Focus on Autism and Other Developmental Disabilities, 13*, pp. 212–220.
2. "Legal Issues," by S. Gorn (pp. 257–274), in *Asperger's Syndrome. Intervening in Schools, Clinics, and Communities,* edited by L.J. Baker and L.A. Welkowitz, 2005. Mahwah, NJ: Erlbaum.

The genetic role is presumed to put in place a predisposition for ASD. However, genes alone cannot explain the recent rapid increases in prevalence.

The common assumption is that autism is related to abnormalities in brain structure or function. According to the ASA (2006):

> Brain scans show differences in the shape and structure of the brain [for children who are autistic] . . . While no one gene has been identified as causing autism, in many families there appears to be a pattern of autism or related disabilities, further supporting a genetic basis to the disorder . . . it also appears that some children are born with a higher susceptibility to autism, but researchers have not yet identified a single "trigger" that causes autism to develop. (p. 4)

Environmental factors that have been hypothesized include toxins, heavy metals, and infections. One area of debate has related to the measles-mumps-rubella (MMR) vaccine. It is within post-hoc case studies that the argument was made based on the presence of Thimersol (mercury preservative) within the MMR vaccine and the possibility that millions of children were exposed to mercury levels above EPA guidelines. The Institute of Medicine concluded that while "biologically plausible" as causative, the theory remains unproven (that is, there is no causal relationship established) (Immunization Safety Review Committee of the Institute of Medicine, 2004).

Prevalence

Autism historically has been considered a low-incidence disability, but the number of children identified over the past few years has increased dramatically (Zirkel, 2002). The incidence of autism varies directly with the definition used. Research from the 1990s indicated that more restricted definitions resulted in approximately 0.7 to 2.3 individuals per 10,000 being identified, while less restrictive definitions resulted in the identification of as many as 7 to 14 per 10,000 (Koegel et al., 1995; Locke, Banken, & Mahone, 1994).

The ASA (2006) most recently indicated that an estimated 1.5 million Americans may have some form of autism, based on a prevalence estimate of 1 in 166 births. Further, the ASA estimated, based on an increase in prevalence of 10–17 percent per year, as many as 4 million Americans may be affected by 2015.

The U.S. Department of Education (2006a) reported that the percentage of children ages six to twenty-one in the schools served under the category of autism was 0.18 percent. Across individual states, the range was from 0.43 percent (Oregon) to 0.07 percent (Colorado).

Figure 9.2 illustrates the changes in prevalence over a ten-year period. Figure 9.3 provides a comparison with other low-incidence categories that, given the trends in terms of increased prevalence of students with autism as reflected in the data presented by the U.S. Department of Education (2005), further raises the question as to whether autism should continue to be considered a low-incidence category. The data in the figure reflect the significant increases, particularly for ages six to eleven, over the ten-year period represented by this graph.

Figure 9.2	**Number of Students with Autism under IDEA**

Percentage of the population receiving special education and related services because of autism, by age group; fall 1992 through fall 2002

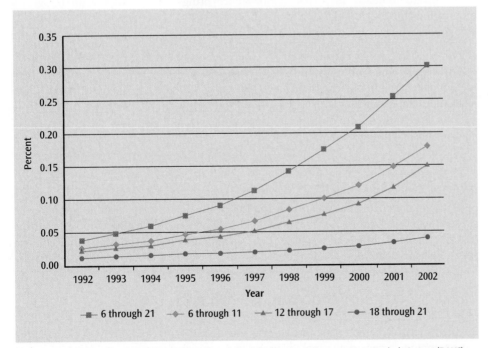

From U.S. Department of Education, 2006b. Office of Special Education Programs, Data Analysis System (DANS), Figure 1.17.

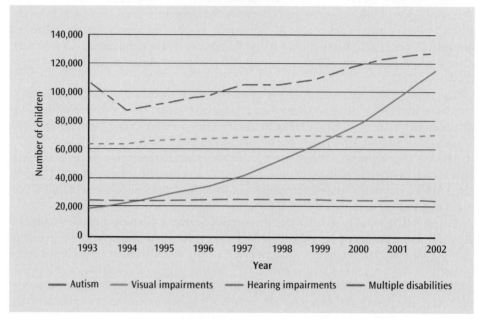

Figure 9.3   **Trend in Numbers of Children Diagnosed with Autism (and Other Low-Incidence Disabilities) Receiving Services under IDEA**

From General Accountability Office, 2005. IDEA data collected for the Department of Education, p. 17.

CONSIDER THIS

Why do you think the prevalence of children identified as having autism has increased so dramatically over the past few years?

The General Accountability Office (GAO) Report (2005) estimated that the annual educational expenditure for students with ASD is approximately $18,790 (1999–2000). Given that this amount is almost triple that for students not receiving special services and 50 percent greater than the average for all students receiving special services, the trend toward dramatic increases in prevalence brings with it significant budgetary implications for the schools.

Byrd and colleagues (2003) identified plausible reasons for dramatic increases in the prevalence (in the state of California). These included:

• Greater awareness of the condition
• General overall population increase
• Definitional changes
• Influx of children from out-of-state
• Prior misdiagnosis (e.g., MR)
• Vaccinations

However, Byrd and colleagues stated that none of these possible reasons could be confirmed.

One popular theory has been that the increase primarily is a result of "diagnostic substitutions" (e.g., autism versus MR or LD). However, Ranta (2006) noted that the ASA has challenged the validity of hypotheses and argued that the data rather confirm that ASD has reached "epidemic proportions."

CROSS-REFERENCE

Review Chapter 7 on children with serious emotional disturbance (SED). Compare the characteristics of children with ASD and those with SED. How are these children similar and different?

Characteristics of Individuals with ASD

A wide variety of characteristics are associated with autism (see Figure 9.4). Some of the more common characteristics include verbal and nonverbal communication impairments (Chan et al., 2005; Dyches, 1998), auditory-based sensory impairments (Orr, Myles, & Carlson, 1998), and problems relating socially to other individuals (ASA, 2006).

Figure 9.4 **Common Characteristics: Autism Spectrum Disorders**

- Insistence on sameness; resistance to change
- Difficulty in expressing needs, using gestures or pointing instead of words
- Repeating words or phrases in place of normal, responsive language
- Laughing (and/or crying) for no apparent reason; showing distress for reasons not apparent to others
- Preference to being alone; aloof manner
- Tantrums
- Difficulty in mixing with others
- Not wanting to cuddle or be cuddled
- Little or no eye contact
- Unresponsive to normal teaching methods
- Sustained odd play
- Spinning objects
- Obsessive attachment to objects
- Apparent oversensitivity or undersensitivity to pain
- No real fears of danger
- Noticeable physical overactivity or extreme underactivity
- Uneven gross/fine motor skills
- Nonresponsive to verbal cues; acts as if deaf, although hearing tests in normal range

From "What Is Autism?" by Autism Society of America, 2005. www.autismsociety.org/site/PageServer?pagename=WhatisAutism.

The challenge of making generalizations is that the individual variance within ASD is so significant. For example, while the characteristics associated with autism are pervasive communication and social disabilities, AS is typically described as follows:

- Limited social interaction and repetitive behaviors.
- Persistent preoccupation with parts of things.
- Significant impairment in social, occupational, or other functioning areas.
- No significant delay in language, self-help, adaptive behavior (other than social), and cognition.

While students classified as having AS share a number of characteristics of other children with autism, they also display some unique features, as noted by Myles and Simpson (1998, p. 3): "Clinical features of Asperger syndrome include social interaction impairments, speech and communication characteristics, cognitive and academic characteristics, sensory characteristics, and physical and motor-skill anomalies."

Behavioral Patterns

Scheuermann and Webber (2002) describe the characteristics of autism by using two broad groups: behavioral deficits and behavioral excesses. Examples of these two groups are as follows:

1. Behavioral deficits
   - Inability to relate to others
   - Lack of functional language
   - Sensory processing deficits
   - Cognitive deficits
2. Behavioral excesses
   - Self-stimulation
   - Resistance to change
   - Bizarre and challenging behaviors
   - Self-injurious behaviors

CEC STANDARDS

CEC 2: Development and Characteristics of Learners

INTASC

INTASC 2: How children learn and develop

PRAXIS

PRAXIS I: Understanding Exceptionalities

Specific to AS, Myles and Simpson (2002) noted that in the social domain, individuals are "typically thought to be socially stiff, socially awkward, emotionally blunted, self-centered, deficient at understanding nonverbal social cues, and inflexible. . . . Although they are well known for their lack of social awareness, many students with AS are aware enough to sense that they are different from their peers. Thus, self-esteem problems and self-concept difficulties are common" (p. 133).

Academic, Linguistic, and Cognitive Considerations

Academic difficulties are commonly noted in students with ASD, although there is wide variance in achievement levels. The U.S. Department of Education (2005) provides summative academic data on a variety of academic tasks. Within these data sets, they note the following: "For the standardized assessments, each student's performance is associated with a percentile score which reflects the proportion of the individuals of that student's age in the general population who received a lower score on that assessment. The [data] indicate the proportion of students whose percentile rank on the assessment fell within a given percentile range (e.g., 0–20, 21–60, 61–100). Thus the data provide comparative samples for students with specific disabilities as compared to the general population" (p. 57). The data are as follows for these specific areas of academic assessment:

1. *Letter-word identification* (Measures the student's reading skills in identifying isolated letters and words. It is not necessary that the student knows the meaning of any words correctly identified.): 49 percent of children with autism fall into the bottom 20 percent of students in the general population while only 19 percent are in the upper 40 percent (p. 57).
2. *Passage comprehension* (Measures the student's skill in reading a short passage and identifying a missing key word; student must exercise a variety of comprehension and vocabulary skills.): 66 percent of students with autism fall into the lower 20 percent and only 8 percent into the upper 40 percent (p. 58).
3. *Calculation* (Measures the student's ability to perform mathematical calculations; student is not required to make any decisions about what operations to use or what data to include.): 49 percent of students with autism fall into the lower 20 percent and 18 percent are in the upper 40 percent (p. 59).
4. *Applied problems* (Measures the ability to analyze and solve problems in mathematics; student must decide not only the appropriate mathematical operations to use but also which of the data to include in the calculations.): 65 percent of students with autism fall into the lowest 20 percent of the general population while only 12 percent are within the upper 40 percent (p. 60).

Although many characteristics associated with autism present as negative academic traits, some children with autism present some positive, as well as unexpected, characteristics. For example, Tirosh and Canby (1993) describe children with autism who also have hyperlexia, which is defined as "an advance of at least one standard deviation (SD) in the reading over the verbal IQ level" (p. 86). For these children, spelling and contextual reading also appeared to be advanced.

Some children with autism display unique splinter skills, or islands of precocity where they display areas of giftedness: "Common splinter skills include (1) calendar abilities, such as being able to give the day of the week for any date you might provide (e.g., May 12, 1896); (2) the ability to count visual things quickly, such as telling how many toothpicks are on the floor when a box is dropped; (3) artistic ability, such as the ability to design machinery; and (4) musical ability, such as playing a piano" (Scheuermann & Webber, 2002, p. 9).

For students with AS, areas of strength include oral expression and reading recognition while difficulties may include oral comprehension, written expression, and mathematics, particularly in the area of problem solving. Myles and Simpson (2002, p. 135)

CONSIDER THIS

How do splinter skills often confuse family members concerning the abilities and capabilities of a child with autism?

CEC STANDARDS

CEC 2: Development and Charcteristics of Learners

caution that "these students often give the impression that they understand more than they do. . . . Their pedantic style, seemingly advanced vocabularies, parrot-like responses, and ability to word call may actually mask the deficits in higher order thinking and comprehension of some students with AS."

According to Barnhill (2006), students with AS often exhibit potential strengths in the areas of grammar, vocabulary, rote memory, absorbing facts, and honesty (often to a fault). At the same time, certain characteristics may have a negative impact on academic performance. These characteristics include insistence on sameness, impairment in social interaction, a restricted range of interests, poor concentration, poor motor coordination, academic difficulties, and emotional vulnerability (Roy, 2004; Safran, 2002b; Williams, 1995).

To summarize the discussion, Table 9.1 shows the similarities and differences of the behavioral characteristics of children with AS and children with autism.

Gender and Ethnicity

One area of note is gender variability. According to the U.S. Department of Education (2005), 83 percent of all children between the ages of six and twelve identified as having autism were male; for ages thirteen to seventeen, the comparable figure is 84.8 percent.

Table 9.1   Behavioral Comparison of Asperger Syndrome and Autism

	Asperger Syndrome	Autistic Syndrome
1. Intelligence measures		
Standardized scores	Average to high average range	Borderline through average range
2. Language		
Development	Normal development	Delayed onset, deficits
Pragmatic language		
a. Verbal	Deficits can be observed	Delayed and disordered
b. Nonverbal	Deficits (e.g., odd eye gaze)	Deficits can be severe
3. Communication		
Expressive	Within normal limits	Deficits can be observed
Receptive	Within normal limits	Deficits can be observed
4. Social responsiveness		
Attachment		
a. Parents	Observed responsiveness	Lack responsiveness
b. Caregivers	Observed responsiveness	Lack responsiveness
c. Peers	Observed responsiveness	Lack responsiveness
Interactions		
a. Initiations to peers	Frequent, poor quality	Minimal frequency
b. Positive responses to peers	Frequent, awkward, and pertains to self-interests	Minimal frequency
c. Symbolic play	No impaired symbolic play	Absence of symbolic play
d. Reciprocal play	Observed but awkward	Minimal frequency
e. Coping	Deficits observed in quality	
f. Friendships	Minimal frequency	Minimal frequency
g. Requests for assistance	Observed but awkward	Minimal frequency
Emotional self-regulation		
a. Emotional empathy	Observed but awkward	Deficits can be observed
b. Emotional responsiveness	Observed but could be extreme	Aloof, indifferent
5. Physical/motor		
a. Gross motor	Observed deficits—controversial	No observed deficits
b. Repetitive behavior	Observed	Observed

From "Asperger Syndrome and Autism: A Literature Review and Meta-Analysis, by E. McLaughlin-Cheng, 1998, *Focus on Autism and Other Developmental Disabilities, 13*, p. 237. Used by permission.

In terms of racial and ethnic composition, the U.S. Department of Education (2006) reported the following ethnic percentage breakdown within the category of autism with comparative data for all students with disabilities across categories provided in parentheses: 0.64 percent for Native Americans/Alaskans (1.15 percent); 4.9 percent for Asians/Pacific Islanders (2.9 percent); 16.5 percent for African Americans (20.4 percent); 10.1 percent for Hispanic (16.0 percent); and 67.5% for European Americans (60.2 percent). By comparing these two sets of data, it can be noted that the percentage of children identified as having autism by ethnic group is somewhat less for each group with the exception of higher school-prevalence rates for Asian/Pacific Islanders and European Americans. Some specific considerations about cultural variance are provided in the "Diversity Forum."

Rett Syndrome

Another condition under the ASD umbrella is named for Dr. Andreas Rett, who first described it in 1966. Rett syndrome is present in 1 in 10,000 to 15,000 female births, representing a genetic disorder on the X chromosome. Young girls develop typically until sometime between six and eighteen months. At that point, key characteristics emerge that include loss of speech and motor skills, repetitive hand movements, seizures, and motor control problems (e.g., in walking and balance).

Barbour (2004) identified the four developmental stages associated with Rett syndrome:

- *Early onset:* Begins ages six to eighteen months; reduced eye contact and interest in toys; hand-wringing
- *Rapid destructive:* begins ages one to four years, can last weeks or months; hand skills and spoken language may be lost; initiating motor movement is difficult
- *Plateau:* Ages two to ten years and can last for years; motor problems and seizures are prominent; behavior may improve along with communication and attention span
- *Late motor deterioration:* Can last for decades; reduced mobility, muscle weakness, rigidity; generally no decline in cognition or communication

The key intervention foci for Rett syndrome are on symptomatic treatment associated with the characteristics discussed above (e.g., medication for seizures). Occupational and physical therapy also remain key considerations in intervention programs.

Strategies for Curriculum and Instruction

Placement Patterns

For preschool students with autism (i.e., ASD) (ages three to five) the U.S. Department of Education (2006) reported during the 2000-2001 academic year that 24.5 percent were served in an early childhood setting; 49.5 percent were served in an early childhood special education setting; 2.1 percent received services in a home-based program; 15.2 percent received part-time services in an early childhood and part-time special education setting; 0.05 percent were served in a residential facility; 5.9 percent were served in a separate school; 1.2 percent were served through Itinerant services provided outside of the home; and 1.6 percent were served in a reverse mainstreaming program.

For students ages six to twenty-one, the same source reported that 24.7 percent were in the regular classroom for 79 percent or more of the day, 17.8 percent were served outside of the regular classroom between 21 and 60 percent of the time, and 45.5 percent were served outside of the regular classroom over 60 percent of the time. Further, 5.8 percent were served in public separate facilities and 4.6 percent in private separate facilities. In terms of residential placement, 1.1 percent were served in public or private residential facilities and 0.4 percent were served within the home or in a hospital environment.

DIVERSITY FORUM

ASD and Multiculturalism

Alicia, a three year old child, has recently been referred for possible early childhood special education services. Her parents have indicated concerns about her developmental progress and her communication skills, behavior, and social interactions are reflective of possible identification of autism. Because of their commitment to family support and independence of social services and local public educational programs, Alicia's family (whose native language is Spanish) had been reluctant to seek assistance until her development delays caused serious concern among friends and other family members.

The importance of multicultural considerations in autism spectrum disorders is highlighted in the work of Dyches, Wilder, Sudweeks, Obiakor, and Algozzine (2004). The premise of these researchers was that "students with multicultural backgrounds and autism are challenged on at least four dimensions: communication, social skills, behavioral repertoires, and culture. The professional literature continues to address the first; it is imperative to now consider the fourth 'multicultural issues'" (p. 221).

In their discussion of multicultural issues in autism, Dyches and her colleagues explore two major concerns: the prevalence of autism across ethnic groups and the ways in which families of different cultures adapt to the challenges of raising children with autism. With regard to prevalence, they stressed the methodological challenges in this area, particularly when research has focused on immigrant and non-immigrant status. The

most readily accessible data set comes from the annual US Department of Education reports on the implementation of IDEA. Using these data as a basis, Dyches et al. noted that the prevalence rates were higher for children who were Black or Asian-Pacific Islander (twice the rate) than for students who were American Indian-Alaskan or Hispanic. White children were between these two groups in terms of prevalence level (approximately 0.09 over two years). The identification rates for the two ethnic groups that had the highest prevalence ranged, over several years, between 0.10 an 0.14 while the two ethnic groups with the lowest percentages were at approximately 0.06.

In terms of family adaptations, Dyches and colleagues provide a detailed discussion of family responses that may be seen as more common within specific ethnic groups. Within this context, they discussed the possibility of negative appraisals occurring to the extent that some cultures may still see autism and other developmental disabilities as the consequence of parental fault, although it can be assumed that these are more traditional and historical views in many instances. Positive appraisals may be included: that a child with a disability may be seen as a blessing or gift from God (e.g., by Latino mothers); that all children are important within the family (e.g., by African American families); that a spiritual orientation toward life influences appraisal as positive (i.e., Native Hawaiian); that functional abilities, even if limited, of

children are important (e.g., within some Native American cultures).

These authors also discussed the question of the supports necessary to raise a child with developmental disabilities in general, and autism in particular. Of significant concern is the strong familial support that is needed in such instances; for many ethnic groups, commitment to familial cohesion is critical for the provision of supports. At the same time, there may be differential reactions to access to organizational support, such as educational and social services. Across ethnic groups, variables that can influence a commitment to accessing such support can include awareness of programs, fear of stigma for labels, preferences for a particular label (autism) as opposed to another label that may be seen as more stigmatizing (mental retardation), and alternative support by other agencies than governmental organizations (e.g., church support).

Questions

1. What special challenges do families face in raising a child with autism? How might these challenges be influenced by cultural background?
2. How can teachers be sensitive to cultural differences in offering to assist with the provision of family supports?

From "Multicultural Issues in Autism," by T. T. Dyches, L. K. Wilder, R. R. Sudweeks, F. E. Obiakor, and B. Algozzine, 2004. *Journal of Autism and Developmental Disabilities, 34,* 211–222.

As noted in a finer-grained analysis by age subgroups, for younger students (ages six to eleven), a larger percentage (27.5 percent) were served primarily in general education-based programs and fewer were served in separate facilities. However, students between the ages of twelve and seventeen and eighteen and twenty-one were more likely to be served in more restrictive settings. Finally, the U.S. Department of Education (2005) indicated that 13 percent of all children with autism spent 100 percent of their time in the general education classroom.

CEC STANDARDS

CEC 5: Learning Environments and Social Interactions

Educational Interventions

Key educational goals for students with ASD include the following:

- To develop basic language and social skills.
- To provide academic instruction consistent with cognitive level.
- To teach functional skills for postschool success.
- To tie instruction to parental education, such as to encompass behavioral interventions to enhance social and functional skills. (Forness, Walker, & Kavale, 2003)

Another goal is to implement effective early intervention programs. Hume, Bellini, and Pratt (2005) stress the importance of effective early intervention practices for students with autism. As they noted, these practices "appear to reduce the debilitating impact of autism [and] young children with autism may make gains more quickly than young children with other severe neuro-developmental disorders. The results of a retrospective study corroborated the belief that children with autism have significantly better outcomes when an intervention begins before age 5" (p. 195).

A number of effective, broad-based educational practices were identified by Iovannone and colleagues (2003). These include:

1. Individualized services and supports for both the family and the child.
2. The systematic instruction of meaningful skills.
3. Reliance on data-based decision-making in educational programs.
4. The creation of structured learning environments.
5. The implementation of specialized curriculum for language and social skills.
6. The application of a functional approach to understanding problem behavior (see Chapter 7).

The Evidence-Based Practice box provides an analysis of each of these core elements of effective interventions. These interventions provide overall guidance for program development.

EVIDENCE-BASED PRACTICE

Appropriate Adaptations for Students with ASD

Yell, Drasgow, and Lowrey (2005) provided a contextual discussion of autism spectrum disorders. Drawing on the research review of Iovannone and colleagues (2003), they outlined the six core elements of effective practices in education for those with autism.

1. **Individualized supports and services:** Must be tailored to meet the unique individual needs and family characteristics of each student. Individualized programming includes (a) considering family preferences when selecting curriculum, (b) developing programming that reflects a student's preferences and interests, and (c) determining the appropriate intensity and level of instruction on the basis of the student's strengths and weaknesses.

2. **Systematic instruction:** Teaching based on identifying desirable learning outcomes, developing specific and focused teaching strategies to achieve these outcomes, consistently implementing the teaching strategies, and using information about student performance to guide daily instructional decisions.

3. **Comprehensible and structured learning environments:** Allow students to predict their daily routine and respond appropriately to behavioral expectations during different activities.

4. **Specific curriculum content:** Must include and emphasize language and social interaction, because these are the primary challenges for students with ASD.

5. **Functional approach to problem behavior:** Represents a movement away from punishment-based approaches that emphasize obedience and compliance and toward instuction that emphasizes useful skill development.

6. **Family involvement:** Improves programming because family members know their child best, spend the most time with him or her, and have an immense influence on their child. It is crucial that they are active participants in developing and implementing their child's educational programming.

From "No Child Left Behind and Students with Autism Spectrum Disorders," by M. L. Yell, E. Drasgow, and K. A. Lowrey, 2005. *Focus on Autism and Other Developmental Disabilities, 20,* pp. 130–139.

In a recent study, Stahmer, Collins, and Palinkas (2005) evaluated the use of these six practices in community early intervention settings. They found their use within these programs was as follows (the first figure is for programs for ages newborn to three, the second for ages three to five): individualized support (70 percent, 67 percent); systematic instruction (50 percent, 83 percent); structured environment (50 percent, 75 percent); specialized curriculum (80 percent, 75 percent); functional approach (70 percent, 67 percent); and family involvement (80 percent, 75 percent). These data provide encouragement for the link between research and practice.

The increase in attention to students with ASD has led to the identification of more specific evidence-based interventions. Odom and colleagues (2003) described proposed interventions that are worthy of consideration as falling into one of these categories:

- *Well-established:* Adult-directed intervention (prompting, scaffolding); differential reinforcement strategies
- *Emerging and effective:* Peer-mediated interventions; visual supports (graphic/photographic activity schedules; Picture Exchange Communication Systems); self-monitoring; involving families
- *Probably efficacious:* Positive behavior support; videotaped modeling of apt behaviors; moderating task characteristics (e.g., child's choice of activities)

No single method is effective with all children who have autism, partly because these children display widely variable characteristics (Heflin & Simpson, 1998). However, several different approaches have shown positive results (Kaplan, 1996). Table 9.2 summarizes selected approaches.

In a 2001 study of interventions in the field of ASD, the National Academy of Sciences reviewed ten general approaches (including those in Table 9.2) and concluded that these programs all had some merit. However, they also reported that any conclusions to be drawn are limited by an inability to ascertain a clear link between the program and the individual's progress as well as methodological issues and the absence of research comparing approaches. The report called for individualized programs that promoted spontaneous, functional communication as well as cognitive and social development in settings that included children who were nondisabled (Interdisciplinary Council on Developmental and Learning Disorders, 2006).

Regardless of the specific intervention used, professionals developing programs for children with autism should ask these questions (Heflin & Simpson, 1998):

1. What are the anticipated outcomes of the programming option?
2. What are the potential risks?
3. How will the option be evaluated?
4. What proof is available that the option is effective?
5. What other options would be excluded if this option is chosen?

Social Stories   One relatively recent intervention is the use of **social stories**. Sansosti and colleagues (2004) noted that social stories were initially developed to help children understand game rules but later they were further developed to address more subtle social rules that may prove problematic for students with autism. Their goal is to clarify social expectations and provide a guide to students for their conduct while promoting self-management in specific life situations.

According to Sansosti and colleagues (2004), social stories identify steps in social situations and facilitate learning because students with ASD often have difficulty reading environmental, social, and behavioral cues. (See Figure 9.5 for sample social stories.) To do so, social stories typically:

- Target a specific problematic social situation
- Identify salient features of context and setting
- Share this information with child and others

CEC STANDARDS

CEC 7: Instructional Strategies

INTASC

INTASC 7: Instructional strategies

PRAXIS

PRAXIS III: Delivery of Services to Students with Disabilities

Table 9.2   **Autism Interventions**

	Lovaas	TEACCH	PECS
Background	Also known as Discrete Trial (DT), Intensive Behavior Intervention (IBI), Applied Behavior Analysis (ABA); DT was earliest form of behavior modification; initial research reported in 1987; initial intent to achieve inclusive kindergarten readiness; has "morphed" into IBI and ABA.	Stands for Treatment and Education of Autistic and Related Communication-Handicapped Children; over thirty-two years empirical data on efficacy of TEACCH approach exists; includes parents as cotherapists; recognizes need for supports from early childhood through adulthood; main focus is on autism rather than behavior.	Stands for Picture Exchange Communication System; derived from need to differentiate between *talking* and *communicating*; combines in-depth knowledge of speech therapy with understanding of communication where student does not typically attach meaning to words and lack of understanding of communication exists; high compatibility with TEACCH.
Goals	Teach child *how to learn* by focusing on developing skills in attending, imitation, receptive/expressive language, preacademics, and self-help.	Provide strategies that support person throughout lifespan; facilitate autonomy at all levels of functioning; can be accommodated to individual needs.	Help child *spontaneously* initiate communicative interaction; help child understand the *function of* communication; develop communicative competency.
How Implemented	Uses ABC model; every trial or task given to the child consists of: **antecedent**—a directive or request for child to perform an action; **behavior**—a response from the child that may include successful performance, noncompliance, no response; **consequence**—a reaction from the therapist, including a range of responses from strong positive reinforcement to faint praise to a negative "No!; **pause**—to separate trials from one another (intertrial interval).	Clearly organized, structured, modified environments and activities; emphasis on visual learning modalities; uses functional contexts for teaching concepts; curriculum is individualized based on individual assessment; uses structure and predictability to promote spontaneous communication.	Recognizes that young children with autism are not strongly influenced by social rewards; training begins with functional acts that bring child into contact with rewards; begins with physically assisted exchanges and proceeds through a hierarchy of eight phases; requires initial ratio of 2:1.
Reported Outcomes	First replications of initial research reporting gains in IQ, language comprehension and expression, adaptive and social skills.	Gains in function and development; improved adaptation and increase in functional skills; learned skills generalized to other environments; North Carolina reports lowest parental stress rates and rate of requests for out-of-home placement, and highest successful employment rates.	Pyramid Educational Consultants report incoming empirical data supporting; increased communicative competency among users (children understanding the *function of* communication); increasing reports of emerging spontaneous *speech*.
Advantages of Approach	Recognizes need for 1:1 instruction; utilizes repetitions of learned responses until firmly imbedded; tends to keep child engaged for increasing periods of time; effective at eliciting verbal production in select children; is a "jump start" for many children, with best outcomes for those in mild to moderate range.	Dynamic model that takes advantage of and incorporates research from multiple fields; model does not remain static; anticipates and supports inclusive strategies; compatible with PECS, Floor Time, OT, PT, selected therapies; addresses subtypes of autism, using individualized assessment and approach; identifies emerging skills, with highest probability of success; modifiable to reduce stress on child and/or family.	Helps to get language started; addresses both the communicative and social deficits of autism; well-suited for preverbal and nonverbal children AND children with a higher performance IQ than verbal IQ; semantics of PECS more like spoken language than signing.
Concerns with Approach	Heavily promoted as THE approach for autism in absence of any comparative research to support claim; no differentiation for subtypes when creating curriculum; emphasizes compliance training, prompt dependence; heavy focus on behavioral approach may ignore underlying neurological aspects of autism, including issues of executive function and attention switching; may overstress child and/or family; costs reported as high as $50,000 per child per year; prohibits equal access.	Belief that TEACCH "gives in" to autism rather than fighting it; seen by some as an exclusionary approach that segregates children with autism; does not place enough emphasis on communication and social development; independent work centers may isolate when there is a need to be with other children to develop social skills.	May suppress spoken language (evidence is to the contrary).
Errors to Avoid	Creating dependency on 1:1; overstressing child or family; interpreting all behaviors as willful rather than neurological manifestations of syndrome; ignoring sensory issues or processing difficulties; failing to recognize when it is time to move to another approach.	Failing to offer sufficient training, consultancy, and follow-up training to teachers for program to be properly implemented; treating TEACCH as a single-classroom approach rather than a comprehensive continuum of supports and strategies; expecting minimally trained teacher to inform and train all other personnel in TEACCH approach; failing to work collaboratively with parents.	Failing to strictly adhere to the teaching principals in Phase I; tendency to rush through Phase I or to use only one trainer; providing inadequate support or follow-up for trainee after attending two-day training; training only one person in approach rather than all classroom personnel; inconsistently implementing in classroom.

Table 9.2 Continued

	Greenspan	Inclusion	Social Stories
Background	Also known as "Floor Time," DIR (Developmental Individual-Difference, Relationship-Based) Model; targets emotional development following developmental model; depends on informed and acute observations of child to determine current level of functioning; has child-centered focus; builds from the child; "Floor Time" is only one piece of a three-part model that also includes spontaneity along with semistructured play, and motor and sensory play.	Initially intended for children with mental retardation and disabilities other than autism; sociological, educational, and political mandates in contrast to psychology as root source for other approaches inclusion defined in three federal laws—PL 94–142, REI, and IDEA	Also known as Social Scripts; developed by Carol Gray in 1991 initially to help student with autism understand rules of a game; was further developed to address understanding subtle social rules of "neurotypical" culture; addresses "Theory of Mind" deficits (the ability to take the perspective of another person).
Goals	Targets personal interactions to facilitate mastery of developmental skills; helps professionals see child as functionally integrated and connected; does not treat in separate pieces for speech development, motor development, etc.	Educate children with disabilities with NT children to the maximum extent possible; educate children with disabilities in the chronological setting they would be in if they had no disability and they lived at home; does not apply separate educational channels except under specific circumstances.	Clarify social expectations for students with ASD; address issues from the student's perspective; redefine social misinterpretations; provide a guide for conduct or self-management in specific social situations.
How Implemented	Teaches in interactive contexts; addresses developmental delays in *sensory modulation, motor planning and sequencing,* and *perceptual processing;* usually done in twenty-minute segments followed by twenty-minute breaks, each segment addressing one each of above-identified delays.	Children with autism typically placed in inclusive settings with 1:1 aide; curriculum modified to accommodate to specific learning strengths and deficits; requires team approach to planning; approach may be selective inclusion (by subject matter or class), partial inclusion (half day included, half day separate instruction), or full, radical inclusion with no exceptions.	Stories or scripts are specific to the person, addressing situations that are problematic for that individual; Social Stories typically comprised of three types of sentences: perspective, descriptive, and directive; types of sentences follow a ratio for frequency of inclusion in the Social Story; Social Story can be read TO or BY the person with autism; introduced far enough in advance of situation to allow multiple readings, but especially *just before* the situation is to occur.
Reported Outcomes	Teaches parents how to engage child in happier, more relaxed ways; hypothetically lays stronger framework for future neurological/cognitive development.	In *certain circumstances,* some children with autism can survive and even become more social in classrooms with NT peers; benefits children who cognitively match classmates.	Stabilization of behavior specific to the situation being addressed; reduction in frustration and anxiety of students; improved behavior when approach is *consistently* implemented.
Advantages of Approach	Addresses emotional development in contrast to other approaches, which tend to focus on cognitive development; avoids drilling in deficit areas, which feeds child's frustrations and highlights inadequacies; is a nonthreatening approach; helps to turn child's actions into interactions.	More opportunities for role modeling and social interaction; greater exposure to verbal communication; opportunities for peers to gain greater understanding of and tolerance for differences; greater opportunities for friendships with typically developing peers.	Developed specifically to address autistic social deficits; tailored to individual and specific needs; is time and cost efficient/flexible.
Concerns with Approach	Does not focus on specific areas for competency; no research to support efficacy for children with autism; approach based on hypotheses, not research; is a more passive approach.	*Automatic* inclusion violates spirit and letter of IDEA; opportunities for successful inclusion begin to plateau by end of third grade as work becomes more abstract and faster paced; increasing use of language-based instruction puts students with autism at great disadvantage; sensory and processing difficulties tend to be insufficiently accommodated; regular education setting not necessarily best learning environment for students with autism; teachers and students in inclusion classrooms are typically ill-prepared to receive student.	Supportive data is anecdotal rather than empirical; benefit depends on skill of writer and writer's understanding of autism, as well as writer's ability to take an autistic perspective.
Errors to Avoid	Attempting to implement approach without training or professional oversight; taking the lead, trying to get the child to do what YOU think he should do; allowing inadequate time; attempting to implement in midst of ongoing activities for other children.	Providing insufficient training, preparation, information, and support to personnel; placing student in settings where level of auditory and visual stimulation is typically too intense; assigning student work in which cognitive demands exceed student's ability to comprehend; depending on support of 1:1 aide; maintaining placement in face of frequent or severe disruptive behaviors; focusing on academics to detriment or exclusion of functional competencies; not offering multiple opportunities to apply functional skills.	Including too many directive sentences in proportion to perspective and descriptive sentences; stating directive sentences in inflexible terms (e.g., "I will do __" rather than "I will try to __"); writing above the person's cognitive developmental age; using complex language; not being specific enough in describing either the situation or the desired behavioral response.

From Autism Society of America, 2003. "Autism Treatments." Available at www.autism-society.org.

Figure 9.5   **Sample Social Story**

Every day we sit in circle.

All the children sit quietly.

Sometimes in circle, I want to scream.

I need to sit quietly and not scream in circle.

It makes my teacher happy when I sit quietly and do not scream. She says, "Good job, Robert!"

From "Teacher-Researcher Partnerships to Improve Social Behavior Through Social Stories," by E. Agosta, J. E. Graetz, M. A. Mastropieri, and T. E. Scruggs, 2004, *Intervention in School and Clinic, 39*, p. 283.

There is limited empirical support to date on social stories and, consequently, interventions cannot be labeled "evidence-based" as yet. However, the approach has merit because it is based on strategies that have already proven effective (e.g., social modeling, task analysis, visual aides, practice with corrective feedback, and priming to provide preview of behaviors before entering social situation to practice) (Sansosti et al., 2004).

PECS   Another approach is to use **picture exchange communication systems (PECS)**. PECS programs are based on teaching children how to exchange picture symbols to make varied social requests, such as to request a type of food, a classroom activity, or refer to a scheduled event (Agosta et al., 2004).

Therefore, PECS use symbols to represent a request that an item, for example, be given, such as with the similar concept of communication boards for those with severe disabilities. In so doing, a related goal is to develop communicative competency. PECS programs have the ability to address both communicative and social deficits. The Phases for using PECS are shown in Figure 9.6. Related information is provided in "Technology Today."

Educational Outcomes

The U.S. Department of Education (2006) provides information on adolescents exiting from special education. These national data indicate that there has been a gradual increase in the number of children with ASD who have graduated with a standard diploma, with an increase from 33.7 percent in 1994 to 51.1 percent in 2002. Conversely, the number of students with autism dropping out of school has decreased from 25.9 percent in 1994 to 17.6 percent in 2002.

While difficulty in social relationships and verbal and nonverbal communication are common characteristics and are coincidentally critical in the workplace, nevertheless there is evidence that individuals with autism can be successful in the community work environment. Further, some characteristics (e.g., memory, tolerance for repetition) may be beneficial for certain types of tasks (Hagner & Cooney, 2005). A key aspect for success is the presence of effective supports (see Chapter 8) in the workplace. It can be generalized that this would also be true for vocational placement programs that may be used for secondary-school level students with autism. Table 9.3 provides a list of key supervision strategies for working with students with autism.

Medical Interventions

Another approach to treatment involves drug therapies. For students with ASD, Broun and Umbarger (2005) noted the following behaviors that impact quality of life, and thus may warrant medical interventions:

- Aggression that has moved beyond what can be tolerated or has become significantly less manageable.

| Figure 9.6 | **Phases in using a Picture Exchange Communication System (PECS)** |

Phase 1
Learn to Spontaneously Request Items

Child learns to exchange a picture for an item

Phase 2
Generalization of Learned Skill

Child is required to move a longer distance to get to a communication partner and to use the skill in a different setting

---

Phase 3
Learn to Discriminate Among Items

Child is required to discriminate among items on a board, making choices based on what he/she wants

---

Phase 4
Focus Moves to Sentence Structure

Child learns to use sentence strips to make longer requests

Phase 5
Extend Sentence Structure Learned in Phase 4

Adjectives and other words are added to the child's repertoire

---

Phase 6
PECS Becomes the Primary Communication System

Child learns to comment on elements in his/her environment using pictures for "I see", "I feel", etc.

From www.polyxo.com/visualsupport/pecs.html

- Self-injurious behavior that poses a threat to her/his health and safety and/or significantly interferes with the activities of daily living.
- Obsessions/compulsions that significantly interfere with the child's participation in the activities of daily living or safety.
- Ongoing, unsafe impulsivity that may include running, climbing, mouthing, or eating inappropriate objects. (p. 1)

Hendren and Martin (2005) aptly describe the current state of affairs with regard to psychotropic medication:

Psychotropic medications can be an important part of an effective treatment plan for individuals with ASD. Generally, a comprehensive treatment plan involves behavioral interventions, education for the family, special education services, and sometimes speech, occupational therapy, and other services as well. Improvement in symptoms

TECHNOLOGY Today

Computerized Activity Schedules and Video Modeling

Stromer and colleagues (2006) have highlighted the use of computerized activity schedules and video modeling with students with ASD and discussed their importance in promoting independence. For example, computerized activity schedules are motivating to students with ASD since time spent on the computer is often used as a reward.

Some students with ASD prefer computerized instruction to that given by a teacher. During receptive language tasks, students learned these tasks more quickly when the lesson was presented using a computer. Video modeling has the distinct advantage of being exactly the same each time, therefore lessening the chances of confusing the student. Video modeling has been used to teach academic skills such as counting and to successfully teach social skills by modeling appropriate social interactions on video.

The use of a computer for scheduling as well as for instructional activities promotes independence for the student. He or she is allowed to proceed at a pace most suitable to his or her needs when using a computer. The visual and auditory cues may also be adjusted to fit the specific need of each learner.

Students are exposed to multiple cues when operating a computer. This experience has been shown to improve stimulus transfer skills in children with ASD. Vocal commentary on activities presented by the computer is also increased in students that are exposed to multiple stimuli by the computer during instruction.

Teachers can use a simple PowerPoint program to create the individual activity schedules and instructional sequences. However, the creation of each program may be somewhat time consuming for the teacher in terms of the initial setup of individualized programs for each student; the ease of adapting the programs afterward negates that disadvantage.

The authors thank Alexandra Barnett for help in reporting on these initiatives.

From "Activity Schedules, Computer Technology, and Teaching Children with Autism Spectrum Disorders," by R. Stromer et al., 2006. *Focus on Autism and Other Developmental Disabilities, 21,* pp. 14–24.

---

as a result of these interventions plus pharmacotherapy can result in . . . better responses from the environment, leading to additional gains for the youngster with ASD. However, although psychiatric medications are widely used in the ASD population, they have not been systematically studied in great detail. Careful monitoring of their use by experienced practitioners and further research are warranted. (p. 75)

Table 9.3   Key Supervision Strategies

Area	Strategy
Job modification	• Maintain a consistent schedule and job duties. • Keep the social demands of the job manageable and predictable. • Provide organizers to help structure and keep track of work. • Add activities to reduce or eliminate unstructured time.
Supervision	• Be direct and specific when giving directions. • Verify that communications are correctly understood. • Assist the employee in learning social rules and interpret social cues encountered on the job. • Explain and help the employee deal with changes on the job.
Coworker relationships and social interactions	• Encourage coworkers to initiate interactions. • Ensure that one or two coworkers play a role in helping to give job-related suggestions and "keep an eye out" for the employee.
Support services	• Provide a sense of familiarity and reassurance until the employee and company staff get to know one another. • Transfer relationships and supports to company employees. • Check in and remain on-call in case problems arise. • Maintain a liaison role for nonwork issues that affect the job.

From " 'I Do That for Everybody': Supervising Employees with Autism," by D. Hagner and B. F. Cooney, 2005, *Focus on Autism and Other Developmental Disabilities, 20,* p. 96.

No specific drugs are recommended for the direct treatment of core symptoms associated with ASD (Forness et al., 2003). Consequently, medical interventions are most often used for secondary symptoms, such as aggression or self-injurious behavior (SIB). The process recommended to address specific symptoms with psychotropic medication is to test one drug at a time and to evaluate its effects by following accepted nondrug practices (e.g., the use of applied behavior analysis methodology). Kalachnik and colleagues (1998, adapted from Schall, 2002) recommended that the use of psychotropic drugs (i.e., any substance prescribed to improve or stabilize mood, mental status, or behavior) should follow these principles:

- Use a multidisciplinary plan and team to coordinate treatment and care.
- Use only in response to a specific hypothesis regarding how the medication will change behavior.
- Obtain informed consent and develop alliances with the person and his or her parents.
- Track outcomes by collecting data on behavioral disorders and quality of life.
- Observe for the presence or absence of side effects.
- Conduct ongoing reviews of the person's clinical status, behavior, and quality of life.
- Strive for administration of the lowest dose possible.

These same authors also identified these "don'ts" related to the use of psychotropic medication:

- Don't use psychotropic drugs in lieu of educational and other services.
- Don't use drugs in quantities that result in a decreased quality of life.
- Don't change drugs and doses frequently.
- Don't use multiple drugs that come from the same pharmaceutical category.
- Don't prescribe medications that are associated with addiction and/or serious side effects.
- Don't prescribe drugs without a regular schedule and eschew the use of drugs on an as-needed basis.

A number of key questions for parents to pose to physicians are listed in Figure 9.7.

Controversial Interventions

As noted by Simpson (2005), the key to successful programming for students with ASD is the use of evidence-based practices. As he noted in this review, reliance on the use of methods that have been untested have proven detrimental to this field. Further, there has been too much dependence on the use of methodologies that are largely unproven and offer "miracle cures" that tend to be unrealistic and related to improbable expectations.

Figure 9.7   **Medication: Questions for Parents to Ask Physicians**

- Why is the person taking medication?
- What behavior changes should occur if medication works?
- About how long should it be before behavior changes occur?
- What adverse side effects may occur?
- What should we do if side effects occur?
- What should we do if the people administering medication forget a dose?
- When and how should the medication be taken?
- When is it necessary or important to call the doctor?
- What information should we bring to our appointment so that the doctor can judge if the drug is working?

From "A Consumer's Guide to Monitoring Psychotropic Medication for Individuals with Autism Spectrum Disorders," by C. Schall, 2002, *Focus on Autism and Other Developmental Disabilities, 17*, p. 231.

CONSIDER THIS

How can the use of procedures that have not yet been validated harm students? Why do some of these ideas become so popular with some educators and family members before they are proven effective?

CONSIDER THIS

What are some problems that may be encountered by general education teachers with which specialists could provide assistance?

CEC STANDARDS

CEC 5: Learning Environments and Social Interactions

INTASC

INTASC 5: Learning Environment

PRAXIS

PRAXIS III: Delivery of Services to Students with Disabilities

TEACHING TIP

Peer buddies can be very useful when a student with autism is included in a general classroom. Peers can serve as excellent role models and provide support for these students.

Nevertheless, a number of such interventions have been widely promoted. The discussion below highlights one such example.

In the 1990s, a major controversy erupted in the education of children with autism over the use of **facilitated communication (FC)**, a process in which a facilitator helps the person with autism (or some other disability related to expressive language) to type or use a keyboard for communication purposes. FC provides an apt illustration of the challenges of miracle cures that have been too common in this field.

Although FC was touted as the key to establishing communication with children with autism, a series of studies cast increasing doubt on its authenticity. The heart of the controversy concerned how to validate the technique. Advocates of the method offered numerous qualitative research studies as proof of success, yet quantitative research raised consistent, significant questions about the program. After reviewing much of the empirical research related to FC, Kaplan (1996) reported that evidence often showed that the facilitator influences the person with autism, though the facilitator may be unaware of it. FC did not turn out to be the miracle many people had hoped it would be.

Facilitated communication provides an excellent case study of breakthroughs and fads that have frequently been touted in the ASD field. In a most apt quote, Simpson (2004, p. 140) noted that "both parents and professionals can be expected to consider using various unproven interventions and treatments. . . . Indeed, one of the most well-defined characteristics of programs and interventions (in ASD) has been the never-ending search for factors or strategies, proven or not, that purportedly restore individuals with autism to normalcy. Of course, who would expect them to not consider approaches that might promise to reclaim children to a typical state!" (e.g., facilitated communication) (p. 140).

The appropriate approach is to continue to identify and use those methods that are based on evidence. Research therefore is a critical component of the continued development of the field of ASD. Parents and teachers need to pay particular attention to the outcomes that are anticipated with a particular methodology, the potential risks that may be associated with this approach, and the ongoing commitment to evaluate the effectiveness of approaches that are being used.

Promoting Inclusion

Growing evidence shows that placing children with autism with their peers who are nondisabled in general education settings, with appropriate supports, can make a significant difference in their behaviors. Personal Spotlight features one professional's perspective on including this group of students.

As Myles and Simpson (2002) noted, students with AS, in particular, are educated primarily in regular classrooms. This placement seems particularly appropriate for these students, and clearly they have the capacity to benefit significantly from academic instruction in general education programs. In fact, contrary to conventional wisdom about inclusion, students with AS may experience more difficulty through inclusion in the nonacademic portions of the day (e.g., lunch, recess) than the academic portions.

One key challenge of the successful inclusion of students with ASD in the general education classroom is the incorporation of key curricular needs into the educational programs for these students. According to the National Research Council (cited in GAO, 2005, p. 33), core instructional objectives should include attention to the following:

- Social skills
- Expressive verbal language, receptive language, nonverbal communications skills
- A functional symbolic communication system, engagement and flexibility in developmentally appropriate tasks and play
- Fine and gross motor skills

Personal Spotlight

A Professional's Opinion on Inclusion

Kim Spence-Cochran is the coordinator of educational and training programs at the University of Central Florida's Center for Autism and Related Disabilities. Kim's research and training interests include alternative communication systems, curriculum development, personnel preparation, family advocacy, and inclusion. As coordinator, Kim deals regularly with the question of the appropriate placement for students with autism. She noted, "I feel very strongly about the inclusion of people with autism spectrum disorders. I am acutely aware that inclusion means different things to different people; my definition consists of each individual getting what he or she needs out of an educational environment with typical peers. It is a process that must be determined carefully based upon each individual's needs.

"I always viewed my classroom as a MASH unit or a 'triage center.' By this, I mean that I felt it was my responsibility to stabilize my students in preparation for them to go out into general education settings. For my students, an intense focus on social skills instruction was required to assist them in successful inclusive situations, as well as in the development of friendships. Additionally, they often required some form of communicative and behavioral support to successfully navigate the school and/or general education classrooms. Along with the skills I taught my students, I often found myself educating other teachers and administrators about the capabilities, gifts, and talents of my students. I have long held the belief that our society would function at a much greater capacity if it were more tolerant of the individual differences among all people."

Kim Spence-Cochran
University of Central Florida

- Cognitive skills (symbolic play and academic skills)
- Conventional/appropriate behaviors
- Independent organizational skills and skills for success in a regular classroom.

Appropriate role models in general education are very important. Peers can provide a basis for students with ASD to understand social situations and develop the ability to respond in a socially appropriate fashion. (See Chapters 6 and 13 for more information on behavior management and social skills instruction.)

An encouraging finding was reported by Boutot and Bryant (2005, p. 14), who found that "students with autism in inclusive settings are [just] as accepted, visible, and members of peer groups, as well as both their peers without disabilities and those with other disabilities."

A promising intervention strategy for children and adults with autism is self-management—implementing a variety of techniques that assist in self-control. See the nearby Evidence-Based Practice box for further information. Ruble and Dalrymple (2002) suggest a variety of environmental supports that can facilitate the success of students with autism in inclusive settings. These are listed in Figure 9.8.

Egel (1989) emphasized two important principles that should inform educational programs for children with autism: the use of functional activities and an effort to make programs appropriate for the student's developmental level and chronological age. Children with autism grow up to be adults with autism; the condition cannot be cured. As a result, educational programs should help them deal with the daily needs that will extend throughout their lives. Educators should ask themselves the following questions:

1. Does the program teach skills that are immediately useful?
2. Will the materials used be available in the student's daily environment?
3. Will learning certain skills make it less likely that someone will have to do the task for the student in the future?

Self-management is a promising intervention strategy for children with autism.

EVIDENCE-BASED PRACTICE

Teaching Self-Management Skills

Teaching students with autism to increase their self-management skills is an area that is appropriate for many of these students. The following provides examples of self-management goals and supports that could help students achieve these goals:

Goal 1: to independently transition from one activity to another using a picture/word schedule
Supports
- Imitate peers
- Learn by observing
- Provide visual supports including schedule for the day, steps in each activity, completion of activity, and time to move

- Train peers in how to use schedule
- Peer models

Goal 2: to stay in bounds at recess
Supports
- Imitate skills
- Learn by observing
- Teach and practice skills
- Use flags to show playground boundaries
- Use peers to model staying within boundaries
- Reinforce appropriate behaviors

Goal 3: to work quietly during individual work time
Supports
- Imitation skills
- Academic ability
- Motivation to do what other students are doing
- Peer models
- Visual reminders about being quiet
- Social story for quiet work
- Positive reinforcement for appropriate behaviors

Adapted from "COMPASS: A Parent-Teacher Collaboration Model for Students with Autism," by L. A. Ruble and M. J. Dalrymple, 2002, *Focus on Autism and Other Developmental Disabilities, 17*, pp. 76–83.

Figure 9.8	**Environmental Supports for Children with Autism**

Communicating to the person (receptive language supports)
- Slow down the pace.
- State positively what to do (e.g., "Let's walk" instead of "Stop running").
- Provide more information in visual format.

Encouraging communication from the person (expressive language supports)
- Pause, listen, and wait.
- Encourage input and choice when possible.
- Provide alternative means, such as written words or pictures, to aid communication.
- Encourage and respond to words and appropriate attempts, rather than to behavior.

Social supports
- Build in time to watch, encourage watching and proximity.
- Practice on specific skills through natural activities with one peer.
- Structure activities with set interaction patterns and roles.
- Provide cooperative learning activities with facilitation.
- Facilitate recruitment of sociable peers to be buddies and advocates.
- Provide opportunity for shared experiences using interests and strengths.

Expanding repertoires of interests and activities
- Capitalize on strengths and individual learning styles.
- Over time, minimize specific fears and frustrations.
- Use rehearsal with visuals.

From "COMPASS: A Parent-Teacher Collaborative Model for Students with Autism," by L. A. Ruble and M. J. Dalrymple, 2002, *Focus on Autism and Other Developmental Disabilities, 17*, p. 76. Used with permission.

Programs for students with autism should also be age appropriate and developmentally appropriate. The individual's chronological age and developmental status must be considered together. Sometimes an incongruence exists between these two realms, making program planning a challenge (McDonnell et al., 1995). In this case, developmentally appropriate materials must be modified to make them as age appropriate as possible. The nearby IEP Goals and Objectives for Cody are developmentally appropriate for her. Developmental levels should also be taken into consideration when implementing classroom adaptations. See Tips for Adapting a Lesson for Cody for examples of the adaptations that might be appropriate for her.

TEACHING TIP

Remember that students with ASD present a wide range of characteristics, strengths, and weaknesses. Treat each child as a unique individual, and do not expect them all to need the same kinds of services.

Special Considerations: AS

Just as there is no single method to teach children with ASD in general, there is also not a preferred educational intervention for children with AS. Teachers must address several issues when dealing with these children and develop effective strategies for each child on an individual basis. Areas that should be considered include using visual strategies, which takes advantage of their more intact learning modality; using structural strategies, such as preparing students for changes in schedules and routines; and providing an instructional sequence that follows a logical progression for learning (Myles & Simpson, 1998).

Safran (2002b) provides the following tips for teachers working with students with AS:

- Carefully structure seating arrangements and group work.
- Provide a safe haven.
- Save the student from himself or herself.
- Prepare for changes in routine.
- Use available resources/make needed accommodations.

*IEP Goals and Objectives for Cody**

For Cody, the second-grader introduced in the opening vignette, appropriate goals and objectives might include the following:

Goal 1:   *To reproduce written materials*
　Objective 1:　*Given a set of letter and word templates, Cody will be able to trace the letters and words with 80 percent accuracy.*
　Objective 2:　*Given a set of letters and words on a piece of paper, Cody will be able to write the letters and words with 80 percent accuracy.*
　Objective 3:　*Given the assignment to write her name and a four-sentence story, Cody will write her name with 100 percent accuracy and the story with 70 percent accuracy.*

Goal 2:   *To participate in group activities*
　Objective 1:　*During a recess game, Cody will be able to remain with a selected group 80 percent of the time without disruptions or leaving the group.*
　Objective 2:　*Given the opportunity to participate in a cooperative learning activity, Cody will do so for at least ten minutes, without any inappropriate behaviors, 80 percent of the time.*

Goal 3:   *To increase expressive vocabulary*
　Objective 1:　*Given an opportunity to express herself verbally, Cody will increase her expressive vocabulary by ten words over a two-week period.*
　Objective 2:　*Given the need to go to the bathroom, Cody will verbally communicate the need to go to the bathroom appropriately 100 percent of the time.*

*Note: IDEA 2004 does not require short-term objectives except for students taking alternative assessments.

Tips for Adapting a Lesson for Cody

Based on the opening vignette, the following adaptations for Cody are appropriate.

Cody's teacher should

- Make sure that Cody is attending before starting instruction.
- Make the instruction clear and brief.
- Make sure the instruction is appropriate and relevant.
- Be consistent with instructions.
- Use effective but not unintended prompts.
- Fade prompts as appropriate.
- Make consequences contingent, immediate, consistent, and clear.
- Positively reinforce appropriate responses.
- Change consequences if they are ineffective.

Adapted from *Autism: Teaching Does Make a Difference* (p. x), by B. Scheuermann and J. Webber, 2002. Belmont, CA: Wadsworth.

- Connect with each other, parents, Internet support groups, and other groups.
- Promote positive peer interactions.
- Capitalize on special interests.
- Don't take it personally.
- Help your classroom become a caring community. (p. 64)

Concluding Thoughts

The dramatic increase in the prevalence along with the complexity of causes and professional debate about effective treatments has dominated the field in recent years. As increased attention has been given to these issues, a national focus has emerged on ASD. The key emphases for the future are outlined in Figure 9.9.

Figure 9.9	**Federal Ten-Year ASD Research Plan**

- Find genetic and nongenetic causes.
- Enhance optimal treatments.
- Develop effective techniques to detect autism as early as possible.
- Develop early intervention programs to prevent autism from developing (so no label by school age).
- Evaluate efficacy of specific medical and behavioral treatments.
- Increase resources to study potential environmental factors.
- Advance knowledge of neuroscience *(to determine brain systems/mechanisms)*.
- Research strategies to improve "real-world" functioning of school-age and older people with autism.
- Understand why the number of children with autism has increased.
- Increase efficiency with which research findings are communicated to others *(e.g., scientists, practitioners, autism community)*.

From "Goals and Activities: Government Develops Research Plan to Combat Autism," *CEC Today, p. 7.*

Summary

- ASD is a pervasive developmental disability that primarily affects social interactions, language, and behavior.
- Although originally thought to be caused by environmental factors, autism is now considered to be caused by organic factors.
- A dramatic increase in the number of students with ASD has occurred in the past decade.
- Although many of the behavioral characteristics displayed by children with AS are similar to those displayed by children with autism, the former generally have higher cognitive development and more typical communication skills.

- A number of specific interventions have been developed for students with ASD.
- Because the field of ASD has witnessed a number of "miracle cures," it is particularly important that evidence-based interventions be used.
- Growing evidence suggests that placing students with autism in general education classrooms results in positive gains.

Questions to Reconsider

Think back to the scenario about Cody that you read at the beginning of this chapter. Would you answer the questions raised there any differently after reading the chapter?

1. Is there a preferred placement for children with autism?

2. What kinds of supports should be available for Cody to facilitate her success in the general education classroom?
3. Is a child ever ready for inclusion, or does the school have to make the placement decision and provide the necessary supports to make it work?

Further Readings

Baker, L. J., & Welkowitz, L. D. (2005). *Asperger's syndrome: Intervening in schools, clinics, and communities.* Mahweh, NJ: Erlbaum.

Barnhill, G. P., & McBride, K. (2002). *Right address wrong planet: Children with Asperger syndrome becoming adults.* Shawnee Mission, KS: Autism Asperger Syndrome Publishing.

Koegel, R. L., & Koegel, L. K. (1995). *Teaching children with autism.* Baltimore, MD: Brookes.

Wetherby, A. M., & Prizant, B. M. (Eds.). (2000). *Autism spectrum disorders: A transactional developmental perspective.* Baltimore, MD: Brookes.

ᴍylabschool
Where the classroom comes to life

Go to Allyn & Bacon's MyLabSchool (www.mylabschool.com) and enter Assignment ID SIM02 into the Assignment Finder. Work through the MLS Simulations, *Accessing the General Education Curriculum: Inclusion for Students with Disabilities, Parts I and II,* which addresses issues related to the inclusion of all students with disabilities. Then consider what you have read in the Simulation along with what you've read in Chapter 9 to answer the following question.

1. How do the issues raised in these simulations relate to students with Autism Spectrum Disorders?

You may also complete the activities included in the simulations and e-mail your responses to your instructor.

Teaching Students with Low-Incidence Disabilities: Sensory Impairments, Traumatic Brain Injury, and Other Severe Disabilities

After reading this chapter, you should be able to:

1. Define and describe students with hearing and vision problems.
2. Define and describe students with traumatic brain injury.
3. Define and describe students with health problems and physical disabilities.
4. Define and describe students with severe mental retardation.
5. Describe various intervention strategies for students with sensory impairments, traumatic brain injury, and other severe disabilities.

Questions to Consider

1. What kind of special skills does Manuel's third-grade classroom teacher need to meet Manuel's educational and social needs?

2. What can Manuel's teacher do to help him improve his social skills?

3. What skills are critical for Manual to have to be successful in higher grades that focus on content topics?

Manuel is nine years old. He was diagnosed with a hearing impairment when he was two-and-a-half years old. While Manuel had appeared to develop typically for the first twelve months, his parents began to realize that he did not seem to respond to noises or voices. He also did not seem to start the "typical" babbling or trying to say words. He was officially diagnosed as having a mild-moderate hearing loss when he was thirty-six months old. At that time he was referred for a preschool special education program where he received half-day services from a special education teacher and daily services from a speech-language pathologist.

Manuel has been included in general education classrooms since kindergarten. He has been wearing a hearing aid since the age of three and can utilize spoken language. Manuel spends thirty minutes a day with a speech-language pathologist, and is beginning to express himself orally fairly effectively. His teacher, Ms. James, and his classmates are able to understand most of what Manuel says. Still, he seems to be isolated from other children and often sits by himself in the lunchroom. Ms. James has implemented a peer support system for Manuel in an effort to get him more included in the social aspects of the classroom. Julie volunteered to serve as Manuel's peer support during classroom activities, and Jeremy serves as his peer support during recess and lunch. These two students have greatly facilitated Manuel's social inclusion.

Manuel is a low-average student. His main difficulties are in reading and written expression, skills directly related to his hearing impairment. He does extremely well in math and really likes science. Manuel's IEP provides him with thirty minutes of resource room time daily, when he receives more intensive support for reading and written expression.

Previous chapters have focused on students with disabilities often considered "high-incidence" disabilities. Learning disabilities, attention deficit disorder, emotional disturbance, and mental retardation occur much more frequently than disabilities described in this chapter. Some special education professionals dichotomize disabilities into high-incidence and low-incidence, depending on the likelihood of occurrence. Disabilities described in this chapter are all considered low-incidence disabilities.

Sensory impairments, including hearing impairments and visual impairments, are typically considered low-incidence disabilities because they do not occur in many children. In addition to these two categories of disabilities, many other conditions that occur relatively rarely in children can result in significant challenges for these students, their families, school personnel, and other professionals. Examples of these conditions include traumatic brain injury (TBI) and a host of physical and health problems that may be present in school-age children, such as cerebral palsy, spina bifida, AIDS, cystic fibrosis, epilepsy, and diabetes.

Many general education classroom teachers will teach their entire careers without encountering children with these problems. However, as a result of IDEA and the inclusion of students with a wide range of disabilities in general education classrooms, at least part of the school day, teachers need to have a general understanding of these conditions and how to support these students in the classroom.

Describing every aspect of hearing impairment, visual impairments, TBI, and other low-incidence disabilities is not possible here. However, this chapter discusses the more common, and in some cases, unique, aspects of these conditions. Table 10.1 shows the number of children in each group served in special education programs during the 2001–2002 school year.

This chapter will provide substantial information on hearing impairments and visual impairments. Other low-incidence conditions, primarily subsumed under the other health impaired and orthopedically impaired categories in IDEA, will be presented more briefly. Finally, although mental retardation has been discussed in a previous chapter, implications of severe MR for schools will also be described.

CEC STANDARDS

CEC 2: Development and Characteristics of Learners

An Overview of Sensory Impairments

The category of sensory impairments includes hearing impairments and visual impairments. Students with sensory impairments may be at a distinct disadvantage in academic settings because of the extent that hearing and vision are used in teaching and

Table 10.1

Number of Students, Ages 6–21, with Visual Impairments, TBI, and Health and Physical Disabilities Served in Public Schools during the 2001–2002 School Year

Source: *Annual Report to Congress on the Implementation of the Individuals with Disabilities Education Act* (p. 25), U.S. Department of Education, 2003. Washington, DC: Author.

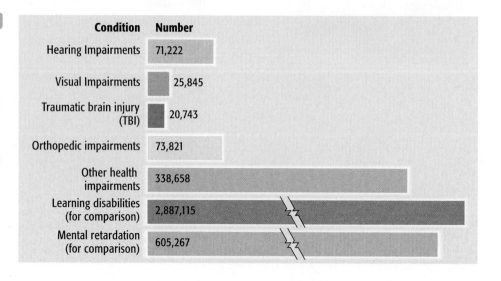

Condition	Number
Hearing Impairments	71,222
Visual Impairments	25,845
Traumatic brain injury (TBI)	20,743
Orthopedic impairments	73,821
Other health impairments	338,658
Learning disabilities (for comparison)	2,887,115
Mental retardation (for comparison)	605,267

learning. Stop to think about the things you do in class; they nearly all include visual or auditory activities. Having limitations in these areas can cause substantial difficulties in the teaching and learning process.

As with all students with special needs, some debate remains regarding the best setting in which to provide services to students with visual and hearing impairments. Whereas many students with sensory impairments were historically served in residential settings, today most students with these conditions are placed in general education settings. While most of these students are capable of handling the academic and social demands of these settings, a variety of accommodations may be needed, ranging from minor seating adjustments to the use of sophisticated equipment for communicating, listening, or navigating, in order for them to be successful (Freiberg, 2005). Students with these impairments may also need the support of additional personnel (e.g., a sign-language interpreter or Braille instructor).

To provide appropriate accommodations, teachers must have accurate information about how to modify their classrooms and adapt instruction to meet students' needs. In addition, they need to understand the psychosocial aspects of these types of disabilities. For some students with severe sensory problems, special consultants may also be needed to assist general education teachers. Ultimately, teachers must feel comfortable and confident that they can address the range of needs these students present.

Sensory impairments are considered low-incidence disabilities since there are not large numbers of these students in the school population. The number of students (ages six to twenty-one) with hearing or visual impairments who were officially identified and provided with special education or related services nationally for the school year 2001–2002 was only 97,067 (see Table 10.1). These are small numbers, considering the total number of students in this age range. Furthermore, these groups represent a very small percentage of all students who are disabled. However, having only one of these students in a classroom may seem overwhelming, as this student may require a variety of modifications in classroom management and in certain instructional practices. Students who have both vision and hearing losses present significant challenges for educators.

Basic Concepts about Hearing Impairment

Hearing impairment is a hidden disability—an observer typically cannot tell from looking at physical features alone that a person's hearing is impaired. However, in any context where communicative skills are needed, hearing limitations become evident. Put yourself in a setting with other people when you cannot hear what is being said. Individuals who are not able to process information audibly are at a distinct disadvantage; students in school who cannot understand spoken language, a primary mode for teaching, must have access to accommodations and appropriate instruction.

Students with a hearing disability pose a variety of challenges to the general classroom teacher. Although their numbers are increasing, relatively few students with profound hearing loss (deafness) are educated in general education settings (U.S. Department of Education, 2005). When these students are placed in general education classes, they need a variety of accommodations, including a sign-language interpreter and high technology.

The number of students who have some degree of hearing loss (i.e., mild to severe) is more noteworthy, because these students can function in general education settings more easily when certain accommodations are provided. To achieve this purpose, it is critical for teachers to understand the nature of hearing impairments and to know how to address the needs associated with these conditions. In addition to these students, other students have minimal hearing losses that are not severe enough to be eligible for special education services; however, they are at a distinct disadvantage in the general education classroom if the teacher does not recognize their problem (Kaderavek & Pakulski, 2002).

INTASC

INTASC 2: How children learn and develop

PRAXIS

PRAXIS I: Understanding Exceptionalities

CONSIDER THIS

Should students whose only disability is hearing or visual impairment be segregated in state residential schools, often many miles away from their families?

CEC STANDARDS

CEC 2: Development Characteristics of Learners

INTASC

INTASC 2: How Children learn and develop

PRAXIS

PRAXIS I: Understanding Exceptionalities

CONSIDER THIS

Do some of the terms used in this chapter—for example, hearing impairment—convey a clear understanding of a particular hearing disability? Which terms in the text are the most descriptive and useful to teachers?

The importance of language acquisition and usage to the development of cognitive abilities and achievement in academic subject areas is unassailable (Polloway, Miller, & Smith, 2003). While the greatest effect of a hearing impairment is on a student's ability to hear someone speak, "its impact on communication development dramatically alters social and academic skill acquisition" (Brackett, 1997, p. 355). Language is a dominant consideration when discussing appropriate education for students with hearing losses (Mayer, Akamatsu, & Stewart, 2002).

The following sections provide basic information on hearing impairments. Teachers who build a solid working knowledge in this area can teach more effectively and communicate more clearly with other professionals and with families.

Hearing Impairment Defined

The number of different terms associated with hearing loss often causes confusion. Three terms are frequently encountered in relation to students with hearing losses, including hearing impairment, deafness, and hard of hearing.

1. *Hearing impairment* is the generic term that has frequently been used to cover the entire range of hearing loss.
2. *Deafness* describes hearing loss that is so severe that speech cannot be understood through the ear alone, with or without aids.
3. *Hard of hearing* describes individuals who have a hearing loss that makes it difficult, but not impossible, to understand speech through the ear alone, with or without a hearing aid. (Moores, 2001)

Some school systems use other terminology, such as audibly impaired, to describe people with hearing loss.

Hearing loss is often measured in decibel (dB) loss. Individuals with losses from 25 to 90 dB are considered hard of hearing, whereas those with losses greater than 90 dB are classified as deaf.

Most schools use the definitions of hearing impairment found in IDEA. The federal definitions of deafness and hearing impairment are as follows:

- *Deafness* means a hearing impairment that is so severe that the child is impaired in processing linguistic information through hearing, with or without amplification, that adversely affects a child's educational performance. (IDEA, 2004)
- *Hearing impairment* means an impairment in hearing, whether permanent or fluctuating, that adversely affects a child's educational performance but that is not included under the definition of deafness in this section. (IDEA, 2004)
- *Minimal hearing loss,* which is not included in the federal definition of hearing impairment but which can cause problems for students, is defined as a loss of between 16 and 25 dB. (Kaderavek & Pakulski, 2002)

Classification of Hearing Impairment

Typically, hearing loss is organized into four different groups: conductive hearing loss (mild loss in both ears); sensorineural hearing loss (caused by sound not being transmitted to the brain); mixed hearing loss; and central auditory hearing loss (Salvia & Ysseldyke, 2004). Table 10.2 summarizes the audiological, communicational, and educational implications for each type of loss. Each specific type and degree of loss poses challenges in learning and communicating.

Prevalence and Causes of Hearing Impairment

Significant hearing impairments affect approximately three to four in every 1,000 births (Hear-It.org, 2006). As noted in Table 10.1, approximately 71,200 students are served in special education programs for students with hearing impairments. This figure

Table 10.2	Symptoms Associated with Conductive Hearing Loss; Unilateral Hearing Loss; Mild, Bilateral Sensorineural Hearing Loss; and Moderate-to-Severe Bilateral Sensorineural Hearing Loss

	Audiological	Communicative	Educational
Conductive Hearing Loss	• Hearing loss 30 dB (range 10–50 dB) • Poor auditory reception • Degraded and inconsistent speech signal • Difficulty understanding under adverse listening conditions • Impaired speech discrimination • Hearing loss overlays developmental requirement for greater stimulus intensity before infants can respond to and discriminate between speech • Inability to organize auditory information consistently	• Difficulty forming linguistic categories (plurals, tense) • Difficulty in differentiating word boundaries, phoneme boundaries • Receptive language delay • Expressive language delay • Cognitive delay	• Lower achievement test scores • Lower verbal IQ • Poorer reading and spelling performance • Higher frequency of enrollment in special support classes in school • Lower measures of social maturity
Unilateral Hearing Loss	• Hearing loss moderate to profound • Impaired auditory localization • Difficulty understanding speech in presence of competing noise • Loss of binaural advantage: binaural summation, binaural release from masking	• Tasks involving language concepts may be depressed	• Lags in academic achievement: reading, spelling, arithmetic • Verbally based learning difficulties • High rate of grade repetition • Self-described: embarrassment, annoyance, confusion, helplessness • Less independence in the classroom
Mild Bilateral Sensorineural Hearing Loss	• Hearing loss 15–20 dB • Speech recognition depressed • Auditory discrimination depressed • Amplification considered: FM systems, classroom amplification	• Potential problems in articulation • Problems in auditory attention • Problems in auditory memory • Problems in auditory comprehension • Possible delays in expressive oral language • Impact on syntax and semantics	• Impact on vocabulary development • Lowered academic achievement: arithmetic problem solving, math concepts, vocabulary, reading comprehension • Educational delays progress systematically with age
Moderate-to-Severe Bilateral Sensorineural Hearing Loss	• Hearing loss 41–90 dB • Noise and reverberation significantly affect listening and understanding • Audiologic management: essentials, amplification recommendations, monitor hearing for: –otitis media –sudden changes in hearing –progressive hearing loss	• Deficits in speech perception • Deficits in speech production (mild-to-moderate articulation problems) • Language deficits from slight to significant: syntax, morphology, semantics, pragmatics • Vocabulary deficits	• Slight to significant deficits in literacy (reading and writing) • Deficits in academic achievement • High rate of academic failure • Immaturity • Feelings of isolation and exclusion • Special education supports needed

From "Hearing Loss and Its Effect," by A. O. Diefendorf (p. 5), in *Hearing Care for Children,* edited by F. N. Martin and J. G. Clark, 1996. Boston: Allyn & Bacon. Used by permission.

Table **10.3**　　**Possible Characteristics of Students with Hearing Impairments**

Area of Functioning	Possible Effects
Psychological	• Intellectual ability range similar to hearing peers • Problems with certain conceptualizations
Communicational	• Poor speech production (e.g., unintelligibility) • Tested vocabulary limited • Problems with language usage and comprehension, particularly abstract topics • Voice quality problems
Social–Emotional	• Less socially mature • Difficulty making friends • Withdrawn behavior—feelings of being an outsider • Possible maladjustment problems • May resent having to wear a hearing aid or use other amplification devices • May be dependent on teacher assistance
Academic	• Achievement levels significantly below those of their hearing peers • Reading ability most significantly affected • Spelling problems • Limited written language production • Discrepancy between capabilities and performance in many academic areas

represents only about 0.11 percent of the total school population (U.S. Department of Education, 2003). Although the number is small of children with hearing impairments significant enough to be eligible for special education, the Centers for Disease Control and Prevention (CDC) have estimated that as many as 15 percent of all children experience some degree of hearing loss (Crawford, 1998). This estimate includes those children with minimal hearing loss that does not result in eligibility for special services (Kaderavek & Pakulski, 2002).

Many different factors can lead to hearing impairments. These include genetic causes (Hear-It.org., 2006); developmental anomalies (Clark & Jaindl, 1996); toxic reaction to drugs, infections, prematurity, and Rh incompatibility (Moores, 2001); birth trauma (Chase, Hall, & Werkhaven, 1996); allergies (Lang, 1998); and noise-induced hearing loss (Haller & Montgomery, 2004). Knowing the specific cause of a hearing impairment is usually not important for school personnel, since the cause rarely affects interventions needed by students.

Characteristics of Students with Hearing Impairment

The characteristics of students with hearing impairment vary greatly. Four categories of characteristics are especially meaningful to the classroom setting: psychological, communicational, academic, and social-emotional. Specific characteristics that fall into each of these general categories are listed in Table 10.2. (Table 10.3 lists characteristics associated with types and degrees of hearing losses.)

Identification, Assessment, and Eligibility

The ease of identifying students with hearing impairment is related to the degree of hearing loss. Students with severe losses are more easily recognized, while those with mild losses may go unrecognized for many years or even their entire school career

(Kaderavek & Pakulski, 2002). The prevalence of hearing loss among children is higher than cited in previous reports because of delayed identification, which often results in serious consequences for children. As noted previously, data indicate that as many as 15 percent of children in the United States have low- or high-frequency hearing loss that is often too mild to allow easy identification (Herer & Reilly, 1999). Teachers should be aware of certain indicators of possible hearing loss and refer students who show these signs for a comprehensive assessment (Stewart & Kluwin, 2001). Teachers should consider referring a student for an evaluation if some of the following behaviors are present (Kaderavek & Pakulski, 2002; Moores, 2001; Stewart & Kluwin, 2001):

- Turns head to position an ear in the direction of the speaker.
- Asks for information to be repeated frequently.
- Uses a loud voice when speaking.
- Pulls or presses on ear.
- Does not respond when spoken to.
- Gives incorrect answers to questions.
- Has frequent colds, earaches, or infections.
- Appears inattentive and daydreams.
- Has difficulty following directions.
- Is distracted easily by visual or auditory stimuli.
- Misarticulates certain speech sounds or omits certain consonant sounds.
- Withdraws from classroom activities that involve listening.
- Has a confused expression on face.
- Has a restricted vocabulary.
- Fidgets or moves about in seat.

A teacher's careful observations and referral can spare a student months or years of struggle and frustration. While all students referred will not be found to have a significant hearing loss, they should be referred so that an assessment can be made to determine which students need additional supports.

Formal Assessment   The assessment of hearing ability requires the use of various audiological techniques. The most common method of evaluating hearing is the use of **pure-tone audiometry**, in which sounds of different frequencies are presented at increasing levels of intensity. This assessment determines the hearing threshold of the student for different frequency pure tones in each ear. Tympanometry screening is another type of formal hearing testing. This type of testing, also known as impedance audiometry, "is designed to detect abnormal conditions, not to detect educationally significant hearing losses" (Salvia & Ysseldyke, 2005, p. 387). The tympanometry screening can detect defects in the middle ear, which could significantly impact education (Salvia & Ysseldyke, 2005).

Informal Assessment   In addition to the formal assessment conducted by audiologists, teachers and other school personnel should engage in informal assessment of students, especially those suspected of having a hearing impairment. Informal assessment focuses on observing students for signs that might indicate a hearing loss. Tables 10.2 and 10.3 list indicators that, if recorded over a period of time, show that a student may need formal assessment.

Eligibility   The eligibility of students for special education and related services is determined by individual state departments of education. Most states follow the federal guidelines for eligibility and add certain levels of decibel loss as criteria. The federal criteria are included in the definitions cited previously. To be eligible under the category of hearing impairment, the students must meet the definitions and must need special education.

Teachers should not be concerned about specific eligibility criteria, but should refer students who display characteristics suggesting the presence of a hearing loss. The evaluation/eligibility committee will be responsible for making the decisions.

TEACHING TIP

Teachers should keep records of students who display these types of behaviors to determine whether there is a pattern that might call for a referral.

CEC STANDARDS

CEC 2: Development and Characteristics of Learners

INTASC

INTASC 2: How children learn and develop

PRAXIS

PRAXIS I: Understanding Exceptionalities

Strategies for Curriculum and Instruction for Students with Hearing Impairments

Students with hearing impairment may present a significant challenge for general education teachers. Language is an important component of instruction and it is difficult for teachers to use standard instructional methods effectively with students who have problems processing language because of hearing losses. Teachers have to rely on supports provided by special education staff and specialists in hearing impairments to meet the needs of these students.

Realities of the General Education Classroom

Students with hearing impairments vary greatly in their need for supports in the general education classroom. Students with mild losses, generally classified as hard of hearing, need minimal supports. In fact, these students resemble their nondisabled peers in most ways. If amplification assistance can enable these students to hear clearly, they will need little specialized instruction (Dagenais et al., 1994).

Students with severe hearing impairments, those classified as deaf, present unique challenges to teachers. Specialized instructional techniques usually involve alternative communication methods; the use of interpreters is typically a necessity for these students. General education teachers must know how to utilize the services of an interpreter to facilitate the success of students with significant hearing losses. They must remember that interpreters are providers of a related service; they are not teachers (Heath, 2006).

Continuum-of-Placement Options Students with hearing impairments are educated in the complete **continuum-of-placement** options, depending on their individual needs. These options range from general education classrooms to residential schools for the deaf. The topic of educational placement for students with hearing impairments has been the most controversial aspect of educating this group of students (Edwards, 1996). As with all students with disabilities, there is no single educational setting that is best for all students with hearing impairments. The placement decision for students with hearing impairments should be based on the unique needs of the student and the IEP process (Edwards, 1996).

Still, the trend continues toward educating more students with hearing impairments in the general education classroom. During the 2000–2001 school year, almost 60 percent of all students with hearing impairments were educated in general education classrooms for at least 40 percent of the school day (U.S. Department of Education, 2003). This figure compares with approximately 44 percent served in the same types of settings during the 1986–1987 school year (U.S. Department of Education, 1989). During the 1999–2000 school year, fewer than 10 percent of these students were educated in residential settings, the most likely placement prior to the passage of Public Law 94–142 (U.S. Department of Education, 2003). The trend, therefore, favors inclusion, which in turn signals a need for supports and services to help students succeed. Types of supports that students with hearing impairments need resemble those needed by students with other disabilities, except for a few services specific to students with hearing problems.

Classroom Adaptations for Students with Hearing Impairments

As mentioned before, the general education setting is appropriate for most students who are hard of hearing and for many students who are deaf. However, this statement is true only if the specific needs of these students are taken into consideration.

CONSIDER THIS

How do educational needs differ for these two students: one with a mild hearing loss who can effectively use a hearing aid and one who is not disabled?

CONSIDER THIS

What are some obvious advantages and disadvantages to the different placement options for students with hearing impairments?

IEP Goals and Objectives for Manuel

Goals and objectives for Manuel, whom you met in the introductory vignette, might include the following. IDEA 2004 does not require objectives. Objectives are provided here to give examples of how interventions might be directed toward goals:

Goal 1: *To improve literacy skills, including reading and writing.*
  Objective 1: *Manuel will improve his reading level by 1.5 grade levels by the end of the year.*
  Objective 2: *Manuel will improve his written expression skills by 1.5 grade levels by the end of the year.*
  Objective 3: *Manuel will improve his comprehension skills by 1.5 grade levels by the end of the year.*

Goal 2: *To develop better social skills.*
  Objective 1: *Manuel will interact with peers during recess at least 50 percent of the time.*
  Objective 2: *Manuel will initiate conversations with peers at least 50 percent of the time during classroom communication time.*
  Objective 3: *Manuel will be selected by three peers as part of a group of ten for different social activities at least once each week.*

The following sections provide recommendations for accommodating these students in general education classrooms. Specific suggestions are also given. Both general recommendations and specific suggestions are clustered under four major areas: management considerations; curricular and instructional accommodations; social-emotional interventions; and technology.

Management Considerations for Students with Hearing Impairments

The effective management of a classroom is critical to maximizing the potential for learning. This important topic is covered in detail in Chapter 14. Attention to classroom management can help include students with various degrees of hearing impairment in general education settings.

CROSS-REFERENCE

Preview the section in Chapter 14 on rules and procedures appropriate for all students with disabilities and for students without disabilities.

Standard Operating Procedures The dimension of standard operating procedures refers to the rules, regulations, and procedures that operate in a classroom. Students who have hearing impairments must be subject to the same requirements as other

---

Tips for Adapting a Lesson for Manuel

Ways to adapt lessons for Manuel:

- Provide reading materials at Manuel's reading and interest level.
- Provide Manuel with the opportunity to use a computer for writing exercises.
- Provide a set of advanced organizers for all students prior to beginning a lesson.
- Make sure that Manuel is listening prior to beginning a lesson or providing instructions.
- Provide Manuel with regular feedback, especially related to his literacy skills.
- Orchestrate opportunities for Manuel to be included in social activities.

CEC STANDARDS

CEC 4: Instructional Strategies

students. Some procedures may have to be modified to accommodate special needs. For instance, students may be allowed to leave their seats to get the attention of a student who cannot hear a spoken communication.

Teachers should always confirm that students understand the rules and procedures developed for the classroom. Teachers may also want to establish a buddy system (i.e., a peer support system). With such a system, a student with normal hearing is assigned to assist the student with a hearing impairment in, for example, following procedures for a fire drill or helping the student take notes during a class lecture.

Physical Considerations for Students with Hearing Impairments   Seating is the major consideration related to the physical setup of the classroom. Teachers need to ensure that students are seated to maximize the use of their residual hearing or to have an unobstructed view of an interpreter. Since information presented visually is extremely helpful to these students, they need to be positioned to take advantage of all visual cues (Berry, 1995). Following are some specific suggestions (Luckner & Denzin, 1998):

INTASC

INTASC 4: Instructional strategies

PRAXIS

PRAXIS III: Delivery of Services to Students with Disabilities

- Seat student in the best place to facilitate attending and participating.
- Seat students in a semicircular arrangement to increase sight lines for student and teacher.
- Position teacher so that student can read lips.
- Position teacher so that he or she faces student when talking.

In addition, make sure that students who use interpreters are seated so that they can easily see the interpreter, the teacher, and any visuals that are used. Unfortunately, seating a student with a hearing loss near the front of the class is rarely the only modification that needs to be made. In contrast to teaching methods of the past, today very little may happen at the front of the room (Crawford, 1998).

CONSIDER THIS

How can teachers use seating as an effective accommodation even when there is a great deal going on in different parts of the room?

Creating a Favorable Environment for Students with Hearing Impairments   As noted in the preceding section, more than preferential seating is necessary for students with a hearing loss. Attention must be given to creating a supportive acoustical environment throughout the classroom. Modifications that can be made to provide an accommodating acoustical environment include (Scott, 1997):

CEC STANDARDS

CEC 5: Learning Environments and Social Interaction

- acoustical ceiling tiles
- carpeting
- thick curtains
- rubber tips on chair and table legs
- proper maintenance of ventilation systems, lighting, doors, and windows

INTASC

INTASC 5: Learning environments

Preinstructional Considerations   Teachers must also carefully plan ahead to deliver instruction in a way that will benefit students with hearing impairments. The following list gives many practical suggestions:

- Allow students to move about the classroom to position themselves for participation in ongoing events.
- Let students use swivel chairs.
- Reduce distracting and competing noise by modifying the classroom environment (e.g., carpeting on floor, corkboard on walls).
- Ensure that adequate lighting is available.
- Provide visual reminders indicating the amount of time left for an activity or until the end of class.
- Use cooperative learning arrangements to facilitate student involvement with hearing peers.
- Include a section of the lesson plan for special provisions for students with hearing impairments.

PRAXIS

PRAXIS III: Delivery of Services to Students with Disabilities

- Acquire or develop visually oriented materials to augment orally presented topics—use overhead projection systems when appropriate.
- Use homework assignment books and make sure that students understand their assignments.

Specific suggestions related to grouping, lesson planning, materials acquisition and adaptation, and homework systems can befound in Chapter 14.

Curricular and Instructional Considerations

All basic elements of effective instructional practice will benefit students with hearing impairment. However, certain specific ideas will enhance their learning experiences.

Communication   Perhaps the most challenging aspect of teaching students whose hearing is impaired is making sure that they participate in communicational activities (i.e., teacher to student, student to teacher, student to student) in the classroom and that they are able to handle the reading and writing demands of the class. Language and communication tend to dominate the teaching of these students (Mayer et al., 2002). Students who have profound hearing loss must rely on alternative methods of communication, such as sign language or lip reading. Because these students typically do not become facile with standard forms of English, they can have significant problems in the areas of reading and writing. Sign language does not follow the grammatical conventions of English.

When students using some form of manual communication, usually **American Sign Language (ASL)**, are in general education classrooms, teachers are not required to learn this language. However, teachers should make an effort to know some of the more common signs and to be able to finger-spell the letters of the alphabet as well as the numbers one to ten. If students can communicate only by using sign language, an interpreter will most likely need to be present. Teachers should know basic information about the role and functions of an interpreter.

Still another form of communication that may be effective is **cued speech** (Stewart & Kluwin, 2001). Cued speech is a system of hand cues that enhances lip-reading. Eight different hand shapes represent consonant sounds and four hand positions represent vowel sounds. Using the hand signs near the lips provides students with cues that help with their lip-reading (Blasi & Priestley, 1998).

Teachers should be conscious of how well they are communicating with their students. The teacher's speech, location, and movement in the classroom can affect the facility with which a student with a hearing impairment can follow a discussion or lecture. The proper use of assistive equipment (e.g., amplification devices) can also make a difference. This topic is covered in a subsequent section.

Transition Planning   Students with hearing impairments must be involved in their transition planning (Garay, 2003). While IDEA requires the involvement of students in the development of their IEP, certain steps must be taken to make this effective for students with hearing impairments. For example, materials need to be provided in writing and an interpreter must be present in cases where an interpreter is necessary for true involvement.

Delivery of Instruction   Teachers need to utilize a host of practices that allow students to learn more effectively and efficiently. One suggestion already mentioned, the use of visually oriented material, is especially valuable for students with hearing problems. The following are additional suggestions:

- Make sure students are attentive.
- Provide short, clear instructions.
- Speak clearly and normally—do not exaggerate the pronunciation of words.

DIVERSITY FORUM

Language, Communication, and Multiple Cultural Identities

Manuel has a large, extended family that is very active in the Mexican American community. He attends many social events that are predominantly in Spanish. Manuel is biliterate and has learned English primarily at school. He attends a Saturday clinic for families with children who are deaf and hard of hearing, where he learned American Sign Language. Manuel's parents enjoy the Saturday clinic where they have become close with another family from Mexico whose older daughter, Yolanda, learned Mexican Sign Language (LSM) prior to coming to the U.S. (Faurot et al., 1999). Yolanda spends one day a week teaching Manuel LSM. Since Manuel has begun learning LSM, he is less motivated to speak English and prefers to use LSM.

Recently, Mr. Cisneros, the bilingual speech-language pathologist who runs the Saturday clinic contacted Manuel's teacher, Ms. James, to discuss his progress. Ms. James shared her concern for Manuel's literacy development. Mr. Cisneros was

surprised because of Manuel's recent acquisition of LSM and connection with a deaf role model. In talking with Ms. James, he began to realize that Manuel was exploring his deaf identity by limiting his use of oral language and only using sign language (Corson, 2001). As a result, Mr. Cisneros recommended the following tips to foster the development of literacy skills:

- Offer reading materials by authors from the same cultural and linguistic background, and on topics and interests relevant to Manuel's experiences.
- Ensure that technology equipment has the capacity to translate materials, allowing him to communicate in his native language.
- Include organizers with key concepts and instructions for upcoming tasks prior to a lesson in his native language or at his English language proficiency level.
- Have an educator/interpreter from the same linguistic and cultural background review his work.

- Orchestrate opportunities for social activities with peers from similar linguistic and cultural backgrounds who are responsive to his interests.

Questions

1. In what way does Manuel's cultural and linguistic background influence his desire to interact with his hearing peers?
2. How can the literacy curriculum and instruction be modified to meet the cultural and linguistic needs of Manuel?

REFERENCES

Faurot, K. et al., (1999). The identity of Mexican sign as a language. Summer Institute of Linguistics. Retrieved on October 6, 2006 at http://www.sil.org/mexico/lenguajes-de-signos/G009i-1dentity-mfs.pdf.

Corson, D. (2001). *Language Diversity and Education*. Mahwah, NJ: Lawrence Erlbaum Associates.

- Keep your face visible to students.
- Avoid frequent movement around the classroom, turning your back on students while talking, and standing in front of a bright light source.
- Use gestures and facial expressions.
- If the student reads speech, male teachers should make sure that their mustache and beard are trimmed to maximize visibility.
- Maintain eye contact with the student, not the interpreter.
- Check with students to confirm that they understand what is being discussed or presented.
- Encourage students to request clarification and to ask questions.
- Identify other speakers by name so that students can more easily follow a discussion among more than one speaker.
- Repeat the comments of other students who speak.
- Paraphrase or summarize discussions at the end of a class session.
- Write information when necessary.
- Have students take responsibility for making themselves understood.
- Provide students with advance organizers, such as outlines of lectures and copies of overhead transparencies.
- Preview new vocabulary and concepts prior to their presentation during a lecture.

- Use the demonstration-guided practice-independent practice paradigm as often as possible (see Polloway & Patton, 1993, for more information).
- Utilize a variety of instructional formats, including demonstrations, experiments, and other visually oriented activities.
- Emphasize the main points covered in a lecture both verbally and visually.
- Use lots of visual aids (e.g., overhead transparencies, slides, diagrams, charts, multimedia) to explain material.
- Provide summaries, outlines, or scripts of videotapes, videodiscs, or films.
- Let students use microcomputers for word processing and for checking their spelling and grammar.

Teaching secondary-level content classes to students with hearing impairments is uniquely challenging. See the nearby Tips for Adapting a Lesson for Manuel.

Coteaching has been shown to be one effective method for teaching students with hearing losses in general education classes. This model encourages general classroom teachers and teachers of students with hearing losses to combine their skills in an inclusive setting. "Coteaching allows teachers to respond to the diverse needs of all students, provides another set of hands and eyes, lowers the teacher–student ratio, and expands the amount of professional expertise that can be directed to student needs" (Luckner, 1999, p. 150).

Social-Emotional Considerations

Classrooms constitute complex social systems. In addition to development of scholastic abilities and academic support skills, personal development is also occurring. Students need to learn how to get along with their peers and authority figures while they learn how to deal with their beliefs and emotions. While the available research suggests that students with hearing impairments develop similarly, socially and emotionally, to their hearing peers (Moores, 2001), teachers still need to be able to help students develop a realistic sense of their abilities, become more responsible and independent, interact appropriately with their peers, and enhance their self-concept and sense of belonging (Luckner, 1994). The following are some specific suggestions:

- Create a positive, supportive, and nurturing classroom environment.
- Encourage class involvement through active participation in classroom activities and interaction in small groups.
- Let students know that you are available if they are experiencing problems and need to talk.
- Help the students with normal hearing understand the nature of hearing impairment and what they can do to assist.
- Practice appropriate interactive skills.
- Encourage and assist students to get involved in extracurricular activities.
- Help them develop problem-solving abilities.
- Help students develop realistic expectations.
- Prepare students for dealing with the demands of life and adulthood.

Technology

Technology has been a boon for individuals with hearing impairments (Stewart & Kluwin, 2001). Simple strategies such as using closed-captioned movies are important (Wurst, Jones, & Luckner, 2005). Students with hearing impairments placed in general education classrooms often use devices to help them to maximize their communication abilities (Easterbrooks, 1999), and they need a supportive environment in which to use these devices (McAnally, Rose, & Quigley, 1999). Teachers need a working knowledge of these devices so that they can ensure that the student benefits from the equipment.

TEACHING TIP

When students in your classroom use assistive listening devices, learn as much about the devices as possible so that you will be able to maximize their use.

Tips for Adapting a Lesson for Manuel

The following are some ways to infuse concepts related to deaf students and self-advocacy throughout the school curriculum for Manuel.

Manuel's teacher should:

- Understand Manuel's strengths and weaknesses.
- Provide written copies of materials that are provided orally.
- Make sure that Manuel understands assignments.
- Encourage Manuel to use oral language and provide positive reinforcement to him when he speaks.
- Implement a buddy system so that Manuel has a partner during social activities.
- Routinely check to ensure that Manuel's hearing aid is working properly.
- Allow Manuel to sit near the front of the class and have students face Manuel when they are talking.
- Encourage Manuel to turn and watch students when they are talking.
- Collaborate with the speech therapist to find out what reinforcing activities can be done in the classroom to improve Manuel's use of oral language.

PRAXIS

PRAXIS II: Delivery of Services to Students with Disabilties

Assistive Listening Devices   Assistive listening devices (ALDs) include hearing aids and other devices that amplify voices and sounds, communicate messages visually, or alert users to environmental sounds (Marschark, Lang, & Albertini, 2002). Children with even small hearing losses, those in the 16- to 25-dB range, may have problems hearing faint or distant speech without some amplification (Iskowitz, 1998).

Hearing aids are the predominant ALDs found in schools. These devices pick up sound with a microphone, amplify and filter it, and then convey that sound into the ear canal through a loudspeaker, also called a receiver (Marschark et al., 2002). They work very well with students who experience mild-to-severe hearing losses (Iskowitz, 1997). Educators must realize that hearing aids amplify sounds; they do not make the sound clearer. Often, students who use hearing aids must have auditory training to learn to use and discriminate the sounds (Deafness.about.com, 2006).

To assist students in maximizing the use of their ALDs, teachers should:

- know what type of ALD a student uses.
- understand how the device works: on/off switch, battery function (e.g., selection, life span, insertion), volume controls.
- be able to determine whether a hearing aid is working properly.
- help students keep their hearing aids functioning properly (e.g., daily cleaning, appropriate storage).
- make sure students avoid getting their hearing aids wet, dropping or jarring them, spraying hairspray on them, and exposing them to extreme heat (Shimon, 1992).
- keep spare batteries on hand.
- ensure that the system is functioning properly.
- be sure that students turn the transmitter off when not engaged in instructional activities to prevent battery loss.
- perform daily troubleshooting of all components of the system (Brackett, 1990).
- make sure background noises are minimized.

Figure 10.1 includes a list of media, materials, and technology available for students with hearing losses. This information should provide teachers with a beginning understanding of how to meet the needs of students with hearing loss. We strongly recommend that teachers consult with a hearing specialist to determine the best possible

Figure 10.1	**Media, Materials, and Technology for Students with Hearing Losses**

Visual Technology, Media, and Materials	• Microcomputers and computer systems such as ENFI • Captioning systems • Computer-assisted notetaking • Videotapes and interactive video discs • Instructional CDs and software • Telecommunication technology • Printed materials, programs, and packages
Auditory Technology, Media, and Materials	• Induction loops • FM systems • Programmable hearing aids • Soundfield amplification systems • Cochlear implants • Instructional CDs, interactive listening developmental program, and software • Audiocassette programs • Computer-based speech training systems

From Bruce, Peyton, & Batson, 1993; Kaplan et al., (1993).

accommodations to provide an appropriate educational environment for students with hearing problems.

Promoting Inclusive Practices for Students with Hearing Impairments

Being an integral part of the inclusive school community is important for students with hearing impairments who receive their educational programs in public schools, especially for those placed in general education classrooms. Simply physically situating students in classrooms does not automatically make them included members of the class. This statement especially holds true for children with hearing impairments who have a very difficult time associating with the "hearing" culture (Andrews & Jordan, 1998). Students with hearing losses may tend to keep to themselves and withdraw from social activities (Hear-it.org., 2006). Therefore, teachers must ensure that these students become part of the community of the school and class and are socially accepted by their peers.

Teachers may have to orchestrate opportunities for interaction between students with hearing impairments and their nondisabled peers. These could include grouping, pairing students for specific tasks, assigning buddies, and establishing a circle of friends. Kluwin (1996) suggests using dialogue journals to facilitate this interaction. Students are paired (one hearing and one nonhearing) to make journal entries and then exchange them. Rather than assign deadlines, allow students to exchange journal entries whenever they want to. You may need to give them ideas appropriate for sharing to get them started. Reward students for making and exchanging journal entries. This approach encourages interactions among students with hearing impairments and their nondisabled peers without using a rigidly structured activity or assignment.

Supports for the General Education Teacher

Students with hearing impairments often create major challenges for general classroom teachers, primarily because of the language barrier that hearing loss often creates. Therefore, teachers must rely on support personnel such as educational consultants who

CONSIDER THIS

Do you think students with hearing impairments can be included and accepted in the classroom by their peers in spite of their differing language skills? Should students with hearing impairments be isolated in institutions with other students who have hearing losses? Why or why not?

CEC STANDARDS

CEC 10: Collaboration

INTASC

INTASC 10: Relationships with School Colleagues

PRAXIS

PRAXIS II: Delivery of Services to Students with Disabilities

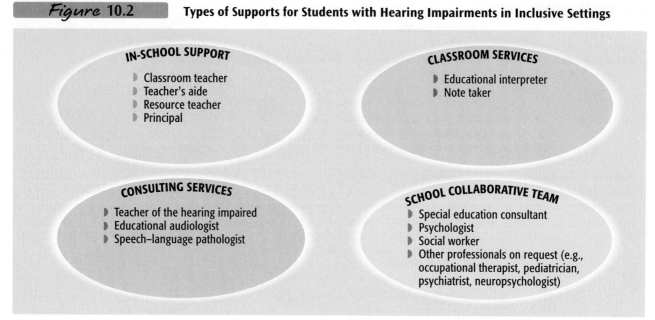

Figure 10.2   **Types of Supports for Students with Hearing Impairments in Inclusive Settings**

From "Educational Management of Children with Hearing Loss," by C. Edwards, p. 306, in *Hearing Care for Children,* edited by F. N. Martin and J. G. Clark, 1996. Boston: Allyn & Bacon. Used by permission.

specialize in the area of hearing impairment, as well as interpreters, audiologists, and medical personnel, to assist them in their efforts to provide appropriate educational programs. Professionals, such as speech-language pathologists, deaf educators, and interpreters can greatly assist general classroom teachers when dealing with students with hearing impairments (Hanks & Velaski, 2003). See Figure 10.2 for potential sources of support.

Basic Concepts about Visual Impairment

Students with visual impairments also pose unique challenges to teachers in general education classrooms. Although the number of students whose vision creates learning-related problems is not large (see Table 10.1), having even one such student in a classroom may require a host of accommodations. Students with visual impairments that cannot be corrected comprise the smallest number of children in any one category served under IDEA (Freiberg, 2005).

Vision plays a critical role in the development of concepts, the understanding of spatial relations, and the use of printed material. In fact, "vision is intimately involved with 70% to 80% of all tasks that occur in our educational programs" (Li, 2004, p. 39). Thus children with visual problems have unique educational needs. For students whose vision is limited, teachers have to use alternative teaching strategies, modified materials, and technology (Downing & Chen, 2003). Teachers may be able to use their usual instructional techniques with some modifications with students who have some functional vision. But for students who have very little or no vision, teachers will need to implement alternative techniques to provide effective educational programs.

General education classes are appropriate settings for many students with visual impairments. However, teachers working with these students need to understand the nature of a particular student's vision problem to be able to choose appropriate accommodative tactics. They need basic information related to four categories: fundamental concepts of vision and visual impairment; signs of possible visual problems; typical characteristics of students with visual problems; and specific accommodative techniques for meeting student needs.

TEACHING TIP

Try using an idea from a children's game to work with children with visual impairments. Just as you would ask a blindfolded child what information he or she needs to make progress in the game, ask the children with visual impairments what assistance or information he or she needs to benefit from your teaching.

Visual Impairments Defined

Because a number of different terms are associated with the concept of visual impairment, confusion regarding the exact meaning of visual terminology is often a problem. These are the most frequently used terms and their definitions:

- *Visual impairment* is a generic term that includes a wide range of visual problems.
- *Blindness* has different meanings depending on context, resulting in some confusion. *Legal blindness* refers to a person's visual acuity and field of vision. It is defined as a visual acuity of 20/200 or less in the person's better eye after correction, or a field of vision of 20 degrees or less. An educational definition of *blindness* implies that a student must use Braille (a system of raised dots that the student reads tactilely) or aural methods to receive instruction (Freiberg, 2005).
- *Low vision* indicates that some functional vision exists to be used for gaining information through written means with or without the assistance of optical, nonoptical, or electronic devices (Freiberg, 2005).

Students with low vision are capable of handling the demands of most classroom settings. However, they will need some modifications to perform successfully. Students who are blind (i.e., have very little or no vision) will need major accommodations to be successful in general education settings.

Classification of Visual Impairments

Visual problems can be categorized in a number of ways. One typical method organizes visual problems as refractive errors (e.g., farsightedness, nearsightedness, and astigmatism); retinal disorders; disorders of the cornea, iris, and lens; and optic nerve problems. In addition to common refractive problems, which usually can be improved with corrective lenses, other visual problems include the following:

- *strabismus*—improper alignment of the eyes
- *nystagmus*—rapid involuntary movements of the eye
- *glaucoma*—fluid pressure buildup in the eye
- *cataract*—cloudy film over the lens of the eye
- *diabetic retinopathy*—changes in the blood vessels of the eye caused by diabetes
- *macular degeneration*—damage to the central portion of the retina, causing central vision loss
- *retinitis pigmentosa*—genetic eye disease leading to total blindness (Smith, 2007)

Tunnel vision denotes a condition caused by deterioration of parts of the retina that leaves the person with central vision only. Individuals who have tunnel vision can see as if they are looking through a long tube; they have little or no peripheral vision.

Regardless of the cause of the visual problem, educators primarily have to deal with its functional result. Educators focus on "what experiences a child needs in order to be able to learn" (Freiberg, 2005, p. 133). Whether the student has usable residual vision is an important issue, as is the time at which the vision problem developed. Students who are born with significant visual loss have a much more difficult time understanding some concepts and developing basic skills than students who lose their vision after they have established certain concepts (Warren, 1994).

Prevalence and Causes of Visual Impairments

Vision problems are common in U.S. society. Fortunately, corrective lenses allow most individuals to see very efficiently. However, many individuals have vision problems that cannot be corrected in this way. As with hearing impairments, the number of individuals who have visual impairments increases with age. In the school-age population, approximately 0.04 percent of students are classified as visually impaired. During the

CONSIDER THIS

Some students who are classified as blind are actually able to read print and do not need to use Braille. Are there descriptors other than blind and low vision that would better describe students with visual impairments for educational purposes?

CEC STANDARDS

CEC 2: Development and Characteristics of Learners

INTASC

INTASC 2: How children learn and develop

PRAXIS

PRAXIS II: Understanding Exceptionalities

CONSIDER THIS

How does the low incidence of visual impairments affect a school's ability to provide appropriate services? How can small systems meet the needs of these children when there may be only one child with a visual impairment in the district?

2001–2002 school year, 25,845 students, ages six to twenty-one, were classified as having visual impairments in the United States (U.S. Department of Education, 2003).

Etiological factors associated with visual impairments include genetic causes, physical trauma, infections, premature birth, anoxia, and retinal degeneration. Retrolental fibroplasia (RLF) was a common cause of blindness in the early 1950s, resulting when premature infants were exposed to too much oxygen in incubators. Once the cause of this problem was understood, it became nearly nonexistent. However, this cause of blindness is reasserting itself as medical science faces the challenge of providing care to infants born more and more prematurely. Blindness sometimes accompanies very premature birth.

Characteristics of Students with Visual Impairments

The most educationally relevant characteristic of students who have visual impairments is the extent of their visual efficiency. More specific characteristics can be categorized as psychological, communicational, academic, and social-emotional. These characteristics are listed in Table 10.4. In a recent study of the physical activity level of students with visual impairments, it was determined that this group of students have low levels of physical activity, for a variety of reasons (Ayvazoglu, Oh, & Kozub, 2006).

Identification, Assessment, and Eligibility

Students with visual impairments can be easily identified if their visual loss is severe. However, many students have milder losses that are much more difficult to identify and may go several years without being recognized. Teachers must be aware of behaviors that could indicate a vision problem. Table 10.5 summarizes possible symptoms of vision problems.

Formal Assessment   Students are screened for vision problems in schools, and when problems are suspected, a more in-depth evaluation is conducted. The typical eye examination assesses two dimensions: visual acuity and field of vision. Visual acuity is most often evaluated by the use of a **Snellen chart**. As Salvia and Yssledyke (2004) note, two versions of this chart are available: the traditional version using alphabetic letters of different sizes, and the other version using the letter E presented in different spatial

Table 10.4   **Possible Characteristics of Students with Visual Impairments**

Area of Functioning	Possible Effects
Psychological	• Intellectual abilities similar to those of sighted peers • Concept development can depend on tactile experiences (i.e., synthetic and analytic touch) • Unable to use sight to assist in the development of integrated concepts • Unable to use visual imagery
Communicational	• Relatively unimpaired in language abilities
Social/Emotional/Behavioral	• May display repetitive, stereotyped movements (e.g., rocking or rubbing eyes) • Socially immature • Withdrawn • Dependent • Unable to use nonverbal cues
Mobility	• Distinct disadvantage in using spatial information • Visual imagery and memory problems with functional implications
Academic	• Generally behind sighted peers

Table 10.5	**Symptoms of Possible Vision Problems**
Behavior	• Rubs eyes excessively • Shuts or covers one eye, tilts head, or thrusts head forward • Has difficulty in reading or in other work requiring close use of the eyes • Blinks more than usual or is irritable when doing close work • Holds books close to eyes • Is unable to see distant things clearly • Squints eyelids together or frowns
Appearance	• Crossed eyes • Red-rimmed, encrusted, or swollen eyelids • Inflamed or watery eyes • Recurring styes
Complaints	• Eyes that itch, burn, or feel scratchy • Cannot see well • Dizziness, headaches, or nausea following close eye work • Blurred or double vision

From *Exceptional Learners: Introduction to Special Education* (9th ed., p. 343), by D. P. Hallahan and J. M. Kauffman, 2003. Boston: Allyn & Bacon. Used by permission.

arrangements and sizes. While these charts can effectively determine the likelihood of children having vision problems, they might not detect near vision problems.

Once students are identified as having possible vision problems, they should be referred for more extensive evaluations. Ophthalmologists, medical doctors, and optometrists (who specialize in evaluating vision and prescribing glasses) are typically involved in this more-extensive evaluation. These specialists determine the specific nature and extent of any vision problem.

Still other formal assessments of vision focus on the ability of students to use their vision. Examples of these types of assessments include functional-vision assessment and learning-media assessment. The learning-media assessment determines the efficiency with which students gather information from sensory modalities; the types of learning media used by students; and the media used for reading and writing (Salvia & Yssledyke, 2004).

Informal Assessment   A great deal of informal assessment should be completed by school personnel. Like that of students with hearing impairments, the informal assessment of students with visual impairments focuses on observation. Teachers and other school personnel note behaviors that might indicate a vision loss or change in the vision of the child. Once students are identified as having a problem, school personnel must be alert to any changes in the student's visual abilities.

Eligibility   Most states adhere to the eligibility guidelines established in IDEA for students with visual impairments. These guidelines focus on the visual acuity of students. Students with a 20/200 acuity or worse, in the better eye with best correction, are eligible as blind students, whereas those with a visual acuity of 20/70 to 20/200 are eligible as low-vision students. As with all students with disabilities served under IDEA, these students must evidence need of special education services to be eligible for them.

Strategies for Curriculum and Instruction for Students with Visual Impairments

Even though students with visual impairments learn similarly to their sighted peers (Bosman, Gompel, Vervloed, & van Bon, 2006), their inability to process visual information efficiently results in their needing specific curricular and instructional modifications. For students with low vision, these modifications may simply mean enlarging printed materials to sufficient size so that the student can see them. For students with little or no vision, modifications must be more extensive.

Realities of the General Education Classroom

Students with visual impairments present a range of needs. Those who are capable of reading print, with modifications, often require minimal curricular changes; those who must read using Braille require significant changes. Teachers should remember that even students who are capable of reading print may need modifications in many day-to-day activities. These may be as simple as ensuring appropriate contrast in printed materials and having students sit in a place that will optimize their vision.

Continuum-of-Placement Options

Like students with hearing impairments, students with visual problems may be placed anywhere on the full continuum of placement options, ranging from general education classrooms to residential schools for students with visual impairments. *The National Agenda for the Education of Children and Youth with Visual Impairments, Including Those with Multiple Disabilities* calls for all schools to offer programs that will give all students a full array of placement options (Corn et al., 1995). Students must be evaluated individually to determine the appropriate educational placement. Although some totally blind students function very well in general education settings, many are placed in residential schools where they receive more extensive services.

The trend for placing students with visual impairment is in the direction of inclusive settings. During the 2000–2001 school year, approximately 70 percent of all students with visual impairments were served in general education classrooms at least 40 percent of each school day. Almost 50 percent were in general classrooms more than 80 percent of the school day. During this same year, fewer than 8 percent were educated in residential schools (U.S. Department of Education, 2003).

Classroom Adaptations for Students with Visual Impairments

Certain classroom accommodations will enhance the quality of programs for students with visual problems. The following sections recommend ways to address the needs of these students, organized according to five categories: general considerations; management considerations; curricular and instructional accommodations; social-emotional interventions; and technology.

General Considerations

When educating students with visual impairments, the unique needs of each student must be considered (Desrochers, 1999). However, some general practices apply for most, if not all, students with these problems. These practices include:

- Ask the student if assistance is needed.
- Do not assume that certain tasks and activities cannot be accomplished without accommodations or modifications.
- Include students with visual impairments in all activities that occur in the class.
- Use seating arrangements to take advantage of any vision the child can use.
- Encourage the use of residual vision.

Remember that many characteristics of students with visual impairments (i.e., intelligence, health) may not be negatively affected by the vision problem.

Children with visual impairments have low levels of physical activity, so school personnel should work to increase activity levels. Since the activity level of children with visual disabilities has been shown to be related to the activity level of parents, school personnel should collaborate with parents to increase the activity level of students (Ayvazoglu et al., 2006).

Management Considerations

A variety of classroom management tactics can be helpful to students who have vision problems. Classroom management is discussed in detail in Chapter 14. When students with vision problems are present, attention needs to be given to standard operating procedures, physical considerations, and preinstructional considerations.

Standard Operating Procedures   The same standards of expected behavior should be applied to all students, including those who have visual problems. However, students with visual limitations may need special freedom to move around the classroom to find the place where they can best see demonstrations or participate in activities.

Physical Considerations   Students with visual problems need to know the physical layout of the classroom so that they can navigate through it without harming themselves. Teachers have to orient these students to the classroom by taking them around the classroom and noting certain features, such as the location of desks, tables, and materials. A clock orientation approach is useful—for example, the front of the class is twelve o'clock, at three o'clock is the teacher's desk, at six o'clock is the reading table, and at nine o'clock is the area for students' coats and backpacks. Appropriate seating is extremely important for students who are able to use their existing vision. Placement of the student's desk, lighting, glare, and distractions should be considered when situating such students in the classroom.

Preinstructional Considerations   Teachers should plan ahead to adapt instruction to the needs of students with visual impairments. Class schedules must allow extra time for students who use large-print or Braille materials, as it takes longer to use these materials.

Test-taking procedures may need to be modified. Modifications might involve preparing an enlarged version of the test, allowing extra time, or arranging for someone to read the test to the student.

Some students may need special instruction in study skills such as note taking, organizational skills, time management, and keyboarding. These become increasingly

EVIDENCE-BASED PRACTICE

Physical Activity of Children with Visual Impairments

Research shows that individuals with visual impairments become less physically active with age. Physical activity among all individuals is linked to a variety of good physical and mental health. Ayvazoglu and colleagues (2006) identified the following ways to increase physical health among children with visual impairments:

- Promote peer involvement in physical activity.

- Ensure safety provisions are in place for family members.
- Provide children with visual impairments with the necessary skills to engage in physical activities.
- Involve family members in the physical activities of children.
- Provide school programs that are supportive of home activities.

- Focus school programs on fitness as well as recreational activities.

Source: "Explaining Physical Activity in Children with Visual Impairments: A Family Systems Approach," by N. R. Ayvazoglu, Hyun-Kyoung Oh, and Francis M. Kozub, 2006, *Exceptional Children, 72,* pp. 235–248.

important as students move to middle school and high school. The following are some specific accommodation suggestions:

- Assign a classmate to assist students who may need help with mobility in emergency situations.
- Teach all students in the class the proper techniques of being a sighted guide.
- In advance, inform staff members at field-trip sites that a student with a visual problem will be part of the visiting group.
- Tell students with visual problems that you are entering or leaving a room so that they are aware of your presence or absence.
- Have all students practice movement patterns that you expect of them, to maintain an orderly classroom.
- Orient students to the physical layout and other distinguishing features of the classroom.
- Maintain consistency in the placement of furniture, equipment, and instructional materials—remove all dangerous obstacles.
- Keep doors to cabinets, carts, and closets closed.
- Assist students in getting into unfamiliar desks, chairs, or other furniture.
- Eliminate auditory distractions.
- Seat students to maximize their usable vision and listening skills—often a position in the front and center part of the room is advantageous.
- Seat students so that they are not looking into a source of light or bothered by glare from reflected surfaces.
- Ensure that proper lighting is available.
- Create extra space for students who must use and store a piece of equipment (e.g., Brailler, notebook computer).
- As a special section of the lesson plan, include notes for accommodating students with visual problems.

Curricular and Instructional Considerations

As the principal agents in delivering instruction, teachers should use techniques that will ensure success for students who have visual problems. A special challenge involves conveying primarily visual material to those who cannot see well. For example, it will require some creativity on the part of the teacher to make a graphic depiction of the circulatory system in a life science book (a two-dimensional illustration) accessible to a student who can see little or not at all. Three-dimensional models or illustrations with raised features might address this need. Teachers have to decide what should be emphasized in the curriculum when students with visual impairments are in their classes. As a result of the wide array of curricular options for these student, teachers must "(a) address the multifaceted educational requisites of their students, (b) ensure that instruction occurs in all areas of greatest need, and (c) ensure that sufficient instructional time is allocated for identified educational priorities" (Lueck, 1999, p. 54).

Materials and Equipment Special materials and equipment can enhance the education of students who have visual impairments. Some materials (e.g., large-print materials) are not appropriate for all and must be considered in light of individual needs. Vision specialists can help teachers select appropriate materials and equipment.

Teachers need to use tactile strategies when teaching students with visual impairments. This may require making tactile adaptations of materials used. Some considerations for developing tactile adaptations include (Downing & Chen, 2003):

1. Identify the objective of the lesson or the instructional concept.
2. Select the materials to convey this concept.
3. Close your eyes and examine the material with your hands.
4. Take a tactile perspective, not visual, when deciding how and what to present.

5. If the entire concept (e.g., house) is too complicated to represent through a tactile adaptation, then select one aspect of the concept (e.g., key) for the tactile representation.
6. Consider the student's previous tactile experiences. What items has he or she examined? How does the student examine materials through the sense of touch?
7. Decide how the item will be introduced to the student.
8. Identify what supports the student needs to tactilely examine the item.
9. Decide what language input (descriptive words) will be used to convey the student's experience of the material. (p. 59)

Classmates can assist students with visual problems in areas such as mobility.

Many materials found in general education classrooms may pose difficulties for students with vision problems. For instance, the size and contrast of print materials have a real effect on students with visual problems. Print size can generally be taken care of with magnification devices; however, little can be done to enhance the poor contrast often found on photocopies. Consider these points when using photocopies:

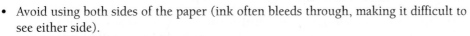

- Avoid using both sides of the paper (ink often bleeds through, making it difficult to see either side).
- Avoid old or light work sheet masters.
- Avoid work sheet masters with missing parts or creases.
- Give the darkest copies of handouts to students with visual problems.
- Do not give a student with a visual impairment a poor copy and say, "Do the best you can with this."
- Copy over lines that are light with a dark marker.
- Make new originals when photocopies become difficult to read.
- Avoid the use of colored inks that may produce limited contrast.
- Do not use colored paper—it limits contrast.

Although large-print materials seem like a good idea, they may be used inappropriately. Barraga and Erin (1992) recommend that these materials be used only as a last resort, since they may not be readily available. They believe that large-print materials should be used only after other techniques (e.g., optical devices or reduction of the reading distance) have been tried.

Teachers also may want to use concrete materials (i.e., realistic representations of actual items). However, concrete representations of large real-life objects may not be helpful for young students, who may not understand the abstract notion of one thing representing another. Teachers must carefully ensure that all instructional materials for students with visual impairments are presented in the appropriate medium for the particular student (Corn et al., 1995).

Various optical, nonoptical, and electronic devices are also available for classroom use. These devices help students by enlarging existing printed images. If these devices are recommended for certain students, teachers will need to learn about them to ensure that they are used properly and to recognize when there is a problem. Teachers should practice the use of optical and electronic devices with students after consultation with a vision specialist.

Some students with more severe visual limitations may use Braille as the primary means of working with written material. They may use instructional materials that are printed in Braille and may also take notes using it. Through the use of computers, a student can write in Braille and have the text converted to standard print. The reverse process is available as well. If a student uses this system of communication, the teacher should consult with a vision specialist to understand how it works.

TEACHING TIP

Have a student who uses a Braille writer demonstrate the Braille code and methods of writing Braille to members of the class so they can understand the learning medium used by their classmate.

Following are some specific accommodation suggestions:

- Call students by name, and speak directly to them.
- Take breaks at regular intervals to minimize fatigue in listening or using a Brailler or optical device.
- Ensure that students are seated properly so that they can see you (if they have vision) and hear you clearly.
- Vary the type of instruction used, and include lessons that incorporate hands-on activities, cooperative learning, or the use of real-life materials.
- Use high-contrast materials, whether on paper or on the chalkboard—dry-erase boards may be preferable.
- Avoid using materials with glossy surfaces and, if possible, dittoed material.
- Use large-print materials only after other methods have been attempted and proved unsuccessful.
- Use environmental connectors (e.g., ropes or railing) and other adaptations for students with visual problems for physical education or recreational activities. (Barraga & Erin, 1992)
- Avoid using written materials with pages that are too crowded.

Social-Emotional Considerations

Although the literature is mixed on whether students with visual impairments are less well adjusted than their sighted peers (Hallahan & Kauffman, 2000), there is evidence that some students with this disability experience social isolation (Huurre, Komulainen, & Aro, 1999). As a result, many students with visual problems will benefit from attention to their social and emotional development. Social skill instruction may be particularly useful (Sacks, Wolffe, & Tierney, 1998). However, because social skills are typically learned through observing others and imitating their behaviors, it is difficult to teach these skills to students who are not able to see.

Concern about emotional development is warranted for all students, including those with visual problems. Teachers should make sure that students know that they are available to talk about a student's concerns. A system can be developed whereby a student who has a visual impairment can signal the need to chat with the teacher. Being accessible and letting students know that someone is concerned about their social and emotional needs are extremely important.

The following are some specific accommodation suggestions:

- Encourage students with visual problems to become independent learners and to manage their own behaviors.
- Create opportunities for students to use tactile learning. (Downing & Chen, 2003)
- Reinforce students for their efforts.
- Help students develop a healthy self-concept.
- Provide special instruction to help students acquire social skills needed to perform appropriately in classroom and social situations.
- Teach students how to communicate nonverbally (e.g., use of hands, etc.).
- Work with students to eliminate inappropriate mannerisms that some students with visual impairments display.

Technology

Like students with hearing impairments, those with visual problems often use technological devices to assist them in their academic work and daily living skills. Low-vision aids include magnifiers, closed-circuit televisions, and monoculars. These devices enlarge print and other materials for individuals with visual impairments.

Assisstive Technology

There are numerous assistive technology devices that can assist individuals with severe disabilities, ranging from very simple to very complex. The following are examples of assistive technology that may help decrease or eliminate challenges encountered by individuals during daily living activities and communication.

Daily living activities

Clock/watch with Braille face

Large-print clock/watch

Audible clock/watch

Tactual control on home appliances

Larger numbers/words on appliances

Knife with cutting guide

Rocking knife

Cooking thermometer with tactual gauge

Spatula with top and bottom blade to grasp items to be turned

Braille or large-print label marker on foods, medicines, etc.

Talking thermometer

Large-button telephone

Talking scale

Talking blood pressure gauge

Magnifying mirror

Label for marking colors, patterns, sizes on clothing items

Needle threader for sewing

Tape measure and ruler with tactual markings

Built-up handles on eating utensils

Built-up sides on plates

Modified handle on toothbrush

Dycem (or other nonslip material to stabilize toys/objects)

Magnifier

Bath seat

Communication

Voice-output communication aid

Laptop computer with voice output

Non-electronic communication aid (pictures in a notebook or wallet, etc)

Braille writer

Slate and stylus (used to write Braille)

Hearing aid

Software that "reads" what is on the monitor

Telecommunications device for the deaf (TDD)

Telephone amplifier

Visual/vibrating alerting signal (for alarm clock, door bell, baby crying, etc.)

Switch (push, lever, joystick, pull) to access computers, etc.

From *An Introduction to Persons with Moderate and Severe Disabilities* (pp. 140–141), by J. J. McDonnell, M. L. Hardman, & A. P. McDonnell, 2005. Boston: Allyn & Bacon. Used with permission.

Many other technological devices are used by students with visual impairments. Refer to the nearby Technology Today box of some of these technological devices. While access to the Internet is relatively easy for students without visual problems, many students with visual impairments may have difficulty. Certain technological devices can make access to the Internet available. Braille printers and speech input/output devices can help achieve access. Access and computer training can give students with visual impairments a vast resource that can have a profound positive impact on their education (Heinrich, 1999).

Promoting Inclusive Practices for Students with Visual Impairments

Students with visual impairments, like those with hearing impairments, need to be part of the school community. Many can be included without special supports. However, for others teachers may need to consider the following (Amerson, 1999; Desrochers, 1999; Torres & Corn, 1990):

Access to Instructional Materials

Rights & Responsibilities

IDEA 2004 adds language related to access to instructional materials. IDEA 1997 did not refer to this topic. Section 612(a)(23) of IDEA 2004 states:

1. States must adopt the National Instructional Materials Accessibility Standard (NIMAS) to provide instructional materials to blind persons or those with disabilities in relation to print.

2. States do not have to coordinate with the National Instructional Materials Access Center (NIMAC), but must assure that they will provide materials to blind or print-disabled individuals in a timely manner.

3. If state coordinates with NIMAC, no later than two years after enactment of IDEA 2004 the state must contract with publishers to provide electronic files of print instructional materials to NIMAC using the NIMAS or must buy materials in specialized formats.

CEC STANDARDS

CEC 4: Instructional Strategies

INTASC

INTASC 4: Instructional strategies

PRAXIS

PRAXIS II: Delivery of Instruction to Students with Disabilities

CONSIDER THIS

Students with visual impairments may not be able to monitor visual cues from peers regarding social behaviors. How can you teach students with visual impairments to understand these visual cues?

- Remember that the student with a visual impairment is but one of many students in the classroom with individual needs and characteristics.
- Use words such as see, look, and watch naturally.
- Introduce students with visual impairments the same way you would introduce any other student.
- Include students with visual impairments in all classroom activities, including physical education, home economics, and so on.
- Encourage students with visual problems to seek leadership and high-visibility roles in the classroom.
- Use the same disciplinary procedures for all students.
- Encourage students with visual problems to move about the room just like other students.
- Use verbal cues as often as necessary to cue the student with a visual impairment about something that is happening.
- Provide additional space for students with visual impairments to store materials.
- Allow students with visual impairments to learn about and discuss with other classmates special topics related to visual loss.
- Model acceptance of visually impaired students as an example to other students.
- Encourage students with visual impairments to use their specialized equipment, such as a Braille writer.
- Discuss special needs of the child with a visual impairment with specialists, as necessary.
- Always tell a person with a visual impairment who you are as you approach.
- Help students avoid inappropriate mannerisms associated with visual impairments.
- Expect the same level of work from students with visual impairments as you do from other students.
- Encourage students with visual impairments to be as independent as possible.
- Treat children with visual impairments as you treat other students in the classroom.
- Provide physical supports for students with concomitant motor problems.
- Include students with visual impairments in outdoor activities and team sports.

In your efforts to promote a sense of community, consider that some students with visual impairments may have different cultural backgrounds than the majority of students in the school. School personnel must be sensitive to different cultural patterns. Bau (1999) noted seven cultural values that could have an impact on the provision of services to students with visual impairments: communication; health beliefs; family structure; attitude toward authority; etiquette; expectations of helping; and time orientation. To communicate clearly with a family that speaks a different language, you may need to use a language interpreter. Being sensitive to the culture and family background of students with visual impairments facilitates the delivery of appropriate services.

Supports for the General Education Teacher

As noted earlier, general education teachers can effectively instruct most students with visual impairments, with appropriate supports. A vision specialist may need to work with students on specific skills, such as Braille; an orientation and mobility instructor can teach students how to travel independently; an adaptive physical education instructor can help modify physical activities for the student with visual impairment.

Counselors, school health personnel, and vocational specialists may also provide support services for general education teachers. School personnel should never forget to include parents in helping develop and implement educational supports for students with visual impairments. In a recent study, McConnell (1999) found that a model program that included family involvement and support greatly assisted adolescents with visual impairments to develop career choices and values. Other ways to enhance the education of students with visual impairments include:

- Get help from others. Teach other students to assist in social as well as academic settings. Call parents and ask questions when you don't understand terminology, equipment, or reasons for prescribed practices.
- Learn how to adapt and modify materials and instruction.
- Learn as much as you can, and encourage the professionals you work with to do the same. Find out about training that may be available and ask to go.
- Suggest that others become informed, especially students. Use your local library and bookstores to find print material that you can read and share. (Viadero, 1989)

Basic Concepts about Traumatic Brain Injury

Traumatic brain injury (TBI) was added to the special education categories under IDEA in 1990. The condition is defined in the law as an acquired injury to the brain caused by an external physical force, resulting in total or partial functional disability or psychosocial impairment, or both, that adversely affects a child's educational performance. The term applies to open or closed head injuries resulting in impairments in one or more areas, such as cognition, language, memory, attention, reasoning, abstract thinking, judgment, problem solving, sensory, perceptual and motor abilities, psychosocial behavior, physical functions, information processing, and speech. The term does not apply to brain injuries that are congenital, degenerative, or induced by birth trauma (IDEA, 2004).

Traumatic brain injury is the most common cause of death and disability among children in the United States. Every year, 14 million individuals in the United States suffer a TBI, with 50,000 dying and an additional 235,000 hospitalized. It has been estimated that every twenty-three seconds, one person suffers a TBI; 5.3 million Americans currently live with TBI (Brain Injury Association of America, 2006). During the 2001–2002 school year, nearly 21,000 students were served in special education programs because of TBI (U.S. Department of Education, 2003). This fact means that many children who suffer from TBI are not in special education, making it even more important that general classroom teachers understand this disability. TBI can result from a wide variety of causes, including falls, vehicle accidents, and even abuse. It can also be caused by lack of oxygen to the brain, infections, tumors, and strokes (Garcia, Krankowski, & Jones, 1998).

The social-emotional and cognitive deficits caused by the injury may persist long after physical capabilities recover. Students with TBI can experience a host of confusing and frustrating symptoms, including cognitive changes; sensory, coordination, and

CEC STANDARDS

CEC 10: Collaboration

INTASC

INTASC 10: Relationships with school colleagues

PRAXIS

PRAXIS II: Delivery of Instruction to Students with Disabilities

CEC STANDARDS

CEC 2: Development and Characteristics of Learners

INTASC

INTASC 2: How children learn and develop

PRAXIS

PRAXIS II: Understanding Exceptionalities

CONSIDER THIS

What can school personnel do to facilitate the transition of children with TBI from hospital and residential settings to public school? What kind of relationship should school personnel and hospital personnel maintain after the transition is completed?

CEC STANDARDS

CEC 4: Instructional Strategies

INTASC

INTASC 4: Instructional strategies

PRAXIS

PRAXIS II: Delivery of Instruction to Students with Disabilities

attention problems; emotional lability; aggressiveness; and depression (Best, 2005). Teachers must guard against minimizing an injury because it presents no visible evidence and many children exhibit typical behaviors.

The prognosis for recovery depends on many variables, including the severity, location, and extent of the injury; immediacy of treatment; chronological age of the individual, and extent of time in a coma (Best, 2005). Later, it will be influenced by the nature of rehabilitative and educational intervention. Some students with TBI will become successful students, while others will have long-term lingering effects of their injury (see Table 10.6).

Classroom Adaptations for Students with TBI

The transition of students with TBI from rehabilitation facilities to school settings needs to be coordinated among a number of people. Intervention involves the efforts of professionals from many different disciplines, including teachers (Bergland & Hoffbauer, 1996). In addition to the injury itself and its implications on functioning and potential learning, students probably will have missed a significant amount of schooling. All these factors can have a significant impact on educational performance. An effective educational program creates a positive attitude about the student's prognosis. Such a program reaches beyond just speaking positively.

Teachers communicate a positive attitude by the type of programming they present and by the level of expectations they establish. Remember to "keep expectations for students' performance high. Often, this means providing students with mild TBI with mul-

Table 10.6	**Persisting Features of Traumatic Brain Injury**
Area of Functioning	**Possible Effects**
Physical/Medical	• Fatigue and reduced stamina • Seizures (5 percent) • Headaches • Problems with regulation of various functions (e.g., growth, eating, body temperature)
Sensory	• Hearing problems (e.g., conductive and/or sensorineural loss) • Vision problems (e.g., blurred vision, visual field defects)
Cognitive	• Memory problems (e.g., storage and retrieval) • Attentional difficulties • Intellectual deficits • Reasoning and problem-solving difficulties
Language-Related	• Word retrieval difficulties • Motor-speech problems (e.g., dysarthria) • Language comprehension deficits (e.g., difficulty listening) • Difficulty acquiring new vocabulary and learning new concepts • Socially inappropriate verbal behavior
Behavioral/Emotional	• Problems in planning, organizing, and problem solving • Disinhibition • Overactivity • Impulsivity • Lack of self-direction • Helplessness or apathy • Inability to recognize one's injury

From *Traumatic Brain Injury in Children and Adolescents: A Sourcebook for Teachers and Other School Personnel* (pp. 71–72), by M. P. Mira, B. F. Tucker, and J. S. Tyler, 1992. Austin, TX: Pro-Ed. Used by permission.

Figure 10.3   **Recommended Instructional Strategies for Children with TBI**

Use a multimodal approach (overheads, videos, hands-on activities) when presenting material and instructions for assignments.

Teach compensatory strategies to students and structure choices.

Begin class with review and overview of topics to be covered.

Provide the student with an outline of the material to be presented, to assist in comprehension.

Emphasize main points and key ideas frequently.

Incorporate repetition into instruction.

Provide specific, frequent feedback on student performance and behavior.

Encourage questions.

Break down large assignments into smaller components.

Use task analyses to determine skill acquisition and maintenance.

Ask the student how he or she could improve learning.

Use a variety of open-ended and multiple-choice questions to encourage independent thinking.

Present difficult material in a simplified fashion, using illustrations or diagrams if possible.

Provide the student with cues when appropriate.

From "Enhancing the Schooling of Students with Traumatic Brain Injury," by L. Keyser-Marcus et al., 2002, *Teaching Exceptional Children, 34,* p. 65. Used with permission.

tiple opportunities for practice that do not carry penalties for inaccuracy" (Hux & Hackley, 1996, p. 162). This will show the students that programs and instruction are designed to support them and not just to give them a grade. They will respond better when programs do not seem punitive.

Under IDEA 2004, TBI is a distinct category of disability, although some students may be provided services under Section 504. If they are identified under IDEA, they will have a written IEP; if served under Section 504, they will have an appropriate accommodation plan. Whatever plan is used, teachers will need to address the specific areas that have been identified as problematic. Figure 10.3 gives ideas for helping students with problems that may result from TBI.

A well-planned program of instruction should focus on "retaining impaired cognitive processes, developing new skills or procedures to compensate for residual deficits, creating an environment that permits effective performance, identifying effective instructional procedures, and improving metacognitive awareness" (Ylvisaker et al., 1994, p. 17). The impact of the injury may require that the student learn compensatory strategies to make up for deficits. Such strategies can address problems with attending, language comprehension, memory, sequencing, and thought organization.

TEACHING TIP

Develop and implement intervention programs based on the student's specific needs. TBI results in a wide variety of deficits resulting in a great diversity of intervention needs.

Orthopedic and Health Impairments

In addition to sensory impairments and TBI, numerous orthopedic and health impairments that occur in children have educational implications. Similar to problems of vision and hearing, orthopedic and health impairments are considered low-incidence disabilities. During the 2001–2002 school year, public schools served 338,658 children

CEC STANDARDS

CEC 2: Development and Characteristics of Learners

PRAXIS

PRAXIS II: Understanding Exceptionalities

CEC STANDARDS

CEC 2: Development and Characteristics of Learners

INTASC

INTASC 2: How children learn and develop

PRAXIS

PRAXIS II: Understanding Exceptionalities

classified as having other health impairment, and 73,821 with orthopedic impairments (U.S. Department of Education, 2003). While these represent fairly large numbers of children, there are many different disabilities within each category. For example, a teacher may be in the classroom for twenty years and never have a child with spina bifida, cerebral palsy, asthma, or childhood cancer. However, when teachers have children with these types of disorders in their classrooms it can pose significant challenges.

Health Impairments   These typically deal with issues that affect stamina and various body systems (Freiberg, 2005). IDEA defines other health impaired as "having limited strength, vitality or alertness, due to chronic or acute health problems such as a heart condition, tuberculosis, rheumatic fever, nephritis, asthma, sickle cell anemia, hemophilia, epilepsy, lead poisoning, leukemia, or diabetes that adversely affects a child's educational performance" [300.7(b)(8)].

Orthopedic Impairments   These include disorders that "hinder physical mobility or the ability to use one or more parts of the skeleton-muscular system of the body" (Freiberg, 2005, p. 169). Orthopedic impairment is defined in IDEA as "a severe orthopedic impairment that adversely affects a child's educational performance. The term includes impairments caused by congenital anomaly (e.g., clubfoot, absence of some member, etc.), impairments caused by disease (e.g., poliomyelitis, bone tuberculosis, etc.), and impairments from other causes (e.g., cerebral palsy, amputations, and fractures or burns, that cause contractures)" [300.7(b)(7)].

Often schools and state education agencies provide support personnel for teachers and students with these types of problems. Therefore, teachers should not have to go it alone when working with students with these disabilities. Behavioral specialists, psychologists, physical therapists, occupational therapists, nurses, and other health personnel are often available to provide services to students and supports to their teachers (Wadsworth & Knight, 1999). The fact that many different professionals are involved in providing services for some of these children may have repercussions for students of certain cultural backgrounds. Individuals from some cultures, for example, prefer to interact with one person at a time, rather than with a team of individuals.

One issue that school personnel must address, especially when dealing with children with health issues, is the use of universal precautions to prevent infection. Some children may have infectious diseases, such as human immunodeficiency virus (HIV), herpes, hepatitis B, or tuberculosis. Schools should have policies for issues related to universal precautions. These policies should include components such as proper use of gloves, proper hand-washing procedures, and blood and bodily fluid clean-up procedures (Edens, Murdick, & Gartin, 2003) (See Figure 10.4 on page 341.)

Another issue that could be faced by educators when dealing with students with health conditions is a **do-not-resuscitate (DNR)** order. There may be some children with life-threatening health conditions where DNR orders are present. When children with DNR orders are in the school, teachers, administrators, and all other school personnel who come into contact with the child need to have appropriate information. DNR orders have to be dealt with on a case-by-case basis; there are no general DNR procedures. The National Education Association (NEA) recommends that schools have specific plans for children who have DNR orders. Considerations for this plan include (Sewall & Balkman, 2002):

1. The DNR must be signed by a physician.
2. The plan should specify actions that should be taken by school personnel.
3. The plan should be reviewed annually.
4. All school personnel involved with the student should be briefed about the plan.
5. Students with the DNR should wear an identification bracelet indicating the DNR order.
6. Training, counseling, and programs on death and dying should be provided for students and school staff.

Low-Incidence Health Problems and Physical Disabilities

As noted in the beginning of this chapter, many health and physical disabilities may be present in children that result in a need for special education and related services. The remainder of this chapter will provide a quick guide to some of these disabilities and some considerations for educators. Teachers who work with children with one of these conditions should refer to a more-thorough reference work to learn more about it. The Further Readings list at the end of this chapter suggests such sources of information.

Asthma

Asthma is the most common chronic illness in children, affecting approximately 3 million children under the age of fifteen (American Academy of Allergy and Immunology, 1991; Bauer et al., 1999). Asthma is the result of the body's antibodies reacting to antigens and causing swelling, mucus secretion, and muscle tightening in the lungs (Best, 2005). This can cause repetitive episodes of coughing, shortness of breath, and wheezing. Dust, cigarette smoke, and animal dander are examples of substances that can trigger an asthma episode. While some asthma is mild and can be controlled by simply inhaling medication, severe attacks can be very dangerous and should be taken seriously by school personnel. Specific suggestions for teachers include:

- Know the signs and symptoms of respiratory distress. (Getch & Neuharth-Pritchett, 1999)
- Ensure that students have proper medications and that they are taken at the appropriate times.
- Allow students to rest when needed, as they often tire easily.
- Eliminate any known allergens found in the classroom.
- Determine what types of physical limitations might have to be set (e.g., restriction of a certain physical activity that can induce attacks), but otherwise encourage students to play games and participate in activities.
- Recognize the side effects of prescribed medication.
- Remain calm if an attack occurs.
- Allow the student to participate in nonstressful activity until an episode subsides.
- Introduce a vaporizer or dehumidifier to the classroom when recommended by the student's physician.
- Work on building up the student's self-image.
- Sensitize other students in the class to the nature of allergic reactions.
- Develop an effective system for helping the student keep up with schoolwork, as frequent absences may occur.

Educators can ask the following questions to determine whether a school is prepared to deal with students with asthma (National Heart, Lung, and Blood Institute, 1998):

1. Is the school free of tobacco smoke all of the time, including during school-sponsored events?
2. Does the school maintain good indoor air quality?
3. Is a school nurse in the school all day, every day?
4. Can children take medicines at school as recommended by their doctor and parents?
5. Does the school have an emergency plan for taking care of a child with a severe asthma attack?
6. Does someone teach school staff about asthma, asthma management plans, and asthma medicines?
7. Do students with asthma have good options for fully and safely participating in physical education class and recess? (p. 168)

CEC STANDARDS

CEC 2: Development and Characteristics of Learners

INTASC

INTASC 2: How children learn and develop

PRAXIS

PRAXIS II: Understanding Exceptionalities

Teachers who have students with cancer should learn about the child's illness from medical personnel.

Childhood Cancer

Childhood cancer occurs in approximately 1 in 330 children before the age of nineteen years, affecting more than 12,500 children and adolescents every year (American Cancer Society, 2002; National Childhood Cancer Foundation, 2003). Childhood cancer can take several different forms, including leukemia, lymphoma, tumors of the central nervous system, bone tumors, tumors affecting the eyes, and tumors affecting various organs (Heller et al., 1996). Treatment of cancer includes chemotherapy, radiation, surgery, and bone marrow transplantation. Whether schools provide appropriate help to students with cancer depends on their understanding of the condition (Spinelli, 2004). Suggestions for teachers and administrators who have students with cancer include:

- Express your concern about a student's condition to the parents and family.
- Learn about a student's illness from hospital personnel and parents.
- Inquire about the type of treatment and anticipated side effects.
- Refer the student for any needed special education services.
- Prepare for a student's terminal illness and possible death.
- Encourage discussion and consideration of future events.
- Allow for exceptions to classroom rules and procedures when indicated (e.g., wearing a baseball cap to disguise hair loss from chemotherapy).
- Be available to talk with a student when the need arises.
- Share information about the student's condition and ongoing status with teachers of the student's siblings.
- Be prepared to deal with issues concerning death and dying with students. Provide information to school staff and parents as needed. (Hoida & McDougal, 1998)
- Facilitate the student's reentry into school after an extended absence.

Cerebral Palsy

Cerebral palsy (CP) is "a group of chronic conditions affecting body movement and muscle coordination." (United Cerebral Palsy, 2006). The condition is caused by brain damage. It primarily affects the ability to control muscles and coordination (UCP, 2006). Cerebral palsy is neither progressive nor communicable (Gersh, 1991; Schleichkorn, 1993). It is also not "curable" in the usual sense of the word, although education, therapy, and applied technology can help people with cerebral palsy lead productive lives. Every year, approximately 5,000 babies are born with CP and an additional 1,200 to 1,500 young children develop the condition (Best & Bigge, 2006). There are several different ways to classify individuals with cerebral palsy; most frequently individuals are classified by location of the disorder and how it affects movement (Best & Bigge, 2006). Table 10.7 describes the different types of cerebral palsy according to two classification systems.

The primary intervention approach for children with cerebral palsy focuses on their physical needs. Physical therapy, occupational therapy, and even surgery often play a part.
Specific suggestions for teachers include:

- Create a supportive classroom environment that encourages participation in every facet of the school day.
- Allow extra time for students to move from one location to another.
- Ask students to repeat verbalizations that may be hard to understand because of their speech patterns.

Table 10.7	Classification of Cerebral Palsy
Topographical Classification System	**Classification System by Motor Symptoms (Physiological)**

A. *Monoplegia:* one limb
B. *Paraplegia:* legs only
C. *Hemiplegia:* one-half of body
D. *Triplegia:* three limbs (usually two legs and one arm)
E. *Quadriplegia:* all four limbs
F. *Diplegia:* more affected in the legs than in the arms
G. *Double hemiplegia:* arms more involved than the legs
	A. Spastic
	B. Athetoid
	  1. Tension
	  2. Nontension
	  3. Dystonic
	  4. Tremor
	C. Rigidity
	D. Ataxia
	E. Tremor
	F. Atonic (rare)
	G. Mixed
	H. Unclassified

From *Understanding Physical, Sensory, and Health Impairments* (p. 95), by K. W. Heller et al., 1996. Pacific Grove, CA: Brooks/Cole. Used by permission.

- Provide many real-life activities.
- Learn the correct way for the student to sit upright in a chair or wheelchair and how to use adaptive equipment (e.g., prone standers).
- Understand the functions and components of a wheelchair and any special adaptive pieces that may accompany it.
- Consider the use of various augmentative communication techniques with students who have severe cerebral palsy. (Musselwhite, 1987)
- Encourage students to use computers that are equipped with expanded keyboards if necessary or other portable writing aids for taking notes or generating written products.
- Consult physical and occupational therapists to understand correct positioning, posture, and other motor function areas.

Assistive technology (AT) can also play a significant role in the education of students with cerebral palsy. The nearby Technology Today provides a means to determine the use of AT in a particular school. After determining its use, school personnel can develop a plan of action to implement appropriate AT supports.

Cystic Fibrosis

Cystic fibrosis is an inherited, fatal disease that results in an abnormal amount of mucus throughout the body, most often affecting the lungs and digestive tract. This results in the blockage of air sacs in the lungs. This causes air to be trapped in the lungs, lungs to over inflate, and lungs to collapse (Best, 2005). It occurs in approximately 1 in 3,500 births (Cystic Fibrosis Foundation, 2006). Although life expectancy for children with cystic fibrosis at one time was only the teens, the current median age of individuals with this condition is 35.1 years (CF Foundation, 2006). Teachers must make sure that children with cystic fibrosis take special medication before they eat. As the disease progresses, it greatly affects stamina and the student's physical condition. Here are some specific suggestions for dealing with students with this disease:

- Prepare students in class for the realities of this disease (e.g., coughing, noncontagious sputum, gas).
- Learn how to clear a student's lungs and air passages, as such assistance may be needed after certain activities.
- Know the medications a student must take and be able to administer them (e.g., enzymes, vitamins).

CEC STANDARDS

CEC 2: Development and Characteristics of Learners

INTASC

INTASC 2: How children learn and develop

PRAXIS

PRAXIS II: Understanding Exceptionalities

TEACHING TIP

Develop some simulation activities for nondisabled students that will help them understand mobility problems. The use of wheelchairs and restricting the use of students' arms or hands will help them understand the problems experienced by some students with CP.

CEC STANDARDS

CEC 2: Development and Characteristics of Learners

Schoolwide Assistive Technology Database Sample

AT Needs	Have	Class/Instructor	Hours of Usage	Hours Available
Books on Tape			Period	Period
1. Our World Today	Yes	1. 7th SS/Brown	1 2 3 4 5 6	1 2 3 4 5 6
2. World History	No	2. 8th Hist/White	1 2 3 4 5 6	1 2 3 4 5 6
3.		3.	1 2 3 4 5 6	1 2 3 4 5 6
4.		4.	1 2 3 4 5 6	1 2 3 4 5 6
Franklin Spellers			Period	Period
1. Set of 35	Yes	1. 6th Eng/Green	1 2 3 4 5 6	1 2 3 4 5 6
2. 20 additional	Yes	2. Individual Checkout	1 2 3 4 5 6	1 2 3 4 5 6
3.		3.	1 2 3 4 5 6	1 2 3 4 5 6
4.		4.	1 2 3 4 5 6	1 2 3 4 5 6
Calculators			Period	Period
1. Set of 35	Yes	1. 6th Math/Black	1 2 3 4 5 6	1 2 3 4 5 6
2. 30 additional	Yes	2. Individual Checkout	1 2 3 4 5 6	1 2 3 4 5 6
3.		3.	1 2 3 4 5 6	1 2 3 4 5 6
4.		4.	1 2 3 4 5 6	1 2 3 4 5 6
Computers			Period	Period
1. IBM	No	1. 6th Eng/Green	1 2 3 4 5 6	1 2 3 4 5 6
2. IBM Lab	Yes	2. Lab/Tann	1 2 3 4 5 6	1 2 3 4 5 6
3.		3.	1 2 3 4 5 6	1 2 3 4 5 6
4.		4.	1 2 3 4 5 6	1 2 3 4 5 6
Software (Title)			Period	Period
1. MS Word	Yes	1. 6th Eng/Green	1 2 3 4 5 6	1 2 3 4 5 6
2. Type to Learn	No	2. Keyboard/Tann	1 2 3 4 5 6	1 2 3 4 5 6
3.		3.	1 2 3 4 5 6	1 2 3 4 5 6
4.		4.	1 2 3 4 5 6	1 2 3 4 5 6
NCR paper/Peer Helper			Period	Period
1. 2 students	Yes	1. 6th Eng/Green	1 2 3 4 5 6	1 2 3 4 5 6
2. 3 students	Yes	2. 7th SS/Brown	1 2 3 4 5 6	1 2 3 4 5 6
3. 1 student	Yes	3. 6th Math/Black	1 2 3 4 5 6	1 2 3 4 5 6
4.		4.	1 2 3 4 5 6	1 2 3 4 5 6
Other			Period	Period
1.		1.	1 2 3 4 5 6	1 2 3 4 5 6
2.		2.	1 2 3 4 5 6	1 2 3 4 5 6
3.		3.	1 2 3 4 5 6	1 2 3 4 5 6
4.		4.	1 2 3 4 5 6	1 2 3 4 5 6

From "Planning and Organizing Assistive Technology Resources in Your School" (p. 53) by B. J. Webb, *Teaching Exceptional Children, 32.* Used with permission.

- Consider restricting certain physical activities.
- Inquire about the therapies being used with the student.
- Support the implementation of special diets if needed.
- Provide opportunities for students to talk about their concerns, fears, and feelings.
- Ensure that the student is included in all class activities to whatever extent is possible.
- Prepare students for the eventual outcome of the disease by discussing death and dying.

Deaf-Blind

Students who have visual impairments or auditory impairments create unique problems for educators. When students present deficits in both sensory areas, resulting in their being deaf-blind, their needs become extremely complex. Although the term deaf-blind continues to be found in federal legislation and regulations, including IDEA, the terms **dual sensory impairment** or **multiple sensory impairments** are considered more appropriate (Marchant, 1992). For purposes of being eligible for special education services under IDEA, deaf-blind is still the label for such students.

Students who are classified as being deaf-blind may be blind or deaf, or they may have degrees of visual and auditory impairments that do not classify as blindness or deafness. "The Helen Keller National Center estimates that about 94% of such individuals have residual hearing or residual sight that can facilitate their educational programs" (Marchant, 1992, p. 114). During the 2000–2001 school year, only 1,320 students nationwide were identified as being deaf-blind and served in special education programs (U.S. Department of Education, 2003).

Obviously, individuals classified as being deaf-blind present a variety of characteristics. While these characteristics represent those exhibited by students who only have visual or hearing impairments, the overlap of these two disabilities results in significant educational needs. Wolfe (1997) suggests the following educational techniques for teachers to use when working with students classified as deaf-blind:

- Use an ecological approach to assessment and skill selection to emphasize functional needs of students.
- Use a variety of prompts, cues, and reinforcement strategies in a systematic instructional pattern.
- Use time-delay prompting, where time between prompts is increased.
- Use groups and cooperative learning strategies.
- Implement environmental adaptations, such as enlarging materials, using contrasting materials, altering seating arrangements, and reducing extraneous noises to maximize the residual hearing and vision of the student.

Diabetes

There are currently more than 20 million children and adults, or 7 percent of the population, with diabetes in the United States. Diabetes is a metabolic disorder in which the pancreas cannot produce sufficient insulin to process food (American Diabetes Association, 2006). Many Americans suffer from **type II**, or **adult-onset**, diabetes. However, the more serious form of diabetes, **type I**, or **insulin-dependent**, occurs in children; approximately one in every 400–500 people under the age of twenty have type I diabetes. Type I diabetes accounts for approximately 5 to 10 percent of all diabetes (Helping the Student, 2003).

Teachers should be alert to possible symptoms of diabetes, including increased thirst, appetite, and urination; weight loss; fatigue; and irritability. Children with type I diabetes must take daily injections of insulin. School personnel must have knowledge of the special dietary needs of these children and understand their need for a daily activity regimen.

INTASC

INTASC 2: How children learn and develop

PRAXIS

PRAXIS II: Understanding Exceptionalities

CEC STANDARDS

CEC 2: Development and Characteristics of Learners

INTASC

INTASC 2: How children learn and develop

PRAXIS

PRAXIS II: Understanding Exceptionalities

CEC STANDARDS

CEC 2: Development and Characteristics of Learners

INTASC

INTASC 2: How children learn and develop

PRAXIS

PRAXIS II: Understanding Exceptionalities.

TEACHING TIP

Be prepared to deal with students with diabetes in your classroom before an emergency develops. Keep a list of symptoms and things to do if a student has too much insulin and if a student has too little insulin readily available.

Action for teachers with students with diabetes in their classroom include (Helping the Student, 2003):

- Participate in the school heath team meetings.
- Work with the school health team to implement written care plans.
- Recognize that a change in the student's behavior could be a symptom of blood glucose changes.
- Be prepared to recognize and respond to the signs and symptoms of hypoglycemia and hyperglycemia.
- Provide a supportive environment for the student.
- Provide classroom accommodations for the student with diabetes.
- Provide instruction to the student if the student misses class.
- Notify parents in advance of changes in school schedule.
- Provide information for substitute teachers.
- Communicate with the school nurse, trained diabetes personnel, or parents regarding any concerns about the student.
- Attend diabetes management training.
- Learn about diabetes.
- Treat the student with diabetes the same as other students.
- Respect the student's confidentiality and right to privacy. (p. 40)

Epilepsy

Epilepsy is a neurological disorder that results in individuals having seizures, which is "a change in sensation, awareness, or behavior brought about by a brief electrical disturbance in the brain" (Epilepsy Foundation, 2006, p. 1). There are several different types of epilepsy, determined by the impact of abnormal brain activity. Table 10.8 describes four types. Approximately 2.7 million people in the United States have epilepsy, among them 326,000 children under the age of fifteen (American Epilepsy Society, 2006). Other facts related to epilepsy include (Epilepsy Foundation, 2006):

Table 10.8	Four Types of Seizures
Generalized (grand mal)	• Sudden cry, fall, rigidity, followed by muscle jerks • Shallow breathing, or temporarily suspended breathing, bluish skin • Possible loss of bladder or bowel control • Usually lasts 2–3 minutes
Absence (petit mal)	• Blank stare, beginning and ending abruptly • Lasting only a few seconds • Most common in children • May be accompanied by blinking, chewing movement • Individual is unaware of the seizure
Simple Partial	• Jerking may begin in one area of body, arm, leg, or face • Cannot be stopped but individual is aware • Jerking may proceed from one area to another area
Complex Partial	• Starts with blank stares, followed by chewing and random activity • Individual may seem unaware or dazed • Unresponsiveness • Clumsy actions • May run, pick up objects, take clothes off, or other activity • Lasts a few minutes • No memory of what occurred

From *Understanding Physical, Sensory, and Health Impairments* (p. 78) by K. W. Heller et al., 1996, Pacific Grove, CA: Brooks/Cole. Used by permission.

- 45,000 children under the age of fifteen develop epilepsy each year.
- Epilepsy occurs in males slightly more than in females.
- Prevalence of epilepsy increases with age.
- Epilepsy occurs more frequently in racial minorities than in Caucasians.

No common characteristics are shared by individuals with epilepsy. The Epilepsy Foundation of America (2006) notes the following significant signs of the disorder: staring spells; ticlike movements; rhythmic movements of the head; purposeless sounds and body movements; head drooping; lack of response; eyes rolling upward; and chewing and swallowing movements. Medical intervention is the primary recourse for individuals with epilepsy. Most people with epilepsy are able to control their seizures with the proper regimen of medical therapy (Agnew, Nystul, & Conner, 1998).

Even people who respond very well to medication have occasional seizures. Therefore, teachers and other school personnel must know what actions to take should a person experience a generalized seizure. Figure 10.4 summarizes the steps that should be taken when a child has a seizure. Teachers, parents, or others need to record behaviors that occur before, during, and after the seizure because they may be important to treatment of the disorder.

HIV and AIDS

Human immunodeficiency virus (HIV) occurs when the virus attacks the body's immune system, leaving an individual vulnerable to infections or cancers. In its later stages, HIV infection becomes **acquired immunodeficiency syndrome (AIDS)**. Two of

CEC STANDARDS

CEC 2: Development and Characteristics of Learners

INTASC

INTASC 2: How children learn and develop

PRAXIS

PRAXIS II: Understanding Exceptionalities

| *Figure* 10.4 | **Steps to Take When Dealing with a Seizure** |

During a generalized tonic-clonic seizure (grand mal), the person suddenly falls to the ground and has a convulsive seizure. It is essential to protect him or her from injury. Cradle the head or place something soft under it, a towel or your hand for example. Remove all dangerous objects. A bystander can do nothing to prevent or terminate an attack. At the end of the seizure, make sure the mouth is cleared of food and saliva by turning the person on his or her side to provide an open airway and allow fluids to drain. If the person assisting remains calm, the person having the seizure will be reassured when he or she regains consciousness.

Breathing almost always resumes spontaneously after a convulsive seizure. Failure to resume breathing signals a complication of the seizure such as a blocked airway, heart attack, or severe head or neck injury. In these unusual circumstances, CPR must start immediately. If repeated seizures occur, or if a single seizure lasts longer than five minutes, the person should be taken to a medical facility immediately. Prolonged or repeated seizures may suggest status epilepticus (nonstop seizures), which requires emergency medical treatment.

When providing seizure first aid for generalized tonic-clonic seizures, these are the key things to remember:

- Keep calm and reassure other people who may be nearby.
- Don't hold the person down or try to stop his or her movements.
- Time the seizure with your watch.
- Clear the area around the person of anything hard or sharp.
- Loosen ties or anything around the neck that may make breathing difficult.
- Put something flat and soft, like a folded jacket, under the head.
- Turn him or her gently onto one side. This will help keep the airway clear. Do not try to force the mouth open with any hard implement or with fingers. It is not true that a person having a seizure can swallow his or her tongue. Efforts to hold the tongue down can injure teeth or jaw.
- Don't attempt artificial respiration except in the unlikely event that a person does not start breathing again after the seizure has stopped.
- Stay with the person until the seizure ends naturally.
- Be friendly and reassuring as consciousness returns.
- Offer to call a taxi, friend, or relative to help the person get home if he or she seems confused or unable to get home by himself or herself.

From "First Aid for Generalized Tonic Clonic (Grand Mal) Seizures." Epilepsy Foundation website. Used with permission.

Figure 10.5 Universal Precautions for Prevention of HIV, Hepatitis B, and Other Blood-Borne Pathogens

The CDC and the Food and Drug Administration (1988) published guidelines designed to protect health-care workers and to ensure the confidentiality of patients with HIV infection. These guidelines include the following information that is useful for classroom teachers.

- Blood should always be handled with latex or nonpermeable disposable gloves. The use of gloves is not necessary for feces, nasal secretions, sputum, sweat, saliva, tears, urine, and vomitus unless they are visibly tinged with blood. Handwashing is sufficient after handling material not containing blood.
- In all settings in which blood or bloody material is handled, gloves and a suitable receptacle that closes tightly and is childproof should be available. Although HIV does not survive well outside the body, all spillage of secretions should be cleaned up immediately with disinfectants. This is particularly important for cleaning up after a bloody nose or a large cut. Household bleach at a dilution of 1:10 should be used. Only objects that have come into contact with blood need to be cleaned with bleach.
- When intact skin is exposed to contaminated fluids, particularly blood, it should be washed with soap and water. Handwashing is sufficient for such activities as diaper change; toilet training; and clean-up of nasal secretions, stool, saliva, tears, or vomitus. If an open lesion or a mucous membrane appears to have been contaminated, AZT therapy should be considered.

From *AIDS Surveillance Report* (p. 7), Centers for Disease Control, 1988. Atlanta, GA: Author. Used by permission.

CONSIDER THIS

Students with HIV and AIDS should not be allowed to attend school because of their potential ability to infect other students. Do you agree or disagree with this statement? Why?

CEC STANDARDS

CEC 2: Development and Characteristics of Learners

INTASC

INTASC 2: How children learn and develop

PRAXIS

PRAXIS II: Understanding Exceptionalities

the fastest-growing groups contracting HIV are infants and teenagers (Johnson & Jefferson-Aker, 2001). HIV/AIDS is transmitted only through the exchange of blood or semen. As of September 1996, 7,472 cases of AIDS in children under age thirteen years were reported to the CDC (Centers for Disease Control, 1997). Students with HIV/AIDS may display a variety of academic, behavioral, and social-emotional problems. Teachers need to take precautions when dealing with children with HIV/AIDS, hepatitis B, or any other blood-borne pathogen. See Figure 10.5 for specific precautions. Some specific suggestions for teachers include:

- Follow the guidelines (universal precautions) developed by the CDC and the Food and Drug Administration for working with HIV-infected individuals (Figure 10.5).
- Ask the student's parents or physician whether there are any special procedures that must be followed.
- Discuss HIV/AIDS with the entire class, providing accurate information, dispelling myths, and answering questions.
- Discuss with students in the class that a student's skills and abilities will change over time if he or she is infected with HIV/AIDS.
- Prepare for the fact that the student may die, especially if AIDS is present.
- Ensure that the student with HIV/AIDS is included in all aspects of classroom activities.
- Be sensitive to the stress that the student's family is undergoing.

Muscular Dystrophy

Muscular dystrophy is a group of disorders characterized by progressive weakness and eventual death of muscle fibers. The most common and most serious form of muscular dystrophy is **Duchenne dystrophy**. In this type of muscular dystrophy, fat cells and connective tissue replace muscle tissue. Symptoms first appear between the ages of two and six years, and progress at varying rates. The condition is genetically transmitted and affects approximately one in every 3,500 male births. Females carry the gene but are not affected (Best, 2005). Teachers must adapt their classrooms to accommodate the physical needs of these students. Most individuals with this form of muscular dystrophy die during young adulthood. Specific suggestions for teachers include:

- Be prepared to help the student deal with the loss of various functions.
- Involve the student in as many classroom activities as possible.
- Using assistive techniques that do not hurt the individual, help the student as needed in climbing stairs or in getting up from the floor.
- Understand the functions and components of wheelchairs.
- Monitor the administration of required medications.
- Monitor the amount of time the student is allowed to stand during the day.
- Be familiar with different types of braces (e.g., short leg, molded ankle-foot) students might use.
- Prepare other students in class for the realities of the disease.

Children in wheelchairs need opportunities for social interactions.

Spina Bifida

Spina bifida is a neural tube defect characterized by bones in the spinal column (vertebrae) not connecting properly. Spina bifida occurs in about 3,000 pregnancies each year; currently there is an estimated 70,000 people in the United States with this disorder (Spina Bifida Association, 2006). There are three different types of spina bifida: spina bifida occulta; meningocele; and myelomeningocele (Best, 2006).

The least serious form of spina bifida is **spina bifida occulta**. In this type, the vertebral column fails to close properly, leaving a hole in the bony vertebrae that protect the delicate spinal column. With this form of spina bifida, surgically closing the opening to protect the spinal column is generally all that is required and does not result in any problems. **Meningocele** is similar to spina bifida occulta in that the vertebral column fails to close properly, leaving a hole in the bony vertebrae. Skin pouches out in the area where the vertebral column is not closed. In meningocele, the outpouching does not contain any nerve tissue. Surgically removing the outpouching and closing the opening usually result in a positive prognosis without any problems. **Myelomeningocele** is the most common and most severe form of spina bifida. It is similar to meningocele but has one major difference: nerve tissue is present in the outpouching. Because nerve tissue is involved, this form of spina bifida generally results in permanent paralysis and loss of sensation. Incontinence is also a possible result of this condition (Best, 2006). School personnel must ensure appropriate use of wheelchairs and make accommodations for limited use of arms and hands.

The primary impact of spina bifida is physical. However, a common characteristic of children with spina bifida that must be addressed by teachers is nonverbal learning disorders (Russell, 2004).

Teachers should do the following when working with a child with spina bifida:

- Inquire about any acute medical needs the student may have.
- Learn about the various adaptive equipment a student may be using (see Baker & Rogosky-Grassi, 1993).
- Maintain an environment that assists the student who is using crutches by keeping floors from getting wet and removing loose floor coverings.
- Understand the use of a wheelchair as well as its major parts.
- Learn how to position these students to develop strength and to keep sores from developing in parts of their bodies that bear their weight or that receive pressure from orthotic devices they are using. Because they do not have sensation, they may not notice the sores themselves. Healing is complicated by poor circulation.
- Understand the process of **clean intermittent bladder catheterization (CIC)**, as some students will be performing this process to become continent and avoid

CONSIDER THIS

Should students who require extensive physical accommodations be placed in the same school, so that all schools and classrooms do not have to be accessible? Defend your response.

TEACHING TIP

Get in a wheelchair and try to move about your classroom to see whether it is fully accessible. Often, areas that look accessible are not.

CEC STANDARDS

CEC 2: Development and Characteristics of Learners

INTASC

INTASC 2: How children learn and develop

PRAXIS

PRAXIS II: Understanding Exceptionalities

urinary tract infections. The process involves insertion of a clean catheter through the urethra and into the bladder, must be done four times a day, and can be done independently by most children by age six.

- Be ready to deal with the occasional incontinence of students. Assure the student with spina bifida that this is not a problem and discuss this situation with other class members.
- Learn how to deal with the special circumstances associated with students who use wheelchairs and have seizures.
- Ensure the full participation of the student in all classroom activities.
- Help the student with spina bifida develop a healthy, positive self-concept.
- Notify parents if there are unusual changes in the student's behavior or personality or if the student has various physical complaints such as headaches or double vision—these may indicate a problem with increased pressure on the brain. (Deiner, 1993)

Tourette Syndrome

CONSIDER THIS

How should students with Tourette syndrome be dealt with when they shout obscenities and display other inappropriate disruptive behaviors?

Tourette syndrome is a neurological disorder that results in multiple motor and verbal tics. The condition is genetically transmitted, with parents having a 50 percent chance of passing the gene to offspring. Tourette syndrome develops before the age of eighteen (Facts about Tourette Syndrome, 2006). The condition occurs in males three times as often as in females, resulting in a prevalence rate for males as high as 1 in 1,000 individuals (Hansen, 1992). Characteristics include various motor tics; inappropriate laughing; rapid eye movements; winks and grimaces; aggressive behaviors; in infrequent cases, mental retardation; mild to moderate incoordination; and peculiar verbalizations (Woodrich, 1998). The condition is manifested in several characteristics that negatively impact educational success, including (Prestia, 2003):

CEC STANDARDS

CEC 2: Development and Characteristics of Learners

- incomplete work
- illegible or poor quality of written work
- inattentive and/or distractible in class
- disorganization of work and work space
- difficulty obtaining and understanding verbal instruction (p. 68)

INTASC

INTASC 2: How children learn and develop

Most important, school personnel should be understanding with children who have Tourette syndrome. Monitoring medication and participating as a member of the interdisciplinary team are important roles for teachers and other school personnel. See the nearby "Evidence-Based Practice" box for suggestions for other interventions.

Severe Cognitive Disabilities

PRAXIS

PRAXIS II: Understanding Exceptionalities

During the past twenty years, the field of special education has dichotomized disabilities into mild and severe. These may have also been described as high incidence and low incidence. Since the category of severe disabilities is broad, it includes individuals with a wide range of characteristics. The one common characteristic shared by this group is the need and dependence on extensive and ongoing supports (Snell & Brown, 2006). Many of the conditions described previously in this chapter could be considered as severe. However, the discussion that follows will focus on students with severe mental retardation.

Mental retardation has been described in Chapter 7. However, the majority of that chapter focused on mild MR. While most individuals with MR are classified as mild, approximately 0.13 percent of the population are classified as having moderate to severe levels of MR (Beirne-Smith, Patton, & Ittenbach, 1994). Moderate to profound levels of MR can be described as having intelligence quotient scores of approximately 0–55. Prior to changing its classification system for MR in 1992, the American Association on Mental Retardation (AAMR) described four levels of mental retardation: mild, moderate, severe, and profound. Individuals with mild MR had IQs ranging from 55 to 70, with the

EVIDENCE-BASED PRACTICE

Interventions for Students with Tourette Syndrome

Research has identified best practices for working with students with Tourette syndrome.

- Break down assignments to avoid overwhelming the student.
- Allow students to use computers to eliminate frustrations and to focus on the content of the work.

- Allow preferential seating.
- Use grid paper to assist students with vertical alignment.
- Use multisensory interventions and instruction.
- Ensure students have ample time to complete work without increasing frustration levels.

- Test in quiet rooms with minimal distractions.
- Ensure a predictable routine for the school day or class period.
- Provide direct teaching of social skills.

From "Tourette's Syndrome; Characteristics and Interventions," by K. Prestia, 2003, *Intervention in School and Clinic, 39*, pp. 67–71.

---

other levels falling below 55. The 1992 revision of the classification manual removed the levels of deficits and created a classification system based on the needed levels of support. The most recent revision of the definition and classification system maintains the concept of levels of support (Taylor et al., 2005). While the prevalence of MR ranges from approximately 1 to 2.3 percent, the majority of students classified as having MR have mild MR. Significantly fewer than 1 percent of the school population would be classified as having more severe levels of MR.

Students with more severe levels of MR, or those requiring extensive supports, display many of the same characteristics as individuals with milder levels of MR, only to a more pronounced level. Characteristics of individuals in this group would include (Taylor et al., 2005):

- adaptive behavior difficulties
- below average academic skills
- weak social skills
- difficulty with transferring/generalizing knowledge
- problems with metacognitive skills
- language development deficits
- memory problems

Most students with severe MR will be placed a great deal of the time in a special education setting. When included in a general education classroom, it is likely that special education supports will be provided. Therefore, general classroom teachers will need to work with and collaborate with special education personnel to develop a team approach for developing and implementing programs for these students.

A critical component of instruction for students with severe disabilities is assessment. While there may be a great deal of commonality among nondisabled students in the same chronological age range, there are significant differences among individuals with severe MR. Therefore, prior to implementing instruction, instructional assessments must be completed. Educators should focus on functional assessments that reflect skills needed by individuals to be as independent as possible. This assessment should be multidimensional, informal, and formal (Taylor et al., 2005).

One area that educators should focus attention on with students who have severe disabilities is making choices. Stafford (2005) notes that while most individuals take making choices for granted, individuals with severe disabilities are often not allowed to make choices or do not know how to make choices. This lack of opportunities to make choices, and the lack of skills in making choices, leads to dependence. Therefore, educators need to implement strategies for teaching choice-making skills to students with severe disabilities.

CEC STANDARDS

CEC 2: Development and Characteristics of Learners

INTASC

INTASC 2: How children learn and develop

PRAXIS

PRAXIS II: Understanding Exceptionalities

EVIDENCE-BASED PRACTICE

Increasing Peer Interactions for Students with Severe Disabilities via Training for Paraprofessionals

Peer interactions among individuals with disabilities and their nondisabled peers can be increased by training paraprofessionals to facilitate such interactions. Four topics in the training activities include:

1. Enhance paraprofessionals' perspective of their social interactions. Paraprofessionals should complete a worksheet to reflect their own social relationships and that of the students they work with.

2. Establish the importance of peer interactions. The importance of peer interactions should be discussed with paraprofessionals.

3. Clarify the paraprofessional's role in facilitating interactions. Discussions about how paraprofessionals could facilitate interactions can help them understand their important role in facilitating such interactions.

4. Increase paraprofessionals' knowledge base. Specific strategies for enhancing interactions should be presented and discussed. Examples of such strategies should be provided.

From "Increasing Peer Interactions for Students with Severe Disabilities via Training for Paraprofessionals," J. N. Causton-Theoharis and K. W. Malmgren, 2005, *Exceptional Children, 71,* pp. 431–444.

CEC STANDARDS

CEC 5: Learning Environments

INTASC

INTASC 5: Learning environments

In inclusive settings, social inclusion can be as much a focus as academic inclusion. Teachers may need to orchestrate opportunities for social interactions. Ohtake (2005) stresses the importance of creating opportunities for students with severe disabilities to participate in team sports. Such involvement will "improve the students' targeted skills, enhance their sense of belonging, and ultimately build friendships with their peers" (p. 27). (See nearby Spotlight and Evidence-Based Practice.) Still another way to make students with severe disabilities feel a part of their inclusive environment is to include them in service learning activities (Kleinert et al., 2005).

Many students with severe disabilities have difficulty communicating. Educators, therefore, should focus on enhancing communication skills among this group of students. Functional communication goals should be established to facilitate this group's participation with their nondisabled peers (Cascella & McNamara, 2005).

Personal Spotlight

Teaching Students with Severe Disabilities

Elizabeth Flippo is one of the strongest supporters of students with severe disabilities you will ever meet. She has taught for 26 years, all in classrooms for children with severe disabilities. Her current classroom is at Springdale High School in Springdale, Arkansas. She has six students, all with severe disabilities. Angelina is an 18-year-old Hispanic with severe autism and mental retardation. Hank is 16 and is classified as having emotional disturbance and mental retardation. Billy, 16 years old, has severe cerebral palsy and mental retardation. Patti is 18 years old and has severe mental retardation; Linda is 15 years old and is classified as having severe autism. Finally, Tommy is 18 years old and has severe autism. All of these students need extensive supports in toileting, daily grooming, and other daily living activities. Several of them also display aggressive behaviors toward each other and their teachers.

Despite the significant challenges presented by her students, Elizabeth says that she loves teaching adolescents with these types of disabilities. The only time most of her students are included with nondisabled peers is during lunch and other social settings. Elizabeth believes that some of these students could be included more had they been placed in more inclusive settings in earlier grade levels. According to Elizabeth, the primary barrier to their being included more is their inappropriate behaviors and aggressiveness.

Elizabeth Flippo
Springdale High School,
Springdale, Arkansas

Classroom teachers will work primarily with special education support personnel when dealing with students with severe MR included in their classrooms. Some general guidelines for teachers include the following:

1. Utilize peer support systems.
2. Participate as a member of an instructional team.
3. Be cognizant of generalization and transfer characteristics.
4. Utilize paraprofessional supports.
5. Differentiate curricula to meet the unique needs of students.
6. Facilitate social interaction between students with severe disabilities and their nondisabled peers.

Summary

Basic Concepts about Hearing Impairment

- Many students with sensory deficits are educated in general education classrooms.
- For students with sensory impairments to receive an appropriate education, various accommodations must be made.
- Students with hearing and visual problems represent a very heterogeneous group.
- Most students with hearing problems have some residual hearing ability.
- The term "hearing impairment" includes individuals with deafness and those who are hard of hearing.

Strategies for Curriculum and Instruction for Students with Hearing Impairments

- The effect of a hearing loss on a student's ability to understand speech is a primary concern of teachers.
- An audiometric evaluation helps to determine the extent of a hearing disorder.
- Several factors should alert teachers to a possible hearing loss in a particular student.

Classroom Adaptations for Students with Hearing Impairments

- Teachers in general education classrooms must implement a variety of accommodations for students with hearing impairments.
- The seating location of a student with hearing loss is critical for effective instruction.
- Specialized equipment, such as hearing aids, may be necessary to ensure the success of students with hearing losses.

Promoting Inclusive Practices for Students with Hearing Impairments

- The most challenging aspect of teaching students with hearing problems is making sure that they participate in the communicational activities that occur in the classroom.
- Teachers need to encourage interaction between students with hearing impairments and their nondisabled classmates (e.g., grouping, assigning buddies).

Basic Concepts about Visual Impairment

- Vision plays a critical role in the development of concepts such as understanding the spatial relations of the environment.
- Teachers must use a variety of accommodations for students with visual disabilities.
- Most students with visual disabilities have residual or low vision.
- Refractive errors are the most common form of visual disability.
- Visual problems may be congenital or occur later in life.

Strategies for Curriculum and Instruction for Students with Visual Impairments

- The most educationally relevant characteristic of students who have visual impairments is the extent of their visual efficiency.
- Special materials may be needed when working with students with visual problems.
- Using large-print and nonglare materials may be sufficient accommodation for many students with visual disabilities.
- Provide ample storage space for students' materials.
- Allow students additional time, as Braille and large-print reading are slower than regular-print reading.

Classroom Adaptations for Students with Visual Impairments

- A very small number of students require instruction in Braille.
- Specialists to teach Braille and develop Braille materials may be needed to successfully place students with visual disabilities in general education classrooms.
- Academic tests may need to be adapted when evaluating students with visual disabilities.
- Facilitate all technology needed by students.

Promoting Inclusive Practices for Students with Visual Impairments

- It is critical that students with visual impairments be socially accepted in their general education classrooms.
- Orchestrate social opportunities for students.

- Encourage students with visual impairments to demonstrate any specialized equipment they may use.

Basic Concepts about TBI

- TBI is one of the newest categories recognized by IDEA as a disability category eligible for special education services.
- Children with TBI exhibit a wide variety of characteristics, including emotional, learning, and behavior problems.

Classroom Adaptations for Students with TBI

- Teachers need to maintain as high a level of expectation as possible for students with TBI.
- Teachers must familiarize themselves with any specific equipment or medications that students with TBI might need and modify the classroom accordingly.

Basic Concepts about Orthopedic and Health Impairments

- Children with physical and health needs are entitled to an appropriate educational program as a result of IDEA.
- Physical and health impairments constitute low-incidence disabilities.
- The severity, visibility, and age of acquisition affect the needs of children with physical and health impairments.
- Students with physical and health problems display a wide array of characteristics and needs.
- Students with physical problems qualify for special education under the orthopedically impaired category of IDEA.
- Students with health problems qualify for special education under the other health impaired category of IDEA.

Basic Concepts about Low-Incidence Health Problems and Physical Disabilities

- Asthma affects many children; teachers primarily need to be aware of medications to control asthma, side effects of medication, and the limitations of students with asthma.
- The survival rates for children with cancer have increased dramatically over the past thirty years.

- Teachers need to be prepared to deal with the emotional issues surrounding childhood cancer, including death issues.
- Children with cancer may miss a good deal of school; the school should make appropriate arrangements in these situations.
- CP is a condition that affects muscles and posture; it can be described by the way it affects movement or which limb is involved.
- Physical therapy is a critical component of treatment for children with CP. Accessibility, communication, and social-emotional concerns are the primary areas that general educators must attend to.
- Cystic fibrosis is a terminal condition that affects the mucous membranes of the lungs.
- Juvenile diabetes results in children having to take insulin injections daily. Diet and exercise can help children manage diabetes.
- Epilepsy is caused by abnormal activity in the brain that is the result of some brain damage or insult.
- Teachers must know specific steps to take in case children have a generalized tonic-clonic seizure in their classrooms.
- Infants and teenagers are two of the fastest-growing groups to contract HIV.
- Teachers need to keep up to date with developments in HIV/AIDS prevention and treatment approaches.
- Muscular dystrophy is a term used to describe several different inherited disorders that result in progressive muscular weakness and may cause death.
- Spina bifida is caused by a failure of the spinal column to close properly; this condition may result in paralysis of the lower extremities.
- Tourette syndrome is a neuropsychiatric disorder that is characterized by multiple motor tics, inappropriate laughter, rapid eye movements, winks and grimaces, and aggressive behavior.

Questions to Reconsider

Think back to the scenario about Manuel that you read at the beginning of this chapter. Would you answer the questions raised there any differently, after reading the chapter itself?

1. What kind of special skills does Manuel's third-grade classroom teacher need in order to meet Manuel's educational and social needs?

2. What can Manuel's teacher do to help him improve his social skills?
3. What skills are critical for Manual to have in order to be successful in higher grades that focus on content topics?

Further Readings

Batshaw, M. L., & Parret, Y. M. (1986). *Children with handicaps: A medical primer.* Baltimore, MD: Brookes.

Blackman, J. A. (Ed.). (1984). *Medical aspects of developmental disabilities in children birth to three.* Rockville, MD: Aspen.

Gillberg, C. (Ed.). (1989). *Diagnosis and treatment of autism.* New York: Plenum Press.

Koegel, R. L., & Koegel, L. K. (1995). *Teaching children with autism.* Baltimore, MD: Brookes.

National Head Injury Foundation. (1988). *An educator's manual: What educators need to know about students with traumatic brain injury.* Southborough, MA: Author.

Pless, I. B. (Ed.). *The epidemiology of childhood disorders.* New York: Oxford Press.

Savage, R. C., & Wolcott, G. F. (Eds.). *Educational dimensions of acquired brain injury.* Austin, TX: Pro-Ed.

Schopler, E., & Mesibov, G. B. (Eds.). *Learning and cognition in autism.* New York: Plenum Press.

Smith, M. D., Belcher, R. G., & Juhrs, P. D. (1995). *A guide to successful employment for individuals with autism.* Baltimore, MD: Brookes.

Wetherby, A. M., & Prizant, B. M. (Eds.). (2000). *Autism spectrum disorders: A transactional developmental perspective.* Baltimore, MD: Brookes.

mylabschool
Where the classroom comes to life

Go to Allyn & Bacon's MyLabSchool (www.mylabschool.com) and enter Assignment ID SPV11 into the Assignment Finder. View the video clip called *Traumatic Brain Injury,* and the video clip called *Physical Disabilities.* Then consider what you have seen along with what you've read in Chapter 10 to answer the following questions.

1. Educational programs for students like Matt, who experienced TBI, should focus on retraining impaired cognitive processes while developing new compensatory skills and providing a supportive environment. If Matt's age permitted him to be in your classroom, how might you support his reentry? Be specific, and support your choices with information from this chapter.

2. Students like Oscar who have paraplegia have many special needs and typically have assigned support staff to aid them. Reflect on and list the issues that might concern you with situations like Oscar's. How might you address these concerns in your classroom?

3. Select another low-incidence disability and briefly describe its characteristics. By doing a key word search for this disability on Research Navigator in *MyLabSchool,* Identify at least one organization that might provide support for you as a teacher of a student with this disability.

You may also answer the questions at the end of these clips and e-mail your responses to your instructor.

Teaching Students with Communication Disorders

After reading this chapter, you should be able to:

1. Define the concept of communication and describe its major components, language, and speech.
2. Describe typical speech and language development in children.
3. Discuss communication disorders, including the different types of disorders and some of their characteristics.
4. Describe various classroom accommodations appropriate for students with speech and language disorders.
5. Discuss language differences that are due to culture and ways that teachers can deal with these differences.
6. Discuss augmentative and alternative communication techniques.
7. Describe trends that are shaping provision of speech therapy services in the schools.

Questions to Consider

1. What should Mr. Parker tell the students in his classroom about stuttering?

2. What could Mr. Parker and Mrs. Woods do to help David better interact with his peers in settings other than the classroom?

3. Should Mr. Parker expect David to give oral reports in front of the class? Why or why not?

4. Why would asking David to "slow down" or "relax" not help him to speak more fluently?

David is an eight-year-old who recently began stuttering in the classroom. At first David's second-grade teacher, Mr. Parker, wasn't concerned because David's dysfluencies were infrequent and short, both in duration and in intensity. But lately, it seems to be becoming more of a problem. Mr. Parker has noticed that David has stopped participating in class and that he doesn't seem to be playing with his friends on the playground as he used to.

Mr. Parker called David's parents to schedule a parent-teacher conference. At the conference, David's parents said that they had also noticed David's stuttering, but that it didn't seem as severe at home as at school. They were very concerned about how David's stuttering might affect his educational, emotional, and behavioral development. They indicated that there was a history of disfluency in their family, and they knew how important it was that David begin receiving therapy as soon as possible.

Mr. Parker and David's parents requested an in-depth evaluation by the school's speech-language pathologist, Mrs. Woods. Mrs. Woods began by chatting with David about his stuttering. David said that he was aware of his stuttering and that he was really embarrassed and ashamed of it. He said that his stuttering was worse when he talked to his friends and when he talked on the phone or with adults with whom he was less familiar. David was clearly upset about his stuttering and even began crying during one part of the interview.

After completing the interview with David as well as the formal assessment, Mrs. Woods scheduled the IEP meeting. At the meeting, she recommended that David begin receiving speech therapy services three times weekly for thirty minutes each session. David would join a small group of two other boys from his school who were also stuttering. Mrs. Woods gave David's parents and Mr. Parker some brochures and pamphlets that provided information about stuttering, speech therapy, and how to help David communicate better in school and at home. The IEP team agreed on David's goals and objectives for the coming school year, and discussed how to modify lessons to help David participate to the fullest extent possible.

For most of us, the ability to communicate is a skill we take for granted. Our communication is effortless and frequent. In one day, we might share a story with family members, discuss problems with our coworkers, ask directions from a stranger on the street, and telephone an old friend. When we are able to communicate easily and effectively, it is natural to participate in both the commonplace activities of daily living and the more enjoyable experiences that enrich our lives.

CONSIDER THIS

How would your life be different if you could not talk? If you could not write? If you could not hear?

However, when communication is impaired, absent, or qualitatively different, the simplest interactions may become difficult or even impossible. Moreover, because the communication skills that most of us use fluently and easily almost always involve personal interactions with others, disorders in speech or language may also result in social problems. For children, these social problems are most likely to occur in school. School is a place not only for academic learning, but also for building positive relationships with teachers and enduring friendships with peers. When a student's communication disorder, however mild, limits these experiences, makes him or her feel different and inadequate, or undermines confidence and self-esteem, the overall impact can be devastating.

Communication problems are often complex. There are many types of communication disorders, involving both speech and language. This chapter describes strategies that teachers can use with students who have such disorders. Suggestions will address specific communication disorders as well as associated problems in socialization and adjustment.

Basic Concepts about Communication Disorders

Communication and Communication Disorders Defined

Speech and **language** are interrelated skills, tools that we use to communicate and learn. Heward (1995) defines the related terms this way:

> Communication is the exchange of information and ideas. Communication involves encoding, transmitting, and decoding messages. It is an interactive process requiring at least two parties to play the roles of both sender and receiver. . . . Language is a system used by a group of people for giving meaning to sounds, words, gestures, and other symbols to enable communication with one another. . . . Speech is the actual behavior of producing a language code by making appropriate vocal sound patterns. Although it is not the only possible vehicle for expressing language (gestures, manual signing, pictures, and written symbols can also be used to convey ideas and intentions), speech is a most effective and efficient method. Speech is also one of the most complex and difficult human endeavors. (pp. 234–236)

CEC STANDARDS

CEC 6: Language

Various cultures develop and use language differently, and the study of language is a complex topic. The **American Speech-Language-Hearing Association (ASHA)** (1982) includes the following important considerations in its discussion of language: language evolves within specific historical, social, and cultural contexts; language is rule-governed behavior; language learning and use are determined by the interaction of biological, cognitive, psychosocial, and environmental factors; and effective use of language for communication requires a broad understanding of human interactions, including associated factors such as nonverbal cues, motivation, and sociocultural roles.

INTASC

INTASC 6: Communication technologies

Because language development and use are such complicated topics, determining what is normal and what is disordered communication is also difficult. According to Emerick and Haynes (1986), a communication difference is considered a disability when:

PRAXIS

PRAXIS II: Understanding Exceptionalities

- the transmission or perception of messages is faulty.
- the person is placed at an economic disadvantage.
- the person is placed at a learning disadvantage.
- the person is placed at a social disadvantage.

- there is a negative impact on the person's emotional growth.
- the problem causes physical damage or endangers the health of the person. (pp. 6–7)

To better understand communication disorders, it is helpful to be familiar with the dimensions of communication and the terms used to describe related disorders.

Types of Communication Disorders In its definition of communicative disorders, ASHA (1982) describes both speech disorders and language disorders. **Speech disorders** include impairments of voice, articulation, and fluency. **Language disorders** are impairments of comprehension or use of language, regardless of the symbol system used. A language disorder may involve the form of language, the content of language, or the function (use) of language. Specific disorders of language form include **phonologic**, **syntactic**, and **morphologic** impairments. **Semantics** refers to the content or meaning of language, and **pragmatics** is the system controlling language function. Figure 11.1 contains the definitions of communication disorders as described by ASHA. The terms in this figure are discussed in more detail later in the chapter. The category of communication disorders is broad in scope and includes a wide variety of problems, some of which may overlap. It is not surprising that this group of disorders includes a large proportion of all students with disabilities.

Prevalence and Causes of Communication Disorders

The second most common disability category of students ages six through twenty-one served under IDEA is speech or language impairment (U.S. Department of Education, 2005). These students have a disorder or delay in their ability to send or receive a message, to articulate clearly or fluently, or to comprehend the pragmatics of social interactions. Because many students have other conditions as their primary disability but still receive speech-language services, the total number of students served by **speech-language pathologists** is about 5 percent of all school-age children, two-thirds of whom are boys. In 2002, students with communication disorders constituted 18.7 percent of all students aged six to twenty-one with disabilities. Provision of services to children with speech or language impairment have increased 9.5 percent since 1991 (U.S. Department of Education, 2002).

Of the more than 1 million students identified as speech or language impaired, about 90 percent (over 900,000) are six to eleven years of age (U.S. Department of Education, 2002). Thirty-four percent of students aged six to eleven who have been identified as requiring special education services are classified as having a speech or language impairment (SLI). For this reason, most of the suggestions in this chapter focus on that age group, although many of the language development activities would also be useful for older students.

Identification, Assessment, and Eligibility

Placement patterns for students with disabilities vary by disability according to students' individual needs. Usually, the milder the disability the less restrictive the placement. Students with SLI are the most integrated of all students with disabilities. Since 1985, most students with SLI have been served in either general education classes or resource rooms. Students with SLI were more likely than students with other disabilities to be educated in regular classes for most of the school day.

During the 2001–2002 school year, 87 percent of students with communication disorders were served in general education classroom placements and 7.5 percent were served in resource rooms (U.S. Department of Education, 2005). The small proportion served in separate classes most likely represents students with severe language delays and disabilities. For classroom teachers, having students with communication disorders

| *Figure* **11.1** | **Definitions of Communication Disorders from ASHA** |

Communication Disorders

A. A *speech disorder* is an impairment of voice, articulation of speech sounds, and/or fluency. These impairments are observed in the transmission and use of the oral symbol system.

  1. A *voice disorder* is defined as the absence or abnormal production of voice quality, pitch, loudness, resonance, and/or duration.

  2. An *articulation disorder* is defined as the abnormal production of speech sounds.

  3. A *fluency disorder* is defined as the abnormal flow of verbal expression, characterized by impaired rate and rhythm, which may be accompanied by struggle behavior.

B. A *language disorder* is the impairment or deviant development of comprehension and/or use of a spoken, written, and/or other symbol system. The disorder may involve (1) the form of language (phonologic, morphologic, and syntactic systems), (2) the content of language (semantic system), and/or (3) the function of language in communication (pragmatic system) in any combination.

  1. Form of language

    a. *Phonology* is the sound system of a language and the linguistic rules that govern the sound combinations.

    b. *Morphology* is the linguistic rule system that governs the structure of words and the construction of word forms from the basic elements of meaning.

    c. *Syntax* is the linguistic rule governing the order and combination of words to form sentences, and the relationships among the elements within a sentence.

  2. Content of language

    Semantics is the psycholinguistic system that patterns the content of an utterance, intent, and meanings of words and sentences.

  3. Function of language

    Pragmatics is the sociolinguistic system that patterns the use of language in communication, which may be expressed motorically, vocally, or verbally.

Communication Variations

A. *Communicative difference/dialect* is a variation of a symbol system used by a group of individuals that reflects and is determined by shared regional, social, or cultural/ethnic factors. Variations or alterations in use of a symbol system may be indicative of primary language interferences. A regional, social, or cultural/ethnic variation of a symbol system should not be considered a disorder of speech or language.

B. *Augmentative communication* is a system used to supplement the communicative skills of individuals for whom speech is temporarily or permanently inadequate to meet communicative needs. Both prosthetic devices and/or nonprosthetic techniques may be designed for individual use as an augmentative communication system.

From "Definitions: Communicative Disorders and Variations," by the American Speech-Language-Hearing Association, 1982, *ASHA, 24,* pp. 949–950. Reprinted by permission of the American Speech-Language-Hearing Association.

in their classes is more the rule than the exception. The Rights & Responsibilities feature highlights the rights of students with speech impairments to related services when they are in the general education classroom.

Because so many students with communication disorders are included in general education classrooms, it is important that teachers be able to identify those students who may have speech or language problems, be familiar with common causes of communication disorders, know when problems are serious enough to require referral to other resources, and have some effective strategies for working with students in the general education environment.

Speech Disorders

This section discusses speech disorders that include problems in phonology, voice, and fluency. The discussion includes a description and definition; a brief explanation of causes; and information related to identifying problems serious enough to require a referral for possible assessment or remediation.

Rights & Responsibilities

The Right to "Related Services" for Students with Speech Impairments

Students with speech impairments are generally served in general education classes. They are usually in need of related services. Related services are "to benefit the student" so that he or she may

- Advance appropriately toward attaining annual goals;
- Be involved and progress in the general curriculum and participate in extracurricular activities and other nonacademic activities; and
- Be educated and participate with other children with disabilities and nondisabled children in those extracurricular

and nonacademic activities. (Turnbull & Turnbull, 2000, p. 193)

Related services include speech pathology and speech–language pathology. IDEA defines these as "identification, diagnosis, and appraisal of specific speech or language impairments; referral to or provision of speech and language, medical, or other services; and counseling and guidance of parents, children, and teachers regarding speech and language impairments" [34 CFR, 300.24(b)(14)].

Articulatory and Phonological Disorders

Articulatory and **phonological disorders** are the most common speech disorders, affecting about 10 percent of preschool and school-age children (ASHA, 2002). The ability to articulate clearly and use the phonological code correctly is a function of many variables, including a student's age, developmental history, oral-motor skills, and culture. Although some articulatory and phonological errors are normal and acceptable at young ages, when students are older these same errors may be viewed as developmentally inappropriate and problematic. However, by the time students begin kindergarten, they should be easily understood by their teacher and their peers. McReynolds (1990) has described the most common types of articulation errors: **distortions, substitutions, omissions,** and **additions** (see Table 11.1).

Causes of Problems in the Phonological System   Articulatory and phonological impairments can be either organic (i.e., having an identifiable physical cause) or functional (i.e., having no identifiable cause). Children with functional disorders account for 99 percent of the articulation caseloads of speech-language pathologists in the schools (ASHA, 1999). Some functional disorders may be related to the student's opportunities to learn appropriate and inappropriate speech patterns, including opportunities to practice appropriate speech, transient hearing loss during early development, and the absence or presence of good speech models. Some functional phonological problems have causes that may be related to complex neurological or neuromuscular deficits and might never be specifically identified. Differences in speech can also be related to cultural and linguistic variables. These differences often do not constitute a speech disorder and will be discussed later in the chapter.

Organic articulatory and phonological disorders are related to the neurological and physical abilities required in the process of producing speech sounds, which is a highly complex activity involving intricate, precise, and rapid coordination of neuromuscular, sensory, and cognitive systems. Organic causes of speech impairments may include hearing loss, cleft palate, dental malformations, or tumors (APA, 2000). Brain damage and related neurological problems may also result in disorders of speech production, such as verbal apraxia and dysarthria. The severity of articulatory and phonological disorders can vary widely, depending in part on the causes of the disorders.

When Articulatory and Phonological Errors are a Serious Problem   Because we know the developmental patterns for normal sound production, we can recognize those

CROSS-REFERENCE

Review Chapter 10 on severe disabilities to see the impact of a hearing loss on articulation skills.

CEC STANDARDS

CEC 6: Language

INTASC

INTASC 6: Communication technologies

PRAXIS

PRAXIS II: Understanding Exceptionalities

Table 11.1   **The Four Kinds of Articulation Errors**

Error Type	Definition	Example
Distortion	A sound is produced in an unfamiliar manner.	Standard: Give the pencil to Sally. Distortion: Give the pencil to Sally. (the /p/ is nasalized)
Substitution	Replace one sound with another sound.	Standard: The ball is red. Substitution: The ball is wed.
Omission	A sound is omitted in a word.	Standard: Play the piano. Omission: P_ay the piano.
Addition	An extra sound is inserted within a word.	Standard: I have a black horse. Addition: I have a balack horse.

From *Human Communication Disorders* (3rd ed., p. 219) by G. H. Shames and E. H. Wiig, 1990, New York: Macmillan. Copyright © 1990 by Macmillan Publishing Company. Reprinted by permission.

CEC STANDARDS

CEC 6: Language

INTASC

INTASC 6: Communication technologies

PRAXIS

PRAXIS II: Understanding Exceptionalities

CONSIDER THIS

How could cultural differences influence a child's development of the specific sounds listed in Figure 11.2?

TEACHING TIP

General classroom teachers should screen all students in their classes, especially during the early elementary grades, to determine which students have articulation problems that might require intervention.

children who are significantly different from the norm. The normal pattern of consonant sound production falls within relatively well-defined age limits (Sander, 1972). For example, children usually master the consonant /p/ sound by age three, but may not produce a correct /s/ sound consistently until age eight. Although young children between ages two and six often make phonological errors as their speech develops, similar errors in older students would indicate a problem. At age three it might be normal for a child to say wabbit instead of rabbit. If a five-year-old consistently makes the same error, it should be considered a problem, and the teacher should refer the student to a speech-language pathologist for evaluation. Figure 11.2 presents this pattern of normal development for production of consonants among speakers of Standard American English.

For a general education teacher, evaluating a student's phonological errors involves looking at the big picture, that is, how well the student is doing in class and whether the disorder is interfering with either overall academic performance or social adjustment. A few commonsense considerations may give some insight into whether the student has a serious problem and what, if anything, should be done about it:

- Take note of how understandable or intelligible the student's speech is.
- Consider how many different errors the student makes.
- Evaluate whether the speech errors may have an impact on the student's ability to read and write.
- Observe whether the articulation errors cause the student problems in socialization or adjustment.
- Consider whether the errors could be due to physical problems.

Voice Disorders

Vocal disturbances in children are actually quite common. **Voice disorders** are characterized by the abnormal vocal quality, pitch, loudness, resonance, or duration, given an individual's age and sex (ASHA, 1993). Because our voices are related to our identities and are an integral part of who we are and how we are recognized, we usually allow for a wide range of individual differences in voice.

There are two basic types of voice disorders: **phonation** and **resonance** (Heward, 1995). **Phonation** refers to the production of sounds by the vocal folds. Humans have two vocal folds, which are located in the larynx and lie side by side. When we speak, healthy vocal folds vibrate, coming together smoothly along the length of their surfaces, separating, and then coming together again. These movements are usually very rapid

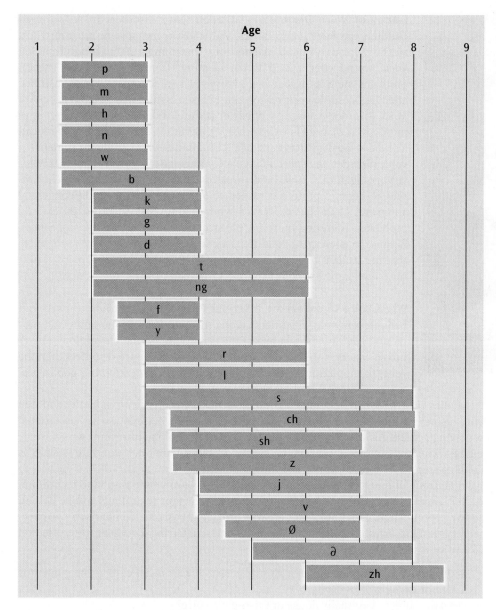

Figure 11.2

Ages at which 90% of All Children Typically Produce a Specific Sound Correctly

Note: Average estimates and upper age limits of customary consonant production. The solid bar corresponding to each sound starts at the median age of customary articulation; it stops at an age level at which 90 percent of all children are customarily producing the sound. The ø symbol stands for the breathed "th" sound, as in *bathroom,* and the ∂ symbol stands for the voiced "th" sound, as in feather (Smith and Luckasson, 1992, p. 168).

From "When Are Speech Sounds Learned?" by E. K. Sander, 1972, *Journal of Speech and Hearing Disorders,* 37, p. 62. Reprinted by permission of the American Speech-Language-Hearing Association.

and are partially controlled by air pressure coming from the lungs. If the vocal folds do not meet and close together smoothly, the voice is likely to sound breathy, hoarse, husky, or strained. Chronic hoarseness is the most common phonatory disorder among children, affecting as many as 38 percent of the school-age population (Hooper, 2004). If a student's vocal folds are too tense or relaxed, or if the voice is produced by vibrating laryngeal structures other than the true vocal folds, the student might demonstrate a pitch disorder. Although pitch disorders occur infrequently in school-age populations, they can sometimes lead to devastating social-emotional consequences.

Disorders of **resonance** usually involve either too many sounds coming out through the air passages of the nose (hypernasality) or the opposite, too little resonance of the nasal passages (hyponasality). Hypernasality sounds like talking through one's nose or with a "twang," and hyponasality sounds like one has a cold or a congested nose. Because resonance is related to what happens to air that travels from the vocal folds into the throat, mouth, and nasal cavity, when there are abnormalities in any of these structures or in the associated musculature, resonance problems can result.

Articulation problems can result in problems in socialization or adjustment.

CONSIDER THIS

How can a student's voice quality affect classroom and peer acceptance? What are some things that teachers can do to influence this impact?

Causes of Voice Disorders Although voice disorders in school-aged children can have many causes, they most commonly result from vocal abuse or misuse, including shouting, screaming, talking loudly, making vocal sound effects, and throat clearing. Common childhood health problems such as upper respiratory tract infections, allergies, asthma, and gastroesophageal reflux can worsen symptoms (Hooper, 2004). Voice disorders caused by abuse or misuse of the vocal folds affect boys more often than girls (ASHA, 2002). Because some voice disorders can also be related to other medical conditions, when students evidence a voice disorder, the speech-language pathologist will refer them to an otolaryngologist (ear, nose, and throat doctor) for evaluation. Some examples of organic problems related to voice disorders include congenital anomalies of the larynx, Reye's syndrome, juvenile arthritis, psychiatric problems, Tourette syndrome, physical trauma to the larynx, and cancer. Because most of these conditions are relatively rare, it may be more likely that the student's voice disorder is a functional problem, perhaps resulting from learned speech patterns (Oyer et al., 1987).

When Voice Disorders are a Serious Problem Classroom teachers can help prevent voice disorders among their students by modeling and promoting healthy voice habits in the classroom, on the playground, and at home. Teachers themselves are at higher risk for voice disorders than the general population and would greatly benefit from adopting good vocal hygiene (Merrill et al., 2004).

Studies have demonstrated that classroom teachers can consistently identify children with disordered and normal voices (Davis & Harris, 1992). A student who is suspected of having a voice disorder should be observed over the course of several weeks, since many symptoms of voice disorders are similar to other temporary conditions such as colds, seasonal allergies, or minor respiratory infections (Oyer et al., 1987). One way to get a meaningful measure of the student's speech during this time is to tape-record him or her several times during the observation period. The tape recordings will be helpful to the speech-language pathologist and will provide a basis for comparison. Teachers might ask themselves the following questions before referring a student for evaluation of a voice disorder:

• Is the student's voice having such an unpleasant effect on others that the student is teased or excluded from activities?
• Does the student habitually abuse or misuse his voice?
• Is there a possibility that the voice disorder is related to another medical condition?
• Does the student's voice problem make him difficult for others to understand?
• Has there been a recent, noticeable change in the student's vocal quality?
• Might the voice quality be related to a hearing loss?

Fluency Disorders

Fluency refers to the pattern of the rate and flow of a person's speech. Normal speech has a rhythm and timing that is regular and steady; however, normal speech patterns also include some interruptions in speech flow. We all sometimes stumble over sounds, repeat syllables or words, mix up speech sounds in words, speak too fast, or fill in pauses with "uh" or "you know." Often normal dysfluencies of speech are related to stressful or demanding situations. When the interruptions in speech flow are so frequent or pervasive that a speaker cannot be understood, when efforts at speech are so intense that they are uncomfortable, or when they draw undue attention, then the dysfluencies are considered a problem (Hallahan & Kauffman, 1995).

Many young children, especially those between ages two and four, demonstrate dysfluencies in the course of normal speech development. Parents and teachers may become concerned about young children's fluency, but most of the dysfluencies of early childhood begin to disappear by age five. The most frequent type of fluency disorder is **stuttering**, which affects about 5 percent of school-age children, three to four times more often boys than girls (Smith & Luckasson, 1992). Cluttering, another type of fluency disorder, occurs infrequently in school-age children. Disturbances of prosody and intonation are rare in children, and are often associated with other, more serious communication problems.

Fluency problems usually consist of blocking, repeating, prolonging, or avoiding sounds, syllables, words, or phrases. In stuttering, these interruptions are frequently obvious to both the speaker and the listener. Often, they are very disruptive to the act of speaking, much more so than disorders of articulation or voice. When the speech dysfluencies occur, listeners may become uncomfortable and look away or try to finish the speaker's words, phrases, or sentences. This discomfort is exacerbated when dysfluent speech is accompanied by unusual gestures, facial contortions, or other movements. Because stuttering can lead to such a pronounced interruption of normal speech and also has a profound impact on listeners, the disorder receives a lot of attention, even though it is not as prevalent as other communication disorders (Hardman et al., 1993).

Causes of Stuttering   Although many causes of stuttering have been suggested over the years, the current thinking among professionals in the field of communication disorders is that there is no one cause for stuttering. Current theories regarding the possible causes of developmental stuttering include factors such as language development, motor skills, personality, and environment.

There seems to be no doubt that the children who stutter are very vulnerable to the attitudes, responses, and comments of their teachers and peers. When considerable attention is focused on normal dysfluencies or when students begin to have negative feelings about themselves because of their stuttering, they may become even more anxious and their stuttering may get worse. Most students who stutter would benefit from intervention by a speech-language pathologist if they hope to avoid a lifelong problem that will affect their ability to communicate, learn, work, and develop positive interpersonal relationships.

When Fluency Disorders are a Serious Problem
Although we know that many children will naturally outgrow their speech dysfluencies, we are unable to predict those children who will not. Therefore, classroom teachers should be sure to refer any children who show signs of dysfluency so they can be evaluated by the speech-language pathologist and, if necessary, receive speech therapy. Teachers should consider the following questions when deciding whether speech dysfluencies are serious:

Stuttering is the most frequent type of fluency disorder, affecting about 2 percent of school-age children, more often boys than girls.

- Are the dysfluencies beginning to occur more often in the student's speech or beginning to sound more effortful or strained?
- Is there a pattern to situations in which the student stutters?
- Is the student experiencing social problems?
- Is the student concerned about his dysfluencies?
- Does the student avoid speaking because he is afraid he may stutter?

CEC STANDARDS

CEC 6: Language

INTASC

INTASC 6: Communication technologies

PRAXIS

PRAXIS II: Understanding Exceptionalities

TEACHING TIP

Teachers who have students who stutter should attempt to reduce the stress on these students and create an accepting atmosphere.

TEACHING TIP

Teachers should keep a log to record instances of stuttering and the activities occurring with the student and the rest of the class when stuttering occurs and when it does not occur.

Classroom Adaptations for Students with Speech Disorders

Build a Positive Classroom Climate

Regardless of the type of speech disorder that students in general education classes demonstrate, it is crucial that teachers make every effort to create a positive, accepting, and supportive climate. The following points are helpful to remember when dealing with children who have speech disorders:

- Talk with the student privately about his or her speech problems. Acknowledge your awareness of the problem, and stress your belief that speech will improve with practice.
- Encourage the student's family to actively support the student's educational and communication goals.
- Do not think of or refer to students with speech disorders in terms of their behaviors ("students," not "stutterers").
- Work closely with the speech-language pathologist, following suggestions and trying to reinforce specific skills.
- Encourage the student.
- Be positive.
- Accept the child just as you would any other student in the class.
- Provide lots of opportunities for students to participate in oral group activities.
- Give students lots of chances to model and practice appropriate speech.
- Maintain eye contact when the student speaks.
- Be a good listener.
- Don't interrupt or finish the student's sentence for him or her.
- When appropriate, educate other students in the class about speech disorders and about acceptance and understanding.
- Reward the child just as you would reward any student.

See Tips for Adapting a Lesson for David for specific recommendations for the student profiled in the chapter-opening vignette.

Help Students Learn to Monitor Their Own Speech

By using simple contract formats, teachers can help students focus on using the skills they learn in speech therapy. After students have had success practicing their communication goals in the therapy setting, they can then practice, monitor their own performance, and earn reinforcement from the teacher or parents whenever specific criteria are met.

Pair Students for Practice

If students are to master speech skills, they will need to practice the skills taught by the speech-language pathologist frequently in many different settings. One way for students to practice specific sounds is to use practice exercises like those in *Read the Picture Stories for Articulation* (Loehr, 2002; Figure 11.3). With a partner, students can use short periods of downtime, such as those between or before classes, to work on their articulation. First, the student is trained in the speech-therapy setting on a specific phoneme in a particular position of words, for example, the initial /s/ sound in seal. After the student has reached 90 percent mastery of the /s/ sound in the beginning of words, she or he then reads a story that is saturated with words beginning with the /s/ sound to a classmate. Each practice session should take no more than five minutes and will provide students with practice that is simple and fun. Both partners should be reinforced for their participation. This practice format can also be used at home with parents.

Tips for Adapting a Lesson for David

Based on the chapter-opening vignette, several adaptations are appropriate for David.

David's teacher should do the following:

- Do not complete sentences for David; be patient and allow him time to get the words out.
- Do not ask David to "slow down" or "relax"; these instructions are not helpful to him.
- During group instruction, call on David fairly early in the discussion and ask David questions that can be answered with relatively few words.
- Speak slowly during group instruction to help slow the pace of all interactions in class.
- Have the same academic expectations for David as for any other student in the class.
- Talk about stuttering with the class and with David just as you would any other matter. It is nothing to be ashamed of.

Figure 11.3   **Sample Form for Articulation Practice**

Sonny the Silly Seal

Target /s/ Words		
seal	sun	sailboat
six	sand	stool
seven	starfish	sticks
sea	circus	

Sonny was a (seal) who loved to sit on the (sand) in the (sun) all day long near his **6** (six) sisters and his best friend Sam the (starfish). Sonny and his

6 (six) sisters would take turns sliding into the (sea) when the (sun) would get too hot. Sonny was the silliest (seal) out of all **7** (seven). He would do silly tricks for his sisters on the (sand) and in the (sea). Sam the (starfish) loved when Sonny would do sommersaults while singing silly songs.

One day, Sonny's friend Sam the (starfish) told him that the (circus) was going to be on the big island

From *Read the Picture Stories for Articulation* (2nd ed., pp. 19–20) by J. Loehr, 2002, Austin, TX: Pro-Ed. Used by permission.

Teach Students Affirmations and Positive Self-Talk

For students with speech disorders, especially stuttering, learning self-confidence and a positive attitude are as important as mastery of specific speech skills. Research has supported the premise that we all talk to ourselves, and the more we talk to ourselves in certain ways, the more we think about ourselves in those same ways. Although negative **self-talk** is common among individuals who have speech disorders, it is possible to change negative patterns to more positive ones.

Affirmations like those suggested by Daly (1991) can help students to build their confidence. The goal of positive self-talk is to replace negative patterns, which might include the statements "I could never do that" or "I can never talk on the phone without stuttering" with positive statements, such as "I am positive and confident. I know that I can handle any speaking situation by being in control of my speech," and "I enjoy saying my name clearly and smoothly when answering the telephone." Whenever a student slips back into a negative frame of mind, encourage him or her to mentally erase the negative ideas and immediately think of something positive. Students should also write their affirmations in their own words, so that they will remember them easily and will more likely use them.

Modify Instruction and Materials

The *Pre-Referral Intervention Manual* (PRIM) (McCarney & Wunderlich, 1988) presents numerous ways to intervene with students who demonstrate speech errors. Some of the suggestions include:

- Set up a system of motivators to encourage students' efforts.
- Highlight material to identify key syllables and words in a passage.
- Give students practice listening so that they can learn to discriminate among sounds, fluent speech patterns, and good vocal habits.
- Tape-record the students' reading so that they can evaluate themselves related to their communication goals.
- Reduce the emphasis on competition. Competitive activities may increase students' stress and result in even more speech errors.

Encourage Parents to Work with Their Children

There are many ways to structure practice activities so that students can work at home with their parents. One program is described in the book *Oral-Motor Activities for School-Aged Children* (Mackie, 1996; Figure 11.4). This series of homework activities is designed to help build the skills that are prerequisite to producing sounds in words. They are designed to be an enjoyable approach to improving the coordination, sensory awareness, and muscle strength needed to produce the sounds of speech. By completing the activities, students assume responsibility for practicing skills learned in the therapy room in other environments. It is suggested that students complete one activity per day and have their parents discuss it with them and provide feedback and guidance.

Teach Students Their Own Strategies

Many of the speech problems that students demonstrate while young can be corrected and modified with therapy. While the therapy is going on, the teacher should focus on giving students strategies for successful learning. The strategies are little "tricks of the trade" that students can use to maximize their academic and social strengths. Some of these strategies also require accommodations on the part of the teacher in structuring situations and requirements.

- Teach them to relax with breathing exercises or mental imagery.

Figure 11.4

Speech Activities That Parents Can Use

From *Oral-Motor Activities for School-Aged Children* by E. Mackie, 1996, Austin: Pro-Ed.

1. What sound are you working on? Write it down. List 10 words with your sound.
   My sound _____

   _____   _____
   _____   _____
   _____   _____
   _____   _____
   _____   _____

2. List the parts of your mouth used to produce your sound.

   _____
   _____
   _____

3. Identify the stability and mobility points needed to produce your sound.

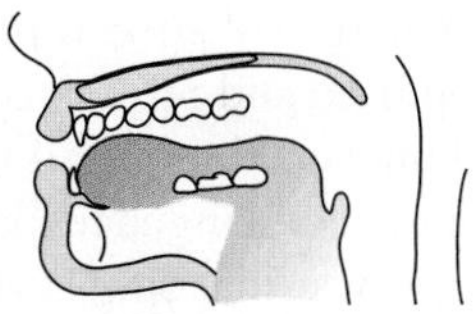

4. Mark the parts of the tongue you need to work on to produce your sound correctly.

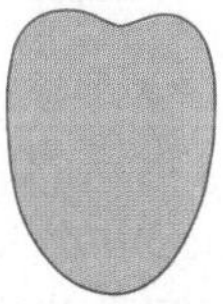

5. Describe what is happening to your mouth when you say your sound incorrectly.

6. Be ready to define the words *stability, mobility,* and *separation (differentiation)* at your next speech session.

Helper _____   Date _____

- Encourage them to participate in groups in which responses do not have to be individually generated.
- Teach them to reinforce themselves by recognizing when they are doing well and by appreciating themselves.
- Let them practice skills with a friend in real situations so that they are not afraid or nervous when it's the "real thing."
- Let them tape-record their own speech and listen carefully for errors so that they can discriminate between correct and incorrect sounds.
- Help them come up with strategies for dealing with specific people or situations that make them nervous (walking away, counting to ten before they speak, deep breathing, etc.).

The IEP Goals and Objectives for David feature includes examples of the strategies recommended for David to try on his own.

Language Disorders

Language is the system we use to communicate our thoughts and ideas to others. Language is a code "whereby ideas about the world are expressed through a conventional system of arbitrary signals for communication" (Lahey, 1988, p. 2). The interrelationships of what we hear, speak, read, and write become our format for sharing information.

For most of us, spoken language is the tool we use to communicate our ideas, but even the most articulate, fluent, pleasant speech would be useless without a language system that enables us to understand and be understood. Language is an integral component of students' abilities in reading, writing, speaking, and listening. Language disorders often have a serious impact on academic performance. In recent years, the emphasis in the field of communication disorders has shifted to encompass an increased focus on language disorders. Results of an epidemiologic study of kindergarten students estimated the overall prevalence rate of developmental language disorders to be 7.4 percent (Tomblin et al., 1997). The prevalence estimate for boys was 8 percent and for girls 6 percent. As many as 50 percent to 80 percent of the children seen by speech-language pathologists in the schools have language disorders (Wiig, 1986).

More important for classroom teachers, however, is that remediation of language disorders will often be as much their responsibility as it is the speech-language pathologist's. Although remediation of speech problems is provided primarily in a therapeutic setting and then supported and reinforced by the classroom teacher, classroom teachers will often direct and manage the overall language development of their students in collaboration with the speech-language pathologist and other special education staff. Recent research has proven that some types of language disorders are best treated collaboratively in the classroom (McGinty & Justice, 2006).

We know that humans can communicate in several ways. Heward (1995) describes a child's process for learning language this way: "A child may learn to identify a familiar object, for example, by hearing the spoken word tree, by seeing the printed word tree, by viewing the sign language gesture for tree, or by encountering a combination of these signals" (p. 235). We generally describe modes of communication as either **receptive language**, which involves receiving and decoding or interpreting language, or **expressive language**, which is the encoding or production of a message. Reading and listening are examples of receptive language; writing and speaking are forms of expressive language.

IEP Goals and Objectives for David*

Goal 1: David will read in a variety of settings with normal fluency.

   Objective 1: Given a short passage to read in the therapy setting, David will read the passage with normal fluency in 75% of trials.

   Objective 2: Given a short passage at home, David will read the passage with normal fluency in 75% of trials.

   Objective 3: Given a short passage in the classroom, David will read the passage with normal fluency in 75% of trials.

Goal 2: David will learn techniques that facilitate fluent speech.

   Objective 1: Given the opportunity to describe and demonstrate breathing techniques in the therapy setting and at home, David will do so appropriately in 70% of the trials.

   Objective 2: Given the opportunity to demonstrate mastery of relaxation techniques in the therapy setting and at home, David will do so successfully in 70% of trials.

   Objective 3: Given the opportunity to demonstrate the use of slow, easy speech in the therapy setting and at home, David will do so successfully in 70% of trials.

   Objective 4: Given the opportunity to demonstrate the use of fluency-facilitating techniques in small groups in the classroom, David will do so successfully in 70% of opportunities.

* IDEA 2004 does not require short-term objectives except for students taking alternative assessments.

As with speech disorders, knowing the normal sequence of language development is important in working with students with language disorders. Some children may be delayed in their development of language but still acquire skills in the same general sequence as other children. Other children may acquire some age-appropriate language skills but have deficits in other specific areas. Table 11.2 shows the normal patterns of language development for children with language disorders and children without language disorders. Although they may refer to these general patterns of language development to judge students' overall progress, teachers should not expect every child to follow this precise sequence on these exact timelines.

Dimensions of Language

Earlier in the chapter, some terminology related to language disorders was introduced. In addition, we refer to the dimensions of language and their related impairments in terms of form, content, and function (or use). Students can demonstrate impairments in any or all of these areas.

Table 11.2 **Language Development for Children with Language Disorders and Without Language Disorders**

Language-Disordered Child			Normally Developing Child		
Age	Attainment	Example	Age	Attainment	Example
27 months	First words	*this, mama, bye bye, doggie*	13 months	First words	*here, mama, bye bye, kitty*
38 months	50-word vocabulary		17 months	50-word vocabulary	
40 months	First two-word combinations	*this doggie more apple this mama more play*	18 months	First two-word combinations	*more juice here ball more TV here kitty*
48 months	Later two-word combinations	*Mimi purse Daddy coat block chair dolly table*	22 months	Later two-word combinations	*Andy shoe Mommy ring cup floor keys chair*
52 months	Mean sentence length of 2.00 words		24 months	Mean sentence length of 2.00 words	
55 months	First appearance of -*ing*	*Mommy eating*	24 months	First appearance of -*ing*	*Andy sleeping*
63 months	Mean sentence length of 3.10 words		30 months	Mean sentence length of 3.10 words	
66 months	First appearance of *is*	*The doggie's mad*	30 months	First appearance of *is*	*My car's gone!*
73 months	Mean sentence length of 4.10 words		37 months	Mean sentence length of 4.10 words	
79 months	Mean sentence length of 4.50 words		37 months	First appearance of indirect requests	*Can I have some cookies?*
79 months	First appearance of indirect requests	*Can I get the ball?*	40 months	Mean sentence length of 4.50 words	

From "Language Disorders in Preschool Children" by L. Leonard, in *Human Communications Disorders: An Introduction* (4th ed.), p. 179, edited by G. H. Shames, E. H. Wiig, and W. A. Second, 1994, New York: Macmillan. Copyright © 1994. Reprinted with permission of Merrill, an imprint of Macmillan Publishing Company.

Form   Form describes the rule systems used in oral language. Three different rule systems are included when we discuss form: **phonology**, **morphology**, and **syntax**.

Phonology is the rule system that governs the individual and combined sounds of a language. Phonological rules vary from one language to another. For example, some of the guttural sounds heard in German are not used in English, and some of the vowel combinations of English are not found in Spanish. The ability to process and manipulate the phonological components of language has been shown to be a critical component in the development of early reading skills.

Morphology refers to the rule system controlling the structure of words. Because the structures of words govern their meanings, comparative suffixes such as -er or -est and plural forms such as the -s that changes *book* to *books* are important. Oyer and colleagues (1987) provide an example of how morphemes (units of meaning) can change a basic word into similar words with many different meanings:

> The word "friend" is composed of one free morpheme that has meaning. One or more bound morphemes may be added, making "friendly," "unfriendly," "friendless," "friendliness," "friendship," and "friendlier." There are rules for combining morphemes into words that must be followed (e.g., "disfriend" is not an allowable word and thus has no meaning). (p. 61)

Syntax is the ordering of words in such a way that they can be understood. Syntax rules determine where words are placed in a phrase or sentence. Just like phonology, syntax rules vary from one language to another. Rules governing negatives, questions, tenses, and compound or simple sentences determine the meanings of word combinations. For example, the same words used in different combinations can mean very different things: "The boy hit the ball" is not the same as "The ball hit the boy."

All these rule systems affect how we use and understand language. Children's abilities to understand and correctly use all these rules related to form develop sequentially as their language skill develops. Language form is important not only in spoken language, but also in written and sign language systems, as well as in augmentative and alternative communication (AAC), discussed later in this chapter.

Content   Content refers to the intent and meaning of language and its rule system; semantics deals with the meaning of words and word combinations. Without specific words to label and describe objects or ideas, our language would have no meaning. When students fail to comprehend concrete and abstract meanings of words, inferences, or figurative expressions, it is difficult for them to understand more subtle uses of language such as jokes, puns, similes, proverbs, or sarcasm. As children mature, they are better able to differentiate meanings of similar words, classify them according to similarities and differences, understand abstract meanings of words, and comprehend figurative language.

Use   When we use language in various social contexts, we follow another set of rules, *pragmatics*. The purpose and setting of our communication as well as the people with whom we are communicating determine the type of language we use. If children are to build and maintain successful relationships with others, it is important that they understand and effectively use skills appropriate to the context. For example, when children speak to adults, it is helpful if they use polite, respectful language; when they speak to their friends, they will most likely use less formal spoken language, demonstrate more relaxed body language, and take turns while talking (Owens, 1984).

The unique language environment of traditional U.S. classrooms places special demands on language use and comprehension that can be particularly challenging to students from diverse cultural and linguistic backgrounds. For example, maintaining eye contact during communication exchanges, naming common objects, and answering "wh" questions are skills at which middle- and upper-class English-speaking children are usually adept, because these skills are valued and supported by their linguistic com-

TEACHING TIP

Teaching students appropriate social skills helps them understand when to modify language in different situations.

munity. However, because these behaviors may not be at all desirable or encouraged in children from communities with a different cultural heritage or linguistic tradition, these children begin their educational career at a distinct disadvantage.

Types and Causes of Language Disorders

Hallahan and Kauffman (1991) have described four basic categories of language disorders: absence of verbal language; qualitatively different language; delayed language development; and interrupted language development. Table 11.3 from Naremore (1980) summarizes these four categories and includes some suspected causes of each. For children who are not deaf, a complete absence of language would likely indicate severe emotional disturbance or a severe developmental disorder. Qualitatively different language is also associated with developmental disorders and emotional disturbance. A good example of this type of problem is the echolalic speech of children with autism, who may repeat speech they hear in a singsong voice and fail to use their spoken language in a meaningful way. Delayed language occurs when a child develops language in the same approximate sequence as other children, but at a slower rate. Causes of delayed language include mental retardation, hearing loss, or lack of stimulation or appropriate experiences. There is also substantial evidence for familial transmission of SLI. The incidence in families with a history of SLI is estimated at 20 percent to 40 percent (Choudhury & Benasich, 2003). Sometimes language development is interrupted by illness or physical trauma. This type of language problem is increasingly common among children as a result of TBI. In general education classrooms, teachers may encounter any or all of these types of language disorders ranging from very mild to severe.

CEC STANDARDS

CEC 6: Language

INTASC

INTASC 6: Communication technologies

PRAXIS

PRAXIS II: Understanding Exceptionalities

Table 11.3   **Types of Language Disorders and Their Causes**

Type	Commonly Suspected Causative Factors or Related Conditions
No Verbal Language Child does not show indications of understanding or spontaneously using language by age 3.	• Congenital or early acquired deafness • Gross brain damage or severe mental retardation/developmental disabilities • Severe emotional disturbance
Quantitatively Different Language Child's language is different from that of nondisabled children at any stage of development—meaning and usefulness for communication are greatly lessened or lost.	• Inability to understand auditory stimuli • Severe emotional disturbance • Learning disability • Mental retardation/developmental disabilities • Hearing loss
Delayed Language Development Language follows normal course of development, but lags seriously behind that of most children who are the same chronological age.	• Mental retardation • Experiential deprivation • Lack of language stimulation • Hearing loss
Interrupted Language Development Normal language development begins but is interrupted by illness, accident, or other trauma; language disorder is acquired.	• Acquired hearing loss • Brain injury due to oxygen deprivation, physical trauma, or infection

Adapted from "Language Disorders in Children" by R. C. Naremore. In *Introduction to Communication Disorders*, p. 224, edited by T. J. Hixon, L. D. Shriberg, and J. H. Saxman, 1980, Englewood Cliffs, NJ: Prentice-Hall. Used by permission.

Indicators of Language Impairments

Some teachers may have an overall sense that a student is demonstrating language problems; others may not notice anything amiss. Wiig and Semel (1984) have identified some indicators of language problems by grade levels.

TEACHING TIP

If you suspect a child of having language problems, keep a record of the problems to better determine if a referral for services is warranted.

- *Primary grades*
  - problems in following verbal directions
  - difficulty with preacademic skills
  - phonics problems
  - poor word-attack skills
  - difficulties with structural analysis
  - problems learning new material
- *Intermediate grades*
  - word substitutions
  - inadequate language processing and production that affects reading comprehension and academic achievement
- *Middle and high school*
  - inability to understand abstract concepts
  - difficulties connecting previously learned information to new material that must be learned independently
  - widening gap in achievement when compared to peers

In addition, teachers can check for linguistic, social, emotional, and academic problems that are related to language disorders (Ratner & Harris, 1994). These problems are shown in Table 11.4.

Children who have language disorders sometimes develop patterns of interaction with peers, teachers, and family members that may result in behavior problems. The behavior problems might seem to have nothing to do with language problems but may in fact have developed in response to inabilities to read, spell, talk, or write effectively.

Classroom Adaptations for Students with Language Disorders

Numerous strategies can be used in general education classrooms to improve students' language skills and remedy language deficits. Consult with the speech-language pathologist and other special education personnel to develop individualized classroom modifications for students with language disorders. The following sections present some ways of structuring learning situations and presenting information to enhance communication.

CEC STANDARDS

CEC 4: Instructional Strategies

Teach Some Prerequisite Imitation Skills

Nowacek and McShane (1993) recommend the following activities:

- Show a picture (of a girl running) and say, "The girl is running."
- Ask the student to repeat a target phrase.
- Positively reinforce correct responses.
- Present a variety of subject/verb combinations until the student correctly and consistently imitates them.

INTASC

INTASC 4: Instructional strategies

Improve Comprehension in the Classroom

Clary and Edwards (1992) suggest some specific activities to improve students' receptive language skills:

PRAXIS

PRAXIS II: Delivery of Services to Students with Disabilities

- *Give students practice in following directions.* Begin with one simple direction, and then increase the length of the list of directions.

Table 11.4		Linguistic, Social, Emotional, and Academic Problems Related to Language Disorders
Linguistic Problems	Language structure	Omissions and distortions of speech sounds
		Omissions of parts of words or word endings
		Sounds or syllables of words out of sequence
		Immature sentence structure
	Language meaning	Difficulty understanding directions and questions
		Confusion of basic concepts and ideas
		Limited vocabulary
		Literal interpretation of figurative language and jokes
		Poor word classification and association skills
	Language use	Difficulty beginning, maintaining, and ending conversations
		Difficulty taking turns in conversations and other classroom activities
		Difficulty understanding the listener's point of view
		Overuse of pauses, fillers, and repetitions in conversation
	Metalinguistics	Difficulty expressing ideas about language
		Poor phonemic awareness skills (rhyming, syllabification, phonics)
Social Problems	Conversational deficits	Poor eye contact
		Inappropriate comments and responses to questions
		Providing insufficient information when describing, relaying information, or giving directions
		Poor social language use (please, thank you)
	Social interaction issues	Poor sense of fair play
		Unable to set limits or boundaries
		Difficulty with new situations
		Difficulty expressing wants, needs, and ideas
Emotional Problems	Personal issues	Poor self-concept
		Low frustration level
		Perseverative and repetitious
	Emotional-interaction issues	Inability to accept responsibility
		Gullible
		Sensitive to criticism
		Poor coping strategies
Academic Problems	Classroom issues	Poor retention of learning
		Problems with organizing and planning
		Difficulty problem solving
		Left/right confusion
		Symbol reversals
		Difficulty expressing known information
		Poor generalization of knowledge to new situations
		Difficulty with higher-level thinking skills (deduction, inference)
		Poor judgment and understanding of cause and effect
		Inability to monitor and self-correct
		Poor memory
	Metacognition	Inability to talk about academic tasks
		Inability to self-regulate behaviors

Adapted from *Understanding Language Disorders: The Impact on Learning* (pp. 171–174) by V. L. Ratner and L. R. Harris, 1994, Eau Claire, WI: Thinking Publications. Reprinted with permission.

- *Have students pair up and practice descriptions.* Place two students at a table separated by a screen. Place groups of identical objects in front of both students. Have one describe one of the objects; the other must determine which object is being described. Reverse roles with new sets of objects.
- *Let students work on categorizing.* Orally present a list of three words. Two should be related in some way. Ask a student to tell which two are related and why (e.g., horse, tree, dog).

CROSS-REFERENCE

When reading Chapters 15 and 16, consider specific activities that could be used to teach listening skills to elementary and secondary students.

The nearby Evidence-Based Practice box provides some additional suggestions for teaching listening skills.

Give Students Opportunities for Facilitative Play

Facilitative play provides modeling for the students so that they can imitate and expand their own use of language. The following is an abbreviated sequence for this type of interaction (Nowacek & McShane, 1993):

- The teacher models self-talk in a play activity. ("I'm making the cars go.")
- The teacher elicits comments from the student and then expands on them. ("Yes, the cars are going fast.")
- The teacher uses "buildups" and "breakdowns" by expanding on a student's ideas, breaking them down, and then repeating them. ("Red car go? Yes, look at the red car. It's going fast on the road. It's going to win the race.")

Encourage Students to Talk with Their Teachers and Peers

Sometimes students who are reluctant to speak require encouragement. In addition to encouraging them with positive social interactions, teachers might also have to structure situations in which students must use language to meet some of their needs in the classroom. The strategies that follow should prompt students to use language when they otherwise might not.

- Place items out of reach so that the child has to ask for them.
- When a child asks for an item, present the wrong item (e.g., the child asks for a spoon and you present a fork).
- Give a child an item that is hard to open so that he or she has to request assistance.
- When performing a task, do one step incorrectly (forget to put the milk in the blender with the pudding mix).
- Make items difficult to find.
- Give students an item that requires some assistance to work with (e.g., an orange that needs peeling).

EVIDENCE-BASED PRACTICE

Teaching Strategies to Help Problem Listeners in the Classroom

- Allow for clarification and repetition of questions during oral tests.
- Avoid use of figurative language and complex or passive sentences.
- Be an interesting speaker—use gestures, facial expressions, movement, and variety in your voice.
- Encourage students to ask questions.
- Identify problem and at-risk listeners and pair them with "study buddies."
- Keep sentence structures simple and direct.

- Limit concentrated listening time to short intervals.
- Make simple adaptations in your classroom to improve the acoustics.
- Reduce noise levels in the classroom during listening tasks.
- Refer problem listeners for hearing screenings.
- Repeat and rephrase.
- Seat problem listeners strategically.
- Speak slowly and pause between thoughts.

- Use advanced organizers and preview questions to help focus listening.
- Use the blackboard and other visual aids.

Adapted from *It's Time to Listen: Metacognitive Activities for Improving Auditory Processing in the Classroom* (2nd ed., pp. 9–15), by P. A. Hamaguchi, 2002, Austin, TX: Pro-Ed.

Use Naturalistic Techniques and Simulated Real-Life Activities to Increase Language Use

Often, the most effective techniques to instill language acquisition and use are those that will be easy for teachers to use and easy for students to generalize to everyday situations. Teachers can encourage generalization by using naturalistic and situational strategies and real-life activities.

- *Naturalistic techniques*
  - Try cloze activities. ("What do you need? Oh, you need paint and a _____. That's right, you need paint and a brush.")
  - Emphasize problem solving. ("You can't find your backpack? What should you do? Let's look on the hook. Is your coat there? What did we do to find your coat? That's right, we looked on the hook.")
  - Use questioning techniques. ("Where are you going? That's right, you are going to lunch.")
- *Simulated real-life activities*
  - Let students role-play a newscast or commercial.
  - Have students write and follow their own written directions to locations in and around the school.
  - Play "social charades" by having students act out social situations and decide on appropriate responses.
  - Have one student teach an everyday skill to another (e.g., how to shoot a basket).
  - Using real telephones, give students opportunities to call each other, and to give, receive, and record messages.

CONSIDER THIS

When using some of these strategies to facilitate the development of students' speech and language skills, what can you do to make it more likely that the student will continue to speak without these strategies?

Encourage Students' Conversational Skills through Story Reading

McNeill and Fowler (1996) give some excellent suggestions for helping students with delayed language development. Since students with language development problems often do not get the results they want through their ordinary conversations, they need more practice. What better way to practice effective language skills than through story reading! Students of all ages enjoy being read to, whether individually or in small groups while students are young, or in larger classes when they are in intermediate or secondary grades.

These authors suggest four specific strategies for teachers to use when reading stories aloud: praise the students' talk; expand on their words; ask open-ended questions; and pause long enough to allow students to initiate speaking. In addition, they emphasize taking turns, so that students have an opportunity to clarify their messages, hear appropriate language models, and practice the unspoken rules of communication.

McNeill and Fowler (1996) also recommend coaching parents in how to give their children opportunities to talk and how to respond when their children do talk. When parents pause, expand on answers, and ask open-ended questions that require more than just "yes" or "no" responses, they can become their children's best teachers.

Use Music and Play Games to Improve Language

Teachers should always try to have some fun with students. Using music and playing games are two ways language can be incorporated into enjoyable activities.

- *Music*
  - Use songs that require students to request items (e.g., rhythm sticks or tambourines passed around a circle).
  - Have picture symbols for common songs so that students can request the ones they like.

- Use props to raise interest and allow students to act out the story (e.g., during "Humpty Dumpty" the student falls off a large ball).
- Use common chants such as "When You're Happy and You Know It," and let students choose the action (e.g., clap your hands).
  - *Games that require language comprehension and expression skills*
    - Play "Simon Says."
    - Play "Musical Chairs" with words rather than music. (Pass a ball around a circle. When the teacher says a magic word, the student with the ball is out.)
    - Use key words to identify and organize students. ("All the boys with red hair stand up. Everyone who has a sister sit down.")
    - Play "Twenty Questions." ("I'm thinking of a person." Students ask yes-or-no questions.)

Arrange Your Classroom for Effective Interactions

For students who have either speech or language problems, the physical arrangement of the classroom can contribute to success. The following guidelines may improve students' language development:

- Give instructions and important information when distractions are at their lowest.

DIVERSITY FORUM

Language Disorder or Language Difference?

Shalisha is an eleven-year-old African American 5th grader who speaks African American English (AAE). Ms. Hertz, Shalisha's teacher, sets aside the first 15 minutes of class for her students to share. Students can tell a story, tell a joke or bring something from home to describe to the class, but Shalisha rarely participates. She feels uncomfortable speaking in front of the class. She contends that Ms. Hertz does not like her because when it is her time to share, Ms. Hertz repeatedly interrupts and corrects her grammar leaving Shalisha confused and frustrated. Ms. Hertz is concerned about Shalisha's expressive language skills; she perceives Shalisha to have poor grammar and incorrect sentence structures and thinks she needs to be assessed by a speech-language pathologist.

Historically, AAE speakers who are not speakers of classroom English (CE) have often been misdiagnosed because they are perceived as having speech and language impairments. One contributing factor is that speech-language referral practices are primarily normed for students who use CE (Green, 2002). Moreover, educators often have difficulty distinguishing disabilities from cultural or linguistic differences. Although some African American students are CE speakers and are socialized similarly to students from the dominant culture, many have different language experiences that shape their use of verbal and non-verbal communication. To prevent misdiagnosis, speech-language referral and assessment and classroom practices should account for these differences.

Ms. Hertz would benefit from knowing that AAE is not linguistically or conceptually inferior to CE and that, in fact, Shalisha's language use is consistent with AAE rules. She can nurture Shalisha's language development by validating and appreciating her language use by (Rickford, 2002):

- Incorporating familiar African American language features into classroom instruction with poetry and African American literature that utilizes AAE.

- Having students develop more accurate views of language by examining data across various dialects, developing hypotheses that describe and predict linguistic phenomena in those dialects, and collecting and comparing data from their own speech communities.

Questions

1. Why is it important to understand the characteristics of Shalisha's dialect (e.g., rules that govern the dialect, common speech patterns, etc.)?
2. Given that it is important to nurture student's language use within the classroom., what are some other ways to incorporate Shalisha's dialect into the curriculum?

REFERENCES

Green, L. (2002). *African American English: A Linguistic Introduction.* Cambridge: University Press.

Rickford, J.R. (2002). Using the vernacular to teach the standard. Stanford University, Department of Linguistics. Retrieved April 4, 2002, from www.stanford.edu/~rickford/papers/VernacularToTeachStandard.html

- Use consistent attention-getting devices, either verbal, visual, or physical cues.
- Be specific when giving directions.
- Write directions on the chalkboard, flip chart, or overhead so that students can refer to them.
- Use students' names frequently when talking to them.
- Emphasize what you're saying by using gestures and facial expressions.
- Pair students with buddies for modeling and support.
- Allow for conversation time in the classroom so that students can share information and ideas.
- Encourage students to use calendars to organize themselves and manage their time. (Breeding, Stone, & Riley, n.d.)

CEC STANDARDS

CEC 5: Learning Environment and Social Interactions

Use Challenging Games with Older Students

Older students may require continued intervention to improve language skills. However, the activities chosen must be appropriate and not seem like "baby" games. Thomas and Carmack (1993) have collected ideas to involve older students in enjoyable, interactive tasks:

INTASC

INTASC 5: Learning Environment

- Read fables or stories with morals. Discuss outcomes and focus on the endings.
- Do "Explain That." Discuss common idiomatic phrases, and help students discover the connection between the literal and figurative meanings (e.g., "She was on pins and needles").
- "Riddlemania" presents riddles to students and has them explain what makes them humorous.
- Have "Sense-Able Lessons." Bring objects to see, taste, hear, and smell, and compile a list of students' verbal comments. (p. 155)

PRAXIS

PRAXIS II: Delivery of Instruction to Students with Disabilities

Modify Strategies to Develop Students' Learning Tools

When facilitating language development for older students, help them develop their own strategies to use in challenging situations (Thomas & Carmack, 1993). Requiring them to use higher-order thinking skills will both require and stimulate higher-level language.

- Pair students to find word meanings. Use partners when working on categories such as synonyms or antonyms. Let students work together to master using a thesaurus.
- Teach students to categorize. Begin with concrete objects that they relate to easily, such as types of cars or names of foods, and then move to more abstract concepts such as feelings or ideas.
- Play reverse quiz games like "Jeopardy!" in which students have to work backward to think of questions for answers. (pp. 155–163)

Work Collaboratively with the Speech–Language Pathologist

LINC (Language IN the Classroom) is a program adapted for use in many school districts (Breeding et al., n.d.). The program philosophy holds that language learning should occur in the child's most natural environment and in conjunction with other content being learned. The development of students' language should relate to their world and should be a learning experience, not a teaching experience.

The purpose of the program is to strengthen the language system of those students in general education classrooms who need to develop coping and compensatory skills to survive academically. Another goal is to transfer language learned from the therapy setting to the classroom, thereby allowing children to learn to communicate, rather than merely talk. The teacher and the speech-language pathologist must both be present for

CEC STANDARDS

CEC 10: Collaboration

INTASC

INTASC 10: Foster relationships

the approach to be successful. The two professionals work together to plan unit lessons that develop language skills in students.

Hiller (1990) presents an example of how LINC works. His elementary school implemented classroom-based language instruction. At the beginning of the program, the speech-language pathologist visited each classroom for a specified amount of time each week (ninety minutes) during the language arts period. The first forty-five minutes were used for an oral language activity, often a cooking activity from the *Blooming Recipes* workbook (Tavzel, 1987). During the second forty-five minutes, students wrote paragraphs. For example, after preparing peanut butter and raisins on celery ("Bumps on a Log"), students responded to the following questions:

1. What was the name of the recipe we made?
2. Where did we do our preparing?
3. Who brought the peanut butter, celery, and raisins?
4. How did we make "Bumps on a Log"?
5. When did we eat "Bumps on a Log"?
6. Why do you think this recipe is called "Bumps on a Log"?

Responses were written on the board or on an overhead transparency. Students copied the responses in paragraph format.

Teachers and speech-language pathologists later extended the activities to teaching language lessons on current topics, team-teaching critical thinking activities during science experiments, and team planning and teaching social studies units. Reports from Hiller's and other schools using LINC programs described better collaboration among professionals, more accurate language referrals, and increased interest in speech-language activities among the entire staff. The nearby Personal Spotlight describes how a speech-language pathologist views collaboration.

Use Storytelling and Process Writing

When children listen to and retell a story, they incorporate it into their oral language repertoire. McKamey (1991) has described a structure for allowing students to retell stories they had heard, to tell stories from their own experience, and to write down and illustrate their oral presentations. In process writing, students are instructed based on what they can already do. This and other balanced literacy approaches often allow students who have had negative language experiences to begin to succeed, to link written and spoken language, and to grow as communicators.

Language Differences

Children's patterns of speech and use of language reflect their culture, socioeconomic status, and gender and may be different from that of some of their peers. It is important not to mistake a language difference for a language disorder, but also a disorder must not be overlooked in a student with language differences. Variations in family structure, child-rearing practices, family perceptions and attitudes, regional dialects, and language and communication styles can all influence students' communication (Wayman, Lynch, & Hanson, 1990).

Acquiring English as a Second Language

Students who are learning English as a second language (ESL) often exhibit error patterns that can look like language disorders when they are, in fact, part of the normal process of second-language acquisition (Roseberry-McKibbin & Brice, 2002). It is crucial that teachers of students who are English-language learners recognize these pat-

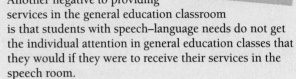

Personal Spotlight

Speech–Language Pathologist

Martha Drennan has been a speech–language pathologist for eight years. She has been employed in both a large, urban district and a small, rural district. Currently she works for the Rison School District in Rison, Arkansas. One of the most significant changes Martha has observed in her field is that many children now receive speech–language services in a general education setting rather than being pulled out for services in a segregated, speech classroom. Martha likes this change. She notes that there are several advantages to providing services to these children in general classrooms rather than pulling them out. Among these advantages are that

- more students can be served because the speech–language pathologist can work with several students at the same time. Often an entire class is the target of a lesson conducted by the speech–language pathologist so that all students benefit.
- some students, especially older ones, do not feel the stigma of receiving services as part of their general education classroom whereas they did when they had to leave the room for speech.

Martha notes that many older students really resent having to go to the speech room. She especially sees serving students in the general education setting as beneficial for this group of students.

Martha Drennan
Rison School District, Rison, AR

Despite benefits, there are also some negative factors associated with this newer service delivery model. Martha said that "some teachers would simply rather teach all the lessons in their classroom themselves because they feel like they do not have the luxury to give another teacher time." Another negative to providing services in the general education classroom is that students with speech–language needs do not get the individual attention in general education classes that they would if they were to receive their services in the speech room.

Overall, Martha is very pleased with serving students with speech and language needs in general education classes. She noted that "virtually all general education teachers are very happy when you go into their classroom and provide a language lesson for all kids." She also stated that the collaboration needed to ensure an effective, smooth lesson requires time for general education teachers and speech–language pathologists to plan, something that seems to always be a problem.

---

terns as language differences rather than communication disorders in order to avoid unnecessary referrals:

- *Interference or transfer:* Students may make errors in English form because of the influence of structures or patterns in their native language.
- *Silent period:* Children who are learning a new language focus on listening to and attempting to understand the new language before trying out what they have learned. This silent period may last as long as a year in very young children and as briefly as a few weeks or months in older children.
- *Code switching or code mixing:* Students use words, phrases, or sentences from one language in the other.
- *Subtractive bilingualism:* As students learn English, they can begin to lose skill and proficiency in their native language if it is not also supported and valued.

Relationship between Communication Style and Culture

Culture has a strong influence on the style of communication. Many areas of communication style can be affected by factors including gender, status, dialect, and age roles; rules governing interruptions and taking turns; use of humor; and how to greet or leave someone (Erickson, 1992). Teachers must be aware of the many manifestations of culture in nonverbal communication as well. Differences in rules governing eye contact, the physical space between speakers, use of gestures and facial expression, and use of silence can cause dissonance between teachers and students of differing cultures.

INTASC

INTASC 6: Communication technologies

PRAXIS

PRAXIS II: Understanding Exceptionalities

Walker (1993) has described how differences such as directness of a conversation, volume of voices, and reliance on verbal (low-context) versus nonverbal (high-context) parts of communication affect attitudes toward the speaker. Teachers can respond to cultural differences in several ways. These suggestions are adapted from Walker (1993) and should be helpful for teachers who want to enhance both overall achievement and communication skills with students who are culturally or linguistically different:

- Try to involve community resources, including churches and neighborhood organizations, in school activities.
- Make home visits.
- Allow flexible hours for conferences.
- Question your own assumptions about human behavior, values, biases, personal limitations, and so on.
- Try to understand the world from the student's perspective.
- Ask yourself questions about an individual student's behavior in light of cultural values, motivation, and worldviews, and how these relate to his or her learning experiences.
- Remind yourself and your students to celebrate and value the cultural and linguistic differences among individuals in their school and community.
- Consult with the speech-language pathologist to understand how to differentiate between students who have language differences and those who have disorders. (p. 2)

Multicultural Considerations in Assessment

Assessment in the area of communication disorders is often complicated, just as it is for students with other disabilities. Because of the increasing numbers of students who are culturally and linguistically different and who require services in ESL or who are **limited English proficient (LEP)**, teachers should consult with personnel in special education, ESL, speech and language services, and bilingual education to obtain appropriate evaluation and programming services. Observation is an important form of assessment, particularly when assessing students who are linguistically different. In the 1999–2000 school year, speech-language pathologists reported that over one-fourth of their students were from a cultural or linguistic group different from their own, and 8.8 percent were English-language learners (Carlson et al., 2002).

Because of the increasing number of students in public schools from cultural or linguistic minority groups, teachers are recognizing the need for information related to learning and communication styles as well as modifications to curriculum and instruction. Although many of these children will never be identified as having a communication disorder, teachers in general education must be aware that differences in language and culture may often impact a student's apparent proficiency in both oral and written communication.

The cultural background of a child will influence many aspects of the style of communication that is used.

Augmentative and Alternative Communication (AAC)

The term **augmentative communication** denotes techniques that supplement or enhance communication by complementing whatever vocal skills the individual already has (Harris & Vanderheiden, 1980). Research has demonstrated that the use of communication devices does not inhibit the development of natural speech. Other individuals (e.g., those who are severely neurologically impaired and cannot speak) must employ techniques that serve in place of speech—in other words, alternative communication. According to Shane and Sauer (1986), the term **alternative communication** applies when "the production of speech for communication purposes has been ruled out" (p. 2). In 2004, almost 49 percent of speech-language pathologists in schools indicated that they served individuals who required AAC (ASHA, 2004).

AAC is a multimodal system consisting of four components (symbols, aids, techniques, and strategies) that can be used in various combinations to enhance communication. Communication techniques used in AAC are usually divided into either aided or unaided forms. Unaided techniques include nonverbal methods used in normal communication and do not require any physical object or entity to express information (e.g., speech, signing, gestures, and facial expressions). Aided communication techniques require a physical object, device, or external support to enable the individual to communicate (e.g., communication boards, charts, and mechanical or electrical devices). Because substantial numbers of individuals lack functional speech secondary to MR, TBI, deafness, neurological disorders, or other causes, there has been increased demand for AAC in recent years. A student's communication skills and needs will change over time, as will the types of technology and methods available to support communication. Thus, the educational team should continually monitor and periodically reevaluate the usefulness of each AAC approach used by their students.

Students who cannot use spoken language may use a basic nonautomated communication device with no electronic parts. Examples include communication boards, charts, frames, and books that can be based on symbols, words, or letters. Typically, this kind of device will contain representations of common objects, words, phrases, or numbers and can be arranged in either an alphabetic or nonalphabetic format (Figure 11.5). Because they are easy to construct and can be modified to fit the student's vocabulary and communication context, nonautomated communication devices are very useful in communicating with teachers, family members, and peers. There are several commercially available sets of symbols, including the *Picture Communication Symbols* (Mayer-Johnson, 1986) and the *Oakland Schools Picture Dictionary* (Kirsten, 1981). Computer software programs that contain picture communication symbols can also be used to generate communication boards, picture schedules, instruction sheets, and other communication tools.

Electronic communication aids encompass a wide variety of capabilities, from simple to complex. Aids that produce voice are known as voice output communication aids, or VOCAs. A large number of different VOCAs are available that vary greatly in their level of sophistication and complexity. They range from aids that speak just one message to aids that provide access to keyboards for virtually unlimited messaging capacity. The voice output may be amplified, digitized, or synthetic speech. Often, a voice synthesizer is used to produce speech output, and written output is produced on printers or displays. Software, which is becoming increasingly sophisticated, can accommodate the many different needs of individuals who cannot produce spoken and/or written language. Some examples of electronic communication aids and their key features are shown in Table 11.5.

CEC STANDARDS

CEC 6: Language

INTASC

INTASC 6: Communication technologies

Figure **11.5**

Communication Board

From *Functional Language Instruction* (p. 87) by C. Cottier, M. Doyle, & K. Gilworth, 1997, Austin, TX: Pro-Ed.

Table 11.5	**Electronic Communication Aids and Their Key Features**

BigMack

A large, colorful, single message digitizer.

Record and re-record a message, song, sound, story line, or choice of up to 20 seconds.

A picture or label can easily be stuck to the large button.

Can be accessed by pressing anywhere on the large button or by a separate switch.

Can be used as a switch to control other devices, toys, or appliances.

Lightwriter SL35

A compact, portable keyboard will speak what is typed into it.

Text messages are displayed on the two-way screen, and synthesized speech is used.

Can be customized for people with more complex needs.

Add-ons such as key guards can be purchased, and a range of models are available.

Reduces keystrokes by using memory and word prediction.

ChatPC

Based on a palmtop Windows CE computer.

Housed in a durable case to give additional protection and additional amplification.

Has a color touch screen, and over a hundred pages of messages can be programmed.

An onscreen keyboard is available, and this speaks out what is typed into it.

3000+ symbols are supplied and can be supplemented with scanned or digital images.

Speech output can be digital or synthetic.

Changes can be made on the device or on a computer and then downloaded.

Dynavox 3100

Touchscreen device offers word layouts, symbol layouts, or a combination of both.

Many preprogrammed page sets, suitable for users with a wide range of ability levels.

Flexible layout can be thoroughly customized.

Symbol-supported word prediction encourages literacy.

DecTalk speech synthesis offers nine different voices.

Can be accessed via touchscreen, mouse, joystick, or switches.

Auditory and visual scanning modes are possible.

Built-in infrared for environmental controls and computer access.

Because recent evidence has shown that everyone can communicate, the focus of contemporary AAC assessment and intervention is on developing and fine-tuning individualized methods that promote functional communication abilities in school, home, and community settings (Sevcik & Romski, 2000). The Technology Today feature on page 379 lists some of the approaches and facilitating strategies for developing an effective team approach to serve students using AAC in the classroom.

Facilitated Communication

Facilitated communication (FC) is a process that has been used with individuals who have developmental disabilities, including autism. First introduced by Rosemary Crossley in Australia, FC usually involves having someone (a facilitator) support the arm or wrist of the person with autism, who then points to pictures, objects, printed letters, and words, or types letters on a keyboard. The keyboard is often connected to a computer so that the individual's words can be displayed or printed (Kirk, Gallagher, & Anastasiow, 1993). Supposedly the support of the facilitator enables the individual to type out words and phrases.

Biklen (1990) has conducted much of the work done in FC and has reported anecdotal success with the procedure. However, results of objective research on the effectiveness of

FC have found no conclusive evidence supporting the method (see Chapter 9). ASHA has issued a position paper on FC that cautions that the validity and reliability of this method have yet to be proven (ASHA, 1995).

Promoting Inclusive Practices for Students with Communication Disorders

Until very recently, the traditional service delivery model for speech therapy included a twice-weekly, thirty-minutes-per-session, pull-out model in which speech-language pathologists worked with students in a small room away from the regular education classroom. Even though this model may still be appropriate with some students some of the time, there are other effective approaches for provision of speech-language therapy services in public school settings. Just as academic services to students with disabilities have become more and more integrated into general education programs, speech-language services are now following more inclusive models. This collaboration between regular and special education staff might involve speech-language pathologists visiting the classroom to work with individual students or with small groups; the teacher and speech-language pathologist teaching alternate lessons or sections of a particular lesson; or professionals coteaching the same lesson at the same time. The following delivery

Developing an Effective Team Approach to Serve Students Using AAC in the Classroom

Approach	Facilitating Strategies
Collaborative teaming	Regularly scheduled team meetings Roles and responsibilities of team members are clearly defined Mutual respect among team members Team members communicate effectively and take a proactive approach Flexible interpretation of traditional roles of team members
Providing access to the curriculum	All team members have a working knowledge of the curriculum Assessment of the student's learning style by each member of the team Vocabulary and support are provided for use of the device across all classroom activities and school events
Cultivating social supports	Facilitate social interactions between the student and his peers Identifying and using natural supports in the classroom Training peers as communication partners Foster the independence and autonomy of the student
AAC system maintenance and operation	Team members are familiar with the basic maintenance, operation, and elements of the AAC device Team members know how to access help and additional resources as necessary Peers are familiarized with the device and regarding how to provide communication support
Building a supportive classroom community	Use of cooperative learning strategies Team teaching between general and special education personnel Working together to support all students in the classroom Promoting appreciation of differences within the classroom

Adapted from "Professional Skills for Serving Students Who Use AAC in General Education Classrooms: A Team Perspective" (pp. 51–56) by G. Soto et al., 2001, *Language, Speech, and Hearing Services in the Schools, 32.*

options have been recommended for the provision of speech and language services in the schools: **direct instruction (pull-out)**, **classroom-based**, **community-based**, and **consultation** (ASHA, 1996). These service-delivery options can be implemented independently or in any combination to best meet the individual needs of the student. Recent evidence suggests that the influence of service-delivery models on the outcomes children achieve varies according to the type of disorder that is being treated.

- The traditional pull-out model is indicated for students who are in particular stages of the intervention process or for those who have very specific communication goals. Pull-out services are often provided within the classroom or in the therapy room, and with individual students or in small groups.
- Classroom-based service-delivery options usually involve a collaborative effort between teachers and speech-language pathologists. This model is particularly appropriate at the preschool and kindergarten levels and in classrooms with large numbers of students who have been identified as having communication disorders or as being at risk. This collaboration can involve the speech-language pathologist providing individual or small group instruction in the classroom or participating in team teaching or coteaching lessons with the classroom teacher.
- The community-based service-delivery model indicates that therapy services are being provided in more natural communication environments such as at home, on the playground, or in other age-appropriate community settings. Providing speech and language therapy in a community-based setting is ideal for students who have pragmatic language disorders, for those who need to generalize new skills to a variety of settings, and for students who are enrolled in vocational programs.
- Consultation is a model of service delivery in which the speech-language pathologist does not provide direct instruction to the student. Instead, the family, teachers, or other school staff are provided with assistance in the form of information, training, or resources to help the student reach specific communication goals. The provision of consultation services is indicated for those students who are working on generalization of communication skills or for those students who are receiving communication programming from other instructional staff.

The following list (Friend, 1992) demonstrates the various roles that members of an educational team might assume to implement speech and language interventions in the school setting:

- There is one primary provider of services to the student.
- One provider (speech-language pathologist) teaches others specific assessment or treatment strategies; other providers (e.g., teacher) implement the strategies.
- One provider provides services; the others assist side by side.
- One provider provides services at a learning center within a large group.
- Two providers implement interventions simultaneously during a codirected lesson (parallel teaching).
- One provider (teacher and curriculum) recommends to other providers suggestions of content and methods to incorporate into intervention; other providers (speech-language pathologists) implement recommendations (supplemental teaching).
- Other roles devised to meet the client's unique needs.

As schools try to maximize the positive impact of professional collaboration, it is important to recognize and overcome the barriers inherent in the process.

The barriers to greater collaboration among speech-language professionals and teachers can include (Kerrin, 1996):

- territorial obstacles ("This is my job; that is your job.")
- time concerns ("When are general education teachers supposed to find the time to meet, plan, and modify?")
- terror ("I'm afraid this new way won't work.")

Fortunately, Kerrin (1996) has also offered some good ideas for overcoming these obstacles. She suggests that team members try the following tips:

- Try to be flexible and creative when scheduling conferences.
- Encourage everyone involved to ask questions.
- Invite speech-language professionals into the classroom.
- Ask for assistance in planning.
- Maintain open, regular communication.
- Keep an open mind, a cooperative spirit, and a sense of humor.

INTASC

INTASC 10: Relationships with school colleagues

PRAXIS

PRAXIS II: Delivery of Services to Students with Disabilities

Future Trends

Several forces are changing the field of communication disorders as practiced in the public schools. First, general education teachers are likely to see more students with moderate to severe disabilities in their classrooms. The movement toward more inclusive environments for students will require classroom teachers to provide more instruction for these students. Moreover, recent legislation and research suggest a shift away from the use of standardized assessment instruments and toward the employment of dynamic, authentic, and curriculum-based assessment methods. The observations and input of the classroom teacher play a crucial role in each of these assessment models.

As a result of expanding knowledge and skills among professionals trained in speech-language pathology, the scope of practice of the profession has been increasing and will continue to do so. In addition to providing services in the more traditional area of oral communication skills, speech-language pathologists now working in the schools are often called on to have expertise in swallowing disorders, Medicaid billing, selecting AAC systems, providing intervention and recommending classroom modifications for children with TBI and other complex neurological disorders, and promoting and enhancing literacy skills (Montgomery & Herer, 1999).

The caseloads of speech-language pathologists are continuing to grow, and there is an ever-increasing demand for services, especially in the area of language disorders. At the same time, there is expected to be an increasing shortage of speech-language pathologists employed to meet these increasing demands. Although pull-out speech-language remediation will still be offered to some students, many of the services will be delivered in an increasingly collaborative and consultative framework, with teachers and speech-language pathologists cooperating and sharing resources. In areas where shortages are particularly acute, schools will need to consider alternate methods of providing services to students with communication disorders. Some methods that might be employed to compensate for shortages in specialty personnel include employment of speech-language pathology assistants, flexible scheduling, cross-disciplinary service provision, peer tutoring, and increased use of natural supports.

The social trends that are shaping U.S. society in general will have an increasing effect on the provision of speech therapy services in the schools. These trends include an increasingly multicultural and multilinguistic society; an increase in the numbers of children living in poverty without access to adequate health care and early intervention services; and the changing role of the school in the community.

Another area of change is the expected continuation of technological advances. Some of the improved technology has already been described here; however, it is virtually impossible to keep up with the rapid improvements in this area. With continued improvements in technology, students with more severe communication disorders will have opportunities to interact with family members, teachers, and peers, perhaps participating in activities that would have seemed impossible ten years ago. Distance learning and telehealth services will become more commonplace, particularly in traditionally underserved areas such as inner-city, geographically remote, and rural schools (Montgomery & Herer, 1994).

Authors' note: The authors would like to express their appreciation to Janice Maxwell, MS, CCC-SLP, for her assistance in providing much of the practical information that was presented in this chapter. Janice is an exemplary speech pathologist and a wonderful friend to teachers in general education.

Summary

Basic Concepts about Communication Disorders

- Although most people take the ability to communicate for granted, communication problems can result in difficulties in even the most simple of interactions and lead to problems in socialization and emotional adjustment. Speech and language are the interrelated, rule-governed skills that we use to communicate.
- About 2 percent of the school-age population has been identified as having speech or language impairments.
- Because most students with speech and language impairments are served in a regular classroom or resource room placement, having students with speech and language disorders in the classroom is more the rule than the exception.

Speech Disorders

- Speech disorders include impairments of phonology, voice, and fluency, with phonological disorders being the most common.
- Speech disorders can either be functional or organic in origin.

Classroom Adaptations for Students with Speech Disorders

- Teachers can make numerous accommodations and modifications for students with speech disorders. For example, building a positive classroom environment is an important accommodation that can make inclusion easier for these students.

Language Disorders

- Language disorders can be expressive or receptive in nature and can affect the form, content, or use of language.
- Disorders of language can be classified into four basic categories: absence of verbal language, qualitatively different language, delayed language development, and interrupted language development.
- Significant language disorders directly impact a student's ability to interact with family, peers, and teachers.

Classroom Adaptations for Students with Language Disorders

- Specific, individualized intervention and instructional modifications (e.g., storytelling, facilitative play, classroom arrangement) are required.

Language Differences

- Individual social and cultural experiences often affect the way in which we use speech and language as tools for communication and learning.

- Teachers should be aware of the influence that culture has on the style and nonverbal aspects of communication.
- Special consideration should be given during assessment of students having diverse cultural and linguistic heritage. Some speech and language differences can be attributed to cultural diversity or environmental factors and are not considered disorders.

Augmentative and Alternative Communication

- All students can communicate.
- AAC options can facilitate the communicative abilities of people with severe speech and language disorders.
- The level and type of technology needed to support AAC methods varies widely.
- Objective research on the FC method has not shown it to be reliable or valid.

Promoting Inclusive Practices for Students with Communication Disorders

- Speech-language pathologists employ a variety of service-delivery models that can be used independently or in combination to meet the individual needs of each student. Most of these models involve some level of professional collaboration and consultation with the classroom teacher.
- The speech-language pathologist can work with the classroom teacher to make necessary modifications to the classroom environment, methodology, and curriculum to accommodate the needs of students with communication disorders in inclusive settings.
- Teachers and therapists need to work as a team to overcome common barriers to greater collaboration.

Future Trends

- The movement toward more inclusive environments for students will require classroom teachers to serve greater numbers of students with moderate and severe communication disorders.
- Increasing caseloads, an expanding scope of practice, and personnel shortages will lead speech-language pathologists to provide many services using collaborative, consultative, and alternative models of service delivery rather than the more traditional "pull-out" approach.
- Technological advances will offer increased options for provision of services to students with severe communication disorders and increased opportunities for students to interact with others and participate in a wider range of activities.

Questions to Reconsider

Think back to the scenario about David that you read at the beginning of this chapter. Would you answer the questions raised there any differently after reading the chapter itself?

1. What should Mr. Parker tell the students in his classroom about stuttering?
2. What could Mr. Parker and Mrs. Woods do to help David better interact with his peers in settings other than the classroom?

3. Should Mr. Parker expect David to give oral reports in front of the class? Why or why not?
4. Why would asking David to "slow down" or "relax" not help him to speak more fluently?

Further Readings

American Speech-Language-Hearing Association. (1996). Inclusive practices for children and youth with communication disorders: Position statement and technical report. *ASHA, 38*(16), 35–44.

American Speech-Language-Hearing Association. (2001). *Roles and responsibilities of speech-language pathologists with respect to reading and writing* (position statement and guidelines). Rockville, MD: Author.

Fahey, K. B., & Reid, D. K. (2000). *Language development, differences, and disorders*. Austin, TX: Pro-Ed.

Kerrin, R. G. (1996). Collaboration: Working with the speech-language pathologist. *Intervention in School and Clinic, 21*, 56–59.

McNeill, J. H., & Fowler, S. A. (1996). Using story reading to encourage children's conversations. *Teaching Exceptional Children, 28*, 43–47.

Miller, R. (1996). *The developmentally appropriate inclusive classroom in early education*. Albany, NY: Delmar.

Parette, P., Hourcade, M., & Van-Biervliet, R. (1993). Selection of appropriate technology for children with disabilities, *Teaching Exceptional Children, 26*, 40–44.

Shames, G. H., Wiig, E. H., & Secord, W. A. (1994). *Human communication disorders: An introduction* (4th ed.). New York: Merrill.

mylabschool

Go to Allyn & Bacon's MyLabSchool (www.mylabschool.com) and enter Assignment ID CS08 in the Assignment Finder. Read the Case Study called *A Broken Arm* and then respond to the questions at the end of it, relying both on the information in the case and on what you have read in this chapter. You may e-mail your responses to your instructor.

Chapter 12

Teaching Students with Special Gifts and Talents

After reading this chapter, you should be able to:

1. Define giftedness.
2. Describe the characteristics of students with gifts and talents.
3. Describe ways to identify and evaluate students with gifts and talents.
4. Discuss the curricular needs of students with gifts and talents.
5. Describe appropriate instructional methods for students with gifts and talents.
6. Identify ways to enhance curriculum and instruction within the general education setting.

Questions to Consider

1. What kinds of challenges can students like Carmen create for teachers and for themselves?

2. How do individuals like Carmen, who are highly gifted, differ from other students who are gifted?

3. Should children like Carmen be included in general education classrooms all the time, separated from time to time, or provided with a completely different curriculum?

Carmen is truly an amazing young woman. She was a student in classes for gifted/talented/creative students for six years, from the first to the sixth grade. Her story provides a glimpse of what giftedness might look like in a student. However, not all students who are gifted display the breadth of exceptionality that Carmen does.

Learning came very easily for Carmen, and she excelled in all subjects. However, mathematics was her personal favorite. When she was in the fifth grade, she successfully completed pre-algebra, and when she was a sixth-grader, Carmen attended a seventh- and eighth-grade gifted mathematics class, where she received the highest grades in algebra. Carmen's writing skills were also well developed. Several of her essays and poems have already been published. When Carmen was a fourth-grader, she presented testimony to a NASA board defending and encouraging the continuation of the junior astronaut program. After completing her first year of junior high school, Carmen was awarded two out of five academic awards given to seventh-grade students at her school for outstanding achievement in science and mathematics. As a tenth-grader, she took the PSAT, and received a perfect score!

Carmen is also musically talented. When she was in second grade, a music specialist who came to school on a weekly basis informed her teacher that Carmen should be encouraged to continue with piano lessons because she demonstrated concert pianist abilities. When Carmen entered junior high school, she took up playing the clarinet in the band. At the end-of-the-year banquet, she received the top honor after being in the band for only one year.

Additionally, Carmen is psychomotorically talented. She is an accomplished gymnast, dances both the hula and ballet, has been a competitive ice-skater (an unusual sport for someone from Hawaii), played soccer for two years on champion soccer teams, and was a walk-on for her junior high's cross-country track team.

Carmen also has artistic strengths, demonstrates leadership abilities, has good social skills, and, wouldn't you know it, is simply beautiful.

Carmen's career goals have remained consistent for a long time. She wants to be either a dentist or an astronaut; she can probably be either one.

Children and youth such as Carmen, who perform or have the potential to perform at levels significantly above those of other students, have special needs as great as those of students whose disabilities demonstrably limit their performance. These needs are notable because most of these students are likely to spend much of their school day in general education settings, if they are attending public schools. As a result, teaching students who are gifted provides challenges to general education teachers that are certainly equal to those associated with meeting the needs of students with other special needs (McGrail, 1998). To feel confident to work with students who are gifted, classroom teachers should have basic information about giftedness and be able to implement some useful techniques for maximizing the educational experiences of these students.

Although there is no general agreement concerning the best way to educate students who are gifted and talented, many professionals argue that such students, especially highly gifted students, benefit from a curricular focus different from that provided in general education. Although some point out that gifted classes and special schools are more effective settings for highly gifted students (Clarkson, 2003), the vast majority of students who are gifted and talented, as noted, spend a considerable amount of time in the general education classroom. As a result, general education teachers are presented with the challenges of working with these students; however these teachers are also privileged to some amazing rewards.

Although a set of exact competencies that general education teachers should have in working with students who are gifted has remained elusive over the years, certain ones have emerged recently. The Council for Exceptional Children (2003) has published a set of suggested standards to help guide the preparation of teachers who will work with students who are gifted and talented. Other sources (National Association for Gifted Children, 1994; Nelson & Prindle, 1992) have provided a general sense of the types of competencies that teachers must possess to successfully address the needs of students in public or private school settings:

- Knowledge and understanding of the cognitive, social, and emotional characteristics, needs, and potential problems of this group of students
- Ability to differentiate curriculum and instruction to meet the needs and interests of these students, including the selection of appropriate methods and materials
- Ability to create an environment in which gifted and talented students can feel challenged, encouraged, and safe
- Knowledge and skills to promote thinking skills, develop creative problem-solving abilities of students, and facilitate independent research

The purpose of the chapter is twofold: to provide basic information about children and youth who are gifted and talented, and to suggest practices for working with these students in inclusive settings. It is important to note that the many topics related to the education of students who are gifted and talented are worthy of discussion; however, the focus of this chapter is to provide useful information for the general education teacher. This chapter is a primer only; confidence and competence in teaching students who are gifted come with study and experience. More in-depth information about teaching students who are gifted can be found elsewhere (Clark, 2006; Colangelo & Davis, 2003; Coleman & Cross, 2001; Davis & Rimm, 1998).

Basic Concepts about Students with Special Gifts and Talents

Students with exceptional abilities continue to be an underidentified, underserved, and too often inappropriately served group. Unlike the situation for students with disabilities, no federal legislation mandates appropriate education for these students. Moreover, states and local school districts vary greatly in the type and quality of services provided.

Students who could benefit from special programming are often not identified because of several factors. Teachers in general education may not be aware of the characteristics that suggest giftedness, as only a few students are "highly" or "exceptionally" gifted and thus fairly recognizable. This oversight is particularly common for those students who differ from the general student populations because of culture, gender, low socioeconomic status, or disability. Historically, ineffective assessment practices have not identified gifted students coming from diverse backgrounds.

For students who are identified as gifted and talented, a common problem is a mismatch between their academic, social, and emotional needs and the programming they receive, especially when they remain in general education settings for much of their instructional day. In many schools, a limited amount of instructional time is devoted to special activities. The point is reflected in the current focus on equity in education associated with the recent educational reform movement and on the need to address students who are below grade level, as accentuated by the No Child Left Behind Act. As Gallagher (1997) notes, "It is this value that leads one to heterogeneous grouping, whereby no one gets any special programming or privileges, and thus all are 'equal'" (p. 17). Furthermore, some gifted programming that exists today (e.g., pull-out options) favors students who are gifted in the linguistic and mathematical areas only. In too many instances, students with gifts and talents do not receive the type of education in the general education classroom that addresses their cognitive, social, and emotional needs and interests.

Services to students with gifts and talents remain controversial, partly because the general public and many school personnel hold misconceptions about these students. Hallahan and Kauffman (2006) highlight some of these misguided beliefs:

■ People with special intellectual gifts are physically weak, socially inept, narrow in interests, and prone to emotional instability or early decline. *Fact:* There are wide individual variations, and most gifted individuals are healthy, well adjusted, socially attractive, and morally responsible.

■ Children with special gifts or talents are usually bored with school and antagonistic toward those who are responsible for their education. *Fact:* Most children with special gifts like school and adjust well to their peers and teachers, although some do not like school and have social or emotional problems.

■ Students who have a true gift or talent for something will excel without special education. They need only the incentives and instruction that are appropriate for all students. *Fact:* Some children with special gifts or talents will perform at a remarkably high level without special education of any kind, and some will make outstanding contributions even in the face of great obstacles to their achievement. But most will not come close to achieving at a level commensurate with their potential unless their talents are deliberately fostered by instruction that is appropriate for their advanced abilities. (p. 499)

The portrayal of individuals who are gifted in movies is noteworthy. As Coleman and Cross (2001) note, too often the portrayal has negative connotations. They described the features of key characters in a number of recent movies, as highlighted in Table 12.1. The problem with negative portrayals of individuals who are gifted is that it leads to inaccurate perceptions and attitudes, ultimately resulting in unfair, and often discriminatory, practices.

Another example of stereotyping that occurs is the use of various terms to describe children, adolescents, and even adults who are gifted and talented. Historically, terms such as "nerd" and "geek" have been used to refer disparagingly to this group of students. What might be an encouraging trend is that these terms may not carry the same virulence that they once did (Cross, 2005). This is most likely due to some very successful and public individuals who might be associated with these terms and who have emerged in positive ways (think Bill Gates).

Many professionals in the field of gifted education find current services unacceptable and are frustrated by the lack of specialized programming for these students (Feldhusen,

CEC STANDARDS

CEC 2: Development and Characteristics of Learners

INTASC

INTASC 2: How children learn and develop

PRAXIS

PRAXIS II: Understanding Exceptionalities

CONSIDER THIS

Why do you think misconceptions about children and adults who are gifted and talented have developed and continue to exist?

Table 12.1		Portrayal of Gifted Characters in Movies
Movie	**Year**	**Portrayal**
Little Man Tate	1991	Dysfunctional
Searching for Bobby Fischer	1993	Dysfunctional
Powder	1995	Frail
Shine	1996	Bespectacled
The Nutty Professor	1996	Idealistic; Misguided
Good Will Hunting	1997	Violent
A Beautiful Mind	2001	Psychiatric problems

From *Being Gifted in School: An Introduction to Development, Guidance, and Teaching* (p. 3), by L. J. Coleman and T. L. Cross, 2001. Waco, TX: Prufrock Press. Copyright 2002 by Prufrock Press. Reprinted by permission.

1997). Undoubtedly, the programming provided in inclusive settings to students who are gifted should be improved. VanTassel-Baska (1997), highlighting key beliefs regarding curriculum theory, remarks that gifted students should be provided with curriculum opportunities that allow them to attain optimum levels of learning. In addition, these curriculum experiences need to be carefully planned, implemented, and evaluated.

"Gifted" Defined

Our understanding of giftedness has changed over time, and the terminology used to describe it has also varied. The term **gifted** is often used to refer to the heterogeneous spectrum of students with exceptional abilities, although some professionals restrict the use of this term only to certain individuals who display high levels of intelligence. Other terms, such as talented and creative, are used to differentiate subgroups of gifted people. An emerging nomenclature is to refer to students as having special gifts and talents.

CEC STANDARDS

CEC 2: Development and Characteristics of Learners

INTASC

INTASC 2: How children learn and develop

PRAXIS

PRAXIS II: Understanding Exceptionalities

Historical Context A number of attempts to define giftedness have been made. One of the earliest efforts, and one that has received a fair amount of attention, is the work of Terman that began in the early 1920s. Collectively the Terman work is titled *Genetic Studies of Genius*, and this research was still being conducted in recent times. Terman and colleagues identified 1,500 individuals with high IQs (i.e., over 140), collected data on their mental and physical traits, and also studied their lives longitudinally (Sears, 1979; Terman, 1926; Terman & Oden, 1959; Tomlinson-Keasey & Little, 1990). The research was important because it represented a major attempt to look closely at individuals who were exceptional and dispelled some early misconceptions relating to high intelligence and neurotic behavior. This work also provided some beginning conceptualizations of giftedness.

As Turnbull and Turnbull (2001) point out, however, Terman's work also led to some misconceptions. First, he equated genius with IQ, thus excluding other areas such as artistic ability. Second, Terman stressed the strong association of genius and genetics, thus precluding that some variability in intelligence can occur due to psychosocial factors and other life-related opportunities.

Throughout the years, other definitional perspectives emerged. Most of these were associated with federal legislation that recognized students who were gifted (e.g., the Elementary and Secondary Education Act; No Child Left Behind Act) or were developed by the U.S. Commissioner of Education (Marland, 1972). Attention was directed to this topic as a function of the creation of various professional organizations as well—

for example, the American Association for the Study of the Gifted in 1946; the National Association for Gifted Children in 1954; and the Association for the Gifted, part of the Council for Exceptional Children, in 1958.

Federal Definition   The current definition of giftedness promoted by the U.S. Department of Education comes from the Jacob K. Javits Gifted and Talented Students Education Act of 1988 (reauthorized in 1994 and incorporated into the No Child Left Behind Act of 2001). Although this legislation is not likely to be funded in 2007 as it had been in the past (National Association for Gifted Children, 2006), and that was not very much, the legislation does provide guidance about how to define this population. It contains many of the key concepts included in previous definitions.

> Children and youth with outstanding talent perform or show the potential for performing at remarkably high levels of accomplishment when compared with others of their age, experience, or environment. These children and youth exhibit high performance capability in intellectual, creative, and/or artistic areas, possess an unusual leadership capacity, or excel in specific academic fields. They require services or activities not ordinarily provided by schools. Outstanding talents are present in children and youth from all cultural groups, across all economic strata, and in all areas of human endeavor. (U.S. Department of Education, 1993, p. 3)

CROSS-REFERENCE
Review the definitions of other categories of disabilities discussed in Chapters 5–11 to compare components of definitions.

A number of interesting observations can be made regarding this definition. First, attention is given to potential—students who have not yet produced significant accomplishments may be considered gifted. Second, there is no mention of giftedness in athletics because this area is already addressed in existing school programs. Third, the need for special services or activities for these students is clearly stated, along with the observation that such intervention is not ordinarily provided. Finally, the fact that students who are gifted come from a range of diverse backgrounds is affirmed.

State Definitions   Since no federal mandates provide for gifted and talented education, it is up to the states to do so. As of June 2004, forty-six states had definitions of who is gifted and talented and four states did not. Of the forty-six states with definitions, twenty-five of them were determined by state legislative action and twenty-one were developed by the education agency for the particular state.

A Developmental Perspective   Attentive to the fact that changes occur with age, Coleman and Cross (2001) propose a definition that is considerate of developmental factors.

> The definition . . . differs from others by proposing a change in the criteria that describe giftedness, accounting for changes in abilities with advancing age in school. The criteria become narrower with increased age. This means that in early grades, giftedness would appear more in the areas of general ability or specific skills; but, as the child moves through the grades, evidence of ability and achievement would manifest within specific areas of study. . . . In this model, preadolescent gifted children have potential or demonstrated high ability in two areas: general cognitive ability and creative ability. Adolescent gifted children have demonstrated ability in abstract thinking, have produced creative works in some worthwhile area, and have demonstrated consistent involvement in activities of either type. (pp. 19–20)

CEC STANDARDS
CEC 2: Development and Characteristics of Learners

This definitional perspective contains elements of the various conceptualizations of giftedness, as discussed in the next section.

INTASC
INTASC 2: How children learn and develop

Other Conceptualizations of Giftedness

Many different ways to understand gifts and talents have been presented in the professional literature. Three of the more popular conceptualizations are highlighted in this section. They include Renzulli's "three-ring" conception of giftedness, Sternberg's "triarchic theory" of intelligence, and Gardner's theory of "multiple intelligences."

PRAXIS
PRAXIS II: Understanding Exceptionalities

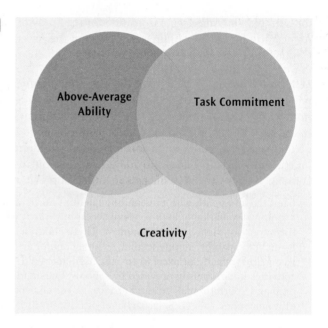

Figure 12.1

Renzulli's Three-Ring Conception of Giftedness

From *What Makes Giftedness?* (Brief #6, p. 10), by J. Renzulli, 1979. Los Angeles: National/State Leadership Training Institute. Reprinted by permission.

Renzulli One way to conceptualize giftedness is to consider the interaction of three interlocking clusters of traits (Renzulli, 1979; Renzulli & Reis, 1991) as essential elements associated with outstanding accomplishments. The three clusters are as follows; their interacting nature is depicted in Figure 12.1.

- High ability—including high intelligence
- High creativity—the ability to formulate new ideas and apply them to the solution of problems
- High task commitment—a high level of motivation and the ability to see a project through to its completion

These criteria are found in the two types of people who are truly gifted and noted in the U.S. Office of Education definition: those who produce and those who perform (Tannebaum, 1997).

Sternberg A popular theory of intellectual giftedness has been developed by Sternberg (1991). His theory includes three types of abilities: analytic giftedness (i.e., ability to dissect a problem and understand its parts); synthetic giftedness (i.e., insight, intuitive creativity, or skill at coping with relatively novel situations); and practical giftedness (i.e., ability to apply aspects of analytical and synthetic strengths to everyday situations). All individuals demonstrate some blend of these three abilities. However, gifted individuals show high ability in one or more of these areas.

Gardner Another perspective, constituting a broad theory of intelligence, has important applications for conceptualizing giftedness and for programming. Gardner and colleagues (Gardner, 1983; Gardner & Hatch, 1989) have developed a very popular model that proposes the idea of **multiple intelligences**. This model currently comprises eight areas of ability. Originally the model included only seven areas, but an eighth area (naturalistic) has been added more recently. Three other "intelligences" have been discussed—they include spiritual intelligence, existential intelligence, and moral intelligence (Smith, 2002). Table 12.2 describes the features of each type of intelligence and provides a possible occupation/role that might be characteristic of a person with a high degree of a given intelligence.

Table 12.2	**Multiple Intelligences**	
Intelligence	**End States**	**Core Components**
Logical–Mathematical	Scientist Mathematician	Sensitivity to, and capacity to discern, logical or numerical patterns; ability to handle long chains of reasoning
Linguistic	Poet Journalist	Sensitivity to the sounds, rhythms, and meanings of words; sensitivity to the different functions of language
Musical	Composer Violinist	Abilities to produce and appreciate rhythm, pitch, and timbre; appreciation of the forms of musical expressiveness
Spatial	Navigator Sculptor	Capacities to perceive the visual-spatial world accurately and to transform one's initial perceptions
Bodily–Kinesthetic	Dancer Athlete	Abilities to control one's body movements and to handle objects skillfully
Interpersonal	Therapist Salesperson	Capacities to discern and respond appropriately to the moods, temperaments, motivations, and desires of other people
Intrapersonal	Person with detailed, accurate self-knowledge	Access to one's own feelings and the ability to discriminate among them and draw upon them to guide behavior; knowledge of one's own strengths, weaknesses, desires, and intelligences
Naturalistic	Naturalist Park ranger	Affinity and appreciation for the wonders of nature

Adapted from "Multiple Intelligences Go to School: Educational Implications of the Theory of Multiple Intelligences," by H. Gardner and T. Hatch, 1989, *Educational Researcher, 18*(8), p. 6. Copyright © 1989 by the American Educational Research Association. Reprinted by permission.

If Gardner's ideas were followed closely, students would be assessed in all areas of intelligence. If found to have strengths in an area, students would be given opportunities to expand their interests, skills, and abilities accordingly. This conceptualization is attractive because it acknowledges some ability areas that are frequently overlooked and it recognizes the importance of different types of intelligences and gives them all equal footing.

Concept of Creativity

Creativity is included as an element of the federal definition of giftedness, and it is a major part of Renzulli's three-ring model. The concept is difficult to pinpoint, yet its importance as it relates to individuals who are gifted makes it a current topic for debate and discussion. As Coleman and Cross (2001) note, this topic has been part of the ongoing discussion of gifted individuals ever since the publication in 1959 of Guilford's seminal work on this topic.

As indicated previously, the concept is somewhat elusive, and no one definition explaining it has become popular. The concept can be characterized by the phrase, "You know it when you see it." Coleman and Cross (2001) aptly describe the state of affairs:

> A single accepted definition of creativity does not exist. In fact, neither is there universal agreement about what relevant attributes are needed to define an act as creative. The difficulty of selecting relevant attributes illustrates the problem of defining creativity. The terms originality and novelty pervade the literature on creativity. They express a quantitative and a qualitative standard, but they fail to say to what criterion a person is being compared. (p. 240)

The concept of creativity continues to receive wide attention, and efforts to better understand it and be able to apply it in meaningful ways within the context of education are warranted. Clark (2002) has created a listing of conditions that facilitate and

CEC STANDARDS

CEC 2: Development and Characteristics of Learners

INTASC

INTASC 2: How children learn and develop

inhibit the development of creativity. This list is useful for developing instructional activities to allow for creative expression.

Prevalence and Origins of Giftedness

The number of students who display exceptional abilities is uncertain. It is, of course, influenced by how giftedness is defined and how it is measured. Figures of 3 percent to 5 percent are typically cited to reflect the extent of giftedness in the school population (National Center for Education Statistics, 1989).

The critical reader should also note the distinction between the number of students served and the number of students who might be gifted. Only certain types of gifted students may be served because of the methods used for identification. Another cautionary note is that such figures generally underestimate the number of gifted students who are ethnically or culturally different, disabled, or female. These subgroups are underrepresented in programs for students with exceptional abilities.

Much professional discussion has focused on what contributes to giftedness in a person. Terman's early work made a strong case for genetics. Without question, research has shown that behavior is greatly affected by genetics. Although this notion is sometimes overemphasized, genetic factors do play a role in giftedness. Most researchers suggest that giftedness results from the interaction between biology and environment. In addition to genetic code, other biological factors, such as nutrition, also have an impact on an individual's development.

The environment in which a child is raised also affects later performance and intellectual abilities. Homes in which significant amounts of stimulation and opportunity to explore and interact with the environment exist, accompanied by high expectations, tend to produce children more likely to be successful scholastically and socially.

Characteristics of Students Who Are Gifted

Students who are gifted demonstrate a wide range of specific aptitudes, abilities, and skills. Though they should not be overgeneralized or considered stereotypical, certain characteristics distinguish students who are gifted or talented. A comprehensive list, depicting the characteristics of gifted students, has been developed by Clark (2006); a summary is presented in Table 12.3.

An interesting phenomenon is the paradoxical negative effect of seemingly desirable behaviors displayed by gifted students. For instance, sincere, excited curiosity about a topic being covered in class can sometimes be interpreted as annoying or disruptive by a teacher or fellow students. Their quick answers or certainty that they are right may be misconstrued as brash arrogance. Such desirable behavior can be misperceived as problem behavior for students who are gifted.

Some characteristics can outright be problematic for students who are gifted. For instance, characteristics such as uneven precocity, interpersonal difficulties (possibly due to cognitive differences), underachievement, nonconformity, perfectionism, and frustration and anger may indeed be negative features (Davis & Rimm, 1998).

Clark (2002) also points out that different levels of ability and performance exist within the ranks of those who are gifted. She distinguishes among students who would be considered typical or moderately gifted, those who are highly gifted, and those who are exceptionally gifted. Carmen, who was introduced at the beginning of the chapter, represents an individual who could be considered highly gifted. Highly gifted students "tend to evidence more energy than gifted individuals; they think faster and are more intent and focused on their interests and they exhibit a higher degree of ability in most of the traits . . . identified with giftedness" (Clark, 2002, p. 63). Clark describes exceptionally gifted as those who "seem to have different value structures . . . tend to be more

Domain	Characteristic

Table 12.3 Differentiating Characteristics of the Gifted

Domain	Characteristic
The Cognitive Function	• Extraordinary quantity of information; unusual retentiveness • Advanced comprehension • Unusual varied interests and curiosity • High level of language development • High level of verbal ability • Unusual capacity for processing information • Accelerated pace of thought processes • Flexible thought processes • Comprehensive synthesis • Early ability to delay closure • Heightened capacity for seeing unusual and diverse relationships, integration of ideas, and disciplines • Ability to generate original ideas and solutions • Early differential patterns for thought processing (e.g., thinking in alternatives; abstract terms; sensing consequences; making generalizations; visual thinking; use of metaphors and analogies) • Early ability to use and form conceptual frameworks • An evaluative approach toward oneself and others • Unusual intensity; persistent goal-directed behavior
The Affective Function	• Large accumulation of information about emotions that have not been brought to awareness • Unusual sensitivity to the expectations and feelings of others • Keen sense of humor—may be gentle or hostile • Heightened self-awareness, accompanied by feelings of being different • Idealism and a sense of justice, which appear at an early age • Earlier development of an inner locus of control and satisfaction • Unusual emotional depth and intensity • High expectations of self and others, often leading to high levels of frustration with self, others, and situations; perfectionism • Strong need for consistency between abstract values and personal actions • Advanced levels of moral judgment • Strongly motivated by self-actualization needs • Advanced cognitive and affective capacity for conceptualizing and solving societal problems • Leadership ability • Solutions to social and environmental problems • Involvement with the metaneeds of society (e.g., injustice, beauty, truth)
The Physical/Sensing Function	• Unusual quantity of input from the environment through a heightened sensory awareness • Unusual discrepancy between physical and intellectual development • Low tolerance for the lag between their standards and their athletic skills • Cartesian split—can include neglect of physical well-being and avoidance of physical activity
The Intuitive Function	• Early involvement and concern for intuitive knowing and metaphysical ideas and phenomena • Open to experiences in this area; will experiment with psychic and metaphysical phenomena • Creative approach in all areas of endeavor • Ability to predict; interest in future

From *Growing Up Gifted* (6th ed.), by Barbara Clark. Copyright 2002 by Merrill/Prentice Hall. Reprinted by permission.

isolated by choice and more invested in concerns of a meta-nature (e.g., universal problems) . . . seldom seek popularity or social acclaim" (p. 63). Both highly gifted and exceptionally gifted students pose significant challenges to educators in meeting their needs within the general education classroom. Most of the discussion in this chapter is directed toward the typical gifted student.

A notable characteristic that has important classroom implications is the gifted student's expenditure of minimum effort while still earning high grades (Reis & Schack,

Rights & Responsibilities

State Programs for Gifted Children

The Individuals with Disabilities Education Act (IDEA) does not include rights for gifted children. Some states, however, do provide programs for this group of students. Examples of state cases involving gifted students include:

1. In a court case in Pennsylvania, *Ellis v. Chester Upland School Dist.,* 651 A.2d 616 (Pa.Cmwlth. 1994), the court ruled that the school did not have to pay out-of-state tuition to a private school for a child who was classified as gifted because the state law did not entitle a gifted student to such services.
2. In the case *Broadley v. Bd. of Educ. of the City of Meriden,* 229 Conn. 1, 639 App.2d 502 (1994), the court ruled that the state of Connecticut did not have to provide special education to gifted children because, even though they were within the broad definition of exceptional children, the law only required special education for children with disabilities.

3. In *Centennial School Dist. v. Commonwealth Dept. of Educ.,* 539 A.2d 785 (Pa.1988), the court ruled that the school district had to provide an IEP and special programs for gifted students because they were classified as exceptional. The court ruled, however, that this requirement did not entitle the student to specialized instruction beyond enrichment.
4. In *Student Roe v. Commonwealth,* 638 F.Supp. 929 (E.D.Pa. 1986), the court ruled that while Pennsylvania law provides for children with an IQ of 130 and above to be admitted to its gifted programs, IDEA did not apply to children unless they had a disability as defined in the act. Therefore, while state law did require some programs for gifted children, this did not result in gifted students being eligible for IDEA protections.

From *Students with Disabilities and Special Education* (14th ed., p. 249), 1997. Burnsville, MN: Oakstone Publishing.

1993). Many gifted students are able to handle the general education curriculum with ease. But the long-term effect of being able to excel without working hard may be a lack of the work habits needed for challenging programs at a later point in time (i.e., advanced placement classes in high school or the curriculum of an upper-tier college).

Identification, Assessment, and Eligibility

General education teachers need to know about the assessment process used to confirm the existence of exceptional abilities. General education teachers play a crucial role in the initial stages of the process, for they are likely to be the first to recognize that a student might be gifted. For this reason, teachers should provide opportunities across the range of ability areas (e.g., multiple intelligences) for students to explore their interests and abilities, particularly at the preschool and elementary levels. Ramos-Ford and Gardner (1997) suggest that such opportunities may help students discover certain abilities that might otherwise go unnoticed.

TEACHING TIP

Classroom teachers need to be alert to students who may be gifted and talented and refer students to appropriate professionals for testing and services.

The assessment process includes a sequence of steps, beginning with an initial referral (i.e., nomination) and culminating with the validation of the nomination by examining existing data and the collection of additional information (Oakland & Rossen, 2005). Schools typically send out announcements to all parents, notifying them that testing to screen for students who are gifted will occur and asking them if they would like for their son or daughter to be considered for this assessment. As mentioned, general education teachers also play a role in identifying gifted students. Efforts to identify children with gifts and talents should begin early. Although some children displaying exceptional abilities may be spotted very early (i.e., preschool years), many are not recognized until they are in school. For this reason, teachers need to be aware of classroom behaviors that gifted students typically display. A listing of such behaviors is provided in Table 12.4.

CEC STANDARDS

CEC 8: Assessment

| *Table* 12.4 | **Classroom Behaviors of Gifted Students** |

Does the child
- Ask a lot of questions?
- Show a lot of interest in progress?
- Have lots of information on many things?
- Want to know why or how something is so?
- Become unusually upset at injustices?
- Seem interested and concerned about social or political problems?
- Often have a better reason than you do for not doing what you want done?
- Refuse to drill on spelling, math, facts, flash cards, or handwriting?
- Criticize others for dumb ideas?
- Become impatient if work is not "perfect"?
- Seem to be a loner?
- Seem bored and often have nothing to do?
- Complete only part of an assignment or project and then take off in a new direction?
- Stick to a subject long after the class has gone on to other things?
- Seem restless, out of seat often?
- Daydream?
- Seem to understand easily?
- Like solving puzzles and problems?
- Have his or her own idea about how something should be done? And stay with it?
- Talk a lot?
- Love metaphors and abstract ideas?
- Love debating issues?

This child may be showing giftedness cognitively.

Does the child
- Show unusual ability in some area? Maybe reading or math?
- Show fascination with one field of interest? And manage to include this interest in all discussion topics?
- Enjoy meeting or talking with experts in this field?

- Get math answers correct, but find it difficult to tell you how?
- Enjoy graphing everything? Seem obsessed with probabilities?
- Invent new obscure systems and codes?

This child may be showing giftedness academically.

Does the child
- Try to do things in different, unusual, imaginative ways?
- Have a really zany sense of humor?
- Enjoy new routines or spontaneous activities?
- Love variety and novelty?
- Create problems with no apparent solutions? And enjoy asking you to solve them?
- Love controversial and unusual questions?
- Have a vivid imagination?
- Seem never to proceed sequentially?

This child may be showing giftedness creatively.

Does the child
- Organize and lead group activities? Sometimes take over?
- Enjoy taking risks?
- Seem cocky, self-assured?
- Enjoy decision making? Stay with that decision?
- Synthesize ideas and information from a lot of different sources?

This child may be showing giftedness through leadership ability.

Does the child
- Seem to pick up skills in the arts—music, dance, drama, painting, etc.—without instruction?
- Invent new techniques? Experiment?
- See minute detail in products or performances?
- Have high sensory sensitivity?

This child may be showing giftedness through visual or performing arts ability.

From *Growing Up Gifted* (6th ed., p. 332), by B. Clark, 2002. Upper Saddle River, NJ: Merrill/Prentice Hall. Copyright 2002 by Pearson Education. Reprinted by permission.

Teachers who recognize behaviors highlighted in Table 12.4 should determine whether a student should be evaluated more comprehensively. Teachers should share their observations with the student's parents. Eventually, teachers may want to nominate the student for gifted services. Oakland and Rossen (2005) suggest that a nomination that "first informs, then educates, and then encourages teachers, parents, and students to become engaged" (p. 61) is most likely to identify a diverse range of students who might have gifts or talents.

Teachers can be involved in the next step in the assessment process as well. After a student has been nominated or referred, teachers should be part of the process of examining existing data. They can assemble information to help determine whether the student should receive special services. The following sources of information can contribute to understanding a student's demonstrated or potential ability: formal test results; informal assessments; interviews with teachers, parents, and peers; and actual student products. For example, a public elementary school may use various screening

INTASC

INTASC 8: Formal and informal assessment

PRAXIS

PRAXIS II: Delivery of Services to Students with Disabilities

instruments to identify gifted students, including a standardized ability test, standardized creativity test, teacher observation form, student portfolio, and parent observation form. This phase should be followed by a set of nondiscriminatory evaluation procedures, as suggested in Table 12.5.

A helpful technique used in many school systems to determine the performance capabilities of students is **portfolio assessment**. Portfolios contain a collection of student-generated products, reflecting the quality of a student's work. They may also contain permanent products such as artwork, poetry, or videotapes of student performance (e.g., theatrical production, dance or music recital).

As VanTassel-Baska, Patton, and Prillaman (1989) point out, students who are culturally different and those who come from socially and economically disadvantaged backgrounds are typically overlooked in the process of identifying students for gifted programs. For the most part, this problem results from entry requirements that stress performance on standardized tests. When students obtain low test scores on standardized instruments that may be biased against them, exclusion results. Oakland and Rossen (2005) recommend the use of local norms over national norms as a way to avert this problem. VanTassel-Baska and colleagues (1989) provide additional recommenda-

Table 12.5 **Nondiscriminatory Evaluation Procedures and Evaluations**

Assessment Measures	Findings That Suggest Giftedness
Individualized intelligence test	Student scores in the upper 2 to 3 percent of the population (most states have cutoff scores of 130 or 132 depending on test). Because of cultural biases of standardized IQ tests, students from minority backgrounds are considered if their IQs do not meet the cutoff but other indicators suggest giftedness.
Individualized achievement test	The student scores in the upper 2 to 3 percent in one or more areas of achievement.
Creativity assessment	The student demonstrates unusual creativity in work products as judged by experts or performs exceptionally well on tests designed to assess creativity. The student does not have to be academically gifted to qualify.
Checklists of gifted characteristics	These checklists are often completed by teachers, parents, peers, or others who know the student well. The student scores in the range that suggests giftedness as established by checklist developers.
Anecdotal records	The student's records suggest high ability in one or more areas.
Curriculum-based assessment	The student is performing at a level beyond peers in one or more areas of the curriculum used by the local school district.
Direct observation	The student may be a model student or could have behavior problems as a result of being bored with classwork. If the student is perfectionistic, anxiety might be observed. Observations should occur in other settings besides the school.
Visual and performing arts assessment	The student's performance in visual or performing arts is judged by individuals with expertise in the specific area. The student does not have to be academically gifted to qualify.
Leadership assessment	Peer nomination, parent nomination, and teacher nomination are generally used. However, self-nomination can also be a good predictor of leadership. Leadership in extracurricular activities is often an effective indicator. The student does not have to be academically gifted to qualify.
Case-study approach	Determination of student's giftedness is based on looking at all areas of assessment described above without adding special weight to one factor.

tions for improving the identification and assessment process:

- Use nontraditional measures for identification purposes.
- Recognize cultural attributes and factors in deciding on identification procedures.
- Focus on strengths in nonacademic areas, particularly in creativity and psychomotor domains. (p. 3)

It has also been difficult to identify and serve students who are twice exceptional—gifted and having a disability or ADHD. For instance, the problems that characterize a learning disability (e.g., problems in language-related areas) often mask high levels of accomplishment in other areas such as drama, art, or music. Special assessment considerations of this unique population are warranted.

After the student has been identified as gifted or talented and begins to participate in special programs or services, ongoing assessment should become part of the student's educational program. Practical and personal needs should be monitored regularly (Del Prete, 1996). Practical concerns, such as progress in academic areas and realization of potential in certain delineated areas, can be evaluated. Nevertheless, the affective needs of students who are gifted (e.g., feeling accepted and developing confidence), which should be addressed as well, may require additional time and effort.

Gifted students are not entitled to receive special services under IDEA, unless, of course, they also have a disability that has a significant impact on their education. As a result, "special education" for gifted students is not guaranteed, even though it should be, and various due-process safeguards, as provided by IDEA, are not applicable to these students and their families.

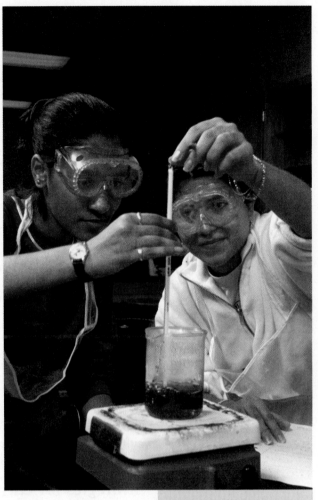

Too few students from minority cultural groups are identified as gifted and talented.

Diversity Issues

As pointed out earlier, diversity issues remain an area of concern in the education of gifted students. Too few students who are culturally different from the majority of their peers are identified and served through programs for gifted students. "Culturally diverse children have much talent, creativity, and intelligence. Manifestations of these characteristics may be different and thus require not only different tools for measuring these strengths, but also different eyes from which to see them" (Plummer, 1995, p. 290). Teachers should look for certain behaviors associated with giftedness in children who come from diverse backgrounds. An example of an observational checklist for accomplishing this task is presented in Figure 12.2.

Even when students from diverse backgrounds have been identified as having special gifts or talents, programming often has not been sensitive to their needs. As Plummer (1995) notes, few programs have the resources (i.e., personnel, materials) available to tap the interests and strengths of these students. Moore and Ford (2005) have raised the issue of retention of students of color in special programs for students with gifts and talents. They point out that too many students of color do not fare well in these programs due to any combination of social and cultural barriers.

Often the general education teacher needs supports to address these students' educational needs in inclusive settings. The twofold challenge for teachers is to respect ethnic

Figure 12.2 — Observational Checklist for Identifying Strengths of Culturally Diverse Students

☐ Ability to express feeling and emotions
☐ Ability to improvise with commonplace materials and objects
☐ Articulateness in role-playing, sociodrama, and storytelling
☐ Enjoyment of and ability in visual arts, such as drawing, painting, and sculpture
☐ Enjoyment of and ability in creative movement, dance, drama, etc.
☐ Enjoyment of and ability in music and rhythm
☐ Use of expressive speech
☐ Fluency and flexibility in figural media
☐ Enjoyment of and skills in group or team activities
☐ Responsiveness to the concrete
☐ Responsiveness to the kinesthetic
☐ Expressiveness of gestures, body language, etc., and ability to interpret body language
☐ Humor
☐ Richness of imagery in informal language
☐ Originality of ideas in problem solving
☐ Problem-centeredness or persistence in problem solving
☐ Emotional responsiveness
☐ Quickness of warmup

From "Identifying and Capitalizing on the Strengths of Culturally Different Children," p. 469, by E. P. Torrance, 1982, in *The Handbook of School Psychology,* edited by C. R. Reynolds and J. B. Gulkin New York: Wiley. Copyright 1982 by John Wiley & Sons. Reprinted by permission.

and cultural differences of students from diverse backgrounds and to integrate diverse cultural topics into the curriculum (Plummer, 1995).

Strategies for Curriculum and Instruction for Students Who Are Gifted

The literature on providing effective services for students with exceptional abilities consistently stresses the need for **differentiated programming**. Very simply, this means that learning opportunities provided to these students must differ according to a student's needs and abilities. Differentiation includes the content of what students learn, the processes used in learning situations, and the final products that students develop. Furthermore, "Difference lies in the depth, scope, pace, and self-directedness of the expectations" (Lopez & Mackenzie, 1993, p. 288).

VanTassel-Baska (1989) notes some of the mistaken beliefs that some educators have about educating students with exceptional abilities:

- A "differentiated" curriculum for the gifted means "anything that is different from what is provided for all learners." *Fact:* A "differentiated" curriculum implies a coherently planned scope and sequence of instruction that matches the needs of students and that typically does differ from the regular education curriculum.
- All experiences provided for gifted learners must be creative and focused on process. *Fact:* Core content areas are important areas of instructional focus.
- One curriculum package will provide what is needed for the entire gifted population. *Fact:* Students need a variety of materials, resources, and courses.
- Acceleration, moving through the curriculum at a more rapid pace, can be harmful because it pushes children socially and leaves gaps in their knowledge. *Fact:* This approach to meeting the needs of students with exceptional abilities is the intervention technique best supported by research. (pp. 13–14)

DIVERSITY FORUM

To Be Young, Gifted and. . .Different

Someday
By Sonny B.
I was identified as gifted in the third grade. . . . I feel that I have had some unique learning experiences, but there has been one drawback—I have been the only Indian in all of the programs that I have participated in. . . . I look forward to participating in an all-Indian program and sharing my experiences with other Indian students like myself.[1]

Students like Sonny—young, talented, and from a cultural heritage different from many of their peers—are often overlooked when schools conduct screenings to identify students who are gifted. Educators often have difficulty recognizing characteristics associated with highly talented students whose languages, cultures, and life experiences are vastly different from their own. For instance, students who are learning English as a second language may not be able to express their creativity and intellectual potential to monolingual English teachers; what is valued and viewed as a gift in the student's culture may be different from what is valued in U.S. public schools and reflected in identification measures and procedures; economic barriers may prevent some children from participating in activities that develop their potential; and students' reactions to a culturally unfamiliar school or classroom climate may make them appear unmotivated.

Identification procedures are more successful in identifying gifted students from these underrepresented groups when (Callahan, 2005):

- Schools have in place a process for ongoing, early identification of students that reflects a broader view of intelligence and giftedness which includes input from the family, community, and teachers;
- Instructional programs are designed to develop all students' gifts and talents;
- The school's curriculum and services are matched to identification criteria and procedures;
- School personnel are sensitive to the cultural and social orientation of the student and family, and collaborate with community members in determining how talent will be defined and identified in the school setting; and
- Assessment tools and activities are multidimensional, authentic, and include input from community members, parents, teachers, and students themselves.

Questions

1. Which of the several models of giftedness would provide the most inclusive guidelines for identifying gifted children from underrepresented groups?
2. How might a focus on talent development improve our ability to identify students from diverse cultural, economic, linguistic, racial and ethnic backgrounds?

REFERENCES
Callahan, C. M. (2005). Identifying gifted students from underrepresented populations. *Theory into Practice,* 44(2), 98–104.
[1]Callahan, C. M., & McIntire, J. A. (1994). *Identifying outstanding talent in American Indian and Alaska Native Students* (p. 3). Washington, DC: Office of Educational Research and Improvement.

Many professionals in the field of gifted education argue that the preferred setting for these students, particularly for highly and exceptionally gifted students, is not the general education classroom; they recommend differentiated programs delivered in separate classes for the greater part, if not all, of the school day. However, in reality students with special gifts and talents are more likely to spend a significant part of their instructional week in general education settings, possibly receiving some differentiated opportunities in a pull-out program.

Continuum-of-Placement Options

A variety of ways exist for providing educational programs to students who are gifted and talented. Figure 12.3 illustrates various options, as developed by Clark (2002), that might be considered for use with different types of gifted learners. Certain options, used more commonly in the public schools settings, include specialized grouping within the general education setting, independent study, various adjunct programs

CROSS-REFERENCE

Review Chapters 5–11 and compare curriculum and instruction modifications suggested for students with other special needs.

CONSIDER THIS

Is the argument for separate programming for gifted students out of phase with the inclusion movement?

EVIDENCE-BASED PRACTICE

Goals for Curricula of Gifted Children

- Include more elaborate, complex, and in-depth study of major ideas, problems, and themes—those that integrate knowledge with and across systems of thought.
- Allow for the development and application of productive thinking skills that enable students to reconceptualize existing knowledge or generate new knowledge.
- Enable students to explore constantly changing knowledge and information,

and to develop the attitude that knowledge is worth pursuing in an open world.
- Encourage exposure to, selection of, and use of appropriate and specialized resources.
- Promote self-initiated and self-directed learning and growth.
- Provide for the development of self-understanding and the understanding of one's relationship to persons, societal institutions, nature, and culture.

- Evaluate students with stress placed on their ability to perform at a level of excellence that demonstrates creativity and higher-level thinking skills.

From *Diverse Populations of Gifted Children* (pp. 15–16), by S. Cline and D. Schwartz, 1999. Columbus, OH: Merrill.

(e.g., mentorships, internships), special classes outside of general education, special schools, and special summer programs. Another option that some families have chosen is to place their son or daughter in a private school that specializes in providing differentiated programming for gifted students. The value of a particular option reflects the extent to which it meets an individual's needs. As Clark (2002) points out, all the options have some merit. None address the needs of all students with exceptional abil-

Figure 12.3

Placement Options for Gifted Students

From *Growing Up Gifted* (6th ed., p. 256), by B. Clark, 2002. Upper Saddle River, NJ: Merrill/Prentice Hall. Copyright 2002 by Pearson Education. Reprinted by permission.

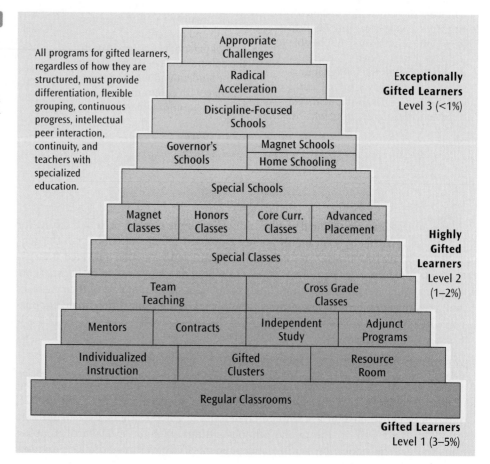

ities; however, the general education classroom as traditionally organized in terms of curriculum and instruction is inadequate for true gifted education. For this reason, school systems should provide a range of programmatic alternatives.

Gifted students who are in general education classrooms for the entire instructional day can have some of their needs met through a variety of special provisions such as enrichment, certain acceleration options, or special grouping. The challenge for teachers is to coordinate these provisions with those required for other students in the classroom. It should be noted that some parents make a conscious decision not to have their gifted children participate in the gifted programming offered by a school. This decision might be made for a number of reasons; sometimes it is made because the quality of the gifted programming is poor.

The idea of inclusion of students with gifts and talents in general education classes has been recognized as a reality for many students. The National Association for Gifted Children (NAGC, 1996) issued the following statement regarding this matter in a position paper on inclusion.

> NAGC maintains that gifted students, like other children with special needs, require a full continuum of educational services to aid in the development of the students' unique strengths and talents. One such option in that continuum of services for gifted students can be the regular classroom (inclusion). In such an inclusive setting there should be well-prepared teachers who understand and can program for these gifted students, and sufficient administrative support necessary to help differentiate the program to their special needs. There should be, for example, staff development to aid the general education teacher in understanding and instructing gifted students, provisions for teacher planning time, allowance for student independent study and access to a specialist in gifted education who can aid in differentiating the curriculum to meet the needs of advanced students.

In many schools, students who have been identified as gifted are pulled out for a specified period of time each day to attend a special class for gifted students. When they are in the general education setting, it may be possible for them to participate in an individualized program of study, apart from the regular curriculum.

Students with special gifts and talents may also participate in various adjunct programs such as mentorships, internships, special tutorials, independent study, and resource rooms—many of which occur outside the regular classroom. For students at the secondary level, spending time in special programming for part of the day, attending heterogeneous classes, or attending a magnet school are other possibilities.

These programmatic options affect the role and responsibilities of the general education teacher. In some situations, the general education teacher will be the primary source of differentiated instruction for these students. In others, the general education teacher may serve as a manager, coordinating the services provided by others. However, it is probable that most teachers will be responsible for providing some level of instruction to these students.

Realities of the General Education Classroom

More attention is being directed to the reality that most gifted students in public school settings will spend a significant amount of time in general education settings. Many innovative and useful techniques exist for addressing the needs of students in these inclusive settings. The section of the chapter on classroom accommodations will highlight many of the techniques. However, cautions remain in regard to meeting the needs of gifted students in general education settings.

In general education settings, students who are gifted or talented are sometimes subject to conditions that diminish the possibility of having their individual needs met. The U.S. Department of Education (1993) has noted the following concerns related to educating gifted students in general education settings:

CEC STANDARDS

CEC 5: Learning Environments and Social Interactions

INTASC

INTASC 5: Learning environment

PRAXIS

PRAXIS II: Delivery of Services to Students with Disabilties

CONSIDER THIS

How should general classroom teachers be prepared to teach students who are gifted?

- *Elementary level*
  - The general education curriculum does not challenge gifted students.
  - Most academically talented students have already mastered up to half of the required curriculum offered to them in elementary school.
  - Classroom teachers do little to accommodate the different learning needs of gifted children.
  - Most specialized programs are available for only a few hours a week. Students talented in the arts are offered few challenging opportunities.
- *Secondary level*
  - Appropriate opportunities in middle schools are scattered and uncoordinated.
  - High school schedules do not meet the needs of talented students (i.e., pacing or content of coverage).
  - The college preparatory curriculum in the United States generally does not require hard work from able students.
  - Small-town and rural schools often have limited resources and are unable to offer advanced classes and special learning opportunities.
  - Specialized schools, magnet schools, and intensive summer programs serve only a fraction of the secondary students who might benefit from them.
  - Dual enrollment in secondary school and college is uncommon.

Other more specific practices that can be problematic for gifted students include the following:

- When involved in group activities (i.e., cooperative learning), gifted students may end up doing all the work (Clinkenbeard, 1991).
- They are often subjected to more stringent grading criteria (Clinkenbeard, 1991).
- When they finish assignments early, they are given more of the same type of work or assigned more of the same types of tasks at the outset (Shaner, 1991).
- They are overused as coteachers to help students who need more assistance.
- Vocabulary use in the average classroom is inappropriate for advanced learners (Clark, 1996).
- Advanced levels of critical thinking are not typically incorporated into lessons (Clark, 1996).
- Instructional materials in general education classrooms are frequently limited in range and complexity (Clark, 1996).
- Problem-solving strategies are not used in classrooms (Gallagher, 1997).

Unfortunately, most general education teachers are not provided with the necessary understanding, skills, and resources to deal appropriately with this population—an issue that will be addressed in more detail later in the chapter. This situation is exacerbated when teachers have to deal with a wide range of abilities and needs in their classrooms. The composition of the general education classroom in many of today's public schools requires a staggering array of competence in providing differentiated instruction and addressing a wide range of social and emotional needs.

In addition, some teachers feel uncomfortable working with students who have exceptional abilities. Figure 12.4 highlights this situation by way of a personal experience. Shaner (1991) remarks that a teacher who is working with a gifted student can be "intimidated by him or her, paralyzed with a fear of not being able to keep up, or threatened by the student's challenges to authority" (pp. 14–15). Teachers are also concerned about being asked questions they are unprepared to answer or challenged on points they may not know well. These are reasonable fears; however, they can be minimized by using these opportunities as a way to increase everyone's knowledge—a teacher's as well—and by understanding how to address gifted students' needs within the general classroom setting.

Differentiated programming for students with exceptional abilities, wherever it occurs, must address individual needs and interests in the context of preparing the students for a

Not long ago, I was invited to go on a "reef walk" with a class of gifted third- and fourth-graders. It was a very educational experience.

While we were wading in shallow water, we came upon a familiar marine organism commonly called a feather duster (tube worm). Forgetting that these students had vocabularies well advanced of their nongifted age peers, I was ready to say something like, "Look how that thing hangs on the rock."

Before I could get my highly descriptive statement out, Eddie, who always amazes us with his comments, offered the following: "Notice how securely anchored the organism is to the stationary coral?"

All I could reply was "Yes. I did."

Figure 12.4

A Personal Experience

Source: _Exceptional Children in Focus_ (p. 216), by J. R. Patton, J. Blackbourn, and K. Fad, 1996. Columbus, OH: Merrill. Used by permission.

world characterized by change and complexity. Reis (1989) suggests that we reassess how we look at gifted education and move away from the content-based nature of most current curriculums to an orientation based on a realistic view of future education.

Approaches to Programming

A number of general approaches exist for designing programs for students who have exceptional abilities. While a variety of options might exist in any given school system, certain options are most commonly used. Many elementary schools rely on a pull-out program to provide enrichment-type experiences for students. The approaches most likely to be used in general education settings involve acceleration, enrichment, and special grouping.

Acceleration   Acceleration refers to practices that introduce content, concepts, and educational experiences to gifted students sooner than for other students. Accelerations can be thought of as a way "in which the learner completes a course of study in less time than ordinarily expected" (Colemon & Cross, 2001, p. 298). This approach presents gifted students with more advanced materials appropriate to their ability and interests. There are many types of accelerative practices, as reflected in the array of options provided by Southern and Jones (1991) in Table 12.6.

All the acceleration options described by Southern and Jones (1991) have relevance for gifted students in general education classrooms. The techniques that have the most direct application in the general education classroom are continuous progress, self-paced instruction, subject-matter acceleration, combined classes, curriculum compacting, and curriculum telescoping. All these practices require teachers to plan and implement instructional activities accordingly.

Other accelerative practices have a more indirect impact on ongoing activities in the general education classroom. Nevertheless, teachers should be aware of them. They include early entrance to school, skipping grades, mentorships, extracurricular programs, concurrent enrollment, advanced placement, and credit by examination.

According to Gallagher and Gallagher (1994), the most common acceleration practices are primary level—early admittance to school, ungraded primary; upper elementary—ungraded classes, grade skipping; middle school—three years in two, senior high classes for credit; and high school—extra load (early graduation), advanced placement (AP). Interestingly, some professionals (Davis, 1996) advocate separate AP classes for

CEC STANDARDS

CEC 4: Instructional Strategies

INTASC

INTASC 4: Instructional strategies

PRAXIS

PRAXIS II: Delivery of Services to Students with Disabilities

Table 12.6   **Range and Types of Accelerative Options**

1. Early entrance to kindergarten or first grade	The student is admitted to school prior to the age specified by the district for normal entry to kindergarten or first grade.
2. Grade skipping	The student is moved ahead of normal grade placement. This may be done during an academic year (placing a third-grader directly into fourth grade), or at year end (promoting a third-grader to fifth grade).
3. Continuous progress	The student is given material deemed appropriate for current achievement as the student becomes ready.
4. Self-paced instruction	The student is presented with materials that allow him or her to proceed at a self-selected pace. Responsibility for selection of pacing is the student's.
5. Subject matter acceleration	The student is placed for a part of a day with students at more advanced grade levels for one or more subjects without being assigned to a higher grade (e.g., a fifth-grader going to sixth grade for science instruction).
6. Combined classes	The student is placed in classes where two or more grade levels are combined (e.g., third- and fourth-grade split rooms). The arrangement can be used to allow younger children to interact with older ones academically and socially.
7. Curriculum compacting	The student is given reduced amounts of introductory activities, drill review, and so on. The time saved may be used to move faster through the curriculum.
8. Telescoping curriculum	The student spends less time than normal in a course of study (e.g., completing a one-year course in one semester, or finishing junior high school in two years rather than three).
9. Mentorships	The student is exposed to a mentor who provides advanced training and experiences in a content area.
10. Extracurricular programs	The student is enrolled in course work or summer programs that confer advanced instruction and/or credit for study (e.g., fast-paced language or math courses offered by universities).
11. Concurrent enrollment	The student is taking a course at one level and receiving credit for successful completion of a parallel course at a higher level (e.g., taking algebra at the junior-high level and receiving credit for high school algebra as well as junior high math credits upon successful completion).
12. Advanced placement	The student takes a course in high school that prepares him or her for taking an examination that can confer college credit for satisfactory performances.
13. Credit by examination	The student receives credit (at high school or college level) upon successful completion of an examination.
14. Correspondence courses	The student takes high school or college courses by mail (or, more recently, through video and audio presentations).
15. Early entrance into junior high, high school, or college	The student is admitted with full standing to an advanced level of instruction (at least one year early).

From *Academic Acceleration of Gifted Children* (Figure 1.1), by W. T. Southern and E. D. Jones, 1991. New York: Teachers College Press. Copyright © 1991 by Teachers College, Columbia University. All rights reserved. Used by permission.

gifted students because their needs differ from those of nongifted students enrolled in AP classes.

Enrichment   Enrichment refers to techniques that provide topics, skill development, materials, or experiences that extend the depth of coverage beyond the typical curriculum. Coleman and Cross (2001) explain enrichment in the following way: "In its broadest interpretation, enrichment encompasses a number of modifications in standard educational practices. In its narrowest interpretation, enrichment means providing interesting and stimulating tributaries to the mainstream of school" (p. 298).

This practice is commonly used in general education classes to address the needs of students who move through content quickly. Many teachers' manuals and guides provide ideas on how to deliver enriching activities to students who finish their work quickly. Comprehensive lesson plans should include a section on "early finishers," which will often include gifted students, so that enriching activities are available for those who complete assignments before the rest of the class.

Some enrichment activities ultimately involve acceleration (Southern & Jones 1991). For instance, whenever topics of an advanced nature are introduced, a form of acceleration is actually being employed. There is, however, a distinction between materials or activities that are accelerated and involve a dimension of difficulty or conceptual complexity and materials or activities that provide variety but do not require advanced skills or understanding.

Special Grouping   Special grouping refers to the practice whereby gifted students of similar ability levels or interests are grouped together for at least part of the instructional day. One commonly cited technique is the use of cluster grouping within the general education classroom. This practice allows for interaction with peers who share a similar enthusiasm, bring different perspectives to topics, and stimulate the cognitive and creative thinking of others in the group.

Classroom Adaptations for Students Who Are Gifted

This section highlights techniques for addressing the needs of students with exceptional abilities who are in general education classes. Teachers who will be working closely with these students are encouraged to consult resources that thoroughly discuss teaching gifted students in general education settings—see Maker (1993), Parke (1989), Ryser and McConnell (2003), Smutny, Walker, and Meckstroth (1997), or Winebrenner (2000).

First and foremost, teachers should strive to create classroom settings that foster conditions in which students with special gifts and talents feel comfortable and are able to realize their potential. Teachers also need to learn about the cognitive, social, and emotional needs of students who are gifted and talented. Furthermore, teachers need a comprehensive long-term plan of education and must enjoy learning experiences that reflect this plan (Kitano, 1993).

Although special opportunities for enrichment, acceleration, and the use of higher-level skills are particularly beneficial to students with special gifts or talents, these opportunities can also be extended to other students when appropriate (Roberts, Ingram, & Harris, 1992). Many students in general education settings will find practices such as integrated programming (combining different subject matter) to be exciting, motivating, and meaningful.

Management Considerations

It is essential to organize and systematically manage the classroom environment. As noted above, teachers must create a psychosocial climate that is open to a "variety of ideas, materials, problems, people, viewpoints, and resources" (Schiever, 1993, p. 209). The learning environment should be safe, accepting, and supportive. It is also useful to design instructional activities that allow for extensive social interactions among all students in the class.

Grouping gifted students for instructional purposes is useful and can be done in a variety of ways. These might include cooperative cluster grouping on the basis of similar abilities or interests, dyads, or seminar-type formats. Gifted students should be afforded an opportunity to spend time with other gifted students, just as competitive

CEC STANDARDS

CEC 7: Instructional Planning

INTASC

INTASC 7: Plans instruction

PRAXIS

PRAXIS II: Delivery of Services to Students with Disabilities

CONSIDER THIS

How can special opportunities for gifted and talented children benefit other students, including those with other special needs?

TEACHING TIP

Pairing gifted students with students who are not gifted can make an excellent learning situation for all students.

tennis players must play opponents with similar or more advanced ability to maintain their skills.

Even though the merits of cooperative learning in classroom settings have been established, heterogeneous cooperative learning arrangements involving gifted students must be managed carefully, as there are some potential pitfalls. Teachers must guarantee that most of the work does not always fall on gifted students in such arrangements. Cooperative learning arrangements can be used effectively but need to be continually monitored to ensure productiveness and fairness.

Teachers should develop effective procedures for planning lessons that include differentiated instruction and for keeping records in terms of monitoring the progress of all students, including gifted students who may be involved in a mix of enrichment and accelerated activities. A differentiated report card may be useful for conveying to parents more information about a gifted student's performance. An example of such a report is shown in Figure 12.5. Qualitative information about student performance that parents will find extremely helpful in understanding the progress of their gifted son or daughter can be communicated through this document.

The following are some specific management-related suggestions on dealing with gifted students:

- Get to know gifted students early in the school year through interviews, portfolios of previous work, child-created portfolios, and dynamic assessment (test-teach-retest) (Smutny et al., 1997).
- Enlist parents as colleagues early in the school year by soliciting information and materials (Smutny et al., 1997).
- Require students with gifts and talents to follow classroom rules and procedures while allowing them to explore and pursue their curiosity when appropriate (Feldhusen, 1993a, 1993b).
- Include gifted students in the development of class procedures that emerge during the course of a school year (e.g., introduction of animals in the room).
- Explain the logic and rationale for certain rules and procedures.
- Use cluster seating arrangements rather than strict rows (Feldhusen, 1993a).
- Identify a portion of the room where special events and activities take place and where stimulating materials are kept.
- Include instructional ideas for gifted students within all lesson plans.
- Let students who are working in independent arrangements plan their own learning activities (Feldhusen, 1993a).
- Use contracts with students who are involved in elaborate independent study projects to maximize communication between teacher and student (Rosselli, 1993).
- Involve students in their own record keeping, thus assisting the teacher and developing responsibility.
- Use periodic progress reports, daily logs, and teacher conferences to monitor and evaluate students who are in independent study arrangements (Conroy, 1993).

Curricular and Instructional Considerations

General education teachers have no choice these days other than to develop instructional lessons that consider a range of abilities and interests. For students with special gifts and talents, instructional activities may be qualitatively, and even quantitatively, different from those assigned to the class in general—or completely different if certain accelerative options are being used.

CEC STANDARDS

CEC 4: Instructional Strategies

Differentiated Instruction   The notion of differentiated instruction, particularly to professionals who have worked in the field of special education for any length of time, is not a new idea. However, the attention that has been given to it in recent years is welcome in

Figure 12.5   **Differentiated-Integrated Curriculum Report**

Differentiated–Integrated Curriculum Report

Student:
Teacher:
Semester/Year:

CONTENT

DISCIPLINES

Area of Study	Broad-Based Theme	Language Arts Enrichment/Acceleration				Math/Science Enrichment		Social Science	Arts	Individual Extension Activities
		Reading	Written Expression	Oral Expression	Spelling	Math	Science	Social Studies/Social Issues	Music/Visual Arts/Performance Arts	

PROCESSES

Research Skills

- Reading for general information
- Creating hypothesis
- Taking notes
- Making an outline
- Reading for supportive evidence
- Writing the thesis
- Using various sources
- Writing bibliography
- Making appendices

Basic Skills

- Brainstorm
- Observe
- Classify
- Interpret
- Analyze
- Evaluate
- Judge

Productive Thinking/Critical Thinking Skills

- Compare
- Categorize
- Synthesize
- Exhibit fluency
- Display flexibility
- Demonstrate originality
- Problem solve

- Elaborate
- Hypothesize
- Exhibit awareness
- Appreciate
- Create
- Redesign
- Prove

PRODUCTS

a variety of ways to communicate and express selves ▲ the opportunity to share information with an audience

☐ Proposed ⎫ in-depth study of
☐ Completed ⎭ student's choice:

From Adapted from S. N. Kaplan by J. Kataoka, revised 1990. Copyright © ASSETS 1986.

TECHNOLOGY Today

Websites That Offer Curriculum, Strategies, and Interventions

- www.kn.pacbell.com/wired/bluewebn (lesson plans and teaching resources)
- www.education-world.com (curriculum ideas)

- www.yahooligans.com (child-safe search engine, links, discussion groups)
- rtec.org (links to six regional technology consortia to support improved teaching)
- www.nyu.edu/projects/mstep/menu. html (lesson plans, activities, and information for math and science teachers)
- www.planemath.com/ (InfoUse with NASA provides student activities in math and aeronautics)

- mathforum.org (database of math lesson plans by topic and grade level)
- www.enc.org (variety of math and science lessons for grades 4–12)

From Quick Guide to the Internet for Special Education, by M. Male and D. Gotthoffer, 2000. Boston: Allyn & Bacon.

INTASC

INTASC 4: Instructional strategies

CONSIDER THIS

How can differentiated instruction be used effectively with students with a variety of different learning needs?

that the underlying constructs have important implications for addressing a range of needs in today's classrooms. A differentiated classroom is "one in which a teacher provides a variety of avenues to content (what is taught), process (activities through which students come to understand what is taught), and products (how a student shows and extends what he or she has learned) in response to the readiness levels, interests, and learning profiles of the full range of academic diversity in the class" (Tomlinson, 1997, p. 34).

When designing instructional activities for the entire class, teachers can use the following series of questions offered by Kitano (1993) to guide planning for gifted students:

- Do the activities include provisions for several ability levels?
- Do the activities include ways to accommodate a variety of interest areas?
- Does the design of activities encourage development of sophisticated products?
- Do the activities provide for the integration of thinking processes with concept development?
- Are the concepts consistent with the comprehensive curriculum plan? (p. 280)

Select Programming Ideas This section provides a number of suggestions for addressing the needs of students with special gifts and talents in general education settings. It is not meant to be an exhaustive list of examples; however, the examples that are provided do show how the needs of these students can be met.

An accelerative technique that can be used effectively with gifted students in general education classes is **curriculum compacting**, which allows students to cover assigned material in ways that are faster or different. As Renzulli, Reis, and Smith (1981) point out, this process involves three phases: the assessment of what students know and the skills they possess; identification of various ways of covering the curricular material; and suggestions for enrichment and accelerative options. Renzulli and colleagues have developed a form to assist teachers in compacting curriculum. This form is presented in Figure 12.6.

Another recommended way to address the needs of gifted students within the context of the general education classroom is to use **enrichment techniques**. Figure 12.7 provides an example of enrichment by showing how the play *Romeo and Juliet* can be taught, keeping in mind the needs of both nongifted and gifted students who are participating in this same lesson. This example developed by Shanley (1993) shows how the content of the play and the activities used by the teacher can be adapted for gifted students.

TEACHING TIP

Nearly all teachers' guides that accompany textbook series for today's schools include suggestions for "extension" activities.

Individual Educational Programming Guide

The Compactor

Name _____ Age _____ Teacher(s) _____

School _____ Grade _____ Parent(s) _____

Individual conference dates and persons participating in planning of IEP

Curriculum areas to be considered for compacting. Provide a brief description of basic material to be covered during this marking period and the assessment information or evidence that suggests the need for compacting.	*Procedures for compacting basic material.* Describe activities that will be used to guarantee proficiency in basic curricular areas.	*Acceleration and/or enrichment activities.* Describe activities that will be used to provide advanced-level learning experiences in each of the regular curricula.

Figure 12.6

Curriculum Compacting Form

From *The Revolving Door Identification Model* (p. 79), by J. Renzulli, S. Reis, and L. Smith, 1981. Mansfield Center, CT: Creative Learning Press. Reprinted with permission from Creative Learning Press, copyright © 1981.

The following are more specific suggestions related to instructional strategies and product differentiation:

- Balance coverage of basic disciplines and the arts (Feldhusen, 1993a).
- Consult teacher/instructor guides of textbook series for ideas for enrichment activities.
- Incorporate Internet-based activities into lessons.
- Acquire an array of different learning-related materials for use with gifted students. These can include textbooks, magazines, artifacts, software, Internet sources, and digital media (CDs, DVDs), as well as other types of media.
- Include time for independent study; use independent study contracts (Pugh, 1999).
- Teach research skills (data-gathering and investigative techniques) to gifted students so they can develop their independent study abilities (Reis & Schack, 1993).
- Use integrated themes for interrelating ideas within and across domains of inquiry (VanTassel-Baska, 1997). This type of curricular orientation can be used for all students in the general education setting, with special activities designed for gifted students.
- Include higher-order thinking skills in lessons (Johnson, 2001; Winocur & Mauer, 1997). For example, include questions that are open-ended and of varying conceptual levels in class discussions (see Table 12.7).
- Allocate time for students to have contact with adults who can provide special experiences and information to gifted students (e.g., mentors).

Figure **12.7** **Adapting Curricular Content for Teaching *Romeo and Juliet***

APPROPRIATE CONTENT FOR REGULAR STUDENTS

1. Discuss qualities of drama that make drama a unique genre of literature.
2. Discuss terms used in discussion of drama, such as aside, soliloquy, prologue, epilogue, dramatic irony, and foreshadowing.
3. Discuss overview of Elizabethan time period, political system, and the role of arts in the society.
4. Distinguish between Shakespeare's time period and setting of the play, giving brief explanation of Verona's social and political characteristics.
5. Discuss structure of Shakespeare's plays, using terms such as act, scene, and line count.
6. Discuss Shakespeare's language and such terms as puns and asides.
7. Discuss main plot, characterization, conflict, and ending of the play.

POSSIBLE ASSIGNMENTS:
a. Write an "updated" scene from *Romeo and Juliet*, stressing the same relationships, but making the scene's setting, names, language more contemporary.
b. Act out the original or rewritten scenes with emphasis on staging considerations.

ROMEO AND JULIET

APPROPRIATE CONTENT FOR GIFTED STUDENTS

1. Arrange students in small group to read play at rate appropriate to level of understanding.
2. Provide reference material dealing with Elizabethan time period, political and social characteristics, English theater, and time period information about Verona and play's setting.
3. Provide reference material on critical analysis of *Romeo and Juliet*.
4. Encourage awareness of concepts found in play, such as decision making, personal identity, interpretation of the law.
5. Complete a Taba Teaching Strategy (Application of Generalization or Resolution of Conflict), stressing concepts as areas for individual research.
6. Facilitate student research and projects on conceptual subject matter from play.

POSSIBLE ACTIVITIES:
a. Visit and interview local agency for counseling youth or counseling for suicide prevention.
b. Become involved in local drama group.
c. Write an original play dealing with similar or related concepts found in *Romeo and Juliet*.

From "Becoming Content with Content" (p. 74), by R. Shanley, in *Critical Issues in Gifted Education: Vol. 1. Defensible Programs for the Gifted,* edited by C. J. Maker, 1993. Austin, TX: Pro-Ed. Used by permission.

- Avoid assigning regular class work missed when gifted students spend time in special programs.
- Manage classroom discussions so that all students have an equal opportunity to contribute, feel comfortable doing so, and understand the nature of the discussion.
- Use standard textbooks and materials carefully, as gifted students will typically be able to move through them rapidly and may find them boring.
- Ensure that gifted students have access to technology, especially various types of software applications (e.g., word processing, spreadsheets, databases, presentation, photo editing) and various interactive/telecommunications options (e-mail, mailing lists, discussion groups, bulletin boards).
- Let students choose from a menu of ways that they can demonstrate their mastery of an assignment. (see Figure 12.8).
- Provide a range of options for demonstrating student mastery of curricular/instructional objectives—for instance, consider a range of options for final product development. See Figure 12.9 for a list of examples.

Career Development Gifted and talented students need to learn about potential careers that await them. They may need to do so at an earlier time than other students because they may participate in accelerated programs that necessitate early decisions about career direction. Students should learn about various career options, the dynamics of different disciplines, and the educational requirements necessary to work in a given discipline.

Teachers can select different ways to address the career needs of students. One way is to ensure that gifted students have access to mentor programs, spending time with adults who are engaged in professional activities that interest them. Another method

Table 12.7	Question Analysis Chart for a Class Discussion on George Washington Carver	
Question Type	**Explanation**	**Example**
1. Data-recall questions	Requires remembering	What was the name given to George Washington Carver's laboratory?
2. Naming questions	Lacks insight	Name ten peanut products developed by George Washington Carver.
3. Observation questions	Requires minimal understanding	What obstacles did George Washington Carver overcome as a black scientist?
4. Control questions	Modifies behavior	How will you remember George Washington Carver's scientific contribution to the farming community?
5. Pseudoquestions	Conveys expected answer	Were George Washington Carver's accomplishments inspirational to black people?
6. Hypothesis-generating questions	Involves speculation	Would George Washington Carver have been famous if he were white?
7. Reasoning questions	Requires rationale	Why did George Washington Carver want to preserve the small family farm?
8. Personal-response questions	Invites personal opinions	What, in your opinion, was George Washington Carver's greatest accomplishment?
9. Discriminatory questions	Requires weighing of pros and cons	Which of George Washington Carver's discoveries was the most significant, those evolving from the sweet potato or the peanut?
10. Problem-solving questions	Demands finding ways to answer questions	If you were to design a memorial for George Washington Carver, what sources would you study for inspiration?

From "Process Differentiation for Gifted Learners in the Regular Classroom: Teaching to Everyone's Needs" (p. 151), by H. Rosselli, in *Critical Issues in Gifted Education: Vol. 3. Programs for the Gifted in Regular Classrooms,* edited by C. J. Maker, 1993. Austin, TX: Pro-Ed. Used by permission.

is to integrate the study of careers into the existing curriculum by discussing various careers when appropriate and by requiring students to engage in some activities associated with different careers. Students can become acquainted with a number of different careers while covering traditional subject areas and through the use of resources like the Occupational Outlook Handbook, which is available online at www.bls.gov/oco/home.htm.

Career counseling and guidance are also recommended. As Hardman and colleagues (1993) point out, because of their multiple exceptional abilities and wide range of interests, some gifted students have a difficult time making career choices or narrowing mentorship possibilities. These students should spend some time with counselors or teachers who can help them make these choices and other important postsecondary decisions.

Social-Emotional Considerations

Gifted students have the same physiological and psychological needs as their peers. In general, high-ability students seem to be as well adjusted as their peers in school (Neihart et al., 2002). In other words, most students with special gifts and talents do not experience more social and emotional problems than other students.

Yet, "The lives of gifted students are both the same as and different from other students' lives" (Cross, 1999, p. 33). They may also be dealing with perplexing concepts that are well ahead of the concerns of their peers. For instance, a gifted fourth-grade girl asked her teacher questions related to abortion—a topic with which she was already dealing conceptually. In addition, gifted students may be dealing with some issues that

CEC STANDARDS

CEC 4: Instructional Strategies

Figure 12.8   **Ways Students Can Select to Demonstrate Mastery**

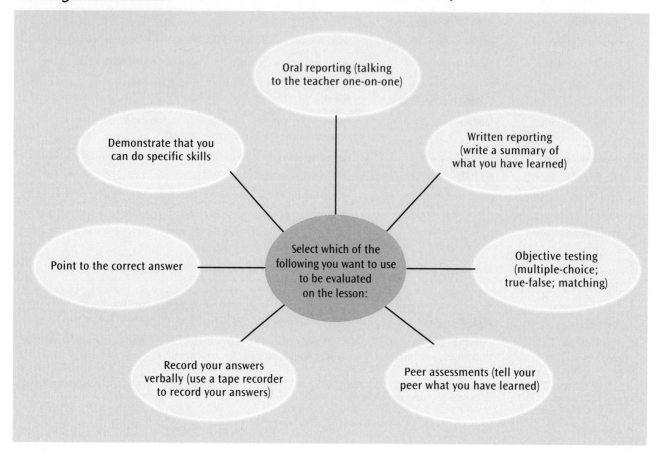

INTASC

INTASC 4: Instructional strategies

PRAXIS

PRAXIS II: Delivery of Instruction to Students with Disabilities

are different from their nongifted peers, such as stress, hypersensitivity, control, perfectionism, underachievement/lack of motivation, coping mechanisms, introversion, peer relationships, need for empathy, self-understanding, and self-acceptance (Smutny et al., 1997).

Perhaps the most important recommendation is for teachers to develop relationships with students that make them feel comfortable discussing their concerns and questions. Teachers can become important resources to gifted students, not only for advice, but also for information. Regularly scheduled individual time with a teacher can have important paybacks for both the student and the teacher.

Teachers may also find it beneficial to schedule weekly room meetings (Feldhusen, 1993b) or class councils (Kataoka, 1987) to identify and address social, procedural, or learning-related problems that arise in the classroom. The group discussion includes articulation of a problem; brainstorming and discussion of possible solutions; selection of an action plan; and implementation, evaluation, and reintroduction of the problem if the action plan is not effective.

The Personal Spotlight highlights one teacher's suggestions for adjusting the curriculum to meet the individual needs of all the students in the classroom. Following are some specific suggestions for dealing with the social-emotional needs of gifted students:

- Know when to refer students to professionals trained to deal with certain types of emotional problems.
- Create a classroom atmosphere that encourages students to take academic risks and allows them to make mistakes without fear of ridicule or harsh negative critique.

Figure 12.9   **Outlet Vehicles for Differentiated Student Products**

Literary
Literary magazine (prose or poetry)
Newspaper for school or class
Class reporter for school newspaper
Collections of local folklore (*Foxfire*)
Book reviews of childrens' books for children, by children
Storytelling
Puppeteers
Student editorials on a series of topics
Kids' page in a city newspaper
Series of books or stories
Classbook or yearbook
Calendar book
Greeting cards (including original poetry)
Original play and production
Poetry readings
Study of foreign languages
Organizer of story hour in local or school library
Comic book or comic book series
Organization of debate society
Monologue, sound track, or script

Mathematical
Contributor of math puzzles, quizzes, games for children's
    sections in newspapers, magazines
Editor/founder of computer magazine or newsletter
Math consultant for school
Editor of math magazine, newsletter
Organizer of metrics conversion movement
Original computer programming
Programming book
Graphics (original use of) films

Media
Children's television show
Children's radio show
Children's reviews (books, movie) on local news shows
Photo exhibit (talking)
Pictorial tour
Photo essay
Designing advertisement (literary magazine)
Slide/tape show on self-selected topic

Artistic
Displays, exhibits
Greeting cards
Sculpture
Illustrated books
Animation
Cartooning

Musical, Dance
Books on life of famous composer
Original music, lyrics

Electronic music (original)
Musical instrument construction
Historical investigation of folk songs
Movement–history of dance, costumes

Historical and Social Sciences
Roving historian series in newspaper
"Remember when" column in newspaper
Establishment of historical society
Establishment of an oral history tape library
Published collection of local folklore and historical
    highlight stories
Published history (written, taped, pictorial)
Historical walking tour of a city
Film on historical topic
Historical monologue
Historical play based on theme
Historical board game
Presentation of historical research topic (World War II, etc.)
Slide/tape presentation of historical research
Starting your own business
Investigation of local elections
Electronic light board explaining historical battle, etc.
Talking time line of a decade (specific time period)
Tour of local historical homes
Investigate a vacant lot
Create a "hall" of local historical figures
Archaeological dig
Arthropological study (comparison of/within groups)

Scientific
Science journal
Daily meteorologist posting weather conditions
Science column in newspaper
Science "slot" in kids television show
Organizer at a natural museum
Science consultant for school
"Science Wizard" (experimenters)
Science fair
Establishment of a nature walk
Animal behavior study
Any prolonged experimentation involving manipulation
    of variables
Microscopic study involving slides
Classification guide to natural habitats
Acid rain study
Future study of natural conditions
Book on pond life
Aquarium study/study of different ecosystems
Science article submitted to national magazines
Plan a trip to national parks (travelogue)
Working model of a heart
Working model of a solar home
Working model of a windmill

From "Differentiating Products for the Gifted and Talented: The Encouragement of Independent Learning," by S. M. Reis and G. D. Schack, in *Critical Issues in Gifted Education: Vol. 3. Programs for the Gifted in Regular Classrooms,* edited by C. J. Maker, 1993. Austin, TX: Pro-Ed. Used by permission.

- Provide time on a weekly basis, if at all possible, for individual sessions with students so that they can share their interests, ongoing events in their lives, or concerns.
- Maintain regular, ongoing communication with the families of gifted students, notifying them of the goals, activities, products, and expectations you have for their children.
- Require, and teach if necessary, appropriate social skills (e.g., appropriate interactions) to students who display problems in these areas.
- Work with parents on the personal development of students.
- Use different types of activities (e.g., social issues) to develop self-understanding and decision-making and problem-solving skills. Rosselli (1993) recommends the use of bibliotherapy (literature that focuses on children with disabilities).
- Teach gifted students how to deal with their "uniqueness."
- Recognize that gifted students may experience higher levels of social pressure and anxiety—for example, peer pressure not to achieve at a high level or lofty expectations originating internally or from others (Del Prete, 1996).

Promoting Inclusive Practices for Students Who Are Gifted

Addressing the needs of students with exceptional abilities in the context of the general education classroom is a monumental challenge. Current realities and probable trends in programming for gifted students suggest that general education will continue to be the typical setting in which they receive instruction. Thus, it is important that educa-

Personal Spotlight

Special Education Teacher

Joy Kataoka has taught students with special needs for ten years. She teaches students with many different types of disabilities, but believes that the most challenging teaching year she had was with students with learning disabilities, some of whom were also gifted. To meet the unique needs of these students, Joy had to develop an approach that met individual student needs while challenging their intellectual advancement. To do this, she selected a differentiated-integrated curriculum, which is a common approach for students classified as gifted. "I selected a broad-based theme that was implemented throughout the entire school year."

Using this model, learning activities and experiences were developed that related to the theme as well as to the basic skill needs of some of the students. For example, one year the theme "change" was chosen. Activities associated with this theme included the study of weather, seasons, the theory of continental drift, the theory of evolution, the Civil Rights movement, and people who made significant contributions to the Civil Rights movement. Conflict resolution in literature and factors that influence change in people were topics that were also included. In addition, students were also engaged in taking a scientific phenomenon, such as lightning, thunder, or rain, and researching how it was represented in mythol-

ogy, examining the scientific explanation, and also looking at how different poets describe the scientific occurrence in poetry.

The implementation of the curriculum required some individualization. Basic concepts were presented to the entire class, and all students participated in class discussions. However, each student was evaluated based on what he or she could successfully accomplish. Gifted students were required to complete projects in much more detail and at a higher level of sophistication than students who were not gifted. However, all students had to meet certain basic or minimum requirements.

Joy noted that "although such a diverse group of learners in one classroom initially presented a challenge, this curricular approach turned out to be the most successful and productive teaching experience in my career." Inclusion often results in having to teach students with diverse needs and abilities. Teachers must analyze the situation and develop an approach that can meet the needs of all students.

Joy Kataoka
Austin, TX

tors enrich the educational experiences of this population in these settings. To do so requires some thoughtful planning and revision to the modus operandi. First, classrooms need to be created where gifted students feel wanted and supported, in addition to having their instructional needs met by appropriate programming. Second, appropriate programming needs to be identified and provided to gifted students who are currently underidentified. Third, it is essential that the necessary supports be provided to general education teachers to achieve desired outcomes for this group of students. Fourth, supports must be offered to parents and families. Last, the way general education teachers are prepared must be examined to ensure that attention is given to the topic of giftedness.

Classroom Climate

The climate of any classroom is determined by the interaction among the teacher, the students in the class, and other regular participants in classroom dynamics; in particular, the teacher plays a leading role in establishing the parameters by which a classroom operates and the foundation for classroom dynamics. The degree to which a classroom becomes a community in which students care for one another and strive to improve the daily experience for everyone will depend on each class's unique dynamics. When a healthy and nurturing classroom context is established, students who are gifted can be important members of the classroom community. In such an environment, their abilities are recognized as assets to the class rather than something to be jealous of, envied, or despised.

To promote acceptance of students with special gifts and talents, teachers should strive to dispel prevailing stereotypes, as perpetuated by myths and misconceptions. Teachers should discuss the uniqueness of these students in terms of the diversity of the classroom, implying that everyone is different. The notion that we all have strengths and weaknesses is also useful.

As noted previously, many of the instructional strategies suggested for gifted students can also be used successfully with nongifted students (Del Prete, 1996). By taking this approach, teachers can accommodate the needs of students with gifts and talents without drawing undue attention to the special programming they are receiving.

Addressing the Needs of Special Populations

It is particularly important to address the needs of students who are typically underidentified as being gifted, such as females, students with disabilities, those who are economically disadvantaged, those who underachieve in school, and those who come from different ethnic or cultural backgrounds. Critical issues related to serving these groups focus on nurturing abilities of students in general education, recognizing their potential and discovering exceptional abilities in academic and nonacademic areas, and providing appropriate interventions.

Some general suggestions for improving the nature of services include:

- *Nurture student development*
  - Create a supportive, caring, nurturing classroom environment, as noted earlier.
  - Establish high expectations for all students in the general education classroom.
  - Encourage all students to do their best.
  - Emphasize that everyone has strengths and areas needing improvement.
  - Identify areas of student interest. This effort often leads to recognition of areas where a student finds some degree of success.
- *Recognize hidden giftedness*
  - Regularly examine the qualitative aspects of students' performance on academic tasks.

CROSS-REFERENCE

Review Chapters 5–11 to determine whether methods of enhancing an inclusive classroom for students with other special needs will be effective with students who are gifted and talented.

CEC STANDARDS

CEC 5: Learning Environment and Social Interactions

INTASC

INTASC 5: Learning environment

PRAXIS

PRAXIS II: Delivery of Instruction to Students with Disabilities

TEACHING TIP

Assigning students who are gifted and talented to be peer tutors can both enhance their acceptance and give them opportunities for leadership.

Methods that are effective with gifted students are also often useful for nongifted students.

- Make sure that certain factors, such as a specific learning-related problem (e.g., memory problems) or English not being the student's first language, do not mask strength in a variety of areas.
- Use a variety of assessment techniques for screening and eligibility determination purposes.
- Seek parent input on students who are very shy and passive in class activities—these students are often overlooked.
- *Provide appropriate services*
  - Consider a student's personal style and cultural background in the selection of various programming options—for instance, heavy reliance on special ability group work may not be the best first choice for some students.
  - Be aware that some enrichment-related activities, while perhaps engaging, may be in conflict with a student's family and personal beliefs.

The needs of gifted females have received more attention over the years. Various lists of suggestions (Silverman, 1986) have been generated to assist teachers, parents, and others to better attend to the needs of this group of students. Reis (2001) examined some of the extant barriers that gifted girls and women still face and provided a list of general recommendations to help gifted girls understand and do something about the external barriers that inhibit their talent development. A selection of some of the recommendations is provided in Table 12.8.

CONSIDER THIS

What other kinds of supports might contribute to the effectiveness of general classroom teachers in meeting the needs of gifted students in their classes?

Support for the General Education Teacher

The responsibility to deliver a quality education to gifted students in general education settings rests on the shoulders of the instructional staff, quite often general education teachers. Given the realities of the general education classroom, teachers face a mighty challenge in meeting the needs of students with special gifts and talents. To maximize the chances of successfully addressing the needs of these students who are in general education settings, Coleman (1998) recommends that schools:

Table 12.8	**Recommendations for Girls and Women**	
Gifted and Talented Girls Should	**Teachers Should**	**Parents, Teachers, and Counselors Should**
Have exposure or personal contact with female role models and mentors who have successfully balanced career and family.	Provide equitable treatment in a nonstereotyped environment and, in particular, provide encouragement.	Form task forces to advocate for programming and equal opportunities and to investigate opportunities for talented, creative girls.
Participate in discussion groups and attend panel discussions in which gifted and talented girls and women discuss the external barriers they have encountered.	Reduce sexism in classrooms and create an avenue for girls to report and discuss examples of stereotyping in schools.	Spotlight achievements of talented females in a variety of different areas; encourage girls and young women to become involved in as many different types of activities, travel opportunities, and clubs as possible.
Pursue involvement in leadership roles and extracurricular activities.	Help creative, talented females appreciate and understand healthy competition.	
Participate in either sports, athletics, and multiple extracurricular activities in areas in which they have an interest.	Group gifted females homogeneously in math/science or within cluster groups of high-ability students in heterogeneous groups.	Encourage girls to take advanced courses in all areas as well as courses in the arts and reinforce successes in these and all areas of endeavor; ensure equal representation of girls in advanced classes.
Discuss issues related to gender and success, such as family issues in supportive settings with other talented girls.	Encourage creativity in girls.	
	Use problem solving in assignments and reduce the use of timed tests and timed assignments within class periods; rather, provide options for untimed work within a reasonable time frame.	Encourage relationships with other creative girls who want to achieve.
Participate in career counseling at an early age and be exposed to a wide variety of career options and talented women who pursue challenging careers in all areas.	Expose girls to other creative, gifted females through direct and curricular experiences—field trips, guest speakers, seminars, role models, books, videotapes, articles, movies.	Maintain options for talented, creative girls in specific groups such as self-contained classes, groups of girls within heterogeneous classes and in separate classes for gifted girls, science and math clubs, or support groups.
	Provide educational interventions compatible with cognitive development and styles of learning (i.e., independent study projects, small group learning opportunities, etc.) and use a variety of authentic assessment tools such as projects and learning centers instead of just using tests.	Consistently point out options for careers and encourage future choices but help girls focus on specific interests and planning for future academic choices, interests, and careers.
	Establish equity in classroom interactions.	
	Provide multiple opportunities for creative expression in multiple modalities.	

Source: "External Barriers Experienced by Gifted and Talented Girls and Women," by S. M. Reis, 2001, *Gifted Child Today, 24*(4) pp. 33–34. Copyright 2001 by Prufrock Press. Reprinted by permission.

- Group students in teachable clusters—groups of six to ten students whose instructional needs are similar.
- Reduce class size.
- Provide additional instructional resources.
- Modify schedules so that there are greater amounts of time available to work with gifted students.
- Provide additional support personnel.
- Require and/or provide training in working with gifted students.

CEC STANDARDS

CEC 4: Instructional Strategies

INTASC

INTASC 4: Instructional strategies

School-based supports such as teacher assistance teams (Chalfant & Van Dusen Pysh, 1993) can also assist with addressing the needs of gifted students. When staffed properly, these teams become a rich resource of experience and ideas for dealing with myriad student needs. Parents also play an important, and often indirect, role in the school-based programs of their children. It is worthwhile to develop parents into good "dance partners" (i.e., to create and maintain positive relationships) in this process (Riley, 1999).

Support for Parents and Families

In addition to the usual suggestion about the importance of establishing a good home–school collaborative arrangement, some parents of gifted students may need additional information and support. Cases exist where parents of highly gifted students did not recognize that their son or daughter might be gifted. These parents are likely to need information about their child as well as information about the different programming that might be available to address their child's needs.

Parents are faced with the same challenges arising from the gifted characteristics that teachers encounter in the classroom. Often these desirable characteristics can become points of contention. Parents can benefit from the advice of teachers in dealing with these student capabilities and in challenging their child at home during the time when the student is not in school.

Parents can also benefit from obtaining information about careers and further education. Most families are very familiar with the college selection process; however, some families are not, particularly those where the parents may not have gone on to postsecondary education.

Teacher Preparation and Professional Development

To be a successful general education teacher of gifted students, a wide range of competencies are needed. A widely recognized set of national standards for teacher preparation is not presently available (Cline & Schwartz, 1999), although some attempts at providing standards are now available (Council for Exceptional Children, 2003). As a result, training programs, where they do exist, may vary widely in terms of the required coursework and the content of courses offered.

Maker (1993) highlighted the following personal features as important in teaching gifted students: commitment; belief that people learn differently; high expectations; organization; enthusiasm; willingness to talk less, listen more; facilitative abilities; creativity; and the ability to juggle. Others have discussed the personal characteristics desirable in teachers of students with special gifts and talents (see Davis & Rimm, 1998) or competencies that are desirable (NAGC, 1994).

It is important to acknowledge that "no one teacher can be expected to have complete expertise in meeting the needs of every type of learner" (Cline & Schwartz, 1999, p. 172). However, general education teachers should be exposed to some basic set of knowledge and skills to better address the needs of gifted students who will be in their classrooms. Research has validated that teachers who have had specialized training in addressing the needs of gifted students are more effective (Hansen & Feldhusen, 1994). A basic list of knowledge/understanding and skills/competencies suggested for general education teachers is provided in Table 12.9.

Final Thought

If the topics and issues presented in this chapter are addressed correctly, we will do a great service to students with exceptional abilities. Furthermore, students with special gifts and talents should be entitled to a set of educational rights, as Clark (2002) has

Table 12.9	What General Education Teachers Need to Know

Knowledge and Understanding	Skills and Competencies
Cognitive and affective differentiating characteristics of gifted learners	Instructional modification techniques
Educational needs of gifted, creative, and talented learners	Instructional design strategies
	Teaching strategy selection
Future studies	Higher-order questioning
Creativity, creative thinking strategies	Creative problem solving
Specific instructional materials and curriculum already designed for basic content areas	Futuring
	Group process
Nature of giftedness, intelligence	Parent conferencing

From "Training Teachers of the Gifted: What Do They Need to Know?" by K. B. Rogers, 1989, *Roeper Review, 11*(3) p. 146. Copyright 1989 by Roeper Review. Reprinted by permission.

suggested, on which efforts to provide appropriate education to this population should be based. Her fifteen educational rights are listed in Figure 12.10. It is only when these conditions are met that teachers will be able to "stimulate the imagination, awaken the desire to learn, and imbue the students with a sense of curiosity and an urge to reach beyond themselves" (Mirman, 1991, p. 59).

Summary

Basic Concepts about Students Who Are Gifted
- Gifted students continue to be an underidentified, underserved, and often inappropriately served segment of the school population. A host of misconceptions exist in the minds of the general public about these individuals.
- Definitional perspectives of giftedness and intellectual abilities vary and contribute to some of the problems related to identification, eligibility, and service delivery. A key component of most definitions is the student's remarkable potential to achieve at levels above that of peers, as well as high ability, high task commitment, and high creativity.
- The notion of multiple intelligences suggests that there are different areas where one can show high ability.
- The identification of gifted students is a complex and multifaceted process. Multiple sources of information are needed to determine whether a student is gifted.
- Gifted students with diverse cultural backgrounds are underrepresented in gifted programs, often because of biased assessment practices. Special effort must be given to serving all students who show promise.

Strategies for Curriculum and Instruction for Students Who Are Gifted
- Most educators of gifted students prefer programs that are typically apart and different from those of nongifted students. The reality, however, is that most gifted students are in general education classes for most of their education.

- The major ways of addressing the needs of gifted students in general education are through the use of acceleration, enrichment, or special grouping.

Classroom Adaptations for Students Who Are Gifted
- The special methods used with gifted students are often effective with other students as well.
- Differentiated instruction and program design are essential to address the needs and interests of students with special gifts and talents.
- The career development needs of gifted students must also be addressed.

Promoting Inclusive Practices for Students Who Are Gifted
- Teachers can do a great deal to promote a sense of community and social acceptance of gifted students in their classrooms. It is difficult to address the needs of gifted students in the context of a large class with a great range of diverse needs.
- Supports to teachers, as well as to parents and families, are needed to effectively address the needs of students who are gifted.
- The probability of successfully helping gifted students reach their potential is contingent on a number of key factors.
- Understanding the needs of special populations of gifted students (females, disabled, economically disadvantaged, underachievers, and those from ethnically and culturally different backgrounds) is essential.

Figure 12.10 **A Declaration of the Educational Rights of the Gifted Child**

It is the right of a gifted child to engage in appropriate educational experiences even when other children of that grade level or age are unable to profit from the experience.

It is the right of a gifted child to be grouped and to interact with other gifted children for some part of their learning experience so that the child may be understood, engaged, and challenged.

It is the right of a gifted child to be taught rather than to be used as a tutor or teaching assistant for a significant part of the school day.

It is the right of a gifted child to be presented with new, advanced, and challenging ideas and concepts regardless of the materials and resources that have been designated for the age group or grade level in which the child was placed.

It is the right of a gifted child to be taught concepts that the child does not yet know instead of relearning old concepts that the child has already shown evidence of mastering.

It is the right of a gifted child to learn faster than age peers and to have that pace of learning respected and provided for.

It is the right of a gifted child to think in alternative ways, produce diverse products, and to bring intuition and innovation to the learning experience.

It is the right of a gifted child to be idealistic and sensitive to fairness, justice, accuracy, and the global problems facing humankind and to have a forum for expressing these concerns.

It is the right of a gifted child to question generalizations, offer alternative solutions, and value complex and profound levels of thought.

It is the right of a gifted child to be intense, persistent, and goal-directed in the pursuit of knowledge.

It is the right of a gifted child to express a sense of humor that is unusual, playful, and often complex.

It is the right of a gifted child to hold high expectations for self and others and to be sensitive to inconsistency between ideals and behavior, with the need to have help in seeing the value in human differences.

It is the right of a gifted child to be a high achiever in some areas of the curriculum and not in others, making thoughtful, knowledgeable academic placement a necessity.

It is the right of a gifted child to have a low tolerance for the lag between vision and actualization, between personal standards and developed skill, and between physical maturity and athletic ability.

It is the right of a gifted child to pursue interests that are beyond the ability of age peers, are outside the grade level curriculum, or involve areas as yet unexplored or unknown.

From *Growing Up Gifted* (6th ed., pp. 19–20), by B. Clark, 2002. Upper Saddle River, NJ: Merrill/Prentice Hall. Copyright 2002 by Pearson Education. Reprinted by permission.

Questions to Reconsider

Think back to the scenario about Carmen that you read at the beginning of this chapter. Would you answer the questions raised there any differently, now that you have read this chapter?

1. What kinds of challenges can students like Carmen create for teachers and for themselves?

2. How do individuals like Carmen, who are highly gifted, differ from other students who are gifted?

3. Should children like Carmen be included in general education classrooms all the time, separated from time to time, or provided with a completely different curriculum?

Further Readings

Baum, S. M., Owen, S. V., & Dixon, J. (1991). *The gifted and learning disabled.* Mansfield Center, CT: Creative Learning Press.

Castellano, J. A., & Díaz, E. I. (2002). *Reaching new horizons: Gifted and talented education for culturally and linguistically diverse students.* Boston: Allyn & Bacon.

Clark, B. (2002). *Growing up gifted* (6th ed.). Upper Saddle River, NJ: Merrill/Prentice Hall.

Cline, S., & Schwartz, D. (1999). *Diverse populations of gifted children.* Boston: Allyn & Bacon.

Colangelo, N., & Davis, G. A. (Eds.). (2003). *Handbook of gifted education* (3rd ed.). Boston: Allyn & Bacon.

Coleman, L. J., & Cross, T. L. (2001). *Being gifted in school: An introduction to development, guidance, and teaching.* Waco, TX: Prufrock Press.

Csikszentmihalyi, M., Rathunde, K., & Whalen, S. (1997). *Talented teenagers: The roots of success and failure.* Cambridge: Cambridge University Press.

Davis, G. A., & Rimm, S. B. (1998). *Education of the gifted and talented* (4th ed.). Boston: Allyn & Bacon.

Delisle, J. R. (2000). *Once upon a mind: The stories and scholars of gifted child education.* Fort Worth, TX: Harcourt Brace.

Gardner, H. (1993). *Multiple intelligences: The theory in practice.* New York: Basic Books.

Heller, K., Monks, F., & Passow, A. H. (Eds.). (1993). *International handbook of research and development of giftedness and talent.* Oxford, UK: Pergamon Press.

Maker, C. J. (Ed.). (1993). *Critical issues in gifted education: Vol. 3. Programs for the gifted in regular classrooms.* Austin, TX: Pro-Ed.

Rogers, K. B. (2002). *Re-forming gifted education: Matching the program to the child.* Scottsdale, AZ: Great Potential Press.

Ryser, G., & McConnell, K. (2003). *Practical ideas that really work for students who are gifted.* Austin, TX: PRO-ED.

Smutny, J. F., Walker, S. Y., & Meckstroth, E. A. (1997). *Teaching young gifted children in the regular classroom: Identifying, nurturing, and challenging ages 4–9.* Minneapolis: Free Spirit.

Subotnik, R. F., & Arnold, K. D. (Eds.). (1994). *Beyond Terman: Contemporary longitudinal studies of giftedness and talent.* Norwood, NJ: Ablex.

VanTassel-Baska, J. (1998). *Gifted and talented learners.* Denver, CO: Love.

Winebrenner, S. (2000). *Teaching gifted kids in the regular classroom: Strategies and techniques every teacher can use to meet the academic needs of the gifted and talented* (rev. ed.). Minneapolis: Free Spirit.

mylabschool

Go to Allyn & Bacon's MyLabSchool (www.mylabschool.com) and enter Assignment ID SPV12 into the Assignment Finder. View the video clip called *Challenging Gifted Learners.* Then consider what you have seen along with what you've read in Chapter 12 to answer the following questions.

1. Find examples in the video clip of students demonstrating some of the intellectual skills common to gifted students: formulating abstractions; processing information in complex ways; showing excitement about new ideas; hypothesizing from evidence; using an extensive vocabulary; being inquisitive. What other characteristics do these students represent that might suggest they are gifted? Use specific examples.

2. What are some advantages and some disadvantages of enrichment or acceleration programs for students identified as gifted and talented? Based on information in this chapter, do you feel such programs are always the best way to support gifted learners? Why or why not?

3. Do you think students who are not identified as gifted would benefit from the kind of instruction shown in the video clip? Explain your position.

You may also answer the questions at the end of the clip and e-mail your responses to your instructor.

Teaching Students Who Are At Risk

After reading this chapter, you should be able to:

1. Define students who are considered to be at risk.
2. Describe the different types of children who are considered at risk for developing learning and behavior problems.
3. Discuss general considerations for teaching at-risk students.
4. Describe specific methods that are effective for teaching at-risk students.

Questions to Consider

1. What types of interventions does Lisa need? What services would you recommend?
2. Should Lisa be considered for special education?
3. What can teachers do with Lisa and students like her to prevent failure?

Lisa is a nine-year-old girl with blond hair and blue eyes. She is currently in third grade; she was kept back once in kindergarten. Mr. Sykes, her teacher, does not know how to help her. He referred Lisa for special education, but the assessment revealed that she was not eligible. Although her intelligence is in the low-average range, she does not have mental retardation or any other qualifying disability. Lisa is shy and very insecure.

Lisa has significant problems in reading and math. Although she seems sharp at times, she is achieving below even her own expected level. Her eyes fill with tears of frustration as she sits at her desk and struggles with her work.

She frequently cries if Mr. Sykes leaves the classroom; she is very dependent on her teacher. She should have a cluster of good friends, but she is a social outcast. Even though on rare occasions a few of the other girls in the classroom will include her, she is typically teased, ridiculed, and harassed by her peers. She has been unable to establish and maintain meaningful relationships with her classmates and adults. Lisa's attempts to win friends are usually couched in a variety of undesirable behaviors, yet she craves attention and friendship. She just does not demonstrate the appropriate social skills requisite of her age.

Lisa lives with her mother and one younger brother in a small apartment. Her mother has been divorced twice and works as a waitress at a local restaurant. Her mother's income barely covers rent, utilities, groceries, and other daily expenses. Occasionally, when Lisa's mother gets the chance to work extra hours at the restaurant, she will do so, leaving Lisa in charge of her brother. Although Lisa's mother appears interested in Lisa's schoolwork, she has been unable to get to a teacher's meeting with Mr. Sykes, even though several have been scheduled. Lisa's mother's interest in helping her daughter with her homework is limited by the fact that Lisa's mother did not complete school and does not have a great command of the content that Lisa is studying.

Mr. Sykes knows that Lisa is not likely to qualify for special education services under IDEA; however, he also recognizes that Lisa could benefit from some assistance, particularly in reading and in social/affective areas.

One thing that can be done for Lisa is prereferral intervention. This option is available in many schools to help general education teachers address the needs of students in their classes who are experiencing problems. These services are called prereferral because they are meant to deal with issues prior to a formal referral to special education. If prereferral interventions are successful, further consideration for special education may not be necessary.

Basic Concepts about Students Who Are At Risk

The movement to include students with special needs in general education has made substantial progress during the past several years. One beneficial result has been the recognition that many students who are not officially eligible for special education services may need, and can benefit from, special interventions and supports. Although certain students like Lisa do not manifest problems severe enough to result in a disability classification, these students are at risk for developing academic and behavior problems that could limit their success in school in the near future and as adults in the more distant future.

Lisa, the student in the chapter-opening vignette, is a good example of a child who is already experiencing some problems that are limiting her ability to succeed in school, and she is very much at risk for developing major academic and behavior problems. In the current system, children like Lisa are not likely to be provided with special education and related services under IDEA or Section 504. The result, too often, is that Lisa and children like her find school to be frustrating and basically an undesirable place to be. Ultimately, these students are likely to drop out of school and experience major problems as adults.

"At Risk" Defined

The term *at risk* can be defined in many ways. It is often used to describe children who have personal characteristics, or who live in families that display characteristics, that are associated with problems in school (Bowman, 1994). Using education as a frame of reference, **at-risk** children and youth are defined as those who are in situations that can lead to academic, personal, and behavioral problems that could limit their success in school and later in life.

Some professionals have championed the idea that a better term to use to describe these students is *placed at risk*. The argument for doing so is that the focus is taken off the student and placed more on situational features that contribute to their educational outcomes not being the same as their peers (Keogh, 2000). The philosophy behind the use of the term "children and youth placed at risk" is articulated by the Center for Research on the Education of Students Placed at Risk (2001): "The philosophy . . . is that students are not inherently at risk but rather are placed at risk of educational failure by many adverse practices and situations" (p. 11). However, while this term is attractive because it refocuses attention away from the individual, this is not to suggest that some at-risk situations are not very much associated with the person (e.g., suicidal tendencies that result from depression). A balance needs to be achieved in the use and implication of the term "at risk."

Students identified as being at risk generally have difficulty learning basic academic skills, exhibit unacceptable social behaviors, and cannot keep up with their peers (Pierce, 1994). They represent a very heterogeneous group (Davis, 1995). Unlike students with disabilities, who have historically been segregated full time or part time from their age peers, students who are considered at risk are typically fully included in educational programs. Unfortunately, rather than receiving appropriate interventions, they have been neglected in the classroom and consigned to failure.

Although often not eligible for special education and related services, students who are at risk need special interventions. Without them, many will be retained year after year, become behavior problems, develop drug and alcohol abuse problems, drop out of school, fail as adults, and possibly even commit suicide (Huff, 1999). School personnel need to recognize students who are at risk for failure and develop appropriate programs to facilitate their success in school and in society. Not doing so will result in losing many of these children, and "to lose today's at-risk students implies [that] society is more than a little out of control itself" (Greer, 1991, p. 390).

Although certain factors can increase the vulnerability of students becoming at risk as we have defined the term, it is important to recognize that this phenomenon is not only associated with students who are poor or educationally disadvantaged in some other way. Barr and Parrett (2001) underscored this point: "any young person may become at risk . . . the risks now facing our youths have become a matter of life and death. It is now clear that students who are at risk are not limited to any single group. They cut across all social classes and occur in every ethnic group" (p. 2).

Prevalence and Factors Related to Being At Risk

Many factors place students at risk for developing school-related problems. These include poverty, homelessness, single-parent homes, death of a significant person, abusive situations, substance abuse, teen pregnancy, sexual identity issues, delinquency, and unrecognized disabilities. The aforementioned topics represent general at-risk situations. Frymier and Gansneder (1989) studied specific factors associated with at risk students and identified and ranked forty-five key indicators. The results of their work are presented in Table 13.1. Although the presence of these factors often makes failure more likely for students, it is critically important not to imply that every student who might possess these factors is at risk for school problem. Likewise, we must refrain from labeling every child who is poor or who lives with a single parent as an at-risk student. Many students are very resilient even when faced with some difficult life situations. Although overly simplistic conclusions should not be drawn concerning students at

Table 13.1	**Factors That Place Students At Risk**

• Attempted suicide during the past year	• Other family members used drugs during past year
• Used drugs or engaged in substance abuse	
• Has been a drug "pusher" during the past year	• Attended three or more schools during past five years
• Sense of self-esteem is negative	• Grades were below C last school year
• Was involved in a pregnancy during the past year	• Was arrested for driving while intoxicated
	• Has an IQ score below 90
• Was expelled from school during the past year	• Parents divorced or separated last year
• Consumes alcohol regularly	• Father is unskilled laborer who is unemployed
• Was arrested for illegal activity	
• Parents have negative attitudes toward education	• Mother is unskilled laborer who is unemployed
• Has several brothers or sisters who dropped out	• Father or mother died during the past year
	• Diagnosed as needing special education
• Was sexually or physically abused last year	• English is not first language
• Failed two courses last school year	• Lives in an inner city, urban area
• Was suspended from school twice last year	• The mother is only parent living in the home
• Student was absent more than twenty days last year	• Is year older than other students in same grade
• Parent drinks excessively and is an alcoholic	• Mother did not graduate from high school
• Was retained in grade (i.e., "held back")	• Father lost his job during the past year
• One parent attempted suicide last year	• Was dropped from athletic team during past year
• Scored below twentieth percentile on standardized test	• Experienced a serious illness or accident

From "Assessing and Predicting Risk among Students in School", p 13, by Frymier, J., Barber, D. Denton, L. T. Johnson-Lewis, M. Ed., Robertson, F., 1992. Final Report Phi Delta Kappa Study of Students at Risk, U. 2 Bloomington, IN. Phi Delta Kappa.

DIVERSITY FORUM

Levels of Instructional Support for Diverse Students

Mrs. Blanco is concerned about her fourth grade student, Joffee, whose family came to the United States as refugees from Somalia when he was six. Social service supports, intense at first, have waned. Joffee's family has moved four times since their arrival, changing schools with each move. His parents work at minimum wage jobs and share a modest apartment with another refugee family. Although all speak fluent English, no adult has more than a third-grade education. Joffee reads at first grade level, and Mrs. Blanco is considering referring him for special education. However, she is concerned that his difficulties also reflect circumstances associated with his family's refugee status.

Like Joffee, many students whose circumstances place them at educational risk may achieve considerably below their potential. A discrepancy between academic potential and achievement may reflect factors other than a disability, including inadequate or inconsistent schooling (Adelman, 1992; Ortiz, 2002). IDEA (2004) provides a "response to intervention" (RTI) model as an alternative to traditional assessment. Typically involving three levels of progressively more intensive interventions, personnel analyze school and classroom practices to ensure that evidence-based teaching is tak-

ing place, and monitor how individual students respond to such instruction. This enables personnel to determine if educational factors, rather than factors intrinsic to the student (e.g., disability) may be responsible for a student's poor achievement (Gresham, 2002).

Schools which serve students from diverse socio-cultural and linguistic backgrounds, must ensure that RTI implementation is based on "what works" with these populations (NCCRESt, 2005). Specifically:

1. The school's instructional practices at all levels of intervention are informed by research that validates these approaches with students from similar socio-cultural and linguistic backgrounds;
2. Educators have consistently high expectations, develop supportive personal relationships with students and families, and provide instruction that is academically challenging, culturally and linguistically relevant, and meaningful; and
3. School-based support systems for students, families, and teachers provide early intervention for struggling learners, and access to resources that enhance teachers' ability to design culturally and linguistically responsive interventions.

Questions

1. For students like Joffee, what do you see as the benefits of using a response-to-intervention model? The challenges?
2. How might teachers gather information about students' sociocultural and linguistic backgrounds, in order to use this information to make instruction relevant and meaningful?

REFERENCES

Adelman, H. (1992). LD: The next 25 years. *Journal of Learning Disabilities,* 25(1), 17–22.

Gresham, Frank M. (2002). Responsiveness to Intervention: An alternative approach to the identification of learning disabilities. In, R. Bradley, L. Danielson, & D. Hallahan (Eds.), *Identification of Learning Disabilities: Research to Practice* (pp.467–507). Mahwah, NJ: Erlbaum.

National Center for Culturally Responsive Education Systems (NCCRESt). (2005). *Cultural Considerations and Challenges in Response-to-Intervention Models: An NCCRESt Position Statement.*

Ortiz, A. A. (2002). Prevention of school failure and early intervention for English Language Learners. In A. J., Artiles, & A. A. Ortiz (Eds.), *English Language Learners with special education needs: Identification, assessment, and instruction* (pp. 31–63). Washington, DC: Center for Applied Linguistics and Delta Systems.

risk, research identifies certain factors as having a clear correlation with school problems, as indicated in Table 13.1.

According to Barr and Parrett (1995), it is possible to predict, with a high degree of accuracy, which students at the third grade are likely to drop out of school at a later point in time. For example, in a government report, McPartland and Slavin (1990) reported that third-graders who read one year below grade level, have been retained in one grade, come from low socioeconomic backgrounds, and attend school with many other poor children have almost no chance of graduating from high school. Figure 13.1 depicts the relationship between these four factors that are such strong predictors of school failure.

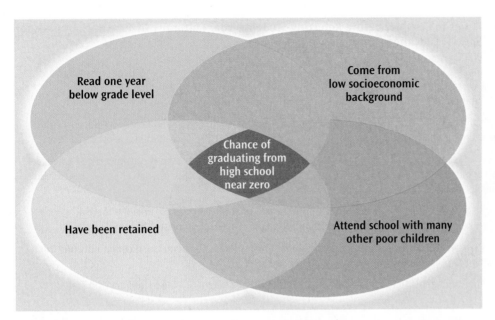

Figure **13.1**

Research on Third-Grade Students

From *Policy Perspectives Increasing Achievement of At-Risk Students at Each Grade Level,* by J. M. McPartland and R. E. Slavin, 1990. Washington, D.C.: U.S. Department of Education. Cited in *Hope at Last for At-Risk Youth* (p. 10), by R. D. Barr and W. H. Parrett, 1995. Boston: Allyn & Bacon. Used by permission.

Even when children are strongly indicated as being at risk, school personnel must be cautious about predicting their actual abilities and potential for achievement. Such care is particularly important when considering students from ethnically, culturally, and linguistically different backgrounds who appear to be experiencing school-related difficulties. Caution must be exercised when initially considering special education referral for students from such backgrounds; some key issues that need to be considered are provided in Table 13.2. Addressing these issues will decrease the likelihood of referring students for special education programs when in-class interventions might be effective.

Select At-Risk Groups

This section explores the challenges that nine at-risk groups present to school-based personnel.

Students Who Grow Up in Poverty

Poverty is a social condition associated with many different kinds of problems. Poverty has been related to crime, physical abuse, and learning, behavior, and emotional problems. Professionals in the field of learning disabilities have begun to realize that poverty can be a significant factor in the etiology of that particular disability (Young & Gerber, 1998). Davis (1993) notes that poverty is the number-one factor that places children at risk for academic failure.

Unfortunately, poverty is a fact of life for many families. The following figures provide an overall picture of current state of affairs, as reported in *Poverty in the United States: 2002* (Proctor & Dalaker, 2003).

- official poverty rate in 2002 was 12.1 percent
- people below the official poverty thresholds numbered 34.6 million—1.7 million higher than in 2001
- poverty rate for children and youth under the age of eighteen was 16.7 percent, representing 12.1 million individuals

CROSS-REFERENCE

For information on the impact of poverty on mental retardation and learning disabilities, review Chapters 5 and 7.

CEC STANDARDS

CEC 2: Development and Characteristics of Learners

Table 13.2	**Issues to Consider before Referring Students from Culturally Diverse Backgrounds for Special Education Programs**

Stage of language development: At what stage of language proficiency, oral and written, is the student in L1 (student's first language) and L2 (student's second language)? What impact have past educational experiences had on language development? Will the environment facilitate further development?

Language skills: What are the particular strengths and weaknesses of the student in oral and written L1 and L2 skills? What curriculum materials and instructional expertise are available to meet the student's needs? What skills are the parents able to work on at home?

Disability/at-risk status: What impact does the student's specific disability or at-risk circumstances have on the acquisition of language skills in L1 and L2 and on other academic skills? Does the teacher have an adequate knowledge base to provide effective services? Does the school have access to community supports?

Age: What impact does the student's age have on the ability to acquire L1 and L2 and to achieve in content areas? Is there a discrepancy between a child's age and emotional maturity? Is the curriculum developmentally appropriate?

Needs of the student: What are the short-term and long-term needs of the student in academic, vocational, and community life? What are the needs of the student in relation to other students in the environment?

Amount of integration: How much time will be spent in L1 and L2 environments? Will the student be able to interact with students who have various levels of ability?

Personal qualities: How might the student's personality, learning style, and interests influence the acquisition of L1 and L2, achievement in content areas, and social–emotional growth? How might personal qualities of the student's peers and teacher influence learning?

From *Assessment and Instruction of Culturally and Linguistically Diverse Students with or At Risk of Learning Problems* (pp. 221–222), by V. Gonzalez, R. Brusca-Vega, and T. Yawkey, 1997. Boston: Allyn & Bacon. Used by permission.

INTASC

INTASC 2: How children learn and develop

PRAXIS

PRAXIS II: Understanding Exceptionalities

- racial distribution was non-Hispanic whites, 8.0 percent; Asians, 10.0 percent; African Americans, 23.9 to 24.1 percent (range due to various ways used to define race); and Hispanics, 21.8 percent
- families living in poverty totaled 7.2 million (9.6 percent of families)
- number of female house-holder families with no husband present in poverty was 3.6 million (26.5 percent)

It is clear from analyzing the data that the highest percentage of any age group that lives in poverty is for those who are eighteen or younger. Figure 13.2 illustrates the different statistics for three age groups. In further examining the data on children under the age of six, the scenario is even more gloomy:

> Children under 6 have been particularly vulnerable to poverty. In 2002, the poverty rate for related children under 6 was 18.5 percent, unchanged from 2001. Of children under 6 living in families with a female householder, no spouse present, 48.6 percent were in poverty, five times the rate of their counterparts in married-couple families (9.7 percent). (Proctor & Dalaker, 2003, p. 7)

Poverty is associated with a range of learning, behavioral, and emotional problems (Adelman & Taylor, 2002) as well as different kinds of disabilities (Smith & Luckasson, 1992), including mental retardation (Beirne-Smith, et al., 2006), learning disabilities (Smith et al., 1997; Young & Gerber, 1998), and various health problems. Poverty is also associated with poor prenatal care, poor parenting, hunger, limited health care, single-parent households, poor housing conditions, and often homelessness (Yamaguchi, Strawser, & Higgins, 1997). Evertson, Emmer, and Worsham (2006) caution that students who live in extreme poverty may lack the basic "going to school" skills that contribute to successful school outcomes.

Elders (2002) remarked that most children who are poor will be members of only one club in their lives—the "Five-H Club." Members carry the following credentials—they are hungry, "healthless," homeless, hugless, and hopeless. Using hyperbole, Elders

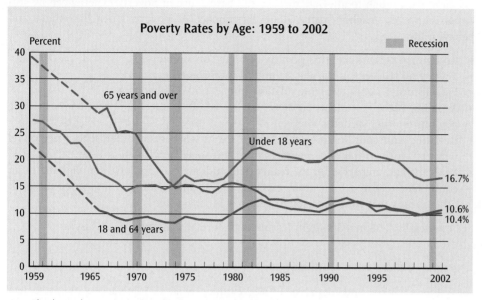

Figure 13.2   **Poverty Rates by Age: 1959 to 2002**

Note: The data points represent the midpoints of the respective years.
Data for people 18 to 64 and 65 and older are not available from 1960 to 1965.

From U.S. Census Bureau, Current Population Survey, 1960–2003 Annual Social and Economic Supplements.

was trying to accentuate some of the key issues confronting many children living in poverty. Most important, all these issues are addressable. Her reference to "hugless" was meant to stress the need in their lives to have an array of people who sincerely care and show it—it was not meant to imply that all children who live in poverty are devoid of love at home. Her point regarding "hope" merely points to the need to provide children and youth with promise and motivation to make changes. Evertson and colleagues (2006) note that "a key to success for these children is a strong, trusting relationship with the teacher in an environment in which they can feel safe, not threatened or stressed" (p. 215).

Hunger   Although many people have a difficult time believing it, thousands of children go to bed hungry every night. "It is estimated that at least 5.5 million children (one in eight children today in the United States) are regularly hungry, while another 6 million other children younger than age twelve are in families living on the edge of poverty and face chronic food shortages" (Davis, 1993, p. 11). Hunger leads to malnutrition, which in turn can result in damage to a developing neurological system. Children who are hungry have a difficult time concentrating on schoolwork and frequently display behavior problems in the classroom. Although free school lunch and breakfast programs have been expanded during the past years, hunger among schoolchildren still remains a significant problem in the United States.

Health Care   Children who grow up in poverty are unlikely to receive adequate health care. Although significant progress with childhood diseases such as polio and whooping cough has been made during the past forty years, the health status of many children today is below that of children in other countries. In 1993, 20.1 percent of poor children had no health insurance (U.S. Department of Commerce, 1995). Poverty appears to be directly associated with many of the health problems experienced by children today (Healthy People 2000, 1992). Just as children who are hungry have difficulties concentrating, children who are unhealthy may miss school and fall behind academically.

CONSIDER THIS

What actions might American society take that could have an impact on the level of poverty? What are some barriers to doing these things?

Implications for School Personnel Unfortunately, teachers and other school personnel cannot do much to alleviate directly the base cause of poverty experienced by students. However, teachers can reduce the impact of poverty on achievement and behavior by:

- Recognizing the impact that poverty can have on students
- Making all students in the classroom feel important
- Establishing a strong, trusting relationship, as noted previously
- Avoiding placing students in situations in which limited family finances become obvious to other students
- Initiating and coordinating with school social workers or other school personnel who can work with family members to secure social services
- Realizing and preparing for the reality that students may not have supplies and other equipment required for certain class activities, and seeking contingency funds or other means that could be used to help pay for these items

> **TEACHING TIP**
>
> A teacher should maintain supplies that all students can use when they do not have the necessary materials.

See the nearby Personal Spotlight feature, which further highlights this issue.

Students Who Are Homeless

As Wilder, Okiakor, and Algozzine (2003) eloquently state, "the success of any society can be ascertained by how it treats its members who have the greatest needs" (p. 9). One area that does not reflect well on current society is the reality of homelessness. A

Personal Spotlight

School Counselor

Sara Gillison has been a school counselor for seven years. During that time, she has generally worked in inner-city schools where poverty is a fact of life for many children. In the two schools where she serves as the elementary counselor, approximately 35 percent of students qualify for a free or reduced-price lunch. Many of the problems that she deals with as the school counselor are related to poverty.

"One of the most difficult things for me to do is identify with these families. Unlike most of my friends growing up, many of the students I see on a daily basis do not have many of the basic things they need. They may not have decent clothes, or even enough to eat at night. I have to try to remember every day that my life experiences are just different and try not to project onto my students and their families the same experiences I have had."

Sara notes that the poverty many of her students experience has a wide-ranging impact on their performances in school. She states, "Many of the children who come from obvious poverty are less likely to be prepared for school every day. They often appear to be tired and uninterested. I wonder, sometimes, how much rest they get at home." She notes that while some poor children do well in school, for most it seems to be a struggle that closely relates to their struggle with everyday life.

Sara Gillison
Lakewood Elementary School, North Little Rock, AR

Sara has had to attempt to understand the impact of poverty on the families she counsels. She notes, "The first time I tried to have a parent conference with a student who was not doing well, I could not understand why the mother or father would not come to a meeting. Finally I realized that not only did they feel uncomfortable because of their personal history of school problems, but also that they did not have transportation. Not having access to personal transportation is not something I used to think of. However, after working with students who come from impoverished backgrounds, one of the first things I try to find out is whether or not the family has a car or access to transportation, and whether or not they have a telephone."

Sara does believe school personnel can deal effectively with children who come from poverty, although it is very difficult. The best advice she can give to teachers and other school people is to try to make these students feel good about themselves and experience success. "Success goes so far with all students," Sara notes, "but for students who are poor, school success can mean the difference between being a failure in life or making it."

tragedy of the new century is the growing number of homeless people in the United States. The number of individuals who do not have homes has risen to epidemic proportions. According to the National Law Center on Homelessness and Poverty (2004), approximately 3.5 million people (1.35 million of them children) are likely to experience homelessness in a given year.

While historically the homeless population has been thought to be made up of aging adults, often with mental illness or alcohol problems, today as many as 39 percent of all homeless persons are children—with 42 percent of these children under the age of five (National Coalition for the Homeless, 2006). "On any given night, it is estimated that between 50,000 and 200,000 children are homeless in the United States" (Davis, 1993, p. 16). The National Coalition for the Homeless (2006) underscored the impact that homelessness has on families:

> Homelessness is a devastating experience for families. It disrupts virtually every aspect of family life, damaging the physical and emotional health of family members, interfering with children's education and development, and frequently resulting in the separation of family members. (p. 1)

More chilling is the realization that homelessness is not a fringe issue (National Center for Homeless Education, 2005)—many of us are not that far away from being homeless. One catastrophe (e.g., a hurricane like Katrina) can change our lives dramatically.

Federal Backdrop   Federal legislation now exists to guide policy and practice throughout the United States. The McKinney-Vento Homeless Assistance Act (2001), which was part of the No Child Left Behind Act of 2001, is a reauthorization of previously enacted legislation (McKinney Homeless Assistance Act of 1987) regarding this population. Following is the definition of "homeless children and youth" under the current law.

(A)   individuals who lack a fixed, regular, and adequate nighttime residence . . ., and
(B)   includes—
   (i) children and youths who are sharing the housing of other persons due to loss of housing, economic hardship, or a similar reason; are living in motels, hotels, trailer parks, or camping grounds due to the lack of alternative accommodations; are living in emergency or transitional shelters; are abandoned in hospitals; or are awaiting foster care placement;
   (ii) children and youths who have a primary nighttime residence that is a public or private place not designed for or ordinarily used as a regular sleeping accommodation for human beings . . .
   (iii) children and youths who are living in cars, parks, public spaces, abandoned buildings, substandard housing, bus or train stations, or similar settings; and
   (iv) migratory children who qualify as homeless for the purposes of this subtitle because the children are living in circumstances described in clauses (i) and (iii). (Section 725, Subtitle B, Title VII)

This act requires that each state have on record a plan for the education of homeless students. Every local school system must designate someone as liaison for homeless students and must provide access to appropriate education for these students.

Presenting Issues   Poverty and the lack of affordable housing are directly associated with homelessness. Today making minimum wage does not provide enough income for one to afford a one- or two-bedroom apartment at fair market rent (federally established standard). This situation has received national attention in the popular literature in books such as *Nickel and Dimed* (Ehrenreich, 2001). The complications that arise when a person is making only minimum wage, may not be employed full time, is a single parent, and has few outside supports are devastating.

As Elders (2002) noted, the key issues and problems of poverty also affect this group of children. The added impact of not having a home greatly compounds problems of

CEC STANDARDS

CEC 2: Development and Characteristics of Learners

INTASC

INTASC 2: How children learn and develop

PRAXIS

PRAXIS II: Understanding Exceptionalities

poverty. Children and youth who are homeless experience health problems, hunger, poor nutrition, academic achievement deficits, depression, and behavioral problems (Yamaguchi et al., 1997). In addition, children who are homeless are usually very embarrassed that they do not have a place to live. The dissolution of families is great as well.

Implications for School Personnel   Although some homeless students are able to stay in a shelter, many live on the streets, in cars, or in other public settings with their parents. Of course, school personnel can do little to find homes for these children. Probably the best advice is to avoid putting students in situations in which their homelessness will result in embarrassment. For example, going around the room after the students' birthday and having everyone tell, in graphic detail, about every gift they received may be very uncomfortable for students who do not even have a home to go to after school.

It is also important to realize that parents of homeless children are very likely to do everything they can to hide the fact that their family is homeless, typically as a precaution to avoid Child Protective Services from removing their children. As a result, they are very unlikely to inform school personnel of significant situations related to a student's life that would be beneficial to know.

We offer the following recommendations to school personnel in regard to students who are homeless and who are attending a particular school.

Figure 13.3   **Common Signs of Homelessness**

Lack of Continuity in Education
- Attendance at many different schools
- Lack of records needed for enrollment
- Gaps in skill development

Poor Health/Nutrition
- Lack of immunizations and/or immunization records
- Unmet medical and dental needs
- Chronic hunger (may hoard food)
- Fatigue (may fall asleep in class)

Transportation and Attendance Problems
- Erratic attendance or tardiness
- Inability to contact parents
- Numerous absences
- Avoidance of class field trips

Poor Hygiene
- Wearing the same clothes for several days
- Lack of shower facility or washers to stay clean

Not Ready for Class
- Lack of basic school supplies
- Concern for the safety of belongings
- Incomplete or missing homework

Social and Behavioral Cues
- Change in behavior
- "Old" beyond years
- Protective of parents
- Poor/short attention span
- Poor self-esteem
- Difficulty or avoidance of making friends
- Difficulty trusting people
- Need for immediate gratification

Reactions/Statements by Parent, Guardian, or Child
- Anger or embarrassment when asked about current address
- Mention of staying with grandparents, other relatives, friends, or in a motel
- Comments such as:
  - "I don't remember the name of my previous school."
  - "We've been moving around a lot."
  - "Our address is new; I can't remember it" (may hide lack of a permanent address).
  - "We're going through a bad time right now."

Note: These are general guidelines. There is significant variability among the school-age homeless population.

Warning signs adapted from flyers developed by the Illinois and Pennsylvania Departments of Education.

From National Center for Homeless Education www.serve.org/nche_web/warning.php

- Realize that a large percentage of homeless students will not attend school on a regular basis.
- Be vigilant and sensitive to students who may be homeless—the students may need services, but their families may fear that to get needed services, discovery is required and the forced breakup of the family may follow. A list of common signs of homelessness is presented in Figure 13.3
- Monitor behavior and progress in the classroom, paying particular attention to physical, health, emotional, and social manifestations.
- Do not expect homework of the same quality as that of children who have homes.
- Become a safe resource for students and their parents.

To work with parents who are homeless, teachers and other school personnel should consider the following:

- Arrange to meet parents at their place of work or at school.
- Offer to assist family members in securing services from available social service agencies.
- Do not require excessive school supplies that many families cannot afford.

Schools can use any of several program models when working with students who are homeless. A description of some of these programs can be found in Table 13.3.

Students in Single-Parent Homes

The nature of the American family has changed dramatically in a relatively short period of time. "During the 1980s, only 6 percent of all U.S. families fit the mold of the 1950s 'Ozzie and Harriet family': a working father, a housewife mother, and two children of public school age" (Davis, 1993, p. 14). The following facts describe the families of the late 1990s:

CONSIDER THIS

What factors found in single-parent homes have an impact on the level of student involvement with schools?

- The percentage of children living in a home with only one parent went from 12.8 percent in 1970 to 27 percent in 1998.
- About 55 percent of African American children live in a home with only one parent.
- Approximately 31 percent of Hispanic children live in a home with only one parent.
- Nearly 70 percent of all children have mothers who work outside the home. (U.S. Census Bureau, 1999)

Figure 13.4 shows the composition of family groups with children, by race, from 1970 to 1998.

Many factors result in children being reared in single-parent homes, including divorce, death of a parent, significant illness of a parent, or a parent being incarcerated. And, as has been stated previously, being raised in a single-parent family does not imply that these families' situations are not healthy, nurturing, and encouraging. The reality is that when single parents are also living at poverty level or have other complications (e.g., substance abuse) in their lives, children and youth are placed at risk.

More than one-quarter of all children live with a single parent, usually a mother.

Children of Divorced Parents   Divorce in the United States is on an upward trend that shows no signs of decreasing. It is estimated that half of all new marriages will end in divorce. Although the birth rate is declining, the number of divorces in which children are involved is increasing (Chiriboga & Catron,

Table 13.3	**Program Models for the Education of Students Who Are Homeless**

Outreach Programs

District-based programs that employ a coordinator whose duties may include:

- maintaining communication among schools, shelters, and social service agencies
- visiting shelters on a daily basis to identify children who may need assistance with school enrollment
- assisting families with referrals to appropriate agencies for accessing necessary services
- providing students with clothing and school supplies
- assisting with school transportation arrangements
- conducting in-service training programs at school sites or to parent groups

District Schools

Schools located in the area of homeless shelters that provide special programs for students who are homeless. Programs include:

- assisting with the school registration process
- assisting with applications for appropriate services, such as free school breakfast and lunch and before- and after-school programs
- providing a free-clothing-and-school-supplies closet located at the school
- assessing the student's present academic levels for appropriate classroom placement
- tutoring and social skills programs for the student

Transition Room in Neighborhood Schools

A classroom located in the student's school that provides a temporary setting for children. Characteristics of the transition room include:

- providing a safe environment where children become acquainted with the school and teachers before moving into their permanent classrooms
- emphasizing the emotional needs of the child
- emphasizing the assessment of academic skills
- establishing good rapport with the family of the child
- providing assistance for the family as necessary
- providing clothing and school supplies as needed

Transition and Shelter Schools

Schools whose specific purpose is to serve students who are homeless. These may be located within a shelter or close to a shelter. When students are functioning well in this setting, they are moved into larger schools in the district. In this setting the goals include:

- providing intense and temporary assistance
- working on basic skills
- providing emotional support to help the children cope with the various levels of stress in their lives
- assisting with the basic needs of clothing, school supplies, food, and health services

After-School Programs

Programs that include all or some of the following:
- one-on-one tutoring
- help with homework
- opportunities to build friendships
- counseling and emotional support
- recreation, field trips, and other leisure activities

From "Children Who Are Homeless: Implications for Educators," by B. J. Yamaguchi, S. Strawser, and K. Higgins, 1997, *Intervention in School and Clinic, 33,* p. 94. Used by permission.

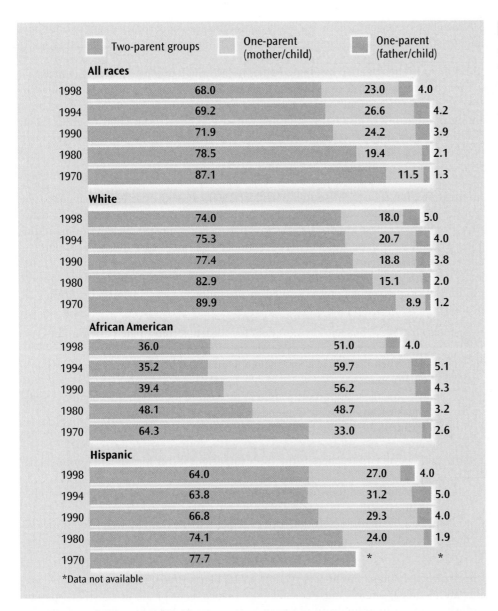

Figure 13.4

Composition of Family Groups with Children, by Race: 1970 to 1998

From *Population Profile of the United States, 1999* (p. ix), by U.S. Department of Commerce, Washington, DC: Bureau of the Census.

1991). Forty-four percent of U.S. children live in a nontraditional family unit, most often headed by a single, working mother (Austin, 1992). Divorce is a disorganizing and reorganizing process, particularly when children are involved, and the process often extends over several years (Morgan, 1985).

Divorce offers the potential for growth and new relationships, but too often it creates only problems for children and youth, and although some children cope very well with the trauma surrounding divorce, many react with major problems (Munger & Morse, 1992). The central dilemma in many divorces is the conflict of interest between the child's need for continuity of the family unit and the parents' decision to break up the family that has provided the child's main supports. Children react in many different ways to divorce, including the following: feeling guilt, developing anxiety, exhibiting social problems, experiencing grief, being angry, and displaying hostility.

Children in Homes Headed by Single Mothers   Most single-parent homes are headed by mothers (see Figure 13.4). The absence of a father figure may have a significant impact on the psychological development of a child (Saintonge, Achille, & Lachance,

TEACHING TIP

Involve school counselors and other support personnel when dealing with the emotional impact of divorce on children.

1993). The absence of the father seems to affect the academic achievement of both boys and girls, with lower achievement correlating with limited presence of the father.

Children in Homes Headed by Single Fathers   Although not nearly as prevalent as single-parent homes headed by mothers, the number of single-parent homes headed by fathers has increased significantly during the past decade. The effects of growing up in a single-parent home headed by a father vary a great deal from child to child. Some studies indicate that fathers are more likely to use other adults in their support networks than are single-parent mothers, and children seem to fare better with a large adult support network than with a limited one (Santrock & Warshak, 1979).

Implications for School Personnel   Children who find themselves in single-parent families as a result of divorce, death, illness, or incarceration require a great deal of support. For many of these children, the school may be their most stable environment during a transitional phase of their lives. School personnel must develop supports to prevent negative outcomes, such as school failure, manifestation of emotional problems, or the development of behavior problems. An interview conducted with children residing in single-parent homes resulted in the following conclusions concerning the positive role schools can play (Lewis, 1992):

- Schools are a place of security and safety for students from single-parent homes.
- Students who lose parents due to death are often treated differently by school personnel than when the loss is from divorce. Unfortunately, the child's needs are similar in both situations.
- Teachers are the most important people in the school for children who are in single-parent homes because of their tremendous influence on self-esteem.
- Students want to be treated just as they were before they became part of a single-parent home.
- Trust with peers and teachers is the most important factor for students from single-parent homes.
- School personnel need to be more sensitive to the new financial situation of families with only one parent.
- Keeping a log or diary is considered an excellent method for children to explore feelings and create opportunities for meaningful discussions.

There are many things schools should and should not do when dealing with students who are from single-parent homes (Wanat, 1992; Figure 13.5). For children whose parents are divorced, schools must consider the involvement of the noncustodial parent. Unfortunately, many schools do not even include spaces for information on forms for students' noncustodial parents (Austin, 1992). To ensure that noncustodial parents are afforded their rights regarding their children, and to actively solicit the involvement of the noncustodial parent, school personnel should:

- Establish policies that encourage the involvement of noncustodial parents
- Maintain records of information about the noncustodial parent
- Distribute information about school activities to noncustodial parents insist that noncustodial parents be involved in teacher conferences
- Structure parent conferences to facilitate the development of a shared relationship between the custodial and noncustodial parents
- Conduct surveys to determine the level of involvement desired by noncustodial parents (Austin, 1992)

Students Who Experience Significant Losses

Although the continued absence of one or both parents through separation or divorce is considered a loss, the loss created by the death of a parent or a sibling can result in significantly more emotionally related problems for children. Unlike children living in ear-

---

TEACHING TIP

Have male staff in the school take the lead in working with single fathers.

CONSIDER THIS

What things could school personnel do to make children from single-parent homes feel more secure?

CROSS-REFERENCE

Review Chapter 4 for due-process requirements of schools, and consider the impact single-parent homes have on these requirements.

Figure 13.5

Some DOs and DON'Ts When Working with Children with Single Parents

From "Meeting the Needs of Single-Parent Children: School and Parent Views Differ," by C. L. Wanat, 1992, *NAASP Bulletin, 76,* p. 47. Used by permission.

Some DOs

- Collect information about students' families.
- Analyze information about students' families to determine specific needs.
- Create programs and practices that address areas of need unique to particular schools.
- Include curricular areas that help students achieve success, such as study skills.
- Provide nonacademic programs such as child care and family counseling.
- Involve parents in determining appropriate roles for school and family.
- Take the initiative early in the year to establish a communication link with parents.
- Enlist the support of both parents, when possible.
- Provide a stable, consistent environment for children during the school day

Some DON'Ts

- Don't treat single parents differently than other parents.
- Don't call attention to the fact that a child lives with only one parent.
- Limit activities such as "father/son" night or other events that highlight the differences in a single-parent home.
- Don't have "room mothers," have "room parents."
- Don't overlook the limitations of single-parent homes in areas such as helping with projects, helping with homework, and so forth.

lier centuries, when extended families often lived together and children actually observed death close at hand (e.g., a grandparent), often in the home environment, children of today are generally insulated from death. Therefore, when death does occur, especially that of a significant person in a child's life, the result can be devastating, often resulting in major problems in school.

Death of a Parent   When a child's parent dies, whether unexpectedly or over the course of a long illness, external events impinge on the child's personality in three main ways (Felner, Ginter, Boike, & Cowan, 1981; Moriarty, 1967; Tennant, Bebbington, & Hurry, 1980):

- The child must deal with the reality of the death itself.
- The child must adapt to the resulting changes in the family.
- The child must contend with the perpetual absence of the lost parent.

Children respond in many different ways to a parent's death. Some responses are guilt, regression, denial, bodily distress, hostile reactions to the deceased, eating disorders, enuresis (incontinence), sleep disturbances, withdrawal, anxiety, panic, learning difficulties, and aggression (Anthony, 1972; Elizer & Kauffman, 1983; Van Eerdewegh, Bieri, Parrilla, & Clayton, 1982). It is also not unusual for sibling rivalry to become very intense and disruptive. Often, extreme family turmoil results from the death of a parent, especially when the parent who dies was the controlling person in the family (Van Eerdewegh et al., 1982).

Death of a Sibling   A sibling plays an important and significant part in family dynamics, so the death of a sibling can initiate a psychological crisis for a child. Sometimes the grief of the parents renders them unable to maintain a healthy parental relationship with the remaining child or children, significantly changing a child's life situation.

When experiencing the death of a sibling, children frequently fear that they will die. When an older sibling dies, the younger child may revert to childish behaviors in hopes of not getting older, thereby averting dying. Older children often react with extreme fear and anxiety, especially if they are ignored by parents during the grieving period. Often these children become preoccupied with the horrifying question about their own future

TEACHING TIP

Involve the school counselor, mental health professionals, and other support personnel when providing information on death and dying; invite these people into the classroom when a student is confronted with this issue.

"Will it happen to me tomorrow, or next week, or next year?" (McKeever, 1983). Children can also develop severe depression when a sibling dies (McKeever, 1983).

CEC STANDARDS

CEC 2: Development and
Characteristics of Learners

Implications for School Personnel   For the most part, the best advice for teachers is to be aware of how the student who experiences loss is doing when in school. Equally important is knowing when to contact the school counselor, if he or she is not already involved in some ongoing work with the student. Some of the issues that may arise require intervention that is outside the training and expertise of most teachers. So, knowing about other school-based and outside school resources is valuable. Some communities are fortunate to have private, nonprofit organizations that have been established to help surviving members of a family deal with the ongoing terminal illness or death of a parent or sibling. School counselors should be aware of such community resources.

INTASC

INTASC 2: How children learn
and develop

Students Who Are Abused and Neglected

PRAXIS

PRAXIS II: Understanding
Exceptionalities

Growing up in an abusive or neglectful family clearly places children at significant risk for a variety of pejorative outcomes, including school failure. Child abuse and neglect occur in families from every socioeconomic level, race, religion, and ethnic background. Family members, acquaintances, or strangers may be the source of the problem. Although there is typically no single cause that leads to abuse or neglect, many factors exist that add to the likelihood of these events occurring. Factors such as poverty, large family size, low maternal involvement with children, low maternal self-esteem, minimal father involvement, and a stepfather in the household are noteworthy (Brown, Cohen, Johnson, & Salzinger, 1998).

The data on the maltreatment of children, as displayed in Figure 13.6 and based on information collected in 2004 (U.S. Department of Health and Human Services, 2006), clearly indicate that the most frequently occurring type of maltreatment is neglect. During 2004, the data reveal that this occurred 7.4 times per 1,000 children. In 2004, 62.4 percent of victims experienced neglect, 17.5 percent experienced physical abuse, 9.7 percent experienced sexual abuse, 7.0 percent experienced psychological maltreatment. It should be noted that these data reflect reported cases and that the actual number of cases of maltreatment are higher due to many cases not being reported and confirmed.

The two major categories addressed in this section are **abuse** and **neglect**. They are different yet are typically covered together in state statutes. Child abuse implies some type of overt inappropriate action that results in negative outcomes for a child or adolescent. Neglect, however, refers to the omission or absence of basic behaviors that should be provided to children and youth and that also result in negative outcomes for the person. Each of these concepts have variations, as discussed below.

A variety of taxonomies exist for categorizing abuse and neglect. Data collected from states by the federal government, as shown in Figure 13.6, are organized into the following categories: physical abuse, neglect, medical neglect, sexual abuse, psychological or emotional maltreatment, and "other" (i.e., allows for variation in state reporting systems). The following discussion, organized around the two major concepts of abuse and neglect, uses the following system.

Abuse: emotional, physical, and sexual
Neglect: physical, educational, emotional, and medical

Abuse   There are three major types of abuse: emotional, physical, and sexual. **Emotional abuse**, sometimes referred to as psychological maltreatment, can be defined as "a pattern of behavior by parents or caregivers that can seriously interfere with a child's cognitive, emotional, psychological, or social development" (American Humane, 2004, p. 1). Emotional abuse, which accompanies all other forms of child abuse, can involve unreasonable demands placed on children by parents, siblings, peers, or teach-

| Figure 13.6 | **Victimization Rates by Maltreatment Type, 2000–2004 Child Maltreatment 2004** |

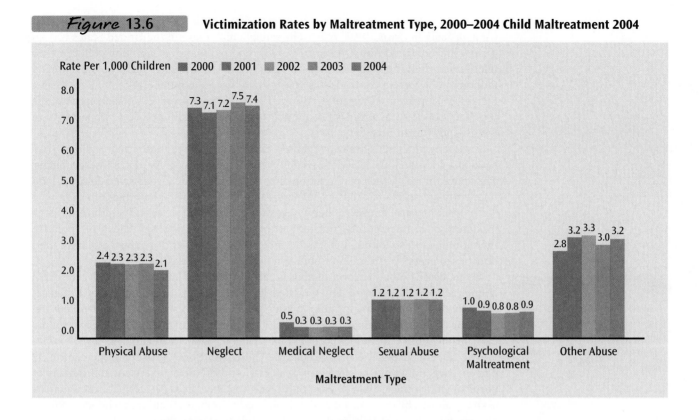

ers, or the failure of parents to provide the emotional support necessary for children to grow and develop (Thompson & Kaplan, 1999). Some examples of emotional abuse might include ignoring, rejecting, isolating, exploiting/corrupting, verbally assaulting, and terrorizing (American Humane, 2004).

Research has revealed that verbal abuse, by itself, can result in lowered self-esteem and school achievement (Solomon & Serres, 1999). Although difficult to identify, emotional abuse has several characteristics that may be exhibited by children who are being emotionally abused. These include:

- absence of a positive self-image
- behavioral extremes
- depression
- psychosomatic complaints
- attempted suicide
- impulsive, defiant, and antisocial behavior
- age-inappropriate behaviors
- inappropriate habits and tics
- enuresis
- inhibited intellectual or emotional development
- difficulty in establishing and maintaining peer relationships
- extreme fear, vigilance
- sleep and eating disorders
- self-destructive tendencies
- rigidly compulsive behaviors (Gargiulo, 1990, p. 22)

Physical abuse is more easily identified than emotional abuse and is defined as "nonaccidental trauma or physical injury caused by punching, beating, kicking, biting, burning, or otherwise harming a child" (*American Humane*, 2003, p. 1). It has also been defined as "any physical injury that has been caused by other than accidental means,

> **CONSIDER THIS**
>
> Think about how being abused would affect you at this point in your life, then transfer those feelings into a young child's perspective. How would these feelings affect the child's school activities?

including any injury which appears to be at variance with the explanation of the injury" (*At Risk Youth in Crisis*, 1991, p. 9). The rate of child abuse in the United States is staggering. Prevent Child Abuse America (1998) reported that over 3 million children were referred for child protective service agencies in the United States in 1997. More than 1 million children were confirmed as victims of abuse. The number of child abuse cases increased 41 percent between 1988 and 1997. Statistics from 2004 indicate that the prevalence of physical abuse is 2.1 out of every 1,000 U.S. children (U.S. Department of Health and Human Services, 2006).

Children who are physically abused are two to three times more likely than nonabused children to experience failing grades and to become discipline problems. They have difficulty with peer relationships, show physically aggressive behaviors, and frequently are substance abusers (Emery, 1989). Studies also show that children who suffer from physical abuse are likely to exhibit social skill deficits, including shyness, inhibited social interactions, and limited problem-solving skills. Deficits in cognitive functioning are also found in greater numbers in students who are abused than in their nonabused peers (Weston, Ludolph, Misle, Ruffins, & Block, 1990).

Sexual abuse is another form of abuse that puts children and youth at risk for school failure. Sexual abuse can be differentiated into three areas: "touching" sexual offenses (e.g., fondling, intercourse); "nontouching" sexual offenses (e.g., indecent exposure, exposing children to pornographic material); and "sexual exploitation" (e.g., prostitution, participating in the creation of pornographic material) (American Humane, 2003, p. 1).

The rate for sexual abuse of girls in the United States ranges from 15 percent to 32 percent, depending on the method of calculation used. Sexual abuse is more likely to occur in girls younger than the age of fifteen (Vogeltanz et al., 1999). Children may be sexually abused by their own families as well as by strangers. Children who are sexually abused not only are at risk for developing problems during their school years, but also will typically manifest problems throughout their adulthood (Silverman, Reinherz, & Giaconia, 1996).

School personnel should be aware of typical physical and behavioral symptoms of sexual abuse:

* Physical injuries to the genital area
* Sexually transmitted diseases
* Difficulty in urinating
* Discharges from the penis or vagina
* Pregnancy
* Aggressive behavior toward adults, especially a child's own parents
* Sexual self-consciousness
* Sexual promiscuity and acting out
* Inability to establish appropriate relationships with peers
* Running away, stealing, and abusing substances
* Using the school as a sanctuary, coming early, and not wanting to go home

Neglect   Neglect refers to situations where a child is exposed to a substantial risk of harm. Neglect is much more difficult to recognize, as no visible physical signs of neglect are evident—unless, of course, physical harm does occur. Signs of neglect are reflected through behaviors. Examples of neglect could include placing a child in an unsupervised situation that could result in bodily injury, failing to seek and obtain proper medical care for a child, or failing to provide adequate food, clothing, or shelter. As mentioned earlier, it is this last element that casts fear into the minds of parents who are homeless. The four major types of neglect, as defined by American Humane (2003), are listed below.

* *Physical neglect:* generally involves the parent or caregiver not providing the child with the basic necessities (e.g., adequate food, clothing, shelter).

CROSS-REFERENCE

Review Chapter 6 on emotional and behavioral disorders, and consider the impact of child abuse on emotional and behavioral functioning.

- *Educational neglect:* failure of a parent or caregiver to enroll a child of mandatory school age in school or provide appropriate home schooling or needed special education training, thus allowing the child or youth to engage in chronic truancy.
- *Emotional neglect:* includes actions such as engaging in chronic or extreme spousal abuse in the child's presence, allowing a child to use drugs or alcohol, refusing or failing to provide needed psychological care, constantly belittling the child, and withholding affection.
- *Medical neglect:* failure to provide appropriate health care for a child (although financially able to do so), thus placing the child at risk of being seriously disabled or disfigured or dying. (pp. 1–2)

Implications for School Personnel   The first thing that school personnel should be prepared to do when dealing with children and youth who might be abused or neglected is to report any incident to the appropriate agencies. In most states, school personnel and other professionals who work with children have a legal, if not a moral, obligation to report suspected child abuse or neglect. In some states, any person who suspects abuse or neglect has a mandate to report it. For instance, Texas statutes (Texas Family Code) include the following mandate:

> Any person having cause to believe that a child's physical or mental health or welfare has been or may be adversely affected by abuse or neglect must report the case to any local or state law enforcement agency and to the Texas Department of Protective and Regulatory Services. (Chapter 34)

Failure to report a case is a punishable offense. The Suspected Child Abuse Network (SCAN) provides a reporting network for referral purposes. School personnel need to understand their responsibility in reporting suspected abuse and know the specific procedures to follow when making such a report. In addition to reporting suspected cases of abuse, schools in general can do the following:

- Work with local government officials to establish awareness of child abuse and neglect as a priority in the community.
- Organize a telephone "hotline" service where parents or other caregivers can call for support when they believe a crisis is impending in their families.
- Offer parent education programs that focus on parenting skills, behavior management techniques, child-care suggestions, and communication strategies.
- Establish a local chapter of Parents Anonymous, a volunteer group for individuals who have a history of abusing their children.
- Develop workshops on child abuse for concerned individuals and disseminate literature on the topic.
- Arrange visits by public health nurses to help families at risk for abuse after the birth of their first child.
- Provide short-term respite day care through a Mother's Day Out program.
- Encourage individuals to serve as foster parents in the community.
- Institute a parent-aide program in which parent volunteers assist single-parent homes by providing support.
- Make structured group therapy available to abuse victims. (Kruczek & Vitanza, 1999)

School-based personnel should consider the following suggestions:

- Provide a safe classroom where students can flourish.
- Be vigilant for the signs of abuse and neglect in students.
- Make yourself recognizable as a person in whom a student can confide very personal information—every student needs someone like this.
- Try not to show any extreme emotion when a student discloses information to you. Remain calm, interested, and reassuring.

CEC STANDARDS

CEC 2: Characteristics and Development of Learners

INTASC

INTASC 2: How children learn and develop

PRAXIS

PRAXIS II: Understanding Exceptionalities

- Report any suspected situations knowing that you are immune from civil or criminal liability as long as the report was made in good faith and without malice.
- Understand that a student who confides in you (i.e., shares very personal information about being abused) in all likelihood will ask you not to tell anyone—and yet you will have to do so. As a result, avoid promising to abide by any preconditions a student may ask of you.
- Understand that initially a student who confided information to you on which you had to take action will feel that you betrayed him or her. For a period of time your relationship with this person will be rough. Ultimately, the student is likely to come around and appreciate what you did.

Students Who Abuse Substances

Substance abuse among children and adolescents results in major problems and places students significantly at risk for school failure (Vaughn & Long, 1999). Students who are abusing substances have a much more difficult time succeeding in school than do their peers. While most people consider substance abuse to relate to the improper use of alcohol and drugs, it can also refer to the use of tobacco, as many health issues are related to tobacco.

Substance abuse among children declined during the late 1980s and early 1990s, then increased again in the late 1990s (*Teen drug use is on the rise again*, 1996; *The condition of education*, 1998). From 2004 to 2005, substance abuse for most drugs decreased or remained stable, according to the National Institute on Drug Abuse (2006). The substance that youth use the most is alcohol. According to data gathered by the National Institute on Drug Abuse (2006), 68.6 percent of high school seniors reported using alcohol during the previous school year. Elders (2002) reported that a third of high school students said that they engaged in binge drinking. Table 13.4 shows the percentage of eighth-graders, tenth-graders, and twelfth-graders using drugs, by type of drug, between 2002 and 2005. The table provides information for four time frames: if ever used during one's lifetime; if used within the past twelve months; if used within the past month; if used daily.

The disturbing fact is that after years of drug abuse education, the use of alcohol and certain drugs has not been significantly influenced. Another more alarming fact about substance abuse is that while the level of use by twelfth-graders has decreased or remained virtually constant, the level of use by younger students (eighth-graders) has increased significantly. For example, in 1991 only 3.2 percent of eighth-graders indicated that they had used marijuana or hashish during the previous thirty days. This number is now reported to be 6.6 percent, as indicated in Table 13.4. Nagel and colleagues (1996) report that boys have a tendency to use illegal drugs slightly more than do girls, but that girls actually use more over-the-counter drugs inappropriately than boys do.

While no factors are always associated with drug use in children and youth, some appear to increase the likelihood of such use. Parental factors—such as drug use by parents, parents' attitudes about drug use, family management styles, and parent-child communication patterns—have an impact on children's drug use (Young, Kersten, & Werch, 1996). Additional cross-pressures—such as the perception of friends' approval or disapproval of drug use, peer pressure to use drugs, and the assessment of individual risk—also play a role (Robin & Johnson, 1996).

Although a great deal of attention has been paid to the impact of marijuana, cocaine, and alcohol abuse on children and youth, only recently has attention been focused on inhalants. Inhalant use increased for every grade level from 1991 to 1995 (*The condition of education*, 1998) and remains at high levels. One of the problems with inhalants is the wide number that can be used by students, many of which are readily available. Examples include cleaning solvents, gasoline, room deodorizers, glue, perfume, wax, and spray paint.

Table 13.4   **Monitoring the Future Study: Trends in Prevalence of Various Drugs for 8th-Graders, 10th-Graders, and 12th-Graders 2002–2005**

Note: [Bracketed figures in the tables below indicate statistically significant changes between 2004 and 2005]

	8th-Graders				10th-Graders				12th-Graders			
	2002	2003	2004	2005	2002	2003	2004	2005	2002	2003	2004	2005
Any Illicit Drug Use												
lifetime	24.5	22.8	21.5	**21.4**	44.6	41.4	39.8	**38.2**	53.0	51.1	51.1	**50.4**
annual	17.7	16.1	15.2	**15.5**	34.8	32.0	31.1	**29.8**	41.0	39.3	38.8	**38.4**
30-day	10.4	9.7	8.4	**8.5**	20.8	19.5	18.3	**17.3**	25.4	24.1	23.4	**23.1**
Marijuana/Hashish												
lifetime	19.2	17.5	16.3	**16.5**	38.7	36.4	35.1	**34.1**	47.8	46.1	45.7	**44.8**
annual	14.6	12.8	11.8	**12.2**	30.3	28.2	27.5	**26.6**	36.2	34.9	34.3	**33.6**
30-day	8.3	7.5	6.4	**6.6**	17.8	17.0	15.9	**15.2**	21.5	21.2	19.9	**19.8**
daily	1.2	1.0	0.8	**1.0**	3.9	3.6	3.2	**3.1**	6.0	6.0	5.6	**5.0**
Inhalants												
lifetime	15.2	15.8	17.3	**17.1**	13.5	12.7	12.4	**13.1**	11.7	11.2	10.9	**11.4**
annual	7.7	8.7	9.6	**9.5**	5.8	5.4	5.9	**6.0**	4.5	3.9	4.2	**5.0**
30-day	3.8	4.1	4.5	**4.2**	2.4	2.2	2.4	**2.2**	1.5	1.5	1.5	**2.0**
Hallucinogens												
lifetime	4.1	4.0	3.5	**3.8**	7.8	6.9	6.4	**5.8**	12.0	10.6	9.7	**8.8**
annual	2.6	2.6	2.2	**2.4**	4.7	4.1	4.1	**4.0**	6.6	5.9	6.2	**5.5**
30-day	1.2	1.2	1.0	**1.1**	1.6	1.5	1.6	**1.5**	2.3	1.8	1.9	**1.9**
LSD												
lifetime	2.5	2.1	1.8	**1.9**	5.0	3.5	2.8	**2.5**	8.4	5.9	4.6	**[3.5]**
annual	1.5	1.3	1.1	**1.2**	2.6	1.7	1.6	**1.5**	3.5	1.9	2.2	**1.8**
30-day	0.7	0.6	0.5	**0.5**	0.7	0.6	0.6	**0.6**	0.7	0.6	0.7	**0.7**
Cocaine												
lifetime	3.6	3.6	3.4	**3.7**	6.1	5.1	5.4	**5.2**	7.8	7.7	8.1	**8.0**
annual	2.3	2.2	2.0	**2.2**	4.0	3.3	3.7	**3.5**	5.0	4.8	5.3	**5.1**
30-day	1.1	0.9	0.9	**1.0**	1.6	1.3	1.7	**1.5**	2.3	2.1	2.3	**2.3**
Crack Cocaine												
lifetime	2.5	2.5	2.4	**2.4**	3.6	2.7	2.6	**2.5**	3.8	3.6	3.9	3.5
annual	1.6	1.6	1.3	**1.4**	2.3	1.6	1.7	**1.7**	2.3	2.2	2.3	1.9
30-day	0.8	0.7	0.6	**0.6**	1.0	0.7	0.8	**0.7**	1.2	0.9	1.0	1.0
Heroin												
lifetime	1.6	1.6	1.6	**1.5**	1.8	1.5	1.5	**1.5**	1.7	1.5	1.5	**1.5**
annual	0.9	0.9	1.0	**0.8**	1.1	0.7	0.9	**0.9**	1.0	0.8	0.9	**0.8**
30-day	0.5	0.4	0.5	**0.5**	0.5	0.3	0.5	**0.5**	0.5	0.4	0.5	**0.5**
Tranquilizers												
lifetime	4.3	4.4	4.0	**4.1**	8.8	7.8	7.3	**7.1**	11.4	10.2	10.6	**9.9**
annual	2.6	2.7	2.5	**2.8**	6.3	5.3	5.1	**4.8**	7.7	6.7	7.3	**6.8**
30-day	1.2	1.4	1.2	**1.3**	2.9	2.4	2.3	**2.3**	3.3	2.8	3.1	**2.9**
Alcohol												
lifetime	47.0	45.6	43.9	**[41.0]**	66.9	66.0	64.2	**63.2**	78.4	76.6	76.8	**75.1**
annual	38.7	37.2	36.7	**[33.9]**	60.0	59.3	58.2	**56.7**	71.5	70.1	70.6	**[68.6]**
30-day	19.6	19.7	18.6	**17.1**	35.4	35.4	35.2	**[33.2]**	48.6	47.5	48.0	**47.0**
daily	0.7	0.8	0.6	**0.5**	1.8	1.5	1.3	**1.3**	3.5	3.2	2.8	**3.1**

Table 13.4		Continued										
	8th-Graders				**10th-Graders**				**12th-Graders**			
	2002	2003	2004	2005	2002	2003	2004	2005	2002	2003	2004	2005
Cigarettes (any use)												
lifetime	31.4	28.4	27.9	[25.9]	47.4	43.0	40.7	**38.9**	57.2	53.7	52.8	[50.0]
30-day	10.7	10.2	9.2	**9.3**	17.7	16.7	16.0	**14.9**	26.7	24.4	25.0	**23.2**
daily	5.1	4.5	4.4	**4.0**	10.1	8.9	8.3	**7.5**	16.9	15.8	15.6	[13.6]
1/2 pack +/day	2.1	1.8	1.7	**1.7**	4.4	4.1	3.3	**3.1**	9.1	8.4	8.0	[6.9]
Smokeless Tobacco												
lifetime	11.2	11.3	11.0	**10.1**	16.9	14.6	13.8	**14.5**	18.3	17.0	16.7	**17.5**
30-day	3.3	4.1	4.1	**3.3**	6.1	5.3	4.9	**5.6**	6.5	6.7	6.7	**7.6**
daily	0.8	0.8	1.0	**0.7**	1.7	1.8	1.6	**1.9**	2.0	2.2	2.8	**2.5**
Steroids												
lifetime	2.5	2.5	1.9	**1.7**	3.5	3.0	2.4	**2.0**	4.0	3.5	3.4	2.6
annual	1.5	1.4	1.1	**1.1**	2.2	1.7	1.5	**1.3**	2.5	2.1	2.5	[1.5]
30-day	0.8	0.7	0.5	**0.5**	1.0	0.8	0.8	**0.6**	1.4	1.3	1.6	[0.9]
MDMA												
lifetime	4.3	3.2	2.8	**2.8**	6.6	5.4	4.3	**4.0**	10.5	8.3	7.5	[5.4]
annual	2.9	2.1	1.7	**1.7**	4.9	3.0	2.4	**2.6**	7.4	4.5	4.0	**3.0**
30-day	1.4	0.7	0.8	**0.6**	1.8	1.1	0.8	**1.0**	2.4	1.3	1.2	**1.0**
Methamphetamine												
lifetime	3.5	3.9	2.5	**3.1**	6.1	5.2	5.3	[4.1]	6.7	6.2	6.2	[4.5]
annual	2.2	2.5	1.5	**1.8**	3.9	3.3	3.0	2.9	3.6	3.2	3.4	[2.5]
30-day	1.1	1.2	0.6	**0.7**	1.8	1.4	1.3	**1.1**	1.7	1.7	1.4	[0.9]
Vicodin												
annual	2.5	2.8	2.5	**2.6**	6.9	7.2	6.2	**5.9**	9.6	10.5	9.3	**9.5**
OxyContin												
annual	1.3	1.7	1.7	**1.8**	3.0	3.6	3.5	**3.2**	4.0	4.5	5.0	**5.5**

From March 2006 National Survey on Drug Use and Health: National Findings. U.S. Department of Health and Human Services.

CEC STANDARDS

CEC 2: Development and Characteristics of Learners

INTASC

INTASC 2: How children learn and develop

PRAXIS

PRAXIS II: Understanding Exceptionalities

Implications for School Personnel   School personnel must be alert to the signs of substance abuse, whether the substance is alcohol, marijuana, inhalants, or some other drug of choice. The following characteristics, though they may not imply abuse in and of themselves, can be associated with substance abuse:

- Inability to concentrate
- Chronic absenteeism
- Poor grades or neglect of homework
- Poor scores on standardized tests not related to IQ or learning disabilities
- Uncooperative and quarrelsome behavior
- Sudden behavior changes
- Shy and withdrawn behavior
- Compulsive behaviors
- Chronic health problems
- Low self-esteem
- Anger, anxiety, and depression
- Poor coping skills
- Unreasonable fears
- Difficulty adjusting to changes

Once a student is identified as having a substance abuse problem, a supportive classroom environment must be provided (Lisnov, Harding, Safer, & Kavenagh, 1998). This includes a structured program to build self-esteem and create opportunities for students to be successful. Referral to professionals who are trained to work with individuals who abuse substances is also recommended. Research has shown that substance-abusing adolescents do not respond positively to lecturing. Rather, successes appear to be related to the development of self-esteem and interventions that are supportive. School personnel involved with students who are substance abusers should consider establishing connections with Alcoholics Anonymous and Narcotics Anonymous to help provide support (Vaughn & Long, 1999).

Students Who Become Pregnant

Teenage pregnancy in the United States remains at a high rate, even though it has decreased in recent years since reaching its peak in 1990. The teenage pregnancy rate in 2000 was 83.6 pregnancies per 1,000 women aged fifteen to nineteen (Alan Guttmacher Institute, 2004).

Breault and Trail (2005) reviewed the research on teenage pregnancy and state that a group of characteristics are associated with a greater likelihood that a young woman may get pregnant. They identified the following factors: external locus of control; self-efficacy; age at onset of sexual experience; socioeconomic status; level of education; mother's level of education; and ethnicity; race, locale, and family history of the teenage mother.

While there are many unfortunate outcomes from teenage pregnancy, including an increased risk that the resulting child will have problems, one of the most prevalent is that the teenage mother will drop out of school (Trad, 1999). In an era of extensive sex education and fear of HIV/AIDS, the continued high levels of teenage pregnancy are surprising. Despite all the information available for adolescents about sex and sexually transmitted diseases (STDs), it appears that many adolescents continue to engage in unprotected sexual activity (Weinbender & Rossignol, 1996).

School personnel should get involved in teenage pregnancy issues before pregnancy occurs. Sex education, information about HIV, and the consequences of unprotected sex should be a curricular focus. Unfortunately, sex education and practices such as distributing free condoms are very controversial, and many schools refuse to get involved in such emotion-laden issues.

> **TEACHING TIP**
>
> Work with school health personnel or state department of education personnel to obtain useful and appropriate teaching materials and suggestions for HIV/AIDS education.

Implications for School Personnel   In addition to having a pregnancy prevention program, school personnel can do the following to intervene in teenage pregnancy situations:

- Provide counseling and parent skills training for girls who become pregnant.
- Develop programs that encourage girls who are pregnant to remain in school—these programs need to include the availability of a school-based child-care program.
- Do not discriminate against students who become pregnant, have children, or are married.
- Work with families of girls who are pregnant to ensure that family support is present.
- Provide counseling support and parent skills training for boys who are fathers.

Students Who Are Gay, Lesbian, Bisexual, or Transgendered

One of the most vulnerable and overlooked groups who might be at risk comprises those students whose sexual identity differs from those around them. Currently referred to in general as LGBT youth, this group includes students who are **gay**, **lesbian**, **bisexual**, or **transgendered**. Statistics point out that these students have experienced some uncomfortable situations when at school. A study conducted by the Gay, Lesbian,

Students whose sexual identity differs from those around them often remain unidentified as at risk.

and Straight Education Network (GLSEN) (2005) found that LGBT youth had experienced the following:

- 75.4 percent had heard derogatory remarks frequently at school
- 37.8 percent were physically harassed
- 17.6 percent were physically assaulted (beaten, punched, kicked)
- LGBT students skipped school five times more often than the general population of students.
- GPAs for students who were physically harassed was half a grade lower than that of LGBT who experienced less harassment.

The home environment for this population may also be an unsafe environment. This is especially true in cases where parents have a difficult time accepting a child who "comes out" or tells family members about this difference. Many LGBT youth experience physical violence at home.

Presenting Issues   Youth who are LGBT come to school feeling that very few, if any, school-based staff understand their situation. To a great extent, they are correct. Most school personnel do lack understanding of their needs and the daily dynamics of their lives at school. Most of the time, this lack of understanding is unintentional; sometimes it is not. This group of students in general is prone to being absent more frequently than their classmates and to dropping out of school more often as a result of their discomfort and lack of safety at school. Positive outcomes are achieved when schools have a staff that is supportive and understanding (GLSEN, 2005).

On a personal level, LGBT youth are at greater risk for depression and attempting suicide. They often feel alienated and isolated. Substance abuse is greater with this group. Furthermore, these students find themselves homeless more often than their straight peers, as they are sometimes thrown out of their homes by parents. It should be noted that some LGBT students report very positive and productive school experiences.

Implications for School Personnel   A number of actions can be taken to improve the climate of acceptance for LGBT youth. Some district-and school-level suggestions include the following:

- Include sexual orientation in all antiharassment and antidiscrimination policies.
- Educate all school-based personnel regarding LGBT issues.
- Commit resources to this issue.
- Have diversity days that include LGBT youth.
- Establish a clear antislur policy.
- Develop and disseminate positive images and resources. (American Civil Liberties Union Freedom Network, n.d.)

Teachers, as mentioned earlier, play a key role. The following suggestions can be helpful to teachers and students who are LGBT:

- Recognize your own attitudes about this topic.
- Refer LGBT youth who are experiencing personal problems to personnel who are more comfortable with this issue, if you are not.
- Recognize your obligations to act on the behalf of LGBT youth when their rights are violated or policies are disregarded (e.g., harassment).
- Create and maintain a safe classroom environment.
- Let students know if you are a "safe" person with whom they can consult if they need to do so.

CEC STANDARDS

CEC 2: Development and Characteristics of Learners

- Create and maintain a classroom environment where diversity is respected and different points of view are welcomed.
- Use language in the classroom that is sexual-orientation neutral.
- Include LGBT topics in the curriculum if at all possible.

INTASC

INTASC 2: How children learn and develop

Students Who Are Delinquents

Students who get into trouble with legal authorities are frequently labeled as *socially maladjusted* or *juvenile delinquents*. Morrison (1997) defines delinquency as "behavior that violates the rules and regulations of the society" (p. 189). Juvenile delinquency often results in school failure; students who are involved in illegal activities often do not focus on school activities. Juvenile delinquency must be considered in conjunction with other factors related to at-risk students, although the relationship of these factors may be difficult to discern. Juvenile delinquency is highly correlated with substance abuse and may be found in higher rates among poor children than among children who are raised in adequate income environments. It is also more prevalent in single-parent homes (Morgan, 1994).

Juvenile delinquency is frequently related to gang activity. Gangs currently represent a major problem for adolescents, especially in large urban areas. In 1997, there were approximately 30,500 gangs in the United States with 816,000 gang members (National Youth Gang Center, 1999). Morgan (1994) cites numerous studies showing that adolescents raised in single-parent homes or homes that sustain a great deal of conflict often join gangs and exhibit other delinquent behaviors. Again, although no single factor leads children to delinquent behaviors, certain factors can indicate high risk. Delinquent behaviors often disrupt school success. School personnel need to work with legal and social service agencies to reduce delinquency and academic failure. In addition, the educational needs of children with disabilities who are in the juvenile justice system must be met the same as for other children with disabilities (Robinson & Rapport, 1999).

PRAXIS

PRAXIS II: Understanding Exceptionalities

Strategies for Curriculum and Instruction for Students Who Are At Risk

There are four primary approaches to dealing with students who are at risk for failure in schools: prevention programs, compensatory education, intervention programs, and transition programs. Figure 13.7 depicts these four orientations.

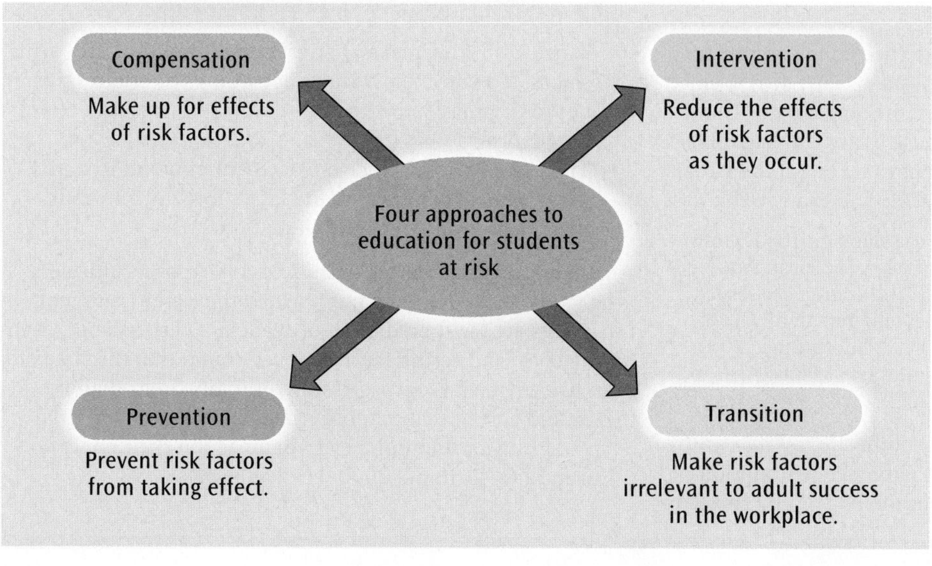

CONSIDER THIS

How can programs like Head Start have an impact on students who are at risk? Should these programs be continuously emphasized? Why or why not?

Figure 13.7

Four Approaches to Education for Students at Risk

From *Teaching in America* (p. 193), by G. S. Morrison, 1997. Boston: Allyn & Bacon. Used by permission.

Prevention programs focus on developing appropriate skills and behaviors that lead to success and, if used, are incompatible with other undesirable behaviors. Prevention programs also attempt to keep certain negative factors from having an impact on students. Drug prevention programs, antismoking educational efforts, and sex education programs are examples of efforts designed to establish responsible behaviors and keep students from developing problem behaviors.

Compensatory education programs "are designed to compensate or make up for existing or past risk factors and their effects in students' lives" (Morrison, 1997, p. 192). Head Start and Chapter I reading programs are examples of efforts to reduce the impact of poverty on children (Morrison, 1997). Reading Recovery, a program that is gaining popularity, has been shown to effectively improve the reading skills of at-risk students (Dorn & Allen, 1995; Ross, Smith, Casey, & Slavin, 1995).

Intervention programs focus on eliminating risk factors. They include teaching teenagers how to be good parents and early intervention programs that target at-risk preschool children (Sexton et al., 1996).

Finally, **transition programs** are designed to help students see the relationship between what they learn in school and how it will be used in the real world. School-to-career programs, which help students move from school to work, are effective transition programs (Morrison, 1997).

After-school programs, along with involvement with various school-sponsored extracurricular activities, provide schools with an opportunity to implement many strategies that are effective with at-risk students. Many students who are at risk for problems face extreme challenges in the afternoon hours following school. "School-age children and teens who are unsupervised during the hours after school are far more likely to use alcohol, drugs, and tobacco, engage in criminal and other high-risk behaviors, receive poor grades, and drop out of school than those children who have the opportunity to benefit from constructive activities supervised by responsible adults" (Safe and Smart, 1998, p. 5). After-school programs combine prevention, intervention, and compensatory programs.

Schools must ensure that they do not discriminate against at-risk students because of their race or socioeconomic status. The use of nondiscriminatory assessment is mandated by IDEA. The nearby Rights & Responsibilities feature focuses on this issue.

CEC STANDARDS

CEC 4: Instructional Strategies

INTASC

INTASC 4: Instructional strategies

PRAXIS

PRAXIS II: Delivery of Services to Students with Disabilities

At-Risk Children's Right to Nondiscriminatory Assessment

Schools are required, under IDEA, to use nondiscriminatory practices when evaluating students, since many at-risk children experience poverty and come from single-parent homes and homes where English is not the primary language. The case law supporting this requirement came out of the *Larry P. v. Riles* case that was first filed in 1972. The court in this case

held that schools no longer may use standardized IQ tests for the purpose of identifying and placing African American children into segregated special education classes for students classified as educable mentally retarded. . . .

The district court found that the Stanford-Binet, Wechsler, and Leiter IQ tests discriminate against African Americans on several grounds.

1. They measure achievement, not ability.
2. They rest on the "plausible but unproven assumption that intelligence is distributed in the population in accor-

dance with a normal statistical curve" and thus are "artificial tools to rank individuals according to certain skills, not to diagnose a medical condition (the presence of retardation)."
3. They "necessarily" lead to placement of more African Americans than Whites into classes for students with mild or moderate mental retardation.

On appeal, the Ninth Circuit Court of Appeals affirmed the lower court decision and rejected the state's argument that tests are good predictors of academic performance, even if they have a discriminatory impact; found that the state did not use any means of diagnosing disability other than IQ tests; and agreed that inappropriate placement of children can result in a profound negative impact on their education (Turnbull & Turnbull, 2000, pp. 153–154).

Characteristics of Effective Programs

Several factors are associated with schools that provide effective programs for students who are at risk. The U.S. Department of Education has noted that some research-based school reform models have been very successful in improving the achievement scores of students who are at risk for school failure. While differing in many respects, successful programs appear to share several characteristics (Tools for Schools, 1998):

CONSIDER THIS

Why have research-based reform models been successful in improving the achievement scores of students who are at risk for failure?

- They provide a clear blueprint with specific instructions for the changes that are to be made by the school in order to improve its educational performance;
- They offer a system of guidance and technical assistance for schools, often by the developer, and, in order to have the widest application, offer instructions on how the model may be scaled up at a large number of sites;
- The changes that the models propose for implementation are comprehensive, involving school organization, social relations (parental involvement, relationships between school staff and student), curriculum and instruction, and educational standards and goals;
- The models are flexible, which allows them to be implemented on variable time scales and with adaptations to meet local circumstances; and
- The model designs are based on up-to-date research on curriculum and the learning environment. (p. 2)

Effective programs are those that see through the myths that have evolved in relation to at-risk students and have become barriers to successful efforts. Barr and Parrett (2001) identified seven myths that must be overcome.

- At-risk youth need slow learning. Fact: They need to be academically challenged like all students.
- At-risk youth should be retained during the early grades until they are ready to move forward. Fact: Research has shown that this can have disastrous effects.
- At-risk youth can be educated with the same expenditures as other students. Fact: Additional programming that might be needed will require additional funds.
- Classroom teachers can adequately address the needs of at-risk youth. Fact: Classroom teachers can contribute, but addressing the needs of at-risk students requires a team effort.
- Some students can't learn. Fact: Reaffirmation of this overriding education theme is often needed.
- The most effective way to improve instruction for at-risk youth is to reduce classroom size. Fact: This is a desirable but not necessary element.
- Students who are having learning difficulties need special education. Fact: A tendency to refer to special education must be balanced with the idea of addressing the needs of at-risk students within the general education classroom with necessary assistance and supports.

Table 13.5 provides a list of factors, culled from research during the past twenty-five years, that have been found to be essential to school programs where at-risk students are learning effectively.

The movement to include students with disabilities in general education classrooms provides an opportunity to meet the needs of at-risk students as well. In an inclusive classroom, students should be educated based on their needs rather than on their clinical labels. In fact, inclusion, rather than separate programming, is supported by the lack of evidence that different teaching techniques are required by students from different disability groups.

The elements that are needed to create and maintain an inclusive classroom (as discussed in Chapter 2), which include specific techniques targeted for a specific population, often benefit everyone. When schools remove labels from students and provide programs based on individual needs, students who are at risk can benefit from the

Table 13.5	**Essential Components of Effective Programs**

Positive School Climate
Choice, commitment, and voluntary participation
Small, safe, supportive learning environment
Shared vision, cooperative governance, and local autonomy
Flexible organization
Community partnerships and coordination of services

Customized Curriculum and Instructional Program
Caring, demanding, and well-prepared teachers
Comprehensive and continuing programs
Challenging and relevant curricula
High academic standards and continuing assessment of student progress
Individualized instruction: personal, diverse, accelerated, and flexible
Successful transitions

Personal, Social, and Emotional Growth
Promoting personal growth and responsibility
Developing personal resiliency
Developing emotional maturity through service
Promoting emotional growth
Promoting social growth

From *Hope Fulfilled for At-Risk and Violent Youth: K–12 Programs That Work* (p. 73), by R. D. Barr and W. H. Parrett, 2001. Boston: Allyn & Bacon. Copyright 2001 by Allyn & Bacon. Reprinted by permission.

strategies and activities supplied for students with various disabilities (Wang, Reynolds, & Walberg, 1994/1995).

Specific Strategies for Students At Risk

CROSS-REFERENCE

Review some of the strategies included in Chapters 5–9 and determine whether any of these methods would be effective with children at risk for school problems.

In addition to the general principles cited earlier, specific programs can prove effective with at-risk students. These include an emphasis on teaching every child to read, accelerated schools, alternative schools, one-on-one tutoring, extended day programs, cooperative learning activities, magnet schools, teen parent programs, vocational-technical programs, mentoring, and school-to-work programs (Barr & Parrett, 2001).

One program that has been used effectively in many schools is mentoring (Slicker & Palmer, 1993). Elementary, middle, and high schools design such programs to provide students with a positive personal relationship with an adult—something that many children and youth lack (Barr & Parrett, 2001). A mentor can be any person of any background who is committed to serving as a support person for a child or youth.

CEC STANDARDS

CEC 4: Instructional Strategies

Mentor programs range in scope from national programs such as Big Brothers/Big Sisters to programs developed by and for specific schools, such as a program wherein adults employed in the community have lunch with students (Friedman & Scaduto, 1995). Programs large and small have proved effective for many children. It is important to ensure that a positive match is made between the mentor and the child. Other features of successful mentor programs are listed in the nearby Evidence-Based Practice feature.

INTASC

INTASC 4: Instructional strategies

Final Thought

PRAXIS

PRAXIS II: Delivery of Services to Students with Disabilities

The population of at-risk children and youth is incredibly diverse. Many different professionals need to get involved in developing and implementing programs for this group of students. Nevertheless, general classroom teachers will continue to play a major role in the lives of students who are at risk. Because teachers and students spend a considerable amount of time together during the week, the importance of the teacher-student relationship is critical. Elders's (2002) thoughts about the key elements that should guide school-based efforts with at risk students serve as a wonderful final thought for this chapter.

> They come to us like a sponge and we must ensure that they leave with four things. We want them to leave with that voice in the ear that can hear all of those less fortunate so that they can have compassion. We want them to leave with a vision in their eye that extends much farther than the eye can see. We want them to have a scroll in their hand, which is a good education, and a song in their heart to carry them through when things get tough, as we know they will. (p. 1)

Mentoring programs can provide at-risk students with positive adult role models.

EVIDENCE-BASED PRACTICE

Components of Effective Mentoring Programs for At-Risk Students

- *Program compatibility:* The program should be compatible with the policies and goals of the organization. In a program for students in a community group, for example, program organizers should work closely with school personnel to ensure that the mentoring they provide complements the student's education.
- *Administrative commitment:* The program must be supported from the top as well as on a grass-roots level. In a school-based program, all school and district administrators, teachers, and staff must provide input and assistance. For a sponsoring business, the president or chief executive officer must view the program as important and worthy of the time and attention of the employees.
- *Proactive:* Ideally the programs should be proactive; that is, not a quick-fix reaction to a crisis. Successful mentoring programs for youth work because they are well thought out, they have specific goals and objectives, and they exist within a larger realm of programs and policies that function together.

- *Participant oriented:* The program should be based on the goals and needs of the participants. These goals will determine the program's focus, recruitment, and training. For example, if the primary aim of a mentoring program is career awareness, students should be matched with successful businesspeople in the youth's area of interest. Activities and workshops should be job related.
- *Pilot program:* The first step should be a pilot program of six to twelve months, with ten to forty participants, in order to work out any problems before expanding to a larger audience. Trying to start out with a large-scale plan that includes more than this number can prove unwieldy and disastrous. In the words of Oregon's guide to mentorship programs, "Think big but start small."
- *Orientation:* An orientation should be provided for prospective participants. It will help determine interest and enthusiasm, as well as give prospective mentors and students an idea of what to expect. In addition, it will provide them with opportunities to help design the program.

- *Selection and matching:* Mentors and their protégés should be carefully selected and matched. Questionnaires are helpful in determining needs, areas of interest, and strengths.
- *Training:* Training must be provided for all participants, including support people, throughout the program. Assuming that because a person is knowledgeable, caring, and enthusiastic he or she will make a good mentor is a mistake. Training must be geared to the specific problems experienced by at-risk youth as well as different styles of communication.
- *Monitoring progress:* The program should be periodically monitored for progress and results to resolve emerging conflicts and problems.
- *Evaluation and revision:* The program should be evaluated with respect to how well goals and objectives are achieved. This can be done using questionnaires, interviews, etc.

From *Mentoring Programs for at-Risk Youth* (pp. 5–6) by National Dropout Prevention Center, 1990, Clemson, SC: Clemson University.

Summary

Basic Concepts about Students Who Are At Risk
- Students who are at risk may not be eligible for special education programs.
- At-risk students include those who are in danger of developing significant learning and behavior problems.

Select At-Risk Groups
- Poverty is a leading cause of academic failure.
- Poverty among children is increasing in the United States.
- Poverty is associated with homelessness, poor health care, hunger, and single-parent households.
- Hunger is a major problem in the United States.
- A sizable percentage of all homeless people are children.
- Students in single-parent homes face major problems in school.
- About 25 percent of all children live in single-parent homes.
- Divorce is the leading reason for which children live in single-parent homes.
- Children react in many different ways to divorce.
- Schools must take into consideration the rights of the noncustodial parent.

- The death of a parent, sibling, or friend can have a major impact on a child and school success.
- Child abuse is a major problem in the United States and causes children to experience major emotional trauma.
- The most common type of child maltreatment is neglect.
- School personnel are required by law to report suspected child abuse.
- Drug use among students is on the increase after several years of decline.
- Teenage pregnancy continues to be a problem, despite the fear of HIV/AIDS and the presence of sex education programs.
- Attention to students who are lesbian, gay, bisexual, or transgendered is needed in schools, as this population still encounters a host of problems.

Strategies for Curriculum and Instruction for Students Who Are At Risk
- Numerous programs and interventions have proved effective in working with at-risk students.

Questions to Reconsider

Think back to the scenario about Lisa that you read at the beginning of this chapter. Would you answer the questions raised there any differently, now that you have read the chapter?

1. What types of interventions does Lisa need? What services would you recommend?

2. Should Lisa be considered for special education?
3. What can teachers do with Lisa and students like her to prevent failure?

Further Readings

Annie E. Casey Foundation. (1998). *1998 kids count data book: Overview.* Baltimore, MD: Author.

Barnes, K. E. (1982). *Preschool screening: The measurement and prediction of children at risk.* Springfield, IL: Thomas.

Barr, J. R., & Parrett, S. (1995). *Hope at last for at-risk youth.* Boston: Allyn and Bacon.

Carnegie Council on Adolescent Development. (1989). *Turning point: Preparing American youth for the 21st century.* New York: Author.

National Education Goals Panel. (1998). *Ready schools.* Washington, DC: Author.

National Law Center on Homelessness and Poverty. (1990). *Shut out: Denial of education to homeless children.* Washington, DC: Author.

Office of Education Research and Improvement. (1988). *Youth indicators, 1988: Trends in the well-being of American youth.* Washington, DC: U.S. Department of Education.

Office of Juvenile Justice and Delinquency Prevention. (1995). *Juvenile offenders and victims: A national report.* Pittsburgh, PA: National Center for Juvenile Justice.

Siccone, F. (1995). *Celebrating diversity: Building self-esteem in today's multi-cultural classrooms.* Boston: Allyn and Bacon.

U.S. Department of Education. (1998). *Tools for schools: From at-risk to excellence.* Washington, DC: Author.

U.S. Department of Education. (1998). *Safe and smart: Making the after-school hours work for kids.* Washington, DC: Author.

U.S. Department of Education. (1999). *The condition of education, 1998.* Washington, DC: Author.

Ysseldyke, J. E., Algozzine, B., & Thurlow, M. L. (2000). *Critical issues in special education* (3rd ed.). Boston: Houghton Mifflin.

(mylabschool**

Where the classroom comes to life

Go to Allyn & Bacon's MyLabSchool (www.mylabschool.com) and enter Assignment ID CS16 into the Assignment Finder. Read the Case Study called *Eric's Last Stand* and respond to the questions at the end of it, relying both on the information in the case and on what you have read in this chapter. You may want to e-mail your responses to your instructor.

Classroom Management and Organization

After reading this chapter, you should be able to:

1. Identify the key components of classroom management.

2. Describe the roles of students, teachers, peers, and family members in promoting a positive classroom climate.

3. Describe ways to increase desirable behaviors, decrease undesirable classroom behaviors, and maintain behaviors over time.

4. Identify self-regulatory approaches and procedures.

5. Identify possible strategies to enhance classroom and personal organization.

This year has been particularly challenging for Jeannie Chung. Jeannie has been teaching fifth grade for ten years, but she cannot recall any year in which her students' needs were more diverse and the tasks of managing the classroom and motivating her students were more challenging.

While many of her students present unique needs, eleven-year-old Sam clearly stands out as the most difficult student in the class. Sam is too frequently out of his seat and often yells out to other students across the room. He has great difficulty staying on task during instructional periods and at times spreads a contagion of misbehavior in the classroom. During large-group language arts lessons, Sam is inattentive and frequently uncooperative. Jeannie is beginning to believe that his high level of inattentive behavior may make it virtually impossible for him to progress and achieve in the general education classroom, although, at the same time, Jeannie does not see him as a candidate for a special class or other pull-out program. Further, his inattentive behavior is gradually resulting in his falling far behind academically. Although it is only November, Jeannie seriously wonders whether this will be a productive year for Sam.

Sam currently receives no special education supports or services. However, Jeannie has referred Sam to the child-study team, and they are pondering suggestions that may be effective within Jeannie's classroom as well as considering a request for a more comprehensive assessment that may elucidate instructional and/or curricular alternatives.

A teacher's ability to manage his or her classroom effectively and efficiently can greatly enhance the quality of the educational experience for all students. Well-organized and well-managed classrooms allow more time for productive instruction for all students, including those with special needs. As Marzano (2003) points out: "Teachers play various roles in a typical classroom, but surely one of the most important is that of classroom manager. Effective teaching and learning cannot take place in a poorly managed classroom." (p. 13)

The overriding theme of the chapter relates back the notion of creating a classroom community, as discussed in Chapter 2. As noted by Kohn (1996), we should strive to "make the classroom a community where students feel valued and respected, where care and trust have taken the place of restrictions and threats" (p. ix). The absence of heavy-handed adult-directed management systems is characteristic of classrooms where students are valued and solid relationships between teachers and students are established (Bender, 2003). When attention is given to preventive action rather than reactive intervention, classrooms run smoothly and without notice. Smith (2004) has referred to this notion as "invisible management" and suggests that, when effective management is operant, it is virtually hard to discern, unless you know what to look for.

This chapter presents a model for thinking about the major dimensions of classroom management, a discussion of these dimensions, and specific pedagogical practices for creating an effective learning environment. Sound organizational and management tactics promote learning for all students and are particularly relevant to the successful inclusion of students with special learning needs. When general and special educators working collaboratively devise management/organizational tactics, the likelihood of establishing an effective learning setting is further enhanced.

Basic Concepts about Classroom Management and Organization

The importance of good classroom management and organization techniques has been affirmed numerous times by professionals in the field of education. Although much attention is given to curricular and instructional aspects of students' educational programs, organizational and management dimensions are typically underemphasized in training programs, educational research, and professional conferences, despite their importance as prerequisites to instruction (Evertson & Weinstein, 2006). This area is consistently identified as most problematic by first-year teachers (Jones, 2006).

The smooth functioning of the general education classroom often represents a challenge for teachers as classrooms become more diverse. Jones and Jones (2007) describe the profile of a typical first grade class as being composed a vast array of students with specific needs that might include any combination or all of the following: a range of disabilities, English language learners, in-school and out-of-school counseling, abusive situations and other unsafe home lives, homelessness, frequent relocation. Students with any of these features in their lives require special attention in school. Evertson and colleagues (2006) accurately articulate the relationship between the diversity found in today's schools and the need for well-run classrooms.

> Students entering the nation's schools come with such widely diverse backgrounds, capabilities, interests, and skills that meeting their needs and finding appropriate learning activities requires a great deal of care and skill. Because one of the first and most basic tasks for the teacher is to develop a smoothly running classroom community where students are highly involved in worthwhile activities that support learning, establishing an effective management system is a first priority. (p. xv)

This particular topic is too important to be overlooked, as attention to the elements described within this chapter can benefit a wide range of students with special needs in the general education classroom. Although reading about classroom management can-

CONSIDER THIS

Does the inclusion of students with special needs result in greater need for good classroom management? If so, why?

CEC STANDARDS

CEC 5: Learning Environments and Social Interactions

INTASC

INTASC 5: Learning environment

PRAXIS

PRAXIS II: Delivery of Services to Students with Disabilities

not take the place of practice and experience, this chapter offers a variety of management strategies to assist both new and experienced educators.

Definition of Classroom Management and Organization

Most definitions describe classroom management as a systematic designing of the classroom environment to create conditions in which effective teaching and learning can occur. This chapter broadly defines the concept as all activities that support the efficient operations of the classroom and that help establish optimal conditions for learning (i.e., creating an effective learning environment). Noting Kohn's (1996) objections to the use of the term "management," because of its origins from business and overtones of directing and controlling, we will still use the term. However, our conceptualization of management and organization is not incompatible with Kohn's overall desire to empower students. A key feature of well-managed classrooms is student choice, empowerment, and growth as a person.

It is important to note, as will be illustrated in the model we have developed to capture the various elements of classroom management, that classroom management is much more that behavior management or disciplinary action. Levin (2003) has defined a disciplinary problem as: "behavior that (1) interferes with the teaching act; (2) interferes with the rights of others to learn; (3) is psychologically or physically unsafe; or (4) destroys property" (p. 4). While disciplinary problems are part of what happens in a classroom and ways to deal with them are needed, the emphasis presented in this chapter is on creating a classroom climate and set of operations that prevent, or minimize, the need to deal with significant disciplinary problems.

Teachers and students may not agree on what good classroom management is, however (see Table 14.1). Hoy and Weinstein (2006) caution that these contrasting views of classroom management may lead to a "downward spiral of mistrust" (p. 209). As a result, effort must be given to better understand what this concept means in the real world of the classroom and to find ways to implement efficient, yet unobtrusive, systems in classrooms.

Table 14.1   Some Likely Contrasting Views of Classroom Management

Teachers' Likely Perceptions	Students' Likely Perceptions
Teachers should always be respected by students	Students should be respected by teachers and teachers have to earn respect
Classrooms should be orderly	Classrooms should allow students to interact with their peers
Rules should always be followed	Rules should be well known and the teacher should enforce them consistently
Students should expect and receive negative consequences when appropriate	Negative consequences should always be meted out fairly and consistently
Students should work for positive reinforcers	Positive reinforcers should be things that students want
Rules should be established by the teacher	Rules should make sense to students and students should help establish them
Teachers always care for their students	Teachers should show that they care for each student
Students should want to learn for the sake of learning	Teachers should motivate students to learn

Comprehensive Model of Classroom Management

Every classroom environment involves a number of elements that have a profound impact on the effectiveness of instruction and learning (Doyle, 1986). Six of these are described briefly here:

1. *Multidimensionality* refers to the wide variety of activities that occur in a classroom within the course of an instructional day.
2. *Simultaneity* refers to the fact that many different events occur at the same time.
3. *Immediacy* refers to the rapid pace at which events occur in classrooms.
4. *Unpredictability* refers to the reality that some events occur unexpectedly and cannot consistently be anticipated, but require attention nonetheless.
5. *Publicness* refers to the fact that classroom events are witnessed by a significant number of students who are very likely to take note of how teachers deal with these ongoing events.
6. *History* refers to the reality that, over the course of the school year, various events (experiences, routines, rules) will shape the evolving dynamics of classroom behavior.

Considering these elements reaffirms the complexity of teaching large numbers of students who have diverse learning needs in our schools today. To address these classroom dynamics, teachers need to be aware and competent to utilize ways to organize and manage their classrooms to maximize the potential opportunities for learning. Figure 14.1 depicts a comprehensive model of classroom organization and management that highlights the multifaceted dimensions of this topic. This particular model of organization and management evolved from one designed by Polloway, Patton, and Serna (2008), reflecting an adaptation of what they identify as "precursors to teaching"

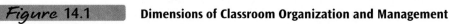

Figure **14.1**   **Dimensions of Classroom Organization and Management**

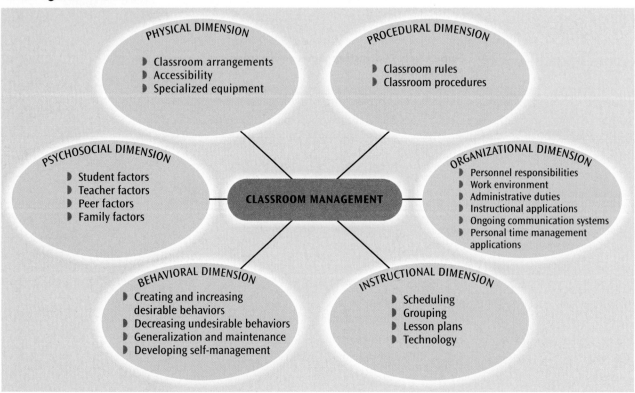

and stresses the comprehensiveness feature by identifying six key areas that need to be considered.

The effective and efficient management of a classroom is based on numerous considerations. To create a positive, supportive, and nurturing environment conducive to learning, teachers must pay attention to psychosocial, procedural, physical, behavioral, instructional, and organizational variables that have a critical impact on learning and behavior. Teachers need to consider much of the content of the dimensional model (see Figure 14.1) discussed in this chapter *before* the beginning of the school year to prevent classroom-related issues from developing.

Prevention will likely be more effective than the crisis intervention that might be needed after issues have become significant disciplinary problems. Prevention takes work, however, and classroom time at the beginning of the year must be dedicated to this task. McEwan (2006) stresses the importance of prevention in her "3 + 3 [equals] 33" rule: "the more consistently you teach your students the routines, rubrics, and rules (3Rs) of your classroom at the beginning of the school year (three weeks), the more productive the rest of your year (thirty-three weeks) will be" (p. 2).

The dynamics of a classroom are determined by many different student factors.

Guiding Principles

The idea that classroom management needs to be comprehensive, as depicted in Figure 14.1, is endorsed by others as well. Jones and Jones (2007) suggest that teachers must demonstrate competence (i.e., knowledge and skills) in fours areas if they are to implement comprehensive classroom management effectively. To these authors, classroom management:

- Should be based on a solid understanding of current research and theory of classroom management and students' personal and psychological needs
- Depends on creating a positive classroom climate and a community of support
- Involves using instructional methods that facilitate optimal learning by responding to the academic needs of individual students and the classroom group
- Involves the ability to use a wide range of counseling and behavioral methods that involve students in examining and correcting their inappropriate behavior (pp. 24–25)

In addition to the points made above, eleven overarching principles guide the development and implementation of comprehensive classroom organization and management procedures:

1. All students must be valued.
2. Meaningful relationships between teachers and students need to be developed and cultivated. (Bender, 2003)
3. Successful management derives from a positive classroom climate.
4. Teachers have control over a number of critical factors that have a major impact on student learning and behavior. (Jones & Jones, 2007)
5. Good classroom organization and management must be planned ahead of time.
6. Affording students choices contributes to effective classroom dynamics.
7. Teachers and students in effective classrooms are considerate of individual differences, including cultural and familial differences (see discussion below).
8. Proactive management (prevention) is preferable to reactive approaches (crisis intervention).
9. Consistency is the key to establishing an effective management program.

CEC STANDARDS

CEC 5: Learning Environments and Social Interactions

INTASC

INTASC 5: Learning environment

PRAXIS

PRAXIS II: Delivery of Services to Students with Disabilities

TEACHING TIP

Teachers need to have a comprehensive behavior-management plan that includes not only consequences for actions by students (reactive elements) but also rules, procedures, and an overall classroom organization approach (proactive elements).

10. Teachers should not feel that they are alone—resources such as other teachers, administrators, and parents can contribute to the successful implementation of a classroom management system.
11. Effective classroom management is "invisible." (Smith, 2004)

Although sound classroom management practices are useful in working with all students, the recommendations provided in this chapter are particularly helpful for students who have special needs and require individualized consideration. Without question, these students struggle to learn in environments that are not well organized and effectively managed.

Cultural Considerations

When developing and implementing a comprehensive classroom management system, teachers must be mindful of the diverse range of students in their classrooms. One of the most overlooked areas of diversity is cultural diversity. Levin (2003) noted two very important points that have to be acknowledged and addressed in regard to students who come from cultural backgrounds different than those of their teachers: (1) schools and classrooms are not culturally neutral or culture free, and (2) because of cultural differences, many children from underrepresented groups experience cultural dissonance or lack of cultural synchronization in school (i.e., teacher and student expectations of appropriate behavior may differ).

Weinstein, Tomlinson-Clarke, and Curran (2004) identified five components that should be part of a *culturally responsive* classroom management system:

- Recognition of one's own ethnocentrism and biases
- Knowledge of students' cultural backgrounds
- Understanding of the broader social, economic, and political context of the U.S. educational system
- Ability and willingness to use culturally appropriate classroom management strategies
- Commitment to building caring classroom communities (p. 27)

Components of Effective Classroom Organization and Management

This section discusses the major elements and subcomponents of classroom management highlighted in the multidimensional model in Figure 14.1.

Psychosocial Dimension

This dimension refers to the psychological and social dynamics of the classroom. Its primary focus is on **classroom climate**, the classroom atmosphere in which students must function.

CEC STANDARDS

CEC 5: Learning Environments and Social Interactions

Student Factors The dynamics of classrooms are influenced by certain student factors. Chief among these factors that can have a remarkable impact on how students behave and react to organizational and management demands are their attitudes about school and their relationships with teachers, other authority figures, and classmates. Fries and Cochran-Smith (2006) note the following factors:

INTASC

INTASC 5: Learning environment

- Home life
- Cultural heritage
- Individual temperament
- Language resources
- Social and interpersonal skills (p. 945)

Other factors that shape student attitudes and behavior include:

- Nature of previous educational experiences
- How they feel about themselves
- Motivation—their own expectations concerning their scholastic futures (i.e., ability of being able to do the task and potential for success)
- Whether they are intrinsically or extrinsically motivated
- Perceived relevance of the instructional tasks
- Emotional factors, including levels of stress

PRAXIS

PRAXIS II: Delivery of Services to Students with Disabilities

Teacher Factors   The psychological atmosphere of any classroom depends in great part on certain teacher factors—some of which are personal and others professional. A teacher's attitudes toward students with special needs can dramatically affect the quality of education that a student will receive during the time he or she is in that teacher's classroom. The type of expectations a teacher holds for students can significantly influence learning outcomes. One's personal philosophy about education, management and discipline, and curriculum/instruction weigh heavily as well. Fries and Cochran-Smith (2006) noted that a teacher's ability "to adapt to the needs of learners" (p. 945) can also make a difference.

Two characteristics identified in classic classroom research enhance a teacher's ability to manage classrooms effectively (Kounin, 1970):

- *With-it-ness:* Overall awareness of what is happening in the classroom.
- *Overlap:* The ability to deal with more than one event simultaneously.

McEwan (2002) defines "with-it-ness" as "the state of being on top of, tuned in to, aware of, and in complete control of three critical facets of classroom life: (1) the management and organization of the classroom; (2) the engagement of students, and (3) the management of time" (p. 48). The concept of overlap requires that the teacher be able to monitor and address a number of activities that are occurring in the classroom at the same time without being distracted, negligent, or acting incorrectly.

One particular set of skills that has bearing on the psychological aspects of the classroom is teacher communication skills. Evertson and colleagues (2006) note that the ability to communicate clearly and effectively with students influences the nature of ongoing dynamics in the classroom. They stress that to become an effective communicator, teachers need to display three related skills: constructive assertiveness (e.g., describing concerns clearly); empathic responding (e.g., listening to the student's perspective); and problem solving (e.g., ability to reach mutually satisfactory resolutions to problems).

Peer Factors   Peers are also key players in forming the psychological and social atmosphere of a classroom, especially among middle- and high-school students. Teachers must understand peer values, pressures, and needs and use this knowledge to benefit students with special needs. Valuable cooperative learning opportunities can evolve based on successful peer involvement strategies. As Kohn (1996) notes, "Communities are built upon a foundation of cooperating throughout the day, with students continually being invited to work, play, and reflect with someone else" (p. 113).

Family-Related Factors   The final component involves a variety of family-related factors. Three major issues, all of which have cultural implications, include family attitudes toward education; level of family support and involvement in the student's education; and the amount of pressure placed on a child by the family. Extremes can be problematic—for example, a family that burdens a student (e.g., a gifted child) with overwhelming pressure to succeed can cause as many difficulties as one that takes limited interest in a child's education.

Efforts should be made to establish relationships with parents and guardians. At the very least, a letter (with correct grammar, punctuation, and spelling) should be sent to each family, describing the nature of the classroom management system. This is particularly important if no other means exists for conveying this information, such as some type of orientation. A benefit of developing a relationship with parents is that the teacher can determine a family's status on the dimensions mentioned in the previous paragraph.

The following recommendations should help create a positive, nurturing environment that contributes to positive outcomes for all students:

- Let students know that you are sensitive to their needs and concerns.
- Understand the family and cultural contexts from which students come.
- Convey enthusiasm about learning and the school experience.
- Create a supportive, safe environment in which students who are different can learn without fear of being ridiculed or threatened.
- Treat all students with fairness.
- Acknowledge all students in some personal way each day to affirm that they are valued within the room.
- Create a learning environment that provides challenge to the students, is built on success, and minimizes failure experiences common to the learning histories of students with disabilities.
- Establish that each student in the classroom has rights (e.g., not to be interrupted when working or responding to a teacher inquiry) and that you expect everyone to respect those rights.
- Instill in students the understanding that they are responsible for their own behavior.
- Convey to students that every student's thoughts and ideas are important.
- Encourage risk taking and support all students (i.e., gifted, average, and disabled) to take on scholastic challenges.
- Share philosophies, management systems, and instructional perspectives with parents or guardians.

Procedural Dimension

As noted in Figure 14.1, the procedural dimension refers to the regulatory operations that are an ongoing part of a classroom. The guidelines discussed here provide direction to school staff and students as to what is expected of all. It is all about expectations!

The teacher must identify all guiding principles, rules, rubrics, procedures, and other regulations before the school year begins and should plan to teach them to students during the first days of the school year. Definitions of the different terms used to describe regulatory functions of the classroom are provided in Table 14.2.

Equally important is preparation for dealing with violations of rules. Immediate and consistent consequences are needed. Various disciplinary techniques can be implemented to ensure that inappropriate behavior is handled effectively. (These will be covered in a subsequent section of this chapter.)

Students with exceptional needs will benefit from being systematically taught the administrative and social rules operative in a classroom. The suggestions provided in this section focus on classroom rules and in-class procedures.

Guiding Principles   Most individuals respond best when they know what is expected of them. Guiding principles provide standards that are in place at all times in the classroom. They can be thought of as "guidelines for life at school" and include very general statements that can be invoked in many different situations. The following are representative examples of guiding principles that are adapted from Smith (2004): treat each other fairly; show respect and responsibility; school is a safe place to learn; our classroom is our community; students have the right to learn and teachers have the right to teach; be safe, kind, and productive.

CEC STANDARDS

CEC 5: Learning Environments and Social Interactions

INTASC

INTASC 5: Learning environment

PRAXIS

PRAXIS II: Delivery of Services to Students with Disabilities

Table 14.2	Regulatory Terminology
Term	**Explanation**
Guiding Principle	• overriding principle that guides behavior • "akin to guidelines . . . more general and often more value-laden than rules" (Smith, 2004, p. 164) • code of conduct • e.g.: "Respect the rights of others"
Rule	• statements that describe expected behavior • apply across different situations • classroom behavior standards (Jones & Jones, 2007) • "what we can and can't live with in our classrooms" (Smith, 2004, p. 165) • e.g.: "Listen when others are speaking"
Rubric	• behaviorally-stated standards indicating different levels of the desired behavior • "continuums of quality or completeness against which teachers and students measure and evaluate behavior" (McEwan, 2006, p. 10)
Procedure	• specific classroom routines • procedures that are executed by either teachers or students (McEwan, 2006, p. 10) • e.g.: "Using the pencil sharpener"

Classroom Rules   Rules provide a general sense of what is expected of students in a classroom setting. Rules can be specific to certain expectations; however, they apply to general classroom situations. The rules that are chosen should be essential to classroom functioning and help create a positive learning environment (Christenson, Ysseldyke, & Thurlow, 1989; Smith & Rivera, 1995).

Reasonable classroom rules, presented appropriately, will be particularly beneficial to students with special needs who are in general education settings, as this process assists in clarifying expectations. Jones and Jones (2007) recommend a sequence of four major steps for developing classroom rules (i.e., classroom behavior standards); three steps are provided in Figure 14.2. Evertson and colleagues (2006) offer four general rules that cover many classroom behaviors: respect and be polite to all people; be prompt and prepared; listen quietly when others are speaking; obey all school rules. Rubrics can be developed for all these rules to assist students in recognizing the continuum of levels at which a rule can be performed along with the acceptable levels for the classroom. Some specific suggestions related to classroom rules are presented in Figure 14.3.

Classroom Procedures   An area of classroom management that can easily be overlooked is the development of logical classroom procedures. Classroom procedures refer to the specific way in which various classroom routines and activities will be performed or the way certain situations will be handled. For example, depending on age, procedures may need to be established for using the pencil sharpener, using the rest room, and entering and leaving the classroom. Figure 14.4 provides a checklist of classroom and school-related routines that should be considered, planned for, presented to students, and practiced during the first days of school. The checklist is an adaptation of a list developed by Smith (2004).

Again, clearly defined procedures are of particular importance, especially for some students with special needs, who may have difficulty attending to details or following instructions. This is one area where adequate consideration of these classroom/school activities can prevent many behavioral-related problems from developing. Failing to

CONSIDER THIS

Why are classroom rules such an important component of classroom management? Describe the likely climate of classrooms with effective rules and those without effective rules.

CEC STANDARDS

CEC 5: Learning Environments and Social Interactions

Figure 14.2   **Steps in Developing Classroom Behavior Standards**

1. Discuss the value of having behavior standards
2. Develop a list of the standards (3-6 Rules)
   a. Positively state standards
   b. Clearly differentiate/separate rules from procedures
   c. Teach the concept of "time, place, and manner"
3. Obtain a commitment to the standards
   a. Have students sign this commitment
   b. Decide if anyone else should sign and commit to supporting these standards
4. Monitor and review the standards
   a. Determine how new students will be involved in understanding and committing to these standards
   b. Review these standards when behavior problems increase or at times you expect students may need a preventive review (prior to having a substitute teacher, following major holidays, etc.)

From *Comprehensive Classroom Management: Creating Communities of Support and Solving Problems* (8th ed.; p. 198), by V. F. Jones and L. S. Jones, 2007. Boston: Allyn & Bacon.

INTASC

INTASC 5: Learning environment

PRAXIS

PRAXIS II: Delivery of Services to Students with Disabilities

address procedural issues in the classroom can cause distress for teachers if not attended to at the beginning of the school year. Teachers are often surprised by the complexity and detail associated with many seemingly trivial areas. The procedures for these areas combine to form the mosaic of one's management system. Here are some suggestions:

- Identify all situations for which a procedure will be needed—refer to the checklist in Figure 14.3 or see Evertson and colleagues (2006, pp. 39–40).
- Develop the procedures collaboratively with the students.
- Explain (describe and demonstrate) each procedure thoroughly.
- Teach each procedure through modeling, guided practice, independent practice and feedback, allowing every student to have an opportunity to practice the procedure and demonstrate learning on an appropriate level.
- Introduce classroom procedures during the first week of school, scheduling priority procedures for the first day and covering others on subsequent days—remember the "3 + 3 = 33" rule. (McEwan, 2006)
- Avoid introducing too many procedures at once.
- Incorporate any school regulation of importance and relevance into classroom procedures instruction (e.g., hall passes, restroom use).

Figure 14.3   **Recommendations for Classroom Rules**

- Develop no more than seven rules for the classroom.
- Involve students in rule setting.
- Keep the rules brief and state them clearly.
- Explain the rules thoroughly and discuss the specific consequences if they are violated.
- State the rules in a positive way—avoid statements that are worded in a negative way, such as "not allowed."
- Post the rules in a location where all students can see.
- Discuss exceptions in advance so that students understand them.
- Teach the rules through modeling and practice and verify that all have been learned.
- Review the rules on a regular basis and when new students join the class.
- Use reminders of rules as a preventive measure for times when possible disruptions are anticipated.

Figure 14.4	**Checklist of Classroom Procedures**

Directions: Develop a procedure that you will teach to your students for the areas listed below that pertain to your classroom. Start by checking the procedures for which you need a specific routine. Then, in the empty column, write out how this routine will work.

Area of Focus	Specific Procedure
<u>Room and hall use</u>: _____ Teacher desk _____ Storage areas _____ Student desks _____ Using the pencil sharpener _____ Using the rest room _____ Using the water fountain _____ Hall pass _____ Going to lockers	
<u>Beginning of class</u>: _____ Students entering the classroom _____ Using cubbies/area for belongings _____ Students who are tardy _____ Absent—excused _____ Absent—unexcused _____ Absent students making up work _____ Starting the lesson _____ Turning in homework _____ Listening to P.A. announcements	
<u>During class instruction</u>: _____ Getting student attention _____ Passing out papers _____ Headings on papers _____ Checking out books to students _____ Passing out classroom supplies/instructional materials _____ Using classroom supplies/instructional materials _____ Collecting classroom/instructional supplies _____ Turning in class work _____ How students ask for help _____ Checking for understanding _____ Hand raising during class discussions _____ Group work _____ Watching videos _____ Sustained silent reading _____ Taking tests _____ Taking quizzes _____ Organizing notebooks _____ Using computers _____ Sharing computers _____ Student involvement in the room _____ Oral reports	

Figure 14.4   (Cont'd)

Area of Focus	Specific Procedure
Ending of class session: _____ Indicating that it is time to end class _____ Students putting their materials away _____ Assigning homework _____ Putting notebooks and other materials in backpacks and backpacks on backs _____ Dismissing class at the end of the period _____ Lining up for recess, lunch, or an assembly _____ Dismissing class at the end of the day _____ Using cubbies	
Special classroom situations and events: _____ Guest speakers _____ Volunteers in the classroom _____ Visitors to the classroom _____ Interruptions or delays _____ Sending students to the office _____ Sending students to another teacher _____ Returning to the room	
Special school-related situations and events: _____ Fire drills _____ Field trips _____ Attending an assembly or other special school event _____ Taking students to a specific area of the school (e.g., library, computer lab) _____ Playground/common area _____ Lunchroom	
Behavior management considerations: _____ Incentive system for desired behavior _____ Consequences for inappropriate behavior _____ Addressing student conflicts with one another _____ Addressing student conflicts with the teacher _____ Classroom community circles	

Adapted from *Conscious Classroom Management: Unlocking the Secrets of Great Teaching* (pp. 83–85), by R. Smith, 2004. San Rafael, CA: Conscious Teaching Publications.

Physical Dimension

CEC STANDARDS

CEC 5: Learning Environments and Social Interations

INTASC

INTASC 5: Learning environment

The physical dimension includes the aspects of the physical environment that teachers can manipulate to enhance the "conditions" for learning. As Doyle (2006) notes, "the data on classroom design and furniture arrangements indicate that different patterns of spatial organization have little effect on achievement but some effect on attitudes and conduct" (p. 106). The physical environment of the classroom does have an impact on behavior and attitudes (McEwan, 2006). For students with certain disabilities, some features of the physical setting may need to be especially arranged to ensure that individual needs are met. This section will address three aspects of the physical dimensions of a classroom: classroom arrangements, accessibility, and specialized equipment.

Classroom Arrangements   Classroom arrangements refer to physical facets of the classroom, including classroom layout (i.e., geography of the room), arrangement of desks, storage, wall use, display areas, and signs. Teachers are encouraged to consider carefully

PRAXIS

PRAXIS II: Delivery of Services to Students with Disabilties

where to seat students who have problems controlling their behaviors, those who experience attention deficit, and students with sensory impairments. Figure 14.5 provides recommendations on seating arrangement. The judicious use of seating arrangements can minimize problems as well as create better learning opportunities for students. Carbone (2001) provides a host of suggestions for arranging the physical dimensions of a general education classroom for addressing the needs of students with ADHD.

Other suggestions for classroom arrangement are listed here:

- Consider establishing areas of the classroom for certain types of activities (e.g., discovery or inquiry learning, independent reading).
- Clearly establish which areas of the classroom, such as the teacher's desk, are off limits—this recommendation is also a procedural one.
- Be sure students can be seen easily by the teacher and that the teacher, or other presenters, can be seen easily by students. (Evertson et al., 2006)
- Begin the year with a more-structured environment, moving to more flexibility after rules and procedures have been established.
- Notify students with visual impairments of changes made to the physical environment.
- Arrange furniture so that teachers and students can move easily around the classroom.
- Direct students' attention to the information to be learned from bulletin boards, if they are used for instructional purposes.
- Establish patterns that students can use in moving around the class and that minimize disruption—keep high-traffic areas free of congestion. (Evertson et al., 2006)
- Keep frequently used teaching materials and student supplies readily accessible. (Evertson et al., 2006)
- Secure materials and equipment that are potentially harmful, if used without proper supervision, such as certain art supplies, chemicals, and science equipment.
- Avoid creating open spaces that have no clear purpose, as they often can become staging areas for problem behaviors. (Rosenberg et al., 1991)
- Provide labels and signs for areas of the room to assist younger or more delayed students in better understanding what and where things are.

Accessibility   The accessibility of the classroom warrants special attention because of legal mandates (e.g., Section 504 of the Rehabilitation Act of 1973). The concept of accessibility, of course, extends beyond physical accessibility; it touches on overall program accessibility for students with special needs. Students who are identified as disabled under IDEA as well as students qualifying as having substantial limitations in a major life function such as walking or learning are able to benefit from needed

---

| *Figure* 14.5 | **Seating Arrangements** |

Seat students with behavior problems first so that they are in close proximity to the teacher for as much of the time as possible.

After more self-control is demonstrated, more distant seating arrangements are possible and desirable.

Locate students for whom visual distractions can interfere with attention to tasks (e.g., learning and attentional problems, hearing impairments, behavior problems) so that these distractions are minimized.

Establish clear lines of vision (a) for students so that they can attend to instruction and (b) for the teacher so that students can be monitored throughout the class period (Rosenberg et al., 1991).

Ensure that students with sensory impairments are seated so that they can maximize their residual vision and hearing.

Consider alternative arrangements of desks (e.g., table clusters) as options to traditional rows.

accommodations. Students with disabilities must be able to use the classroom like other students and the room must be free of potential hazards. Most of the time, making a classroom physically accessible is neither difficult nor costly. Specific suggestions for creating an accessible classroom include the following:

- Ensuring that the classroom is accessible to students who use wheelchairs, braces, crutches, or other forms of mobility assistance—this involves doorways, space to move within the classroom, floor coverings, learning centers, microcomputers, chalkboards or dry-erase boards, bookshelves, sinks, tables, desks, and any other areas or physical objects that students use.
- Guaranteeing that the classroom is free of hazards (e.g., low-hanging mobiles or plants) that could injure students who have a visual impairment.
- Labeling storage areas and other parts of the classroom for students with visual impairments by using raised lettering or Braille.
- Paying special attention to signs identifying hazards by providing nonverbal cautions for nonreaders.

Specialized Equipment   Some students with disabilities require the use of specialized equipment, such as wheelchairs, hearing aids and other types of amplification systems, communication devices, adaptive desks and trays, prone standers (i.e., stand-up desks), and medical equipment. This equipment allows programmatic accessibility and, in many instances, access to the general education curriculum. These types of assistive devices were introduced earlier in the book so that teachers may understand how the equipment works, how it should be used, and what classroom adaptations will need to be made to accommodate the student using it. Other students in the classroom should be introduced to the special equipment as well. Instructional lessons on specific pieces of equipment will not only be helpful in creating an inclusive environment, but may also provide a basis for curricular tie-ins in areas including health and science. Suggestions include the following:

- Identify the special equipment that will be used in the classroom prior to the arrival of the student who needs it.
- Learn how special equipment and devices work and how to identify problems or malfunctions.
- Find out how long students need to use time-specified equipment or devices.
- Structure lessons and other learning activities with the knowledge that some students will be using specialized equipment or materials.

Behavioral Dimension

The ability to create and maintain appropriate behaviors and to manage inappropriate behaviors that may disrupt the learning environment are important components of classroom management. As stressed previously, dealing with inappropriate behavior is only part of a comprehensive behavior management program. Management systems should also include techniques for developing new behaviors or increasing desirable behaviors within the students' repertoire. Moreover, a sound program must ensure that behaviors learned or changed will be maintained over time and generalized (e.g., demonstrated in different contexts). It must also teach self-control and self-regulatory mechanisms.

Recently more attention has been given to behavior that goes beyond the typical emphasis on external behavioral tactics. For instance, Bender (2003) promotes the concept of "relational discipline."

> Relational discipline focuses squarely on the relationship between the teacher and the student, and various tactics and strategies are implemented within that broader context. For it is this relationship, rather than the specific disciplinary tactics that are used, that forms the basis for appropriate classroom behavior and that eventually develops into self-discipline. (p. 3)

CROSS-REFERENCE

Review Chapter 10 on students with low-incidence disabilities. Consider the implications of equipment needed in the classroom by these groups of students.

CONSIDER THIS

IDEA requires that attention be given to positive behavioral interventions.

Related to the notion that relationship is important, Bender points out that "behavioral interventions practices" (i.e., disciplinary tactics) must be understood from a developmental perspective. Differential techniques must be considered in terms of age-related needs and predominant influences operative at a given age. Figure 14.6 illustrates these points. Bender notes that few disciplinary systems have, to any reasonable extent, built on the influence of peer groups with older students.

Given the importance of the behavioral dimension, most general educators will probably work regularly with special educators to develop effective programs for students with disabilities and for students with behavioral problems. To provide a flavor of the areas for possible emphasis, Etscheidt and Bartlett (1999) identified the following sample factors:

- *Skill training:* Could the student be involved in social skill instruction? Does the student need counseling?
- *Behavior management plan:* Does the student need a behavior management plan that describes a reinforcement system, supportive signals, and corrective options?
- *Self-management:* Could the student use self-monitoring of target behaviors?
- *Peer support:* Could peers help monitor and/or redirect behavior? Could peers take notes, help prepare for exams, and so on?
- *Classwide systems:* Could the teacher implement an interdependent group contingency for the class? Could a "circle of friends" be initiated? (p. 171)

Behavior-Management Plans   When behaviors need to be developed or when certain behaviors interfere with the learning of a student or that of his or her classmates, the development of a behavior-management plan might be necessary. Figure 14.7 describes the basic components of a behavior-management plan based on functional assessment procedures. Behavior-management plans are much like behavior-intervention plans that are required by IDEA in certain situations.

The concept of BIPs was introduced in Chapter 4 and explored in more detail in Chapter 7 for its particular relevance to students with emotional and behavioral problems. This planning process, mandated under IDEA for any student displaying serious behavioral problems, is built on the idea of understanding the functions of behavior prior to designing ways to address it. Most behavioral plans will include intervention ideas discussed in this section. A number of sources can be consulted for more details about how to conduct a functional behavioral assessment and develop an appropriate BIP (see Fad, Patton, & Polloway, 2006; McConnell, Hilvitz, & Cox, 1998; Simpson, 1998; and Zurkowski, Kelly, & Griswold, 1998).

Positive Behavioral Supports   Because research confirms the effectiveness of behavioral techniques for promoting learning in students with special needs (see Lloyd, Forness, & Kavale, 1998), the ability to develop a behavior-management plan and implement interventions must be part of a teacher's repertoire. Today, professionals in the area of behavior management have been stressing the need to implement positive

CEC STANDARDS

CEC 4: Instructional Strategies

INTASC

INTASC 4: Instructional strategies

PRAXIS

PRAXIS II: Delivery of Services to Students with Disabilities

CEC STANDARDS

CEC 7: Instructional Planning

INTASC

INTASC 7: Plans instruction

PRAXIS

PRAXIS II: Delivery of Services to Students with Disabilities

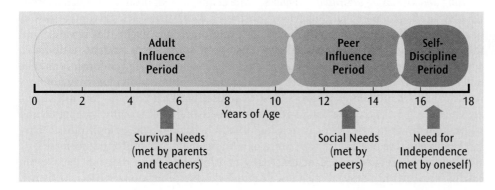

Figure 14.6

Relational Discipline

From *Relational Discipline: Strategies for In-Your-Face Kids* (p. 35) by W. N. Bender, 2003. Boston: Allyn & Bacon. Copyright 2003 by Pearson Education. Reprinted by permission.

> *Figure* 14.7   **Components of a Behavior Management Plan**
>
> **Conduct a Functional Assessment**
> 1. Collect information.
> • Identify and define the target behavior.
> • Identify events/circumstances associated with the problem behavior.
> • Determine potential function(s) of the problem behavior.
> 2. Develop hypothesis statements about the behavior.
> • Events/circumstances associated with the problem behavior.
> • Function/purpose of the behavior.
>
> **Develop an Intervention (Based on Hypothesis Statements)**
> 1. Teach alternative behavior.
> 2. Modify events/circumstances associated with the problem behavior.

From Using Functional Assessment to Develop Effective, Individualized Interventions for Challenging Behaviors (p. 46) by L. F. Johnson and G. Dunlap, 1993, *Teaching Exceptional Children, 25.* Used by permission.

TEACHING TIP

Students should be involved in selecting positive reinforcers to make sure that they are indeed attractive to the student.

behavioral interventions and supports. This emphasis has been accompanied by a de-emphasis on the use of more negative and punitive tactics.

As Horner (2000) notes, "Positive behavior support involves the assessment and reengineering of environments so people with problem behaviors experience reductions in (these behaviors) and increased social [and] personal quality in their lives. . . . It is an approach that blends values about the rights of people with disabilities with the practical science about how learning and behavior change occur" (p. 181).

The essential element of positive behavior support is the emphasis on fixing environments rather than focusing just on changing the behavior of individuals. Thus, the key element is to design schools and curricula to prevent problem behaviors from occurring and thus make them "irrelevant, inefficient, and ineffective" (Horner, 2000, p. 182). As discussed in Chapter 7, the basis for effective positive behavior support programs is the use of functional behavior assessment that identifies classroom events that serve to predict the occurrence of problem behaviors and function to maintain positive behaviors (Horner, 2000). Thus, the reader is encouraged to consider the remaining behavioral reduction strategies discussed in this chapter in light of the need to balance the focus on the individual with the more significant focus on designing a curriculum and operating a classroom in ways in which behavioral disturbances are minimized and students with special needs are more accepted members of the classroom.

Not all facets of behavior management can be covered in sufficient detail in this chapter. However, the following sections provide recommendations that should guide practice in increasing desirable behaviors, decreasing undesirable behaviors, promoting generalization and maintenance, and enhancing self-management.

CONSIDER THIS

Some people argue that contracts, as well as other forms of positive reinforcement, amount to little more than bribery. Do you agree or disagree? Why?

Creating and increasing desirable behaviors   The acquisition of desired new behaviors—whether academic, personal, behavioral, social, or vocational—is a classroom goal. A new desired behavior can be affirmed with a **reinforcer**, any event that rewards, and thus strengthens, the behavior it follows. **Positive reinforcement** presents a desirable consequence for performance of an appropriate behavior. Positive reinforcers can take different forms; however, what serves as reinforcement for one individual may not hold true for another. Reinforcers can consist of praise, physical contact, tangible items, activities, or privileges. The use of reinforcement is the most socially acceptable and instructionally sound tactic for increasing desired behaviors. The goal of most behavioral regimens is to internalize the nature of reinforcement (i.e., self-reinforcement).

Controversy about the use of externally controlled systems that rely heavily on extrinsic rewards has brewed for a few years now. Some professionals (Deci, Koestner,

CEC STANDARDS

CEC 4: Instructional Strategies

DIVERSITY FORUM

Positive Behavior Supports through Culturally Responsive Social Skills Curriculum

Shawn is a biracial fourth-grader living with his grandparents where he attends an historically low performing urban school. He currently receives inclusion services in Mr. Grisanti's classroom as a student with emotional/behavior disorders. A social worker, Tara, was assigned to Shawn and to advise Mr. Grisanti. Shawn's behavior has escalated in the past year, and he does not appear to respond to behavioral interventions implemented by the teacher. In meeting with Shawn, Tara discovered that his father was killed and his mother left him with his grandparents as a result of a drug addiction.

As teachers, it is important to address students' cultural backgrounds and social-emotional needs when implementing behavioral assessments and interventions. Through his conversations with Tara and Shawn's grandparents, Mr. Grisanti realized that he needed to re-think his approach to Shawn's challenging behaviors. With Tara's encouragement, he began to learn more about a comprehensive and responsive approach to developing social skills (Cartledge, & Milburn, 1996; Salend, & Taylor, 2002). Teachers who use this approach:

- *Obtain multiple forms of data from a variety of perspectives to gain background information on each student.* During his meeting with Shawn's grandparents Mr. Grisanti learned that Shawn had a passionate interest in science.
- *Determine the target behavior(s) to be taught in collaboration with the student, family, and professionals.* It was agreed that Shawn would learn alternative strategies to respond to difficult situations such as teasing, peer pressure, etc. He would also receive counseling services to address the recent loss of his father and abandonment by his mother.
- *Incorporate students' cultural and linguistic backgrounds and interests into the social skills curriculum and instruction.* With Shawn's involvement, Mr. Grisanti developed scripts using his dialect to role-play alternative responses. He also sup-ported Shawn's learning in the target social skill areas through a variety of media (e.g., books, poetry, documentary, etc) that included experiences familiar to him. Finally, Shawn enrolled in an after-school academy to support his interests and abilities in science.

Questions

1. To ensure a culturally responsive behavior analysis, why is it important to have multiple forms of data from a variety of perspectives?
2. How could you engage your students in creating culturally responsive scripts to role-play alternative responses to difficult social situations?

REFERENCES

Cartledge, G. & Milburn, J. F. (Eds.) (1996). *Cultural Diversity and Social Skills Instruction.* Champaign, IL: Research Press.

Salend, S. J., & Taylor, L. S. (2002). Cultural perspectives: Missing pieces in the functional assessment process. *Intervention in School and Clinic,* 38(2), 104–112.

& Ryan, 1999; Kohn, 1993) argue that the use of external rewards interferes with the development of intrinsic systems of reinforcement. Extrinsic systems of reward can be used incorrectly (e.g., rewards are provided haphazardly) and can indeed interfere with the development of more intrinsic motivation. Landrum and Kauffman's (2006) response to this controversy provides two very important points: (1) the research data do not support the idea that rewards are to be assiduously avoided, and (2) in the absence of intrinsic motivation to complete academic tasks or behave as expected in school, nothing is to be gained and much is to be lost by refusing to use extrinsic rewards to reinforce desired conduct (p. 67).

Three basic principles must be followed for positive reinforcement to be most effective: it must be meaningful to the student; contingent on the proper performance of a desired behavior; and presented immediately. In other words, for positive reinforcement to work, students must find the reinforcement desirable in some fashion; understand that it is being given as a result of the behavior demonstrated; and receive it soon after they do what was asked. Principles for the use of positive reinforcement are presented in Figure 14.8. Generally, attention to the systematic nature of the reinforcement program should parallel the severity of a student's intellectual, learning, or behavioral problem. All too often, teachers do not pay close enough attention to the principles that

INTASC

INTASC 4: Instructional strategies

PRAXIS

PRAXIS II: Delivery of Instruction to Students with Disabilities

| *Figure* 14.8 | **Implementing Positive Reinforcement Techniques** |

Determine what reinforcements will work for particular students:

- Ask the child by using direct formal or informal questioning or by administering an interest inventory or reinforcement survey.
- Ask those knowledgeable about the student (e.g., parents, friends, or past teachers).
- Observe the student in the natural environment as well as in a structured observation (e.g., arranging reinforcement alternatives from which the student may select).

Select meaningful reinforcers that are easy and practical to deliver in classroom settings (Idol, 1993).

"Catch" students behaving appropriately, and provide them with the subsequent appropriate reinforcement (referred to as the differential reinforcement of behavior incompatible with problem behavior). Begin this technique early so that students experience the effects of positive reinforcement.

Use the Premack (1959) principle ("Grandma's law": "eat your vegetables and then you can have dessert") regularly.

Use reinforcement techniques as the student makes gradual progress in developing a desired behavior that requires the mastery of numerous substeps (reinforce each successive approximation). This concept is called shaping.

Demonstrate to a student that certain behaviors will result in positive outcomes by reinforcing nearby peers.

have been noted, and, as a result, do not implement techniques with any power. Another potential problem is that some powerful positive behavioral interventions cannot be implemented because of such factors as cost or complexity (Bender, 2003).

The first illustrative application of the principle of positive reinforcement is **contingency contracting**, a concept introduced by Homme (1969). With this method, the teacher develops contracts with students that state what behaviors (e.g., academic work, social behaviors) students are to complete or perform, and what consequences (e.g., reinforcement) the instructor will provide. These contracts are presented as binding agreements between student and teacher. To be most effective, contracts should initially reward imperfect approximations of the behavior; provide frequent reinforcement; reward accomplishment rather than obedience; and be fair, clear, and positive. Figure 14.9 shows an example of a contract for a secondary school student.

Group contingencies, which are set up for groups of students rather than for individuals, provide excellent alternatives for managing behavior and actively including students with special needs in the general education classroom. There are three types:

- *Dependent contingencies:* All group members share in the reinforcement if one individual achieves a goal (i.e., the "hero" strategy).
- *Interdependent contingencies:* All group members are reinforced if all collectively (or all individually) achieve the stated goal.
- *Independent contingencies:* Individuals within the group are reinforced for individual achievement toward a goal.

Whereas independent contingencies are commonly used, the other two forms are less widely seen in the classroom. The dependent strategy is sometimes referred to as a "hero approach" because it singles out one student's performance for attention. Although it can be abused, such an approach may be particularly attractive for a student who responds well to peer attention. A student with special needs may feel more meaningfully included in class when his or her talents are recognized in this way.

Others may feel reinforced and accepted as part of a group when interdependent contingencies are employed. The most common use of an interdependent strategy is the "good behavior game." Because it is most often used as a behavioral reduction intervention, it is discussed later in the chapter.

The benefits of group-oriented contingencies (or peer-mediated strategies, as they are often called) include the involvement of peers, the ability of teachers to enhance

Contract

_____ will demonstrate the following appropriate behaviors
(Student's name)

in the classroom:

1. Come to school on time.
2. Come to school with homework completed.
3. Complete all assigned work in school without prompting.
4. Ask for help when necessary by raising hand and getting teacher's attention.

_____ will provide the following reinforcement:
(Teacher's name)

1. Ten tokens for the completion of each of the above four objectives. Tokens for the first two objectives will be provided at the beginning of class after all homework assignments have been checked. Tokens for objectives 3 and 4 will be provided at the end of the school day.
2. Tokens may be exchanged for activities on the Classroom Reinforcement Menu at noon on Fridays.

_____   _____
Student's signature   Teacher's signature

                                                      _____
                                                      Date

Figure 14.9

Sample Contract between Student and Teacher

From _Behavior Management: Applications for Teachers and Parents_ (p. 189), by T. Zirpoli and G. Melloy, 1993. Columbus, OH: Merrill. Used by permission.

motivation, and increased efficiency for the teacher. In some instances, students will raise questions of fairness concerning group contingency programs. Those who typically behave appropriately may feel that they are being penalized for the actions of others if reinforcement occurs only when the whole group evidences a desired behavior. You can assure them that, ultimately, they and everyone else will benefit from group success with particular guidelines or goals. Two resources—one for young students (_Practical Ideas That Really Work with Students Who Are Disruptive, Defiant, and Difficult: Preschool through Grade 4,_ [McConnell, Ryser, & Patton, 2002a]) and the other for older students (_Practical Ideas That Really Work with Students Who Are Disruptive, Defiant, and Difficult: Grades 5–12_ [McConnell, Ryser, & Patton, 2002b])—include many practical ideas for using individual and group contingencies.

Decreasing Undesirable Behaviors   Every teacher will face situations involving undesirable behaviors that require behavior reduction techniques. Most undesirable behavior will represent minor infractions that will require straightforward, fairly easy-to-administer interventions; some behaviors will be more disruptive, defiant, or disturbing, and will require more intrusive and complex responses. For these more severe behaviors, knowledge of the "acting-out cycle" (Colvin, 1993) and responding during the early stages will prevent the behavior from escalating or minimize the impact of the behavior on classroom dynamics. This cycle includes the following seven sequential phases: calm, triggers, agitation, acceleration, peak, de-escalation, and recovery. This section will focus more on dealing with less-severe behaviors that are typical of almost all classrooms.

Teachers can select from a range of techniques; however, it is usually best to begin with the least intrusive interventions (Smith & Rivera, 1995) and more neutrally oriented ones. A recommended sequence of reduction strategies is depicted in Figure 14.10. As teachers consider reductive strategies, they are cautioned to keep records, develop plans of action, and follow state and local guidelines.

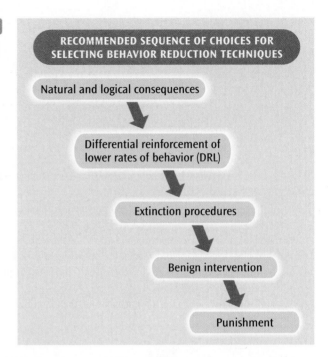

Figure 14.10

Recommended Sequence of Selected Behavior Reduction Techniques

The use of natural and logical consequences can help children and adolescents learn to be more responsible for their behaviors (West, 1986, 1994). These principles are particularly important for students with special needs who often have difficulty seeing the link between their behavior and the resulting consequences.

With **natural consequences**, the situation itself provides the contingencies for a certain behavior. For example, if a student forgets to return a permission slip to attend an off-campus event, the natural consequence is that the student is not allowed to go and must remain at school. Thus, rather than intervening in a given situation, the teacher allows the situation to teach the student. Natural consequences are an effective ways to teach common sense and responsibility (West, 1994).

In **logical consequences**, there is a logical connection between inappropriate behavior and the consequences that follow. If a student forgets lunch money, a logical consequence might be that money must be borrowed from someone else. The uncomfortable consequence is the hassle or embarrassment of requesting financial assistance. These tactics can help students recognize that their own behavior has created the discomfort and not something the teacher has done to them. When using this approach, teachers should clarify to students that they are responsible for their own behaviors. Logical consequences relate the disciplinary response directly to the inappropriate behavior.

The next option on the continuum is the use of **differential reinforcement**. A number of variations of this researched-based technique exist, such as *differential reinforcement of alternative behaviors (DRA)*, *differential reinforcement of incompatible behavior (DRI)*, *differential reinforcement of other behavior (DRO)*, and *differential reinforcement of lower rates of behavior (DRL)*. This last technique will be discussed in below.

The DRL technique uses positive reinforcement strategies as a behavior reduction tool. A teacher using this procedure provides appropriate reinforcement to students for displaying lower rates of a certain behavior that has been targeted for reduction. It is important to remember that the goal should be to decrease the frequency or duration of the unwanted behavior.

An example of this technique used with groups of students is the "good behavior game" (originally developed by Barrish, Saunders, & Wolf, 1969), in which student teams receive reinforcement if the number of occurrences of inappropriate behaviors

CONSIDER THIS

What are some advantages of using a DRL approach when working on a complex behavior, rather than simply reinforcing the student only after a targeted behavior has completely disappeared?

remains under a preset criterion. Tankersley (1995) provides a good overview of the use of the good behavior game:

> First, teachers should define target behaviors that they would like to see improved and determine when these behaviors are most problematic in their classrooms. Criteria for winning must be set and reinforcers established; the students should be taught the rules for playing. Next, the classroom is divided into teams and team names are written on the chalkboard. If any student breaks a rule when the game is in effect, the teacher makes a mark by the name of the team of which the disruptive student is a member. At the end of the time in which the game is played, any team that has fewer marks than the preestablished criterion wins. Members of the winning team(s) receive reinforcers daily. In addition, teams that meet weekly criterion receive reinforcers at the end of the week. (p. 20)

Here are additional considerations:

- Understand that undesirable behaviors will still occur and must be tolerated until target levels are reached.
- Reduce the criterion level after students have demonstrated stability at the present level.
- Avoid making too great a jump between respective criterion levels to ensure that students are able to meet the new demands.

Tankersley (1995) stresses the value of this strategy in noting that it "can be very effective in changing students' behaviors, can lead to improved levels of academic skills . . ., can reduce the teacher's burden of incorporating several individual contingency systems for managing behavior, . . . [makes] use of natural supports available in the classroom, [and] can help promote generalization" (p. 26).

The next reduction option involves **extinction procedures**. In this technique, the teacher withholds reinforcement for a behavior. Over time, such action, in combination with the positive reinforcement of related desirable behaviors, should extinguish the inappropriate behavior. One example is for the teacher to cease responding to student misbehavior. For some situations, it will be necessary to involve a student's peers in the extinction process to eliminate a behavior because the peers' actions are controlling the relevant reinforcers. The following are additional suggestions:

> **TEACHING TIP**
>
> When attempting to reduce an inappropriate behavior by ignoring it, teachers must remember to positively reinforce behaviors that are desired.

- Analyze what is reinforcing the undesirable behavior, and isolate the reinforcer(s) before initiating this procedure.
- Understand that the extinction technique is desirable because it does not involve punishment, but it will take time to be effective.
- Do not use this technique with behaviors that require immediate intervention (e.g., fighting).
- Recognize that the withholding of reinforcement is likely to induce an increase ("spiking" effect) in the occurrence of the undesirable behavior—as students intensify their efforts to receive the reinforcement they are used to getting—and may produce an initial aggressive response.
- Provide reinforcement to students who demonstrate appropriate incompatible behaviors (e.g., taking turns versus interrupting).

The fourth option is the use of behavior reduction techniques that border on being punishment but are so unobtrusive that they can be considered **benign tactics**. These suggestions are consistent with a concept developed by Cummings (1983), called the "law of least intervention," and that of Evertson and colleagues (2006), called "minor interventions." The main idea is to eliminate disruptive behaviors quickly with a minimum of disruption to the classroom or instructional routine. Table 14.3 includes a list of benign tactics for reducing undesirable behavior that is based on four types of prompts: physical, gestural, visual, and verbal.

> **TEACHING TIP**
>
> Being physically close to students who often display behavior problems is a powerful method of reducing inappropriate behaviors.

The last option in this reduction hierarchy and the one that is most intrusive and less attractive, is the use of **punishment**. It is the least preferable option because it involves

Table 14.3   **Benign Tactics for Reducing Undesirable Behavior**

Type of Prompt	Specific Tactic
Physical	• Position yourself physically near students who are likely to create problems (proximity control). • Touch a student's shoulder gently to convey your awareness that the student is behaving in some inappropriate (albeit previously identified) way. • Place a note (e.g., post-it) on the student's desk — it does not have to have anything written on it, if the student understands the intent (Jones & Jones, 2007). • Remove seductive objects (Levin & Nolan, 2003).
Gestural	• Use subtle and not-so-subtle gestures to stop undesirable behaviors (e.g., pointing, head shaking, finger spelling). • Use hand signals to indicate any number of messages.
Visual/auditory	• Establish eye contact and maintain it for a while with a student who is behaving inappropriately. This results in no disruption to the instructional routine. • Use sound signals — from simple devices to get student attention (Smith, 2004).
Verbal	• Redirect behavior in unobtrusive ways (i.e., not embarrassing to an individual student) that are directed to the whole class or through the use of humor. • Ask students, as a group, to look at the teacher — Note: cultural implications of this suggestion must be considered (Smith, 2004). • Stop talking for a noticeable length of time to redirect student attention. • Call on students who are not attending, but ask them questions that they can answer successfully. • Give the student a choice. • Try nonpunitive time out — ask the student if they would like to do something that will remove them from the situation for a short, defined period of time — thus, accomplishing a change of activity that might be needed (Levin & Nolan, 2003). • Use an "I-Message" — e.g., I feel concerned that. . . .; I hear you say that . . . • Avoid sarcasm and confrontation.
Instructional	• Change the pace of the classroom activity (Levin & Nolan, 2003). • Increase interest by using humor (Jones & Jones, 2007). • Use "interest boosting" — i.e., showing interest in the student's work (Levin & Nolan, 2003). • Provide needed re-instruction — if the student clearly is struggling (Evertson et al., 2006).

the presentation of something unpleasant or the removal of something pleasant as a consequence of the performance of an undesirable behavior.

Much controversy has arisen in regard to the use of punishment. Those who espouse a positive behavioral supports attitude would argue strongly against the use of punishers. Punishment should be considered only as a last resort. However, in situations in which a more immediate cessation of undesirable behaviors is required, punishment may be necessary. Because of their potency, punishment strategies should be weighed carefully; they can interfere with the learning process if not used sparingly and appropriately. Given that all teachers are likely to use punishment at some point, the key is to ensure that it is used appropriately.

Three punishment techniques are commonly used in classrooms: **reprimands, time-out,** and **response cost.** For these forms of punishment to work, it is critical that they be applied immediately after the occurrence of the undesirable behavior and that students understand why they are being applied. An overview of these techniques is provided in Table 14.4.

A reprimand represents a type of punishment in which an unpleasant condition (verbal reprimand from the teacher) is presented to the student. The following are some specific ways to use this type of technique:

• Do not let this type of interchange dominate your interactions with students.
• Look at the student and talk in a composed way.

Table 14.4	Three Commonly Used Punishment Techniques		
Type	**Definition**	**Advantages**	**Disadvantages**
Reprimand	A verbal statement or nonverbal gesture that expresses disapproval	Easily applied with little or no preparation required No physical discomfort to students	Sometimes not effective Can serve as positive reinforcement if this is a major source of attention
Response Cost	A formal system of penalties in which a reinforcer is removed contingent on the occurrence of an inappropriate behavior	Easily applied with quick results Does not disrupt class activities No physical discomfort to students	Not effective once student has "lost" all reinforcers Can initially result in some students being more disruptive
Time-Out	Limited or complete loss of access to positive reinforcers for a set amount of time	Fast-acting and powerful No physical discomfort to students	Difficult to find secluded areas where students would not be reinforced inadvertently May require physical assistance to the time-out area Overuse can interfere with educational and prosocial efforts

From *Student Teacher to Master Teacher* (p. 149), by M. S. Rosenberg, L. O'Shea, and D. J. O'Shea, 1991. New York: Macmillan. Reprinted by permission.

- Do not verbally reprimand a student from across the room. Get close to the student, maintain a degree of privacy, and minimize embarrassment.
- Let the student know exactly why you are concerned.
- Convey to the student that it is the behavior that is the problem and not him or her.

With time-out a student is removed from a situation in which he or she typically receives positive reinforcement, thus being prevented from enjoying something pleasurable. Different ways are available to remove a student from a reinforcing setting: students are allowed to observe the situation from which they have been removed (contingent observation); students are excluded from the ongoing proceedings entirely (exclusion time-out); and students are secluded in a separate room (seclusion time-out). The first two versions are most likely to be considered for use in general education classrooms. The following suggestions are extremely important if time-out is to be used appropriately.

- Confirm that the ongoing situation from which a student is going to be removed is indeed reinforcing; if not, this technique will not serve as a punisher and rather may be a form of positive reinforcement.
- Ensure that the time-out area is devoid of reinforcing elements. If it is not a neutral setting, this procedure will fail.
- Do not keep students in time-out for long periods of time (i.e., more than ten minutes) or use it frequently (e.g., daily), as students will miss significant amounts of instructional time.
- As a rule of thumb with younger children, never allow time-out periods to extend beyond one minute for every year of the child's age (up to a maximum of ten minutes).
- Use a timer to ensure accuracy in the length of time-out.

TEACHING TIP

To ensure proper compliance, teachers must always be aware of state or local guidelines when using time out for reducing student behavior.

A time-out can be an effective reinforcement of the need for appropriate behavior.

- Incorporate this procedure as one of the classroom procedures explained and taught at the beginning of the school year.
- Consider using a time-out system in which students are given one warning before being removed.
- Signal to the student when it is appropriate to return.
- Do not use this technique with certain sensitive students.
- Keep records on frequency, reason for using, and amount of time placed when using seclusion time-out procedures.

Response cost involves the loss of something the student values, such as privileges or points. It is a system in which a penalty or fine is levied for occurrences of inappropriate behavior. The following are some specific suggestions:

- Explain clearly to students how the system works and how much one will be fined for a given offense.
- Make sure all penalties are presented in a nonpersonal manner.
- Confirm that privileges that are lost are indeed reinforcing to students.
- Make sure that all privileges are not lost quickly, resulting in a situation in which a student may have little or no incentive to behave appropriately.
- Tie in this procedure with positive reinforcement at all times.

Generalization and Maintenance   After behaviors have been established at acceptable levels, the next stages involve transferring what has been learned to new contexts and maintaining established levels of performance. Teachers often succeed in teaching students certain behaviors but fail to help them apply the skills to new situations or retain them over time. Teaching appropriate behaviors and then hoping that students will be able to use various skills at some later time is detrimental to many students with special needs because a core difficulty they experience is performing independently in the classroom.

Teachers need to program for generalization, the wider application of a behavior skill, by giving students opportunities to use new skills in different settings, with different people, and at different times. Students often need help to identify the cues that should trigger the performance of an acquired behavior, action, or skill.

To maintain their skills, students also need to practice what they have learned previously. Instructional planning should allow time for students to determine how well they have retained what they have learned. This time usually can be provided during seatwork activities or other arrangements.

Suggestions for generalization and maintenance include:

- Create opportunities for students to practice in different situations what they have learned.
- Work with other teachers to provide additional opportunities.
- Place students in situations that simulate those that they will encounter in the future, both within school and in other areas of life.
- Show students how these skills or behaviors will be useful to them in the future.
- Prompt students to use recently acquired skills in a variety of contexts.
- Maintain previously taught skills by providing ongoing practice or review.

As noted previously, the use of positive behavior supports has become more popular in working with students with special needs, particularly because of its effectiveness and its emphasis on the environment rather than the individual. A key to behavioral generalization and maintenance, therefore, is to focus beyond the student and ensure that the learning environment is designed in such a way that students can use their newly acquired skills effectively to become accepted and active members of the classroom while enhancing their learning opportunities. In addition, key elements of generalization and maintenance relate to self-management strategies, which become essential in work with adolescents.

Self-Management   Ultimately, we want all students to be able to manage their own behaviors without external direction, as this ability is a requirement of functioning independently in life. Special attention needs to be given to those who do not display independent behavioral control and thus must develop student-regulated strategies—interventions that, though initially taught by the teacher, are intended to be implemented independently by the student. Bender (2003) refers to this end state as the "self-discipline" phase.

CONSIDER THIS

Why is it important to teach students to manage their own behaviors without external guidance from teachers? How can self-management assist students with disabilities in their inclusion in the community?

An interesting contraction exists regarding the development of student responsibility for their own behavior. While a strong research base exists for such instruction (Marzano, 2003), it does not occur very often within the K through 12 experience of most students (Shapiro & Cole, 1994). Marzano feels this occurs because providing this type of instruction "goes beyond the traditional duties of a classroom teacher" (p. 79). This situation is further exacerbated in today's schools with heightened attention to addressing the content and performance standards of the curriculum.

The concept of self-management is an outgrowth of cognitive behavior modification, a type of educational intervention for students with disabilities in use since the 1980s, that stresses active thinking about behavior. Shapiro, DuPaul, and Bradley-Klug (1998) provide a good overview of self-management:

> It is helpful to conceptualize self-management interventions as existing on a continuum. At one end, the intervention is completely controlled by the teacher . . .; this individual provides feedback regarding whether the student's behavior met the desired criteria and administers the appropriate consequences for the behavior. At the other end, the student engages in evaluating his or her own behavior against the criteria for performance, without benefit of teacher . . . input. The student also self-administers the appropriate consequences. In working with students with behavior problems, the objective should be to move a student as far toward the self-management side of the continuum as possible. Although some of these students may not be capable of reaching levels of independent self-management, most are certainly capable of approximating this goal. (p. 545)

Fiore, Becker, and Nerro (1993) state the rationale for such interventions: "Cognitive-behavioral [intervention] is . . . intuitively appealing because it combines behavioral techniques with cognitive strategies designed to directly address core problems of impulse control, higher order problem solving, and self-regulation" (p. 166). Whereas traditional behavioral interventions most often stress the importance of teacher monitoring of student behavior, extrinsic reinforcement, and teacher-directed learning, cognitive interventions instead focus on teaching students to monitor their own behavior, to engage in self-reinforcement, and to direct their own learning in strategic fashion (Dowdy, Patton, Smith, & Polloway, 1997).

Such approaches have become particularly popular with students with learning and attentional difficulties because they offer the promise of:

- Increasing focus on selective attention
- Modifying impulsive responding
- Providing verbal mediators to assist in academic and social problem-solving situations
- Teaching effective self-instructional statements to enable students to "talk through" tasks and problems
- Providing strategies that may lead to improvement in peer relations. (Rooney, 1993)

While using self-management strategies with students with special needs in inclusive settings has been far more limited than studies of using them in pull-out programs, the moderate to strong positive outcomes reported in research are encouraging (McDougall, 1998).

Student-regulated strategies form the essence of self-management. Although variations exist in how these are defined and described, the components listed in Figure 14.11 represent the central aspects of self-management.

Figure 14.11

Components of Self-Management

From *Guide to Attention Deficits in the Classroom* (p. 162), by C. A. Dowdy, J. R. Patton, T. E. C. Smith, and E. A. Polloway, 1998. Austin, TX: Pro-Ed. Used by permission.

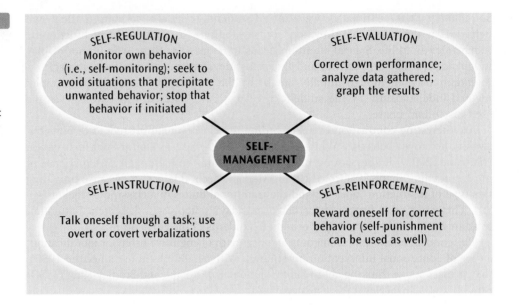

CONSIDER THIS

Do you engage in any self-monitoring techniques? If so, how do you use them? How effective are they?

Two components with particular utility for general education teachers are self-monitoring and self-instruction. **Self-monitoring**, a technique in which students observe and record their own behavior, has been commonly employed with students with learning problems. Lloyd, Landrum, and Hallahan (1991) note that self-monitoring was initially seen as an assessment technique, but as individuals observed their own behavior, the process also resulted in a change in behavior. Self-monitoring of behavior, such as attention, is a relatively simple technique that has been validated with children who have learning disabilities, mental retardation, multiple disabilities, attention deficits, and behavior disorders; it has also been profitable for nondisabled students (McDougall, 1998; Lloyd et al., 1991; Prater, Joy, Chilman, Temple, & Miller, 1991). Increased attention, beneficial to academic achievement, has been reported as a result.

A common mechanism for self-monitoring was developed by Hallahan, Lloyd, and Stoller (1982). It involves using a tape-recorded tone that sounds at random intervals (e.g., every forty-five seconds), and a self-recording sheet. Each time the tone sounds, children ask themselves whether they are paying attention and then mark the "yes" or the "no" box on the tally sheet. Students are often not accurate in their recording, nevertheless positive changes in behavior have been observed in many research studies. While self-monitoring procedures may prove problematic for one teacher to implement alone, a collaborative approach within a cooperative teaching arrangement offers much promise.

Teachers should consider ways to creatively use self-monitoring in their classrooms as an adjunct to other ongoing management strategies. McDougall (1998) offers this unique suggestion:

> Practitioners . . . could train students to use tactile cues to mediate self-management in much the same manner that students use visually cued, audio-cued, or covert self-monitoring. Tactile cues such as those produced by vibrating pagers might be a functional option for (a) students who have difficulty responding to visual and auditory cues, (b) students with multiple, profound, or sensory disabilities, (c) situations in which audio or visual cues might distract other students, and (d) students who wish to maintain privacy when self-monitoring. (p. 317)

Self-instruction represents another useful intervention. Pfiffner and Barkley (1991) describe components of a self-instruction program as follows:

Self-instructions include defining and understanding the task or problem, planning a general strategy to approach the problem, focusing attention on the task, selecting an answer or solution, and evaluating performance. In the case of successful performance, self-reinforcement (usually in the form of a positive self-statement, such as "I really did a good job") is provided. In the case of an unsuccessful performance, a coping statement is made (e.g., "Next time I'll do better if I slow down") and errors are corrected. At first, an adult trainer typically models the self-instructions while performing a task. The child then performs the same task while the trainer provides the self-instructions. Next, the child performs the task while self-instructing aloud. These overt verbalizations are then faded to covert self-instructions. (p. 525)

Clear, simple self-instruction strategies form an appropriate beginning for interventions with students with learning or attentional difficulties in the general education classroom. Such approaches are likely to enhance success. Pfiffner and Barkley (1991) recommend the STAR program, in which "children learn to Stop, Think ahead about what they have to do, Act or do the requested task while talking to themselves about the task, and Review their results" (p. 529).

Detailed and systematic procedures have been developed for implementing self-management strategies. Some basic recommendations follow:

- Allocate sufficient instructional time to teach self-management to students who need it.
- Establish a sequence of activities that move by degrees from teacher direction to student direction and self-control.
- Include objectives relevant to improved behavior and enhanced learning (e.g., increased attention yields reading achievement gains).
- Provide strategies and assistive materials (e.g., self-recording forms) for students to use.
- Model how effective self-managers operate. Point out actual applications of the elements of self-management (as highlighted in Figure 14.5), and give students opportunities to practice these techniques with your guidance.
- Provide for the maintenance of learned strategies and for generalization to other settings in and out of school.

Instructional Dimension

In general, teachers need to provide instruction that fulfills the objectives set by school standards and that matches the needs of their students. Levin and Nolan (2003) recommend that "students need to be assigned tasks that are moderately challenging but within their capability" (p. 16). Carter and Doyle (2006) suggest that students do better with familiar tasks—that is, "tasks that are typical or recognizable, have a clearly defined product and explicit grading criteria, and have been routinized in class" (p. 383)—than they do with novel work.

All the dimensions discussed in this chapter relate to the broad concern for instructional outcomes. However, certain aspects of instruction are closely related to sound organizational and management practices, such as scheduling, transitions, grouping, lesson planning, and technology, and can have a significant impact on quality of instruction.

Scheduling   Scheduling involves the general temporal arrangement of events for both the entire day (i.e., master schedule) and a specific class period. This section focuses on the latter. The importance of a carefully planned schedule cannot be overemphasized. This is particularly true in classrooms that include students with special needs.

The thoughtful scheduling of a class period can contribute greatly to the amount of time that students can spend actively engaged in learning. It can also add to the quality of what is learned. For instance, a science lesson might include the following components:

- Transitional activities (into the classroom)
- Attention-getting and motivating techniques

CROSS-REFERENCE

Review Chapter 5 on learning disabilities to see how self-monitoring and self-instructional techniques are used with students with learning disabilities.

CEC STANDARDS

CEC 4: Instructional Strategies

INTASC

INTASC 4: Instructional strategies

PRAXIS

PRAXIS II: Delivery of Services to Students with Disabilities

Rights & Responsibilities

Disciplinary Issues and Federal Law

Under PL 94–142, relevant state statues, and IDEA, students with disabilities were protected from arbitrary suspension or expulsion in instances in which their behavioral difficulty was determined to be related to their disability. This provision was promoted as a major victory for the rights of students with disabilities because it decreased the likelihood that they could be denied a free, appropriate public education. The unforeseen side effect was that the protection of the rights of an individual came to be perceived as a potential threat to school discipline, in general, and to the safety and security of other students, teachers, and staff by creating a two-tiered system of discipline.

The extent of serious behavioral problems associated with students with disabilities has been a controversial issue. Nevertheless, a distinct minority of such students may present troublesome behaviors that challenge a school's ability to effectively educate all children and youth. As a result, it is not surprising that when possible amendments to the IDEA were discussed, concern was focused on determining the balance between the rights of students with disabilities and the needs for an orderly learning environment in the schools.

The legal resolution of this debate was the incorporation of a requirement for specific practices within the new regulations under PL 105–17 (1997 amendments to IDEA). Foremost among these were the establishment of clearer guidelines for the removal of students with disabilities from the regular school setting, the need for a functional behavioral assessment, and the establishment of a requirement for the development of a behavioral intervention plan for individual students who present challenging behaviors within the school setting. The final regulations issued in March 1999 reaffirmed the use of these procedures.

Adapted from *Behavioral Intervention Planning* (p. 27), by K. Fad, J. R. Patton, and E. A. Polloway, 2000. Austin, TX: Pro-Ed. Used by permission.

- Data-gathering techniques
- Data-processing techniques
- Closure activities
- Transitional activities (to the next class period)

All components support the instructional goal for the day. Reminders or cues from the teacher can augment such a system. The following are some specific suggestions:

- Provide time reminders (visual and audible) for students during the class period so that they know how much time is available.
- Plan for transitions (see next section).
- Require students to complete one activity or task before moving on to the next.
- Vary the nature of class activities to keep students engaged and to create a stimulating instructional tempo and pace.
- Minimize noninstructional time when students are not academically engaged.

Scheduling involves planning for class period transitions. Efficient transitions can minimize disruptions, maximize the amount of time allocated to instructional tasks, and maintain desired conditions of learning. Structured approaches to transitions will be particularly helpful to students with special needs. Several ways to ease transitions follow:

- Model appropriate transitions between activities. (Rosenberg et al., 1991)
- Let students practice appropriate transition skills.
- Use specific cues (e.g., blinking lights, a buzzer, teacher signal) to signal students that it is time to change instructional routine.

CROSS-REFERENCE

See Chapter 15 for more information on using grouping strategies for students with disabilities.

Grouping Grouping refers to how students are organized for instructional purposes. The need to place students into smaller group arrangements depends on the nature of the curricular area or the goal of a specific lesson. Evertson and colleagues (2006) discuss seven ways to group students for instruction: whole group, small teacher-led group, small cooperative group, small noncompetitive group, student pairs, individualized instruction, and centers or stations. Each of these formats has advantages and disadvantages for students and teachers.

For students with special needs, the main concern within a group setting is attention to individual needs. Using innovative grouping arrangements and providing different cooperative learning opportunities allow for variety in the instructional routine for students with special needs. Some specific suggestions follow:

- Give careful consideration to the makeup of groups.
- Make sure that group composition is not constant. Vary membership as a function of having different reasons for grouping students.
- Use different grouping arrangements that are based on interest or for research purposes. (Wood, 1996)
- Use cooperative learning arrangements on a regular basis, as this approach, if structured properly, facilitates successful learning and socialization.
- Determine the size of groups based on ability levels: the lower the ability, the smaller the size of the group. (Rosenberg et al., 1991)
- Use mixed-ability groups when cooperative learning strategies are implemented to promote the active involvement of all students.

Lesson Planning Lesson plans help teachers prepare for instruction. Many teachers start out writing very detailed lesson plans and eventually move to less comprehensive formats. However, some teachers continue to use detailed plans throughout their teaching careers, as they find the detail helpful in providing effective instruction. Detailed planning is frequently needed for lessons that must be modified to be appropriate for gifted students or students with disabilities. Six research-based components of lessons include: lesson introduction, clarity, coached practice, closure, solitary practice, and review (Levin & Nolan, 2003). Other key elements of lesson planning that should be considered are options for early finishers, specific accommodations that some students may require, and techniques for evaluation. Suggestions for developing lesson plans follow:

CEC STANDARDS

CEC 7: Instructional Planning

- Create interest in and clarify the purpose of lessons. This concern is particularly important for students with special needs.
- Consider the importance of direct instruction to help students acquire an initial grasp of new material.
- Assign independent practice, some of which can be accomplished in class and some of which should be done as homework.
- Plan activities for students who finish early. Such planning might be particularly useful for gifted students.
- Anticipate problems that might arise during the course of the lesson, and identify techniques for dealing with them.

INTASC

INTASC 7: Plans instruction

PRAXIS

PRAXIS II: Delivery of Services to Students with Disabilities

Evertson and colleagues (2006) have developed a checklist for planning for instruction (see Figure 14.12). The checklist provides a nice way to ensure that key issues related to an instructional lesson are considered prior to actual instruction. This type of reminder is extremely useful for beginning teachers.

Technology The application of technology to curriculum and instruction is widespread today. From a management perspective, teachers must consider a number of variables when deciding to use technology. While more software choices are available commercially these days, the selection of software that is appropriate for students and that relates to instructional objectives requires effort and knowledge. Some suggestions follow:

- Consider accessibility needs of students with disabilities.
- Obtain necessary input and output devices for students who require such hardware.

Figure 14.12   **Planning for Instruction**

Check When Complete	Before the Lesson Ask Yourself	Notes
☐	A. What are the most important concepts or skills to be learned?	_____
☐	B. What kind of learning is your goal (memorization, application, appreciation)? Have you communicated this to your students?	_____
☐	C. What learning style is targeted by this lesson? Are you varying learning modalities?	_____
☐	D. Are there difficult words or concepts that need extra explanation?	_____
☐	E. How will you help students make connections to previous learning?	_____
☐	F. What activities will you plan to create interest in the lesson?	_____
☐	G. How will you make transitions between activities?	_____
☐	H. What materials will be needed? Will students need to learn how to use them?	_____
☐	I. What procedures will students need to know to complete the activities?	_____
☐	J. How much time will you allocate for the lesson? For different parts of the lesson?	_____
☐	K. If activities require that students work together, how will groups be formed? How will you encourage productive work in groups?	_____
☐	L. What examples and questioning strategies will you use? Prepare a list of examples for explanations and list higher-order questions.	_____
☐	M. How will you know during and after the lesson what students understand?	_____
☐	N. What are some presentation alternatives if students have trouble with concepts (peer explanation, media, etc.)?	_____
☐	O. Are there extra- or special-help students?	_____
☐	P. How will you make sure that all students participate?	_____
☐	Q. How will you adjust the lesson if time is too short or too long?	_____
☐	R. What kind of product, if any, will you expect from students at the end of the lesson?	_____
☐	S. What will students do when they finish?	_____
☐	T. How will you evaluate students' work and give them feedback?	_____
☐	U. How will the concepts you present be used by students in future lessons?	_____

From *Classroom Management for Elementary Teachers* (7th ed.; pp. 112–113), by C. M. Evertson, E. T. Emmer, and M. E. Worsham, 2006. Boston: Allyn & Bacon.

- Determine whether websites are considerate of students with disabilities.
- Make sure that websites are appropriate.
- Consider the use of Internet filters.
- Design lessons that utilize computers in ways that are engaging.
- Teach students dos and don'ts of using e-mail and the Internet (e.g., giving out private information).

Organizational Dimension

The increased diversity in today's general education classrooms has created numerous new challenges for the teacher. Some have likened the current classroom to a "one-room schoolhouse," in which the classroom teacher must respond to the unique needs of many students. This section acknowledges how time management in the areas of personnel interactions, the work environment, administrative duties, instructional applications, ongoing communication systems, and personal applications can promote success. The nearby Personal Spotlight describes how one teacher uses time management techniques.

Personnel Responsibilities In the typical general education classroom, teachers regularly interact with special education teachers, other classroom teachers, professional support staff (e.g., speech-language pathologists, school psychologists), paraeducators, teacher trainees, volunteers, and peer tutors. To enhance personnel interactions, teachers should consider these recommendations:

- Establish good initial working relationships with support personnel.
- Clarify the supports professional personnel are providing to students in your class. See the nearby Evidence-Based Practice feature for more ideas.
- Clarify the roles of these people and the classroom teachers as collaborators for instructional and behavioral interventions.
- Establish the roles and responsibilities of aides, volunteers, and trainees.
- Determine the level of expertise of paraeducators, and discuss with them specific activities that they can perform and supports they can provide to students.
- Delegate noninstructional (and, as appropriate, instructional) duties to classroom aides when these assistants are available.

Personal Spotlight

Third-Grade Teacher

Karen Weeks Canfield is a third-grade teacher. As such, she has to deal with a very heterogeneous group of children. Some children in Karen's room have identified disabilities and receive special education for part of the day; some appear to be at risk for developing problems; and others seem to be your "typical nine-year-old." Karen notes that "with so many types of teaching, and with parents involved in the classroom in various ways, attention to organization is critical."

Karen uses several methods to help herself stay organized. Without a certain level of organization, she believes that teaching would be an impossible task. Some of Karen's methods for staying organized are these:

1. Completing forms as soon as she receives them so they do not get lost "in the shuffle."
2. Not taking part in conversations during the school day that do not benefit herself or her students in some way.
3. Grading all papers the same day that they are turned in.
4. Using a correspondence file for all students so she has a record of all of her communications with parents—both good communication and negative communication.
5. Using a "to do" list for her planning periods.

These organizational tips help Karen manage her classroom more efficiently. Without such strategies, she believes that she would have to spend a great deal of time at home doing schoolwork, which would take away time from her family.

Karen notes that "being a well-organized teacher affects not only my job performance, but the students' performance as well. The days that I am less organized are the days that the students seem to be 'crazy.' I don't think it's a coincidence. I am constantly looking for ways to make the most out of a priceless commodity—time."

Karen Weeks Canfield

Lynchburg Public Schools, Lynchburg, VA

EVIDENCE-BASED PRACTICE

Collaboration: Ways to Involve Other Personnel in Management

1. The school principal or administrator can
   • Supply any necessary equipment or materials
   • Provide flexibility in staffing patterns
   • Show support for the teacher's actions.
2. The school guidance counselor can
   • Provide individual counseling sessions
   • Work with other students who may be reinforcing the inappropriate behavior of the disruptive student
   • Offer the teacher information about what may be upsetting to the student.
3. The school nurse can
   • Review the student's medical history for possible causes of difficulties

   • Recommend the possibility and practicality of medical or dietary intervention
   • Explain the effects and side effects of any medication the student is taking or may take in the future.
4. The school psychologist can
   • Review the teacher's behavior management plan and make recommendations for changes
   • Observe the student in the classroom and in other settings to collect behavioral data and note possible environmental instigators
   • Provide any useful data on the student that may have been recently collected, e.g., test scores, behavioral observations, etc.

5. The social worker can
   • Provide additional information about the home environment
   • Schedule regular visits to the home
   • Identify other public agencies that may be of assistance.
6. Other teachers can
   • Provide curricular and behavior management suggestions that work for them
   • Offer material resources
   • Provide carryover and consistency for the tactics used.

From *The Special Educator's Handbook* (p. 119), by D. L. Westling and M. A. Koorland, 1989. Boston: Allyn & Bacon. Used by permission.

• In cases in which a paraeducator accompanies a child with a disability in the general education classroom, develop a comprehensive plan with the special education teacher for involving this assistant appropriately.

Work Environment   The work environment refers to the immediate work area used by teachers—usually the desk and files. Teachers must consider how to utilize work areas and how to organize them. For instance, a teacher's desk may be designated as off-limits to all students or may be used for storage only or as a work area. Suggestions for establishing a work environment are listed here:

• Keep the teacher's desk organized and free of stacks of papers.
• Organize files so that documents and information can be retrieved easily and quickly.
• Use color-coded systems for filing, if possible.

Administrative Duties   Along with instructional duties, teaching includes numerous administrative duties. Two of the most time-demanding activities are participating in meetings and handling paperwork, including various forms of correspondence. The presence of students with special needs will increase such demands. The following are some strategies for handling paperwork:

• Prepare form letters for all necessary events (e.g., permissions, notifications, status reports, memo formats, reimbursement requests).
• Prepare master copies of various forms that are used regularly (e.g., certificates and awards, record sheets, phone conversation sheets).
• Keep notes of all school-related phone conversations with parents, teachers, support staff, administrators, or any other people.
• Handle most paperwork only once.
• Make the most of meetings—request an agenda and ask that meetings be time-limited and be scheduled at times that are convenient.

TEACHING TIP

Teachers must develop their own time-management strategies; adopting strategies that are effective for other teachers may or may not be effective for you.

Instructional Applications Some additional instructional applications of time-management techniques are provided here, focusing on materials and technology that can make the job of teaching easier. The most attractive piece of equipment available to teachers is the microcomputer. With the appropriate software, teachers can greatly reduce the amount of time spent on test generation, graphic organizers, behavior management planning, and so on. The following are some specific suggestions:

- Use self-correcting materials with students to reduce the amount of time required to correct student work.
- Use grade-book programs for recording student scores and determining grades.
- Use computers to generate a variety of instructionally related materials (tests, graphic organizers, puzzles).
- Give students computer-generated calendars that include important dates.

Ongoing Communication Systems As was pointed out earlier in the chapter, communication with parents or guardians is essential. Establishing a home–school communication system prior to the start of the school year and making it operational as soon as school begins is highly recommended. Many of the following suggestions are taken from ideas identified by Jones and Jones (2007).

- Obtain parental support for student support and positive classroom behaviors via introductory letter, phone call, home visit, or "back-to-school" night.
- Maintain teacher–parent communication throughout the year via Friday envelopes (work completed during the week), newsletters, progress reports.
- Create a website that provides various types of information—be sure to include homework assignments and important dates (e.g., when projects are due, when quizzes and tests are scheduled).

Personal Time-Management Applications Since it is impossible to completely divorce the management of one's personal time from management of professional time, it is worthwhile considering various time-management tactics that have a more personal application but can affect one's efficiency and effectiveness in the classroom as well. Some basic recommendations are provided here:

- Use a daily to-do list.
- Break down major tasks into smaller pieces and work on them.
- Avoid getting overcommitted.
- Work during work time. This might mean avoiding situations at school in which long social conversations will cut into on-task time.
- Avoid dealing with trivial activities if important ones must be addressed.
- Use idle time (e.g., waiting in lines) well. Always be prepared for these situations by having reading material or other portable work available.

The efficient management of one's professional and personal time can pay off in making day-to-day demands less overwhelming. Thus, the efforts to become a better time manager are certainly worthwhile.

Summary

Basic Concepts about Comprehensive Classroom Management and Organization

- Comprehensive classroom management includes all teacher-directed activities that support the efficient operations of the classroom and establish optimal conditions for learning.

- The key elements of the classroom environment that have a significant effect on instruction and learning include multidimensionality, simultaneity, immediacy, unpredictability, publicness, and history, while the key principles of successful management are careful planning, proactive strategies, consistency, awareness, and overlapping.

Components of Effective Classroom Organization and Management

- Classroom rules provide a general sense of what is expected of students.
- Rules should be essential for classroom functioning and for the development of a positive learning environment.
- Classroom procedures should include the specific ways in which certain activities or situations will be performed.
- Effective physical management includes classroom arrangement, accessibility, seating, and the use of specialized equipment.
- Desirable behaviors are increased through the use of positive reinforcement.
- Undesirable behaviors can be reduced through a variety of reduction strategies.

- Hierarchy of options would include (from least to most restrictive) natural and logical consequences, differential reinforcement, extinction, benign tactics, reprimands, response costs, and time-out.
- Successful educational programs help students develop self-management strategies.
- Instructional management includes careful attention to scheduling, transitions, grouping, and lesson plans.
- Successful teachers are organized and engage in the careful management of time. Technology can assist teachers in time management.
- Teachers need to take the student's culture into consideration when dealing with management issues.

Questions to Reconsider

Think back to the scenario about Sam and his teacher, Jeannie, at the beginning of this chapter. Would you answer the questions raised there any differently, now that you have read the chapter?

1. What recommendations would you give Jeannie for focusing on Sam's behavior and its consequences?

2. Which procedures can Jeannie use to significantly increase Sam's attention-to-task behaviors?
3. How can Sam's peers be involved in a comprehensive behavior management program?
4. How can cooperative teaching facilitate successful intervention in the inclusive classroom?

Further Readings

Christian, B. T. (1999). *Outrageous behavior modification.* Austin, TX: Pro-Ed.

Evertson, C. M., Emmer, E. T., & Worsham, M. E. (2006). *Classroom management for elementary teachers* (7th ed.). Boston: Allyn & Bacon.

Emmer, E. T., Evertson, C. M., & Worsham, M. E. (2006). *Classroom management for secondary teachers* (7th ed.). Boston: Allyn & Bacon.

Fad, K. M., Patton, J. R., & Polloway, E. A. (2006). *Behavioral intervention planning* (3rd ed.). Austin, TX: Pro-Ed.

Jones, V. F., & Jones, L. S. (2007). *Comprehensive classroom management: Creating communities of support and solving problems* (8th ed.). Boston: Allyn & Bacon.

Kaplan, J. S., & Carter, J. (1999). *Beyond behavior modification: A cognitive-behavioral approach to behavior management in the school* (3rd ed.). Austin, TX: Pro-Ed.

Koegel, L. K., Koegel, R. L., & Dunlap, G. (eds.). (1996). *Positive behavioral support.* Baltimore, MD: Brookes.

Lavelle, L. (1998). *Practical charts for managing behavior.* Austin, TX: Pro-Ed.

Levin, J., & Nolan, J. F. (2003). *What every teacher should know about classroom management.* Boston: Allyn & Bacon.

McConnell, K., Reyser, G., & Patton, J. R. (2002a). *Practical ideas that really work for disruptive, defiant, and difficult students: Preschool through grade 4.* Austin, TX: Pro-Ed.

McConnell, K., Reyser, G., & Patton, J. R. (2002b). *Practical ideas that really work for disruptive, defiant, and difficult students: Grades 5 through 12.* Austin, TX: Pro-Ed.

McEwan, E. K. (2006). *How to survive and thrive in the first three weeks of school.* Thousand Oaks, CA: Corwin Press.

Scott, J. R., & Meyer, L. H. (eds.). (1999). *Behavioral intervention: Principles, models, and practices.* Baltimore, MD: Brookes.

Smith, R. (2004). *Conscious classroom management: Unlocking the secrets of great teaching.* San Rafael, CA: Conscious Teaching Publications.

(mylabschool
Where the classroom comes to life

Go to Allyn & Bacon's MyLabSchool (www.mylabschool.com) and enter Assignment ID SPV7 into the Assignment Finder. Review the video clip called *Attention Deficit/Hyperactivity Disorder*. Now enter Assignment ID SPV10 and review the video clip called *Behavior Disorder*. Consider what you have seen along with what you have read in Chapter 14 to answer the following questions.

1. The two video clips show several students with significant behavioral problems. This chapter offers a number of interventions and strategies for helping children achieve age-appropriate classroom behavior.
   - What interventions and/or strategies might you use with Eric? Why?
   - What interventions and/or strategies might you use with Nick? Why?

2. Most public schools have support staff to help with students who have special needs, such as a school psychologist, social worker, or nurse. How might you involve these specialists in your classroom efforts to instruct students with special needs?

You may also answer the questions at the end of the clip and e-mail your responses to your instructor.

Now enter Assignment ID CS02 in the Assignment Finder and read the Case Study called *Encouraging Appropriate Behavior*. Select two cases from the case bank about students with special needs. Read the cases and respond to the questions raised at the end of them, relying both on the information in the case and on what you have read in this chapter. You may want to e-mail your responses to your instructor.

Teaching Students with Special Needs in Elementary Schools

After reading this chapter, you should be able to:

1. Describe the impact of inclusion on elementary students with disabilities.
2. Define the concept of comprehensive curriculum for students at the elementary level.
3. Identify curricular content considerations for academic, social skills, and transitional instruction.
4. Describe ways that collaboration can enhance inclusion in elementary schools.
5. Identify appropriate instructional adaptations.

Questions to Consider

1. How can Tamara and Adria develop effective collaboration strategies that will take advantage of their own talents and meet the needs of their students?

2. How can they resolve their ongoing questions about approaches for instruction for beginning readers in general and for those with learning difficulties?

3. What curriculum adaptations can be made to more effectively meet the needs of students with special needs in this classroom?

Tamara Nance was told by one of her college professors that the elementary classrooms of the new millennium were becoming increasingly similar to the "one-room schoolhouses of the turn of the twentieth century," encompassing a diversity of learning needs that had never been greater. Tamara was excited by this challenge and, in her first year of teaching, often reflected on this comment.

Tamara is teaching a class of second-graders in a self-contained general education class. She has responsibility for twenty-two eager students for all subjects except art, music, health, and physical education. She has found their diversity to be exciting and somewhat overwhelming.

Naturally, one of her greatest concerns has been in the area of language arts. After doing some informal observations and after reading the records of her students, she realized during the second week of the academic year that the ability levels of her students ranged greatly; two students were virtual nonreaders, whereas five pupils were functioning significantly above grade level in terms of their academic achievement.

It has become apparent to Tamara that these students do not all learn in the same way, but she continues to struggle to find approaches that will meet the needs of this diverse classroom. She is fortunate to be working two hours a day during her language arts instructional block with Adria Nunez, a special education teacher who is certified in learning disabilities.

This opening vignette illustrates a point that is consistent with the discussion throughout the book: elementary school presents unique challenges and unique opportunities for young students with special needs who are included in general education. In elementary school, the similarity of educational objectives and content for all students is at its greatest. Thus, there is an excellent opportunity for students with special needs to prosper in general education with the appropriate supports in place.

CONSIDER THIS

Inclusive classrooms are more common at the elementary level than at the secondary. Why do you think this statement is true?

Elementary school also offers an important beginning point for students with disabilities to profit from positive interactions with their peers who are not disabled. Preparation for successful life beyond the school setting requires the ability to learn, live, and work with a diversity of individuals. Thus, inclusion offers benefits both to students who are disabled and to their nondisabled peers. There is clearly no better time for inclusion to commence than in early childhood and throughout the primary and elementary grades.

The trend toward inclusion is reflected in Table 15.1. This analysis from Hoover and Patton (2005) reflects the changes in professional perspectives that have occurred over the past several decades. Furthermore, it highlights the core rationales for inclusive classrooms and the focus of curriculum.

Table **15.1**   **Trends in Educational Placements of Special Education Students in Elementary and Secondary Schools**

Predominant Theme	Primary Placement(s)	Prevailing Thought toward Education	Predominant View toward Curriculum
Separate special education is needed.	Self-contained classroom	Students who cannot benefit from general education would be best served in special classrooms.	Specialized curriculum and techniques are needed to effectively educate individuals with disabilities.
Effectiveness of separate special classrooms is questioned.	Self-contained classroom	Educators are questioning the practice and effects of educating students with disabilities in separate special classes.	The need for special curriculum and techniques for many students with disabilities is being questioned.
Education for many students with special needs does not occur in separate classrooms.	Resource rooms with some education in general education classrooms	Many learners may benefit from education in general education classrooms, requiring only some education in a special classroom.	Selected aspects of the general education curriculum are appropriate for learners with special needs.
Students with special needs may be educated appropriately in general education classrooms.	General education classrooms with some education in resource rooms	The least restrictive environment for many students termed "disabled" is education in the general education classroom.	Many students may benefit from the general education curriculum if proper adaptations and modifications are provided.
Students with disabilities should achieve full inclusion into general education.	Full integration into general education classrooms	The education of all students with disabilities is best achieved in the general education setting.	Continued expansion of integrated programs and curricula can be implemented in inclusive education settings.
Many diverse needs are to be met in inclusive settings.	Reaffirmation of full inclusion and full integration for students with special needs	The inclusive education setting is responsible for meeting an ever-increasing range of diverse needs.	Curriculum and instruction must be differentiated in collaborative ways to meet all diverse needs in the classroom.

Adapted from *Curriculum Adaptations for Students with Learning and Behavior Problems: Principles and Practices for Differentiating Instruction* (p. 29), by J. J. Hoover and J. R. Patton, 2005. Austin, TX: Pro-Ed.

Consistent with the trend reflected in Table 15.1, many young students with disabilities will receive a significant portion, or all, of their instruction in the general education classroom. According to the U.S. Department of Education (2006), 58.1 percent of all students with disabilities (ages six to eleven) were served in general education for at least 79 percent of the school day, while an additional 23.6 percent were in regular classes for 40–79 percent of the day. Only 15.9 percent were served in more restrictive settings within the regular school or in separate school and/or residential settings (2.4 percent). These data reflect a clear trend across recent years. Thus, beginning at the elementary level, careful attention must be given by all teachers to these students' educational needs.

The two critical questions in education are the question of curriculum (what?) and instruction (how?). Effective school programs begin with considerations of what is the information that students need to learn and how best can they learn that information. The primary purpose of this chapter is to address these two concerns. The initial section outlines core curriculum considerations. The discussion that follows emphasizes instructional strategies that provide the means for achieving learning goals.

General Curricular Considerations

Four general considerations provide a foundation for curriculum development. These include emphases on the general education (standards-based) curriculum, the need for a multitiered model of curriculum, universal design for learning, and the importance of comprehensive curriculum.

The curriculum for virtually all elementary students with special needs will be based on the **standards of learning**, as required in general by NCLB and as dictated by the particular state. The adoption of such standards, as consistent with the No Child Left Behind Act, has transformed the focus of educational programs for children with special needs. Table 15.2 provides an outline of key elements of standards-based education.

The core of the standards-based reform movement in recent years has been the focus on **content and performance standards**. As Pemberton, Rademacher, Tyler-Wood, and Cereijo (2006) note, "content standards define the knowledge and skills of students or what students should know and be able to accomplish as a result of their educational experiences. Performance standards define how well students should demonstrate the knowledge and skills" (pp. 283–284).

Providing further clarification, Wehmeyer (in press) referenced the work of the Committee on Goals 2000 and the Inclusion of Students with Disabilities (1997) in noting several ways in which standards could be made defensible for use with students with disabilities. Wehmeyer noted that content standards must reflect those skills that are critical to the success of students after leaving school; that these standards should be appropriate based on the age of the students; and that the standards-based curriculum should be taught to students with special needs while not effectively impacting on their opportunity to be taught, and acquire, functional behaviors and skills that are critical for community success.

The emphases in standards-based curriculum and the need for students with special needs to have access to the general curriculum have provided the impetus for multitiered models for curriculum development. The model developed by Hoover and Patton (2006) defines the three tiers as follows:

1. *High-quality core instruction:* This tier refers to empirically validated and systematic instruction embedded in a challenging curriculum in the general education classroom. Universal design for learning (see above) and differentiated instruction (as discussed earlier in Chapter 12), for example, provide guidelines for vehicles to successfully implement tier-one interventions. For most elementary students, this is the core curriculum they will follow.

CONSIDER THIS

Although general educators can rarely offer a truly "comprehensive curriculum," collaborative efforts with special educators can effect a more broad-based program. How can this work?

CEC STANDARDS

CEC 7: Instructional Planning

INTASC

INTASC 7: Plans instruction

PRAXIS

PRAXIS II: Delivery of Services to Students with Disabilities

CEC STANDARDS

CEC 7: Instructional Planning

Table 15.2	Elements of Standards-Based Education and Curriculum

Element	Description
Assessment closely linked to the curriculum	A significant alignment exists between the curriculum being taught and the skills and knowledge being assessed.
Comparison to standards, not other students	Standards-based curriculum emphasizes the development of standards, and the assessment reflects the level of proficiency for each student. Thus, the assessment compares students' proficiency levels with established standards and not with other students.
Alternative assessments used	Assessment of standards-based curriculum may include a variety of assignment strategies, such as constructed response, writing essays, authentic and real-life problem solving, or rubrics.
Achieving proficiency	NCLB requires that states and school systems annually monitor progress toward helping all students achieve proficiency of the standards, rather than simply reporting grouped, grade-level scores.
Application of results	Standards-based assessment results can be used to determine graduation requirements, hold educators accountable, and adapt curriculum. Results are no longer simply reported; rather, they are used for program improvement and documentation of progress toward full proficiency.
Inclusion of all students	Standards-based curriculum is designed to challenge all students to increase their expectations and proficiency levels. This includes English language learners and students with disabilities.

From *Curriculum Adaptations for Students with Learning and Behavior Problems: Principles and Practices for Differentiating Instruction* (p. 21), by J. J. Hover and J. R. Patton, 2006. Austin, TX: Pro-Ed.

INTASC

INTASC 7: Plans instruction

PRAXIS

PRAXIS II: Delivery of Instruction to Students with Disabilities

2. *High-quality, targeted supplemental instruction:* The focus of the second tier is to provide supplemental supports in addition to the core program. Such instruction could be provided in the general education classroom or through a variety of pull-out programs such as resource rooms. Specific examples of such programs are those that are identified as general education supports programs. For many elementary students with special needs, this tier will provide the instructional supports they require. The discussion later in the chapter on adaptations provides numerous such examples.

3. *High-quality intensive intervention:* The third tier is more consistent with the traditional concept of special education as modified to reflect scientifically validated instructional programs to teach relevant curricular content. Such programs typically are offered to students with more significant disabilities and may more often be delivered in specialized settings. Examples include certain remedial programs. However, many of these curricular goals can be achieved in general education as well.

The third key emphasis is the importance of **universal design** for learning. This concept, with its roots in architectural design, was introduced in Chapter 2. It is important to note here how this design relates to standards for learning.

A number of practices are consistent with this concept and are relatively straightforward and intuitive (Acrey, Johnstone, & Milligan, 2005). As a consequence, teachers are encouraged to design the learning environment by using basic original principles for universal design and architecture as a model (e.g., considering ways in which to make lessons more accessible to all in the same way that buildings can be made so).

To meet the needs of all students, including those with special needs, a curriculum that is based on universal design principles should be open-ended rather than close-ended. As Wehmeyer (in press) notes: "Close-ended standards are specific and require narrowly defined outcomes or performance indicators. Open-ended standards do not restrict the ways in which students exhibit knowledge with skills and focus more on the expectations that students will interact with the content, ask questions, manipulate materials, make observations, and then communicate their knowledge in a variety of ways."

For all students, any consideration of curriculum also should include an outcomes orientation. Therefore, our concept of curriculum, even at the elementary level, must embrace consideration for the preparation for life after the completion of K–12 schooling. As a result, even though curriculum design is preordained by state standards in general education programs, it is nevertheless important to consider the concept of comprehensive curriculum. The concept takes into account the reality that students are enrolled in school on a time-limited basis. Educators must consider what will happen to their students in the future and consider the environments that students will need to adapt to in order to function successfully. Thus, curriculum design should be predicated on a focus on these subsequent environments (e.g., middle school, high school, college, community). The degree to which this subsequent-environments attitude permeates general education will significantly affect the ultimate success of students with disabilities taught in such settings (Polloway, Patton, & Serna, 2008).

An elementary-level comprehensive curriculum therefore should reflect responsiveness to the needs of the individual at the current time, the importance of achieving maximum interaction with peers while addressing critical curricular needs, and attention to relevant forthcoming transitional needs (e.g., transition from elementary to middle school) (Polloway et al., 2008).

Curricular Emphases

Elementary students in general, and certainly most students with disabilities, primarily need scientifically validated instruction in reading, writing, and mathematics to maximize their academic achievement. These needs can typically be met by a developmental approach to instruction, supplemented as needed by a remedial focus for students who experience difficulty. In addition, students with special needs will also benefit from a curriculum that addresses social skills and transitional needs. In the sections that follow, an overview of principles and practices related to these curricular areas is provided.

Reading Instruction

Reading problems are the foremost concern for all elementary teachers working in inclusive classrooms. Young students with special needs commonly experience difficulties in both the decoding processes inherent in word recognition and in reading comprehension. In a general sense, educators have responded to the need for quality instruction by selecting one (or a combination) of the three common approaches in elementary-level reading and language arts programs: **basal series, direct instruction,** and **whole language.**

Basal series, or graded class-reading texts, are the most typical means of teaching reading and, for that matter, other curricular domains including spelling and math, in the elementary school. Most reading basals are intended to meet developmental needs in reading. However, there is a multiplicity of programs, and it would be impossible to typify the focus of all basal series. Polloway, Miller, and Smith (2003) note that such series have both advantages and disadvantages. They note that on the positive side, basals contain inherent structure and sequence, a controlled vocabulary, a wide variety of teaching activities, and materials that provide preparation for the teacher. Weaknesses, however, include possible inappropriate pacing for an individual child, a common concern for certain skills to the exclusion of others, and the encouragement of group instructional orientation.

Direct instruction (i.e., the directive teaching of skills) has often been associated with a remedial perspective, although it clearly has played a significant preventive role as well. Often it has been tied to a focus on basic skills, which has typically constituted the core of most elementary special education curricula. In the area of reading, direct instruction programs are most often associated with a strong initial emphasis on decoding skills. Basic skills programs typically are built on the development of phonological awareness (i.e., a sensitivity to the sounds inherent in our language system) and subsequently phonetic analysis instruction. Research on beginning reading emphasizes the critical importance of children developing sound-symbol correspondences as a basis for subsequent reading success.

Whole language approaches (i.e., programs that primarily emphasize meaning in the beginning of the reading process) at the primary and elementary level dramatically increased in popularity in the 1990s. They embrace a more holistic view of learning than does direct instruction, which tends to be oriented much more to specific skills acquisition. Whole language programs attempt to break down barriers within the area of language arts between reading, writing, and speaking, as well as barriers between reading and other curricular areas, by stressing an integrated approach to learning. Polloway and colleagues (2008) provide examples of whole language instruction:

- orally sharing stories by the teacher
- sustained silent reading
- silent reading time segments in which students write responses to what they are reading and share this with other students or with the teacher in individual conferences
- language experience activities in which children write stories in a group or individually to be used for future reading experiences
- time set aside for large-group writing instruction followed by students' writing, revising, editing, and sharing their own writing
- reading and writing activities that involve a content area theme such as science or social studies (pp. 16–17)

The nearby Evidence-Based Practice boxes provide lists of effective practices for reading instruction, in general, and for reading comprehension in particular.

> ### CONSIDER THIS
>
> The emphasis on meaning and the integration of the language arts make whole language approaches particularly attractive for use with students with special needs. Why do you think these approaches are effective?

EVIDENCE-BASED PRACTICE

Teaching Reading with Emphasis on Word Recognition

- Develop balanced programs that emphasize both decoding skills and comprehension skills.
- Determine whether students have sufficient phonological awareness skills to be able to use phonetic analysis as a decoding strategy.
- Develop phonological awareness skills by enhancing students' ability to differentiate, analyze, and blend sounds, and to tie this effort to word study.
- Teach word meanings directly and complement students' ability to recognize words with the ability to understand their meaning.
- Teach phonetic analysis conventions that have high levels of utility (i.e., have applicability to multiple words

such as the "silent e" rule and the "two vowels together" format).

- Teach students word structures by providing opportunities for them to take advantage of structural analyses skills to focus on prefixes, suffixes, contractions, and compound words.
- Teach students to use context to enhance word recognition and comprehension. However, use caution in placing significant weight on contextual analysis because of the difficulties presented as students engage in reading with more difficult vocabulary. As this occurs, phonetic cues are likely to be more effective than context cues.
- Teach students to use a strategy for attacking unknown words in print so

they can determine if it is important that they be able to say the word accurately (such as may not be the case with a proper noun), use phonetic analysis skills, and structural analysis, for example.

- Ensure that students have ample opportunity to read and encounter words, concepts, and knowledge through print.
- Provide motivational strategies for struggling readers that can relate to extrinsic strategies, such as the use of reinforcement, and intrinsic strategies related to student interest and self-management.
- Ensure that skills instruction is explicit, intensive, and ongoing to result in the acquisition, maintenance, and generalization of skills.

EVIDENCE-BASED PRACTICE

Teaching Reading Comprehension

- **Comprehension monitoring:** Readers learn how to be conscious of their understanding during reading and learn procedures to deal with problems in understanding as they arise.
- **Cooperative learning:** Readers work together to learn strategies in the context of reading.
- **Graphic and semantic organizers:** Readers learn to present graphically the meanings and relationships of the ideas that underlie the words in the text.

- **Story structure:** Readers learn to ask and answer "who, what, where, when, and why" questions about the plot and map out the timeline, characters, and events in stories.
- **Question answering:** Readers answer questions posed by the teacher and are given feedback on the correctness of their answers.
- **Question generation:** Readers ask "what, when, were, why, what will happen, how, and who" questions.

- **Summarization:** Readers attempt to identify and write the main idea that integrates the other meanings of the text into a coherent whole.
- **Multiple-strategy teaching:** Readers use several of these procedures and interact with the teacher over the text.

Adapted from The National Reading Panel, 2000, pp. 4–6.

Writing

Elementary-age children with special needs commonly experience problems with writing, especially with written expression. It is essential that they be given ample opportunities to write and that appropriate attention be given to handwriting and spelling (see Polloway, Miller, & Smith, 2003, for a full discussion of writing instruction). The nearby Evidence-Based Practice box provides a list of practices associated with effective writing instruction.

Mathematics

Mathematics represents a third potentially challenging academic area for students with disabilities. The development of both **computational skills** and **problem-solving abilities** forms the foundation of successful math instruction and learning. In the area of computation, teachers should focus first on the students' conceptual understanding of a particular skill and then on the achievement of automaticity with the skill (see Figure 15.1 for an effective approach to achieve these goals).

Problem solving can be particularly difficult for students with disabilities and thus warrants special attention. For learners with special needs, and for many other students as well, instruction in specific problem-solving strategies can greatly enhance math understanding. After a problem-solving strategy has been selected or designed, the strategy's steps should be taught and followed systematically so that students learn to reason through problems and understand problem-solving processes (see Figure 15.2). The nearby Evidence-Based Practice box provides a list of recommendations for effective practice.

The potential benefits of including students with special needs in general education classrooms to study core academic areas also extend to other academic areas. Subjects such as science, social studies, health and family life, and the arts offer excellent opportunities for social integration, while effective instructional strategies can lead to academic achievement. Cooperative teaching (discussed later in the chapter) presents an excellent instructional alternative in these areas because it combines the expertise and resources of the classroom teacher with the talents of the special education teacher, rather than requiring them each to develop separate curricula in these respective curricular areas.

CEC STANDARDS

CEC 7: Instructional Planning

INTASC

INTASC 7: Plans instruction

PRAXIS

PRAXIS II: Delivery of Services to Students with Disabilities

Figure 15.1 **Interactive Unit Model**

Group A: Geometry (8 students)	Group B: Fractions (10 students)	Group C: Addition (5 students)
15 minutes — Manipulate/Manipulate* *Input:* Teacher walks the perimeter of a geometric shape. *Output:* Learner does the same.	**Display/Write** *Input:* Write the fraction that names the shaded part. *Output:* Learner writes ½	**Write/Write** *Input:* $\begin{array}{r} 3 \\ +\,2 \\ \hline \end{array}$ Write the answer. *Output:* Learner writes 5
15 minutes — Display/Identify *Input:* From the choices, mark the shape that is the same as the first shape. *Output:* Learner marks	**Manipulate/Say*** *Input:* Teacher removes portion of shape and asks learner to name the part. *Output:* Learner says, "One fourth"	**Display/Write** *Input:* Write the number there is in all. *Output:* Learner writes 5
15 minutes — Write/Identify *Input:* Circle Mark the shape that shows the word. *Output:* Learner marks Circle	**Write/Write** *Input:* one half Write this word statement as a numeral. *Output:* Learner writes ½	**Say/Say*** *Input:* Teacher says, "I am going to say some addition items. Six plus six. Tell me the answer." *Output:* Learner says, "Twelve"

From *Developmental Teaching of Mathematics for the Learning Disabled* (p. 246), by J. F. Cawley (Ed.), 1984. Austin, TX: Pro-Ed. Copyright 1984 by Pro-Ed Inc. Used by permission.

Figure 15.2

Problem-Solving Strategy for Mathematics

Source: *Strategies for Teaching Learners with Special Needs* (7th ed., p. 328), by E. A. Polloway, J. R. Patton, and L. Serna, 2001. Columbus, OH: Merrill. Used by permission.

S	**SAY**	the problem to yourself (repeat).
O	**OMIT**	any unnecessary information from the problem.
L	**LISTEN**	for key vocabulary indicators.
V	**VOCABULARY**	Change vocabulary to math concepts.
E	**EQUATION**	Translate problem into a math equation.
I	**INDICATE**	the answer.
T	**TRANSLATE**	the answer back into the context of the word problem.

Social Skills Instruction

As discussed in earlier chapters, virtually all students identified with intellectual disabilities or emotional and behavioral disorders, and many with learning disabilities, have difficulties related to the development of social skills. The challenge for classroom teachers is to find ways to incorporate this focus in their classes, such as by seeking assistance from a special education teacher or a counselor. Because performance in the social domain is often predictive of success or failure in inclusive settings, the development of social skills should not be neglected. All educators agree about the importance of social competence, but, as discussed in Chapter 8, concern remains about the modest effects that social skills instruction have demonstrated in research (Kavale, 2001b). The nearby Evidence-Based Practice box presents a series of recommendations for practice.

A second consideration involves selecting a social adjustment program that promotes both social skills and social competence. Whereas social skills facilitate individual

CEC STANDARDS

CEC 7: Instructional Planning

INTASC

INTASC 7: Plans instruction

EVIDENCE-BASED PRACTICE

Teaching Mathematics

- Base instruction on a concrete/semiconcrete/abstract model in which initial instruction of a new skill is grounded in an understanding that comes through concrete representation and in which students learn to use visual representations (semiconcrete) to enhance skills and more abstract math to facilitate automaticity inclusive of accuracy and speed (e.g., through the reliance on numerals and mathematical symbols).
- Ensure that prerequisite skills have been achieved in sequential fashion in mathematics (i.e., students should have 1-to-1 correspondence before counting and should have effective counting skills before addition).
- Use math attack strategies as ways to learn, recall, and apply basic skills related to specific math operations (such as through the use of mnemonics to recall ways to perform multiplication, long division, and algebraic equations).
- Teach problem-solving strategies that enable students to attack word problems and reach solutions (see, for example, Figure 15.2).
- Place word problems in the context of real-life settings in which students are not directly cued as to the correct algorithm (operation) to be used, but rather are challenged to think about the task.
- Present word problems that include distracters or extraneous information to teach students how to focus on relevant aspects for problem solutions.
- Develop graduated word problems, such as through a matrix approach that enables students to enhance their skills in terms of the language structure of problems, the computational challenges, and the presence or absence of distracters, for example.

Science class offers an excellent opportunity for social integration of students with special needs.

interpersonal interactions, social competence involves the broader ability to use skills at the right times and places, showing social perception, cognition, and judgment of how to act in different situations (Sargent, 1991). A focus limited to specific skill training may make it difficult for the child to maintain the specific social skills or transfer them to various settings. Table 15.3 outlines a typical sequence within a social skills curriculum.

Third, a decision must be made as to who will teach social skills. Often initial instruction occurs in pull-out programs (e.g., resource rooms) with generalization plans developed for transfer to the general education classroom. For inclusive classrooms, a useful strategy is the use of the complementary instructional model of cooperative teaching (see Chapter 2).

Transitional Needs

In addition to the academic and social components of the curriculum, career education and transition form an important emphasis even for younger children. For all elementary students, career awareness and a focus on facilitating movement between levels of schooling (i.e., vertical transitions) are curricular essentials. Figure 15.3 outlines key vertical transitions and also illustrates the concept of horizontal transitions (i.e., from more- to less-restrictive settings).

Transition from Preschool to Primary School   Research on students moving from preschool programs into school settings has identified variables that predict success in school. Four such variables include early academic (i.e., readiness) skills, social skills,

---

EVIDENCE-BASED PRACTICE

Teaching Writing Skills

- Establish a writing environment where students understand that there is an audience for their work that includes teachers, other students, and individuals beyond the classroom.
- Encourage legible handwriting styles as alternatives to formal styles that may otherwise be taught to young children but abandoned by middle school. A helpful approach is to encourage a mixed script with cursive and manuscript forms blended together.
- After legibility has been achieved, focus instruction on maintenance through attention to continued legible work.
- Relate spelling instruction to emphases within the reading curriculum to take advantage of, for example, words that

have significant personal interest, words from linguistic families, and words that are important for all writing efforts (i.e., high frequency words).
- Beyond initial instruction, emphasize handwriting and spelling as tool subjects that can be improved in conjunction with writing skills.
- Avoid having students monitor errors only while writing and emphasize the importance of expression of ideas and error monitoring to take place during the postwriting stage.
- Teach writing through a process approach in which students learn the importance of, and strategies related to, prewriting, drafting, and postwriting (i.e., editing, revising) stages.

- Use learning strategies to promote student independence such as in areas inclusive of error monitoring and sentence, paragraph, and composition generation.
- Provide text structures, such as graphic organizers, to provide a model for students to follow in writing.
- Use student–teacher conferences to review student work and make recommendations for changes as related to both the craft (structure, mechanics) and content (ideas, themes) of written work.
- Have students write often so that they have an opportunity to develop skills and to reinforce interest.

EVIDENCE-BASED PRACTICE

Teaching Social Skills

- Emphasize social competence as the key focus of instruction.
- Use social skills curricula with caution and evaluate success on an ongoing basis, because of the limited efficacy data on most programs.
- Determine the specific social skills that will enhance performance both within and beyond the school setting, and focus instruction on these areas. Develop targeted behaviors and skills that are important for all students to learn.
- Place priority on skills that are most needed for immediate interactions in

the classroom in order to enhance the likelihood of successful inclusion. These may include skills such as taking turns, asking for assistance, following directions, and interacting positively with adults and peers.
- Emphasize self-management or self-control strategies that are cognitively based and require students to think about their actions.
- Collect data on student behavior to determine the effectiveness of instructional, teacher management, and student self-management interventions, and make modifications as needed.

- Develop positive behavioral support programs that are applicable across individuals within the classroom and, if possible, throughout the school.
- Develop a collaborative plan that includes involvement of general education teachers, special education teachers, school counselors, and school psychologists as needed.

---

responsiveness to instructional styles, and responsiveness to the structure of the school environment (Polloway et al., 1992). Analyzing the new school environment can help a teacher determine the skills a student will need to make this crucial adjustment.

Academic readiness skills have traditionally been cited as good predictors of success at the primary school level. Examples include the ability to recognize numbers and letters, grasp a writing utensil, count to ten, and write letters and numbers. Yet a clear delineation between academic readiness and academic skills is not warranted. Rather, to use reading as an example, it is much more productive to consider readiness as inclusive of examples of early reading skills, or what has been termed emergent literacy. Programming in this area should focus on academic activities that advance the processes of learning to read, write, or calculate.

Social skills consistent with the developmental attributes of other five- and six-year-olds are clearly important to success in the elementary school. It is particularly critical that students be able to function in a group. Thus, introducing small-group instructional activities in preschool programs prepares students to function in future school situations.

Developing responsiveness to instructional styles is another challenge for the young child. Since the instructional arrangement in the preschool program may vary significantly from that of the kindergarten or first-grade school program, providing instructional experiences that the student can generalize to the new school setting will be helpful; some learning activities in the preschool class should approximate those of kindergarten to provide the preparation.

Responsiveness to the daily learning environment is a fourth concern. Changes may include new transportation arrangements, extended instructional time, increased expectations of individual independence, and increased class size resulting in a reduction in individual attention. Teachers may set up opportunities for the preschoolers to visit kindergarten classes to familiarize them with the future environment.

Increasingly, public schools have provided prekindergarten programs for young children, particularly those deemed at risk for later school difficulties. In addition, federal law requires that young children identified as having disabilities be provided special education programs, with the actual years of eligibility and the nature of the service delivery program determined by individual state guidelines. The discussion, herein,

INTASC

INTASC 7: Plans instruction

PRAXIS

PRAXIS II: Delivery of Services to Students with Disabilities

TEACHING TIP

Teachers should accept responsibility to prepare students for their next school-life challenge or transition (e.g., preschool to elementary school, middle school to secondary school).

CEC STANDARDS

CEC 5: Learning Environments and Social Interactions

INTASC

INTASC 5: Learning environment

Table 15.3	**Sample Social Skills Curriculum Sequence**
Session 1	Listening Meeting people—introducing self, introducing others Beginning a conversation Listening during a conversation Ending a conversation Joining an ongoing activity
Session 2	Asking questions appropriately Asking favors appropriately Seeking help from peers and adults Following directions
Session 3	Sharing Interpreting body language Playing a game successfully
Session 4	Suggesting an activity to others Working cooperatively Offering help
Session 5	Saying "Thank you" Giving and accepting a compliment Rewarding self
Session 6	Apologizing Understanding the impact your behavior has on others Understanding others' behavior

From *Managing Attention Disorders in Children: A Guide for Practitioners.* (pp. 342–343), by S. Goldstein and M. Goldstein, 1990. New York: John Wiley. Used by permission.

PRAXIS

PRAXIS II: Delivery of Services to Students with Disabilities

does not focus on the needs of preschoolers with disabilities or those at risk, but the particular discussions on areas such as listening, following directions, and cooperative learning are equally applicable for young children as they are for those at the elementary school level.

Transition Curricular Considerations Career education in general, and life-skills education in particular, have become major emphases among secondary school teachers, especially those who work with students who have disabilities. Yet life-skills concepts should also be incorporated into elementary and middle school programs (Patton & Cronin, 1993; Patton & Dunn, 1998). Table 15.4 provides a matrix of topics that may be incorporated into an elementary-level life-skills curriculum. Even programs for young children should be designed to encourage positive long-term outcomes for all students.

Concepts and topics related to life skills can be integrated into existing subject areas, thus broadening the curriculum without the necessity of creating a new subject. This purpose can be accomplished in three ways. The first approach, augmentation, uses career–education oriented materials to supplement the existing curriculum. The second approach infuses relevant career-education topics into the lessons laid out in the existing curriculum.

Transition to Middle School Elementary students with disabilities need to be prepared for movement to middle school or junior high school. To successfully make this vertical transition, students need an organized approach to their work, time-management and study skills, note-taking strategies, homework strategies, and the ability to use lockers.

TEACHING TIP

Integrated curricular approaches also can enable gifted students to extend their learning beyond the curriculum.

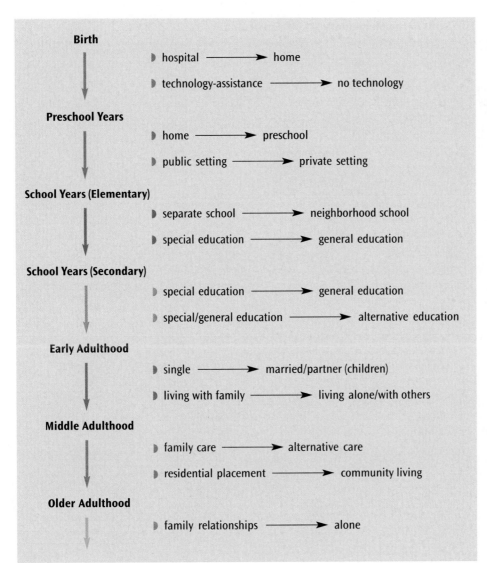

Figure 15.3

Vertical and Horizontal Transitions

From *Transition from School to Young Adulthood: Basic Concepts and Recommended Practices* (p. 2), by J. R. Patton and C. Dunn, 1998. Austin, TX: Pro-Ed. Used by permission.

Wenz-Gross and Siperstein (1998) similarly focused on transitional issues relative to students' success at the middle school level. They concluded that interventions for students in middle school should emphasize developing coping skills for academic demands, peer stress, and relationships with teachers. Helping students develop time-management and organizational skills should also be a focus. To do so, teachers and parents should help these students prioritize multiple tasks and integrate and master the information needed at the middle school level.

Students need to strengthen interpersonal skills so they can build more positive peer relationships. To assist students in these areas, schools should start before middle school and add emphasis in this area in middle school, when peer relationships become so important. Students also need to be empowered to better deal with the problems experienced by adolescence.

A variety of instructional strategies may assist in the transition process: having middle school faculty visit elementary classes to discuss programs and expectations; viewing videotaped middle school classes; and taking field trips to the middle school to get a sense of the physical layout, the changing of classes, and environmental and pedagogical

Table 15.4   **Life Skills in the Elementary School Curriculum**

	Consumer Economics	Occupational Knowledge	Health	Community Resources	Government and Law
Reading	Look for ads in the newspaper for toys.	Read books from library on various occupations.	Read the school lunch menu.	Find television listing in the *TV Guide*.	Read road signs and understand what they mean.
Writing	Write prices of items to be purchased.	Write the specific tasks involved in performing one of the classroom jobs.	Keep a diary of food you eat in each food group each day.	Complete an application to play on a Little League team.	Write a letter to the mayor inviting him/her to visit your school.
Speaking, Writing, Viewing	Listen to bank official talk about savings accounts.	Call newspaper in town to inquire about delivering papers in your neighborhood.	View a film on brushing teeth.	Practice the use of the 911 emergency number.	Discuss park playground improvements with the mayor.
Problem Solving	Decide if you have enough coins to make a purchase from a vending machine.	Decide which job in the classroom you do best.	Role-play what you should do if you have a stomachache.	Role-play the times you would use the 911 emergency number.	Find the city hall on the map. Decide whether you will walk or drive to it.
Interpersonal Relations	Ask for help finding items in a grocery store.	Ask a student in the class to assist you with a classroom job.	Ask the school nurse how to take care of mosquito bites.	Call the movie theater and ask the show times of a movie.	Role-play being lost and asking a police officer for help.
Computation	Compute the cost of a box of cereal with a discount coupon.	Calculate how much you would make on a paper route at $3 per hour for 5 hours per week.	Compute the price of one tube of toothpaste if they are on sale at three for $1.	Compute the complete cost of going to the movie (admission, food, transportation).	Compute tax on a candy bar.

From "Curricular Considerations: A Life Skills Orientation," by J. R. Patton, M. E. Cronin, E. A. Polloway, D. R. Hutchison, and G. A. Robinson, 1989, in *Best Practices in Mild Mental Retardation*, edited by G. A. Robinson, J. R. Patton, E. A. Polloway, and L. Sargent, p. 31. Reston, VA: CEC-MR. Used by permission.

factors (Jaquish & Stella, 1986). Cooperative planning and follow-up between both general and special education teachers at the two school levels will smooth the transition. Further attention to transition into high school and into the community and/or postsecondary environments is provided in Chapter 16.

Instructional Strategies

To successfully implement the curriculum, teachers should focus on strategies that are scientifically validated and produce significant gains in academic achievement. To be consistent with IDEA (2004) and NCLB (2002), effective instruction has now been defined as those practices that are research-based and empirically validated (Boardman, Arguelles, Vaughn, Hughes, & Klingner, 2005; Yell, Katsiyannis, & Shiner, 2006).

While a variety of strategies are needed to reach this objective, three primary foci are to provide excellent instruction, to assess programs continuously, and to ensure instruction is intensive enough to guarantee learning. With regard to the first two, especially in reference to students with learning disabilities, Lloyd and Hallahan (2005) noted that "reasonably informed people . . . argue strongly for explicit, systematic instruction that focuses on teaching students strategies for completing academic tasks and that includes monitoring of progress so instruction can be adjusted to maximize progress" (p. 135).

Deshler (2005), through addressing his remarks directly to adolescents, succinctly stated the third point in noting:

> Intensive instruction involves helping students maintain a high degree of attention and response during instructional sessions that are scheduled as frequently and consistently as possible. In other words, a key factor affecting learning is both the amount of time and instruction and how effectively each instructional moment is used to engage students in activities that contribute to their learning. Intensity during instruction is achieved by progressive pacing, frequent question-answer interactions, and frequent activities that require a physical response (e.g., pointing, writing, raising hands, repeating). Intensity can also be achieved through reflective or open-ended questions if the activities are focused on a process that engages interest and maintains the student's attention. (pp. 123–124)

In inclusive elementary school environments, instruction also must be based on the realities of that environment. Successful programs thus reflect collaborative practices—both between teachers and among students. These concerns are discussed below. Following these sections on professional collaboration and cooperative learning, the succeeding section addresses curricular and instructional adaptations—necessary considerations in the elementary classroom.

Professional Collaboration

The successful elementary classroom is a model of collaboration. Both teachers and students benefit from supports from their peers. This section addresses both professional collaboration; the next section focuses on peer-mediated collaborative learning.

As noted in Chapters 1 and 2, professional collaboration is a key component of effective elementary schools and a necessity for successful inclusion. Collaboration can occur in IEP meetings through cooperative teaching and within the prereferral (or child study) process.

Cooperative teaching (see also Chapter 2) potentially can help prevent or correct the learning problems of any student while effecting the remediation of identified deficits for students with disabilities. Cooperative teaching, perhaps the best vehicle for attaining successful inclusive classrooms, truly provides **supported education**, the school-based equivalent of supported work in which students are placed in the least-restrictive environment and provided with the necessary support (e.g., by the special educator) to be successful. The nearby Personal Spotlight describes one approach to helping new teachers learn how to collaborate with other professionals.

Another key area for collaboration is through the prereferral process (also referred to as child-study or teacher assistance teams). According to Buck, Fad, Patton, and Polloway (2003), prereferral is best conceptualized as a problem-solving process aimed at meeting the needs of students who exhibit learning or behavioral problems. The process is typically carried out within a school by a team made up of various school personnel and sometimes joined by parents.

The objective of the prereferral process is to meet the challenges presented by students within the context of their classrooms. Teams review student cases and develop instructional and/or behavioral strategies to resolve problems. As Buck, Williams, Patton, and Polloway (in press) note, several assumptions are inherent in this team approach:

- Problems can be solved more effectively when they are clearly defined.
- Members of a team often can objectively perceive a student problem better than the referring teacher, who may be emotionally involved in the situation.
- A team of professionals is better able to develop intervention strategies than are one or two professionals.
- Many of the problems students have are complex and require the expertise of professionals from varied backgrounds and disciplines.

INTASC

INTASC 4: Instructional strategies

PRAXIS

PRAXIS II: Delivery of Services to Students with Disabilities

CEC STANDARDS

CEC 10: Collaboration

INTASC

INTASC 10: Fosters relationships

PRAXIS

PRAXIS II: Delivery of Services to Students with Disabilities

Personal Spotlight

Teacher Educator

Val Sharpe
Hood College,
Frederick, MD

Val Sharpe has taught in many educational settings. She notes: "It is the ongoing process of change in order to meet the needs of students with disabilities that has afforded me the opportunity for diversification as an educator." As a teacher educator, Val and her colleagues (e.g., Roberta Strosnider) have developed a "hands on" approach to teaching methods courses in a professional development school (PDS) setting at Hood College.

During the teacher-training process, the future special educator is exposed to a variety of learning theories, adaptations, and modifications designed to facilitate instruction and enhance concept mastery. Within the PDS, the student is provided with multiple opportunities to practice these theories, adaptations, and modifications with children in the classroom setting. Initially, the Hood faculty teach a concept through modeling and incorporating the necessary adaptations and strategies that facilitate learning. The next step is for the student to practice teaching this concept to other future educators. Once the student acquires mastery of the concept, the student teaches this concept to children. This is the stage when the future educator is introduced to the collaborative process.

Val feels it necessary for future educators to be afforded the opportunity to become acquainted with this process through the implementation of various reality-based activities. After teaching the prerequisite skills and successful ingredients involved in the collaborative process, Val has students actively participate in this process using the following vehicles:

1. Students become knowledgeable about a variety of learning theories, adaptations, and modifications, and their implementation.
2. Students complete a collaborative work sheet.
3. Students are given an assignment to teach a lesson to a group of children within an inclusive setting. Using the

collaboration process, decisions are made regarding appropriate topics for the lesson, as well as the necessary adaptations needed to facilitate the learning process. Via the collaborative process, the students then decide on the topic and develop a lesson plan. The lesson is then taught to the children. The implemented lesson is evaluated by the children, students, PDS teachers, and college supervisor.
4. Students reflect on this venture by referring back to their collaborative work sheet as well as discussing this experience with their classmates.

Throughout the student-teaching practicum, Val enables the students to utilize the collaborative process. These future educators are required to collaborate with parents in the form of a conference, collaborate with other teachers with regard to lesson development and implementation, collaborate with administrators in terms of scheduling and school policy, and collaborate with the multidisciplinary team in developing an IEP.

This hands-on approach to the collaborative process enables the future teacher to practice this process in a variety of settings. It is beneficial because it helps them make connections about the collaborative process. This approach incorporates the elements of good instructional practices through the use of modeling, repetition, guided practice, independent practice, and reflection. Future educators become familiar with the collaborative process and become comfortable using this process.

- Most learning and behavior problems are not indicative of a disability. With environmental manipulations, such problems can be reduced and eliminated without the need for special education services.

The prereferral process usually occurs in three stages:

1. A teacher or other school staff notices that a student is having difficulty in one or more areas (e.g., academics, social behavior, truancy).
2. The prereferral team attempts to analyze the student's difficulties.
3. Once the problem has been clearly defined, the prereferral team develops strategies to resolve the student's difficulties. In some cases, the team members may provide assistance to the teacher as he or she attempts to implement these strategies in the classroom.

Collaborative Learning

Cooperative Learning (CL) is a key means of facilitating the successful inclusion of students with disabilities in general education classrooms. CL is categorized by classroom techniques that involve students in group learning activities, in which recognition and reinforcement are based on group, rather than individual, performance. Heterogeneous small groups work together to achieve a group goal, and an individual student's success directly affects the success of other students (Slavin, 1987).

A variety of formats can be used to implement cooperative learning. These include peer tutoring and group projects of various types.

Classwide peer tutoring is one peer tutoring program that is effective in inclusive settings.

Peer Tutoring   Peer teaching, or peer tutoring, is a relatively easy-to-manage system of cooperative learning. It can benefit both the student being tutored and the tutor. Specific activities that lend themselves to peer tutoring include reviewing task directions, drill and practice, recording material dictated by a peer, modeling of acceptable or appropriate responses, and providing pretest practice (such as in spelling).

A research-based approach for using students as instructors is classwide peer tutoring, instructional strategies that involve students being taught by peers who previously were trained and are then supervised by teachers. Maheady, Harper, and Mallette (2003) identified the four primary components of *classwide peer tutoring (CWPT)* as follows: "competing teams; a highly structured tutoring procedure; daily point earning and public posting of people performance; and direct practice in the implementation of instructional activities. In using CWPT, the teacher's role changes from primary 'deliverer' of instruction to facilitator and monitor of peer-teaching activities" (p. 1).

CWPT is intended to be a reciprocal tutoring approach. That is, students assume roles as both tutor and also tutee during individual instructional sessions. Further, the sessions are highly structured by the teacher to ensure that students are on task and focused on key instructional content.

As summarized by Seeley (1995), CWPT involves the following arrangements:

CEC STANDARDS

CEC 10: Collaboration

INTASC

INTASC 10: Fosters relationships

PRAXIS

PRAXIS II: Delivery of Services to Students with Disabilities

- Classes are divided into two teams that engage in competitions typically of one to two weeks' duration.
- Students work in pairs, both tutoring and being tutored on the same material in a given instructional session.
- Partners reverse roles after fifteen minutes.
- Typical subjects tutored include math, spelling, vocabulary, science, and social studies.
- Teachers break down the curriculum into manageable subunits.
- Students accumulate points for their team by giving correct answers and by using correct procedures, and they receive partial credit for corrected answers.
- Individual scores on master tests are added to the team's total.

CWPT has been positively evaluated in terms of enhancing content learning, promoting diversity and integration, and freeing teachers to prepare for other instructional activities (King-Sears & Bradley, 1995; Maheady et al., 2003; Simmons, Fuchs, Hodge, & Mathes, 1994).

Another example of a successful peer tutoring approach is *peer-assisted learning strategies (PALS)*, described by Mathes and Torgesen (1998). In PALS, beginning readers are assisted in learning through paired instruction in which each member of the pair takes turns serving as a coach and a reader. The first coach is the reader who is at a higher achievement level who listens to, comments on, and reinforces the other student before the roles are reversed. These researchers found that the use of this approach enhanced students' reading by promoting careful attention to saying and hearing sounds, sounding out words, and reading stories. They recommended using the approach three times a week for approximately sixteen weeks with each session lasting thirty-five minutes. The PALS program complements general education instruction by enhancing the academic engaged time of each student.

Kroeger and Kouche (2006) provided an example of a successful application of PALS to middle school students in math. As they note, the benefits reflect "a world of students discussing and talking through math problems, regardless of ability levels or past experiences in math classes . . . . PALS is an effective intervention to increase engagement and opportunities to respond for all students" (p. 12).

Group Projects   Group projects allow students to pool their knowledge and skills to complete an assignment. The task is assigned to the entire group, and the goal is to develop a single product reflecting the contributions of all members. For example, in social studies, a report on one of the fifty states might involve making individual students responsible for particular tasks: drawing a map, sketching an outline of state history, collecting photos of scenic attractions, and developing a display of products from that state. The benefits of groups are enhanced when they include high, average, and low achievers.

The *jigsaw format* is an approach that involves giving all group members individual tasks to be completed before the group can reach its goal. Each individual studies a portion of the material and then shares it with other members of the team. For example, Salend (1990) discussed an assignment related to the life of Dr. Martin Luther King Jr. in which each student was given a segment of his life to research (e.g., religious beliefs, protest marches, opposition to the Vietnam war). The students then had to teach others in their group the information from the segment they had mastered. In using this approach, teachers are cautioned to oversee the individual assignments within the group project and keep in mind the importance of distributing student expertise over aspects of the assignment.

Cooperative learning strategies offer much promise as inclusive practices. These approaches have been used successfully with low, average, and high achievers to promote the acquisition of academic and social skills and to enhance independence. The fact that CL appears to be effective in general education and special education classrooms would seem to support the benefits of its use with heterogeneous populations (McMaster & Fuchs, 2002). Cooperative learning also can enhance the social adjustment of students with special needs by helping to create natural support networks involving nondisabled peers, such as within the "circle of friends" approach discussed in Chapter 8.

At the same time, teachers should keep in mind that CL approaches are not the single solution for resolving the academic challenges faced by students with special needs. As McMaster and Fuchs (2002) conclude, the state of research in this area is such that CL is best seen as a "promising instructional strategy (rather than as) an unqualified effective approach" (p. 116). Thus, as with many classroom interventions, teachers are encouraged to assess the effectiveness of CL if they use it as a tool to promote the successful inclusion of students with special needs.

Instructional and Curricular Adaptations

In general, students with disabilities profit directly from the same types of teaching strategies that benefit all students. In particular, certain research-validated interventions that reflect adaptations in the classroom are associated with successful learning outcomes for students with learning disabilities and other special needs. To promote successful inclusion, adaptations will frequently be needed both in terms of curriculum and instruction.

Wehmeyer (in press) notes that curriculum adaptations included "efforts to modify the representation of the curriculum content or to modify the student's engagement with the curriculum to enhance and progress" (p. 8). The complementary concept of instructional adaptation refers to ways in which teachers can design and deliver instruction and seek student responses to reflect learning in varied ways that enhance success for students with special needs. The discussion below addresses both curriculum and instructional adaptations.

Vaughn, Gersten, and Chard (2000) note that all students benefit when best practices for students with disabilities are used. They identify three general instructional features that stand out as producing the most significant impact on learning:

CEC STANDARDS

CEC 4: Instructional strategies

INTASC

INTASC 4: Instructional strategies

PRAXIS

PRAXIS II: Delivery of Services to Students with Disabilities

- Control of task difficulty (i.e., sequencing examples and problems to maintain high levels of student success).
- Teaching students in small interactive groups of six or fewer students.
- Directed response questioning (i.e., involves the use of procedures . . . that promote "thinking aloud" about text being read, mathematical problems to be solved, or about the process of composing a written essay or story). (p. 101)

The focus of this section is on specific adaptations that will enhance learning for students with special needs. These reflect efforts to support students and promote academic achievement. In addition, it is important to note that "the need to adapt curricula increases as the variability of student abilities and learner characteristics increases" (Hoover & Patton, 2005, p. 43).

It is useful to have a common set of definitions to build upon in discussing classroom adaptations. Polloway and colleagues (2002) provide the following differentiation between two types of adaptations. **Accommodations** refer to changes in input and output processes in teaching and assessment, such as in the format of instructional presentations, as well as test practice and preparation activities. The concept of **modifications** refers to changes in content or standards. In curricular areas, modifications could involve changes in content or skill expectations for different groups of students. As a general pattern, Polloway and colleagues (2002) report that teachers indicate a greater willingness to consider accommodations, while they express more reluctance to consider the implementation of modifications.

Adaptations made to instructional programs in the general education classroom then form the keys to successful inclusion. As the traditional saying goes, special education is not necessarily special, it is just good teaching, and good teaching often means making appropriate modifications and accommodations.

A key component of successful inclusion is the teacher acceptability of specific interventions to accommodate the needs of students with disabilities. Polloway, Bursuck, and colleagues (1996) used the term "teacher acceptability" to refer to the likelihood that certain specific classroom interventions will be acceptable to the general education teacher. Thus it may include, for example, the helpfulness, desirability, feasibility, and fairness of the intervention, as well as how other students will perceive it in a particular setting. As Witt and Elliott (1985) note, the "attractiveness" of an intervention is important: if the treatment is not deemed acceptable, it is unlikely to be implemented.

In a review of research on adaptations, Scott, Vitale, and Masten (1998) summarize the types of adaptations that have been researched for their effectiveness. They use the qualifiers "typical" to refer to specific examples that are routine, minor, or applicable to an entire class, and "substantial" to refer to those that are tailored to the needs of individual students. Their categories (as adapted) are as follows:

- Adapting instruction: typical (concrete classroom demonstrations, monitoring classroom understanding); substantial (adjusting the pace to individual learners, giving immediate individual feedback, using multiple modalities)
- Adapting assignments: typical (providing models); substantial (breaking tasks into small steps, shortening assignments, lowering difficulty levels)

- Teaching learning skills: typical (study skills, note-taking techniques); substantial (learning strategies, test-taking skills)
- Altering instructional materials: substantial (using alternative materials, taping textbooks, using supplementary aids)
- Modifying curriculum: substantial (lowering difficulty of course content)
- Varying instructional grouping: substantial (using peer tutoring, using cooperative groups)
- Enhancing behavior: typical (praise, offering encouragement); substantial (using behavioral contracts, using token economies, frequent parental contact)
- Facilitating progress monitoring: typical (read tests orally, give extended test-taking time, give frequent short quizzes, provide study guides); substantial (retaking tests, obtaining direct daily measures of academic progress, modifying grading criteria) (p. 107)

Table 15.5 presents the findings of Scott and colleagues (1998) relative to research on specific accommodations and modifications.

Table 15.5	**Representative Examples of Instructional Adaptations**
Munson, 1986–1987 (elementary)	1. Simplify/supplement the curriculum 2. Provide concrete materials 3. Change papers, worksheets 4. Shorten assignments 5. Provide peers for individual instruction
Johnson & Pugach, 1990 (elementary)	1. Adjust performance expectations in the student's problem area to increase the likelihood that the student will succeed 2. Use peer tutors, volunteers, or aides to work with student physically 3. Use alternative textbook or materials 4. Talk with school psychologist, special education teachers, counselor, or other special education personnel about ways to work on the student's academic problem 5. Give additional explicit oral or written instructions to the student
Ysseldyke, Thurlow, Wotruba, & Nania, 1990 (K–12)	1. Alter instruction so student can experience success 2. Use different materials to instruct failing student 3. Adjust lesson pace to meet student's rate of mastery 4. Inform student frequently of his or her instructional needs 5. Use alternative methods to instruct failing student
Bacon & Schulz, 1991 (K–12)	1. Use lower-level workbooks or worksheets 1. Provide volunteer tutor (adult) 2. Provide note takers 3. Use taped lectures 4. Provide hands-on activities, manipulatives
Schumm & Vaughn, 1991 (K–12)	1. Establish personal relationship with mainstreamed student 2. Adapt daily plans 3. Use alternative materials 4. Pair with classmate 5. Modify long-term curriculum goals
Whinnery, Fuchs, & Fuchs, 1991 (1–6)	1. Regroup students for language arts across grades into homogeneous groups 2. Regroup students for language arts within grades into homogeneous groups 3. Use resource staff in classroom for the lowest language arts groups 4. Establish mixed-ability student partners with low- and high-ability pairs 5. Cover the same basic instructional activities each day with the lowest language arts group

Table 15.5	**Continued**
Fuchs, Fuchs, & Bishop, 1992 (elementary)	1. Vary goals 2. Use alternative materials 3. Alter teaching activities 4. Vary groupings 5. Adjust schedule
Schumm & Vaughn, 1992 (K–12)	1. Plan or make adaptations in the curriculum 2. Plan or make adaptations to tests 3. Make adaptations while the student is working
Blanton, Blanton, & Cross, 1994 (elementary)	1. Provide extra time for the student's reading instruction 2. Provide instruction for the student in smaller steps 3. Use computer-assisted instruction 4. Make use of teacher-directed reading instruction 5. Use peer tutors, volunteers, or aides to work with student physically
Schumm, Vaughn, & Saumell, 1994 (K–12)	1. Preview textbook with students 2. Read textbook aloud to students 3. Write abridged versions of textbooks 4. Provide questions to guide reading 5. Model effective reading strategies
Polloway, Epstein, Bursuck, Jayanthi, & Cumblad, 1994 (K–12)	1. Adjust length of assignment 2. Evaluate on the basis of effort, not performance 3. Provide extra-credit opportunities 4. Check more frequently with student about assignments and expectations 5. Allow alternative response formats
Schumm, Vaughn, Gordon, & Rothlein, 1994 (K–12)	1. Vary group composition (e.g., small group, large group, whole class) for main-streamed students 2. Adapt daily planning for mainstreamed students 3. Use frequent checks with individual students to monitor the progress of main-streamed students
Bender, Vail, & Scott, 1995 (elementary–middle)	1. Suggest particular methods of remembering 2. Provide peer tutoring to assist slow learners 3. Use reading materials that highlight the topic sentence and main idea for slow learners 4. Use several test administration options, such as oral tests or extended-time tests 5. Use advance organizers to assist students in comprehension of difficult concepts
Schumm, Vaughn, Haager, McDowell, Rothlein, & Saumell, 1995 (K–12)	1. Preplan lesson(s) experiences for students with LD 2. Monitor a lesson and make adaptations in response to the progress of students with LD 3. Postplan for later lessons (e.g., reteach a lesson)
Jayanthi, Bursuck, Polloway, & Epstein, 1996 (K–12)	1. Prepare tests that are typewritten rather than handwritten 2. Give shorter, more frequent tests rather than fewer, more comprehensive tests 3. Change the setting in which the student takes the test 4. Allow students to dictate their responses 5. Limit the number of matching items to ten
Bursuck, Polloway, Plante, Epstein, Jayanthi, & McConeghy, 1996 (K–12)	1. Base grades on amount of improvement an individual makes 2. Award separate grades for process (e.g., effort) and product (e.g., tests) 3. Adjust grades according to student's ability 4. Base grades on less content than for the rest of the class 5. Base grades on a modified grading scale (e.g., from 93 to 100 = A to 90 to 100 = A)

From "Implementing Instructional Adaptations for Students with Disabilities in Inclusive Classrooms: A Literature Review," by B. J. Scott, M. R. Vitale, and W. G. Masten, 1998, *Remedial and Special Education, 19,* pp. 111–112. Used by permission.

The specific modifications and accommodations for students with disabilities in elementary classes, discussed next, will likely vary in terms of teacher acceptability. Many adaptations will prove beneficial to all students, not only to those with special needs. Teachers are encouraged to select strategies that appear applicable to a given situation and then evaluate their effectiveness. "Tips for Adapting an Elementary Lesson Plan" illustrates the use of adaptations.

Adaptations for Instructional Lessons

Numerous important instructional areas present challenges for learners with special needs. In this section, we address several key areas of concern.

To facilitate learning, teachers must consider vehicles for the effective presentation of content to enhance successful listening. Adaptations in this area typically prove beneficial to all students. Some specific considerations include relating information to students' prior experiences and providing an overview before beginning; limiting the number of concepts introduced at a given time; and reviewing lessons before additional content is introduced.

In many instances, instructional tasks, assignments, or materials may be relevant and appropriate for children with disabilities but may present problematic reading demands. Teachers should consider options for adapting the task or the textual materials. Several suggestions that illustrate ways to assist students in processing reading content are:

- Previewing reading material with students to assist them in establishing purpose, activating prior knowledge, budgeting time, and focusing attention.
- preteaching vocabulary to ensure that students can use them rather than simply recognize them.
- Using graphic organizers (e.g., charts, graphs) to provide an orientation to reading tasks or to supplement them.

Adaptations can also enhance the ability of children to meet the written language demands of the inclusive classroom. For example, teachers can:

- allow children to select the most comfortable method of writing (i.e., cursive or manuscript).
- let students type or tape-record answers.
- provide the student with a copy of lecture notes, PowerPoint slides, or detailed outlines to guide notetaking.

Another key area is enhancing children's ability to follow instructions and complete work assignments. The following suggestions are adapted from *CEC Today* (1997):

- Get the student's attention before giving directions.
- Use alerting cues.
- Give one direction at a time.
- Quietly repeat the directions to the student after they have been given to the entire class.
- Check for understanding by having the student repeat the directions.
- Break up tasks into workable and obtainable steps, and include due dates.
- Post requirements necessary to complete each assignment.
- Check assignments frequently. (p. 15)

One type of adaptation warrants particular attention. Graphic organizers, advance organizers that provide visual models for presenting curricular content, have been widely promoted as a particularly efficacious approach to content learning by students with special needs (Wehmeyer, in press). As such, the widespread use of graphic organizers has become an important aspect of the application of universal design for learning, which was discussed earlier in the chapter. Strangman, Hall, and Meyer (n.d.) defined a

Tips for Adapting an Elementary Lesson Plan

Topic: Oral dictation of story endings

Objective: Given one story read orally, the students will dictate a new story ending with 80 percent mastery.

1. Review of previous lesson: "Yesterday we completed orally reading the story *My Friend Bear* by Jez Alborough."

2. Advance organizer: "Today we will dictate our own story endings for the story that I will read to the class. We will first play a game with partners, and then we will orally retell the new story endings."

3. Motivator, introduction, command for attention, and obtaining commitment to learn: "Have you ever been listening to a story being read to you, and the ending of the story was not the one you wanted? You can change that problem! Today, we will practice making up our own story endings. I am going to read a story to you, and you will tell me how you think the story should end."

4. Direct instruction: Reread the story *My Friend Bear*. Stop before reading the end. Tell the students that they will now make up their own ending instead of reading the ending of the book. Be sure to "think out loud" when modeling. For example: "I do not like the way that story ends. Instead of having the bear and the boy both walking away from each other, I am going to have the bear go home with the boy. Can you think of anything else?" Brainstorm with the students, and provide feedback when they give answers. Orally model the ending of the story.

5. Guided practice and feedback: "We will now practice orally dictating our own story endings." Put the students into groups of two, and give each group a game board, dice, tape recorder, pennies for playing pieces, and short story cards. Have them brainstorm for possible new story endings for the stories (previously read) listed on the cards. Closely supervise each group. Have each student orally dictate a new story ending. Use a tape recorder to record responses.

6. Independent practice and feedback: Have each student pick the name of a story out of a box. Instruct each student to think of a new ending to the story that he or she picked. Have the students orally tell the teacher their new story endings.

7. Adaptations to lesson: To successfully include students with special needs in the lesson, use the following strategies:
   - Stop periodically while giving instruction to ensure understanding; ask questions to verify.
   - Provide prompts about possible points to consider in developing endings.
   - Establish dyads in which the student with a disability is paired with a supportive peer.
   - After the pair creates a story, be sure the child with special needs has a chance to dictate a portion of the story.
   - Add pictures to the story cards to cue meaning.

8. Techniques for student evaluation: The teacher will read one story orally. The students will dictate new story endings (can be done with the use of a tape recorder). The teacher will use a checklist to check for student understanding.

9. Summary and transition to next lesson: "Today we learned that we can change the endings of stories by making our own endings. We orally dictated new story endings. Tomorrow, we will review oral dictation of story endings. We will then begin work on making new story endings that can be orally presented to the entire class."

The authors thank Stacy Roberts of the University of Alabama, Birmingham, for contributing this sample lesson plan, which we have adapted.

graphic organizer as "a visual and graphic display that depicts the relationships between facts, terms, and/or ideas within a learning task. Graphic organizers are also sometimes referred to as knowledge maps, concept maps, story maps, cognitive organizers, advance organizers, or concept diagrams" (p. 2).

Graphic organizers can be developed for content in any instructional area. For example, graphic organizers can provide outlines for note taking from lectures; a template for organizing reports and speeches for oral presentation in class; a format for deriving key content information from reading assigned as homework; and a prompt to assist students in monitoring their own errors in writing as part of a proofreading strategy. The material that follows in the text provide a wealth of examples of graphic organizers. For instance, semantic maps in reading and paragraph development models in writing are particularly useful applications of graphic organizers.

Cultural Diversity Considerations

Educators need to consider issues related to cultural diversity when working with elementary-age students with special needs. Students who come from different language backgrounds and whose families reflect values that differ from those of the majority culture must be treated with sensitivity and respect. Thus, teachers should often make adaptations to instruction so that it reflects effective responses to multicultural considerations.

Considerations of linguistic and cultural diversity must inform all aspects of curriculum design and should be reflected in instructional practices. The continued overrepresentation of minority children in high-incidence special education categories underscores the importance of this focus (e.g., Oswald et al., 1999). Because

DIVERSITY FORUM

Scaffolding Learning for Diverse Students with Disabilities

Mrs. Jones is a second grade teacher in a rural school district in the Midwest that has recently experienced an influx of immigrant families due to the opening of a poultry plant. Ms. Jones began the school year learning more about her students and their families to include important holidays and traditions, family composition, work schedules, and cultural patterns of behavior. She learned about the process of acculturation and second language acquisition to understand the social emotional experiences of her students. To ensure that her students have full access to the general education curriculum, Ms. Jones infused content from students' experiences and used various scaffolding strategies to support comprehension. She has noticed that all students, including her students with disabilities are responding well to her efforts.

The No Child Left Behind Act (2001) and IDEA (2004) require that all teachers are highly qualified and provide access to the general education curriculum for all learners in special education. Given the diversity among students in general and special edu-

cation, it has become increasingly important for teachers to understand different models of curriculum and instruction that meet the needs of all learners. For example, instructional scaffolds can provide temporary supports which make learning accessible and enable students to become independent learners. Ms. Jones used four types of scaffolding (Santamaria, Fletcher, & Bos, 2002):

1. *Mediated Scaffolds* make new information more accessible; e.g., pair students with peers, educational staff, and/or adults;
2. *Task Scaffolds* adjust tasks by breaking them down into manageable parts and/or provide more time for each component so that the student can generate information independently and meet mastery.
3. *Materials Scaffolds* facilitate learning through the use of assistive technology and manipulatives (e.g., advanced organizers, story maps, paragraph frames, and sentence starters).
4. *Comprehensible Input Scaffolds* make concepts comprehensible and

meaningful to the learner through language modifications (e.g., include the use of literal or concrete vocabulary, familiar terms, and native language/dialect).

Questions

1. Select one of the scaffolding techniques above in connection with a general education lesson, and create examples of ways to scaffold instruction for English language learners in Ms. Jones' general education classroom.
2. What are ways you can support the general education teacher in creating curriculum and instruction that is accessible to English language learners with disabilities?

REFERENCES
Santamaria, L. J., Fletcher, T. V., & Bos, C. S. (2002). Effective pedagogy for English language learners in inclusive classrooms. In A. J. Artiles & A. A. Ortiz (Eds.). *English language learners with special needs: Identification, assessment, and instruction* (Chapter 6). McHenry, Il: Center for Applied Linguistics & by Delta Systems.

TECHNOLOGY Today

Virtual Technology in the Special Education Classroom

Smedley and Higgins (2005) advocate the use of virtual technology to bring the world to students with disabilities. One of their examples is through the use of "virtual field trips." Through this approach, teachers can take advantage of the various benefits of such trips without the concerns of preparation time, scheduling, funding, transportation, and liability. Some examples from their list of online virtual field trips to selected locations are provided below:

Expedition online: Students may take virtual field trips to caves, volcanoes, and glaciers around the world.

Virtual field trips: During these virtual experiences, a class may pair up with another class in a different location with one group serving as the host.

CTI: Students tour art galleries and museums as well as visit Europe, Asia, America, and Antarctica.

Hidden New York: This website highlights twelve little-known areas around New York City.

Since virtual field trips and other types of simulations are generally delivered using several modalities, students with and without disabilities can use diverse learning approaches while participating in these activities. In addition, a computer-delivered course of instruction allows students to work at their own pace. Such virtual excursions also encourage students to focus on

the most pertinent topics or details prior to an in-class lesson or an actual field trip.

While the application of technology obviously offers students many additional opportunities to learn and interact with the world around them, teachers should be aware that technology use presents challenges as well. One potential challenge is that both teachers and students will require additional training in the appropriate use of each simulation or software program. Despite such challenges, virtual programs and other forms of computer technology continue to offer all students an opportunity to learn using multiple modalities and to demonstrate their unique strengths.

From "Virtual Technology: Bringing the World into the Special Education classroom," by T. M. Smedley and K. Higgins, 2005, *Intervention in School and Clinic, 41,* pp. 114–119.

---

students with special needs benefit from direct, hands-on approaches to such topics, teachers should introduce specific activities that promote cultural awareness and sensitivity to develop students' appreciation of diversity at the elementary level and then lay the foundation for subsequent programming at the middle and secondary school level.

An excellent resource for building a multicultural focus in the curriculum is through the use of the Internet. "Technology Today" presents an innovative approach to web use.

Adapting the Classroom Environment

Two key considerations are time and physical arrangement. Time is a critical element and can be associated with special challenges for students with disabilities. Thus, adapting deadlines and other requirements can help promote success. When handled properly, these adaptations need not impinge on the integrity of the assignments or place undue burdens on the classroom teacher. Other examples include:

- reviewing with students to reinforce routines
- providing each student with a copy of the schedule
- increasing the amount of time allowed to complete assignments or tests
- teaching time-management skills

Changes in the classroom arrangement can also help children with special needs. Some specific examples include establishing a climate that fosters positive social interactions between students, using study carrels, and establishing high- and low-frequency areas for class work (thus using the Premack principle to allow students to move to "fun" areas contingent on work completion in more academically rigorous areas).

CROSS-REFERENCE

See also the discussion on classroom arrangement in Chapter 14.

CEC STANDARDS

CEC 5: Learning Environments and Social Interactions

INTASC

INTASC 5: Learning environments

PRAXIS

PRAXIS II: Delivery of Services

Figure 15.4	**Homework Communication Problems Noted by Elementary Teachers**

Note: Items were ranked by general education teachers from most to least serious.

1. Do not know enough about the abilities of students with disabilities who are mainstreamed in their classes.
2. Do not know how to use special education support services or teachers to assist students with disabilities about homework.
3. Lack knowledge about the adaptations that can be made to homework.
4. Are not clear about their responsibility to communicate with special education teachers about the homework of students with disabilities.
5. Are not aware of their responsibility to communicate with parents of students with disabilities about homework.

From "Homework Communication Problems: Perspectives of General Education Teachers," by M. H. Epstein, E. A. Polloway, G. H. Buck, W. D. Bursuck, L. M. Wissinger, F. Whitehause, and M. Jayanthi, 1997, *Learning Disabilities Research and Practice, 12,* pp. 221–227. Used by permission.

Developing Effective Homework Programs

CONSIDER THIS

The importance of homework adaptations to the successful inclusion of students with special needs has been confirmed in numerous research studies. How important do you think they are? Why?

Homework is an essential element of education, and educational reforms have led to its increased use by elementary general education teachers. Traditional research on the effectiveness of homework as an instructional tool suggests that it leads to increased school achievement for students in general, with particular benefits in the area of habit formation for elementary students (Cooper, 1989; Walberg, 1991).

Homework for students with disabilities presents several dilemmas for general education teachers. Epstein and colleagues (1997) recognized that communication concerning homework is often negatively affected by the inadequate knowledge base of general education teachers. Figure 15.4 presents typical problems (ordered from most- to least-serious by teachers) in this area.

Polloway, Epstein, Bursuck, Jayanthi, and Cumblad (1994) asked teachers to rate specific strategies that were most helpful to students with disabilities. Figure 15.5 summarizes these responses; each column reflects teachers' ratings from most to least helpful.

Patton and colleagues (2001) reviewed the research on collaboration concerning homework and identified recommended practices that are respectively school-based, teacher-directed, parent-initiated, and student-regulated. These are listed in Table 15.6.

Developing Responsive Grading Practices

CROSS-REFERENCE

Grading issues become more problematic at the secondary level; see Chapter 16 for more information.

The assignment of grades is an integral aspect of education. Grading serves multiple purposes in contemporary education, as summarized in Table 15.7. Thus, grading practices have been subject to frequent evaluation and review, generating a number of problematic issues.

In a national survey of teachers, Bursuck and colleagues (1996) found that approximately 40 percent of general educators shared responsibilities for grading with special education teachers. This collaboration is timely because existing grading systems make success challenging for students who are disabled.

Further, these same researchers reported that elementary teachers evaluated adaptations and indicated that adaptations allowing for separate grades for process and product and grades indexed against student improvement were particularly helpful, whereas passing students "no matter what" or basing grades on effort alone was not; this finding is consistent with the distinction of accommodations versus modifications made by Polloway and colleagues (2002) noted earlier in this chapter. Figure 15.6 presents Bursuck and colleagues (1996) ranking of grading adaptations.

| Figure 15.5 | Teachers' Ratings of Helpfulness of Homework Adaptations and Practices |

Most Helpful

- Communicate clear consequences about successfully completing homework.
- Begin assignment in class, and check for understanding.
- Communicate clear expectations about the quality of homework completion.
- Use a homework assignment sheet or notebook.
- Communicate clear consequences about failure to complete homework.
- Give assignments that are completed entirely at school.
- Begin assignment in class without checking for understanding.
- Assist students in completing the assignment.
- Make adaptations in assignment.
- Talk to students about why the assignment was not completed.
- Require corrections and resubmission.
- Call students' parents.
- Keep students in at recess to complete the assignment.
- Keep students after school to complete the assignment.
- Lower students' grades.
- Put students' names on board.
- Give praise for completion.
- Provide corrective feedback in class.
- Give rewards for completion.
- Monitor students by charting performance.
- Record performance in grade book.
- Provide additional teacher assistance.
- Check more frequently with student about assignments and expectations.
- Allow alternative response formats (e.g., oral or other than written).
- Adjust length of assignment.
- Provide a peer tutor for assistance.
- Provide auxiliary learning aids (e.g., calculator, computer).
- Assign work that student can do independently.
- Provide a study group.
- Provide extra-credit opportunities.
- Adjust (i.e., lower) evaluation standards.
- Adjust due dates.
- Give fewer assignments.

Least Helpful

From "A National Survey of Homework Practices of General Education Teachers," by E. A. Polloway, M. H. Epstein, W. Bursuck, M. Jayanthi, and C. Cumblad, 1994," *Journal of Learning Disabilities, 27,* p. 504. Used by permission.

A related issue is the feasibility of specific adaptations in general education. Bursuck and colleagues (1996) assessed this question by determining whether teachers actually use these same adaptations with students without disabilities. As implied by Figure 15.6, three of the four adaptations deemed most helpful for students with disabilities (i.e., grading on improvement, adjusting grades, giving separate grades for process and product) were also seen as feasible because they were used by 50 percent or more of the teachers (regardless of grade level) with nondisabled students. Basing grades on less content and passing students no matter what are frowned on in both general and special education.

Questions of fairness also influence the discussion on grading (e.g., Are adaptations in grading made only for students with disabilities really fair to other students?). Bursuck and colleagues (1996) report that only 25 percent of general education teachers

Table 15.6	**Recommended Homework Practices**

School-based
- Require frequent written communication from teachers to parents.
- Schedule parent–teacher meetings in the evening.
- Provide release time for teachers to communicate with parents.
- Establish telephone hotlines.
- Establish after-school sessions to provide extra help.
- Institute peer tutoring programs.

Teacher-directed
- Require and teach students to use homework assignment books.
- Assess students' skills related to homework completion.
- Involve parents and students in the homework process from the beginning of the school year.
- Establish an ongoing communication system with parents to convey information related to homework assignments.
- Coordinate homework assignments with other teachers.
- Present assignments clearly and provide timely feedback.
- Teach students techniques for managing their time more effectively.

Parent-initiated
- Discuss homework assignments with their children daily.
- Attend parent–teacher conferences.
- Communicate views, concerns, and observations about homework to teacher(s) or other school personnel.
- Provide support to their child when doing homework by creating and maintaining an appropriate homework environment.

Student-regulated
- Demonstrate a range of self-advocacy skills including the ability to ask for help when needed.
- Become an interdependent learner.
- Manage time more effectively.

From "Home–School Collaboration about Homework: What Do We Know and What Should We Do?" by J. R. Patton, M. Jayanthi, and E. A. Polloway, 2001, *Reading & Writing Quarterly, 17*, p. 233.

thought such adaptations were fair. Those who believed they were fair noted that students should "not be punished" for an inherent problem such as a disability, that adaptations for effort are appropriate because the students are "fighting uphill battles," and that adaptations allow students to "be successful like other kids."

Those teachers who thought adaptations unfair indicated that other students experience significant learning problems even though they have not been formally identified, that some students have extenuating circumstances (e.g., divorce, illness) that necessitate adaptations, and that all students are unique and deserve individual consideration (i.e., students both with and without disabilities may need specific adaptations). Finally, a minority of general educators believe that because classes have standards to uphold, all students need to meet those standards without adaptations (Bursuck et al., 1996).

Polloway and colleagues (2008) suggest these overall considerations about grading:

- Plan for special and general education teachers to meet regularly to discuss student progress.
- Emphasize the acquisition of new skills as a basis for grades assigned, thus providing a perspective on the student's relative gains.
- Investigate alternatives for evaluating content that has been learned (e.g., oral examinations for poor readers in a science class).

Table 15.7	**Purposes of Grading**
1. Achievements:	To certify and measure mastery of curricular goals and specific skills (e.g., learning standards).
2. Progress:	To indicate progress in learning over a specific period of time.
3. Effort:	To acknowledge and indicate the effort a student puts forth in learning.
4. Comparison:	To compare students in terms of their competence, progress, and effort.
5. Instructional planning:	To identify students' learning strengths and needs, and to group students for instruction.
6. Program effectiveness:	To examine the efficacy of the instructional program.
7. Motivation:	To motivate students to learn, to reward learning, and to promote self-esteem.
8. Communication:	To provide feedback to students, families, and others.
9. Educational and career planning:	To aid students, families, and school districts in determining the courses and educational services needed by students, placing students who enter the school district from another school district, and planning for the future (e.g., facilitate student advisement and career planning).
10. Eligibility:	To determine eligibility for graduation and promotion, and rank students in terms of their eligibility for certain programs and awards (e.g., honors programs, participation in extracurricular activities, grants, scholarships, rankings for college admission).
11. Accountability:	To provide measures of student achievement to the community, employers, legislators, and educational policy makers (e.g., grades provide employers with a point of reference concerning the aptitude and job skills of prospective employees).

Adapted from "Grading Students in Inclusive Settings," by S. Salend and L. G. Duhaney, 2002, *Teaching Exceptional Children, 34,* pp. 13–14.

- Engage in cooperative grading agreements (e.g., grades for language arts might reflect performance both in the classroom and the resource room).
- Use narrative reports as a key portion of, or adjunct to, the report card. These reports can include comments on specific objectives within the student's IEP.
- Develop personalized grading plans for students. (Munk & Bursuck, 2001, 2004)

The nearby Evidence-Based Practice box on effective grading practices provides additional perspectives.

Figure 15.6	**Elementary Teachers' Ratings of Helpfulness of Grading Adaptations for Students with Disabilities**

Note: Numbers in parentheses refer to general education teachers' rankings of adaptations from **most likely to least likely to be used** with nondisabled students.

Most Helpful
1. Grades are based on the amount of improvement an individual makes. (1)
2. Separate grades are given for process (e.g., effort) and product (e.g., tests). (3)
3. Grades are based on meeting IEP objectives. (9)
4. Grades are adjusted according to student ability. (2)
5. Grading weights are adjusted (e.g., efforts on projects count more than tests). (4)
6. Grades are based on meeting the requirements of academic or behavioral contracts. (5)
7. Grades are based on less content than the rest of the class. (7)
8. Students are passed if they make an effort to pass. (6)
9. Grades are based on a modified grading scale (e.g., from 93 to 100 = A, 90 to 100 = A). (8)

Least Helpful
10. Students are passed no matter what. (10).

Adapted from "Report Card Grading Practices and Adaptations," by W. D. Bursuck, E. A. Polloway, L. Plante, M.H. Epstien, M. Jayanthi, and J. McConeghy, 1996, *Exceptional Children, 62,* pp. 301–318. Used by permission.

EVIDENCE-BASED PRACTICE

Effective Grading Practices

Grading is a critical element of successful inclusion. Salend and Duhaney (2002) provided a series of recommendations, which include the following:

- **Communicating expectations and grading guidelines:** Student performance is enhanced when teachers clearly communicate their expectations to students and families and share their grading guidelines and criteria with them.
- **Informing students and families regarding grading progress on a regular basis:** Providing students and their families with ongoing information concerning current performance and grades helps all involved parties understand the grading guidelines. Ongoing sharing of students' grading progress facilitates the modifications of instructional programs so that students and families are not surprised by the grades received at the end of the grading period. It also prompts students to examine their effort, motivation, and attitudes, and their impact on their performance and grades.
- **Using a range of assignments that address students' varied learning needs, strengths, and styles:** Rather than assigning grades based solely on test performance or a limited number of assignments, many teachers determine students' grades by weighing a variety of student assignments (e.g., tests, homework, projects, extra credit, class participation, attendance, behavior, and other factors).
- **Employing classroom-based assessment alternatives to traditional testing:** Whereas grades are frequently

determined by students' performance on tests, they also can be established on classroom-based assessment techniques, such as performance assessment, portfolio assessment, and curriculum-based measurement. By using performance assessment, teachers grade students on authentic products (e.g., creating and making things, solving problems, responding to stimulations) that demonstrate their skills, problem-solving abilities, knowledge, and understanding of the learning standards. Similarly, student portfolios and curriculum-based measurements that are linked to the learning standards serve as tools for grading students and guiding the teaching and learning process.

- **Providing feedback on assignments and grading students after they have learned something rather than while they are learning it:** Before grading students on an assignment or a test, teachers should provide a range of appropriate learning activities and give nongraded assignments that help students practice and develop their skills. As students work on these assignments, teachers should give them feedback and additional instructional experiences to improve their learning of the material, which is then assessed when they have completed the learning cycle.
- **Avoiding competition and promoting collaboration:** While grading on a curve results in a consistent grade distribution, it hinders the teaching and learning process by promoting competition

among students. Therefore, educators minimize competition by grading students in reference to specific learning criteria and refraining from posting grades. Teachers also promote collaboration among students by structuring learning and assessments activities so that students work together and are graded cooperatively.

- **Designing valid tests and providing students with appropriate testing accommodations:** Teachers enhance the value of their tests and promote student performance by developing valid tests and providing students with appropriate testing accommodations. In designing valid tests, teachers select the content of the test so that it relates to the learning standards, the manner in which the content was taught, and the amount of class time devoted to the topics on the test. Teachers also carefully examine the format and readability of their tests and provide students with the testing accommodations outlined on their IEPs.
- **Teaching test-taking to students:** Instruction in test-taking skills helps students perform at their optimal levels by reducing testing anxiety and assisting them in feeling comfortable with the format of the test.

Adapted from "Grading Students in Inclusive Settings," by S. Salend and L. G. Duhaney, 2002, *Teaching Exceptional Children, 34*(3), pp. 13–14.

Summary

General Curriculum Considerations

- The curriculum for elementary students with disabilities should meet their current and long-term needs, facilitate their interactions with nondisabled peers, and facilitate their transition into middle school.

Curriculum Emphases

- Reading instruction should reflect emphases on both decoding skills and whole language to provide a comprehensive, balanced program.
- Math instruction should provide students with concrete and abstract learning opportunities and should stress the development of problem-solving skills.
- Teachers should select programs and strategies that focus on the social skills most needed by students in their classrooms.
- Life-skills instruction should be a part of the elementary curriculum through the use of augmentation, infusion, or an integrated curriculum.

Instructional Strategies

- Cooperative teaching involves a team approach in which teachers share their talents in providing class instruction to all students. This requires a commitment to planning, time, and administrative support to reach its potential for success.
- Instructional adaptations should be evaluated against their "teacher acceptability" (e.g., helpfulness, feasibility, desirability, and fairness).
- Listening is a skill that requires conscious effort on the part of students and planned intervention strategies on the part of teachers.
- Reading tasks can be adapted through a variety of instructional strategies, such as clarifying intent, highlighting content, modifying difficulty level, and using visual aids.
- Written responses can be facilitated through modification of the response requirement.
- Cooperative learning affords teachers a unique opportunity to involve students with disabilities in classroom activities.
- Adaptations in class schedules or classroom arrangements should be considered to enhance the learning of students with disabilities.
- Educational programs should be designed to reflect the importance of motivation.
- Homework creates significant challenges for students with special needs; these should be addressed by using intervention strategies.
- Classroom grading practices should be flexible enough to facilitate inclusion.

Further Readings

Buck, G. H., Williams, K., Patton, J. R., & Polloway, E. A. (in press). *Prereferral intervention resource guide*. Austin, TX: Pro-Ed.

Hoover, J.J., & Patton, J.R. (2005). *Curriculum adaptations for students with learning and behavior problems: Principles and practices for differentiating instruction*. Austin, TX: Pro-Ed.

Polloway, E. A., Patton, J. R., & Serna, L. (2008). *Strategies for teaching learners with special needs* (9th ed.). Columbus, OH: Merrill.

Scruggs, T. E., & Mastropieri, M. (2006). *The inclusive classroom: Strategies for effective instruction* (3rd ed.). Upper Saddle River, NJ: Pearson Education.

mylabschool
Where the c assroom comes to ife

Go to Allyn & Bacon's MyLabSchool (www.mylabschool.com) and enter Assignment ID SPV5 in the Assignment Finder. View the video clip called *Inclusion in Early Childhood Education*. Then consider what you have seen along with what you've read in Chapter 15 to answer the following questions.

1. Although this video clip focuses on preschool inclusion, do you see strategies at work here that would be equally useful in the elementary grades? Why do you think these strategies would be useful for somewhat older children? What strategies would not be useful in elementary classrooms, if any? Why? Be specific.

2. Many states have a special education category called *developmentally delayed* that can be used to identify students needing services up to age nine. Why would states have such a category? How might it be useful to you as an elementary school teacher?

3. As a student with special needs moves from preschool to elementary school, how might the benefits and limitations of inclusion change for that student? How might a teacher's focus change?

You may also answer the questions at the end of the clip and e-mail your responses to your instructor.

Teaching Students with Special Needs in Secondary Schools

After reading this chapter, you should be able to:

1. Describe the demands of a secondary education setting.

2. Discuss the curricular options available in most secondary schools.

3. Discuss the transition planning process for students with disabilities.

4. Identify and describe the key elements of effective instruction.

5. Discuss the role of general education and special education teachers in ensuring successful secondary school programs for students with special needs.

6. Identify accommodations and modications that can facilitate learning for secondary school students.

7. Identify and give examples of study skills and learning strategies that can enhance school performance for adolescent learners.

Jim just turned seventeen years old. While he seemed extremely happy about reaching this milestone in his life, his personality began to change. He gradually went from an easy-going eleventh-grade student to one who was more oppositional, lashing out occasionally at other students and teachers. Although he had always been close to his parents, they were having similiar problems at home. He wanted to stay in his room most of the time and was unusually resistant to helping around the house or talking about what was going on at school. He sat for hours pretending to do homework without making much progress; grades began to drop. In the past Jim had welcomed his parents' assistance in reading difficult content material, but now when they tried to help, he became aggitated and refused the assistance. During a teacher–parent conference, it was decided that Jim needed counseling. After a bit of cajoling, an appointment was scheduled; and several sessions later, the counselor was able to get Jim to express his feelings. He was becoming overwhelmed by all of the "unknowns" in his life!

His driving test was coming up and he was afraid he would not be able to pass the written test, especially the part where he had to read a map. He had passed only the math and science portions of the exit exam; now reading and language were scheduled in the spring and he questioned whether he could make high enough scores to pass. Also, could he pass the academic courses that he needs to graduate? Would he go to college? What should he major in? Would someone be available to help in college, like his teachers and parents have helped in high school? At least now the IEP team—and Jim—had the concerns identified. What could be done to help?

In a family session, Jim agreed to continue meeting with the counselor to explore these feelings, and a midyear IEP meeting was scheduled including the counselor, general and special education teachers, parents, a vocational rehabilitation counselor, and Jim. The teacher agreed to teach Jim skills in self-advocacy so he could access agencies and develop a network of support in his upcoming life after high school. The vocational rehabilitation counselor agreed to send Jim for a vocational assessment to determine his strengths, interests, and challenges. She also suggested that during the school breaks for the remaining year and a half, Jim job-shadow adults whose jobs held an interest for him. His parents agreed to work more with Jim on driving to obtain his permanent license, and the school assigned a driving instructor to add support and assist Jim in requesting accommodations for taking the written driving test. Insightful counselors, teachers, and parents, and a "relieved" student, turned this story into a positive ending. The transition portion of Jim's IEP is presented nearby.

Jim's IEP: Transition Components

Unique educational needs, characteristics, and measured present levels of academic achievement and functional performance (PLOPs).	Special education, related services and supplemental aids and services (based on peer-reviewed research to the extent practicable); assistive technology and modifications or personnel support.	Measurable annual goals and short-term objectives (progress markers),[1] including academic and functional goals to enable students to be involved in and make progress in the general curriculum and to meet other needs resulting from the disability.
(Including how the disability affects student's ability to participate and progress in the general curriculum.)	(Including anticipated starting date, frequency, duration, and location for each.)	(Including progress measurement method for each goal.)

Instruction

Self-advocacy PLOP: Jim is unaware of his legal rights under Section 504 and ADA, and he is unable to request appropriate accommodations he would need in given situations, such as a large lecture class. He becomes embarrassed and anxious when discussing his disability and its affects on his school performance, and he becomes angry or tries to change the subject.

Community

Driver's license PLOP: Jim has been driving for a year on a learner's permit and is concerned that he cannot pass the written test required for his license, although he is confident of all his driving and related skills except map reading.

Employment and other

Not needed at this time. Jim intends to enroll in the computer network support program at Leland Community College (LCC) and is on track for a regular diploma. He is a tech lab assistant this year and is doing very well.

1. Small group instruction from special ed teacher in relevant rights, procedures, and remedies under Section 504, ADA, and IDEA

   - Role playing in describing needed accommodations to employers, professors, and other adult life figures of authority.
   - Services to begin Tuesday, Sept. 15; two thirty-minute sessions weekly until goals are met.
   - (L&R) Protection and Advocacy will assist teacher and provide materials at no cost. (Verified by phone—M. Adams)
   - LCC Office of Disability Services will meet with Jim to set up an accommodation plan. (Verified by phone—S. Holvey)

2. Within two weeks from the date of this IEP, the driver training instructor will inform Jim about accommodations available in the state, if any, for licensing people with reading disabilities. Then she and Jim will develop a plan to follow through and that plan will be added to this IEP no later than Oct. 10.

   - (L&R) DMV will assist instructor and will provide information on test accommodations. (Verified by phone—J. Hill)
   - Instruction in map reading and route highlighting.

Goal 1: Given a twenty-five-item objective test over basic rights and procedures under Section 504 and ADA, Jim will pass with a score of 75 percent or better.

Goal 2: In hypothetical role-play scenarios of disability-based discrimination, Jim will calmly and accurately explain to an employer, professor, or other representative of the postschool world his rights and remedies under Section 504 and ADA.

Goal 3: Given a real-world meeting with the Director of Disability Services at LCC, Jim will describe the effect of his disability in a school situation and will explain what accommodations help him to meet expectations.

Goal 4: Jim will become a competent driver in Jefferson state and will take the licensing exam on March 15. By March 1, given a practice exam administered under real-world conditions, Jim will score at least 70 percent.

Goal 5: Given a city map, Jim will accurately highlight six common routes he routinely follows and four routes he will use next year, when he is attending LCC, e.g., from his home to the mall, from his home to LCC, etc.

From *Better IEPs: How To Develop Legally Correct and Educationally Useful Programs* (p. 145), by B. D. Bateman and M. A. Linden, 2006, Verona, WI: Attainment.

[1]For students who take an alternative assessment and are assessed against other than grade level standards, the IEP **must** include short-term objectives (progress markers). For other students, the IEP **may** include short-term objectives. The IEP **must** for all students clearly articulate how the student's progress will be measured; and that progress must be reported to parents at designated intervals.

Secondary school can be a stressful setting for students with and without disabilities. Significant differences exist between elementary and secondary settings in terms of organizational structure, curricula, and learner characteristics. These differences create special challenges for successful inclusion. Certainly one concern is the gap found between the demands of the classroom setting and academics and the ability of many students with disabilities. Academically, this gap widens; many students with disabilities exhibit limited basic skills, study skills, and strategies, and therefore experience difficulty in performing higher-level cognitive tasks. Figure 16.1 provides a list of the demands placed on students in a secondary setting.

A second concern is that teachers are often trained primarily as content specialists, yet are expected to present complex material in such a way that a diverse group of students can master the information (Masters, Mori, & Mori, 1999). Secondary teachers are more likely to focus on teaching the content than on individualizing instruction to meet the unique needs of each student. Further, because there may be reluctance to change grading systems or make other accommodations, it may become difficult for students with disabilities to experience success in general education settings.

A third challenge is the general nature of adolescence. Adolescence is a difficult and trying time for all young people. For students with disabilities, the developmental period is even more challenging. Problems such as a lack of motivation associated with adolescence are exacerbated by the presence of a disability (Masters et al., 1999).

A fourth problem is the current movement to reform schools. For example, these changes may mean that all students will have to take more math and science courses or achieve a passing grade on a minimum competency test; such requirements may prove difficult to meet for many students who experience learning and behavior problems.

Regardless of the difficulties associated with placing adolescents with special needs in general education programs, more students with disabilities are going to depend on classroom teachers to help develop and provide appropriate educational programs. Therefore, classroom teachers in secondary schools must be prepared to offer specialized instruction and modified curricula in order for these special students to benefit from their placement in general education settings.

CONSIDER THIS

Without the quick response of the IEP team, what do you predict might have happened to Jim and his family?

CONSIDER THIS

Do special education support staff need different skills at the secondary level than they need in elementary schools? If so, what are some of the differences?

TEACHING TIP

Special education teachers might want to provide a staff development session to general classroom teachers outlining the purposes of an inclusive program and provide some success stories. Ensure that classroom teachers know that they have some supports.

Figure 16.1   **Secondary Setting Demands**

- Students need to be able to read a wide variety of content areas independently with fluidity and speed.
- Students are expected to have prerequisite content knowledge and skills.
- Students need to be able to learn from teachers who use lecture as their standard format and use a fast pace for introduction of new material.
- Students need to be able to learn with less contact time with the teachers than they had in elementary school (e.g., 50 minutes/day versus 350 minutes/day).
- Students need to have strong written language skills.
- Students need to be able to work independently with little immediate feedback or correction.
- Students need to be able to determine the importance of what is being said and take notes in a format that can be used later for review.
- Students need to be able to break a long-term task into parts, and complete each part prior to the due date.
- Students need to be able to keep track of their materials, their class requirements, and their schedules.
- Students are expected to pass high-stakes testing.

From *Teaching Students with Mild and High-Incidence Disabilities at the Secondary Level* (2nd ed., p. 6), by E. J. Sabornie and L. U. deBettencourt, 2004. Upper Saddle River, NJ: Merrill.

CONSIDER THIS

Describe some of the reforms made in secondary schools and their impact on providing services to students with special needs. For example, how does increasing graduation requirements affect students with special needs?

CEC STANDARDS

CEC 7: Instructional Planning

INTASC

INTASC 7: Plans instruction

PRAXIS

PRAXIS II: Delivery of Services to Students with Disabilities

Secondary School Curricula

More curricular differentiation has been advocated at the secondary level to accommodate the individual needs and interests of the wide variety of students attending comprehensive high schools in the United States. At the same time, most high schools have a general curriculum that all students must complete to obtain a diploma. This curriculum, generally prescribed by the state education agency, includes science, math, social studies, and English. Often, state and local education agencies add areas such as art education, sexuality, drug education, and foreign languages to the required general curriculum.

Students have opportunities to choose curricular alternatives, which are usually related to postschool goals. For example, students planning to go to college choose a college preparatory focus that builds on the general curriculum with higher-level academic courses and often the study of a language. This college preparatory option helps prepare students for the rigorous courses found at college. Other students choose a vocational program, designed to help prepare them for specific job opportunities after high school. Still other students choose a general curriculum, with some course choices for students who would be willing to enter a variety of job fields not requiring postsecondary training. The curricular focus that students choose should be an important consideration because the decision could have long-term implications after the student exits school.

The educational reform movements of the 1980s, the 1990s, and Goals 2000 have had a direct impact on the secondary curriculum. Schools have begun to offer, and in some cases require, more science and math courses. Also, in many states and districts students must successfully complete high school competency examinations before they are eligible for graduation. Students who do not pass these exams may receive a certificate of attendance or completion instead of a diploma. These changes seem to have had a positive effect on students in general education, since their graduation rate continues to climb. Newburger and Curry (1999) report that the national high school completion rate, including those earning the General Educational Development (GED) certificate and those completing an adult education program, is 90 percent. Unfortunately, these changes have not resulted in more positive outcomes for students with special needs.

Special Education Curriculum in Secondary Schools

CONSIDER THIS

In the 1950s, a high school diploma was a valuable asset in the labor market. In the 2000s, a diploma is considered essential for the labor force or further training or education (National Center for Education Statistics, 2001).

The curriculum for students with disabilities is the most critical programming consideration in secondary schools. Even if students have excellent teachers, if the curriculum is inappropriate to meet their needs, then the teaching may be ineffective and students will not benefit from their education. The high school curriculum for students with disabilities must be comprehensive. That is, it must:

- Be responsive to the needs and interests of individual students.
- Facilitate maximum integration with nondisabled peers.
- Facilitate socialization.
- Focus on the students' transition to postsecondary settings.

Determining Curricular Needs of Students

TEACHING TIP

Teachers must remember that students with disabilities can be successful in an academic curriculum. The curricular needs of each student should be assessed before any conclusions are drawn about the student's program of study.

The curriculum for any student should be based on an appraisal of desired long-term outcomes and an assessment of current needs and selected to meet the individual needs of students. However, the dropout data for students with disabilities suggests that the needs of many of these students are not being met. The 23rd Annual Report to Congress on the Implementation of IDEA (U.S. Department of Education, 2002) reported that 28.9 percent of all students with disabilities, aged fourteen and older, dropped out of school. Unlike their nondisabled peers, data suggests that individuals with disabilities who drop out of school seldom obtain their GED or attend an adult program (Center for Adult Learning and Educational Credentials, 1999). The report also shows differences by exceptionlity. For example, the report revealed only 9.5 percent of students with autism and 11.8 percent of the visually impaired dropped out compared to 27.1 percent of students with learning diabilities, 24.9 percent of students with mental retardation, and 50.6 percent of students with emotional disturbance.

Unfortunately, school dropout rate is also tied to negative adult outcomes. In 2001 the National Bureau of Labor Statistics showed that adults with less educaition were less likely to be employed than adults with more educaiton. Only 32 percent of individuals with disabilities (ages eighteen to sixty-four) work part time or full time, compared to 81 percent of their nondisabled peers (National Organization on Disability, 2000). Therefore, regardless of the efforts made in secondary schools to meet the individual needs of students with disabilities, many of these students seem unprepared to achieve success as young adults.

To ensure that students have the optimum chance at success in their lives after high school, transition planning is an essential responsibility and legal requirement (see the Rights & Responsibility feature). The transition IEP helps individuals and their families focus on the future, building a bridge to futher vocational training, a community or four-year college education, or obtaining employment and living as independently as possible in a community. Figure 16.2 contains interview questions that can assist the team in determing preferences and needs leading to transition goals.

A team of professionals participate in developing the plan, but the student should be an active participant and, when possible, should lead the IEP meeting. His or her role might include planning the meeting, sending invitations, preparing the room, presenting his or her interests and goals, proposing activities, and interacting with parents and other team members to identify the objectives and activities that will most likely lead to the desired outcome (Steere & Cavaioulo, 2002). Figure 16.3 contains an outline of ten training sessions that can be used to teach students with disabilities the basics of leading their own transition IEP. Teachers can then hold mock IEP meetings and use this form to grade student performance and provide feedback before the day of the actual meeting. Reviewing these steps will help you visualize the IEP development process.

The overriding goal of the IEP and ITP for secondary students is to achieve personal fulfillment as an adult. To be successful, students need to identify and use all services and supports available to them. These steps lead to the acquisition of usable skills and knowledge and to the identification of adult service agencies that will help them meet the demands of adulthood at their maximum potential.

CONSIDER THIS

What are some things that schools could do to increase the number of students with disabilities who stay in school and graduate? Should schools do these things?

CEC STANDARDS

CEC 7: Instructional Planning

INTASC

INTASC 7: Plans instruction

PRAXIS

PRAXIS II: Delivery of Services to Students with Disabilities

TEACHING TIP

Teachers and other school personnel must include students with disabilities and their family members in planning for the future.

Rights & Responsibilities

Legal Requirements Related to Transition

In 1990, with the reauthorization of the Individuals with Disabilities Education Act, transition became a critical mandate and component of the law. This mandate requires that schools provide a process for planning for students' attainment of future postschool outcomes through the development of an appropriate educational course of study. IDEA 2004 describes this as a results-oriented process that is focused on improving the functional and academic achievement of the child to facilitate his movement from school to postschool activities. The adult postschool outcomes that are described in transition IEPs focus on the areas of employment, postsecondary education and training, community living, adult continuing education, and adult services.

Figure 16.2   **Sample Interview Questions**

Profile and Family Life
- Tell me about yourself (age, where you live, etc.).
- Tell me about your family.
- Do your parents work?
- What kind of work does your father/mother do?
- Do you have brothers or sisters who work?
- What kind of work do they do?
- Have you always lived here, or did you move here?
- Tell me about the neighborhood that you live in.

Interests and Hobbies
- What do you like to do in your free time?
- What are your hobbies and interests?
- What do you like to do on weekends?
- Tell me about some enjoyable vacations that you have had.

School
- What are your favorite subjects in school?
- What are your least favorite subjects?
- Who are your friends in school?
- What do you like best about school? What do you like least?
- Are you involved in any extracurricular activities?

Finances
- Do you have a bank account?
- Do you earn an allowance?
- Do you know how to write a check?
- Do you know how to use a credit card/debit card?
- Do you know about costs such as electric service, phone service, and gas?

Mobility
- How do you get around your community?
- Where do you like to go?
- Do you have a driver's license or are you planning on getting one?

Employment
- Have you ever had a job?
- If you were going to get a summer job, what kind of job would you look for?
- What skills do you feel that you could build a career on?
- What are your interests in terms of employment?

Postsecondary Education
- Are you planning to go to college?
- If so, have you considered a major?
- Did anyone else in your family go to college?
- Have you ever visited a college campus?

Community Living
- Do you know how to cook?
- Do you do any chores at home? If so, what chores?
- Do you know how much it costs to rent an apartment?
- Do you like living with others?
- Do you like privacy?
- Do you know what to do if there is an emergency in your home?

Future Aspirations
- What do you see yourself doing in five years?
- What careers do you plan on exploring, and why?
- What steps do you feel you need to take now to help prepare you for your future career?
- Who could help you take the steps you described in the previous question, and how might they help you?

From *Growing Up: Transition to Adult Life for Students with Disabilities* (pp 37–38), by D. E. Steere, E. Rose, and D. Cavaiuolo, 2007. Boston: Allyn & Bacon.

CEC STANDARDS

CEC 4: Instructional Strategies

PRAXIS

PRAXIS II: Instructional Strategies

Recent studies suggest that many states have been too slow in implementing transition service requirements and have failed to meet minimal levels of compliance (Johnson et al., 2002). Many challenges face educators as they try to implement methods to meet transition service needs of students with disabilities. High expectations must be maintained and students must remain on a full curriculum track, with additional opportunities as appropriate in vocational education, community work experience, service learning, and adult living skills (Johnson, 2002). A survey by Dunn, Chambers, and Rabren (2004) found that only 54 percent of students interviewed who had dropped out of school reported that school prepared them for what they wanted to do after high school; this was compared to 80 percent of students who did not drop out. Often when the curriculum fails a student, a favorite teacher can make the difference; however, these interviewers reported that 23 percent of the students who had dropped out responded that no one was helpful during their high school program. Only 8 percent of those who did not drop out were unable to identify a helpful person.

Figure 16.3   **Checklist for Self-Determination Skills**

UNIT 1

Lesson 1. Begin meeting: 3 points available
1. State the purpose
   a. to review goals
   b. to state progress toward goals   _____
   c. to set new goals   _____

Lesson 2. Introduce everyone: 5 points available
1. Parents   _____
2. Local education area representative   _____
3. General education teacher   _____
4. Vocational teacher   _____
5. Special education teacher   _____

Lesson 3. Review past goals and performances: 3 points available
1. State past goals   _____
2. Discuss how you did on these goals   _____
3. Ask others for feedback on your performance   _____

Lesson 4. Ask for others' feedback: 3 points available
1. Acknowledge that feedback can be written (e.g., a test score), verbal (e.g., a comment),
   or physical (e.g., a frown or smile)   _____
2. Recognize that feedback gives information about your actions   _____
3. Understand that feedback tells you how good your actions need to be to accomplish your goal   _____
Unit 1 Total Points (14 total points available)   _____

UNIT 2

Lesson 5. State your school and transition goals: 12 points available
1. Education: Explain what goal you want to meet in school
   a. Identify your interests   _____
   b. Identify your skills   _____
   c. Identify your limits   _____
2. Employment: Explain what goal you want to meet toward getting a job
   a. Identify your interests   _____
   b. Identify your skills   _____
   c. Identify your limits   _____
3. Personal: Explain any goal you may want to meet in the area of hobbies, fun/recreation, relationships, health
   a. Identify your interests   _____
   b. Identify your skills   _____
   c. Identify your limits   _____
4. Housing, daily living, and community participation
   a. Identify your interests   _____
   b. Identify your skills   _____
   c. Identify your limits   _____

Lesson 6. Ask questions if you don't understand: 3 points available
1. Use eye contact   _____
2. Use a polite and respectful tone of voice   _____
3. Ask for help if you don't know how to ask a question   _____

Lesson 7. Deal with differences in opinion: 4 points available
1. **L**isten to and restate the other person's opinion   _____
2. **U**se a respectful tone of voice   _____
3. **C**ompromise, or **C**hange your opinion, if needed   _____
4. **K**now and state the reasons for your opinion   _____
Unit 2 Total Points (19 total points available)   _____

Figure 16.3 **Continued**

UNIT 3
Lesson 8. State the support you will need to reach your goal: **6 points available**
1. Explain what help you will need in school (1 point)
   a. small groups   ___
   b. individual help   ___
   c. study guides   ___
   d. extra time   ___
2. Explain what help you will need on the job (1 point)   ___
   a. transportation   ___
   b. job coach/buddy   ___
   c. hygiene   ___
   d. social skills   ___
3. Explain what help you will need with personal issues (1 point)   ___
   a. hobbies   ___
   b. relationships   ___
   c. fun/recreation   ___
   d. health   ___
4. Explain what help you will need with (3 points)   ___
   a. housing   ___
   b. daily living   ___
   c. community participation   ___

Lesson 9. Summarize your current goals: **3 points available**
1. State your goals in your own words   ___
2. State what actions you will take to meet your goals   ___
3. Tell how you will receive feedback   ___

Lesson 10. Close meeting: **3 points available**
1. Good eye contact   ___
2. Use a pleasant tone of voice   ___
3. Thank everyone for coming   ___
Unit 3 Total Points (12 total points available)   ___

From "Effects of the *Self-Directed IEP* on Student Participation in Planning Meetings," by S. A. Arndt, M. Konrad, & D. W. Test, *Remedial and Special Education,* *27*(4), pp. 197 & 198.

CONSIDER THIS

Factors that may keep a child in school are his or her perception of a "helpful class" or a "helpful person." Are you up to the challenge?

Several have questioned the the impact that heavy teacher workloads have had on the educational experiences of students. Conderman and Katsiyannis (2002) found that special education teachers were required to hold a variety of roles to meet the needs of students. In the course of a day, a teacher might teach a content class in a self-contained setting, serve as a resource teacher to support students struggling in a general education class, oversee vocational placements and transition plans, teach social skills and/or strategies for learning, coteach with a general education teacher in a different subject matter, and remediate basic skills for a required exit exam.

It is no wonder that there are many references in the literature to teacher burnout and attrition that will eventually impact student achievement (Wasburn-Moses, 2005). School personnel must prioritize the research needed to streamline teacher responsibilities and roles so that teachers can stay dedicated and physically and mentally healthy. One thing that can help is the collaboration between special and general education and other agencies to meet the needs of students. It is important for teachers to understand the roles of these agencies and the services available. The most commonly accessed adult agencies and their potential contributions for students going to postsecondary education or employment, as well as those needing assistance with independent living, are shown in Table 16.1.

DIVERSITY FORUM

Planning for the Future: Self-Determination and Transition

Susan, now 16 years old, receives special education services in the category of mild mental retardation (see Chapter 7). Her family has emphasized self-determination and independence throughout her development, consistent with their Navajo values and beliefs. Ms. Applegate, a European American teacher, is drafting transition goals for Susan's IEP meeting. She is concerned about the availability of employment because the rural locale is economically depressed. Ms. Applegate has connections with small business owners in her town (about 40 miles from the high school) who are interested in employing young adults with disabilities. Although Ms. Applegate will invite a vocational rehabilitation program representative to the meeting, she is unsure whether the family is interested in these services and/or opportunities.

Transition planning and instruction include ongoing assessment of students' preferences, strengths, and needs, yet few existing tools help teachers gather culturally relevant information (Sittlington & Clark, 2006). Culturally responsive communication and collaboration requires teachers to identify values that are foundational to the educational system, as well as those that reflect the student's family and community (Harry, Kalyanpur, & Day, 1999). This can be accomplished through personal communication, by providing multiple opportunities for informal assessments, and by actively learning about cultural beliefs and practices of students' larger communities. While Ms. Applegate knows that individuals with cognitive disabilities frequently benefit from specialized training and compensatory strategies provided by job coaches and vocational rehabilitation counselors (Beirne-Smith, Patton, & Kim, 2006), conversations with Susan and her parents would help inform her decision to invite other professionals to the IEP meeting. Although this is a preferred transition planning practice (Cozzens, Dowdy, & Smith, 1999), doing so may affect the family's comfort level or participation. As differences between priorities of school and home emerge, teachers must explicitly acknowledge and show respect for families' cultural practices and beliefs while adapting the transition plan to this value system. Teachers must also provide information so that individuals and families can make informed decisions about their future.

Questions

1. What are some naturally occurring opportunities for the teacher to communication with Susan's family about transition-related issues and provide informal assessment of preferences, strengths, and needs?
2. How might the teacher increase personal knowledge of Susan's community's practices and beliefs with regard to adulthood, employment, and individuals with disabilities?

REFERENCES

Beirne-Smith, M., Patton, J. R., & Kim, S. H. (2006). *Mental retardation.* Allyn & Bacon: Upper Saddle River, NJ.

Cozzens, G., Dowdy, C. A., & Smith, T. E. C. (1999). *Adult agencies: Linkages for adolescents in transition.* Austin, TX: Pro-Ed.

Harry, B., Kalyanpur, M., & Day, M. (1999). *Building cultural reciprocity with families.* Baltimore: Paul H. Brookes.

Sittlington, P. L., & Clark, G. M. (2006). *Transition education and services for students with disabilities* (4th ed.). Allyn & Bacon: Boston.

Programs for Students in Secondary Schools

Most secondary students with disabilities are currently included in general education classrooms for at least a portion of each school day. A recent U.S. Department of Education (2002) survey indicated that 70 percent of students with disabilities, aged twelve to seventeen, were served in either resource rooms or regular classrooms. Therefore, the responsibility for these students becomes a joint effort between general education classroom teachers and special education personnel (Walther-Thomas et al., 2000). Unfortunately, many of these students do not experience success in the general classroom setting. They frequently fail classes, become frustrated and act out, and may even drop out of school because they are not prepared to meet the demands placed on them by secondary teachers. There are numerous reasons why many students with disabilities fail in secondary classes:

CEC STANDARDS

CEC 7: Instructional Planning

- Lack of communication between special education personnel and classroom teachers
- Discrepancies between the expectations of classroom teachers and the abilities of students

Table 16.1   **Common Community Agencies and the Transition Services They May Offer**

Agency/Program* (Purpose and Funding Source)	Examples of Employment Services	Examples of Postsecondary Education Services	Examples of Adult and Independent Living Services
Vocational Rehabilitation Agency assists people with cognitive, sensory, physical, or emotional disabilities to attain employment and increased independence. Funded by federal and state money, VR agencies typically operate regional and local offices. VR services typically last for a limited period of time and are based on an individual's rehabilitation plan. If needed, an individual with disabilities can request services at a later time, and a new rehabilitation plan will be developed.	• Vocational guidance and counseling • Medical, psychological, vocational, and other types of assessments to determine vocational potential • Job development, placement, and follow-up services • Rehabilitation, technological services and adaptive devices, tools, equipment, and supplies	• Apprenticeship programs, usually in conjunction with Department of Labor • Vocational training • College training toward a vocational goal as part of an eligible student's financial aid package	• Housing or transportation supports needed to maintain employment • Interpreter services • Orientation and mobility services
Mental Health and Mental Retardation Agencies provide a comprehensive system of services responsive to the needs of individuals with mental illness or mental retardation. Federal, state, and local funding are used to operate regional offices; local funding is often the primary source. Services are provided on a sliding payment scale.	• Supported and sheltered employment • Competitive employment support for those who need minimal assistance		• Case management services to access and obtain local services • Therapeutic recreation, including day activities, clubs, and programs • Respite care • Residential services (group homes and supervised apartments)
Independent Living Centers help people with disabilities to achieve and maintain self-sufficient lives within the community. Operated locally, ILCs serve a particular region. ILCs may charge for classes, but advocacy services are typically available at no cost.	• Information and referral services • Connecting students with mentors with disabilities	• Advocacy training • Connecting students with mentors with disabilities	• Advocacy training • Auxiliary social services (e.g., maintaining a list of personal care attendants) • Peer counseling services • Housing assistance • Training in skills of independent living (attendant management, housing, transportation, career development) • Information and referral services • Connecting with mentors
Social Security Administration operates the federally funded program that provides benefits for people of any age who are unable to do substantial work and have a severe mental or physical disability. Several programs are offered for people with disabilities, including Social Security Disability Insurance (SSDI), Supplemental Security Income (SSI), Plans to Achieve Self-Support (PASS), Medicaid, and Medicare.	Work incentive programs which may include: • Cash benefits while working (e.g., student-earned income) • Medicare or Medicaid while working • Help with any extra work expenses the individual has as a result of the disability • Assistance to start a new line of work	• Financial incentives for further education and training	• Medical benefits • Can use income as basis for purchase or rental of housing

*Names of agencies or programs may differ slightly from state to state.

From *Transition Planning: A Team Effort* (pp. 4–5), by S. H. de Fur, 1999. Washington, DC: NICHCY.

- Students' lack of understanding about the demands of the classroom
- Classroom teachers' lack of understanding about students with disabilities
- Special education personnel's lack of knowledge about working with classroom teachers
- School policies that are inflexible

Regardless of the reasons why some students with disabilities do not achieve success in general education settings, the fact remains that the majority will be taught in inclusive settings. Therefore, classroom teachers and special education personnel must work together to increase the chances that these students will be successful. Figure 16.4 displays the frequent mismatch between the characteristics of students with disabilities and the academic and setting demands of high school, as well as the need for instructional interventions that will be described later in the chapter.

Roles of Personnel

As noted, the responsibility for educating students with disabilities in public schools is shared by general classroom teachers and special education personnel. Therefore, educators must improve their skills at working together to help students with various learning and behavior problems.

General Education Teachers The primary role of general classroom teachers is to assume the responsibility for students with disabilities in particular classes or subject areas. Most classroom teachers present information using one general technique, but

INTASC

INTASC 7: Plans instruction

PRAXIS

PRAXIS II: Delivery of Services to Students with Disabilities

CONSIDER THIS

The roles of general educators and special educators must change for effective inclusion to occur. What are some potential barriers to these changes, and how can they be overcome?

INSTRUCTIONAL CONDITIONS

Learning Characteristics

▶ Academic deficits
▶ Learning strategy deficits
▶ Study skill deficits
▶ Thinking deficits
▶ Social interaction problems
▶ Motivation problems

Academic Demands

▶ Acquire information written at secondary level
▶ Gain information through lectures
▶ Demonstrate knowledge through tests
▶ Express information in writing
▶ Use problem-solving strategies
▶ Work independently
▶ Be motivated to learn

Setting Realities

▶ Coverage of large amounts of content
▶ Use of difficult texts
▶ Limited opportunities for academic interactions
▶ Classes of diverse learners
▶ Emphasis on achieving students
▶ Limited planning and teaching time

ESSENTIAL SERVICES

Learning Strategies

▶ Techniques, principles, or rules that enable students to learn, to solve problems, and to complete tasks independently

Content Enhancements

▶ Devices and teaching routines that help teachers present content in a learner-friendly manner to help students identify, organize, comprehend, and recall critical information.

Study Skills Techniques

▶ Specific techniques and devices to help students acquire, retain, and express knowledge

Figure 16.4

Instructional Conditions and Essential Services for Students with Learning Problems

From *Teaching Students with Learning Problems* (6th ed., p. 532), by C. D. Mercer and A. R. Mercer, 2001. Upper Saddle River, NJ: Merrill.

CEC STANDARDS

CEC 7: Instructional Planning

INTASC

INTASC 7: Plans instruction

PRAXIS

PRAXIS II: Delivery of Services to Students with Disabilities

they will probably have to expand their instructional activities when dealing with students with disabilities. Various accommodations and adaptations in instructional techniques and materials will be discussed later in the chapter.

Classroom teachers have general responsibilities that apply to students with and without disabilities. These include managing the classroom environment, providing instruction at an appropriate level and pace, using an appropriate curriculum, and evaluating student success and modifying instruction as appropriate. For students with disabilities, general classroom teachers have the added responsibility of participating on an interdisciplinary team.

When teaching content courses, such as history and science, teachers should give students with disabilities the same opportunities to learn that they give other students, remembering that the students with special needs would not be placed in the general classroom setting if an interdisciplinary team had not determined that they could benefit from that environment. In addition, teachers should ensure that all students have an opportunity to answer questions and a good chance to achieve at least moderate success in classroom activities. This is not a call for teachers to "give" students with disabilities passing grades, only a requirement that students with disabilities receive an equal chance at being successful.

Within the classroom, teachers can do several things that will facilitate the success of students with disabilities. They must remember that students with disabilities, as well as those without disabilities, have different learning styles and needs, and therefore require, from time to time, some alteration of instruction. However, some basic principles of good teaching apply to all students. These are listed in the nearby "Evidence-Based Practice" box. Effective teachers have to individualize their efforts, constantly evaluating the impact of their teaching efforts. (See Figure 16.5 for a guide for these reflections.)

Teachers must think carefully about how realistic their expectations are of students. Schumm, Vaughn, and Leavell (1994) developed the planning pyramid that allows teachers to identify different degrees of learning to address individual needs and abilities; the philosophy is that all students will learn something but not all students will learn everything. In Figure 16.6 you see a learning pyramid developed for a science class by Watson and Houtz (2002) for culturally and linguistically diverse students. A lesson plan presented later in the chapter demonstrates how contengency plans can be developed to assist struggling students to benefit from the general education curriculum being presented.

Classroom teachers should also do all they can to work effectively with special education professionals. Open communication and dialogue among classroom teachers and special education personnel is crucial if inclusion is to be successful. Communication among all individuals providing services to students with disabilities is the most important factor related to the success of inclusion (Walther-Thomas et al., 2000).

Collaborative Role of the Special Education Teacher

The special education teacher plays an important role in the successful inclusion of students with disabilities in secondary schools. In addition to collaborating with general educators, the special education teacher must prepare students for the challenges that occur daily in the general education environment and equip them for future challenges that await them in their lives after high school. Above all, special education teachers play a major support role for general classroom teachers. They should communicate regularly with classroom teachers and provide assistance through consultation or through direct instruction.

The specific roles of the special education teacher discussed further include counseling students for the personal crises that may occur daily and preparing students for content classes, the high school graduation exam, postsecondary education, independent living, and, ultimately, employment. Special education teachers, general teachers, and individuals from other agencies often collaborate in performing these roles.

General education teachers are primarily responsible for students with special needs in their classrooms.

Figure 16.5   **Questions for Evaluating the Instructional Process**

- *Student motivation* Am I creating a context in which learning is valued?
- *Student attention* Am I creating an environment in which students can and are encouraged to attend to the learning task?
- *Encouragement* Am I creating a setting in which students are encouraged to take risks and be challenged by learning?
- *Modeling* Are the students given the opportunity to watch, listen, and talk to others so that they can see how the knowledge or skill is learned?
- *Activating prior knowledge* Am I getting the students to think about what they already know about a skill or topic, and are they given the opportunity to build upon that information in an organized fashion?
- *Rate, amount, and manner of presentation* Are the new skills and knowledge being presented at a rate and amount that allows the students time to learn, and in a manner that gives them enough information yet does not overload them?
- *Practice* Are the students given ample opportunity to practice?
- *Feedback* Are the students given feedback on their work so they know how and what they are learning?
- *Acquisition* Are the students given the opportunity to learn skills and knowledge until they feel comfortable with them and to the point they do or know something almost automatically?
- *Maintenance* Are the students given the opportunity to continue to use their skills and knowledge so that they can serve as tools for further learning?
- *Generalization* Are the students generalizing the skills and knowledge to other tasks, settings, and situations? Are the students, other teachers, or parents seeing the learning?
- *Application* Are the students given the opportunity to apply their skills and knowledge in new and novel situations, thereby adapting their skills to meet the new learning experiences?

From *Strategies for Teaching Students with Learning and Behavior Problems* (5th ed., p. 26), by C. S. Bos and S. Vaughn, 2002. Boston: Allyn & Bacon.

Counseling for Daily Crises   Adolescence is a difficult time of change for all children; for children with disabilities, the period is even more challenging as they carry the joy and sorrow of adolescence as well as the stigma of a disability (Sabornie & deBettencourt, 2004). In U.S. society, students face the challenge of identifying carreer and life goals during a time of tremendous physical and social changes. They also experience more exposure to drugs and alcohol as well as the possibility of school drop out, sexually transmitted diseases, depression, pregnancy, and AIDS. The increased tension,

CROSS-REFERENCE

Review Chapters 5 to 11 and reflect on how different disabilities influence preparation for high school content courses.

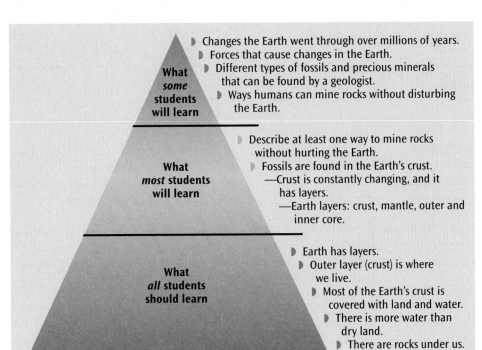

Figure 16.6

A Learning Pyramid for a Science Class

From "Teaching Science: Meeting the Academic Needs of Culturally and Linguistically Diverse Students," by S. M. R. Watson and L. E. Houtz, 2002, *Intervention in School and Clinic*, 37(5), p. 270.

EVIDENCE-BASED PRACTICE

What Instructional Practices Are Best?

Kauffman, Mostert, Trent, and Hallahan (2002) suggest that good teaching (best instructional practice) is characterized by the following (and they provide a mnemonic, consisting of the first letters of each point—CLOCS-RAM—(for remembering the points)

1. *Clarity*—The student must know exactly what to do (i.e., have no doubt about what is expected).
2. *Level*—The student must be able to do the task with a high degree of accuracy (i.e., be able to get *at least* 80 percent correct), but the task must be challenging (i.e., the student should not easily get 100 percent correct repeatedly).
3. *Opportunities*—The student must have frequent opportunities to respond (i.e., be actively engaged in the task a high percentage of the time).

4. *Consequences*—The student must receive a meaningful reward for correct performance (i.e., the consequences of correct performance must be frequent and perceived as desirable by the student).
5. *Sequence*—The tasks must be presented in logical sequence so that the student gets the big idea (i.e., steps must be presented and learned in order that the knowledge or skill is built on a logical progression or framework of ideas, which is a systematic curriculum).
6. *Relevance*—The task must be relevant to the student's life and, if possible, the student understands how and why it is useful (i.e., the teacher attempts to help the student see why the task is important in the culture).

7. *Application*—The teacher helps the student learn how to learn and remember by teaching memory and learning strategies and applying knowledge and skills to everyday problems (i.e., teaches generalizations, not just isolated skills, and honors the student's culture).
8. *Monitoring*—The teacher continuously monitors student progress (i.e., records and charts progress and always knows and can show what the student has mastered and the student's place or level in a curriculum or sequence of tasks).

From *Managing Classroom Behavior: A Reflective Case-Based Approach*, (3rd ed., p. 7), by J. M. Kauffman et al., 2002. Boston: Allyn & Bacon. Copyright © 2002 by Pearson Education. Reprinted by permission of the publisher.

CEC STANDARDS

CEC 4: Instructional Strategies

INTASC

INTASC 4: Instructional strategies

PRAXIS

PRAXIS II: Delivery of Services to Students with Disabilities

TEACHING TIP

Teachers need to evaluate each student to determine the level of skills necessary for success in postsecondary settings and develop plans to improve weak areas.

frustration, and depression can lead to a variety of behavior and emotional problems or suicide, the third leading cause of death among adolescents and the leading cause of death in college students (Aseltine & DeMartino, 2004).

Special education teachers need to collaborate with general educators to help students deal with these problems. One innovative program being tried to increase access to the general education program and provide a support system for students with moderate or severe disabilities is the peer support program (Copeland et al., 2004). A student with a disability and a student without are partnered for shared activities that might be academic (e.g., tutoring functional academics and life skills) or nonacademic (e.g., "hanging out" between classes and attending sporting events). The nondisabled peers report that the experience improved their knowledge of disabilities and allowed them to develop a friendship rather than simply offering help. It also gave them experience in advocating for someone else, gave them feelings of accomplishment, and was fun. The effect for students with disabilities is a decrease in alienation, a common problem for adolescents, especially those with disabilities (Brown, Higgins, & Paulsen, 2003). It is important for teachers to develop a nonthreatening classroom atmosphere where anxiety about learning is reduced and open lines of communication are maintained (Schloss, Schloss, & Schloss, 2007).

Preparing for High School Content Classes The special education teacher should be aware of factors such as classroom teacher expectations, teaching styles, and the demands of the learning environment. One way special education teachers can help students deal with the "general education world" is to teach them how to self-advocate. To do so, students need to understand their specific learning problems. Therefore, special education teachers may need to have a discussion with their students about the nature of specific disabilities.

When working with students with disabilities in general education classrooms, the role of the special educator expands to include informing the general educator as to the unique abilities and challenges presented by each student, providing ongoing support and collaboration for the student and teacher, and frequent monitoring to ensure that the arrangement is satisfactory for both the student and the teacher.

Lenz and Deshler (2004) propose that effective teaching is based on making meaningful connections between teachers and students, students and students, and students and the content they need to learn. They challenge teachers to understand what their students already know as a result of prior learning as well as their life experiences, and to select content that is based on the general education standards but that is relevant to their future life goals. Finally they recommend compensating for students' learning problems by using evidence-based teaching methods to enhance instruction and explicitly teaching students how to use and develop learning strategies so students learn how to learn. These strategies have been highlighted throughout the text and will be addressed again later in this chapter. An example of an effective strategy to help students perform at their maximum level in class is presented in Figure 16.7.

Preparing for the High School Graduation Exam   Passing a high school graduation exam as a requirement for receiving a regular diploma began in many states in the 1980s as part of the national reform movements in education. By 2000 twenty-three states required a passing score on an "exit exam" to earn a high school diploma, and an additional seven expected to require one by 2003 (Disability Rights Advocates, 2001). Students with disabilities may or may not be required to take the exam, depending on state regulations and local school district policies. In some states, students with disabilities are granted a regular high school diploma without having to complete the examination; in others, students with disabilities who do not pass the graduation exam are given a certification of attendance or completion, even if they have passed all required classes. This is often the time that families and educators wish that remediation of basic skills had been continued as these struggling readers are further penalized in trying to pass science, social studies, and even math sections. Figure 16.8 shows the steps of an evidence-based strategy that can be used to help students break down multisyllable words into smaller, more readable segments.

Special education teachers, in conjunction with classroom teachers, have two roles regarding the high school graduation exam. On one hand, they are obligated to help the student prepare for the exam if it is the decision of the IEP team that the student should be prepared to take the exam. On the other hand, the special education teacher and classroom teachers may choose to focus on convincing the student and parents that time could more appropriately be spent on developing functional skills rather than on preparing for the graduation exam.

Preparing for Postsecondary Training   Students with disabilities should absolutely be encouraged to aim for a postsecondary education if they have the ability and motivation. One survey reported differences in posititve outcomes in employment rates, salaries, and employment satisfaction between students with learning disabilities with and without postsecondary degrees (Madaus et al., 2003). The National Council on Disability (2004) emphasized this in its 2002–2003 progress report:

> With unemployment among persons with disabilities remaining stubbornly high despite a variety of federal initiatives and public-private partnerships designed to improve the situation, and with long-term job prospects and income potential for people without college education looking increasingly grim, it should be more apparent than ever before that, wherever possible, higher education is key to the economic prospects and aspirations for independence of youth with disabilities. (p. 68)

Postsecondary education does not have to mean attending a four-year institution. A community college, vocational-technical school, trade school, or some other form of postsecondary education and training are other possibilities. Figure 16.9 provides the pros and cons of postsecondary options and community living. Teachers, both general and special education, need to inform students about future employment trends and

Figure 16.7

Sample Hierarchic Flowchart Used to Teach Class Preparation

From "Graphic Organizers: Tools to Build Behavioral Literacy and Foster Emotional Competency," by M. L. Rock, 2004, *Intervention in School and Clinic, 40*(1), p. 24.

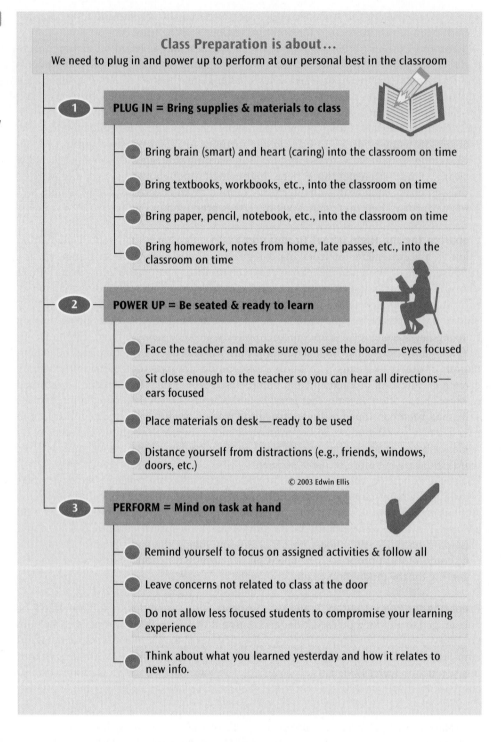

Class Preparation is about…
We need to plug in and power up to perform at our personal best in the classroom

1 PLUG IN = Bring supplies & materials to class

- Bring brain (smart) and heart (caring) into the classroom on time
- Bring textbooks, workbooks, etc., into the classroom on time
- Bring paper, pencil, notebook, etc., into the classroom on time
- Bring homework, notes from home, late passes, etc., into the classroom on time

2 POWER UP = Be seated & ready to learn

- Face the teacher and make sure you see the board—eyes focused
- Sit close enough to the teacher so you can hear all directions—ears focused
- Place materials on desk—ready to be used
- Distance yourself from distractions (e.g., friends, windows, doors, etc.)

© 2003 Edwin Ellis

3 PERFORM = Mind on task at hand

- Remind yourself to focus on assigned activities & follow all
- Leave concerns not related to class at the door
- Do not allow less focused students to compromise your learning experience
- Think about what you learned yesterday and how it relates to new info.

help them select a realistic career with employment potential. A variety of reports regarding the importance of education in the future for students with and without disabilities have concluded the following higher levels of academic achievement will be required and very few jobs will be available for individuals deficient in reading, writing, and math. Technology will also play an increasing role for all individuals.

For Jim in the opening vignette, the possibility of going to a new school at the post-secondary level was terrifying. His parents had been instrumental in getting services set up in high school and suddenly everyone was talking to him about self-advocacy.

| Figure 16.8 | **Strategy Chart Showing the Steps Used in Strategy Instruction** |

Overt Strategy
1. Circle the word parts (prefixes) at the beginning of the word.
2. Circle the word parts (suffixes) at the end of the word.
3. Underline the letters representing vowel sounds in the rest of the word.
4. Say the parts of the word.
5. Say the parts fast.
6. Make it a real word.

Example

reconstruction

From "Decoding and fluency: Foundation skills for struggling older readers," by A. L. Archer, M. M. Gleason, and V. L. Vachon, 2003, *Learning Disability Quarterly, 26,* p. 95.

Luckily the IEP team picked up on his concerns and wrote the training needed into the IEP. Refer to the portion of Jim's IEP that addresses self-advocacy as well as Jim's other transitional needs. Other ideas that are helpful in preparation for postsecondary education are summarized by Schloss and colleagues (2007):

1. Identify the match between the student's academic and career goals and the programs available at two- and four-year colleges and technical programs.
2. Consider the entrance requirements carefully. Some schools have open admission with a high school diploma, and others require a minimum grade point average and specific scores on entrance exams.

| Figure 16.9 | **Location Pros and Cons** |

Pros	Cons
Four-Year College/University	
Wide array of coursework	Less prevalent
Many clubs/organizations	Admissions and application process
Social sciences/medical departments	Tuition
Stable student population	Attitudinal barriers
Residential possibilities	
Community College	
Open-door policies	Transient student population
Nontraditional students	Limited access to potential peer support
Proximity	Space may be limited
Fellow graduates as peers	Attitudinal barriers
Lower costs (tuition walved)	
Community Settings	
Natural setting for students not going to college	Lack of access to same-age peers
Access to employment sites	May lead to segregated experiences
Daily living or social activities	Transportation barriers
Doesn't preclude possible college connections	

From *Transitional Services for Students with Significant Disabilities in College and Community Settings: Strategies for Planning, Implementation and Evaluation,* p. 19 by M. Grigal, D. A. Neubert, and M. S. Moon, 2005, Austin, TX: Pro Ed.

3. Consider the size of the campus. Navigating smaller campuses may be easier, and they may be able to offer more individualized services. A larger campus may offer more extracurricular activities and a wider variety of courses.
4. Examine the cost and help the student and parents to identify financial resources.
5. Encourage families to meet with the director of the Office for Students with Disabilities to discuss services, policies, and procedures to document the disability and request appropriate accommodations. Students must also be taught self-advocacy skills so they can self-identify with their professors. (Madaus & Shaw, 2004)
6. Arrange for the student to shadow currently enrolled students.
7. Consider living arrangements available and begin to work with students and families to prepare for more independent living if the student will be leaving home.

Preparing for Independent Living   Independent living is a realistic goal for the vast majority of individuals with disabilities; however, for them to live successfully in today's complex, automated world, direct instruction in certain independent living skills may be required. This is also important in a student's transition program. The following areas may be problematic for people with disabilities:

CEC STANDARDS

CEC 7: Instructional Planning

- Sexuality
- Managing personal finances
- Developing and maintaining social networks
- Maintaining a home
- Managing food
- Employment
- Transportation
- Self-confidence and self-esteem
- Organization
- Time management

INTASC

INTASC 7: Plans for instruction

Special education teachers as well as general education teachers can help students with disabilities achieve competence in these areas. Although published materials are available to guide instruction in these areas, creative teachers can use community resources, gathering real materials from banks, libraries, restaurants, the local courthouse, and so forth, for developing their own program. These authentic life skills can then be infused into subjects such as math, science, or English to add interest and relevance for all students.

PRAXIS

PRAXIS II: Delivery of Services to Students with Disabilities

Preparing for Employment   The ultimate goal of all education is the employment of graduates at their maximum vocational potential. The passage of the Americans with Disabilities Act (ADA) in 1990 has made that dream a reality for millions of people with disabilities. The law encompasses areas of employment, transportation, public accommodations, and telecommunications, and prohibits discrimination against individuals with disabilities. ADA requires employers to make "reasonable accommodations" to assist people with disabilities in performing their jobs. Supported employment initiatives (i.e., providing job coaches to support workers on the job) have emerged as particularly powerful tools. Teachers need to help students prepare for employment by teaching them the necessary skills for vocational success. Inclusive vocational and technical programs present a unique opportunity to offer students both a functional curriculum and integration with nondisabled peers. These programs can provide appropriate entry into work-study programs, business apprenticeships, and technical and trade school programs. Figure 16.10 provides a sequence of preemployment activities that led to successful employment for one student.

Teachers must be sure that students with disabilities can communicate their strengths and limitations to persons in postsecondary and future employment settings. These self-advocacy skills will empower individuals to seek employment and independent living opportunities on their own. In best practice, encouragement and devel-

| *Figure 16.10* | **Student Employment Goal** |

Student Name: Dwayne Rodgers   School Year: 2005–2006

Student Goal 1: To obtain paid employment in an office setting

Upon entry: Dwayne had worked in a fast-food establishment, making $5.15 an hour, and had previous unpaid work experience in the public library.

October: Dwayne took an interest inventory. Dwayne and his coordinator reviewed the results of the inventory and talked about Dwayne's preferred job characteristics and goals. Dwayne wants to learn how to be a receptionist in an office setting.

December: Dwayne visited three office settings (medical, dental, business) to job shadow a receptionist. Dwayne enjoyed the business office setting the most and determined that support would be needed in typing and filing.

February: Dwayne interviewed for two jobs and was hired by Malcolm Industries as a part-time receptionist, making $5.15 an hour. He works three days a week for four hours a day. He received on-the-job training and support from the job coach daily.

May: Dwayne continues his schedule at Malcolm Industries and plans to increase his hours over the summer. His job coach now checks in twice a month, and Dwayne has received his first evaluation and a small pay raise (to $5.35 an hour).

Outcome: Dwayne successfully achieved his goal and hopes to maintain this job through his remaining school year. He has expressed interest in expanding his job duties to include filing microfiche and learning data entry.

From *Transitional Services for Students with Significant Disabilities in College and Community Settings: Strategies for Planning, Implementation and Evaluation*, p. 53, by M. Grigal, D. A. Neubert, and M. S. Moon, 2005. Austin TX: Pro Ed.

opment of self-determination or self-advocacy shills begins in elementary school. Table 16.2 provides a list of activities that can promote these skills. Many of these can be carried out with parents or teachers in multiple contexts (Test et al., 2005).

The nearby Personal Spotlight highlights a young adult with a learning disability who has become a strong self-advocate.

Methods to Facilitate Students' Success in General Education Classes

Students with disabilities traditionally have been placed in general education classrooms for instruction when they were determined to have the requisite academic ability necessary for success. With the advent of the inclusion movement, however, students with disabilities are often placed in such classes for other reasons. For most of these students, success can be engineered by teachers using evidence-based teaching practices and developing contingency strategies for assisting students still needing assistance. Some students will require the implementation of accommodations or adaptations; other students can achieve success when taught to use effective study skills and learning strategies.

Evidence-Based Teaching Strategies

The evidence-based teaching strategies that have been shared throughout this text are critical for students with disabilities to benefit from their educational placement. Even if the IEP goals and general education curricular standards are a perfect match, an ineffective teacher can stop progress. Of particular importance is the behavioral support techniques and a comprehensive lesson plan that includes the components backed by research. Figure 16.11 provides the format for a written lesson plan for secondary students. These plans should be written out in long form until the process becomes second nature. Figure 16.12 demonstrates a written lesson plan with the contingency plans that could be used to address learning needs at several levels.

Table 16.2   **Section II Items of the Survey Instruments by Grade Level**

Level	Items
Elementary	1. Provide opportunities to choose from several different strategies for a task. 2. Ask the child to reconsider choices made in the recent past, in light of those choices' subsequent consequences. 3. Encourage the child to "think aloud" with you, saying the steps the child is taking to complete a task or solve a problem. 4. Provide opportunities for the student to talk about how he or she learns and help him or her test out his or her answer. 5. Provide opportunities for the child to systematically evaluate his or her work. 6. Help the child set simple goals and check to see whether he or she is reaching the goals.
Secondary	1. Provide opportunities for the student to make decisions that have an important impact on his or her academic goals, such as what program and what courses the student wants to take. 2. Provide opportunities for the student to make decisions that have an important impact on his or her career, such as what the student wants to do after finishing high school. 3. Provide opportunities for the student to make decisions that have an important impact on his or her schedule. 4. Make it easy for the student to see the link between the goals her or she sets for himself or herself and the daily decisions he or she makes. 5. Provide guidance in breaking the student's long-term goals into a number of objectives. 6. Lead the student through planning activities to determine the steps to take to progress toward goals. 7. Assist the student in realistically recognizing and accepting weaknesses in key skills. 8. Assist the student in requesting academic and social supports from teachers.

From "A conceptual framework of self-advocacy for students with disabilities," by D. W. Test et al., 2005, *Remedial and Special Education,* p. 59. Austin, TX: Pro-Ed.

Student and Football Player

Bill Flowers is a winner on and off the football field! "Some people get academic gifts; my gift is athletics," he said. Bill's goal is to be a professional football player like his dad and brother, but he knows he must work hard to attain that goal. Hard work is not new to Bill. In high school he practiced football before and after school; his coach talked about his impressive work ethic, noting that Bill was always looking for someone to throw to him. As a result, he was named Player of the Year for his area, Back of the Year by the Sports Writers Association, and Alabama's Player of the Year by Gatorade.

With learning disabilities, Bill has had to work as hard off the field as on. He attended a special school in Miami for children with special needs, where his fellow students were learning disabled, mentally retarded, and physically challenged. In high school, he went to tutors for two years to help him "pass math" and prepare for the graduation exam and the ACT. He didn't want the academic challenges to stand in his way. His high school teachers provided testing in distraction-reduced settings and with extended time.

Currently in college, Bill says college has been easier in some ways because of the note-taker who has been pro-vided as an accommodation. His ADHD makes it really hard to listen and take notes; plus, he said his notes looked like "chicken scratch" when he tried to read them later. With the note-taker he can keep his mind on the lecture and learn while the professor talks. As a result, he now takes most of his tests with the class. College is still a real challenge, but Bill is confident that things will turn out for the best.

Bill Flowers
Student, University of Mississippi

When asked about his successes, Bill always gives credit to others—his family, teachers, tutors, coaches, and other players. He is also very religious, and he feels that he was given a learning disability to make him a better person. He uses his setbacks as challenges to conquer, and he wants his story to help others who may not see their disability as a gift and to help those who haven't learned to see the gifts in every person.

Name:

Grade:

Teacher:

Date:

Objectives of the Lesson:

Procedures used in the Lesson (include contingency plans):

Accomodations or Modifications Necessary:

Figure 16.11

Format for Lesson Plan for Secondary Students

Adaptations: Accommodations and Modifications

In most instances, general education teachers are responsible for making accommodations or modifications to help students with disabilities achieve in the secondary school. Unfortunately, even though most general education teachers view adaptations as desirable and reasonable, they often do not implement them. In Table 16.3 Lenz and Deshler (2004) provide accommodations as well as modifications that can be made during the major components of a lesson plan. Figure 16.13 provides a checklist teachers can use for further ideas, documentation, and evaluation of options implemented for accommodating learning needs.

Adaptations should be designed to offer the least amount of alteration of the regular programming that will still allow the student to benefit from instruction. This approach is fair to nondisabled students and provides the students with disabilities with a realistic sense of their abilities and limitations. If too many adaptations are made, some students may be set up for failure in college or in other academically demanding environments. Students with too many accommodations may also begin to feel that they bring very little to the class; this feeling can further damage an already fragile self-concept. Modifications used in settings or classes designed to prepare an individual for a future job or postsecondary training program should reflect real conditions present in these future environments and realistic adaptations.

Homework, Grading, and Testing

Homework, grading, and testing stand out as important considerations in students' success within secondary school classrooms. They have become more significant in light of trends toward making academic standards more rigorous and toward accountability in general education classrooms. Higher expectations for student performance in general education classes and the emphasis on national achievement tests affect testing and grading. This section explores these problem areas, focusing on adaptations to facilitate student success.

Homework   Problems in homework often become more pronounced at the secondary level. Given that students typically have four to six teachers, assignments represent a

CEC STANDARDS

CEC 4: Instructional Strategies

INTASC

INTASC 4: Instructional strategies

PRAXIS

PRAXIS II: Delivery of Services to Students with Disabilities

CROSS-REFERENCE

Review Chapters 5 to 11 to determine specific accommodations suggested for children with different disabilities.

Figure 16.12 **Contingency Plans Included in a Written Lesson Plan**

Objective

Given ten word problems involving addition and subtraction, the student will use a calculator to compute the answer with 100 percent accuracy.

Procedures

1. Review previous work, describe today's activity, and emphasize how this skill will be useful to students.
2. Read a sample problem with the class. Determine the correct operation. Turn on the calculator. Show how to enter the first number, the operation sign, the second number, and the equal sign. Identify and record the answer.
3. Repeat with another problem requiring a different operation.
4. Show the class a third problem using a transparency on the overhead projector.
   a. Call on a student to read the problem out loud.
      Contingency: For a student unable to read parts of the problem, read it for him or her; then have the student repeat it.
   b. Determine the correct operation.
      Contingency: Students unable to determine the operation will be provided a list of key words and phrases that provide hints. For example, "How much more?" indicates subtraction.
   c. Turn on the calculator.
      Contingency: Use a red marker to highlight the "on" button for students unable to locate it.
   d. Enter the first digit of the first number.
      Contingency 1: Students unable to determine which number should be entered first will be assisted in setting up the problem on paper first.
      Contingency 2: Students unable to determine which digit of a number should be entered first will be told to enter the digits as they are softly repeated out loud.
   e. Enter the operation sign.
      Contingency: Students unable to locate the operation sign will be referred to a sample problem on the board and asked to match the sign written on the board with the button on the calculator.
   f. Enter the equal sign.
      Contingency: Use a blue marker to highlight the "[=]" button for students unable to locate it.
   g. Record the answer.
5. Repeat with another problem presented to the entire group.
6. Provide a worksheet with ten word problems to those who needed no assistance during the teacher-directed activity.
   Contingency: Continue to work in a small group with those who experienced difficulty.
7. If time permits, allow students who have mastered the skill to go "Christmas shopping" using a catalog from a department store. Tell them they have $200 to spend. They must keep track of their expenses.
   Contingency: Have students previously engaged in small group instruction complete the worksheet containing ten problems. Be available to provide assistance.

From *Instructional Methods for Secondary Students with Learning and Behavior Problems* (4th ed., p. 85), by P. I. Schloss, M. A. Schloss, and C. N. Schloss, 2007. Boston: Allyn & Bacon.

CONSIDER THIS

Should teachers who refuse to make accommodations for students with different learning needs in their classes be required to make such efforts? What are the consequences for students included in classrooms where teachers refuse to make accommodations?

significant hurdle for middle and high school students with disabilities. Although the amount of homework assigned provides a challenge, the unique difficulties of students with disabilities are underscored by the types of problems they are likely to have. Just as the characteristics of each exceptionality described in previous chapters can have a negative impact on classroom performance, they create additional challenges as students attempt to complete work without the guidance of a teacher, the modeling of a peer, or the structure of a classroom.

Polloway and colleagues (2005) suggest that although homework can pose a special challenge for students with disabilities and their families, effective intervention techniques have been identified. Teachers and parents can work together to implement these procedures that can increase students' success with homework and ultimately have a positive effect on school achievement. Following is a list of homework practices that are organized as management, assignment, and student considerations, and parent involvement.

Management considerations
- Assess a student's homework skills to identify potential problems

Table 16.3	**Curriculum or Instruction Adaptations**	
Stage of Instruction	**Accommodations (Examples)**	**Modifications (Examples)**
Initial Instruction	• Clear overheads/graphic organizer • Partners repeat or read to each other • Teacher uses signals • Study guide/guided notes • Highlighted text • Teacher position/proximity to particular students	• Different study guide (partially filled out) • Different text • Introduce different but related skill
Guided Practice	• Notated/highlighted/more structured assignment or activity • Teacher/student model • Partners do/check • Partners tutor • Frequent checks by teacher • Alter pace	• Different assignment or activity on same skill or content • Different assignment or activity on related skill or content • Physical guidance by teacher/paraeducator/peer
Independent Practice	• Slower transition from guided practice • More structure	• Do less of same task • Different task • Teach parent/sibling to coach • Do with a partner
Evaluation	• Test under different conditions (more time, different location, test read to student) • Same rubric or standard but different tasks • Portfolio • Mastery standard, but vary time allowed to mastery • Evaluation based on more than curriculum mastery	• Evaluation of different objectives/different outcomes

From *Teaching Content to All: Evidence-Based Inclusive Practices in Middle and Secondary Schools* (p. 315), by B. K. Lenz and D. D. Deshler, 2004. Boston: Allyn & Bacon.

- Assign homework early in the year and on a regular basis.
- Present clear instuctions: State the purpose, give directions, identify the format and materials to be used and an estimate of how long the assignment should take, clarify how the assigment will be graded.
- Use an incentive program. (Figure 16.14 shows a homework pass that can be given for turning in homework. When the specified number is collected, a homework assignment can be skipped.)
- Use assignment notebooks and have parents sign off on work.

Assignment considerations
- Give the purpose of each assignment and establish relevance.
- Select activities appropriate for independent work.
- Use homework adaptations such as shorter assignments that cover the same content, extended due dates, grades based on effort not accuracy or only one component of the assignment, assign group homework.

Student considerations
- Teach study skills such as time management and dictionary skills.
- Consider student preferences on homework assignments.
- Help students develop self-management behaviors

Parental involvement
- Support and reinforce skills learned at school.
- Create environment for homework that occurs at same time daily in a distraction reduced setting with all needed materials available.
- Provide ongoing encouragement and support.

CEC STANDARDS

CEC 7: Instructional Planning

INTASC

INTASC 7: Plans for instruction

PRAXIS

PRAXIS II: Delivery of Services to Students with Disabilities

TEACHING TIP

These accommodations are helpful for all students, including those without disabilities who do not need specialized instruction.

Figure 16.13	**Checklist of Options for Accommodating Learning Needs**

Student _____ Teacher _____ Date(s) _____

[Circle accommodations attempted; mark successful accommodations with plus (+), unsuccessful with minus (–)]

Classroom
Design constructive learning environment.

Preferential seating (specifiy): _____				
Group size:	___1–1 w/teacher	___1–1 w/peer	___Small group	___Large group
Need for movement:	___Little	___Average	___High	
Distraction management:	___Carrels	___Headsets	___Seating	___Other
Noise:	___None	___Quiet	___Moderate	
Lighting:	___Dim	___Average	___Bright	
Temperature:	___Warm	___Average	___Cool	
Other (specify): _____				

Schedule
Arrange productive learning schedule.

Peak time:	___Early morning	___Late morning	___Midday	___Afternoon
Lesson length:	___5–10 min.	___15–20 min.	___25–30 min.	___30+ min.
Variation needed:	___Little	___Some	___Average	___Much
Extra time needed:	___Little	___Some	___Average	___Much
Other (specify): _____				

Lessons
Use best stimulus/response format.

Stimulus Format

Visual:	___Observe	___Read
Auditory:	___Oral	___Discuss
Touch:	___Hold	___Feel
Model:	___Coach	___Demonstrate
Multisensory:	___Combination	

Response Format

Choose:	___Point	___Mark
Tell:	___Restate	___Explain
Write:	___Short answer	___Essay
Word process:	___Some	___All
Show:	___Demonstrate	___Make

Other (specify): _____

Materials
Make constructive material adjustments.

___Vary stimulus/response	___Vary directions	___Vary sequence
___Highlight essential content	___Use partial content	___Add steps
___Expand practice	___Add self-checking	___Add Supplements
___Segment	___State key concepts in margins	(see below)

Other (specify): _____

Supplements
Provide supplementary aids to facilitate learning.

Instructional Strategies	*Materials*	*Assignments*	*Human Resources*
___Advance organizers	___Adaptive/assistive devise	___Adapted testing	___Co-teacher
___Charted progress	___Audiotapes of text	___Advance assignment	___Cooperative group
___Checklist of steps	___Calculator	___Alternate assignments	___Instructional coach
___Computer activities	___Captioned films	___Extended time	___Interpreter
___Evaluation checklists	___Coded text	___Extra practice	___Peer advocate
___Graphic organizers	___Computer programs	___Outlined tasks	___Peer notetaker
___Modeling	___Games for practice	___Partial outlines	___Peer prompter
___Mnemonic guides	___Highlighted text	___Question guides	___Peer tutor
___Multisensory techniques	___Key term definitions	___Reference access	___Personal attendant
___Organization charts	___Large print texts	___Scripted practice	___Study buddy
___Repeated readings	___Manipulatives	___Segmented tasks	___Volunteer tutor
___Scripted demonstrations	___Math number charts	___Shortened assignments	
___Self-questioning	___Multiple text	___Simplified directions	*Management Strategies*
___Strategy posters	___Parallel text	___Simplified tasks	___Charted performance
___Verbal rehearsal	___Simplified text	___Structured notes	___Checklists
___Video modeling	___Summaries	___Study guides	___Contracts
___Visual imagery	___Video enactments	___Timed practice	___Extra reinforcement
___Other	___Other	___Other	___Other
_____	_____	_____	_____
_____	_____	_____	_____

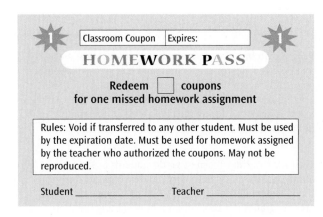

Figure 16.14

Example of a Homework Pass Used for Reinforcement

From *Successful Inclusive Teaching* (3rd ed., p. 389), by J. S. Choate, 2000. Boston: Allyn & Bacon.

Grading   The challenges of inclusion of adolescents with disabilities are perhaps most clearly reflected in the area of grading. School systems should develop a diverse committee to study the best practices in grading that support mastery of academic standards and meet legal guidelines to develop a policy for the entire system (Salend & Duhaney, 2002). Figure 16.15 provides optional grading systems that might be adopted for different purposes. Munk and Bursuck (2001) and Salend and Duhaney (2002) propose the following eleven purposes for grades (cited in Schloss et al., 2007):

1. Document achievement of curricular goals and specific skills.
2. Measure progress over time.
3. Measure effort put into learning.
4. Make comparisons among students.
5. Determine program effectivness.
6. Motivate students to succeed and learn.
7. Identify student strengths and weaknesses for planning instruction.
8. Communicate and provide feedback to families.
9. Factor into educational and career planning.
10. Determine eligibility for programs, graduation, awards, and promotions.
11. Provide accountability to the community, legislators, employers, and educational policy makers.

Testing   The inclusion movement has raised concerns regarding how students with special needs will be assessed. Simple adaptations can make the difference between taking a test successfully or poorly. For example, reading a test to a student who is a very poor reader gives the student a chance to display knowledge or skills. If such students have to read the questions themselves, test results will reflect students' poor reading skills and fail to assess knowledge of a particular content area. Teachers can address this situation in the following ways:

- Have another student, teacher, or aide read the test to the student.
- Use technology to scan and read text.
- Give the student additional time to complete the test. The extra time gives the student a chance to read the material first to identify the words and again for better comprehension.
- Reword the test to include only words that are within the student's reading vocabulary.

A full consideration of adaptations in testing, however, extends beyond the consideration of reading ability. Other ways that teachers can make tests more accessible to students is to use the COLA checklist (Figure 16.16), a strategy developed by Rotter (2006) to guide development of written material presented to students.

CONSIDER THIS

Should school policies regarding homework be altered to increase the likelihood of success for students with disabilities, or should these students be required to follow a rigid policy designed for all students? Why or why not?

CONSIDER THIS

In what ways can self-advocacy and self-determination affect young adults with disabilities? Should schools teach self-advocacy skills to adolescents with disabilities? Why or why not?

CONSIDER THIS

If alternative grading requirements are used with students with disabilities, should these students be eligible for honor roll, honors programs, and so forth? Why or why not?

CONSIDER THIS

Should standardized tests play such an important role in public schools? How does the expansion of these tests affect students with disabilities?

Figure 16.15   **Grading Systems**

✓ **Numeric/Letter Grades:** Teachers assign numeric or letter grades based on students' performance on tests or specific learning activities.

✓ **Checklists/Rating Scales:** Teachers develop checklists and rating scales that delineate the benchmarks associated with their courses and evaluate each student according to mastery of these benchmarks. Some school districts have revised their grading systems by creating rating scales for different grade levels. Teachers rate students on each skill, using a scale that includes "not yet evident," "beginning," "developing," and "independent."

✓ **Anecdotal/Descriptive and Portfolio Grading:** Teachers write descriptive comments regarding students' skills, learning styles, effort, attitudes, and growth, and strategies to improve student performance. These comments can be included with examples of students' work as part of portfolio grading.

✓ **Pass/Fail Systems:** Minimum course competencies are specified and students who demonstrate mastery receive a "P" grade, while those who fail to meet the minimum standards are given an "F" grade. Some schools have modified the traditional pass/fail grading system to include such distinctions as honors (HonorP), high pass (HP), pass (P), and low pass (LP).

✓ **Mastery Level/Criterion Systems:** Students and teachers meet to divide the material into a hierarchy of skills and activities, based on an assessment of individual needs and abilities. After completing the learning activities, students take a post-test or perform an activity to demonstrate mastery of the content. When students demonstrate mastery, they receive credit for that accomplishment and repeat the process with the next skill to be mastered.

✓ **Progressive Improvement Grading:** Students take exams and engage in learning activities, and receive feedback and instruction based on their performance throughout the grading period. Only performance on cumulative tests and learning activities during the final weeks of the grading period, however, are used to determine students' grades.

✓ **Multiple Grading:** Teachers grade students in the areas of ability, effort, and achievement. Students' report cards can then include a listing of the three grades for each content area, or grades can be computed by weighting the three areas.

✓ **Level Grading:** Teachers use a numeric subscript to indicate the level of difficulty at which the students' grades are based. For example, a grade of B6 can be used to note that a student is working in the B range at the sixth-grade level. Subscript systems can also be devised to indicate whether students are working at grade level, above grade level, or below grade level.

✓ **Contract Grading:** Teachers and students agree on a contract outlining the learning objectives; the amount, nature, and quality of the products students must complete; and the procedures for evaluating student products and assigning a grade.

✓ **Individualized Education Program (IEP) Grading:** Teachers assign grades that acknowledge students' progress in meeting the students' IEP goals and performance criteria.

Source: "Grading Students in Inclusive Settings," by S. J. Salend & L. G. Duhaney, 2002, *Teaching Exceptional Children,* January/February, p. 11.

CEC STANDARDS

CEC 8: Assessment

INTASC

INTASC 8: Formal and informal assessment

The following examples are additional techniques that can be used to adapt measurement instruments and assessment procedures:

- Using information about performance outside school in making evaluations.
- Administering frequent short tests, rather than a few long tests.
- Dividing tests or tasks into smaller, simpler sections or steps.
- Developing practice items or pretest trials using the same response format as the test.
- Considering the appropriateness of the instrument or procedure in terms of age or maturity.
- Giving open-book or open-note tests.
- Reducing the number of test items or removing items that require more abstract reasoning or have high levels of difficulty.
- Using different levels of questions for different students.
- Having a student develop a product or packet of materials that show knowledge and understanding of the content of a unit (portfolio assessment).

- Providing alternative projects or assignments.
- Videotaping a student performing a task and then playing it back to him or her to show skills learned and areas needing improvement.
- Using a panel of students to evaluate one another on task performance.
- Allowing students to type answers.
- Allowing students to use a computer during testing.
- Allowing small groups to work together on a task to be evaluated (such as a project or test).
- Using short written or verbal measures on a daily or weekly basis to provide more feedback on student progress.
- Increasing the amount of time allowed to complete the test.
- Altering the types of responses to match a student's strengths (written, oral, short answer, or simple marking).
- Having a student review the course or unit content verbally so that he or she is not limited to test item recall.
- Limiting the number of formal tests by using checklists to observe and record learning.
- Assessing participation in discussions.
- Giving extra credit for correction of mistakes.

A survey of middle school students' opinions found that preferred modifications were open-notes or open-book tests, practice questions for study, and multiple choice

CROSS-REFERENCE

Review Chapters 5 to 11 and determine specific testing adaptations that might be necessary with students with different types of disabilities.

Figure 16.16

The COLA Checklist

C	Contrast	There is plenty of white space around important information and answer spaces.	
		Color of the text is in clear contrast from background (this includes avoiding the use of pencil or lightly printed dittos).	
		Color, underlining, dark borders, and/or highlights are used to point out critical information, such as directions.	
		Bold font is used infrequently, for highlighting important information only.	
O	Orientation	Important information, such as directions, is in the top-left position.	
		All information reads from left to right, top to bottom.	
		Material is aligned to the left.	
L	Lettering	Material is printed, not handwritten.	
		The same clear font is used throughout.	
		The font is big enough to read easily at the typical viewing distance.	
		The material uses upper- and lowercase letters as they would typically appear in print. (No use of all caps or small caps fonts.)	
		Italicized fonts are not used.	
A	Artwork	Artword is used only to support information and not to make the paper "pretty."	
		The page is not too "busy," and pictures are not distracting.	
		Artwork is culturally sensitive	

From "Creating Instructional Materials for All Pupils: Try Cola", (p. 281) by K. Rotter, 2006, *Intervention in School and Clinic, 4115,* pp. 273–282.

CROSS-REFERENCE

Refer to Chapter 15 for information regarding treatment acceptability.

TEACHING TIP

A high stakes assessment is one in which the results are used to make decisions with significant consequences. For example: a standardized test that must be "passed" before a student can graduate.

CEC STANDARDS

CEC 4: Instructional Strategies

INTASC

INTASC 4: Instructional strategies

PRAXIS

PRAXIS II: Delivery of Services to Students with Disabilities

instead of essay. Their least preferred modifications were having the teacher read the test, tests with fewer questions, and tests covering less material (Nelson et al., 2000). Bolt and Thurlow (2004) offer several suggestions for identifying the most appropriate accommodations that will have the greatest impact on the performance of students:

1. Be sure that the accommodation does not compromise the purpose of the test. For example, a math or science test could be read to a student but a test of reading comprehension could not be.
2. Choose the least intrusive options. For example, if a poor reader can function with extra time, he or she should not be given a reader.
3. Let students get used to the accommodation before using it during a "high stakes assessment."
4. Individuals providing the accommodation should be trained; for example, no prompts or cues should be given unless specified.
5. Monitor the effectiveness of the accommodation. One student was given extended time on a test, but the extra time was during the loud break time of the other 100 students taking the test!

For students to perform successfully on tests, they will need to learn individual test-taking and organizational strategies that are often difficult for students with disabilities. Such strategies are typically subsumed within the area of study skills, discussed in the next section.

Study Skills and Learning Strategies

Teachers' accommodations are insufficient to guarantee that students with special needs will be successful. Students must develop their own skills and strategies to help them overcome, or compensate for, a disability. Understanding how to use study skills will greatly enhance their chances for being successful in future academic, vocational, or social activities. Classroom teachers can help students acquire a repertoire of study skills. Study skills are tools that students can use to assist them with independent learning.

Many students have an innate ability in these areas. For example, some students are good readers, adept at comprehension, and able to read quickly; other students find it easy to memorize facts. These students may not need instruction in study skills. For other students, however, study skills represent an "invisible curriculum" that must be taught directly if they are to be successful. For example, the study skill of listening is critical in most educational settings because teachers provide so much information verbally. If students are not able to attend to auditory information, they will miss a great deal of content. Following is a list of ways to help secondary students prepare to study; study; and follow up after studying developed by Lambert and Nowacek (2006):

Preparing to study
- Explain that it's easier to study during the daytime, expecially during study halls and time provided in class.
- Assist students in deciding on a routine time and a distraction-reduced, well-lit area at home for study.
- Help students identify needed materials for study (e.g., study guides, texts, notes, planners, pencils).
- Teach students to develop a study agenda, beginning with hardest items as soon as they are assigned.
- Help students learn to break difficult and long-term assignments into shorter parts with time lines identified that can be checked off as they are completed.
- Remind students to use positive self-talk, reminding themselves that they "can do" instead of "can't do."

Studying in the content areas

- Show students how to prioritize and focus, not jumping from one subject to another without completion.
- Encourage them to study for fifty minutes (using a timer is helpful) and then take a ten-minute break.
- Teach chapter previewing skills, looking first at title, subheads, graphics, and questions to be answered.
- Teach the paraphrasing strategy where the main ideas are developed for each subhead.
- Teach students to use graphic organizers to summarize information and show relationships (see Figure 16.17)
- Teach students to identify what they do not understand and find a solution (e.g. look on web, in reference book, or ask student or teacher)
- Remind them to keep up the positive self-talk ("This is working! I am really making progress.").

Following up after studying

- Help students keep material needed later in organized notebooks or separate folders.
- Have students establish a habit of writing three questions to discuss in class from what they read or studied and putting homework in notebooks and backpacks.
- Encourage students to reflect on what they have learned and relate the new information to what they have already learned.
- Teach students to reward themselves with a favorite activity after working.

Figure 16.17 **PROJECT Strategy Steps and an Assignment Sheet Example**

PROJECT Strategy Steps
Prepare your form.
Record and ask.
Organize.
　　Break the assignment into parts.
　　Estimate the number of study sessions.
　　Schedule the sessions.
　　Take your materials home.
Jump to it.
Engage in the work.
Check your work.
Turn in your work.

Subject (Read) Book　　　　　　Partner John

Eng.　Answer　　　　　　Phone 583-8888

(Write) Report – 2 pgs.

Other

A
B
C
D
E

\# of parts 5　　　　\# of study sessions 10

Due 4/18　　　　Done 4/17

From "Effects of Instruction in an Assignment Completion Strategy on the Homework Performance of Students with Learning Disabilities in General Education Classes," by C. A. Hughes et al., 2002, *Learning Disabilities Research and Practice, 17*, 1–18. Copyright 2002 by Blackwell Publishing. Reprinted by permission.

Closely related to study skills are learning strategies—specific steps to use to guide learning before, during, and after active learning to acquire and use new information and solve problems ("learning to learn"). Learning strategies were cited as "an essential component of high-quality reading intruction" in the No Child Left Behind Act of 2001. Reading comprehension, error monitoring in writing, problem solving in math, and test preparation are just a few of the important skills that can be developed and strengthened through strategy training. A comprehensive source on numerous strategies for learning (and their use) is provided by Lenz and Deshler (2004).

Examples of learning strategies include:

- SCROL (Grant, 1993) is a strategy that helps students learn how to use textbook headings to improve comprehension. There are five steps in the strategy (Scholes, 1998):
  1. *Survey* the heading. Read each heading and subheading and answer the following questions: What do I already know about this topic? What do I expect the author to include in this section?
  2. *Connect* the parts of the reading. How are the headings related to each other? Write down words from the headings that provide connections between them.
  3. *Read* the text. As you read, look for words or phrases that provide important information about the headings. Stop to make sure you understand the major ideas and supporting details at the end of each section. Reread if you don't understand.
  4. *Outline* the major ideas and supporting details in the section. Try to do this without looking back.
  5. *Look back* at the text to check the accuracy of your outline. Correct your outline as needed. (p. 111)
- The COPS strategy (Schumaker et al., 1981) is an error-monitoring strategy for writing. The acronym stands for four tasks:
  1. Capitalization.
  2. Overall appearance (e.g., neatness, appropriate margins).
  3. Punctuation.
  4. Spelling. (p. 11)

Efforts to validate the use of specific strategies within inclusive classrooms have been ongoing for many years and cover a variety of purposes. Although many are used to make content learning more efficient, teachers have been able to develop their own strategies to assist their students in a variety of areas. The range of uses of learning strategies is limited only by one's creativity. Another exciting aspect of instruction in strategies is its potential to benefit students with and without disabilities in inclusive classrooms (Keith & Lenz, 2004).

Summary

Secondary School Curricula
- Important differences exist between elementary and secondary settings in terms of organizational structure, curriculum, and learner characteristics.
- From a curricular perspective, integrating students with disabilities into general classes is more challenging at the secondary level than at the elementary level.
- The period of adolescence adds to the problems experienced by students with disabilities.

Programs for Students in Secondary Schools
- Curricular options for students at the secondary level with particular relevance for students with disabilities include basic skills, social skills, tutoring, learning strategies, vocational skills, and life skills.
- ITPs are required by law, and their effectiveness is critical for successful life after high school for individuals with disabilities.
- Classroom teachers and special education teachers must collaborate to ensure effective secondary school programs.
- Special education teachers must be avalaible if needed to help prepare students for academic content classes.
- Transition to the life after high school is a major endeavor for students with disabilities.

Methods to Facilitate Students' Success in General Education Classes

- Adaptations are accommodations or modifications that are changes that teachers can make to facilitate the success of students with disabilities.
- Specific challenges for successful inclusion occur in the areas of homework, grading, and testing.
- Study skills can help students with disabilities achieve success in general and special education classes.
- Learning strategies enable students to achieve independence as they "learn how to learn."

Questions to Reconsider

Think back to the scenario about Jim that you read at the beginning of this chapter. Would you answer the questions raised there any differently, now that you have read the chapter?

1. What adolescent characteristics is Jim displaying?
2. What role did Jim's parents play in developing Jim's problems and solutions?

3. How did the legal requirement for a transition component of the IEP help Jim?
4. What could parents and teachers have done throughout Jim's school years to help prepare him to understand and address his transition challenges more effectively?

Further Readings

Grigal, M., Neubert, D. A., & Moon, M. S. (2005). *Transition services for students with significant disabilities in college and community settings: Strategies for planning, implementation, and evaluation.* Austin, TX: Pro-Ed.

Johnson, D. et al., (2002). Current challenges facing secondary education and transition services: What research tells us. *Exceptional Children, 68*(4), 519–531.

Lenz, B. K. & Deshler, D. D. (2004). *Teaching content to all: Evidence-based inclusive practices in middle and secondary schools.* Boston: Allyn & Bacon.

Miller, S. P. (2001). *Validated practices for teaching students with diverse needs and abilities.* Boston: Allyn & Bacon.

Prater, M. A. (2000). Using juvenile literature with portrayals of disabilities in your classroom. *Intervention in School and Clinic, 35*(3), 167–176.

Steere, D. E., Rose, E., & Cavaiuolo, D. (2007). *Growing up: Transition to adult life for students with disabilities.* Boston: Allyn & Bacon.

Sullivan, P. (2003). Connecting IEP objectives to general curriculum and instruction. *Middle School Journal, 34*(4), 47–52.

Trainor, A. A., Patton, J. R., & Clark, G. M. (2005). *Case studies in assessment for transition planning.* Austin, TX: Pro-Ed.

Wehman, P., & Kregel, J. (Eds.) (1998). *More than a job: Securing satisfying careers for people with disabilities.* Baltimore, MD: Brookes.

Website: Adolescent Autonomy Checklist to help keep track of a child's skills at home, in the community, leisure time, and for the future is available at www.depts.washington.edu/healthtr/Timeline/timeline_int=str.htm.

ᴍylabschool
Where the classroom comes to life

Go to Allyn & Bacon's MyLabSchool (www.mylabschool.com) and enter Assignment ID SPV9 into the Assignment Finder. View the video clip called *Visual Impairment*. Then consider what you have seen along with what you've read in Chapter 16 to answer the following questions.

1. What special accommodations do Kyle's teacher and family make to enable him to function both in and out of school? Provide specific examples. Using information from this chapter, briefly explain the importance of social skill strategies for successful inclusion of secondary students with disabilities.

Now enter Assignment ID SPV7 and review the video clip called *Learning Disabilities.*

2. Using the information in this chapter and in the video clip, suggest a curricular program that would be appropriate for Bridget's goal of going to college. How might her high school choices help her overcome the fear that she will never be able to get or keep a job?

3. Make a list of Bridget's deficits or areas of difficulty as noted in the video clip. Based on what you have read in this text, what inclusion strategies would you suggest as a focus for Bridget's teachers?

You may also answer the questions at the end of these clips and e-mail your responses to your instructor.

Sample IEP for an Elementary Student

INDIVIDUALIZED EDUCATION PROGRAM

STUDENT'S NAME: Betty

DOB _____12/15/1996_____ SCHOOL YEAR ____2006____ - ____2007____ GRADE ____4____ - _____

IEP INITIATION/DURATION DATES   FROM   08/14/06   TO   05/26/07

THIS IEP WILL BE IMPLEMENTED DURING THE REGULAR SCHOOL TERM UNLESS NOTED IN EXTENDED SCHOOL YEAR SERVICES.

STUDENT PROFILE

Betty will be entering the fourth grade at Smallville Elementary School in the fall. She will be included in all general education classes with accommodations. At this time she is exhibiting fewer hyperactive behaviors and is able to focus and remain on task with supports during the school day. Betty has been experiencing difficulty in achieving grade level academic content standards in the area of math. Currently, she is working toward third grade standards.

Betty takes great pride in her work. All assigned tasks are generally completed when she is provided with additional time to complete assignments. She also requires additional time to take tests.

Achievement test scores indicate Betty is on grade level in reading and below average in the area of math, particularly in the area of spatial problems. On the *Stanford 10* and the *Alabama Reading & Mathematics Test* (ARMT), Betty solved addition and subtraction problems, including word problems. She was also able to divide whole numbers and make change up to $1.00. She had difficulty completing geometric problems. Betty could not specify locations on a coordinate grid or analyze data. She appears to have difficulty with spatial problems and transferring items from a concrete form to an abstract form. Betty's problems in math affect her ability to comprehend the required content (graphs, angles and spatial problems) at her current grade level.

Her teachers report she gets along well with her peers. She does not initiate responses in class, but will respond upon request.

Betty's parents are very involved in her academic work. They assist with homework and have provided tutoring when needed. Betty is involved in many community and church activities. Betty's parents are concerned with her academic performance and lack of self-esteem.

> **TAKE NOTE**
> A narrative of the student's strengths and weaknesses is a better way of describing the student than simply listing test scores.

INDIVIDUALIZED EDUCATION PROGRAM

STUDENT'S NAME: Betty

SPECIAL INSTRUCTIONAL FACTORS

ITEMS CHECKED "YES" WILL BE ADDRESSED IN THIS IEP:	YES	NO

- Does the student have behavior, which impedes his/her learning or the learning of others?   [ ]   [x]
- Does the student have limited English proficiency?   [ ]   [x]
- Does the student need instruction in Braille and the use of Braille?   [ ]   [x]
- Does the student have communication needs (deaf or hearing impaired only)?   [ ]   [x]
- Does the student need assistive technology devices and/or services?   [ ]   [x]
- Does the student require specially designed P.E.?   [ ]   [x]
- Is the student working toward alternate achievement standards and participating in the Alabama Alternate Assessment?   [ ]   [x]
- Are transition services addressed in this IEP?   [ ]   [x]

CROSS-REFERENCE

Review chapters 6 and 15 to determine specific needs of students with these kinds of learning issues.

TRANSPORTATION AS A RELATED SERVICE

Does the student require transportation as a related service?   [ ] YES   [x] NO

Does the student need accommodations or modifications for transportation?   [ ] YES   [x] NO

    If YES, check any transportation accommodations/modifications that are needed.

    [ ]   Bus driver is aware of student's behavioral and/or medical concerns

    [ ]   Wheelchair lift

    [ ]   Restraint system

    Specify: _____

    [ ]   Other

    Specify: _____

NONACADEMIC and EXTRACURRICULAR ACTIVITIES

Will the student have the opportunity to participate in nonacademic/extracurricular activities with his/her nondisabled peers?

[x]   YES

[ ]   YES, with supports. Describe: _____

[ ]   NO. Explanation must be provided: _____

METHOD/FREQUENCY FOR REPORTING PROGRESS OF ATTAINING GOALS TO PARENTS

Annual Goal Progress reports will be sent to parents each time report cards are issued every _____**9.0**_____ week(s).

TAKE NOTE

Parents must be notified of the progress being made by their children on the same schedule that parents of nondisabled children receive notification.

INDIVIDUALIZED EDUCATION PROGRAM

STUDENT'S NAME: Betty

AREA: Math

PRESENT LEVEL OF ACADEMIC ACHIEVEMENT AND FUNCTIONAL PERFORMANCE:

Betty has not attained all of the third grade content standards in math. She is able to compare (M.3.1.1) and order numbers (M 3.1.2) less than 100, solve addition and subtraction problems and simple word problems (M.3.2). She has difficulty working problems involving spatial relationships and geometric patterns. Betty's lack of knowledge in the areas of spatial and geometric relationships negatively affects achieving grade-level math geometry standards.

MEASURABLE ANNUAL GOAL related to meeting the student's needs:
At the end of 36 weeks, Betty will identify geometric representations for points, lines, perpendicular lines, parallel lines, angles and rays (M.3.8) on weekly classroom tests an average of 9 out of 10 times.

TAKE NOTE

Annual goals should be directly related to present level of performance.

TYPE(S) OF EVALUATION FOR ANNUAL GOAL:

[X] Curriculum Based Assessment   [X] Teacher/Text Test   [ ] Teacher Observation   [ ] Grades
[ ] Data Collection   [X] State Assessment(s)   [X] Work Samples
[ ] Other: _____
[ ] Other: _____

DATE OF MASTERY: _____

SPECIAL EDUCATION AND RELATED SERVICE(S): (Special Education, Supplementary Aids and Services, Program Modifications, Accommodations Needed for Assessments, Related Services, Assistive Technology, and Support for Personnel.)

Type of Service(s)	Anticipated Frequency of Service(s)	Amount of time	Beginning/ Ending Date	Location of Service(s)
Special Education Special education and general education teachers will plan lessons and activities using the Curriculum Guide: Mathematics.	Weekly	55 min.	08/14/06 to 05/26/07	General Education Classroom
Special education teacher will re-teach lesson in small group.	Daily	20 min.	08/14/06 to 05/26/07	General Education Classroom
Supplementary Aids and Services Betty needs extra time for classroom assignments in mathematics.	Daily	55 min.	08/14/06 to 05/26/07	General and Special Education Classroom
Betty needs a peer helper to assist with classroom activities in mathematics.	Daily	55 min.	08/14/06 to 05/26/07	General Education Classroom
Program Modifications				
Accommodations Needed for Assessments Betty will have extended time on test.	Weekly	55 min.	08/13/06 to 05/26/07	Special Education Classroom
Betty will receive study guides for tests in mathematics.	Weekly	10 min.	08/13/06 to 05/26/07	General Education Classroom
Related Services				
Assistive Technology				
Support for Personnel				

TAKE NOTE

Specific services that the school will provide to assist the student in achieving goals and objectives must be listed.

INDIVIDUALIZED EDUCATION PROGRAM

STUDENT'S NAME: Betty

GENERAL FACTORS

HAS THE IEP TEAM CONSIDERED::	YES	NO
• The strengths of the child?	[X]	[ ]
• The concerns of the parents for enhancing the education of the child?	[X]	[ ]
• The results of the initial or most recent evaluations of the child?	[X]	[ ]
• As appropriate, the results of performance on any State or districtwide assessments?	[X]	[ ]
• The academic, developmental, and functional needs of the child?	[X]	[ ]
• The need for extended school year services?	[X]	[ ]

LEAST RESTRICTIVE ENVIRONMENT

Does this student attend the school (or for a preschool-age student, participate in the environment) he/she would attend if non-disabled?   [X] YES [ ] NO

If no, justify:

Does this student receive all special education services with non-disabled peers?   [ ] YES [X] NO

If no, justify (justification may not be solely because of needed modifications in the general curriculum):
Betty requires intensive instruction and frequent feedback in mathematics in an environment free of distractions.

> **TAKE NOTE**
> The team must consider the least restrictive setting for each student and justify why a lesser restrictive setting is not used.

[X]   **6-21 YEARS OF AGE**   [ ]   **3-5 YEARS OF AGE**
(Select one from the drop-down box.)
02-99%-80%of the day inside Gen Ed Environment

Secondary LRE (only if LRE above is Private School-Parent Placed)

COPY OF IEP

Was a copy of the IEP given to parent at the IEP meeting?
   [X] Yes   [ ] No
If no, date sent to parent: _____

COPY OF *SPECIAL EDUCATION RIGHTS*

Was a copy of the *Special Education Rights* given to parent at the IEP meeting?   [X] Yes   [ ] No
If no, date sent to parent: _____

Date copy of **amended** IEP provided/sent to parent   _____

THE FOLLOWING PEOPLE ATTENDED AND PARTICIPATED IN THE MEETING TO DEVELOP THIS IEP

Position	Signature	Date
Parent	*	4/26/06
Parent	*	4/26/06
LEA Representative	*	4/26/06
Special Education Teacher	*	4/26/06
General Education Teacher	*	4/26/06
Student		
Career/Technical Education Rep		
Other Agency Representative		

INFORMATION FROM PEOPLE NOT IN ATTENDANCE

Position	Name	Date

Sample IEP for a Middle School Student

INDIVIDUALIZED EDUCATION PROGRAM

STUDENT'S NAME: Robert _____

DOB _____ 03/25/1993 _____   SCHOOL YEAR _____ 2006 _____ - _____ 2007 _____ GRADE ___ 8 ___ - _____

IEP INITIATION/DURATION DATES   FROM   08/15/06   TO   05/14/07

THIS IEP WILL BE IMPLEMENTED DURING THE REGULAR SCHOOL TERM UNLESS NOTED IN EXTENDED SCHOOL YEAR SERVICES.

STUDENT PROFILE

Robert is in the eighth grade at Lincoln Middle School and is in foster care. His foster parents are concerned about Robert's academic and behavioral performance. They are also worried about Robert's lack of appropriate socialization with age-appropriate peers and adults.

Robert has a strong interest in sports and has indicated a desire to play varsity basketball. Currently, he is the trainer for the junior varsity basketball and football teams. A career inventory indicates interests in music and computers.

Robert has moved many times. His birth parents changed locations for various reasons. Since entering school, Robert has lived with four foster families. Records indicate that extreme violence was witnessed while living with his birth parents.

Robert has made significant progress academically although he is functioning below grade level in reading. He will work quietly and intently on a task when he knows exactly what to do and has a high chance of success. He may lose interest after awhile but, if the task is short he will complete it.

Robert is included in all eighth grade general education classes for his core subjects with accommodations. His assessments indicate that he is on eighth grade level in the area of math. He is reading on sixth grade level and reading comprehension is an area of concern. Therefore, he will receive intensive reading instruction in the special education room on a daily basis to close the gaps in reading. Grades for the 2005-2006 school year are poor in all subjects due to behavioral difficulties in the general education classroom. Robert does not complete his class assignments or homework on a consistent basis.

Teachers report that in the general education classroom, Robert continues to make inappropriate gestures that annoy his classmates, speaks very negatively to others, and exhibits impulsive behaviors (i.e. destroying or breaking objects without provocation). He is also noncompliant with reasonable requests and suggestions from adults. At this time, Robert's behavioral and academic difficulties adversely affect his full participation in the general education environment.

A psychiatrist diagnosed Robert with Attention Deficit/Hyperactivity Disorder (ADHD) when he was in the third grade. The school psychologist has reported elevated scales on the Behavior Assessment System for Children-2 (BASC-2) in anxiety and depression. Robert's foster mother reports he receives medication each morning before school to help control his impulsive behaviors. It is clear that supportive behavioral interventions are required to work in conjunction with medication to achieve positive results. Robert will continue to receive mental health counseling focusing on cognitive behavior modification (CBM) for one hour once a week after school. School personnel, the Department of Human Resources and Mental Health will work collaboratively at least once a month to address Robert's academic and behavioral concerns.

TAKE NOTE

A narrative of the student's strengths and weaknesses is a better way of describing the student than simply listing test scores.

INDIVIDUALIZED EDUCATION PROGRAM

STUDENT'S NAME: Robert

SPECIAL INSTRUCTIONAL FACTORS

ITEMS CHECKED "YES" WILL BE ADDRESSED IN THIS IEP: YES   NO
- Does the student have behavior, which impedes his/her learning or the learning of others?   [x]   [ ]
- Does the student have limited English proficiency?   [ ]   [x]
- Does the student need instruction in Braille and the use of Braille?   [ ]   [x]
- Does the student have communication needs (deaf or hearing impaired only)?   [ ]   [x]
- Does the student need assistive technology devices and/or services?   [ ]   [x]
- Does the student require specially designed P.E.?   [ ]   [x]
- Is the student working toward alternate achievement standards and participating in the Alabama Alternate Assessment?   [ ]   [x]
- Are transition services addressed in this IEP?   [ ]   [x]

CROSS-REFERENCE

Review chapters 6 and 16 to determine when transition services must be addressed in IEPs

TRANSPORTATION AS A RELATED SERVICE

Does the student require transportation as a related service?   [ ]   YES   [x]   NO

Does the student need accommodations or modifications for transportation?   [ ]   YES   [x]   NO

    If YES, check any transportation accommodations/modifications that are needed.
- [ ]   Bus driver is aware of student's behavioral and/or medical concerns
- [ ]   Wheelchair lift
- [ ]   Restraint system
      Specify: _____

- [ ]   Other
      Specify: _____

NONACADEMIC and EXTRACURRICULAR ACTIVITIES

Will the student have the opportunity to participate in nonacademic/extracurricular activities with his/her nondisabled peers?

[x]   YES

[ ]   YES, with supports. Describe: _____

_____

[ ]   NO. Explanation must be provided: _____

_____

METHOD/FREQUENCY FOR REPORTING PROGRESS OF ATTAINING GOALS TO PARENTS

Annual Goal Progress reports will be sent to parents each time report cards are issued every _____**9.0**_____ week(s).

TAKE NOTE

Parents must be notified of the progress being made by their children on the same schedule that parents of nondisabled children receive notification.

INDIVIDUALIZED EDUCATION PROGRAM

STUDENT'S NAME: Robert

AREA: Reading

PRESENT LEVEL OF ACADEMIC ACHIEVEMENT AND FUNCTIONAL PERFORMANCE:

Robert can comprehend fifth-grade literary/recreational materials. He uses a wide range of strategies and skills to gain meaning, summarize passages, and draw conclusions to comprehend fifth-grade functional and textual reading materials (R.5.4.3). He cannot interpret literary elements (R.6.2) in sixth-grade material. Robert's difficulty reading text material affects his progress in understanding content and achieving grade-level standards.

MEASURABLE ANNUAL GOAL related to meeting the student's needs:

By the end of the fourth grading period. Robert will be able to define conflict and personification (R.6.2.1) and identify the main idea in 6th grade reading material (R.6.2.2) with 80 percent accuracy.

> **TAKE NOTE**
>
> Annual goals should be directly related to present level of performance.

TYPE(S) OF EVALUATION FOR ANNUAL GOAL:

[X] Curriculum Based Assessment   [X] Teacher/Text Test   [ ] Teacher Observation   [ ] Grades
[ ] Data Collection   [X] State Assessment(s)   [X] Work Samples
[ ] Other: _____
[ ] Other: _____

DATE OF MASTERY: _____

SPECIAL EDUCATION AND RELATED SERVICE(S): (Special Education, Supplementary Aids and Services, Program Modifications, Accommodations Needed for Assessments, Related Services, Assistive Technology, and Support for Personnel.)

Type of Service(s)	Anticipated Frequency of Service(s)	Amount of time	Beginning/ Ending Date	Location of Service(s)
Special Education The special education teacher will provide intensive reading instruction using a research-based reading program.	Daily	30 min.	08/15/06 to 12/13/06	Special Education Classroom
Supplementary Aids and Services The general education teachers will use the following accommodations in all subjects: provide a seat in front of the classroom; provide notes; and allow more time to complete assignments.	Daily	90 min.	08/15/06 to 05/14/07	General Education Classroom
Program Modifications				
Accommodations Needed for Assessments Tests in assigned curriculum requiring reading may be read by the general or special education teacher allowing extended time for completion.	Weekly	60 min.	08/15/06 to 05/14/07	General Education Classroom
Related Services				
Assistive Technology				
Support for Personnel				

> **TAKE NOTE**
>
> Specific services that the school will provide to assist the student in achieving goals and objectives must be listed.

INDIVIDUALIZED EDUCATION PROGRAM

STUDENT'S NAME: Robert

AREA: Reading

PRESENT LEVEL OF ACADEMIC ACHIEVEMENT AND FUNCTIONAL PERFORMANCE:

Robert can comprehend fifth-grade literary/recreational materials. He uses a wide range of strategies and skills to gain meaning, summarize passages, and draw conclusions to comprehend fifth-grade functional and textual reading materials (R.5.4.3). He cannot apply reading strategies (R.6.3) to comprehend sixth-grade material. Robert's difficulty reading text material affects his progress in understanding content and achieving grade-level standards.

MEASURABLE ANNUAL GOAL related to meeting the student's needs:

By the end of the fourth grading period. Robert will identify the essential information in 6th grade reading material (R.6.3.4) with 80 percent accuracy.

TYPE(S) OF EVALUATION FOR ANNUAL GOAL:

[ ] Curriculum Based Assessment [ ] Teacher/Text Test [X] Teacher Observation [ ] Grades
[X] Data Collection [ ] State Assessment(s) [ ] Work Samples
[ ] Other: _____
[ ] Other: _____

DATE OF MASTERY: _____

SPECIAL EDUCATION AND RELATED SERVICE(S): (Special Education, Supplementary Aids and Services, Program Modifications, Accommodations Needed for Assessments, Related Services, Assistive Technology, and Support for Personnel.)

Type of Service(s)	Anticipated Frequency of Service(s)	Amount of time	Beginning/ Ending Date	Location of Service(s)
Special Education The special education teacher will provide intensive reading instruction using a research-based reading program.	Daily	30 min.	12/14/06 to 02/09/07	Special Education Classroom
Supplementary Aids and Services				
Program Modifications				
Accommodations Needed for Assessments				
Related Services				
Assistive Technology				
Support for Personnel				

TAKE NOTE

Person(s) responsible for addressing goals and objectives should be included in the IEP.

INDIVIDUALIZED EDUCATION PROGRAM

STUDENT'S NAME: Robert

AREA: Reading

PRESENT LEVEL OF ACADEMIC ACHIEVEMENT AND FUNCTIONAL PERFORMANCE:
Robert can comprehend fifth-grade literary/recreational materials. He uses a wide range of strategies and skills to gain meaning, summarize passages, and draw conclusions to comprehend fifth-grade functional and textual reading materials (R.5.4.3). He cannot recognize the use of text elements (R.6.4) in sixth-grade materials. Robert's difficulty reading text material affects his progress in achieving grade-level standards.

MEASURABLE ANNUAL GOAL related to meeting the student's needs:
By the end of the fourth grading period, Robert will identify main idea (R.6.4.1), cause and effect sentences (R.6.4.3), and define persuasive techniques (R.6.4.4) in 6th grade reading material with 80 percent accuracy.

TYPE(S) OF EVALUATION FOR ANNUAL GOAL:

[X] Curriculum Based Assessment   [X] Teacher/Text Test   [ ] Teacher Observation   [ ] Grades
[ ] Data Collection   [X] State Assessment(s)   [X] Work Samples
[ ] Other: _____
[ ] Other: _____

DATE OF MASTERY: _____

SPECIAL EDUCATION AND RELATED SERVICE(S): (Special Education, Supplementary Aids and Services, Program Modifications, Accommodations Needed for Assessments, Related Services, Assistive Technology, and Support for Personnel.)

Type of Service(s)	Anticipated Frequency of Service(s)	Amount of time	Beginning/ Ending Date	Location of Service(s)
Special Education The special education teacher will provide intensive reading instruction using a research-based reading program.	Daily	30 min.	02/10/07 to 05/14/07	Special Education Classroom
Supplementary Aids and Services				
Program Modifications				
Accommodations Needed for Assessments				
Related Services				
Assistive Technology				
Support for Personnel				

CROSS-REFERENCE

Refer to Chapter 4 on the IEP process.

INDIVIDUALIZED EDUCATION PROGRAM

STUDENT'S NAME: Robert

AREA: Behavior

PRESENT LEVEL OF ACADEMIC ACHIEVEMENT AND FUNCTIONAL PERFORMANCE:
Teachers report that in the general education classroom, Robert annoys his classmates by making inappropriate gestures, negative comments to others, and destroys or breaks objects for no apparent reason at least twice a week. However, when Robert is participating in athletics, he can control negative outbursts and demonstrates appropriate social skills. Robert's impulsive behavior interferes with completion of assignments and participating in the general education environment.

MEASURABLE ANNUAL GOAL related to meeting the student's needs:
By the end of the fourth grading period. Robert will interact appropriately with age-appropriate peers and adults in a variety of settings 4 out of 5 times a week.

TYPE(S) OF EVALUATION FOR ANNUAL GOAL:

[ ]	Curriculum Based Assessment	[ ]	Teacher/Text Test	[X]	Teacher Observation	[ ]	Grades
[X]	Data Collection			[ ]	State Assessment(s)	[ ]	Work Samples
[X]	Other: Behavior Charts						
[ ]	Other:						

DATE OF MASTERY:

SPECIAL EDUCATION AND RELATED SERVICE(S): (Special Education, Supplementary Aids and Services, Program Modifications, Accommodations Needed for Assessments, Related Services, Assistive Technology, and Support for Personnel.)

Type of Service(s)	Anticipated Frequency of Service(s)	Amount of time	Beginning/ Ending Date	Location of Service(s)
Special Education The special education teacher will assist Robert with monitoring/charting a self-evaluation system for appropriate behaviors in the classroom	Daily	5 min.	08/15/06 to 05/14/07	General Education Classroom
Supplementary Aids and Services General education teachers in all classes will sign the self-evaluation form if they agree with his ratings of identified behaviors in all subjects.	Daily	5 min.	08/15/06 to 05/14/07	General Education Classroom
Program Modifications				
Accommodations Needed for Assessments				
Related Services The school counselor will provide individual counseling focusing on building self-esteem and social skills.	Weekly	30 min.	08/15/06 to 05/14/07	Counselor's Office
Assistive Technology				
Support for Personnel General education teachers will be trained on the use of the self-evaluation system.	Once	30	08/14/06 to 08/14/06	General Education Classroom

TAKE NOTE

Accommodations and modifications in general education classrooms are common components of IEPs for secondary students

CROSS-REFERENCE

Review Chapter 2 for the roles of special education and general education teachers in inclusive settings.

INDIVIDUALIZED EDUCATION PROGRAM

STUDENT'S NAME: Robert

GENERAL FACTORS

HAS THE IEP TEAM CONSIDERED::   YES   NO

- The strengths of the child?   [X]   [ ]
- The concerns of the parents for enhancing the education of the child?   [X]   [ ]
- The results of the initial or most recent evaluations of the child?   [X]   [ ]
- As appropriate, the results of performance on any State or districtwide assessments?   [X]   [ ]
- The academic, developmental, and functional needs of the child?   [X]   [ ]
- The need for extended school year services?   [X]   [ ]

LEAST RESTRICTIVE ENVIRONMENT

Does this student attend the school (or for a preschool-age student, participate in the
environment) he/she would attend if non-disabled?   **[X] YES [ ] NO**
If no, justify:

Does this student receive all special education services with non-disabled peers?   **[ ] YES [X] NO**
If no, justify (justification may not be solely because of needed modifications in the general curriculum):
Robert needs individual guidance on using appropriate classroom behaviors and intensive reading instruction in an environment with very few distractions.

| **[X] 6-21 YEARS OF AGE** | **[ ] 3-5 YEARS OF AGE** |

(Select one from the drop-down box.)
02-99%-80%of the day inside Gen Ed Environment

Secondary LRE (only if LRE above is Private School-Parent Placed)

> **TAKE NOTE**
> The team must consider the least restrictive setting for each student and justify why a lesser restrictive setting is not used.

COPY OF IEP

Was a copy of the IEP given to parent at the IEP meeting?
  [X] Yes   [ ] No
If no, date sent to parent: _____

COPY OF *SPECIAL EDUCATION RIGHTS*

Was a copy of the *Special Education Rights* given to parent
at the IEP meeting?   **[X]** Yes   [ ] No
If no, date sent to parent: _____

Date copy of **amended** IEP provided/sent to parent _____

THE FOLLOWING PEOPLE ATTENDED AND PARTICIPATED IN THE MEETING TO DEVELOP THIS IEP

Position	Signature	Date
Parent	*	4/24/06
LEA Representative	*	4/24/06
Special Education Teacher	*	4/24/06
General Education Teacher	*	4/24/06
Student	*	4/24/06
School Counselor		4/24/06
Mental Health Counselor		4/24/06
Family Service Worker		4/24/06

INFORMATION FROM PEOPLE NOT IN ATTENDANCE

Position	Name	Date

Sample IEP for a Secondary School Student

INDIVIDUALIZED EDUCATION PROGRAM

STUDENT'S NAME: Sam

DOB 05/05/1989   **SCHOOL YEAR** 2006 - 2007   **GRADE** 12 - _____

IEP INITIATION/DURATION DATES   FROM 08/10/06   **TO** 05/25/07

THIS IEP WILL BE IMPLEMENTED DURING THE REGULAR SCHOOL TERM UNLESS NOTED IN EXTENDED SCHOOL YEAR SERVICES.

STUDENT PROFILE

Sam is in the 12th grade at Morris High School. He is currently pursuing a regular high school diploma. During 2005-2006, Sam received accommodations and special education support in all of his core academic general education classes. He took and passed 11th grade English, Geometry, Biology, and U.S. History.

Sam is experiencing difficulty in the area of reading comprehension. Scores on achievement tests, curriculum based assessments, and the reading section of the Alabama High School Graduation Exam (AHSGE), indicate a deficit in the area of reading comprehension. Sam passed all sections of the AHSGE except for reading. Sam received reading accommodations for the other sections of the AHSGE. Sam's low level of reading comprehension is impacting his academic performance in all classes. Poor organizational skills also impact Sam's ability to complete and turn in assignments on time. A transition assessment identified organizational skills as a need for improvement. Through a parent interview, Sam's mother expressed concerns about Sam's lack of organizational skills and need for transition assistance.

Sam is a client of Vocational Rehabilitation Services. He received a vocational evaluation in 2005-2006. The Interest Inventory completed as part of the vocational evaluation showed Sam has a high preference for working with computers.

A transition assessment administrated by Sam's special education teacher indicates his greatest needs are in the area of post-secondary education and personal management. Sam attends a Transition Service class one period a day to address academic and transition needs. The career interest/aptitude inventory showed Sam has the ability to pursue a career in or relating to computers. Currently, Sam plans to attend Morris Junior College to pursue a career in computers. Sam will take the college entrance exams and complete the necessary applications for Morris Junior College and/or other junior colleges or technical schools as part of his postsecondary education preparation.

During the 10th grade, Sam obtained a drivers license. He worked at Best Buy during the summer to earn money to pay for a car. Sam continues to work at Best Buy after school.

A Summary of Performance (SOP) will be completed at the end of 12th grade in order to help facilitate Sam's transition to Postsecondary Education and linkage with other agencies.

TAKE NOTE

A narrative of the student's strengths and weaknesses is a better way of describing the student than simply listing test scores.

INDIVIDUALIZED EDUCATION PROGRAM

STUDENT'S NAME: Sam

SPECIAL INSTRUCTIONAL FACTORS

ITEMS CHECKED "YES" WILL BE ADDRESSED IN THIS IEP: YES   NO

- Does the student have behavior, which impedes his/her learning or the learning of others?   [ ]   [x]
- Does the student have limited English proficiency?   [ ]   [x]
- Does the student need instruction in Braille and the use of Braille?   [ ]   [x]
- Does the student have communication needs (deaf or hearing impaired only)?   [ ]   [x]
- Does the student need assistive technology devices and/or services?   [ ]   [x]
- Does the student require specially designed P.E.?   [ ]   [x]
- Is the student working toward alternate achievement standards and participating in the
  Alabama Alternate Assessment?   [ ]   [x]
- Are transition services addressed in this IEP?   [x]   [ ]

CROSS-REFERENCE
Review chapters 6 and 16 to determine when transition services must be addressed in IEPs

TRANSPORTATION AS A RELATED SERVICE

Does the student require transportation as a related service?   [ ]   YES   [x]   NO
Does the student need accommodations or modifications for transportation?   [ ]   YES   [x]   NO

    If YES, check any transportation accommodations/modifications that are needed.
    [ ]   Bus driver is aware of student's behavioral and/or medical concerns
    [ ]   Wheelchair lift
    [ ]   Restraint system
          Specify: _____
          _____

    [ ]   Other
          Specify: _____
          _____

NONACADEMIC and EXTRACURRICULAR ACTIVITIES

Will the student have the opportunity to participate in nonacademic/extracurricular activities with his/her nondisabled peers?

[x]   YES
[ ]   YES, with supports. Describe: _____
_____
[ ]   NO. Explanation must be provided: _____
_____

TAKE NOTE
Parents must be notified of the progress being made by their children on the same schedule that parents of nondisabled children receive notification.

METHOD/FREQUENCY FOR REPORTING PROGRESS OF ATTAINING GOALS TO PARENTS

Annual Goal Progress reports will be sent to parents each time report cards are issued every _____9.0_____ week(s).

INDIVIDUALIZED EDUCATION PROGRAM

STUDENT'S NAME: Sam

EXIT OPTIONS

[ ]   Alabama High School Diploma   [ ]   Alabama Occupational Diploma   **Anticipated Date of Exit:**
    with Advanced Academic Endorsement   [ ]   Graduation Certificate
[X]   Alabama High School Diploma   [ ]   Other:

May	2007
Month	Year

PROGRAM CREDIT TO BE EARNED

For each course taken, indicate program credit to be earned.	ENGLISH	MATH	SCIENCE	SOCIAL STUDIES	Transition Service Class	Computer Class	Art Graphic Design	
Alabama High School Diploma with Advanced Academic Endorsement								
Alabama High School Diploma	1	1	1	1	1	1	1	
Alabama Occupational Diploma								
Graduation Certificate								

TRANSITION

(Beginning not later than the first IEP to be in effect when the student is 16 and updated annually thereafter)

Transition Assessments (Check the assessment(s) used to determine the student's measurable transition goals: (*Check all that apply.*)

[X]   Student Interview   [ ]   Student Survey   [ ]   Work Samples   [X]   Vocational Assessment
[ ]   Interest Inventory   [X]   Parent Interview   [ ]   Other:

Transition Goals
Postsecondary Education/Employment Goal:
Student will be prepared to participate in postsecondary education/training based on completion of graduation requirements and submission of application for enrollment.
If **Other** is selected, specify:

Community/Independent Living Goal:
Student will be prepared to participate in community activities and live independently based on independent living skill level achieved and identification of community/living options.
If Other is selected, specify:

Transition Services   **(Based on this student's strengths, preferences, and interests the following coordinated transition services will be addressed this year.)**

[ ]   Vocational Evaluation (VE)   [X]   Personal Management (PM)   [ ]   Community Participation (CP)
[ ]   Employment Development (ED()   [ ]   Transportation (T)   [ ]   Medical (M)
[X]   Postsecondary Education (PE)   [ ]   Living Arrangements (LA   [ ]   Linkages to Agencies (L)
[ ]   Financial Management (FM)   [ ]   Advocacy/Guardianship (AG)   [ ]   Other: _____

TRANSITION OF RIGHTS

(Beginning not later than the IEP that will be in effect when the student reaches 18 years of age.)
Date student was informed that the rights under the IDEA will transfer to him/her at the age of 19:   05/18/06

TAKE NOTE
Transition goals must be addressed when students reach the age of 16.

INDIVIDUALIZED EDUCATION PROGRAM

STUDENT'S NAME: Sam

AREA: Reading

PRESENT LEVEL OF ACADEMIC ACHIEVEMENT AND FUNCTIONAL PERFORMANCE:
Sam's spoken vocabulary is a relative strength. He averages 6 out of 10 reading comprehension questions correctly on 11th grade classroom assessments. Sam has difficulty using context clues to confirm implied meaning of unfamiliar vocabulary in functional text (R.11.3.2). His difficulty with reading comprehension negatively affects his ability to glean information from written materials.

MEASURABLE ANNUAL GOAL related to meeting the student's needs:
At the end of 36 weeks, Sam will be able to interpret and analyze charts and tables in textual informational and functional materials (R12.2.2) with 90% accuracy on classroom assessments and worksheets within time limits in his assigned curriculum.

TYPE(S) OF EVALUATION FOR ANNUAL GOAL:

[X] Curriculum Based Assessment [X] Teacher/Text Test [ ] Teacher Observation [ ] Grades

[ ] Data Collection [X] State Assessment(s) [ ] Work Samples

[ ] Other: _____

[ ] Other: _____

DATE OF MASTERY: _____

SPECIAL EDUCATION AND RELATED SERVICE(S): (Special Education, Supplementary Aids and Services, Program Modifications, Accommodations Needed for Assessments, Related Services, Assistive Technology, and Support for Personnel.)

Type of Service(s)	Anticipated Frequency of Service(s)	Amount of time	Beginning/ Ending Date	Location of Service(s)
Special Education Special education teacher will pre-teach vocabulary words.	1 time per week	20 min.	08/10/06 to 05/25/07	Special Education Classroom
Special education teacher will re-teach lessons in small group.	2 times per week	20 min.	08/10/06 to 05/25/07	General Education Classroom
Special and general education teachers will plan lessons and activities.	1 time per week	15 min.	08/10/06 to 05/25/07	General Education Classroom
Supplementary Aids and Services Sam needs extra time for classroom assignments.	Daily	55 min.	08/10/06 to 05/25/07	Special Education Classroom
Read directions and provide peer helper to assist with classroom assignments and activities.	Daily	55 min.	08/10/06 to 05/25/07	General Education Classroom
Program Modifications				
Accommodations Needed for Assessments Sam will have tests read orally and extended time on tests.	Weekly	55 min.	08/10/06 to 05/25/07	Special Education Classroom
Sam will receive a study guide for all classroom assessments.	Weekly	55 min.	08/10/06 to 05/25/07	General Education Classroom
Related Services				
Assistive Technology				
Support for Personnel				

TAKE NOTE
Annual goals should be directly related to present level of performance

TAKE NOTE
Specific services that the school will provide to assist the student in achieving goals and objectives must be listed.

INDIVIDUALIZED EDUCATION PROGRAM

STUDENT'S NAME: Sam

AREA: Organizational Skills

PRESENT LEVEL OF ACADEMIC ACHIEVEMENT AND FUNCTIONAL PERFORMANCE:
Sam is able to keep up with events on his personal calendar. Sam is unable to organize his assignments and class notebook for each academic class. He loses assignments, both classroom and homework. He is unable to complete projects. Sam's difficulty with organization negatively affects his progress in completing assignments and projects to meet grade level standards.

MEASURABLE ANNUAL GOAL related to meeting the student's needs:
At the end of 36 weeks, Sam will implement a system for organizing his assignments and notebooks, as developed and monitored by his special education teacher, for each class 90% of the time.

TYPE(S) OF EVALUATION FOR ANNUAL GOAL:

[ ]   Curriculum Based Assessment   [ ]   Teacher/Text Test   [X]   Teacher Observation   [ ]   Grades

[ ]   Data Collection   [ ]   State Assessment(s)   [X]   Work Samples

[ ]   Other: _____

[ ]   Other: _____

DATE OF MASTERY: _____

SPECIAL EDUCATION AND RELATED SERVICE(S): (Special Education, Supplementary Aids and Services, Program Modifications, Accommodations Needed for Assessments, Related Services, Assistive Technology, and Support for Personnel.)

Type of Service(s)	Anticipated Frequency of Service(s)	Amount of time	Beginning/ Ending Date	Location of Service(s)
Special Education Special education teacher will help develop system, check notebooks and calendar. Special education teacher will plan and consult with the general education teacher to ensure that all assignments are in notebook.	Daily Daily	20 min. 20 min.	8/10/06 to 5/25/07 8/10/05 to 5/25/07	Special Education Classroom General Education Classroom
Supplementary Aids and Services Provide copy of notes and list of vocabulary words for all classes.	Daily	20 min.	8/25/06 to 5/25/07	General Education Classroom
Program Modifications				
Accommodations Needed for Assessments				
Related Services				
Assistive Technology				
Support for Personnel				

TAKE NOTE

Person(s) responsible for addressing goals and objectives should be included in the IEP.

INDIVIDUALIZED EDUCATION PROGRAM

STUDENT'S NAME: Sam
_____

GENERAL FACTORS

HAS THE IEP TEAM CONSIDERED::	YES	NO
• The strengths of the child?	[x]	[ ]
• The concerns of the parents for enhancing the education of the child?	[x]	[ ]
• The results of the initial or most recent evaluations of the child?	[x]	[ ]
• As appropriate, the results of performance on any State or districtwide assessments?	[x]	[ ]
• The academic, developmental, and functional needs of the child?	[x]	[ ]
• The need for extended school year services?	[x]	[ ]

LEAST RESTRICTIVE ENVIRONMENT

Does this student attend the school (or for a preschool-age student, participate in the environment) he/she would attend if non-disabled?   [x] YES [ ] NO
If no, justify:

Does this student receive all special education services with non-disabled peers?   [ ] YES [x] NO
If no, justify (justification may not be solely because of needed modifications in the general curriculum):
Due to Sam's inability to read at grade level and organize he will require intensive reading instruction and guidance with developing organizational skills.

[x] **6-21 YEARS OF AGE**	[ ] **3-5 YEARS OF AGE**

(Select one from the drop-down box.)
02-99%-80%of the day inside Gen Ed Environment
Secondary LRE (only if LRE above is Private School-Parent Placed)

TAKE NOTE
The team must consider the least restrictive setting for each student and justify why a lesser restrictive setting is not used.

## COPY OF IEP	## COPY OF *SPECIAL EDUCATION RIGHTS*
Was a copy of the IEP given to parent at the IEP meeting?	Was a copy of the *Special Education Rights* given to parent at the IEP meeting?
[x] Yes [ ] No	**[x]** Yes [ ] No
If no, date sent to parent: _____	If no, date sent to parent: _____
Date copy of **amended** IEP provided/sent to parent _____	

THE FOLLOWING PEOPLE ATTENDED AND PARTICIPATED IN THE MEETING TO DEVELOP THIS IEP

Position	Signature	Date
Parent	*	05/18/06
Parent	*	05/18/06
LEA Representative	*	05/18/06
Special Education Teacher	*	05/18/06
General Education Teacher	*	05/18/06
Student	*	05/18/06
Career/Technical Education Rep	*	05/18/06
Other Agency Representative	*ADRS	05/18/06

INFORMATION FROM PEOPLE NOT IN ATTENDANCE

Position	Name	Date

References

Abell, M. M., Bauder, D. K., & Simmons, T. J. (2005). Access to the general curriculum. *Intervention, 41*(2), 76–81.

Acrey, C., Johnstone, C., & Milligan, C. (2005). Using universal design to unlock the potential for academic achievement of at-risk learners. *Teaching Exceptional Children, 38*(2), 22–31.

Ad Hoc Committee on Terminology and Classification. (2001, September–October). Request for comments on proposed new edition of *Mental Retardation: Definition, Classification, and Systems of Supports. American Association on Mental Retardation News and Notes, 14*(5), 1, 9–12.

Agosta, J., & Melda, K. (1996). Supporting families who provide care at home for children with disabilities. *Exceptional Children, 62,* 271–282.

Agosti, J. E., Graetz, M. A., Mastropieri, M. A., & Scruggs, T. E. (2004). Teacher–researcher partnerships. *Intervention, 39,* 280–285.

Agrawal, A. (2001). The stammering brain. *Science Now.* Washington, DC: American Association for the Advancement of Science.

Alber, S. R., Heward, W. L., & Hippler, B. J. (1999). Teaching middle school students with learning disabilities to recruit positive teacher attention. *Exceptional Children, 65,* 253–270.

Alexander, K., & Alexander, M. D. (2001). *American public school law* (5th ed.). Belmont, CA: Wadsworth/Thomson Learning.

Algozzine, B. (2001). Effects of interventions to promote self-determination for individuals with disabilities. *Review of Educational Research, 71,* 219–277.

Algozzine, R., Serna, L., & Patton, J. R. (2001). *Childhood behavior disorders: Applied research and educational practices* (2nd ed.). Austin, TX: Pro-Ed.

Allen, K. E. (1992). *The exceptional child: Mainstreaming in early childhood education* (2nd ed.). Albany, NY: Delmar.

Allsopp, D. H., Santos, K. E., & Linn, R. (2000). Collaborating to teach pro-social skills. *Intervention in School and Clinic, 33,* 142–147.

American Academy of Pediatrics. (1988). *Learning disabilities and children: What parents need to know.* Elk Grove Village, IL: Author.

American Association on Mental Retardation. (1992). *Mental retardation: Definition, classification, and systems of supports* (9th ed.). Washington, DC: Author.

American Association on Mental Retardation. (2002). *Mental retardation: Definition, classification, and systems of supports* (10th ed.). Washington, DC: Author.

American Foundation for the Blind. (1998). *AFB directory of services for blind and visually impaired persons in the United States and Canada* (27th ed.). New York: Author.

American Humane (2003). *Protecting Children, 18*(1–2).

American Humane (2004). *Protecting Children, 18*(3).

American Psychiatric Association. (2000). *Diagnostic and statistical manual of mental disorders (DSM-IV-TR)* (4th ed. rev.). Washington, DC: Author.

American Speech–Language–Hearing Association. (2006). *2006 schools survey report: Current issues.* Rockville, MD: Author.

American Speech–Language–Hearing Association. (1982). Definitions: Communicative disorders and variations. *Journal of Speech, Language, and Hearing Research 24,* 949–950.

American Speech–Language–Hearing Association. (1995, March). Position statement—Facilitated communication. *Journal of Speech, Language, and Hearing Research 37* (Suppl. 14), 12.

American Speech–Language–Hearing Association. (1996, May). Cultural differences in communication and learning styles. Retrieved September 23, 2002 from http://professional.asha.org/resources/multicultural/reading_2.cfm. Compiled by the Multicultural Issues Board, Rockville, MD: Author.

American Speech–Language–Hearing Association. (1999). Terminology pertinent to fluency and fluency disorders. *Guidelines, 41,* 29–36.

American Speech–Language–Hearing Association. (2000). *What's language? What's speech?* Rockville, MD: Author.

American Speech–Language–Hearing Association. (2002a). *Communication facts: Incidence and prevalence of communication disorders and hearing loss in children (2002 edition).* Retrieved June 29, 2002 from http://professional.asha.org/resources/factsheets/children.cfm.

American Speech–Language–Hearing Association. (2002b). *Roles and responsibilities of speech–language pathologists with respect to reading and writing.* Rockville, MD: Author.

Anastopoulos, A. D., Smith, J. M., & Wien, E. E. (1998). Counseling and training parents. In R. A. Barkley (Ed.), *Attention-deficit/hyperactivity disorder: A handbook for diagnosis and treatment* (2nd ed.). New York: Guilford Press.

Anderson, J. A., Kutash, K., & Duchnowski, A. J. (2001). A comparison of the academic progress of students with ED and students with LD. *Journal of Emotional and Behavioral Disorders, 9,* 106–115.

Angold, A., Erkali, A., Egger, H. L., & Costell, J. E. (2000). Stimulant treatment for children: A community perspective. *Journal of the American Academy of Child and Adolescent Psychiatry, 39*(8), 975–987.

Anhalt, K., McNeil, C. B., & Bahl, A. B. (1998). The ADHD classroom kit: A whole-classroom approach for managing disruptive behavior. *Psychology in the Schools, 35*(1), 67–79.

Anthony, S. (1972). *The discovery of death in childhood and after.* New York: Basic Books.

Arc (1993, November/December). Second national status report on inclusion reveals slow progress. *ARC Newsletter,* p. 5.

Arc (1995). Report finds nation's schools still failing at inclusion. *The Arc Today, 44*(4), 1, 4.

Archer, A. & Gleason, M. (2002). *Skills for school success: Book 5.* North Billerica, MA: Curriculum Associates, Inc.

Archer, A. L., Gleason, M. M., & Vachon, V. L. (2003). Decoding and fluency foundation skills for struggling readers. *Learning Disabilities Quarterly, 26,* 89–101.

Arndt, S. A., Konrad, M., & Test, D. W. (2006). Effects of the *Self-Directed IEP* on student participation in planning meetings, *Remedial and Special Education, 27*(4), 194–207.

Arnold, L. E. (1999). Treatment alternative for attention-deficit/hyperactivity disorder (ADHD). *Journal of Attention Disorders, 3*(1), 30–48.

Aseltine, R. H. & DeMartino, R. (2004). An outcome evaluation of the SOS Suicide Prevention program. *American Journal of Public Health, 94,* 446–451.

ASHA Ad Hoc Committee on Service Delivery in the Schools. (1993, March). Definitions of communication disorders and variations. *Journal of Speech, Language, and Hearing Research, 35* (Suppl. 10), 40–41.

At-risk youth in crisis: A handbook for collaboration between schools and social services. (1991). Albany, OR: Linn-Benton Education Service Digest.

Austin, J. F. (1992). Involving noncustodial parents in their student's education. *NASSP Bulletin, 76,* 49–54.

Austin, V. L. (2001). Teachers' beliefs about co-teaching. *Remedial and Special Education, 22,* 245–255.

Austin, V. L. (2003). Pharmacological interventions for students with ADD. *Intervention in School and Clinic, 38*(5), 289–296.

Autism Society of America (2000). *Advocate, 33,* 3.

Autism Society of America (2002). *Advocate, 35,* 2.

Ayvazoglu, N. R., Oh, H., & Kozub, F. MJ. (2006). Explaining physical activity in children with visual impairments: A family systems approach. *Exceptional Children, 72,* 235–248.

Babkie, A. M. (2006). Be proactive in managing classroom behavior. *Intervention in School and Clinic, 41*(3), 184–187.

Babkie, A. M., & Provost, M. C. (2002). Select, write, and use metacognition strategies in the classroom. *Intervention, 37,* 172–175.

Bacon, E. H., & Schulz, J. B. (1991). A survey of mainstreaming practices. *Teacher Education and Special Education, 14*(2), 144–149.

Baker, B. L., Brightman, A. J., Blacher, J. B., Heifetz, L. J., Hinshaw, S. P., & Murphy, D. M. (1997). *Steps to independence: Teaching everyday skills to children with special needs.* Baltimore, MD: Brookes.

Banks, J. (1992). A comment on "Teacher perceptions of the Regular Education Initiative." *Exceptional Children, 58,* 564.

Barbour, C. B. (2005). A problem-solving model for special education's storms. *School Administration, 62*(2), 50–55.

Baren, M. (2000). *Hyperactivity and attention disorders in children: A guide for parents.* San Ramon, CA: Health Information Network.

Barkley, R. A. (1991). *Attention deficit hyperactivity disorder: A clinical workbook.* New York: Guilford Press.

Barkley, R. A. (1997). *Defiant children: A clinician's manual for assessment and parent training.* New York: Guilford Press.

Barkley, R. A. (2000). *Taking charge of ADHD: The complete, authoritative guide for parents* (rev. ed.). New York: Guilford Press.

Barnes, K. E. (1982). *Preschool screening: The measurement and prediction of children at risk.* Springfield, IL: Thomas.

Barnhill, G.P. (2006). *Right address...wrong planet: Children with Autism Spectrum Disorder becoming adults.* Shawnee, KS: Autism Asperger Publishing Co.

Barr, R. D., & Parrett, W. H. (1995). *Hope at last for at-risk youth.* Boston: Allyn and Bacon.

Barr, R. D., & Parrett, W. H. (2001). *Hope fulfilled for at-risk and violent youth: K–12 programs that work* (2nd ed.). Boston: Allyn and Bacon.

Barraga, N. C., & Erin, J. N. (1992). *Visual handicaps and learning* (3rd ed.). Austin, TX: Pro-Ed.

Barrish, H. H., Saunders, M., & Wolf, M. M. (1969). Good-behavior game: Effects of individual contingencies for group consequences on disruptive behavior in a classroom. *Journal of Applied Behavior Analysis, 2,* 119–124.

Bateman, B. D., & Linden, M. A. (2007). *Better IEPs: How to develop legally correct and educationally useful programs.* Verona, WI: Attainment.

Bau, A. M. (1999). Providing culturally competent services to visually impaired persons. *Journal of Visual Impairment & Blindness, 93,* 291–297.

Bauer, E. J., Lurie, N., Yeh, C., & Grant, E. N. (1999). Screening for asthma in an inner city elementary school in Minneapolis, MN. *Journal of School Health, 69,* 12–16.

Bauwens, J., & Hourcade, J. J. (1995). *Cooperative teaching: Re-building the schoolhouse for all students.* Austin, TX: Pro-Ed.

Bauwens, J., Hourcade, J., & Friend, M. (1989). Cooperative teaching: A model for general and special education integration. *Remedial and Special Education, 10*(2), 17–22.

Beigel, A. R. (2000). Assistive technology assessment: More than a device. *Intervention in School and Clinic, 55*(4), 237–243.

Beirne-Smith, M., Ittenbach, R. F., & Patton, J. R. (2006). *Mental retardation* (7th ed.). Upper Saddle River, NJ: Prentice-Hall/Merrill.

Bender, W. N. (1995). *Learning disabilities: Characteristics, identification, and teaching strategies* (2nd ed.). Boston: Allyn and Bacon.

Bender, W. N. (2001a). *Learning disabilities: Characteristics, identification, and teaching strategies* (4th ed.). Boston: Allyn and Bacon.

Bender, W. N. (2001b). Previous school violence by identified kids in trouble. *Intervention, 37,* 105–111.

Bender, W. N. (2003). *Relational discipline: Strategies for in-your-face kids.* Boston: Allyn and Bacon.

Bender, W. N., Vail, C. D., & Scott, K. (1995). Teachers attitudes toward mainstreaming. *Journal of Learning Disabilities, 28*(2), 84–90.

Bergland, M., & Hoffbauer, D. (1996). New opportunities for students with traumatic brain injury: Transition to postsecondary education. *Teaching Exceptional Children, 28,* 54–57.

Best, S. J. (2006). Physical disabilities. In S. J. Best, K. W. Heller, & J. L. Bigge (Eds.), *Teaching individuals with physical or multiple disabilities* (5th ed., pp. 31–58). Columbus, OH: Pearson/Merrill.

Best, S. J. (2006). Health impairments and infectious diseases. In S. J. Best, K. W. Heller, & J. L. Bigge (Eds.), *Teaching individuals with physical or multiple disabilities* (5th ed., pp. 59–85). Columbus, OH: Pearson/Merrill.

Best, S. J. & Bigge, J. L. (2006). Cerebral palsy. In S. J. Best, K. W. Heller, & J. L. Bigge (Eds.), *Teaching individuals with physical or multiple disabilities* (5th ed., pp. 87–109). Columbus, OH: Pearson/Merrill.

Beukelman, D. R., & Mirenda, P. (1998). *Augmentative and alternative communication* (2nd ed.). Baltimore, MD: Brookes.

Biederman, J., Faraone, S. V., Mick, E., Spencer, T., Wilens, T., Kiely, K. I., et al. (1995). High risk for attention-deficit/hyperactivity disorder of parents with childhood onset of the disorder: A pilot study. *American Journal of Psychiatry, 152,* 431–435.

Biklen, D. (1990). Communication unbound: Autism and praxis. *Harvard Educational Review, 60*(3), 291–314.

Biklen, D., Morton, M. W., Gold, D., Berrigan, C., & Swaminathan, S. (1992). Facilitated communication: Implications for individuals with autism. *Topics in Language Disorders, 2,* 23.

Blackman, H. P. (1989). Special education placement: Is it what you know or where you live? *Exceptional Children, 55,* 459–462.

Blanton, L. P., Blanton, S. D., & Cross, F. L. (1994). An exploratory study of how general and special education teachers think and make instructional decisions about students with special needs. *Teacher Education and Special Education, 17*(1), 62–74.

Blatt, B. (1987). *The conquest of mental retardation.* Austin, TX: Pro-Ed.

Bloom, T. (1996). Assistive listening devices. *The Hearing Journal, 49,* 20–23.

Boardman, A. G., Arguelles, M., Vaughn, S., Hughes, M., & Klinger, J. (2005). Special education teachers' views of research-based practices. *Journal of Special Education, 39*(3), 168–180.

Bolt, S. E., & Thurlow, M. L. (2004). Five of the most frequently allowed testing accommodations in state policy: Synthesis of research. *Remedial and Special Education, 25,* 141–152.

Bos, C.S. & Vaughn, S. (2002). *Strategies for teaching students with learning and behavior problems* (5th ed.). Boston: Allyn and Bacon.

Bowman, B. T. (1994). The challenge of diversity. *Phi Delta Kappan, 76,* 218–224.

Brandes, J. A. (2005). Partner with parents. *Intervention in School and Clinic, 41,* 52–54.

Breeding, M., Stone, C., & Riley, K. (n.d.) *LINC: Language in the classroom.* Unpublished manuscript. Abilene, TX: Abilene Independent School District.

Brice, A. E. (2002). *The Hispanic child: Speech, language, culture, and education.* Boston: Allyn and Bacon.

Brody, J., & Good, T. (1986). Teacher behavior and student achievement. In M. C. Wittrock (Ed.), *Handbook of research on teaching* (pp. 328–375). New York: Macmillan.

Brolin, D. E. (1989). *Life-centered career education.* Reston, VA: CEC.

Broun, L., & Umbarger, G. (2005). *Considerations on the use of medications with people who have autism spectrum disorder.* Position Paper. Division on Developmental Disabilities.

Brown, D. L., & Moore, L. (1992). The Bama bookworm program: Motivating remedial readers to read at home with their parents. *Teaching Exceptional Children, 24,* 17–20.

Brown, J., Cohen, P., Johnson, J. G., & Salzinger, S. (1998). A longitudinal analysis of risk factors for child maltreatment: Findings of a 17-year prospective study of officially recorded and self-reported child abuse and neglect. *Child Abuse & Neglect, 22,* 1065–1078.

Brown, M. R., Higgins, K., & Paulsen, K. (2003). Adolescent alienation: What is it and what can educators do about it? *Intervention in School and Clinic, 39*(1), 3–9.

Bryan, T. (1999). Reflections on a research career: It ain't over til it's over. *Exceptional Children, 65*(4), 438–447.

Bryan, T., Bay, M., & Donahue, M. (1988). Implications of the learning disabilities definition for the regular education initiative. *Journal of Learning Disabilities, 21*(1), 23–27.

Bryan, T., Bay, M., Lopez-Reyna, N., & Donahue, M. (1991). Characteristics of students with learning disabilities: A summary of the extant database and its implications for educational programs. In J. W. Lloyd, N. N. Singh, & A. C. Repp (Eds.), *The regular education initiative: Alternative perspectives* (pp. 121–131). Sycamore, IL: Sycamore.

Bryan, T., Burstein, K., & Ergul, C. (2004). The social-emotional side of learning disabilities: A science-based presentation of the art. *Learning Disabilities Quarterly, 27*(1), 45–51.

Bryan, T. A., & Sullivan-Burstein, K. (1998). Teacher selected strategies for improving homework completion. *Remedial and Special Education, 19,* 263–273.

Bryant, D. P., & Bryant, B. R. (2003). Vocabulary instruction for students with learning disabilities. *Learning Disability Quarterly, 26*(2), 117–128.

Bryant, D. P., Patton, J. R., & Vaughn, S. (2002). *Step-by-step guide for including students with disabilities in statewide assessment.* Austin, TX: Pro-Ed.

Bryant, D. P., Ugel, N., Thompson, S., & Hamff, A. (1999). Instructional strategies for content-area reading instruction. *Intervention in School and Clinic, 34*(5), 293.

Buck, G. H., Bursuck, W. D., Polloway, E. A., Nelson, J., Jayanthi, M., & Whitehouse, F. A. (1996). Homework-related communication problems: Perspectives of special educators. *Journal of Emotional and Behavioral Disorders, 4,* 105–113.

Buck, G. H., Fad, K., Patton, J. R., & Polloway, E. A. (2003). *Pre-referral intervention resource guide*. Austin, TX: Pro-Ed.

Buck, G. H., Polloway, E. A., Kirkpatrick, M. A., Patton, J. R., & Fad, K. (1999). Developing intervention plans: A sequential approach. *Intervention, 36*, 3–9.

Buck, G. H., Polloway, E. A., Patton, J. R., & McConnell, K. (in press). *The pre-referral guide*. Austin, TX: Pro-Ed.

Buck, G. H., Wilcox-Cook, K., Polloway, E. A., & Smith-Thomas, A. (2002). *Pre-referral intervention processes: A survey of practices*. Manuscript submitted for publication.

Budgar, L. (2001). Say again: Stuttering may be more than a case of nerves. *Psychology Today, 34*(6), 16.

Bullock, L. (1992). *Exceptionalities in children and youth*. Boston: Allyn and Bacon.

Bullock, L. M., Zagar, E. L., Donahue, C. A., & Pelton, G. B. (1985). Teachers' perceptions of behaviorally disordered students in a variety of settings. *Exceptional Children, 52*, 123–130.

Bureau of Labor Statistics, U.S. Department of Labor. *Occupational Outlook Handbook, 2006–07 Edition: Speech–Language Pathologists*. Retrieved October 8, 2006 from http://www.bls.gov/oco/ocos099.htm.

Burnley, G. D. (1993). A team approach for identification for an attention deficit hyperactivity disorder child. *The School Counselor, 40*, 228–230.

Burns, B. J., Hoagwood, K., & Maultsby, L. T. (1999). Improving outcomes for children and adolescents with serious emotional and behavioral disorders: Current and future directions. In M. H. Epstein, K. Kutash, & A. Duchnowski (Eds.), *Outcomes for children and youth with behavioral and emotional disorders in their families: Programs and evaluation of best practices* (pp. 685–707). Austin, TX: Pro-Ed.

Burstein, K., Chao, P., Bryant, T., & Erqul, C. (2006). Family-centered interventions for young children at-risk for language and behavior problems. *Early Childhood Education Journal, 34*(2), 147–153.

Burstein, N., Sears, S., Wilcoxen, A., Cabello, B., Spagra, M. (2004). Moving toward inclusive practices. *Remedial and Special Education, 25*(2), 104–116.

Bursuck, W., Harniss, M. K., Epstein, M. H., Polloway, E. A., Jayanthi, M., & Wissinger, L. M. (in press). Solving communication problems about homework: Recommendations of special education teachers. *Learning Disabilities Research & Practice*.

Bursuck, W., Munk, D., & Olson, M. (1999). The fairness of report card grading adaptations: What do students with and without disabilities think? *Remedial and Special Education, 20*, 84–92, 105.

Bursuck, W., Polloway, E., Epstein, M., & Jayanthi, M. (n.d.). *Recommendations of general education teachers regarding communication problems about homework and students with disabilities*. Manuscript in preparation.

Bursuck, W. D., Polloway, E. A., Plante, L., Epstein, M. H., Jayanthi, M., & McConeghy, J. (1996). Report card grading and adaptations: A national survey of classroom practices. *Exceptional Children, 62*, 301–318.

Bussing, R., Zima, B., Perwien, A. R., Belin, T. R., & Widawski, M. (1998). Children in special education programs: Attention deficit hyperactivity disorder, use of services, and unmet needs. *American Journal of Public Health 88*(6), 880–886.

Butera, G., Klein, H., McMullen, L., & Wilson, B. (1998). A statewide study of FAPE and school discipline policies. *The Journal of Special Education, 32*, 108–114.

Callahan, C. M., & McIntire, J. A. (1994). *Identifying outstanding talent in American Indian and Alaska native students*. Washington, DC: Office of Educational Research and Improvement.

Callahan, K., Redemacher, R., & Hildreth, T. A. (1998). The effectiveness of parent participation in strategies to improve homework performance of students at risk. *Remedial and Special Education, 19*, 131–141.

Cantrell, M. L. (1992). Guest editorial. *Journal of Emotional and Behavioral Problems, 1*, 4.

Cantu, N. (1993). OCR clarifies evaluation requirements for ADD. *The Special Educator, 9*(1), 11–12.

Carbone, E. (2001). Arranging the classroom with an eye (and ear) to students with ADHD. *Teaching Exceptional Children, 34*, 72–81.

Carlson, E., Brauen, M., Klein, S., Schroll, K., & Willig, S. (2002). *SPeNSE: Key findings*. Retrieved October 8, 2006 from *http://www.spense.org/Results.html*.

Carnegie Council on Adolescent Development. (1989). *Turning point: Preparing American youth for the 21st century*. New York: Carnegie.

Carnine, D., Silbert J., & Kameenui, E. J. (1990). *Direct instruction reading* (2nd ed.). Columbus, OH: Merrill.

Caroley, J. F., & Foley, T. E. (2001). Enhancing the quality of mathematics for students with learning disabilities: Illustrations from subtraction learning disabilities. *Learning Disabilities: A Multidisciplinary Journal, 12*(2), 47–59.

Carpenter, S. L., & McKee-Higgins, E. (1996). Behavior management in inclusive classrooms. *Remedial and Special Education, 17*, 195–203.

Carr, E. G., Dozier, C. L., Patel, M. R. (2002). Treatment of automatic resistance to extinction. *Research in Developmental Disabilities, 23*, 61–78.

Carroll, D. (2001). Consider paraeducator training roles and responsibilities. *Teaching Exceptional Children, 34*, 60–64.

Cascella, P. W., & McNamara, K. (2005). Empowering students with severe disabilities to actualize communication skills. *Teaching Exceptional Children, 37*, 38–43.

Cawley, J. (1984). *Developmental teaching of mathematics for the learning disabled*. Austin, TX: Pro-Ed.

Center for Teaching and Learning. (1986). Thirty years of NICHD research: What we now know about how children learn to read. *Effective School Practices, 15*(3), 33–46.

Centers for Disease Control. (1988). *AIDS surveillance report*. Atlanta, GA: Author.

Centers for Disease Control. (1997). AIDS among children—United States, 1996. *Journal of School Health, 67*, 175–177.

Chalfant, J. C., & Van Dusen Pysh, R. L. (1993). Teacher assistance teams: Implications for the gifted. In C. J. Maker (Ed.), *Critical issues in gifted education:. Programs for the gifted in regular classrooms* (Vol. 3, pp. 32–48). Austin, TX: Pro-Ed.

Chamberlain, S. P. (2003). An interview with Evelyn Green and Perry Green. *Intervention in School and Clinic, 38*(5), 297–0306.

Chamberlain, S. P. (2005). Recognizing and responding to cultural differences in the education of culturally and linguistically diverse learners. *Intervention in School and Clinic, 40*(4), 195–211.

Chamberlain, S. P. (2006). An interview with Don Deshler: Perspectives on teaching students with learning disabilities. *Intervention in School and Clinic, 41*(5), 302–306.

Chan, A. S., Cheung, J., Leung, W. W., Cheung, R., & Chueng, M. (2005). Verbal expression and comprehension deficits in young children with autism. *Focus on Autism and Other Developmental Disabiliteis 20*(2), 117–124.

Cheney, C. O. (1989). The systematic adaptation of instructional materials and techniques for problem learners. *Academic Therapy, 25*, 25–30.

Chiriboga, D. A., & Catron, L. S. (1991). *Divorce*. New York: University Press.

Choate, J. S. (2002). *Successful inclusive teaching: Proven ways to determine and correct special needs* (3rd ed.). Boston: Allyn and Bacon.

Choudhury, N., & Benasich, A. A. (2003). A family aggregation study: the influence of family history and other risk factors on language development. *Journal of Speech Language, Hearing Research, 46*(2): 261–272.

Christenson, S. L., Ysseldyke, J. E., & Thurlow, M. L. (1989). Critical instructional factors for students with mild handicaps: An integrative review. *Remedial and Special Education, 10*(5), 21–31.

Christian, B. T. (1999). *Outrageous behavior model*. Austin, TX: Pro-Ed.

Christiansen, J., & Vogel, J. R. (1998). A decision model for grading students with disabilities. *Teaching Exceptional Children, 31*(2), 30–35.

Clark, B. (2002). *Growing up gifted: Developing the potential of children at home and at school* (6th ed.). Upper Saddle River, NJ: Merrill/Prentice-Hall.

Clark, J. G., & Jaindl, M. (1996). Conductive hearing loss in children: Etiology and pathology. In F. N. Martin & J. G. Clark (Eds.), *Hearing care for children* (pp. 45–72). Boston: Allyn and Bacon.

Clark, S. G. (2000). The IEP process as a tool for collaboration. *Teaching Exceptional Children, 33*, 56–66.

Clarkson, W. P. Beautiful minds. *American School Board Journal, 190*(8), 24–28.

Clary, D. L., & Edwards, S. (1992). Spoken language. In E. A. Polloway, J. R. Patton, J. S. Payne, & R. A. Payne (Eds.), *Strategies for teaching learners with special needs* (4th ed., pp. 185–285). Columbus, OH: Merrill.

Clayton, J., Burdge, M., Denham, A., Kleinert, H. L., & Kearns, J. (2006). A four-step process for accessing the general curriculum for students with significant cognitive disabilities. *Teaching Exceptional Children, 38*, 20–27.

Cline, S., & Schwartz, D. (1999). *Diverse populations of gifted children*. Boston: Allyn and Bacon.

Clinkenbeard, P. R. (1991). Unfair expectations: A pilot study of middle school students' comparisons of gifted and regular classes. *Journal for the Education of the Gifted, 15*, 56–63.

Cohen, L. G., & Spenciner, L. J., (2007). *Assessment of children and youth with special needs*. Boston: Allyn & Bacon.

Colangelo, N., & Davis, G. A. (Eds.). (1997). *Handbook of gifted education* (2nd ed.). Boston: Allyn and Bacon.

Colangelo, N., & Davis, G. A. (Eds.). (2003). *Handbook of gifted education* (3rd ed.). Boston: Allyn and Bacon.

Colarusso, R. P., Keel, M. C., & Dangel, H. L. (2001). A comparison of eligibility criteria and their impact on minority representation in learning disabilities programs. *Learning Disabilities Research and Practice, 16*(1), 1–17.

Coleman, L. J., & Cross, T. L. (2001). *Being gifted in school: An introduction to developing, guidance, and teaching*. Austin, TX: Pro-Ed.

Coleman, M. C., & Webber, J. (2002). *Emotional and behavioral disorders: Theory and practice* (4th ed.). Boston: Allyn and Bacon.

Collins, B. C., Hendricks, T. B., Fetko, K., & Land, L. A. (2002). Student-2-student learning in inclusive classrooms. *Teaching Exceptional Children, 34,* 56–61.

Conderman, G., Ikan, P. A., & Hatcher, R. E. (2000). Student-led conferences in inclusive settings. *Intervention in School and Clinic, 36,* 22–26.

Conderman, G., & Katsiyannis, A. (2002). Instructional issues in secondary special education. *Remedial and Special Education, 23,* 163–171.

Condition of education. (1990). Washington, DC: Office of Educational Research and Improvement.

Conroy, E. (1993). Strategies for counseling with parents. *Elementary School Guidance and Counseling, 29,* 60–66.

Conte, R. (1991). Attention disorders. In B. Y. L. Wong (Ed.), *Learning about learning disabilities* (pp. 55–101). New York: Academic Press.

Conyers, C., Martin, T.L., Martin, G.L., & Yu, D. (2002). The 1983 AAMR Manual, the 1992 AAMR Manual, or the Developmental Disabilities Act: Which Do Researchers Use? *Education and Training in Mental Retardation and Developmental Disabilities, 37*(3), 310–316.

Cooper, H. (1989). *Homework.* White Plains, NY: Longman.

Copeland, S. R., Hughes, C., Carter, E. W., Guth, C., Presley, J. A. Williams, et al. (2004). Increasing access to general education: Perspectives of participants in a high school peer support program. *Remedial and Special Education, 25*(6), 341–351.

Cotler, S. (1986). Epidemiology and outcome. In J. M. Reisman (Ed.), *Behavior disorders in infants, children, and adolescents* (pp. 196–211). New York: Random House.

Council for Exceptional Children. (1992). *Children with ADD: A shared responsibility.* Reston, VA: Author.

Council for Exceptional Children. (1997a). A disability or a gift? *CEC Today, 4*(3), 7.

Council for Exceptional Children. (1997b). Effective accommodations for students with exceptionalities. *CEC Today, 4*(3), 1, 9, 15.

Council for Exceptional Children. (1999). The hidden problem among students with exceptionalities—depression. *CEC Today, 5*(5), 1, 5, 15.

Council of Administrators in Special Education. (1992). *Student access: Section 504 of the Rehabilitation Act of 1973.* Reston, VA: Author.

Coutinho, M. J. & Oswald, D. P. (2005). State variation in gender disproportional in special education: Findings and recommendations, *Remedial and Special Education, 26*(1), 7–15.

Coutinho, M. J., & Repp, A. C. (1999). *Inclusion: The integration of students with disabilities.* Belmont, CA: Wadsworth.

Coyne, M.D., Zipoli, R.P., & Ruby, M.F. (2006). Beginning reading instruction for students at-risk for reading disabilities. *Intervention, 41*(3) 161–168.

Cozzins, G., Dowdy, C. A., & Smith, T. E. C. (1999). *Adult agencies.* Austin: TX: Pro-Ed.

Craig, C., Hough, D. L., & Churchwell, C. (2001). A statewide study on the literacy of students with visual impairments. *Journal of Visual Impairments and Blindness, 96,* 452–455.

Craig, S., Hull, K., Haggart, A. G., & Crowder, E. (2001). Storytelling addressing the literacy needs of diverse learners. *Teaching Exceptional Children, 33*(5), 46–51.

Cramer, S. (1998). *Collaboration: A successful strategy for special education.* Boston: Allyn and Bacon.

Crane, L. (2002). *Mental retardation: A community integration approach.* Belmont, CA: Thomson Publishing.

Crawford, H. (1998). Classroom acoustics: Creating favorable environments for learning. *ADVANCE for Speech-Language Pathologists & Audiologists, 36,* 25–27.

Crawford, V. (2002). *Embracing the monster: Overcoming the challenges of hidden disabilities.* Baltimore, MD: Brookes.

Crews, W. D., Bonaventura, S., Hay, C. L., Steele, W. K., & Rowe, F. B. (1993). Gilles de la Tourette disorder among individuals with severe or profound mental retardation. *Mental Retardation, 31,* 25–28.

Cross, T. L. (2005). Moving the discussion from patholoty to context: An interview with Laurence J. Coleman. *Roeper Review, 28*(1), p. 5.

Cullinan, D., & Epstein, M. (1985). Teacher related adjustment problems. *Remedial and Special Education, 6,* 5–11.

Cullinan, D. & Sabornie, E. J. (2004). Characteristics of emotional disturbance in middle and high school students. *Journal of Emotional and Behavioral Disorders, 12*(3), 157–167.

Cummings, C. (1983). *Managing to teach.* Edmonds, WA: Teaching Inc.

Cunningham, A. E., & Stanovich, K. E. (1997). Early reading acquisition and its relationship to reading ability ten years later. *Developmental Psychology, 33,* 934–945.

Dabkowski, D. M. (2004). Encouraging active parent participation in IEP team meetings. *Teaching Exceptional Children, 36,* 34–39.

Dagenais, P. A., Critz-Crosby, P., Fletcher, S. G., & McCutcheon, M. J. (1994). Comparing abilities of children with profound hearing impairments to learn consonants using electropalatography or traditional aural–oral techniques. *Journal of Speech and Hearing Research, 37,* 687–699.

Daly, D. A. (1991, April). *Multi-modal therapy for fluency clients: Strategies that work.* Paper presented at the Spring Convention of the Texas Speech-Language-Hearing Association, Houston, TX.

Davis, C. N., & Harris, T. B. (1992). Teachers' ability to accurately identify disordered voices. *Language, Speech, and Hearing Services in Schools, 23,* 136–140.

Davis, G. A., & Rimm, S. B. (1998). *Education of the gifted and talented* (4th ed.). Boston: Allyn and Bacon.

Davis, J. (1996). Two different flight plans: Advanced placement and gifted programs—different and necessary. *Gifted Child Today, 19*(2), 32–36, 50.

Davis, W. E. (1993). *At-risk children and educational reform: Implications for educators and schools in the year 2000 and beyond.* Orono, ME: College of Education, University of Maine.

Davis, W. E. (1995). Students at risk: Common myths and misconceptions. The *Journal of At-Risk Issues, 2,* 5–10.

deBettencourt, L. U. (1987). How to develop parent relationships. *Teaching Exceptional Children, 19,* 26–27.

Del Prete, T. (1996). Asset or albatross? The education and socialization of gifted students. *Gifted Child Today, 19*(2), 24–25, 44–49.

Delpit, L. (2006). Lessons from teachers. *Journal of Teacher Education, 57,* 220–231.

Denning, C. B., Chamberlain, J. A., & Polloway, E. A. (2000). An evaluation of state guidelines for mental retardation: Focus on definition and classification practices. *Education and Training in Mental Retardation and Developmental Disabilities, 35,* 135–144.

Denbo, S. J., & Beaulieu, L. M. (2002). *Improving schools for African Americans: A reader for educational leaders.* Springfield, IL: Charles C. Thomas.

Deno, E. (1970). Special education as development capital. *Exceptional Children, 55,* 440–447.

Deno, S. L., Foegen, A., Robinson, S., & Espin, C. (1996). Commentary: Facing the realities of inclusion for students with mild disabilities. *Journal of Special Education, 30,* 345–357.

Deshler, D. (2005). Adolescents with learning disabilities. *Learning Disabilities Quarterly, 28*(2), 122–123.

Deshler, D., & Schumaker, J. B. (1988). Learning strategies: An instructional alternative for low-achieving adolescents. *Exceptional Children, 52,* 83–89.

Deshler, D. D., Ellis, E. S., & Lenz, B. K. (1996). *Teaching adolescents with learning disabilities: Strategies and methods* (2nd ed.). Denver, CO: Love.

Deshler, D. D., & Lenz, B. K. (1989). The strategies instructional approach. *International Journal of Disability, Development, and Education, 36*(3), 203–224.

Desrochers, J. (1999). Vision problems—How teachers can help. *Young Children, 54,* 36–38.

Devlin, S. D., & Harber, M. M. (2004). Collaboration among parents and professionals with discrete trial training in the treatment for autism. *Education and Training in Developmental Disabilities, 39,* 291–300.

Diana v. State Board of Education, C-70-37 R.F.P. (N.D., California, Jan. 7, 1970, and June 18, 1972).

Diefendorf, A. O. (1996). Hearing loss and its effects. In F. N. Martin & J. G. Clark (Eds.), *Hearing care for children* (pp. 3–18). Boston: Allyn and Bacon.

Disability Rights Advocates (2001). *Do no harm: High stakes testing and students with learning disabilities.* Oakland, CA: Author.

Dobbs, F., & Black P., (2004). Assistive technology use and stigma. *Education and Training in Developmental Disabilities, 39*(3), 216–217.

Dobbs, R. F., Primm, E. B., & Primm, B. (1991). Mediation: A common sense approach for resolving conflicts in education. *Focus on Exceptional Children, 24,* 1–12.

Dorn, L., & Allen, A. (1995). Helping low-achieving first-grade readers: A program combining reading recovery tutoring and small-group instruction. *Journal of School Research and Information, 13,* 16–24.

Dover, W. F. (2005). Consult and support students with special needs in inclusive classrooms. *Intervention, 41,* 36–38.

Dowdy, C. A. (1998). Strengths and limitations inventory: School version. In C. A. Dowdy, J. R. Patton, T. E. C. Smith, & E. A. Polloway (Eds.), *Attention deficit/hyperactivity disorder in the classroom: A practical guide for teachers.* Austin, TX: Pro-Ed.

Dowdy, C. A., Carter, J., & Smith, T. E. C. (1990). Differences in transitional needs of high school students with and without learning disabilities. *Journal of Learning Disabilities, 23*(6), 343–348.

Dowdy, C. A., Patton, J. R., Smith, T. E. C., & Polloway, E. A. (1998). *Attention deficit/hyperactivity disorders in the classroom.* Austin, TX: Pro-Ed.

Downing, J. A. (2002). Individualized behavior contracts. *Intervention, 37,* 164–172.

Downing, J. E., & Chen, D. (2003). Using tactile strategies with students who are blind and have severe disabilities. *Teaching Exceptional Children, 36,* 56–61.

Downing, J. E., & Eichinger, J. (2003). Creating learning opportunities for students with severe disabilities in inclusive classrooms. *Teaching Exceptional Children, 36,* 26–31.

Doyle, W. (1986). Classroom organization and management. In M. C. Wittrock (Ed.), *Handbook of research and teaching* (3rd ed., pp. 392–431). New York: Macmillan.

Drasgow, E., Yell, M. L., & Robinson, T. (2001). Developing legally correct and educationally appropriate IEPs. *Remedial and Special Education, 22,* 359–373.

Drug use increasing. (1992). *Youth Today, 1,* 27–29.

Duane, D. D., & Gray, D. B. (Eds.) (1991). *The reading brain: The biological basis of dyslexia.* Parkton, MD: York.

Duhaney, L. M. G., & Salend, S. J. (2000). Parental perceptions of inclusive educational placements. *Remedial and Special Education, 21,* 121–128.

Dunn, C., Chambers, D., & Rabren, K. (2004). *Remedial and Special Education, 25*(5), 314–323.

Dunn, L. M. (1968). Special education for the mildly handicapped: Is much of it justifiable? *Exceptional Children, 35,* 5–22.

Dunst, C. J., Johanson, C., Trivette, C. M., & Hamby, D. (1991). Family-oriented early intervention policies and practices: Family-centered or not? *Exceptional Children, 58,* 115–126.

DuPaul, G. J., & Eckert, T. L. (1998). Academic interventions for students with attention-deficit/hyperactivity disorder: A review of the literature. *Reading and Writing Quarterly, 14*(1), 59–83.

Dyches, T. (1998). The effectiveness of switch training on communication of children with autism and severe disabilities. *Focus on Autism and Other Developmental Disabilities, 13,* 151–162.

Easterbrooks, S. R. (1999). *Adapting regular classrooms for children who are deaf/hard of hearing.* Paper presented at the Council for Exceptional Children Convention, Minneapolis, MN.

Eaves, R. C. (1992). Autism. In P. J. McLaughlin & P. Wehman (Eds.), *Developmental disabilities* (pp. 68–80). Boston: Andover Medical.

Edmunds, A. L. (1999). Cognitive credit cards: Acquiring learning strategies. *Teaching Exceptional Children, March/April,* 68–73.

Edwards, C. (1996). Educational management of children with hearing loss. In F. N. Martin & J. G. Clark (Eds.), *Hearing care for children* (pp. 303–315). Boston: Allyn and Bacon.

Egel, A. L. (1989). Finding the right educational program. In M. D. Powers (Ed.), *Children with autism: A parent's guide.* New York: Woodbine House.

Eggert, L. L., & Herting, J. R. (1993). Drug involvement among potential dropouts and "typical" youth. *Journal of Drug Education, 23,* 31–55.

Elders, J. (2002). Keynote address. 57th Annual Conference of the Association for Supervision and Curriculum Development, San Antonio, TX.

Elias, J. J. (2004). The connection between social-emotional learning and learning disabilities: Implications for intervention, *Learning Disabilities Quarterly, 27*(1), 53–63.

Elizer, E., & Kauffman, M. (1983). Factors influencing the severity of childhood bereavement reactions. *American Journal of Orthopsychiatry, 53,* 393–415.

Elksnin, L. K., Bryant, D. P., Gartland, D., King-Sears, M., Rosenberg, M. S., Scanlon, D., et al. (2001). LD summit: Important issues for the field of learning disabilities. *Learning Disability Quarterly, 24,* 297–305.

Elksnin, L. K., & Elksnin, N. (1998). Teaching social skills to students with learning and behavioral problems. *Intervention in School and Clinic, 33,* 131–140.

Ellenwood, A. E., & Felt, D. (1989). Attention-deficit/hyperactivity disorder: Management and intervention approaches for the classroom teacher. *LD Forum, 15,* 15–17.

Emerick, L. L., & Haynes, W. O. (1986). *Diagnosis and evaluation in speech pathology* (3rd ed.). Englewood Cliffs, NJ: Prentice-Hall.

Emery, R. E. (1989). Family violence. *American Psychologist, 44,* 321–327.

Engelmann, S., & Carnine, D. (1982). *Theory of instruction.* New York: Irvington.

Epilepsy Foundation of America. (1992). *Seizure recognition and observation: A guide for allied health professionals.* Landover, MD: Author.

Epstein, M. H. (1999). The development and the validation of a scale to assess the emotional and behavioral strengths of children–adolescents. *Remedial and Special Education, 20,* 258–262.

Epstein, M. H., & Charma, J. (1998). *Behavioral and emotional rating scale: A strength-based approach to assessment.* Austin, TX: Pro-Ed.

Epstein, M. H., Kutash, K., & Duchnowski, A. (2005). *Outcomes for children and youth with behavioral and emotional disorders and their families: Programs and evaluation of best practices.* Austin, TX: Pro-Ed.

Epstein, M. H., Munk, D. D., Bursuck, W. D., Polloway, E. A., & Jayanthi, M. M. (1999). Strategies for improving home-school communication problems about homework for students with disabilities: Perceptions of general educators. *Journal of Special Education, 33,* 166–176.

Epstein, M. H., Nelson, J. R., Trout, A. L., Mooney, P. (2005). Achievement and ED: Academic status and intervention research in outcomes for children and youth with emotional and behavioral disorders and their families. In M. H. Epstein, M. Kurash, and L. Duchnowski. *Outcomes for children and youth with emotional and behavioral disorders* (2nd ed.). Austin, TX: Pro-Ed.

Epstein, M. H., Patton, J. R., Polloway, E. A., & Foley, R. (1992). Educational services for students with behavior disorders: A review of individualized education programs. *Teacher Education and Special Education, 15,* 41–48.

Epstein, M. H., Polloway, E. A., Buck, G. H., Bursuck, W. D., Wissinger, L. M., Whitehouse, F., et al. Homework-related communication problems: Perspectives of general education teachers. *Learning Disabilities Research and Practice, 12,* 221–227.

Epstein, M. H., Polloway, E. A., Bursuck, W., Jayanthi, M., & McConeghy, J. (1996). *Recommendations for effective homework practices.* Manuscript in preparation.

Epstein, M. H., Polloway, E. A., Foley, R. M., & Patton, J. R. (1993). Homework: A comparison of teachers' and parents' perceptions of the problems experienced by students identified as having behavioral disorders, learning disabilities, or no disabilities. *Remedial and Special Education, 14*(5), 40–50.

Erickson, J. G. (1992, April). *Communication disorders in multicultural populations.* Paper presented at the Texas Speech–Language–Hearing Association Annual Convention, San Antonio, TX.

Erwin, E. J. (1993). The philosophy and status of inclusion. *The Lighthouse,* 1–4.

Etscheidt, S.K. (2006). Progress monitoring: Legal issues and recommendations for IEP teams. *Teaching Exceptional Children, 38,* 56–60.

Etscheidt, S. K., & Bartlett, L. (1999). The IDEA amendments: A four-step approach for determining supplementary aids and services. *Exceptional Children, 65,* 163–174.

Evertson, C. M., Emmer, E. T., & Worsham, M. E. (2006). *Classroom management Elementary teachers* (7th ed.). Boston: Allyn and Bacon.

Evertson, C. M., Emmer, E. T., Clements, B. J., Sanford, J. P., & Worsham, M. E. (2003). *Classroom management for elementary teachers* (6th ed.). Englewood Cliffs, NJ: Prentice-Hall.

Evertson, C. M., Emmer, E. T., Clements, B. J., Sanford, J. P., & Worsham, M. E. (2006). *Classroom management for elementary teachers* (4th ed.). Englewood Cliffs, NJ: Prentice-Hall.

Fad, K., Patton, J. R., & Polloway, E. A. (2006). *Behavioral intervention planning: Completing a functional behavioral assessment and developing a behavioral intervention plan* (2nd ed.). Austin, TX: Pro-Ed.

Faraone, S. V. & Doyle, A. E. (2001). The nature and heritability of attention-deficit/hyperactivity disorder. *Child and Adolescent Psychiatric Clinics of North America, 10,* 299–316.

Favazza, P. C., Phillipsen, L., Kumar, P. (2000). Measuring and promoting acceptance of young children with disabilities. *Exceptional Children, 66,* 491–508.

Federal Register, 42, 42478.

Federal Register, 58, 48952.

Fedorowitz, C., Benezra, E., MacDonald, W., McElgunn, B., Wilson, A., & Kaplan, B. (2001). Neurological brains of learning disabilities: An update. *Learning Disabilities Association Multidisciplinary Journal, 11,* 1–74.

Feiring, C., Taska, L., & Lewis, M. (1999). Age and gender differences in children's and adolescents' adaptation to sexual abuse. *Child Abuse & Neglect, 23,* 115–126.

Feldhusen, H. J. (1993a). Individualized teaching of the gifted in regular classrooms. In C. J. Maker (Ed.), *Critical issues in gifted education: Programs for the gifted in regular classrooms* (Vol. 3, pp. 263–273). Austin, TX: Pro-Ed.

Feldhusen, H. J. (1993b). Synthesis of research on gifted youth. *Educational Leadership, 22,* 6–11.

Feldhusen, J. F. (1999). Programs for the gifted few or talent development for the many. *Phi Delta Kappan, 79,* 735–738.

Felner, R., Ginter, M., Boike, M., & Cowan, E. (1981). Parental death or divorce and the school adjustment of young children. *American Journal of Community Psychology, 9,* 181–191.

Ficker-Terrill, C. (2001, May–June). Perhaps the time has come to change our name. *American Association on Mental Retardation News and Notes, 14*(3), 3.

Final regulations for IDEA. (1999). Washington, DC: U.S. Government Printing Office.

Finn, C. E., Rotherham, A. J., Hokanson, C. R. (2002). *Rethinking special education for a new century.* Washington, DC: Fordham Foundation.

Fiore, T. A., Becker, E. A., & Nerro, R. C. (1993). Educational interventions for students with attention deficit disorder. *Exceptional Children, 60,* 163–173.

Fisher, D., Frey, N., & Thousand, J. (2003). What do special educators need to know and be prepared to do for inclusive schooling to work? *Teacher Education and Special Education, 26*(1), 42–50.

Fisher, S., Clark, G. M., & Patton, J. R. (in press). *Understanding occupational vocabulary.* Austin, TX: Pro-Ed.

Fisher, D., Pumpian, I., & Sax, C. (1998). Parent and caregiver impressions of different educational models. *Remedial and Special Education, 19,* 173–180.

Fitzgerald, J. L., & Watkins, M. W. (2006). Parents' rights in special education: The readability of procedural safeguards. *Exceptional Children, 72,* 497–510.

Fleming, J. L., Monda-Amaya, L. E., (2001). Process variables critical for team effectiveness. *Remedial and Special Education, 22,* 158–171.

Fletcher, J. M., Lyon, G. R., Barnes, M., Stuebing, K. K., Francis, D. J., Olson, R. K., et al. (2001). *Classification of learning disabilities: An evidence-based evaluation.* Paper presented at the LD Summit, Washington, D.C.

Flick, G. L. (1998). Managing AD/HD in the classroom minus medication. *Education Digest, 63*(9), 50–56.

Foorman, B. R., & Torgeson, J. (2001). Critical elements of classroom and small group instruction promoting reading success in all children. *Research and Practice, 16,* 203–212.

Ford, A., Pugach, M. C., & Otis-Wilborn, A. (2001). Preparing general educators to work well with students who have disabilities: What's reasonable at the preservice level? *Learning Disability Quarterly, 24,* 275–285.

Forness, S. R. (1999). Stimulant medication revisited: Effective treatment of children with attention deficit disorder. *Journal of Emotional and Behavior Problems, 7,* 230–233.

Forness, S. R. (2001). Special education and related services: What have we learned from meta-analysis? *Exceptionality, 9,* 185–197.

Forness, S. R., & Kavale, K. A. (1988). Planning for the needs of children with serious emotional disturbance: The National Mental Health and Special Education Coalition. *Behavior Disorders, 13,* 127–133.

Forness, S. R., & Polloway, E. A. (1987). Physical and psychiatric diagnoses of pupils with mild mental retardation currently being referred for related services. *Education and Training in Mental Retardation, 22,* 221–228.

Forness, S. R., Sweeney, D. P., & Toy, K. (1996). Psychopharmacologic medication: What teachers need to know. *Beyond Behavior, 7*(2) 4–11.

Forness, S. R., Walker, H. M., Kavale, K. A. (2003). Psychiatric disorders and treatments. *Teaching Exceptional Children, 36*(2), 42–49.

Foster-Johnson, L., & Dunlap, G. (1993). Using functional assessment to develop effective, individualized interventions for challenging behaviors. *Teaching Exceptional Children, 56,* 44–52.

Fowler, M. (1992a). Attention deficit disorder (NICHY briefing paper). Washington, DC: National Information Center for Children and Youth with Disabilities.

Fowler, M. (1992b). *C.H.A.D.D. educators manual: An in-depth look at attention deficit disorder for an educational perspective.* Fairfax, VA: CASET Associates, Ltd.

Fox, P., & Emerson, E. (2001). Socially valid outcomes of intervention for people with MR and challenging behavior: Views of different stakeholders. *Journal of Positive Behavior Interventions, 3*(3), 183–189.

Francis, D. J., Fletcher, J. M., Stuebing, K. K., Lyon, G. R., Shaywitz, B. A., & Shaywitz, S. E. (2005). Psychometric approaches to the identification of LD: IQ and achievement scores are not sufficient, *Journal of Learning Disabilities, 38*(2), 98–108.

French, N., & Gerlach, K. (1999). Paraeducators: Who are they and what do they do? *Teaching Exceptional Children, 32,* 65–69.

Friend, M. (1992). *Visionary leadership for today's schools.* Kansas City, KS: Center for Leadership Development.

Friend, M. (2000). Myths and misunderstandings about professional collaboration. *Remedial and Special Education, 21,* 130–132.

Friend, M. F., & Bursuck, W. D. (1999). *Including students with special needs: A practical guide for classroom teachers.* Boston: Allyn and Bacon.

Friend, M. F., & Bursuck, W. D. (2002). *Including students with special needs: A practical guide for classroom teachers* (3rd ed.) Boston: Allyn and Bacon.

Frymier, J., & Gansneder, B. (1989). The Phi Delta Kappa study of students at risk. *Phi Beta Kappan,. 71*(2), 142–146.

Fuchs, D., & Fuchs, L. S. (1994–1995). Sometimes separate is better. *Educational Leadership, 52,* 22–24.

Fuchs, D., & Fuchs, L.S. (2005). Peer assistance learning strategies. *Journal of Special Education, 39*(1) 34–44.

Fuchs, L. S., & Fuchs, D. (2001). Helping teachers formulate sound test accommodation decisions for students with learning disabilities. *Learning Disability Research and Practice, 16*(3), 174–181.

Fuchs, L. S., Fuchs, D., & Bishop, N. (1992). Instructional adaptations for students at-risk. *Journal of Educational Research, 86*(2), 66–74

Fuchs, D., Mock, D., Morgan, P. L., & Young, C. L. (2003). Responsiveness-to-intervention: Definitions, evidence, and implications for the learning disabilities construct. *Learning Disabilities Research and Practice, 18*(3), 157–171.

Fulk, B. M., & King, K. (2001). Classwide peer tutoring at work. *Teaching Exceptional Children, 34,* 49–54.

Fulk, B. M., & Montgomery-Grymes, D. J. (1994). Strategies to improve student motivation. *Intervention in School and Clinic, 30*(1), 28–33.

Furner, J. M., Dubby, M. L. Equity for all students. *Intervention, 38*(2), 67–74.

Furner, J. M., Yahya, N., & Duffy, M. A. (2005). Teach mathematics: Strategies to reach all students. *Intervention in School and Clinic, 41*(1), 16–23.

Gable, R. A., Arllen, N. L., & Hendrickson, J. M. (1994). Use of students with emotional/behavioral disorders as behavior change agents. *Education and Treatment of Children, 17,* 267–276.

Gallegos, A. Y., & Gallegos, M. L. (1990). A student's perspective on good teaching: Michael. *Intervention in School and Clinic, 26,* 14–15.

Garay, S. V. (2003). Listening to the voices of deaf students. *Teaching Exceptional Children, 35,* 56–61.

Garcia, J.N., & deCaso, A. M. (2004). Effects of a motivational intervention for improving the writing of children with learning disabilities. *Learning Disabilities Quarterly, 27,* 141–159.

Garcia, N., & deCaso, A. M. (2004). Effects of a motivational intervention for improving the writing of children with learning disabilities. *Learning Disability Quarterly, 27,* 141–159.

Garcia, S. B., & Guerra, P. L. (2004). Deconstructing deficit thinking: Working with educators to create more equitable learning environments. *Education and Urban Society, 36*(2), 150–168.

Gardner, H. (1983). *Frames of mind: The theory of multiple intelligences.* New York: Basic Books.

Gardner, H. (1993). *Multiple intelligences: The theory in practice.* New York: Basic Books.

Gardner, H., & Hatch, T. (1989). Multiple intelligences go to school: Educational implications of the theory of multiple intelligences. *Educational Researcher, 18*(8), 4–9.

Gargiulo, R. M. (1990). Child abuse and neglect: An overview. In R. L. Goldman & R. M. Gargiulo (Eds.), *Children at risk* (pp. 1–35). Austin, TX: Pro-Ed.

Gargiulo, R. M. (2003). *Special education in contemporary society.* Belmont, CA: Wadsworth.

Gargiulo, R. S., O'Sullivan, P., Stephens, D. G., & Goldman, R. (1989–1990). Sibling relationships in mildly handicapped children: A preliminary investigation. *National Forum of Special Education Journal, 1,* 20–28.

Garrick Duhaney, L. M. (2000). Culturally sensitive strategies for violence prevention. *Multicultural Education, 7*(4), 10–17.

Garrick Duhaney, L. M. (2003). A practical approach to managing the behaviors of students with ADD. *Intervention in School and Clinic, 38*(5), 267–279.

Gartin, B. C., & Murdick, N. L. (2001). A new IDEA mandate: The use of functional assessment of behavior and positive behavior supports. *Remedial and Special Education, 22,* 344–349.

Gartin, B. C., & Murdick, N. L. (2005). IDEA 2004: The IEP. *Remedial and Special Education, 26*(6), 327–331.

Gartland, D. (1994). Content area reading: Lessons from the specialists. *LD Forum, 19*(3), 19–22.

Gay, G. (2002). Preparing for culturally responsive teaching. *Journal of Teacher Education. 53*(2), 106–116.

Gay, I. (2003). The teacher makes it more explanable. *Reading Teacher, 56*(8), 812–814.

Gay, Lesbian, and Straight Education Network. (1999). *GLSEN's national school climate survey.* Washington, DC: Author.

General Accounting Office. (2005). IDEA data collected for the Department of Education.

Gerstein, R., Brengleman, S., & Jimenez, R. (1994). Effective instruction for culturally and linguistically diverse students: A reconceptualization. *Focus on Exceptional Children, 27*(1), 1–6.

Gersten, R., Jordan, N. C., & Flojo, J. R. (2005). Early identification and intervention for students with math difficulties. *Journal of Learning Disabilities, 38*(4), 293–304.

Getch, Y. Q., & Neuhart-Pritchett, S. (1999). Children with asthma: Strategies for educators. *Teaching Exceptional Children, 31,* 30–36.

Getty, L. A., & Summy, S. E. (2004). The course of due process. *Teaching Exceptional Children, 36,* 40–43.

Giangreco, M. F., Dennis, R., Cloninger, C., Edelman, S., & Schattman, R. (1993). I've counted Jon: Transformational experiences of teachers educating students with disabilities. *Exceptional Children, 59,* 359–372.

Giangreco, M. F., Dennis, R. E., & Edelman, S. W. (1994). *Creativity and collaborative teaming. A practical guide to employment. Remedial and Special Education, 15*(5), 288–296.

Giangreco, M. F., Edelman, S. W., Broer, S. M., & Doyle, M. B. (2001). Paraprofessional support of students with disabilities: Literature from the past decade. *Exceptional Children, 68,* 45–63.

Gillberg, C. (Ed.). (1989). *Diagnosis and treatment of autism.* New York: Plenum Press.

Ginsberg, R., Gerber, P. J., & Reiff, H. B. (1994). Employment success for adults with learning disabilities. In P. Gerber & H. Reiff (Eds.), *Learning disabilities in adulthood* (pp. 204–213). Stoneham, MA: Andover Medical Publishers.

Goldstein, S., & Goldstein, M. (1990). *Managing attention disorder in children: A guide for practitioners.* New York: John Wiley & Sons.

Gollnick, D. M., & Chinn, P.C. (2006). *Multicultural education in a pluralistic society* (7th ed.). Upper Saddle River, NJ: Prentice Hall.

Gomez, C.R., & Baird, S. (2005). Identifying early indicators for autism in self-regulated difficulties. *Journal of Autism and Other Developmental Disabilities, 20*(2), 106–116.

Gonzalez, V., Brusca-Vega, R., & Yawkey, T. (1997). *Assessment and instruction of culturally diverse students.* Boston: Allyn and Bacon.

Graham, S., Harris, K. R. & MacArthur, C. (2006) Cognitive strategy instruction. In C. MacArthur, S. Graham, & J. Ditgerald, (Eds.). *Handbook for writing research* (pp. 187–207). New York: Guildford.

Grant, J. (1993). Hearing-impaired children from Mexican-American homes. *Volta Review, 95*(5), 212–218.

Green, L. (2002). *African-American English.* Cambridge, UK: University Press.

Greenbaum, P. E., Dedrick, R. F., Friedman, R. M., Kutash, K., Brown, E. C., Lardieri, S. P., et al. (1998). National adolescent and child treatment study (NACTS): Outcomes for children with serious emotional behavioral disturbance. In M. H. Epstein, K. Kutash, & A. Duchnowski (Eds.), *Outcomes for children and youth with emotional and behavioral disorders and their families: Programs and evaluation of best practices* (pp. 21–54). Austin, TX: Pro-Ed.

Greenspan, S. (1996, October 11). *Everyday intelligence and a new definition of mental retardation.* Presented at Fifth Annual MRDD Conference, Austin, TX.

Greenspan, S. (in press). Functional concepts in mental retardation: Finding the natural essence of an artificial category. *Exceptionality.*

Greenwood, C. R., Arrega-Mayer, C., Utley, C. A., Gavin, B., & Terry, L. (2001). Classwide peer tutoring management system: Application with elementary-level English language learners. *Remedial and Special Education, 22,* 34–47.

Greer, J. V. (1991). At-risk students in the fast lanes: Let them through. *Exceptional Children, 57,* 390–391.

Gregory, R. J. (2004). *Psychological testing: History, principles, and applications* (4th ed.). Boston: Pearson.

Gresham, F. M. (1984). Social skills and self-efficacy for exceptional children. *Exceptional Children, 51,* 253–261.

Gresham, F. M. (2002). Responsiveness to Intervention. In Bradley, Danielson, & Hallahan (Eds.). Identification of Learning Disabilities: Research to Practice. Mahwah, NJ: Erlbaum.

Grigol, M., Neubert, D. A., & Moon, M. S. (2005). *Strategies for planning, implementation and evaluation.* Austin, TX: Pro-Ed.

Griswold, D. E., Barnhill, G. P., Myles, B. S. (2002). Asperger's syndrome and academic achievement. *Focus on Autism and Other Developmental Disabilities, 17,* 94–102.

Grosenick, J. K., George, N. L., George, M. P., & Lewis, T. J. (1991). Public school services for behaviorally disordered students: Program practices in the 1980s. *Behavioral Disorders, 16,* 87–96.

Grossman, H. J. (1983). *Classification in mental retardation.* Washington, DC: American Association on Mental Deficiency.

Guyer, B. (2000). Reaching and teaching the adolescent. In B. D. Guyer (Ed.), *ADHD: Achieving success in school and in life.* Boston: Allyn and Bacon.

Guyer B. D. (2002). So you have a learning disability: Do you have what it takes to succeed in college? *LDA Newsbriefs,* May/June, 3–5.

Hagner, D., & Cooney, B. F. (2005). I do that for everybody. *Focus on Autism and Other Developmental Disabilities, 20,* 92–99.

Haight, S. L., Patriarca, L. A., Burns, M. K. (2001). A statewide analysis of the eligibility criteria and procedures for determining learning disabilities. *Learning Disabilities, 11,* 39–46.

Hall, T. E., Wolfe, P. S., & Bollig, A. A. (2003). The home-to-school notebook: An effective communication strategy for students with severe disabilities. *Teaching Exceptional Children, 36,* 68–73.

Hallahan, D. P., & Kauffman, J. M. (2000). *Exceptional children: Introduction to special education* (8th ed.). Boston: Allyn and Bacon.

Hallahan, D. P., & Kauffman, J. M. (2003). *Exceptional children: Introduction to special education* (9th ed.). Boston: Allyn and Bacon.

Hallahan, D. P., Kauffman, J. M., & Lloyd, J. W. (1996). *Introduction to learning disabilities.* Boston: Allyn and Bacon.

Hallahan, D. P., Kauffman, J. M., & Lloyd, J. W. (1999). *Introduction to learning disabilities* (2nd ed.). Boston: Allyn and Bacon.

Hallahan, D. P., & Keogh, D. P. (2001). *Research and global perspectives in learning disabilities: Essays in honor of William M. Cruickshank.* Mahwah, NJ: Lawrence Erlbaum Associates.

Hallahan, D. P., Lloyd, J. W., Kauffman, J. M., Weiss, M. P., & Martinez, E. A. (2005). *Learning disabilities: Foundations, characteristics, and effective teaching* (3rd ed.). Boston: Allyn & Bacon.

Hallahan, D. P., Lloyd, J. W., & Stoller, L. (1982). *Improving attention with self-monitoring: A manual for teachers.* Charlottesville, VA: University of Virginia Press.

Hallahan, D. P., & Mercer, C. D. (2001). *Learning disabilities: Historical perspectives.* Paper presented at the 2001 LD Summit: Building a Foundation for the Future. Available on-line from www.air.org/ ldsummit.

Halvorsen, A. T., & Neary, T. (2001). *Building inclusive schools: Tools and strategies for success.* Boston: Allyn and Bacon.

Hamaguchi, P. A. (2002). *It's time to listen: Metacognitive activities for improving auditory processing in the classroom* (2nd ed.) Austin, TX: Pro-Ed.

Hammill, D. (2004). What we know about correlates of reading. *Exceptional Children, 70*(4), 453–468.

Hammill, D. D., & Bryant, B. R. (1991). The role of standardized tests in planning academic instruction. In H. L. Swanson (Ed.), *Handbook on the assessment of learning disabilities.* Austin, TX: Pro-Ed.

Hammill, D. D., & Bartel, N. R. (1995). *Teaching students with learning and behavior problems.* Austin, TX: Pro-Ed.

Hamre-Nietupski, S., Ayres, B., Nietupski, J., Savage, M., Mitchell, B., & Bramman,

H. (1989). Enhancing integration of students with severe disabilities through curricular infusion: A general/special educator partnership. *Education and Training in Mental Retardation, 24,* 78–88.

Hanks, J. A., & Velaski, A. (2003). A summertime collaboration between speech-language pathology and deaf education. *Teaching Exceptional Children, 36,* 58–62.

Hanson, M. J., Horn, E., & Sandall, S. (2001). After pre-school inclusion: Children's educational pathways over the early school years. *Exceptional Children, 68,* 65–83.

Hardman, M. L., Drew, C. J., Egan, M. W., & Wolf, B. (2005). *Human exceptionality: Society, school, and family* (8th ed.). Boston: Allyn and Bacon.

Harniss, M. K., & Epstein, M. H. (2005) Strength-based assessment in children's mental health. In M. H. Epstein, K. Kutash, & A. J. Duchnowski (Eds.), *Outcomes for children and youth with emotional and behavioral disorders and their families* (2nd ed., pp. 125–141). Austin, TX: Pro-Ed.

Harris, D., & Vanderheiden, G. C. (1980). Augmentative communication techniques. In R. L. Schiefelbusch (Ed.), *Nonspeech language and communication: Analysis and intervention* (pp. 259– 302). Austin, TX: Pro-Ed.

Harris, K. C. (1998). *Collaborative elementary teaching: A casebook for elementary special and general educators.* Austin, TX: Pro-Ed.

Harrison, P. & Oakland, T (2003). Adaptive Behavior Assessment System, 2nd Ed. San Antonio, TX: Harcourt Assessment.

Hasselbring, T., & Goin, L. (1993). Integrated media and technology. In E. A. Polloway & J. R. Patton (Eds.), *Strategies for teaching learners with special needs* (5th ed., pp. 145–162). Columbus, OH: Macmillan.

Healthy People 2000. (1992). Washington, DC: U.S. Government Printing Office.

Heaton, S., & O'Shea, D. J. (1995). Using mnemonics to make mnemonics. *Teaching Exceptional Children, 28*(1), 34–36.

Heflin, L. J., & Simpson, R. (1998). The interventions for children and youth with autism: Prudent choices in a world of extraordinary claims and promises: Part II. *Focus on Autism and Other Developmental Disabilities, 13,* 212–220.

Heward, W. L. (1995). *Exceptional children: An introductory survey of special education* (4th ed.). New York: Macmillan.

Heward, W. L. (2000). *Exceptional children: An introduction to special education* (7th ed.). Englewood Cliffs, NJ: Prentice-Hall.

Hietsch, D. G. (1986). Father involvement: No moms allowed. *Teaching Exceptional Children, 18,* 258–260.

Higgins, E. L., Raskind, M. H., Goldberg, R. J., & Herman, K. L. (2002). Stages of acceptance of learning disabilities: The impact of labeling. *Learning Disability Quarterly, 25,* 3–18.

Hill, M., Szefler, S. J., & Larsen, G. L. (1998). Asthma pathogenesis and the implications for therapy in children. *Pediatric Clinics of North America, 39,* 1205–1222.

Hiller, J. F. (1990). Setting up a classroom-based language instruction program: One clinician's experience. *Texas Journal of Audiology and Speech Pathology, 16*(2), 12–13.

Hilton, A. (1990). *Parental reactions to having a disabled child.* Paper presented at annual International Conference of the Council for Exceptional Children.

Hoagwood, K., Kelleher, K. J., Feil, M., & Comer, D. M. (2000). Treatment services for children with ADHD: A national perspective. *Journal of the American Academy of Child and Adolescent Psychiatry, 39*(2), 198–206.

Hobbs, T., & Westling, D. L. (1998). Promoting successful inclusion. *Teaching Exceptional Children, 34,* 10–14.

Hobson v. Hansen, 269 F. Supp. 401 (D.DC 1967).

Hollingsworth, H. L. (2001). We need to talk: Communication strategies for effective collaboration. *Teaching Exceptional Children, 33,* 4–8.

Hooper, C. R. (2004). Treatment of voice disorders in children. *Language, Speech, and Hearing Services in Schools, 35,* 320–326.

Hoover, J. J. (1988). Implementing a study skills program in the classroom. *Academic Therapy, 24,* 471–476.

Hoover, J. J. (1990). Curriculum adaptations: A five-step process for classroom implementation. *Academic Therapy, 25,* 407–416.

Hoover, J. J., & Patton, J. R. (1995). *Teaching students with learning problems to use study skills: A teacher's guide.* Austin, TX: Pro-Ed.

Hoover, J. J., & Patton, J. R. (2004). Differentiating standards-based education for students with diverse needs. *Remedial and Special Education, 25*(2), 74–78.

Hoover, J. J. & Patton, J. R. (2005). Differentiating curriculum and instruction for English-language learners with special needs. *Intervention in School and Clinic, 40*(4), 231–235.

Hoover, J. J., & Patton, J. R. (2006). *Curriculum adaptations for students with learning and behavior problems* (3rd ed.). Austin, TX: Pro-Ed.

Horner, R. H. (2000). Positive behavior supports. In M. L. Wehmeyer & J. R. Patton (Eds.), *Mental retardation in the 21st century* (pp. 181–196). Austin, TX: Pro-Ed.

Hoy, C., & Gregg, N. (1994). *Assessment: The special educator's role.* Pacific Grove, CA: Brooks/Cole.

Huff, C. R. (1999). *Comparison of criminal behaviors of youth gangs and at-risk youth.* Washington, DC: Department of Justice National Institute of Justice.

Hughes, C., Copeland, S. R., Guth, C., Rung, L. L., Hwang, B., Kleeb, G., et al.

(2001). General education students' perspectives on their involvement in a high school peer buddy program. *Education and Training in Mental Retardation and Developmental Disabilities, 36,* 343–355.

Hume, K., Bellini, L., & Pratt, R. (2005). The usage and perceived outcomes of early intervention and early childhood programs for young children with autism. *Topics in Early Childhood Education, 25*(4), 195–207.

Hunt, P., Doering, K., & Hirose-Hatae, A. (2001). Across-program collaboration to support students with and without disabilities in general education classrooms. *Journal of the Association for Persons with Severe Handicaps, 26,* 240–256.

Hunt, P., Hirose-Hatae, A., & Doering, K. (2000). "Communication" is what I think everyone is talking about. *Remedial and Special Education, 21,* 305–317.

Hutton, A. M. & Caron, S. L. (2005). Experiences of families with children with autism in rural New England. *Focus on Autism and Other Developmental Disabilities, 20,* 180–189.

ICD-10: International statistical classification of diseases and related health problems (1992). (10th rev. ed.). Geneva, Switzerland: World Health Organization.

Idol, L. (2006). Toward inclusion of special education students in general education: A program evaluation of eight schools. *Remedial and Special Education, 27*(2), 77–94.

Individuals with Disabilities Education Act. (1997). Washington, DC: U.S. Government Printing Office.

Infusini, M. (1994). From the patient's point of view. *The Journal of Cognitive Rehabilitation, 12,* 4–5.

International Dyslexia Association (Summer, 2004). *Controversial therapy based on insufficient evidence.* Statement printed by permission in *LDA Newsbriefs* (July/August, 2004), p. 9.

Janota, J. O. (2004). *2004 Schools survey.* Rockville, MD: ASHA.

Jaquish, C., & Stella, M. A. (1986). Helping special students move from elementary to secondary school. *Counterpoint, 7*(1), 1.

Jayanthi, M., Bursuck, W., Epstein, M. H., & Polloway, E. A. (1997). Strategies for successful homework. *Teaching Exceptional Children, 30*(1), 4–7.

Jayanthi, M., Bursuck, W. D., Polloway, E., & Epstein, M. (1996). Testing adaptations for students with disabilities: A national survey of classroom practices. *Journal of Special Education, 30,* 99–115.

Jayanthi, M., Nelson, J. S., Sawyer, V., Bursuck, W. D., & Epstein, M. H. (1994). Homework-communication problems among parents, general education, and special education teachers: An exploratory study. *Remedial and Special Education, 16*(2), 102–116.

Jensen, P. S. (2000). Commentary: The NIH ADHD consensus statement: Win, lose, or draw? *Journal of the American Academy of Child and Adolescent Psychiatry, 39*(2), 194–197.

Jensen, P. S., Kettler, L., Roper, M., Sloan, M. T., Dulcan, M. K., Hoven, C., et al. (1999). Are stimulants over prescribed? Treatment of ADHD in four US communities. *Journal of the American Academy of Child and Adolescent Psychiatry, 38*(7), 797–804.

Johnson, A. (2001). How to use thinking skills to differentiate curricula for gifted and highly creative students. *Gifted Child Today, 24*(4), 58–63.

Johnson, D. J. (1999). The language of instruction. *Learning Disabilities: A Multidisciplinary Journal 9*(2), 1–7.

Johnson, D. R., Stodden, R. A., & Emanuel, E. J. (2002). Curricular challenges facing secondary education and transition services. *Exceptional Children, 68,* 519–531.

Johnson, E., & Arnold, N. (2004). Validating an alternative assessment. *Remedial and Special Education, 25*(5), 266–275.

Johnson, G., & Jefferson-Aker, C. R. (2001). HIV/AIDS prevention: Effective instructional strategies for adolescents with mild mental retardation. *Teaching Exceptional Children, 33,* 28–32.

Johnson, L. F., & Dunlap, G. (1993). Using functional assessment to develop individual interventions. *Teaching Exceptional Children, 25,* 44–47.

Johnson, L. J., & Pugach, M. C. (1990). Classroom teachers views of intervention strategies. *Journal of Special Education, 24*(1), 68–75.

Jones, V. F., & Jones, L. S. (1995). *Comprehensive classroom management* (4th ed.). Boston: Allyn and Bacon.

Jones, V. F., & Jones, L. S. (2007). *Comprehensive classroom management* (8th ed.). Boston: Allyn and Bacon.

Kaderavek, J. N., & Pakulski, L. A. (2002). Minimal hearing loss is not minimal. *Teaching Exceptional Children, 34,* 14–18.

Kamradt, B., Gilbertson, S.A., & Lynn N. (2005). Wraparound Milwaukee. In M. Epstein, J. Kurash, & L. Duchnowski (Eds.), *Outcomes for Children and Youth with Emotional and Behavioral Disorders.* Austin, TX: Pro-Ed.

Kaplan, P. S. (1996). *Pathways for exceptional children: School, home, and culture.* St. Paul, MN: West.

Kataoka, J. C., & Patton, J. R. (1989). Integrated curriculum. *Science and Children, 16,* 52–58.

Katims, D. S. (2001). Literacy assessment of students with mental retardation: An exploratory investigation. *Education and Training in Mental Retardation and Developmental Disabilities, 36*(4), 363–372.

Katsiyannis, A., Hodge, J., & Lanford, A. (2000). Paraeducators: Legal and practice considerations. *Remedial and Special Education, 21,* 297–304.

Katsiyannis, A., Landrum, T. J., & Vinton, L. (1997). Practical guidelines for monitoring treatment of Attention-Deficit/Hyperactivity Disorder. *Prevention of School Failure, 41*(3) 132–136.

Katsiyannis, A., & Maag, J. W. (2001). Manifestation determination as a golden fleece. *Exceptional Children, 68,* 89–96.

Katsiyannis, A., Yell, M. L., & Bradley, R. (2001). Reflections on the 25th anniversary of the Individuals with Disabilities Education Act. *Remedial and Special Education, 22,* 324–334.

Katsiyannis, A., Zhang, D., & Zhang, H. (2002). Placement and exit patterns for students with mental retardation: An analysis of national trends. *Education and Training in Mental Retardation and Developmental Disabilities, 37,* 134–145.

Kauffman, J. M. (2005). *Characteristics of emotional and behavioral disorders of children and youth* (8th ed.). Upper Saddle River, NJ: Prentice-Hall.

Kauffman, J. M., & Landrum, T. J. (2006). *Children and youth with emotional and behavioral disorders: A history of their education.* Austin, TX: Pro-Ed.

Kauffman, J. M., Lloyd, J. W., Baker, J., & Riedel, T. M. (1995). Inclusion of all students with emotional or behavioral disorders? Let's think again. *Phi Delta Kappan, 76*(8), 542–546.

Kauffman, J. M., Mostert, M. P., Trent, S. C., & Hallahan, D. P. (2002). Managing classroom behavior: A reflective case-based approach (3rd ed.). Boston: Allyn & Bacon.

Kauffman, J. M., & Wong, K. L. H. (1991). Effective teachers of students with behavioral disorders: Are generic teaching skills enough? *Behavioral Disorders, 16,* 225–237.

Kavale, K. A. (2001a). Decision making in special education: The function of meta-analysis. *Exceptionality, 9,* 245–268.

Kavale, K. A., (2001b). *Discovering models in the identification of learning disabilities.* Executive summary. Washington, DC: LD Summit.

Kavale, K. A., & Forness, S. R. (1996). Treating social skill deficits in children with learning disabilities: A meta-analysis of the research. *Learning Disability Quarterly, 19*(1), 2–13.

Kavale, K. A., & Forness, S. R. (1999). The future of research and practice in behavior disorders. *Journal of Behavior Disorders, 24,* 305–318.

Kavale, K. A., & Forness, S. R. (2000). History, rhetoric, and reality: Analysis of the inclusion debate. *Remedial and Special Educaiton, 21,* 279–296.

Kavale, K. A., Holdnack, J. A., & Mostert, M. P. (2006). Responsiveness to intervention and the identification of specific learning disability: A critique and alternative proposal. *Learning Disability Quarterly, 29,* 113–27.

Kavale, K. A., & Mostert, M. P. (2004). Social skills interventions for individuals with learning disabilities. *Learning Disabilities Quarterly, 27*(1), 31–43.

Keith, B., & Lenz, B. (2004). Creating school-wide conditions for high quality learning strategies classroom. *Intervention, 41*(5), 261–268.

Kerr, L., Delaney, B., Clarke, S., Dunlap, G, & Childs, K. (2001). Improving the classroom behavior of students with emotional and behavioral disorders using individualized curricular modifications. *Journal of Emotional and Behavioral Disorders, 9,* 239–247.

Kerrin, R. G. (1996). Collaboration: Working with the speech–language pathologist. *Intervention in School and Clinic, 32*(1), 56–59.

Keyser-Marcus, L., et al. (2002). Enhancing the schooling of students with traumatic brain injury. *Teaching Exceptional Children, 34,* 62–65.

Killoran, J., Templeman, T. P., Peters, J., & Udell, T. (2001). Identifying paraprofessional competencies for early intervention and early childhood special education. *Teaching Exceptional Children, 34,* 68–73.

King-Sears, M. E. (2001a). Institutionalizing peer-mediated instruction and interventions in schools. *Remedial and Special Education, 22,* 89–101.

King-Sears, M. E. (2001b). Three steps for gaining access to the general education curriculum for learners with disabilities. *Intervention in School and Clinic, 37,* 67–76.

King-Sears, M. E., & Bradley, D. F. (1995). Classwide peer tutoring. *Preventing School Failure, 40*(1), 27–31.

King-Sears, M. E., & Cummings, C. S. (1996). Inclusive practices of classroom teachers. *Remedial and Special Education, 17,* 217–225.

Kirk, R., & Even, B. (2001). Disability or difference: Reflections on learning. *New Teacher Advocate 9*(1), 12–15.

Kirk, S. A. (1962). *Educating exceptional children.* Boston: Houghton Mifflin.

Kirk, S. A., Gallagher, J. J., & Anastasiow, A. (2000). *Educating exceptional children* (8th ed.). Boston: Houghton Mifflin.

Kirsten, I. (1981). *The Oakland picture dictionary.* Wauconda, IL: Don Johnston.

Klassen, R. (2002). A question of calibration: A review of the self-efficacy beliefs of students with learning disabilities. *Learning Disabilities Quarterly, 25,* 88–102.

Kluwin, T. N. (1996). Getting hearing and deaf students to write to each other through dialogue journals. *Teaching Exceptional Children, 28,* 50–53.

Knitzer, J., Steinberg, Z., & Fleisch, B. (1990). *At the schoolhouse door.* New York: Bank Street College of Education.

Koegel, R. L., & Koegel, L. K. (1995). *Teaching children with autism.* Baltimore, MD: Brookes.

Koenig, A. J., & Holbrook, M. C. (1995). *Learning media assessment of students with visual impairments: A resource guide for teachers* (2nd ed.). Austin, TX: Pro-Ed.

Kohn, A. (1996a). *Beyond discipline: From compliance to community.* Washington, DC: Association for Supervision and Curriculum Development.

Kohn, A. (1996b). What to look for in the classroom. *Educational Leadership, 54,* 54–55.

Kollins, S. H., Barkley, R. A., & DuPaul, G. J. (2001). Use and management of medications for children diagnosed with attention deficit hyperactivity disorder (ADHD). *Focus on Exceptional Children, 33*(5), 1–23.

Koppang, A. (2004). Curriculum mapping: Building collaboration and communication. *Intervention in School and Clinic, 39*(3), 154–161.

Korinek, L., & Polloway, E. A. (1993). Social skills: Review and implications for instruction for students with mild mental retardation. In R. A. Gable & S. F. Warren (Eds.), *Advances in mental retardation and developmental disabilities* (Vol. 5, pp. 71–97). London, UK: Jessica Kingsley.

Korinek, L., Walther-Thomas, C., McLaughlin, V. L., & Williams, B. T. (1999). *Intervention in School and Clinic, 35,* 3–8.

Kounin, J. (1970). *Discipline and group management in classrooms.* New York: Holt, Rinehart & Winston.

Krauss, M. W. (1990). New precedent in family policy: Individualized family service plan. *Exceptional Children, 56,* 388–395.

Kravolek, E., & Buell, J. (2000). *The end of homework: How homework disrupts families, overburdens children, and limits learning.* Boston: Beacon Press.

Kruczek, T., & Vitanza, S. (1999). Treatment effects with an adolescent abuse survivor's group. *Child Abuse & Neglect, 23,* 477–485.

Kubler-Ross, E. (1969). *On death and dying.* New York: Macmillan.

Lahey, M. (1988). *Language disorders and language development.* New York: Macmillan.

Lake, J. F., & Billingsley, B. S. (2000). An analysis of factors that contribute to parent–school conflict in special education. *Remedial and Special Education, 21,* 240–250.

Lamar-Dukes, P., & Dukes, C. (2005). Consider the roles and responsibilities of the inclusion support teacher. *Intervention, 41*(1), 55–59.

Lambert, M. A., & Nowacek, J. (2006). Help high school students improve their study skills. *Intervention in School and Clinic, 41*(4), 241–243.

Lambros, K. M., Ward, S. L., Bocian, K. M., MacMillan, D. L., & Gresham, F. M. (1998). Behavioral profiles of children at-risk for emotional and behavioral disorders: Implications for assessment and classification. *Focus on Exceptional Children, 30*(5), 1–16.

Lang, L. (1998). Allergy linked to common ear infection. *ADVANCE for Speech-Language Pathologists and Audioligists, 36,* 8–9.

Langerock, N. L. (2000). A passion for action research. *Teaching Exceptional Children, 33,* 26–34.

Larry P. v. Riles, C-71-2270 (RFP, District Court for Northern California 1972).

Larson, S. A. Lakin, K. C., Anderson, L., Kwak, N., Lee, J. H., & Anderson, D. (2001). Prevalence of mental retardation and developmental disabilities: Estimates from the 1994/1995 National Health Interview Survey Disability Supplements. *American Journal on Mental Retardation, 106,* 231–252.

Lawrence, V., Houghton, S., Tannock, R., Douglas, G., Durkin, K., & Whiting, K. (2002). ADHD outside the laboratory: Boys' executive function performance on tasks in video-game play and on a visit to the zoo. *Journal of Abnormal Psychology, 30,* 447–462.

Lee, S. H., Palmer, S. B., Turnbull, A. P., & Wehmeyer, M. L. (2006). A model for parent–teacher collaboration to promote self-determination in young children with disabilities. *Teaching Exceptional Children, 38,* 36-41.

Lenz, B. K., Deshler, D. D., & Kissam, B. R. (2004). *Teaching content to all: Evidence-based inclusive practices in middle and secondary schools.* Boston: Allyn and Bacon.

Leo, J. (2002, January/February). American preschoolers on Ritalin. *Society,* pp. 52–60.

Lerner, J. W. (2000). *Learning disabilities: Theories, diagnosis, and teaching strategies* (4th ed.) Boston: Houghton Mifflin.

Levin, J., & Nolan, J. F. (2000). *Principles of classroom management* (3rd ed.). Boston: Allyn and Bacon.

Lewis, T. J., & Sugai, G. (1999). Effective behavior support: A systems approach to proactive school-wide management. *Focus on Exceptional Children, 31*(6), 1–24.

Li, A. (2004). Classroom strategies for improving and enhancing visual skills in students with disabilities. *Teaching Exceptional Children, 36,* 38–42.

Lipsky, D. K., & Gartner, A. (1996). The evaluation of inclusive programs. *NCERI Bulletin, 2,* 1–7.

Lisnov, L., Harding, C. G., Safer, L. A., & Kavanagh, J. (1998). Adolescents' perceptions of substance abuse prevention strategies. *Adolescence, 33,* 301–312.

Lloyd, J. W., & Hallahan, D. F. (2005). Going forward: How the field of learning disabilities has and will contribute to education. *Learning Disability Quarterly, 28*(2), 133–138.

Lloyd, J. W., Landrum, T., & Hallahan, D. P. (1991). Self-monitoring applications for classroom intervention. In G. Stoner, M. R. Shinn, & H. M. Walker (Eds.), *Interventions for achievement and behavior problems* (pp. 201–213). Washington, DC: NASP.

Locke, M. N., Banken, L. L., & Mahone, T. E. (1994). *Adapting early childhood curriculum for children with special needs.* New York: Merrill.

Loehr, J. (2002). *Read the picture stories for articulation* (2nd ed.). Austin, TX: Pro-Ed.

Logan, K. R., Hansen, C. D., Nieminen, P. K., & Wright, E. H. (2001). Student support teams: Helping students succeed in general education classrooms or working to place students in special education? *Education and Training in Mental Retardation and Developmental Disabilities, 36,* 280–292.

Lopez, R., & MacKenzie, J. (1993). A learning center approach to individualized instruction for gifted students. In C. J. Maker (Ed.), *Critical issues in gifted education: Programs for the gifted in regular classrooms* (Vol. 3, pp. 282–295). Austin, TX: Pro-Ed.

Luckasson, R. (2002). *Mental retardation: Definition, classification and systems of supports.* Washington, DC: American Association on Mental Retardation.

Luckasson, R., Coulter, D., Polloway, E. A., Reis, S., Schalock, R., Snell, et al. (1992). *Mental retardation: Definition, classification, and systems of supports.* Washington, DC: American Association on Mental Retardation.

Luckasson, R., Schalock, R., Snell, M., & Spitalnik, D. (1996). The 1992 AAMR definition and preschool children: Response from the committee on terminology and classification. *Mental Retardation, 34,* 247–253.

Luckner, J. (1994). Developing independent and responsible behaviors in students who are deaf or hard of hearing. *Teaching Exceptional Children, 26,* 13–17.

Luckner, J. (1999). An example of two coteaching classrooms. *American Annals of the Deaf, 44,* 24–34.

Luckner, J., & Denzin, D. (1998). In the mainstream: Adaptions for students who are deaf or hard of hearing. *Perspectives in Education and Deafness, 17,* 8–11.

Lyon, G. R. (1995). Research initiatives in learning disabilities: Contributions from scientists supported by the National Institutes of Child Health and Human Development. *Journal of Child Neurology, 10*(1), 5120–5126.

Lyon, G. R., Fletcher, J. M., Shaywitz, S. E., Shaywitz, B. A., Torgesen, J. K., Wood, et al. (2001). Rethinking learning disabilities. In C. E. Finn, A. J. Rotherham, & C. R. Hokanson, Jr. (Eds.), *Rethinking special education for a new century* (pp. 259–287). Washington, DC: Thomas B. Fordham Foundation.

Lytle, R. K., & Bordin, J. (2001). Enhancing the IEP team: Strategies for parents and professionals. *Teaching Exceptional Children, 33,* 40–44.

Mackie, E. (1996). *Oral-motor activities for school aged-children.* Austin, TX: Pro-Ed.

MacMillan, D. L., & Forness, S. R. (1998). The role of IQ in special education placement decisions: Primary and determinative or peripheral and inconsequential? *Remedial and Special Education, 19,* 239–253.

MacMillan, D. L., & Siperstein, G. N. (2001). *Learning disabilities as operationally defined by schools.* Paper presented at the 2001 LD Summit: Building a Foundation for the Future, Washington, DC.

Madaus, J. (2006). Employment outcomes of university graduates with Learning Disabilities. *Learning Disabilities Quarterly, 29,* 19–30.

Madaus, J. W., Ruban, L. M., Foley, T. E., & McGuire, J. M. (2003). *Learning Disabilities Quarterly, 26,* 159–169.

Madaus, J. W., & Shaw, S. F. (2004). Section 504: Differences in the regulations for secondary and postsecondary education. *Intervention in School and Clinic, 40*(2), 81–87.

Magiera, K., & Zigmond, N. (2005). Co-teaching in middle school classrooms. *Learning Disabilities Research and Practice, 20*(2), 79–85.

Maheady, L., Harper, G. F., & Mallette, B. (2001). Peer-mediated instruction and interventions and students with mild disabilities. *Remedial and Special Education, 22,* 4–14.

Maheady, L., Harper, G., & Mallette, B. (2003). Preparing preservice teachers to implement class wide peer tutoring. *Teacher Education and Special Education, 27*(4), 408–418.

Maker, C. J. (1993). Gifted students in the regular education classroom: What practices are defensible and feasible? In C. J. Maker (Ed.), *Critical issues in gifted education: Programs for the gifted in regular classrooms* (Vol. 3, pp. 413–436). Austin, TX: Pro-Ed.

Malott, R. W., Whaley, D. L., & Malott, M. E. (1997). *Elementary principles of behavior* (3rd ed.). Upper Saddle River, NJ: Prentice-Hall.

Marcotte, D., Fortin, L., Potvin, P., & Papillon, M. (2002). Gender differences in depressive symptoms during adolescence: Role of gender-typed characteristics, self-esteem, body image, stressful life events, and pubertal status. *Journal of Emotional and Behavioral Disorders, 10,* 29–42.

Marland, S. P. (1992). *Education of the gifted and talented: Report to the Congress by the U.S. Commissioner of Education and background papers submitted to the U.S. Office of Education* (2 volumes, pp. 79–118). Washington, DC: U.S. Government Printing Office.

Marston, D., & Magnusson, D. (1985). Implementing curriculum-based measurement in special and regular education settings. *Exceptional Children, 52,* 266–276.

Marston, D., Muyskens, P., Lau, M. (2003). Problem-solving model for decision-making with high incidence disabilities. *Learning Disabilities Research and Practice, 18*(3), 187–200.

Martin, J. E., Van Dycke, J. L., Greene, B. A., Gardner, J. E., Christensen, W. R., Woods, L. L., et al. (2006). Direct observation of teacher-directed IEP meetings: Establishing the need for student IEP meeting instruction. *Exceptional Children, 72,* 187–200.

Marzano, R. J. (2003). *Classroom management that works.* Alexandria, VA: ASCD.

Masi, G., Mucci, M., & Favilla, L. (1999). Depressive symptoms in adolescents with mild mental retardation. *Education and Training in Mental Retardation and Developmental Disabilities, 34,* 223–226.

Mastropieri, M. A., & Scruggs, T. E. (1994). *Effective instruction for special education* (2nd ed.). Austin, TX: Pro-Ed.

Mastropieri, M. A., & Scruggs, T. E. (1997). Best practices in promoting reading comprehension in students with learning disabilities: 1976 to 1996. *Remedial and Special Education, 18,* 197–218.

Mastropieri, M. A., & Scruggs, T. E. (2000). *The inclusive classroom: Strategies for effective instruction.* Columbus, OH: Merrill.

Mastropieri, M. A., & Scruggs, T. E. (2001). Promoting inclusion in secondary classrooms. *Learning Disability Quarterly, 24,* 265–274.

Mastropieri, M. A., Scruggs, T. E., & Graetz, J. E. (2003). Reading comprehension instruction for secondary students: Challenges for struggling students and teachers. *Learning Disabilities Quarterly, 26*(2), 103–116.

Mastropieri, M. A., Sweda, J., & Scruggs, T. E. (2000). Putting mnemonic strategies to work in an inclusive classroom. *Learning Disabilities Research and Practice, 15*(2), 69–74.

Mather, N., Bos, C., & Babur, N. (2001). Perceptions and knowledge of pre-service and in-service teachers about early literacy instruction. *Journal of Learning Disabilities, 34,* 472–482.

Mathes, P., & Torgesen, J. (1998, November). *Early reading basics: Strategies for teaching reading to primary-grade students who are at risk for reading and learning disabilities.* Paper presented at the Annual Council for Learning Disabilities Conference, Albuquerque, NM.

McConaughy, S. H., & Wadsworth, M. E. (2000). Life history reports of young adults previously referred for mental health services. *Journal of Emotional and Behavioral Disorders, 8,* 202–215.

McConnell, J. (1999). Parents, adolescents, and career planning for visually impaired students. *Journal of Visual Impairment and Blindness, 93,* 498–515.

McConnell, K. (2001). Placement. In R. Algozzine, L. Serna, & J. R. Patton (Eds.), *Childhood behavior disorders: Applied research and educational practice* (pp. 309–330). Austin, TX: Pro-Ed.

McConnell, K., Patton, J. R., & Polloway, E. A. (2006). *BIP-III.* Austin: Pro-Ed.

McConnell, K., Ryser, G., & Patton, J. R. (2002a). *Practical ideas that really work for disruptive, defiant, and difficult students: Preschool through grade 4.* Austin, TX: Pro-Ed.

McConnell, K., Ryser, G., & Patton, J. R. (2002b). *Practical ideas that really work for disruptive, defiant, and difficult students: Grades 5 through 12.* Austin, TX: Pro-Ed.

McConnell, M. E., Hilvitz, P. B., & Cox, C. J. (1998). Functional assessment: A systematic process for assessment and intervention in general and special education classrooms. *Intervention in School and Clinic, 34,* 10–20.

McCordle, P., Cooper, J., Houle, G. R., Karp, N., & Paul-Brown, D. (2001). Next steps in research and practice. *Learning Disabilities Research and Practice, 16*(4), 250–254.

McCormick, L., Noonan, M. J., Ogata, V., & Heck, R. (2001). Co-teaching relationship and program quality: Implications for preparing teachers for inclusive preschool settings. *Education and Training in Mental Retardation and Developmental Disabilities, 36,* 119–132.

McDonnell, J. J., Hardman, M. L., & McDonnell, A. P. (2005). *An introduction to persons with moderate and severe disabilities.* Boston: Allyn & Bacon.

McDougall, D. (1998). Research on self-management techniques used by students with disabilities in general education settings: A descriptive review. *Remedial and Special Education, 19,* 310–320.

McEachlin, J. J., Smith, T., & Lovaas, O. I. (1993). Long-term outcome for children with autism who received early intensive behavioral treatment. *American Journal on Mental Retardation, 97,* 359–372.

McEnvoy, M. A., Shores, R. E., Wehby, J. H., Johnson, S. M., & Fox, J. J. (1990). Special education teachers' implementation of procedures to promote social interaction among children in integrated settings. *Education and Training in Mental Retardation, 25,* 267–276.

McEvoy, A., & Welker, R. (2000). Antisocial behavior and academic failures and school climate: A critical review. *Journal of Emotional and Behavioral Disorders, 8,* 24–33.

McEwan, E.K. (2006). How to survive and thrive in the first three weeks of school. Thousand Oaks, CA: Corwin Press.

McGinty, A. S., & Justice, L. M. (2006). Classroom-based versus pullout speech-language intervention: A review of the experimental evidence. *EBP Briefs, 1*(1), 1–25.

McGrail, L. (1998). Modifying regular classroom curricula for high-ability students. *Gifted Child Today, 21,* 36–39.

McKamey, E. S. (1991). Storytelling for children with learning disabilities: A first-hand account. *Teaching Exceptional Children, 23,* 46–48.

McKeever, P. (1983). Siblings of chronically ill children: A literature review with implications for research and practice. *American Journal of Orthopsychiatry, 53,* 209–217.

McLaughlin-Cheng, E. (1998). The Asperger syndrome and autism: A literature review and meta-analysis. *Focus on Autism and Other Developmental Disabilities, 13,* 234–245.

McMaster, K. N., & Fuchs, D. (2002). Effects of cooperative learning on the academic achievement of students with learning disabilities. *Learning Disabilities Research and Practice, 17,* 107–117.

McNamara, J. K., & Wong, B. (2003). Memory for everyday information in students with learning disabilities. *Journal of Learning Disabilities, 36*(5), 394–406.

McNeill, J. H., & Fowler, S. A. (1996). Using story reading to encourage children's conversations. Teaching Exceptional Children, 28(2), 43–47.

McPartland, J. M., & Slavin, R. E. (1990). *Policy persepctives increasing achievement of at-risk students.* Washington: DC: U.S. Department of Education.

McReynolds, L. (1990). Functional articulation disorders. In G. H. Shames & E. H. Wiig (Eds.), *Human communication disorders: An introduction* (2nd ed.) (pp. 139–182). Columbus, OH: Merrill.

Meyer, D. (2001). Meeting the unique concerns of brothers and sisters of children with special needs. *Insight, 51,* 28–32.

Miller, R. J. (1995). Preparing for adult life: Teaching students their rights and responsibilities. *CEC Today, 1*(7), 12.

Miller, S. P. (2002). *Validated practices for teaching students with diverse needs.* Boston: Allyn & Bacon.

Miller, S. P., Mercer, C. D., & Dillon, A. S. (1992). CSA: Acquiring and retaining math skills. *Intervention in School and Clinic, 28,* 105–110.

Montague, M., McKinney, J. D., & Hocutt, L. (1994). Assessing students for attention deficit disorder. *Intervention in School and Clinic, 29*(4), 212–218.

Montgomery, D. J. (2005). Communicating without harm: Strategies to enhance parent-teacher communication. *Teaching Exceptional Children, 37,* 50–55.

Montgomery, J. R., & Herer, G. R. (1994). Future watch: Our schools in the 21st century. *Language, Speech, and Hearing Services in the Schools, 25,* 130–135. American Speech–Language–Hearing Association.

Montgomery, W. (2001). Creating culturally responsive, inclusive classrooms. *Teaching Exceptional Children, 33,* 4–9.

Moores, D. (2001). *Educating the deaf: Psychology, principles, and practices* (6th ed.). Columbus, OH: Merrill.

Morgan, S. (1985). *Children in crisis: A team approach in the schools.* Austin, TX: Pro-Ed.

Morgan, S. R. (1994a). *At-risk youth in crises: A team approach in the schools* (2nd ed.). Austin, TX: Pro-Ed.

Morgan, S. (1994b). *Children in crisis: A team approach in the schools* (2nd ed.). Austin, TX: Pro-Ed.

Moriarty, D. (1967). *The loss of loved ones.* Springfield, IL: Charles C Thomas.

Morris, S. (2002). Promoting social skills among students with nonverbal learning disabilities. *Teaching Exceptional Children, 34,* 66–70.

Morrison, G. S. (2006). *Teaching in America* (4th ed.). Boston: Allyn & Bacon.

MTA Cooperative Group. (1999). A 14-month randomized clinical trial of treatment strategies for attention-deficit/hyperactivity disorder. *Archives of General Psychiatry, 56,* 1073–1086.

Munden, A. C., & Archelus, J. (2001). *The ADHD Handbook: A guide for parents and professionals.* New York: Jessica Kingsley.

Mundschenk, N. A., & Foley, R. M. (1997). Collaborative activities and competencies of secondary schools special educators: A national survey. *Teacher Education in Special Education, 20,* 47–60.

Munger, R., & Morse, W. C. (1992). When divorce rocks a child's world. *The Educational Forum, 43,* 100–103.

Munk, D. D., & Bursuck, W. D. (2001). Preliminary findings on personalized grading plans for middle school students with learning disabilities. *Exceptional Children, 67,* 211–234.

Munk, D. D., Bursuck, W. D., Epstein, M. H., Jayanthi, M., Nelson, J., & Polloway, E. A. (2001). Homework communication problems: Perspectives of special and general education parents. *Reading and Writing Quarterly, 17,* 189–203.

Munson, S. M. (1986–1987). Regular education teachers modifications for mainstreamed handicapped students. *Journal of Special Education, 20*(4), 10–18.

Murdick, N. L., Gartin, B. C., & Crabtree, T. (2007). *Special education law.* Columbus, OH: Merrill.

Murray, C., & Greenberg, M. T. (2006). Examining the importance of social relationships and social contexts in the lives of children with high incidence disabilities. *Journal of Special Education, 39*(4), 220–233.

Myles, B. S., & Simpson, R. L. (1998). Aggression and violence by school-age children and youth: Under the aggression cycle and prevention/intervention strategies. *Intervention in School and Clinic, 33,* 259–264.

Nagel, L., McDougall, D., & Granby, C. (1996). Students' self-reported substance use by grade level and gender. *Journal of Drug Education, 26,* 49–56.

Naremore, R. C. (1980). Language disorders in children. In T. J. Hixon, L. D. Shriberg, & J. H. Saxman (Eds.), *Introduction to communication disorders* (pp. 111–132). Englewood Cliffs, NJ: Prentice-Hall.

National Association for the Deaf. (2002). Information Center. Retrieved September 20, 2002 from http://www.nad.org.

National Association for the Gifted (2006). *Legislative Update.* p. 1.

National Cancer Foundation. (1997). *Cancer risk report.* Washington, DC: Author.

National Center for Education Statistics. (1989). *Digest of educational statistics, 1989.* Washington, DC: U.S. Department of Education, Office of Research and Improvement.

National Center for Education Statistics. (1991). *The condition of education, 1991 edition.* Washington, DC: Author.

National Center for Education Statistics. (2001, November). *Statistical analysis report: Dropout rates in the United States: 2000.* Washington, DC: U.S. Department of Education, Office of Educational Research and Improvement.

National Center for Responsive Education. (2005). Technical Reports, quarter three and four. Washington, D.C,: U.S. Department of Education.

National Center on Child Abuse and Neglect. (1986). *Status of child abuse in the United States.* Washington, DC: Author.

National Coalition for the Homeless. (1999). *Homeless families with children (fact sheet 7).* Washington, DC: Author.

National Education Goals Panel. (1998). *Ready schools.* Washington, DC: Author.

National Head Injury Foundation. (1988). *An educator's manual: What educators need to know about students with traumatic brain injury.* Southborough, MA: Author.

National Heart, Lung, and Blood Institute. (1998). How asthma friendly is your school? *Journal of School Health, 68,* 167–168.

National Information Center for Children and Youth with Handicaps. (1990). *Children with autism.* Washington, DC: Author.

National Information Center for Children and Youth with Handicaps. (1991). *The education of children and youth with special needs: What do the laws say?* Washington, DC: Author.

National Institutes of Health. (2000). Consensus and development conference statement: Diagnosis and treatment of attention-deficit/hyperactivity disorder. *Journal of the American Academy of Child and Adolescent Psychiatry, 39(2),* 182–193.

National Joint Committee on Learning Disabilities. (1988). Letter to NJCLD member organizations.

National Joint Committee on Learning Disabilities. (2005,June). Responsiveness to intervention and learning disabilities: A report prepared by the National Joint Committee on Learning Disabilities. *Learning Disabilities Quarterly, 28,* 249–260.

National Law Center on Homelessness and Poverty. (1990). *Shut out: Denial of education to homeless children.* Washington, DC: Author.

National Minority AIDS Education and Training Center. (1999). *Cultural competency resources.* Retrieved October 30, 2002 from http://www.nmaetc.org.

National Reading Panel. (2000). *Report of the National Reading Panel: Teaching children to read.* Washington, DC: National Institute of Child Health and Human Development.

National study on inclusion: Overview and summary report. National Center on Educational Restructuring Inclusion, 1–8.

Neito, S. (1996). *Affirming diversity* (2nd ed.). White Plains, NY: Longman.

Nelson, J. R., Benner, G. J., & Cheney, D. (2005). An investigation of the language skills of students with emotional disturbance served in public schools. *Journal of Special Education, 39(2),* 97–105.

Nelson, J. S. (2000). Using the nominal group technique for homework communication decisions. *Remedial and Special Education, 23(6),* 379–386.

Nelson, K. C., & Prindle, N. (1992). Gifted teacher competencies: Ratings by rural principals and teachers. *Journal of the Education of the Gifted, 15,* 357–369.

Nelson, L. G. L., Summers, J. A., & Turnbull, A. P. (2004) Boundaries in family-professional relationships. *Remedial and Special Education, 25,* 153–165.

No Child Left Behind Act. 34 CFR Part 200 (2001).

Nowacek, E. J., & McShane, E. (1993). Spoken language. In E. A. Polloway & J. R. Patton (Eds.), *Strategies for teaching learners with special needs* (5th ed., pp. 183–205). Columbus, OH: Merrill.

Nyman McMaster, K., & Fuchs, D. (2002). Effects of cooperative learning on the academic achievement of students with learning disabilities: An update of Tateyama-Sniezek's review. *Learning Disabilities Research and Practice, 17,* 107–117.

Obenchain, K. M., & Abernathy, T. V. (2003). Build community and empower students. *Intervention in School and Clinic, 39(1),* 55–60.

Odom, S. L., Brown, W. H., & Frey, T. (2003). Evidence-based practices for young children with autism. *Focus on Autism and Other Developmental Disabilities, 18(3),* 166–175.

Office of Educational Research. (1998). *Tools for schools: From at-risk to excellence.* Washington, DC: Office of Educational Research.

Office of Education Research and Improvement. (1988). *Youth indicators, 1988: Trends in the well-being of American youth.* Washington, DC: U.S. Department of Education.

Office of Juvenile Justice and Delinquency Prevention. (1995). *Juvenile offenders and victims: A national report.* Pittsburgh, PA: National Center for Juvenile Justice.

Ohtake, Y. (2004). Meaningful inclusion for all students in team sports. *Teaching Exceptional Children, 37,* 22–26.

O'Leary (2006). New and improved transition services–Individuals with Disabilities Education Improvement Act of 2004, LDA Newsbriefs, 41(1), 1–5.

Olson, J. L., & Platt, J. M. (1996). *Teaching children and adolescents with special needs* (2nd ed). Englewood Cliffs, NJ: Merrill.

Orr, T. J., Myles, B. S., & Carlson, J. R. (1998). The impact of rhythmic entertainment on a person with autism. *Focus on Autism and Other Developmental Disabilities, 13,* 163–166.

Ortiz, A. A., (2002). Prevention of school failure and early identification. In A. J. Artiles & A. A. Orgiz (Eds.), *English language learners with special needs.* Washington, DC: Center for Applied Linguistics.

Oswald, D. P., Coutinho, M. J., Best, A. M., & Singh, N. N. (1999). Ethnic representation in special education: The influence of school-related economic and demographic values. *The Journal of Special Education, 32,* 194–206.

Overton, T. (2006). Promoting academic success through environmental assessment. *Intervention, 39,* 147–153.

Owens, R. E., Jr. (1984). *Language development: An introduction.* Columbus, OH: Merrill.

Oyer, H. J., Crowe, B., & Haas, W. H. (1987). *Speech, language, and hearing disorders: A guide for the teacher.* Boston: Little, Brown.

Palmer, D. S., Borthwick-Duffy, S. A., & Widaman, K. (1998). Parents perceptions of inclusive practices for their children with significant cognitive disabilities. *Exceptional Children, 64,* 271–279.

Palmer, D. S., Fuller, K., Arora, T., & Nelson, M. (2001). Taking sides: Parent views on inclusion for their children with severe disabilities. *Exceptional Children, 67,* 467–484.

Palmer, S. B., Wehmeyer, M. L., & Gipson, K. (2004). Providing access to the general curriculum by teaching self-determination skills. *Exceptional Children, 70(4),* 427–435.

Pancheri, C., & Prater, M. A. (1999). What teachers and parents should know about Ritalin. *Teaching Exceptional Children, March/April),* 20–26.

Pandiani, J. A., Schacht, L. M., & Banks, S. M. (2001). After children's services: A longitudinal study of significant life events. *Journal of Emotional and Behavioral Disorders, 9,* 131–138.

Parke, B. N. (1989). *Gifted students in regular classrooms.* Boston: Allyn and Bacon.

Patton, J. R. (1994). Practical recommendations for using homework with students with learning disabilities. *Journal of Learning Disabilities, 27,* 570–578.

Patton, J. R., Blackburn, J., & Fad, K. (2001). *Focus on exceptional children* (8th ed.). Columbus, OH: Merrill.

Patton, J. R., & Cronin, M. E. (1993). *Life skills instruction for all students with disabilities.* Austin, TX: Pro-Ed.

Patton, J. R., Cronin, M. E., & Wood, J. D. (1999). *Infusing real-life topics into extracurriculuar activities.* Austin, TX: Pro-Ed.

Patton, J. R., & Dunn, C. R. (1998). *Transition from school to adult life for students with special needs: Basic concepts and recommended practices.* Austin, TX: Pro-Ed.

Patton, J. R., Jayanthi, M., & Polloway, E. A. (2001). Home-school collaboration about homework. *Reading and Writing Quarterly, 17,* 230–236.

Patton, J. R., & Keyes, D. W. (in press). Death penalty issues. *Exceptionality.*

Patton, J. R., Polloway, E. A., & Smith, T. E. C. (2000). Educating students with mild mental retardation. In M. L. Wehmeyer & J. R. Patton (Eds.), *Mental retardation in the 21st century.* Austin, TX: Pro-Ed.

Patton, J. R., Polloway, E. A., Smith, T. E. C., Edgar, E., Clark, G. M., & Lee, S. (1996). Individuals with mild mental retardation: Postsecondary outcomes and implications for educational policy. *Education and Training in Mental Retardation and Developmental Disabilities, 31,* 77–85.

Peck, A. & Scarpati, S. (2004). Techniques for program support. *Teaching Exceptional Children, 39(1),* 4.

Pemberton, J. B. (2003). Communicating academic progress as an integral part of assessment. *Teaching Exceptional Children, 35,* 16–20.

Pemberton, J. B., Rademacher, J. A., Tyler-Wood, T., & Careijo, M. V. (2006). Aligning assessments with state curricular standards. *Intervention, 41(5),* 283–289.

Pfiffner, L., & Barkley, R. (1991). Educational placement and classroom management. In R. Barkley (Ed.), *Attention deficit hyperactivity disorder: A handbook for diagnosis and treatment* (pp. 498–539). New York: Guilford Press.

Physicians' Desk Reference (1994). Oravell, NJ: Medical Economics Company.

Physicians' Desk Reference (1999). Oravell, NJ: Medical Economics Company.

Pickett, A. L., & Gerlach, K. (1997). *Paraeducators.* Austin, TX: Pro-Ed.

Pierangelo, R. & Giuliani, G. (2006). *Learning disabilities: A practical approach to foundations, assessment, diagnosis, and teaching.* Boston: Allyn and Bacon.

Pierce, C. (1994). Importance of classroom climate for at-risk learners. *Journal of Educational Research, 88,* 37–44.

Plummer, D. L. (1995). Serving the needs of gifted children from a multicultural perspective. In J. L. Genshaft, M. Bireley, & C. L. Hollinger (Eds.), *Serving gifted and talented students: A resource for school personnel* (pp. 285–300). Austin, TX: Pro-Ed.

Pocock, A., Lambros, S., Karvonen, M., Test, D. W., Algozzine, B., Wood, W., et al (2002). Successful strategies for promoting self-advocacy among students with learning disabilities: The LEAD Group. *Intervention in School and Clinic, 37*(4), 209–216.

Podemski, R. S., Marsh, G. E., Smith, T. E. C., & Price, B. J. (1995). *Comprehensive administration of special education.* Columbus, OH: Merrill.

Polloway, E. A. (1984). The integration of mildly retarded students in the schools: A historical review. *Remedial and Special Education, 5*(4), 18–28.

Polloway, E. A. (1997). Developmental principles of the Luckasson et al. AAMR definition: A retrospective. *Education and Training in Mental Retardation and Developmental Disabilities, 32,* 174–178.

Polloway, E. A. (2004). The profession of learning disabilities: Progress and promises. *Learning Disability Quarterly, 25,* 103–112.

Polloway, E. A. (2005). Perspectives on mild retardation: The status of a category of exceptionality. In J. J. Hoover (Eds.), *Current issues in special education* (pp. 35–46). Boulder, CO: BUENO Center.

Polloway, E.A. (Ed.). (in press). Mild mental retardation: The forgotten disability. *Exceptionality.*

Polloway, E. A., Bursuck, W., & Epstein, M. H. (1999). Testing adaptations in the general education classroom. *Reading and Writing Quarterly, 17*(3), 181–187.

Polloway, E. A., Bursuck, W. D., & Epstein, M. H. (2001). Homework for students with learning disabilities: The challenge of home-school communication. *Reading and Writing Quarterly, 17,* 181–187.

Polloway, E. A., Bursuck, W., Jayanthi, M., Epstein, M., & Nelson, J. (1996). Treatment acceptability: Determining appropriate interventions within inclusive classrooms. *Intervention in School and Clinic, 31,* 133–144.

Polloway, E. A., Epstein, M. H., Bursuck, W. D. (2002). Homework for students with learning disabilities. *Reading and Writing Quarterly, 17,* 181–187.

Polloway, E. A., Epstein, M. H., Bursuck, W. D., Jayanthi, M., & Cumblad, C. (1994). Homework practices of general education teachers. *Journal of Learning Disabilities, 27,* 500–509.

Polloway, E. A., Epstein, M. H., Bursuck, W. D., Roderique, T. W., McConeghy, J., & Jayanthi, M. (1994). Classroom grading: A national survey of policies. *Remedial and Special Education, 15*(2), 162–170.

Polloway, E. A., & Jones-Wilson, L. (1992). Principles of assessment and instruction. In E. A. Polloway & T. E. C. Smith (Eds.), *Language instruction for students with disabilities* (pp. 87–120). Denver, CO: Love.

Polloway, E. A., Miller, L., & Smith, T. E. C. (2003). *Language instruction for students with disabilities* (3rd ed.). Denver, CO: Love.

Polloway, E. A., Patton, J. R., Epstein, M. H., & Smith, T. E. C. (1989). Comprehensive curriculum: Program design for students with mild handicaps. *Focus on Exceptional Children, 21*(8), 1–12.

Polloway, E. A., Patton, J. R., Payne, J. S., & Payne, R. A. (1989). *Strategies for teaching learners with special needs* (5th ed). Columbus, OH: Merrill.

Polloway, E. A., Patton, J. R. , & Serna, L. (2008). *Strategies for teaching learners with special needs* (9th ed.). Columbus, OH: Merrill.

Polloway, E. A., Patton, J. R., Smith, J. D., & Roderique, T. W. (1992). Issues in program design for elementary students with mild retardation: Emphasis on curriculum development. *Education and Training in Mental Retardation, 27,* 142–150.

Polloway, E. A., Patton, J. R., Smith, T. E. C., & Buck, G. H. (1997). Mental retardation and learning disabilities: Conceptual issues. *Journal of Learning Disabilities, 30,* 219–231.

Polloway, E. A., & Smith, J. D. (1988). Current status of the mild mental retardation construct: Identification, placement, and programs. In M. C. Wang, M. C. Reynolds, & H. J. Walberg (Eds.), *The handbook of special education: Research and practice* (Vol. II, pp. 1–22). Oxford, UK: Pergamon Press.

Polloway, E. A., & Smith, J. D. (2001). Biological sources of mental retardation and efforts for prevention. In Beirne-Smith, M., Ittenbach, R. F., & Patton, J. R. *Mental retardation* (6th ed., pp. 150–195). Upper Saddle River, NJ: Prentice-Hall/ Merrill.

Polloway, E. A., & Smith, J. D. (2006). Inclusion of people with mental retardation and other developmental disabilities in the community. *Mental Retardation, 44*(2), 100–111.

Polloway, E. A., Smith, J. D., Chamberlain, J., Denning, C., & Smith, T. E. C. (1999). Levels of deficit vs. levels of support in mental retardation classification. *Education and Training in Mental Retardation and Development Disabilities, 34,* 48–59.

Polloway, E. A., Smith, J. D., Patton, J. R., & Smith, T. E. C. (1996). Historic changes in mental retardation and developmental disabilities. *Education and Training in Mental Retardation and Developmental Disabilities, 31,* 3–2.

Polloway, E. A., & Smith, J. E. (1982). *Teaching language skills to exceptional learners.* Denver, CO: Love.

Polloway, E. A., & Smith, T. E. C. (2000). *Language instruction for students with disabilities.* Denver, CO: Love.

Popp, R. A. (1983). Learning about disabilities. *Teaching Exceptional Children, Winter,* 78–81.

Powers, M. D. (1989). *Children with autism: A parent's guide.* New York: Woodbine House.

Prasse, D.P. (2006). Legal supports for problem-solving systems. *Remedial and Special Education, 27,* 7–14.

Prater, M. A. (1992). Increasing time-on-task in the classroom. *Intervention in School and Clinic, 28*(1), 22–27.

Prater, M. A., Joy, R., Chilman, B., Temple, J., & Miller, S. R. (1991). Self-monitoring of on-task behavior by adolescents with learning disabilities. *Learning Disability Quarterly, 14,* 164–177.

Prouty, V., & Fagan, M. (1997). *Language strategies for children.* Eau Claire, WI: Thinking Publications.

Public Law 94–142 (1975). *Federal Register, 42,* 42474–42518.

Public Law 101–476 (1990). *Federal Register, 54,* 35210–35271.

Pugach, M. C., & Warger, C. L. (2001). Curriculum matters. *Remedial and Special Education, 22,* 194–196.

Pugh, K. R., Mencl, W. E., Jenner, A. R., Lee, J. R., Katz, L., Frost, S. J., et al. (2001). Neuroimaging studies of reading development and reading disability. *Learning Disabilities Research and Practice, 16*(4), 240–249.

Pugh, S. (1999). Working with families of individual students. *Gifted Children Today, 22,* 26–31.

Quay, H., & Peterson, D. (1987). *Revised behavior problem checklist.* Coral Gables, FL: University of Miami.

Quinn, M. M., Kavale, K. A., Mathur, S. R., Rutherford, R. B., Jr., & Forness, S. R. (1999). A meta-analysis of social skill interventions for students with emotional and behavioral disorders. *Journal of Emotional and Behavioral Disorders, 7,* 54–64.

Ramos-Ford, V., & Gardner, H. (1997). Giftedness from a multiple intelligences perspective. In N. Colangelo & G. A. Davis (Eds.), *Handbook of gifted education* (2nd ed., pp. 54–66). Boston: Allyn and Bacon.

Rankin-Erickson, J. L., & Pressley, M. (2000). A survey of instructional practices of special education teachers nominated as effective teachers of literacy. *Learning Disabilities Research and Practice, 15*(4), 206–225.

Rapp, W. H. (2005). Inquiry-based environments for individuals with exceptional learning needs. *Remedial and Special Education, 26*(5), 297–310.

Raskind, M. H., Goldberg, R. J., Higgins, E. L., & Herman, K. L. (2002). Teaching life success to students with learning disabilities: Lessons learned from a 20-year study. *Intervention in Schools and Clinic, 37*(4), 201–208.

Raskind, W. W. (2001). Current understanding of the genetic basis of reading and spelling differences. *Learning Disabilities Quarterly, 24,* 141–157.

Ratner, V. L., & Harris, L. R. (1994). *Understanding language disabilities: The impact of language.* Eau Claire, WI: Thinking Publications.

Rea, P. J., McLaughlin, V. L., & Walther-Thomas, C. (2002). Outcomes for students with learning disabilities in inclusive and pullout programs. *Exceptional Children, 68,* 203–222.

Reeve, R. E. (1990). ADHD: Facts and fallacies. *Intervention in School and Clinic, 26,* 71–78.

Reid, R., & Nelson, J. R. (2002). The utility, acceptability, and practicality of functional behavioral assessment for students with high-incidence problem behaviors. *Remedial and Special Education, 23,* 15–23.

Reis, S. M. (1989). Reflections on policy affecting the education of gifted and talented students. *American Psychologist, 44,* 399–408.

Reis, S. M. (2001). External barriers experienced by gifted and talented girls. *Gifted Children Today, 24,* 31–36.

Reis, S. M., & Schack, G. D. (1993). Differentiating products for the gifted and talented: The encouragement of independent learning. In C. J. Maker (Ed.), *Critical issues in gifted education: Programs for the gifted in regular classrooms* (Vol. 3, pp. 161–186). Austin, TX: Pro-Ed.

Renzulli, J. S. (1979). *What makes giftedness: A reexamination of the definition of the gifted and talented.* Ventura, CA: Ventura County Superintendent of Schools Office.

Renzulli, J. S., & Reis, S. M. (1985). *The schoolwide enrichment model: A comprehensive plan for educational excellence.* Mansfield Center, CT: Creative Learning Press.

Renzulli, J. S., & Reis, S. M. (1997). The schoolwide enrichment model: New directions for developing high-end learning. In N. Colangelo & G. A. Davis (Eds.), *Handbook of gifted education* (2nd ed.). Boston: Allyn and Bacon.

Renzulli, J. S., Reis, S. M., & Smith, L. M. (1981). *The revolving door identification model.* Wethersfield, CT: Creative Learning Press.

Research identifies opportunities and offers solutions for improving family involvement. (2001). *Research Connections, Fall*(9), 2–5.

Reschly, D. (1988). Incorporating adaptive behavior deficits into instructional programs. In G. A. Robinson, J. R. Patton, E. A. Polloway, & L. R. Sargent (Eds.), *Best practices in mental disabilities* (Vol. 2, pp. 53–80). Des Moines, IA: Iowa State Department of Education.

Reschly, D. J. & Hosp, J. L. (2004). State SLD identification policies and practices. *Learning Disabilities Quarterly, 27*(4), 197–213.

Richards, T. L. (2001). Functional magnetic resonance imaging and spectroscopic imaging of the brain: Application of fMRI and fMRS to reading disabilities and education. *Learning Disabilities Quarterly, 24*(3), 189–203.

Rieck, W. A., & Wadsworth, D. E. (1999). Foreign exchange: An inclusion strategy. *Intervention, 35,* 22–28.

Riley, T. (1999). The role of advocacy: Creating change for gifted children throughout the world. *Gifted Child Today, 22,* 44–47.

Riggs, C. G. (2001). Work effectively with paraeducators in inclusive settings. *Intervention in School and Clinic, 37,* 114–117.

Roach, V. (1995). Supporting inclusion: Beyond the rhetoric. *Phi Delta Kappan, 77,* 295–299.

Robin, A. L. (1998). *ADHD in adolescents: Diagnosis and treatment.* New York: Guilford Press.

Robin, S. S., & Johnson, E. O. (1996). Attitude and peer cross pressure: Adolescent drug and alcohol use. *Journal of Drug Education, 26,* 69–99.

Robinson, C. S., Manchetti, B. M., & Torgesen, J. K. (2002). Toward a two-factor theory of one type of mathematics disability. *Learning Disabilities Research and Practice, 17,* 81–89.

Robinson, S. M., Braxdale, C. T., & Colson, S. E. (1988). Preparing dysfunctional learners to enter junior high school: A transitional curriculum. *Focus on Exceptional Children, 18*(4), 1–12.

Robinson, L. M., Skaer, T. L., Sclar, D. A., & Galin, R. S. (2002). Is attention deficit hyperactivity disorder increasing among girls in the U.S.? *CNS Drugs, 16,* 129–137.

Rock, E. E., Rosenberg, M. S., & Carran, D. T. (1995). Variables affecting the reintegration rate of students with serious emotional disturbance. *Exceptional Children, 6,* 254–268.

Rooney, K. (1993). *Attention deficit hyperactivity disorder: A videotape program.* Richmond, VA: State Department of Education.

Rooney, K. J. (1995). Dyslexia revisited: History, educational philosophy, and clinical assessment applications. *Intervention in School and Clinic, 31*(1), 6–15.

Roseberry-McKibbins, C. & Brice, A. (2002). Choice of language instruction: One or two? *Teaching Exceptional Children, 33,* 10–16.

Rosenberg, M. S., O'Shea, L., & O'Shea, D. J. (1991). *Student teacher to master teacher: A handbook for preservice and beginning teachers of students with mild and moderate handicaps.* New York: Macmillan.

Rosenberg, M. S., Wilson, R., Maheady, L., & Sindelar, P. (1992). *Educating students with behavior disorders.* Boston: Allyn and Bacon.

Ross, S. M., Smith, L. J., Casey, J., & Slavin, R. E. (1995). Increasing the academic success of disadvantaged children: An examination of alternative early intervention programs. *American Educational Research Journal, 32,* 773–800.

Rosselli, H. (1993). Process differentiation for gifted learners in the regular classroom: Teaching to everyone's needs. In C. J. Maker (Ed.), *Critical issues in gifted education: Programs for the gifted in regular classrooms* (Vol. 3, pp. 139–155). Austin, TX: Pro-Ed.

Rossow, A., & Hess, C. (2001). Engaging students in meaningful reading: A professional development journey. *Teaching Exceptional Children, 33,* 15–20.

Rotter, K. (2006). Creating instructional materials for all pupils: Try COLA. *Intervention in School and Clinic, 41*(5), 273–282.

Roy, N., Merrill, R. N., Thibeault, S., Gray, S. D., & Smith, E. M. (2004). Voice disorders in teachers and the general population: effects on work performance, attendance, and future career choices. *Journal of Speech, Language, Hearing Research, 47*(3): 542–551.

Ruble, L. A., & Dalrymple, M. J. (2002). COMPASS: A parent–teacher collaboration model for students with autism. *Focus on Autism and Other Developmental Disabilities, 17,* 76–83.

Rueda, R., Monzo, L., Shapiro, J., Gomez, J., & Blacher, J. (2005). Cultural models of transition: Latina mothers of young adults with developmental disabilities. *Exceptional Children, 71,* 401–414.

Rylance, B. J. (1998). Predictors of post-high school employment for youth identified as severely emotionally disturbed. *The Journal of Special Education, 32,* 184–192.

Ryser, G., & McConnell, K. (2003). *Scales for diagnosing attention deficit/hyperactivity disorder.* Austin, TX: Pro-Ed.

Sabatino, D. A. (1987). Preventive discipline as a practice in special education. *Teaching Exceptional Children, 19,* 8–11.

Sabornie, E. J. & deBettencourt, L. U. (2004). *Teaching students with mild and high-incidence disabilities at the secondary level* (2nd ed.). Upper Saddle River, NJ: Merrill.

Safford, P. L., & Safford, E. J. (1998). Visions of the special class. *Remedial and Special Education, 19,* 229–238.

Safran, J. S. (2002). A practical guide to research on Asperger's syndrome. *Intervention in School and Clinic, 37,* 283–293.

Saintonge, S., Achille, P. A., & Lachance, L. (1998). The influence of big brothers on the separation-individuation of adolescents from single-parent families. *Adolescence, 33,* 343–352.

Salend, S. J. (1994). *Effective mainstreaming: Creating inclusive classrooms* (2nd ed.). Columbus, OH: Merrill/Prentice-Hall.

Salend, S. J. (1999). Facilitating friendships among diverse students. *Intervention in School and Clinic, 35,* 9–15.

Salend, S. J. (2000). Parental perceptions of inclusive placement. *Remedial and Special Education, 21,* 121–128.

Salend, S. J. (2001). *Creating inclusive classrooms: Effective and reflective practices* (4th ed.). Columbus, OH: Merrill/Prentice Hall.

Salend, S. J. (2004). Fostering inclusive values in children: What families can do. *Teaching Exceptional Children, 37,* 64–68.

Salend, S., & Duhaney, L. G. (1999). The impact of inclusion on students with and without disabilities and their education. *Remedial and Special Education, 20,* 114–126.

Salend, S., & Duhaney, L. G. (2002). Grading students in inclusive settings. *Teaching Exceptional Children, 34,* 13–14.

Salend, S. J., Elhoweris, H., & van Garderen, D. (2003). Educational interventions for students with ADHD. *Intervention in School and Clinic, 38*(5), 280–288.

Salend, S. J., & Garrick Duhaney, L. M. (2005). Understanding and addressing the disproportionate representation students of color in special education. *Intervention, 40*(4), 213–221.

Salend, S. J., Gordon, J., & Lopez-Vona, K. (2002). Evaluating cooperative teaching teams. *Intervention in School and Clinic, 37,* 195–200.

Salend, S. J. & Melland, J. (2002). Evaluating cooperative teaching teams. *Intervention in School and Clinic, 37,* 195–200.

Salend, S.J. & Rohena, E. (2002) Students with attention deficit disorders: An overview. *Intervention in School and Clinic, 38*(5), 259–266.

Salvia, J., & Ysseldyke, J. E. (1998). *Assessment* (8th ed.). Boston: Houghton Mifflin.

Sander, E. K. (1972). When are speech sounds learned? *Journal of Speech and Hearing Disorders, 37,* 62.

Sanders, R., Colton, M., & Roberts, S. (1999). Child abuse fatalities and cases of extreme concern: Lessons from reviews. *Child Abuse and Neglect, 23,* 257–273.

Sansoti, F. J., Powell-Smith, K. A., & Kincaid, D. (2004). A research synthesis of social story interventions for children with autism. *Journal of Autism and Other Developmental Disabilities, 19*(4), 194–204.

Santrock, J. W., & Warshak, R. A. (1979). Father custody and social development in boys and girls. *Journal of Social Issues, 35,* 112–125.

Sargent, L. R. (1991). *Social skills for school and community.* Reston, VA: CEC-MR.

Savage, R. C. (1997). Integrating the rehabilitation and education services for school–age children. *Journal of Head Trauma Rehabilitation, 12,* 11–20.

Savage, R. C., & Wolcott, G. F. (Eds.) (1994). *Educational dimensions of acquired brain injury.* Austin, TX: Pro-Ed.

Scahill, L. & Schwab-Stone, M. (2000). Epidemiology of ADHD in school-age children. *Child and Adolescent Psychiatric Clinics of North America, 9,* 541–555.

Scanlon, D., & Melland, D. F. (2002). Academic and participant profiles of school-age dropouts with and without disabilities. *Exceptional Children, 68,* 239–258.

Schaffner, C. B., & Buswell, B. E. (1996). Ten critical elements for creating inclusive and effective school communities. In S. Stainback & W. Stainback (Eds.), *Inclusion: A guide for educators* (pp. 49– 65). Baltimore, MD: Brookes.

Schall, C. (2002). A consumer's guide to monitoring medication for individuals with ASD. *Focus on Autism and Other Developmental Disabilities, 17,* 228–235.

Schalock, R. (2001, May–June). Consortium on language presents phase one report. *American Association on Mental Retardation News and Notes, 14*(3), 1, 4–6.

Scheuerman, B., & Webber, J. (2002). *Autism: Teaching does make a difference.* Belmont, CA: Wadsworth.

Schiever, S. W. (1993). Differentiating the learning environment for gifted students. In C. J. Maker (Ed.), *Critical issues in gifted education: Programs for the gifted in regular classrooms* (Vol. 3, pp. 201–214). Austin, TX: Pro-Ed.

Schloss, P., Schloss, A., & Shloss, C.N. (2007). *Instructional methods for secondary students with learning and behavior problems.* Boston: Allyn and Bacon.

Scholes, C. (1998). General science: A diagnostic teaching unit. *Intervention, 34*(2), 107–114.

Schuck, S. E. B., & Crinella, F. M. (2005). Why children with ADHD do not have low IQs. *Journal of Learning Disabilities, 38*(3), 262–280.

Schulte, A., & Olson, R. (2001). Rethinking learning disabilities. In C. E. Finn, A. J. Rotherham, & C. R. Hokanson, Jr. (Eds.), *Rethinking special education for a new century.* Washington, DC: Thomas B. Fordham Foundation.

Schulz, J. B., & Carpenter, C. D. (1995). *Mainstreaming exceptional students: A guide for classroom teachers.* Boston: Allyn and Bacon.

Schumaker, J. B., Deshler, D. D., Allen, G. R., Warner, M. M., & Denton, P. H. (1981). Multipass: A learning strategy for improving reading comprehension. *Learning Disability Quarterly, 5(3),* 295–304.

Schumm, J. S., & Vaughn, S. (1991). Grouping for reading instruction. *Journal of Learning Disabilities, 25(5),* 66–74.

Schumm, J. S., & Vaughn, S. (1992). Reflections on planning for mainstreamed special education students. *Exceptionality, 3(2),* 121–127.

Schumm, J. S., & Vaughn, S., & Leavell (1994). Getting ready for inclusion. *Learning Disabilities Research and Practice, 10(3),* 169–179.

Schumm, J. S., & Vaughn, S., & Saumell (1994). Responsible inclusion for students with learning disabilities. *Journal of Learning Disabilities, 28(5),* 264–270.

Schumm, J. S., & Vaughn, S., Gordon, & Rothlein, L. (1994). General education teachers' beliefs, skills, and practices in planning for mainstreamed students with learning disabilities. *Teacher Education and Special Education, 17(3),* 22–37.

Schumm, J. S., & Vaughn, S., Haager, McDowell, Rothlein, L., & Saumell (1995). General education teacher planning: What can students with learning disabilities expect? *Exceptional Children, 61(4),* 335–352.

Scott, B. J., Vitale, M. R., & Masten, W. G. (1998). Implementing instructional adaptations for students with disabilities in inclusive classrooms: A literature review. *Remedial and Special Education, 19,* 106–119.

Scott, T. M., & Nelson, M. C. (1998). Confusion and failure in facilitating generalized social responding in the school setting: Sometimes 2 + 2 = 5. *Behavioral Disorders, 23,* 264–275.

Scruggs, T. E., & Mastropieri, M. A. (1994). Successful mainstreaming in elementary science classes: A qualitative study of three reputational cases. *American Educational Research Journal, 31,* 785–811.

Scruggs, T. E., & Mastropieri, M. A. (1996). Teacher perceptions of mainstreaming/inclusion, 1958–1995: A research synthesis. *Exceptional Children, 63,* 59–74.

Scruggs, T. E. & Mastropieri, M. A. (2000). The effectiveness of mnemonic instruction for students with learning and behavior problems: An update and research synthesis. *Journal of Behavioral Education, 10,* 163–173.

Searcy, S., & Meadows, N. B. (1994). The impact of social structures on friendship development for children with behavior disorders. *Education and Treatment of Children, 17,* 255–268.

Sears, P. S. (1978). The Terman genetic studies of genius, 1922–1972. In A. H. Passow (Ed.), *The gifted and the talented: Their education and development* (Vol. 78, pp. 75–96). Chicago: University of Chicago Press.

Seeley, K. (1995). Classwide peer tutoring. Unpublished manuscript, Lynchburg College, VA.

Seery, M. E., Davis, P. M., & Johnson, L. J. (2000). Seeing eye to eye: Are parents and professionals in agreement about the benefits of preschool inclusion? *Remedial and Special Education, 21,* 368–378.

Semrul-Clikerman, M., Steingard, R. J., Filipek, P., Biederman, J., Bekken, K., and Renshaw, P. F. (2000). Using MRI to examine brain–behavior relationships in males with attention-deficit hyperactivity disorder. *Journal of the American Academy of Child and Adolescent Psychiatry, 39(4),* 477–484.

Sevcik, R. A., & Romski, M. (2000). *AAC: More than three decades of growth and development.* Washington, DC: American Speech–Language–Hearing Association.

Sexton, D., Snyder, P., Wolfe, B., Lobman, M., Stricklin, S., & Akers, P. (1996). Early intervention inservice training strategies: Perceptions and suggestions from the field. *Exceptional Children, 62,* 485–496.

Shane, H. C., & Sauer, M. (1986). *Augmentative and alternative communication.* Austin, TX: Pro-Ed.

Shaner, M. Y. (1991). Talented teachers for talented students. *G/C/T, 22,* 14–15.

Shanker, A. (1994–1995). Educating students in special programs. *Educational Leadership, 52,* 43–47.

Shapiro, E. S., DuPaul, G. J., & Bradley-Klug, K. L. (1998). Self-management as a strategy to improve the classroom behavior of adolescents with ADHD. *Journal of Learning Disabilities, 31,* 545–555.

Shea, T. M., & Bauer, A. M. (1991). *Parents and teachers of children with exceptionalities: A handbook for collaboration.* Boston: Allyn and Bacon.

Sileo, T. W., Sileo, A. P., & Prater, M. A. (1996). Parent and professional partnerships in special education: Multicultural considerations. *Intervention in School & Clinic, 31,* 145–153.

Silver, L. B. (1995). Controversial therapies. *Journal of Child Neurology, 10(1),* 96–100.

Silver, L. B. (1999). *Attention deficit hyperactivity disorder: A clinical guide to diagnosis and treatment for health and mental health.* Washington, DC: American Psychiatric Press.

Silver, L. B. (2000). Alternative treatment for ADHD. In B. P. Guyer (Ed.), *ADHD: Achieving success in school and in life.* Boston: Allyn and Bacon.

Silver, L. B. (2002). What does it mean to have LD? *LDA Newsbriefs,* p. 3.

Silver, L. B. (2003, September/October). Another claim of a treatment for learning disabilities. Should you consider it? *LDA Newsbriefs,* pp. 4, 12.

Silverman, A. B., Reinherz, H. Z., & Giaconia, R. M. (1996). The long-term sequelae of child and adolescent abuse: A longitudinal community study. *Child Abuse and Neglect, 20,* 709–723.

Silverman, L. K. (1986). What happens to the gifted girl? In C. J. Maker (Ed.), *Critical issues in gifted education: Defensible programs for the gifted* (Vol. 1, pp. 43–89). Austin, TX: Pro-Ed.

Simmons, D., Fuchs, D., Hodge, J., & Mathes, P. (1994). Importance of instructional complexity and role reciprocity to classwide peer tutoring. *Learning Disabilities Research and Practice, 9,* 203–212.

Simpson, R. (1996). *Working with parents and families of exceptional children and youth* (3rd ed.). Austin, TX: Pro-Ed.

Simpson, R. (1998). Behavior modification for children and adolescents with exceptionalities. *Intervention in School and Clinic, 33,* 219–226.

Simpson, R. (2001). ABA and students with autism spectrum disorders. *Focus on Autism and Developmental Disabilities, 16,* 68–71.

Simpson, R. (2004). Evidence-based practices and students with autism spectrum disorder. *Journal of Autism and Other Developmental Disabilities, 20(3),* 140–149.

Skiba, R., Grizzle, K., & Minke, K. M. (1994). Opening the floodgates? The social maladjustment exclusion and state SED prevalence rates. *Journal of School Psychology, 32,* 267–283.

Skoto, B. G., Koppebnhaver, D. A., & Erickson, K. A. (2004). Parent reading behaviors and communication outcomes in girls with Rett syndrome. *Exceptional Children, 70,* 145–166.

Smedley, T. M., & Higgins, K. (2005). Virtual technology: Bringing the world into the special education room. *Intervention, 41(2),* 114–119.

Smith, T. J., & Adams G. (2006). The effects of comorbidity AD/HD and learning disabilities on parent-reported behavioral and academic outcomes in children. *Learning Disabilities Quarterly, 29(2),* 17–21.

Smith, C. R. (1994). *Learning disabilities: The interaction of learner, task, and setting* (3rd ed.). Boston: Allyn and Bacon.

Smith, C. R. (1998). From gibberish to phoneme awareness: Effective decoding instruction. *Teaching Exceptional Children, 30,* 20–25.

Smith, C. R. (2004). *Learning Disabilities: The interaction of students and their environments.* Boston: Allyn & Bacon.

Smith, D. D., & Luckasson, R. (1995/1998). *Introduction to special education: Teaching in an age of challenge.* Boston: Allyn and Bacon.

Smith, R. (2004). *Conscious classroom management: Unlocking the secrets of great teaching* (pp. 83–87). San Rafael, CA: Conscious Teaching Publications.

Smith, D. D., & Rivera, D. P. (1993). *Effective discipline* (2nd ed.). Austin, TX: Pro-Ed.

Smith, D. D., & Rivera, D. P. (1995). Discipline in special and regular education. *Focus on Exceptional Children, 27(5),* 1–14.

Smith, J. D. (1994). The revised AAMR definition of mental retardation: The MRDD position. *Education and Training in Mental Retardation and Developmental Disabilities, 29,* 179–183.

Smith, J. D. (1995). Inclusive school environments and students with disabilities in South Carolina: The issues, the status, the needs. *Occasional Papers, 1,* 1–5.

Smith, J. W., & Smith, S. B. (2002). Technology for organizing and presenting digital information. *Intervention in School and Clinic, 37,* 306–310.

Smith, M. D., Belcher, R. G., & Juhrs, P. D. (1995). *A guide to successful employment for individuals with autism.* Baltimore, MD: Brookes.

Smith, P. M. (1997). You are not alone: For parents when they learn that their child has a disability. *NICHY News Digest, 2,* 2–5.

Smith, R. (2004). *Conscious classroom management.* San Rafael, CA: Conscious Teaching Publications.

Smith, S. W. (1990a). A comparison of individualized education programs (IEPs) of students with behavioral disorders and learning disabilities. *Journal of Special Education, 24,* 85–100.

Smith, S. W. (1990b). Individualized education programs (IEPs) in special education: From intent to acquiescence. *Exceptional Children, 57,* 6–14.

Smith, S. W., & Simpson, R. L. (1989). An analysis of individualized education programs (IEPs) for students with behavior disorders. *Behavioral Disorders, 14,* 107–116.

Smith, T. E. C. (1990). *Introduction to education* (2nd ed.). St. Paul, MN: West.

Smith, T. E. C. (2001). Section 504, the ADA, and public schools: What educators need to know. *Remedial and Special Education, 21,* 335–343.

Smith, T. E. C. (2002). Section 504: Basic requirements for schools. *Intervention in School and Clinic, 37,* 2–6.

Smith, T. E. C. (2005). IDEA 2004: Another round in the reauthorization process. *Remedial and Special Education, 26,* 314–319.

Smith, T. E. C., & Dowdy, C. A. (1992). Future-based assessment and intervention and mental retardation. *Education and Training in Mental Retardation, 27,* 23–31.

Smith, T. E. C., Dowdy, C. A., Polloway, E. A., & Blalock, G. (1997). *Children and adults with learning disabilities.* Boston: Allyn and Bacon.

Smith, T. E. C., Finn, D. M., & Dowdy, C. A. (1993). *Teaching students with mild disabilities.* Ft. Worth, TX: Harcourt Brace Jovanovich.

Smith, T. E. C., Gartin, B. C., Murdick, N. L., & Hilton, A. (2006). *Families and children with special needs*. Columbus, OH: Merrill.

Smith, T. E. C., & Hendricks, M. D. (1995). *Prader-Willi syndrome: Practical considerations for educators*. Little Rock, AR: Ozark Learning.

Smith, T. E. C., & Hilton, A. (1994). Program design for students with mental retardation. *Education and Training in Mental Retardation and Developmental Disabilities, 29*, 3–8.

Smith, T. E. C., & Patton, J. R. (2007). *Section 504 and public schools* (2nd ed.). Austin, TX: Pro-Ed.

Smith, T. E. C., Price, B. J., & Marsh, G. E. (1986). *Mildly handicapped children and adults*. St. Paul, MN: West.

Smutny, J. F., Walker, S. Y., & Meckstroth, E. A. (1997). *Teaching young gifted children in the regular classroom: Identifying, nurturing, and challenging ages 4–9*. Minneapolis, MN: Free Spirit.

Snell, M.E., Brown, F. (2006). *Instruction of students with severe disabilities*. (6th ed.). Columbus, OH: Pearson/Merrill.

Solomon, C. R., & Serres, F. (1999). Effects of parental verbal aggression on children's self-esteem and school marks. *Child Abuse & Neglect, 23*, 339–351.

Soto, G., Muller, E., Hunt, P., and Goetz, L. (2001). Professional skills for serving students who use AAC in general education classrooms: A team perspective. *Language, Speech, and Hearing Services in the Schools, 32*, 51–56.

Southern, W. T., & Jones, E. D. (1991). Academic acceleration: Background and issues. In W. T. Southern & E. D. Jones (Eds.), *Academic acceleration of gifted children* (pp. 1–17). New York: Teachers College Press.

Sprinthall, N. A., & Collins, W. A. (1995). *Adolescent psychology: A developmental view*. New York: McGraw-Hil.

Squires, E. C., & Reetz, L. J. (1989). Vocabulary acquisition activities. *Academic Therapy, 14*, 589–592.

Stafford, A. M. (2005). Choice making: A strategy for students with severe disabilities. *Teaching Exceptional Children, 37*, 12–16.

Stahmer, A. C., Collins, N. M., & Palinkas, L. A. (2005). Early intervention practices for children with autism: Descriptions for community providers. *Journal of Autism and Other Developmental Disabilities, 20*(2), 66–79.

Stainback, S., Stainback, W., East, K., & Sapon-Shevin, M. (1994). A commentary on inclusion and the development of a positive self-identity by people with disabilities. *Exceptional Children, 60*, 486–490.

Steere, D. E., Rose, E., & Cavaiuolo (2007). *Growing up: Transition to adult life for students with disabilities*. Boston: Allyn & Bacon.

Steere, M. L., & Cavaoulo, S. D. (2002). Local school boards under review: Their role and effectiveness inrelation to students academic achievement. *Review of Educational Research, 72*(4), 229–278.

Stewart, D. A., & Kluwin, T. N. (2001). *Teaching deaf and hard of hearing students*. Boston: Allyn and Bacon.

Storey, K. (1993). A proposal for assessing integration. *Education and Training in Mental Retardation and Developmental Disabilities, 28*, 279–286.

Stormont-Spurgin, J. (1997). I lost my homework: Strategies for improving organization in students with ADHD. *Intervention in School and Clinic, 32*(5), 270–274.

Stover, D. (1992). The at-risk students schools continue to ignore. *The Education Digest, May*, 37–40.

Strangman, N., Hall, T., & Meyer, A. (nd). Graphic organizers and implications for universal design for learning (Cooperative Agreement No. H324H990004). National Center on Accessing the General Curriculum: US Department of Education/Office of Special Education Programs.

Strichart, S. S. & Mangrum, C. T. (2002). *Teaching learning strategies and study skills to students with learning disabilities, attention deficit disorders, or special needs* (3rd ed.). Boston: Allyn & Bacon

Stromer, R., Kimball, J. W., Kinney, E. M., & Taylor, B. A. (2006). Activity schedules and teaching chidlren with ASD. *Focus on Autism and Other Developmental Disabilities, 21*, 14–24.

Summers, M., Bridge, J., & Summers, C. R. (1991). Sibling support groups. *Teaching Exceptional Children, 23*, 20–25.

Summers, J.A., Hoffman, L., Marquis, J., Turnbull, K. A., Poston, D., Nelson, L.L. (2005). Measuring the quality of family-professional partnerships in special education services. *Exceptional Children, 72*, 65–81.

Swain, K. D., Friehe, M. M., & Harrington, J. M. (2004). Teaching listening strategies in the inclusive classroom. *Intervention in School and Clinic, 40*(1), 48–54.

Swanson, H. L. (2000). Are working memory differences in readings with learning disabilities hard to change? *Journal of Learning Disabilities, 33*, 551–566.

Tabassam, W., & Grainger, J. (2002). Self-concept, attributional style, and self-efficacy beliefs of students with learning disabilities with and without ADHD. *Learning Disabilities Quarterly, 25*, 141–151.

Tankersley, M. (1995). A group-oriented management program: A review of research on the good behavior game and implications for teachers. *Preventing School Failure, 40*, 19–28.

Tannenbaum, A. J. (1997). The meaning and making of giftedness. In N. Colangelo & G. A. Davis (Eds.), *Handbook of gifted education* (2nd ed.). Boston: Allyn and Bacon.

Tavzel, C. S., & Staff of LinguiSystems. (1987). *Blooming recipes*. East Moline, IL: LinguiSystems.

Taylor, R. L. (2000). *Assessment of individuals with mental retardation*. San Diego: Singular.

Taylor, R. L., Richards, S. B., & Brady, M. P. (2005). *Mental retardation: Historical perspectives, current practices, and future directions*. Boston: Allyn & Bacon.

Tennant, C., Bebbington, P. R., & Hurry, J. (1980). Parental death in childhood and risk of adult depressive disorders: A review. *Psychological Medicine, 10*, 289–299.

Terman, L. M. (1925). *Genetic studies of genius (Vol. 1): Mental and physical traits of a thousand gifted children.*. Stanford, CA: Stanford University Press.

Terman, L. M., & Oden, M. H. (1959). *Genetic studies of genius (Vol. 5): The gifted group at mid-life*. Stanford, CA: Stanford University Press.

Test, D. W., Fowler, C. H., Wood, W. M., Brewer, D. M., & Eddy, S. (2005). *Remedial and Special Education, 26*(1), 42–54.

Test, D. W., Mason, C., Hughes, C., Konrad, M., Neale, M., & Wood, W. M. (2004). Student involvement in individualized education program meetings. *Exceptional Children, 70*, 391–411.

Thomas, P. J., & Carmack, F. F. (1993). Language: The foundation of learning. In J. S. Choate (Ed.), *Successful mainstreaming: Proven ways to detect and correct special needs* (pp. 148–171). Boston: Allyn and Bacon.

Tirosh, E., & Canby, J. (1993). Autism with hyperlexia: A distinct syndrome? *American Journal on Mental Retardation, 98*, 84–92.

Tomblin, J. B., Records, N. L., Buckwalter, P., Zhang, X., Smith, E., & O'Brien, M. (1997). Prevalence of specific language impairment in kindergarten children. *Journal of Speech, Language, Hearing Research, 40*, 1245–1260.

Tomlinson-Keasey, C., & Little, T. D. (1990). Predicting educational attainment, occupational achievement, intellectual skill, and personal adjustment among gifted men and women. *Journal of Educational Psychology, 82*, 442–455.

Tovey, R. (1995). Awareness programs help change students' attitudes towards their disabled peers. *Harvard Educational Letter, 11*(6), 7–8.

Trad, P. V. (1999). Assessing the patterns that prevent teenage pregnancy. *Adolescence, 34*, 221–238.

Trainer, A. A. (2005). Self-determination perceptions and behaviors of diverse students with LD during the transition planning process. *Journal of Learning Disabilities, 38*(3), 233–249.

Truscott, S. D., Cohen, C. E., & Sams, D. P. (2005). The curriculum states of pre-referral intervention teams. *Remedial and Special Education, 26*(3), 130–140.

Tsal, Y., Shalev, & Mevorach, C. (2005). The diversity of attention deficits in ADHD: The prevalence of four cognitive factors in ADHD versus controls. *Journal of Learning Disabilities, 38*(2), 142–157.

Turnbull, A. P., Strickland, B., & Hammer, S. E. (1978). IEPs: Presenting guidelines for development and implementation. *Journal of Learning Disabilities, 11*, 40–46.

Turnbull, A. P., & Turnbull, H. R. (1997). *Families, professionals, and exceptionality: A special partnership*. Columbus, OH: Merrill.

Turnbull, H. R. (1993). *Free appropriate public education: The law and children with disabilities*. (4th ed.). Denver, CO: Love.

Turnbull, H. R. (1998). *Free appropriate public education: The law and children with disabilities* (5th ed.). Denver, CO: Love.

Turnbull, H. R., Pereira, L., & Blue-Banning, M. (2000). Teachers as friendship facilitators. *Teaching Exceptional Children, 32*, 66–70.

Turnbull, H. R., & Turnbull, A. P., (1986). *Families, professionals, and exceptionality: A special partnership*. Columbus, OH: Merrill.

Turnbull, H. R., & Turnbull, A. P. (2000). *Free appropriate public education* (6th ed.). Denver, CO: Love.

Turnbull, H. R., Turnbull, A. P., Shank, S., Smith, S., & Lead, D. (2002). *Exceptional lives: Special education in today's schools* (3rd ed.). Upper Saddle, NJ: Merrill.

Uess, M. L., Drasgow, E., & Lowery, K. A. (2005). NCLB and students with autism. *Focus on Autism and other Developmental Disabilities, 20*, 130–139.

Uhing, B. M., Mooney, P., & Ryser, G. R. (2005). Differences in strength assessment scores for youth with and without emotional disturbance. *Journal of Emotional and Behavioral Disorders, 13*(3), 181–187.

Ulrich, M. E., & Bauer, A. M. (2003). Levels of awareness: A closer look at communication between parents and professionals. *Teaching Exceptional Children, 35*, 20–24.

U.S. Department of Commerce. (1993). *Poverty in the United States: 1992*. Washington, DC: Author.

U.S. Department of Commerce. (1995). *Population Profile of the United States, 1995*. Washington, DC: Author.

U.S. Department of Education. (1989). *11th annual report to Congress on the implementation of IDEA*. Washington, DC: Author.

U.S. Department of Education. (1990). *12th annual report to Congress on the implementation of the Education of the Handicapped Act*. Washington, DC: Author.

U.S. Department of Education. (1990, January 9). Reading and writing proficiency remains low. *Daily Education News,* pp. 1–7.

U.S. Department of Education. (1991, September 16). *Memorandum: Clarification of policy to address the needs of children with attention deficit disorders within general and/or special education.* Washington, DC: Author.

U.S. Department of Education. (1993). *15th annual report to Congress on the implementation of IDEA.* Washington, DC: Author.

U.S. Department of Education. (1994). *16th annual report to Congress on the Implementation of the Individuals with Disabilities Education Act.* Washington, DC: Author.

U.S. Department of Education. (1996). *18th annual report to Congress on the implementation of IDEA.* Washington, DC: Author.

U.S. Department of Education. (1997). New report links fathers' involvement with children's success. *Community Update, 52,* 3.

U. S. Department of Education. (1998a). *Safe and smart: Making the after-school hours work for kids.* Washington, DC: Author.

U.S. Department of Education. (1998b). *20th annual report to Congress on the implementation of the Individuals with Disabilities Education Act.* Washington, DC: Author.

U. S. Department of Education. (1999). *The condition of education, 1998.* Washington, DC: Author.

U.S. Department of Education. (2002). *23rd annual report to Congress on the implementation of the Individuals with Disabilities Education Act.* Washington, DC: Author.

U.S. Department of Education. (2006). *25th annual report to Congress on the implementation of the Individuals with Disabilities Education Act.* Washington, DC: Author.

U.S. Department of Education, Office of Special Education and Rehabilitative Services, Office of Special Education Programs. (2005). *26th Annual (2004) Report to Congress on the Implementation of the Individuals with Disabilities Education Act (Vol. 1).*

U.S. Department of Health and Human Services, Center for Disease Control and Prevention. (2002). *Attention deficit disorder and learning disabilities: United States 1997–1998* (DHHS Publication No. PHS 2002–1534). Hyattsville, MD: Author.

U.S. Office of Education. (1977). Assistance to states for education of handicapped children: Procedures for evaluating specific learning disabilities. *Federal Register, 42,* 65082–65085.

U.S. Office of Education. (1999, March 12). Assistance to the states for the education of children with disabilities and the early intervention program for infants and toddlers with disabilities; final regulations. *Federal Register, 64*(48) 12406–12458.

Valente, S. (2001). Treating attention deficit hyperactivity disorder. *Nurse Practitioner, 26*(9), 14–29.

Van Eerdewegh, M. M., Bieri, M. D., Parrilla, R. H., & Clayton, P. J. (1982). The bereaved child. *British Journal of Psychiatry, 140,* 23–29.

Van Garderen, D., & Whittaker, C., (2006). Planning different multicultural instruction in secondary classes. *Teaching Exceptional Children, 44,* 12–15.

Van Laarhoven, T., Coutinho, M., Van Laarhoven-Myers, T., & Repp, A. C. (1999). Assessment of the student instructional setting, and curriculum to support successful integration. In M. J. Coutinho & A. C. Repp (Eds.), *Inclusion: The integration of students with disabilities.* Belmont, CA: Wadsworth Publishing.

VanTassel-Baska, J. (1989). Appropriate curriculum for gifted learners. *Educational Leadership, 47,* 13–15.

VanTassel-Baska, J. (1998). *Gifted and talented learners.* Denver, CO: Love.

VanTassel-Baska, J., Patton, J., & Prillaman, D. (1989). Disadvantaged gifted learners at-risk for educational attention. *Focus on Exceptional Children, 22*(3), 1–16.

Vaughn, C., & Long, W. (1999). Surrender to win: How adolescent drug and alcohol users change their lives. *Adolescence, 34,* 9–22.

Vaughn, S., Bos, C. S., & Schumm, J. S. (2000). *Teaching exceptional, diverse, and at-risk students in the general education classroom* (2nd ed.). Boston: Allyn and Bacon.

Vaughn, S., Gersten, R., & Chard, D. J. (2000). The underlying message in learning disabilities intervention research: Findings from research synthesis. *Exceptional Children, 67,* 99–114.

Vogeltanz, N. D., Wilsnack, S. C., Harris, T. R., Wilsnack, R. W., Wonderlich, S. A., & Kristjanson, A. F. (1999). Prevalence and risk factors for childhood sexual abuse in women: National survey findings. *Child Abuse & Neglect, 23,* 579–592.

Volkmar, F. R. (2005). *Handbook on autism* (3rd ed.). New York: Wiley.

Voltz, D., Brazil, N., & Ford, A. (2001). What matters most in inclusive education. *Intervention in School and Clinic, 37,* 23–30.

Wagner, J., & James, A. (2006). Pilot study of school counselors preparedness to serve students with disabilities. *Journal of School Health, 76,* 387–392.

Walberg, H. J. (1991). Does homework help? *School Community Journal, 1*(1), 13–15.

Walker, B. (1993, January). *Multicultural issues in education: An introduction.* Paper presented at Cypress–Fairbanks Independent School District In-Service, Cypress, TX.

Walker, H., Golly, A., McLane, J. Z., & Kimmich, M., (2005). The Oregon first step to success report. *Journal of Emotional and Behavior Disorders, 13,* 160–173.

Walker, J. E., & Shea, T. M. (1988). *Behavior management: A practical approach for educators* (4th ed.). New York: Merrill/Macmillan.

Walker, J. E., & Shea, T. M. (1995). *Behavior management: A practical approach for educators* (6th ed.). Columbus, OH: Merrill.

Walther-Thomas, C., Korinek, L., McLaughlin, V. L., & Williams, B. T. (2000). *Collaboration for inclusive education.* Boston: Allyn and Bacon.

Wanat, C. L. (1992). Meeting the needs of single-parent children: School and parent views differ. *NASSP Bulletin, 76,* 43–48.

Wang, M. C., & Gordon, E. W. (Eds.). (1994). *Educational resilience in inner-city America.* Hillsdale, NJ: Erlbaum.

Wang, M. C., Reynolds, M. C., & Walberg, H. J. (1994–1995). Serving students at the margins. *Educational Leadership, 52,* 12–17.

Warren, S. F. (2000). The future of early communication in language intervention. *Topics in Early Childhood Special Education, 20,* 33–37.

Warren, S. F. (2000, May–June). Mental retardation: Curse, characteristic, or coin of the realm? *American Association on Mental Retardation News and Notes, 13*(3), 1, 10–11.

Wasburn-Moses, L. (2005). Roles and responsibilities of secondary special education teachers in an age of reform. *Remedial and Special Education, 26*(3), 1512–158.

Watson, S. M., & Houtz, L. E. (2002). Teaching science: Meeting academic and cultural needs of students. *Intervention in School and Clinic, 37,* 268–278.

Wayman, K., Lynch, E., & Hanson, M. (1990). Home-based early childhood services: Cultural sensitivity in a family systems approach. *Topics in Early Childhood Special Education, 10*(4), 65–66.

Webber, J. (1997). Responsible inclusion: Key components for success. In P. Zionts (Ed.), *Effective inclusion of students with behavior and learning problems.* Austin, TX: Pro-Ed.

Webber, J., & Scheuermann, B. (1991). Accentuate the positive. . .Eliminate the negative! *Teaching Exceptional Children, 24,* 14–17.

Wehby, J. H., Symons, F. J., Canale, J. A., & Go, F. J. (1998). Teaching practices in classrooms for students with emotional and behavioral disorders: Discrepancies between recommendations and observations. *Behavioral Disorders, 24,* 51–56.

Wehmeyer, M. L. (in press). Universal design for learning, access to the general education curriculum, and students with mild mental retardation. *Exceptionality.*

Wehmeyer, M. (1993). Self-determination as an educational outcome. *Impact, 6*(4), 16–17, 26.

Wehmeyer, M. (1994). Perceptions of self-determination and psychological empowerment of adolescents with mental retardation. *Education and Training in Mental Retardation and Developmental Disabilities, 29,* 9–21.

Wehmeyer, M. L., Garner, N., Yeager, D., Lawrence, M., & Davis, A. K. (2006). Infusing self-determination into 18–21 services for students with intellectual or developmental disabilities: A multi-state, multiple component model. *Education and Training in Developmental Disabilities, 41,* 23–13.

Wehmeyer, M. L., Lattin, D., & Agran, M. (2001). Achieving access to the general education curriculum for students with mental retardation: A curriculum decision-making model. *Education and Training in Mental Retardation and Developmental Disabilities, 36,* 327–342.

Wehmeyer, M. L., Morningstar, M., & Husted, D. (1999). *Family involvement in transition planning and implementation.* Austin, TX: Pro-Ed.

Wehmeyer, M. L., & Patton, J. R. (2000). *Mental retardation in the 21st century.* Austin, TX: Pro-Ed.

Weinbender, M. L. M., & Rossignol, A. M. (1996). Lifestyle and risk of premature sexual activity in a high school population of Seventh-Day Adventists: Valuegenesis 1989. *Adolescence, 31,* 265–275.

Wenz-Gross, M., & Siperstein, G. N. (1998). Students with learning problems at risk in middle school: Stress, social support, and adjustment. *Exceptional Children, 65,* 91–100.

Werts, M. G., Harris, S., Tillery, C. Y., & Roark, R. (2004). What parents tell us about paraeducators. *Remedial and Special Education, 25,* 232–239.

Wesson, C. L., & Deno, S. L. (1989). An analysis of long-term instructional plans in reading for elementary resource room students. *Remedial and Special Education, 10*(1), 21–28.

West, G. K. (1986). Parenting without guilt. Springfield, IL: Thomas.

West, G. K. (1994, Nov. 10). Discipline that works: Part 1. *The News and Daily Advance,* 3–4.

West, G. K. (2000). *The Shelbys need help: A choose-your-own-solutions guidebook for parents.* Atascadero, CA: Impact.

West, G. K. (2002). *Parent education programs and benefits for parents of children with disabilities.* Unpublished manuscript, Lynchburg College, Lynchburg, VA.

Westling, D. L., & Koorland, M. A. (1988). *The special educator's handbook.* Boston: Allyn and Bacon.

Wetherby, A. M., & Prizant, B. M. (Eds.). (2000). *Autism spectrum disorders: A transactional developmental perspective*. Baltimore, MD: Brookes.

Weyandt, L. L. (2001). *An ADHD primer*. Boston: Allyn and Bacon.

White, C. C., Lakin, K. C., Bruininks, R. H., & Li, X. (1991). *Persons with mental retardation and related conditions in state-operated residential facilities: Year ending June 30, 1989, with longitudinal trends from 1950 to 1989*. Minneapolis, MN: University of Minnesota, Institute on Community Integration.

Wicks-Nelson, R., & Israel, A. C. (1991). *Behavior disorders of childhood*. Englewood Cliffs, NJ: Prentice-Hall.

Wiedemeyer, D., & Lehman, J. (1991). House plan: Approach to collaborative teaching and consultation. *Teaching Exceptional Children, 23(3)*, 6–10.

Wiederholt, J. L., & Bryant, B. (1986). *Gray oral reading test—Revised*. Austin, TX: Pro-Ed.

Wiener, J., Schneider, B. (2002). A multi-source exploration of friendship patterns of children with and without LD. *Journal of Abnormal Child Psychology, 30*, 127–141.

Wiig, E. H. (1986). Language disabilities in school-age children and youth. In G. H. Shames & E. H. Wiig (Eds.), *Human communication disorders* (2nd ed., pp. 331–383). Columbus, OH: Merrill.

Wiig, E. H., & Semel, E. (1984). *Language assessment and intervention for the learning disabled* (2nd ed.). Columbus, OH: Merrill.

Wilens, T. E., Biederman, J., & Spencer, T. J. (2002). Attention deficit/hyperactivity disorder across the lifespan. *Annual Review of Medicine, 53*, 113–131.

Will, M. C. (1984). Educating children with learning problems: A shared responsibility. *Exceptional Children, 52*, 411–415.

Williams, S. (2002). How speech-feedback and work prediction software can help students write. *Teaching Exceptional Children, 34*, 72–76.

Wilson, J. (2005). Interrupting the failure cycle. *Voices from the Middle, 12*, 25–30.

Winebrenner, S. (1992). *Teaching gifted kids in the regular classroom: Strategies and techniques every teacher can use to meet the academic needs of the gifted and talented*. Minneapolis, MN: Free Spirit.

Winocur, S. L., & Mauer, P. A. (1997). Critical thinking and gifted students: Using IMPACT to improve teaching and learning. In N. Colangelo and G. A. Davis (Eds.), *Handbook of gifted education* (2nd ed., pp. 308–317). Boston: Allyn and Bacon.

Winzer, M. A., & Mazurek, K. (1998). *Special education in multicultural contexts*. Upper Saddle River, NJ: Prentice Hall.

Witt, J. C., & Elliott, S. N. (1985). Acceptability of classroom management strategies. In T. R. Kratochwill (Ed.), *Advances in school psychology* (Vol. 4, pp. 251–288). Hillsdale, NJ: Erlbaum.

Wolfe, P. S. (1997). Deaf-blindness. In P. Wehman (Ed.), *Exceptional individuals* (pp. 357–381). Austin, TX: Pro-Ed.

Wolfe, P. S. & Hall, T. E. (2003). Making inclusion a reality for students with severe disabilities. *Teaching Exceptional Children, 35*, 56–61.

Wood, D. K., & Frank, A. R. (2000). Using memory-enhancing strategies to learn multiplication facts. *Teaching Exceptional Children, 32*, 78–82.

Wood, J. W. (1984). *Adapting instruction for the mainstream*. Columbus, OH: Merrill.

Wood, J. W. (1996). *Adapting instruction for mainstreamed and at-risk students* (3rd ed.). New York: Merrill.

Wood, M. (1998). Whose job is it anyway? Educational roles in inclusion. *Exceptional Children, 64*, 181–196.

Wurst, D., Jones, D., & Luckner, J. (2005). Promoting literacy development with students who are deaf, hard-of-hearing, and hearing. *Teaching Exceptional Children, 37*, 56–60.

Yamaguchi, B. J., Strawser, S., & Higgins, K. (1997). Children who are homeless: Implications for educators. *Intervention in School and Clinic, 33*, 90–98.

Yell, M. L., Drasgow, E., & Lowery, K. A. (2006). NCLB and students with autism spectrum disorder. *Journal of Autism and Other Developmental Disabilities, 20(3)*, 130–139.

Yell, M. L., Katsiyannis, A., & Shiner, J. G. (2006). The No Child Left Behind Act, adequate yearly progress, and students with disabilities. *Teaching Exceptional Children, 38(4)*, 32–39.

Yell, M. L., Rogers, D., & Rogers, E. L. (1998). The legal history of special education: What a long, strange trip it's been! *Remedial and Special Education, 19*, 219–228.

York, J., Vandercook, T., MacDonald, C., Heise-Neff, C., & Caughey, E. (1992). Feedback about integrating middle-school students with severe disabilities in general education classes. *Exceptional Children, 58*, 244–258.

Young, G., & Gerber, P. J. (1998). Learning disabilities and poverty: Moving towards a new understanding of learning disabilities as a public health and economic-risk issue. *Learning Disabilities, 9*, 1–6.

Young, M. E., Kersten, L., & Werch, T. (1996). Evaluation of patient-child drug education program. *Journal of Drug Education, 26*, 57–68.

Ysseldyke, J. E., Algozzine, B., & Thurlow, M. L. (2000). *Critical issues in special education* (3rd ed.). Boston: Houghton Mifflin.

Ysseldyke, J. E., Thurlow, M. L., Wotruba, J. W., & Nania, L. T. (1990). Special education student teacher ratios for mildly handicapped children. *Journal of Special Education, 23(1)*, 27–36.

Zabel, R. H., & Zabel, M. K. (1996). *Classroom management in context*. Boston: Houghton Mifflin.

Zentall, S. (2006). *ADHD and education: Foundations, characteristics, methods, and collaboration*. Upper Saddle River, NJ: Merrill Prentice Hall.

Zhang, D. (2001a). The effectiveness of "Next STEP" on the self-determination skills of students with learning disabilities. *Career Development for Exceptional Individuals, 24*, 121–132.

Zhang, D. (2001b). Self-determination and inclusion: Are students with mild mental retardation more self-determined in regular classrooms? *Education and Training in Mental Retardation and Developmental Disabilities, 36(4)*, 357–362.

Zionts, P. (1997). *Inclusion strategies for students with learning and behavior problems*. Austin, TX: Pro-Ed.

Zirkell, P. (1999). Districts should use caution in determing substantive obligation for services to Section 504 students. *Section 504 Compliance Advisor, 3*, 3–4.

Zirpoli, T., & Melloy, G. (1993). *Behavior management: Applications for teachers and parents*. Columbus, OH: Merrill.

Zucker, S. H., & Polloway, E. A. (1987). Issues in identification and assessment in mental retardation. *Education and Training in Mental Retardation, 22*, 69–76.

Zurkowski, J. K., Kelly, P. S., & Griswold, D. E. (1998). Discipline and IDEA 1997: Instituting a new balance. *Intervention in School and Clinic, 34*, 3–9.

Name Index

Page numbers followed by the letters *f* or *t* indicate figures or tables, respectively.

Subject Index

Page numbers followed by the letters *f, p,* or *t* indicate figures, photos, or tables, respectively.

595

Council for Exceptional Children (CEC) Special Education Content Standards

Standard 1: Foundations

Special educators understand the field as an evolving and changing discipline based on philosophies, evidence-based principles and theories, relevant laws and policies, diverse and historical points of view, and human issues that have historically influenced and continue to influence the field of special education and the education and treatment of individuals with exceptional needs both in school and society. Special educators understand how these influence professional practice, including assessment, instructional planning, implementation, and program evaluation. Special educators understand how issues of human diversity can impact families, cultures, and schools, and how these complex human issues can interact with issues in the delivery of special education services. They understand the relationships of organizations of special education to the organizations and functions of schools, school systems, and other agencies. Special educators use this knowledge as a ground upon which to construct their own personal understandings and philosophies of special education.

Standard 2: Development and Characteristics of Learners

Special educators know and demonstrate respect for their students first as unique human beings. Special educators understand the similarities and differences in human development and the characteristics between and among individuals with and without exceptional learning needs (ELN)[1]. Moreover, special educators understand how exceptional conditions can interact with the domains of human development and they use this knowledge to respond to the varying abilities and behaviors of individual's with ELN. Special educators understand how the experiences of individuals with ELN can impact families, as well as the individual's ability to learn, interact socially, and live as fulfilled contributing members of the community.

Standard 3: Individual Learning Differences

Special educators understand the effects that an exceptional condition[2] can have on an individual's learning in school and throughout life. Special educators understand that the beliefs, traditions, and values across and within cultures can affect relationships among and between students, their families, and the school community. Moreover, special educators are active and resourceful in seeking to understand how primary language, culture, and familial backgrounds interact with the individual's exceptional condition to impact the individual's academic and social abilities, attitudes, values, interests, and career options. The understanding of these learning differences and their possible interactions provide the foundation upon which special educators individualize instruction to provide meaningful and challenging learning for individuals with ELN.

Standard 4: Instructional Strategies

Special educators posses a repertoire of evidence-based instructional strategies to individualize instruction for individuals with ELN. Special educators select, adapt, and use these instructional strategies to promote challenging learning results in general and special curricula[3] and to appropriately modify learning environments for individuals with ELN. They enhance the learning of critical thinking, problem solving, and performance skills of individuals with ELN, and increase their self-awareness, self-management, self-control, self-reliance, and self-esteem. Moreover, special educators emphasize the development, maintenance, and generalization of knowledge and skills across environments, settings, and the lifespan.

Beginning special educators demonstrate their mastery this standard through the mastery of the CEC Common Core Knowledge and Skills, as well as through the appropriate CEC Specialty Area(s) Knowledge and Skills for which the program is preparing candidates.

Standard 5: Learning Environments and Social Interactions

Special educators actively create learning environments for individuals with ELN that foster cultural understanding, safety and emotional well being, positive social interactions, and active engagement of individuals with ELN. In addition, special educators foster environments in which diversity is valued and individuals are taught to live harmoniously and productively in a culturally diverse world. Special educators shape environments to encourage the independence, self-motivation, self-direction, personal empowerment, and self-advocacy of individuals with ELN. Special educators help their general education colleagues integrate individuals with ELN in regular environments and engage them in meaningful learning activities and interactions. Special educators use direct motivational and instructional interventions with individuals with ELN to teach them to respond effectively to current expectations. When necessary, special educators can safely intervene with individuals with ELN in crisis. Special educators coordinate all these efforts and provide guidance and direction to paraeducators and others, such as classroom volunteers and tutors.

Standard 6: Language

Special educators understand typical and atypical language development and the ways in which exceptional conditions can interact with an individual's experience with and use of language. Special educators use individualized strategies to enhance language development and teach communication skills to individuals with ELN. Special educators are familiar with augmentative, alternative, and assistive technologies to support and enhance communication of individuals with exceptional needs. Special educators match their communication methods to an individual's language proficiency and cultural and linguistic differences. Special educators provide effective language models, and they use communication strategies and resources to facilitate understanding of subject matter for individuals with ELN whose primary language is not English.

Standard 7: Instructional Planning

Individualized decision-making and instruction is at the center of special education practice. Special educators develop long-range individualized instructional plans anchored in both general and special curricula. In addition, special educators systematically translate these individualized plans into carefully selected shorter-range goals and objectives taking into consideration an individual's abilities and needs, the learning environment, and a myriad of cultural and linguistic factors. Individualized instructional plans emphasize explicit modeling and efficient guided practice to assure acquisition and fluency through maintenance and generalization. Understanding of these factors as well as the implications of an individual's exceptional condition, guides the special educator's selection, adaptation, and creation of materials, and the use of powerful instructional variables. Instructional plans are modified based on ongoing analysis of the individual's learning progress. Moreover, special educators facilitate this instructional planning in a collaborative context including the individuals with exceptionalities, families, professional colleagues, and personnel from other agencies as appropriate. Special educators also develop a variety of individualized transition plans, such as transitions from preschool to elementary school and from secondary settings to a variety of postsecondary work and learning contexts. Special educators are comfortable using appropriate technologies to support instructional planning and individualized instruction.

Standard 8: Assessment

Assessment is integral to the decision-making and teaching of special educators and special educators use multiple types of assessment information for a variety of educational decisions. Special educators use the results of assessments to help identify exceptional learning needs and to develop and implement individualized instructional programs, as well as to adjust instruction in response to ongoing learning progress. Special educators understand the legal policies and ethical principles of measurement and assessment related to referral, eligibility, program planning, instruction, and

---

[1]"Individual with exceptional learning needs" is used throughout to include individuals with disabilities and individuals with exceptional gifts and talents.

[2]"Exceptional Condition" is used throughout to include both single and co-existing conditions. These may be two or more disabling conditions or exceptional gifts or talents coexisting with one or more disabling condition.

[3]"Special Curricula" is used

placement for individuals with ELN, including those from culturally and linguistically diverse backgrounds. Special educators understand measurement theory and practices for addressing issues of validity, reliability, norms, bias, and interpretation of assessment results. In addition, special educators understand the appropriate use and limitations of various types of assessments. Special educators collaborate with families and other colleagues to assure non-biased, meaningful assessments and decision-making. Special educators conduct formal and informal assessments of behavior, learning, achievement, and environments to design learning experiences that support the growth and development of individuals with ELN. Special educators use assessment information to identify supports and adaptations required for individuals with ELN to access the general curriculum and to participate in school, system, and statewide assessment programs. Special educators regularly monitor the progress of individuals with ELN in general and special curricula. Special educators use appropriate technologies to support their assessments.

Beginning special educators demonstrate their mastery of this standard through the mastery of the CEC Common Core Knowledge and Skills, as well as through the appropriate CEC Specialty Area(s) Knowledge and Skills for which the preparation program is preparing candidates.

Standard 9: Professional and Ethical Practice
Special educators are guided by the profession's ethical and professional practice standards. Special educators practice in multiple roles and complex situations across wide age and developmental ranges. Their practice requires ongoing attention to legal matters along with serious professional and ethical considerations. Special educators engage in professional activities and participate in learning communities that benefit individuals with ELN, their families, colleagues, and their own professional growth. Special educators view themselves as lifelong learners and regularly reflect on and adjust their practice. Special educators are aware of how their own and oth-

ers attitudes, behaviors, and ways of communicating can influence their practice. Special educators understand that culture and language can interact with exceptionalities, and are sensitive to the many aspects of diversity of individuals with ELN and their families. Special educators actively plan and engage in activities that foster their professional growth and keep them current with evidence-based best practices. Special educators know their own limits of practice and practice within them.

Beginning special educators demonstrate their mastery of this standard through the mastery of the CEC Common Core Knowledge and Skills, as well as through the appropriate CEC Specialty Area(s) Knowledge and Skills for which the preparation program is preparing candidates.

Standard 10: Collaboration
Special educators routinely and effectively collaborate with families, other educators, related service providers, and personnel from community agencies in culturally responsive ways. This collaboration assures that the needs of individuals with ELN are addressed throughout schooling. Moreover, special educators embrace their special role as advocate for individuals with ELN. Special educators promote and advocate the learning and well being of individuals with ELN across a wide range of settings and a range of different learning experiences. Special educators are viewed as specialists by a myriad of people who actively seek their collaboration to effectively include and teach individuals with ELN. Special educators are a resource to their colleagues in understanding the laws and policies relevant to Individuals with ELN. Special educators use collaboration to facilitate the successful transitions of individuals with ELN across settings and services.

Beginning special educators demonstrate their mastery of this standard through the mastery of the CEC Common Core Knowledge and Skills, as well as through the appropriate CEC Specialty Area(s) Knowledge and Skills for which the preparation program is preparing candidates.

PRAXIS II Special Education Knowledge-Based Core Principles (0351)

I. Understanding Exceptionalities
- Theories and principles of human development and learning, including research and theories related to human development; theories of learning; social and emotional development; language development; cognitive development; and physical development, including motor and sensory
- Characteristics of students with disabilities, including medical/ physical; educational; social; and psychological
- Basic concepts in special education, including definitions of all major categories and specific disabilities; causation and prevention of disability; the nature of behaviors, including frequency, duration, intensity, and degrees of severity; and classification of students with disabilities, including classifications as represented in IDEA and labeling of students.

II. Legal and Societal Issues
- Federal laws and landmark legal cases related to special education (for example, PL94-142, PL101476 [IDEA], Section 504, ADA, Rowley re: program appropriateness, Tatro re: related services, Honig re: discipline)
- Issues related to school, family, and/or community, such as teacher advocacy for students and families, including advocating for educational change and developing student self-advocacy; family participation and support systems; public attitudes toward individuals with disabilities; and cultural and community influences

III. Delivery of Services to Students with Disabilities
- Conceptual approaches underlying the delivery of services to students with disabilities (for example, medical, psychodynamic, behavioral, cognitive, sociological, eclectic)
- Professional roles and responsibilities of teachers of students with disabilities (for example, teacher as a collaborator with other teachers, parents, community groups, and outside agencies); teacher as a multi disciplinary team member; teacher's role in selecting appropriate environments and providing appropriate services to students; knowledge and use of professional literature, research (including classroom research), and professional organizations and associations; and reflecting on one's own teaching

- Assessment, including how to modify, construct, or select and conduct nondiscriminatory and appropriate informal and formal assessment procedures; how to interpret standardized and specialized assessment results; how to use evaluation results for various purposes, including monitoring instruction and IEP/ ITP development; and how to prepare written reports and communicate findings to others
- Placement and program issues (including continuum of services; mainstreaming; integration; inclusion; least restrictive environment; noncategorical, categorical, and cross-categorical programs; related services; early intervention; community-based training; transition of students into and within special education placements; postschool transitions; and access to assistive technology)
- Curriculum and instruction, including the IEP/ITP process; instructional development and implementation (for example, instructional activities, curricular materials, resources and equipment, working with classroom personnel, tutoring and the use of technology); teaching strategies and methods (for example , direct instruction, cooperative learning, diagnostic prescriptive method); instructional format and components (for example, individualized instruction , small- and large-group instruction, modeling, drill and practice); and areas of instruction (such as academics, study and learning skills, social, self-care, and vocational skills)
- Management of the learning environment , including behavior management (for example, behavior analysis—identification and definition of antecedents, target behavior, and consequent events, data-gathering procedures, selecting and using behavioral interventions); classroom organization/management (for example, providing the appropriate physical-social environment for learning — expectations, rules, consequences, consistency, attitudes, lighting, seating, access, and strategies for positive interactions, transitions between lessons and activities); grouping of students; and effective and efficient documentation (such as parent/teacher contacts and legal records)

INTASC's Model Standards for Licensing General and Special Education Teachers of Students with Disabilities: A Resource for State Dialogue

Principle 1

The teacher understands the central concepts, tools of inquiry, Structures of the discipline(s) he or she teaches and can create learning experiences that make these aspects of subject matter meaningful for students.

Implications for students with disabilities: Both general and special education teachers demonstrate an understanding of the primary concepts and ways of thinking and knowing in the content areas they teach as articulated in INTASC subject matter principles and other professional, state, and institutional standards. They understand the underlying values and implications of disability legislation and special education policies and procedures as they relate to their roles and responsibilities in supporting the educational needs of students with disabilities. All teachers provide equitable access to and participation in the general curriculum for students with disabilities.

Principle 2

The teacher understands how children learn and develop, and can provide learning opportunities that support the intellectual, social and personal development of each learner.

Implications for students with disabilities: Both general and special education teachers understand that all children have similar patterns of learning and development that vary individually within and across cognitive, social, emotional and physical areas. They recognize that children with disabilities may exhibit greater individual variation in learning and development than students without disabilities, and that a disability often influences development and functioning in more than one area. Teachers use knowledge of the impact of disabilities on learning and development to optimize learning opportunities for each student.

Principle 3

The teacher understands how students differ in their approaches to learning and creates instructional opportunities that are adapted to diverse learners.

Implications for students with disabilities: Students with disabilities come from a variety of cultures, languages, classes, and ethnicities. Disability, like other aspects of diversity, may affect a student's approach to learning and a teacher's approach to teaching. Teachers understand students with disabilities within the broader context of their families, cultural backgrounds, socioeconomic classes, languages, communities and peer/social groups.

Principle 4

The teacher understands and uses a variety of instructional strategies to encourage students' development of critical thinking, problem solving, and performance skills.

Implications for students with disabilities: Ensuring that students with disabilities can participate successfully in the general curriculum requires teachers to tailor their instructional strategies to the particular learning needs of individual students. General and special education teachers use a variety of instructional strategies and technologies and know how to modify and adapt the general curriculum to accommodate individual students' needs. Students with disabilities who have goals related to an expanded curriculum will also need specialized instruction to achieve those goals.

Principle 5

The teacher uses an understanding of individual and group motivation and behavior to create a learning environment that encourages positive social interaction, active engagement in learning, and self-motivation.

Implications for students with disabilities: Students' affiliation and acceptance within a community is an important basis for developing social responsibility, self-esteem and positive peer relations. Students learn more effectively when they are valued members of a learning community in which everyone can grow and learn. Teachers welcome students with disabilities and take deliberate action to ensure that they are included as members of the learning community. Teachers may also need to structure activities that specifically foster engagement, self-motivation and independent learning in students with disabilities.

Principle 6

The teacher uses knowledge of effective verbal, nonverbal, and media communication technologies to foster active inquiry, collaboration, and supportive interaction in the classroom.

Implications for students with disabilities: Students with disabilities often have communication or language delays or disorders associated with their disabilities. They may require multiple and alternative modes of communication. Teachers set a high priority on establishing a safe and comfortable environment in which students with disabilities are encouraged and supported to use language and contribute their ideas. They teach language and communication skills, make accommodations to promote effective communication, and encourage and support the use of technology to promote learning and communication.

Principle 7

The teacher plans instruction based on knowledge of subject matter, students, the community and curriculum goals.

Implications for students with disabilities: While students with disabilities often pursue the same learning goals within the general curriculum and benefit from instruction in a manner that is similar to that of their non-disabled peers, they may require adjustments in goals, teaching strategies or supports. Some students with disabilities may require an expanded curriculum that may include areas such as functional life skills, communication skills, or behavior/social skills. Planning for students with disabilities requires an individualized plan of instruction and is a collaborative process that involves special and general educators, the student (when appropriate), families, and other professionals.

Principle 8

The teacher understands and uses formal and informal assessment strategies to evaluate and ensure the continuous intellectual, social and physical development of the learner.

Implications for students with disabilities: Individualized comprehensive assessments are required for students with disabilities and are used to determine eligibility for special education services, to plan individualized instruction, and to monitor and evaluate student performance. It is also expected that students with disabilities will participate in the overall assessment programs of the classroom, school district, and state, and that they may require accommodations to demonstrate their knowledge and skills. In addition, some students with disabilities may require assessments related to achievement in an expanded curriculum (i.e. alternate assessments).

Principle 9

The teacher is a reflective practitioner who continually evaluates the effects of his/her choices and actions on others (students, parents, and other professionals in the learning community) and who actively seeks out opportunities to grow professionally.

Implications for students with disabilities: Teacher reflection is essential for designing, monitoring and adapting instruction for all students, including students with disabilities Teachers reflect on their knowledge of the learning strengths and needs of individual students with disabilities, and question and evaluate the appropriateness and effectiveness of their instructional choices and practices for building on those strengths and meeting those needs. Based on their data-based reflections, teachers engage in actions that consistently support and promote the achievement of students with disabilities.

Principle 10

The teacher fosters relationships with school colleagues, families, and agencies in the larger community to support students' learning and well being

Implications for students with disabilities: Families, schools and communities are important contexts for teaching, learning, and development. Teachers advocate for students with disabilities to receive the support they need to be successful in the general curriculum and to achieve the goals of their individual education plans. They collaborate with each other, with other professionals, and with families to ensure that students with disabilities are valued members of the classroom, school, and larger communities.